CONSTITUTIONAL LAW FOR A CHANGING AMERICA

INSTITUTIONAL POWERS AND CONSTRAINTS

FIFTH EDITION

LEE EPSTEIN
Washington University

THOMAS G. WALKER
Emory University

CQ PRESS

A DIVISION OF
CONGRESSIONAL QUARTERLY INC.
WASHINGTON, D.C.

In honor of our parents
Ann and Kenneth Spole
Josephine and George Walker

CQ Press
1255 22nd St., N.W., Suite 400
Washington, D.C. 20037
Phone, 202-729-1900
Toll-free, 1-866-4CQ-PRESS (1-866-427-7737)
www.cqpress.com

∞ The paper used in this publication exceeds the requirements of the American National Standard for Information Sciences—Permanence of Paper for Printed Library Materials, ANSI Z39.48-1992.

Cover design: Naylor Design Inc., Washington, D.C.
Interior Design: Kachergis Book Design, Pittsboro, North Carolina
Composition: BMWW, Baltimore, Maryland

Printed and bound in the United States of America

08   07   06   05   04   5   4   3   2   1

LIBRARY OF CONGRESS CATALOGING-IN-PUBLICATION DATA
   Epstein, Lee, date
    Constitutional law for a changing America : institutional powers and constraints / Lee Epstein, Thomas G. Walker.— 5th ed.
    p. cm.
    ISBN 1-56802-822-9 (alk. paper)
    1. Constitutional law—United States—Cases. I. Walker, Thomas G. II. Title.
    KF4548 .E67 2004
    342.73—dc22

                                            2003025320

CONTENTS

CHRONOLOGICAL TABLE OF CASES

TABLES, FIGURES, AND BOXES

PREFACE

Twelve years have passed since *Constitutional Law for a Changing America: Institutional Powers and Constraints* made its debut in a discipline already supplied with many fine casebooks by law professors, historians, and social scientists. We believed then, as we do now, that there was a need for a fresh approach because, as political science professors who regularly teach courses on public law, and as scholars concerned with judicial processes, we saw a growing disparity between what we taught and what our research taught us.

We had adopted books for our classes that focused primarily on Supreme Court decisions and how the Court applied the resulting legal precedents to subsequent disputes, but as scholars we understood that to know the law is to know only part of the story. A host of political factors—internal and external—influence the Court's decisions and shape the development of constitutional law. Among the more significant forces at work are the ways lawyers and interest groups frame legal disputes, the ideological and behavioral propensities of the justices, the politics of judicial selection, public opinion, and the positions elected officials take, to name just a few.

Because we thought no existing book adequately combined the lessons of the legal model with the influences of the political process, we wrote one. In most respects, our book follows tradition: readers will find, for example, that we include the classic cases that best illustrate the development of constitutional law. But our focus is different, as is the appearance of this volume. We emphasize the arguments raised by lawyers and interest groups

and the politics surrounding litigation, for example, and include tables and figures on Court trends, profiles of influential justices and organizations, and other materials that bring out the rich legal, social, and political contexts in which the Court reaches its decisions. As a result, students and instructors will find this work both similar to and different from casebooks they may have read before.

Integrating traditional teaching and research concerns was only one of our goals. Another was to animate the subject of public law. As instructors, we find our subject inherently interesting—to us public law is exciting stuff. The typical constitutional law book, however, could not be less inviting in design, presentation, or prose. That kind of book can only dampen enthusiasm. We have written a book that we hope mirrors the excitement we feel for our subject.

Along with cases excerpted in the traditional manner, we have included descriptions of the events that led to the suits, photographs of litigants, and relevant exhibits from the cases. Moreover, finding ourselves increasingly confronted with questions from students about the fate of particular litigants—for example, what happened to Fred Korematsu?—and hearing the same from colleagues elsewhere, we decided to attach "Aftermath" boxes to a select set of cases. In addition to providing human interest material, they can lead to interesting discussions about the impact of decisions on the lives of "ordinary" Americans. We hope these materials demonstrate to students that Supreme Court cases involve real people engaged in real disputes and are not merely legal names and citations.

Readers will also find material designed to enhance their understanding of the law, such as information on the Supreme Court decision-making process, the structure of the federal judiciary, and briefing court cases. Also included are a glossary of legal terms and brief biographical information on each justice. Finally, to broaden students' perspective on the U.S. legal system, we have added boxes on the laws and legal practices of other countries. Students and instructors can use these to compare and contrast U.S. Supreme Court decisions over issues such as judicial review, privileges and immunities for legislators, and the separation of powers system with policies developed in other countries. This material has inspired lively debates in our classes, and we hope it will in yours as well.

In preparing this fifth edition, we have strengthened the distinctive features of the earlier versions by making changes at two levels of the book—chapters and cases. We thoroughly updated individual chapters to include significant opinions since publication of the previous edition. Where relevant, we also updated the narrative to take into account recent events in the legal and political environments. The chapter on the separation of powers, for example, now includes a full discussion of the government's war on terrorism. We supply documents detailing Congress's authorization for the use of military force against Iraq and identify steps President George W. Bush has taken in response, as well as others for which he has not obtained congressional approval. Some of these, of course, implicate the authority of the ordinary courts, such as the establishment of military tribunals to try noncitizens suspected of terrorism. The Supreme Court has not yet ruled on these corresponding issues (though September 11–related cases are now making their way to the High Court), but during World War II, in *Ex parte Quirin*, it permitted a military commission to try the "Nazi saboteurs" who landed on Long Island intending to attack manufacturing and transportation sites. In light of the current relevance of this case, we have excerpted it in the section on presidential war powers.

Finally, we made a change in our presentation of the case material. As professors who regularly teach courses on rights, liberties, and justice we are the first to acknowledge that no one book—not even our own!—can possibly contain excerpts of each and every significant Supreme Court decision; the constraints of space and semesters simply prohibit that. As a result, we had to make choices—often hard ones. Recognizing that some instructors would enjoy greater flexibility in deciding the cases on which to focus, we have created a case archive located at www.cqpress.com/college/clca.htm. Through this archive professors and students can access important decisions that we do not include in the book. But we do more than provide full-text versions online. We have excerpted each decision to match the focus and streamlining we provide for cases in the book. Cases included in the archive are identified in the text in bold italic type; they also are listed in Appendix 10. Currently, as the appendix indicates, the archive houses about seventy cases relevant to *Institutional Powers and Constraints*, as well as hundreds pertaining to our *Rights, Liberties, and Justice* and *Short Course* volumes. We will keep it current, and will add important decisions as the Court hands them down. Our intention to keep the text up to date is still intact. Each year we will post on the companion Web site important opinions issued by the Court since the book's publication.

Also worth noting, we retained and enhanced other features pertaining to case presentation that have proved to be useful. We continue to excerpt concurring and dissenting opinions; in fact, virtually all cases analyzed in the text now include one or the other or both. Although these opinions lack the force of precedent, they are useful in helping students to see alternative points of view. We also provide universal resource locators (URLs) to the full text of the opinions and, where available, to a Web site containing oral arguments in many landmark cases. We took this step because we recognize how rewarding it can be to read decisions in their entirety and to listen to oral arguments. Doing so, we believe, helps students to develop an important skill—differentiating between viable and less-viable arguments. Finally, we continue to retain the historical flavor of the decisions, reprinting verbatim the original language used in the *U.S. Reports* to introduce the justices' writings. Students will see that during most of its history the Court used the term "Mr." to refer to justices, as in "Mr. Justice Holmes delivered the opinion of the Court" or "Mr. Justice Harlan, dissenting." In 1980 the Court dropped the "Mr." This point may seem minor, but we think it is evidence that the justices, like other Americans, updated their usage to reflect fundamental changes in American society—in this case, the emergence of women as a force in the legal profession and shortly thereafter on the Court itself.

ACKNOWLEDGMENTS

Although the first edition of this volume was published only twelve years ago, it had been in the works for many more. During those developmental years, numerous people provided guidance, but none as much as Joanne Daniels, a former editor at CQ Press. It was Joanne who conceived the idea of a constitutional law book that would be accessible, sophisticated, and contemporary. And it was Joanne who brought that concept to our attention and helped us develop it into a book. We are forever in her debt.

Because this new edition charts the same course as the first four, we remain grateful to all of those who had a hand in the previous editions. They include David Tarr and Jeanne Ferris at CQ Press, Jack Knight at Washington University, Joseph A. Kobylka of Southern Methodist University, Jeffrey A. Segal of the State University of New York at Stony Brook, and our many colleagues who reviewed and commented on them: Judith A. Baer, Ralph Baker, Lawrence Baum, John Brigham, Gregory A. Caldeira, Bradley C. Canon, Robert A. Carp, Phillip J. Cooper, Sue Davis, John Fliter, John B. Gates, Edward V. Heck, Kevin McGuire, Wayne McIntosh, John A. Maltese, Susan Mezey, Richard J. Pacelle Jr., C. K. Rowland, Donald R. Songer, and Harry P. Stumpf. We are also grateful to the many scholars who took time out of their busy schedules to write us with suggestions, including (again) Gregory Caldeira, as well as Akiba J. Covitz, Alec C. Ewald, Leslie Goldstein, and Neil Snortland. Most of all, we wish to acknowledge the contributions of our editor at CQ Press, Brenda Carter, who has seen *Constitutional Law for a Changing America* through all five editions. There are many things we could say about Brenda—all positive— but perhaps this best summarizes our feelings: we cannot think of one editor, not one, in this business with whom we would rather work. Somehow she knows exactly when to steer us and when to steer clear. Also working with us on this fifth edition was Charisse Kiino, another wonder-

ful editor at CQ. Charisse too was terrific about keeping us on our toes but not stepping (too hard) on them.

We remain indebted to Carolyn Goldinger. She worked as our copy editor on the first four editions, and her imprint remains, without exaggeration, *everywhere.* She made our prose more accessible, questioned our interpretation of certain events and opinions—and was all too often right—and made our tables and figures understandable. Talia Greenberg, our copy editor for this edition, picked up where Carolyn left off, tightening the narrative, urging us to add (and eliminate) material where appropriate, and detecting numerous inconsistencies and repetitions. We are extremely grateful for all her hard work and patience. We also thank Lorna Notsch for her superior organizational skills.

Many thanks also go to Jeffrey A. Segal for his frank appraisal of the earlier works and his willingness to discuss even half-baked ideas for changes; to Judith Baer and Leslie Goldstein for their help with the revision of the discrimination chapter and their answers to innumerable e-mail messages; to Jack Knight for his comments on the drafts of several chapters; and to Harold J. Spaeth for his wonderful data set.

Our home institutions provided substantial support, not complaining when presented with astronomical telephone bills, postal fees, and copying expenses. For this and all the moral support they provide, we thank all of our colleagues and staffs.

Finally, we acknowledge the support of our friends and families. We are forever grateful to our former professors for instilling in us their genuine interest in and curiosity about things judicial and legal, and to our parents for their unequivocal support.

As we were working on this edition we learned that the *Constitutional Law for a Changing America* volumes had won the 2003 award for teaching and mentoring presented by the Law and Courts section of the American Political Science Association. Each and every one of the editors and scholars we thank above deserves credit for whatever success our books have enjoyed. Any errors of omission or commission, though, remain our sole responsibility. We encourage students and instructors alike to comment on the book and to inform us of any errors. Contact us at: *epstein@artsci.wustl.edu* or *polstw@emory.edu.*

PART I
THE U.S. CONSTITUTION

AN INTRODUCTION TO THE
U.S. CONSTITUTION

1. UNDERSTANDING THE
U.S. SUPREME COURT

AN INTRODUCTION TO THE U.S. CONSTITUTION

ACCORDING TO President Franklin Roosevelt, "Like the Bible, it ought to be read again and again." [1] Sen. Henry Clay said it "was made not merely for the generation that then existed, but for posterity—unlimited, undefined, endless, perpetual posterity." [2] Justice Hugo Black carried one with him virtually all the time. The object of all this admiration? The U.S. Constitution. To be sure, the Constitution has its flaws and its share of detractors, but most Americans take great pride in their charter. And why not? It is, after all, the world's oldest written constitution.

In what follows, we provide a brief introduction to the document—in particular, the circumstances under which it was written, the basic principles underlying it, and some controversies surrounding it. This material may not be new to you, but, as the balance of this book is devoted to Supreme Court interpretation of the Constitution, we think it is worth reviewing.

THE ROAD TO THE U.S. CONSTITUTION

While the fledgling United States was fighting for its independence from England, it was being run (and the war conducted) by the Continental Congress. Although this body had no formal authority, it met in session from 1774 through the end of the war in 1781, establishing itself as a "de facto" government. But it may have been something more than that. About a year into the Revolution-

ary War, Congress took steps toward nationhood. On July 2, 1776, it passed a resolution declaring the "United Colonies free and independent states." Two days later, on July 4, it formalized this proclamation in the Declaration of Independence, in which the nation's Founders used the term United States of America for the first time. [3] But even before the adoption of the Declaration of Independence, the Continental Congress had selected a group of delegates to make recommendations for the formation of a national government. Composed of representatives of each of the thirteen colonies, this committee labored for several months to produce a proposal for a national charter, the Articles of Confederation. [4] Congress passed the proposal and submitted it to the states for ratification in November 1777. Ratification was achieved in March 1781, when Maryland—a two-year holdout—gave its approval.

Despite being the nation's first written charter, the Articles of Confederation changed the way the government operated very little: the articles merely institutionalized practices that had developed prior to 1774. For example, rather than provide for a compact between the people and the government, the 1781 charter institutionalized "a league of friendship" among the states, one that rested on strong notions of state sovereignty. This is not to suggest that the charter failed to provide for a central government. As we can see in Figure I-1, which depicts

---

1. Quoted in Michael Kammen, ed., *The Origins of the American Constitution* (New York: Penguin Books, 1986), vii.
2. Speech to the Senate, January 29, 1850.

3. The text of the Declaration of Independence is available at: *www.constitution.org/usdeclar.htm.*
4. The full text of the Articles of Confederation is available at: *www.yale.edu/lawweb/avalon/artconf.htm.*

FIGURE I-1   The Structure and Powers of Government under the Articles of Confederation

The States

Congress

Had the Power to	Lacked Power to
Declare war and make peace	Provide for effective treaty-making
Enter into treaties and alliances	power and control of foreign relations;
Establish and control armed forces	it could not compel states to respect
Requisition men and money from states	treaties
Regulate coinage	Compel states to meet military quotas;
Borrow money and issue bills of credit	it could not draft soldiers
Fix uniform standards of weight and	Regulate interstate and foreign commerce;
measurement	it left each state free to set up its own tariff
Create admiralty courts	system
Create a postal system	Collect taxes directly from the people; it had
Regulate Indian affairs	to rely on states to collect and forward
Guarantee citizens of each state the rights	taxes
and privileges of citizens in the several	Compel states to pay their share of govern-
states when in another	ment costs
Adjudicate disputes between states upon	Provide and maintain a sound monetary
state petition	system or issue paper money; this was
	left up to the states, and monies in
	circulation differed tremendously in value

Committee of the States

(Composed of representatives of all the states to act in the name of Congress between sessions)

Officers

(Congress appointed officers to do some of the executive work)

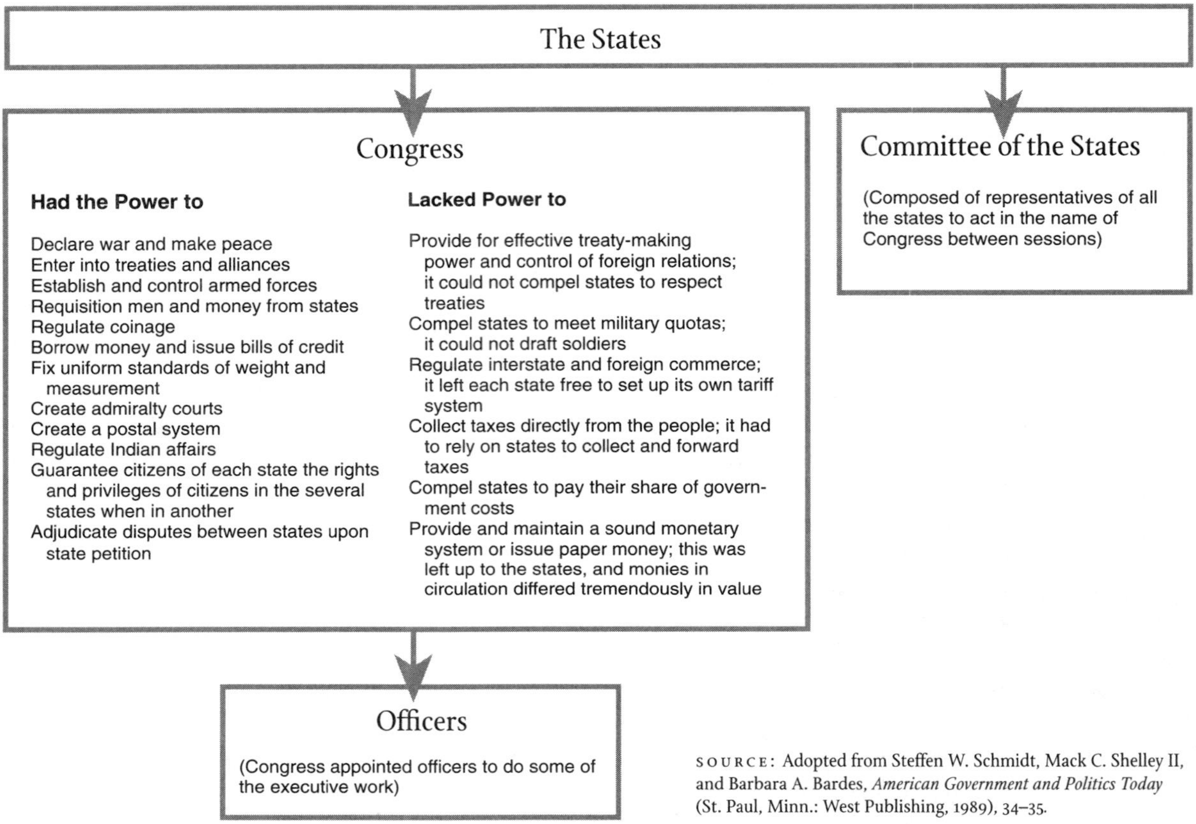

SOURCE: Adopted from Steffen W. Schmidt, Mack C. Shelley II, and Barbara A. Bardes, *American Government and Politics Today* (St. Paul, Minn.: West Publishing, 1989), 34–35.

the structure and powers of government, the articles created a national governing apparatus, however simple and weak. There was a one-house legislature but no formal federal executive or judiciary. And although the legislature had some power, most notably in the area of foreign affairs, it derived its authority from the states that had created it, not the people.

The condition of the United States under the Articles of Confederation was not entirely satisfactory. Analysts have pointed out weaknesses of the Articles of Confederation, including the following:

Because it allowed Congress only to requisition funds and not to tax, the federal government was virtually broke. Between 1781 and 1783 the national legislature requested $10 million

from the states and received only $1.5 million. Given the foreign debts the United States had accumulated during the war, this problem was particularly troublesome.

Because Congress lacked any concrete way to regulate foreign commerce, treaties between the United States and other countries were of limited value. Some European nations (for example, England and Spain) took advantage by imposing restrictions on trade that made it difficult for America to export goods.

Because the government lacked coercive power over the states, mutual cooperation among them quickly dissipated. They engaged in trading practices that hurt one another economically. In short, the states acted more like thirteen separate countries than a union or even a confederation.

Because the exercise of most national authority required the approval of nine states and the passage of amendments required unanimity, the articles stymied Congress. Indeed, given the divisions among the states at the time, the approval of nine states for any action of substance was rare, and the required unanimity for amendment was never obtained.

Nevertheless, the government accomplished many notable objectives during the years the Articles of Confederation were in effect: it brought the Revolutionary War to a successful end and paved the way for the 1783 Treaty of Paris, which helped make the United States a presence on the international scene. Moreover, the charter served an important purpose. It prevented the states from going their separate ways until a better system could be put into place.

Still, the articles' shortcomings were becoming more and more apparent. By the mid-1780s, several dissidents, including James Madison of Virginia and Alexander Hamilton of New York, had held a series of meetings to arouse interest in revising the system of government. At one, held in Annapolis in September 1786, they urged the states to send delegations to another meeting scheduled for the following May in Philadelphia. Their plea could not have come at a more opportune time. Just the month before, in August 1786, a former Revolutionary War captain, Daniel Shays, had led disgruntled farmers in an armed rebellion in Massachusetts. They were protesting the poor state of the economy, particularly as it affected farmers.

Shays's Rebellion was suppressed by state forces, but it was seen as yet another sign that the Articles of Confederation needed amending. In February 1787 Congress issued a call for a convention to reevaluate the current national system. It was clear, however, that Congress did not want a new charter; in fact, it stated that the delegates were to meet "for the sole and express purpose of revising the Articles of Confederation."

Despite these words, the fifty-five delegates who gathered in Philadelphia quickly realized that they would be doing more than "revising" the articles: they would be framing a new charter. We can attribute this change in purpose, at least in part, to the Virginia delegation. When the Virginians arrived in Philadelphia on May 14, the day the convention was supposed to start, only they and the Pennsylvania delegation were there. Although lacking a quorum, the Virginia contingent used the eleven-day delay to its advantage, crafting a series of proposals. The Virginians called for a wholly new government structure, composed of a strong three-branch national government empowered to lead the nation.

Known as the Virginia Plan, these proposals were formally introduced to the delegates May 29, just four days after the convention began. And, although it was the target of a counterproposal submitted by the New Jersey delegation, the Virginia Plan set the tone for the convention. It served as the basis for many of the ensuing debates and, as we shall see, for the Constitution itself (see Table I-1).

The delegates had much to accomplish during the convention period. Arguments between large states and small states over the structure of the new government and its relationship to the states threatened to deadlock the meeting. Indeed, it is almost a miracle that the delegates were able to frame a new constitution, which they did in just four months. One can speculate that the Founders succeeded in part because they were able to close their meetings to the public, a feat almost inconceivable today. A contemporary convention of the states would be a media circus. Moreover, it is hard to imagine that delegates from fifty states could agree even to frame a new charter, much less do it in four months.

The difficulties facing such an enterprise bring up an important issue. A modern constitutional convention would be hard pressed to reach consensus because the delegates would bring with them diverse interests and aims. What about back in 1787? Who were the Framers and what were their motives? If, as had been recorded, they were such a fractious bunch, how could they have reached accord so rapidly?

These questions have been the subject of lively debates among scholars. Many agree with historian Melvin I. Urofsky, who wrote of the Constitutional Convention, "Few gatherings in the history of this or any other country could boast such a concentration of talent." And, "despite [the Framers'] average age of forty-two [they] had extensive experience in government and were fully conversant with political theories of the Enlightenment." [5]

5. Melvin I. Urofsky, *A March of Liberty* (New York: Knopf, 1988), 89.

TABLE 1-1　The Virginia Plan, the New Jersey Plan, and the Constitution

Item	Virginia Plan	New Jersey Plan	Constitution
Legislature	Two houses	One house	Two houses
Legislative representation	Both houses based on population	Equal for each state	One house based on population; one house with two votes from each state
Legislative power	Veto authority over state legislation	Authority to levy taxes and regulate commerce	Authority to levy taxes and regulate commerce; authority to compel state compliance with national policies
Executive	Single; elected by legislature for a single term	Plural; removable by majority of state legislatures	Single; chosen by electoral college; removal by national legislature
Courts	National judiciary elected by legislature	No provision	Supreme Court appointed by executive, confirmed by Senate

The Framers were, to be sure, an impressive group. Thirty-three had served in the Revolutionary War, forty-two had attended the Continental Congress, and two had signed the Declaration of Independence; two would go on to serve as U.S. presidents, sixteen as governors, and two as chief justices of the United States.

Still, there are those who would take issue with Urofsky's statement. Because the Framers were a relatively homogeneous lot—all white men, many of whom had been educated at the country's best schools—some suggest that the document they produced was biased in various ways. For example, in 1987 Justice Thurgood Marshall said that the Constitution was "defective from the start," that its first words—"We the People"—excluded "the majority of American citizens," because it left out blacks and women. He further alleged that the Framers "could not have imagined, nor would they have accepted, that the document they were drafting would one day be construed by a Supreme Court to which had been appointed a woman and the descendent of an African slave." [6] Along the same lines is the point of view expressed by historian Charles Beard in his controversial work, *An Economic Interpretation of the Constitution of the United States*, which depicts the Framers as self-serving. Beard says the Constitution was an "economic document" devised to protect the "property interests" of those who wrote it.

Various scholars have refuted these allegations; Beard's work, in particular, has been largely negated by other studies.[7] Still, by today's standards it is impossible to deny that the original Constitution was a racist and sexist document or that the Framers wrote it in a way that benefited their class.

Given these charges, how has the Constitution survived for so long, particularly as the U.S. population has become increasingly heterogeneous? The answer lies in part with the Supreme Court, which generally has analyzed the document in light of its contemporary context. That is, some justices have viewed the Constitution as a living document and have sought to adapt it to the times. In addition, the Founders provided for an amending process to keep the document alive. That we can alter the Constitution to fit changing needs and expectations is obviously important. For example, the original document held a slave to be three-fifths of a person for the purposes of representation, and a slave had no rights of

6. Quoted in the *Washington Post*, May 7, 1987. See also Thurgood Marshall, "Reflections on the Bicentennial of the United States Constitution," *Harvard Law Review* 101 (1987): 1–5.

7. See, for example, Robert E. Brown's *Charles Beard and the Constitution* (Princeton, N.J.: Princeton University Press, 1956). Brown concludes that "we would be doing a grave injustice to the political sagacity of the Founding Fathers if we assumed that property or personal gain was their only motive" (p. 198).

citizenship at all. In the aftermath of the Civil War, the country recognized the outrageousness of such a provision and added three amendments to alter the status of blacks and provide full equality under law.

This is not to suggest that controversies surrounding the Constitution no longer exist. To the contrary, charges abound that the document has retained an elitist or otherwise biased flavor. Some argue that the amending process is too cumbersome, that it is too slanted toward the will of the majority. Others point to the Supreme Court as the culprit, asserting that its interpretation of the document—particularly at certain points in history—has reinforced the biases of the Framers.

Throughout this volume, you will have many opportunities to evaluate these controversies. They will be especially evident in cases involving economic liberties—those that ask the Court, in some sense, to adjudicate claims between the privileged and the underdogs in society. For now, let us consider some of the basic features of that controversial document—the U.S. Constitution.

UNDERLYING PRINCIPLES OF THE CONSTITUTION

Table I-1 sets forth the basic proposals considered at the convention and how they got translated into the Constitution. What it does not show are the fundamental principles underlying, but not necessarily explicit in, the Constitution. Three are particularly important: the separation of powers/checks and balances doctrine, which governs relations among the branches of government; federalism, which governs relations between the states and the national government; and individual rights and liberties, which govern relations between the government and the people.

Separation of Powers/Checks and Balances

One of the fundamental weaknesses of the Articles of Confederation was its failure to establish a strong and authoritative federal government. It created a national legislature, but that body had few powers, and those it did have were kept in check by the states. The new Constitution overcame this deficiency by creating a national government with three branches—the legislature, the executive, and the judiciary—and by providing each with significant power and authority within its sphere. Moreover, the three newly devised institutions were constitutionally and politically independent from one another.

The specific powers that each branch was given are spelled out in Articles I, II, and III of the Constitution. Section 8 of Article I is especially explicit, empowering Congress to lay and collect taxes, to regulate commerce, and so forth. Nonetheless, many questions have arisen over the scope of these powers as they are wielded by all three institutions. Consider a few examples:

Article I provides Congress with various authority over the U.S. military, for example, to provide and maintain a navy, to raise and support armies. But it does not specifically empower Congress to initiate and operate a draft. Does that omission mean that Congress may not do so?

Article II provides the president with the power to "nominate, and by and with the Advice and Consent of the Senate, [to] appoint . . . Officers of the United States," but it does not specifically empower the president to fire such officers. May the president independently dismiss appointees, or is the "advice and consent" of the Senate also necessary?

Article III provides the federal courts with the authority to hear cases involving federal laws. But it does not specifically empower these courts to strike down such laws if they are incompatible with the Constitution. Does that mean federal courts lack the power of judicial review?

These examples illustrate just a handful of the questions involving institutional powers the U.S. Supreme Court has addressed.

But institutional powers are only one side of the coin. The other side—constraints on those powers—is also worthy of consideration. As depicted in Figure I-2, the Framers not only endowed each branch with distinct power and authority over its own sphere, but also provided explicit checks on the exercise of those powers such that each branch can impose limits on the primary functions of the others. The Framers also made the institutions responsible to different sets of constituencies. They took these steps—creating an intricate system of checks and balances—because they feared the concentration of powers in a single branch.

Although this system has worked successfully, it too has produced numerous constitutional questions, many

FIGURE 1-2 The Separation of Powers/Checks and Balances

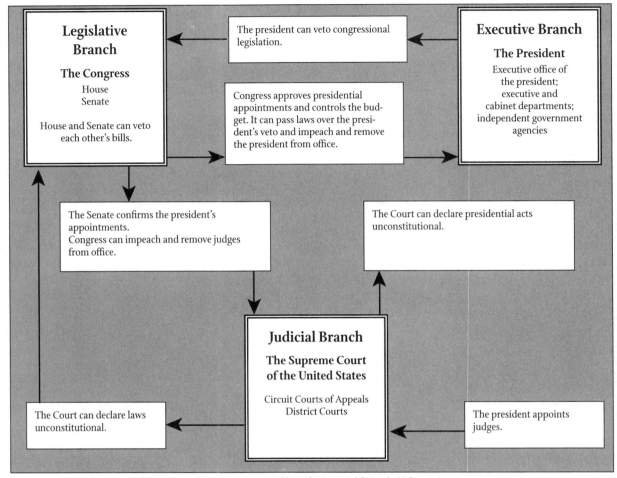

Legislative Branch

The Congress

House
Senate

House and Senate can veto each other's bills.

The president can veto congressional legislation.

Congress approves presidential appointments and controls the budget. It can pass laws over the president's veto and impeach and remove the president from office.

Executive Branch

The President
Executive office of the president; executive and cabinet departments; independent government agencies

The Senate confirms the president's appointments.
Congress can impeach and remove judges from office.

The Court can declare presidential acts unconstitutional.

Judicial Branch

The Supreme Court of the United States

Circuit Courts of Appeals
District Courts

The Court can declare laws unconstitutional.

The president appoints judges.

SOURCE: Janet A. Flammang et al., *American Politics in a Changing World* (Pacific Grove, Calif.: Brooks/Cole, 1990), 41.

of which become apparent when we have a politically divided government, such as a Democratic president and a Republican Congress, and one or the other is seeking to assert its authority. What is truly interesting about such cases is that they continue to appear at the Court's doorstep; despite the passage of more than two hundred years, the justices have yet to resolve all the "big" constitutional questions. During the past few decades the Court addressed many, including:

May Congress call for the creation of a commission, with members, including judges, to be appointed by the president, that would create mandatory sentencing guidelines for federal judges and that would be located within the judicial branch?

May Congress write into laws legislative veto provisions by which to nullify actions of the executive branch?

May Congress pass legislation requiring the attorney general to appoint an independent counsel to investigate allegations of wrongdoing within the executive branch?

In the cases and narrative that follow, you will develop an understanding of how the Court has addressed these and many other questions relating to the separation of powers/checks and balances system.

Federalism

Another flaw in the Articles of Confederation was the way they envisioned the relationship between the federal government and the states. As already noted, the national legislature was not only weak, it was more or less an apparatus controlled by the states. They had set up the Articles of Confederation and, therefore, they empowered Congress.

The U.S. Constitution overcame this liability in two ways. First, it created three branches of government, all with significant authority. Second, it set out a plan of operation for the exercise of state and federal power. Called federalism, it works today under the following constitutional guidelines:

The Constitution grants certain legislative, executive, and judicial powers to the national government. Those not granted to the national government are reserved to the states.

The Constitution makes the national government supreme. The Constitution, all laws passed pursuant to it, and treaties are the supreme law of the land. American citizens, most of whom are also state citizens, and state officials owe their primary allegiance to the national government.

The Constitution denies some powers to both national and state governments, some only to the national government, and still others only to the state governments.

By making the national government supreme in its spheres of authority, the Constitution corrected a defect in the Articles of Confederation. Nevertheless, and in spite of the best efforts of the Framers to spell out the nature of federal-state relations, the Constitution left open many questions. For example, the Constitution authorizes Congress to lay and collect taxes but is unclear as to whether the states also may exercise powers that are reserved to the federal government. States are not expressly prohibited from collecting taxes. Therefore, may Congress and the states both operate taxing systems?

As you know, the answer to this question is yes. However, why that is the case is not explicitly answered by the Constitution. As a result, elected government bodies through legislation and courts through interpretation have defined the specifics of state-federal relations. The Supreme Court, in particular, by defining the boundaries of federal and state power, has helped shape the contours of American federalism.

Individual Rights and Liberties

For many of the Framers, the most important purpose of the new Constitution was to safeguard individual rights and liberties. They created a limited government that would wield only those powers delegated to it and that could be checked by its own component parts—the states and the people. The majority of the Founders felt it unnecessary to load the Constitution with specific individual rights, such as those later spelled out in the Bill of Rights. As Alexander Hamilton put it, "The Constitution is itself . . . a Bill of Rights." Under it, the government could exercise only those functions specifically bestowed upon it; all other rights remained with the people. He and others felt that a list of rights might even be dangerous because it would inevitably leave some out.

For this reason and possibly others—for example, some argue that the Framers were too exhausted to continue—the Constitution was sent to the states without a bill of rights. That omission became the source of major controversy and served as the vehicle by which states exacted a compromise over the Constitution's ratification.

By January 1788, four states had ratified the Constitution, but then the pace began to slow. A movement opposed to ratification was growing in size and marshaling arguments to deter state convention delegates. What these opponents, the so-called Anti-Federalists, most feared was the Constitution's new balance of powers. They believed that strong state governments provided the best defense against the accumulation of too much power by the national government but that the Constitution tipped the scales the other way. These fears were countered by the self-labeled Federalists, who favored ratification of the Constitution.

Although the Federalists' arguments and writings took many forms, among the most important was a series of eighty-five articles published in New York newspapers under the pen name *Publius*. Written by John Jay, James Madison, and Alexander Hamilton, *The Federalist*

Papers—as we shall see throughout this book—continue to provide great insight into the objectives and intent of the nation's Founders.[8]

Debates between the Federalists and their opponents were often highly philosophical, with emphasis on the appropriate roles and powers of national institutions. Yet, within the states, ratification drives were full of the stuff of ordinary politics—making deals. The Massachusetts ratifying convention provides a case in point. After three weeks of debate among delegates, Federalist leaders realized that they would achieve victory only if they could attain Gov. John Hancock's support. They called on Hancock at home and proposed that he endorse ratification on condition that a series of amendments be tacked on for consideration by Congress. The governor agreed so long as he would become president of the United States if Virginia failed to ratify or George Washington refused to serve. Or he would accept the vice presidency. With the deal cut, Hancock went to the convention to propose a compromise—the ratification of the Constitution with amendments. The delegates went along with the plan, making Massachusetts the sixth state to ratify.[9]

This compromise—the call for a bill of rights—caught on, and Madison began to advocate it whenever close votes were likely. As it turned out, he and other Federalists needed to mention the point quite often: of the nine states ratifying after January 1788, seven recommended that the new Congress consider amendments. New York and Virginia probably would not have agreed to the Constitution without such an addition, and Virginia called for a second constitutional convention for this purpose. Other states began revising their own wish lists of specific rights they wanted put into the document.[10]

The Federalists realized that if they did not accede to state demands, either the Constitution would not be ratified or a new constitutional convention would be necessary. Since neither alternative was particularly attractive,

it was agreed to amend the document as soon as the new government came into power. And with that promise came the ratification of the Constitution by the requisite number of states just a year after it had been drafted.

The eventual ratification of the Bill of Rights, on December 15, 1791, quieted those who had voiced objections. But the guarantees it contained continue to serve as fodder for debate and, most relevant here, for Supreme Court litigation. Many of these debates involve the construction of specific guarantees, such as free speech and free exercise of religion, under which individuals seek relief when governments allegedly infringe upon their rights. They also involve clashes between the authority of the government to protect the safety, health, morals, and general welfare of citizens and the right of individuals not to be deprived of their liberty without due process of law. For example, may government force employers to pay their employees a certain wage, or does that requirement infringe on the employer's liberty? May government force homeowners to vacate their houses if it needs the property to construct a road and is willing to pay the "fair market value," or does that interfere with a right contained in the Fifth Amendment? The answers to this question and others like it reveal the contours of government power in relation to individual rights.

READINGS

Ackerman, Bruce. *We the People, Volume I: Foundations.* Cambridge: Harvard University Press, 1991.

Amar, Akhil Reed. *The Bill of Rights: Creation and Reconstruction.* New Haven: Yale University Press, 1998.

Anastapolo, George. *The Constitution of 1787: A Commentary.* Baltimore: Johns Hopkins University Press, 1989.

Anderson, Thornton. *Creating the Constitution: The Convention of 1787 and the First Congress.* University Park: Pennsylvania State University Press, 1993.

Bailyn, Bernard. *The Ideological Origins of the American Revolution.* Cambridge: Harvard University Press, 1967.

Beard, Charles A. *An Economic Interpretation of the Constitution.* New York: Macmillan, 1935.

Brown, Robert E. *Charles Beard and the Constitution.* Princeton, N.J.: Princeton University Press, 1956.

Cogan, Neil, ed. *The Complete Bill of Rights: The Drafts, Debates, Sources, and Origins.* New York: Oxford University Press, 1997.

Cornell, Saul. *The Other Founders: Anti-Federalism and Dissension Tradition in America, 1788–1828.* Chapel Hill: University of North Carolina Press, 1999.

---

8. *The Federalist Papers* are available at: *http:memory.loc.gov/const/fed/fedpapers.html.*

9. Joseph T. Keenan, *The Constitution of the United States* (Chicago: Dorsey Press, 1988), 32–33.

10. Alpheus T. Mason, *The States Rights Debate,* 2nd ed. (New York: Oxford University Press, 1972), 92–93.

Ellis, Joseph. *Founding Brothers: The Revolutionary Generation.* New York: Knopf, 2000.

Farber, Daniel A., and Suzanna Sherry. *A History of the American Constitution.* St. Paul, Minn.: West Publishing, 1990.

Farrand, Max. *The Framing of the Constitution of the United States.* New Haven: Yale University Press, 1913.

Grofman, Bernard, and Donald Wittman. *The Federalist Papers and the New Institutionalism.* Flemington, N.J.: Agathon Press, 1989.

Jensen, Merrill. *The New Nation: A History of the United States During the Confederation, 1781–1789.* New York: Knopf, 1950.

Kramnick, Isaac, ed. *The Federalist Papers.* New York: Penguin, 1987.

Levy, Leonard W. *Origins of the Bill of Rights.* New Haven: Yale University Press, 1999.

Levy, Leonard W., and Dennis J. Mahoney, eds. *The Framing and Ratification of the Constitution.* New York: Macmillan, 1987.

Main, Jackson Turner. *The Anti-Federalists: Critics of the Constitution, 1781–1788.* New York: W. W. Norton, 1974.

Marshall, Thurgood. "Reflections on the Bicentennial of the United States Constitution." *Harvard Law Review* 101 (1987): 1–5.

McDonald, Forrest. *E Pluribus Unum.* Boston: Houghton Mifflin, 1965.

Rakove, Jack. *Original Meanings: Politics and Ideas in the Making of the Constitution.* New York: Knopf, 1996.

Riker, William H. *The Strategy of Rhetoric: Campaigning for the American Constitution.* New Haven: Yale University Press, 1996.

Roche, John P. "The Founding Fathers: A Reform Caucus in Action." *American Political Science Review* 55 (1961): 799–816.

Rutland, Robert Allen. *The Birth of the Bill of Rights, 1776–1791.* Boston: Northeastern University Press, 1997.

Smith, David G. *The Convention and the Constitution.* New York: St. Martin's Press, 1965.

Warren, Charles. *The Making of the Constitution.* Boston: Little, Brown, 1928.

Wood, Gordon S. *The Creation of the American Republic.* Chapel Hill: University of North Carolina Press, 1969.

CHAPTER 1

UNDERSTANDING THE U.S. SUPREME COURT

THIS BOOK is devoted to narrative and opinion excerpts showing how the U.S. Supreme Court has interpreted the Constitution. As a student approaching constitutional law, perhaps for the first time, you may think it is odd that the subject requires 657 pages of text. After all, in length, the Constitution and the amendments to it could fit easily into many Court decisions. Moreover, the document itself—its language—seems so clear.

First impressions, however, can be deceiving. Even apparently clear constitutional scriptures do not necessarily lend themselves to clear constitutional interpretation. For example, according to Article I, Section 2, the president "shall be Commander in Chief of the Army and Navy of the United States." Sounds simple enough; but could you, based on those words, answer the following questions, all of which have been posed to the Court?

• May the president, during times of war, order a blockade of certain American ports?
• May Congress delegate to the president the power to order an arms embargo against nations at war?
• May the president, during times of war, order that "traitors" be tried by military tribunals rather than civilian courts?
• May the president, during times of international crisis, authorize the creation of military camps to intern potential "traitors" to prevent sabotage?

What these and other questions arising from the different guarantees contained in the Constitution illustrate is that a gap sometimes exists between the document's words and reality. Although the language seems explicit, its meaning can be elusive and difficult to follow. Accordingly, justices have developed various approaches to resolving disputes.

But, as Figure 1-1 shows, a great deal happens before the justices actually decide cases. We begin our discussion with a brief overview of the steps depicted in the figure. Next, we consider explanations for the choices justices make at the final and most important stage, the resolution of disputes.

PROCESSING SUPREME COURT CASES

During the 2002–2003 term more than 8,255 cases arrived at the Supreme Court's doorstep, but the justices decided, with a written opinion, only 84.[1] The disparity between the number of parties that want the Court to resolve their disputes and the number the Court agrees to resolve raises some important questions: How do the justices decide which cases to hear? What happens to the cases it rejects? Those it agrees to resolve? We address these and other questions by describing how the Court processes its cases.

---

1. Data courtesy of the clerk of the U.S. Supreme Court.

FIGURE 1-1 The Processing of Cases

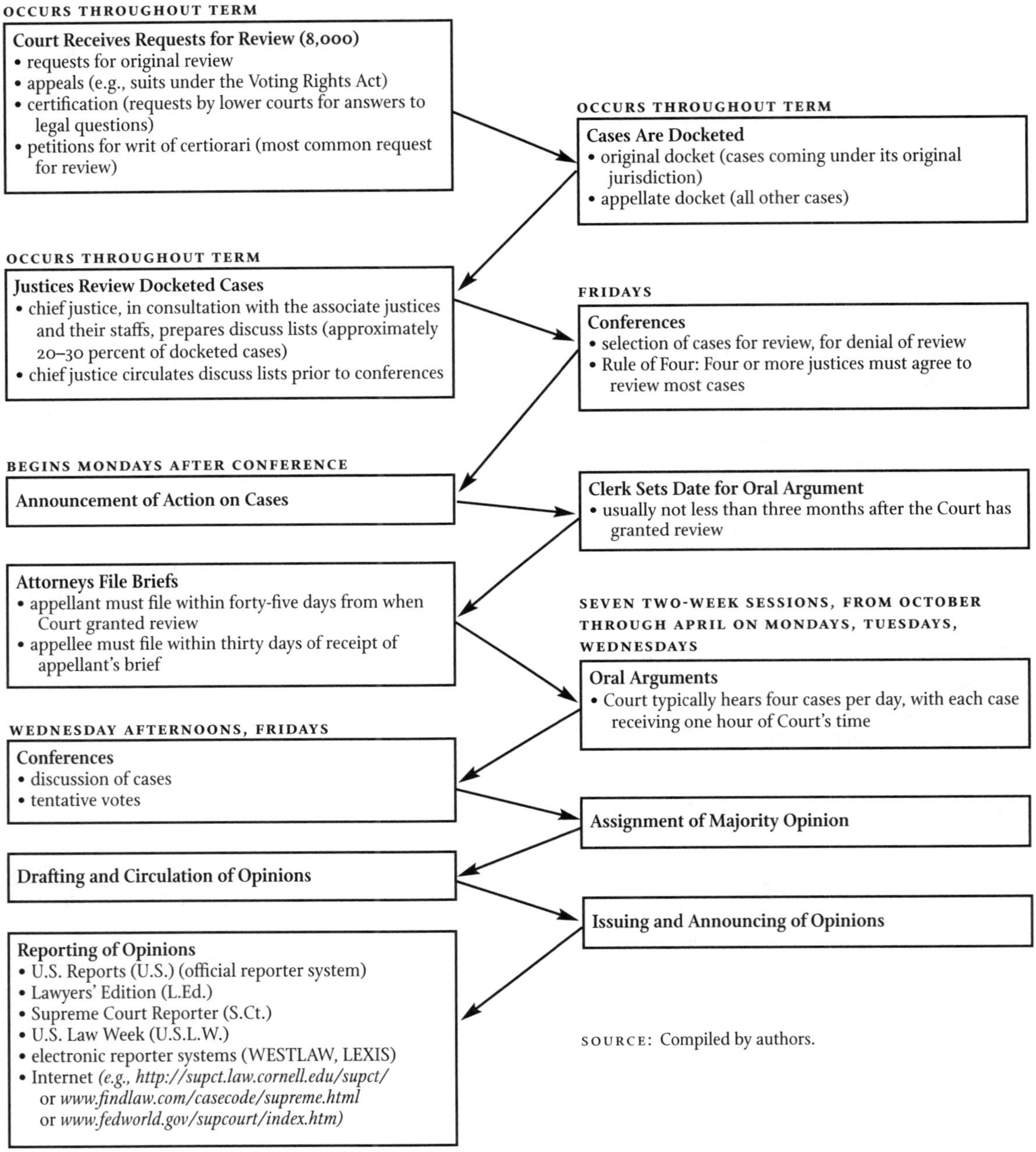

OCCURS THROUGHOUT TERM

Court Receives Requests for Review (8,000)
- requests for original review
- appeals (e.g., suits under the Voting Rights Act)
- certification (requests by lower courts for answers to legal questions)
- petitions for writ of certiorari (most common request for review)

OCCURS THROUGHOUT TERM

Cases Are Docketed
- original docket (cases coming under its original jurisdiction)
- appellate docket (all other cases)

OCCURS THROUGHOUT TERM

Justices Review Docketed Cases
- chief justice, in consultation with the associate justices and their staffs, prepares discuss lists (approximately 20–30 percent of docketed cases)
- chief justice circulates discuss lists prior to conferences

FRIDAYS

Conferences
- selection of cases for review, for denial of review
- Rule of Four: Four or more justices must agree to review most cases

BEGINS MONDAYS AFTER CONFERENCE

Announcement of Action on Cases

Clerk Sets Date for Oral Argument
- usually not less than three months after the Court has granted review

Attorneys File Briefs
- appellant must file within forty-five days from when Court granted review
- appellee must file within thirty days of receipt of appellant's brief

SEVEN TWO-WEEK SESSIONS, FROM OCTOBER THROUGH APRIL ON MONDAYS, TUESDAYS, WEDNESDAYS

Oral Arguments
- Court typically hears four cases per day, with each case receiving one hour of Court's time

WEDNESDAY AFTERNOONS, FRIDAYS

Conferences
- discussion of cases
- tentative votes

Assignment of Majority Opinion

Drafting and Circulation of Opinions

Issuing and Announcing of Opinions

Reporting of Opinions
- U.S. Reports (U.S.) (official reporter system)
- Lawyers' Edition (L.Ed.)
- Supreme Court Reporter (S.Ct.)
- U.S. Law Week (U.S.L.W.)
- electronic reporter systems (WESTLAW, LEXIS)
- Internet (e.g., http://supct.law.cornell.edu/supct/ or www.findlaw.com/casecode/supreme.html or www.fedworld.gov/supcourt/index.htm)

SOURCE: Compiled by authors.

Deciding to Decide: The Supreme Court's Caseload

As the figures for the 2002–2003 term indicate, the Court heard and decided only 1 percent of the cases it received. This percentage is quite low, but it follows the general trend in Supreme Court decision making: the number of requests for review has increased dramatically over the last century, but the number of cases the Court formally decides each year has not increased. So, for example, in 1930 the Court agreed to decide 159 of the 726 disputes pending before it. Six decades later, in 1990, the number of cases granted review fell to 141, but the sum total of pending disputes had risen to 6,302—or nearly nine times greater than the 1930 figure.[2]

How do these cases get to the Supreme Court? How do the justices decide which will get a formal review and which will be rejected? Why do they make the choices that they do? Let us consider each of these questions, for they are fundamental to an understanding of judicial decision making.

How Cases Get to the Court: Jurisdiction and the Routes of Appeal. Cases come to the Court in one of four ways: either by a request for review under the Court's original jurisdiction or by three appellate routes—appeals, certification, and petitions for writs of certiorari (*see Figure 1-1*). Chapter 2 explains more about the Court's original jurisdiction, as it is central to understanding the landmark case of *Marbury v. Madison* (1803). Here, it is sufficient to note that original cases are those that have not been heard by any other court. Article III of the Constitution authorizes such suits in cases involving ambassadors from foreign countries and those to which a state is a party. But, because congressional legislation permits lower courts to exercise concurrent authority over most cases meeting Article III requirements, the Supreme Court does not have exclusive jurisdiction over them. Consequently, the Court normally accepts, on its original jurisdiction, only those cases in which one state is suing another (usually over a disputed boundary) and sends

the rest back to the lower courts for an initial ruling. That is why, in recent years, original jurisdiction cases comprise only a tiny fraction of the Court's overall docket—between one and five cases per term.

Most cases reach the Court under its appellate jurisdiction, meaning that a lower federal or state court has already rendered a decision and one of the parties is asking the Supreme Court to review that decision. As Figure 1-2 shows, such cases typically come from one of the U.S. courts of appeals or state supreme courts. The U.S. Supreme Court, the nation's highest tribunal, is the court of last resort.

To invoke the Court's appellate jurisdiction, litigants can take one of three routes, depending on the nature of their dispute: appeal as a matter of right, certification, and certiorari. Cases falling into the first category (normally called "on appeal") involve issues Congress has determined are so important that a ruling by the Supreme Court is necessary. Before 1988 these included cases in which a lower court declared a state or federal law unconstitutional or in which a state court upheld a state law challenged as violating the U.S. Constitution. Although the justices were supposed to decide such appeals, they often found ways to deal with them more expediently—by either failing to consider them or issuing summary decisions (shorthand rulings). Finally, in 1988, at the Court's urging, Congress virtually eliminated "mandatory" appeals. Today the Court is legally obliged to hear only those few cases (typically involving the Voting Rights Act) appealed from special three-judge district courts.

A second, rarely used, route to the Court is certification. Under the Court's appellate jurisdiction and by an act of Congress, lower appellate courts can file writs of certification, asking the justices to respond to questions aimed at clarifying federal law. Because only judges may use this route, very few cases come to the Court this way. Moreover, the justices may accept a question certified to them or dismiss it.

That leaves the third and most common appellate path, a request for a writ of certiorari (from the Latin meaning "to be informed"). In a petition for a writ of certiorari, the litigants desiring Supreme Court review ask

---

2. Data are from Lee Epstein, Jeffrey A. Segal, Harold J. Spaeth, and Thomas G. Walker, *The Supreme Court Compendium: Data, Decisions, and Developments,* 3rd ed. (Washington, D.C.: CQ Press, 2003), Tables 2-5 and 2-6.

FIGURE 1-2 The American Court System

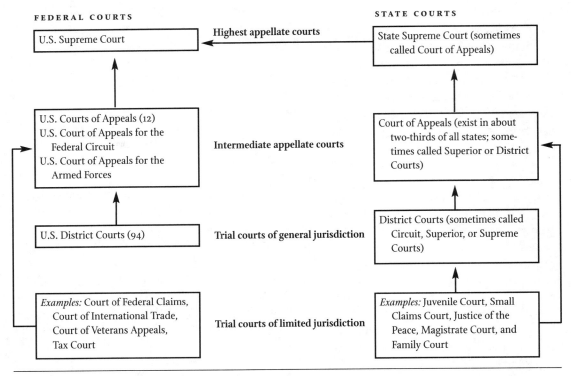

FEDERAL COURTS

STATE COURTS

U.S. Supreme Court — **Highest appellate courts** — State Supreme Court (sometimes called Court of Appeals)

U.S. Courts of Appeals (12)
U.S. Court of Appeals for the Federal Circuit
U.S. Court of Appeals for the Armed Forces — **Intermediate appellate courts** — Court of Appeals (exist in about two-thirds of all states; sometimes called Superior or District Courts)

U.S. District Courts (94) — **Trial courts of general jurisdiction** — District Courts (sometimes called Circuit, Superior, or Supreme Courts)

Examples: Court of Federal Claims, Court of International Trade, Court of Veterans Appeals, Tax Court — **Trial courts of limited jurisdiction** — *Examples:* Juvenile Court, Small Claims Court, Justice of the Peace, Magistrate Court, and Family Court

SOURCE: Compiled by authors.

the Court, literally, to become "informed" about their cases by requesting the lower court to send up the record. Most of the eight thousand or so cases that arrive each year come as requests for certiorari. The Court, exercising its ability to choose the cases to review, grants "cert" to about 1 percent of the petitions. Granting cert means that the justices have decided to give the case full review; denying cert means that the decision of the lower court remains in force.

In sum, while Article III of the Constitution enables the Court to decide cases that have not been heard by any other court, the vast majority of disputes that reach the justices have already been resolved by another judicial body. But there are other ways to design a legal system. For example, in societies that have created a single constitutional court that tribunal may have a judicial monopoly on interpreting matters of constitutional law; it may be the only forum in which citizens can bring constitutional claims *(see Box 1-1)*.

How Does the Court Decide? The Case Selection Process. Regardless of the specific design of a legal system, in many countries jurists must confront the task of "deciding to decide," that is, choosing which cases, among many hundreds or even thousands, they will actually resolve. The U.S. Supreme Court is no exception, with the job of "deciding to decide"—or identifying those cases to which it will grant cert—presenting something of a mixed blessing to the justices. Selecting the approximately one hundred cases to review from the large number of requests is an arduous undertaking that requires the justices or their law clerks to look over hundreds of thousands of pages of briefs and other memoranda.

BOX 1-1   THE AMERICAN LEGAL SYSTEM IN GLOBAL PERSPECTIVE

THE AMERICAN legal system can be described as *dual, parallel,* and (for the most part) *three tiered.* It is dual because both one federal system and fifty state systems coexist, each ruling on disputes falling under its particular purview. This does not mean, however, that state courts never hear cases involving claims made under the U.S. Constitution or that federal courts necessarily shun cases arising out of state law. In fact, the U.S. Supreme Court can review cases involving federal questions on which state supreme courts have ruled and can strike down state laws if they are incompatible with the U.S. Constitution. Similarly, many cases arising from state law and heard in state courts also contain federal issues that must be resolved.

Differences exist among the states, but most today roughly parallel the federal system. Trial courts—the lowest rungs on the ladder—are the entry points into the system *(see Figure 1-2).* In the middle of the ladder are appellate courts, those that upon request review the records of trial court proceedings. Finally, both have supreme courts, bodies that provide final answers to legal questions in their own domains.

Although a supreme court sits atop each ladder, the U.S. Supreme Court plays a unique role—it is the apex of both state and federal court systems. Because it can hear cases and ultimately overturn the rulings of federal and state court judges, it is presumably *the* authoritative legal body in the United States.

Many nations have created legal systems that, to greater or lesser extents, resemble the American system. For example, Japan, whose constitutional document was largely drafted by Americans, also has a three-tiered structure. Cases begin at the district (trial) court level, move to high courts (Japan's version of mid-level appellate courts) and, finally, to the Supreme Court.[1] But other nations—first Germany and Italy, and later Belgium, Portugal, South Africa, Spain, and most of the countries of Eastern Europe—took a much different approach. In these countries, the highest court is not a supreme court but a single constitutional court, which has a judicial monopoly on interpreting matters of constitutional law. These constitutional courts are not a part of the "ordinary" court system; litigants do not typically petition the justices to review decisions of lower courts. Rather, when judges confront a law whose constitutionality they doubt, they are obliged to send the case directly to the constitutional court. This tribunal receives evidence on the constitutional issue, sometimes gathers evidence on its own, hears arguments, perhaps consults sources that counsel overlooked, and hands down a decision. But, unlike in the United States, the constitutional court does not decide the case because it has not heard a case; it has only addressed a question of constitutional interpretation. Although the court publishes an opinion justifying its ruling and explaining the controlling principles, the case still must be decided by regular tribunals. In some countries—for example, Germany, Italy, and Russia—public officials also may bring suits in their constitutional court to challenge the legitimacy of legislative, executive, or judicial acts, and, under some circumstances, private citizens may start similar litigation. Where judicial action is challenged, the constitutional court in effect reviews a decision of another court, but the form of the action is very different from an appeal in the United States.

This type of court system is often called "centralized" because the power of judicial review—that is, the power to review government acts for their compatibility with the nation's constitution and strike down those acts that are not compatible—rests in one constitutional court; other courts are typically barred from exercising judicial review, although they may refer constitutional questions to the constitutional tribunal. In contrast, the U.S. system is deemed "decentralized" because ordinary courts—not just supreme courts—can engage in judicial review, We shall return to this distinction in Chapter 2 *(see Box 2-1).*

---

1. Japan has summary courts with jurisdiction over minor civil and criminal cases. District courts (trial courts of general jurisdiction) can hear civil appeals from summary courts. For more details, see Herbert Jacob, ed., *Courts, Law, and Politics* (New Haven: Yale University Press, 1996), chap. 6.

However, the ability to exercise discretion frees the Court from one of the major constraints on judicial bodies: the lack of agenda control. The justices may not be able to reach out and propose cases for review the way members of Congress can propose legislation, but the enormous number of petitions ensures that they can resolve at least some issues important to them.

Many scholars have tried to determine what makes a case "certworthy," that is, worthy of review by the Supreme Court. Before we review some of their findings, let us consider the case selection process itself. The original pool of about eight thousand petitions faces several checkpoints along the way *(see Figure 1-1, page 14)*, which significantly reduce the amount of time the Court, acting as a collegial body, spends on deciding what to decide. The staff members in the office of the Supreme Court clerk act as the first gatekeepers. When a petition for certiorari arrives, the clerk's office examines it to make sure it is in proper form, that it conforms to the Court's precise rules. For example, briefs must "be produced on paper that is opaque, unglazed, 6⅛ by 9¼ inches in size, and not less than 60 pounds in weight, and shall have margins of at least three fourths of an inch on all sides." Exceptions are made for litigants who cannot afford to pay the Court's fees. The rules governing these petitions, known as in forma pauperis briefs, are somewhat looser, allowing indigents to submit briefs on 8½ by 11-inch paper. The Court's major concern, or so it seems, is that the document "be legible." [3] The clerk's office gives all acceptable petitions an identification number, called a "docket number," and forwards copies to the chambers of the individual justices. Each justice reviews the petitions, making independent decisions about which cases he or she feels are worthy of a full hearing. Some have their clerks read and summarize all the petitions; most use the "certiorari pool system" in which clerks from different chambers collaborate in reading and then writing memoranda on the petitions.[4] Either way, the justices use their clerks' reports as a basis to make case selection decisions.

During this process, the chief justice plays a special role, serving as yet another checkpoint on petitions. Before the justices meet to make case selection decisions, the chief circulates a "discuss list," containing those cases he feels worthy of full Court consideration; any justice may add cases to this list but may not subtract any. About 20 percent to 30 percent of the cases that come to the Court make it to the list and are actually discussed by the justices in conference. The rest are automatically denied review, and the lower court decision stands.[5]

This much we know. Because the Court's conferences are attended only by the justices and held in private, we cannot say precisely what transpires. We can offer only a rough picture based on scholarly writings, the comments of justices, and our examination of the private papers of a few retired justices. These sources tell us that the discussion of each petition begins with the chief justice presenting a short summary of the facts and, typically, stating his vote. The associate justices, who sit at a rectangular table in order of seniority, then comment on each petition, with the most senior justice speaking first and the newest member last. The associate justices usually provide some indication of how they will vote on the merits of the case if it is accepted. Indeed, as Figure 1-3 shows, the justices record certiorari and merits votes in their docket books. But, given the large number of petitions, the justices apparently discuss few cases in detail.

By tradition, the Court adheres to the so-called Rule of Four: it grants certiorari to those cases receiving the affirmative vote of at least four justices. The Court identifies the cases accepted and rejected on a "certified orders list," which is released to the public. For cases granted certiorari or in which probable jurisdiction is noted, the clerk informs participating attorneys, who then have specified time limits in which to turn in their written legal arguments (briefs), and the case is scheduled for oral argument.

---

3. Rules 33 and 39 of the Rules of the Supreme Court of the United States. All Supreme Court rules are available at: *www.law.cornell.edu/rules/supct/overview.html.*

4. Supreme Court justices are authorized to hire four law clerks each. Typically, these clerks are outstanding recent graduates of the nation's top law schools.

5. For information on the discuss list, see Gregory A. Caldeira and John R. Wright, "The Discuss List: Agenda Building in the Supreme Court," *Law and Society Review* 24 (1990): 807–836.

FIGURE 1-3 A Page from Justice Brennan's Docket Books

	HOLD FOR	CERT.		JURISDICTIONAL STATEMENT				MERITS		MOTION		ABSENT	NOT VOTING
		G	D	N	POST	DIS	AFF	REV	AFF	G	D		
Burger, Ch. J.			✓					✓	✓				
Brennan, J.		✓	✓										
Stewart, J.		✓						✓					
White, J.								✓	✓				
Marshall, J.			✓										
Blackmun, J.		✓	✓					✓					
Powell, J.		✓						✓					
Rehnquist, J.								✓	✓				
Stevens, J.			✓										

SOURCE: Dockets of Justice William J. Brennan Jr., Manuscript Division, Library of Congress, Washington, D.C.
    NOTE: In the CERT. column, G = grant the petition; D = deny the petition. In the MERITS column, REV = reverse the decision of the court below; AFF = affirm the decision of the court below.

Considerations Affecting Case Selection Decisions. In this section, we consider the path of the cases the Court agrees to decide. But first, we take up an equally intriguing issue—two sets of factors scholars have identified as affecting the Court's review decision: legal considerations and political considerations.[6]

Legal considerations are listed in Rule 10, which the Court has established to govern the certiorari decision-making process:

Review on a writ of certiorari is not a matter of right, but of judicial discretion. A petition for a writ of certiorari will be granted only for compelling reasons. The following, although neither controlling nor fully measuring the Court's discretion, indicate the character of the reasons the Court considers:

(a) a United States court of appeals has entered a decision in conflict with the decision of another United States court of appeals on the same important matter; has decided an important federal question in a way that conflicts with a decision by a state court of last resort; or has so far departed from the ac-

cepted and usual course of judicial proceedings, or sanctioned such a departure by a lower court, as to call for an exercise of this Court's supervisory power;

(b) a state court of last resort has decided an important federal question in a way that conflicts with the decision of another state court of last resort or of a United States court of appeals;

(c) a state court or a United States court of appeals has decided an important question of federal law that has not been, but should be, settled by this Court, or has decided an important federal question in a way that conflicts with relevant decisions of this Court.

A petition for a writ of certiorari is rarely granted when the asserted error consists of erroneous factual findings or the misapplication of a properly stated rule of law.

To what extent do the considerations outlined in Rule 10 affect the Court? The answer is mixed. On the one hand, the Court seems to follow its dictates. In particular, the presence of actual conflict between or among federal courts, a major concern of Rule 10, substantially increases the likelihood of review; if actual conflict is present in a case, there is a 33 percent chance that the Court will grant review—as compared with the usual 1–2 percent certiorari rate.[7] On the other hand, as political scientists Gregory A. Caldeira and John R. Wright explain, Rule 10 is not all that helpful in understanding "how the Court

6. Some scholars have noted a third set: procedural considerations. These emanate from Article III, which—under the Court's interpretation—places constraints on the ability of federal tribunals to hear and decide cases. These constraints are reviewed in Chapter 2. Here we note the two that are particularly important for the review decision: the case must be appropriate for judicial resolution in that it presents a real "case" and "controversy" (justiciability) and the appropriate person must bring the case (standing). Unless these procedural criteria are met, the Court—at least theoretically—will deny review. It is worth noting, however, that because most petitions meet these criteria, they are not especially useful in helping the justices make their case selection decisions.

7. See Gregory A. Caldeira and John R. Wright, "Organized Interests and Agenda Setting in the U.S. Supreme Court," *American Political Science Review* 82 (1988): 1109–1127.

makes gatekeeping decisions." [8] The Court may use the existence of actual conflict as a threshold (cases that do not present conflict *may* be rejected); it does not accept all cases with conflict because there are too many. [9]

The legal considerations listed in Rule 10 may act as constraints on the justices' behavior, but they do not necessarily further our understanding of what occurs in cases meeting the criteria. That is why scholars have looked elsewhere—to *political* factors that may influence the Court's case selection process. Three are particularly important. The first is the U.S. solicitor general (SG), the attorney who represents the U.S. government before the Supreme Court. Simply stated, when the SG files a petition, the Court is very likely to grant certiorari. In fact, the Court accepts about 70 percent to 80 percent of the cases in which the federal government is the petitioning party.

Scholars have posited a number of reasons for the solicitor general's success as a petitioner. One is that the Court is cognizant of the SG's special role. A presidential appointee whose decisions often reflect the administration's philosophy, the SG also represents the interests of the United States. As the nation's highest court, the Supreme Court cannot ignore these interests. In addition, the justices rely on the solicitor general to act as a filter; that is, they expect the SG to examine carefully the cases to which the government is a party and bring only the most important to their attention. Finally, because solicitors general are involved in so much Supreme Court litigation, they acquire a great deal of knowledge about the Court that other litigants do not. They are "repeat players" who know the "rules of the game" and can use them to their advantage. For example, they know how to structure their petitions to attract the attention and interest of the justices.

The second political factor is the amicus curiae (friend of the court) brief. These briefs may be filed by interest groups at the certiorari stage before the Court makes its selection decision *(see Box 1-2)*. Research by Caldeira and Wright shows that amicus briefs significantly enhance a case's chance to be heard, and multiple briefs have a greater effect. [10] Another interesting finding of their study is that even when groups file *in opposition* to granting certiorari, they increase—rather than decrease—the probability that the Court will hear the case.

What can we make of these findings? Most important is this: although the justices may not be strongly influenced by the arguments contained in these briefs (if they were, why would briefs in opposition to certiorari have the opposite effect?), they seem to use them as cues. In other words, because amicus curiae briefs filed at the certiorari stage are somewhat uncommon—less than 10 percent of all petitions are accompanied by amicus briefs—they single out a case, to draw the justices' attention. If major organizations are sufficiently interested in an appeal to file briefs in support of (or against) Court review, then the petition for certiorari is probably worth the justices' serious consideration.

In addition, we have strong reasons to suspect that a third political factor—the ideology of the justices—affects actions on certiorari petitions. Researchers tell us that the justices during the liberal period under Chief Justice Earl Warren (1953–1969) were more likely to grant review to cases in which the lower court reached a conservative decision so that they could reverse, while those of the moderately conservative Court during the years of Chief Justice Warren Burger (1969–1985) took liberal results to reverse. It would be difficult to believe that the current justices would be any less likely than their predecessors to vote on the basis of their ideology. Scholarly studies also suggest that justices engage in strategic voting behavior at the cert stage. In other words, justices are forward thinking; they consider the implications of their cert vote for the later merits stage, asking themselves: If I vote to grant a particular petition, what are the odds of my position winning down the road? As one justice explained his calculations, "I might think the Nebraska Supreme Court made a horrible decision, but I wouldn't want to take the case, for if we take the case and affirm it, then it would become precedent." [11]

8. Ibid., 1115.

9. In fact, during any given term, the Court rejects hundreds of cases in which real conflicts exist. See Lawrence Baum, *The Supreme Court*, 7th ed. (Washington, D.C.: CQ Press, 2001), 111.

10. Caldeira and Wright, "Organized Interests and Agenda Setting."

11. Quoted in H. W. Perry, *Deciding to Decide* (Cambridge: Harvard University Press, 1991), 200.

BOX 1-2 THE AMICUS CURIAE BRIEF

The amicus curiae practice probably originates in Roman law. A judge would often appoint a *consilium* (officer of the court) "to advise him on points on which he [was] in doubt."[1] That may be why the term amicus curiae translates from the Latin as "friend of the court." But today it is the rare amicus who is a friend of the court. Rather, contemporary briefs almost always are a friend of a party, supporting one side over the other at the certiorari and merits stages. Consider the brief filed in *United States v. Virginia* (1996), the cover of which is reprinted here. In that case, the National Women's Law Center and other organizations supported the federal government's request to have the Court hear the case. They, along with the United States, believed that the court below erred when it allowed the state of Virginia to maintain a single-sex admissions policy at Virginia Military Institute. These groups were anything but neutral participants.

How does an organization become an amicus curiae participant in the Supreme Court of the United States? Under the Court's rules, groups wishing to file an amicus brief at the cert or merits stage must obtain the written consent of the parties to the litigation (the federal and state governments are exempt from this requirement). If the parties refuse to give their consent, the group can file a motion with the Court asking for its permission. The Court today almost always grants these motions.

---

1. Frank Covey Jr., "Amicus Curiae: Friend of the Court," *De Paul Law Review* 9 (1959): 33.

In the
Supreme Court of the United States
October Term, 1994
June 26, 1995
NO. 94-1941

————•————

United States of America, *Petitioner*

— v. —

Commonwealth of virginia, et al., *Respondents.*

————

ON PETITION FOR A WRIT OF CERTIORARI TO THE UNITED STATES
COURT OF APPEALS FOR THE FOURTH CIRCUIT

————

BRIEF OF AMICI CURIAE NATIONAL WOMEN'S LAW CENTER, AMERICAN CIVIL LIBERTIES UNION, THE AMERICAN ASSOCIATION OF UNIVERSITY WOMEN, B'NAI B'RITH WOMEN, CENTER FOR ADVANCEMENT OF PUBLIC POLICY, CENTER FOR WOMEN POLICY STUDIES, COALITION OF LABOR UNION WOMEN, CONNECTICUT WOMEN'S EDUCATION AND LEGAL FUND, EQUAL RIGHTS ADVOCATES, FEDERALLY EMPLOYED WOMEN, INC., NATIONAL COUNCIL OF JEWISH WOMEN, INC., NATIONAL COUNCIL OF NEGRO WOMEN, NATIONAL EDUCATION ASSOCIATION, THE NATIONAL GAY AND LESBIAN TASK FORCE, NATIONAL ORGANIZATION FOR WOMEN, THE NATIONAL WOMAN'S PARTY, NATIONAL WOMEN'S CONFERENCE COMMITTEE, NATIONAL WOMEN'S POLITICAL CAUCUS, NOW LEGAL DEFENSE AND EDUCATION FUND, TRIAL LAWYERS FOR PUBLIC JUSTICE, WOMEN EMPLOYED, WOMEN'S LAWPROJECT, AND THE WOMEN'S LEGAL DEFENSE FUND IN SUPPORT OF THE PETITION

Marcia D. Greenberger, Deborah L. Brake
National Women's Law Center, 11 Dupont Circle, Suite 800,
Washington, D.C. 20036

Sara L. Mandelbaum, Steven R. Shapiro, Janet Gallagher
American Civil Liberties Union, 132 W. 43rd Street, New York, NY 10036

Robert N. Weiner, *Counsel for Record,* Walter J. Rockler,
Peter G. Neiman, Mark Eckenwiler, Arnold & Porter
555 12th Street, N.W., Washington, D.C. 20004
(202) 942-5000
Counsel for Amici Curiae

The Role of Attorneys

Once the Supreme Court agrees to decide a case, the clerk of the Court informs the parties. The parties have two methods of presenting their side of the dispute to the justices—written and oral arguments.

Written Arguments. Written arguments, called briefs, are the major vehicles for parties to Supreme Court cases to document their positions. Under the Court's rules, the appealing party (known as the appellant or petitioner) must submit its brief within forty-five days of the time the Court grants certiorari; the opposing party (known as the appellee or respondent) has thirty days after receipt of the appellant's brief to respond with arguments urging affirmance of the lower court ruling.

The Court has specific rules covering the presentation and format of the briefs. For example, the briefs of both parties must be submitted in forty copies and not exceed fifty pages in length. Rule 24 outlines the material that briefs must contain, such as a description of the questions presented for review, a list of the parties, and a statement describing the Court's authority to hear the case.

The clerk sends the briefs to the justices, who normally study them before oral argument. Written briefs are important because the justices may use them to formulate the questions they ask the lawyers representing the parties. The briefs also serve as a permanent record of the positions of the parties, available to the justices for consultation after oral argument when they decide the case outcome. A well-crafted brief can place into the hands of the justices arguments, legal references, and suggested remedies that later may be incorporated into the opinion.

In addition to the briefs submitted by the parties to the suit, Court rules allow interested persons, organizations, and government units to participate as amici curiae on the merits—just as they are permitted to file such briefs at the review stage. Those wishing to submit friend of the court briefs must obtain the written permission of the parties or the Court. Only the federal government and state governments are exempt from this requirement (*see Box 1-2, page 21*).

Oral Arguments. Attorneys also have the opportunity to present their cases orally before the justices. Each side has thirty minutes to convince the Court of the merits of its position and to field questions the justices may raise. The justices are allowed to interrupt the attorneys at any time with comments and questions, as an exchange between Justice Byron White and Sarah Weddington, the attorney representing Jane Roe in *Roe v. Wade* (1973), indicates. White got the ball rolling when he asked Weddington to respond to an issue her brief had not addressed: whether abortions should be performed during all stages of pregnancy or should somehow be limited. The following discussion ensued:

WHITE: And the statute doesn't make any distinction based upon at what period of pregnancy the abortion is performed?

WEDDINGTON: No, Your Honor. There is no time limit or indication of time, whatsoever. So I think—

WHITE: What is your constitutional position there?

WEDDINGTON: As to a time limit—

WHITE: What about whatever clause of the Constitution you rest on—Ninth Amendment, due process . . . —that take you right up to the time of birth?

WEDDINGTON: It is our position that the freedom involved is that of a woman to determine whether or not to continue a pregnancy. Obviously I have a much more difficult time saying that the State has no interest in late pregnancy.

WHITE: Why? Why is that?

WEDDINGTON: I think that's more the emotional response to a late pregnancy, rather than it is any constitutional—

WHITE: Emotional response by whom?

WEDDINGTON: I guess by persons considering the issue outside the legal context, I think, as far as the State—

WHITE: Well, do you or don't you say that the constitutional—

WEDDINGTON: I would say constitutional—

WHITE: —right you insist on reaches up to the time of birth, or—

WEDDINGTON: The Constitution, as I read it . . . attaches protection to the person at the time of birth.

In the Court's early years, there was little doubt about the importance of such exchanges, of oral arguments in general. Because attorneys did not always prepare written briefs, the justices relied on orals to learn about the cases and to help them marshal their arguments for the next stage. Moreover, orals were considered important public events, with the most prominent attorneys of the day participating. Arguments often went on for days: *Gibbons v. Ogden* (1824), the landmark Commerce Clause case, was argued for five days, and *McCulloch v. Maryland* (1819), the litigation challenging the constitutionality of the national bank, took nine days to argue.

Scholars, lawyers, and judges have questioned the effectiveness of oral argument and its role in decision making. Chief Justice Earl Warren maintained that they made little difference to the outcome. Once the justices have read the briefs and studied related cases, most have relatively firm views on how the case should be decided, and orals change few minds. Justice William J. Brennan Jr., however, maintained that they are extremely important because they help justices to clarify core arguments. Orals may not be good predictors of the Court's final votes, but they provide some indication of what the justices believe to be the central issues of the case. In addition, we should not forget the symbolic importance of the oral argument stage: it is the only part of the Court's decision-making process that occurs in public.

It is unlikely that this debate will ever be resolved, but you now have the opportunity to form your own opinion. Political scientist Jerry Goldman has made the oral arguments of many cases available on the World Wide Web *(www.oyez.org/oyez/frontpage)*. Throughout the book, you will find the URLs (universal resource locators) of the specific pages to which you can navigate to listen to arguments in the cases you are reading.

The Supreme Court Decides: Some Preliminaries

After the Court hears oral arguments, it meets in a private conference to discuss the case and to take a preliminary vote. Following is a description of the Court's conference procedures, along with two events that happen after the conference: the assignment of the opinion of the Court and the opinion circulation period.

The Conference In these days of "government in the sunshine" the Court stands alone in its insistence that its decisions take place in a private conference, with no one in attendance except the justices. Congress has agreed to this demand by exempting the federal courts from open government and freedom of information legislation. There are two basic reasons. First, the Supreme Court—which, unlike Congress, lacks an electoral connection—is supposed to base its decisions on factors other than public opinion. Opening up deliberations to press scrutiny, for example, might encourage the justices to take notice of popular sentiment, which is not supposed to influence them. Or so the argument goes. Second, although in conference the Court reaches tentative decisions on cases, the opinions explaining the decisions remain to be written. This process can take many weeks or even months, and it is not until the opinions have been written, circulated, and approved that the decision is final. Because the decisions can have a major impact on politics and the economy, any party having advance knowledge of case outcomes could use that information for unfair business and political advantage.

The system works so well that, with only a few exceptions, the justices have not experienced information leaks, and it is impossible to know precisely what occurs in the deliberation of any particular case. We can, however, piece together the procedures and the general nature of the Court's discussions from the papers of retired justices and the comments of others. We have learned the following. First, we know that the chief justice presides over the deliberations. He calls up the case for discussion and then presents his views on the issues and how the case should be decided. The remaining justices state their views and votes in order of seniority.

The level and intensity of discussion, as Justice Brennan's notes from conference deliberations reveal, differ from case to case. In some, it appears that the justices had very little to say. The chief presented his views, and the rest noted their agreement. In others, every Court member had something to add. Whether the discussion is subdued or lively, it is unclear to what extent conferences affect the final decisions. It would be unusual for a justice to enter the conference room without having reached a tentative position on the cases to be discussed; after all, he or she has read the briefs and listened to oral arguments. But the conference is the first opportunity the justices have to review cases as a group and size up the positions of their colleagues. This sort of information, as we shall see, may be important as the justices begin the process of crafting and circulating opinions.

Opinion Assignment. The conference typically leads to a tentative outcome and vote. What happens at this point is critical because it determines who assigns the writing of the opinion of the Court—the Court's only authoritative policy statement, the only one that establishes precedent. Under Court norms, the chief justice assigns the writing of the opinion when he votes with the majority. The chief may decide to write the opinion or assign it to one of the other justices who voted with the majority. When the chief justice votes with the minority, the assignment task falls to the most senior member of the Court who voted with the majority.

In making these assignments, the chief justice (or the senior associate in the majority) takes many factors into account. Forrest Maltzman and Paul J. Wahlbeck examined the opinion assignments of Chief Justice Rehnquist.[12] These scholars discovered that the chief tries to equalize the distribution of the Court's workload. This concern makes sense: the Court will not run efficiently, given the burdensome nature of opinion writing, if some justices are given many more assignments than others. The research also suggests that Rehnquist takes into account the justices' particular areas of expertise. He recognizes that some of his colleagues have more knowledge of particular areas of the law than others, and he tends to assign accordingly. By encouraging specialization, Rehnquist may be increasing the quality of opinions and reducing the time to write them. Finally, Maltzman and Wahlbeck noted that when a case was decided by a one-vote margin, Rehnquist assigns the opinion to a moderate member of the majority rather than to an extreme member. His reasoning seems clear: if the writer in a close case drafts an opinion with which other members of the majority are uncomfortable, the opinion may drive justices to the other side, causing the majority to become a minority. Rehnquist tries to minimize this risk by asking justices squarely in the middle of the majority coalition to write.

Opinion Circulation. Regardless of the factors the chief considers in making assignments, one thing is clear: the opinion writer is a critical player in the opinion circulation phase, which eventually leads to the final decision of the Court. The writer begins the process by circulating an opinion draft to the others.

Once the justices receive the first draft of the opinion, they have many options. First, they can join the opinion, meaning that they agree with it and want no changes. Second, they can ask the opinion writer to make changes, that is, *bargain* with the writer over the content of and even the disposition—to reverse or affirm the lower court ruling—offered in the draft. The following memo sent from Brennan to White is exemplary: "I've mentioned to you that I favor your approach to this case and want if possible to join your opinion. If you find the following suggestions . . . acceptable, I can join you."[13]

Third, they can tell the opinion writer that they plan to circulate a dissenting or concurring opinion. A dissenting opinion means that the writer disagrees with the disposition the majority opinion reaches and with the rationale it invokes; a concurring opinion generally agrees with the disposition but not with the rationale. Finally, justices can tell the opinion writer that they await further writings, meaning that they want to study various dissents or concurrences before they decide what to do.

As justices circulate their opinions and revise them—the average majority opinion undergoes three to four revisions in response to colleagues' comments—many different opinions on the same case, at various stages of development, will be floating around the Court over the course of several months. Because this process is replicated for each case the Court decides with a formal written opinion, it is possible that scores of different opinions may be working their way from office to office at any point in time.

Eventually, the final version of the opinion is reached, and each justice expresses a position in writing or by signing an opinion of another justice. This is how the final vote is taken. When all of the justices have declared themselves, the only remaining step is for the Court to announce its decision and the vote to the public.

---

12. "May It Please the Chief? Opinion Assignments in the Rehnquist Court," *American Journal of Political Science* 40 (1996): 421–443.

13. Memorandum from Justice Brennan to Justice White, 12/9/76, re: 75-104, *United Jewish Organizations v. Carey.*

SUPREME COURT DECISION MAKING: THE ROLE OF LAW

So far, we have examined the processes the justices follow to reach decisions on the disputes brought before them. We answered basic questions about the institutional procedures the Court uses to carry out its responsibilities. The questions we did not address were why the justices reach particular decisions and what forces play a role in determining their choices. As you might imagine, there is no shortage of responses to these questions. They can be roughly categorized into two groups. One focuses on the role of the law in determining how justices interpret the Constitution, emphasizing, among other things, the importance of its words, the intent of the Framers, and precedent (or previously decided constitutional rulings). The other emphasizes the role of politics, stressing, again among other factors, the particular ideological views of the justices, the mood of the public, and the political preferences of the executive and legislative branches.

Often commentators define these two sides as "should" versus "do." That is, they say the justices *should* interpret the Constitution in line with, say, the language of the text of the document or in accord with precedent. That is because justices are supposed to shed all of their personal biases, preferences, and partisan attachments when they take their seats on the bench. But, it is argued, justices *do not* shed these biases, preferences, and attachments; rather, their decisions often reflect the justices' own politics or the political views of those around them.

To the extent that approaches grounded in law originated to answer the question of how justices *should* decide pending disputes, we understand why the difference between the two groups is often cast in terms of "should" versus "do." But, for several reasons, we ask you to think about whether, in fact, the justices actually do use these "should" approaches to reach decisions, and not merely to camouflage their politics. One reason is that the justices themselves often say they look to the intent of the Framers, the words of the Constitution, previously decided cases, and other "law" approaches to resolve disputes because they consider them appropriate criteria for reaching decisions. Another is that some scholars express

agreement with the justices, arguing that Court members cannot follow their own personal preferences, the whims of the public, or other nonlegally relevant factors "if they are to have the continued respect of their colleagues, the wider [legal] community, citizens, and leaders." Rather, they "must be principled in their decision-making process." [14] Whether they are principled in their decision making is for you to determine as you read the cases to come. First, however, it is necessary to have some sense of approaches grounded in law—or what some call modes of constitutional interpretation—that the justices frequently say they employ. In what immediately follows, we consider seven of the most important and describe the philosophies that support their use: original intent or understanding, textualism, polls of other jurisdictions, logical reasoning, stare decisis, balancing approaches, and cost-benefit analysis.

Original Intent or Understanding

It was more than two hundred years ago that the Supreme Court first invoked the term *the intention of the Framers.* In *Hylton v. United States* (1796) the Court said, "It was . . . obviously the intention of the framers of the Constitution, that Congress should possess full power over every species of taxable property, except exports. The term taxes, is generical, and was made use of to vest in Congress plenary authority in all cases of taxation." [15] In *Hustler Magazine v. Falwell* (1988) the Court used the same grounds to find that cartoon parodies, however obnoxious, constitute expression protected by the First Amendment.

Undoubtedly, justices over the years have frequently looked to the intent of the Framers to reach conclusions about the disputes before them.[16] But why? What possible relevance could the Framers' intentions have for

14. Ronald Kahn, "Institutional Norms and Supreme Court Decision-Making: The Rehnquist Court on Privacy and Religion," in *Supreme Court Decision-Making: New Institutionalist Approaches,* ed. Cornell W. Clayton and Howard Gillman (Chicago: University of Chicago Press, 1999), 176.

15. Example cited by Boris I. Bittker in "The Bicentennial of the Jurisprudence of Original Intent: The Recent Past," *California Law Review* 77 (1989): 235.

16. Given the subject of this volume, we deal here exclusively with the intent of the Framers of the U.S. Constitution and its amendments, but one also could apply this approach to statutory construction by considering the intent of those who drafted the laws in question.

today's controversies? Advocates of this approach offer several answers. First, they assert that the Framers acted in a calculated manner; that is, they knew what they were doing, so why should we disregard their precepts? One adherent said, "Those who framed the Constitution chose their words carefully; they debated at great length the most minute points. The language they chose meant something. It is incumbent upon the Court to determine what that meaning was." [17]

Second, if they scrutinize the intent of the Framers, justices can deduce "constitutional truths," which they can apply to cases. Doing so, proponents argue, would produce neutral principles of law and eliminate value-laden decisions.[18] Consider an example involving nation-state relations. Suppose the federal government enacted legislation forcing states to pay their employees a minimum wage. Justices could look at such a law in several ways. One who favors states' rights might conclude that the Tenth Amendment, which says, "The Powers not delegated to the United States by the Constitution . . . are reserved to the States," bars the federal government from interfering with the relationship between a state and its employees. A jurist who favors a strong national government might reach the opposite conclusion. They disagree because their policy orientations dictate different outcomes. According to the original intent school of thought, however, neither is using proper jurisprudence: policy or ideological preferences should not creep into law. Therefore, originalists favor an examination of the Framers' intent as a way to keep the law value neutral. As scholar Raoul Berger writes:

For a "proper understanding" of federalism, nowhere mentioned in the Constitution, we must look at the explanations of the Founders, what is characterized as the "original intention." That canon of construction is centuries old, as the Court itself pointed out, saying "[t]he intention of the lawmaker is the law," rising even above the text.[19]

Finally, supporters of this mode of analysis argue that it fosters stability in law. They assert that the law today is far too fluid; it changes with the ideological whims of the justices, creating havoc for those who must implement and interpret Court decisions. Lower court judges, lawyers, and even ordinary citizens do not know if today's rights will exist tomorrow. Following a jurisprudence of original intent would eliminate such confusion because it provides a principle that justices would consistently follow.

Many Supreme Court opinions contemplate the original intent of the Framers, and at least one justice on the current Court—Clarence Thomas—regularly invokes originalism to answer a wide range of questions, from limits on campaign spending to the appropriate balance of power between the states and the federal government.[20]

Such a jurisprudential course would have angered Thomas's predecessor, Thurgood Marshall, who did not believe that the Constitution was "forever 'fixed' at the Philadelphia Convention." Nor did Marshall find "the wisdom, foresight, and sense of justice exhibited by the framers"—in light of the 1787 Constitution's treatment of women and blacks—"particularly profound." [21]

Marshall is far from the only critic of an originalist approach to the Constitution; it has generated many others over the years. One reason for the controversy is that the doctrine became highly politicized in the 1980s. Those who advocated it, particularly Edwin Meese, an attorney general in President Ronald Reagan's administration, and defeated Supreme Court nominee Robert Bork, were widely viewed as conservatives who were using the doctrine to attain their own ideological ends.

Others joined Marshall, however, in raising several more concrete objections to this jurisprudence. Justice Brennan in 1985 argued that if the justices employed only this approach, the Constitution would lose its applicability and be rendered useless:

We current Justices read the Constitution in the only way that we can: as Twentieth Century Americans. We look to the history of the time of the framing and to the intervening history

17. Edwin Meese III, Address before the American Bar Association, July 9, 1983, Washington, D.C.

18. See, for example, Robert Bork, "Neutral Principles and Some First Amendment Problems," *Indiana Law Journal* 47 (1971): 1–35.

19. Raoul Berger, *Federalism: The Founders' Design* (Norman: University of Oklahoma Press, 1987), 15–16.

20. By the same token, many scholars advocate originalism. For a particularly intelligent defense, see Keith E. Whittington, *Constitutional Interpretation: Textual Meaning, Original Intent, and Judicial Review* (Lawrence: University Press of Kansas, 1999).

21. Thurgood Marshall, "Reflections on the Bicentennial of the United States Constitution," *Harvard Law Review* 101 (1987): 1.

of interpretation. But the ultimate question must be, what do the words of the text mean in our time. For the genius of the Constitution rests not in any static meaning it might have had in a world that is dead and gone, but in the adaptability of its great principles to cope with current problems and current needs.[22]

Another criticism is that the Constitution embodies not one intent, but many. Political scientists Jeffrey A. Segal and Harold J. Spaeth pose some interesting questions: "Who were the Framers? All fifty-five of the delegates who showed up at one time or another in Philadelphia during the summer of 1787? Some came and went.... Some probably had not read [the Constitution]. Assuredly, they were not all of a single mind." [23]

Finally, from which sources should justices divine the original intentions of the Framers? They could look at the records of the constitutional debates and at the Founders' journals and papers, but some of what passes for "records" of the Philadelphia convention is jumbled, even forged.[24] During the debates, the secretary became confused and thoroughly botched the minutes; and James Madison, who took the most complete and probably the most reliable notes on what was said, edited them after the convention adjourned.

Those who rely on the original intent might claim that the condition of the historic record is less a barrier to their approach. The popular debate on ratification was full; millions of pamphlets (heavily outnumbering the entire population) argued for and against the new political system. This mass of literature, however, demonstrates not one but maybe dozens of understandings of what the new constitution would mean. In other words, they often fail to provide a single clear message. Justice Robert H. Jackson made this point when he wrote:

Just what our forefathers did envision, or would have envisioned had they foreseen modern conditions, must be divined from materials almost as enigmatic as the dreams Joseph was called upon to interpret for Pharaoh. A century and a half of partisan debate and scholarly specification yields no net result but only supplies more or less apt quotations from respected sources on each side of any question. They largely cancel each other.[25]

Textualism I: Literalism

On the surface, textualism resembles the doctrine of original intent: it puts a premium on the Constitution. But this is where the similarity ends. In an effort to prevent the infusion of new meanings from sources outside the text of the Constitution, adherents of original intent seek to deduce constitutional truths by examining the *intended* meanings behind the words. Textualists look no further than the words of the Constitution to reach decisions. Justice Antonin Scalia *(see Box 1-3)* explained the differences between the approaches in a 1996 speech:

I belong to a school, a small but hardy school, called "textualists" or "originalists." That used to be "constitutional orthodoxy" in the United States. The theory of originalism treats a constitution like a statute, and gives it the meaning that its words were understood to bear at the time they were promulgated. You will sometimes hear it described as the theory of original intent. You will never hear me refer to original intent, because as I say I am first of all a textualist, and secondly an originalist. If you are a textualist, you don't care about the intent, and I don't care if the framers of the Constitution had some secret meaning in mind when they adopted its words. I take the words as they were promulgated to the people of the United States, and what is the fairly understood meaning of those words.[26]

Under Scalia's brand of textualism, it is fair game for justices to go beyond the literal meaning of the words and consider what they would have ordinarily meant to the people of that time—a type of textual analysis to which we return presently. To other textualists, whom we might call pure textualists or *literalists*, it is only the

22. William J. Brennan Jr., Address to the Text and Teaching Symposium, Georgetown University, October 12, 1985, Washington, D.C.

23. Jeffrey A. Segal and Harold J. Spaeth, *The Supreme Court and the Attitudinal Model Revisited* (New York: Cambridge University Press, 2002), 68. See also William Anderson, "The Intention of the Framers: A Note on Constitutional Interpretation," *American Political Science Review* 49 (1955): 340–352.

24. We adopt the next few sentences from Walter F. Murphy, C. Herman Pritchett, and Lee Epstein, *Courts, Judges, and Politics*, 5th ed. (New York: McGraw-Hill, 2002).

25. *Youngstown Sheet & Tube Co. v. Sawyer* (1952).

26. Antonin Scalia, "A Theory of Constitutional Interpretation," Remarks at The Catholic University of America, Washington, D.C., October 18, 1996.

BOX 1-3 ANTONIN SCALIA (1986–)

Antonin Scalia was the first person of Italian ancestry to be appointed to the Supreme Court and the first Roman Catholic since William J. Brennan Jr. was named in 1956. He was born March 11, 1936, in Trenton, New Jersey, to Eugene Scalia, a professor of Romance languages who had emigrated from Italy, and Catherine Panaro Scalia, a schoolteacher whose parents also had emigrated from Italy. Scalia grew up in Queens, where he attended Jesuit schools.

Scalia graduated from Georgetown University and Harvard Law School. The year he graduated from law school, he married Maureen McCarthy. Scalia spent seven years in private practice in Cleveland, Ohio, with the law firm of Jones, Day, Reavis, and Pogue, but left practice to teach at the University of Virginia School of Law in the late 1960s. Early in his career, he developed a strong individual style marked by a keen legal intellect and a certain whimsicality. He made playful use of language, would sometimes sing at public appearances, and liked to entertain friends with his piano playing.

Scalia was drawn to government service during the Nixon administration, which he joined in 1971 as general counsel of the White House Office of Telecommunications Policy. From that post, he became chairman of the Administrative Conference of the United States, and in 1974 he joined the Justice Department as assistant attorney general in charge of the Office of Legal Counsel, the same post William H. Rehnquist held from 1969 to 1971.

Scalia remained in that position through the Nixon and Ford administrations. He returned to teaching and held posts at Georgetown University Law School, the University

of Chicago Law School, and Stanford University Law School. He was then named by President Reagan to the U.S. Court of Appeals for the District of Columbia Circuit in 1982.

Scalia developed a reputation as an outspoken conservative with very definite views of the law. He believed the power of the courts was limited. He also took a strong interest in the interpretation of statutes, arguing that the only legitimate guide for judges is the actual text of a statute and its related provisions. In 1986 Reagan promoted him to the U.S. Supreme Court.

True to his pattern on the appeals court, Scalia has established himself as one of the most conservative members of the Supreme Court. He is not willing to acknowledge any individual right not clearly set forth in the language of the Constitution. In *Webster v. Reproductive Health Services* (1989) and *Cruzan v. Director, Missouri Department of Health* (1990), to cite two examples, Scalia rejected any constitutional basis for the right to an abortion or the right to refuse life-sustaining treatment. In 1996 he wrote an angry dissent in *Romer v. Evans*, arguing that Colorado voters had the right to amend their state constitution to ban any local ordinances attempting to protect homosexuals. Seven years later, his equally angry dissent in *Lawrence v. Texas* accused the justices of bending to the whims of a "law-profession culture that has largely signed on to the so-called homosexual agenda."

SOURCE: Adapted from Joan Biskupic and Elder Witt, *Guide to the U.S. Supreme Court*, 3rd ed. (Washington, D.C.: Congressional Quarterly, 1997), 957–958.

words in the constitutional text, and the words alone, that justices ought consider.

And it is this distinction—between original intent and literalism—that can lead to some extraordinary differences in case outcomes. Consider, for example, a case dealing with congressional hearings on subversive activ-

ity aimed at the overthrow of the U.S. government. Suppose that during the course of its investigation Congress orders a witness, a member of a radical organization, to answer questions about her and others' activities. The witness declines to do so on the ground that the First Amendment protects political speech. Originalists would say that "speech advocating the violent overthrow is . . . not [protected] 'political speech' as that term must be defined by a Madisonian system of government." [27] They would argue that Congress could compel the witness to testify. Pure literalists would scrutinize the words of the First Amendment—"Congress shall make no law . . . abridging the freedom of speech"—and read them literally: no law means no law. Therefore, any government action infringing on speech, even a law that prohibits expression advocating the overthrow of the government, would violate the First Amendment.

Original intent and literalism sometimes overlap. When it comes to the right to privacy, particularly its use to create other rights, such as legalized abortion, *some* original intent adherents and literalists would reach the same conclusion: it does not exist. The former would argue that it was not the intent of the Framers to confer privacy; the latter, that because the Constitution fails to guarantee explicitly this right, Americans do not automatically possess it.

Although strains of literalism run through the opinions of many justices, Hugo Black is most closely associated with this view. During his thirty-four-year tenure on the Court, Justice Black reiterated the literalist philosophy. His own words best describe his position:

My view is, without deviation, without exception, without any ifs, buts, or whereases, that freedom of speech means that government shall not do anything to people . . . either for the views they have or the views they express or the words they speak or write. Some people would have you believe that this is a very radical position, and maybe it is. But all I am doing is following what to me is the clear wording of the First Amendment. . . . As I have said innumerable times before I simply believe that "Congress shall make no law" means Congress shall make no law. . . . Thus we have the absolute command of the First Amendment that no law shall be passed by Congress abridging freedom of speech or the press.[28]

As this statement indicates, Black applied literalism most often to cases involving the First Amendment, but he also invoked it to examine other kinds of constitu-

tional disputes. In *Youngstown Sheet & Tube Co. v. Sawyer* (1952), the Court was asked to determine whether President Harry S. Truman could order the secretary of commerce to seize the nation's steel mills, which because of an impending strike were under threat of being shut down. Truman argued that, with the United States at war in Korea, the action was necessary "to avert a national catastrophe." Even so, Black refused to relent. Indeed, his response for the majority was classic literalism: "It is clear that if the President had the authority to issue the order he did, it must be found in some provision of the Constitution. . . . The order cannot properly be sustained [because] . . . the Constitution limits his functions in the lawmaking process to the recommending of laws he thinks wise and the vetoing of laws he thinks bad."

Why did Black advocate literalism? Like original intent adherents, he viewed it as a value-free form of jurisprudence. If justices looked only at the words of the Constitution, their decisions would not reflect ideological or political values, but rather those of the document. Black's opinions provide good illustrations. Although he almost always supported claims of free *speech* against government challenges, he refused to extend constitutional protection to *expression* that was not precisely speech. For example, he asserted that activities such as flag burning and the wearing of armbands, even if designed to express political views, fell outside of the speech protected by the First Amendment.

Moreover, literalists maintain that their approach is superior to the doctrine of original intent. They say that some provisions of the Constitution are so transparent that, were the government to violate them, justices could "almost instantaneously and without analysis identify the violation"; they would not need to undertake an extensive search to uncover the Framers' understanding.[29] Often-cited examples include the "mathematical" provisions of the Constitution, such as the command that the president's term be four years, and that the president be at least thirty-five years old.

---

27. Bork, "Neutral Principles," 31.
28. Hugo L. Black, *A Constitutional Faith* (New York: Knopf, 1969), 45–46.

29. We draw this material and the related discussion to follow from Mark V. Tushnet, "A Note on the Revival of Textualism," *Southern California Law Review* 58 (1985): 683–700.

Despite the seeming logic of these justifications and the high regard scholars have for Black, many have actively attacked his brand of jurisprudence. Some assert that it led him to take some rather odd positions, particularly in cases involving the First Amendment. For example, most analysts and justices—even those considered liberal—agree that obscene materials fall outside of First Amendment protection and that states can prohibit their dissemination. But, in opinion after opinion, Black clung to the view that no publication could be banned on the grounds that it was obscene.

A second objection is that literalism can result in inconsistent outcomes. For example, is it really sensible for Black to hold that obscenity is constitutionally protected, while other types of expression, such as desecration of the flag, are not? There were times when even Black could not abide by his own approach. During World War II he allowed President Franklin D. Roosevelt to issue an order "excluding all persons of Japanese descent" from certain designated areas on the West Coast, but recall that later he would hold that President Truman lacked authority to seize the nation's steel mills. How did he justify the earlier decision? He said, "Because we are at war with the Japanese Empire . . . and . . . because Congress, reposing its confidence in this time of war in our military leaders—as inevitably it must—determined that they should have the power to do just that." [30] The decision may have been reasonable to many in the context of the times, but certainly it is difficult to justify under a literal reading of the Constitution.

Segal and Spaeth raise yet a third problem with literalism: it supposes a precision in the English language that does not exist. Not only may words, including those used by the Framers, have multiple meanings, but also the meanings themselves may be contrary. For example, the common legal word *sanction,* as Segal and Spaeth note, means to punish *and* to approve.[31] How, then, would a literalist construe it?

Finally, even when the words are crystal clear, literalism may not be on firm ground. Despite the precision of the mathematical provisions, Frank Easterbrook has suggested that they, like all the others, are loaded with "reasons, goals, values, and the like." [32] The Framers might have imposed the presidential age limit "as a percentage of average life expectancy"—to ensure that presidents have a good deal of practical political experience before ascending to the presidency and little opportunity to engage in politicking after they leave—or "as a minimum number of years after puberty"—to guarantee that they are sufficiently mature but not to unduly limit the pool of eligible candidates. Seen in this way, the words "thirty-five Years" in the Constitution may not have much value: they may be "simply the framers' shorthand for their more complex policies, and we could replace them by 'fifty years' or 'thirty years' without impairing the integrity of the constitutional structure." [33] More generally, as Justice Oliver Wendell Holmes Jr. once put it, "A word is not a crystal, transparent and unchanged, it is the skin of a living thought and may vary greatly in color and content according to the circumstances and the time in which it is used." [34]

Textualism II: Meaning of the Words

As we noted above, advocates of textual approaches suggest that justices need look no further than the words of the Constitution to reach decisions. But as we also suggested, adherents do not necessarily approach the task of interpreting the "words" in the same way. While Black claimed to be loath to go beyond the literal meaning of the words, Scalia is not so reticent. Indeed, under his "meaning of the words" brand of textualism, it is appropriate for justices to ask what the words would have ordinarily meant to the people of that time.[35]

Seen in this way, the "meaning of the words" approach to constitutional interpretation has its roots in both literalism and originalism: it emphasizes the words of the Constitution at the time the Framers wrote them. But there are differences. While literalists stress the words

30. *Korematsu v. United States* (1944).

31. Segal and Spaeth, *The Supreme Court and the Attitudinal Model Revisited,* 54.

32. Frank Easterbrook, "Statutes' Domains," *University of Chicago Law Review* 50 (1983): 536.

33. Tushnet, "A Note on the Revival of Textualism," 686.

34. *Towne v. Eisner* (1918).

35. See his "Originalism: The Lesser Evil," *University of Cincinnati Law Review* 57 (1989): 849–866.

themselves, this mode highlights their meaning; and while originalism focuses on the intent behind phrases, at least some variants of the meaning of the words approach emphasize "lexicographic skill"—asking justices to interpret the words of the Constitution according to their meaning at the time they were written.[36]

The merits of this approach are similar to those of literalism and originalism. By focusing on how the Framers defined their own words and then applying their definitions to disputes over those constitutional provisions containing them, this approach seeks to generate value-free and ideology-free jurisprudence. Indeed, one of the most important developers of this approach, William W. Crosskey, specifically embraced it to counter "sophistries" of the "living-document" view of the Constitution.[37]

Chief Justice Rehnquist's opinion in *Nixon v. United States* (1993) provides a particularly good illustration of the value of this approach. Here, the Court considered a challenge to the procedures the Senate used to impeach a federal judge, Walter L. Nixon Jr. Rather than having the entire Senate try the case, a special twelve-member committee heard it and reported to the full body. Nixon argued that this procedure violated Article I of the Constitution, which states, "The Senate shall have the sole power to try all Impeachments." But before he addressed Nixon's claim, Rehnquist sought to determine whether courts had any business resolving such disputes. He used a meaning of the words approach to consider the word *try* in Article I:

Petitioner argues that the word "try" in the first sentence imposes by implication an additional requirement on the Senate in that the proceedings must be in the nature of a judicial trial. . . . There are several difficulties with this position which lead us ultimately to reject it. The word "try," both in 1787 and later, has considerably broader meanings than those to which petitioner would limit it. Older dictionaries define try as "[t]o examine" or "[t]o examine as a judge." See 2 S. Johnson, A Dictionary of the English Language (1785). In more modern usage the term has various meanings. For example, try can mean "to examine or investigate judicially," "to conduct the trial of," or

"to put to the test by experiment, investigation. . . ." Webster's Third New International Dictionary (1971).

Like the other modes we have examined, the meaning of the words approach is not without its critics. One objection is similar to that leveled at originalism: it is too static. Political scientist C. Herman Pritchett noted that like originalism, it can "make a nation the prisoner of its past, and reject any constitutional development save constitutional amendment." [38]

Another criticism is that it may be just as difficult for justices to establish the meaning of words as it is to establish the original intent behind them. Attempting to understand what the Framers meant by each word can be a far more daunting task in the run-of-the-mill case than it was for Rehnquist in *Nixon*. It might even require the development of a specialized dictionary, which could take years of research to compile and still not have any value—determinate or otherwise. Besides, scholars argue, even if we could create a dictionary that would help shed light on the meaning of particular words, it would tell us little about the significance of such constitutional phrases as "due process of law" or "cruel and unusual punishment."

This last criticism becomes even more poignant when we consider that Crosskey did, in fact, develop "a specialized dictionary of the eighteenth-century word-usages, and political and legal ideas." He believed that such a work was "needed for a true understanding of the Constitution." But some scholars have been skeptical of the understandings, many of which were highly "unorthodox," to which it led him.[39] The same charge has been leveled at a more recent work on textualism, *The Bill of Rights: Creation and Reconstruction* by Akhil Reed Amar.[40]

Where does Professor Amar's textualism lead him? It should make us a bit suspicious that it leads him to disagree with what

36. David W. Rohde and Harold J. Spaeth, *Supreme Court Decision Making* (San Francisco: W. H. Freeman, 1976), 41.

37. W. W. Crosskey, *Politics and the Constitution in the History of the United States* (Chicago: University of Chicago Press, 1953), 1172–1173.

38. C. Herman Pritchett, *Constitutional Law of the Federal System* (Englewood Cliffs, N.J.: Prentice-Hall, 1984), 37.

39. Bittker, "The Bicentennial of the Jurisprudence of Original Intent," 237–238. Some applauded Crosskey's conclusions. Charles E. Clark, for example, in "Professor Crosskey and the Brooding Omnipresence of Erie-Tompkins," *University of Chicago Law Review* 21 (1953): 24, called it "a major scholastic effort of our times." Others were appalled. See Julius Goebel Jr., "Ex Parte Clio," *Columbia Law Review* 54 (1954): 450, who wrote, "[M]easured by even the least exacting of scholarly standards, [the work] is in the reviewer's opinion without merit."

40. Yale University Press (1998).

he calls "mainstream scholars" on almost every controversial constitutional question. Indeed, in some areas—especially criminal procedure—he stands virtually alone against a broad consensus. Can conventional wisdom have been so wrong for so long? Perhaps it was, and perhaps it takes Professor Amar's strong textualism to expose the errors. But . . . law is an incrementalist discipline, and we ought to mistrust a thesis that blinds us with its novelty and brilliance.[41]

Polls of Other Jurisdictions[42]

As well as originalism, textualism, or other historical approaches, a justice might probe English traditions or early colonial or state practices to determine how public officials of the times—or later—interpreted similar words or phrases. The Supreme Court has frequently used such evidence. For instance, when *Wolf v. Colorado* (1949) presented the Court with the question whether the Fourth Amendment barred use in state courts of evidence obtained through an unconstitutional search, Justice Felix Frankfurter surveyed the law in all the states and in ten jurisdictions within the British Commonwealth. He used this poll to bolster a conclusion that, while the Constitution forbade unreasonable searches and seizures, it did not prohibit state officials from using such questionably obtained evidence against a defendant.

In 1952, however, when *Rochin v. California* confronted the justices with the question whether a state could use evidence it had obtained from a defendant by pumping his stomach—evidence admissible in the overwhelming majority of states at that time—Frankfurter declined to call the roll. Instead, he declared that gathering evidence by a stomach pump was "conduct that shocks the conscience" whose fruits could not be used in either state or federal courts. When in 1961 *Mapp v. Ohio* overruled *Wolf* and held that state courts must *exclude* all unconstitutionally obtained evidence, the justices again surveyed the field. For the Court, Justice Tom C. Clark said, "While in 1949 almost two-thirds of the States were opposed to the exclusionary rule, now, despite the *Wolf* Case, more than half of those since passing upon it, by

their own legislative or judicial decision, have wholly or partly adopted or adhered to the [rule]."

The point of this set of examples is not that Frankfurter or the Court were inconsistent but that the method itself—while it offers insights—is, according to some commentators, far from foolproof. First of all, the Constitution of 1787 as it initially stood and has since been amended rejects many English and some colonial and state practices. Second, even a steady stream of precedents from the states may mean no more than the fact that judges, too busy to give the issue much thought, imitated each other under the rubric of stare decisis. Third, if justices are searching for original intent or understanding, it is difficult to imagine the relevance of what was in the minds of people in the eighteenth century to state practices in the twentieth and twenty-first centuries. Polls are useful if we want to know what other judges, now and in the recent past, have thought about the Constitution, writ large or small. Nevertheless, they say nothing about the correctness of those thoughts—and the correctness of a lower court's interpretation may be precisely the issue before the Supreme Court.

Despite these criticisms, the Supreme Court continues to take into account the practices of other U.S. jurisdictions, just as courts in other societies occasionally look to their counterparts elsewhere—including the U.S. Supreme Court—for guidance. The South African ruling in *The State v. Makwanyane* (1995) provides a vivid example. To determine whether the death penalty violated its nation's constitution, the republic's Constitutional Court surveyed practices elsewhere, including those in the United States. At the end of the day, the justices decided not to follow the path taken by the U.S. Supreme Court, ruling instead that their constitution prohibited the state from imposing capital punishment. Rejection of U.S. practice was made all the more interesting in light of a speech delivered by Justice Harry Blackmun, only a year before *Makwanyane*.[43] In that address, Blackmun chastised his colleagues for failing to take into account a decision of the South African high court dismissing a prosecution against

41. Suzanna Sherry, "Textualism and Judgment," *George Washington Law Review* 66 (1998): 1148.

42. We adopt the material in this section from Murphy, Pritchett, and Epstein, *Courts, Judges, and Politics*, 540–542.

43. "Justice Blackmun Addresses the ASIL Annual Dinner," American Society of International Law Newsletter, March 1994.

a person kidnapped from a neighboring country. This ruling, Blackmun argued, was far more faithful to international conventions than the one his Court had reached in *United States v. Alvarez-Machain* (1992), which permitted U.S. agents to abduct a Mexican national.

Alvarez-Machain aside, there does seem to be an increasing tendency for American justices to consider the rulings of courts abroad and practices elsewhere as they interpret the U.S. Constitution. This trend is particularly evident in opinions regarding capital punishment, wherein justices opposed to this form of retribution often point to the nearly one hundred countries that have abolished the death penalty.

Whether this practice will become more widespread or filter into other legal areas is an intriguing question, and one likely to cause debate among the justices. While some support efforts to expand their horizons beyond U.S. borders, others apparently agree with Justice Scalia, who has argued that "the views of other nations, however enlightened the Justices of this court may think them to be, cannot be imposed upon Americans through the Constitution." [44]

Logical Reasoning

Unlike originalism, the meaning of the words approach, or even variants of attempts to poll other jurisdictions, logical reasoning is not necessarily dependent on historical interpretations of particular constitutional provisions. Rather, it suggests that judges should engage in reasoned analysis. Such an analysis often takes the form of a syllogism—a type of logic in which justices draw a conclusion from two assumed premises, major and minor.

Chief Justice John Marshall's opinion in *Marbury v. Madison* provides an often-cited example of logical reasoning in action:

MAJOR PREMISE: A law repugnant to the Constitution is void.
MINOR PREMISE: This law is repugnant to the Constitution.
CONCLUSION: Therefore, this law is void.

The beauty of logical analysis, as this example illustrates, is that the resulting decision takes on an objective, perhaps even a scientific, aura. In other words, Marshall's syllogism suggests that anybody with a logical mind would reach the same conclusion. But is this necessarily so? Consider another syllogism:

MAJOR PREMISE: Sweden has many storks.
MINOR PREMISE: Storks deliver babies.
CONCLUSION: Therefore, Sweden has many babies.

We know that storks do not deliver babies, and therein lies the major problem with logical reasoning: because it can be undertaken in the absence of any factual analysis, almost any conclusion can result. To see this, compare the two syllogisms. If we assume that the major premises of both are accurate, then the soundness of their conclusions rests with the factual accuracy of the minor premises. Obviously, storks do not deliver babies, but is Marshall's minor premise any more believable or logically driven? Put another way, can logic reveal whether a particular law is repugnant to the Constitution?

To many the answer is no. As Justice Holmes put it:

The life of the law has not been logic: it has been experience. The felt necessities of the time, the prevalent moral and political theories, intuitions of public policy, avowed or unconscious, even the prejudices which judges share with their fellow-men, have had a good deal more to do than the syllogism in determining the rules by which men should be governed. [45]

Stare Decisis

Translated from Latin, stare decisis means "let the decision stand." What the term suggests is that, as a general rule, jurists should decide cases on the basis of previously established precedent. In shorthand terms, judicial tribunals should honor prior rulings.

The benefits of this approach are fairly evident. If justices rely on past cases to resolve current cases, some scholars argue, the law they generate becomes predictable and stable. Justice Harlan F. Stone acknowledged the value of precedent in a somewhat more ironic way: "The rule of stare decisis embodies a wise policy because it is

---

44. *Thompson v. Oklahoma* (1987); see also his dissent in *Atkins v. Virginia* (2002).

45. *The Common Law,* quoted by Max Lerner in *The Mind and Faith of Justice Holmes* (New York: Modern Library, 1943), 51–52.

often more important that a rule of law be settled than that it be settled right." [46] The message, however, is the same: if the Court adheres to past decisions, it provides some direction to all who labor in the legal enterprise. Lower court judges know how they should and should not decide cases; lawyers can frame their arguments in accord with the lessons of past cases; legislators understand what they can and cannot enact or regulate, and so forth.

Precedent, then, can be an important and useful factor in Supreme Court decision making. Along these lines, it is interesting to note that the Court rarely reverses itself—it has done so less than three hundred times over its entire history. Even modern-day Courts, as Table 1-1 shows, have been loath to overrule precedents. In the nearly fifty terms covered in the table, the Court has overturned only 129 precedents, or about 2.6 per term. What is more, the justices almost always cite previous rulings in their decisions; indeed, it is the rare Court opinion that does not mention other cases.[47] Finally, several scholars have verified that precedent helps to explain Court decisions in some areas of the law. In one study, analysts found that the Court reacted quite consistently to legal doctrine presented in more than fifteen years of death penalty litigation. Put differently, using precedent from past cases, the researchers could correctly categorize the outcomes (for or against the death penalty) in 75 percent of sixty-four cases decided since 1972.[48] Scholarly work considering precedent in search and seizure litigation had similar success.[49]

Despite these data, we should not conclude that the justices necessarily follow this approach. Many allege that judicial appeal to precedent often is mere window dressing, used to hide ideologies and values, rather than a substantive form of analysis. There are several reasons for this allegation.

TABLE 1-1 Precedents Overruled, 1953–2001 Terms

Court Era (Terms)	Number of Terms	Number of Overruled Precedents	Average Number of Overrulings Per Term
Warren Court (1953–1968)	16	42	2.6
Burger Court (1969–1985)	17	47	2.8
Rehnquist Court (1986–)	16	40	2.5

SOURCE: U.S. Supreme Court Database, with orally argued citation as the unit of analysis. The table includes cases in which the majority opinion formally altered precedent, as well as those in which the Court claimed that a precedent was no longer good law. For more details on the data, see Harold J. Spaeth's documentation to the U.S. Supreme Court Judicial Database, available at: *www.polisci.msu.edu/pljp/index.html.*

First, the Supreme Court has generated so much precedent that it is usually possible to find support for any conclusion. By way of proof, turn to any page of any opinion in this book and you probably will find the writers—both for the majority and the dissenters—citing precedent.

Second, it may be difficult to locate the rule of law emerging in a majority opinion. To decide whether a previous decision qualifies as a precedent, judges and commentators often say, one must strip away the nonessentials of a case and expose the basic reasons for the Supreme Court's decision. This process is generally referred to as "establishing the principle of the case," or the ratio decidendi. Other points made in a given opinion—obiter dicta (any expression in an opinion that is unnecessary to the decision reached in the case or that relates to a factual situation other than the one actually before the court)—have no legal weight, and judges are not bound by it. It is up to courts to separate the ratio decidendi from dicta. This task can be difficult, but it provides a way for justices to skirt precedent with which they do not agree. All they need to do is declare parts of it to be dicta. Or justices can brush aside even the ratio decidendi when it suits their interests. Because the Supreme Court, at least today, is so selective about the cases

46. *United States v. Underwriters Association* (1944).

47. See Jack Knight and Lee Epstein, "The Norm of Stare Decisis," *American Journal of Political Science* 40 (1996): 1018–1035.

48. Tracey E. George and Lee Epstein, "On the Nature of Supreme Court Decision Making," *American Political Science Review* 86 (1992): 323–337.

49. Jeffrey A. Segal, "Predicting Supreme Court Cases Probabilistically: The Search and Seizure Cases, 1962–1984," *American Political Science Review* 78 (1984): 891–900.

it decides, it probably would not take a case for which clear precedent existed. Even in the past, two cases that were precisely identical probably would not be accepted. What this means is that justices can always deal with "problematic" ratio decidendi by distinguishing the case at hand from those that have already been decided.

A scholarly study of the role of precedent in Supreme Court decision making offers a third reason. Two political scientists hypothesized that if precedent matters, it ought to affect the subsequent decisions of members of the Court. If a justice dissented from a decision establishing a particular precedent, the same justice would not dissent from a subsequent application of the precedent. But that was not the case. Of the eighteen justices included in the study, only two occasionally subjugated their preferences to precedent.[50]

Finally, and most interesting, many justices recognize the limits of stare decisis in cases involving constitutional interpretation. Indeed, the justices often say that, when constitutional issues are involved, stare decisis is a less rigid rule than it might normally be. This view strikes some as prudent, for the Constitution is difficult to amend and judges make mistakes—or come to see problems quite differently as their perspectives change. As Justice Black once said:

Ordinarily it is sound policy to adhere to prior decisions but this practice has quite properly never been a blind, inflexible rule. Courts are not omniscient. Like every other human agency, they too can profit from trial and error, from experience and reflection. As others have demonstrated, the principle commonly referred to as stare decisis has never been thought to extend so far as to prevent the courts from correcting their own errors. . . . Indeed, the Court has a special responsibility where questions of constitutional law are involved to review its decisions from time to time and where compelling reasons present themselves to refuse to follow erroneous precedents; otherwise mistakes in interpreting the Constitution are extremely difficult to alleviate and needlessly so.[51]

In fact, of the 129 precedents overruled between the 1953 and 2001 terms *(see Table 1-1),* about two-thirds involved constitutional issues.[52]

Balancing Approaches

The modes of analysis we have examined so far are not, for the most part, case specific, meaning that conclusions reached by literalists and original intent advocates, for example, on points of law would not waiver with the facts of a given case. The original intent advocates would always hold that the First Amendment does not protect speech advocating the violent overthrow of the government, and the literalists would always reach the opposite conclusion, regardless of the controversy at hand. Supporters of a balancing approach take a position that is more case specific than philosophical; that is, in each case they balance the interests of the individual against those of the government. Their decisions can vary because at times an individual's activity outweighs the government's interest in prohibiting it, while at other times the reverse holds true.

The balancing approach, however, is not monolithic. Some justices take a strict view of balancing, giving the interests of individuals and governments equal weight. They justify doing so on constitutional and philosophical grounds, saying, for example, that while the First Amendment protects individual speech, the text of the Constitution gives legislatures the power to enact laws that may sometimes interfere with speech. The Court, according to this view, should initially give equal weight to both and then balance them to determine which should fall. Justice John Marshall Harlan's opinion in *Barenblatt v. United States* (1959) demonstrates this theory in practice. Among the issues raised was whether a congressional committee could question an individual about his political beliefs and associations. Lloyd Barenblatt alleged that he could refuse to answer such questions because they infringed on his First Amendment rights. Harlan wrote:

Where First Amendment rights are asserted to bar governmental interrogation, resolution of the issue always involves a

50. Jeffrey A. Segal and Harold J. Spaeth, "The Influence of Stare Decisis on the Votes of U.S. Supreme Court Justices," *American Journal of Political Science* 40 (1996): 971–1002.

51. *Green v. United States* (1958).

52. We computed this figure from the U.S. Supreme Court Judicial Database.

balancing by the courts of the competing private and public interests at stake in the particular circumstances shown.

He held that, in this instance, the scale favored the government over Barenblatt.

Balancing also can take at least two other forms. While some opinions, such as Harlan's in *Barenblatt,* weigh equally the claims of governments and individuals, others give preference to one above the other. In accordance with a philosophy of judicial restraint, Justice Frankfurter often balanced government interests versus individual interests but with a finger on the scale: he gave preference to the state over the individual. He did so in the belief that a body made up of unelected judges should not lightly overturn laws passed by legislatures composed of representatives elected by the populace. In his view,

the framers of the Constitution denied . . . legislative powers to the federal judiciary. They chose instead to insulate the judiciary from the legislative function. They did not grant to this Court supervision over legislation. . . . The removal of unwise laws from the statute books . . . lies not to the court but to the ballot and to the processes of democratic government.[53]

In contrast to Frankfurter's perspective is the preferred freedoms position, which also balances interests, but tips the scale to favor the individual's rights and liberties. Although this approach is most often associated with First Amendment freedoms, the Supreme Court also has invoked it to adjudicate disputes involving economic liberties. For example, in *Lochner v. New York* (1905) the justices examined a state law that established maximum work hours for bakery employees. New York defended its law as a valid exercise of its police powers, its ability to legislate in the best interests of its citizens. An employer challenged the law as a violation of his liberty to enter into a contract with his employees. Writing for the majority, Justice Rufus W. Peckham acknowledged the need for the Court to balance these interests, but to do so with a bias in favor of the individual. He wrote:

Statutes of the nature of that under review, limiting the hours in which grown and intelligent men may labor to earn their living, are mere meddlesome interferences with the rights of the individual, and they are not saved from condemnation by the claim that they are passed in the exercise of the police power.

The holding in *Lochner* has since been overruled, and now the government may regulate employees' work hours. But the logic of balancing rights with a bias in favor of the individual is still invoked, only today it is more often in conjunction with rights and liberties enumerated in the first ten amendments.

Debates over this mode of analysis generally have centered on views about the role of the Supreme Court in a democratic society.[54] Those opposed to the equal balancing of Harlan and to the judicial restraint of Frankfurter contend that each ignores the Court's role of protecting minority interests. According to this argument, the Court, because it is not elected, is in the best position to protect groups and individuals who hold unpopular views. As Justice Brennan wrote in *NAACP v. Button* (1963),

Groups which find themselves unable to achieve their objectives through the ballot frequently turn to the courts. . . . And, under the conditions of modern government, litigation may well be the sole practicable avenue open to a minority to petition for redress of grievances. . . . For such a group, association for litigation may be the most effective form of political association.

Brennan opposed doctrines like absolute balancing because they almost always lead to decisions in favor of the majority. Consider the outcome in *Barenblatt:* Would it have been possible for Justice Harlan to weigh the interests of all against those of one man and reach any other conclusion?

Frankfurter and others chastise adherents of a position giving special treatment to individual rights and liberties. In Frankfurter's view, that posture is "mischievous" because its application gives the Court too much power. When Congress and other legislative bodies enact laws that reflect the will of the people, why should the Court—composed of unelected officials—strike them down? In this light, the Court should be seen as part of the ruling regime, willing to reflect its wishes.

---

53. *West Virginia State Board of Education v. Barnette* (1943).

54. For more specific criticisms of balancing, see Laurent B. Frantz, "The First Amendment in the Balance," *Yale Law Journal* 71 (1962): 1424–1450. On the preferred freedoms approach, see Frankfurter's dissent in *Kovacs v. Cooper* (1949).

Cost-Benefit Analysis

Balancing might also tie in with cost-benefit analysis. Justices often appraise alternative rulings by forecasting their consequences. These estimates can, of course, influence choices among plausible constitutional interpretations. And here we might have, if not balancing, an effort to maximize benefits and minimize costs.

One of the recurrent issues the Supreme Court confronted during much of the twentieth century concerned application of the exclusionary rule, which forbids use in criminal proceedings of evidence secured in violation of the Fourth Amendment. Claims that the rule hampers the conviction of criminals have affected judicial attitudes, as Justice White frankly admitted in *United States v. Leon* (1984): "The substantial social costs exacted by the exclusionary rule for the vindication of Fourth Amendment rights have long been a source of concern." In *Leon* a majority of the justices applied a "cost-benefit" calculus to justify a "good faith" seizure by police on an invalid search warrant.

When you encounter cases that engage in this sort of analysis, you might ask a question raised by some critics of the approach: By what account of values should judges weigh costs and benefits, and how do they take into account the different people whom a decision may simultaneously punish and reward?

SUPREME COURT DECISION MAKING: THE ROLE OF POLITICS

So far in our discussion we have not mentioned the justices' ideologies, their political party affiliations, or their personal views on various public policy issues. The reason is that legal approaches to Supreme Court decision making do not admit that these factors play a role in the way the Court arrives at its decisions. Instead, they suggest that justices divorce themselves from their personal and political biases and settle disputes based upon the law. The approaches we consider below posit a quite different vision of Supreme Court decision making. They argue that the forces that drive the justices are anything but legal in composition and that it is unrealistic to expect justices to shed all their preferences and values and to ignore public opinion when they put on their black robes. Rather, under the black robes there are people like all of us whose (largely political) biases and partisan attachments are strong and pervasive.

Justices usually do not admit that they are swayed by the public or that they vote according to their ideologies. Therefore, our discussion of the role politics plays in Supreme Court decision making is distinct from that of the role of law. Here you will find little in the way of supporting statements from Court members, for it is an unusual justice indeed who admits to following anything but precedent, the intent of the Framers, the words of the Constitution, and the like in deciding cases. Instead, we have included the results of decades of research by scholars who think that political and other extralegal forces shape judicial decisions. We organize these approaches into three categories: preference-based, strategic, and external forces. See if you think these scholarly accounts are persuasive.

Preference-Based Approaches

As a class, preference-based approaches see the justices as rational decision makers who hold certain values they would like to see reflected in the outcomes of Court cases. The two most prevalent preference-based approaches stress the importance of judicial attitudes and roles.

Judicial Attitudes. Attitudinal approaches emphasize the importance of the justices' political ideologies. Typically, scholars examining the ideologies of the justices discuss the degree to which a justice is conservative or liberal—as in "Justice X holds conservative views on issues of criminal law" or "Justice Y holds liberal views on free speech." This school of thought maintains that when a case comes before the Court each justice evaluates the facts of the dispute and arrives at a decision consistent with his or her personal ideology.

One of the first scholars to study the importance of the justices' personal attitudes was Pritchett.[55] Examining

55. C. Herman Pritchett, *The Roosevelt Court* (New York: Macmillan, 1948); and Pritchett, "Divisions of Opinion Among Justices of the U.S. Supreme Court, 1939–1941," *American Political Science Review* 35 (1941): 890–898.

FIGURE 1-4 Percentage of U.S. Supreme Court Cases with at Least One Dissenting Opinion, 1800–2001 Terms

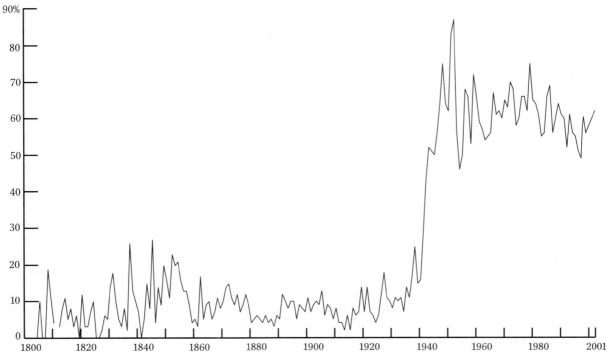

SOURCE: Lee Epstein, Jeffrey A. Segal, Harold J. Spaeth, and Thomas G. Walker, *The Supreme Court Compendium: Data, Decisions, and Developments*, 3rd ed. (Washington, D.C.: CQ Press, 2003), Table 3-2.

the Court during the 1930s and 1940s, Pritchett observed that dissent had become an institutionalized feature of judicial decisions *(see Figure 1-4)*. If precedent and other legal factors drove Court rulings, why did various justices interpreting the same legal provisions consistently reach different results? Pritchett concluded that the justices were not following precedent but were "motivated by their own preferences." [56]

Pritchett's findings touched off an explosion of research on the influence of attitudes on Supreme Court decision making.[57] Much of this scholarship describes how liberal or conservative the various justices were and

56. Pritchett, *The Roosevelt Court*, xiii.
57. The classic works in this area are Pritchett, *The Roosevelt Court;* Glendon Schubert, *The Judicial Mind* (Evanston, Ill: Northwestern University Press, 1965); and Rohde and Spaeth, *Supreme Court Decision Making.* For a lucid, modern-day treatment, see Segal and Spaeth, *The Supreme Court and the Attitudinal Model Revisited,* chaps. 3 and 8.

attempts to predict their voting behavior based on their attitudinal preferences. To understand some of these differences, consider Table 1-2, which presents the voting records of the present chief justice, William Rehnquist, and his two immediate predecessors, Warren Burger and Earl Warren. The data report the percentage of times each voted in the liberal direction in two different issue areas: civil liberties and economic liberties.

The data show dramatic differences among these three important jurists, especially in civil liberties. Cases in this category include disputes over issues such as the First Amendment freedoms of religion, speech, and press, the right to privacy, the rights of the criminally accused, and illegal discrimination. The liberal position is a vote in favor of the individual who is claiming a denial of these basic rights. Warren supported the liberal side almost 80 percent of the time, but Burger and Rehnquist

TABLE 1-2 Liberal Voting of the Chief Justices, 1953–2001 Terms

| | Issue Areas | | | |
| | Civil Liberties | | Economics | |
	Number of Cases	Percentage Liberal	Number of Cases	Percentage Liberal
Warren	771	78.6%	442	81.9%
Burger	1,429	29.6	424	42.5
Rehnquist	2,127	21.8	666	43.1

SOURCES: Lee Epstein, Jeffrey A. Segal, Harold J. Spaeth, and Thomas G. Walker, *The Supreme Court Compendium: Data, Decisions, and Developments,* 3rd ed., (Washington, D.C.: CQ Press, 2003), Table 6-2.

NOTE: The data in this table are based on decisions reached during the following tenures: Earl Warren, 1953–1968; Warren Burger, 1969–1985; William Rehnquist, 1972–2001.

did so in less than 30 percent of such cases. Economics cases involve challenges to the government's authority to regulate the economy. The liberal position supports an active role by the government in controlling business and economic activity. Here, too, the three justices show different ideological positions. Warren is the most liberal of the three, ruling in favor of government regulatory ac-

tivity in better than 80 percent of the cases, while Burger and Rehnquist support such government activity in less than half. These data are typical of the findings of most such studies. Within given issue areas, individual justices tend to show consistent ideological predispositions.

Moreover, we often hear that a particular Court is ideologically predisposed toward one side or the other. For example, on October 5, 1999, the *New York Times* described Justice Anthony Kennedy as "a member of the Court's conservative majority" on certain kinds of criminal justice disputes; three years later, on May 29, 2002, it ran a story claiming that "Chief Justice William Rehnquist and his fellow conservatives have made no secret of their desire to alter the balance of federalism, shifting power from Washington to the states." Sometimes an entire Court era is described in terms of its political preferences, such as the "liberal" Warren Court or the "conservative" Rehnquist Court. Figure 1-5 confirms that these labels have some basis in fact. Looking at the two lines from left to right, from the 1950s through 2001, note the downward trend, indicating the increased conservatism of the Court in economics and civil liberties cases.

FIGURE 1-5 Court Decisions on Economics and Civil Liberties, 1953–2001 Terms

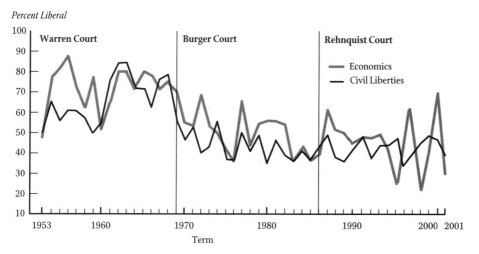

SOURCES: Jeffrey A. Segal and Harold J. Spaeth, *The Supreme Court Compendium: Data, Decisions, and Developments,* 3rd ed., (Washington, D.C.: CQ Press, 2003), Table 3-8.

How valuable are the ideological terms used to describe particular justices or Courts in helping us understand judicial decision making? On the one hand, knowledge of justices' ideologies can lead to fairly accurate predictions about their voting behavior. Suppose, for example, that the Rehnquist Court hands down a decision dealing with the death penalty and that the vote in the case is 7–2 in favor of the criminal defendant. The most conservative members of the Court on death penalty cases are Justices Antonin Scalia and Clarence Thomas—they almost always vote against the defendant. If we predicted that Scalia and Thomas cast the dissenting votes in our hypothetical death penalty case, we would almost certainly be right.[58]

On the other hand, preference-based approaches are not foolproof. First, how do we know if a particular justice is liberal or conservative? The answer typically is that we know a justice is liberal or conservative because he or she casts liberal or conservative votes. Scalia favors conservative positions on the Court because he is a conservative, and we know he is a conservative because he favors conservative positions in the cases he decides. This is circular reasoning indeed. Second, knowing that a justice is liberal or conservative or that the Court decided a case in a liberal or conservative way does not tell us much about the Court's (or the country's) policy positions. To say that *Roe v. Wade* is a liberal decision is to say little about the policies governing abortion in the United States. If it did, this book would be nothing more than a list of cases labeled liberal or conservative. But such labels would give us no sense of two hundred years of constitutional interpretation.

Finally, we must understand that ideological labels are occasionally time dependent, that they are bound to particular historical eras. In *Muller v. Oregon* (1908) the Supreme Court upheld a state law that set a maximum number on the hours women (but not men) could work. How would you, as a student in the twenty-first century, view such an opinion? You probably would classify it as conservative because it seems to patronize and protect

women. But in the early 1900s most considered *Muller* a liberal ruling because it allowed the government to regulate business.

A related problem is that some decisions do not fall neatly on a single conservative-liberal dimension. Exemplary is *Wisconsin v. Mitchell* (1993), in which the Court upheld a state law that increased the sentence for crimes if the defendant "intentionally selects the person against whom the crime is committed" on the basis of race, religion, national origin, sexual orientation, and other similar criteria. Is this ruling liberal or conservative? If you view the law as penalizing racial or ethnic hatred, you would likely see it as a liberal decision. However, if you see the law as treating criminal defendants more harshly and penalizing a person because of what he or she believes or says, the ruling is conservative.

Judicial Role. Another concept within the preference-based category is the judicial role, which scholars have defined as norms that constrain the behavior of jurists.[59] Some students of the Court argue that each justice has a view of his or her role, a view that is based far less on political ideology and far more on fundamental beliefs of what a good judge should do or what the proper role of the Court should be. Some scholars claim that jurists vote in accordance with these role conceptions.

Analysts typically discuss judicial roles in terms of activism and restraint. An activist justice believes that the proper role of the Court is to assert independent positions in deciding cases, to review the actions of the other branches vigorously, to strike down unconstitutional acts willingly, and to impose far-reaching remedies for legal wrongs whenever necessary. Restraint-oriented justices take the opposite position. Courts should not become involved in the operations of the other branches unless absolutely necessary. The benefit of the doubt should be given to actions taken by elected officials. Courts should impose remedies that are narrowly tailored to correct a specific legal wrong.

Based on these definitions, we might expect to find activist justices more willing than their opposites to strike

---

58. We adopt this example from Jeffrey A. Segal and Harold J. Spaeth, *The Supreme Court and the Attitudinal Model* (New York: Cambridge University Press, 1993), 223.

59. See James L. Gibson, "Judges' Role Orientations, Attitudes, and Decisions," *American Political Science Review* 72 (1978): 917–924.

TABLE 1-3 Votes in Support of and Opposition to Decisions Declaring Legislation Unconstitutional: The Current Court

Justice	All Laws	%	Federal Laws Only	%
Breyer	35/24	59.3	13/31	41.9
Ginsburg	42/24	63.6	15/16	48.4
Kennedy	106/7	93.8	25/2	92.6
O'Connor	143/46	75.7	38/8	82.6
Rehnquist	146/186	44.0	38/21	64.4
Scalia	87/39	69.0	29/9	76.3
Souter	66/18	78.6	21/12	63.6
Stevens	244/49	83.3	29/22	56.9
Thomas	59/21	73.8	26/6	81.3
TOTALS	928/415	69.1	234/127	64.8

SOURCE: Lee Epstein, Jeffrey A. Segal, Harold J. Spaeth, and Thomas G. Walker, *The Supreme Court Compendium: Data, Decisions, and Developments*, 3rd ed. (Washington, D.C.: CQ Press, 2003), Table 6-8.

NOTE: Figures to the left of the slash indicate the number of votes cast in favor of striking down legislation; figures to the right indicate the number of votes in favor of upholding the legislation. Percentages indicate the percentage of cases in which the justice voted with the majority to declare legislation unconstitutional.

down legislation. Therefore, a natural question to ask is this: To what extent have specific jurists practiced judicial activism or restraint? The data in Table 1-3 address this question by reporting the votes of justices on the current Court in cases in which the majority declared federal, state, or local legislation unconstitutional. Note the wide variation among the justices, even for those who sat together and therefore heard many of the same cases. For example, compare Justice John Paul Stevens's rate of 83 percent (meaning that he almost always voted with the majority to strike down laws) with Chief Justice Rehnquist's 44 percent—a difference of nearly 40 percentage points, despite the fact that Stevens's and Rehnquist's service on the Court has overlapped by twenty-eight years.

Even more interesting may be the behavior of Justice Frankfurter, who served on the Court between 1939 and 1962. In many Supreme Court opinions, Frankfurter declared his adherence to the doctrine of judicial restraint. But relevant data suggest otherwise. During his last nine years on the bench, Frankfurter voted with the majority to overturn federal laws in 76.6 percent of the sixty-four cases in which he participated.

The Frankfurter example should make clear that what justices say they do and what they actually do may be two different things. It also illustrates a less obvious point: judicial activism and restraint do not necessarily equal judicial liberalism and conservatism. An activist judge need not be liberal, and a judge who practices restraint need not be conservative. As for Frankfurter, scholars argue that in his voting behavior he was "a staunch economic conservative" who was willing to strike down laws that impinged on his policy preferences.[60] Among the twenty-seven justices who served on the Court between 1953 and 1996, only three—Harlan, Charles E. Whittaker, and Thomas—supported liberal outcomes in economic cases at a rate lower than Frankfurter's 39 percent. In other words, in some areas of the law, Frankfurter was a conservative activist.

It is also true that so-called liberal Courts are no more likely to strike down legislation than are conservative Courts. Figure 1-6 shows the number of federal, state, and local laws struck down since 1789. Note the relatively high numbers of statutes declared unconstitutional during the 1920s, 1970s, and 1980s, all periods of relative conservatism on the Court. Such activism calls into question a strong relationship between ideology and judicial role.

We have shown that one can use measures, such as the number of laws struck down, to assess the extent to which justices practice judicial activism or restraint. But does this information help us understand Supreme Court decision making? This question is difficult to answer because few scholars have studied the relationship between roles and voting in a systematic way.

The paucity of scholarly work on judicial roles leads to a criticism of the approach: it is virtually impossible to separate roles from attitudes. When Justice Frankfurter voted to uphold an economically conservative law, can we conclude that he was practicing restraint? The answer, quite clearly, is no. It may have been his conservative attitude toward economic cases—not restraint—that led him to uphold the law. Another criticism of role approaches

60. See Segal and Spaeth, *The Supreme Court and the Attitudinal Model*, 236–237.

FIGURE 1-6 Provisions of Federal, State, and Local Laws and Ordinances Held Unconstitutional by the Supreme Court, 1789–1989

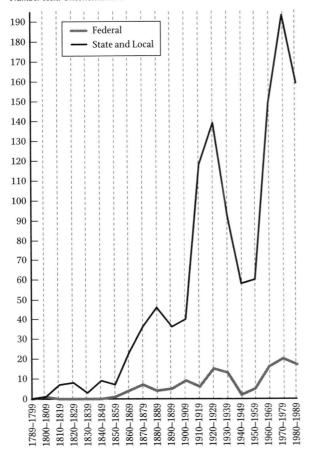

Number Held Unconstitutional

SOURCE: Harold W. Stanley and Richard G. Niemi, *Vital Statistics on American Politics*, 5th ed. (Washington, D.C.: CQ Press, 1995), 286.

NOTE: We do not include data for the most recent decade as it is not complete. Stanley and Niemi report that the Court struck down three federal laws and thirty-one state and local laws between 1990 and 1994.

is similar to that leveled at attitudinal factors—they tell us very little about the resulting policy in a case. Again, to say that *Roe v. Wade* was an activist decision because it struck down abortion laws nationwide is to say nothing about the policy content of the opinion.

Strategic Approaches

Strategic accounts of judicial decisions rest on a few simple propositions: justices may be primarily seekers of legal policy (as the attitudinal adherents claim) or they may be motivated by jurisprudential principles (as approaches grounded in law suggest), but they are not unconstrained actors who make decisions based solely on their own ideological attitudes or jurisprudential desires. Rather, justices are strategic actors who realize that their ability to achieve their goals—whatever those goals might be—depends on a consideration of the preferences of other relevant actors (such as their colleagues and members of other political institutions), the choices they expect others to make, and the institutional context in which they act. Scholars have termed this a "strategic" account because the ideas it contains are derived from the rational choice paradigm, on which strategic analysis is based and as it has been advanced by economists and political scientists working in other fields. Accordingly, we can restate the strategic argument in this way: we can best explain the choices of justices as strategic behavior and not merely as a response to ideological or jurisprudential values.[61]

Such arguments about Supreme Court decision making seem to be sensible: a justice can do very little alone. It takes a majority vote to decide a case and a majority agreeing on a single opinion to set precedent. Under such conditions, human interaction is important, and case outcomes—not to mention the rationale of decisions—can be influenced by the nature of relations among the members of the group.

Although scholars have not considered strategic approaches to the same degree that they have studied judicial attitudes, a number of influential works point to their importance. Research started in the 1960s and continuing today into the private papers of the former justices consistently has shown that through intellectual persuasion, effective bargaining over opinion writing, in-

61. For more details on this approach, see Lee Epstein and Jack Knight, *The Choices Justices Make* (Washington, D.C.: CQ Press, 1998).

formal lobbying, and so forth, justices have influenced the actions of their colleagues.[62]

How does strategic behavior manifest itself? One possibility is in the frequency of vote changes. During the deliberations that take place after oral arguments, the justices discuss the case and vote on it. These votes do not become final until the opinions are completed and the decision is made public (see Figure 1-1, page 14). Research has shown that between the initial vote on the merits of cases and the official announcement of the decision at least one vote switch occurs more than 50 percent of the time.[63] This figure indicates that justices change their minds—perhaps reevaluating their initial positions or succumbing to the persuasion of their colleagues—which seems inexplicable if we believe that justices are simply liberals or conservatives and always vote in accord with their preferences.

Vote shifts are just one manifestation of the interdependence of the Court's decision-making process. Another is the revision of opinions that occurs in almost every Court case.[64] As opinion writers try to accommodate their colleagues' wishes, their drafts may undergo five, ten, even fifteen revisions. Bargaining over the content of an opinion is important because it can significantly alter the policy ultimately expressed. A clear example is *Griswold v. Connecticut* (1965), in which the Court considered the constitutionality of a state law that prohibited the dissemination of birth control devices and information, even to married couples. In his initial draft of the majority opinion, Justice William O. Douglas

struck down the law on the ground that it interfered with the First Amendment's right of association. A memorandum from Justice Brennan convinced Douglas to alter his rationale and to establish the foundation for a right to privacy. "Had the Douglas draft been issued as the *Griswold* opinion of the Court, the case would stand as a precedent on the freedom of association," rather than serve as the landmark ruling it became.[65]

Although strategic approaches have their uses, *Griswold* points to a problem. To date, scholarly treatments have been ad hoc or case specific—we do not know whether a case like *Griswold* represents the rule or the anomaly. Until analysts begin to study interdependent decision making more systematically, which manuscript collections such as Marshall's, Brennan's, and Lewis F. Powell's make possible, the general value of this approach will remain unknown.

External Factors

In addition to internal bargaining, strategic approaches (as well as others) also take account of political pressures that come from outside the Court. We consider three sources of such influence: public opinion, partisan politics, and interest groups. While reading about these sources of influence, keep in mind that one of the fundamental differences between the Supreme Court and the political branches is that there is no direct electoral connection between the justices and the public. Once appointed, justices may serve for life. They are not accountable to the public and are not required to undergo any periodic reevaluation of their decisions. So why would they let the stuff of ordinary partisan politics, such as public opinion and interest groups, influence their opinions?

Public Opinion. To address this question, let us first look at public opinion as a source of influence on the Court. We know that the president and members of Congress are always trying to find out what the people are thinking. Conducting and analyzing public opinion polls is a never-ending task, and there is good reason for this

62. Walter F. Murphy, *Elements of Judicial Strategy* (Chicago: University of Chicago Press, 1964); David J. Danelski, "The Influence of the Chief Justice in the Decisional Process of the Supreme Court," in *The Federal Judicial System,* ed. Thomas P. Jahnige and Sheldon Goldman (New York: Holt, Rinehart, and Winston, 1968); J. Woodford Howard, "On the Fluidity of Judicial Choice," *American Political Science Review* 62 (1968): 43–56; Epstein and Knight, *The Choices Justices Make;* Forest Maltzman, Paul J. Wahlbeck, and James Spriggs, *Crafting Law on the Supreme Court: The Collegial Game* (New York: Cambridge University Press, 2000).

63. Saul Brenner, "Fluidity on the Supreme Court, 1956–1967," *American Journal of Political Science* 26 (1982): 388–390; Brenner, "Fluidity on the United States Supreme Court: A Re-examination," *American Journal of Political Science* 24 (1980): 526–535; Forest Maltzman and Paul J. Wahlbeck, "Strategic Considerations and Vote Fluidity on the Burger Court," *American Political Science Review* 90 (1996): 581–592.

64. Epstein and Knight, *The Choices Justices Make,* chap. 3.

65. See Bernard Schwartz, *The Unpublished Opinions of the Warren Court* (New York: Oxford University Press, 1985), chap. 7.

activity. The political branches are supposed to represent the people, and the incumbents' reelection prospects can be jeopardized by straying too far from what the public wants. But federal judges—including Supreme Court justices—are not dependent upon pleasing the public to stay in office, and they do not serve in the same kind of representative capacity that legislators do.

Does that mean that the justices are not affected by public opinion? Some scholars claim that the answer, for at least three reasons, is no. First, because justices are political appointees, nominated and approved by popularly elected officials, it is logical that they reflect, however subtly, the views of the majority. It is probably true that an individual radically out of step with either the president or the Senate would not be nominated, much less confirmed. Second, the Court, at least occasionally, views public opinion as a legitimate guide for decisions. It has even gone so far as to incorporate that dimension into some of its jurisprudential standards. For example, in evaluating whether certain kinds of punishments violate the Eighth Amendment's prohibition against cruel and unusual punishment, the Court proclaimed that it would look toward "evolving standards of decency," as defined by public sentiment.[66] The third reason relates to the Court as an institution. Put simply, the justices have no mechanism for enforcing their decisions. Instead, they depend on other political officials to support their positions and on general public compliance, especially when controversial Court opinions have ramifications beyond the particular concerns of the parties to the suit.

Certainly, we can think of particular cases that lend support to these claims—cases in which the Court seems to have embraced public opinion, especially under conditions of extreme national stress. One example occurred during World War II. In *Korematsu v. United States* (1944) the justices endorsed the government's program to remove all Japanese Americans from the Pacific Coast states and relocate them to inland detention centers. It seems clear that the justices were swept up in the same wartime apprehensions as the rest of the nation. But it is

equally easy to summon examples of the Court handing down rulings that fly in the face of what the public wants. The most obvious example occurred after Franklin D. Roosevelt's 1932 election to the presidency. By choosing Roosevelt and electing many Democrats to Congress, the voters sent a clear signal that they wanted the government to take vigorous action to end the Great Depression. The president and Congress responded with many laws—the so-called New Deal legislation—but the Court remained unmoved by the public's endorsement of Roosevelt and his legislation. In case after case, at least until 1937, the justices struck down many of the laws and administrative programs designed to get the nation's economy moving again.

More systematic research, scrutinizing the correspondence between various measures of public opinion and trends in Court decisions, have yielded equally mixed results. On one end of the spectrum are studies by political scientists Thomas Marshall, William Mishler, and Reginald S. Sheehan. Marshall finds that, at the very least, Court rulings do not deviate significantly from the views of the citizenry: "When a clear-cut poll majority or plurality exists, over three-fifths of the Court's decisions reflect the polls. By all arguable evidence the modern Supreme Court appears to reflect public opinion about as accurately as other policy makers." [67] Mishler and Sheehan go even further, suggesting that changes in the public's ideological mood have a causal effect on Court decisions: The justices "are broadly aware of fundamental trends in the ideological tenor of public opinion, and . . . at least some justices, consciously or not, may adjust their decisions at the margins to accommodate such fundamental trends." [68]

On the other end of the spectrum are those scholars who remain unconvinced of the role of public opinion in Court decision making. In part, this disbelief emanates from a concern about the nature of the research that has

---

66. *Trop v. Dulles* (1958).

67. Thomas Marshall, *Public Opinion and the Supreme Court* (New York: Unwin Hyman, 1989), 97.
68. William Mishler and Reginald S. Sheehan, "The Supreme Court as a Counter-Majoritarian Institution? The Impact of Public Opinion on Supreme Court Decisions," *American Political Science Review* 87 (1993): 89.

been conducted. Helmut Norpoth and Jeffrey A. Segal, for example, criticized Mishler and Sheehan's research.[69] In reexamining that study's methodology, they reasoned: "Does public opinion influence Supreme Court decisions? If the model of influence is of the sort where the justices set aside their own (ideological) preferences and abide by what they divine as the vox populi, our answer is a resounding no." What Norpoth and Segal find instead is that Court appointments made by Richard Nixon in the early 1970s caused a "sizable ideological shift" in the direction of Court decisions *(see Figure 1-5)*. The entry of conservative justices created the illusion that the Court was echoing public opinion; it was not that sitting justices modified their voting patterns to conform to the changing views of the public.

This finding reinforces yet another criticism of this approach: that public opinion affects the Court only indirectly through presidential appointments, and not through the justices' reading of public opinion polls. This distinction is important, for if justices were truly influenced by the public, their decisions would change with the ebb and flow of opinion. But if they merely share their appointing president's ideology, which must mirror the majority of the citizens *at the time of the president's election*, their decisions will remain constant over time. They would not fluctuate, as public opinion often does.

At the end of the day, the question of whether public opinion affects Supreme Court decision making remains an open one. This is reinforced by the most recent research, which tends to reach conclusions somewhat between Mishler and Sheehan on one side and Segal and Norpoth on the other. As the authors of one of these studies note, "Commenting on Mishler and Sheehan, Norpoth and Segal argue that the role of public opinion on Court decisions is wholly indirect through the election-nomination-confirmation process. Mishler and Sheehan claim a direct public opinion influence. Our results . . . leave us in the middle of this debate. We believe that there is a trace of influence for both processes, but our results are too weak to leave us confident about the matter." [70]

Partisan Politics. Public opinion is not the only political factor that might influence the justices. As Jonathan Casper wrote, we cannot overestimate "the importance of the political context in which the Court does its work." In his view, the statement that the Court follows the election returns "recognizes that the choices the Court makes are related to developments in the broader political system." [71] In other words, the political environment has an effect on Court behavior. In fact, many assert that the Court is responsive to the influence of partisan politics, both internally and externally.

On the inner workings of the Court, social scientists long have argued that political creatures inhabit the Court, that justices are not simply neutral arbiters of the law. Since 1789, the beginning of constitutional government in the United States, those who have ascended to the bench have come from the political institutions of government or, at the very least, have affiliated with a particular political party. Judicial scholars recognize that justices bring with them the philosophies of those partisan attachments. Just as the members of the present Court tend to reflect the views of the Republican Party or Democratic Party, so too did the justices who came from the ranks of the Federalists and Jeffersonians. As one might expect, justices who affiliate with the Democratic Party tend to be more liberal in their decision making than those who are Republicans. Some commentators, of course, say that *Bush v. Gore* (2000), in which the Supreme Court issued a ruling that virtually ensured that George W. Bush would be the ultimate victor of the presidential election of 2000, provides an example *(see Chapter 13)*. In that case, five of the Court's Republicans "voted" for Bush, while its two Democrats "voted" for Gore.

69. Helmut Norpoth and Jeffrey A. Segal, "Popular Influence in Supreme Court Decisions," *American Political Science Review* 88 (1994): 711–716.

70. James A. Stimson, Michael B. MacKuen, and Robert S. Erikson, "Dynamic Representation," *American Political Science Review* 89 (September 1995): 556. For a succinct review of this literature, see Bradley C. Canon and Charles A. Johnson, *Judicial Policies*, 2nd ed. (Washington, D.C.: CQ Press, 1999), 196–197.

71. Jonathan Casper, *The Politics of Civil Liberties* (New York: Harper and Row, 1972), 293.

Political pressures from the outside also can affect the Court. Although the justices have no electoral connection or mandate of responsiveness, the other institutions of government have some influence on judicial behavior, and, naturally, the direction of that influence reflects the partisan composition of those branches. The Court has always had a complex relationship with the president, a relationship that provides the president with several possible ways to influence judicial decisions. The president has some direct links with the Court, including (1) the power to nominate justices and shape the Court; (2) personal relationships with sitting justices, including Franklin Roosevelt's with James Byrnes, Lyndon Johnson's with Abe Fortas, and Richard Nixon's with Warren Burger; and (3) the notion that the president, having been elected within the previous four years, may carry a popular mandate, reflecting the preferences of the people, which would affect the environment within which the Court operates.

A less direct source of influence is the executive branch, which operates under the president's command. The bureaucracy can assist the Court in implementing its policies, or it can hinder the Court by refusing to do so, a fact of which the justices are well aware. As a judicial body, the Supreme Court cannot implement or execute its own decisions. It often must depend on the executive branch to give its decisions legitimacy through action. The Court, therefore, may act strategically, anticipating the wishes of the executive branch and responding accordingly to avoid a confrontation that could threaten its legitimacy. *Marbury v. Madison*, in which the Court enunciated the doctrine of judicial review, is the classic example *(see Chapter 2 for an excerpt)*. Some scholars suggest that the justices knew if they ruled a certain way, the Jefferson administration would not carry out their orders. Because the Court felt that such a failure would threaten the legitimacy of judicial institutions, it crafted its opinion in a way that would not force the administration to take any action but would send a message about its displeasure with the administration's politics.

Another indirect source of presidential influence is the U.S. solicitor general. We have already discussed the SG's success as a petitioning party, and the office can have an equally pronounced effect at the merits stage. In fact, data indicate that, whether acting as an amicus curiae or as a party to a suit, the SG's office is generally able to convince the justices to adopt its preferred positions.[72]

Presidential influence is also demonstrated in the kinds of arguments a solicitor general brings into the Court. That is, solicitors general representing Democratic administrations tend to present more liberal arguments; those from the ranks of the Republican Party, more conservative arguments. The transition from the first Bush administration to the Clinton administration provides an interesting illustration. Bush's solicitor general had filed amicus curiae briefs—many of which took a conservative position—in a number of cases heard by the Court during the 1993–1994 term. Drew S. Days III, Clinton's first solicitor general, rewrote at least four of those briefs to reflect the new administration's more liberal posture. For example, Days argued that the Civil Rights Act of 1991 should be applied retroactively, whereas the Bush administration suggested that it should not be. In another case, Days claimed trial attorneys could not systematically challenge prospective jurors on the basis of sex; his predecessor argued that such dismissals were constitutional.

Congress, too—or so some argue—can influence Supreme Court decision making. Like the president, the legislature has many powers over the Court the justices cannot ignore.[73] Some of these resemble presidential powers—the Senate's role in confirmation proceedings, the implementation of judicial decisions—but there are others. Congress can restrict the Court's jurisdiction to hear cases, enact legislation or propose constitutional amendments to recast Court decisions, and hold judicial salaries constant. To forestall a congressional attack, the Court might accede to legislative wishes. Often-cited examples include the Court's willingness to defer to the Radical Republican Congress after the Civil War and to approve New Deal legislation after Roosevelt proposed his Court-packing plan in 1937. Some argue that these examples represent anomalies, not the rule. The Court,

---

72. See Epstein et al., *Supreme Court Compendium*, Tables 7-15 and 7-16.
73. See William N. Eskridge Jr., "Overriding Supreme Court Statutory Interpretation Decisions," *Yale Law Journal* 101 (1991): 331–455.

they say, has no reason to respond strategically to Congress because it is so rare that the legislature threatens, much less takes action, against the judiciary. Only once has Congress retaliated against the Court by removing its jurisdiction over a class of cases—and that occurred more than a hundred years ago. This argument needs to be kept in mind as you read the cases that pit the Court against Congress and the president.

Interest Groups. In *Federalist* No. 78, Alexander Hamilton wrote that the U.S. Supreme Court was "to declare the sense of the law" through "inflexible and uniform adherence to the rights of the constitution and individuals." Despite this expectation, Supreme Court litigation has become political over time. We see manifestations of politics in virtually every aspect of the Court's work, from the nomination and confirmation of justices to the factors that influence their decisions, but perhaps the most striking example of this politicization is the incursion of organized interest groups into the judicial process.

Naturally, interest groups may not attempt to persuade the Supreme Court the same way lobbyists deal with Congress. It would be grossly improper for the representatives of an interest group to approach a Supreme Court justice directly. Instead, as already mentioned, interest groups try to influence Court decisions by submitting written legal arguments called amicus curiae briefs *(see Box 1-2, page 21)*. This procedure allows interest groups to make their views known to the Court, even when the group is not a direct party to the litigation.

These days, it is a rare case before the U.S. Supreme Court that does not attract such submissions. On average, organized interests in recent years filed at least one amicus brief in well over 85 percent of all cases decided by full opinion between 1986 and 2002.[74] In fact, during a typical term in the 1990s, 4.5 amici cosigned each friend of the court brief, for a total of about 1,800 organizational participants. Some cases, particularly those involving such controversial issues as abortion and affirmative action, have attracted even wider participation. In addition to participating as amici, groups are sponsoring cases—that is, providing litigants with attorneys and the money necessary to pursue their cases—in record numbers.

The explosion of interest group participation in Supreme Court litigation raises two questions. First, why do groups go to the Court? The answer is obvious: they want to influence the Court's decisions. But groups also go to the Supreme Court to achieve other, subtler, ends. One is the setting of institutional agendas: by filing amicus curiae briefs at the case-selection stage or by bringing cases to the Court's attention, organizations seek to influence the justices' decisions on which disputes to hear. Group participation also may serve as a counterbalance to other interests that have competing goals. So, for example, if Planned Parenthood, a pro-choice group, observes Life Legal Defense Foundation, a pro-life group, filing an amicus curiae brief in an abortion case (or vice versa), it too may enter the dispute to ensure that its side is represented in the proceedings. Finally, groups go to the Court to publicize their causes and their organizations. The NAACP Legal Defense Fund's legendary litigation campaign to end school segregation provides an excellent example. It resulted not only in a favorable policy decision in *Brown v. Board of Education* (1954), but also it established the LDF as the foremost organizational litigant of this issue.

The second question is this: Can groups influence the outcomes of Supreme Court decisions?[75] This question has no simple answer. When interest groups participate on both sides, it is reasonable to speculate that one or more exerted some intellectual influence or at least that intervention of groups on the winning side neutralized the arguments of those who lost. To be sure of how much influence any group or private party exerted, a researcher would have to interview all the justices who participated in the decision—and they do not grant such interviews—because a citation to a brief may indicate only that a justice is seeking support for a conclusion he or she had already reached.

We can be more certain that many cases would not get into any court, much less the U.S. Supreme Court, without the help of an interest group. Therefore, we can

74. Lee Epstein et al., *Supreme Court Compendium*, Table 7-25.

75. We adopt some of this material from Pritchett, Murphy, and Epstein, *Courts, Judges, and Politics*, chap. 6.

say that, because judges have to wait for cases to come before them, groups help set the judicial agenda. It may be that many judges, especially judges on appellate courts, look on interest groups as sources of important information that otherwise would not come to their attention. Gregory A. Caldeira and John R. Wright's research on amici participation at the agenda-setting stage supports this contention.[76] The growing percentage of U.S. Supreme Court opinions that cite amici's arguments reinforces the point. During the Warren Court, the justices cited amicus curiae briefs in about 40 percent of their opinions; that figure rose to 66 percent for Burger Court justices; and to 68 percent for the Rehnquist Court.[77] It thus seems clear that the justices—now more than ever—are at least learning enough from amici briefs to cite them in their opinions.

Once having gained the attention of a court, attorneys for some groups, such as the Women's Rights Project of the American Civil Liberties Union and the NAACP, are often more experienced and their staffs are more adept at research than counsel for what Marc Galanter calls "one-shotters." [78] For the NAACP, Thurgood Marshall would orchestrate help from allied groups, allocating the task of making specific arguments to each, and enlisting sympathetic social scientists to muster supporting data. Before going to the Supreme Court for oral argument, he would sometimes have a practice session with friendly law professors, each one playing the role of a particular justice and trying to pose the sorts of questions that a justice would be likely to ask. That type of preparation can pay off, but it need not be decisive. During oral arguments in *Regents of the University of California v. Bakke* (1978), a case involving admission of minority students to medical school, Allan Bakke's attorney displayed ignorance of constitutional law and curtly told one justice who tried to help him that he would like to argue the case his own way. Despite this poor performance, Bakke won.

On the other hand, there is strong evidence suggesting that attorneys working for interest groups are no more successful than private counsel. One study paired similar cases decided by the same district court judge, the same year, with the only major difference being that one case was sponsored by a group, the other brought by attorneys unaffiliated with an organized interest. Despite Galanter's contentions about the obstacles confronting one-shotters, the study found no major differences between the two.[79]

In short, the debate over the influence of interest groups continues, and it is a debate that you will have ample opportunity to consider. Within the case excerpts we often provide information on the arguments of amici and attorneys so that you can compare these points with the justices' opinions.

CONDUCTING RESEARCH ON THE SUPREME COURT

As you can see, there is considerable disagreement in the scholarly and legal communities about how justices should interpret the Constitution, and even why they decide cases the way they do. These approaches show up in many of the Court's opinions in this book. Remember that the opinions here are excerpts, designed to highlight the most important points of the various majority, dissenting, and concurring opinions. Occasionally, you may want to read the decisions in their entirety. Following is an explanation of how to locate opinions and other kinds of information on the Court and its members.

Locating Supreme Court Decisions

U.S. Supreme Court decisions are published by various reporters. The four major reporters are: *U.S. Reports, Lawyers' Edition, Supreme Court Reporter,* and *U.S. Law Week.* All contain the opinions of the Court, but they vary in the kinds of ancillary material they provide. For example, as Table 1-4 shows, the *Lawyers' Edition* contains excerpts of the briefs of attorneys submitted in orally argued cases, *U.S. Law Week* provides a topical index of cases on the Court's docket, and so forth.

76. Caldeira and Wright, "Organized Interests and Agenda Setting."

77. See Epstein et al., *Supreme Court Compendium: Data, Decisions, and Developments,* Table 7-27.

78. "Why the 'Haves' Come Out Ahead: Speculations on the Limits of Social Change," *Law and Society Review* 9 (1974): 95.

79. Lee Epstein and C. K. Rowland, "Debunking the Myth of Interest Group Invincibility in the Court," *American Political Science Review* 85 (1991): 205–217.

TABLE 1-4 Reporting Systems

Reporter/Publisher	Form of Citation (terms)	Description
United States Reports Government Printing Office	Dall. 1–4 (1790–1800) Cr. 1–15 (1801–1815) Wheat. 1–12 (1816–1827) Pet. 1–16 (1828–1843) How. 1–24 (1843–1861) Bl. 1–2 (1861–1862) Wall. 1–23 (1863–1875) U.S. 91– (1875–)	Contains official text of opinions of the Court. Includes tables of cases reported, cases and statutes cited, miscellaneous materials, and subject index. Includes most of the Court's decisions. Court opinions prior to 1875 are cited by the name of the Reporter of the Court. For example, Dall. stands for Alexander J. Dallas, the first reporter.
United States Supreme Court Reports, Lawyers' Edition Lawyers' Cooperative Publishing Company	L. Ed. L. Ed. 2d	Contains official reports of opinions of the Court. Additionally, provides per curiam and other decisions not found elsewhere. Summarizes individual majority and dissenting opinions and counsel briefs.
Supreme Court Reporter West Publishing Company	S. Ct.	Contains official reports of opinions of the Court. Contains annotated reports and indexes of case names. Includes opinions of justices in chambers. Appears semi-monthly.
United States Law Week Bureau of National Affairs	U.S.L.W.	Weekly periodical service containing full text of Court decisions. Includes four indexes: topical, table of cases, docket number table, and proceedings section. Contains summary of cases filed recently, journal of proceedings, summary of orders, arguments before the Court, argued cases awaiting decisions, review of Court's work, and review of Court's docket.

SOURCES: Lee Epstein, Jeffrey A. Segal, Harold J. Spaeth, and Thomas G. Walker, *The Supreme Court Compendium: Data, Decisions, and Developments*, 3rd ed. (Washington, D.C.: CQ Press, 2003), Table 2-9. Dates of reporters are from Joan Biskupic and Elder Witt, *Guide to the U.S. Supreme Court*, 3rd ed. (Washington, D.C.: Congressional Quarterly, 1997), 826.

Locating cases within these reporters is easy if you know the case *citation*. Case citations, as the table shows, take different forms, but they all work in roughly the same way. To see how, turn to page 268 to find an excerpt of *Mistretta v. United States* (1989). Directly under the case name is a citation: 488 U.S. 361, which means that *Mistretta v. United States* appears in volume 488, page 361, of *U.S. Reports*.[80] The first set of numbers is the volume number; the U.S. is the form of citation for *U.S. Reports;* and the second set of numbers is the starting page of the case.

80. In this book, we list only the *U.S. Reports* cite because it is the official record of Supreme Court decisions. It is the only reporter published by the federal government; the three others are privately printed. Almost every law library has *U.S. Reports*. If your college does not have a law school, check with your librarians. If they have any Court reporter, it is probably *U.S. Reports*.

Mistretta v. United States also can be located in the three other reporters. The citations are as follows:

> *Lawyers' Edition:* 102 L. Ed. 2d 714 (1989)
> *Supreme Court Reporter:* 109 S. Ct. 647 (1989)
> *U.S. Law Week:* 57 U.S.L.W. 4102 (1989)

Note that the abbreviations vary by reporter, but they parallel the *U.S. Reports* in that the first set of numbers is the volume number, and the second set is the starting page number.

If you do not know the citation, try to find out the year the case was decided. With this information, you can check the index of the appropriate volume of the *U.S. Reports (see Appendix 6)* or of the other reporters.

In addition to these print volumes, Supreme Court opinions are available in various electronic forms. First, several companies maintain databases of the decisions of federal and state courts, along with a wealth of other information. In some institutions these services—LEXIS-NEXIS and Westlaw—are available only to law school students. Check with your librarians to see if your school provides access to other students, perhaps via Academic Universe (a subset of the LEXIS-NEXIS service). Second, the Legal Information Institute (LII) at Cornell Law School (www.law.cornell.edu), FindLaw (www.findlaw.com/casecode/supreme.html), and FedWorld (www.fedworld.gov/supcourt/index.htm)—to name just three—index Supreme Court opinions and offer an array of indices and search capabilities. You can read the opinions from your browser (for example, Netscape Navigator), have them e-mailed to you, or download them immediately. The LII site contains cases decided since 1990; it also houses an archive of selected historically important Court opinions (http://supct.law.cornell.edu/supct/cases/ name.htm); FindLaw's site contains Supreme Court opinions dating back to 1893; FedWorld has more than seven thousand cases from 1937 to 1975. If a case we have excerpted is located in these archives, we have noted the URL after the case citation.

Locating Other Information on the Supreme Court and Its Members

As you might imagine, there is no shortage of reference material on the Court. Four good (print) starting points are:

1. *The U.S. Supreme Court: A Bibliography* is an annotated bibliography of scholarly writings on the Court.[81] Entries cover the development of the Court, its work, various areas of the law, and the justices.

2. *The Supreme Court Compendium: Data, Decisions, and Developments*, third edition, contains information on the following dimensions of Court activity: the Court's development, review process, opinions and decisions, judicial background, voting patterns, and impact.[82] You will find data as varied as the number of cases the Court decided during a particular term, the votes in the Senate on Supreme Court nominees, and the law schools the justices attended.

3. *Guide to the U.S. Supreme Court*, third edition, provides a fairly detailed history of the Court. It also summarizes the holdings in landmark cases and provides brief biographies of the justices.[83]

4. *The Oxford Companion to the Supreme Court of the United States* is an encyclopedia, containing entries on the justices, important Court cases, the amendments to the Constitution, and so forth.[84]

The U.S. Supreme Court also gets a great deal of attention on the World Wide Web. The Legal Information Institute (www.law.cornell.edu) is particularly useful. In addition to Supreme Court decisions, the LII contains links to various documents (such as the U.S. Code and state statutes) and to a vast array of legal indexes and libraries. If you are unable to find the material you are looking for here, you may locate it by clicking on one of the links.

Another worthwhile site is the home page of the Law and Courts Section of the American Political Science Association (www.law.nyu.edu/lawcourts). Devoted to promoting interest in teaching and research in the areas of law and the judicial process, this site contains links to papers, data sources, and other Web sites relating to law and courts.

As already mentioned, you can listen to selected oral arguments of the Court at the Oyez Project site (www.oyez.org/oyez/frontpage). Oyez contains audio files of Supreme Court oral arguments for selected constitutional cases decided since the 1950s. For those cases included in the archive, we provide the URLs.

Finally, in 2000 the Court put up its own Web site (www.supremecourtus.gov). There you will find historical information about the Court, as well as opinions, orders, and the Court's current calendar.

81. Fenton S. Martin and Robert U. Goehlert, *The U.S. Supreme Court: A Bibliography* (Washington, D.C.: Congressional Quarterly, 1990).
82. Epstein et al., *Supreme Court Compendium*.
83. Joan Biskupic and Elder Witt, *Guide to the U.S. Supreme Court*, 3rd ed. (Washington, D.C.: Congressional Quarterly, 1997).
84. Kermit Hall, ed., *The Oxford Companion to the Supreme Court of the United States* (New York: Oxford University Press, 1992).

These are just a few of the many sites—perhaps hundreds—that contain information on the federal courts. To find others, invoke search engines, such as Yahoo *(www.yahoo.com)* or AltaVista *(www.altavista. com)*, which are vehicles for locating legal and other resources that the sites listed above may not contain. Enter the search word(s), and the engine will match the term against its database of Web sites. If you want to limit your search to legal resources, invoke one of Yahoo's or AltaVista's specific search index mechanisms—for example, Government: Law, Legal Research *(www.yahoo. com/Government/Law/Legal_Research)*. From there, you can conduct general searches or further limit your search to one of the following categories: Academic Papers, Cases, Companies, Institutes, Journals, or Libraries.

There is at least one other important electronic source of information on the Court—Harold J. Spaeth's computer-dependent U.S. Supreme Court Judicial Databases. They provide a wealth of data beginning with the Vinson Court (1946 term) to the present. Among the many attributes of Court decisions coded by Spaeth are the names of the courts making the original decision, the identities of the parties to the cases, the policy context of a case, and the votes of each justice. You can obtain the databases and accompanying documentation, free of charge *(www.polisci.msu.edu/pljp/)*. The databases also are available to faculty, staff, and students at colleges and universities that are members of the Inter-University Consortium for Political and Social Science Research in Ann Arbor, Michigan.

In this chapter, we have examined Supreme Court procedures and attempted to shed some light on how and why justices make the choices they do. Our consideration of preference-based factors, for example, highlighted the role ideology plays in Court decision making, and our discussion of political explanations emphasized public opinion and interest groups. After reading this chapter, you may have concluded that the justices are relatively free to go about their business as they please. But, as we shall see in the next chapter, that is not necessarily so. Although Court members have a good deal of power and the freedom to exercise it, they also face considerable institutional obstacles. It is to the subjects of judicial power and constraints that we now turn.

READINGS

Ackerman, Bruce. *We the People.* Cambridge: Harvard University Press, 1991.

Alexander, Larry, ed. *Constitutionalism: Philosophical Foundations.* Cambridge: Cambridge University Press, 1998.

Amar, Akhil Reed. *The Bill of Rights: Creation and Reconstruction.* New Haven: Yale University Press, 1998.

Barber, Sotirios. *On What the Constitution Means.* Baltimore: Johns Hopkins University Press, 1984.

Baum, Lawrence. *The Puzzle of Judicial Behavior.* University of Michigan Press, 1997.

———. *The Supreme Court,* 7th ed. Washington, D.C.: CQ Press, 2001.

Bickel, Alexander. *The Least Dangerous Branch of Government.* Indianapolis: Bobbs-Merrill, 1962.

Biskupic, Joan, and Elder Witt. *Guide to the U.S. Supreme Court,* 3rd ed. Washington, D.C.: Congressional Quarterly, 1997.

Bobbitt, Philip. *Constitutional Interpretation.* Cambridge: Basil Blackwell, 1991.

Bork, Robert. "Neutral Principles and Some First Amendment Problems." *Indiana Law Journal* 47 (1971): 1–35.

Brenner, Saul, and Harold J. Spaeth. *Stare Indecisis: The Alteration of Precedent on the Supreme Court, 1946–1992.* New York: Cambridge University Press, 1995.

Burt, Robert A. *The Constitution in Conflict.* Cambridge: Belknap Press, 1992.

Caldeira, Gregory A., and John R. Wright. "The Discuss List: Agenda Building in the Supreme Court." *Law and Society Review* 24 (1990): 807–836.

———. "Organized Interests and Agenda Setting in the U.S. Supreme Court." *American Political Science Review* 82 (1988): 1109–1127.

Canon, Bradley C., and Charles A. Johnson. *Judicial Policies: Implementation and Impact,* 2nd ed. Washington, D.C.: CQ Press, 1998.

Carter, Lief H. *Contemporary Constitutional Lawmaking.* New York: Pergamon Press, 1985.

———. *An Introduction to Constitutional Interpretation: Cases in Law and Religion.* New York: Longman, 1991.

———. *Reason in Law,* 4th ed. New York: HarperCollins, 1994.

Casper, Jonathan. *The Politics of Civil Liberties.* New York: Harper and Row, 1972.

Clayton, Cornell W., and Howard Gillman, eds. *Supreme Court Decision-Making: New Institutionalist Approaches.* Chicago: University of Chicago Press, 1999.

Crapanzano, Vincent. *Serving the Word: Literalism in America from the Pulpit to the Bench.* New York: New Press, 2000.

Crosskey, W. W., and William Jeffrey Jr. *Politics and the Constitution in the History of the United States.* Chicago: University of Chicago Press, 1980.

Duxbury, Neil. *Patterns of American Jurisprudence.* Oxford: Clarendon Press, 1995.

Dworkin, Ronald. *Taking Rights Seriously.* Cambridge: Harvard University Press, 1977.

Epstein, Lee, and Jack Knight. *The Choices Justices Make.* Washington, D.C.: CQ Press, 1998.

Epstein, Lee, Jeffrey A. Segal, Harold J. Spaeth, and Thomas G. Walker. *The Supreme Court Compendium: Data, Decisions, and Developments,* 3rd ed. Washington, D.C.: CQ Press, 2003.

Epstein, Lee, Thomas G. Walker, and William Dixon. "On the Mysterious Demise of Consensual Norms in the United States Supreme Court." *Journal of Politics* 50 (1988): 361–389.

Fallon, Richard H., Jr. *Implementing the Constitution.* Cambridge: Harvard University Press, 2001.

Farber, Daniel A., and Suzanna Sherry. *Desperately Seeking Certainty.* Chicago: University of Chicago Press, 2002.

Fisher, Louis. *Constitutional Dialogues.* Princeton: Princeton University Press, 1988.

Gibson, James L. "Judges' Role Orientations, Attitudes, and Decisions." *American Political Science Review* 72 (1978): 911–924.

Gillman, Howard. *The Constitution Besieged: The Rise and Demise of Lochner Era Police Powers Jurisprudence.* Durham: Duke University Press, 1993.

———. *The Votes That Counted.* Chicago: University of Chicago Press, 2001.

Goldstein, Leslie Friedman. *In Defense of the Text.* Savage, Md.: Rowman and Littlefield, 1991.

Goodhart, Arthur L. "Determining the Ratio Decidendi of a Case." *Yale Law Journal* 40 (1930): 161–183.

Halpern, Stephen C., and Charles M. Lamb, eds. *Supreme Court Activism and Restraint.* Lexington, Mass.: D. C. Heath, 1982.

Howard, J. Woodford. "On the Fluidity of Judicial Choice." *American Political Science Review* 62 (1968): 43–56.

Kahn, Ronald. "Institutional Norms and Supreme Court Decision-Making: The Rehnquist Court on Privacy and Religion." In *Supreme Court Decision-Making: New Institutionalist Approaches.* Ed. Cornell W. Clayton and Howard Gillman. Chicago: University of Chicago Press, 1999.

———. *The Supreme Court and Constitutional Theory.* Lawrence: University Press of Kansas, 1994.

Knight, Jack, and Lee Epstein. "The Norm of Stare Decisis." *American Journal of Political Science* 40 (1996): 1018–1035.

Lawrence, Susan E. *The Poor in Court.* Princeton: Princeton University Press, 1990.

Lee, Thomas R. "Stare Decisis in Historical Perspective: From the Founding Era to the Rehnquist Court." *Vanderbilt Law Review* 52 (1999): 647–734.

Levinson, Sanford V. *Constitutional Faith.* Princeton: Princeton University Press, 1988.

Levy, Leonard W. *Origins of the Bill of Rights.* New Haven: Yale University Press, 1999.

Lynch, Joseph M. *Negotiating the Constitution: The Earliest Debates over Original Intent.* Ithaca: Cornell University Press, 1999.

Maltzman, Forrest, and Paul J. Wahlbeck. "May It Please the Chief? Opinion Assignments in the Rehnquist Court." *American Journal of Political Science* 40 (1996): 421–443.

———. "Strategic Policy Considerations and Voting Fluidity on the Burger Court." *American Political Science Review* 90 (1996): 581–592.

Maltzman, Forrest, Paul J. Wahlbeck, and James Spriggs. *Crafting Law on the Supreme Court: The Collegial Game.* New York: Cambridge University Press, 2000.

Marshall, Thomas. *Public Opinion and the Supreme Court.* New York: Unwin Hyman, 1989.

Marshall, Thurgood. "Reflections on the Bicentennial of the United States Constitution." *Harvard Law Review* 101 (1987): 1–5.

Martin, Fenton S., and Robert U. Goehlert. *The U.S. Supreme Court: A Bibliography.* Washington, D.C.: Congressional Quarterly, 1990.

McCloskey, Robert G. *The American Supreme Court.* Chicago: University of Chicago Press, 1960.

McGuire, Kevin T. *The Supreme Court Bar: Legal Elites in the Washington Community.* Charlottesville: University Press of Virginia, 1993.

Mishler, William, and Reginald S. Sheehan. "The Supreme Court as a Counter-Majoritarian Institution? The Impact of Public Opinion on Supreme Court Decisions." *American Political Science Review* 87 (1993): 87–101.

Moore, Wayne D. *Constitutional Rights and the Powers of the People.* Princeton: Princeton University Press.

Murphy, Walter J. *Elements of Judicial Strategy.* Chicago: University of Chicago Press, 1964.

Murphy, Walter J., C. Herman Pritchett, and Lee Epstein. *Courts, Judges, and Politics.* New York: Macmillan, 2002.

Norpoth, Helmut, and Jeffrey A. Segal. "Popular Influence in Supreme Court Decisions." *American Political Science Review* 88 (1994): 711–716.

Pacelle, Richard L., Jr. *The Transformation of the Supreme Court's Agenda.* Boulder: Westview Press, 1991.

Perry, H. W., Jr. *Deciding to Decide: Agenda Setting in the United States Supreme Court.* Cambridge: Harvard University Press, 1991.

Perry, Michael J. *The Constitution in the Courts: Law or Politics?* New York: Oxford University Press, 1994.

Porto, Brian L. *The Craft of Legal Reasoning.* Fort Worth: Harcourt Brace, 1998.

Posner, Richard. *The Problems of Jurisprudence.* Cambridge: Harvard University Press, 1990.

Powell, Jefferson H. "The Original Understanding of Original Intent." *Harvard Law Review* 91 (1985): 885–947.

Powell, Lewis F., Jr. "What Really Goes on at the Supreme Court." *American Bar Association Journal* 66 (1980): 721–723.

Pritchett, C. Herman. *The Roosevelt Court.* New York: Macmillan, 1948.

Provine, Doris Marie. *Case Selection in the United States Supreme Court.* Chicago: University of Chicago Press, 1980.

Rehnquist, William. "The Notion of a Living Constitution." *Texas Law Review* 54 (1976): 693–706.

Segal, Jeffrey A. "Predicting Supreme Court Cases Probabilistically: The Search and Seizure Cases, 1962–1984." *American Political Science Review* 78 (1984): 891–900.

Segal, Jeffrey A., and Harold J. Spaeth. *The Supreme Court and the Attitudinal Model.* New York: Cambridge University Press, 1993.

———. *The Supreme Court and the Attitudinal Model Revisited.* New York: Cambridge University Press, 2003.

Shaman, Jeffrey M. *Constitutional Interpretation: Illusion and Reality.* Westport, Conn.: Greenwood Press, 2001.

Sherry, Suzanna. "Textualism and Judgment." *George Washington Law Review* 66 (1998): 1148–1152.

Slotnick, Elliot F. "Who Speaks for the Court? Majority Opinion Assignment from Taft to Burger." *American Journal of Political Science* 23 (1979): 60–77.

Smith, Rogers M. "Political Jurisprudence, The 'New Institutionalism,' and the Future of Public Law." *American Political Science Review* 82 (1988): 89–108.

Spaeth, Harold J., and Jeffrey A. Segal. *Majority Rule or Minority Will.* New York: Cambridge University Press, 1999.

Stearns, Maxwell L. *Constitutional Process: A Social Choice Analysis of Supreme Court Decision Making.* Ann Arbor: University of Michigan Press, 2000.

Sunstein, Cass R. *The Partial Constitution.* Cambridge: Harvard University Press, 1993.

Tribe, Laurence H., and Michael C. Dorf. *On Reading the Constitution.* Cambridge: Harvard University Press, 1991.

Tushnet, Mark V. "A Note on the Revival of Textualism." *Southern California Law Review* 58 (1985): 683–700.

van Geel, T. R. *Understanding Supreme Court Opinions.* New York: Longman, 1991.

Wahlbeck, Paul J., James F. Spriggs, and Forrest Maltzman. "Marshalling the Court: Bargaining and Accommodation on the United States Supreme Court." *American Journal of Political Science* 42 (1998): 294–315.

Walker, Thomas G., and Lee Epstein. *The Supreme Court of the United States: An Introduction.* New York: St. Martin's Press, 1992.

Wasby, Stephen L. *The Supreme Court in the Federal Judicial System,* 4th ed. Chicago: Nelson-Hall, 1993.

Wechsler, Herbert. "Toward Neutral Principles of Constitutional Law." *Harvard Law Review* 43 (1959): 1–35.

Wellington, Harry H. *Interpreting the Constitution: The Supreme Court and the Process of Adjudication.* New Haven: Yale University Press, 1990.

Whittington, Keith E. *Constitutional Interpretation: Textual Meaning, Original Intent, and Judicial Review.* Lawrence: University Press of Kansas, 1999.

PART II
INSTITUTIONAL AUTHORITY

STRUCTURING THE FEDERAL SYSTEM

STRUCTURING THE FEDERAL SYSTEM

ONE OF THE first things anyone learns in an American government course is that two concepts undergird our constitutional system. The first is the separation of powers doctrine, under which each of the branches has a distinct function: the legislature makes the laws, the executive implements those laws, and the judiciary interprets them. The second is the notion of checks and balances: each branch of government imposes limits on the primary function of the others. For example, the Supreme Court may interpret laws and even strike them down as being in violation of the Constitution. But congressional committees can introduce legislation to override the Court's decision; if they do, Congress must act by either adopting the committees' recommendation, enacting a different version of it, or rejecting it. If Congress takes action, then the president has the option of vetoing the law. If that happens, Congress must decide whether to override the president's veto. Seen in this way, the rule of checks and balances inherent in the system of separation of powers suggests that policy in the United States emanates not from the separate actions of the branches of government but from the interaction among them.

A full understanding of the basics of institutional powers and constraints thus requires a consideration of three important subjects. First, we must investigate the separation of powers doctrine and why the Framers adopted it, a subject we take up in the following pages. Second, because of the unique role the judiciary plays in the American government system, we need to understand how the Court has interpreted its own powers (located in Article III) and the constraints on those powers, as well as those of Congress (Article I) and the president (Article II). We consider these matters in Chapters 2, 3, and 4. Finally, we need to understand how the Court has dealt with situations when the various institutions take on roles other than those ascribed to them in the Constitution (such as when the legislature exerts executive powers and vice versa) or when the Constitution is ambiguous about which branch has what powers (such as the power to make war). Chapter 5 takes up these important topics.

THE ORIGINS OF THE SEPARATION OF POWERS/CHECKS AND BALANCES SYSTEM

Even a casual comparison of the Articles of Confederation with the Constitution reveals major differences in the way the two documents structured the national government (*see Figure 1-1, page 14*). Under the articles, the powers of government were concentrated in the legislature, a unicameral Congress, in which the states had equal voting powers. There was no executive or judicial branch separate and independent from the legislature. Issues of separation of powers and checks and balances were not particularly relevant to the articles, largely because the national government had too little power to abuse it. The states were capable of checking anything the central government proposed, and they provided whatever restraints the newly independent nation needed.

The government under the Articles of Confederation failed at least in part because it lacked sufficient power and authority to cope with the problems of the day. The requirements for amending the document were so restrictive that fundamental change within the articles proved impossible. When the Constitutional Convention met in Philadelphia in 1787, the delegates soon concluded that the articles had to be scrapped and replaced with a charter that would provide more effective power for the national government. The country had experienced conditions of economic decline, crippling taxation policies, interstate barriers to commerce, and isolated but alarming insurrections among the lower economic classes. The Framers saw a newly structured national government as the only method of dealing with the problems besetting the nation in the aftermath of the Revolution.

But allocating significant power to the national government was not without its risks. Many of the Framers feared the creation of a federal power capable of dominating the states and abusing individual liberties. It was apparent to all that the new government would have to be structured in a way that the potential for abuse and excess would be minimized. The concept of the separation of powers and its twin, the idea of checks and balances, appealed to the Framers as the best way to accomplish these necessary restraints.

The theory of separation of powers was not new to the Framers. They were introduced to it by the political philosophy of the day and by their own political experiences. The theories of James Harrington and Charles de Montesquieu were particularly influential in this respect. Harrington (1611–1677) was an English political philosopher whose emphasis on the importance of property found a sympathetic audience among the former colonists. Harrington's primary work, *Oceana*, published in 1656, was a widely read description of a model government. Incorporated into Harrington's ideal state was the notion that government powers ought to be divided into three parts. A Senate made up of the intellectual elite would propose laws; the people, guided by the Senate's wisdom, would enact the laws; and a magistrate would execute the laws. This system, Harrington argued, would impose an important balance that would maintain a stable government and protect property rights.

Harrington's concept of a separation of powers was less well developed than that later proposed by Montesquieu (1689–1755), a French political theorist. Many scholars consider his *Spirit of the Laws* (1748), widely circulated during the last half of the eighteenth century, to be the classic treatise on the separation of powers philosophy. Montesquieu was concerned about government abuse of liberty. In his estimation, liberty could not long prevail if too much power accrued to a single ruler or a single branch of government. He flatly warned, "When the legislative and executive powers are united in the same person, or the same body of magistrates, there can be no liberty. . . . Again, there is no liberty if the judicial power be not separated from the legislative and executive." Although Montesquieu's message was directed at the citizens of his own country, he found a more receptive audience in the United States.

The influence of these political thinkers was reinforced by the Framers' political experiences. The settlers had come to the New World largely to escape the abuses of the European governments. The treatment of the colonies by George III taught them that executives were not to be trusted with too much power. The colonists also feared an independent and powerful judiciary, especially if it were not answerable to the people. While the legislature was undoubtedly the institution in which the Framers had the most confidence, they knew it too had the potential of exceeding its proper bounds. The English experience during the reign of Oliver Cromwell was lesson enough that muting the power of the king did not necessarily lead to the elimination of government abuse. What the Framers sought was balance, a system in which each branch of government would be strong enough to keep excessive power from flowing into the hands of any other single branch. This necessary balance, as John Adams pointed out in his *Defense of the Constitutions of Government of the United States of America* (1787–1788), would also have the advantage of being able to keep the power-hungry aristocracy in check and prevent the majority from taking away rights from the minority.

SEPARATION OF POWERS
AND THE CONSTITUTION

The debates at the Constitutional Convention and the various plans that were presented for the delegates' consideration all focused on the issue of dividing government power among the three branches as well as between the national government and the states. A general fear of a concentration of power permeated all the discussions. James Madison noted, "The truth is, all men having power ought to be distrusted to a certain degree." The Framers' solution to the exceedingly difficult problem of expanding government power, while at the same time reducing the probability of abuse, was found in their proposed new Constitution of the United States.

Although the term *separation of powers* is nowhere to be found in the document, the Constitution plainly adopts the central tenets of the theory. A reading of the first lines of each of the first three articles makes this point clearly.

All legislative Powers herein granted shall be vested in a Congress of the United States, which shall consist of a Senate and House of Representatives. [Article I]

The executive Power shall be vested in a President of the United States of America. [Article II]

The judicial Power of the United States, shall be vested in one supreme Court, and in such inferior Courts as the Congress may from time to time ordain and establish. [Article III]

In the scheme of government incorporated into the Constitution, the legislative, executive, and judicial powers each resided in a separate branch of government. Unless otherwise specified in the document, each branch was limited to the political function granted to it, and that function could not be exercised by either of the other two branches.

In addition to the separation concept, the Framers placed into the Constitution a number of mixed powers. That is, while the document reserves certain functions for specific branches, it also provides explicit checks on the exercise of those powers. As a consequence, each branch of government imposes limits on the primary functions of the others. A few examples illustrate this point.

Congress has the right to pass legislation, but the president may veto the bills passed by Congress.

The president may veto bills passed by Congress, but the legislature may override the president's veto.

The president may make treaties with foreign powers, but the Senate must vote its approval of those treaties.

The president is commander in chief of the army and navy, but Congress must pass legislation to raise armies, regulate the military, and declare war.

The president may nominate federal judges, but the Senate must confirm them.

The judiciary may interpret the law and even strike down laws as being in violation of the Constitution, but Congress may pass new legislation or propose constitutional amendments.

Congress may pass laws, but the executive must enforce them.

In addition to these offsetting powers, the Framers structured each branch so that the criteria and procedures for selecting the officials of each institution differed, as did their tenures. Consequently, each branch has a slightly different source of political power. In the original scheme these differences were even more pronounced than they are today.

For example, in the original version of the Constitution, the two houses of Congress were politically dependent upon different selection processes. Members of the House were, as they are today, directly elected by the people, and the seats were apportioned among the states on the basis of population. With terms of only two years, the representatives were required to go back to the people for review on a frequent and regular basis. Senators, on the other hand, were, and still are, representatives of whole states, with each state having two members in the upper chamber. But senators originally were selected by the state legislatures, a system that was not changed until the Seventeenth Amendment, which imposed popular election of senators, was ratified in 1913. The six-year, staggered terms of senators were intended to make the upper house less immediately responsive to the volatile nature of public opinion.

The Constitution dictated that the president be selected by an electoral college, a group of political elites selected by the people or their representatives who would exercise judgment in casting their ballots among presidential candidates. Although the electors over time have ceased to perform any truly independent selection function, presidential selection remains a step away from direct popular election. The president's four-year term places the office squarely between the tenures conferred on representatives and senators. The original Constitution placed no limits on the number of terms a president could serve, but a traditional two-term limit was observed until 1940 and was then imposed by constitutional amendment in 1951.

Differing altogether from the other two branches is the judiciary, which was assigned the least democratic selection system. The people have no direct role in the selection or retention of federal judges. Instead, the president nominates individuals for the federal bench, and the Senate confirms them. Once in office, federal judges serve for terms of good behavior, removable against their will only through impeachment. The intent of the Framers was to make the judiciary independent. To do so they created a system in which judges would not depend on the mood of the masses or on a single appointing power. Furthermore, judges would be accountable only to their own philosophies and consciences, with no periodic review or reassessment required.

Through a division of powers, an imposition of checks, and a variation in selection and tenure requirements, the Framers hoped to achieve the balanced government they desired. This structure, they thought, would be the greatest protection against abuses of power and government violations of personal liberties and property rights. Many delegates to the Constitutional Convention considered this system of separation of powers a much more effective method of protecting civil liberties than the formal pronouncements of a bill of rights.

Most political observers would conclude that the Framers' invention has worked remarkably well. As the government has evolved through the years, the relative strengths of the branches have changed back and forth. At certain times, for example, the judiciary was excep-

tionally weak, such as during the pre-Marshall era and before the Civil War. At other times, however, the judiciary has been criticized as being too powerful, such as when it repeatedly blocked New Deal legislation in the 1930s or expanded civil liberties during the Warren Court era. The executive also has led the other branches in political power. Beginning with the tenure of Franklin Roosevelt, for example, and extending into the 1970s, references were often made to the "imperial presidency." But when one branch gains too much power and abuses occur, as in the case of Richard Nixon and the Watergate crisis, the system tends to reimpose the balance intended by the Framers.

CONTEMPORARY THINKING ON THE CONSTITUTIONAL SCHEME: SEPARATION OF POWERS GAMES

As you read the four chapters in this part and consider the original understandings of the separation of powers doctrine, you may also want to take into account contemporary thinking about the relationships among the three branches of government. The past decade or so has witnessed a resurgence of interest in this area of study, with scholars offering novel frameworks to examine federal policy making.

Among the most intriguing are the "separation of powers games" offered by law professor William Eskridge and political scientists John Ferejohn and Barry Weingast, among others.[1] These games typically operate under some simple assumptions about the goals of the various institutions of government and the way the political process works. According to this school of thought, the aims of the institutions of government are to see the government's policy—for our purposes, the ultimate state of the law—reflect their positions. Or, to put it in

1. William N. Eskridge Jr., "Reneging on History: Playing the Court/Congress/President Civil Rights Game," *California Law Review* 79 (1991): 613–684; Eskridge, "Overriding Supreme Court Statutory Interpretation Decisions," *Yale Law Journal* 101 (1991): 331–455; John A. Ferejohn and Barry Weingast, "Limitation of Statutes: Strategic Statutory Interpretation," *International Review of Law and Economics* 12 (1992): 263–279. See also Jack Knight and Lee Epstein, *The Choices Justices Make*, Washington, D.C.: CQ Press, 1998; and Pablo T. Spiller and Rafael Gely, "Congressional Control or Judicial Independence: The Determinants of U.S. Supreme Court Labor-Relations Decisions," *RAND Journal of Economics* 23 (1992): 463–492.

FIGURE II-1   The Supreme Court as a *Strategic* National Policy Maker

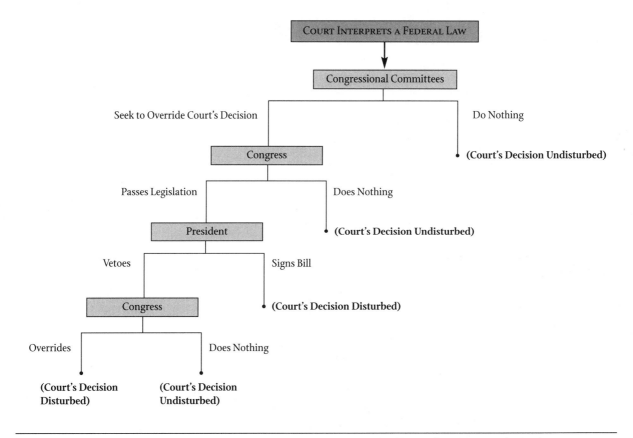

SOURCE: Lee Epstein, Jack Knight, and Andrew Martin, "The Supreme Court as a *Strategic* National Policy Maker," *Emory Law Journal* 50 (2001): 593.

more technical terms, the branches want policy set as close as possible to their ideal or most preferred point. The problem—and here is where assumptions about the nature of the process, including the separation of powers doctrine, come in—is that the political institutions do not make policy in isolation from one another. Rather, policy is set (or the game is played out) along the lines set out in Figure II-1. In this example, the Supreme Court makes the first "move" when it interprets a congressional statute, a constitutional provision, and so forth. Congressional committees and other "gatekeepers" (majority party leaders) then must decide whether they want to introduce legislation or a constitutional amendment to override the Court's decision; if they do, Congress must act by adopting the gatekeepers' recommendation, adopting a different version of it, or rejecting it. If Congress acts by passing legislation, then the president has the option of vetoing the law; the last move rests again with Congress, which must decide whether to override the president's veto.[2]

2. In Figure II-1 we depict a sequence in which the Court makes the first "move" and Congress the last. Of course, it is possible to lay out other sequences and to include other (or different) actors. For example, we could construct a scenario in which the Court moves first; congressional committees and Congress again go next, but this time they propose a constitutional amendment (rather than a law); and the states (not the president) have the last turn by deciding whether or not to ratify the amendment.

From these premises about the institutions' goals and about the sequence of play, perhaps you can see why the separation of powers doctrine is so important. Think about it this way. If the Supreme Court were the only American institution, it would merely set policy at its preferred point; it would not need to consider the positions of congressional gatekeepers, Congress as a whole, or the president. We know, however, that the Court is but one of several players in the game; therefore, it may take into account the preferences of others. If it sets the policy too far away from the position of, say, Congress, it could face an override. The legislature might attempt to overturn the Court's decision or "punish" the justices in other ways.

The last statement raises an interesting point: although the separation of powers games proposed by Eskridge and others were designed to cover instances of statutory interpretation, where it is clear that Congress and the president can modify Court decisions, some have suggested that they may be applicable (though perhaps in a different form) to constitutional interpretation as well.[3] The reason is that, as we consider in some detail in the next chapter, the other branches possess various powers through which they can modify constitutional decisions or invoke various mechanisms to sanction the Court.

As we explore these various checks on the Court, and, more generally, the constitutional separation of powers/ checks and balances system, keep in mind these contemporary studies of the system of separation of powers. To what extent do the justices' perceptions of Congress and the president influence their decisions? You will have ample opportunity to think about this question, for in the coming pages we also examine the significant political and legal clashes among the executive, legislative, and judicial branches, focusing on how the justices of the Supreme Court have interpreted and applied the Constitution to settle disputes. Throughout these constitutional

controversies, fundamental issues of institutional powers and the constraints placed on those powers have taken center stage.

READINGS

Black, Charles L., Jr. *Structure and Relationship in Constitutional Law.* Baton Rouge: Louisiana State University Press, 1969.

Burgess, Susan R. *Contest for Constitutional Authority.* Lawrence: University Press of Kansas, 1992.

Campbell, Colton C., and John F. Stack Jr., eds. *Congress Confronts the Court: The Struggle for Legitimacy and Authority in Lawmaking.* Lanham, Md.: Rowman & Littlefield, 2001.

Casper, Gerhard. "An Essay in Separation of Powers: Some Early Versions and Practices." *William & Mary Law Review* 30 (1989): 211–261.

Epstein, Lee, Jack Knight, and Andrew Martin. "The Supreme Court as a *Strategic* National Policy Maker." *Emory Law Journal* 50 (2001): 583–612.

Eskridge, William N., Jr. "Reneging on History: Playing the Court/ Congress/President Civil Rights Game." *California Law Review* 79 (1991): 613–684.

Eskridge, William N., Jr., and John A. Ferejohn. "The Article I, Section 7 Game." *Georgetown Law Journal* 80 (1992): 523–563.

Farber, Daniel A., and Philip P. Frickey. *Law and Public Choice.* Chicago: University of Chicago Press, 1991.

Ferejohn, John A., and Barry Weingast. "Limitation of Statutes: Strategic Statutory Interpretation." *International Review of Law and Economics* 12 (1992): 263–279.

Fisher, Louis. *Constitutional Dialogues: Interpretation as Political Process.* Princeton, N.J.: Princeton University Press, 1988.

Fisher, Louis, and Neal Devins. *Political Dynamics of Constitutional Law,* 3rd ed. St. Paul, Minn.: West, 2001.

Gwyn, William B. *The Meaning of the Separation of Powers.* New Orleans: Tulane University Press, 1965.

Knight, Barbara B. *Separation of Powers in the American Political System.* Fairfax, Va.: George Mason University Press, 1989.

Knight, Jack, and Lee Epstein. "On the Struggle for Judicial Supremacy." *Law and Society Review* 30 (1996): 87–120.

Kurland, Philip B. *Watergate and the Constitution.* Chicago: University of Chicago Press, 1978.

Meernik, James, and Joseph Ignagni. "Judicial Review and Coordinate Construction of the Constitution." *American Journal of Political Science* 41 (1997): 447–467.

Pocock, J. G. A. *The Political Works of James Harrington.* New York: Cambridge University Press, 1977.

Richter, Melvin. *The Political Theory of Montesquieu.* New York: Cambridge University Press, 1977.

Rosenberg, Gerald N. "Judicial Independence and the Reality of Political Power." *Review of Politics* 54 (1992): 369–398.

Vanderbilt, Arthur T. *The Doctrine of the Separation of Powers and Its Present Day Significance.* Lincoln: University of Nebraska Press, 1953.

Vile, M. J. C. *Constitutionalism and the Separation of Powers.* Oxford: Clarendon Press, 1967.

3. See Lee Epstein, Jack Knight, and Andrew Martin, "The Supreme Court as a *Strategic* National Policy Maker," *Emory Law Journal* 50 (2001): 583–612; Louis Fisher, "Congressional Checks on the Judiciary," in *Congress Confronts the Court: The Struggle for Legitimacy and Authority in Lawmaking,* ed. Colton C. Campbell and John F. Stack (2001); James Meernik and Joseph Ignagni, "Judicial Review and Coordinate Construction of the Constitution," *American Journal of Political Science* 41 (1997), 463–492; and Gerald N. Rosenberg, "Judicial Independence and the Reality of Political Power," *Review of Politics* 54 (1992), 369–398.

CHAPTER 2
THE JUDICIARY

ETWEEN 1932 and 1983 Congress attached legislative veto provisions to more than two hundred laws. Although these provisions took different forms, among the more common were those that authorized one house of Congress to invalidate a decision of the executive branch. For example, under the Immigration and Nationality Act, Congress gave the U.S. attorney general power to suspend the deportation of aliens. However, it reserved the authority to veto, by a majority vote in either house, any such suspension.

In *Immigration and Naturalization Service v. Chadha* (1983) the Court held that this device violated specific clauses as well as general principles contained in the U.S. Constitution. In doing so, as Justice Byron R. White wrote in his dissent, the Court sounded the "death knell" for the legislative veto.[1]

In many ways, the Court's action was less than startling. For nearly two centuries federal courts have exerted the power of judicial review, the power to review acts of government to determine their compatibility with the U.S. Constitution. And, despite the fact that the Constitution does not explicitly give them such power, the courts' authority to do so has been challenged only occasionally. Today we take for granted the notion that federal courts may review government actions and strike them down if they violate constitutional mandates.

Nevertheless, when courts do exert this power, as the U.S. Supreme Court did in *Chadha*, they provoke controversy. Look at it from this perspective: Congress, composed of officials we *elect*, passed these legislative veto provisions, which were then rendered invalid by a Supreme Court of nine *unelected* justices. Such an occurrence strikes some people as quite odd, perhaps even antidemocratic. Why should we Americans allow a branch of government over which we have no electoral control to review and nullify the actions of the government officials we elect to represent us?

The alleged antidemocratic nature of judicial review is just one of many controversies surrounding the practice. In this chapter, we review others—both in theory and in practice. First, however, we explore the circumstances leading to the adoption of Article III, which outlines the contours of judicial power. To understand the cases that follow—all of which examine the parameters of the judiciary's authority—it is important to consider the framing of Article III. Next, we turn to the development of judicial review in the United States. Many of the early justifications for the practice are still fueling contemporary debates.

Judicial review is the primary weapon, the check that federal courts have on other branches of government. Because this power can be awesome in scope, many tend to emphasize it to the neglect of factors that constrain its use, as well as other checks on the power of the Court. In the second and third parts of this chapter, we explore the limits on judicial power.

---

1. It is worth noting that this is true in theory but not in practice. Since *Chadha*, Congress has passed more than two hundred new laws containing legislative vetoes. See Louis Fisher, "The Legislative Veto: Invalidated, It Survives," *Law and Contemporary Problems* 5/6 (1993): 288; and Chapter 3 of this volume for more details.

ESTABLISHMENT OF
THE FEDERAL JUDICIARY

The federal judicial system is built on a foundation created by two major statements of the 1780s: Article III of the U.S. Constitution and the Judiciary Act of 1789. In this section, we consider both, with an emphasis on their content and the debate they provoked. Note, in particular, the degree to which the major controversies reflect more general concerns about federalism. Designing and fine-tuning the U.S. system of government required many compromises over the balance of power between the federal government and the states, and Article III and the Judiciary Act are no exceptions.

Article III

The Framers of the Constitution spent days upon days debating the contents of Article I (dealing with the legislature) and Article II (centering on the executive), but they had comparatively little trouble drafting Article III. Indeed, it caused the least controversy of any major constitutional provision. Why? One reason is that the states and Great Britain had well-entrenched court systems, and the Founders had firsthand knowledge of the workings of courts—knowledge they lacked about the other political institutions they were establishing. Second, thirty-four of the fifty-five delegates to the Constitutional Convention were lawyers or had some training in the law. They held a common vision of the *general* role courts should play in the new polity.[2]

That vision was expressed by Alexander Hamilton in Federalist Paper No. 78, one of a series of papers designed to garner support for the ratification of the Constitution *(see Appendix 2)*. Hamilton specifically referred to the judiciary as the "least dangerous branch" of government; he (and virtually all of the Founders) saw the courts as legal, not political, bodies. He wrote: "If judges should be disposed to exercise *will* instead of *judgment*, the consequences would equally be the substitution of their pleasure to that of the legislative body." To ensure that judges did not become legislators, the Framers agreed on the

need for judicial independence—a goal they sought to accomplish by giving jurists life tenure rather than subjecting them to periodic public checks through the electoral process. They also concurred on the need to block Congress from reducing a federal judge's compensation during terms of continuous service. The Compensation Clause, located in Article III, also implicates judicial independence: the Framers hoped to prohibit members of the legislature upset with court decisions from punishing judges by cutting their pay.[3]

That the Framers shared a fundamental view of the role of the federal judiciary does not mean that they agreed on all the specifics. They had many debates over the structure of the American legal system. They agreed that there would be at least one federal court, the Supreme Court of the United States, but disagreed over the establishment of federal tribunals inferior to the Supreme Court. The Virginia Plan, which served as the basis for many of the proposals debated at the Convention, suggested that Congress should establish lower federal courts. Delegates who favored a strong national government agreed with this plan, with some wanting to use Article III to create such courts.

But delegates favoring states' rights over those of the national government vehemently objected to the creation of any federal tribunals, other than the U.S. Supreme Court. As one put it, "The people will not hear of such an innovation. The states will revolt at such encroachments."[4] Instead of creating new federal courts, they proposed that the existing state courts should hear

---

2. See Daniel A. Farber and Suzanna Sherry, *A History of the American Constitution* (St. Paul, Minn.: West Publishing, 1990), 51.

3. Compensation Clause cases are relatively rare, but one such dispute, *United States v. Hatter,* came before the Court in 2001. Here the justices considered whether the Clause prohibits the government from collecting certain Medicare and Social Security taxes from eight federal judges who were all appointed prior to 1983—before Congress extended the taxes to federal employees. Writing for the Court, Justice Breyer concluded that the Compensation Clause "does not prevent Congress from imposing a 'nondiscriminatory tax laid generally' upon judges and other citizens, but it does prohibit taxation that singles out judges for specially unfavorable treatment. Consequently, we conclude that Congress may apply the Medicare tax—a nondiscriminatory tax—to then-sitting federal judges. The special retroactivity-related Social Security rules that Congress enacted in 1984, however, effectively singled out then-sitting federal judges for unfavorable treatment. Hence, we conclude that the Clause forbids the application of the Social Security tax to those judges."

4. Quoted in Farber and Sherry, *A History of the American Constitution,* 56.

cases in the first instance, with an allowance for appeals to the U.S. Supreme Court. "This dispute," as Justice Hugo L. Black wrote, "resulted in compromise. One 'supreme Court' was created by the Constitution, and Congress was given the power to create other federal courts." [5] In other words, Article III does not establish a system of lower federal courts; rather, it gives Congress the option of doing so.

The First Congress (with its Federalist majority) took full advantage of Section 1 by immediately passing the Judiciary Act of 1789, which established lower federal courts. That Congress would take such an action was not a surprise: the majority of the Founders anticipated the law because much of Article III—specifically Section 2, the longest part—defines the jurisdiction of these federal courts that did not yet exist. By spelling out their jurisdiction, the Framers provided the courts with the authority to hear cases involving certain subjects or brought by certain parties. The Framers also defined the jurisdiction of the U.S. Supreme Court. Its jurisdiction was defined in terms of original and appellate authority *(see Box 2-1)*.

A second area of debate at the 1787 convention was the appointment of federal judges. Again, the Virginia Plan's suggestion—that Congress appoint these judges—served as the focus of debate. Some of the delegates wanted the language of Article III to reflect the Virginia Plan, while others suggested that appointments be left to the Senate. Benjamin Franklin argued that perhaps lawyers should decide who should sit on the courts. After all, Franklin joked, the lawyers would select "the ablest of the profession in order to get rid of him, and share his practice among themselves." [6] Finally, the delegates decided that the appointment power should be given to the president, with the "advice and consent" of the Senate. Accordingly, the power to appoint federal judges is located in Article II rather than Article III. That, of course, does not mean that the Senate lacks a role in the process: since 1789, it has read "advice and consent" to mean that it must approve presidential nominees by a majority vote. And it has taken that role quite seriously, rejecting

5. *Atlantic Coast Line R. R. Co. v. Brotherhood of Locomotive Engrs.* (1970).
6. Quoted in Farber and Sherry, *A History of the American Constitution*, 55.

BOX 2-1 JURISDICTION OF THE FEDERAL COURTS AS DEFINED IN ARTICLE III

Jurisdiction of the Lower Federal Courts

Subjects Falling Under Their Authority
- **Cases involving the U.S. Constitution, federal laws, and treaties**
- **Cases affecting ambassadors, public ministers, and consuls**
- **Cases of admiralty and maritime jurisdiction**

Parties Falling Under Their Authority
- **United States**
- **Controversies between two or more states**
- **Controversies between a state and citizens of another state[a]**
- **Controversies between citizens of different states**
- **Controversies between citizens of the same state claiming lands under grants of different states**
- **Controversies between a state, or the citizens thereof, and foreign states, citizens, or subjects**

Jurisdiction of the Supreme Court

Original Jurisdiction
- **Cases affecting ambassadors, public ministers, and consuls**
- **Cases to which a state is a party**

Appellate Jurisdiction
- **Cases falling under the jurisdiction of the lower federal courts, "with such Exceptions, and under such Regulations as the Congress shall make."**

a. In 1795, this was modified by the Eleventh Amendment, which removed from federal jurisdiction those cases in which a state is sued by the citizens of another state.

TABLE 2-1 Presidential Nominees to the Supreme Court Rejected by the Senate

President	Nominee	Date of Nomination by President	Date of Rejection	Vote	Reasons
Washington	John Rutledge	July 1, 1795	December 15, 1795	10–14	Candidate's political views; mental health questions raised
Madison	Alexander Wolcott	February 4, 1811	February 13, 1811	9–24	Candidate's performance as a customs' collector
Tyler	John C. Spencer	January 9, 1844	January 31, 1844	21–26	Partisan politics
Polk	George W. Woodward	December 23, 1845	January 22, 1846	20–29	Questions about candidate's political views
Buchanan	Jeremiah S. Black	February 5, 1861	February 21, 1861	25–26	Partisan politics; candidate's political views
Grant	Ebenezer R. Hoar	December 15, 1869	February 3, 1870	24–33	Candidate's political views
Cleveland	William B. Hornblower	September 19, 1893	January 15, 1894	24–30	Opposition from home state senator
Cleveland	Wheeler H. Peckham	January 22, 1894	February 16, 1894	32–41	Opposition from home state senator
Hoover	John J. Parker	March 21, 1930	May 7, 1930	39–41	Questions about candidate's views toward civil rights and labor unions
Nixon	Clement Haynsworth Jr.	August 18, 1969	November 21, 1969	45–55	Ethical improprieties; opposition from labor and civil rights groups
Nixon	G. Harrold Carswell	January 19, 1970	April 8, 1970	45–51	Undistinguished judicial record; opposition from civil rights groups
Reagan	Robert H. Bork	July 1, 1987	October 23, 1987	42–58	Candidate's political views; opposition from the liberal interest group community

SOURCES: Joan Biskupic and Elder Witt, *CQ's Guide to the Supreme Court*, 3rd ed. (Washington, D.C.: Congressional Quarterly, 1997); Lee Epstein, Jeffrey A. Segal, Harold J. Spaeth, and Thomas G. Walker, *The Supreme Court Compendium: Data, Decisions, and Developments*, 3rd ed. (Washington, D.C.: CQ Press, 2003), Table 4–13; and Gregory A. Caldeira and John R. Wright, "Lobbying for Justice," in *Contemplating Courts*, ed. Lee Epstein (Washington, D.C.: CQ Press, 1995).

NOTE: This table includes only nominees rejected, with a vote, by the Senate. It excludes the sixteen that were withdrawn, postponed, or not acted upon.

outright 12 of the 148 Supreme Court nominees over the past two centuries—a greater number (proportionately speaking) than any other presidential appointees requiring senatorial approval *(see Table 2-1)*.[7]

Another source of debate was the proposal by James Madison for the creation of a Council of Revision, which would be composed of Supreme Court justices and the president of the United States and have the power to veto

legislative acts. But each time this was proposed, the delegates voted to defeat it. In *Marbury v. Madison* (1803), the first case we excerpt in this chapter, Chief Justice John Marshall in essence articulated such veto power for the Court. Those who take a dim view of Marshall's decision occasionally point to the delegates' rejection of the Council of Revision as proof that Marshall skirted the Founders' intent.

At the end of the section on *Marbury v. Madison*, we consider debates over Marshall's holding. Here, we underscore that Article III—for the reasons just stated—did not establish any federal courts other than the U.S. Supreme Court. It was left up to Congress to create (or

7. All in all, of the 148 nominees to the Court, 28 failed to obtain confirmation. The other 16 were withdrawn, postponed, or not acted upon. For data on all nominations, see Lee Epstein, Jeffrey A. Segal, Harold J. Spaeth, and Thomas G. Walker, *The Supreme Court Compendium: Data, Decisions, and Developments*, 3rd ed. (Washington, D.C.: CQ Press, 2003), Table 4-13.

FIGURE 2-1 The Federal Court System under the Judiciary Act of 1789

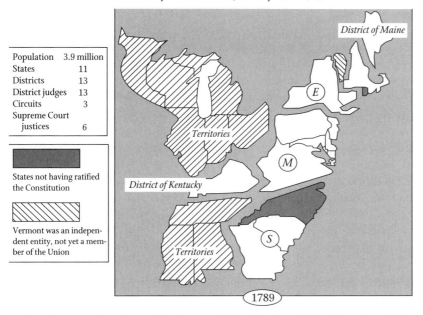

Population   3.9 million
States   11
Districts   13
District judges 13
Circuits   3
Supreme Court
   justices   6

States not having ratified
the Constitution

Vermont was an indepen-
dent entity, not yet a member of the Union

SOURCE: Russell R. Wheeler and Cynthia Harrison, *Creating the Federal Judicial System* (Washington, D.C.: Federal Judicial Center, 1989), 5.

not) more federal courts. Dominated by Federalists, the First Congress did create new courts, to give some "flesh" to the "skeleton" that was Article III.[8]

Judiciary Act of 1789

The Judiciary Act of 1789 is a long and relatively complex law that, at its core, had two purposes. First, it sought to establish a federal court structure, which it accomplished by providing for a Supreme Court, circuit courts, and district courts. Under the law, the Supreme Court was to have one chief justice and five associate justices. That the Court initially had only six members illustrates an important point: Congress, not the U.S. Constitution, determines the number of justices on the Supreme Court. It has been fixed at nine since 1869.

As Figure 2-1 shows, the act also created thirteen district courts. Each of the eleven states that had ratified the Constitution received a court, with separate tribunals created for Maine and Kentucky, which were then parts of Massachusetts and Virginia, respectively. District courts, then as now, were presided over by one judge. But the three newly established circuit courts were quite extraordinary in composition. Congress grouped the district courts—except Kentucky and Maine—geographically into the eastern, middle, or southern circuit and put one district court judge and two Supreme Court justices in charge of each. In other words, three judges would hear cases in the circuits. Today, courts of appeals continue to hear cases in panels of three, but district court judges or Supreme Court justices do not sit on these panels. Instead, the president now appoints judges specifically to the courts of appeals.

A second goal of the Judiciary Act was to specify the jurisdiction of the federal courts. Section 2 of Article III speaks broadly about the authority of federal courts, giving them jurisdiction over cases involving particular parties or subjects or, in the case of the Supreme Court, original and appellate jurisdiction *(see Box 2-1, page 65)*. The

8. Russell R. Wheeler and Cynthia Harrison, *Creating the Federal Judicial System* (Washington, D.C.: Federal Judicial Center, 1989), 2.

Judiciary Act provided more specific information, defining the parameters of authority for each of the newly established courts and for the U.S. Supreme Court. The district courts were to serve as trial courts, hearing cases involving admiralty issues, forfeitures and penalties, petty federal crimes, and minor U.S. civil cases. Congress recognized that some of these courts would be busier than others and fixed judicial salaries accordingly. For example, Delaware judges received only $800 for their services, while their counterparts in South Carolina, a coastal state that would generate many admiralty disputes, earned $1,800.[9]

Unlike today, the circuit courts were trial courts with jurisdiction over cases involving citizens from different states and major federal criminal and civil cases. Congress also gave them limited appellate authority to hear major civil and admiralty disputes coming out of the district courts.

Finally, the 1789 act contained several important provisions concerning the jurisdiction of the U.S. Supreme Court. Section 13 reiterated the Court's authority over suits in the first instance (its original jurisdiction) and gave the justices appellate jurisdiction over major civil disputes, those involving more than $2,000—a good deal of money back then. Section 13 also spoke about the Court's authority to issue writs of mandamus, which command a public official to carry out a particular act or duty: "The Supreme Court . . . shall have the power to issue . . . writs of *mandamus*, in cases warranted by the principles and usages of law, to any courts appointed, or persons holding office, under the authority of the United States." This matter may seem trivial, but, as we shall see, the Court's interpretation of this particular provision formed the centerpiece of *Marbury v. Madison*.

Another part of the act, Section 25, expanded the Court's appellate authority under Article III, enabling it to review certain kinds of cases coming out of the states. Specifically, the Supreme Court could now hear appeals from the highest state courts if those tribunals upheld a state law against claims that the law violated the Constitution or denied some claim based on the U.S. Constitution, federal laws, or treaties.

At first glance, the components of the 1789 act—its establishment of a federal court system and of rules governing that system—appear to favor the Federalists' position. Recall that Anti-Federalist delegates at the Constitutional Convention did not want the document even to mention lower federal tribunals, much less to give Congress the authority to establish them. The 1789 act does that and more: it goes so far as to give the Supreme Court the power to review state supreme court cases—surely an Anti-Federalist's worst nightmare! But it would be a mistake to believe that the act did not take into account the position taken by states' rights advocates. For example, the 1789 act used state lines as the boundaries for the district and circuit courts, even though there were other ways the boundaries could have been defined.[10] That Congress tied the boundaries to the states may have been a concession to the Anti-Federalists who wanted the judges of the federal courts to feel a part of the state's legal and political culture.

Whichever side won or lost, passage of the 1789 Judiciary Act was a defining moment in American legal history. It established the first federal court system, one that is strikingly similar to that in effect today. And, as the following pages reveal, it paved the way for three landmark constitutional cases—*Marbury v. Madison*, *Martin v. Hunter's Lessee*, and **Cohens v. Virginia**—all of which centered on judicial review, the major power of the federal judiciary.

JUDICIAL REVIEW

Judicial review is the most powerful tool of federal courts and there is evidence that the Framers intended for courts to have it *(see page 89)*, but it is not mentioned in the Constitution. Early in U.S. history, federal courts claimed it for themselves. In *Hylton v. United States* (1796), Daniel Hylton challenged the constitutionality of a 1793 federal tax on carriages. According to Hylton, the act violated the constitutional mandate that direct taxes must be apportioned on the basis of population. With

9. Ibid., 6.

10. As Wheeler and Harrison note: "The creators of the federal judiciary might have established separate judicial administrative divisions that would ensure roughly equal allocation of workload and would be subject to realignment to maintain the allocation" (ibid.).

only three justices participating, the Court upheld the act. But even by considering it, the Court in effect used its authority to review acts of Congress.

In 1803, however, the Court invoked judicial review to strike down legislation deemed incompatible with the U.S. Constitution. That decision came in the landmark case *Marbury v. Madison*. How does Chief Justice Marshall justify the Court's power to strike down legislation in light of the failure of the newly framed Constitution to confer on it judicial review?

Marbury v. Madison

1 CR. (5 U.S.) 137 (1803)
http://supct.law.cornell.edu/supct/cases/name.htm
Vote: 4 (Chase, Marshall, Paterson, Washington)

0

Opinion of the Court: Marshall
Not participating: Cushing, Moore

When voting in the presidential election of 1800 was over, it was apparent that Federalist president John Adams had lost after a long and bitter campaign, but it was not known who had won.[11] The voting resulted in a tie between Republican candidate Thomas Jefferson and his running mate, Aaron Burr, and the election had to be settled in the House of Representatives. In February 1801 the House elected Jefferson. Because the Federalists had lost both the presidential election and their majority in Congress, they took steps to maintain control of the third branch of government, the judiciary. The lame-duck Congress enacted the Circuit Court Act of 1801, which created six new circuit courts and several district courts to accommodate the new states of Kentucky, Tennessee, and Vermont. These new courts required judges and support staff such as attorneys, marshals, and clerks. As a result, during the last six months of his term in office, Adams made more than two hundred nominations, with sixteen

judgeships (the "midnight appointments") approved by the Senate during his last two weeks in office.

An even more important opportunity arose in December 1800, when the third chief justice of the United States, Federalist Oliver Ellsworth, resigned so that Adams—not Jefferson—could name his replacement. Adams first offered the post to John Jay, who had served as the first chief justice before leaving to take the more prestigious office of governor of New York. When Jay refused, Adams turned to his secretary of state, John Marshall, an ardent Federalist. Marshall was confirmed by the Senate in January 1801, while he continued as secretary of state.

In addition, the Federalist Congress passed the Organic Act of 1801, which authorized Adams to appoint forty-two justices of the peace for the District of Columbia. It was this seemingly innocuous law that set the stage for the dramatic case of *Marbury v. Madison*. In the confusion of the Adams administration's last days in office, Marshall, the outgoing secretary of state, failed to deliver some of these commissions. When the new administration came into office, James Madison, the new secretary of state, acting under orders from Jefferson, refused to deliver at least five commissions.[12] Indeed, some years later, Jefferson explained the situation in this way:

I found the commissions on the table of the Department of State, on my entrance into office, and I forbade their delivery. Whatever is in the Executive offices is certainly deemed to be in the hands of the President, and in this case, was actually in my hands, because when I countermanded them, there was as yet no Secretary of State.[13]

As a result, in 1801 William Marbury and three others who were denied their commissions went directly to the Supreme Court and asked it to issue a writ of mandamus ordering Madison to deliver the commissions. Marbury could take his case directly to the Court because Section

11. For analyses of the events surrounding *Marbury*, see Jack Knight and Lee Epstein, "On the Struggle for Judicial Supremacy," *Law and Society Review* 30 (1996): 87–120; Dean Alfange Jr., "*Marbury v. Madison* and Original Understandings of Judicial Review: In Defense of Traditional Wisdom," *Supreme Court Review* (1994): 329–446.

12. Historical accounts differ, but it seems that Jefferson decreased the number of Adams's appointments to justice of the peace positions to thirty from forty-two. Twenty-five of the thirty appointees received their commissions, but five—including William Marbury—did not. See Francis N. Stites, *John Marshall* (Boston: Little, Brown, 1981), 84.

13. Quoted in Charles Warren, *The Supreme Court in United States History*, vol. 1 (Boston: Little, Brown, 1922), 244.

BOX 2-2   JOHN MARSHALL (1801–1835)

THE ELDEST of fifteen children, John Marshall was born September 24, 1755, in a log cabin on the Virginia frontier. His father, descended from Welsh immigrants, was an assistant surveyor to George Washington and member of the Virginia House of Burgesses. His mother was the daughter of an educated Scottish clergyman.

As a youth, Marshall's main teacher was his father, who introduced him to English literature and Blackstone's *Commentaries on the Laws of England.*

During the Revolutionary War, young Marshall participated in the siege of Norfolk as a member of the Culpeper Minute Men and was present at Brandywine, Monmouth, Stony Point, and Valley Forge as a member of the third Virginia Regiment. He left the Continental Army with the rank of captain in 1781.

Marshall was self-taught in the law; his only formal instruction came in 1780 when he attended George Wythe's course of law lectures at the College of William and Mary. He was admitted to the bar that same year and gradually developed a lucrative practice.

On January 3, 1783, Marshall married Mary Willis Ambler, daughter of the Virginia state treasurer, and established a home in Richmond. The couple had ten children, only six of whom survived to maturity. Marshall spent many years caring for his wife, who suffered from a chronic illness. She died December 25, 1831.

From 1796 until about 1806, Marshall's life was dominated by the pressures of meeting debts incurred by a land investment he had made. It has been speculated that his need for money motivated him to write *The Life of George Washington,* which appeared in five volumes from 1804 to 1807. He later condensed the work into a schoolbook, but it proved not to be the answer to his financial difficulties.

MARSHALL was elected to the Virginia House of Delegates from Fauquier County in 1782 and 1784. He reentered the House in 1787 and was instrumental in Virginia's ratification of the new U.S. Constitution. At the state ratifying convention he focused on the need for judicial review. By 1789 Marshall was considered to be a leading Federalist in the state.

Marshall refused many appointments in the Federalist administrations of George Washington and John Adams. In 1797 he agreed to serve as one of three special envoys sent to smooth relations with France. This mission, known as the "XYZ Affair," failed when French diplomats demanded a bribe as a condition for negotiation. Congress, however, was greatly impressed by the stubborn resistance of the American emissaries, and Marshall received a generous grant as a reward for his participation.

In 1799 Washington persuaded Marshall to run for the U.S. House of Representatives as a Federalist from Richmond. His career in the House was brief, however, for in 1800 he became secretary of state under Adams. At one point, Marshall served as the effective head of government.

Chief Justice Oliver Ellsworth resigned in 1800, and Adams offered the position to John Jay, who had been the Court's first chief justice. Jay declined, and the Federalists urged Adams to elevate Associate Justice William Paterson. But on January 20, 1801, Adams nominated Marshall instead. The Senate confirmed Marshall January 27 by a voice vote.

As the primary founder of the American system of constitutional law, including the doctrine of judicial review, Marshall participated in more than 1,000 Supreme Court decisions, writing more than 500 of them himself. In 1807 he presided over the treason trial of Aaron Burr in the Richmond circuit court, locking horns with Thomas Jefferson, who sought an absolute conviction. Burr was acquitted.

When Marshall died in Philadelphia on July 6, 1835, the Liberty Bell cracked as it tolled in mourning.

SOURCE: Adapted from Joan Biskupic and Elder Witt, *Guide to the U.S. Supreme Court,* 3rd ed. (Washington, D.C.: Congressional Quarterly, 1997), 869–870.

13 of the 1789 Judiciary Act gives the Court the power to issue writs of mandamus to anyone holding federal office.

In this volatile political climate, Marshall, now serving as chief justice, was perhaps in the most tenuous position of all. On the one hand, he had been a supporter of the Federalist Party, which now looked to him to "scold" the Jefferson administration. On the other, Marshall wanted to avoid a confrontation between the Jefferson administration and the Supreme Court, which not only seemed imminent but also could end in disaster for the struggling nation. In fact, Jefferson and his party were so annoyed with the Court for agreeing to hear the *Marbury* dispute that they began to consider impeaching Federalist judges—with two justices (Samuel Chase and Marshall himself) high on their lists. Note, too, the year in which *Marbury* was handed down by the Court; the case was not decided until two years after Marbury filed suit because Congress and the Jefferson administration had abolished the 1802 term of the Court.

The following opinion of the court was delivered by the CHIEF JUSTICE.

Opinion of the Court.

The peculiar delicacy of this case, the novelty of some of its circumstances, and the real difficulty attending the points which occur in it, require a complete exposition of the principles, on which the opinion to be given by the court, is founded.

These principles have been, on the side of the applicant, very ably argued at the bar. In rendering the opinion of the court, there will be some departure in form, though not in substance, from the points stated in that argument.

In the order in which the court has viewed this subject, the following questions have been considered and decided.

1st. Has the applicant a right to the commission he demands?

2dly. If he has a right, and that right has been violated, do the laws of his country afford him a remedy?

3dly. If they do afford him a remedy, is it a *mandamus* issuing from this court?

The first object of enquiry is,

1st. Has the applicant a right to the commission he demands? . . .

In order to determine whether he is entitled to this commission, it becomes necessary to enquire whether he has been appointed to the office. For if he has been appointed, the law continues him in office for five years, and he is entitled to the possession of those evidences of office, which, being completed, became his property. . . .

These are the clauses of the constitution and laws of the United States, which affect this part of the case. They seem to contemplate three distinct operations:

1st. The nomination. This is the sole act of the President, and is completely voluntary.

2d. The appointment. This is also the act of the President, and is also a voluntary act, though it can only be performed by and with the advice and consent of the senate.

3d. The commission. To grant a commission to a person appointed, might perhaps be deemed a duty enjoined by the constitution. "He shall," says that instrument, "commission all the officers of the United States.". . .

This is an appointment made by the President, by and with the advice and consent of the senate, and is evidenced by no act but the commission itself. In such a case therefore the commission and the appointment seem inseparable; it being almost impossible to shew an appointment otherwise than by proving the existence of a commission; still the commission is not necessarily the appointment; though conclusive evidence of it.

But at what stage does it amount to this conclusive evidence? . . .

If it should be supposed, that the solemnity of affixing the seal, is necessary not only to the validity of the commission, but even to the completion of an appointment, still when the seal is affixed the appointment is made, and the commission is valid. No other solemnity is required by law; no other act is to be performed on the part of government. All that the Executive can do to invest the person with his office, is done; and unless the appointment be then made, the Executive cannot make one without the cooperation of others. . . .

In considering this question, it has been conjectured that the commission may have been assimilated to a deed, to the validity of which, delivery is essential.

This idea is founded on the supposition that the commission is not merely *evidence* of an appointment, but is itself the actual appointment; a supposition by no means unquestionable. But for the purpose of examining this objection fairly, let it be conceded, that the principle, claimed for its support, is established.

The appointment being, under the constitution, to be made by the President *personally*, the delivery of the deed of appointment, if necessary to its completion, must be made by the President also. It is not necessary that the livery should be made personally to the grantee of the office: It never is so made. The law would seem to contemplate that it should be made to the secretary of state, since it directs the secretary to affix the seal to the commission *after* it shall have been signed by the President. If then the act of livery be necessary to give validity to the commission, it has been delivered when executed and given to the secretary for the purpose of being sealed, recorded, and transmitted to the party.

But in all cases of letters patent, certain solemnities are required by law, which solemnities are the evidences of the validity of the instrument. A formal delivery to the person is not among them. In cases of commissions, the sign manual of the President, and the seal of the United States, are those solemnities. This objection therefore does not touch the case.

It has also occurred as possible, and barely possible, that the transmission of the commission, and the acceptance thereof, might be deemed necessary to complete the right of the plaintiff.

The transmission of the commission, is a practice directed by convenience, but not by law. It cannot therefore be necessary to constitute the appointment which must precede it, and which is the mere act of the President. If the Executive required that every person appointed to an office, should himself take means to procure his commission, the appointment would not be the less valid on that account. The appointment is the sole act of the President; the transmission of the commission is the sole act of the officer to whom that duty is assigned, and may be accelerated or retarded by circumstances which can have no influence on the appointment. A commission is transmitted to a person already appointed; not to a person to be appointed or not, as the letter enclosing the commission should happen to get into the post office and reach him in safety, or to miscarry. . . .

If the transmission of a commission be not considered as necessary to give validity to an appointment; still less is its acceptance. The appointment is the sole act of the President; the acceptance is the sole act of the officer, and is, in plain common sense, posterior to the appointment. As he may resign, so may he refuse to accept: but neither the one, nor the other, is capable of rendering the appointment a non-entity.

That this is the understanding of the government, is apparent from the whole tenor of its conduct.

A commission bears date, and the salary of the officer commences from his appointment; not from the transmission or acceptance of his commission. When a person, ap-

pointed to any office, refuses to accept that office, the successor is nominated in the place of the person who has declined to accept, and not in the place of the person who had been previously in office, and had created the original vacancy.

It is therefore decidedly the opinion of the court, that when a commission has been signed by the President, the appointment is made; and that the commission is complete, when the seal of the United States has been affixed to it by the secretary of state. . . .

The discretion of the Executive is to be exercised until the appointment has been made. But having once made the appointment, his power over the office is terminated in all cases, where, by law, the officer is not removable by him. The right to the office is *then* in the person appointed, and he has the absolute, unconditional, power of accepting or rejecting it.

Mr. Marbury, then, since his commission was signed by the President, and sealed by the secretary of state, was appointed; and as the law creating the office, gave the officer a right to hold for five years, independent of the Executive, the appointment was not revocable; but vested in the officer legal rights, which are protected by the laws of his country.

To withhold his commission, therefore, is an act deemed by the court not warranted by law, but violative of a vested legal right.

This brings us to the second enquiry; which is,

2dly. If he has a right, and that right has been violated, do the laws of his country afford him a remedy?

The very essence of civil liberty certainly consists in the right of every individual to claim the protection of the laws, whenever he receives an injury. One of the first duties of government is to afford that protection. . . .

The government of the United States has been emphatically termed a government of laws, and not of men. It will certainly cease to deserve this high appellation, if the laws furnish no remedy for the violation of a vested legal right.

If this obloquy is to be cast on the jurisprudence of our country, it must arise from the peculiar character of the case. . . .

The conclusion . . . is, that where the heads of departments are the political or confidential agents of the Executive, merely to execute the will of the President, or rather to act in cases in which the Executive possesses a constitutional or legal discretion, nothing can be more perfectly clear than that their acts are only politically examinable. But where a specific duty is assigned by law, and individual rights depend upon the performance of that duty, it seems equally clear that the individual who considers himself injured, has a right to resort to the laws of his country for a remedy.

If this be the rule, let us enquire how it applies to the case under the consideration of the court.

The power of nominating to the senate, and the power of appointing the person nominated, are political powers, to be exercised by the President according to his own discretion. When he has made an appointment, he has exercised his whole power, and his discretion has been completely applied to the case. If, by law, the officer be removable at the will of the President, then a new appointment may be immediately made, and the rights of the officer are terminated. But as a fact which has existed cannot be made never to have existed, the appointment cannot be annihilated; and consequently if the officer is by law not removable at the will of the President; the rights he has acquired are protected by the law, and are not resumable by the President. They cannot be extinguished by executive authority, and he has the privilege of asserting them in like manner as if they had been derived from any other source.

The question whether a right has vested or not, is, in its nature, judicial, and must be tried by the judicial authority. If, for example, Mr. Marbury had taken the oaths of a magistrate, and proceeded to act as one; in consequence of which a suit had been instituted against him, in which his defence had depended on his being a magistrate; the validity of his appointment must have been determined by judicial authority.

So, if he conceives that, by virtue of his appointment, he has a legal right, either to the commission which has been made out for him, or to a copy of that commission, it is equally a question examinable in a court, and the decision of the court upon it must depend on the opinion entertained of his appointment.

That question has been discussed, and the opinion is, that the latest point of time which can be taken as that at which the appointment was complete, and evidenced, was when, after the signature of the president, the seal of the United States was affixed to the commission.

It is then the opinion of the court,

William Marbury

John Marshall

James Madison

Thomas Jefferson

1st. That by signing the commission of Mr. Marbury, the president of the United States appointed him a justice of peace, for the county of Washington in the district of Columbia; and that the seal of the United States, affixed thereto by the secretary of state, is conclusive testimony of the verity of the signature, and of the completion of the appointment; and that the appointment conferred on him a legal right to the office for the space of five years.

2dly. That, having this legal title to the office, he has a consequent right to the commission; a refusal to deliver which, is a plain violation of that right, for which the laws of his country afford him a remedy.

It remains to be enquired whether,

3dly. He is entitled to the remedy for which he applies. . . .

The act to establish the judicial courts of the United States authorizes the supreme court "to issue writs of mandamus, in cases warranted by the principles and usages of law, to any courts appointed, or persons holding office, under the authority of the United States."

The secretary of state, being a person holding an office under the authority of the United States, is precisely within the letter of the description; and if this court is not authorized to issue a writ of mandamus to such an officer, it must be because the law is unconstitutional, and therefore absolutely incapable of conferring the authority, and assigning the duties which its words purport to confer and assign.

The constitution vests the whole judicial power of the United States in one supreme court, and such inferior courts as congress shall, from time to time, ordain and establish. This power is expressly extended to all cases arising under the laws of the United States; and consequently, in some form, may be exercised over the present case; because the right claimed is given by a law of the United States.

In the distribution of this power it is declared that "the supreme court shall have original jurisdiction in all cases affecting ambassadors, other public ministers and consuls, and those in which a state shall be a party. In all other cases, the supreme court shall have appellate jurisdiction."

It has been insisted, at the bar, that as the original grant of jurisdiction, to the supreme and inferior courts, is general, and the clause, assigning original jurisdiction to the supreme court, contains no negative or restrictive words; the power remains to the legislature, to assign original jurisdiction to that court in other cases than those specified in the article which has been recited; provided those cases belong to the judicial power of the United States.

If it had been intended to leave it in the discretion of the legislature to apportion the judicial power between the supreme and inferior courts according to the will of that body, it would certainly have been useless to have proceeded further than to have defined the judicial power, and the tribunals in which it should be vested. The subsequent part of the section is mere surplussage, is entirely without meaning, if such is to be the construction. If congress remains at liberty to give this court appellate jurisdiction, where the constitution has declared their jurisdiction shall be original; and original jurisdiction where the constitution has declared it shall be appellate; the distribution of jurisdiction, made in the constitution, is form without substance.

Affirmative words are often, in their operation, negative of other objects than those affirmed; and in this case, a negative or exclusive sense must be given to them or they have no operation at all.

It cannot be presumed that any clause in the constitution is intended to be without effect; and therefore such a construction is inadmissible, unless the words require it.

If the solicitude of the convention, respecting our peace with foreign powers, induced a provision that the supreme court should take original jurisdiction in cases which might be supposed to affect them; yet the clause would have proceeded no further than to provide for such cases, if no further restriction on the powers of congress had been intended. That they should have appellate jurisdiction in all other cases, with such exceptions as congress might make, is no restriction; unless the words be deemed exclusive of original jurisdiction.

When an instrument organizing fundamentally a judicial system, divides it into one supreme, and so many inferior courts as the legislature may ordain and establish; then enumerates its powers, and proceeds so far to distribute them, as to define the jurisdiction of the supreme court by declaring the cases in which it shall take original jurisdiction, and that in others it shall take appellate jurisdiction; the plain import of the words seems to be, that in one class of cases its jurisdiction is original, and not appellate; in the other it is appellate, and not original. If any other construction would render the clause inoperative, that is an additional reason for rejecting such other construction, and for adhering to their obvious meaning.

To enable this court then to issue a mandamus, it must be shewn to be an exercise of appellate jurisdiction, or to be necessary to enable them to exercise appellate jurisdiction.

It has been stated at the bar that the appellate jurisdiction may be exercised in a variety of forms, and that if it be the will of the legislature that a mandamus should be used for that purpose, that will must be obeyed. This is true, yet the jurisdiction must be appellate, not original.

It is the essential criterion of appellate jurisdiction, that it revises and corrects the proceedings in a cause already instituted, and does not create that cause. Although, therefore, a mandamus may be directed to courts, yet to issue such a writ to an officer for the delivery of a paper, is in effect the same as to sustain an original action for that paper, and therefore seems not to belong to appellate, but to original jurisdiction. Neither is it necessary in such a case as this, to enable the court to exercise its appellate jurisdiction.

The authority, therefore, given to the supreme court, by the act establishing the judicial courts of the United States, to issue writs of mandamus to public officers, appears not to be warranted by the constitution; and it becomes necessary to enquire whether a jurisdiction, so conferred, can be exercised.

The question, whether an act, repugnant to the constitution, can become the law of the land, is a question deeply interesting to the United States; but, happily, not of an intricacy proportioned to its interest. It seems only necessary to recognise certain principles, supposed to have been long and well established, to decide it.

That the people have an original right to establish, for their future government, such principles as, in their opinion, shall most conduce to their own happiness, is the basis, on which the whole American fabric has been erected. The exercise of this original right is a very great exertion; nor can it, nor ought it to be frequently repeated. The principles, therefore, so established, are deemed fundamental. And as the authority, from which they proceed, is supreme, and can seldom act, they are designed to be permanent.

This original and supreme will organizes the government, and assigns, to different departments, their respective powers. It may either stop here; or establish certain limits not to be transcended by those departments.

The government of the United States is of the latter description. The powers of the legislature are defined, and limited; and that those limits may not be mistaken, or forgotten, the constitution is written. To what purpose are powers limited, and to what purpose is that limitation committed to writing, if these limits may, at any time, be passed by those intended to be restrained? The distinction, between a government with limited and unlimited powers, is abolished, if those limits do not confine the persons on whom they are imposed, and if acts prohibited and acts allowed, are of equal obligation. It is a proposition too plain to be contested, that the constitution controls any legislative act repugnant to it; or, that the legislature may alter the constitution by an ordinary act.

Between these alternatives there is no middle ground. The constitution is either a superior, paramount law, unchangeable by ordinary means, or it is on a level with ordinary legislative acts, and like other acts, is alterable when the legislature shall please to alter it.

If the former part of the alternative be true, then a legislative act contrary to the constitution is not law: if the latter part be true, then written constitutions are absurd attempts, on the part of the people, to limit a power, in its own nature illimitable.

Certainly all those who have framed written constitutions contemplate them as forming the fundamental and paramount law of the nation, and consequently the theory of every such government must be, that an act of the legislature, repugnant to the constitution, is void.

This theory is essentially attached to a written constitution, and is consequently to be considered, by this court, as one of the fundamental principles of our society. It is not therefore to be lost sight of in the further consideration of this subject.

If an act of the legislature, repugnant to the constitution, is void, does it, notwithstanding its invalidity, bind the courts, and oblige them to give it effect? Or, in other words, though it be not law, does it constitute a rule as operative as if it was a law? This would be to overthrow in fact what was established in theory; and would seem, at first view, an absurdity too gross to be insisted on. It shall, however, receive a more attentive consideration.

It is emphatically the province and duty of the judicial department to say what the law is. Those who apply the rule to particular cases, must of necessity expound and interpret that rule. If two laws conflict with each other, the courts must decide on the operation of each.

So if a law be in opposition to the constitution; if both the law and the constitution apply to a particular case, so that the court must either decide that case conformably to the law, disregarding the constitution; or conformably to the constitution, disregarding the law; the court must determine which of these conflicting rules governs the case. This is of the very essence of judicial duty.

If then the courts are to regard the constitution; and the constitution is superior to any ordinary act of the legislature; the constitution, and not such ordinary act, must govern the case to which they both apply.

Those then who controvert the principle that the constitution is to be considered, in court, as a paramount law, are reduced to the necessity of maintaining that courts must close their eyes on the constitution, and see only the law.

This doctrine would subvert the very foundation of all written constitutions. It would declare that an act, which, according to the principles and theory of our government, is entirely void; is yet, in practice, completely obligatory. It would declare, that if the legislature shall do what is expressly forbidden, such act, notwithstanding the express prohibition, is in reality effectual. It would be giving to the legislature a practical and real omnipotence, with the same breath which professes to restrict their powers within narrow limits. It is prescribing limits, and declaring that those limits may be passed at pleasure.

That it thus reduces to nothing what we have deemed the greatest improvement on political institutions—a written constitution—would of itself be sufficient, in America, where written constitutions have been viewed with so much reverence, for rejecting the construction. But the peculiar expressions of the constitution of the United States furnish additional arguments in favour of its rejection.

The judicial power of the United States is extended to all cases arising under the constitution.

Could it be the intention of those who gave this power, to say that, in using it, the constitution should not be looked into? That a case arising under the constitution should be decided without examining the instrument under which it arises?

This is too extravagant to be maintained.

In some cases then, the constitution must be looked into by the judges. And if they can open it at all, what part of it are they forbidden to read, or to obey?

There are many other parts of the constitution which serve to illustrate this subject.

It is declared that "no tax or duty shall be laid on articles exported from any state." Suppose a duty on the export of cotton, of tobacco, or of flour; and a suit instituted to recover it. Ought judgment to be rendered in such a case? ought the judges to close their eyes on the constitution, and only see the law?

The constitution declares that "no bill of attainder or *ex post facto* law shall be passed."

If, however, such a bill should be passed and a person should be prosecuted under it; must the court condemn to death those victims whom the constitution endeavours to preserve?

"No person," says the constitution, "shall be convicted of treason unless on the testimony of two witnesses to the same overt act, or on confession in open court."

Here the language of the constitution is addressed especially to the courts. It prescribes, directly for them, a rule of evidence not to be departed from. If the legislature should change that rule, and declare *one* witness, or a confession *out* of court, sufficient for conviction, must the constitutional principle yield to the legislative act?

From these, and many other selections which might be made, it is apparent, that the Framers of the constitution contemplated that instrument, as a rule for the government of *courts*, as well as of the legislature.

Why otherwise does it direct the judges to take an oath to support it? This oath certainly applies, in an especial manner, to their conduct in their official character. How immoral to impose it on them, if they were to be used as the instruments, and the knowing instruments, for violating what they swear to support!

The oath of office, too, imposed by the legislature, is completely demonstrative of the legislative opinion on this subject. It is in these words, "I do solemnly swear that I will administer justice without respect to persons, and do equal right to the poor and to the rich; and that I will faithfully and impartially discharge all the duties incumbent on me as according to the best of my abilities and understanding, agreeably to *the constitution*, and laws of the United States."

Why does a judge swear to discharge his duties agreeably to the constitution of the United States, if that constitution forms no rule for his government? if it is closed upon him, and cannot be inspected by him?

If such be the real state of things, this is worse than solemn mockery. To prescribe, or to take this oath, becomes equally a crime.

It is also not entirely worthy of observation, that in declaring what shall be the supreme law of the land, the constitution itself is first mentioned; and not the laws of the United States generally, but those only which shall be made in pursuance of the constitution, have that rank.

Thus, the particular phraseology of the constitution of the United States confirms and strengthens the principle, supposed to be essential to all written constitutions, that a law repugnant to the constitution is void; and that courts, as well as other departments, are bound by that instrument.

The rule must be discharged.

Many scholars consider Marshall's opinion in *Marbury* absolutely stunning, even brilliant. As the great legal scholar Edward S. Corwin wrote:

Regarded merely as a judicial decision, the decision of *Marbury v. Madison* must be considered as most extraordinary, but regarded as a political pamphlet designed to irritate an enemy [Jefferson] to the very limit of endurance, it must be regarded a huge success.[14]

To see Corwin's point, we only have to think about the way the chief justice dealt with a most delicate political situation. By ruling against Marbury—who never did receive his judicial appointment *(see Box 2-3)*—Marshall avoided a potentially devastating clash with the new president; but, by exerting the power of judicial review, he sent a clear signal to Jefferson that the Court had a major role to play in the American government. Other scholars, however, point out that judicial review emerged, not because of some brilliant strategic move by Marshall in the face of intense political opposition, but because it was politically viable at the time. According to these scholars, Jefferson favored the establishment of judicial

---

14. Edward S. Corwin, "The Establishment of Judicial Review-II," *Michigan Law Review* 9 (1911): 292.

BOX 2-3   AFTERMATH . . .
MARBURY V. MADISON

FROM meager beginnings, William Marbury gained political and economic influence in his home state of Maryland and become a strong supporter of John Adams and the Federalist Party. Unlike others of his day who rose in wealth through agriculture or trade, Marbury's path to prominence was banking and finance. At age thirty-eight, he saw his appointment to be a justice of the peace as a public validation of his rising economic status and social prestige. Marbury never received his judicial position; instead, he returned to his financial activities, ultimately becoming the president of a bank in Georgetown. He died in 1835, the same year as Chief Justice John Marshall.

Other participants in the famous decision played major roles in the early history of our nation. Thomas Jefferson, who refused to honor Marbury's appointment, served two terms as chief executive, leaving office in 1809 as one of the nation's most revered presidents. James Madison, the secretary of state who carried out Jefferson's order depriving Marbury of his judgeship, became the nation's fourth president, serving from 1809 to 1817. Following the *Marbury* decision, Chief Justice Marshall led the Court for an additional thirty-two years. His tenure was marked with fundamental rulings expanding the power of the judiciary and enhancing the position of the federal government relative to the states. He is rightfully regarded as history's most influential chief justice.

Although the *Marbury* decision established the power of judicial review, it is ironic that the Marshall Court never again used its authority to strike down a piece of congressional legislation. In fact, it was not until *Scott v. Sandford* (1857), more than two decades after Marshall's death, that the Court once again invalidated a congressional statute.

SOURCES: John A. Garraty, "The Case of the Missing Commissions," in John A. Garraty, *Quarrels that Have Shaped the Constitution* (New York: Harper and Row, 1962); David F. Forte, "Marbury's Travail: Federalist Politics and William Marbury's Appointment as Justice of the Peace," *Catholic University Law Review* 45 (1996): 349–402.

review and Marshall realized this. So Marshall simply took the rational course of action: deny Marbury his commission (which Jefferson desired) and articulate judicial review (a move which Jefferson also approved).[15]

Either way, the decision helped to establish John Marshall's reputation as perhaps the greatest justice in Supreme Court history *(see Box 2-2, page 70)*. As will be shown throughout this book, *Marbury* was just the first in what would be a long line of seminal Marshall decisions. But most important here, *Marbury* firmly established the Court's authority to review and strike down government actions that were incompatible with the Constitution. In Marshall's view, such authority, while not explicit in the Constitution, was clearly intended by the Framers of that document. Was he correct? His opinion makes a plausible argument, but some judges and scholars have suggested otherwise. We review their assertions later in this chapter *(see pages 88–93)*.

For now, though, it is worth noting that contemporary Courts not only accept *Marbury* but continue to invoke its logic. Consider, for example, the Court's decision in **City of Boerne v. Flores** (1997). At issue was the Religious Freedom Restoration Act of 1993 (RFRA), which Congress passed by overwhelming majorities in response to an earlier Court decision, *Employment Division v. Smith* (1990). The RFRA directed the Court to adopt a particular standard of law in constitutional cases involving the Free Exercise Clause of the First Amendment—a standard the Court had rejected in *Smith*.

In striking down Congress's effort at constitutional interpretation, the Court did not hesitate to cite *Marbury v. Madison*:

Our national experience teaches that the Constitution is preserved best when each part of the government respects both the Constitution and the proper actions and determinations of the other branches. When the Court has interpreted the Constitution, it has acted within the province of the Judicial Branch, which embraces the duty to say what the law is. *Marbury v. Madison*. When the political branches of the Government act against the background of a judicial interpretation of

15. For more on this view, see Knight and Epstein, "On the Struggle for Judicial Supremacy."

the Constitution already issued, it must be understood that in later cases and controversies the Court will treat its precedents with the respect due them under settled principles, including stare decisis, and contrary expectations must be disappointed. RFRA was designed to control cases and controversies, such as the one before us; but as the provisions of the federal statute here invoked are beyond congressional authority, it is this Court's precedent, not RFRA, which must control.

Three years later, in **Dickerson v. United States** (2000), the Court reiterated this message. At issue was a law Congress enacted in 1968 that was designed to overturn the Court's decision in *Miranda v. Arizona* (1966)—the decision that established the now-famous Miranda warnings: "You have the right to remain silent; anything you say can and will be used against you. . . ." Once the justices held that *Miranda* announced a constitutional rule, they concluded that the 1968 congressional law was unconstitutional: "Congress may not legislatively supersede our decisions interpreting and applying the Constitution. See, e.g., *City of Boerne v. Flores* (1997)."

It is not only current U.S. Supreme Court justices who continue to cite *Marbury* with approval. Many countries have written judicial review into their constitutions, refusing to leave its establishment to chance *(see Box 2-4)*.

Judicial Review of State Court Decisions

In *Marbury* the Court addressed only the power to review acts of the federal government. Could the Court also exert judicial review over the states? According to Section 25 of the 1789 Judiciary Act, indeed, it could. Recall from our discussion of the act that Congress authorized the Court to review appeals from the highest state courts, if those tribunals upheld a state law against challenges of unconstitutionality or denied some claim based on the U.S. Constitution, federal laws, or treaties. But the mere existence of this statute did not necessarily mean that either state courts or the Supreme Court would follow it. Because Section 25 expanded the Supreme Court's jurisdiction, it was always possible that the justices might question Congress's authority to do so, even though it involved appellate, not original, jurisdiction.

More important was the potentially hostile reaction from the states, which in the 1780s and 1790s zealously guarded their power from federal encroachment. Even if

the Court were to take advantage of its ability to review state court decisions, it was more than likely that such tribunals would disregard its rulings. Keep these issues in mind as you read *Martin v. Hunter's Lessee*, an important case in which the Court asserted its power to review state court decisions.

Martin v. Hunter's Lessee

1 WHEAT. (14 U.S.) 304 (1816)
http://supct.law.cornell.edu/supct/cases/name.htm
Vote: 6 (Duvall, Johnson, Livingston, Story, Todd, Washington)
   0

Opinion of the Court: Story
Concurring opinion: Johnson
Not participating: Marshall

Before the Revolutionary War, Lord Fairfax, a British loyalist, inherited a large tract of land in Virginia. When the war broke out, Fairfax, too old and frail to make the journey back to England, remained in Virginia. He died there in 1781 and left the property to his nephew, Denny Martin, a British subject residing in England, with the stipulation that Martin change his name to Fairfax.

The inheritance was complicated by a 1781 Virginia law, which specified that no "enemy" could inherit land. Virginia confiscated Fairfax's (also known as Martin's) property and began proceedings to sell it. Because he believed he had rightfully inherited the land, Martin also began to sell off tracts—among the purchasers were John Marshall and his brother—resulting in a suit contesting title.

A lower Virginia state court upheld Martin's claim, but the highest court in Virginia reversed. When the case, *Fairfax's Devisee v. Hunter's Lessee* (1813), was appealed to the U.S. Supreme Court, only four justices heard it; Chief Justice Marshall recused himself due to the potential conflict of interest. In a 3–1 decision the Court upheld Fairfax's claim, finding that the Virginia statute was unconstitutional because it conflicted with the 1783 Treaty of Paris in which Congress promised to recommend to the states that they restore confiscated property to loyalists.

BOX 2-4   JUDICIAL REVIEW IN GLOBAL PERSPECTIVE

JUDICIAL AUTHORITY to invalidate acts of coordinate branches is not unique to the United States, although it is fair to say that the prestige of the U.S. Supreme Court has provided a model and incentive for other countries. By the middle of the nineteenth century, the Judicial Committee of the British Privy Council was functioning as a kind of constitutional arbiter for colonial governments within the British Empire—but not for the United Kingdom itself. Then Canada in the late nineteenth century and Australia in the first years of the twentieth created their own systems of constitutional review.

In the nineteenth century Argentina also modeled its Corte Suprema on that of the United States and even instructed its judges to pay special attention to precedents of the American tribunal. In the twentieth century Austria, Ireland, India, and the Philippines adopted judicial review, and variations of this power can be found in Norway, Switzerland, much of Latin America, and some countries in Africa.

After World War II the three defeated Axis powers—Italy, Japan, and West Germany—all institutionalized judicial review in their new constitutions. This development was due in part to a revulsion against their recent experiences with unchecked political power and in part to the influence of American occupying authorities. Japan, where the constitutional document was largely drafted by Americans, follows the decentralized model of the United States: the power of constitutional review is diffused throughout the entire judicial system.[1] Any court of general jurisdiction can declare a legislative or executive act invalid.

Germany and Italy, and later Belgium, Portugal, and Spain, followed a centralized model first adopted in the Austrian constitution of 1920. Each country has a single constitutional court (although some sit in divisions or senates) that has a judicial monopoly on reviewing acts of government for their compatibility with their constitutions. The most a lower court judge can do when a constitutional issue is raised is to refer the problem to the specialized constitutional court. *(See Box 1-2, page 21.)*

After the Berlin Wall collapsed in 1989 and the Soviet Union disintegrated soon after, many East European republics looked to judges' interpreting a constitutional text with a bill of rights to protect their new-found liberties. Most opted for centralized systems of constitutional review, establishing ordinary tribunals and a separate constitutional court. They made this choice despite familiarity with Chief Justice John Marshall's argument for a decentralized court system in *Marbury;* namely, all judges may face the problem of a conflict between a statute or executive order, on the one hand, and the terms of a constitutional document on the other. If judges cannot give preference to the constitutional provision over ordinary legislation or an executive act, they violate their oath to support the constitution.

The experience of these tribunals has been quite varied. The German Constitutional Court, for example, is largely regarded as a success story. In its first thirty-eight years, that tribunal invalidated 292 Bund (national) and 130 Land (state) laws, provoking frequent complaints that it "judicializes" politics.[2] The Court, however, has survived these attacks and has gone on to create a new and politically significant jurisprudence in the fields of federalism and civil liberties. The Russian Constitutional Court stands (or teeters) in stark contrast. It too began to make extensive use of judicial review to strike down government acts but quickly paid a steep price: In 1993 President Boris Yeltsin suspended the Court's operations; it did not resume its activities until nearly two years later.

1. Walter F. Murphy and Joseph Tanenhaus, eds., *Comparative Constitutional Law* (New York: St. Martin's Press, 1977), chaps. 1–6; C. Neal Tate and Torbjörn Vallinder, eds., *The Global Expansion of Judicial Power: The Judicialization of Politics* (New York: New York University Press, 1995).

2. Donald P. Kommens, *The Constitutional Jurisprudence of the Federal Republic of Germany,* 2nd ed. (Durham: Duke University Press, 1997), 52.

SOURCE: Adapted from C. Herman Pritchett, Walter F. Murphy, and Lee Epstein, *Courts, Judges and Politics* (New York: McGraw-Hill, 2002), chap. 6.

The U.S. Supreme Court ordered the Virginia Supreme Court to carry out its ruling. In response, the Virginia court, which did not consider itself subordinate to the Supreme Court, held hearings to determine whether it should comply. Eventually, it not only declined to follow the order but also struck down Section 25 of the Judiciary Act of 1789 as unconstitutional. The Virginia Supreme Court's decision was then appealed to the U.S. Supreme Court in the case of *Martin v. Hunter's Lessee*. Here the justices considered the question of whether Congress could expand their appellate jurisdiction, as it had done in Section 25.

STORY, J., delivered the opinion of the court.

The questions involved in this judgment are of great importance and delicacy. Perhaps it is not too much to affirm, that, upon their right decision, rest some of the most solid principles which have hitherto been supposed to sustain and protect the constitution itself. The great respectability, too, of the court whose decisions we are called upon to review, and the entire deference which we entertain for the learning and ability of that court, add much to the difficulty of the task which has so unwelcomely fallen upon us. . . .

Before proceeding to the principal questions, it may not be unfit to dispose of some preliminary considerations which have grown out of the arguments at the bar.

The constitution of the United States was ordained and established, not by the states in their sovereign capacities, but emphatically, as the preamble of the constitution declares, by "the people of the United States." There can be no doubt that it was competent to the people to invest the general government with all the powers which they might deem proper and necessary; to extend or restrain these powers according to their own good pleasure, and to give them a paramount and supreme authority. As little doubt can there be, that the people had a right to prohibit to the states the exercise of any powers which were, in their judgment, incompatible with the objects of the general compact; to make the powers of the state governments, in given cases, subordinate to those of the nation, or to reserve to themselves those sovereign authorities which they might not choose to delegate to either. The constitution was not, therefore, necessarily carved out of existing state sovereign-

ties, nor a surrender of powers already existing in state institutions, for the powers of the states depend upon their own constitutions; and the people of every state had the right to modify and restrain them, according to their own views of policy or principle. On the other hand, it is perfectly clear that the sovereign powers vested in the state governments, by their respective constitutions, remained unaltered and unimpaired, except so far as they were granted to the government of the United States.

These deductions do not rest upon general reasoning, plain and obvious as they seem to be. They have been positively recognised by one of the articles in amendment of the constitution, which declares, that "the powers not delegated to the United States by the constitution, nor prohibited by it to the states, are reserved to the *states* respectively, or *to the people.*"

The government, then, of the United States, can claim no powers which are not granted to it by the constitution, and the powers actually granted, must be such as are expressly given, or given by necessary implication. On the other hand, this instrument, like every other grant, is to have reasonable construction, according to the import of its terms; and where a power is expressly given in general terms, it is not to be restrained to particular cases, unless that construction grow out of the context expressly, or by necessary implication. The words are to be taken in their natural and obvious sense, and not in a sense unreasonably restricted or enlarged.

The constitution unavoidably deals in general language. It did not suit the purposes of the people, in framing this great charter of our liberties, to provide for minute specifications of its powers, or to declare the means by which those powers should be carried into execution. It was foreseen that this would be a perilous and difficult, if not an impracticable, task. The instrument was not intended to provide merely for the exigencies of a few years, but was to endure through a long lapse of ages, the events of which were locked up in the inscrutable purposes of Providence. It could not be foreseen what new changes and modifications of power might be indispensable to effectuate the general objects of the charter; and restrictions and specifications, which, at the present, might seem salutary, might, in the end, prove the overthrow of the system itself. Hence its powers are expressed in general terms, leaving to the legislature,

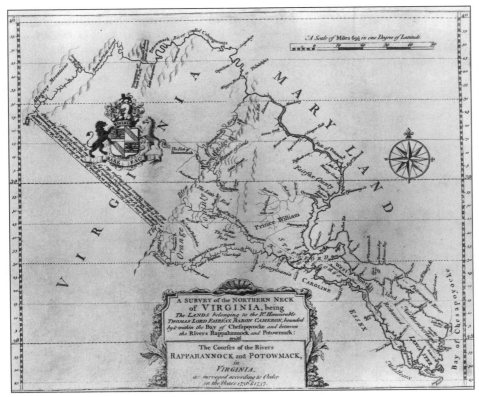

Martin v. Hunter's Lessee (1816) involved land in Virginia that the state had confiscated from a Loyalist during the Revolutionary War. Justice Story wrote the landmark opinion establishing the Supreme Court's authority to reverse state court decisions involving federal laws or constitutional rights.

from time to time, to adopt its own means to effectuate legitimate objects, and to mould and model the exercise of its powers, as its own wisdom, and the public interests, should require.

With these principles in view, principles in respect to which no difference of opinion ought to be indulged, let us now proceed to . . . the consideration of the great question as to the nature and extent of the appellate jurisdiction of the United States. . . . [A]ppellate jurisdiction is given by the constitution to the supreme court in all cases where it has not original jurisdiction; subject, however, to such exceptions and regulations as congress may prescribe. It is, therefore, capable of embracing every case enumerated in the constitution, which is not exclusively to be decided by way of original jurisdiction. But the exercise of appellate jurisdiction is far from being limited by the terms of the constitution to the supreme court. There can be no doubt that congress may create a succession of inferior tribunals, in each of which it may vest appellate as well as original juris-

diction. The judicial power is delegated by the constitution in the most general terms, and may, therefore, be exercised by congress under every variety of form, of appellate or original jurisdiction. And as there is nothing in the constitution which restrains or limits this power, it must, therefore, in all other cases, subsist in the utmost latitude of which, in its own nature, it is susceptible.

As, then, by the terms of the constitution, the appellate jurisdiction is not limited as to the supreme court, and as to this court it may be exercised in all other cases than those of which it has original cognizance, what is there to restrain its exercise over state tribunals in the enumerated cases? The appellate power is not limited by the terms of the third article to any particular courts. The words are, "the judicial power (which includes appellate power) shall extend *to all cases*," &c., and "in all other cases before mentioned the supreme court shall have appellate jurisdiction." It is the *case*, then, and not *the court*, that gives the jurisdiction. If the judicial power extends to the case, it will be in vain to search in the letter of the constitution for any qualification as to the tribunal where it depends. It is incumbent, then, upon those who assert such a qualification to show its existence by necessary implication. If the text be clear and distinct, no restriction upon its plain and obvious import ought to be admitted, unless the inference be irresistible.

If the constitution meant to limit the appellate jurisdiction to cases pending in the courts of the United States, it would necessarily follow that the jurisdiction of these courts would, in all the cases enumerated in the constitution, be exclusive of state tribunals. How otherwise could the jurisdiction extend to *all* cases arising under the constitution, laws, and treaties of the United States, or *to all cases* of admiralty and maritime jurisdiction? If some of these cases might be entertained by state tribunals, and no appellate jurisdiction as to them should exist, then the appellate power would not extend to *all*, but to *some*, cases. If state tribunals might exercise concurrent jurisdiction over all or some of the other classes of cases in the constitution without control, then the appellate jurisdiction of the United States might, as to such cases, have no real existence, contrary to the manifest intent of the constitution. Under such circumstances, to give effect to the judicial power, it must be construed to be exclusive; and this not only when the *casus faederis* should arise directly, but when it should arise, incidentally, in cases pending in state courts. This construction would abridge the jurisdiction of such court far more than has been ever contemplated in any act of congress.

On the other hand, if, as has been contended, a discretion be vested in congress to establish, or not to establish, inferior courts at their own pleasure, and congress should not establish such courts, the appellate jurisdiction of the supreme court would have nothing to act upon, unless it could act upon cases pending in the state courts. Under such circumstances it must be held that the appellate power would extend to state courts; for the constitution is peremptory that it shall extend to certain enumerated cases, which cases could exist in no other courts. Any other construction, upon this supposition, would involve this strange contradiction, that a discretionary power vested in congress, and which they might rightfully omit to exercise, would defeat the absolute injunctions of the constitution in relation to the whole appellate power. . . .

It must, therefore, be conceded that the constitution not only contemplated, but meant to provide for cases within the scope of the judicial power of the United States, which might yet depend before state tribunals. It was foreseen that in the exercise of their ordinary jurisdiction, state courts would incidentally take cognizance of cases arising under the constitution, the laws, and treaties of the United States. Yet to all these cases the judicial power, by the very terms of the constitution, is to extend. It cannot extend by original jurisdiction if that was already rightfully and exclusively attached in the state courts, which (as has been already shown) may occur; it must, therefore, extend by appellate jurisdiction, or not at all. It would seem to follow that the appellate power of the United States must, in such cases, extend to state tribunals; and if in such cases, there is no reason why it should not equally attach upon all others within the purview of the constitution.

It has been argued that such an appellate jurisdiction over state courts is inconsistent with the genius of our governments, and the spirit of the constitution. That the latter was never designed to act upon state sovereignties, but only upon the people, and that if the power exists, it will materially impair the sovereignty of the states, and the independence of their courts. We cannot yield to the force of this reasoning; it assumes principles which we cannot admit, and draws conclusions to which we do not yield our assent.

It is a mistake that the constitution was not designed to operate upon states, in their corporate capacities. It is crowded with provisions which restrain or annul the sovereignty of the states in some of the highest branches of their prerogatives. The tenth section of the first article contains a long list of disabilities and prohibitions imposed upon the states. Surely, when such essential portions of state sovereignty are taken away, or prohibited to be exercised, it cannot be correctly asserted that the constitution does not act upon the states. The language of the constitution is also imperative upon the states as to the performance of many duties. It is imperative upon the state legislatures to make laws prescribing the time, places, and manner of holding elections for senators and representatives, and for electors of president and vice president. And in these, as well as some other cases, congress have a right to revise, amend, or supersede the laws which may be passed by state legislatures. . . . The courts of the United States can, without question, revise the proceedings of the executive and legislative authorities of the states, and if they are found to be contrary to the constitution, may declare them to be of no legal validity. Surely the exercise of the same right over judicial tribunals is not a higher or more dangerous act of sovereign power.

Nor can such a right be deemed to impair the independence of state judges. It is assuming the very ground in controversy to assert that they possess an absolute independence of the United States. In respect to the powers granted to the United States, they are not independent; they are expressly bound to obedience by the letter of the constitution; and if they should unintentionally transcend their authority, or misconstrue the constitution, there is no more reason for giving their judgments an absolute and irresistible force, than for giving it to the acts of the other coordinate departments of state sovereignty. . . .

It is further argued, that no great public mischief can result from a construction which shall limit the appellate power of the United States to cases in their own courts: first, because state judges are bound by an oath to support the constitution of the United States, and must be presumed to be men of learning and integrity; and, secondly, because congress must have an unquestionable right to remove all cases within the scope of the judicial power from the state courts to the courts of the United States, at any time before final judgment, though not after final judgment. As to the first reason—admitting that the judges of the state courts are, and always will be, of as much learning, integrity, and wisdom, as those of the courts of the United States, (which we very cheerfully admit), it does not aid the argument. It is manifest that the constitution has proceeded upon a theory of its own, and given or withheld powers according to the judgment of the American people, by whom it was adopted. We can only construe its powers, and cannot inquire into the policy or principles which induced the grant of them. The constitution has presumed (whether rightly or wrongly we do not inquire) that state attachments, state prejudices, state jealousies, and state interests, might sometimes obstruct, or control, or be supposed to obstruct or control, the regular administration of justice. . . .

This is not all. A motive of another kind, perfectly compatible with the most sincere respect for state tribunals, might induce the grant of appellate power over their decisions. That motive is the importance, and even necessity of *uniformity* of decisions throughout the whole United States, upon all subjects within the purview of the constitution. Judges of equal learning and integrity, in different states, might differently interpret a statute, or a treaty of the United States, or even the constitution itself: If there were no revising authority to control these jarring and discordant judgments, and harmonize them into uniformity, the laws, the treaties, and the constitution of the United States would be different in different states, and might, perhaps, never have precisely the same construction, obligation, or efficacy, in any two states. The public mischiefs that would attend such a state of things would be truly deplorable; and it cannot be believed that they could have escaped the enlightened convention which formed the constitution. What, indeed, might then have been only prophecy, has now become fact; and the appellate jurisdiction must continue to be the only adequate remedy for such evils. . . .

On the whole, the court are of opinion, that the appellate power of the United States does extend to cases pending in the state courts; and that the 25th section of the judiciary act, which authorizes the exercise of this jurisdiction in the specified cases, by a writ of error, is supported by the letter and spirit of the constitution. We find no clause in that instrument which limits this power; and we dare not interpose a limitation where the people have not been disposed to create one. . . .

It is the opinion of the whole court, that the judgment of the court of appeals of Virginia, rendered on the mandate in this cause, be reversed, and the judgment of the district court, held at Winchester, be, and the same is hereby, affirmed.

With these words, the justices may have presumed that the issue was settled, but after they announced *Martin*, Virginia continued its assaults on the authority of the Supreme Court to review state actions. The issue was not fully resolved until the case of *Cohens v. Virginia* (1821). The Cohen brothers were tried and convicted in Virginia for selling tickets for the District of Columbia lottery, a lottery that was authorized by an act of Congress but not by Virginia law. When the Cohens alleged that the federal law superseded the Virginia statute, the Supreme Court was again compelled to review a Virginia court's interpretation of a congressional act.

As in *Marbury*, the Court was faced with a difficult political situation. Virginia had refused to comply with the Court's earlier decision in *Martin*. The state's attorneys, including Philip P. Barbour, who later would serve on the

U.S. Supreme Court, continued to argue that the Court could not review state court decisions because the states were sovereign entities. In particular, they turned to the Eleventh Amendment. That amendment overturned a 1793 Supreme Court decision, *Chisholm v. Georgia*, which had upheld the right of citizens of one state to bring suit, in the Supreme Court, against another state. The amendment says, "The Judicial power of the United States shall not be construed to extend to any suit in law or equity, commenced or prosecuted against one of the United States by Citizens of another State, or by Citizens or Subjects of any Foreign State." The attorneys argued that these words prohibited the Supreme Court from hearing appeals by citizens against their own states—regardless of what Section 25 said and even if the appeal involved a congressional act (as was the case here). But, writing for a unanimous Court, Chief Justice Marshall disagreed:

The constitution and laws of a State, so far as they are repugnant to the constitution and laws of the United States, are absolutely void. These States are constituent parts of the United States. They are members of one great empire—for some purposes sovereign, for some purposes subordinate.

In a government so constituted, is it unreasonable that the judicial power should be competent to give efficacy to the constitutional laws of the legislature? . . .

We think it is not. We think that in a government acknowledgedly supreme, with respect to objects of vital interest to the nation, there is nothing inconsistent with sound reason, nothing incompatible with the nature of government, in making all its departments supreme, so far as respects those objects, and so far as is necessary to their attainment. The exercise of the appellate power over those judgments of the State tribunals which may contravene the constitution or laws of the United States, is, we believe, essential to the attainment of those objects.

By so ruling, Marshall reinforced the constitutionality of Section 25 of the Judiciary Act, held that the Eleventh Amendment did not preclude the Supreme Court from exercising jurisdiction over a federal question raised on appeal by citizens against their own states (in accord with Section 25), and ended the immediate dispute with Virginia. But neither *Martin* nor *Cohens* fully resolved questions concerning the role of federal courts vis-à-vis their state counterparts; nor did they end state challenges to the Court's authority.

In Chapter 6 we have more to say about issues relating to federal court review of state court decisions. Here we only wish to outline the basic contours of three (*see Box 2-5*). The first centers directly on the Supreme Court and specifically its jurisdiction to hear appeals from state courts. Even after Congress, in 1916 and 1925, gave the Court discretion over whether or not to hear many sorts of disputes, it maintained provisions obligating the justices to review state court decisions invalidating a federal law or validating a state law challenged as inconsistent with federal law. Finally, in 1988, under pressure from the justices themselves, Congress eliminated these mandatory appeals, giving the Court nearly complete discretion over all state court decisions involving federal law. And, it is worth noting, the Supreme Court is quite selective about the kinds of state court decisions it will hear. Beginning with **Murdock v. City of Memphis** (1875), the Court has said that it will not review decisions interpreting state statutes and constitutional provisions unless the state court's interpretation implicates issues of federal law; in other words, the justices believe that state courts should be the final arbiters of the meaning of their own laws and constitutions. This traditional view is called the "adequate and independent state grounds" test: the Court will refrain from reviewing state court interpretations of state constitutions and law unless those decisions involve issues of federal law.[16]

The second is more general, centering on the supervisory powers of federal courts over their state counterparts and state officials. As Box 2-5 shows, they can issue injunctions to prevent state officials from implementing unconstitutional state laws; they can also review state court convictions via the habeas corpus procedure (petitions filed by people in custody to challenge their detention and to request a court to release them).

Finally, Congress has, on occasion, made other exceptions to the Eleventh Amendment. And, as we imply in Box 2-5, from *Cohens* through the 1980s, in case after case the Court permitted these exceptions. For example, in

16. Because we discuss this approach in some detail in Chapter 6, we want only to note here that this test is not as clear as it might seem because, occasionally, state court opinions rely on both federal and state law. So the question often emerges as to whether these kinds of "ambiguous" decisions do or do not rest on adequate and independent state grounds.

BOX 2-5   SUPERVISION OF FEDERAL COURTS OVER THE STATES

Jurisdiction of Supreme Court over State Court Decisions: Highlights

• *Section 25 of the 1789 Judiciary Act.* Gave Court authority to review decisions from the highest state courts, if those tribunals upheld a state law against challenges of unconstitutionality or denied some claim based on the U.S. Constitution, federal laws, or treaties.

• *Murdock v. City of Memphis (1875).* Court will not review decisions interpreting state statutes and constitutional provisions unless the state court's interpretation implicates issues of federal law; in other words, the justices believe that state courts should be the final arbiters of the meaning of their own law and constitutions. This traditional view is called the "adequate and independent state grounds" test: the Court will refrain from reviewing state court interpretations of state constitutions and law unless those decisions involve issues of federal law.

• *Congressional Act of 1914.* Opened the door to discretionary review by allowing Court to review by certiorari state court decisions in favor of rights claimed under federal law; previously (e.g., under Section 25 of the 1789 act) only state court decisions denying a right had been reviewable.

• *Administration of Justice Improvements Act of 1988.* Eliminated virtually all of the Court's nondiscretionary jurisdiction. Court no longer obligated to review state court decisions involving federal law.

Other Mechanisms for Federal Court Supervision of States: Some Examples

• *Injunctions.* Beginning with the 1824 case of *Osborn v. Bank of United States,* the Court has said that federal courts may issue injunctions to prevent state officials from enforcing unconstitutional state provisions. The power of federal courts to do so was, during the Warren Court era, quite broad, but more recent Courts have limited it. In *Younger v. Harris* (1971), for example, the justices said that federal courts should not enjoin state officials from enforcing their

laws unless continued enforcement would irreparably harm the individual seeking the enjoinment.

• *Habeas Corpus Petitions.* Provide federal courts with the ability to review state court convictions. Decisions of the Warren Court era loosened the requirements for filing habeas corpus petitions in federal courts; decisions of the Rehnquist Court *(see Table 6-7)* have restricted the scope of habeas corpus review, thereby reducing the supervisory role of federal courts.

• *Congressional Exceptions to the Eleventh Amendment.* While the Eleventh Amendment bars states from being sued in federal court without their express consent (see, e.g., *Edelman v. Jordan,* 1974), the Supreme Court has allowed Congress to make exceptions to this rule.[1] In recent years, however, the Court has cut back on some of these. See the text for more details. For example, in *Fitzpatrick v. Bitzer* (1976), the Court held that because the Fourteenth Amendment expressly gives Congress the power to enforce the amendment "by appropriate legislation," Congress could abrogate the Eleventh Amendment immunity from suit when attempting to enforce the Fourteenth. Similarly, in *Pennsylvania v. Union Gas Co.* (1989), a divided Court held that the Commerce Clause of Article I permitted Congress to make an exception to the Eleventh Amendment's grant of immunity, stating that the power to regulate interstate commerce would be "incomplete without the authority to render States liable in damages." In the 1996 case of *Seminole Tribe of Florida v. Florida,* however, the Court overruled *Union Gas.* Writing for the Court, Chief Justice Rehnquist held, "Even when the Constitution vests in Congress complete law-making authority over a particular area, the Eleventh Amendment prevents congressional authorization of suits by private parties against unconsenting States."

---

1. Daniel A. Farber et al. point to *Cohens* as starting this line of exceptions: "The Marshall Court gave the [Eleventh] amendment a stingy reading, finding in *Cohens v. Virginia* that the Eleventh Amendment does not preclude Supreme Court jurisdiction over a federal question raised upon appeal by a citizen against his own state." *Constitutional Law* (St. Paul: West, 1993), 1091.

Fitzpatrick v. Bitzer (1976), the Court held that because the Fourteenth Amendment expressly gives Congress the power to enforce the amendment "by appropriate legislation," Congress could abrogate the Eleventh Amendment immunity from suit when attempting to enforce the Fourteenth. Similarly, in *Pennsylvania v. Union Gas Co.* (1989), a divided Court held that the Commerce Clause of Article I permitted Congress to make an exception to the Eleventh Amendment's grant of immunity, stating that the power to regulate interstate commerce would be "incomplete without the authority to render States liable in damages." But, as we also imply in Box 2-5, contemporary Courts have seriously cut back on these exceptions—much to the delight of those who support increased power for the states vis-à-vis the federal government. The first notable change came in the 1996 case of *Seminole Tribe of Florida v. Florida*, in which the Court overruled *Union Gas*. Writing for the Court, Chief Justice William H. Rehnquist held, "Even when the Constitution vests in Congress complete law-making authority over a particular area, the Eleventh Amendment prevents congressional authorization of suits by private parties against unconsenting States." In other words, the Court asserted that Article I of the Constitution does not permit Congress to abrogate the states' sovereign immunity from suits commenced or prosecuted in the federal courts. Three years later, the justices pushed *Seminole Tribe* even further, when they ruled in *Alden v. Maine* (1999) that Congress cannot subject nonconsenting states to private suits for damages even in their own courts. This trend has generally continued, with the Court, among other holdings, ruling that Congress cannot make states liable for suits brought by state employees under federal age and disability discrimination acts (*Kimel v. Florida Board of Regents*, 2000; *Board of Trustees of University of Alabama v. Garrett*, 2001). In the 2003 case of *Nevada Department of Human Resources v. Hibbs*, however, the Court appeared to buck the trend when it held that state employees may bring suit under the federal Family and Medical Leave Act of 1993, which enables employees to take up to twelve workweeks of unpaid leave annually for the onset of a "serious health condition" in the employee's spouse and for other reasons.

In Chapter 6 we have more to say about sovereign immunity and other matters pertaining to the relationship between federal courts and the states; these have been areas of focus for the current Court as well as the causes of acrimonious debates among the justices. Indeed, underlying *Bush v. Gore* (2000) (excerpted on pages 190–200), in which the justices effectively decided the outcome of the presidential election of 2000, are important questions about the ability and desirability of federal court review of state court decisions.

Again, we turn to these and related questions in Chapter 6. But one clear implication of even this brief discussion is that the relationship between federal courts and the states has changed over time, as a result of various Court rulings and congressional enactments. One thing that has not changed since the days of *Martin* and *Cohens*, however, is that states continue, on occasion, to challenge the authority of the Supreme Court to "interfere" in their business. And they have developed a variety of techniques to do so—as reactions to *Brown v. Board of Education* (1954) indicate. In the wake of that decision, which told states that they could not maintain segregated public schools, came the following responses (to name just a few):[17]

- Speech. Public statements in defiance of the Court, such as Alabama governor George Wallace's often-cited remark: "I draw the line in the dust and toss the gauntlet before the feet of tyranny and I say segregation now, segregation tomorrow, segregation forever." Or Mississippi senator James Eastland's claim that the South "will not abide by or obey this legislative decision by a political court."

- Legislation. One hundred thirty-six laws and state constitutional amendments to preserve segregation in the South, reflecting the sentiment that "as long as we can legislate, we can segregate." Examples include the Alabama legislature's declaration that the decision was null and void; a Louisiana law that denied promotion or

---

17. These are from Gerald N. Rosenberg, *The Hollow Hope* (Chicago: University of Chicago Press, 1991); Richard Kluger, *Simple Justice* (New York: Knopf, 1975); and Bradley C. Canon and Charles A. Johnson, *Judicial Policies: Implementation and Impact*, 2nd ed. (Washington, D.C.: CQ Press, 1999).

graduation to students of desegregated schools; and a Mississippi act that simply prohibited students from attending desegregated schools.

• The Southern Manifesto. A 1957 statement signed by ninety-six members of Congress from the South, which said: "We pledge ourselves to use all lawful means to bring about the reversal of [*Brown*]. . . ."

• Threats of violence. In 1957 Gov. Orville Faubus of Arkansas had members of the National Guard stand at the entrance of Little Rock Central High School to prevent black students from entering. He and other state officials claimed that they were not bound by *Brown*. This incident led to *Cooper v. Aaron* (1958), in which the justices took the opportunity to reaffirm their commitment to Marshall's words in *Marbury:* "It is emphatically the province and the duty of the judicial department to say what the law is."

Judicial Review: Some Controversies

The reactions to *Brown* were extreme; the typical Supreme Court decision—even one that overrules a state law—does not elicit such blatant defiance. Still, these sorts of actions are suggestive: as we know from the Court's opinion in *City of Boerne, Marbury* firmly established the power of federal courts to exert judicial review over national actions, and *Martin* and *Cohens* over state actions. In short, while specific decisions have often met fierce resistance, the Court's role as a principal, though certainly not always final, constitutional interpreter is now so firmly established that it can precipitate the resignation of a president, as it did in *Nixon v. United States* (1974) (excerpted on pages 108–111); or the election of a president, as it did in *Bush v. Gore.* At one swoop, it can declare more than two hundred federal statutory provisions unconstitutional, as it did in *Immigration and Naturalization Service v. Chadha* (1983) (excerpted on pages 273–276); or invalidate almost every law in the country regulating abortion, as it did in *Roe v. Wade* (1973).

But what these and other momentous decisions did not do, and perhaps could not do, was put an end to the controversies surrounding judicial review.

Some of the complaints with *Marbury* emerged while Marshall was still on the bench. Jefferson, for one, griped about the decision until his last days. In an 1823 letter he wrote,

This practice of Judge Marshall, of travelling out of his case to prescribe what the law would be in a moot case not before the court, is very irregular and very censurable. . . . [In *Marbury v. Madison*] the Court determined at once, that being an original process, they had no cognizance of it; and therefore the question before them was ended. But the Chief Justice went on to lay down what the law would be, had they jurisdiction of the case, to wit: that they should command the delivery. The object was clearly to instruct any other court having the jurisdiction, what they should do if *Marbury* should apply to them. Besides the impropriety of this gratuitous interference, could anything exceed the perversion of law? . . . *Yet this case of Marbury and Madison is continually cited by bench and bar, as if it were settled law, without any animadversion on its being merely an obiter dissertation of the Chief Justice.* (Emphasis added.)[18]

Strong words from one of our nation's most revered presidents!

But Jefferson was not the last to complain about Marshall's opinion. Some critics pick apart specific aspects of the ruling, as Jefferson did. He argued that once Marshall ruled that the Court did not have jurisdiction to hear the case, he should have dismissed it. Another criticism of Marshall's opinion is that Section 13 of the 1789 Judiciary Act—which *Marbury* held unconstitutional—did not actually expand the Supreme Court's original jurisdiction. If this is so, then Marshall "had nothing to declare unconstitutional!" [19]

Other debates center on the Court's holding; in particular, on what legal scholar Alexander Bickel called the "countermajoritarian difficulty": given our nation's fundamental commitment to a representative form of government, why should we allow a group of unelected of-

18. Quoted by Andrew A. Lipscomb in *The Writings of Thomas Jefferson*, vol. 15 (Washington, D.C.: Thomas Jefferson Memorial Association, 1905), 447–448.
19. Jeffrey A. Segal and Harold J. Spaeth, *The Supreme Court and the Attitudinal Model* (Cambridge: Cambridge University Press, 1993), 16. A counterargument is that people of the day must have considered Section 13 as expanding the Court's original jurisdiction, or else why would Marbury have brought his suit directly to the Supreme Court?

ficials to override the wishes of the people, as expressed by their elected officials?[20] In other words, while most Americans now accept the fact that courts have the power of judicial review, many legal analysts still argue over whether they should. Let us consider some of the theoretical debates surrounding judicial review, debates that political scientist David Adamany puts into five categories: Framers' intent, judicial restraint, democratic checks on the Court, public opinion, and protection of minority rights.[21]

Framers' Intent. Perhaps the oldest debate concerns whether the Framers intended the federal courts to exercise judicial review. Chief Justice Marshall's affirmative view was a major justification in *Marbury* and *Cohens*, and there is some historical evidence to support it. Most important is that the Framers had knowledge of judicial review. Although Marshall often is credited with its first full enunciation, there is evidence that the concept originated in England in *Dr. Bonham's Case* (1610). At issue here was an act of Parliament that enabled physicians of the London College to authorize medical licenses and to punish those practicing without one. Convicted of violating the act, Dr. Bonham appealed his case to England's high court, the King's Bench. Writing for the court, Lord Chief Justice Sir Edward Coke struck down the act, noting in dictum, "It appears in our books, that in many cases, the common law will control acts of Parliament, and sometimes adjudge them to be utterly void." Coke's resounding declaration of the authority of the court to void parliamentary acts came at a critical point in British history. At a time when King James I was claiming tremendous authority, the court, in an otherwise trivial case, took the opportunity to assert its power.

By the early 1700s the concept of judicial review had fallen out of favor in England. Coke's writings, however, had a profound impact on the development of the American legal system, as best illustrated by the *Writs of As-sistance Case* (1761), involving the legality of sweeping search warrants issued by the British Parliament in the name of the king. In arguing against such writs, James Otis, a Boston lawyer, relied on Coke's opinion in *Bonham* as precedent for his request. Otis lost the case, but his argument was not forgotten. Between 1776 and 1787, eight of the thirteen colonies incorporated judicial review into their constitutions, and by 1789 various state courts had struck down as unconstitutional eight acts passed by their legislatures.

This background makes the question of why the Framers left judicial review out of the Constitution even more perplexing. Some historians argue that the Framers omitted it because they did not want to heighten controversy over Article III by inserting judicial review, not because they opposed the practice. To the contrary, they may have implicitly accepted it. First, historians have established that more than half of the delegates to the Constitutional Convention approved of judicial review, including those generally considered to be the most influential. Second, in *The Federalist Papers* Hamilton adamantly defended the concept, arguing that one branch of government must safeguard the Constitution and that the courts would be in the best position to undertake that important responsibility.

Even with all this evidence, many still argue that the Framers did not intend for courts to review acts of the other branches. In support of this view, some point to the Framers' rejection of the proposed Council of Revision, which would have been composed of Supreme Court justices and the president and permitted to veto legislative acts. Others note that even though some states adopted judicial review, their courts rarely exercised the power. When they did, public outcries typically followed, indicating that support for judicial review was not widespread. What, then, can we conclude about the intent of the Framers with regard to judicial review? Perhaps legal scholar Edward S. Corwin said it best: "The people who say the framers intended it are talking nonsense, and the people who say they did not intend it are talking nonsense." [22]

20. Alexander Bickel, *The Least Dangerous Branch of Government* (New York: Bobbs-Merrill, 1962).

21. David Adamany, "The Supreme Court," in *The American Courts: A Critical Assessment*, ed. John B. Gates and Charles A. Johnson (Washington, D.C.: CQ Press, 1991).

22. Quoted in ibid., 13.

Judicial Restraint. Another controversy surrounding judicial review involves the notion of judicial restraint. Many legal analysts and justices have asserted that courts generally should defer to the elected institutions of government and avoid conflicts with those branches. An early statement of this position came in *Eakin v. Raub* (1825), in which John Gibson, a Pennsylvania Supreme Court justice, took issue with the *Marbury* decision. Because Gibson's opinion provides an important counterpoint to Marshall's arguments in *Marbury*, we have included an excerpt from it. As you read it, consider whether you agree with Gibson's call for judicial restraint in light of the *Marbury* opinion.

Eakin v. Raub

12 SARGENT & RAWLE 330 (PA. 1825)

John Gibson was a well-regarded judge who served on the Pennsylvania Supreme Court for thirty-seven years and nearly obtained a seat on the U.S. Supreme Court. His dissent in *Eakin v. Raub* is not significant because it came in a case of any great moment—indeed, the facts are not particularly important. But even today scholars maintain that it provides one of the finest rebuttals of Marshall's opinion in *Marbury v. Madison*.[23]

GIBSON, J., dissenting.

I am aware, that a right to declare all unconstitutional acts void, without distinction as to either state or federal constitution, is generally held as a professional dogma; but I apprehend, rather as a matter of faith than of reason. It is not a little remarkable, that although the right in question has all along been claimed by the judiciary, no judge has ventured to discuss it, except Chief Justice Marshall; and if the argument of a jurist so distinguished for the strength of his ratiocinative powers be found inconclusive, it may fairly be set down to the weakness of the position which he attempts to defend. . . .

The constitution is said to be a law of superior obligation; and consequently, that if it were to come into collision

23. Melvin I. Urofsky, ed., *Documents of American Constitutional History*, vol. 1 (New York: Knopf, 1989), 183–185.

with an act of the legislature, the latter would have to give way; this is conceded. But it is a fallacy, to suppose, that they can come into collision *before the judiciary*.

The constitution and the *right* of the legislature to pass the act, may be in collision; but is that a legitimate subject for judicial determination? If it be, the judiciary must be a peculiar organ, to revise the proceedings of the legislature, and to correct its mistakes; and in what part of the constitution are we to look for this proud preeminence? It is by no means clear, that to declare a law void, which has been enacted according to the forms prescribed in the constitution, is not a usurpation of legislative power. It is an act of sovereignty; and sovereignty and legislative power are said by Sir William *Blackstone* to be convertible terms. It is the business of the judiciary, to interpret the laws, not scan the authority of the lawgiver; and without the latter, it cannot take cognizance of a collision between a law and the constitution. So that, to affirm that the judiciary has a right to judge of the existence of such collision, is to take for granted the very thing to be proved.

But it has been said to be emphatically the business of the judiciary, to ascertain and pronounce what the law is; and that this necessarily involves a consideration of the constitution. It does so: but how far? If the judiciary will inquire into anything beside the form of enactment, where shall it stop? There must be some point of limitation to such an inquiry; for no one will pretend, that a judge would be justifiable in calling for the election returns, or scrutinizing the qualifications of those who composed the legislature.

It will not be pretended, that the legislature has not, at least, an equal right with the judiciary to put a construction on the constitution; nor that either of them is infallible; nor that either ought to be required to surrender its judgment to the other. Suppose, then, they differ in opinion as to the constitutionality of a particular law; if the organ whose business it first is to decide on the subject, is not to have its judgment treated with respect, what shall prevent it from securing the preponderance of its opinion by the strong arm of power? The soundness of any construction which would bring one organ of the government into collision with another, is to be more than suspected; for where collision occurs, it is evident, the machine is working in a way the framers of it did not intend. . . .

But the judges are sworn to support the constitution, and are they not bound by it as the law of the land? The oath to support the constitution is not peculiar to the judges, but is taken indiscriminately by every officer of the government, and is designed rather as a test of the political principles of the man, than to bind the officer in the discharge of his duty: otherwise, it were difficult to determine, what operation it is to have in the case of a recorder of deeds, for instance, who, in the execution of his office, has nothing to do with the constitution. But granting it to relate to the official conduct of the judge, as well as every other officer, and not to his political principles, still, it must be understood in reference to supporting the constitution, *only as far as that may be involved in his official duty;* and consequently, if his official duty does not comprehend an inquiry into the authority of the legislature, neither does his oath. . . .

But do not the judges do a *positive* act in violation of the constitution, when they give effect to an unconstitutional law? Not if the law has been passed according to the forms established in the constitution. The fallacy of the question is, in supposing that the judiciary adopts the acts of the legislature as its own; whereas, the enactment of a law and the interpretation of it are not concurrent acts, and as the judiciary is not required to concur in the enactment, neither is it in the breach of the constitution which may be the consequence of the enactment; the fault is imputable to the legislature, and on it the responsibility exclusively rests.

Twenty years after *Raub*, Gibson had a change of heart. In an 1845 opinion he suggested that state courts should exercise judicial review over the acts of political institutions located within their jurisdictions.[24] But if we take *Raub* on its face, the use of judicial review belies this notion of judicial restraint for which Gibson clamors. Recall the legislative veto case described earlier in this chapter. By even considering the issue, the Court placed itself squarely in the middle of an executive-legislative dispute; when it nullified the veto, it showed no deference to the wishes of the legislature. To this argument, supporters of judicial review point to Marshall's decision in *Marbury*, Hamilton's assertion in *The Federalist Papers*, and so forth. They suggest that the government needs an umpire who will act neutrally and fairly in interpreting the constitutional strictures.

Again, the question of which position is correct has no absolute answer, only opinion. But what we do know is that U.S. Supreme Court justices—with a few exceptions, such as Felix Frankfurter—have not taken seriously the dictate of judicial restraint or, at the very least, have not let it interfere in their voting.[25] Even those who profess a basic commitment to judicial deference have tended to allow their attitudes and values to dictate their decisions. Still, there is a persistent tendency to equate judicial restraint with conservatism and judicial activism with liberalism. Former president Ronald Reagan often asserted the need for judicial restraint, saying that, if he could, he would appoint a Court of Felix Frankfurters. But many note that what Reagan really wanted was a Court that would defer to legislatures if the laws in question reflected conservative values and would overturn them otherwise.

Democratic Checks. A third controversy involves what Adamany calls "democratic checks on the Court." Although we consider these in some detail in the final section of this chapter (where we look at political constraints on the Court), let us take a moment to outline the two sides of this debate. According to one side, judicial review is defensible on the ground that the Supreme Court—while lacking an explicit electoral connection—is subject to potential checks from the elected branches. That is, if the Court overturns government acts in a way repugnant to the best interests of the people, Congress, the president, and even the states have a number of recourses. Acting in different combinations they can, for example, ratify a constitutional amendment to overturn a decision, change the size of the Court, or remove the Court's appellate jurisdiction.

Moreover, some scholars suggest that the elected branches do not even need to take direct action against the justices to influence their decisions: the mere fact that the legislature has weapons to use against the judiciary may influence the justices.[26] In other words, if the

---

24. See ibid., 183.

25. But see Segal and Spaeth, who argue that Frankfurter was "nothing more than a stalwart economic conservative who, along with his other economically oriented colleagues, used judicial restraint and judicial activism with equal facility to achieve his substantial policy objectives" (*Supreme Court and the Attitudinal Model*, 318).

26. See generally, William N. Eskridge Jr., "Overriding Supreme Court Statutory Interpretation Decisions," *Yale Law Journal* 101 (1991): 331–455.

justices care about the ultimate state of the law, they might seek to accommodate the wishes of Congress rather than face the wrath of the legislators, which could lead to the reversal of a ruling.

It is the existence of congressional threat—not its actual invocation—that may affect how the Court rules in a given case. This dynamic, in the eyes of some analysts, may explain why the justices rarely strike down acts of Congress. To see the point, consider *Mistretta v. United States* (1989), in which the Supreme Court scrutinized a law that sought to minimize judicial discretion in sentencing *(see pages 268–271)*. The law created a sentencing commission charged with promulgating guidelines for federal judges to follow in handing down criminal sentences. Although some lower court judges refused to adopt the guidelines, arguing that they undermined judicial independence, the Supreme Court upheld the law. It is possible that the justices upheld the law because they agreed with it ideologically, because precedent led them to that conclusion, and so forth. But it also may be true that the justices feared a congressional backlash—a fear that was sufficiently real for them to act in accord with legislative wishes.

The problem with these arguments, in the eyes of some analysts, is twofold. First, explicit checks on the part of elected branches are very rarely invoked: only four amendments have overturned Court decisions; the Court's size has not been changed since 1869; and only once has Congress removed the Court's appellate jurisdiction. Second, although there are clearly some constitutional cases in which justices have voted in accord with congressional preferences (rather than with their own when those preferences are different, to avoid a backlash), those may be the exceptions, not the rules. After all, some ask, why would the Court fear Congress when it so rarely takes action against it? *City of Boerne* well illustrates the point: in rendering their opinion, the majority did not seem particularly concerned with the fact that the law had received substantial legislative support.

Public Opinion. A fourth debate surrounding judicial review concerns public opinion and the Court. Those who support judicial review point to two aspects of the Court's relationship with the public. First, they argue

that Court decisions are usually in harmony with public opinion; that is, even though the Court faces no real pressure to do so, it generally "follows the elections." Therefore, Americans need not fear that the Court will usurp their power because it does not exercise the power in a countermajoritarian fashion.

Empirical evidence, however, is mixed. After conducting an extensive investigation of the relationship of public opinion and the Court, Thomas R. Marshall concluded that "the evidence suggests that the modern Court has been an essentially majoritarian institution. Where clear poll margins exist, three-fifths to two-thirds of Court rulings reflect the polls."[27] Yet, as he and others concede, the Court at times has handed down decisions well out of line with public preferences, such as its prohibition of prayer in school and its short-lived ban on the death penalty.[28]

Second, even if the Court is occasionally out of sync with the public, judicial review is important: when the Court reviews and affirms government acts, it can play the role of republican schoolmaster—educating the public and conferring legitimacy on those acts. But evidence suggests that the Court does not and cannot serve this function, that too few people actually know about any given Court decision and, even if they do know, they do not necessarily shift their ideas to conform to the Court's opinions.

Research by Charles H. Franklin and Liane Kosaki provides an interesting example of the last point.[29] They examined whether the Court's decision in *Roe v. Wade* (1973) changed citizens' opinions on abortion, reasoning that if the Court acted as a republican schoolmaster then the public would adopt more liberal attitudes. Their data indicate, however, that no such change occurred. Instead, those who supported abortion rights before *Roe* became more liberal, while those opposed became more

27. Thomas R. Marshall, *Public Opinion and the Supreme Court* (Boston: Unwin Hyman, 1989), 192.

28. For an excellent review of this literature, see Gregory A. Caldeira, "Courts and Public Opinion," in *The American Courts*.

29. Charles H. Franklin and Liane Kosaki, "The Republican Schoolmaster: The U.S. Supreme Court, Public Opinion, and Abortion," *American Political Science Review* 83 (1989): 751–771; see also Timothy R. Johnson and Andrew D. Martin, "The Public's Conditional Response to Supreme Court Decisions," *American Political Science Review* 92 (1998): 299–310.

pro-life. In other words, the Court's decision served to so-lidify existing views and not to change attitudes.

Role of the Court. A final controversy—perhaps the most hotly debated—concerns what role the Supreme Court should play in the American system of government. Those who support judicial review assert that the Court must have this power if it is to fulfill its most important constitutional assignment: protection of minority rights. By their very nature—the fact that they are elected—legislatures and executives reflect the interests of the majority. Those interests may take action that is blatantly unconstitutional. So that the majority cannot tyrannize a minority, it is necessary for the one branch of government that lacks any electoral connection to have the power of judicial review. This is a powerful argument, the truth of which has been demonstrated many times throughout our history. For example, when the legislatures of southern states continued to enact segregation laws, it was the U.S. Supreme Court that struck them down as violative of the Constitution.

This position also has its share of problems. One is that it conflicts with the notion of the Court as a body that defers to the elected branches. Another is that empirical evidence suggests that some Supreme Courts have not used judicial review in this manner. According to Robert Dahl, many of the acts struck down by the Supreme Court before the 1960s were those that harmed a "privileged class," not disadvantaged minorities.[30] We have seen similar decisions by the Rehnquist Court as well. For example, in *City of Richmond v. J. A. Croson Co.* (1989), the justices struck down a city affirmative action program designed to help minority interests.

Judicial Review in Action

These controversies are important to the extent that they place the subject of judicial review into a theoretical context for debate. But they present debates that probably never will be resolved: as one side finds support for its position, the other always seems to follow suit.

Let us consider instead several issues arising from the way the Court actually has exercised the power of judicial review: the number of times it has invoked the power to strike laws, and the significance of those decisions. As Lawrence Baum suggests, investigation of these issues can help us achieve a better understanding of judicial review and place it in a realistic context.[31] First, how often has the Court overturned a federal, state, or local law or ordinance? Figure 1-6 *(page 42)* depicts those numbers over time. The data seem to indicate that the Court has made frequent use of the power, striking down close to 1,500 government acts since 1790. However, as Baum notes, those acts are but a "minute fraction" of the laws enacted at various levels of government. Between the 1790s and 1990s, for example, Congress passed more than 60,000 laws, with the Court striking far less than 1 percent of them.

The more important question, then, may be that of significance: Does the Court tend to strike down important laws or relatively minor laws? Using the case of *Scott v. Sandford (see Chapter 6)* as an illustration, some argue that the Court, in fact, often strikes significant legislation. Undoubtedly, that opinion had major consequences. By ruling that Congress could not prohibit slavery in the territories and by striking down a law, the Missouri Compromise (which had already been repealed), the Court fed the growing divisions between the North and South, providing a major impetus for the Civil War. The decision also tarnished the prestige of the Court and the reputation of Chief Justice Roger B. Taney.

But how representative is *Scott?* Some other Court opinions striking down government acts have been almost as important; those nullifying state abortion and segregation laws, the federal child labor acts, and many pieces of New Deal legislation come to mind. But Baum astutely notes, "many of the Court's decisions declaring statutes unconstitutional have been unimportant."[32] Consider *Monongahela Navigation Co. v. United States* (1893). Here the Court struck down, on Fifth Amendment grounds, a law concerning the amount of money to be paid by the United States to companies for the "purchase or condemnation of a certain lock and dam in the Monongahela River."

30. Robert Dahl, "Decision-Making in a Democracy: The Supreme Court as a National Policy-Maker," *Journal of Public Law* 6 (1957): 279–295.

31. Lawrence Baum, *The Supreme Court*, 7th ed. (Washington, D.C.: CQ Press, 2001), 194–202.

32. Ibid., 195.

Despite the rather ambiguous record, we can reach three conclusions about the Court's use of judicial review. First, although the Court has struck down some important acts of government—thereby demonstrating its muscle to the other branches and the states—it has not interfered with a good deal of their policy efforts. It is no wonder, then, that scholars believe "While judicial review allows the Court to play a major role in policy making, it certainly has not made the Court the dominant national policy maker." [33] Second, it is not necessarily the Court's use of judicial review that is significant. Rather, as is true with the presidential veto, the threat of its invocation may be its power. In either case, it is clear that without the power of judicial review, the Court's role in our system of government would be far different and, perhaps, far slimmer than it is now.

Finally, given all the attention paid to judicial review, it is easy to forget that the power of courts to exercise it and their judicial authority, more generally, has substantial limits. In the next sections, we consider two: those that emanate from Article III and those that stem from the separation of powers system.

CONSTRAINTS ON JUDICIAL POWER: ARTICLE III

Article III—or the Court's interpretation of it—places three major constraints on the ability of federal tribunals to hear and decide cases: courts must have authority to hear a case (jurisdiction); the case must be appropriate for judicial resolution (justiciability); and the appropriate party must be bringing the case (standing). In what follows, we review doctrine surrounding these constraints. As you read this discussion, consider not only the Court's interpretation of its own limits but also the justifications it offers. Note, in particular, how fluid these can be: some Supreme Courts tend to favor loose constructions of the rules, while others are anxious to enforce them. What factors might explain these different tendencies? Or, to put it another way, to what extent do these constraints limit the Court's authority?

Jurisdiction

According to Chief Justice Salmon P. Chase, "Without jurisdiction the court cannot proceed at all in any cause. Jurisdiction is power to declare the law, and when it ceases to exist, the only function remaining to the court is that of announcing the fact and dismissing the cause." [34] In other words, a court cannot hear a case unless it has the authority—the jurisdiction—to do so.

Article III, Section 2, defines the jurisdiction of U.S. federal courts. Lower courts have the authority to hear disputes involving particular parties and subject matter. The U.S. Supreme Court's jurisdiction is divided into original and appellate: the former are classes of cases that originate in the Court; the latter are those it hears after a lower court.

To what extent does jurisdiction actually constrain the federal courts? *Marbury v. Madison* provides some answers, although contradictory, to this question. Chief Justice Marshall informed Congress that it could not alter the original jurisdiction of the Court. Having reached this conclusion, perhaps Marshall should have merely dismissed the case on the ground that the Court lacked authority to hear it, but that is not what he did.

The issue of appellate jurisdiction is a bit more complex. Article III explicitly states that for those cases over which the Court does not have original jurisdiction, it "shall have appellate Jurisdiction . . . with such Exceptions, and under such Regulations as the Congress shall make." In other words, the Exceptions Clause seems to give Congress authority to alter the Court's appellate jurisdiction.

Has the Supreme Court allowed Congress to do so? We know from *Martin v. Hunter's Lessee* and *Cohens v. Virginia* that the Court has allowed Congress to expand its appellate jurisdiction; in those cases, the Court upheld the *additions* made to its appellate jurisdiction under Section 25 of the Judiciary Act *(see also Box 2-5)*. The question the Court addresses in *Ex parte McCardle* is a bit different. Here the justices must determine whether Congress can use its power under the Exceptions Clause to *re-*

33. Ibid., 201.

34. *Ex parte McCardle* (1869).

move the Court's appellate jurisdiction over a particular category of cases.

Ex parte McCardle

7 WALL. (74 U.S.) 506 (1869)
http://supct.law.cornell.edu/supct/cases/name.htm
Vote: 8 (Chase, Clifford, Davis, Field, Grier, Miller, Nelson, Swayne)

0

Opinion of the Court: Chase

After the Civil War the Radical Republican Congress imposed a series of restrictions on the South.[35] Known as the Reconstruction laws, they in effect placed the region under military rule. Journalist William McCardle opposed these measures and wrote editorials urging resistance to them. As a result, he was arrested for publishing allegedly "incendiary and libelous articles" and held for a trial before a military tribunal, established under Reconstruction.

Because he was a civilian, not a member of any militia, McCardle alleged that he was being illegally held. He petitioned for a writ of habeas corpus under an 1867 act, which stipulated that federal courts had the power to grant writs of habeas corpus in all cases where any person may be restrained of his or her liberty in violation of the Constitution, laws, or treaties of the United States. When this effort failed, McCardle appealed to the U.S. Supreme Court, on which the 1867 act had conferred appellate jurisdiction in such cases.

In early March 1868 *McCardle* "was very thoroughly and ably [presented] upon the merits" to the U.S. Supreme Court. It was clear to most observers that "no Justice was still making up his mind": the Court's sympathies, as was widely known, lay with McCardle.[36] But before the justices issued their decision, Congress, on March 27, 1868, enacted a law repealing the 1867 Habeas

Corpus Act and removing the Supreme Court's authority to hear appeals emanating from it. This move was meant to punish the Court or, at the very least, to send it a strong message. Two years before *McCardle*, in 1866, the Court had invalidated Abraham Lincoln's use of military tribunals in certain areas, and Congress did not want to see the Court take similar action in this dispute.[37] The legislature felt so strongly on this issue that after President Andrew Johnson vetoed the 1868 repealer act, Congress overrode the veto.

The Court responded by redocketing the case for oral arguments in March 1869. During the arguments and in its briefs, the government made its position clear: "When the jurisdiction of a court to determine a case or a class of cases depends upon a statute and that statute is repealed, the jurisdiction ceases absolutely." In short, the government contended that the Court no longer had authority to hear the case and should dismiss it.

THE CHIEF JUSTICE delivered the opinion of the court.

It is unnecessary to consider whether, if Congress had made no exceptions and no regulations, this court might not have exercised general appellate jurisdiction under rules prescribed by itself. From among the earliest Acts of the first Congress, at its first session, was the Act of September 24th, 1789, to establish the judicial courts of the United States. That Act provided for the organization of this court, and prescribed regulations for the exercise of its jurisdiction. . . .

The exception to appellate jurisdiction in the case before us . . . is not an inference from the affirmation of other appellate jurisdiction. It is made in terms. The provision of the Act of 1867, affirming the appellate jurisdiction of this court in cases of habeas corpus, is expressly repealed. It is hardly possible to imagine a plainer instance of positive exception.

We are not at liberty to inquire into the motives of the Legislature. We can only examine into its power under the Constitution; and the power to make exceptions to the appellate jurisdiction of this court is given by express words.

What, then, is the effect of the repealing Act upon the case before us? We cannot doubt as to this. Without jurisdiction the court cannot proceed at all in any cause. Jurisdiction is power to declare the law, and when it ceases to

35. See Lee Epstein and Thomas G. Walker, "The Role of the Supreme Court in American Society: Playing the Reconstruction Game," in *Contemplating Courts*, ed. Lee Epstein (Washington, D.C.: CQ Press, 1995), 315–346.

36. Charles Fairman, *History of the Supreme Court of the United States*, Volume VII: *Reconstruction and Reunion* (New York: Macmillan, 1971), 456.

37. That action came in *Ex parte Milligan* (1866), discussed in Chapter 5.

TABLE 2-2 A Sample of Congressional Proposals Aimed at Eliminating the U.S. Supreme Court's Appellate Jurisdiction

Issue	Supreme Court Decision Provoking Proposal	Proposal
Communist infiltration/ Security programs	*Schware v. Board of Bar Examiners* (1957) in which the Supreme Court refused to allow states to use "inferences regarding moral character" (i.e., past association with a subversive cause) to exclude applicants for admission to the bar.	1958 proposal to eliminate the Court's appellate jurisdiction over any "regulation pertaining to the admission of persons to the practice of law."
Criminal confessions	*Miranda v. Arizona* (1966) in which the Court required police to read those under arrest a series of rights.	1968 proposal to remove the Court's jurisdiction to hear state cases involving the admissibility of confessions.
School busing	*Swann v. Charlotte-Mecklenburg County* (1971) in which the Court permitted district courts to fashion their own school desegregation plans, which may include the busing of students to other schools.	During the 1970s and 1980s many proposals were offered to curb the Court's authority to hear busing cases and to limit the authority of courts to order busing.
School prayer	*Engel v. Vitale* (1962) and *Abington School District v. Schempp* (1963), which eliminated voluntary and mandatory prayer in school.	Several proposals, with a major effort coming in 1979, to eliminate the Supreme Court's as well as all other federal courts' ability to hear any cases involving voluntary school prayer.
Abortion	*Roe v. Wade* (1973) in which the Supreme Court struck down state laws criminalizing abortion. *Roe* legalized abortion during the first two trimesters of pregnancy.	During the 1970s and 1980s several proposals to remove the Court's authority to hear abortion cases.

SOURCE: Adopted from Gerald Gunther and Kathleen M. Sullivan, *Constitutional Law*, 13th ed. (Westbury, N.Y.: Foundation Press, 1997), 83–85.

exist, the only function remaining to the court is that of announcing the fact and dismissing the cause. And this is not less clear upon authority than upon principle. . . .

It is quite clear, therefore, that this . . . court cannot proceed to pronounce judgment in this case, for it has no longer jurisdiction of the appeal; and judicial duty is not less fitly performed by declining ungranted jurisdiction than in exercising firmly that which the Constitution and the laws confer. . . .

The appeal of the petitioner in this case must be dismissed for want of jurisdiction.

As we can see, the Court acceded and declined to hear the case. *McCardle* suggests that Congress has the authority to remove the Court's appellate jurisdiction as it deems necessary. Since *McCardle*, however, Congress has only considered, but not enacted, legislation—at least

legislation aimed directly at the Court—to limit the Court's appellate jurisdiction. Table 2-2 lists some of the proposals members of Congress have offered. As noted, many involve controversial issue areas—abortion, prayer in school, busing—leading to the conclusion that modern Congresses are no different from the one that passed the 1868 repealer act: they would like to use the Exceptions Clause as a political tool, as a way to restrain the Court, but they have yet to do so successfully.

In spite of *McCardle*, there are several reasons to believe that the Court might not uphold the sorts of proposals depicted in Table 2-2. One is that *McCardle* was something of an odd case. According to many scholars, the Court had no choice but to acquiesce to Congress if it wanted to retain its legitimacy in post–Civil War America. The pressures of the day, rather than the Constitution or the beliefs of the justices, may have led to the decision.

Another reason is that a case subsequent to *McCardle* cast some doubt on the precedent it seemed to set. In *United States v. Klein* (1872) the Court considered an 1870 law in which Congress sought to impinge on the president's authority to issue executive amnesties. In particular, it required those who wished to recover property taken by the government during the Civil War to prove their loyalty, even if they had received a presidential pardon. Moreover, the law withdrew the U.S. Supreme Court's (and a lower appellate court's) jurisdiction to hear such cases. Although the justices acknowledged that the Exceptions Clause gave Congress the right to remove their appellate jurisdiction "in a particular class of cases," it could not do so only as "a means to an end." That is, in previous cases, the Court had stated that the president had the power to grant pardons. Therefore, Congress was using the Exceptions Clause to skirt those decisions. If the Court allowed this, it would then permit Congress to "prescribe rules of decision to the Judicial Department . . . in cases pending before it," in violation of constitutional mandates requiring the separation of powers.

Still, *Klein* did not settle the issue. Compare, for example, the views of three twentieth-century justices. In 1949 Justice Frankfurter wrote, "Congress need not give this Court any appellate power; it may withdraw appellate jurisdiction once conferred and it may do so even while a case is sub judice" [before a judge].[38] A year later, former justice Owen J. Roberts, who apparently thought Frankfurter's assertion was correct, proposed an amendment to the Constitution that would have deprived Congress of the ability to remove the Court's appellate jurisdiction.[39] Yet, in 1962, Justice William O. Douglas remarked, "There is a serious question whether the *McCardle* case could command a majority view today."[40]

Whether the Court would allow Congress to use the Exceptions Clause remains an open question until such litigation occurs. Until then, Chief Justice Chase perhaps summed up the situation best when he noted that use of the Exceptions Clause was "unusual and hardly to be justified except upon some imperious public exigency."[41]

Justiciability

According to Article III, judicial power of the federal courts is restricted to "cases" and "controversies." Taken together, these words mean that a litigation must be justiciable—appropriate or suitable for a federal tribunal to hear or to solve. As Chief Justice Earl Warren asserted, cases and controversies

are two complementary but somewhat different limitations. In part those words limit the business of federal courts to questions presented in an adversary context and in a form historically viewed as capable of resolution through the judicial process. And in part those words define the role assigned to the judiciary in a tripartite allocation of power to assure that the federal courts will not intrude into areas committed to the other branches of government. Justiciability is the term of art employed to give expression to this dual limitation placed upon federal courts by the case-and-controversy doctrine.[42]

Although Warren also suggested that "justiciability is itself a concept of uncertain meaning and scope," he elucidated several characteristics of litigation that would render it nonjusticiable. In this section, we treat five: advisory opinions, collusion, mootness, ripeness, and political questions. In the following section we deal with another concept related to justiciability—standing to sue.

Advisory Opinions. A few states and some foreign countries require judges of the highest court to advise the executive or legislature, when so requested, as to their views on the constitutionality of a proposed policy. Since the time of Chief Justice John Jay, however, federal judges in the United States have refused to issue advisory opinions. They do not render advice in hypothetical suits because if litigation is abstract, it possesses no real controversy. The language of the Constitution does not prohibit advisory opinions as opinions, but the Framers rejected a proposal that would have permitted the other branches of government to request judicial rulings "upon important questions of law, and upon solemn occasions."

---

38. *National Mutual Insurance Co. v. Tidewater Transfer Co.* (1949).

39. See his "Now is the Time: Fortifying the Supreme Court's Independence," *American Bar Association Journal* 35 (1949): 1. The Senate approved the amendment in 1953, but the House tabled it. Cited in Gerald Gunther, *Constitutional Law*, 12th ed. (Westbury, N.Y.: Foundation Press, 1991), 45.

40. *Glidden Co. v. Zdanok* (1962).

41. *Ex parte Yerger* (1869).

42. *Flast v. Cohen* (1968).

Madison was critical of this proposal on the ground that the judiciary should have jurisdiction only over "cases of a Judiciary Nature." [43]

The Supreme Court agreed. In July 1793 Secretary of State Thomas Jefferson asked the justices if they would be willing to address questions concerning the appropriate role America should play in the ongoing British-French war. Jefferson wrote that President George Washington "would be much relieved if he found himself free to refer questions [involving the war] to the opinions of the judges of the Supreme Court in the United States, whose knowledge . . . would secure us against errors dangerous to the peace of the United States." [44] Less than a month later the justices denied Jefferson's request, with a reply written directly to the president:

We have considered [the] letter written by your direction to us by the Secretary of State [regarding] the lines of separation drawn by the Constitution between the three departments of government. These being in certain respects checks upon each other, and our being judges of a court in the last resort, are considerations which afford strong arguments against the propriety of our extra-judicially deciding the questions alluded to, especially as the power given by the Constitution to the President, of calling on the heads of departments for opinions, seems to have been *purposely* as well as expressly united to the *executive* departments. [45]

With these words, the justices sounded the death knell for advisory opinions: they would violate the separation of powers principle embedded in the Constitution. The subject has resurfaced only a few times in U.S. history; in the 1930s, for example, President Franklin Roosevelt considered a proposal that would require the Court to issue advisory opinions on the constitutionality of federal laws. But Roosevelt quickly gave up on the idea at least in part because of its dubious constitutionality.

Nevertheless, scholars still debate the Court's 1793 letter to Washington. Some agree with the justices' logic. Others assert that more institutional concerns were at work; perhaps the Court—out of concern for its institutional legitimacy—did not want to become embroiled in "political" disputes at this early phase in its development. Whatever the reason, all subsequent Courts have followed that 1793 precedent: requests for advisory opinions to the *U.S. Supreme Court* present nonjusticiable disputes. [46]

But this does not mean that justices have not found other ways of offering advice. [47] They have, for example, sometimes offered political leaders informal suggestions in private conversations or correspondence. [48] Furthermore, justices of the Supreme Court have often given advice in an institutional but indirect manner. The Judiciary Act of 1925, which granted the Court wide discretion in controlling its docket, was largely drafted by Justice Willis Van Devanter. Chief Justice William Howard Taft and several associate justices openly lobbied for its passage, "patrolling the halls of Congress," as Taft put it. In 1937, when the Senate was considering President Roosevelt's Court-packing plan, opponents arranged for Chief Justice Charles Evans Hughes to send a letter to Sen. Burton K. Wheeler, advising him that increasing the number of justices would impede rather than facilitate the Court's work and that the justices' sitting in separate panels to hear cases—a procedure that increasing the number of justices was supposed to allow—would probably violate the constitutional command that there be one Supreme Court. Like other recent chief justices, William H. Rehnquist has sent an annual report on the state of the judiciary to Congress explaining not only what kind of legislation he deems good for the courts but also the likely impact of proposed legislation on the federal judicial system.

Finally, justices have occasionally used their opinions to provide advice to decision makers. In *Regents of the University of California v. Bakke* (1978), for instance, the Court held that a state medical school's version of affirmative action had deprived a white applicant of equal

43. Quoted by Farber and Sherry in *A History of the American Constitution*, 65.

44. The full text of Jefferson's letter is in Henry M. Hart Jr. and Albert M. Sacks, *The Legal Process*, ed. William N. Eskridge Jr. and Philip P. Frickey (Westbury, N.Y.: Foundation Press, 1994), 630–632.

45. Quoted in ibid., 637.

46. We emphasize the Supreme Court because some state courts do, in fact, issue advisory opinions.

47. We adopt some of the material to follow from C. Herman Pritchett, Walter F. Murphy, and Lee Epstein, *Courts, Judges, and Politics* (New York: McGraw-Hill, 2002), chap. 6.

48. See, for example, Stewart Jay, *Most Humble Servants: The Advisory Role of Early Judges* (New Haven: Yale University Press, 1997).

protection of the laws by rejecting him in favor of minority applicants whom the school ranked lower on all the relevant academic criteria. But, in his opinion, Justice Lewis F. Powell Jr. proffered the advice that the kind of affirmative action program operated by Harvard University would be constitutionally acceptable.

Collusive Suits. A second corollary of justiciability is collusion. The Court will not decide cases in which the litigants (1) want the same outcome, (2) evince no real adversity between them, or (3) are merely testing the law. Indeed, Chief Justice Taney once said that collusion is "contempt of the court, and highly reprehensible." [49]

Why the Court deems collusive suits nonjusticiable is well illustrated in *Muskrat v. United States* (1911). At issue here were several federal laws involving land distribution and appropriations to Native Americans. To determine whether these laws were constitutional, Congress enacted a statute authorizing David Muskrat and other Native Americans to challenge the land distribution law in court. This legislation also ordered the courts to give priority to Muskrat's suit and allowed the attorney general to defend his claim. Furthermore, Congress agreed to pay Muskrat's legal fees if his suit was successful. When the dispute reached the U.S. Supreme Court, it dismissed it. Justice William Day wrote:

[T]here is neither more nor less in this [litigation] than an attempt to provide for a judicial determination, final in this court, of the constitutional validity of an act of Congress. Is such a determination within the judicial power conferred by the Constitution, as the same has been interpreted and defined in the authoritative decisions to which we have referred? We think it is not. That judicial power, as we have seen, is the right to determine actual controversies arising between adverse litigants, duly instituted in courts of proper jurisdiction. The right to declare a law unconstitutional arises because an act of Congress relied upon by one or the other of such parties in determining their rights is in conflict with the fundamental law. The exercise of this, the most important and delicate duty of this court, is not given to it as a body with revisory power over the action of Congress, but because the rights of the litigants in justiciable controversies require the court to choose between the fundamental law and a law purporting to be enacted within constitutional authority, but in fact beyond the power delegated to the legislative branch of the Government. This attempt to obtain a judicial declaration of the validity of the act of Congress is not presented in a "case" or "controversy," to which, under the Constitution of the United States, the judicial power alone extends. It is true the United States is made a defendant to this action, but it has no interest adverse to the claimants. The object is not to assert a property right as against the Government, or to demand compensation for alleged wrongs because of action upon its part. The whole purpose of the law is to determine the constitutional validity of this class of legislation, in a suit not arising between parties concerning a property right necessarily involved in the decision in question, but in a proceeding against the Government in its sovereign capacity, and concerning which the only judgment required is to settle the doubtful character of the legislation in question.

The Court, however, has not always followed the *Muskrat* precedent. Indeed, several collusive suits resulted in landmark decisions, including *Pollock v. Farmers' Loan and Trust Co.* (1895), in which the Court declared the federal income tax unconstitutional. The litigants in this dispute, a bank and a stockholder in the bank, both wanted the same outcome—the demise of the tax. *Carter v. Carter Coal Co.* (1936) is also exemplary. Here the Court agreed to resolve a dispute over a major piece of New Deal legislation despite the fact that the litigants, a company president and the company, which included the president's father, both wanted the same outcome—the eradication of the legislation.

Why did the justices resolve these disputes? "The Court's decision to hear or dismiss such a test case," Joan Biskupic and Elder Witt claim, "usually turns on whether it presents an actual conflict of legal rights susceptible to judicial resolution." [50] In other words, the Court might overlook some element of collusion if the suit presents a real controversy or the potential for one. Other scholars are more skeptical. The temptation to set "good" public policy (or strike down "bad" public policy) is sometimes too strong for the justices to follow their own rules.

Mootness. In general, the Court will not decide cases in which the controversy is no longer live by the time it reaches the Court's doorstep. *DeFunis v. Odegaard* (1974) provides an example. Rejected for admission to the

---

49. *Lord v. Veazie* (1850).

50. Joan Biskupic and Elder Witt, *Guide to the U.S. Supreme Court*, 3rd ed. (Washington, D.C.: Congressional Quarterly, 1997), 300.

University of Washington Law School, Marco DeFunis Jr. brought suit against the school, alleging that it had engaged in reverse discrimination because it had denied him a place but accepted statistically less-qualified minority students. In 1971 a trial court found merit in his claim and ordered that the university admit him. While DeFunis was in his second year of law school, the state's high court reversed the trial judge's ruling. He then appealed to the U.S. Supreme Court. By that time, DeFunis had registered for his final quarter in school. In a *per curiam* opinion, the Court refused to rule on the merits of DeFunis's claim, asserting that it was moot:

Because [DeFunis] will complete his law school studies at the end of the term for which he has now registered regardless of any decision this Court might reach on the merits of this litigation, we conclude that the Court cannot, consistently with the limitations of Art. III of the Constitution, consider the substantive constitutional issues tendered by the parties.

Still, the rules governing mootness are a bit fuzzier than the *DeFunis* opinion characterized them. A well-known case is *Roe v. Wade* (1973), in which the Court legalized abortions performed during the first two trimesters of pregnancy. Norma McCorvey, also known as Roe, was pregnant when she filed suit in 1970. When the Court handed down the decision in 1973, she had long since given birth and put her baby up for adoption. But the justices did not declare this case moot.

Why not? What made *Roe* different from *DeFunis*? The justices provided two legal justifications. First, DeFunis brought the litigation in his own behalf; *Roe* was a class action—a lawsuit brought by one or more persons who represent themselves and all others similarly situated. Second, DeFunis had been admitted to law school, and he would "never again be required to run the gauntlet." Roe could become pregnant again; that is, pregnancy is a situation "capable of repetition, yet evading review." Are these reasonable points? Or is it possible, as some suspect, that the Court developed them to avoid particular legal issues? In either case, it is clear that mootness may be a rather slippery concept, open to interpretation by different justices and Courts.

Ripeness. Ripeness is the flip side of mootness. Whereas moot cases are brought too late, "unripe" cases are those that are brought too early. In other words, under existing Court interpretation, a case is nonjusticiable if the controversy is premature—has insufficiently gelled—for review. *United Public Workers v. Mitchell* (1947) is an often-cited example. In this case, government workers challenged the Hatch Act of 1940, which prohibits some types of federal employees from participating in political campaigns. But only one of the appellants had actually violated the act; the rest simply expressed an interest in working on campaigns. According to the justices, only the one employee had a ripe claim because "the power of courts, and ultimately of this Court to pass upon the constitutionality of acts of Congress arises only when the interests of the litigants require the use of this judicial authority for their protection against actual interference. A hypothetical threat is not enough. We can only speculate as to the kinds of political activity the appellants desire to engage in."

The justices echoed the sentiment of *Mitchell* in *International Longshoreman's Union v. Boyd* (1954). This case involved a 1952 federal law mandating that all aliens seeking admission into the United States from Alaska be "examined" as if they were entering from a foreign country. Believing that the law might affect seasonal American laborers working in Alaska temporarily, a union challenged the law. Writing for the Court, Justice Frankfurter dismissed the suit. In his view,

Appellants in effect asked [the Court] to rule that a statute the sanctions of which had not been set in motion against individuals on whose behalf relief was sought, because an occasion for doing so had not arisen, would not be applied to them if in the future such a contingency should arise. That is not a lawsuit to enforce a right; it is an endeavor to obtain a court's assurance that a statute does not govern hypothetical situations that may or may not make the challenged statute applicable. Determination of the . . . constitutionality of the legislation in advance of its immediate adverse effect in the context of a concrete case involves too remote and abstract an inquiry for the proper exercise of the judicial function.

Political Questions. Another type of nonjusticiable suit involves a political question. Chief Justice Marshall stated in *Marbury v. Madison:*

The province of the court is, solely, to decide on the rights of individuals, not to inquire how the executive, or executive officers, perform duties in which they have a discretion. Questions in their nature political, or which are, by the constitution and laws, submitted to the executive, can never be made in this court.

In other words, there is a class of questions that may be constitutional in nature but that the Court will not address because they are better solved by other branches of government.

But what exactly constitutes a political question? The Court took its first stab at addressing this question in **Luther v. Borden** (1849). This case has its origins in the 1840s when some Rhode Island citizens sought to persuade the legislature to change suffrage requirements (which mandated the ownership of property as a criterion for voting) or to hold a convention for the purpose of writing a constitution (which Rhode Island did not have; it was still operating under its royal charter from King Charles II). When the government rejected these proposals, these citizens wrote their own constitution and created their own government. Meanwhile, the existing government issued a proclamation placing the entire state under martial law, and the governor warned citizens not to support the new constitution. He even contacted President John Tyler for help in suppressing the rebellion. Although Tyler did not send in federal troops, he agreed to do so if war broke out.

Eventually, the existing government managed to suppress the rebels, but one of them, Martin Luther, sued. Luther asserted that the Rhode Island Charter violated Article IV, Section 4, of the U.S. Constitution, which states: "The United States shall guarantee to every State in the Union a Republican Form of Government, and shall protect each of them against Invasion; and on Application of the Legislature or of the Executive (when the Legislature cannot be convened) against Domestic violence." Luther asked the Court to declare the charter government illegitimate and to supplant it with the new constitution.

The Supreme Court, however, refused to go along with Luther. Writing for the majority, Chief Justice Taney held that the Court should avoid deciding any question arising out of the Guarantee Clause because such questions are inherently "political." He based the opinion largely on the words of Article IV, which he believed governed relations between the states and the federal government, not governments and courts. In other words, because the clause omits mention of the Court, it is enforceable only by the president or Congress.

For the next hundred years or so, the Court maintained Taney's position: any case involving the Guarantee Clause constituted a nonjusticiable dispute. In the 1940s an issue came before the Court that presented it with an opportunity to rethink *Luther*. The issue was reapportionment, the way the states draw their legislative districts.

Under the U.S. Constitution, each state is allotted a certain number of seats in the House of Representatives based on the population of the state. Once that number has been determined, it is up to the state to map out the congressional districts. Article I specifies:

Representatives . . . shall be apportioned among the several States which may be included within this Union, according to their respective Numbers. . . . The actual Enumeration shall be made within three Years after the first Meeting of the Congress of the United States, and within every subsequent Term of ten Years, in such Manner as they shall by Law direct. The Number of Representatives shall not exceed one for every thirty Thousand, but each State shall have at Least one Representative.

Article I makes clear that a ten-year census determines the number of representatives each state receives. But no guidelines exist as to how those representatives are to be allocated or apportioned within a given state.

As population shifts occurred within states about the middle of the twentieth century, some redrew their congressional district lines. For most states, the new maps meant creating greater parity for urban centers as citizens moved out of rural areas. Others, however, ignored these shifts and refused to reapportion seats. Over time, the results of their failure to do so became readily apparent. It was possible for two districts within the same state, with large differences in populations, each to elect one member to the House.

Because malapportionment generally had the greatest effect on urban voters, grossly undervaluing their voting power, reform groups representing their interests began to bring litigation to force legislatures to reapportion. In one of the most important of these efforts, *Colegrove v.*

Green (1946), they did so under Article IV. They argued that the failure to reapportion legislative districts deprived some voters of their right to a republican form of government. By way of proof, plaintiffs indicated that a large statistical discrepancy existed between the voting power of urban and rural dwellers because the Illinois legislature had not reapportioned since 1901.

Writing for the Court, Justice Frankfurter dismissed *Colegrove*. He invoked the logic of *Luther v. Borden* to hold that the question of legislative reapportionment within states was left open by the Constitution. If the Court intervened in this matter, it would be acting in a way "hostile to a democratic system." Put in different terms, reapportionment constituted a "political thicket" into which "courts ought not enter."

Less than two decades later, however, in *Baker v. Carr* (1962), the Court did, in fact, enter this thicket, holding that reapportionment was a justiciable issue.[51] What brought about this change? And, more relevant here, what meaning does *Baker* have for the political question doctrine? In particular, does it overrule *Luther,* or does it merely change its interpretative context?

Baker v. Carr

369 U.S. 186 (1962)
http://laws.findlaw.com/US/369/186.html
Vote: 6 (Black, Brennan, Clark, Douglas, Stewart, Warren)
*   2 (Frankfurter, Harlan)*
Opinion of the Court: Brennan
Concurring opinions: Clark, Douglas, Stewart
Dissenting opinions: Frankfurter, Harlan
Not participating: Whittaker

As a result of the Court's decision in *Colegrove*, states that had not reapportioned since the turn of the century were under no federal constitutional mandate to do so, and disparities between the voting power of urban and rural citizens continued to grow. Figure 2-2 shows that a rural vote for the Tennessee legislature counted nearly four times as much as an urban vote.

51. To hear oral arguments in this case, navigate to: *www.oyez.org/oyez/frontpage.*

FIGURE 2-2 Map of Districts in Tennessee, 1901 and 1950

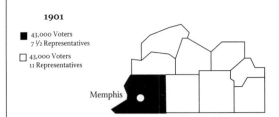

1901

■ 43,000 Voters
7 ½ Representatives

□ 43,000 Voters
11 Representatives

Memphis

Battle of the ballot: In 1901 Memphis, Tennessee, had as many people as eight nearby counties together and elected nearly the same number of representatives.

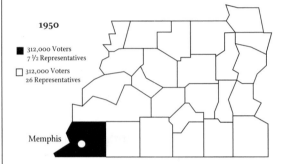

1950

■ 312,000 Voters
7 ½ Representatives

□ 312,000 Voters
26 Representatives

Memphis

By 1950 Memphis's population equaled that of twenty-four counties. Under the state constitution the city should have gained more representatives, but did not; so the rural vote counted almost four times as much as the urban. Reviewing city voters' complaint that this situation denied them equal protection of the laws, the Court in 1962 held that judges should hear and decide such claims under the Fourteenth Amendment (**Baker v. Carr**). Chief Justice Earl Warren looked back upon this decision as the most important and influential in his sixteen years on the Court. It opened the way to enunciation (in **Reynolds v. Sims**) of the "one person, one vote" principle and its enforcement by court order in many related cases across the nation.

SOURCE: *Equal Justice Under Law* (Washington, D.C.: Foundation of the Federal Bar Association, 1965), 108.

Naturally, many citizens and organizations wanted to force legislatures to reapportion, but under *Colegrove* they could not do so using the Guarantee Clause. They looked, therefore, to another section of the Constitution, the Fourteenth Amendment's Equal Protection Clause, which says, no state shall "deny to any person within its jurisdiction the equal protection of the laws." From this clause, they made the argument that the failure to reapportion led to unequal treatment of voters.

Although this strategy represented a clever legal attempt to reframe the issue of reapportionment, when attorneys sought to apply it to the Tennessee situation, a lower federal district court dismissed their suit.[52] Relying on *Colegrove* and other cases, that court held reapportionment to constitute a political question on which it could not rule.

MR. JUSTICE BRENNAN delivered the opinion of the Court.

In holding that the subject matter of this suit was not justiciable, the District Court relied on *Colegrove v. Green* . . . [and related cases]. The court stated: "From a review of these decisions there can be no doubt that the federal rule . . . is that the federal courts . . . will not intervene in cases of this type to compel legislative reapportionment." We understand the District Court to have read the cited cases as compelling the conclusion that since the appellants sought to have a legislative apportionment held unconstitutional, their suit presented a "political question" and was therefore nonjusticiable. We hold that this challenge to an apportionment presents no nonjusticiable "political question." The cited cases do not hold the contrary.

Of course the mere fact that the suit seeks protection of a political right does not mean it presents a political question. Such an objection "is little more than a play upon words." Rather, it is argued that apportionment cases, whatever the actual wording of the complaint, can involve no federal constitutional right except one resting on the guaranty of a republican form of government, and that complaints based

on that clause have been held to present political questions which are nonjusticiable.

We hold that the claim pleaded here neither rests upon nor implicates the Guaranty Clause and that its justiciability is therefore not foreclosed by our decisions of cases involving that clause. The District Court misinterpreted *Colegrove v. Green* and other decisions of this Court on which it relied. . . . To show why we reject the argument based on the Guaranty Clause, we must examine the authorities under it. But because there appears to be some uncertainty as to why those cases did present political questions, and specifically as to whether this apportionment case is like those cases, we deem it necessary first to consider the contours of the "political question" doctrine. . . .

We have said that "In determining whether a question falls within [the political question] category, the appropriateness under our system of government of attributing finality to the action of the political departments and also the lack of satisfactory criteria for a judicial determination are dominant considerations." The nonjusticiability of a political question is primarily a function of the separation of powers. Much confusion results from the capacity of the "political question" label to obscure the need for case-by-case inquiry. Deciding whether a matter has in any measure been committed by the Constitution to another branch of government, or whether the action of that branch exceeds whatever authority has been committed, is itself a delicate exercise in constitutional interpretation, and is a responsibility of this Court as ultimate interpreter of the Constitution. To demonstrate this requires no less than to analyze representative cases and to infer from them the analytical threads that make up the political question doctrine. We shall then show that none of those threads catches this case.

Foreign relations: There are sweeping statements to the effect that all questions touching foreign relations are political questions. Not only does resolution of such issues frequently turn on standards that defy judicial application, or involve the exercise of a discretion demonstrably committed to the executive or legislature; but many such questions uniquely demand single-voiced statement of the Government's views. Yet it is error to suppose that every case or controversy which touches foreign relations lies beyond judicial cognizance. Our cases in this field seem invariably to show a discriminating analysis of the particular question

52. For more on this, see Richard C. Cortner, "Strategies and Tactics of Litigants in Constitutional Cases," *Journal of Public Law* 17 (1968): 287–307; and Cortner, *The Apportionment Cases* (Knoxville: University of Tennessee Press, 1970).

posed, in terms of the history of its management by the political branches, of its susceptibility to judicial handling in the light of its nature and posture in the specific case, and of the possible consequences of judicial action. For example, though a court will not ordinarily inquire whether a treaty has been terminated, since on that question "governmental action . . . must be regarded as of controlling importance," if there has been no conclusive "governmental action" then a court can construe a treaty and may find it provides the answer. Though a court will not undertake to construe a treaty in a manner inconsistent with a subsequent federal statute, no similar hesitancy obtains if the asserted clash is with state law. . . .

Dates of duration of hostilities: Though it has been stated broadly that "the power which declared the necessity is the power to declare its cessation, and what the cessation requires," here too analysis reveals isolable reasons for the presence of political questions, underlying this Court's refusal to review the political departments' determination of when or whether a war has ended. Dominant is the need for finality in the political determination, for emergency's nature demands "A prompt and unhesitating obedience." Moreover, "the cessation of hostilities does not necessarily end the war power. It was stated in *Hamilton v. Kentucky Distilleries & W. Co.* that the war power includes the power 'to remedy the evils which have arisen from its rise and progress' and continues during that emergency." But deference rests on reason, not habit. The question in a particular case may not seriously implicate considerations of finality—e.g., a public program of importance (rent control) yet not central to the emergency effort. Further, clearly definable criteria for decision may be available. In such case the political question barrier falls away. . . .

Validity of enactments: In *Coleman v. Miller* [1939] this Court held that the questions of how long a proposed amendment to the Federal Constitution remained open to ratification, and what effect a prior rejection had on a subsequent ratification, were committed to congressional resolution and involved criteria of decision that necessarily escaped the judicial grasp. Similar considerations apply to the enacting process: "The respect due to coequal and independent departments," and the need for finality and certainty about the status of a statute contribute to judicial reluctance to inquire whether, as passed, it complied with all requisite formalities. . . .

It is apparent that several formulations which vary slightly according to the settings in which the questions arise may describe a political question, although each has one or more elements which identify it as essentially a function of the separation of powers. Prominent on the surface of any case held to involve a political question is found a textually demonstrable constitutional commitment of the issue to a coordinate political department; or a lack of judicially discoverable and manageable standards for resolving it; or the impossibility of deciding without an initial policy determination of a kind clearly for nonjudicial discretion; or the impossibility of a court's undertaking independent resolution without expressing lack of the respect due coordinate branches of government; or an unusual need for unquestioning adherence to a political decision already made; or the potentiality of embarrassment from multifarious pronouncements by various departments on one question.

Unless one of these formulations is inextricable from the case at bar, there should be no dismissal for nonjusticiability on the ground of a political question's presence. The doctrine of which we treat is one of "political questions," not one of "political cases." The courts cannot reject as "no lawsuit" a bona fide controversy as to whether some action denominated "political" exceeds constitutional authority. The cases we have reviewed show the necessity for discriminating inquiry into the precise facts and posture of the particular case, and the impossibility of resolution by any semantic cataloguing.

But it is argued that this case shares the characteristics of decisions that constitute a category not yet considered, cases concerning the Constitution's guaranty, in Art. IV, §4, of a republican form of government. A conclusion as to whether the case at bar does present a political question cannot be confidently reached until we have considered those cases with special care. We shall discover that Guaranty Clause claims involve those elements which define a "political question," and for that reason and no other, they are nonjusticiable. In particular, we shall discover that the nonjusticiability of such claims has nothing to do with their touching upon matters of state governmental organization.

Republican form of government: . . . Clearly, several factors were thought by the Court in *Luther* [v. *Borden*] to make the question there "political": the commitment to the other branches of the decision as to which is the lawful state government; the unambiguous action by the President, in recognizing the charter government as the lawful authority; the need for finality in the executive's decision; and the lack of criteria by which a court could determine which form of government was republican.

But the only significance that *Luther* could have for our immediate purposes is in its holding that the Guaranty Clause is not a repository of judicially manageable standards which a court could utilize independently in order to identify a State's lawful government. The Court has since refused to resort to the Guaranty Clause—which alone had been invoked for the purpose—as the source of a constitutional standard for invalidating state action. . . .

Just as the Court has consistently held that a challenge to state action based on the Guaranty Clause presents no justiciable question so has it held, and for the same reasons, that challenges to congressional action on the ground of inconsistency with that clause present no justiciable question. . . .

We come, finally, to the ultimate inquiry whether our precedents as to what constitutes a nonjusticiable "political question" bring the case before us under the umbrella of that doctrine. A natural beginning is to note whether any of the common characteristics which we have been able to identify and label descriptively are present. We find none: The question here is the consistency of state action with the Federal Constitution. We have no question decided, or to be decided, by a political branch of government coequal with this Court. Nor do we risk embarrassment of our government abroad, or grave disturbance at home if we take issue with Tennessee as to the constitutionality of her action here challenged. Nor need the appellants, in order to succeed in this action, ask the Court to enter upon policy determinations for which judicially manageable standards are lacking. Judicial standards under the Equal Protection Clause are well developed and familiar, and it has been open to courts since the enactment of the Fourteenth Amendment to determine, if on the particular facts they must, that a discrimination reflects no policy, but simply arbitrary and capricious action.

This case does, in one sense, involve the allocation of political power within a State, and the appellants might conceivably have added a claim under the Guaranty Clause. Of course, as we have seen, any reliance on that clause would be futile. But because any reliance on the Guaranty Clause could not have succeeded it does not follow that appellants may not be heard on the equal protection claim which in fact they tender. True, it must be clear that the Fourteenth Amendment claim is not so enmeshed with those political question elements which render Guaranty Clause claims nonjusticiable as actually to present a political question itself. But we have found that not to be the case here. . . .

We conclude then that the nonjusticiability of claims resting on the Guaranty Clause which arises from their embodiment of questions that were thought "political," can have no bearing upon the justiciability of the equal protection claim presented in this case. Finally, we emphasize that it is the involvement in Guaranty Clause claims of the elements thought to define "political questions," and no other feature, which could render them nonjusticiable. . . .

. . . [T]he complaint's allegations of a denial of equal protection present a justiciable constitutional cause of action upon which appellants are entitled to a trial and a decision. The right asserted is within the reach of judicial protection under the Fourteenth Amendment.

The judgment of the District Court is reversed and the cause is remanded for further proceedings consistent with this opinion.

Reversed and remanded.

MR. JUSTICE CLARK, concurring.

I believe it can be shown that this case is distinguishable from earlier cases dealing with the distribution of political power by a State, that a patent violation of the Equal Protection Clause of the United States Constitution has been shown, and that an appropriate remedy may be formulated. . . .

Although I find the Tennessee apportionment statute offends the Equal Protection Clause, I would not consider intervention by this Court into so delicate a field if there were any other relief available to the people of Tennessee. But the majority of the people of Tennessee have no "practical opportunities for exerting their political weight at the polls" to correct the existing "invidious discrimination." Tennessee has no initiative and referendum. I have searched diligently for other "practical opportunities" present under the law. I find none other than through the federal courts. The majority of the voters have been caught up in a legislative straitjacket. Tennessee has an "informed, civically militant electorate" and "an aroused popular conscience," but it does not sear "the conscience of the people's representatives."

This is because the legislative policy has riveted the present seats in the Assembly to their respective constituencies, and by the votes of their incumbents a reapportionment of any kind is prevented. The people have been rebuffed at the hands of the Assembly; they have tried the constitutional convention route, but since the call must originate in the Assembly it, too, has been fruitless. They have tried Tennessee courts with the same result, and Governors have fought the tide only to flounder. It is said that there is recourse in Congress and perhaps that may be, but from a practical standpoint this is without substance. To date Congress has never undertaken such a task in any State. We therefore must conclude that the people of Tennessee are stymied and without judicial intervention will be saddled with the present discrimination in the affairs of their state government.

MR. JUSTICE FRANKFURTER, whom MR. JUSTICE HARLAN joins, dissenting.

The present case involves all of the elements that have made the Guarantee Clause cases non-justiciable. It is, in effect, a Guarantee Clause claim masquerading under a different label. But it cannot make the case more fit for judicial action that appellants invoke the Fourteenth Amendment rather than Art. IV, §4, where, in fact, the gist of their complaint is the same—unless it can be found that the Fourteenth Amendment speaks with greater particularity to their situation. We have been admonished to avoid "the tyranny of labels." Art. IV, §4, is not committed by express constitutional terms to Congress. It is the nature of the controversies arising under it, nothing else, which has made it judicially unenforceable. Of course, if a controversy falls within judicial power, it depends "on how he [the plaintiff] casts his action," whether he brings himself within a jurisdictional statute. But where judicial competence is wanting, it cannot be created by invoking one clause of the Constitution rather than another. . . .

Here appellants['] . . . complaint is that the basis of representation of the Tennessee Legislature hurts them. They assert that "a minority now rules in Tennessee," that the apportionment statute results in a "distortion of the constitutional system," that the General Assembly is no longer "a body representative of the people of the State of Tennessee," all "contrary to the basic principle of represen-

tative government. . . ." Accepting appellants' own formulation of the issue, one can know this handsaw from a hawk. Such a claim would be non-justiciable not merely under Art. IV. §4, but under any clause of the Constitution, by virtue of the very fact that a federal court is not a forum for political debate.

But appellants, of course, do not rest on this claim *simpliciter*. In invoking the Equal Protection Clause, they assert that the distortion of representative government complained of is produced by systematic discrimination against them, by way of "a debasement of their votes. . . ." Does this characterization, with due regard for the facts from which it is derived, add anything to appellants' case?

At first blush, this charge of discrimination based on legislative underrepresentation is given the appearance of a more private, less impersonal claim, than the assertion that the frame of government is askew. Appellants appear as representatives of a class that is prejudiced as a class, in contradistinction to the polity in its entirety. However, the discrimination relied on is the deprivation of what appellants conceive to be their proportionate share of political influence. This, of course, is the practical effect of any allocation of power within the institutions of government. Hardly any distribution of political authority that could be assailed as rendering government nonrepublican would fail similarly to operate to the prejudice of some groups, and to the advantage of others, within the body politic. It would be ingenuous not to see, or consciously blind to deny, that the real battle over the initiative and referendum, or over a delegation of power to local rather than state-wide authority, is the battle between forces whose influence is disparate among the various organs of government to whom power may be given. No shift of power occurs that but works a corresponding shift in political influence among the groups composing a society.

What, then, is this question of legislative apportionment? Appellants invoke the right to vote and to have their votes counted. But they are permitted to vote and their votes are counted. They go to the polls, they cast their ballots, they send their representatives to the state councils. Their complaint is simply that the representatives are not sufficiently numerous or powerful—in short, that Tennessee has adopted a basis of representation with which they are dissatisfied. Talk of "debasement" or "dilution" is circular talk. One cannot speak of "debasement" or "dilution" of the value of a vote until there is first defined a standard of reference as to what a vote should be worth. What is actually asked of the Court in this case is to choose among competing bases of representation—ultimately, really, among competing theories of political philosophy—in order to establish an appropriate frame of government for the State of Tennessee and thereby for all the States of the Union.

In such a matter, abstract analogies which ignore the facts of history deal in unrealities; they betray reason. This is not a case in which a State has, through a device however oblique and sophisticated, denied Negroes or Jews or red-headed persons a vote, or given them only a third or a sixth of a vote. . . . What Tennessee illustrates is an old and still widespread method of representation—representation by local geographical division, only in part respective of population—in preference to others, others, forsooth, more appealing. Appellants contest this choice and seek to make this Court the arbiter of the disagreement. They would make the Equal Protection Clause the charter of adjudication, asserting that the equality which it guarantees comports, if not the assurance of equal weight to every voter's vote, at least the basic conception that representation ought to be proportionate to population, a standard by reference to which the reasonableness of apportionment plans may be judged.

To find such a political conception legally enforceable in the broad and unspecific guarantee of equal protection is to rewrite the Constitution. See *Luther v. Borden*. Certainly, "equal protection" is no more secure a foundation for judicial judgment of the permissibility of varying forms of representative government than is "Republican Form." Indeed since "equal protection of the laws" can only mean an equality of persons standing in the same relation to whatever governmental action is challenged, the determination whether treatment is equal presupposes a determination concerning the nature of the relationship. This, with respect to apportionment, means an inquiry into the theoretic base of representation in an acceptably republican state. For a court could not determine the equal-protection issue without in fact first determining the Republican-Form issue, simply because what is reasonable for equal-protection purposes will depend upon what frame of government, basically, is allowed. To divorce "equal protection" from "Republican Form" is to talk about half a question. . . .

Manifestly, the Equal Protection Clause supplies no clearer guide for judicial examination of apportionment methods than would the Guarantee Clause itself. Apportionment, by its character, is a subject of extraordinary complexity, involving—even after the fundamental theoretical issues concerning what is to be represented in a representative legislature have been fought out or compromised—considerations of geography, demography, electoral convenience, economic and social cohesions or divergencies among particular local groups, communications, the practical effects of political institutions like the lobby and the city machine, ancient traditions and ties of settled usage, respect for proven incumbents of long experience and senior status, mathematical mechanics, censuses compiling relevant data, and a host of others. Legislative responses throughout the country to the reapportionment demands of the 1960 Census have glaringly confirmed that these are not factors that lend themselves to evaluations of a nature that are the staple of judicial determinations or for which judges are equipped to adjudicate by legal training or experience or native wit. And this is the more so true because in every strand of this complicated, intricate web of values meet the contending forces of partisan politics. The practical significance of apportionment is that the next election results may differ because of it. Apportionment battles are overwhelmingly party or intra-party. It will add a virulent source of friction and tension in federal-state relations to embroil the federal judiciary in them.

Baker is significant for a number of reasons. One is that it opened the window for judicial resolution of reapportionment cases, which continue to appear on the Court's docket. Another reason—more relevant here—is that, unlike *Luther*, it established a clear doctrinal base for determining political questions. Note, however, that the definition does not dismiss the logic of *Luther* entirely; it just reworks it a bit. More to the point, Justice William J. Brennan quite clearly says that claims invoking the Guarantee Clause possess the attributes of a political question (under his definition) and, thus, are nonjusticiable.

Nor did *Baker* lead to the demise of the political question doctrine. Over the years, the Court has used the doctrine to dismiss a range of substantive disputes, particularly those involving international relations. For example, in *Goldwater v. Carter* (1979), which presented a challenge to President Jimmy Carter's unilateral termination of a U.S. treaty with Taiwan, Justice Rehnquist held that the case presented a political question. In his view, it involved a foreign policy matter on which the Constitution provided no definitive answer. As such, it "should be left for resolution by the Executive and Legislative branches."

In the 1993 case of *Nixon v. United States*, however, the Court relied heavily on *Baker v. Carr* to examine a domestic issue—the impeachment of a federal judge who claimed that the Senate used unconstitutional procedures in trying his case.[53] As you read *Nixon*, take note of how the modern-day Court applied the political question doctrine. Also consider the mode of constitutional analysis it used; Chief Justice Rehnquist's opinion serves as an interesting example of the Court searching for the plain "meaning of the words" and the intent of the Framers in interpreting a constitutional provision.

Nixon v. United States

506 U.S. 224 (1993)
http://laws.findlaw.com/US/506/224.html
Vote: 9 (Blackmun, Kennedy, O'Connor, Rehnquist, Scalia,
    Souter, Stevens, Thomas, White)
    0

Opinion of the Court: Rehnquist
Concurring opinions: Souter, Stevens, White

Walter L. Nixon Jr. was appointed a U.S. district court judge for the Southern District of Mississippi by President Lyndon Johnson in 1968. In 1984 federal prosecutors began to investigate Judge Nixon's relationship with Hattiesburg entrepreneur Wiley Fairchild. They suspected that Fairchild had allowed Nixon to participate in a sweetheart oil and gas deal in return for Nixon's intervention in behalf of Fairchild's son, Drew, who was under state indictment for drug trafficking. Nixon, testifying before a federal grand jury, denied that he had discussed Drew Fairchild's case with the local district attorney or had intervened in any other way in the young man's be-

half. In 1986 Nixon stood trial in a federal court for committing perjury in his grand jury testimony and for accepting an illegal gratuity. The jury acquitted Nixon of the illegal gratuity charge but convicted him on two counts of lying to the grand jury. He received a five-year prison term. Nixon, asserting his innocence on all charges, refused to resign from the bench and continued to receive his salary while serving his sentence.

The Judicial Conference of the United States, the policy-making body of the federal judiciary, recommended to the House of Representatives that Nixon be impeached. Impeachment is the only constitutionally permitted method of removing a federal judge from office. Following an investigation by the Judiciary Committee, the House voted 417–0 to impeach Nixon for "high crimes and misdemeanors." The case then went to the Senate for trial. That body invoked its own rule, Impeachment Rule XI, under which the presiding officer appoints a committee of senators to "receive evidence and take testimony." Pursuant to this rule, a special twelve-member bipartisan committee was appointed to hear the case and report to the full Senate.

As part of the deliberative process, the Senate committee examined briefs submitted by Nixon and the House impeachment managers, heard from ten witnesses, and allowed Nixon to "make a personal appeal." After four days of hearings, the committee recommended that Nixon be removed from office. In November 1989 the Senate voted 89–8 and 78–19 to convict Nixon on two articles of impeachment stemming from his grand jury testimony. The conviction officially stripped Nixon of his judgeship, even though by that time he had received an estimated $286,500 in salary since his federal court conviction.

Nixon responded by claiming in a federal lawsuit that Senate Rule XI violated the Constitution. He argued that the Senate procedure of having a committee—rather than the full Senate—hear his case violated Article I, Section 3, Clause 6, of the Constitution, which states that the "Senate shall have the sole power to try all Impeachments." The committee procedure, he alleged, prohibited the full Senate from participating in the evidentiary hearings. Unsuccessful in the lower courts, Nixon pursued his case to the U.S. Supreme Court.

---

53. To hear oral arguments in this case, navigate to: *www.oyez.org/oyez/frontpage.*

CHIEF JUSTICE REHNQUIST delivered the opinion of the Court.

Petitioner Walter L. Nixon, Jr., asks this Court to decide whether Senate Rule XI, which allows a committee of Senators to hear evidence against an individual who has been impeached and to report that evidence to the full Senate, violates the Impeachment Trial Clause, Art. I, §3, cl. 6. That Clause provides that the "Senate shall have the sole power to try all Impeachments." But before we reach the merits of such a claim, we must decide whether it is "justiciable," that is whether it is a claim that may be resolved by the courts. We conclude that it is not. . . .

A controversy is nonjusticiable—i.e., involves a political question—where there is a "textually demonstrable constitutional commitment of the issue to a coordinate political department; or a lack of judicially discoverable and manageable standards for resolving it. . . ." *Baker v. Carr* (1962). But the courts must, in the first instance, interpret the text in question and determine whether and to what extent the issue is textually committed. As the discussion that follows makes clear, the concept of a textual commitment to a coordinate political department is not completely separate from the concept of a lack of judicially discoverable and manageable standards for resolving it; the lack of judicially manageable standards may strengthen the conclusion that there is a textually demonstrable commitment to a coordinate branch.

In this case, we must examine Art. I, §3, cl. 6, to determine the scope of authority conferred upon the Senate by the Framers regarding impeachment. It provides:

"The Senate shall have the sole Power to try all Impeachments. When sitting for that Purpose, they shall be on Oath or Affirmation. When the President of the United States is tried, the Chief Justice shall preside: And no Person shall be convicted without the Concurrence of two thirds of the Members present."

The language and structure of this Clause are revealing. The first sentence is a grant of authority to the Senate, and the word "sole" indicates that this authority is reposed in the Senate and nowhere else. The next two sentences specify requirements to which the Senate proceedings shall conform: the Senate shall be on oath or affirmation, a two-thirds vote is required to convict, and when the President is tried the Chief Justice shall preside.

Petitioner argues that the word "try" in the first sentence imposes by implication an additional requirement on the Senate in that the proceedings must be in the nature of a judicial trial. From there petitioner goes on to argue that this limitation precludes the Senate from delegating to a select committee the task of hearing the testimony of witnesses, as was done pursuant to Senate Rule XI. " '[T]ry' means more than simply 'vote on' or 'review' or 'judge.' In 1787 and today, trying a case means hearing the evidence, not scanning a cold record." Petitioner concludes from this that courts may review whether or not the Senate "tried" him before convicting him.

There are several difficulties with this position which lead us ultimately to reject it. The word "try," both in 1787 and later, has considerably broader meanings than those to which petitioner would limit it. Older dictionaries define try as "to examine" or "to examine as a judge." See 2 S. Johnson, *A Dictionary of the English Language* (1785). In more modern usage the term has various meanings. For example, try can mean "to examine or investigate judicially," "to conduct the trial of," or "to put to the test by experiment, investigation, or trial." *Webster's Third New International Dictionary* (1971). Petitioner submits that "try," as contained in T. Sheridan, *Dictionary of the English Language* (1796), means "to examine as a judge; to bring before a judicial tribunal." Based on the variety of definitions, however, we cannot say that the Framers used the word "try" as an implied limitation on the method by which the Senate might proceed in trying impeachments. "As a rule the Constitution speaks in general terms, leaving Congress to deal with subsidiary matters of detail as the public interests and changing conditions may require. . . ."

The conclusion that the use of the word "try" in the first sentence of the Impeachment Trial Clause lacks sufficient precision to afford any judicially manageable standard of review of the Senate's actions is fortified by the existence of the three very specific requirements that the Constitution does impose on the Senate when trying impeachments: the members must be under oath, a two-thirds vote is required to convict, and the Chief Justice presides when the President is tried. These limitations are quite precise, and their nature suggests that the Framers did not intend to impose additional limitations on the form of the Senate proceedings by the use of the word "try" in the first sentence.

Petitioner devotes only two pages in his brief to negating the significance of the word "sole" in the first sentence of Clause 6. As noted above, that sentence provides that "the Senate shall have the sole Power to try all Impeachments." We think that the word "sole" is of considerable significance.

Indeed, the word "sole" appears only one other time in the Constitution—with respect to the House of Representatives' "*sole* Power of Impeachment." Art. I, §2, cl. 5 (emphasis added). The common sense meaning of the word "sole" is that the Senate alone shall have authority to determine whether an individual should be acquitted or convicted. The dictionary definition bears this out. "Sole" is defined as "having no companion," "solitary," "being the only one," and "functioning . . . independently and without assistance or interference." *Webster's Third New International Dictionary* (1971). If the courts may review the actions of the Senate in order to determine whether that body "tried" an impeached official, it is difficult to see how the Senate would be "functioning . . . independently and without assistance or interference."

Nixon asserts that the word "sole" has no substantive meaning. To support this contention, he argues that the word is nothing more than a mere "cosmetic edit" added by the Committee of Style after the delegates had approved the substance of the Impeachment Trial Clause. There are two difficulties with this argument. First, accepting as we must the proposition that the Committee of Style had no authority from the Convention to alter the meaning of the Clause, we must presume that the Committee's reorganization or rephrasing accurately captured what the Framers meant in their unadorned language. That is, we must presume that the Committee did its job. This presumption is buttressed by the fact that the Constitutional Convention voted on, and accepted, the Committee of Style's linguistic version. . . . Second, carrying Nixon's argument to its logical conclusion would constrain us to say that the second to last draft would govern in every instance where the Committee of Style added an arguably substantive word. Such a result is at odds with the fact that the Convention passed the Committee's version, and with the well-established rule that the plain language of the enacted text is the best indicator of intent. . . .

The history and contemporary understanding of the impeachment provisions support our reading of the constitutional language. The parties do not offer evidence of a single word in the history of the Constitutional Convention or in contemporary commentary that even alludes to the possibility of judicial review in the context of the impeachment powers. This silence is quite meaningful in light of the several explicit references to the availability of judicial review as a check on the Legislature's power with respect to bills of attainder, *ex post facto* laws, and statutes.

The Framers labored over the question of where the impeachment power should lie. Significantly, in at least two considered scenarios the power was placed with the Federal Judiciary. Indeed, Madison and the Committee of Detail proposed that the Supreme Court should have the power to determine impeachments. Despite these proposals, the Convention ultimately decided that the Senate would have "the sole Power to Try all Impeachments." Art. I, §3, cl. 6. According to Alexander Hamilton, the Senate was the "most fit depositary of this important trust" because its members are representatives of the people. The Supreme Court was not the proper body because the Framers "doubted whether the members of the tribunal would, at all times, be endowed with so eminent a portion of fortitude as would be called for in the execution of so difficult a task" or whether the Court "would possess the degree of credit and authority" to carry out its judgment if it conflicted with the accusation brought by the Legislature—the people's representative. In addition, the Framers believed the Court was too small in number: "The awful discretion, which a court of impeachments must necessarily have, to doom to honor or to infamy the most confidential and the most distinguished characters of the community, forbids the commitment of the trust to a small number of persons."

There are two additional reasons why the Judiciary, and the Supreme Court in particular, were not chosen to have any role in impeachments. First, the Framers recognized that most likely there would be two sets of proceedings for individuals who commit impeachable offenses—the impeachment trial and a separate criminal trial. In fact, the Constitution explicitly provides for two separate proceedings. The Framers deliberately separated the two forums to avoid raising the specter of bias and to ensure independent judgments. . . . Certainly judicial review of the Senate's "trial" would introduce the same risk of bias as would participation in the trial itself.

Second, judicial review would be inconsistent with the Framers' insistence that our system be one of checks and balances. In our constitutional system, impeachment was designed to be the only check on the Judicial Branch by the Legislature. . . . Judicial involvement in impeachment proceedings, even if only for purposes of judicial review, is counterintuitive because it would eviscerate the "important constitutional check" placed on the Judiciary by the Framers.

Nevertheless, Nixon argues that judicial review is necessary in order to place a check on the Legislature. Nixon fears that if the Senate is given unreviewable authority to interpret the Impeachment Trial Clause, there is a grave risk that the Senate will usurp judicial power. The Framers anticipated this objection and created two constitutional safeguards to keep the Senate in check. The first safeguard is that the whole of the impeachment power is divided between the two legislative bodies, with the House given the right to accuse and the Senate given the right to judge. This split of authority "avoids the inconvenience of making the same persons both accusers and judges; and guards against the danger of persecution from the prevalency of a factious spirit in either of those branches." The second safeguard is the two-thirds supermajority vote requirement. Hamilton explained that "as the concurrence of two-thirds of the senate will be requisite to a condemnation, the security to innocence, from this additional circumstance, will be as complete as itself can desire."

In addition to the textual commitment argument, we are persuaded that the lack of finality and the difficulty of fashioning relief counsel against justiciability. See *Baker v. Carr*. We agree with the Court of Appeals that opening the door of judicial review to the procedures used by the Senate in trying impeachments would "expose the political life of the country to months, or perhaps years, of chaos." This lack of finality would manifest itself most dramatically if the President were impeached. The legitimacy of any successor, and hence his effectiveness, would be impaired severely, not merely while the judicial process was running its course, but during any retrial that a differently constituted Senate might conduct if its first judgment of conviction were invalidated. Equally uncertain is the question of what relief a court may give other than simply setting aside the judgment of conviction. Could it order the reinstatement of a convicted federal judge, or order Congress to create an additional judgeship if the seat had been filled in the interim? . . .

We agree with Nixon that courts possess power to review either legislative or executive action that transgresses identifiable textual limits. . . . But we conclude, after exercising that delicate responsibility, that the word "try" in the Impeachment Clause does not provide an identifiable textual limit on the authority which is committed to the Senate.

For the foregoing reasons, the judgment of the Court of Appeals is

Affirmed.

JUSTICE SOUTER, concurring in the judgment.

Whatever considerations feature most prominently in a particular case, the political question doctrine is "essentially a function of the separation of powers," existing to restrain courts "from inappropriate interference in the business of the other branches of Government," and deriving in large part from prudential concerns about the respect we owe the political departments. Not all interference is inappropriate or disrespectful, however, and application of the doctrine ultimately turns, as Learned Hand put it, on "how importunately the occasion demands an answer."

This occasion does not demand an answer. The Impeachment Trial Clause commits to the Senate "the sole Power to try all Impeachments.". . . Other significant considerations confirm a conclusion that this case presents a nonjusticiable political question: the "unusual need for unquestioning adherence to a political decision already made," as well as "the potentiality of embarrassment from multifarious pronouncements by various departments on one question." As the Court observes, judicial review of an impeachment trial would under the best of circumstances entail significant disruption of government.

One can, nevertheless, envision different and unusual circumstances that might justify a more searching review of impeachment proceedings. If the Senate were to act in a manner seriously threatening the integrity of its results, convicting, say, upon a coin toss, or upon a summary determination that an officer of the United States was simply " 'a bad guy,' " judicial interference might well be appropriate. In such circumstances, the Senate's action might be so far beyond the scope of its constitutional authority, and the consequent impact on the Republic so great, as to merit a judicial response despite the prudential concerns that would ordinarily counsel silence. "The political question doctrine, a tool for maintenance of governmental order, will not be so applied as to promote only disorder." *Baker* [v. *Carr*].

The Court handed Judge Nixon a stinging defeat, and his circumstances did not improve much after the case *(see Box 2-6)*. More generally, the Court ruled that the

**BOX 2-6   AFTERMATH . . .
WALTER NIXON**

In March 1986 federal district court judge Walter L. Nixon Jr. was convicted of two counts of perjury for lying to a grand jury. He was sentenced to five years in prison. When his last appeal proved unsuccessful, Nixon entered a federal minimum security prison at Eglin Air Force Base in Florida. He served sixteen months before being released to a New Orleans halfway house in July 1989. Four months later, just eighteen days after the Senate removed him from office, Nixon was released on five-years' probation.

Nixon had not heard any cases since his indictment in 1985 but, proclaiming his innocence, refused to resign from office. From 1985 until his removal by the Senate in 1989, Nixon was paid his $89,500 annual salary, even though he spent part of that time in a federal prison. The removal formally ended his tenure as a federal judge and terminated his salary. At about the same time, the Mississippi Supreme Court disbarred Nixon from the practice of law.

In 1990 Mississippi wildlife officials discovered Nixon and a former game warden in a field that was baited to attract wild turkeys. In Nixon's possession was a 12-gauge automatic shotgun. Nixon was charged with conspiracy to hunt wild birds with the aid of bait, a misdemeanor. More important was the possession of a firearm, which violated the terms of his parole. The United States Parole Commission ordered Nixon to return to prison for four months; the punishment was relatively light because the shotgun had never been taken out of its zipped case.

Nixon's efforts to return to the practice of law were ultimately successful. In May 1993 the Mississippi Supreme Court considered Nixon's petition to be reinstated. The state bar association opposed the request, arguing that Nixon lacked the required moral character to practice law. However, a parade of public officials, including three former governors and three former state supreme court justices, urged the court to be lenient. The justices agreed to reactivate Nixon's license to practice law once he passed the state bar examination. Chief Justice Armis Hawkins said, "This petitioner has been whipped enough." Nixon passed and was readmitted to the practice of law in September 1993.

SOURCES: *Los Angeles Times*, May 21, 1993; *Memphis Commercial Appeal*, October 3, 1990; *New York Times*, April 28, 1990, September 26, 1993; *Washington Post*, February 7, 1986; *Washington Times*, November 22, 1989; various UPI reports.

procedures used by Congress to handle impeachments are not subject to judicial review. The Constitution grants the Senate the sole power to try all impeachments, and how the Senate organizes itself to discharge that duty constitutes a political question. Even so, note Justice David Souter's caveat: the Court might not be so hesitant to review impeachment procedures if those procedures "[threaten] the integrity of its results." But Justice John Paul Stevens, in a brief concurring opinion, disagreed: "Respect for a coordinate Branch of the Government forecloses any assumption that improbable hypotheticals like those mentioned by Justice Souter . . . will ever occur."

Despite the ruling in *Nixon*, some scholars continue to believe that the Court has weakened the political questions doctrine over the last four decades. By way of proof, they point to *Bush v. Gore* (2000) (excerpted on pages 190–200) and suggest the Court should have dismissed it as raising a political question. To these observers, *Bush* is just the last in a line of cases beginning with *Baker* that signaled a "weakening of the traditional 'political questions doctrine' and the expanded application of the equal protection clause to voting rights and democratic process." If this is so, should we regard this as a dangerous move on the Court's part—one reflecting "a broader conservative inclination to impose order on democratic politics"?[54]

Standing to Sue

Another constraint on federal judicial power is standing: if the party bringing the litigation is not the appropriate party, the courts will not resolve the dispute. Put in somewhat different terms, "not every person with the money to bring a lawsuit is entitled to litigate the legality or constitutionality of government action in the federal courts."[55] Rather, as Justice Brennan noted in *Baker*, Article III requires that litigants demonstrate "such a personal stake in the outcome of the controversy as to assure that concrete adverseness which sharpens the presentation of issues upon which the Court so largely depends for illumination of difficult constitutional questions."

In most private disputes, the litigants have no difficulty demonstrating a personal stake or injury. The more

54. See Howard Gillman, *The Votes That Counted* (Chicago: University of Chicago Press, 2001), 202.

55. C. Herman Pritchett, *The American Constitution* (New York: McGraw-Hill, 1959), 145.

interesting constitutional questions have arisen in those suits that involve parties wishing to challenge some government action on the ground that they are taxpayers. Such claims raise an important question: Does the mere fact that one pays taxes provide a sufficiently personal stake in litigation, sufficient enough to meet the requirement for standing?

The Court first addressed this question in *Frothingham v. Mellon* (1923). At issue was the Sheppard-Towner Maternity Act of 1921, in which Congress provided federal aid to the states to fund programs designed to reduce infant mortality rates. Although many progressive groups had lobbied for the law, other organizations viewed it as an unconstitutional intrusion into the family and into the rights of states, as they believed the Tenth Amendment of the Constitution guaranteed. They decided to challenge it and enlisted one among their ranks, Harriet Frothingham, to serve as a plaintiff. She was not receiving Sheppard-Towner Maternity Act aid; she was a taxpayer who did not want to see her tax dollars spent on the program. Her attorneys argued that she had sufficient grounds to bring suit.

The Court did not agree, holding that Frothingham lacked standing to bring the litigation. Justice George Sutherland wrote for the majority:

If one taxpayer may champion and litigate such a cause, then every other taxpayer may do the same, not only in respect of the statute here under review but also in respect of every other appropriation act and statute whose administration requires the outlay of public money, and whose validity may be questioned. The bare suggestion of such a result, with its attendant inconveniences, goes far to sustain the conclusion which we have reached, that a suit of this character cannot be maintained.

He also outlined an approach to standing:

The party . . . must be able to show not only that the statute is invalid but that he has sustained or is immediately in danger of sustaining some direct injury as the result of its enforcement, and not merely that he suffers in some indefinite way in common with people generally.

For the next forty years, *Frothingham* served as a major bar to taxpayer suits. Unless litigants could demonstrate that a government program injured them or threatened to do so—beyond the mere expenditure of tax dollars—they could not bring suit. In *Flast v. Cohen*, however, the Court substantially relaxed that rule. Why? With what did the Court replace it?[56]

Flast v. Cohen

392 U.S. 83 (1968)
http://laws.findlaw.com/US/392/83.html
*Vote: 8 (Black, Brennan, Douglas, Fortas, Marshall, Stewart,
    Warren, White)*
    1 (Harlan)
Opinion of the Court: Warren
Concurring opinions: Douglas, Fortas, Stewart
Dissenting opinion: Harlan

Seven taxpayers sought to challenge federal expenditures made under the Elementary and Secondary Education Act of 1965. Under this law, states could apply to the federal government for grants to assist in the education of children from low-income families. They could, for example, obtain funds for the acquisition of textbooks, school library materials, and so forth. The taxpayers alleged that some of the funds disbursed under this act were used to finance "instruction in reading, arithmetic, and other subjects and for guidance in religious and sectarian schools." Such expenditures, they argued, violated the First Amendment's prohibition on religious establishment.

A three-judge district court dismissed their complaint. It reasoned that because the plaintiffs had suffered no real injury and because their only claim of standing rested "solely on their status as federal taxpayers," they failed to meet the criteria established in *Frothingham*.

MR. CHIEF JUSTICE WARREN delivered the opinion of the Court.

Standing is an aspect of justiciability and, as such, the problem of standing is surrounded by the same complexities and vagaries that inhere in justiciability. Standing has been called one of "the most amorphous [concepts] in the entire domain of public law." Some of the complexities peculiar to standing problems result because standing "serves, on occasion, as a shorthand expression for all the various elements of

56. To hear oral arguments in this case, navigate to: *www.oyez.org/oyez/ frontpage.*

justiciability." In addition, there are at work in the standing doctrine the many subtle pressures which tend to cause policy considerations to blend into constitutional limitations.

Despite the complexities and uncertainties, some meaningful form can be given to the jurisdictional limitations placed on federal court power by the concept of standing. The fundamental aspect of standing is that it focuses on the party seeking to get his complaint before a federal court and not on the issues he wishes to have adjudicated. The "gist of the question of standing" is whether the party seeking relief has "alleged such a personal stake in the outcome of the controversy as to assure that concrete adverseness which sharpens the presentation of issues upon which the court so largely depends for illumination of difficult constitutional questions." *Baker v. Carr* (1962). In other words, when standing is placed in issue in a case, the question is whether the person whose standing is challenged is a proper party to request an adjudication of a particular issue and not whether the issue itself is justiciable. . . .

A taxpayer may or may not have the requisite personal stake in the outcome, depending upon the circumstances of the particular case. Therefore, we find no absolute bar in Article III to suits by federal taxpayers challenging allegedly unconstitutional federal taxing and spending programs. There remains, however, the problem of determining the circumstances under which a federal taxpayer will be deemed to have the personal stake and interest that impart the necessary concrete adverseness to such litigation so that standing can be conferred on the taxpayer *qua* taxpayer consistent with the constitutional limitations of Article III.

. . . We have noted that, in deciding the question of standing, it is not relevant that the substantive issues in the litigation might be nonjusticiable. However . . . it is both appropriate and necessary to look to the substantive issues for another purpose, namely, to determine whether there is a logical nexus between the status asserted and the claim sought to be adjudicated. . . .

The nexus demanded of federal taxpayers has two aspects to it. First, the taxpayer must establish a logical link between that status and the type of legislative enactment attacked. Thus, a taxpayer will be a proper party to allege the unconstitutionality only of exercises of congressional power under the taxing and spending clause of Art. I, §8, of the Constitution. It will not be sufficient to allege an incidental expenditure of tax funds in the administration of an essentially regulatory statute. . . . Secondly, the taxpayer must es-

tablish a nexus between that status and the precise nature of the constitutional infringement alleged. Under this requirement, the taxpayer must show that the challenged enactment exceeds specific constitutional limitations imposed upon the exercise of the congressional taxing and spending power and not simply that the enactment is generally beyond the powers delegated to Congress by Art. I, §8. When both nexuses are established, the litigant will have shown a taxpayer's stake in the outcome of the controversy and will be a proper and appropriate party to invoke a federal court's jurisdiction.

The taxpayer-appellants in this case have satisfied both nexuses to support their claim of standing under the test we announce today. Their constitutional challenge is made to an exercise by Congress of its power under Art. I, §8, to spend for the general welfare, and the challenged program involves a substantial expenditure of federal tax funds. In addition, appellants have alleged that the challenged expenditures violate the Establishment and Free Exercise Clauses of the First Amendment. Our history vividly illustrates that one of the specific evils feared by those who drafted the Establishment Clause and fought for its adoption was that the taxing and spending power would be used to favor one religion over another or to support religion in general. James Madison, who is generally recognized as the leading architect of the religion clauses of the First Amendment, observed in his famous Memorial and Remonstrance Against Religious Assessments that "the same authority which can force a citizen to contribute three pence only of his property for the support of any one establishment, may force him to conform to any other establishment in all cases whatsoever." The concern of Madison and his supporters was quite clearly that religious liberty ultimately would be the victim if government could employ its taxing and spending powers to aid one religion over another or to aid religion in general. The Establishment Clause was designed as a specific bulwark against such potential abuses of governmental power, and that clause of the First Amendment operates as a specific constitutional limitation upon the exercise by Congress of the taxing and spending power conferred by Art. I, §8.

The allegations of the taxpayer in *Frothingham v. Mellon* were quite different from those made in this case, and the result in *Frothingham* is consistent with the test of taxpayer standing announced today. The taxpayer in *Frothingham* attacked a federal spending program and she, therefore, established the first nexus required. However, she lacked standing because her constitutional attack was not based on an allegation that Congress, in enacting the Maternity Act of 1921, had breached a specific limitation upon its taxing and spending power. . . . In essence, Mrs. Frothingham was attempting to assert the States' interest in their legislative prerogatives and not a federal taxpayer's interest in being free of taxing and spending in contravention of specific constitutional limitations imposed upon Congress' taxing and spending power.

We have noted that the Establishment Clause of the First Amendment does specifically limit the taxing and spending power conferred by Art. I, §8. Whether the Constitution contains other specific limitations can be determined only in the context of future cases. However, whenever such specific limitations are found, we believe a taxpayer will have a clear stake as a taxpayer in assuring that they are not breached by Congress. Consequently, we hold that a taxpayer will have standing consistent with Article III to invoke federal judicial power when he alleges that congressional action under the taxing and spending clause is in derogation of those constitutional provisions which operate to restrict the exercise of the taxing and spending power. The taxpayer's allegation in such cases would be that his tax money is being extracted and spent in violation of specific constitutional protections against such abuses of legislative power. Such an injury is appropriate for judicial redress, and the taxpayer has established the necessary nexus between his status and the nature of the allegedly unconstitutional action to support his claim of standing to secure judicial review. Under such circumstances, we feel confident that the questions will be framed with the necessary specificity, that the issues will be contested with the necessary adverseness and that the litigation will be pursued with the necessary vigor to assure that the constitutional challenge will be made in a form traditionally thought to be capable of judicial resolution. We lack that confidence in cases such as *Frothingham* where a taxpayer seeks to employ a federal court as a forum in which to air his generalized grievances about the conduct of government or the allocation of power in the Federal System.

While we express no view at all on the merits of appellants' claims in this case, their complaint contains sufficient allegations under the criteria we have outlined to give them standing to invoke a federal court's jurisdiction for an adjudication on the merits.

Reversed.

MR. JUSTICE HARLAN, dissenting.

The problems presented by this case are narrow and relatively abstract, but the principles by which they must be resolved involve nothing less than the proper functioning of the federal courts, and so run to the roots of our constitutional system. The nub of my view is that the end result of *Frothingham v. Mellon* was correct, even though, like others, I do not subscribe to all of its reasoning and premises. Although I therefore agree with certain of the conclusions reached today by the Court, I cannot accept the standing doctrine that it substitutes for *Frothingham*, for it seems to me that this new doctrine rests on premises that do not withstand analysis. Accordingly, I respectfully dissent.

It is desirable first to restate the basic issues in this case. The question here is not, as it was not in *Frothingham*, whether "a federal taxpayer is without standing to challenge the constitutionality of a federal statute." It could hardly be disputed that federal taxpayers may, as taxpayers, contest the constitutionality of tax obligations imposed severally upon them by federal statute. Such a challenge may be made by way of defense to an action by the United States to recover the amount of a challenged tax debt or to a prosecution for willful failure to pay or to report the tax. Moreover, such a challenge may provide the basis of an action by a taxpayer to obtain the refund of a previous tax payment.

The lawsuits here and in *Frothingham* are fundamentally different. They present the question whether federal taxpayers *qua* taxpayers may, in suits in which they do not contest the validity of their previous or existing tax obligations, challenge the constitutionality of the uses for which Congress has authorized the expenditure of public funds. These differences in the purposes of the cases are reflected in differences in the litigants' interests. An action brought to contest the validity of tax liabilities assessed to the plaintiff is designed to vindicate interests that are personal and proprietary. The wrongs alleged and the relief sought by such a plaintiff are unmistakably private; only secondarily are his interests representative of those of the general population. I take it that the Court, although it does not pause to examine the question, believes that the interests of those who as taxpayers challenge the constitutionality of public expenditures may, at least in certain circumstances, be similar. Yet this assumption is surely mistaken. . . .

It seems to me clear that public actions . . . may involve important hazards for the continued effectiveness of the federal judiciary. Although I believe such actions to be within the jurisdiction conferred upon the federal courts by Article III of the Constitution, there surely can be little doubt that they strain the judicial function and press to the limit judicial authority. There is every reason to fear that unrestricted public actions might well alter the allocation of authority among the three branches of the Federal Government. It is not, I submit, enough to say that the present members of the Court would not seize these opportunities for abuse, for such actions would, even without conscious abuse, go far toward the final transformation of this Court into the Council of Revision which, despite Madison's support, was rejected by the Constitutional Convention. I do not doubt that there must be "some effectual power in the government to restrain or correct the infractions" of the Constitution's several commands, but neither can I suppose that such power resides only in the federal courts. We must as judges recall that, as Mr. Justice Holmes wisely observed, the other branches of the Government "are ultimate guardians of the liberties and welfare of the people in quite as great a degree as the courts." The powers of the federal judiciary will be adequate for the great burdens placed upon them only if they are employed prudently, with recognition of the strengths as well as the hazards that go with our kind of representative government.

Presumably the Court recognizes at least certain of these hazards, else it would not have troubled to impose limitations upon the situations in which, and purposes for which, such suits may be brought. Nonetheless, the limitations adopted by the Court are, as I have endeavored to indicate, wholly untenable. This is the more unfortunate because there is available a resolution of this problem that entirely satisfies the demands of the principle of separation of powers. This Court has previously held that individual litigants have standing to represent the public interest, despite their lack of economic or other personal interests, if Congress has appropriately authorized such suits. Any hazards to the proper allocation of authority among the three branches of the Government would be substantially diminished if public actions had been pertinently authorized by Congress and the President. I appreciate that this Court does not ordinarily await the mandate of other branches of the Government, but it seems to me that the extraordinary character of public actions, and of the mischievous, if not dangerous, consequences they involve for the proper functioning of our constitutional system, and in particular of the federal courts,

makes such judicial forbearance the part of wisdom. It must be emphasized that the implications of these questions of judicial policy are of fundamental significance for the other branches of the Federal Government.

Such a rule could readily be applied to this case. Although various efforts have been made in Congress to authorize public actions to contest the validity of federal expenditures in aid of religiously affiliated schools and other institutions, no such authorization has yet been given.

This does not mean that we would, under such a rule, be enabled to avoid our constitutional responsibilities, or that we would confine to limbo the First Amendment or any other constitutional command. The question here is not, despite the Court's unarticulated premise, whether the religious clauses of the First Amendment are hereafter to be enforced by the federal courts; the issue is simply whether plaintiffs of an additional category, heretofore excluded from those courts, are to be permitted to maintain suits. The recent history of this Court is replete with illustrations, including even one announced today, that questions involving the religious clauses will not, if federal taxpayers are prevented from contesting federal expenditures, be left "unacknowledged, unresolved, and undecided."

Accordingly, for the reasons contained in this opinion, I would affirm the judgment of the District Court.

Flast did not overrule *Frothingham;* in fact, the Court was careful to indicate that had the 1968 ruling been applied to *Frothingham*, the plaintiff still would have been unable to attain standing. But *Flast* substantially revised the 1923 precedent. If taxpayers could indicate a logical link between their status and the legislation, and one between their status and a specific constitutional infringement, then they might have standing.

Flast symbolized what was at that time a general trend toward lowering barriers to access to federal courts. Twenty-two years earlier, Congress had passed the Administrative Procedure Act of 1946, which, among other things, provided that any person "suffering legal wrong because of agency action, or adversely affected or aggrieved within the meaning of a relevant statute, is entitled to judicial review thereof." Congress had been reacting to pressure from the American Bar Association and business organizations concerned about regulation by federal administrative agencies; but other groups have been able to use this statute. *Association of Data Processing Service Organizations v. Camp* (1970) gave this provision a broad interpretation by specifically rejecting the old standing test of a "recognized legal interest."

But the days of easing standing requirements have apparently come to an end *(see Box 2-7)*. During the last three decades, a majority of the justices have been restoring strict standing requirements and limiting access to federal courts. They have, for example, read *Flast* rather narrowly, restricting its reach to precisely the kind of suit at issue there—a challenge to the use of federal funds allegedly in violation of the First Amendment's ban against establishment of religion. Such a reading has led some scholars to suggest that current doctrine governing standing now resembles *Frothingham* rather than *Flast*.

Those who hold that view may be overstating the case, because when parties have clearly met the *Flast* standing requirements, the Court has permitted them to bring suit. *Bowen v. Kendrick* (1988) provides a case in point. Here, taxpayers and others challenged the constitutionality, under the Religion Establishment Clause, of the Adolescent Family Life Act of 1981, which provides federal grants to agencies and groups for services and research in the area of premarital adolescent sexual relations and pregnancy. The Court had no hesitation in ruling that the parties had standing:

In *Flast v. Cohen*, we held that federal taxpayers have standing to raise Establishment Clause claims against exercises of congressional power under the taxing and spending power of Article I, §8, of the Constitution. Although we have considered the problem of standing and Article III limitations on federal jurisdiction many times since then, we have consistently adhered to *Flast* and the narrow exception it created to the general rule against taxpayer standing established in *Frothingham v. Mellon*. Accordingly, in this case there is no dispute that appellees have standing to raise their challenge to the AFLA on its face.

Still, it is true that standing, like the other "constraints" on judicial power—jurisdiction and justiciability—is open to interpretation. Various opinions filed in the case of **Raines v. Byrd** (1997) shore up this point. Substantively, *Raines* involved the Line Item Veto Act of 1996, which gave the president the ability to cancel certain tax and spending benefits after they were signed into law. As a threshold matter, however, the justices had to decide whether the six members of Congress, who had brought the suit, had standing to challenge the law.

Writing for the majority, Chief Justice Rehnquist concluded that they did not: "These individual members of Congress do not have a sufficient 'personal stake' in this dispute and have not alleged a sufficiently concrete injury to have established Article III standing." In a dissenting opinion, Justice Stevens took issue with Rehnquist's conclusion:

The Line Item Veto Act purports to establish a procedure for the creation of laws that are truncated versions of bills that have been passed by the Congress and presented to the President for signature. If the procedure were valid, it would deny every Senator and every Representative any opportunity to vote for or against the truncated measure that survives the exercise of the President's cancellation authority. Because the opportunity to cast such votes is a right guaranteed by the text of the Constitution, I think it clear that the persons who are deprived of that right by the Act have standing to challenge its constitutionality.

A year later, in *Clinton v. City of New York* (1998), the justices found that the litigants did have standing to challenge the Act, and decided the case on its merits *(see Chapter 4)*. But the very fact that these justices, in *Raines*, could reach such different conclusions underscores the notion that standing—like the other constraints on judicial power (justiciability and jurisdiction)—may be more fluid than it appears and than the Court sometimes lets on. Hence, Article III may place certain limits on the power of the federal judiciary. However, its language is vague enough to allow for a good deal of judicial latitude.

In the final analysis, then, we are left with many questions centering on judicial power and Article III's constraints on its exercise. We shall ask just one. Box 2-8 is an excerpt from Justice Louis D. Brandeis's concurring opinion in *Ashwander v. Tennessee Valley Authority* (1936), in which he outlined the constraints on judicial decision making we reviewed in this section. Given the cases and material you have just read, to what extent are those limitations substantial constraints on the Court or open to interpretation?

BOX 2-7   STANDING TO SUE IN THE AFTERMATH OF *FLAST*

Examples of Cases Limiting Standing Concepts

United States v. Richardson (1974)

Question: Does a taxpayer have standing to challenge a congressional law allowing the CIA to avoid a public "accounting of agency expenditures" as a violation of Article I, Section 9?

The Court: Richardson fails to meet the criteria established in *Flast* and "neatly . . . falls within the *Frothingham* holding." Because the law was not enacted under Article I, Section 8, the taxpayer cannot demonstrate a "logical nexus" between his status and the law. Moreover, the Court noted that the suit rested on an impermissible "generalized grievance" because "the impact on the [plaintiff] is plainly undifferentiated and common to all members of the public."

Schlesinger v. Reservists Committee to Stop the War (1974)

Question: Do members of an organization (and taxpayers) have standing to launch an attack on the Vietnam War? In particular, can they challenge the fact that members of Congress have commissions in the military reserves, as a violation of Article I, Section 6?

The Court: No. They have suffered an insufficiently concrete injury. Further, the suit does not meet *Flast's* nexus test because they did not challenge an Article I, Section 8, power.

Valley Forge Christian College v. Americans United for Separation of Church and State (1982)

Question: Can an organization challenge, on First Amendment grounds, a decision by the Department of Health, Education and Welfare—made under a congressional law—to transfer surplus government property to a religious college?

The Court: No. The organization failed to demonstrate some personal injury. And, the suit was a challenge to an administrative agency's actions, not to Congress's. The organization fails the *Flast* nexus test.

Lujan v. Defenders of Wildlife (1992)

Question: Do members of an environmental organization have standing to challenge the Interior Department's reinterpretation of the Endangered Species Act of 1973, which said that the law would no longer be applied to federally financed projects overseas?

The Court: No. The environmentalists have failed to show how Interior's policy would produce "imminent" injury to them.

Raines v. Byrd (1997)

Question: Do members of Congress have standing to challenge the Line Item Veto Act of 1996, which gives the president the ability to cancel certain tax and spending benefits after they have been signed into law?

The Court: No. The members of Congress did not have a sufficient personal stake in the dispute, nor did they allege a sufficiently concrete injury.

Examples of Cases Expanding Standing Concepts

Sierra Club v. Morton (1972)

Question: Does an interest group have standing to bring a suit seeking to restrain the federal government from approving the development of a ski resort in a valley of a national park?

The Court: No. The group failed to demonstrate sufficient injury to it or its members. However, the Court expanded the concept of injury to include harm to "aesthetic and environmental well-being."

United States v. SCRAP (1973)

Question: Does an interest group have standing to challenge an order of the Interstate Commerce Commission on the grounds that the order adversely affected the environment and the economic interests and recreational pursuits of the organization and its members?

The Court: Yes. The allegations made by SCRAP, though unproven, were sufficient to indicate that perceptible harm might occur. Moreover, SCRAP demonstrated a more "attenuated line of causation to the eventual injury" than did the Sierra Club in *Morton*.

Arlington Heights v. Metropolitan Housing Corporation (1977)

Question: Does a developer have standing to challenge a town's refusal to rezone an area (from a single-family to multifamily category) as racially discriminatory, despite the fact that zoning was not the only obstacle to its housing project? Does an individual black plaintiff have standing to challenge the town's decision on the grounds that he would want to live in the proposed housing project?

The Court: Yes to both questions. Both plaintiffs had specific, not "generalized," complaints. And, both had indicated a "fairly traceable" causal link between the injury and the town's denial sufficient to demonstrate an "actionable causal relationship."

BOX 2-8   JUSTICE BRANDEIS, CONCURRING IN *ASHWANDER V. TENNESSEE VALLEY AUTHORITY*

IN 1936 Justice Louis D. Brandeis delineated, in a concurring opinion in *Ashwander v. Tennessee Valley Authority*, a set of Court-formulated rules useful in avoiding constitutional decisions. A portion of his opinion setting forth those rules, minus case cites and footnotes, follows:

The Court developed, for its own governance in the cases confessedly within its jurisdiction, a series of rules under which it has avoided passing upon a large part of all the constitutional questions pressed upon it for decision. They are:

1. The Court will not pass upon the constitutionality of legislation in a friendly, non-adversary, proceeding, declining because to decide such questions "is legitimate only in the last resort, and as a necessity in the determination of real, earnest and vital controversy between individuals. It never was the thought that, by means of a friendly suit, a party beaten in the legislature could transfer to the courts an inquiry as to the constitutionality of the legislative act."

2. The Court will not "anticipate a question of constitutional law in advance of the necessity of deciding it." "It is not the habit of the Court to decide questions of a constitutional nature unless absolutely necessary to a decision of the case."

3. The Court will not "formulate a rule of constitutional law broader than is required by the precise facts to which it is to be applied."

4. The Court will not pass upon a constitutional question although properly presented by the record, if there is also present some other ground upon which the case may be disposed of. This rule has found most varied application. Thus, if a case can be decided on either of two grounds, one involving a constitutional question, the other a question of statutory construction or general law, the Court will decide only the latter. Appeals from the highest court of a state challenging its decision of a question under the Federal Constitution are frequently dismissed because the judgment can be sustained on an independent state ground.

5. The Court will not pass upon the validity of a statute upon complaint of one who fails to show that he is injured by its operation. Among the many applications of this rule, none is more striking than the denial of the right of challenge to one who lacks a personal or property right. Thus, the challenge by a public official interested only in the performance of his official duty will not be entertained. . . .

6. "The Court will not pass upon the constitutionality of a statute at the instance of one who has availed himself of its benefits."

7. "When the validity of an act of the Congress is drawn in question, and even if a serious doubt of constitutionality is raised, it is a cardinal principle that this Court will first ascertain whether a construction of the statute is fairly possible by which the question may be avoided."

CONSTRAINTS ON JUDICIAL POWER: THE SEPARATION OF POWERS/CHECKS AND BALANCES SYSTEM

Whatever you believe is the answer to the question just posed, one thing is clear: many traditional accounts of the constraints on Supreme Court decision making begin and end with Article III. But, in recent years, scholars have argued that when it comes to making decisions, the justices are constrained in another way: if the justices want to generate enduring policy, they must be attentive to the preferences of the elected institutions and the actions they expect them to take.[57]

57. We adapt this discussion from Lee Epstein and Jack Knight, *The Choices Justices Make* (Washington, D.C.: CQ Press, 1998), chap. 5.

This claim flows from the logic of the framework underlying the U.S. Constitution—the separation of powers/ checks and balances system. As we explained earlier, that system and the informal rules that have evolved over time (such as the power of judicial review) endow each branch of government with significant powers and authority over its sphere. At the same time, it provides explicit checks on the exercise of those powers such that each branch can impose limits on the primary functions of the others. So, for example, the judiciary may interpret the law and even strike down laws as being in violation of the Constitution, but Congress can pass new legislation, which the president may sign or veto.

Seen in this way, the rule of checks and balances inherent in the system of separation of powers provides justices (and all other government actors) with important information: *policy in the United States emanates not from the separate actions of the branches of government but from the interaction among them.* For any set of actors to make authoritative policy—be they justices, legislators, or executives—they may have to take into account this institutional constraint by formulating expectations about the preferences of the other relevant actors and what they expect them to do when making their own choices.[58]

This general claim requires some clarification. Although it may be true that the separation of powers system operates across a range of substantive issues, many argue that the system imposes a more significant constraint on powers of the statutory, rather than of the constitutional, variety.[59] It is easy to understand the rationale behind this claim because when the Court construes a federal law Congress can, by a simple majority vote, overturn or modify the justices' interpretation. For example, in *Grove City College v. Bell* (1984), the Court held that Title IX of the 1972 Education Amendments, which prohibits sex discrimination in any "program or activity" receiving federal aid, applies only to the particular program receiving the aid, not to every program at an institution. Congress believed the Court had misconstrued its intent in Title IX, which was for Title IX to have an institutionwide scope. In 1988 the legislature made this clear to the Court by enacting a new law that essentially overruled *Grove City*.[60]

58. Some argue that the constraint imposed by the separation of powers system subsumes Article III constraints. In *Constitutional Law* (St. Paul: West, 1993), 1028, Daniel A. Farber, William N. Eskridge Jr., and Philip P. Frickey note that the political questions doctrine centers on the notion that the branches have distinct responsibilities. Others suggest—as we did above—that it comes directly from the words of Article III.

59. For a somewhat different point of view—one suggesting that the constraint is equally operative in constitutional cases—see Lee Epstein, Jack Knight, and Andrew Martin, "The Supreme Court as a *Strategic* National Policy Maker," *Emory Law Journal* 50 (2001): 583–612; Harry Stumpf, "Congressional Responses to Supreme Court Rulings: The Interaction of Law and Politics," *Journal of Public Law* 14 (1965): 377–395; and James Meernik and Joseph Ignagni, "Judicial Review and Coordinate Construction of the Constitution," *American Journal of Political Science* 41 (1997): 447–467.

60. See William N. Eskridge Jr., "Reneging on History?" *California Law Review* 79 (1991): 613–684. Congress's action in *Grove City* was not all that unusual; indeed, between 1967 and 1990, Congress disturbed some 120 Court decisions.

The sheer number of overrides raises an interesting question: If the Court takes into account government preferences and likely actions when

Cases involving constitutional interpretation present a different situation. Although the separation of powers system endows Congress and the president with weapons they can deploy against the Court, they do not deploy them very often. This point is important because the mere infrequency of congressional responses to constitutional decisions (coupled with the difficulty involved in overturning them) means that justices may be less attentive to the preferences and likely actions of other government actors in constitutional disputes than in statutory ones.

We can offer three reasons why we would not expect the Court to completely ignore the external constraint imposed by the separation of powers system in constitutional cases. First, the other branches of government have the power to alter constitutional policy established by the Court. Although the Rehnquist Court has shut down efforts to do so through simple legislation—with *City of Boerne* and *Dickerson v. United States* clear illustrations—they can propose constitutional amendments to overturn Court decisions. This constraint on the Court is especially effective because, once an amendment is part of the Constitution, it is "constitutional," and the justices are bound by it. By the same token, once the amendment process is set in motion, the Court has been reluctant to interfere.

Consider *Coleman v. Miller* (1939), a case to which Justice Brennan made specific reference in his *Baker* opinion. Here the Court considered the actions of the Kansas legislature over the Child Labor Amendment. Proposed by Congress in 1924, the amendment stated, "The Congress shall have power to limit, regulate, and prohibit the labor of persons under eighteen years of age." In January 1925 Kansas legislators rejected the Child Labor Amendment. The issue arose again, however, when the state senate reconsidered the amendment in January 1937. At that time, the legislative body split, 20–20, with the lieutenant governor casting the decisive vote in favor of the

it reaches decisions, why does it occasionally produce inefficacious policy (that is, decisions that Congress or the president later overturns)? One explanation is that the Court fails to take account of the external constraint imposed by the separation of powers systems. Another is that the Court believes its decisions can provide information to the legislature—information that, in turn, can lead members of Congress to reevaluate their positions. Finally, it is quite possible that the Court simply does not know with certainty what other government actors will do. In these situations, the justices can only make estimates, which may be wrong.

amendment. Members of the Kansas legislature (mostly those who had opposed the proposal) challenged the 1937 vote on two grounds: they questioned the ability of the lieutenant governor to break the tie and, more generally, the reconsideration of an amendment that previously had been rejected. Writing for the Court, Chief Justice Charles Evans Hughes refused to address these points. Rather, he asserted that the suit raised a political question. In his words, "the ultimate authority" over the amendment process was Congress, not the Court.

It is worth reiterating that Congress does not often propose constitutional amendments or even legislation to override the Court. Only four times has Congress succeeded in overriding the Court with a constitutional amendment, and attempts to overrule by simple legislation may be equally rare.[61] And when the legislature has attempted to direct the justices on how to adjudicate constitutional cases, they may decline to do so—as the majority's reaction in City of Boerne and Dickerson v. United States indicates. The more general point, however, is this: because Congress has, in the past, overridden the Court, there is no reason for justices to believe that the legislature would not do so in the future. This threat may be sufficient to constrain the justices, even in constitutional disputes.

A second reason the Court may take into account the preferences and likely actions of the other branches in constitutional disputes stems from the U.S. Constitution itself. That document provides the elected institutions with general weapons they can use to "punish" justices for their (constitutional) policy decisions. Congress, for example, can hold judicial salaries constant, impeach justices, change the size of the Court, and make "exceptions" to the Court's appellate jurisdiction. And these weapons can have an effect on the doctrine the Court produces. To see this point, we need only to reconsider

Ex parte McCardle. Perhaps in an effort to protect the Court's institutional legitimacy, the justices eschewed their most preferred position—to rule in favor of McCardle. Instead, they dismissed the suit, thereby lending credence to the notion that Congress can remove the Court's appellate jurisdiction as it deems necessary.

Although McCardle is the exception in that the government rarely deploys these weapons, their mere existence may serve to constrain policy-oriented justices from acting on their preferences. The best-known example may be Marbury v. Madison. Certainly, Chief Justice Marshall—himself an Adams appointee—wanted to give Marbury his appointment. But, at the same time, Marshall was well aware of the serious repercussions of ordering the administration to do so. Jefferson made no secret of his disdain for Marshall, and with impeachment of the chief justice a distinct possibility in the president's (and Marshall's) mind, Marshall was confronted with a dilemma: vote his sincere political preferences and risk the institutional integrity of the Court (not to mention his own job), or act in a sophisticated fashion with regard to his political preferences (refuse to give Marbury his commission) and elevate judicial supremacy (establish judicial review) in a way that Jefferson could accept. Perhaps not so surprisingly, Marshall chose the latter course of action.

Finally, government actors can refuse, implicitly or explicitly, to implement particular constitutional decisions, thereby decreasing the Court's ability to create efficacious policy. Immigration and Naturalization Service v. Chadha, which we discussed at the beginning of this chapter, provides a case in point. Theoretically speaking, Chadha nullified on constitutional grounds the practice of legislative vetoes, that is, congressional rejection of policies produced by executive agencies. In practice, however, Congress has passed more than two hundred new laws containing legislative vetoes since Chadha, and agencies continue to pay heed when Congress rejects their policies. The problem, so it seems, was that the Court fashioned a rule that was "unacceptable" to the other branches of government and, as a result, one that has been "eroded by open defiance and subtle evasion." [62] Why the Court

---

61. But see Meernik and Ignagni, "Judicial Review and Coordinate Construction of the Constitution," 447. They argue that, contrary to what some scholars have suggested, "Congress often does reverse Supreme Court [constitutional] rulings." They claim that of the 569 cases in which the Court rendered unconstitutional a federal law, a state law, or executive order, Congress made 125 attempts to override by constitutional amendment or by statute. Of these, Congress succeeded in reversing the Court in 41. But it is uncertain whether Congress was attempting a reinterpretation of the Constitution, as it did in the Religious Freedom Restoration Act, or trying to correct a constitutional defect identified by the Court.

62. Fisher, "The Legislative Veto: Invalidated, It Survives," 288.

would establish such an inefficacious rule is open to speculation, but the relevant point is simple enough: once the Court reached its decision, it had to depend on Congress to implement it. Because Congress failed to do so, the Court was unable to set long-term policy.

In sum, Article III is not the only source of constraint on the Court's power. Although those that emanate from the separation of powers system may play a greater role in cases involving statutory, rather than constitutional, interpretation, they seem to have had some effect in constitutional disputes—as *McCardle* illustrates. What it and many other cases you will read in this book demonstrate is that justices, in their quest to create efficacious policy, occasionally consider how other government actors will respond. If they are not attentive in this fashion, then a *Chadha*-like situation may result, in which other branches fail to comply with Court policy or seek to overturn it.

READINGS

Barkow, Rachel E. "More Supreme Than Court? The Fall of the Political Question Doctrine and the Rise of Judicial Supremacy." *Columbia Law Review* 102 (2002): 237–334.

Berger, Raoul. "Standing to Sue in Public Actions." *Yale Law Journal* 78 (1969): 816–840.

Bickel, Alexander M. *The Least Dangerous Branch.* New York: Bobbs-Merrill, 1962.

Burbank, Stephen B., and Barry Friedman, eds. *Judicial Independence at the Crossroads: An Interdisciplinary Approach.* Thousand Oaks, Calif.: Sage Publications, 2002.

Canon, Bradley C. "Defining the Dimensions of Judicial Activism." *Judicature* 66 (1983): 236–247.

Casper, Jonathan D. "The Supreme Court and National Policy Making." *American Political Science Review* 70 (1976): 50–63.

Choper, Jesse H. *Judicial Review and the National Political Process.* Chicago: University of Chicago Press, 1980.

Clinton, Robert Lowry. *Marbury v. Madison and Judicial Review.* Lawrence: University Press of Kansas, 1989.

Cover, Robert M. "The Origins of Judicial Activism in the Protection of Minorities." *Yale Law Journal* 91 (1982): 1287–1316.

Dahl, Robert. "Decision Making in a Democracy: The Supreme Court as a National Policy-Maker." *Journal of Public Law* 6 (1957): 279–295.

Ely, John Hart. *Democracy and Distrust.* Cambridge: Harvard University Press, 1980.

Epstein, Lee, Jack Knight, and Andrew Martin. "The Supreme Court as a *Strategic* National Policy Maker." *Emory Law Journal* 50 (2001): 583–612.

Fisher, Louis. *Constitutional Dialogues.* Princeton: Princeton University Press, 1988.

Franck, Thomas M. *Political Questions/Judicial Answers: Does the Rule of Law Apply to Foreign Affairs?* Princeton: Princeton University Press, 1992.

Funston, Richard. *A Vital National Seminar.* Palo Alto, Calif.: Mayfield, 1978.

Gettleman, Marvin E. *The Dorr Rebellion: A Study in American Radicalism, 1833–1849.* New York: Random House, 1973.

Gillman, Howard. *The Votes That Counted.* Chicago: University of Chicago Press, 2001.

Grofman, Bernard, ed. *Political Gerrymandering and the Courts.* New York: Agathon Press, 1990.

Gunther, Gerald. "The Subtle Vices of the Passive Virtues—A Comment on Principle and Expediency in Judicial Review." *Columbia Law Review* 64 (1964): 1–25.

Henkin, Louis. "Is There a 'Political Question' Doctrine?" *Yale Law Journal* 85 (1976): 597–625.

Langer, Laura. *Judicial Review in State Supreme Courts: A Comparative Study.* Albany: State University of New York Press, 2002.

Lasser, William. *The Limits of Judicial Power.* Chapel Hill: University of North Carolina Press, 1988.

Meernik, James, and Joseph Ignagni. "Judicial Review and Coordinate Construction of the Constitution." *American Journal of Political Science* 41 (1997): 447–467.

Murphy, Walter F. *Congress and the Court.* Chicago: University of Chicago Press, 1962.

Nelson, William E. *Marbury v. Madison: The Origins and Legacy of Judicial Review.* Lawrence: University Press of Kansas, 2000.

Orren, Karen. "Standing to Sue: Interest Group Conflict in the Federal Courts." *American Political Science Review* 70 (1976): 723–741.

Peretti, Terri Jennings. *In Defense of a Political Court.* Princeton: Princeton University Press, 1999.

Radcliffe, James E. *The Case-or-Controversy Provision.* University Park: Pennsylvania State University Press, 1978.

Rathjen, Gregory J., and Harold J. Spaeth. "Access to the Federal Courts: An Analysis of Burger Court Policy Making." *American Journal of Political Science* 23 (1979): 360–382.

Rosenberg, Gerald N. "Judicial Independence and the Reality of Political Power." *Review of Politics* 54 (1992): 369–398.

Rowland, C. K., and Bridgett Todd. "Where You Stand Depends on Who Sits: Platform Promises and Judicial Gatekeeping in the Federal District Courts." *Journal of Politics* 53 (1991): 175–185.

Schuckman, John S. "The Political Background of the Political Question Doctrine: The Judges and the Dorr War." *American Journal of Legal History* 16 (1972): 111–125.

Strum, Philippa. *The Supreme Court and Political Questions.* Tuscaloosa: University of Alabama Press, 1974.

Sunstein, Cass R. *One Case at a Time: Judicial Minimalism on the Supreme Court.* Cambridge: Harvard University Press, 1999.

Tate, C. Neal, and Torbjrn Vallinder, eds. *The Global Expansion of Judicial Power: The Judicialization of Politics.* New York: New York University Press, 1995.

Van Alstyne, William. "A Critical Guide to *Marbury v. Madison.*" *Duke Law Journal* 1969 (1969): 1–48.

Wolfe, Christopher. *Judicial Activism.* Pacific Grove, Calif.: Brooks/Cole, 1991.

———. *The Rise of Modern Judicial Review.* New York: Basic Books, 1986.

CHAPTER 3
THE LEGISLATURE

A RTICLE I of the U.S. Constitution is its longest and most explicit. The Founders spelled out in great detail the powers Congress did and did not have over its own operations and its authority to make laws. Reading through Article I, we might conclude that it could not be the source of much litigation. After all, given its specificity, how much room for interpretation could there be?

For cases involving Congress's authority over its internal affairs, this assumption would be accurate. The Supreme Court has heard relatively few cases touching upon the first seven sections of Article I, which deal with the various qualifications for membership in Congress, the ability of the chambers to punish members, and certain privileges enjoyed by the members. In those on which the Court has ruled, it generally, though not always, has given the legislature great latitude over its own business.

That assumption, however, is incorrect when we consider cases that deal directly with Congress's most basic power, the enactment of laws, and with its role in American government. Article I, Section 8, enumerates specifically the substantive areas in which Congress may legislate. But is it too specific, failing to foresee how congressional powers might need to be exercised in areas it does not cover? For example, Section 8 provides Congress with the power to borrow and coin money, but not with the authority to make paper money for the payment of debts. Since 1792 congressional committees have held investigations and hearings, but no clause in Section 8

authorizes them to do so. In general, the Supreme Court has had to determine whether legislative action that is not explicitly covered in Article I falls within Congress's authority, and that is why the Court so often has examined statutes passed by Congress.

There is another reason. As we saw earlier, and as we shall see throughout this book, basic (and purposeful) tensions were built into the design of the government. Disputes occur between the branches of the federal government, between the federal government and the states, and between governments and individuals. Emanating from the basic principles underlying the structure of government—federalism, the separation of powers, and checks and balances—these conflicts have provided the stuff of myriad legal disputes, and the Court has been right in the middle of many of them.

This chapter examines how the justices have interpreted Article I of the Constitution.[1] It is divided into three sections: the first provides a historical overview of Article I, the second explores cases involving Congress's authority over its own structure and operations, and the third looks at the sources and scope of its lawmaking power.

ARTICLE I: HISTORICAL OVERVIEW

Many factors led the colonists in America to rebel against England. An important one, sometimes neglected

---

1. This chapter focuses generally on the scope of Article I and related issues. In Chapter 5, we consider relationships between Congress and the executive.

in treatments of the American Revolution, was the different ways the British and the colonists thought about legislative bodies such as Parliament. The British viewed legislatures as "deliberative bodies whose allegiance was to the nation rather than specific constituencies."[2] Underlying this view is the notion of "virtual" representation: "since the *interests* of all British citizens were represented in Parliament, the *citizens* themselves did not need to be." Therefore, the British reasoned, the colonists did not have to vote for members of Parliament because they were "virtually represented" within it. The Americans took a quite different stance. To them, legislators "were nothing more and nothing less than agents of their constituents." As John Adams wrote in 1776, the ideal legislature "should be in miniature an exact portrait of the people at large. It should think, feel, reason and act like them."

During the founding period, the American states created legislatures that reflected some of Adams's views of representation. Most states provided for very short terms of office, with elections typically occurring every other year. They also mandated that legislatures have open sessions and publish their proceedings. Finally, many states actually gave their inhabitants the right to "instruct" their representatives on how to vote on certain issues. These and other measures were designed to keep legislators responsive to their constituents. Concerns about representation at the federal level also were present, as were suspicions about a powerful national government like England's. The unicameral Congress that had been created under the Articles of Confederation had few important powers, and many of those it had, it could not exercise without state compliance, which often was lacking *(see Figure 1-1, page 4)*.

The problems Congress and the nation faced under the Articles of Confederation made it clear to the delegates attending the Constitutional Convention of 1787 that a very different kind of legislature was necessary if the United States was to endure. But what form would that legislature take? And what powers would it have?

These questions produced a great deal of discussion during the convention; indeed, debates over the structure and powers of Congress occupied more than half of the Framers' time.

Structure and Composition of Congress

The Virginia Plan set the tone for the Constitutional Convention and became the backbone for Article I. Essentially, the plan called for a bicameral legislature, with the number of representatives in each house apportioned on the basis of state population. Under this scheme, the lower house (now the House of Representatives) would be elected by the people; the upper house (the Senate) would be chosen by the lower based on recommendations from state legislatures.

The Framers dealt with two aspects of the Virginia Plan with relative ease. Almost all agreed on the need for a bicameral legislature. Accord on this point was not surprising; by 1787 only four states had a one-house legislature. The plan for selecting the upper house provoked more discussion. Some thought that having the lower house elect the upper would make the Senate subservient to the House and upset the delicate checks and balances system. Instead, the delegates agreed that the Senate should be selected by state legislatures. (The Seventeenth Amendment to the Constitution, ratified in 1913, changed this method of selection; senators, like representatives, are now elected by the people.)

The third aspect of the Virginia Plan—the composition of the houses of Congress—generated some of the most acrimonious debates of the convention. As historians Alfred Kelly, Winfred Harbison, and Herman Belz put it:

Would the constituent units be the states, represented equally by delegates chosen by state legislatures, as the small-state group desired? Or would the constituent element be the people of the United States . . . with representation in both chambers apportioned according to population, as the large-state group wished?[3]

2. The discussion in this paragraph has been adopted from Daniel A. Farber and Suzanna Sherry, *A History of the American Constitution* (St. Paul, Minn.: West Publishing, 1990), 110–111.

3. Alfred H. Kelly, Winfred A. Harbison, and Herman Belz, *The American Constitution: Its Origins and Development*, 7th ed. (New York: W. W. Norton, 1991), 90.

On one level, the answer to this question involved the straightforward motivation of self-interest. Naturally, the large states wanted both chambers to be based on population because they would send more representatives to the new Congress. The smaller states thought all states should have equal representation in both houses and regarded their plan as the only way to avoid tyranny by a majority. On another level, the issue of composition went to the core of the Philadelphia enterprise. The approach advocated by the small states would signify the importance of the states in the new system of government, while that put forth in the Virginia Plan would suggest that the federal government received its power directly from the people rather than from the states and was truly independent.

It is no wonder, then, that the delegates had so much trouble resolving this issue: it defined the basic character of the new government. In the end they took the course of action that characterized many of their decisions—they agreed to disagree. Specifically, the delegates reached a compromise under which the House of Representatives would be constituted on the basis of population, and the Senate would have two delegates from each state.

Reaching this compromise was crucial to the success of the convention. Without it, the delegates may have left without framing a constitution. But because the Founders split the difference between the demands of the small and large states, they never fully dealt with the critical underlying issue: Do the people or the states empower the federal government? The impact of this lingering question on the development of the country is addressed in Chapter 6. Here, we note that this question not only has been at the center of many disputes brought to the Supreme Court but also was a leading cause of the Civil War.

This compromise has also led to more specific controversies, centering on the very nature of representation. We know that in drafting Article I, the Framers clearly intended that representation in the House of Representatives would be based on population. Each state was allotted at least one representative, with additional seats based on the number of persons residing within its boundaries. The exact number of representatives per state was to be determined by a census of the population (beginning within three years of the first Congress and continuing every ten years thereafter) and calculated by adding the number of "free persons" and "three-fifths of all other persons" (read: slaves). Passage of the Fourteenth Amendment changed this formula so that blacks would be fully counted. But even that did not end debates over representation because, when the number of representatives reached 435 in the early 1900s, Congress decided that it should be no larger.

The fixed size of the House generated the reapportionment controversies we considered briefly in the previous chapter. Recall that, as population shifts occurred within states in the middle of the twentieth century, some redrew their congressional district lines. For most, the new maps meant creating greater parity for urban centers as citizens moved out of rural areas. Other states, however, ignored these shifts and refused to reapportion seats. Over time, the results of their failure to do so became readily apparent. It was possible for two districts within the same state, with large differences in population, each to elect one member to the House. Beginning with *Baker v. Carr* (1962), the Court heard a series of challenges to legislative malapportionment, eventually creating the "one man, one vote" principle. This holds that "as nearly as is practicable one man's vote in a congressional election is to be worth as much as another's." [4]

With the articulation of this principle, the Court settled some controversies: so long as the one person, one vote principle is observed, the Supreme Court generally has allowed states freedom in constructing representational districts for members of the House of Representatives. But other controversies arose with time. Particularly heated today are debates centering on the extent to which states can or should take race into account when they reapportion their districts. According to some analysts, creating districts with a high concentration of minority voters is the only way to increase minority representation in Congress. Others, including some civil rights

4. *Wesberry v. Sanders* (1964).

advocates, however, have criticized such efforts, arguing that they do not offer real opportunities for increased minority representation. Even if the number of minority representatives grew to approximate their proportion in the general population, so the argument goes, they would still be too small in number to have any real clout in the legislature. These critics claim that only through changes in representational and institutional rules can minorities achieve political influence at the national level.[5] What is beyond debate is that the number of minority members of the House remains relatively small.

Powers of Congress

With the possible exception of reapportionment and term limits for members of Congress *(see pages 135–143)*, Americans today rarely debate issues concerning the structure and composition of Congress: most of us simply accept the arrangements outlined in the Constitution. Instead, we tend to concern ourselves with what Congress does or does not do, with its ability to change our lives—sometimes dramatically—through the exercise of its lawmaking powers. Should Congress increase taxes? Pass health care reform? Provide aid for the homeless? Such questions—not structural points—generate heated debate among Americans.

In 1787 the situation was reversed. While the Framers fiercely debated issues involving the makeup of the legislature, they generally agreed over the particular powers it would have. This consensus probably reflected their experience under the Articles of Confederation: severe economic problems due in no small part, as the Framers knew, to "congressional impotence."[6]

To correct these problems, Article I, Section 8, which lists seventeen specific powers given to Congress by the delegates, contains many provisions relating to the economy. Consider, for example, the problem of raising money. Under the Articles of Confederation the legislature could not collect taxes from the people; instead it had to rely on the less-than-dependable states to collect and forward taxes (between 1781 and 1783, the legislature requested $10 million from the states but received less than $2 million). In response, the first power given to Congress in the newly minted Constitution was to "lay and collect taxes." In all, six of the seventeen specific congressional powers enumerated in Section 8 deal with economic issues. The rest center on foreign relations, the military, and internal matters, such as the creation of courts, post offices, and so forth.

While the Framers agreed on these powers, two others provoked heated discussions. The first concerned a proposal in the Virginia Plan to give Congress veto authority over state legislation. This idea had the strong support of James Madison, who argued that "the propensity of the States to pursue their particular interests in opposition to the general interest . . . will continue to disturb the system, unless effectually controuled." Madison and others who supported the veto proposal were once again reacting to the problems produced by the Articles of Confederation. Because the federal government lacked coercive power over the states, mutual cooperation among them was virtually nonexistent. They engaged in practices that hurt one another economically and, in general, acted more like thirteen separate countries than a union or even a confederation. But the majority of delegates thought that a congressional veto would "disgust all the States." Accordingly, they compromised with Article VI, the Supremacy Clause, which made the Constitution, U.S. laws, and treaties "the supreme law of the land," binding all judges in all the states to follow them.

The second source of controversy was this question: Would Congress be able to exercise powers that were not listed in Article I, Section 8, or was it limited to those explicitly enumerated? Some analysts would argue that the last clause of Article I, Section 8, the Necessary and

---

5. For three decades the Supreme Court has wrestled with the constitutional propriety of states purposefully drawing legislative district lines to ensure representation for minorities. During the 1970s and 1980s the Court gave considerable leeway to state legislatures to take race into account. In the 1990s, however, the Court changed course sharply. In a series of cases, the justices ruled that the Constitution is violated when district lines are explainable only in terms of race and when racial factors clearly dominate more traditional districting criteria. For a full discussion of this issue, see Lee Epstein and Thomas G. Walker, *Constitutional Law for a Changing America: Rights, Liberties, and Justice*, 5th ed. (Washington, D.C.: CQ Press, 2004), chap. 13.

6. Farber and Sherry, *A History of the American Constitution*, 134.

Proper Clause, addressed this question by granting Congress the power "To make all Laws which shall be necessary and proper for carrying into Execution the foregoing Powers." But is that interpretation correct? Even after they agreed on the wording of that clause (with little discussion), the delegates continued to raise the issue in various debates. Delegate James McHenry of Maryland wrote about a conversation that occurred on September 6: "Spoke to Gov. Morris Fitzsimmons . . . to insert a power . . . enabling the legislature to erect piers for protection of shipping in winter. . . . Mr. Gov.: thinks it may be done under the words of the 1 clause 1 sect 7 art. amended—'and provide for the common defense and general welfare.'" [7] In other words, Fitzsimmons was arguing that one of Congress's enumerated powers (to provide for the common defense and general welfare) implied the power to erect piers. Under this argument, then, Congress could assert powers beyond those that were enumerated.

A majority of the Founders may have agreed with Fitzsimmons. Because the question of congressional power is central to understanding the role Congress plays in American society, we shall return to it. At this point, however, we consider the Court's interpretation of the first parts of Article I, which lay out the structure of Congress and its authority over its own affairs.

CONGRESSIONAL AUTHORITY OVER INTERNAL AFFAIRS: INSTITUTIONAL INDEPENDENCE AND INTEGRITY

While the Framers were debating Congress's structure and composition, they were also thinking about ways to safeguard the independence and integrity of the institution. Included in Article I are provisions dealing with the ability of the chambers to control who joins them and to punish those who do not behave in accord with their norms. Another section, the Speech or Debate Clause, protects members from "harassment" by other institutions.

How would the Supreme Court interpret these provisions? The information presented in Table 3-1 provides one way to start to address this question. Although we often think about the Court and Congress as wholly separate entities, they are connected in an interesting way. As Table 3-1 shows, almost half of all those who have sat on the Supreme Court have had some prior state or federal legislative experience. From this, we might conclude that those justices would empathize with the claims of Congress regarding the need for authority over its own affairs; indeed, the Court generally has acceded to legislative wishes—but not always. As you read what follows, think about the reasons the Court offers for its decisions. Further, take note of the various coalitions emerging on different Courts. Do the justices with legislative experience exhibit a greater willingness to defer to Congress than those who never were legislators?

Membership in Congress: Seating and Discipline

In addition to specifying the structure and composition of Congress, Article I contains the requirements that must be met by all prospective members of the institution:

• A senator must be at least thirty years old and have been a citizen of the United States not less than nine years (Section 3, Clause 3);

• A representative must be at least twenty-five years old and have been a citizen not less than seven years (Section 2, Clause 2);

• Every member of Congress must be, when elected, an inhabitant of the state that he or she is to represent (Section 2, Clause 2, and Section 3, Clause 3);

• No one may be a member of Congress who holds any other "Office under the United States" (Section 6, Clause 2).

Finally, Section 3 of the Fourteenth Amendment states that no person may be a senator or a representative who, having previously taken an oath as a member of Congress to support the Constitution, has engaged in rebellion against the United States or given aid or comfort to its enemies, unless Congress has removed such disability by a two-thirds vote of both houses.

7. Ibid., 141.

TABLE 3-1 U.S. Supreme Court Justices with Federal or State Legislative Experience

Justice	Federal House	Federal Senate	State	Court Service
John Rutledge			S.C. (1776–78; 98–99)	1789–91
John Blair Jr.			Va. (1766–70)	1789–96
Thomas Johnson			Md. (1780, 86, 87)	1792–93
William Paterson		1789–90	N.J. (1775–76)	1793–1806
Samuel Chase			Md. (1776–84)	1796–1811
Oliver Ellsworth		1789–96	Conn. (1773–76)	1796–1800
Bushrod Washington			Va. (1787)	1798–1829
Alfred Moore			N.C. (1782, 1792)	1799–1804
John Marshall	1799–1800		Va. (1782–85; 87–90; 95–96)	1801–35
William Johnson			S.C. (1794–98)	1804–34
Henry B. Livingston			N.Y. (3 sessions)	1806–23
Joseph Story	1808–09		Mass. (1805–08)	1811–45
Gabriel Duvall	1794–96		Md. (1787–94)	1811–35
Smith Thompson			N.Y. (1800)	1823–43
Robert Trimble			Ky. (1802)	1826–28
John McLean	1813–16			1829–61
Henry Baldwin	1817–22			1830–44
James M. Wayne	1829–35		Ga. (1815–16)	1835–67
Roger B. Taney			Md. (1799–1800; 16–21)	1836–64
Philip P. Barbour	1814–25		Va. (1812–14)	1836–41
John McKinley	1837	1826–31; 1837	Ala. (1820, 1831, 1836)	1837–52
Peter Daniel			Va. (1809–12)	1841–60
Levi Woodbury		1825–31; 41–45	N.H. (1825)	1846–51
Benjamin R. Curtis			Mass. (1849–51)	1851–57
John A. Campbell			Ala. (1837, 1843)	1853–61
Nathan Clifford	1839–43		Maine (1830–34)	1858–81
Noah H. Swayne			Ohio (1830, 1836)	1862–81
David Davis		1877–85	Ill. (1845–47)	1862–77
Stephen J. Field			Calif. (1850–51)	1863–97
Salmon P. Chase		1849–55		1864–73
William Strong	1847–51			1870–80
Ward Hunt			N.Y. (1839)	1873–82
Morrison R. Waite			Ohio (1850–52)	1874–88
William B. Woods			Ohio (1858–62)	1880–87
Stanley Matthews		1877–79	Ohio (1855–58)	1881–89
Lucius Q. C. Lamar	1857–60; 73–77	1877–85	Ga. (1853)	1888–93
Melville W. Fuller			Ill. (1863–64)	1888–1910
Howell E. Jackson		1881–86	Tenn. (1880)	1893–95
Edward D. White		1891–94	La. (1874)	1894–1921
Joseph McKenna	1885–92		Calif. (1875–76)	1898–1925
William Moody	1895–1902			1906–10
Willis Van Devanter			Wyo. (1888)	1910–37
Joseph R. Lamar			Ga. (1886–89)	1910–16
Mahlon Pitney	1895–99		N.J. (1899–1901)	1912–22
George Sutherland	1901–03	1905–17	Utah (1896–1900)	1922–38
Hugo L. Black		1927–37		1937–71
Stanley Reed			Ky. (1912–16)	1938–57
James F. Byrnes	1911–25	1931–41		1941–42
Harold H. Burton		1941–45	Ohio (1929)	1945–58
Fred M. Vinson	1924–29			1946–53
Sherman Minton		1935–41		1949–56
Sandra Day O'Connor			Ariz. (1969–75)	1981–

SOURCE: Adapted from Joan Biskupic and Elder Witt, *Guide to the U.S. Supreme Court*, 3rd ed. (Washington, D.C.: Congressional Quarterly, 1997), 179.

TABLE 3-2   Duly Elected Members of Congress Excluded

Chamber (Year)	Member-Elect (Party-State)	Grounds for Exclusion
Senate (1793)	Albert Gallatin (D-Pa.)	Citizenship
House (1823)	John Bailey (Ind.-Mass.)	Residence
House (1867)	John Y. Brown (D-Ky.)	Loyalty
House (1867)	John D. Young (D-Ky.)	Loyalty
House (1867)	John A. Wimpy (Ind.-Ga.)	Loyalty
House (1867)	W. D. Simpson (Ind.-S.C.)	Loyalty
Senate (1867)	Phillip F. Thomas (D-Md.)	Loyalty
House (1870)	Benjamin F. Whittemore (R-S.C.)	Malfeasance
House (1900)	Brigham H. Roberts (D-Utah)	Polygamy
House (1919)	Victor L. Berger (Socialist-Wis.)	Sedition
House (1920)	Victor L. Berger (Socialist-Wis.)	Sedition
House (1967)	Adam C. Powell Jr. (D-N.Y.)	Misconduct

SOURCE: Congressional Quarterly, *Guide to Congress*, 5th ed. (Washington, D.C.: CQ Press, 2000), 919, 921.

With only a few exceptions, these standards qua standards have not caused much controversy or litigation. Some legal questions, however, have arisen with respect to their relationship to Article I, Section 5, which reads: "Each House shall be the Judge of the Elections, Returns and Qualifications of its own Members." Several interpretations are possible. One is that this clause ought to be read in conjunction with the Article I requirements for members. That is, Congress cannot deny a duly elected person a seat in the institution unless that person fails to meet the specified criteria. Another interpretation is that Congress is free to develop additional qualifications, independent of those specified elsewhere.[8]

For the better part of the nation's history, the Court stayed away from such disputes, even though Congress occasionally acted as if it could add qualifications or ignore them when they were not met. For example, during the Civil War, Congress enacted the Test Oath Law of 1862, which required incoming members to "swear . . . that they had never voluntarily borne arms against the United States." Moreover, as shown in Table 3-2, both the House and the Senate have refused to seat properly elected individuals, sometimes on extraconstitutional grounds. The Senate excluded Phillip Thomas on loyalty grounds when it was discovered that he had given money to his son when he became a soldier in the Confederate army. The House refused to seat Brigham H. Roberts because he had been convicted of violating an antipolygamy law.

Investigating the Roberts case, a congressional committee concluded that the Framers "had not foreclosed the right of Congress to establish qualifications for membership other than those mentioned in the Constitution."[9] As Table 3-2 shows, both houses subscribed to this theory. The question of whether the Supreme Court would follow suit remained largely unaddressed until 1969. In that year, the Court decided *Powell v. McCormack*, in which it squarely responded to Congress's traditional approach to seating qualifications. What was the nature of that response?[10] Did the Court simply defer to Congress's wishes?

---

8. Note that this controversy—over the *exclusion* of duly elected members—stems from the first paragraph of Article I, §5. There is not much debate over whether Congress can *censure* or *expel* sitting members. The second paragraph of Article I, §5, is clear on this point: "Each House may determine the Rules of its Proceedings, punish its Members for disorderly Behaviour, and, with the Concurrence of two thirds, expel a member." Although the Supreme Court has not dealt directly with any dispute involving the punishment of members, such as censure or expulsion, it has suggested that this is a broad privilege, best left to the judgment of the individual chambers. See, for example, *In re Chapman* (1897). This kind of action is not something Congress takes with any regularity, particularly disciplining through expulsion; since 1787 it has censured twenty-six members and expelled nineteen.

9. Congressional Quarterly, *Guide to Congress*, 5th ed. (Washington, D.C.: CQ Press, 2000), 920.

10. To hear oral arguments in this case, navigate to: *www.oyez.org/oyez/frontpage.*

Rep. Adam Clayton Powell Jr. gives an impromptu news conference January 9, 1967. That was the year the House of Representatives voted to exclude him from its chambers, even though he had been duly elected to office. In *Powell v. McCormack* (1969) the Court held that because Powell met the constitutional standards for membership, the House could not refuse to seat him.

Powell v. McCormack

395 U.S. 486 (1969)
http://laws.findlaw.com/US/395/486.html
Vote: 7 (Black, Brennan, Douglas, Harlan, Marshall, Warren,
  White)
  1 (Stewart)
Opinion of the Court: Warren
Concurring opinion: Douglas
Dissenting opinion: Stewart

Rep. Adam Clayton Powell Jr. was one of the most interesting and controversial people ever to serve in the U.S. Congress.[11] As pastor of the Abyssinian Baptist Church in Harlem, among the nation's largest congregations, Powell had been a force within that New York City community since the 1930s. This influence only increased when he was elected to the House in 1944 (he received nominations from both the Democratic and Republican parties), and he continued to be reelected by wide margins for the next twenty-five years.

Powell never had problems with his constituents, but his relations with his colleagues were another matter. By the early 1960s he had acquired sufficient seniority to chair the House Committee on Education and Labor, but he had become unpopular. Other House members disliked his opulent, unconventional lifestyle, his unpredictable leadership, and his use of the media to suit his political ends. Moreover, by that time, Powell had become entangled in various legal controversies; for example, he refused to pay damages assessed against him in a defamation of character suit and actively sought to avert efforts to compel him to pay.

The 89th Congress (1965–1966) launched an inquiry into Powell's activities. This investigation yielded two major violations of House rules: Powell had used federal monies to fly a woman staff member with him on trips to his vacation home in the Bahamas and to pay his former wife a salary of $20,000, even though she did not work in either his district or Washington office, in accordance with law. Despite the fact that he had been reelected in November 1966, the House refused to seat Powell pending further investigation.

Four months later, in March 1967, the new investigation reached two conclusions: (1) from a constitutional standpoint, Powell met the requirements for office: he was older than twenty-five, had been a citizen of the United States for seven years, and was an inhabitant of New York; and (2) Powell had sought to evade the fine associated with the defamation of character offense, had misused public funds, and had filed false expenditure reports. The committee recommended that Powell be seated as a member of Congress but that he be censured

---

11. We derive our account of this case largely from Thomas G. Walker, *American Politics and the Constitution* (North Scituate, Mass.: Duxbury Press, 1978), 132.

by the House, fined $40,000, and deprived of his seniority. The House, however, rejected that recommendation and instead adopted by a vote of 307–116 a resolution that excluded Powell from the House and directed Speaker John McCormack to notify the governor of New York that the seat was vacant.

Powell, not one to accept such a decision lying down, responded. He and thirteen constituents filed a lawsuit against McCormack and other members of Congress, claiming that Congress's refusal to seat him violated the letter of the Constitution. In other words, because he met the requirements for office, the House had no choice but to seat him. In his view, Article I, Section 5—"Each House shall be the judge of the Elections, Returns and Qualifications of its own Members"—was not implicated: it gave Congress no authority to exclude members who met the constitutional standards for office.

McCormack's attorneys thought otherwise. In their opinion and in accord with institutional tradition, the Court should read separately the Qualifications Clause and Section 5. They argued that the House has the authority to exclude members, even if they meet constitutional standards. They also asserted that the case presented a political question, which the Court should refrain from answering. Their reasoning? Article I, Section 5, shows a "textually demonstrable constitutional commitment" to the House of the "adjudicatory power" to determine Powell's qualifications. In other words, "the House, and the House alone, has power to determine who is qualified to be a member." This was not, under the political questions argument, an appropriate issue for the Court to consider.[12]

MR. CHIEF JUSTICE WARREN delivered the opinion of the Court.

Respondents maintain that even if this case is otherwise justiciable, it presents only a political question. It is well established that the federal courts will not adjudicate political

questions. In *Baker v. Carr*, we noted that political questions are not justiciable primarily because of the separation of powers within the Federal Government. After reviewing our decisions in this area, we concluded that on the surface of any case held to involve a political question was at least one of the following formulations:

"a textually demonstrable constitutional commitment of the issue to a coordinate political department; or a lack of judicially discoverable and manageable standards for resolving it; or the impossibility of deciding without an initial policy determination of a kind clearly for nonjudicial discretion; or the impossibility of a court's undertaking independent resolution without expressing lack of the respect due coordinate branches of government; or an unusual need for unquestioning adherence to a political decision already made; or the potentiality of embarrassment from multifarious pronouncements by various departments on one question."

Respondents' . . . contention is that this case presents a political question because under Art. I, §5, there has been a "textually demonstrable constitutional commitment" to the House of the "adjudicatory power" to determine Powell's qualifications. Thus it is argued that the House, and the House alone, has power to determine who is qualified to be a member.

In order to determine whether there has been a textual commitment to a coordinate department of the Government, we must interpret the Constitution. In other words, we must first determine what power the Constitution confers upon the House through Art. I, §5, before we can determine to what extent, if any, the exercise of that power is subject to judicial review. Respondents maintain that the House has broad power under §5, and, they argue, the House may determine which are the qualifications necessary for membership. On the other hand, petitioners allege that the Constitution provides that an elected representative may be denied his seat only if the House finds he does not meet one of the standing qualifications expressly prescribed by the Constitution. . . .

In order to determine the scope of any "textual commitment" under Art. I, §5, we necessarily must determine the meaning of the phrase to "be the Judge of the Qualifications of its own Members." Petitioners argue that the records of the debates during the Constitutional Convention; available commentary from the post-Convention, pre-ratification period; and early congressional applications of Art. I, §5, support their construction of the section. Respondents insist, however, that a careful examination of the pre-Convention

---

12. McCormack's attorneys also made a number of more procedurally based claims. For example, after Powell initiated the suit, he was reelected to office. This time the House decided to seat him. Therefore, they argued, the dispute was moot. The Court disagreed and ruled on the merits of Powell's claims. But see Justice Stewart's dissent.

practices of the English Parliament and American colonial assemblies demonstrates that by 1787, a legislature's power to judge the qualifications of its members was generally understood to encompass exclusion or expulsion on the ground that an individual's character or past conduct rendered him unfit to serve. When the Constitution and the debates over its adoption are thus viewed in historical perspective, argue respondents, it becomes clear that the "qualifications" expressly set forth in the Constitution were not meant to limit the long-recognized legislative power to exclude or expel at will, but merely to establish "standing incapacities," which could be altered only by a constitutional amendment. Our examination of the relevant historical materials leads us to the conclusion that petitioners are correct and that the Constitution leaves the House without authority to exclude any person, duly elected by his constituents, who meets all the requirements for membership expressly prescribed in the Constitution. . . .

Relying heavily on Charles Warren's analysis of the Convention debates, petitioners argue that the proceedings manifest the Framers' unequivocal intention to deny either branch of Congress the authority to add to or otherwise vary the membership qualifications expressly set forth in the Constitution. We do not completely agree, for the debates are subject to other interpretations. However, we have concluded that the records of the debates, viewed in the context of the bitter struggle for the right to freely choose representatives which had recently concluded in England and in light of the distinction the Framers made between the power to expel and the power to exclude, indicate that petitioners' ultimate conclusion is correct.

The Convention opened in late May 1787. By the end of July, the delegates adopted, with a minimum of debate, age requirements for membership in both the Senate and the House. The Convention then appointed a Committee of Detail to draft a constitution incorporating these and other resolutions adopted during the preceding months. . . .

On August 10, the Convention considered the Committee of Detail's proposal that the "Legislature of the United States shall have authority to establish such uniform qualifications of the members of each House, with regard to property, as to the said Legislature shall seem expedient." The debate on this proposal discloses much about the views of the Framers on the issue of qualifications. For example,

James Madison urged its rejection, stating that the proposal would vest

"an improper & dangerous power in the Legislature. The qualifications of electors and elected were fundamental articles in a Republican Govt. and ought to be fixed by the Constitution. If the Legislature could regulate those of either, it can by degrees subvert the Constitution. A Republic may be converted into an aristocracy or oligarchy as well by limiting the number capable of being elected, as the number authorized to elect. . . . It was a power also, which might be made subservient to the views of one faction agst. another. Qualifications founded on artificial distinctions may be devised, by the stronger in order to keep out partizans of [a weaker] faction."

Significantly, Madison's argument was not aimed at the imposition of a property qualification as such, but rather at the delegation to the Congress of the discretionary power to establish any qualifications. . . .

In view of what followed Madison's speech, it appears that on this critical day the Framers were facing and then rejecting the possibility that the legislature would have power to usurp the "indisputable right [of the people] to return whom they thought proper" to the legislature. Oliver Ellsworth, of Connecticut, noted that a legislative power to establish property qualifications was exceptional and "dangerous because it would be much more liable to abuse." Gouverneur Morris then moved to strike "with regard to property" from the Committee's proposal. His intention was "to leave the Legislature entirely at large." Hugh Williamson, of North Carolina, expressed concern that if a majority of the legislature should happen to be "composed of any particular description of men, of lawyers for example, . . . the future elections might be secured to their own body." Madison then referred to the British Parliament's assumption of the power to regulate the qualifications of both electors and the elected and noted that "the abuse they had made of it was a lesson worthy of our attention. They had made the changes in both cases subservient to their own views, or to the views of political or Religious parties." Shortly thereafter, the Convention rejected both Gouverneur Morris' motion and the Committee's proposal. Later the same day, the Convention adopted without debate the provision authorizing each House to be "the judge of the . . . qualifications of its own members."

One other decision made the same day is very important to determining the meaning of Art. I, §5. When the delegates reached the Committee of Detail's proposal to empower each House to expel its members, Madison "observed that the right of expulsion . . . was too important to be exercised by a bare majority of a quorum: and in emergencies [one] faction might be dangerously abused." He therefore moved that "with the concurrence of two-thirds" be inserted. With the exception of one State, whose delegation was divided, the motion was unanimously approved without debate, although Gouverneur Morris noted his opposition. The importance of this decision cannot be overemphasized. None of the parties to this suit disputes that prior to 1787 the legislative powers to judge qualifications and to expel were exercised by a majority vote. Indeed, without exception, the English and colonial antecedents to Art. I, §5, cls. 1 and 2, support this conclusion. Thus, the Convention's decision to increase the vote required to expel, because that power was "too important to be exercised by a bare majority," while at the same time not similarly restricting the power to judge qualifications, is compelling evidence that they considered the latter already limited by the standing qualifications previously adopted. . . .

The debates at the state conventions also demonstrate the Framers' understanding that the qualifications for members of Congress had been fixed in the Constitution. Before the New York convention, for example, Hamilton emphasized: "The true principle of a republic is, that the people should choose whom they please to govern them. Representation is imperfect in proportion as the current of popular favor is checked. This great source of free government, popular election, should be perfectly pure, and the most unbounded liberty allowed." In Virginia, where the Federalists faced powerful opposition by advocates of popular democracy, Wilson Carey Nicholas, a future member of both the House and Senate and later Governor of the State, met the arguments that the new Constitution violated democratic principles with the following interpretation of Art. I, §2, cl. 2, as it respects the qualifications of the elected: "It has ever been considered a great security to liberty, that very few should be excluded from the right of being chosen to the legislature. This Constitution has amply attended to this idea. We find no qualifications required except those of age and residence, which create a certainty of their judgment being matured, and of being attached to their state.". . .

As clear as these statements appear, respondents dismiss them as "general statements . . . directed to other issues." They suggest that far more relevant is Congress' own understanding of its power to judge qualifications as manifested in post-ratification exclusion cases. Unquestionably, both the House and the Senate have excluded members-elect for reasons other than their failure to meet the Constitution's standing qualifications. For almost the first 100 years of its existence, however, Congress strictly limited its power to judge the qualifications of its members to those enumerated in the Constitution.

Congress was first confronted with the issue in 1807, when the eligibility of William McCreery was challenged because he did not meet additional residency requirements imposed by the State of Maryland. In recommending that he be seated, the House Committee of Elections reasoned:

"The committee proceeded to examine the Constitution, with relation to the case submitted to them, and to find that qualifications of members are therein determined, without reserving any authority to the State Legislatures to change, add to, or diminish those qualifications; and that, by that instrument, Congress is constituted the sole judge of the qualifications prescribed by it, and are obliged to decide agreeably to the Constitutional rules. . . ." (1807).

Lest there be any misunderstanding of the basis for the committee's recommendation, during the ensuing debate the chairman explained the principles by which the committee was governed:

"The Committee of Elections considered the qualifications of members to have been unalterably determined by the Federal Convention, unless changed by an authority equal to that which framed the Constitution at first; that neither the State nor the Federal Legislatures are vested with authority to add to those qualifications, so as to change them. . . . Congress, by the Federal Constitution, are not authorized to prescribe the qualifications of their own members, but they are authorized to judge of their qualifications; in doing so, however, they must be governed by the rules prescribed by the Federal Constitution, and by them only. These are the principles on which the Election Committee have made up their report, and upon which their resolution is founded."

The chairman emphasized that the committee's narrow construction of the power of the House to judge qualifications was compelled by the "fundamental principle in a free government," that restrictions upon the people to choose their own representatives must be limited to those "absolutely necessary for the safety of the society." At the conclusion of a lengthy debate, which tended to center on the more narrow issue of the power of the States to add to the standing qualifications set forth in the Constitution, the House agreed by a vote of 89 to 18 to seat Congressman McCreery.

There was no significant challenge to these principles for the next several decades. They came under heavy attack, however, "during the stress of civil war [but initially] the House of Representatives declined to exercise the power [to exclude], even under circumstances of great provocation." The abandonment of such restraint, however, was among the casualties of the general upheaval produced in war's wake. From that time until the present, congressional practice has been erratic; and on the few occasions when a member-elect was excluded although he met all the qualifications set forth in the Constitution, there were frequently vigorous dissents. Even the annotations to the official manual of procedure for the 90th Congress manifest doubt as to the House's power to exclude a member-elect who has met the constitutionally prescribed qualifications.

Had these congressional exclusion precedents been more consistent, their precedential value still would be quite limited. That an unconstitutional action has been taken before surely does not render that same action any less unconstitutional at a later date. Particularly in view of the Congress' own doubts in those few cases where it did exclude members-elect, we are not inclined to give its precedents controlling weight. The relevancy of prior exclusion cases is limited largely to the insight they afford in correctly ascertaining the draftsmen's intent. Obviously, therefore, the precedential value of these cases tends to increase in proportion to their proximity to the Convention in 1787. And, what evidence we have of Congress' early understanding confirms our conclusion that the House is without power to exclude any member-elect who meets the Constitution's requirements for membership.

Had the intent of the Framers emerged from these materials with less clarity, we would nevertheless have been compelled to resolve any ambiguity in favor of a narrow construction of the scope of Congress' power to exclude members-elect. A fundamental principle of our representative democracy is, in Hamilton's words, "that the people should choose whom they please to govern them." As Madison pointed out at the Convention, this principle is undermined as much by limiting whom the people can select as by limiting the franchise itself. In apparent agreement with this basic philosophy, the Convention adopted his suggestion limiting the power to expel. To allow essentially that same power to be exercised under the guise of judging qualifications, would be to ignore Madison's warning, and some of Congress' own post–Civil War exclusion cases, against "vesting an improper & dangerous power in the Legislature." Moreover, it would effectively nullify the Convention's decision to require a two-thirds vote for expulsion. Unquestionably, Congress has an interest in preserving its institutional integrity, but in most cases that interest can be sufficiently safeguarded by the exercise of its power to punish its members for disorderly behavior and, in extreme cases, to expel a member with the concurrence of two-thirds. In short, both the intention of the Framers, to the extent it can be determined, and an examination of the basic principles of our democratic system persuade us that the Constitution does not vest in the Congress a discretionary power to deny membership by a majority vote.

For these reasons, we have concluded that Art. I, §5, is at most a "textually demonstrable commitment" to Congress to judge only the qualifications expressly set forth in the Constitution. Therefore, the "textual commitment" formulation of the political question doctrine does not bar federal courts from adjudicating petitioners' claims. . . .

. . . Thus, there is no need to remand this case to determine whether he was entitled to be seated in the 90th Congress. Therefore, we hold that, since Adam Clayton Powell, Jr., was duly elected by the voters of the 18th Congressional District of New York and was not ineligible to serve under any provision of the Constitution, the House was without power to exclude him from its membership. . . .

It is so ordered.

MR. JUSTICE STEWART, dissenting.

I believe that events which have taken place since certiorari was granted in this case on November 18, 1968, have rendered it moot, and that the Court should therefore refrain from deciding the novel, difficult, and delicate constitutional questions which the case presented at its inception.

The essential purpose of this lawsuit by Congressman Powell and members of his constituency was to regain the seat from which he was barred by the 90th Congress. That purpose, however, became impossible of attainment on January 3, 1969, when the 90th Congress passed into history and the 91st Congress came into being. On that date, the petitioners' prayer for a judicial decree restraining enforcement of House Resolution No. 278 and commanding the respondents to admit Congressman Powell to membership in the 90th Congress became incontestably moot.

The petitioners assert that actions of the House of Representatives of the 91st Congress have prolonged the controversy raised by Powell's exclusion and preserved the need for a judicial declaration in this case. I believe, to the contrary, that the conduct of the present House of Representatives confirms the mootness of the petitioners' suit against the 90th Congress. Had Powell been excluded from the 91st Congress, he might argue that there was a "continuing controversy" concerning the exclusion attacked in this case. And such an argument might be sound even though the present House of Representatives is a distinct legislative body rather than a continuation of its predecessor, and though any grievance caused by conduct of the 91st Congress is not redressable in this action. But on January 3, 1969, the House of Representatives of the 91st Congress admitted Congressman Powell to membership, and he now sits as the Representative of the 18th Congressional District of New York. With the 90th Congress terminated and Powell now a member of the 91st, it cannot seriously be contended that there remains a judicial controversy between these parties over the power of the House of Representatives to exclude Powell and the power of a court to order him reseated.

Chief Justice Earl Warren's holding in *Powell* is indisputable: because Powell was duly elected and because he met the constitutional standards for membership, the House could not refuse to seat him. *(For Powell's fate after the Court's decision, see Box 3-1.)* As Warren emphatically noted, "Congress is limited to the standing qualifications prescribed in the Constitution." Note that Warren, on the basis of the intent of the Framers of the Constitution, rejected McCormack's political question argument. But how would you square his decision with Chief Justice William H. Rehnquist's in *Nixon v. United States* (1993), discussed in Chapter 2? Are the two reconcilable or contradictory?

Another question to ask yourself about *Powell* concerns its relevance for one of the more interesting contemporary debates about Article I: Does the U.S. Constitution give states the power to enact term limits for

---

BOX 3-1   AFTERMATH . . . ADAM CLAYTON POWELL JR.

WHILE the House of Representatives debated what to do with him, Adam Clayton Powell Jr. spent most of 1967 on the island of Bimini in the Bahamas. He was unable to return to New York because of his refusal to pay court-ordered damages in a 1963 libel case and a pending contempt of court charge. He ultimately raised sufficient funds to satisfy the judgment and settled the contempt matter.

He ran for his vacated congressional seat in a special election in April 1967 and again in November 1968 regular elections, winning overwhelmingly both times. In January 1969, as the Supreme Court was about to hear arguments in the lawsuit challenging his 1967 exclusion from Congress, the House agreed to seat Powell, but stripped him of his seniority and fined him $25,000 for misuse of funds. As a result, Powell lost his position as chair of the House Committee on Education and Labor, a primary source of his political power.

About this same time Powell was diagnosed with cancer. Weakened by treatments for the disease, he ran for reelection in 1970, but was defeated by a 150-vote margin in the Democratic primary by Charles Rangel. The loss ended Powell's quarter century of service in Congress. In 1971 Powell, in declining health, retired from the pulpit of Harlem's Abyssinian Baptist Church and wrote his autobiography. He died on April 4, 1972, in Miami, Florida, at age sixty-four.

SOURCE: *American National Biography*, vol. 17 (New York: Oxford University Press, 1999), 773–775.

---

members of the U.S. Congress? Opponents of term limits point to Article I's qualification clauses and use *Powell* to argue that those clauses fix the requirements for office—requirements that neither Congress nor the states may alter. Supporters, as noted below, offer a number of counterarguments to *Powell*. In 1995 the Supreme Court entered the fray in *U.S. Term Limits, Inc. v. Thornton*.[13]

13. To hear oral arguments in this case, navigate to: *www.oyez.org/oyez/frontpage.*

U.S. Term Limits, Inc. v. Thornton

514 U.S. 779 (1995)
http://laws.findlaw.com/US/514/779.html
Vote: 5 (Breyer, Ginsburg, Kennedy, Souter, Stevens)
      4 (O'Connor, Rehnquist, Scalia, Thomas)
Opinion of the Court: Stevens
Concurring opinion: Kennedy
Dissenting opinion: Thomas

In 1990 Colorado became the first state to limit terms for federal officeholders. Subsequently, twenty-three additional states passed term limit initiatives. *Thornton* involved one of those initiatives. It originated in Arkansas, where in 1992 voters approved an amendment to the state constitution (Amendment 73), prohibiting from the ballot anyone seeking reelection who previously had served two terms in the U.S. Senate or three terms in the U.S. House of Representatives. It permitted anyone to be elected as a write-in candidate, presumably as a way of allowing for the reelection of a popular incumbent.

Arkansas voters approved the amendment in 1992, and it was to apply to all persons seeking reelection after January 1, 1993. But, about two months before that date, the League of Women Voters and various citizens of Arkansas, including U.S. representative Ray Thornton, filed suit asking a state court to declare the amendment unconstitutional. Among the arguments they made in this court and later in the Arkansas Supreme Court was that Amendment 73 violated Article I of the U.S. Constitution. In particular, based on *Powell v. McCormack*, they claimed that the federal Constitution establishes the sole qualifications for federal office, and the states may not alter them. In response, the state and U.S. Term Limits, an organization supporting the amendment, made a number of arguments. First, they pointed to Section 4 of Article I, which says: "The Times, Places and Manner of holding Elections for Senators and Representatives, shall be prescribed in each State by the Legislature thereof." In their view, this section—and not the Qualifications Clauses—was applicable because term limits seek to regulate access to the ballot, not qualifications for office. Second, they suggested that *Powell* spoke only

about the ability of the U.S. House of Representatives, not of the states, to set qualifications. Finally, because the Constitution does not explicitly prohibit the states from setting qualifications for office, it is a power reserved to them under the Tenth Amendment.

The Arkansas courts disagreed. The lower court struck down the amendment as a violation of Article I of the U.S. Constitution and, in 1994, the Arkansas Supreme Court affirmed. According to the justices, "The qualifications clauses fix the sole requirement for congressional service. This is not a power left to the states." With this defeat in hand, amendment proponents appealed to the U.S. Supreme Court, which agreed to hear the case.

In the meantime, the notion of term limits was moving even further into the national spotlight. In the Contract with America, a majority of Republicans seeking election in 1994 promised that they would guarantee a vote on a term limits initiative if their party gained control of the House. This pledge made political sense: about 80 percent of Americans favored placing limits on congressional tenures.

After they gained control of Congress, the Republican leadership tried to make good on the promise. In March 1995, before the Supreme Court issued its opinion in *Thornton*, the House considered four constitutional amendment proposals. Although they differed in their specific provisions, each would have limited the number of terms that senators and representatives could serve. Because these proposals were framed as constitutional amendments, a two-thirds vote was required for any one to gain approval. After several days of debate, the House voted. None of the proposals obtained sufficient support to pass. Not surprisingly, the members of the House were unwilling to pass self-imposed limits on the number of terms they could serve.

Despite these losses, the Republican leaders still hoped that the Supreme Court would decide *Thornton* in favor of state term limit initiatives. It was ironic that Republicans pinned their hopes on the Court because they had deliberately chosen the constitutional amendment route (as opposed to a term limits law) to supersede an anti–term limits Supreme Court ruling. But, when the

Court issued its opinion on May 22, 1995, it was clear that the Republican leadership had suffered another setback: in a 5–4 decision, the justices struck down Arkansas's Amendment 73.

As you read the majority opinion, compare it with Chief Justice Warren's in *Powell v. McCormack*: Does the rationale used by the majority in *Thornton* square with the reasoning in *Powell?* Also pay close attention to the way that both the majority and dissenting opinions deal with the intent of the Framers. Is *Thornton* yet another example of the difficulty of applying this mode of analysis to actual cases? Finally, consider this question: Do you think the Court would have arrived at a different answer had the House mustered the votes to propose a term-limits amendment?

JUSTICE STEVENS delivered the opinion of the Court.

Today's cases present a challenge to an amendment to the Arkansas State Constitution that prohibits the name of an otherwise-eligible candidate for Congress from appearing on the general election ballot if that candidate has already served three terms in the House of Representatives or two terms in the Senate. The Arkansas Supreme Court held that the amendment violates the Federal Constitution. We agree with that holding. Such a state-imposed restriction is contrary to the "fundamental principle of our representative democracy," embodied in the Constitution, that "the people should choose whom they please to govern them." *Powell v. McCormack* (1969). Allowing individual States to adopt their own qualifications for congressional service would be inconsistent with the Framers' vision of a uniform National Legislature representing the people of the United States. If the qualifications set forth in the text of the Constitution are to be changed, that text must be amended. . . .

As the opinions of the Arkansas Supreme Court suggest, the constitutionality of Amendment 73 depends critically on the resolution of two distinct issues. The first is whether the Constitution forbids States from adding to or altering the qualifications specifically enumerated in the Constitution. The second is, if the Constitution does so forbid, whether the fact that Amendment 73 is formulated as a ballot access restriction rather than as an outright disqualification is of constitutional significance. Our resolution of these issues draws upon our prior resolution of a related but distinct issue: whether Congress has the power to add to or alter the qualifications of its Members.

Twenty-six years ago, in *Powell v. McCormack*, we reviewed the history and text of the Qualifications Clauses in a case involving an attempted exclusion of a duly elected Member of Congress. The principal issue was whether the power granted to each House in Art. I, §5, to judge the "Qualifications of its own Members" includes the power to impose qualifications other than those set forth in the text of the Constitution. In an opinion by Chief Justice Warren for eight Members of the Court, we held that it does not. Because of the obvious importance of the issue, the Court's review of the history and meaning of the relevant constitutional text was especially thorough. We therefore begin our analysis today with a . . . statement of what we decided in that case. . . .

Powell . . . establishes two important propositions: first, that the "relevant historical materials" compel the conclusion that, at least with respect to qualifications imposed by Congress, the Framers intended the qualifications listed in the Constitution to be exclusive; and second, that that conclusion is equally compelled by an understanding of the "fundamental principle of our representative democracy . . . 'that the people should choose whom they please to govern them.' "

Petitioners argue somewhat half-heartedly that the narrow holding in *Powell*, which involved the power of the House to exclude a member pursuant to Art. I, §5, does not control the more general question whether Congress has the power to add qualifications. *Powell*, however, is not susceptible to such a narrow reading. Our conclusion that Congress may not alter or add to the qualifications in the Constitution was integral to our analysis and outcome. Only two Terms ago we confirmed this understanding of *Powell* in *Nixon v. United States* (1993). After noting that the three qualifications for membership specified in Art. I, §2, are of "a precise, limited nature" and "unalterable by the legislature," we explained:

"Our conclusion in *Powell* was based on the fixed meaning of 'qualifications' set forth in Art I, §2. The claim by the House that its power to 'be the Judge of the Elections, Returns and Qualifications of its own Members' was a textual commitment of unreviewable authority was defeated by the existence of this separate provision specifying the only qualifications which might be imposed for House membership."

Unsurprisingly, the state courts and lower federal courts have similarly concluded that *Powell* conclusively resolved the issue whether Congress has the power to impose additional qualifications.

In sum, after examining *Powell's* historical analysis and its articulation of the "basic principles of our democratic system," we reaffirm that the qualifications for service in Congress set forth in the text of the Constitution are "fixed," at least in the sense that they may not be supplemented by Congress.

Our reaffirmation of *Powell*, does not necessarily resolve the specific questions presented in these cases. For petitioners argue that whatever the constitutionality of additional qualifications for membership imposed by Congress, the historical and textual materials discussed in *Powell* do not support the conclusion that the Constitution prohibits additional qualifications imposed by States. In the absence of such a constitutional prohibition, petitioners argue, the Tenth Amendment and the principle of reserved powers require that States be allowed to add such qualifications.

Before addressing these arguments, we find it appropriate to take note of the striking unanimity among the courts that have considered the issue. None of the overwhelming array of briefs submitted by the parties and amici has called to our attention even a single case in which a state court or federal court has approved of a State's addition of qualifications for a member of Congress. To the contrary, an impressive number of courts have determined that States lack the authority to add qualifications. . . . This impressive and uniform body of judicial decisions . . . indicates that the obstacles confronting petitioners are formidable indeed.

Petitioners argue that the Constitution contains no express prohibition against state-added qualifications, and that Amendment 73 is therefore an appropriate exercise of a State's reserved power to place additional restrictions on the choices that its own voters may make. We disagree for two independent reasons. First, we conclude that the power to add qualifications is not within the "original powers" of the States, and thus is not reserved to the States by the Tenth Amendment. Second, even if States possessed some original power in this area, we conclude that the Framers intended the Constitution to be the exclusive source of qualifications for members of Congress, and that the Framers thereby "divested" States of any power to add qualifications. . . .

Contrary to petitioners' assertions, the power to add qualifications is not part of the original powers of sovereignty that the Tenth Amendment reserved to the States. Petitioners' Tenth Amendment argument misconceives the nature of the right at issue because that Amendment could only "reserve" that which existed before. As Justice Story recognized, "the states can exercise no powers whatsoever, which exclusively spring out of the existence of the national government, which the constitution does not delegate to them. . . . No state can say, that it has reserved, what it never possessed.". . .

With respect to setting qualifications for service in Congress, no such right existed before the Constitution was ratified. The contrary argument overlooks the revolutionary character of the government that the Framers conceived. Prior to the adoption of the Constitution, the States joined together under the Articles of Confederation. In that system, "the States retained most of their sovereignty, like independent nations bound together only by treaties." After the Constitutional Convention convened, the Framers were presented with, and eventually adopted a variation of, "a plan not merely to amend the Articles of Confederation but to create an entirely new government with a National Executive, National Judiciary, and a National Legislature." In adopting that plan, the Framers envisioned a uniform national system, rejecting the notion that the Nation was a collection of States, and instead creating a direct link between the National Government and the people of the United States. In that National Government, representatives owe primary allegiance not to the people of a State but to the people of a Nation. . . .

In short, as the Framers recognized, electing representatives to the National Legislature was a new right, arising from the Constitution itself. The Tenth Amendment thus provides no basis for concluding that the States possess reserved power to add qualifications to those that are fixed in the Constitution. Instead, any state power to set the qualifications for membership in Congress must derive not from the reserved powers of state sovereignty, but rather from the delegated powers of national sovereignty. In the absence of any constitutional delegation to the States of power to add qualifications to those enumerated in the Constitution, such a power does not exist.

Even if we believed that States possessed as part of their original powers some control over congressional qualifications, the text and structure of the Constitution, the relevant historical materials, and, most importantly, the "basic principles of our democratic system" all demonstrate that the Qualifications Clauses were intended to preclude the States from exercising any such power and to fix as exclusive the qualifications in the Constitution.

Much of the historical analysis was undertaken by the Court in *Powell*. There is, however, additional historical evidence that pertains directly to the power of States. That evidence, though perhaps not as extensive as that reviewed in *Powell*, leads unavoidably to the conclusion that the States lack the power to add qualifications.

The available affirmative evidence indicates the Framers' intent that States have no role in the setting of qualifications. In Federalist Paper No. 52, dealing with the House of Representatives, Madison addressed the "qualifications of the electors and the elected." Madison first noted the difficulty in achieving uniformity in the qualifications for electors, which resulted in the Framers' decision to require only that the qualifications for federal electors be the same as those for state electors. Madison argued that such a decision "must be satisfactory to every State, because it is comfortable to the standard already established, or which may be established, by the State itself." Madison then explicitly contrasted the state control over the qualifications of electors with the lack of state control over the qualifications of the elected:

"The qualifications of the elected, being less carefully and properly defined by the State constitutions, and being at the same time more susceptible of uniformity, have been very properly considered and regulated by the convention. A representative of the United States must be of the age of twenty-five years; must have been seven years a citizen of the United States; must, at the time of his election be an inhabitant of the State he is to represent; and, during the time of his service must be in no office under the United States. Under these reasonable limitations, the door of this part of the federal government is open to merit of every description, whether native or adoptive, whether young or old, and without regard to poverty or wealth, or to any particular profession of religious faith." . . .

We also find compelling the complete absence in the ratification debates of any assertion that States had the power to add qualifications. In those debates, the question whether to require term limits, or "rotation," was a major source of controversy. The draft of the Constitution that was submitted for ratification contained no provision for rotation. In arguments that echo in the preamble to Arkansas' Amendment 73, opponents of ratification condemned the absence of a rotation requirement, noting that "there is no doubt that senators will hold their office perpetually; and in this situation, they must of necessity lose their dependence, and their attachments to the people." Even proponents of ratification expressed concern about the "abandonment in every instance of the necessity of rotation in office." At several ratification conventions, participants proposed amendments that would have required rotation.

The Federalists' responses to those criticisms and proposals addressed the merits of the issue, arguing that rotation was incompatible with the people's right to choose. . . . Hamilton argued that the representatives' need for reelection rather than mandatory rotation was the more effective way to keep representatives responsive to the people, because "when a man knows he must quit his station, let his merit be what it may, he will turn his attention chiefly to his own emolument."

Regardless of which side has the better of the debate over rotation, it is most striking that nowhere in the extensive ratification debates have we found any statement by either a proponent or an opponent of rotation that the draft constitution would permit States to require rotation for the representatives of their own citizens. If the participants in the debate had believed that the States retained the authority to impose term limits, it is inconceivable that the Federalists would not have made this obvious response to the arguments of the pro-rotation forces. The absence in an otherwise freewheeling debate of any suggestion that States had the power to impose additional qualifications unquestionably reflects the Framers' common understanding that States lacked that power.

In short, if it had been assumed that States could add additional qualifications, that assumption would have provided the basis for a powerful rebuttal to the arguments being advanced. The failure of intelligent and experienced advocates to utilize this argument must reflect a general agreement that its premise was unsound, and that the power to add qualifications was one that the Constitution denied the States. . . .

Our conclusion that States lack the power to impose qualifications vindicates the same "fundamental principle of our representative democracy" that we recognized in *Powell*, namely that "the people should choose whom they please to govern them."

... [T]he *Powell* Court recognized that an egalitarian ideal—that election to the National Legislature should be open to all people of merit—provided a critical foundation for the Constitutional structure. This egalitarian theme echoes throughout the constitutional debates. In Federalist Paper No. 57, for example, Madison wrote:

"Who are to be the objects of popular choice? Every citizen whose merit may recommend him to the esteem and confidence of his country. No qualification of wealth, of birth, of religious faith, or of civil profession is permitted to fetter the judgment or disappoint the inclination of the people.". . .

Similarly, we believe that state-imposed qualifications, as much as congressionally imposed qualifications, would undermine the second critical idea recognized in *Powell*: that an aspect of sovereignty is the right of the people to vote for whom they wish. Again, the source of the qualification is of little moment in assessing the qualification's restrictive impact.

Finally, state-imposed restrictions, unlike the congressionally imposed restrictions at issue in *Powell*, violate a third idea central to this basic principle: that the right to choose representatives belongs not to the States, but to the people. . . .

The Framers deemed this principle critical when they discussed qualifications. For example, during the debates on residency requirements, [Gouverneur] Morris noted that in the House, "the people at large, not the States, are represented." Similarly, George Read noted that the Framers "were forming a National Government and such a regulation would correspond little with the idea that we were one people." James Wilson "enforced the same consideration.". . .

Petitioners attempt to overcome this ... evidence against the States' power to impose qualifications by arguing that the practice of the States immediately after the adoption of the Constitution demonstrates their understanding that they possessed such power. One may properly question the extent to which the States' own practice is a reliable indicator of the contours of restrictions that the Constitution imposed on States, especially when no court has ever upheld a state-imposed qualification of any sort. . . . But petitioners' argument is unpersuasive even on its own terms. At the time of the Convention, "almost all the State Constitutions required members of their Legislatures to possess considerable property." Despite this near uniformity, only one State, Virginia, placed similar restrictions on members of Congress, requiring that a representative be, inter alia, a "freeholder." Just 15 years after imposing a property qualification, Virginia replaced that requirement with a provision requiring that representatives be only "qualified according to the constitution of the United States.". . .

In sum, the available historical and textual evidence, read in light of the basic principles of democracy underlying the Constitution and recognized by this Court in *Powell*, reveal the Framers' intent that neither Congress nor the States should possess the power to supplement the exclusive qualifications set forth in the text of the Constitution.

Petitioners argue that, even if States may not add qualifications, Amendment 73 is constitutional because it is not such a qualification, and because Amendment 73 is a permissible exercise of state power to regulate the "Times, Places and Manner of Holding Elections." We reject these contentions.

Unlike §1 and §2 of Amendment 73, which create absolute bars to service for long-term incumbents running for state office, §3 merely provides that certain Senators and Representatives shall not be certified as candidates and shall not have their names appear on the ballot. They may run as write-in candidates and, if elected, they may serve. Petitioners contend that only a legal bar to service creates an impermissible qualification, and that Amendment 73 is therefore consistent with the Constitution. . . .

We need not decide whether petitioners' narrow understanding of qualifications is correct because, even if it is, Amendment 73 may not stand. As we have often noted, " 'constitutional rights would be of little value if they could be ... indirectly denied.' " The Constitution "nullifies sophisticated as well as simple-minded modes" of infringing on Constitutional protections.

In our view, Amendment 73 is an indirect attempt to accomplish what the Constitution prohibits Arkansas from accomplishing directly. As the plurality opinion of the Arkansas Supreme Court recognized, Amendment 73 is an "effort to dress eligibility to stand for Congress in ballot access clothing," because the "intent and the effect of Amendment 73 are to disqualify congressional incumbents from further service." We must, of course, accept the State Court's view of the purpose of its own law: we are thus authoritatively informed that the sole purpose of §3 of Amendment 73 was to attempt to achieve a result that is forbidden by the Federal Constitution. Indeed, it cannot be seriously contended that the intent behind Amendment 73 is other than to prevent the election of incumbents. The preamble of Amendment 73 states explicitly: "The people of Arkansas . . . herein limit the terms of elected officials." Sections 1 and 2 create absolute limits on the number of terms that may be served. There is no hint that §3 was intended to have any other purpose.

Petitioners do, however, contest the Arkansas Supreme Court's conclusion that the Amendment has the same practical effect as an absolute bar. They argue that the possibility of a write-in campaign creates a real possibility for victory, especially for an entrenched incumbent. One may reasonably question the merits of that contention. Indeed, we are advised by the state court that there is nothing more than a faint glimmer of possibility that the excluded candidate will win. Our prior cases, too, have suggested that write-in candidates have only a slight chance of victory. But even if petitioners are correct that incumbents may occasionally win reelection as write-in candidates, there is no denying that the ballot restrictions will make it significantly more difficult for the barred candidate to win the election. In our view, an amendment with the avowed purpose and obvious effect of evading the requirements of the Qualifications Clauses by handicapping a class of candidates cannot stand. . . .

The merits of term limits, or "rotation," have been the subject of debate since the formation of our Constitution, when the Framers unanimously rejected a proposal to add such limits to the Constitution. The cogent arguments on both sides of the question that were articulated during the process of ratification largely retain their force today. Over half the States have adopted measures that impose such limits on some offices either directly or indirectly, and the Nation as a whole, notably by constitutional amendment, has imposed a limit on the number of terms that the President may serve. Term limits, like any other qualification for office, unquestionably restrict the ability of voters to vote for whom they wish. On the other hand, such limits may provide for the infusion of fresh ideas and new perspectives, and may decrease the likelihood that representatives will lose touch with their constituents. It is not our province to resolve this longstanding debate.

We are, however, firmly convinced that allowing the several States to adopt term limits for congressional service would effect a fundamental change in the constitutional framework. Any such change must come not by legislation adopted either by Congress or by an individual State, but rather—as have other important changes in the electoral process—through the Amendment procedures set forth in Article V. The Framers decided that the qualifications for service in the Congress of the United States be fixed in the Constitution and be uniform throughout the Nation. That decision reflects the Framers' understanding that Members of Congress are chosen by separate constituencies, but that they become, when elected, servants of the people of the United States. They are not merely delegates appointed by separate, sovereign States; they occupy offices that are integral and essential components of a single National Government. In the absence of a properly passed constitutional amendment, allowing individual States to craft their own qualifications for Congress would thus erode the structure envisioned by the Framers, a structure that was designed, in the words of the Preamble to our Constitution, to form a "more perfect Union."

The judgment is affirmed.

It is so ordered.

JUSTICE THOMAS, with whom THE CHIEF JUSTICE, JUSTICE O'CONNOR, and JUSTICE SCALIA join, dissenting.

It is ironic that the Court bases today's decision on the right of the people to "choose whom they please to govern them." Under our Constitution, there is only one State whose people have the right to "choose whom they please" to represent Arkansas in Congress. The Court holds, however, that neither the elected legislature of that State nor the people themselves (acting by ballot initiative) may prescribe any qualifications for those representatives. The majority therefore defends the right of the people of Arkansas to "choose whom they please to govern them" by invalidating a provision that won nearly 60% of the votes cast in a direct election and that carried every congressional district in the State.

I dissent. Nothing in the Constitution deprives the people of each State of the power to prescribe eligibility requirements for the candidates who seek to represent them in Congress. The Constitution is simply silent on this question. And where the Constitution is silent, it raises no bar to action by the States or the people.

Because the majority fundamentally misunderstands the notion of "reserved" powers, I start with some first principles. Contrary to the majority's suggestion, the people of the States need not point to any affirmative grant of power in the Constitution in order to prescribe qualifications for their representatives in Congress, or to authorize their elected state legislators to do so.

Our system of government rests on one overriding principle: all power stems from the consent of the people. To phrase the principle in this way, however, is to be imprecise about something important to the notion of "reserved" powers. The ultimate source of the Constitution's authority is the consent of the people of each individual State, not the consent of the undifferentiated people of the Nation as a whole. . . .

When they adopted the Federal Constitution, of course, the people of each State surrendered some of their authority to the United States (and hence to entities accountable to the people of other States as well as to themselves). They affirmatively deprived their States of certain powers and they affirmatively conferred certain powers upon the Federal Government. Because the people of the several States are the only true source of power, however, the Federal Government enjoys no authority beyond what the Constitution confers: the Federal Government's powers are limited and enumerated. In the words of Justice Black, "the United States is entirely a creature of the Constitution. Its power and authority have no other source."

In each State, the remainder of the people's powers—"the powers not delegated to the United States by the Constitution, nor prohibited by it to the States,"—are either delegated to the state government or retained by the people. The Federal Constitution does not specify which of these two possibilities obtains; it is up to the various state constitutions to declare which powers the people of each State have delegated to their state government. As far as the Federal Constitution is concerned, then, the States can exercise all powers that the Constitution does not withhold from them. The Federal Government and the States thus face different default rules: where the Constitution is silent about the exercise of a particular power—that is, where the Constitution does not speak either expressly or by necessary implication—the Federal Government lacks that power and the States enjoy it.

These basic principles are enshrined in the Tenth Amendment, which declares that all powers neither delegated to the Federal Government nor prohibited to the States "are reserved to the States respectively, or to the people." With this careful last phrase, the Amendment avoids taking any position on the division of power between the state governments and the people of the States: it is up to the people of each State to determine which "reserved" powers their state government may exercise. . . .

The majority begins by announcing an enormous and untenable limitation on the principle expressed by the Tenth Amendment. According to the majority, the States possess only those powers that the Constitution affirmatively grants to them or that they enjoyed before the Constitution was adopted; the Tenth Amendment "could only 'reserve' that which existed before." From the fact that the States had not previously enjoyed any powers over the particular institutions of the Federal Government established by the Constitution, the majority derives a rule precisely opposite to the one that the Amendment actually prescribes: " 'The states can exercise no powers whatsoever, which exclusively spring out of the existence of the national government, which the constitution does not delegate to them.' "

. . . Given the fundamental principle that all governmental powers stem from the people of the States, it would simply be incoherent to assert that the people of the States could not reserve any powers that they had not previously controlled.

The Tenth Amendment's use of the word "reserved" does not help the majority's position. If someone says that the power to use a particular facility is reserved to some group, he is not saying anything about whether that group has previously used the facility. He is merely saying that the people who control the facility have designated that group as the entity with authority to use it. The Tenth Amendment is similar: the people of the States, from whom all governmental powers stem, have specified that all powers not prohibited to the States by the Federal Constitution are reserved "to the States respectively, or to the people."

The majority is therefore quite wrong to conclude that the people of the States cannot authorize their state governments to exercise any powers that were unknown to the States when the Federal Constitution was drafted. Indeed, the majority's position frustrates the apparent purpose of the Amendment's final phrase. The Amendment does not pre-empt any limitations on state power found in the state constitutions, as it might have done if it simply had said that the powers not delegated to the Federal Government are reserved to the States. But the Amendment also does not prevent the people of the States from amending their state constitutions to remove limitations that were in effect when the Federal Constitution and the Bill of Rights were ratified. . . .

I take it to be established, then, that the people of Arkansas do enjoy "reserved" powers over the selection of their representatives in Congress. . . . Whatever one might think of the wisdom of this arrangement, we may not override the decision of the people of Arkansas unless something in the Federal Constitution deprives them of the power to enact such measures.

The majority settles on "the Qualifications Clauses" as the constitutional provisions that Amendment 73 violates. . . . [T]he Qualifications Clauses are merely straightforward recitations of the minimum eligibility requirements that the Framers thought it essential for every Member of Congress to meet. They restrict state power only in that they prevent the States from abolishing all eligibility requirements for membership in Congress. . . .

. . . To the extent that they bear on this case, the records of the Philadelphia Convention affirmatively support my unwillingness to find hidden meaning in the Qualifications Clauses, while the surviving records from the ratification debates help neither side. As for the postratification period, five States supplemented the constitutional disqualifications in their very first election laws. The historical evidence thus refutes any notion that the Qualifications Clauses were generally understood to be exclusive. Yet the majority must establish just such an understanding in order to justify its position that the Clauses impose unstated prohibitions on the States and the people. In my view, the historical evidence is simply inadequate to warrant the majority's conclusion that the Qualifications Clauses mean anything more than what they say.

The decision in *U.S. Term Limits v. Thornton*, coupled with the *Powell* ruling, authoritatively settled the issue of qualifications for congressional office. The Constitution's age, residency, and citizenship requirements are a complete statement of congressional eligibility standards. Neither Congress nor the states may add to or delete from those requirements. According to the Court, such alterations on members of the federal legislature could be imposed only by constitutional amendment.

The term limit question, however, remained a hot political topic—so much so that at least one state took direct action to circumvent the Court's decision. In response to *Thornton*, voters in Missouri adopted an amendment (Article VIII) to their state constitution with the aim of bringing about a "congressional term limits amendment" to the federal constitution. Article VIII required that the words DISREGARDED VOTERS' INSTRUCTION ON TERM LIMITS be put on the ballot near the name of any incumbent who had not supported proposed term limits, and that the words DECLINED TO PLEDGE TO SUPPORT TERM LIMITS be printed on the ballot near the names of nonincumbents who refused to take a pledge in support of term limits. Donald Gralike, a nonincumbent candidate for the U.S. House of Representatives, challenged Missouri's Article VIII on federal constitutional grounds. And, in the case of *Cook v. Gralike* (2001), he prevailed before the U.S. Supreme Court. Writing for the Court, Justice John Paul Stevens relied on the logic of his majority opinion in *Thornton* to conclude that this was an unconstitutional effort on the part of a state to add qualifications for office.

Speech or Debate Clause

The Constitution provides mechanisms for Congress to discipline its members, but it also contains a safeguard against harassment or intimidation. Article I, Section 6, specifies:

The Senators and Representatives . . . shall in all Cases, except Treason, Felony, and Breach of the Peace, be privileged from Arrest during their Attendance at the Session of their respective Houses, and in going to and returning from the same; and for any Speech or Debate in either House, they shall not be questioned in any other Place.

Called the Speech or Debate Clause, this privilege of membership emanates from British practice. The English Parliament, during its struggles with the Crown, asserted that its members were immune from arrest during its sessions, and the English Bill of Rights embodies this guarantee. The importance of the Speech or Debate Clause's protection is undeniable: without it, a president could order the arrest of, or otherwise intimidate, members of Congress who disagreed with the administration. The

Framers thought the statement was necessary "to protect the integrity of the legislative process by insuring the independence of individual legislators." [14] Other countries apparently share this sentiment. Whether in their constitutions or by law, many democracies throughout the world provide similar protection for their legislators (see Box 3-2).

The language of Section 6 of the U.S. Constitution has generated two kinds of constitutional questions: What is protected, and who is protected? Its reach was first addressed by the Court in *Kilbourn v. Thompson* (1881). In *Kilbourn* the Court dealt primarily with the scope of congressional investigations, but it also noted that the clause extends to

written reports presented . . . by its committees, to resolutions offered, which, though in writing, must be reproduced in speech, and to the act of voting, whether it is done vocally or by passing between the tellers. In short, to things generally done in a session [of Congress] by one of its members in relation to the business before it.

With only some minor modifications, *Kilbourn* remained the Court's most significant statement on the Speech or Debate Clause until 1972, when *Gravel v. United States* was decided. This case had important implications for both dimensions of Section 6: Who and what are protected? [15]

Gravel v. United States

408 U.S. 606 (1972)
http://laws.findlaw.com/US/408/606.html
Vote: 5 (Blackmun, Burger, Powell, Rehnquist, White)
    4 (Brennan, Douglas, Marshall, Stewart)
Opinion of the Court: White
Dissenting opinions: Brennan, Douglas
Dissenting in part: Stewart

On June 29, 1971, Sen. Mike Gravel, D-Alaska, held a public meeting of the Subcommittee on Buildings and Grounds of which he was the chair. Before the hearing

---

BOX 3-2   PRIVILEGES AND IMMUNITIES FOR LEGISLATORS IN GLOBAL PERSPECTIVE

M OST democracies provide protection for legislators similar to the U.S. Constitution's Speech or Debate Clause, but these countries have put their own twists on it. In Austria, for example, legal action may be taken against members of parliament (MPs) only if the matter is unconnected with political activity. If it is connected, the state or other authority must get the permission of the MP's chamber before it brings action. Belgium provides its MPs with full immunity from arrest, unless the MP is caught in the act or his or her chamber approves. Moreover, parliament can vote to prohibit the arrest while it is in session.

Brazil and Israel go one step further. Brazil's members of Congress enjoy immunity over a full range of offenses—from homicides to libel. Only by a vote of a majority of the member's house can that immunity be stripped (which almost never occurs), and only the Supreme Court can try legislators. An Israeli law of 1951 covers parliamentary immunity: members of its legislature "shall not be held civilly or criminally responsible, and shall be immune from legal action," for a range of behavior pertaining to or having as its purpose "the fulfillment of his mandate as a member" of the legislature. Apparently, the law is phrased so broadly that it gives members a great deal of protection. And, as is the case in other countries, members are absolutely immune from arrest unless they are caught committing a crime. Authorities cannot hold the member for more than ten days unless the legislature revokes the member's immunity.

Some countries do provide mechanisms for redress for people who feel they have been hurt by legislators. Australia provides an interesting example. Although members of its Parliament are immune from defamation suits for statements they make on the floor, its Senate allows people to request that body to allow them to reply to the statement in the Senate's published record.

SOURCE: George Thomas Kurian, *World Encyclopedia of Parliaments and Legislatures* (Washington, D.C.: Congressional Quarterly, 1998).

---

14. *United States v. Brewster* (1972).
15. To hear arguments in this case, navigate to: *www.oyez.org/oyez/frontpage.*

began, Gravel made a statement about the Vietnam War, noting that it was "relevant to his subcommittee . . . because of its effects upon the domestic economy and . . . the lack of federal funds to provide for adequate public facilities." He then read portions of a classified government document, now known as the Pentagon Papers, which provided details of U.S. involvement in the war. After he finished, Gravel introduced the forty-seven-volume document into the committee's record and "arranged, without any personal profit to himself, for its verbatim publication by Beacon Press," a publishing division of the Unitarian Universalist Association. At the time, there were also reports in the press that members of Gravel's staff had talked with Howard Webber, director of MIT Press, about possible publication of the documents.

The Justice Department began an investigation to determine how the Pentagon Papers were released. It requested a district court judge to convene a grand jury, which in turn subpoenaed Dr. Leonard Rodberg, an aide to Senator Gravel; Webber; and, later, the publisher of Beacon Press. Rodberg and Gravel asked the court to quash the subpoena. In their view, U.S. attorneys "intended to interrogate Dr. Rodberg" about "the actions of Senator Gravel and his aides in making available" the Pentagon Papers. Such interrogation, they argued, would violate the Speech or Debate Clause because its scope extended to aides. As Gravel's attorney later noted, "Given the realities of the modern-day legislative process, congressmen must seek the advice and assistance of persons outside the immediate staff." Forcing Rodberg to testify would be tantamount to having Gravel do so: they were both protected. He made a similar claim when prosecutors sought to force Webber and the publisher of Beacon Press to testify. In particular, he asserted that his arrangements for private publication of the documents also came under the protection of the Speech or Debate Clause, since those documents had been introduced in Congress.

At first, the government rejected all those claims; it even argued that Gravel's actions remained outside of constitutional protections. By the time the case reached the Supreme Court, however, the government had limited its arguments to Gravel's aide and the publisher. It asserted that the language of the Speech or Debate Clause, past precedents, and the intent of the Framers all pointed to the same conclusion: its reach covered neither congressional aides nor arrangements with private publishers, even for material introduced into a subcommittee record. *Gravel v. United States* presented the Court with the two classic questions: Who and what are covered under the Speech or Debate Clause?

Opinion of the Court by MR. JUSTICE WHITE. . . .

[T]he United States strongly urges that because the Speech or Debate Clause confers a privilege only upon "Senators and Representatives," Rodberg himself has no valid claim to constitutional immunity from grand jury inquiry. In our view, both courts below correctly rejected this position. We agree with the Court of Appeals that for the purpose of construing the privilege a Member and his aide are to be "treated as one.". . . [I]t is literally impossible, in view of the complexities of the modern legislative process, . . . for Members of Congress to perform their legislative tasks without the help of aides and assistants; the day-to-day work of such aides is so critical to the Members' performance that they must be treated as the latter's alter egos; and that if they are not so recognized, the central role of the Speech or Debate Clause—to prevent intimidation of legislators by the Executive and accountability before a possibly hostile judiciary—will inevitably be diminished and frustrated. . . .

Rather than giving the clause a cramped construction, the Court has sought to implement its fundamental purpose of freeing the legislator from executive and judicial oversight that realistically threatens to control his conduct as a legislator. We have little doubt that we are neither exceeding our judicial powers nor mistakenly construing the Constitution by holding that the Speech or Debate Clause applies not only to a Member but also to his aides insofar as the conduct of the latter would be a protected legislative act if performed by the Member himself. . . .

The United States fears the abuses that history reveals have occurred when legislators are invested with the power to relieve others from the operation of otherwise valid civil and criminal laws. But these abuses . . . are for the most part obviated if the privilege applicable to the aide is viewed . . . as the privilege of the Senator, and invocable only by the Senator or by the aide on the Senator's behalf, and if in all events the privilege available to the aide is confined to those services that would be immune legislative conduct if performed by the Senator himself. This view places beyond the Speech or Debate Clause a variety of services characteristically performed by aides for Members of Congress, even though within the scope of their employment. It likewise provides no protection for criminal conduct threatening the security of the person or property of others, whether performed at the direction of the Senator in preparation for or in execution of a legislative act or done without his knowledge or direction. Neither does it immunize Senator or aide from testifying at trials or grand jury proceedings involving third-party crimes where the questions do not require testimony about or impugn a legislative act. Thus our refusal to distinguish between Senator and aide in applying the Speech or Debate Clause does not mean that Rodberg is for all purposes exempt from grand jury questioning.

We are convinced also that the Court of Appeals correctly determined that Senator Gravel's alleged arrangement with Beacon Press to publish the Pentagon Papers was not protected speech or debate within the meaning of Art. I, §6, cl. 1, of the Constitution. . . .

The heart of the Clause is speech or debate in either House. Insofar as the Clause is construed to reach other matters, they must be an integral part of the deliberative and communicative processes by which Members participate in committee and House proceedings with respect to the consideration and passage or rejection of proposed legislation or with respect to other matters which the Constitution places within the jurisdiction of either House. As the Court of Appeals put it, the courts have extended the privilege to matters beyond pure speech or debate in either House, but "only when necessary to prevent indirect impairment of such deliberations."

Here, private publication by Senator Gravel through the cooperation of Beacon Press was in no way essential to the deliberations of the Senate; nor does questioning as to private publication threaten the integrity or independence of the Senate by impermissibly exposing its deliberations to executive influence. The Senator had conducted his hearings; the record and any report that was forthcoming were available both to his committee and the Senate. Insofar as we are advised, neither Congress nor the full committee ordered or authorized the publication. We cannot but conclude that the Senator's arrangements with Beacon Press were not part and parcel of the legislative process. . . .

The Speech or Debate Clause does not in our view extend immunity to Rodberg, as a Senator's aide, from testifying before the grand jury about the arrangement between Senator Gravel and Beacon Press or about his own participation, if any, in the alleged transaction, so long as legislative acts of the Senator are not impugned. . . .

Rodberg's immunity . . . extends only to legislative acts as to which the Senator himself would be immune. The grand jury, therefore, if relevant to its investigation into the possible violations of the criminal law, . . . may require from Rodberg answers to questions relating to his or the Senator's arrangements, if any, with respect to republication or with respect to third-party conduct under valid investigation by the grand jury, as long as the questions do not implicate legislative action of the Senator. Neither do we perceive any constitutional or other privilege that shields Rodberg, any more than any other witness, from grand jury questions relevant to tracing the source of obviously highly classified documents that came into the Senator's possession and are the basic subject matter of inquiry in this case, as long as no legislative act is implicated by the questions.

Because the Speech or Debate Clause privilege applies both to Senator and aide, it appears to us that paragraph one of the order, alone, would afford ample protection of the privilege if it forbade questioning any witness, including Rodberg: (1) concerning the Senator's conduct, or the conduct of his aides, at the June 29, 1971, meeting of the subcommittee; (2) concerning the motives and purposes behind the Senator's conduct, or that of his aides, at that meeting; (3) concerning communications between the Senator and his aides during the term of their employment and related to said meeting or any other legislative act of the Senator; (4) except as it proves relevant to investigating possible third-party crime, concerning any act, in itself not criminal, performed by the Senator, or by his aides in the course of their employment, in preparation for the subcommittee hearing. We leave the final form of such an order to the Court of Appeals in the first instance, or, if that court prefers, to the District Court.

The judgment of the Court of Appeals is vacated and the cases are remanded to that court for further proceedings consistent with this opinion.

So ordered.

MR. JUSTICE STEWART, dissenting in part.

The Court . . . decides . . . that a Member of Congress may, despite the Speech or Debate Clause, be compelled to testify before a grand jury concerning the sources of information used by him in the performance of his legislative duties, if such an inquiry "proves relevant to investigating possible third-party crime." In my view, this ruling is highly dubious in view of the basic purpose of the Speech or Debate Clause—"to prevent intimidation [of members of Congress] by the executive and accountability before a possibly hostile judiciary."

Under the Court's ruling, a Congressman may be subpoenaed by a vindictive Executive to testify about informants who have not committed crimes and who have no knowledge of crime. Such compulsion can occur, because the judiciary has traditionally imposed virtually no limitations on the grand jury's broad investigatory powers; grand jury investigations are not limited in scope to specific criminal acts, and standards of materiality and relevance are greatly relaxed. But even if the Executive had reason to believe that a Member of Congress had knowledge of a specific probable violation of law, it is by no means clear to me that the Executive's interest in the administration of justice must always override the public interest in having an informed Congress. Why should we not, given the tension between two competing interests, each of constitutional dimensions, balance the claims of the Speech or Debate Clause against the claims of the grand jury in the particularized contexts of specific cases? And why are not the Houses of Congress the proper institutions in most situations to impose sanctions upon a Representative or Senator who withholds information about crime acquired in the course of his legislative duties?

MR. JUSTICE BRENNAN, with whom MR. JUSTICE DOUGLAS, and MR. JUSTICE MARSHALL, join, dissenting.

My concern is with the narrow scope accorded the Speech or Debate Clause by today's decision. I fully agree with the Court that a Congressman's immunity under the Clause must also be extended to his aides if it is to be at all effective. The complexities and press of congressional business make it impossible for a Member to function without the close cooperation of his legislative assistants. Their role as his agents in the performance of official duties requires

that they share his immunity for those acts. The scope of that immunity, however, is as important as the persons to whom it extends. In my view, today's decision so restricts the privilege of speech or debate as to endanger the continued performance of legislative tasks that are vital to the workings of our democratic system.

In holding that Senator Gravel's alleged arrangement with Beacon Press to publish the Pentagon Papers is not shielded from extra-senatorial inquiry by the Speech or Debate Clause, the Court adopts what for me is a far too narrow view of the legislative function. The Court seems to assume that words spoken in debate or written in congressional reports are protected by the Clause, so that if Senator Gravel had recited part of the Pentagon Papers on the Senate floor or copied them into a Senate report, those acts could not be questioned "in any other Place." Yet because he sought a wider audience, to publicize information deemed relevant to matters pending before his own committee, the Senator suddenly loses his immunity and is exposed to grand jury investigation and possible prosecution for the republication. The explanation for this anomalous result is the Court's belief that "Speech or Debate" encompasses only acts necessary to the internal deliberations of Congress concerning proposed legislation. "Here," according to the Court, "private publication by Senator Gravel through the cooperation of Beacon Press was in no way essential to the deliberations of the Senate." Therefore, "the Senator's arrangements with Beacon Press were not part and parcel of the legislative process."

Thus, the Court excludes from the sphere of protected legislative activity a function that I had supposed lay at the heart of our democratic system. I speak, of course, of the legislator's duty to inform the public about matters affecting the administration of government. That this "informing function" falls into the class of things "generally done in a session of the House by one of its members in relation to the business before it," *Kilbourn v. Thompson* (1881), was explicitly acknowledged by the Court in *Watkins v. United States* (1957). In speaking of the "power of the Congress to inquire into and publicize corruption, maladministration or inefficiency in agencies of the Government," the Court noted that "from the earliest times in its history, the Congress has assiduously performed an 'informing function' of this nature."

We need look no further than Congress itself to find evidence supporting the Court's observation in *Watkins*. Congress has provided financial support for communications between its Members and the public, including the franking privilege for letters, telephone and telegraph allowances, stationery allotments, and favorable prices on reprints from the Congressional Record. Congressional hearings, moreover, are not confined to gathering information for internal distribution, but are often widely publicized, sometimes televised, as a means of alerting the electorate to matters of public import and concern. The list is virtually endless, but a small sampling of contemporaneous hearings of this kind would certainly include the Kefauver hearings on organized crime, the 1966 hearings on automobile safety, and the numerous hearings of the Senate Foreign Relations Committee on the origins and conduct of the war in Vietnam. In short, there can be little doubt that informing the electorate is a thing "generally done" by the Members of Congress "in relation to the business before it.". . .

Unlike the Court, therefore, I think that the activities of Congressmen in communicating with the public are legislative acts protected by the Speech or Debate Clause. I agree with the Court that not every task performed by a legislator is privileged; intervention before Executive departments is one that is not. But the informing function carries a far more persuasive claim to the protections of the Clause. It has been recognized by this Court as something "generally done" by Congressmen, the Congress itself has established special concessions designed to lower the cost of such communication, and, most important, the function furthers several well-recognized goals of representative government. To say in the face of these facts that the informing function is not privileged merely because it is not necessary to the internal deliberations of Congress is to give the Speech or Debate Clause an artificial and narrow reading unsupported by reason.

Gravel provided some guidance for legislators: the Speech or Debate Clause gave similar protection to the senator and the aide, but that protection was not absolute. Both could be questioned for activities that had no direct connection to or "impinged upon" the legislative process.

Despite the specificity of the Court's ruling, it did not put an end to controversies under the Speech or Debate Clause. Indeed, as illustrated in Table 3-3, in the 1970s the Court decided several important issues that were left open by *Gravel*. In *United States v. Helstoski* (1979) the justices refused to allow prosecutors to introduce evidence into a court proceeding against a former member of Congress involving legislative activities. ***Hutchinson v. Proxmire*** (1979), however, was a defeat for congressional authority. Here the Court examined a dispute arising when Sen. William Proxmire, D-Wis., on the floor of the Senate and later in a newsletter and on television, labeled Ronald R. Hutchinson's federally funded research virtually worthless and a waste of taxpayer money. Hutchinson brought a libel suit against Proxmire, and, when the case reached the Court, the justices addressed the issue of whether the Speech or Debate Clause immunized the senator from a libel proceeding on the ground that he had first made the remarks on the chamber's floor. The Court held that it did not:

A speech by Proxmire in the Senate would be wholly immune and would be available to other Members of Congress and the public in the Congressional Record. But neither the newsletters nor the press release was "essential to the deliberations of the Senate," and neither was part of the deliberative process.

SOURCES AND SCOPE OF LEGISLATIVE POWERS

As noted earlier, Article I, Section 8, contains a virtual laundry list of Congress's powers. These enumerated powers, covered in seventeen clauses, establish congressional authority to regulate commerce, to lay and collect taxes, to establish post offices, and so forth. The enumerated powers pose few constitutional problems: those that the Constitution names, Congress clearly has.

But questions have arisen over other aspects of congressional power. First, does the legislative branch have powers beyond those specified by the Constitution? Despite the fact that the Framers left this question unaddressed, as noted in Table 3-4, the Court has not hesitated to answer it affirmatively, suggesting that Congress possesses implied, inherent, and amendment-enforcing

TABLE 3-3 Speech or Debate Clause Cases after *Gravel v. United States*

Case	Legal Question	Court's Response
United States v. Brewster (1972)	Does the Speech or Debate Clause protect members from prosecution for alleged bribery to perform a legislative act?	The Speech or Debate Clause protects members from inquiry into legislative acts; it does not protect all conduct relating to the legislative process.
Doe v. McMillan (1973)	Does the Speech or Debate Clause protect members of Congress (and their staff) and other persons who were involved in the investigating, disseminating, and distributing of a report of the D.C. school system, which identified, by name, specific children and did so in a negative way?	The Speech or Debate Clause offers absolute immunity to members of Congress and staff, but not to individuals who, acting under congressional authority, distributed the materials.
Eastland v. U.S. Servicemen's Fund (1975)	Does the Speech or Debate Clause protect members of Congress against a suit brought by an organization to stop the implementation of a subpoena ordering a bank to produce certain records?	The Speech or Debate Clause offers absolute protection because the activities fall within the "legitimate legislative" sphere.
Davis v. Passman (1979)	Does the Speech or Debate Clause protect a member of Congress against charges of sex discrimination?	The Supreme Court decided the case on Fifth Amendment grounds and reached no result on the member of Congress's claim that he was protected by the Speech or Debate Clause.
United States v. Helstoski (1979)	Does the Speech or Debate Clause protect a member of Congress against prosecution (for accepting bribes), when evidence introduced in that action hinges on past legislative acts?	The Speech or Debate Clause does not permit the introduction of evidence involving past legislative acts.
Hutchinson v. Proxmire (1979)	Does the Speech or Debate Clause protect a member of Congress from a civil suit in response to negative statements made to the press and in newsletters about a government grant awardee's research?	The Speech or Debate Clause does not protect a member of Congress from a libel judgment when information is disseminated to the press and the public through newsletters.

powers in addition to those listed in Article I. In this section, we examine the cases in which the Court located those sources.

We also focus on a second, more complex, question: What constraints are there on Congress's ability to exercise these powers? For example, the Court has permitted Congress to conduct hearings and investigations, but it also has asserted that the power is not unlimited, that certain restrictions apply.

As you read the next cases, keep in mind not only the sources of legislative power but also its scope. How has the Court sought to constrain Congress and, more important, why? What pressures have been brought to bear on the justices in making their decisions?

Enumerated and Implied Powers

The Constitution's specific list of congressional powers leaves no doubt that Congress has these powers. In *Gibbons v. Ogden* (1824), when the Court was asked to interpret one of them, the power to regulate interstate commerce, Chief Justice John Marshall said:

The words [of the Constitution] are, "Congress shall have power to regulate commerce with foreign nations, and among the several States. . . ." The subject to be regulated is commerce, and

TABLE 3-4 The Sources of Congressional Power

Power[a]	Defined	Example
Enumerated powers	Those that the Constitution expressly grants	See Article I, Section 8. Includes the power to borrow money, raise armies, regulate commerce.
Implied powers	Those that may be inferred from power expressly granted	Read Article I, Section 8, Clauses 2–17, in conjunction with Clause 18, the Necessary and Proper Clause. For example, the enumerated power of raising and supporting armies leads to the implied power of operating a draft.
Inherent powers	Those powers that do not depend on constitutional grants but grow out of the very existence of the national government	Encompasses field of foreign affairs. That is, foreign affairs powers are those that the national government would have even if the Constitution was silent, because they are powers that all nations have under international law. For example, the federal government can issue orders prohibiting U.S. businesses from selling arms to particular nations.
Amendment-enforcing powers	Those powers contained in some constitutional amendments that provide Congress with the ability to enforce them	Amendments 13, 14, and 15, for example, state that Congress shall have the power to enforce the article by "appropriate legislation."

SOURCE: Adopted from J. W. Peltason, *Understanding the Constitution*, 14th ed. (Fort Worth, Texas: Harcourt Brace, 1997), 20–21.
    a. Some analysts suggest that Congress also possesses resulting powers (those that result when several enumerated powers are added together) and inherited powers (those that Congress inherited from the British Parliament).

our constitution being . . . *one of enumeration, and not of definition*, to ascertain the extent of the power, it becomes necessary to settle the meaning of the word. (Emphasis added.)

In these two sentences, Marshall asserted that Congress indeed has the enumerated power to regulate commerce, but that the Court needed to define what that power entails. This point is important because, as we shall see later, the fact that a power is written into the Constitution does not necessarily make the Court's task easier: often it must define how Congress can and cannot make use of that power. For now, we can conclude that virtually no debate ever occurs over whether, in fact, Congress has the powers contained in Article I, Section 8.

Necessary and Proper Clause. Where debate has occurred is over the question of whether Congress has more powers, or was intended to have more powers, than those specifically granted. And if so, how broad should they be? Those who look to the plain language of the Constitution or to the intent of the Framers would find few concrete answers, although both camps would

point to the same clause. Article I, Section 8, Clause 18, provides that Congress shall have the power "to make all Laws which shall be necessary and proper for carrying into Execution the foregoing Powers, and all other Powers vested by this Constitution in the Government of the United States, or in any Department or Officer thereof."

Called by various names—the Necessary and Proper Clause, the Elastic Clause, or the Sweeping Clause—this provision was the subject of heated debate early in the nation's history. Many affiliated with the Federalist Party, which favored a strong national government, argued for a loose construction of the clause. In their view, the Framers inserted it into the Constitution to provide Congress with some "flexibility"; in other words, Congress could exercise powers beyond those listed in the Constitution, those that were "necessary and proper" for implementing legislative activity. The Jeffersonians asserted the need for a strict interpretation of the clause; in their view, it constricted congressional powers, rather than expanded them. In other words, congressional exercise of power under the Necessary and Proper Clause could be only that power necessary to carry out its enumerated functions.

Which view would the Supreme Court adopt? Would it interpret the Necessary and Proper Clause strictly or loosely? This was one of two major questions at the core of *McCulloch v. Maryland* (1819), which many consider the Court's most important explication of congressional powers.[16] Indeed, some suggest that this opinion was Chief Justice Marshall's finest. As you read this case, consider not only the Court's holding, but also the language and logic of *McCulloch*. Why is it such an extraordinary statement?

McCulloch v. Maryland

4 WHEAT. (17 U.S.) 316 (1819)
http://supct.law.cornell.edu/supct/cases/name.htm
Vote: 6 (Duvall, Johnson, Livingston, Marshall, Story,
 Washington)

o

Opinion of the Court: Marshall
Not participating: Todd

Although we now take for granted the ability of the federal government to operate a banking system—today called the Federal Reserve System—in the eighteenth century and into the nineteenth, this topic was a political battleground. The first sign of controversy came as early as 1790, when George Washington's secretary of the Treasury, Alexander Hamilton, asked Congress to adopt a comprehensive economic plan for the new nation. Among the proposals was the creation of a Bank of the United States, which would receive deposits, disburse funds, and make loans; Congress responded with a bill authorizing the first federal bank.

When the bill arrived at President Washington's desk, however, he did not sign it immediately. He wanted to ascertain whether in fact Congress could create a bank since it lacked explicit constitutional authority to do so. To this end he asked Hamilton, Secretary of State Thomas Jeffer-

son, and Attorney General Edmund Randolph for their opinions on the bank's constitutionality.

Box 3-3 provides excerpts of Hamilton's and Jefferson's responses. We offer them not only because they reached different conclusions—Hamilton argued that it was constitutional, Jefferson that it was not—but also because they represent the classic competing theories of congressional power. Moreover, they illustrate the limits of the Framers' intent mode of constitutional interpretation. Does it seem odd that just four years after the writing of the Constitution, two of the nation's foremost leaders could have such different views? In his argument, Hamilton, in fact, noted that there was a "conflicting recollection" of a convention debate highly relevant to the bank issue.[17] In the end, the president was persuaded by Hamilton and signed the bill. Congress then created the first Bank of the United States in 1791, chartering it for a twenty-year period.

Nevertheless, the bank controversy did not disappear. As we illustrate in Figure 3-1, which superimposes the bank's history (and that of its successor) against political and economic events, it is clear why the bank remained in the spotlight. Most important was that it became a symbol of the loose-construction, nationally oriented Federalist Party, which had lost considerable power from its heyday in the 1790s. Indeed, by the turn of the century, a strict-construction approach to congressional power was among the primary ideas endorsed by the Federalists' competitors, the Jeffersonian Republicans. To no one's surprise, and despite the fact that the bank had done an able job, the Republican Congress refused to renew its charter in 1811.

After the War of 1812, it became apparent even to the Republicans that Congress should recharter the bank. During the war, the lack of a national bank for purposes of borrowing money and transferring funds became a source of embarrassment to the administration. Moreover, with the absence of a federal bank, state-chartered institutions flooded the market with worthless notes,

16. The other question involved federalism. See Chapter 6.

17. One scholar notes that the Framers rejected a proposal that would have allowed Congress to establish corporations; in fact, they did so in part because of the possibility that Congress would create banks. See Jethro Lieberman, *Milestones!* (St. Paul, Minn.: West Publishing, 1976), 19. Still, Hamilton argued that debate was unclear.

BOX 3-3 **JEFFERSON AND HAMILTON ON THE BANK OF THE UNITED STATES**

Thomas Jefferson

To take a single step beyond the boundaries . . . specially drawn around the powers of Congress, is to take possession of a boundless field of power, no longer susceptible of any definition.

The incorporation of a bank, and other powers assumed by this bill have not, in my opinion, been delegated to the U.S. by the Constitution.

I. They are not among the powers specially enumerated, for these are

1. A power to *lay taxes* for the purpose of paying the debts of the U.S. But no debt is paid by this bill, nor any tax laid. . . .

2. "to borrow money." But this bill neither borrows money, nor ensures the borrowing of it. . . .

3. "to regulate commerce with foreign nations, and among the states, and with the Indian tribes." To erect a bank, and to regulate commerce, are very different acts. . . .

II. Nor are they within either of the general phrases, which are the two following.

1. "To lay taxes to provide for the general welfare of the U.S." that is to say "to lay taxes *for the purpose* of providing for the general welfare." For the laying of taxes is the *power* and the general welfare the *purpose* for which the power is to be exercised. They are not to lay taxes ad libitum *for any purpose they please;* but only to *pay the debts or provide for the welfare of the Union.* In like manner they are not *to do anything they please* to provide for the general welfare, but only *to lay taxes* for that purpose. To consider the latter phrase, not as describing the purpose of the first, but as giving a distinct and independent power to do any act they please, which might be for the good of the Union, would render all the preceding and subsequent enumerations of power completely useless. It would reduce the whole instrument to a single phrase, that of instituting a Congress with power to do whatever would be for the good of the U.S. and as they would be the sole judges of the good or evil, it would be also a power to do whatever evil they pleased. . . . Certainly no such universal power was meant to be given them. It was intended to lace them up straitly within the enumerated powers, and those without which, as means, these powers could not be carried into effect. It is known that the very power now proposed *as a means*, was rejected *as an end*, by the Convention which formed the constitution. . . .

2. The second general phrase is "to make all laws *necessary* and proper for carrying into execution the enumerated powers." But they can all be carried into execution without a bank. A bank therefore is not *necessary*, and consequently not authorised by this phrase.

It has been much urged that a bank will give great facility, or convenience in the collection of taxes. Suppose this were true: yet the constitution allows only the means which are "necessary" not those which are merely "convenient" for effecting the enumerated powers. If such a latitude of construction be allowed to this phrase as to give any non-enumerated power, it will go to every one, for there is no one which ingenuity may not torture into a *convenience, in some way or other,* to *some one* of so long a list of enumerated powers. It would swallow up all the delegated powers, and reduce the whole to one phrase as before observed. Therefore it was that the constitution restrained them to the *necessary* means, that is to say, to those means without which the grant of the power would be nugatory.

OPINION AS TO THE CONSTITUTIONALITY OF THE BANK OF THE UNITED STATES (1791)

Alexander Hamilton

Now it appears to the Secretary of the Treasury that this *general principle* is *inherent* in the very *definition* of government, and *essential* to every step of the progress to be made by that of the United States, namely: That every power vested in a government is in its nature *sovereign,* and includes, by *force* of the *term,* a right to employ all the *means* requisite and fairly applicable to the attainment of the *ends* of such power, and which are not precluded by restrictions and exceptions specified in the Constitution, or not immoral, or not contrary to the *essential ends* of political society.

This principle, in its application to government in general, would be admitted as an axiom; and it will be incumbent upon those who may incline to deny it, to prove a distinction, and to show that a rule which, in the general system of things, is essential to the preservation of the social order, is inapplicable to the United States. . . .

This general and indisputable principle puts at once an end to the *abstract* question, whether the United States have power to erect a corporation; that is to say, to give a *legal* or *artificial capacity* to one or more persons, distinct from the *natural.* For it is unquestionably incident to *sovereign power* to erect corporations, and consequently to *that* of the United States, in *relation* to the *objects* intrusted to the management of the government. . . .

Another argument made use of by the Secretary of State is, the rejection of a proposition by the Convention to empower Congress to make corporations, either generally, or for some special purpose.

What was the precise nature or extent of this proposition, or what the reasons for refusing it, is not ascertained by any authentic document, or even by accurate recollection. . . .

But whatever may have been the nature of the proposition, or the reasons for rejecting it, it includes nothing in respect to the real merits of the question. The Secretary of State will not deny that, whatever may have been the intention of the framers of a constitution or of a law, that intention is to be sought for in the instrument itself, according to the usual and established rules of construction. Nothing is more common than for laws to *express* and *effect* more or less than was intended. If, then, a power to erect a corporation in any case be deducible, by fair inference, from the whole or any part of the numerous provisions of the Constitution of the United States, arguments drawn from extrinsic circumstances, regarding the intention of the Convention, must be rejected. . . .

To establish such a right, it remains to show the relation of such an institution to one or more of the specified powers of the government. Accordingly it is affirmed that it has a relation, more or less direct, to the power of collecting taxes, to that of borrowing money, to that of regulating trade between the States, and to those of raising and maintaining fleets and armies. To the two former the relation may be said to be immediate; and in the last place it will be argued, that it is clearly within the provision which authorizes the making of all *needful rules and regulations* concerning the *property* of the United States, as the same has been practised upon the government.

A bank relates to the collection of taxes in two ways—*indirectly,* by increasing the quantity of circulating medium and quickening circulation, which facilitates the means of paying directly, [and] by creating a *convenient species* of medium in which they are to be paid. . . .

SOURCE: Melvin I. Urofsky, ed., *Documents of American Constitutional and Legal History,* vol. I (New York: Knopf, 1989), 132–139.

FIGURE 3-1 The History of the First and Second Banks of the United States

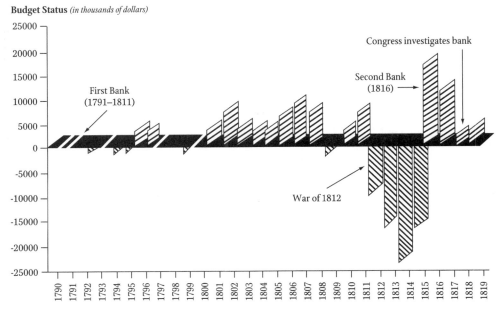

Budget Status *(in thousands of dollars)*

SOURCE: Data from U.S. Department of Commerce, *Historical Statistics of the United States* (Washington, D.C.: U.S. Bureau of the Census, 1975), 1104.

contributing to economic problems throughout the country. Amid renewed controversy and cries for strict constructionism, Congress in 1816 created the second Bank of the United States, granting it a twenty-year charter and $35 million in capital.

Some scholars have suggested that a challenge to the new bank was inevitable, primarily because the Supreme Court had never decided whether the first bank was constitutional. It is possible, however, that litigation would not have materialized had the second bank performed its function as well as its predecessor did, but it did not. It flourished during the postwar economic boom, mainly because it was fiscally aggressive and encouraged speculative investing. These practices caught up to bank officials when, in 1818, in anticipation of a recession, they began calling in the bank's outstanding loans. As a result, they brought down banks throughout the South and West, which had overextended themselves. To make matters worse, accusations of fraud and embezzlement were rampant within several of the bank's eighteen branches,

particularly in Maryland, Pennsylvania, and Virginia. Among those most seriously implicated was James McCulloch, the cashier of the Baltimore branch bank and its main lobbyist in Washington. According to some accounts, his illegal financial schemes had cost the branch more than $1 million.

As a result of these allegations, Congress began to hold hearings on the bank. In addition, some states reacted by attempting to regulate branches located within their borders. For example, Maryland mandated that branches of the bank in the state pay either a 2 percent tax on all bank notes or a fee of $15,000. When a state official came to collect from the Baltimore branch, McCulloch refused to pay and, by refusing, set the stage for a monumental confrontation between the United States and Maryland on not one, but two, major issues. The first involved the bank itself: Did Congress, in the absence of an explicit constitutional authorization, have the power to charter the bank? Second, did the state exceed its powers by seeking to tax a federal entity?

By the time the case reached the Supreme Court, it was clear that something significant was going to happen. The Court reporter noted that *McCulloch* involved "a constitutional question of great importance." The justices waived their rule that permitted only two attorneys per side "and allowed three each." [18] Oral arguments took nine days.

Both sides were ably represented. Some commentators praise Daniel Webster's oratory for the federal government's side as extraordinary, but it was former attorney general and Maryland senator William Pinkney with whom the Court was most taken. Justice Joseph Story said later, "I never, in my whole life, heard a greater speech." [19] The gist of his arguments (and those of his colleagues) was familiar stuff; Pinkney largely reiterated Hamilton's original defense of the bank, particularly his interpretation of the Necessary and Proper Clause.

Maryland's legal representation may have appeared less astute. According to one account, "it has been rumored" that one of the state's lawyers, Attorney General Luther Martin, "was drunk when he made his two-day-long argument. If he was, it apparently did not affect his acuity." For his side, he reiterated parts of Jefferson's argument against the bank, added some on the subject of states' rights, and read some of the speeches John Marshall had delivered at the Virginia convention.[20]

CHIEF JUSTICE MARSHALL delivered the opinion of the court.

The constitution of our country, in its most interesting and vital parts, is to be considered; the conflicting powers of the government of the Union and of its members, as marked in that constitution, are to be discussed; and an opinion given, which may essentially influence the great operations of the government. No tribunal can approach such a question without a deep sense of its importance, and of the awful responsibility involved in its decision. But it must be decided peacefully, or remain a source of hostile legislation,

perhaps of hostility of a still more serious nature; and if it is to be so decided, by this tribunal alone can the decision be made. On the Supreme Court of the United States has the constitution of our country devolved this important duty.

The first question . . . is, has Congress power to incorporate a bank? . . .

This government is acknowledged by all to be one of enumerated powers. The principle, that it can exercise only the powers granted to it, would seem too apparent to have required to be enforced by all those arguments which its enlightened friends, while it was depending before the people, found it necessary to urge. That principle is now universally admitted. But the question respecting the extent of the powers actually granted, is perpetually arising, and will probably continue to arise, as long as our system shall exist. . . .

Among the enumerated powers, we do not find that of establishing a bank or creating a corporation. But there is no phrase in the instrument which, like the articles of confederation, excludes incidental or implied powers; and which requires that everything granted shall be expressly and minutely described. Even the 10th amendment, which was framed for the purpose of quieting the excessive jealousies which had been excited, omits the word "expressly," and declares only that the powers "not delegated to the United States, nor prohibited to the states, are reserved to the states or to the people;" thus leaving the question, whether the particular power which may become the subject of contest has been delegated to the one government, or prohibited to the other, to depend on a fair construction of the whole instrument. . . . A constitution, to contain an accurate detail of all the subdivisions of which its great powers will admit, and of all the means by which they may be carried into execution, would partake of a prolixity of a legal code, and could scarcely be embraced by the human mind. It would probably never be understood by the public. Its nature, therefore, requires, that only its great outlines should be marked, its important objects designated, and the minor ingredients which compose those objects be deduced from the nature of the objects themselves. That this idea was entertained by the framers of the American constitution, is not only to be inferred from the nature of the instrument, but from the language. Why else were some of the limitations, found in the ninth section of the 1st article, introduced? It is also, in some degree, warranted by their

---

18. Quoted in Fred W. Friendly and Martha J. H. Elliot, *The Constitution: That Delicate Balance* (New York: Random House, 1984), 256.

19. Quoted in Lieberman, *Milestones!* 122.

20. Farber and Sherry, *A History of the American Constitution*, 251.

having omitted to use any restrictive term which might prevent its receiving a fair and just interpretation. In considering this question, then, we must never forget that it is a constitution we are expounding.

Although, among the enumerated powers of government, we do not find the word "bank" or "incorporation," we find the great powers to lay and collect taxes; to borrow money; to regulate commerce; to declare and conduct a war; and to raise and support armies and navies. The sword and the purse, all the external relations, and no inconsiderable portion of the industry of the nation, are entrusted to its government. It can never be pretended that these vast powers draw after them others of inferior importance, merely because they are inferior. Such an idea can never be advanced. But it may with great reason be contended, that a government, entrusted with such ample powers, on the due execution of which the happiness and prosperity of the nation so vitally depends, must also be entrusted with ample means for their execution. The power being given, it is the interest of the nation to facilitate its execution. It can never be their interest, and cannot be presumed to have been their intention, to clog and embarrass its execution by withholding the most appropriate means. . . .

The government which has a right to do an act, and has imposed on it the duty of performing that act, must, according to the dictates of reason, be allowed to select the means; and those who contend that it may not select any appropriate means, that one particular mode of effecting the object is excepted, take upon themselves the burden of establishing that exception. . . .

But the constitution of the United States has not left the right of Congress to employ the necessary means for the execution of the powers conferred on the government to general reasoning. To its enumeration of powers is added that of making "all laws which shall be necessary and proper, for carrying into execution the foregoing powers, and all other powers vested by this constitution, in the government of the United States, or in any department thereof."

The counsel for the State of Maryland have urged various arguments, to prove that this clause, though in terms a grant of power, is not so in effect; but is really restrictive of the general right, which might otherwise be implied, of selecting means for executing the enumerated powers. . . .

The word "necessary" is considered as controlling the whole sentence, and as limiting the right to pass laws for the execution of the granted powers, to such as are indispensable, and without which the power would be nugatory. That it excludes the choice of means, and leaves to Congress, in each case, that only which is most direct and simple.

Is it true that this is the sense in which the word "necessary" is always used? Does it always import an absolute physical necessity, so strong that one thing, to which another may be termed necessary, cannot exist without that other? We think it does not. If reference be had to its use, in the common affairs of the world, or in approved authors, we find that it frequently imports no more than that one thing is convenient, or useful, or essential to another. To employ the means necessary to an end, is generally understood as employing any means calculated to produce the end, and not as being confined to those single means, without which the end would be entirely unattainable. . . . This word, . . . like others, is used in various senses; and, in its construction, the subject, the context, the intention of the person using them, are all to be taken into view.

Let this be done in the case under consideration. The subject is the execution of those great powers on which the welfare of a nation essentially depends. It must have been the intention of those who gave these powers, to insure, as far as human prudence could insure, their beneficial execution. This could not be done by confiding the choice of means to such narrow limits as not to leave it in the power of Congress to adopt any which might be appropriate, and which were conducive to the end. This provision is made in a constitution intended to endure for ages to come, and, consequently, to be adapted to the various crises of human affairs. To have prescribed the means by which government should, in all future time, execute its powers, would have been to change, entirely, the character of the instrument, and give it the properties of a legal code. It would have been an unwise attempt to provide, by immutable rules, for exigencies which, if foreseen at all, must have been seen dimly, and which can be best provided for as they occur. To have declared that the best means shall not be used, but those alone without which the power given would be nugatory, would have been to deprive the legislature of the capacity to avail itself of experience, to exercise its reason, and to accommodate its legislation to circumstances. . . .

The baneful influence of this narrow construction on all the operations of the government, and the absolute impracticability of maintaining it without rendering the government incompetent to its great objects, might be illustrated by numerous examples drawn from the constitution, and from our laws. . . .

In ascertaining the sense in which the word "necessary" is used in this clause of the constitution, we may derive some aid from that with which it is associated. Congress shall have power "to make all laws which shall be necessary and proper to carry into execution" the powers of the government. If the word "necessary" was used in that strict and rigorous sense for which the counsel for the state of Maryland contend, it would be an extraordinary departure from the usual course of the human mind, as exhibited in composition, to add a word, the only possible effect of which is to qualify that strict and rigorous meaning; to present to the mind the idea of some choice of means of legislation not straightened and compressed within the narrow limits for which gentlemen contend.

But the argument which most conclusively demonstrates the error of the construction contended for by the counsel for the state of Maryland, is founded on the intention of the convention, as manifested in the whole clause. To waste time and argument in proving that without it Congress might carry its powers into execution, would be not much less idle than to hold a lighted taper to the sun. As little can it be required to prove, that in the absence of this clause, Congress would have some choice of means. That it might employ those which, in its judgment, would most advantageously effect the object to be accomplished. That any means adapted to the end, any means which tended directly to the execution of the constitutional powers of the government, were in themselves constitutional. This clause, as construed by the state of Maryland, would abridge, and almost annihilate this useful and necessary right of the legislature to select its means. That this could not be intended, is, we should think, had it not been already controverted, too apparent for controversy. We think so for the following reasons:

1st. The clause is placed among the powers of Congress, not among the limitations on those powers.

2d. Its terms purport to enlarge, not to diminish the powers vested in the government. . . .

We admit, as all must admit, that the powers of the government are limited, and that its limits are not to be transcended. But we think the sound construction of the constitution must allow to the national legislature that discretion, with respect to the means by which the powers it confers are to be carried into execution, which will enable that body to perform the high duties assigned to it, in the manner most beneficial to the people. Let the end be legitimate, let it be within the scope of the constitution, and all means which are appropriate, which are plainly adapted to that end, which are not prohibited, but consist with the letter and spirit of the constitution, are constitutional.

That a corporation must be considered as a means not less usual, not of higher dignity, not more requiring a particular specification than other means, has been sufficiently proved. If we look to the origin of corporations, to the manner in which they have been framed in that government from which we have derived most of our legal principles and ideas, or to the uses to which they have been applied, we find no reason to suppose that a constitution, omitting, and wisely omitting, to enumerate all the means for carrying into execution the great powers vested in government, ought to have specified this. Had it been intended to grant this power as one which should be distinct and independent, to be exercised in any case whatever, it would have found a place among the enumerated powers of the government. But being considered merely as a means, to be employed only for the purpose of carrying into execution the given powers, there could be no motive for particularly mentioning it. . . .

If a corporation may be employed indiscriminately with other means to carry into execution the powers of the government, no particular reason can be assigned for excluding the use of a bank, if required for its fiscal operations. To use one, must be within the discretion of Congress, if it be an appropriate mode of executing the powers of government. That it is a convenient, a useful, and essential instrument in the prosecution of its fiscal operations, is not now a subject of controversy. All those who have been concerned in the administration of our finances, have concurred in representing the importance and necessity; and so strongly have they been felt, that statesmen of the first class, whose previous opinions against it had been confirmed by every circumstance which can fix the human judgment, have yielded those opinions to the exigencies of the nation. Under the confederation, Congress, justifying the measure by its necessity, transcended perhaps its powers to obtain the advantage of a bank; and our own legislation attests the universal conviction of the utility of this measure. The time has passed away when it can be necessary to enter into any discussion in order to prove the importance of this instrument, as a means to effect the legitimate objects of the government.

But, were its necessity less apparent, none can deny its being an appropriate measure; and if it is, the degree of its necessity, as has been very justly observed, is to be discussed in another place. Should Congress, in the execution of its powers, adopt measures which are prohibited by the constitution; or should Congress, under the pretext of executing its powers, pass laws for the accomplishment of objects not entrusted to the government, it would become the painful duty of this tribunal, should a case requiring such a decision come before it, to say that such an act was not the law of the land. But where the law is not prohibited, and is really calculated to effect any of the objects entrusted to the government, to undertake here to inquire into the degree of its necessity, would be to pass the line which circumscribes the judicial department, and to tread on legislative ground. This court disclaims all pretensions to such a power. . . .

After the most deliberate consideration, it is the unanimous and decided opinion of this court that the act to incorporate the bank of the United States is a law made in pursuance of the constitution, and is a part of the supreme law of the land.

As we can see, Marshall fully adopted Hamilton's reasoning and the government's claims. Some even felt his opinion was a virtual transcript of the oral arguments presented by the federal attorneys. Given that Marshall issued *McCulloch* just three days after the case had been presented, it is more likely, as others suspect, that he wrote the opinion the previous summer.

Either way, *McCulloch* stands as a landmark decision. By holding that Congress has powers beyond those enumerated, that it has implied powers, Marshall set into law a largely Hamiltonian version of congressional authority:

Let the end be legitimate, let it be within the scope of the constitution, and all means which are appropriate, which are plainly adapted to that end, which are not prohibited, but consist with the letter and spirit of the constitution, are constitutional.

And in so doing, he might very well have accomplished his stated objective: to allow the Constitution "to endure for ages to come."

The immediate reaction to Marshall's opinion was interesting in that it focused less on the portion we have dealt with here—congressional powers—and more on the federalism dimension, which we take up in Chapter 6. Nonetheless, the long-term effect of his interpretation of the Necessary and Proper Clause has been significant: Congress now exercises many powers not named in the Constitution but implied from it.

Power to Investigate. Of all the implied powers now asserted by Congress, the power to investigate merits close examination. Many think it is one of the major congressional powers. As Woodrow Wilson noted: "The informing function of Congress should be preferred even to its legislative function." Another president, Harry Truman, concurred: "The power of investigation is one of the most important powers of Congress. The manner in which that power is exercised will largely determine the position and prestige of the Congress in the future." In addition, the scope of congressional authority in this area has been the subject of some rather interesting, perhaps conflicting, and most definitely controversial, Supreme Court opinions.

What has never been controversial, however, is that Congress has the ability to conduct investigations. After all, to legislate effectively requires the gathering of information to determine if new laws are necessary and, if so, how the new statutes can best be written. Although this power is not an enumerated power, there is little question that legislatures can hold inquiries. Some analysts refer to it as an incidental power that legislatures have by virtue of being legislatures. Others call it an inherited power that the British Parliament willed to Congress or, alternatively, an implied power. In any event, Congress took advantage of this privilege virtually from the beginning, holding its first investigation in 1792. Since then no period in our history has been without investigations.

If the power of Congress to investigate is so well entrenched, what is controversial about the practice? There are several answers. Questions arise over the scope of the power—into what subjects may Congress inquire? May Congress summon witnesses and punish, by holding in contempt, those who do not cooperate with the investigating body? If so, what rights do witnesses have? One argument is that the power to call and punish witnesses may be implied from the inherent nature of legislative authority. Congress is, by definition, the lawmaking institution, and an inherent quality of such an institution is the power to investigate. To function, therefore, it is necessary for Congress to have the authority to summon witnesses and punish those who do not comply, and both chambers have always availed themselves of this authority. As early as 1795 Congress jailed for contempt a man who had tried to bribe a member of Congress. The Supreme Court theoretically approved of the contempt practice as early as 1821, in *Anderson v. Dunn*. But it was not until *Kilbourn v. Thompson* (1881) that the justices attempted to provide firm answers to the questions of Congress's power to summon and punish witnesses and on the scope of congressional investigations.

Kilbourn involved a House investigation into a private banking firm. An important witness, Hallett Kilbourn, refused to produce documents demanded by the inquiring committee. By a House order, Kilbourn was held in contempt and jailed. When he was released, he sued various officials and representatives for false arrest. In his view, the investigation was not legitimate because it concerned private, not public, matters and, as such, he would resist "the naked, arbitrary power of the House to investigate private businesses in which nobody but me and my customers have concern." [21]

The Supreme Court agreed. In what some have called a rather narrow ruling on legislative powers, the justices said that Congress could punish witnesses only if the inquiry itself was within the "legitimate cognizance" of the institution. With this ruling, the Court seemed to establish several limits on the scope of investigations. Inquiries (1) must not "invade areas constitutionally reserved to the courts or the executive"; (2) must deal "with subjects on which Congress could validly legislate"; and (3) must suggest, in the resolutions authorizing the investigation, a "congressional interest in legislating on that subject." [22] In general, then, *Kilbourn* said that Congress could hold inquiries only into subjects that are

21. Quoted in *Guide to Congress*, 5th ed., 252.
22. See C. Herman Pritchett, *Constitutional Law of the Federal System* (Englewood Cliffs, N.J.: Prentice-Hall, 1984), 191.

specifically grounded within its constitutional purview and, in particular, that the "private affairs of individuals," where the inquiry could result in "no valid legislation," did not fall into that category.

Four decades later the Court was once again called on to examine the scope of congressional investigative authority. As you read *McGrain v. Daugherty* (1927), consider its ruling in light of *Kilbourn*. Some think that the justices substantially reworked the 1881 holding. Do you agree? If so, what did they change?

McGrain v. Daugherty

273 U.S. 135 (1927)
http://laws.findlaw.com/US/273/135.html
Vote: 8 (Brandeis, Butler, Holmes, McReynolds, Sanford, Sutherland, Taft, Van Devanter)
0
Opinion of the Court: Van Devanter
Not participating: Stone

In 1922 Congress began an investigation of a huge scandal known as Teapot Dome. It involved the alleged bribery of public officials by private companies to obtain leasing rights to government-held oil reserves, including the Teapot Dome reserves in Wyoming. Initial inquiries centered on employees of the Department of the Interior, but Congress soon turned its attention to the Justice Department. It was thought that Attorney General Harry M. Daugherty was involved in fraudulent activities because he failed to prosecute wrongdoers. A Senate committee ordered the attorney general's brother, Mally S. Daugherty, to appear before it and to produce documents. Mally Daugherty was a bank president, and the committee suspected that he was involved in the scandal.

This suspicion grew stronger with the resignation of the attorney general and the subsequent refusal of his brother to appear before the committee. The Senate had Mally arrested. He, in turn, challenged the committee's authority to compel him—through arrest—to testify against his brother. Picking up on one of the limits of investigation emanating from *Kilbourn*, Mally's lawyer argued that "the arrest of Mr. Daugherty is the result of an

Members of the Senate investigating committee that sought to compel testimony from Mally Daugherty. From left, Burton K. Wheeler, George Moses, Smith Brookhart, Andrieus Jones, and Henry Ashurst.

attempt of the Senate to vest its committee with judicial power."

The U.S. government's brief was written by Attorney General Harlan Stone, who had since been appointed a justice on the Court deciding the case. The brief also used *Kilbourn* to frame its arguments: "The investigation ordered by the Senate, in the course of which the testimony of the Appellee [Daugherty] and the production of books and records of the bank of which he is President were required, was legislative in its character."

MR. JUSTICE VAN DEVANTER delivered the opinion of the Court.

We have given the case earnest and prolonged consideration because the principal questions involved are of unusual importance and delicacy. . . .

The first of the principal questions—the one which the witness particularly presses on our attention—is . . . whether the Senate—or the House of Representatives . . .— has power . . . to compel a private individual to appear before it or one of its committees and give testimony needed to enable it efficiently to exercise a legislative function belonging to it under the Constitution.

The Constitution provides for a Congress consisting of a Senate and House of Representatives and invests it with "all legislative powers" granted to the United States, and with power "to make all laws which shall be necessary

and proper" for carrying into execution these powers and "all other powers" vested by the Constitution in the United States or in any department or officer thereof. . . . But there is no provision expressly investing either house with power to make investigations and exact testimony to the end that it may exercise its legislative function advisedly and effectively. So the question arises whether this power is so far incidental to the legislative function as to be implied.

In actual legislative practice, power to secure needed information by such means has long been treated as an attribute of the power to legislate. It was so regarded in the British Parliament and in the colonial Legislatures before the American Revolution; and a like view has prevailed and been carried into effect in both houses of Congress and in most of the state Legislatures. . . .

. . . The state courts quite generally have held that the power to legislate carries with it by necessary implication ample authority to obtain information needed in the rightful exercise of that power, and to employ compulsory process for the purpose. . . .

[This Court has decided several cases that] are not decisive . . . [but] definitely settle two propositions . . . : One, that the two houses of Congress . . . possess, not only such powers as are expressly granted to them by the Constitution, but such auxiliary powers as are necessary and appropriate to make the express powers effective; and the other, that neither house is invested with "general" power to inquire into private affairs and compel disclosures, but only with such limited power of inquiry as is shown to exist when the rule of constitutional interpretation just stated is rightly applied. . . .

We are of opinion that the power of inquiry—with process to enforce it—is an essential and appropriate auxiliary to the legislative function. . . . A legislative body cannot legislate wisely or effectively in the absence of information respecting the conditions which the legislation is intended to affect or change; and where the legislative body does not itself possess the requisite information . . . recourse must be had to others who do possess it. Experience has taught that mere requests for such information often are unavailing, and also that information which is volunteered is not always accurate or complete; so some means of compulsion are essential to obtain what is needed. All this was true before and when the Constitution was framed and adopted. In that period the power of inquiry—with enforcing process—was regarded and employed as a necessary and appropriate attribute of the power to legislate—indeed, was treated as inhering in it.

Thus there is ample warrant for thinking, as we do, that the constitutional provisions which commit the legislative function to the two houses are intended to include this attribute to the end that the function may be effectively exercised.

The contention is earnestly made on behalf of the witness that this power of inquiry, if sustained, may be abusively and oppressively exerted. If this be so, it affords no ground for denying the power. The same contention might be directed against the power to legislate, and of course would be unavailing. We must assume, for present purposes, that neither house will be disposed to exert the power beyond its proper bounds, or without due regard to the rights of witnesses. But if, contrary to this assumption, controlling limitations or restrictions are disregarded, the decision . . . in *Kilbourn v. Thompson* . . . point[s] to admissible measures of relief. And it is a necessary deduction from the decision . . . that a witness rightfully may refuse to answer where the bounds of the power are exceeded or the questions are not pertinent to the matter under inquiry.

Attorney General Harry M. Daugherty, whose brother Mally S. Daugherty refused to appear before the Senate to answer questions concerning the Teapot Dome Scandal, in which both were implicated. In *McGrain v. Daugherty* the Court affirmed congressional power to investigate, even without an explicitly stated legislative purpose.

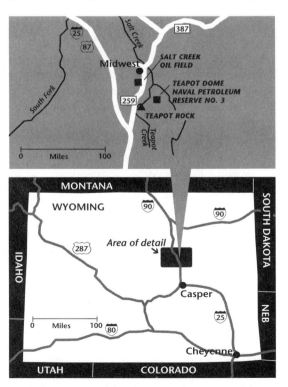

Map of Wyoming and detail showing the location of the U.S. Navy's oil reserves that, along with reserves in Elk Hills, California, were illegally leased to a private oil company.

We come now to the question whether it sufficiently appears that the purpose for which the witness's testimony was sought was to obtain information in aid of the legislative function. . . .

We are of opinion that . . . it sufficiently appears . . . that the object of the investigation and of the effort to secure the witness's testimony was to obtain information for legislative purposes.

It is quite true that the resolution directing the investigation does not in terms avow that it is intended to be in aid of legislation; but it does show that the subject to be investigated was . . . one on which legislation could be had and would be materially aided by the information which the investigation was calculated to elicit. This becomes manifest when it is reflected that the functions of the Department of Justice, the powers and duties of the Attorney General and the duties of his assistants, are all subject to regulation by congressional legislation, and that the department is maintained and its activities are carried on under such appropriations as in the judgment of Congress are needed from year to year.

The only legitimate object the Senate could have in ordering the investigation was to aid it in legislating; and we think the subject-matter was such that the presumption should be indulged that this was the real object. An express avowal of the object would have been better; but in view of the particular subject-matter was not indispensable. . . .

We conclude that the investigation was ordered for a legitimate object; that the witness wrongfully refused to appear and testify before the committee and was lawfully attached; [and] that the Senate is entitled to have him give testimony pertinent to the inquiry, either at its bar or before the committee.

McGrain is significant for two reasons. First, it firmly established Congress's power to inquire and to enforce that power with the ability to punish as an implied power. The Court said: "Experience has taught that mere requests for such information often are unavailing . . . so some means of compulsion are essential to obtain what is needed." This statement was an important affirmation of a long-standing practice. Since 1795 congressional committees had often invoked their power to punish, issuing more than 380 contempt citations over the years.

When a committee does so, and, if the parent chamber approves by a simple majority, the case is forwarded to a U.S. attorney for possible prosecution. Still, in *McGrain*, the justices were unwilling to allow a virtually limitless use of that power. Although they had backed away from the rigid stance of *Kilbourn*, they continued to assert its basic underpinning: Congress could not inquire, generally speaking, into private affairs. Second, and perhaps more important, *McGrain* provides some insight into another controversial area of congressional inquiries: the rights of witnesses. Even as it ruled against Daugherty, the Court held that witnesses may refuse to answer "where the bounds of the power are exceeded or the questions are not pertinent to the matter under inquiry."

This window of opportunity for witnesses to refuse to testify became quite important during World War II and in the postwar period when, out of fear of an influx of foreign ideologies into the United States, Congress embarked on a new type of investigation: the "inquisitorial panel." In short, the goal of congressional hearings on subversive activities was "exposure," not necessarily "information."

As discussed in Box 3-4, this kind of "investigation" is similar to those held in the 1930s by the House Special Committee to Investigate Un-American Activities and in the 1940s and 1950s by Sen. Joseph McCarthy and by the House Un-American Activities Committee (HUAC). The latter were especially controversial. At that time, the fear of communism was so pervasive that even being called to testify before McCarthy or HUAC created such suspicion that individuals lost their jobs, were placed on blacklists, and so forth. Moreover, many witnesses were sufficiently scared of being branded communist sympathizers or supporters that they refused to testify or asserted a constitutional protection against so doing, which resulted in an unusually high number of contempt citations. Between 1792 and 1942, Congress had issued 108 citations; from 1945 to 1957, fourteen committees presented 226 contempt citations to their respective chambers. HUAC alone held 144 "uncooperative" witnesses in contempt.[23]

---

23. Congressional Quarterly, *Guide to Congress*, 3rd ed. (Washington, D.C.: Congressional Quarterly, 1982), 163.

BOX 3-4 INVESTIGATIONS OF "UN-AMERICANISM"

ONE OF THE MOST significant expansions of congressional investigative powers beyond direct legislative matters was the study of subversive movements after World War II. Instead of pursuing traditional lines of congressional inquiry—government operations and national social and economic problems—committees probed into the thoughts, actions, and associations of individuals and institutions.

The House Committee on Un-American Activities was the premier example of these investigative panels. The committee was abolished in January 1975, ending thirty years of controversy over its zealous pursuit of subversives. Its long survival surprised many observers. From the outset the panel, renamed the Internal Security Committee in 1969, was attacked by liberals and civil libertarians. Throughout the 1960s it withstood court suits challenging the constitutionality of its mandate and attempts in the House to end its funding. The death blow finally came when the House Democratic Caucus, by voice vote in January 1975, transferred its functions to the House Judiciary Committee.

EARLY HISTORY

The first congressional investigation of un-American activities was authorized September 19, 1918, toward the close of World War I. That original mandate was to investigate the activities of German brewing interests. The investigation, conducted by the Senate Judiciary Committee, was expanded in 1919 to cover "any efforts . . . to propagate in this country the principles of any party exercising . . . authority in Russia . . . and . . . to incite the overthrow" of the U.S. government.

The House on May 12, 1930, set up a Special Committee to Investigate Communist Activities in the United States—the Fish Committee, so called after its chairman, Rep. Hamilton Fish Jr., R-N.Y. On March 20, 1934, the House created a Special Committee on Un-American Activities, under Chairman John W. McCormack, D-Mass. On May 26, 1938, three years after McCormack's committee submitted its report, which covered Nazi as well as communist activities in the United States, the House set up another Special Committee on Un-American Activities, under Chairman Martin Dies Jr., D-Texas. The committee, whose chairman was avowedly anti-communist and anti-New Deal, was given a broad mandate to investigate subversion.

Dies focused his early investigations on organized labor groups, especially the Congress of Industrial Organizations, and set a tactical pattern that would guide the permanent Un-American Activities Committee, which was created in 1945.

Friendly witnesses, who often met in secret with Dies as a one-man subcommittee, accused hundreds of people of supporting communist activities, but few of the accused were permitted to testify in rebuttal. The press treated Dies's charges sensationally, a practice that was to continue after World War II.

The Dies Committee was reconstituted in succeeding Congresses until 1945. That January, at the beginning of the Seventy-ninth Congress, it was renamed the House Committee on Un-American Activities and made a standing committee.

The next five years marked the peak of the committee's influence. In 1947 it investigated communism in the motion picture industry, with repercussions that lasted almost a decade. Its hearings resulted in the Hollywood blacklist that kept many writers and actors suspected of communist leanings out of work.

The committee's investigation in 1948 of State Department official Alger Hiss, and Hiss's subsequent conviction for perjury, established communism as a leading political issue and the committee as an important political force. The case against Hiss was vigorously developed by a young member of the committee, Richard Nixon.

The committee's tactics during this period included extensive use of contempt citations against unfriendly witnesses, some of whom pleaded their Fifth Amendment right against self-incrimination. In 1950, for example, the House voted fifty-nine contempt citations, of which fifty-six had been recommended by the committee.

SENATE INVESTIGATIONS

In the early 1950s the Un-American Activities Committee was overshadowed by Senate investigations conducted by Joseph R. McCarthy, R-Wis., chairman (1953–1954) of the Senate Government Operations Committee's Permanent Investigations Subcommittee. McCarthy's investigation into alleged subversion in the U.S. army—televised nationwide in 1954—intensified concern over the use by Congress of its investigating powers and led to his censure by the Senate in 1954.

During the same period, the Senate Judiciary Committee's Internal Security Subcommittee, established in 1951, also investigated subversive influences in various fields, including government, education, labor unions, the United Nations, and the press.

SOURCE: *Guide to Congress*, 4th ed., ed. Mary Cohn (Washington, D.C.: Congressional Quarterly, 1991), 240.

The House Un-American Activities Committee holds a press conference December 3, 1948, after a closed session. Standing are two committee investigators. Seated are several reporters and, left to right, Richard Nixon, R-Calif., John Rankin, D-Miss., and John McDowell, R-Pa.

In the late 1950s the Supreme Court decided two major cases involving the rights of witnesses to refuse to answer questions. While reading *Watkins v. United States* (1957) and *Barenblatt v. United States* (1959), think about this question: Did the Court treat the cases consistently?[24] If not, what difference do you see?

Watkins v. United States

354 U.S. 178 (1957)
http://laws.findlaw.com/US/354/178.html
Vote: 6 (Black, Brennan, Douglas, Frankfurter, Harlan,
       Warren)
    1 (Clark)
Opinion of the Court: Warren
Concurring opinion: Frankfurter
Dissenting opinion: Clark
Not participating: Burton, Whittaker

24. To hear oral arguments in these cases, navigate to: *www.oyez.org/oyez/frontpage.*

When the House Un-American Activities Committee was made a standing committee in 1945, Congress defined its authority in Rule XI as follows:

The Committee on Un-American Activities, as a whole or by subcommittee, is authorized to make from time to time investigations of (1) the extent, character, and objects of un-American propaganda activities in the United States, (2) the diffusion within the United States of subversive and un-American propaganda that is instigated from foreign countries or of a domestic origin and attacks the principle of the form of government as guaranteed by our Constitution, and (3) all other questions in relation thereto that would aid Congress in any necessary remedial legislation.

In the early 1950s HUAC took that mandate to mean that it could call witnesses to testify about Communist Party infiltration into American society and their involvement in that organization.

Watkins v. United States crystallized when the committee invoked a favorite modus operandi: asking a witness before it to "name names," to implicate others as Communist Party members. Two witnesses told the committee that John T. Watkins, who had been involved in various labor organizations such as the United Electrical, Radio and Machine Workers and the United Auto Workers, was not only a Communist Party member but also a recruiter for the party.

When the committee subpoenaed Watkins in April 1954, he readily answered these allegations. Among his responses was the following:

I would like to make it clear that for a period of time from approximately 1942 to 1947 I cooperated with the Communist Party and participated in Communist activities to such a degree that some persons may honestly believe that I was a member of the party.

I have made contributions upon occasions to Communist causes. I have signed petitions for Communist causes. I attended caucuses at [a] . . . convention at which Communist Party officials were present.

Since I freely cooperated with the Communist Party I have no motive for making the distinction between cooperation and membership except for the simple fact that it is the truth. I never carried a Communist Party card. I never accepted discipline and indeed on several occasions I opposed their position.

The government conceded that in addressing questions pertaining to his own activities, it could "hardly . . . imagine" a more "complete and candid statement."

But it alleged that Watkins went astray because he refused to answer questions about the activities of others. When the committee read a list of names, some of whom Watkins knew, and asked him to say whether they had been Communist Party members, Watkins stated:

I refuse to answer certain questions that I believe are outside the proper scope of your committee's activities. I will answer any questions which this committee puts to me about myself. I will also answer questions about those persons whom I knew to be members of the Communist Party and whom I still believe are. I will not, however, answer any questions with respect to others with whom I associated in the past. I do not believe that any law in this country requires me to testify about persons who may in the past have been Communist Party members or otherwise engaged in Communist Party activity but who to my best knowledge and belief have long since removed themselves from the Communist movement.

Watkins then questioned the pertinency of the inquiries into others' activities to the committee's work:

I do not believe that such questions are relevant to the work of this committee, nor do I believe that this committee has the right to undertake the public exposure of persons because of their past activities. I may be wrong, and the committee may have this power, but until and unless a court of law so holds and directs me to answer, I most firmly refuse to discuss the political activities of my past associates.

At that point, the committee chair responded to Watkins's question relating to pertinency:

This committee is set up by the House of Representatives to investigate subversion and subversive propaganda and to report to the House of Representatives for the purpose of remedial legislation.

The House of Representatives has by a very clear majority . . . directed us to engage in that type of work, and so we do, as a committee of the House of Representatives, have the authority, the jurisdiction, to ask you concerning your activities in the Communist Party, concerning your knowledge of any persons who are members of the Communist Party or who have been members of the Communist Party, and so, Mr. Watkins, you are directed to answer the question propounded to you by counsel.

When Watkins once again refused to respond, the chair of the committee reported the matter to the full House, which held Watkins in contempt and presented the case to a U.S. attorney for criminal prosecution. Watkins was found guilty of "contempt of Congress," fined $100, and given a one-year suspended prison sentence.

In his brief to the Supreme Court, Watkins's lawyer made two interrelated arguments centering on the committee's authority. First, he complained that "the very idea of congressional committee exposure for the sake of exposure unrelated to a legislative purpose is incompatible with our constitutional system." Second, he suggested that the questions his client refused to answer fell beyond "the language of the Committee's authorization" in part because that "authorization is so vague and indefinitive of purpose" as to deprive Watkins of his rights.

MR. CHIEF JUSTICE WARREN delivered the opinion of the Court.

We start with several basic premises on which there is general agreement. The power of the Congress to conduct investigations is inherent in the legislative process. . . . No inquiry is an end in itself; it must be related to, and in furtherance of, a legitimate task of the Congress. Investigations conducted solely for the personal aggrandizement of the investigator or to "punish" those investigated are indefensible.

It is unquestionably the duty of all citizens to cooperate with the Congress in its efforts to obtain the facts needed for intelligent legislative action. . . . This, of course, assumes that the constitutional rights of witnesses will be respected by the Congress as they are in a court of justice. The Bill of Rights is applicable to investigations as to all forms of governmental action. . . .

Abuses of the investigative process may imperceptibly lead to abridgment of protected freedoms. The mere summoning of a witness and compelling him to testify, against his will, about his beliefs, expressions or associations is a measure of governmental interference. And when those forced revelations concern matters that are unorthodox, unpopular, or even hateful to the general public, the reaction in the life of the witness may be disastrous. This effect is even more harsh when it is past beliefs, expressions or associations that are disclosed and judged by current standards rather than those contemporary with the matters exposed. Nor does the witness alone suffer the consequences. Those who are identified by witnesses and thereby placed in the same glare of publicity are equally subject to public stigma, scorn and obloquy. Beyond that, there is the more subtle and immeasurable effect upon those who tend to adhere to the most orthodox and uncontroversial views and associations in order to avoid a similar fate at some future time. That this impact is partly the result of non-governmental activity by private persons cannot relieve the investigators of their responsibility for initiating the reaction. . . .

Accommodation of the congressional need for particular information with the individual and personal interest in privacy is an arduous and delicate task for any court. We do not underestimate the difficulties that would attend such an undertaking. It is manifest that despite the adverse effects which follow upon compelled disclosure of private matters, not all such inquiries are barred. *Kilbourn v. Thompson* teaches that such an investigation into individual affairs is invalid if unrelated to any legislative purpose. . . .

Petitioner has earnestly suggested that the difficult questions of protecting these rights from infringement by legislative inquiries can be surmounted in this case because there was no public purpose served in his interrogation. His conclusion is based upon the thesis that the Subcom-

mittee was engaged in a program of exposure for the sake of exposure. . . .

The Government contends that the public interest at the core of the investigations of the Un-American Activities Committee is the need by the Congress to be informed of efforts to overthrow the Government by force and violence so that adequate legislative safeguards can be erected. From this core, however, the Committee can radiate outward infinitely to any topic thought to be related in some way to armed insurrection. The outer reaches of this domain are known only by the content of "un-American activities.". . .

An excessively broad charter, like that of the House Un-American Activities Committee, places the courts in an untenable position if they are to strike a balance between the public need for a particular interrogation and the right of citizens to carry on their affairs free from unnecessary governmental interference. It is impossible in such a situation to ascertain whether any legislative purpose justifies the disclosures sought and, if so, the importance of that information to the Congress in furtherance of its legislative function. The reason no court can make this critical judgment is that the House of Representatives itself has never made it. . . .

Absence of the qualitative consideration of petitioner's questioning by the House of Representatives aggravates a serious problem, revealed in this case, in the relationship of congressional investigating committees and the witnesses who appear before them. Plainly these committees are restricted to the missions delegated to them, i.e., to acquire certain data to be used by the House or the Senate in coping with a problem that falls within its legislative sphere. No witness can be compelled to make disclosures on matters outside that area. This is a jurisdictional concept of pertinency drawn from the nature of a congressional committee's source of authority. . . . When the definition of jurisdictional pertinency is as uncertain and wavering as in the case of the Un-American Activities Committee, it becomes extremely difficult for the Committee to limit its inquiries to statutory pertinency. . . .

The problem attains proportion when viewed from the standpoint of the witness who appears before a congressional committee. He must decide at the time the questions are propounded whether or not to answer. . . .

It is obvious that a person compelled to make this choice is entitled to have knowledge of the subject to which the interrogation is deemed pertinent. . . .

The statement of the Committee Chairman in this case, in response to petitioner's protest, was woefully inadequate to convey sufficient information as to the pertinency of the questions to the subject under inquiry. Petitioner was thus not accorded a fair opportunity to determine whether he was within his rights in refusing to answer, and his conviction is necessarily invalid under the Due Process Clause of the Fifth Amendment.

We are mindful of the complexities of modern government and the ample scope that must be left to the Congress as the sole constitutional depository of legislative power. Equally mindful are we of the indispensable function, in the exercise of that power, of congressional investigations. The conclusions we have reached in this case will not prevent the Congress, through its committees, from obtaining any information it needs for the proper fulfillment of its role in our scheme of government. . . . It is only those investigations that are conducted by use of compulsory process that give rise to a need to protect the rights of individuals against illegal encroachment. A measure of added care on the part of the House and the Senate in authorizing the use of compulsory process and by their committees in exercising that power would suffice. That is a small price to pay if it serves to uphold the principles of limited, constitutional government without constricting the power of the Congress to inform itself.

Reversed and remanded.

MR. JUSTICE FRANKFURTER, concurring.

I deem it important to state what I understand to be the Court's holding. Agreeing with its holding, I join its opinion. . . .

To turn to the immediate problem before us, the scope of inquiry that a committee is authorized to pursue must be defined with sufficiently unambiguous clarity to safeguard a witness from the hazards of vagueness in the enforcement of the criminal process against which the Due Process Clause protects. The questions must be put with relevance and definiteness sufficient to enable the witness to know whether his refusal to answer may lead to conviction for criminal contempt and to enable both the trial and the appellate courts readily to determine whether the particular circumstances justify a finding of guilt.

While implied authority for the questioning by the Committee, sweeping as was its inquiry, may be squeezed out of the repeated acquiescence by Congress in the Committee's inquiries, the basis for determining petitioner's guilt is not thereby laid. Prosecution for contempt of Congress presupposes an adequate opportunity for the defendant to have awareness of the pertinency of the information that he has denied to Congress. And the basis of such awareness must be contemporaneous with the witness' refusal to answer and not at the trial for it. Accordingly, the actual scope of the inquiry that the Committee was authorized to conduct and the relevance of the questions to that inquiry must be shown to have been luminous at the time when asked and not left, at best, in cloudiness. The circumstances of this case were wanting in these essentials.

MR. JUSTICE CLARK, dissenting.

It may be that at times the House Committee on Un-American Activities has, as the Court says, "conceived of its task in the grand view of its name." And, perhaps, as the Court indicates, the rules of conduct placed upon the Committee by the House admit of individual abuse and unfairness. But that is none of our affair. So long as the object of a legislative inquiry is legitimate and the questions propounded are pertinent thereto, it is not for the courts to interfere with the committee system of inquiry. To hold otherwise would be an infringement on the power given the Congress to inform itself, and thus a trespass upon the fundamental American principle of separation of powers. The majority has substituted the judiciary as the grand inquisitor and supervisor of congressional investigations. It has never been so. . . .

I think the Committee here was acting entirely within its scope and that the purpose of its inquiry was set out with "undisputable clarity." In the first place, [its charter] must be read as a whole, not dissected. It authorized investigation into subversive activity, its extent, character, objects, and diffusion. While the language might have been more explicit than using such words as "un-American," or phrases like "principle of the form of government," still these are fairly well understood terms. We must construe them to give them meaning if we can. Our cases indicate that rather than finding fault with the use of words or phrases, we are bound to presume that the action of the legislative body in granting authority to the Committee was with a legitimate object "if [the action] is capable of being so construed." Before we can deny the authority "it must be obvious that" the Committee has "exceeded the bounds of legislative power." The fact that the Committee has often been attacked has caused close scrutiny of its acts by the House as a whole and the House has repeatedly given the Committee its approval. "Power" and "responsibility" have not been separated. But the record in this case does not stop here. It shows that at the hearings involving Watkins, the Chairman made statements explaining the functions of the Committee. And, furthermore, Watkins' action at the hearing clearly reveals that he was well acquainted with the purpose of the hearing. It was to investigate Communist infiltration into his union. This certainly falls within the grant of authority from [its charter] and the House has had ample opportunity to limit the investigative scope of the Committee if it feels that the Committee has exceeded its legitimate bounds.

The Court makes much of petitioner's claim of "exposure for exposure's sake" and strikes at the purposes of the Committee through this catch phrase. But we are bound to accept as the purpose of the Committee [as stated in its charter] together with the statements of the Chairman at the hearings involved here. Nothing was said of exposure. The statements of a single Congressman cannot transform the real purpose of the Committee into something not authorized by the parent resolution. The Court indicates that the questions propounded were asked for exposure's sake and had no pertinency to the inquiry. It appears to me that they were entirely pertinent to the announced purpose of the Committee's inquiry. Undoubtedly Congress has the power to inquire into the subjects of communism and the Communist Party. As a corollary of the congressional power to inquire into such subject matter, the Congress, through its committees, can legitimately seek to identify individual members of the Party.

The pertinency of the questions is highlighted by the need for the Congress to know the extent of infiltration of communism in labor unions. This technique of infiltration was that used in bringing the downfall of countries formerly free but now still remaining behind the Iron Curtain. . . . If the parties about whom Watkins was interrogated were Communists and collaborated with him, as a prior witness indicated, an entirely new area of investigation might have been opened up. Watkins' silence prevented the Committee from learning this information which could have been vital

to its future investigation. The Committee was likewise entitled to elicit testimony showing the truth or falsity of the prior testimony of the witnesses who had involved Watkins and the union with collaboration with the Party. If the testimony was untrue a false picture of the relationship between the union and the Party leaders would have resulted. For these reasons there were ample indications of the pertinency of the questions.

Barenblatt v. United States

360 U.S. 109 (1959)
http://laws.findlaw.com/US/360/109.html
Vote: 5 (Clark, Frankfurter, Harlan, Stewart, Whittaker)
    4 (Black, Brennan, Douglas, Warren)
Opinion of the Court: Harlan
Dissenting opinions: Black, Brennan

On February 25, 1953, a subcommittee of HUAC, operating under the same authority it had before the *Watkins* case (Rule XI), initiated a series of hearings called "Communist Methods of Infiltration (Education)." Before the hearings got under way, HUAC's chair stated that their purpose would be to "ascertain the character, extent and objects of Communist Party activities . . . carried on by [teachers] who are subject to the directives and discipline of the Communist Party." More generally, he observed that:

It has been fully established in testimony before congressional committees and before the courts of our land that the Communist Party of the United States is part of an international conspiracy which is being used as a tool or weapon by a foreign power to promote its own foreign policy and which has for its object the overthrow of the governments of all non-Communist countries, resorting to the use of force and violence, if necessary.

Among those testifying before the committee was Francis X. T. Crowley, who admitted that while he was a graduate student at the University of Michigan in 1950 he had belonged to a club with links to the Communist Party. He also told the committee that Lloyd Barenblatt, with whom he had shared an apartment, had been a member as well. Based on that information, in June 1954 the committee subpoenaed Barenblatt to testify before it. Since 1950 Barenblatt had been a psychology instructor at Vassar, but after he received the subpoena, the college refused to renew his contract. So it was an unemployed Barenblatt who appeared before HUAC.

Barenblatt told the committee that he had been a teaching fellow at Michigan, as Crowley had testified. He also admitted that he knew Crowley. But he refused to answer five questions about his activities:

1. Are you now a member of the Communist Party?
2. Have you ever been a member of the Communist Party?
3. Now, you have stated you knew Francis Crowley. Did you know Francis Crowley as a member of the Communist Party?
4. Were you ever a member of the Haldane Club of the Communist Party while at the University of Michigan?
5. Were you a member while a student of the University of Michigan Council of Arts, Sciences, and Professions?

The House held him in contempt for unlawfully refusing to answer these questions, and a U.S. attorney sought and obtained a conviction against him.

On appeal to the Supreme Court, Barenblatt's American Civil Liberties Union lawyers raised three claims: First, "on the basis of . . . *Watkins*, it is clear that the language of the legislation purportedly granting investigative authority to the House Committee was not sufficiently definite and specific to constitute a delegation of power, and thus there is a complete lack of authority in the Committee to investigate by compulsory process." In other words, they reiterated Warren's reasoning in *Watkins* that first, the authority of the committee rested on a rule (Rule XI) that was too vague; second, the questions lacked pertinence; and third, the questions infringed on Barenblatt's First Amendment right to expression and association.

In response, the government argued that although the Court in *Watkins* "criticized the Committee's authorizing resolution," it did not invalidate it. And now the Court must wake up to the fact that Congress was quite serious about investigating communist infiltration, with the functions primarily falling to HUAC. As the government claimed:

The Supreme Court upheld the conviction of Lloyd Barenblatt, left, for contempt of Congress. Barenblatt had refused to testify about his beliefs and his membership in a university club. Shown at a rally November 5, 1959, with Willard Uphaus, another defendant, Barenblatt thanked the ACLU and other organizations that helped him fight his case.

Whatever justification there may be for criticism of [HUAC's] authorizing resolution on its face on grounds of vagueness and imprecision, the resolution comes before the Court, not in its bare terms alone, but with a "persuasive gloss of legislative history" . . . which shows beyond a doubt that there is one subject, above all others, which the House of Representatives has desired and does desire this Committee continuously to investigate and periodically to report on to it. That subject is Communism, in its various aspects and facets, and the menace posed by that system and ideology to American government and institutions.

MR. JUSTICE HARLAN delivered the opinion of the Court.

Once more the Court is required to resolve the conflicting constitutional claims of congressional power and of an individual's right to resist its exercise. The congressional power in question concerns the internal process of Congress in moving within its legislative domain; it involves the utilization of its committees to secure "testimony needed to enable it efficiently to exercise a legislative function belonging to it under the Constitution." (*McGrain v. Daugherty*) . . . The scope of the power of inquiry, in short, is as penetrating and far-reaching as the potential power to enact and appropriate under the Constitution. . . .

At the outset it should be noted that Rule XI authorized this Subcommittee to compel testimony within the framework of the investigative authority conferred on the Un-American Activities Committee. Petitioner contends that *Watkins v. United States* nevertheless held the grant of this power in all circumstances ineffective because of the vagueness of Rule XI in delineating the Committee jurisdiction to which its exercise was to be appurtenant. . . .

The *Watkins* case cannot properly be read as standing for such a proposition. A principal contention in *Watkins* was that the refusals to answer were justified because the requirement . . . that the questions asked be "pertinent to the question under inquiry" had not been satisfied. This Court reversed the conviction solely on that ground, holding that Watkins had not been adequately apprised of the subject matter of the Subcommittee's investigation or the pertinency thereto of the questions he refused to answer. . . .

Petitioner also contends, independently of *Watkins*, that the vagueness of Rule XI deprived the Subcommittee of the right to compel testimony in this investigation into Communist activity. . . . Granting the vagueness of the Rule, we may not read it in isolation from its long history in the House of Representatives. Just as legislation is often given meaning by the gloss of legislative reports, administrative interpretation, and long usage, so the proper meaning of an authorization to a congressional committee is not to be derived alone from its abstract terms unrelated to the definite content furnished them by the course of congressional actions. The Rule comes to us with a "persuasive gloss of legislative history," which shows beyond doubt that in pursuance of its legislative concerns in the domain of "national security" the House has clothed the Un-American Activities Committee with pervasive authority to investigate Communist activities in this country. . . .

In light of this . . . history it can hardly be seriously argued that the investigation of Communist activities generally, and the attendant use of compulsory process, was beyond the purview of the Committee's intended authority under Rule XI. . . .

Undeniably a conviction for contempt under 2 U.S.C. §192 cannot stand unless the questions asked are pertinent to the subject matter of the investigation. *Watkins v. United States*. But the factors which led us to rest decision on this ground in *Watkins* were very different from those involved here.

In *Watkins* the petitioner had made specific objection to the Subcommittee's questions on the ground of pertinency; the question under inquiry had not been disclosed in any illuminating manner; and the questions asked the petitioner were not only amorphous on their face, but in some instances clearly foreign to the alleged subject matter of the investigation—"Communism in labor."

. . . What we deal with here is whether petitioner was sufficiently apprised of "the topic under inquiry" thus authorized "and the connective reasoning whereby the precise questions asked relate[d] to it." In light of his prepared memorandum of constitutional objections there can be no doubt that this petitioner was well aware of the Subcommittee's authority and purpose to question him as it did. . . . The subject matter of the inquiry had been identified at the commencement of the investigation as Communist infiltration into the field of education. Just prior to petitioner's appearance before the Subcommittee, the scope of the day's hearings had been announced as "in the main communism in education and the experiences and background in the party by Francis X. T. Crowley. It will deal with activities in Michigan, Boston, and in some small degree, New York.". . . [P]etitioner refused to answer questions as to his own Communist Party affiliations, whose pertinency of course was clear beyond doubt. . . .

Our function, at this point, is purely one of constitutional adjudication in the particular case and upon the particular record before us, not to pass judgment upon the general wisdom or efficacy of the activities of this Committee in a vexing and complicated field.

The precise constitutional issue confronting us is whether the Subcommittee's inquiry into petitioner's past or present membership in the Communist Party transgressed the provisions of the First Amendment, which of course reach and limit congressional investigations.

. . . [T]he protections of the First Amendment, unlike a proper claim of the privilege against self-incrimination under the Fifth Amendment, do not afford a witness the right to resist inquiry in all circumstances. Where First Amendment rights are asserted to bar governmental interrogation resolution of the issue always involves a balancing by the courts of the competing private and public interests at stake in the particular circumstances shown. These principles were recognized in the *Watkins* case. . . .

The first question is whether this investigation was related to a valid legislative purpose, for Congress may not constitutionally require an individual to disclose his political relationships or other private affairs except in relation to such a purpose.

That Congress has wide power to legislate in the field of Communist activity in this Country, and to conduct appropriate investigations in aid thereof, is hardly debatable. The existence of such power has never been questioned by this Court. . . . Justification for its exercise in turn rests on the long and widely accepted view that the tenets of the Communist Party include the ultimate overthrow of the Government of the United States by force and violence, a view which has been given formal expression by the Congress. . . .

Nor can we accept the further contention that this investigation should not be deemed to have been in furtherance of a legislative purpose because the true objective of the Committee and of the Congress was purely "exposure." So long as Congress acts in pursuance of its constitutional power, the Judiciary lacks authority to intervene on the basis of the motives which spurred the exercise of that power. . . . The constitutional legislative power of Congress in this instance is beyond question.

Finally, the record is barren of other factors which in themselves might sometimes lead to the conclusion that the individual interests at stake were not subordinate to those of the state. . . .

We conclude that the balance between the individual and the governmental interests here at stake must be struck in favor of the latter, and that therefore the provisions of the First Amendment have not been offended.

MR. JUSTICE BLACK, with whom THE CHIEF JUSTICE and MR. JUSTICE DOUGLAS concur, dissenting.

It goes without saying that a law to be valid must be clear enough to make its commands understandable. For obvious reasons, the standard of certainty required in criminal statutes is more exacting than in noncriminal statutes. This is simply because it would be unthinkable to convict a man for violating a law he could not understand. This Court has recognized that the stricter standard is as much required in criminal contempt cases as in all other criminal cases, and has emphasized that the "vice of vagueness" is es-

pecially pernicious where legislative power over an area involving speech, press, petition and assembly is involved. In this area the statement that a statute is void if it "attempts to cover so much that it effectively covers nothing," takes on double significance. For a statute broad enough to support infringement of speech, writings, thoughts and public assemblies, against the unequivocal command of the First Amendment necessarily leaves all persons to guess just what the law really means to cover, and fear of a wrong guess inevitably leads people to forego the very rights the Constitution sought to protect above all others. Vagueness becomes even more intolerable in this area if one accepts, as the Court today does, a balancing test to decide if First Amendment rights shall be protected. It is difficult at best to make a man guess—at the penalty of imprisonment—whether a court will consider the State's need for certain information superior to society's interest in unfettered freedom. It is unconscionable to make him choose between the right to keep silent and the need to speak when the statute supposedly establishing the "state's interest" is too vague to give him guidance.

Measured by the foregoing standards, Rule XI cannot support any conviction for refusal to testify. . . .

The First Amendment says in no equivocal language that Congress shall pass no law abridging freedom of speech, press, assembly or petition. The activities of this Committee, authorized by Congress, do precisely that, through exposure, obloquy and public scorn. See *Watkins v. United States.* The Court does not really deny this fact but relies on . . . [t]he notion that despite the First Amendment's command Congress can abridge speech and association if this Court decides that the governmental interest in abridging speech is greater than an individual's interest in exercising that freedom. . . .

I do not agree that laws directly abridging First Amendment freedoms can be justified by a congressional or judicial balancing process. There are, of course, cases suggesting that a law which primarily regulates conduct but which might also indirectly affect speech can be upheld if the effect on speech is minor in relation to the need for control of the conduct. With these cases I agree. But we did not in [previous cases] even remotely suggest that a law directly aimed at curtailing speech and political persuasion could be saved through a balancing process. Neither these cases, nor any others, can be read as allowing legislative bodies to pass laws abridging freedom of speech, press and association merely because of hostility to views peacefully expressed in a place where the speaker had a right to be. Rule XI, on its face and as here applied, since it attempts inquiry into beliefs, not action—ideas and associations, not conduct—does just that.*

To apply the Court's balancing test under such circumstances is to read the First Amendment to say "Congress shall pass no law abridging freedom of speech, press, assembly and petition, unless Congress and the Supreme Court reach the joint conclusion that on balance the interest of the Government in stifling these freedoms is greater than the interest of the people in having them exercised." This is closely akin to the notion that neither the First Amendment nor any other provision of the Bill of Rights should be enforced unless the Court believes it is reasonable to do so. Not only does this violate the genius of our written Constitution, but it runs expressly counter to the injunction to Court and Congress made by Madison when he introduced the Bill of Rights. "If they [the first ten amendments] are incorporated into the Constitution, independent tribunals of justice will consider themselves in a peculiar manner the guardians of those rights; they will be an impenetrable bulwark against every assumption of power in the Legislative or Executive; they will be naturally led to resist every encroachment upon rights expressly stipulated for in the Constitution by the declaration of rights." Unless we return to this view of our judicial function, unless we once again accept the notion that the Bill of Rights means what it says and that this Court must enforce that meaning, I am of the opinion that our great charter of liberty will be more honored in the breach than in the observance.

---

*I do not understand the Court's opinion in *Watkins v. United States* to approve the type of balancing process adopted in the Court's opinion here. We did discuss in that case "the weight to be ascribed to . . . the interest of the Congress in demanding disclosures from an unwilling witness." As I read, and still read, the Court's discussion of this problem in *Watkins* it was referring to the problems raised by *Kilbourn v. Thompson*, which held that legislative committees could not make roving inquiries into the private business affairs of witnesses. The Court, in *Kilbourn*, held that the courts must be careful to insure that, on balance, Congress did not unjustifiably encroach on an individual's private business affairs. Needless to say, an individual's right to silence in such matters is quite a different thing from the public's interest in freedom of speech and the test applicable to one has little, if anything, to do with the test applicable to the other.

But even assuming what I cannot assume, that some balancing is proper in this case, I feel that the Court after stating the test ignores it completely. At most it balances the right of the Government to preserve itself, against Barenblatt's right to refrain from revealing Communist affiliations. Such a balance, however, mistakes the factors to be weighed. . . . [I]t completely leaves out the real interest in Barenblatt's silence, the interest of the people as a whole in being able to join organizations, advocate causes and make political "mistakes" without later being subjected to governmental penalties for having dared to think for themselves. It is this right, the right to err politically, which keeps us strong as a Nation. For no number of laws against communism can have as much effect as the personal conviction which comes from having heard its arguments and rejected them, or from having once accepted its tenets and later recognized their worthlessness. Instead, the obloquy which results from investigations such as this not only stifles "mistakes" but prevents all but the most courageous from hazarding any views which might at some later time become disfavored. This result, whose importance cannot be overestimated, is doubly crucial when it affects the universities, on which we must largely rely for the experimentation and development of new ideas essential to our country's welfare. It is these interests of society, rather than Barenblatt's own right to silence, which I think the Court should put on the balance against the demands of the Government, if any balancing process is to be tolerated. Instead they are not mentioned, while on the other side the demands of the Government are vastly overstated and called "self preservation." It is admitted that this Committee can only seek information for the purpose of suggesting laws, and that Congress' power to make laws in the realm of speech and association is quite limited, even on the Court's test. Its interest in making such laws in the field of education, primarily a state function, is clearly narrower still. Yet the Court styles this attenuated interest self-preservation and allows it to overcome the need our country has to let us all think, speak, and associate politically as we like and without fear of reprisal. Such a result reduces "balancing" to a mere play on words. . . .

Finally, I think Barenblatt's conviction violates the Constitution because the chief aim, purpose and practice of the House Un-American Activities Committee, as disclosed by its many reports, is to try witnesses and punish them because they are or have been Communists or because they refuse to admit or deny Communist affiliations. The punishment imposed is generally punishment by humiliation and public shame. . . .

The same intent to expose and punish is manifest in the Committee's investigation which led to Barenblatt's conviction. The declared purpose of the investigation was to identify to the people of Michigan the individuals responsible for the, alleged, Communist success there. The Committee claimed that its investigation "uncovered" members of the Communist Party holding positions in the school systems in Michigan; that most of the teachers subpoenaed before the Committee refused to answer questions on the ground that to do so might result in self-incrimination, and that most of these teachers had lost their jobs. . . . It then stated that "the Committee on Un-American Activities approves of this action. . . ." The Court, today, barely mentions these statements, which, especially when read in the context of past reports by the Committee, show unmistakably what the Committee was doing. I cannot understand why these reports are deemed relevant to a determination of a congressional intent to investigate communism in education, but irrelevant to any finding of congressional intent to bring about exposure for its own sake or for the purposes of punishment.

I do not question the Committee's patriotism and sincerity in doing all this. I merely feel that it cannot be done by Congress under our Constitution. For, even assuming that the Federal Government can compel witnesses to testify as to Communist affiliations in order to subject them to ridicule and social and economic retaliation, I cannot agree that this is a legislative function. Such publicity is clearly punishment, and the Constitution allows only one way in which people can be convicted and punished. As we said in [*United States v.*] *Lovett* [1946], "Those who wrote our Constitution well knew the danger inherent in special legislative acts which take away the life, liberty or property of particular named persons because the legislature thinks them guilty of conduct which deserves punishment. They intended to safeguard the people of this country from punishment without trial by duly constituted courts." Thus if communism is to be made a crime, and Communists are to be subjected to "pains and penalties," I would still hold this conviction bad, for the crime of communism, like all others, can be punished only by court and jury after a trial with all judicial safeguards. . . .

Ultimately all the questions in this case really boil down to one—whether we as a people will try fearfully and futilely to preserve democracy by adopting totalitarian methods, or whether in accordance with our traditions and our Constitution we will have the confidence and courage to be free.

To return to our initial question: Did the Court treat the claims of *Barenblatt* and *Watkins* consistently? The majority in *Barenblatt* went to great lengths to indicate that it did, indeed, that *Barenblatt* amounted to nothing more or less than a "clarification" of *Watkins*. But many legal analysts, not to mention Justice Hugo L. Black's eloquent dissent, suggest that at minimum the justices backed away from *Watkins*, and others say that *Barenblatt* signaled a reversal of sorts of the earlier ruling.

If it was a reversal, how can we explain the shift, which occurred within a two-year period? There are two possibilities. The first takes us back to our discussion in Chapter 2 about constraints on the Court imposed by the separation of powers system. On this account, *Barenblatt* constituted "a strategic withdrawal" because at the time the Court was under a good deal of pressure from the public and Congress.[25] In particular, *Watkins* and other "liberal" decisions on subversive activity and on discrimination, such as *Brown v. Board of Education* (1954), made the Court the target of numerous congressional proposals. A few even sought to remove the Court's jurisdiction to hear cases involving subversive activities. According to some observers, the justices felt the heat and acceded to congressional pressure.

Another explanation is that personnel changes produced a more conservative Court, that *Barenblatt* was simply part of a trend ushered in by President Dwight Eisenhower's appointments of Charles Whittaker and Potter Stewart. By way of support, scholars point to the voting alignments in the two cases and to the general trend in the disposition of civil liberties cases. As Walter F. Murphy noted, during the 1956 term, which included *Watkins*, the Court ruled in favor of the civil liberties claim in

---

25. C. Herman Pritchett, *Congress versus the Supreme Court* (Minneapolis: University of Minnesota Press, 1961), 12.

74 percent of the cases; that figure fell to 59 percent and 51 percent in the 1957 and 1958 terms, respectively.[26]

Either way, the explanations indicate the susceptibility of the Court to political influences outside and inside its chambers. As the dangers associated with the cold war began to ebb, the justices again evinced a change of heart on the rights of witnesses. In case after case in the 1960s, they reversed the convictions of many whom Congress had cited for contempt. But its most significant decision involved not Congress, but a state legislature. In *Gibson v. Florida Legislative Investigating Commission* (1963) the Court reversed the contempt conviction of a leader in the National Association for the Advancement of Colored People (NAACP) who refused to provide a committee with the organization's membership records. Theodore R. Gibson argued that doing so would abridge his First Amendment rights. The Supreme Court distinguished this dispute from *Barenblatt*, noting that the state had not sufficiently linked the NAACP to subversive activities and, therefore, had provided no compelling reason for wanting the membership lists. More generally, the Court said:

[T]his Court's prior holdings demonstrate that there can be no question that the State has power adequately to inform itself—through legislative investigation, if it so desires—in order to act and protect its legitimate and vital interests. . . . It is no less obvious, however, that the legislative power to investigate, broad as it may be, is not without limit. . . . [W]e hold . . . that groups which themselves are neither engaged in subversive or other illegal or improper activities nor demonstrated to have any substantial connections with such activities are to be protected in their [First Amendment rights].

In essence, the Court sought to strike a balance between the rights of individuals and those of legislatures, no easy task because of the substantive nature of the power to investigate. Certainly, as HUAC's activities illustrate, there are ample opportunities for abuse. But, when Congress invokes the investigation power in a responsible manner, it can serve as an important check on abuses of the system made by other actors. We have only to consider congressional hearings into the Watergate scandal, which we shall examine in Chapter 4, to see the truth in this.

Inherent Powers

As we have seen, Congress has not only enumerated powers but also powers that can be implied or inferred from, or are incidental to, its role as the lawmaking institution. In addition, many analysts argue that Congress has certain inherent powers that are neither explicit nor even implied by the Constitution, but which somehow attach themselves to sovereign states *(see Table 3-4, page 150)*.

As Justice Story defined them, inherent powers are those that result "from the whole mass of the powers of the National Government, and from the nature of political society, [not as] a consequence or incident of the powers specifically enumerated."[27] For example, as noted earlier, some analysts suggest that the congressional power to investigate is an inherent, rather than implied, power. The argument suggests that Congress is the law-making body, and an inherent quality of such an institution is the power to investigate.

Although theorists had long espoused this concept, it found its way into constitutional law in *United States v. Curtiss-Wright Export Corp.* (1936). As you read this case, pay particular attention to Justice George Sutherland's explication of inherent powers. How does he define them? More important, how does he square the existence of inherent powers with the idea of a government based on enumeration? Keep in mind that during the Harding presidency Sutherland gained substantial international policy-making experience; he represented the administration during a conference on the Limitation of Naval Armaments in 1921 and served as counsel in arbitration between the United States and Norway over shipping. How might this experience have affected his resolution of this dispute?

---

26. Walter F. Murphy, *Congress and the Supreme Court* (Chicago: University of Chicago Press, 1962), 246.

27. Joseph Story, *Commentaries on the Constitution*, vol. III (New York: Da Capo Press, 1970; reprint of 1833 edition), 124.

BOX 3-5   GEORGE SUTHERLAND (1922–1938)

GEORGE SUTHERLAND was born March 25, 1862, in Buckinghamshire, England, and brought to the United States the following year by his parents. His father, a recent convert to the Church of Jesus Christ of Latter-day Saints, settled his family in Springville in the Utah Territory. The senior Sutherland soon deserted the Mormons, but the family remained in Utah. George Sutherland learned the value of thrift and hard work in his childhood—he left school at age twelve to help support the family. By the time he was sixteen, however, he had saved enough money to enroll at Brigham Young Academy in

Provo. After three years there, he spent a year working for the company building the Rio Grande Western Railroad and in 1883 entered the University of Michigan Law School. He studied law for only one year before returning to Provo to start his law practice. He married Rosamund Lee of Beaver, Utah, on June 18, 1883. The couple had two daughters and one son.

AFTER TEN years in Provo, Sutherland in 1893 moved to Salt Lake City. The next year he helped found the Utah Bar Association. When the territory achieved statehood in 1896, Sutherland, running as a Republican, was elected to the first state Senate. In 1900 he was elected to the U.S. House of Representatives. He declined to run for a second term in the House but was elected in 1904 to the U.S. Senate, serving from 1905 to 1917.

During his first term in the Senate, Sutherland endorsed several reform measures, including the Pure Food and Drug Act (1906), the Postal Savings Act (1910), and a compensation bill for workers injured in interstate commerce (1911–

1912). He also played a major role in the revision and codification of federal criminal statutes. Among legislative programs he opposed were statehood for Arizona and New Mexico (1912)—because their constitutions provided for recalls, initiatives, and referenda—the Federal Reserve Act (1913), the Sixteenth Amendment (1913), the Clayton Antitrust Act (1914), and the Federal Trade Commission Act (1914). He also opposed the nomination of Louis D. Brandeis to the Supreme Court.

In 1916 Sutherland failed in his attempt to be renominated by the Utah Republican Party. He stayed in Washington, D.C., practiced law, and remained in touch with former Senate colleague Warren Harding. Sutherland developed into one of Harding's closest advisers and worked on his successful presidential campaign in 1920. Soon thereafter Sutherland represented the Harding administration as chair of the advisory committee to the Washington Conference for the Limitation of Naval Armaments in 1921 and as counsel in arbitration between Norway and the United States over matters of shipping.

President Harding named Sutherland to the Supreme Court when Justice John H. Clarke unexpectedly resigned to work for the cause of world peace. He was confirmed by voice vote the same day he was nominated, September 5, 1922. Sutherland retired from the Court January 17, 1938, and died in Stockbridge, Massachusetts, July 18, 1942.

SOURCE: Joan Biskupic and Elder Witt, *Guide to the U.S. Supreme Court*, 3rd ed. (Washington, D.C.: Congressional Quarterly, 1997), 924–925.

United States v. Curtiss-Wright Export Corp.

299 U.S. 304 (1936)
http://laws.findlaw.com/US/299/304.html
Vote: 7 (Brandeis, Butler, Cardozo, Hughes, Roberts,
Sutherland, Van Devanter)
1 (McReynolds)
Opinion of the Court: Sutherland
Not participating: Stone

After Charles Lindbergh's 1927 transatlantic flight, the aviation industry began to boom. Americans were convinced that "flying . . . would take its place as the new mode of transportation." [28] As a result, many new companies, including Curtiss-Wright, formed to build aircraft.

Although it started off on a strong footing, Curtiss-Wright soon fell prey to the Great Depression: between 1930 and 1931, it lost $13 million. To avoid going bankrupt, it looked beyond the United States into the foreign market, where money still could be made. However, Curtiss-Wright was not selling its wares to other private companies, but to foreign governments involved in military conflicts and in need of war planes.

The company found a ready buyer in Bolivia, which since 1932 had been at war with Paraguay over the Chaco, a region east of Bolivia. Landlocked Bolivia was determined to take control of the Chaco to gain access to the Atlantic Ocean. It became an excellent customer of Curtiss-Wright's, buying thirty-four planes in the early 1930s. The Chaco war, in turn, enabled the company to survive the Depression.

Things began to turn sour in 1934. Books and articles appeared attacking companies like Curtiss-Wright as "merchants of death." More important, the League of Nations wanted to put an end to the Chaco war and asked the United States to help. In response, President Franklin Roosevelt asked Congress to enact a resolution enabling him to prohibit the sale of arms to the warring countries, and on May 28, 1934, Congress did so.

28. We adopt this and what follows from Robert A. Divine, "The Case of the Smuggled Bombers," in *Quarrels That Have Shaped the Constitution* by John A. Garraty (New York: Harper and Row, 1987).

[I]f the President finds that the prohibition of the sale of arms and munitions of war in the United States to those countries now engaged in armed conflict in the Chaco may contribute to the reestablishment of peace between those countries, and if after consultation with the governments of other American Republics and with their cooperation, as well as that of such other governments as he may deem necessary, he makes proclamation to that effect, it shall be unlawful to sell, except under such limitations and exceptions as the President prescribes, any arms or munitions of war in any place in the United States to the countries now engaged in that armed conflict, or to any person, company, or association acting in the interest of either country, until otherwise ordered by the President or by Congress.

Whoever sells any arms or munitions of war . . . shall . . . be punished by a fine not exceeding $10,000 or by imprisonment not exceeding two years, or both.

Shortly after the resolution was enacted, Roosevelt issued an order embargoing weapon sales to Bolivia and Paraguay. Curtiss-Wright refused to comply with the order and tried to get around it by disguising bombers as passenger planes. Eventually, it got caught and was charged with violating the order.

The company challenged the government's action. Among its arguments when the case reached the Court, the most pertinent was the contention that the 1934 resolution was invalid because it gave "uncontrolled" lawmaking "discretion" to the president. On this score, the company's reasoning appeared strong: in *Panama Refining Company v. Ryan* (1935) the Court had struck down a congressional act on the ground that the legislature had delegated lawmaking authority to the president without sufficient guidelines *(see Box 5-1, page 266)*. In the company's view, the 1934 resolution was no different from the law struck down in *Panama*.

The U.S. government tried to distinguish the facts in this case from those in the 1935 decision. The government pointed out that the congressional delegation of power in *Panama*, as we shall see, involved domestic, not international, affairs. This distinction was important because "from the beginning of the government, in the conduct of foreign affairs, Congress has followed the practice of conferring upon the President power similar to that conferred by the present resolution." By way of example, U.S. attorneys indicated that as early as 1794, Congress had given the president the "duty of determining" when embargoes should be laid "upon vessels in ports of the United States bound for foreign ports."

MR. JUSTICE SUTHERLAND delivered the opinion of the Court.

It is contended that by the Joint Resolution, the going into effect and continued operation of the resolution was conditioned (a) upon the President's judgment as to its beneficial effect upon the reestablishment of peace between the countries engaged in armed conflict in the Chaco; (b) upon the making of a proclamation, which was left to his unfettered discretion, thus constituting an attempted substitution of the President's will for that of Congress; (c) upon the making of a proclamation putting an end to the operation of the resolution, which again was left to the President's unfettered discretion; and (d) further, that the extent of its operation in particular cases was subject to limitation and exception by the President, controlled by no standard. In each of these particulars, appellees urge that Congress abdicated its essential functions and delegated them to the Executive.

Whether, if the Joint Resolution had related solely to internal affairs it would be open to the challenge that it constituted an unlawful delegation of legislative power to the Executive, we find it unnecessary to determine. The whole aim of the resolution is to affect a situation entirely external to the United States, and falling within the category of foreign affairs. The determination which we are called to make, therefore, is whether the Joint Resolution, as applied to that situation, is vulnerable to attack under the rule that forbids a delegation of the law-making power. In other words, assuming (but not deciding) that the challenged delegation, if it were confined to internal affairs, would be invalid, may it nevertheless be sustained on the ground that its exclusive aim is to afford a remedy for a hurtful condition within foreign territory?

It will contribute to the elucidation of the question if we first consider the differences between the powers of the Federal government in respect of foreign or external affairs and those in respect of domestic or internal affairs. That there are differences between them, and that these differences are fundamental, may not be doubted.

The two classes of powers are different, both in respect of their origin and their nature. The broad statement that the Federal government can exercise no powers except those specifically enumerated in the Constitution, and such implied powers as are necessary and proper to carry into effect the enumerated powers, is categorically true only in respect of our internal affairs. In that field, the primary purpose of the Constitution was to carve from the general mass of legislative powers *then possessed by the states* such portions as it was thought desirable to vest in the Federal government, leaving those not included in the enumeration still in the states. That this doctrine applies only to powers which the states had, is self-evident. And since the states severally never possessed international powers, such powers could not have been carved from the mass of state powers but obviously were transmitted to the United States from some other source. During the colonial period, those powers were possessed exclusively by and were entirely under the control of the Crown. By the Declaration of Independence, "the Representatives of the United States of America" declared the United [not the several] Colonies to be free and independent states, and as such to have "full Power to levy War, conclude Peace, contract Alliances, establish Commerce and to do all other Acts and Things which Independent States may of right do."

As a result of the separation from Great Britain by the colonies, acting as a unit, the powers of external sovereignty passed from the Crown not to the colonies severally, but to the colonies in their collective and corporate capacity as the United States of America. Even before the Declaration, the colonies were a unit in foreign affairs, acting through a common agency—namely the Continental Congress, composed of delegates from the thirteen colonies. That agency exercised the powers of war and peace, raised an army, created a navy, and finally adopted the Declaration of Independence. Rulers come and go; governments end and forms of government change; but sovereignty survives. A political society cannot endure without a supreme will somewhere. Sovereignty is never held in suspense. When, therefore, the external sovereignty of Great Britain in respect of the colonies ceased, it immediately passed to the Union. . . .

The Union existed before the Constitution, which was ordained and established among other things to form "a more perfect Union." Prior to that event, it is clear that the Union, declared by the Articles of Confederation to be "perpetual," was the sole possessor of external sovereignty, and in the Union it remained without change save in so far as the

Constitution in express terms qualified its exercise. The Framers' Convention was called and exerted its powers upon the irrefutable postulate that though the states were several their people in respect of foreign affairs were one. . . .

It results that the investment of the Federal government with the powers of external sovereignty did not depend upon the affirmative grants of the Constitution. The powers to declare and wage war, to conclude peace, to make treaties, to maintain diplomatic relations with other sovereignties, if they had never been mentioned in the Constitution, would have vested in the Federal government as necessary concomitants of nationality. Neither the Constitution nor the laws passed in pursuance of it have any force in foreign territory unless in respect of our own citizens . . . and operations of the nation in such territory must be governed by treaties, international understandings and compacts, and the principles of international law. As a member of the family of nations, the right and power of the United States in that field are equal to the right and power of the other members of the international family. Otherwise, the United States is not completely sovereign. . . .

Practically every volume of the United States Statutes contains one or more acts or joint resolutions of Congress authorizing action by the President in respect of subjects affecting foreign relations, which either leave the exercise of the power to his unrestricted judgment, or provide a standard far more general than that which has always been considered requisite with regard to domestic affairs. . . .

The result of holding that the joint resolution here under attack is void and unenforceable as constituting an unlawful delegation of legislative power would be to stamp this multitude of comparable acts and resolutions as likewise invalid. And while this court may not, and should not, hesitate to declare acts of Congress, however many times repeated, to be unconstitutional if beyond all rational doubt it finds them to be so, an impressive array of legislation such as we have just set forth, enacted by nearly every Congress from the beginning of our national existence to the present day, must be given unusual weight in the process of reaching a correct determination of the problem. A legislative practice such as we have here, evidenced not by only occasional instances, but marked by the movement of a steady stream for a century and a half of time, goes a long way in the direction of proving the presence of unassailable ground for the constitutionality of the practice, to be found in the origin and history of the power involved, or in its nature, or in both combined. . . .

The uniform, long-continued and undisputed legislative practice just disclosed rests upon an admissible view of the Constitution which, even if the practice found far less support in principle than we think it does, we should not feel at liberty at this late day to disturb.

We deem it unnecessary to consider, seriatim, the several clauses which are said to evidence the unconstitutionality of the Joint Resolution as involving an unlawful delegation of legislative power. It is enough to summarize by saying that, both upon principle and in accordance with precedent, we conclude there is sufficient warrant for the broad discretion vested in the President to determine whether the enforcement of the statute will have a beneficial effect upon the reestablishment of peace in the affected countries; whether he shall make proclamation to bring the resolution into operation; whether and when the resolution shall cease to operate and to make proclamation accordingly; and to prescribe limitations and exceptions to which the enforcement of the resolution shall be subject.

Reversed.

Curtiss-Wright was a landmark ruling. As we shall see in Chapter 5, the decision ran directly counter to what the Court was doing in other areas of the law. At the same time it was striking down many segments of Roosevelt's New Deal, in part on the ground that the laws were unconstitutional delegations of power, here the Court upheld congressional authority to delegate power. Why it did so brings us to another important, and for present purposes more relevant, aspect of the decision: the distinction between foreign and domestic affairs. Sutherland justified the delegation of power here on the ground that it involved external affairs, while the Court's rulings on the New Deal programs involved domestic programs.

In this dichotomy the majority found the concept of inherent powers. In its view, the U.S. Constitution transferred some domestic powers from the states to the federal government, leaving some with the states or the people. That is why Congress cannot exercise authority over internal affairs beyond that which is explicitly enumerated or can be implied from that document. In contrast, no such transfer occurred or could have occurred for authority over foreign affairs. Because the states never had such power to begin with, they could not have bestowed it on the federal government. Rather, "authority over foreign affairs is an inherent power, which attaches automatically to the federal government as a sovereign entity, and derives from the Constitution only as the Constitution is the creator of that sovereign entity." [29] It is not Congress specifically but the federal government that enjoys complete authority over foreign relations, which is an inherent power of sovereign nations, one that is derived not from their charters but from their status. Louis Henkin summarized:

Foreign affairs are national affairs. The United States is a single nation-state, and it is the United States (not the States of the Union, singly or together) that has relations with other nations, and the United States Government that conducts these relations and makes foreign policy. [30]

What are we to make of the majority opinion? Some support certainly exists for its distinction between domestic and foreign affairs. We will explore this subject in greater detail in Chapters 4 and 5, but here we can say that some of the Framers would have approved of *Curtiss-Wright*. As Hamilton wrote in Federalist Paper No. 23, "The circumstances that endanger the safety of nations are infinite, and for this reason no constitutional shackles can wisely be imposed on the power to which the care of it is committed." The idea, in short, was not novel, and Sutherland had espoused it during his Senate career.

But *Curtiss-Wright* also has been the subject of some criticism. Historians and legal scholars assert that Sutherland's historical analysis was inaccurate: "There is evidence that, after independence, at least some of the erstwhile colonies . . . considered themselves sovereign, independent states." [31] More relevant here, however, is the argument that the entire notion of "inherent powers" cannot possibly conform with theories underlying the Constitution. The Tenth Amendment states: "The powers not delegated to the United States by the Constitu-

tion, nor prohibited by it to the States, are reserved to the States respectively, or to the people." Can it be that this language applies only to domestic powers and not foreign affairs? *Curtiss-Wright* seems to teach this lesson, and it makes some analysts squirm.

Even so, Sutherland's opinion remains authoritative doctrine. Its conceptualization of the federal government's inherent power over foreign affairs provides that entity with considerable leeway. And it is a doctrine to which the Court continues, generally speaking, to subscribe.

Amendment-Enforcing Power

Many discussions of congressional powers end with those powers inherent to sovereign nations. But it is important to understand, especially today, another source of legislative authority—amendment-enforcing power—because Congress makes frequent use of it as a basis for legislation. Today, seven constitutional amendments (the eighth, the Eighteenth Amendment, was repealed in 1933) contain some variant of the following language: Congress shall have power to enforce, by appropriate legislation, the provisions of this article. For example, the first section of the Fifteenth Amendment says, "The right of citizens of the United States to vote shall not be denied . . . on account of race," and this statement is followed by an enforcement provision. Presumably, the writers of this Reconstruction amendment intended, at the very least, to implement its mandate; that is, Congress could pass legislation forbidding states to deny blacks the right to vote.

Many states, particularly in the South, however, continued to impose barriers such as literacy tests, poll taxes, grandfather clauses, and primary rules aimed at excluding blacks from voting. Throughout the 1950s Congress invoked its enforcement power under the Fifteenth Amendment to enact legislation to end these practices. The 1957 Civil Rights Act, for example, prohibited attempts to intimidate or prevent persons from voting in general or primary elections for federal offices, empowered the attorney general to seek an injunction when an individual was deprived or about to be deprived of the right to vote, gave the district courts jurisdiction over such proceedings, and provided that any person cited for

---

29. Pritchett, *Constitutional Law of the Federal System*, 305.
30. Louis Henkin, *Foreign Affairs and the Constitution* (New York: W. W. Norton, 1975), 15.
31. Ibid., 23.

TABLE 3-5 White and Nonwhite Voter Registration Statistics, 1960, 1964, 1970, 1998

| | Percentage of Voting-Age Population Registered to Vote | | | | | | | |
| | 1960 | | 1964 | | 1970 | | 1998 | |
State	Whites	Nonwhites	Whites	Nonwhites	Whites	Nonwhites	Whites	Nonwhites
Alabama	63.6	13.7	70.7	23.0	85.0	66.0	74.1	74.3
Arkansas	60.9	38.0	71.7	54.4	74.1	82.3	65.9	51.8
Florida	69.3	39.4	84.0	54.4	65.5	55.3	61.1	50.4
Georgia	56.8	29.3	74.5	44.0	71.7	57.2	62.0	64.1
Louisiana	76.9	31.3	80.4	32.0	77.0	57.4	75.2	69.5
Mississippi	63.9	5.2	70.7	6.7	82.1	71.0	75.2	71.3
North Carolina	92.1	39.1	92.5	46.8	68.1	51.3	65.6	57.4
South Carolina	57.1	13.7	78.5	38.8	62.3	56.1	67.9	68.0
Tennessee	73.0	59.1	72.9	69.4	78.5	71.6	63.9	64.8
Texas	42.5	35.5	53.2	57.7	78.5	72.6	59.7	62.1
Virginia	46.1	23.1	55.9	45.7	62.0	57.0	63.5	53.6
Averages	61.1	29.2	73.2	43.3	64.5	62.0	63.5	61.5

SOURCES: *Revolution in Civil Rights* (Washington, D.C.: Congressional Quarterly, 1965), 43, 74; and Lee Epstein, Jeffrey A. Segal, Harold J. Spaeth, and Thomas G. Walker, *The Supreme Court Compendium: Data, Decisions, and Developments*, 3rd ed. (Washington, D.C.: CQ Press, 2003); U.S. Census Bureau *(www.census.gov.).*
    NOTE: 1998 average is for entire South.

contempt should be defended by counsel and allowed to compel witnesses to appear. Another act, passed three years later, enabled judges to appoint "referees" to help blacks register to vote.

Few analysts ever seriously questioned the constitutionality of these laws. Under the Fifteenth Amendment, Congress seemed to have the authority to ensure that states did not deny the right to vote, and, because these acts were aimed at accomplishing that end, they were deemed appropriate under the language of Section 2 of the amendment. But in the mid-1960s voting rights advocates clamored for stronger measures. They claimed that the existing congressional legislation was inadequate, and that the legal suits it authorized the attorney general to undertake were too expensive and not all that successful. Court rulings alone were insufficient to prompt major changes, they argued, because many local governments maintained nondiscriminatory voting laws but administered them in a discriminatory fashion. The South, in other words, was following the letter, but not the spirit, of the laws. Voter registration figures for 1960 and 1964 support this observation: a far lower percent-

age of voting-age nonwhites than of whites was registered to vote (see Table 3-5).

Data of the sort displayed in Table 3-5 convinced Congress that a more aggressive policy was required. The result was the Voting Rights Act of 1965—the most comprehensive, some say drastic, measure yet. Not only was it directed at eliminating every ingenious device designed to restrict suffrage racially, but also it gave the federal government extraordinary power to regulate elections. If a state or a political subdivision had used barriers to voting prior to 1964, or if less than 50 percent of its voting-age population was registered to vote or had voted in the 1964 election—conditions known as the "triggering formula"—the government could send in federal examiners who, in turn, could order state officials to "register all persons found qualified to vote." Moreover, states under the triggering formula were required to receive "preclearance" from the attorney general or a district court before they could enact new voting laws.

The Voting Rights Act of 1965 marked a dramatic change from earlier laws. As we noted, in previous legislation, Congress was simply providing mechanisms to enforce existing rights. Now it was issuing sanctions against states (the preclearance requirements) and allowing the attorney general to take action against certain areas, despite the fact that no judicial body had found the states to be engaging in unconstitutional activity.

Did Congress's power to enforce amendments support such legislation? Was it appropriate under the amendment's language? Given that the act constituted a drastic intrusion of the federal government into state operations, it is not surprising that it was quickly challenged as an unconstitutional use of congressional power. As you read *South Carolina v. Katzenbach*, consider the Court's response, and not just its reaction to the 1965 act.[32] How did it resolve the larger issue of the scope of Congress's amendment-enforcing power?

South Carolina v. Katzenbach

383 U.S. 301 (1966)
http://laws.findlaw.com/US/383/301.html
Vote: 8 (Brennan, Clark, Douglas, Fortas, Harlan, Stewart,
    Warren, White)
    1 (Black)
Opinion of the Court: Warren
Concurring/dissenting opinion: Black

In accordance with the Voting Rights Act of 1965, the director of the Census Bureau sent the following notice to the attorney general in August 1965:

I have determined that in each of the following States less than 50 per centum of the persons of voting age residing therein voted in the presidential election of November 1964: Alabama, Alaska, Georgia, Louisiana, Mississippi, South Carolina, [and] Virginia.

These seven states, as well as parts of several others, met the criteria for coverage under the Voting Rights Act's remedial provisions.

Rather than accede to the federal government, South Carolina asked the U.S. Supreme Court, under its original jurisdiction, to find the act unconstitutional. South Carolina argued that the legislation was not appropriate to enforce the Fifteenth Amendment, that it infringed on states' rights, and that it had the effect of treating states in an unequal manner. Five of the other six states coming under the act's purview—Alaska did not participate—filed amicus curiae briefs in support of South Carolina.

In defense of the law, U.S. government attorneys, including Attorney General Nicholas Katzenbach and Solicitor General Thurgood Marshall, who would later serve on the Court, argued, "Section 2 of the Fifteenth Amendment confers upon Congress power to enact all legislation reasonably adapted to the objective of preventing abridgment of the right to vote on account of race or color." Nineteen states, mostly in the East and Midwest, submitted an amicus curiae brief supporting the U.S. government.[33] In contrast to their southern counterparts, which supported South Carolina's states' rights position, they argued that "although a state has power to determine the qualifications for voting, such power may not be used to violate the Fourteenth and Fifteenth Amendments." The brief further stated, "Congress has power to enact appropriate legislation precluding the states from denying the right to vote on the basis of color."

MR. CHIEF JUSTICE WARREN delivered the opinion of the Court.

The Voting Rights Act was designed by Congress to banish the blight of racial discrimination in voting, which has infected the electoral process in parts of our country for nearly a century. The Act creates stringent new remedies for voting discrimination where it persists on a pervasive scale, and in addition the statute strengthens existing remedies for pockets of voting discrimination elsewhere in the country. Congress assumed the power to prescribe these remedies from §2 of the Fifteenth Amendment, which authorizes the National Legislature to effectuate by "appropriate" measures the constitutional prohibition against racial discrimination in voting. We hold that the sections of the Act which are properly before us are an appropriate means for carrying out Congress' constitutional responsibilities and are

---

32. To hear oral arguments in this case, navigate to: *www.oyez.org/oyez/frontpage.*

33. California and Illinois filed separate amicus curiae briefs in support of the act.

consonant with all other provisions of the Constitution. We therefore deny South Carolina's request that enforcement of these sections of the Act be enjoined.

The constitutional propriety of the Voting Rights Act of 1965 must be judged with reference to the historical experience which it reflects. Before enacting the measure, Congress explored with great care the problem of racial discrimination in voting. . . .

Two points emerge vividly from the voluminous legislative history of the Act contained in the committee hearings and floor debates. First: Congress felt itself confronted by an insidious and pervasive evil which had been perpetuated in certain parts of our country through unremitting and ingenious defiance of the Constitution. Second: Congress concluded that the unsuccessful remedies which it had prescribed in the past would have to be replaced by sterner and more elaborate measures in order to satisfy the clear commands of the Fifteenth Amendment. . . .

. . . [P]rovisions of the Voting Rights Act of 1965 are challenged on the fundamental ground that they exceed the powers of Congress and encroach on an area reserved to the States by the Constitution. . . .

The objections to the Act which are raised under these provisions may therefore be considered only as additional aspects of the basic question presented by the case. Has Congress exercised its powers under the Fifteenth Amendment in an appropriate manner with relation to the States?

The ground rules for resolving this question are clear. The language and purpose of the Fifteenth Amendment, the prior decisions construing its several provisions, and the general doctrines of constitutional interpretation, all point to one fundamental principle. As against the reserved powers of the States, Congress may use any rational means to effectuate the constitutional prohibition of racial discrimination in voting. . . . We turn now to a more detailed description of the standards which govern our review of the Act.

Section 1 of the Fifteenth Amendment declares that "[t]he right of citizens of the United States to vote shall not be denied or abridged by the United States or by any State on account of race, color, or previous condition of servitude." This declaration has always been treated as self-executing and has repeatedly been construed, without further legislative specification, to invalidate state voting qualifications or procedures which are discriminatory on their face or in practice. See . . . *Smith v. Allwright* [1944]; *Gomillion*

v. Lightfoot [1960]; *Louisiana v. United States* [1965]. Those decisions have been rendered with full respect for the general rule . . . that States "have broad powers to determine the conditions under which the right of suffrage may be exercised." The gist of the matter is that the Fifteenth Amendment supersedes contrary exertions of state power. "When a State exercises power wholly within the domain of state interest, it is insulated from federal judicial review. But such insulation is not carried over when state power is used as an instrument for circumventing a federally protected right."

South Carolina contends that the cases cited above are precedents only for the authority of the judiciary to strike down state statutes and procedures—that to allow an exercise of this authority by Congress would be to rob the courts of their rightful constitutional role. On the contrary, §2 of the Fifteenth Amendment expressly declares that "Congress shall have power to enforce this article by appropriate legislation." By adding this authorization, the Framers indicated that Congress was to be chiefly responsible for implementing the rights created in §1. "It is the power of Congress which has been enlarged. Congress is authorized to *enforce* the prohibitions by appropriate legislation. Some legislation is contemplated to make the [Civil War] amendments fully effective." Accordingly, in addition to the courts, Congress has full remedial powers to effectuate the constitutional prohibition against racial discrimination in voting.

Congress has repeatedly exercised these powers in the past, and its enactments have repeatedly been upheld. . . . On the rare occasions when the Court has found an unconstitutional exercise of these powers, in its opinion Congress had attacked evils not comprehended by the Fifteenth Amendment.

The basic test to be applied in a case involving §2 of the Fifteenth Amendment is the same as in all cases concerning the express powers of Congress with relation to the reserved powers of the States. Chief Justice Marshall laid down the classic formulation, 50 years before the Fifteenth Amendment was ratified:

"Let the end be legitimate, let it be within the scope of the constitution, and all means which are appropriate, which are plainly adapted to that end, which are not prohibited, but consist with the letter and spirit of the constitution, are constitutional." *McCulloch v. Maryland* [1819].

The Court has subsequently echoed his language in describing each of the Civil War Amendments:

"Whatever legislation is appropriate, that is, adapted to carry out the objects the amendments have in view, whatever tends to enforce submission to the prohibitions they contain, and to secure to all persons the enjoyment of perfect equality of civil rights and the equal protection of the laws against State denial or invasion, if not prohibited, is brought within the domain of congressional power." *Ex parte Virginia* [1880].

This language was again employed, nearly 50 years later, with reference to Congress' related authority under §2 of the Eighteenth Amendment.

We therefore reject South Carolina's argument that Congress may appropriately do no more than to forbid violations of the Fifteenth Amendment in general terms—that the task of fashioning specific remedies or of applying them to particular localities must necessarily be left entirely to the courts. Congress is not circumscribed by any such artificial rules under §2 of the Fifteenth Amendment. In the oft-repeated words of Chief Justice Marshall, referring to another specific legislative authorization in the Constitution, "This power, like all others vested in Congress, is complete in itself, may be exercised to its utmost extent, and acknowledges no limitations, other than are prescribed in the constitution." *Gibbons v. Ogden* [1824]. . . .

After enduring nearly a century of widespread resistance to the Fifteenth Amendment, Congress has marshalled an array of potent weapons against the evil, with authority in the Attorney General to employ them effectively. Many of the areas directly affected by this development have indicated their willingness to abide by any restraints legitimately imposed upon them. We here hold that the portions of the Voting Rights Act properly before us are a valid means for carrying out the commands of the Fifteenth Amendment. Hopefully, millions of non-white Americans will now be able to participate for the first time on an equal basis in the government under which they live. We may finally look forward to the day when truly "[t]he right of citizens of the United States to vote shall not be denied or abridged by the United States or by any State on account of race, color, or previous condition of servitude."

The bill of complaint is dismissed.

Bill dismissed.

MR. JUSTICE BLACK, concurring and dissenting.

Though . . . I agree with most of the Court's conclusions, I dissent from its holding that every part of §5 of the Act is constitutional. Section 4 (a), to which §5 is linked, suspends for five years all literacy tests and similar devices in those States coming within the formula of §4(b). Section 5 goes on to provide that a State covered by §4(b) can in no way amend its constitution or laws relating to voting without first trying to persuade the Attorney General of the United States or the Federal District Court for the District of Columbia that the new proposed laws do not have the purpose and will not have the effect of denying the right to vote to citizens on account of their race or color. I think this section is unconstitutional on at least two grounds.

(a) The Constitution gives federal courts jurisdiction over cases and controversies only. If it can be said that any case or controversy arises under this section which gives the District Court for the District of Columbia jurisdiction to approve or reject state laws or constitutional amendments, then the case or controversy must be between a State and the United States Government. But it is hard for me to believe that a justifiable controversy can arise in the constitutional sense from a desire by the United States Government or some of its officials to determine in advance what legislative provisions a State may enact or what constitutional amendments it may adopt. If this dispute between the Federal Government and the States amounts to a case or controversy it is a far cry from the traditional constitutional notion of a case or controversy as a dispute over the meaning of enforceable laws or the manner in which they are applied. And if by this section Congress has created a case or controversy, and I do not believe it has, then it seems to me that the most appropriate judicial forum for settling these important questions is this Court acting under its original Art. III, §2, jurisdiction to try cases in which a State is a party. At least a trial in this Court would treat the States with the dignity to which they should be entitled as constituent members of our Federal Union. . . .

(b) My second and more basic objection to §5 is that Congress has here exercised its power under §2 of the Fifteenth Amendment through the adoption of means that conflict with the most basic principles of the Constitution. As the Court says the limitations of the power granted under §2 are the same as the limitations imposed on the exercise of any of the powers expressly granted Congress by the Constitution. The classic formulation of these constitutional limitations was stated by Chief Justice Marshall when he said in *McCulloch v. Maryland*, "Let the end be legitimate, let it be within the scope of the constitution, and all means which are appropriate, which are plainly adapted to that end, *which are not prohibited, but consist with the letter and spirit of the constitution*, are constitutional." (Emphasis added.) Section 5, by providing that some of the States cannot pass state laws or adopt state constitutional amendments without first being compelled to beg federal authorities to approve their policies, so distorts our constitutional structure of government as to render any distinction drawn in the Constitution between state and federal power almost meaningless. One of the most basic premises upon which our structure of government was founded was that the Federal Government was to have certain specific and limited powers and no others, and all other power was to be reserved either "to the States respectively, or to the people." Certainly if all the provisions of our Constitution which limit the power of the Federal Government and reserve other power to the States are to mean anything, they mean at least that the States have power to pass laws and amend their constitutions without first sending their officials hundreds of miles away to beg federal authorities to approve them. Moreover, it seems to me that §5 which gives federal officials power to veto state laws they do not like is in direct conflict with the clear command of our Constitution that "The United States shall guarantee to every State in this Union a Republican Form of Government." I cannot help but believe that the inevitable effect of any such law which forces any one of the States to entreat federal authorities in far-away places for approval of local laws before they can become effective is to create the impression that the State or States treated in this way are little more than conquered provinces. And if one law concerning voting can make the States plead for this approval by a distant federal court or the United States Attorney General, other laws on different subjects can force the States to seek the advance approval not only of the Attorney General but of the President himself or any other chosen members of his staff. It is inconceivable to me that such a radical degradation of state power was intended in any of the provisions of our Constitution or its Amendments. Of course I do not mean to cast any doubt whatever upon the indisputable power of the Federal Government to invalidate a state law once enacted and operative on the ground that it intrudes into the area of supreme federal power. But the Federal Government has heretofore always been content to exercise this power to protect federal supremacy by authorizing its agents to bring lawsuits against state officials once an operative state law has created an actual case and controversy. A federal law which assumes the power to compel the States to submit in advance any proposed legislation they have for approval by federal agents approaches dangerously near to wiping the States out as useful and effective units in the government of our country. I cannot agree to any constitutional interpretation that leads inevitably to such a result. . . .

In this and other prior Acts Congress has quite properly vested the Attorney General with extremely broad power to protect voting rights of citizens against discrimination on account of race or color. Section 5 viewed in this context is of very minor importance and in my judgment is likely to serve more as an irritant to the States than as an aid to the enforcement of the Act. I would hold §5 invalid for the reasons stated above with full confidence that the Attorney General has ample power to give vigorous, expeditious and effective protection to the voting rights of all citizens.

The Court's standard for evaluating amendment-enforcing power, the words *appropriate legislation*, is not so different from the one it uses to adjudicate under the Necessary and Proper Clause. Indeed, not only does Chief Justice Warren cite *McCulloch v. Maryland* with approval, but also his logic reflects Marshall's. Compare Marshall's words, "Let the end be legitimate, let it be within the scope of the constitution, and all means which are appropriate . . . are constitutional," with Warren's: "Congress may use any rational means to effectuate the constitutional prohibition of racial discrimination in voting."

Katzenbach was an important opinion in two regards. First, it upheld the Voting Rights Act, which in turn had a marked effect on closing the gap between white and black voter registration rates; today, throughout the United States, blacks and whites are registered to vote at near equal levels, 60.2 percent and 63.9 percent, respectively (compare also 1964 and 1998 in Table 3-5). Second, and more relevant here, *Katzenbach* greatly enhanced Congress's amendment-enforcing power, placing it on the same plane as implied powers. But, just as is true for implied powers, the amendment-enforcing power is not without limits. The Court made this very clear in **City of Boerne v. Flores** (1997). At issue here was the Religious

Freedom Restoration Act of 1993 (RFRA), which Congress passed by overwhelming majorities in response to the Court's decision in *Employment Division v. Smith* (1990). RFRA directed the Court to adopt a particular standard of law in constitutional cases involving the Free Exercise clause of the First Amendment—a standard the Court had rejected in *Smith*—and that would presumably make it easier for people believing that a government had violated their free exercise rights to prevail in court. In passing some parts of RFRA, Congress relied on the Fourteenth Amendment's enforcement provision. To the United States, which entered the case as an amicus curiae, this use was perfectly permissible because Congress was protecting one of the liberties guaranteed by the Fourteenth Amendment's Due Process Clause, the free exercise of religion.

The Supreme Court disagreed. Although it acknowledged that "Congress can enact legislation under §5 [of the Fourteenth Amendment] enforcing the constitutional right to the free exercise of religion," it held that

the design of the Amendment and the text of §5 are inconsistent with the suggestion that Congress has the power to decree the substance of the Fourteenth Amendment's restrictions on the states. Legislation which alters the meaning of the Free Exercise Clause cannot be said to be enforcing the Clause. Congress does not enforce a constitutional right by changing what the right is. It has been given the power "to enforce," not the power to determine what constitutes a constitutional violation. Were it not so, what Congress would be enforcing would no longer be, in any meaningful sense, the "provisions of [the Fourteenth Amendment]."

The Court also rejected claims that RFRA was a proper exercise of Congress's remedial or preventive power under the enforcement clause of the Fourteenth Amendment. Along these lines, among the features that distinguished it from the Voting Rights Act at issue in *Katzenbach* was, first, a very different sort of congressional record on the need for the legislation: "A comparison between RFRA and the Voting Rights Act is instructive. In contrast to the record which confronted Congress and the judiciary in the voting rights cases, RFRA's legislative record lacks examples of modern instances of generally applicable laws passed because of religious bigotry." Second, "the reach and scope of RFRA distinguish it from

other measures passed under Congress' enforcement power, even in the area of voting rights. In *South Carolina v. Katzenbach*, the challenged provisions were confined to those regions of the country where voting discrimination had been most flagrant"; in the case of RFRA, no such limits existed. The act "is not designed to identify and counteract state laws likely to be unconstitutional because of their treatment of religion."

City of Boerne is an interesting case, but, in some ways, it is distinct from the Court's other decisions dealing with the sources and scope of congressional power. On the whole, with a few scattered exceptions—*City of Boerne* being one—the Court has allowed Congress a good deal of leeway in exercising enumerated and extraconstitutional power, especially in disputes involving that body's power to regulate its own affairs and to enact legislation, even if a law intrudes on state operations. Where the Court has wavered and at times has reined Congress in, is over its authority vis-à-vis the other national institutions. In *City of Boerne* the Court was protecting its own authority, but more usually it is the executive's. In other words, during certain periods of the nation's history, the Court has taken a hard line on the separation of powers doctrine, limiting both friendly and unfriendly relations between Congress and the president.

In Chapter 5, we explore Court rulings in both areas. But before you can understand executive-legislative relations, it is important to establish as strong a grasp of Article II as you now have of Article I. Accordingly, in the next chapter we turn to the Court's interpretation of executive powers.

READINGS

Adler, David Gray, and Larry N. George, eds. *The Constitution and the Conduct of American Foreign Policy*. Lawrence: University Press of Kansas, 1996.

Colton, Campbell C., and John F. Stack Jr., eds. *Congress Confronts the Court: The Struggle for Legitimacy and Authority in Lawmaking*. Lanham, Md.: Rowman & Littlefield, 2001.

Currie, David P. *The Constitution in Congress: The Federalist Period, 1789–1801*. Chicago: University of Chicago Press, 1997.

Davidson, Chandler, and Bernard Grofman, eds. *Quiet Revolution in the South: The Impact of the Voting Rights Act 1965–1990*. Princeton, N.J.: Princeton University Press, 1994.

Elliott, Ward E. Y. *The Rise of Guardian Democracy: The Supreme Court's Role in Voting Rights Disputes, 1845–1969.* Cambridge: Harvard University Press, 1974.

Goodman, Walter. *The Committee: The Extraordinary Career of the House Committee on Un-American Activities.* New York: Farrar, Straus, and Giroux, 1968.

Gunther, Gerald, ed. *John Marshall's Defense of McCulloch v. Maryland.* Stanford: Stanford University Press, 1969.

Henkin, Louis. *Constitutionalism, Democracy, and Foreign Affairs.* New York: Columbia University Press, 1992.

———. *Foreign Affairs and the United States Constitution.* New York: Oxford University Press, 1996.

Katzmann, Robert A. *Courts and Congress.* Washington, D.C.: Brookings Institution, 1997.

Katzmann, Robert A., ed. *Judges and Legislators: Toward Institutional Comity.* Washington, D.C.: Brookings Institution, 1988.

Lawson, Steven F. *Black Ballots: Voting Rights in the South, 1944–1969.* Lanham, Md.: Lexington Books, 1999.

Lofgren, Charles A. "U.S. v. Curtiss-Wright Export Corporation: An Historical Reassessment." *Yale Law Journal* 83 (1973): 1–32.

McGeary, M. Nelson. *The Development of Congressional Investigative Power.* New York: Columbia University Press, 1940.

Murphy, Walter F. *Congress and the Court.* Chicago: University of Chicago Press, 1962.

Pritchett, C. Herman. *Congress versus the Supreme Court, 1957–1960.* Minneapolis: University of Minnesota Press, 1961.

Schmidhauser, John R., and Larry L. Berg. *The Supreme Court and Congress.* New York: Free Press, 1972.

Warren, Charles. *Congress, the Constitution, and the Supreme Court.* Boston: Little, Brown, 1935.

CHAPTER 4

THE EXECUTIVE

THE FRAMERS would have great trouble recognizing today's presidency. The sentiment of the Philadelphia Convention was that the Articles of Confederation were flawed because they did not provide for an executive, but few delegates would have supported the far-reaching powers wielded by modern presidents. After what they had suffered under the British monarch, many delegates had serious reservations about awarding too much authority to the executive branch. Those who supported the New Jersey Plan envisioned a plural executive in which two individuals would share the chief executive position as insurance against excessive power accruing to a single person. The Framers would be amazed at the vast military resources over which the president serves as commander in chief, to say nothing of the hundreds of departments, agencies, and bureaus that constitute the executive branch.

The rather loose wording of Article II has permitted this astonishing growth in the presidency. The article has neither the detail nor the precision of the Framers' Article I description of the legislature; instead, it is dominated by issues of selection and removal, and less attention is devoted to powers and limitations. The wording is quite broad. For example, presidents are given the undefined "executive power" of the United States and are admonished to take care that the laws are "faithfully executed." Other grants of authority, such as the president's role as "Commander in Chief of the Army and Navy" and the preferential position given the chief executive in matters of foreign policy, allow for significant expansion.

The presidency also has grown in response to the world's changing conditions. As American society became more complex, the number of areas requiring government action has mushroomed. Overwhelmed by these responsibilities, Congress has delegated to the executive branch authority that was not anticipated by the Framers. In addition, the expanding importance of defense and foreign policy has demanded a more powerful presidency.

As these changes took place, the Supreme Court was frequently called upon to umpire disputes over the constitutional limits of executive authority. This chapter explores how the justices have interpreted Article II of the Constitution. It is divided into four sections. The first provides an overview of Article II; the second takes up the Supreme Court's general response to questions concerning presidential power; the third considers the domestic powers of the president; and the fourth explores the role of the president in foreign affairs.

ARTICLE II: BASIC CONSIDERATIONS

When the Framers gathered in Philadelphia in 1787, they were uncertain about how to create an executive for the new nation.[1] On the one hand, they knew all too well the dangers of a strong executive. Indeed, widespread dissatisfaction with the British system led states, during

---

1. We adopt some of this discussion from Daniel A. Farber and Suzanna Sherry, *A History of the American Constitution* (St. Paul, Minn.: West Publishing, 1990), 79–81. This book contains excerpts of the debates over Article II.

the period from 1776 to 1778, to adopt constitutions that established weak governorships. State executives were often given short terms of office, with few powers, which were sometimes shared with a council. On the other hand, by 1787 some states had become sufficiently dissatisfied with their weak governorships that they strengthened them. During the war with Britain, it had become apparent that state executives were too inexperienced and politically constrained to maintain an effective effort. Therefore, by the time the Framers met, a range of executive systems existed in the states—from those that remained weak to those that were quite strong.

Which tack would the Founders take? To address this question, let us consider the two aspects of the executive with which the Framers grappled: the structure of the presidency and executive powers.

The Structure of the Presidency

At the constitutional convention, the vast majority of discussions over Article II concerned not the powers of the executive but the structure of the institution. The Framers debated everything about the presidency, including selection, removal, tenure, and succession.

The Selection of the President. The selection of the president was discussed at length at the convention, and several mechanisms were considered, including, notably, selection by the national legislature. In the end the Framers devised a novel solution: the Electoral College. Until then, the executives of most nations had been chosen by bloodline, military power, or legislative selection *(see Box 4-1)*. No other country had experimented with a system like the Electoral College apparatus created at the Philadelphia Convention. Perhaps because it had never been tried, the system, as we shall see, was plagued with defects that required correction over time.

The Framers designed the Electoral College system to allow the general electorate to have some influence on the selection of the chief executive without resorting to direct popular election. The original blueprint called for each state to select presidential electors equal in number to the state's delegates to the Senate and House of Representatives. The Constitution empowered the state legislatures to decide the method of choosing the electors. Pop-

---

BOX 4-1   THE AMERICAN PRESIDENCY IN GLOBAL PERSPECTIVE

THE METHOD FOR SELECTING the president generated a good deal of discussion at the 1787 constitutional convention. Several mechanisms were considered and rejected, including, notably, selection by the national legislature. In the end the Framers devised a novel solution: slates of electors equal to the congressional delegation of each state would elect the president.

Even today, in many countries (especially in Western Europe but also in Israel and Japan), executives are not chosen in elections separate from those of the legislative branch. In these parliamentary systems, executives may be the leaders of parties that win legislative elections or are chosen by an elected legislature, as in Germany and the United Kingdom. Sometimes leaders continue to hold seats in the parliament. This practice is forbidden by the U.S. Constitution, which states that "no Person holding any Office under the United States, shall be a Member of either House during his Continuance in Office."

Under the parliamentary system, if the electorate votes the ruling regime in the legislature out of office, the executive also changes. Moreover, the executive is typically accountable to such a legislature: the membership may remove a leader after a vote of no confidence. Because of its importance, many nations have developed elaborate procedures for considering motions of no confidence. In Italy, for example, the parliament cannot debate a no-confidence motion for more than three days; and it must be signed by at least one-tenth of the members of one house. In Germany the legislature can dissolve parliament, thereby removing the chancellor, but only if they select a new chancellor at the same time.

SOURCE: George Thomas Kurian, *World Encyclopedia of Parliaments and Legislatures* (Washington, D.C.: Congressional Quarterly, 1998).

---

ular election was always the most common method, but in the past some state legislatures voted for the electors. Article II disqualifies those who hold federal office, but otherwise there are no specified qualifications for being an elector. The Electoral College system was based on the theory that the states would select their most qualified citizens, who would exercise their best judgment in the selection of the president.

The Constitution mentions only three qualifications for presidential eligibility—citizenship, age, and residency. First, Article II requires that only individuals who are natural-born citizens may become president.[2] Naturalized citizens—those who attain citizenship after birth—may not hold the nation's highest office. Second, to be president a person must have reached the age of thirty-five. Third, the president must have been a resident of the United States for fourteen years. Although the original version of the Constitution made no mention of qualifications for vice president, this oversight was corrected with the 1804 ratification of the Twelfth Amendment, which says that no person can serve as vice president who is not eligible to be president.

Under the original procedures detailed in Article II, the electors were to assemble in their respective state capitals on election day and cast votes for their presidential preferences. Each elector had two votes, no more than one of which could be cast for the candidate from the elector's home state. These votes were then sent to the federal capital, where the president of the Senate opened them. The candidate receiving the most votes would be declared president, if the number of votes received was a majority of the number of electors. Article II anticipated two possible problems with this procedure. First, because the electors each cast two votes, it was possible for the balloting to result in a tie between two candidates. In this event, the Constitution stipulated that the House of Representatives should select one of the two. Second, if multiple candidates sought the presidency, it would be possible that no candidate would receive the required majority. In this case the House was to decide among the top five finishers in the Electoral College voting. In settling such disputed elections, each state delegation was to cast a single vote, rather than allowing the individual members to vote independently.

2. The Constitution also allowed individuals who were citizens at the time the Constitution was adopted to be eligible to hold the presidency.

In the original scheme the vice president was selected right after the president. The formula for choosing the vice president was simple—the vice president was the presidential candidate who received the second highest number of electoral votes. If two or more candidates tied for second in the Electoral College voting, the Senate would select the vice president from among them.

The first two elections took place with no difficulty. In 1789 George Washington received one ballot from each of the 69 electors who participated and was elected president. John Adams became vice president because he got the next highest number of electoral votes (34). History repeated itself in the election of 1792, with Washington receiving one vote from each of the 132 electors. Adams again gathered the next highest number of votes (77) and returned to the vice presidency.

The first defects in the electoral system became apparent with the election of 1796. By this time political parties had begun to develop, and this election was a contest between the incumbent Federalists and the Democratic-Republicans. With Washington declining to run for a third term, John Adams became the Federalist candidate, and Thomas Jefferson was the choice of those who wanted political change. When the ballots were counted, Adams had won the presidency with seventy-one electoral votes, and Jefferson, with sixty-eight, became vice president. For the first time, the nation had a divided executive branch, with the president and vice president of different political parties.

Matters got even worse with the 1800 election. The Democratic-Republicans were now the more popular of the two major parties, and they backed Jefferson for president and Aaron Burr for vice president. The electors committed to the Democratic-Republican Party candidates each cast one ballot for Jefferson and one for Burr. Although it was clear which man was running for which office, the method of selection did not allow for such distinctions. The result was that Jefferson and Burr each received seventy-three votes, and the election moved to the House of Representatives for settlement. Each of the sixteen states had a single vote, and a majority was required for election. On February 11, 1801, the first vote in the House was taken. Jefferson received eight votes, and Burr six. Two states, Maryland and Vermont, were unable to register a preference because their state delegations were evenly divided. Votes continued to be taken over the next several days, until finally, on February 17, after thirty-six ballots, Jefferson received the support of ten state delegations and was named president, with Burr becoming vice president.

It was clear that the Constitution required changing to avoid such situations. Congress proposed the Twelfth Amendment in 1803, and the states ratified it the next year. The amendment altered the selection system by separating the offices of president and vice president. Rather than casting two votes for president, electors would vote for a presidential candidate and then vote separately for a vice presidential candidate. The House and Senate continued to settle presidential and vice presidential elections in which no candidate received a majority, although the procedures for such elections also were modified by the amendment.

Presidential and vice presidential elections are still governed by the Twelfth Amendment. However, the evolution of political parties and the reduction in the degree of independence exercised by presidential electors have made huge changes in the way the system operates. The Electoral College persists. Although there has always been a degree of support for replacing it with direct popular election, proponents of this reform have never achieved enough strength to prompt Congress or the state legislatures to propose the necessary constitutional amendment. Historically, opposition to popular election has come from the smaller states, which enjoy more influence within the Electoral College system than they would under popular election reforms.

Until recently, most Americans were not concerned with reforming the presidential selection system. In modern times the Electoral College system had not produced a result at odds with the popular vote, and many Americans had relatively little knowledge of how the system actually worked. All of this changed with the presidential election of 2000. *(See Box 4-2, page 199.)* Texas governor George W. Bush assumed the presidency after capturing a majority of the Electoral College votes, although his opponent, Vice President Al Gore, narrowly

won the popular vote. The election was so close that the result was not known until weeks after the balloting, when a Supreme Court decision in *Bush v. Gore* (2000) settled the final issues that determined the outcome. The publicity over this disputed election served as a national civics lesson in how the U.S. president is selected and led to a widespread public debate on election reform. Consider the issue of reform as you read the excerpt below. Also consider another hotly debated question surrounding the case: To what degree did the justices allow their partisan preferences to enter into the decision? This question has arisen, in part, because the five justices in the majority—all Republicans—cast their "ballots" in favor of the presidential candidate of their party, while the two Democrats on the Court (Justices Breyer and Ginsburg) "voted" for Gore.

Bush v. Gore

531 U.S. 98 (2000)
http://laws.findlaw.com/US/531/98.html
Vote: 5 (Kennedy, O'Connor, Rehnquist, Scalia, Thomas)
*   4 (Breyer, Ginsburg, Souter, Stevens)*
Opinion of the Court: Per Curiam
Concurring opinion: Rehnquist
Dissenting opinions: Breyer, Ginsburg, Souter, Stevens

The presidential election of November 7, 2000, was one of the closest races in American history. On election night it became clear that the battle between Republican governor George W. Bush of Texas and Democratic vice president Al Gore of Tennessee for the 270 electoral votes necessary for victory would be decided by the outcome in the state of Florida.

First vote counts in Florida gave Governor Bush a lead of some 1,780 votes out of six million cast. This narrow margin triggered an automatic machine recount held on November 10. The results gave Bush a victory, but the margin had slipped to a scant 250 votes, with absentee overseas ballots still to be counted. By this time charges and countercharges of voting irregularities led to lawsuits and political protests. As the various issues sorted themselves out over the ensuing days, the outcome of the

In the aftermath of the contested 2000 presidential election, voting officials in Florida struggled with the task of examining individual punch card ballots in an attempt to discern the electoral choices of the voters. The ballot recounts were stopped by the Supreme Court's decision in *Bush v. Gore*, thus assuring that George W. Bush would win the presidency.

election appeared to hinge on one major issue: large numbers of undercounted ballots in a select number of traditionally Democratic counties. Undercounted ballots were those for which vote-counting machines did not register a presidential preference. In many cases such undercounting was the result of a failure by the voter to pierce completely the computer punchcard ballot. In other cases, machine malfunction may have been the cause. Gore supporters demanded a hand recount of the undercounted ballots.

Three statutory deadlines imposed obstacles for the labor-intensive and time-consuming manual recounts. First, Florida law directed the secretary of state to certify the election results by November 18. Second, federal law provided that if all controversies and contests over a state's electors were resolved by December 12, the state's

slate would be considered conclusive and beyond challenge (the so-called "safe harbor" provision). And third, federal law set December 18 as the date the electors would cast their ballots.

As the manual recounts proceeded, it became clear that the process would not be completed prior to the November 18 deadline for certification. Florida's Republican secretary of state, Katherine Harris, announced her intention to certify the vote on November 18 regardless of the ongoing recounts. Gore forces went to court to block Harris from doing so. A unanimous Florida Supreme Court, emphasizing that every cast vote should be counted, ruled that the recounts should continue and extended the certification date to November 26. Believing the Florida court had exceeded its authority, Bush's lawyers appealed this decision to the U.S. Supreme Court. On December 4 the justices set aside the Florida court's certification extension and asked it to explain the reasoning behind its decision (*Bush v. Palm Beach County Canvassing Board*, 2000). In the meantime, Secretary Harris on November 26 certified George W. Bush as winning the state by 537 votes.

Four days after the U.S. Supreme Court's decision, the Florida high court, in response to an appeal by Vice President Gore, ordered a new statewide manual recount of all undervotes to begin immediately. The recounts were to be conducted by local officials guided only by the instruction to determine voter intent on each ballot. Governor Bush appealed this decision to the U.S. Supreme Court. On December 9, the justices scheduled the case for oral argument and ordered the recounts to stop pending a final decision.

Two major issues dominated the case. First, did the Florida State Supreme Court violate federal law by altering the election procedures in place prior to the election? Second, did the Florida Supreme Court violate the Equal Protection Clause of the Fourteenth Amendment when it ordered a recount to take place without setting a single uniform standard for determining vote intent?

A badly divided Supreme Court issued its ruling on December 12. The majority opinion focuses on the Equal Protection claim. The concurring and dissenting opinions include a wide range of views on the issues presented and debate what remedies should be imposed for any constitutional or statutory violations found.

PER CURIAM.

The closeness of this election, and the multitude of legal challenges which have followed in its wake, have brought into sharp focus a common, if heretofore unnoticed, phenomenon. Nationwide statistics reveal that an estimated 2% of ballots cast do not register a vote for President for whatever reason, including deliberately choosing no candidate at all or some voter error, such as voting for two candidates or insufficiently marking a ballot. In certifying election results, the votes eligible for inclusion in the certification are the votes meeting the properly established legal requirements.

This case has shown that punch card balloting machines can produce an unfortunate number of ballots which are not punched in a clean, complete way by the voter. After the current counting, it is likely legislative bodies nationwide will examine ways to improve the mechanisms and machinery for voting.

The individual citizen has no federal constitutional right to vote for electors for the President of the United States unless and until the state legislature chooses a statewide election as the means to implement its power to appoint members of the Electoral College. U.S. Const., Art. II, §1. This is the source for the statement in *McPherson v. Blacker* (1892) that the State legislature's power to select the manner for appointing electors is plenary; it may, if it so chooses, select the electors itself, which indeed was the manner used by State legislatures in several States for many years after the Framing of our Constitution. History has now favored the voter, and in each of the several States the citizens themselves vote for Presidential electors. When the state legislature vests the right to vote for President in its people, the right to vote as the legislature has prescribed is fundamental; and one source of its fundamental nature lies in the equal weight accorded to each vote and the equal dignity owed to each voter. The State, of course, after granting the franchise in the special context of Article II, can take back the power to appoint electors.

The right to vote is protected in more than the initial allocation of the franchise. Equal protection applies as well to the manner of its exercise. Having once granted the right to vote on equal terms, the State may not, by later arbitrary and disparate treatment, value one person's vote over that of another. . . .

There is no difference between the two sides of the present controversy on these basic propositions. Respondents say that the very purpose of vindicating the right to vote justifies the recount procedures now at issue. The question before us, however, is whether the recount procedures the Florida Supreme Court has adopted are consistent with its obligation to avoid arbitrary and disparate treatment of the members of its electorate.

Much of the controversy seems to revolve around ballot cards designed to be perforated by a stylus but which, either through error or deliberate omission, have not been perforated with sufficient precision for a machine to count them. In some cases a piece of the card—a chad—is hanging, say by two corners. In other cases there is no separation at all, just an indentation.

The Florida Supreme Court has ordered that the intent of the voter be discerned from such ballots. For purposes of resolving the equal protection challenge, it is not necessary to decide whether the Florida Supreme Court had the authority under the legislative scheme for resolving election disputes to define what a legal vote is and to mandate a manual recount implementing that definition. The recount mechanisms implemented in response to the decisions of the Florida Supreme Court do not satisfy the minimum requirement for non-arbitrary treatment of voters necessary to secure the fundamental right. Florida's basic command for the count of legally cast votes is to consider the "intent of the voter." This is unobjectionable as an abstract proposition and a starting principle. The problem inheres in the absence of specific standards to ensure its equal application. The formulation of uniform rules to determine intent based on these recurring circumstances is practicable and, we conclude, necessary.

The law does not refrain from searching for the intent of the actor in a multitude of circumstances; and in some cases the general command to ascertain intent is not susceptible to much further refinement. In this instance, however, the question is . . . how to interpret the marks or holes or scratches on an inanimate object, a piece of cardboard or paper which, it is said, might not have registered as a vote during the machine count. The factfinder confronts a thing, not a person. The search for intent can be confined by specific rules designed to ensure uniform treatment.

The want of those rules here has led to unequal evaluation of ballots in various respects. As seems to have been acknowledged at oral argument, the standards for accepting or rejecting contested ballots might vary not only from county to county but indeed within a single county from one recount team to another.

The record provides some examples. A monitor in Miami-Dade County testified at trial that he observed that three members of the county canvassing board applied different standards in defining a legal vote. And testimony at trial also revealed that at least one county changed its evaluative standards during the counting process. Palm Beach County, for example, began the process with a 1990 guideline which precluded counting completely attached chads, switched to a rule that considered a vote to be legal if any light could be seen through a chad, changed back to the 1990 rule, and then abandoned any pretense of a *per se* rule, only to have a court order that the county consider dimpled chads legal. This is not a process with sufficient guarantees of equal treatment. . . .

The State Supreme Court ratified this uneven treatment. It mandated that the recount totals from two counties, Miami-Dade and Palm Beach, be included in the certified total. The court also appeared to hold *sub silentio* that the recount totals from Broward County, which were not completed until after the original November 14 certification by the Secretary of State, were to be considered part of the new certified vote totals even though the county certification was not contested by Vice President Gore. Yet each of the counties used varying standards to determine what was a legal vote. Broward County used a more forgiving standard than Palm Beach County, and uncovered almost three times as many new votes, a result markedly disproportionate to the difference in population between the counties.

In addition, the recounts in these three counties were not limited to so-called undervotes but extended to all of the ballots. The distinction has real consequences. A manual recount of all ballots identifies not only those ballots which show no vote but also those which contain more than one, the so-called overvotes. Neither category will be counted by the machine. This is not a trivial concern. At oral argument, respondents estimated there are as many as 110,000 overvotes statewide. As a result, the citizen whose ballot was not read by a machine because he failed to vote for a candidate in a way readable by a machine may still have his vote counted in a manual recount; on the other hand, the citizen who marks two candidates in a way discernable by the machine will not have the same opportunity to have his vote count, even if a manual examination of the ballot would reveal the requisite indicia of intent. Furthermore, the citizen who marks two candidates, only one of which is discernable by the machine, will have his vote counted even though it should have been read as an invalid ballot. The State Supreme Court's inclusion of vote counts based on these variant standards exemplifies concerns with the remedial processes that were under way.

That brings the analysis to yet a further equal protection problem. The votes certified by the court included a partial total from one county, Miami-Dade. The Florida Supreme Court's decision thus gives no assurance that the recounts included in a final certification must be complete. Indeed, it is respondent's submission that it would be consistent with the rules of the recount procedures to include whatever partial counts are done by the time of final certification, and we interpret the Florida Supreme Court's decision to permit this. This accommodation no doubt results from the truncated contest period established by the Florida Supreme Court in *Bush I*, at respondents' own urging. The press of time does not diminish the constitutional concern. A desire for speed is not a general excuse for ignoring equal protection guarantees.

In addition to these difficulties the actual process by which the votes were to be counted under the Florida Supreme Court's decision raises further concerns. That order did not specify who would recount the ballots. The county canvassing boards were forced to pull together ad hoc teams comprised of judges from various Circuits who had no previous training in handling and interpreting ballots. Furthermore, while others were permitted to observe, they were prohibited from objecting during the recount.

The recount process, in its features here described, is inconsistent with the minimum procedures necessary to protect the fundamental right of each voter in the special instance of a statewide recount under the authority of a single state judicial officer. Our consideration is limited to the present circumstances, for the problem of equal protection in election processes generally presents many complexities.

The question before the Court is not whether local entities, in the exercise of their expertise, may develop different systems for implementing elections. Instead, we are presented with a situation where a state court with the power to assure uniformity has ordered a statewide recount with minimal procedural safeguards. When a court orders a statewide remedy, there must be at least some assurance that the rudimentary requirements of equal treatment and fundamental fairness are satisfied.

Given the Court's assessment that the recount process underway was probably being conducted in an unconstitutional manner, the Court stayed the order directing the recount so it could hear this case and render an expedited decision. The contest provision, as it was mandated by the State Supreme Court, is not well calculated to sustain the confidence that all citizens must have in the outcome of elections. The State has not shown that its procedures include the necessary safeguards. The problem, for instance, of the estimated 110,000 overvotes has not been addressed. . . .

Upon due consideration of the difficulties identified to this point, it is obvious that the recount cannot be conducted in compliance with the requirements of equal protection and due process without substantial additional work. It would require not only the adoption (after opportunity for argument) of adequate statewide standards for determining what is a legal vote, and practicable procedures to implement them, but also orderly judicial review of any disputed matters that might arise. In addition, the Secretary of State has advised that the recount of only a portion of the ballots requires that the vote tabulation equipment be used to screen out undervotes, a function for which the machines were not designed. If a recount of overvotes were also required, perhaps even a second screening would be necessary. Use of the equipment for this purpose, and any new software developed for it, would have to be evaluated for accuracy by the Secretary of State, as required by [Florida law].

The Supreme Court of Florida has said that the legislature intended the State's electors to "participat[e] fully in the federal electoral process," as provided in 3 U.S.C. §5. That statute, in turn, requires that any controversy or contest that is designed to lead to a conclusive selection of electors be completed by December 12. That date is upon us, and there is no recount procedure in place under the State Supreme Court's order that comports with minimal constitutional standards. Because it is evident that any recount seeking to meet the December 12 date will be unconstitutional for the reasons we have discussed, we reverse the judgment of the Supreme Court of Florida ordering a recount to proceed.

Seven Justices of the Court agree that there are constitutional problems with the recount ordered by the Florida Supreme Court that demand a remedy. The only disagreement is as to the remedy. Because the Florida Supreme Court has said that the Florida Legislature intended to obtain the safe-harbor benefits of 3 U.S.C. §5, JUSTICE BREYER's proposed remedy—remanding to the Florida Supreme Court for its ordering of a constitutionally proper contest until December 18—contemplates action in violation of the Florida election code, and hence could not be part of an "appropriate" order authorized by [Florida law].

None are more conscious of the vital limits on judicial authority than are the members of this Court, and none stand more in admiration of the Constitution's design to leave the selection of the President to the people, through their legislatures, and to the political sphere. When contending parties invoke the process of the courts, however, it becomes our unsought responsibility to resolve the federal and constitutional issues the judicial system has been forced to confront.

The judgment of the Supreme Court of Florida is reversed, and the case is remanded for further proceedings not inconsistent with this opinion. . . .

CHIEF JUSTICE REHNQUIST, with whom JUSTICE SCALIA and JUSTICE THOMAS join, concurring.

We join the *per curiam* opinion. We write separately because we believe there are additional grounds that require us to reverse the Florida Supreme Court's decision.

We deal here not with an ordinary election, but with an election for the President of the United States. . . .

In most cases, comity and respect for federalism compel us to defer to the decisions of state courts on issues of state law. . . . But there are a few exceptional cases in which the Constitution imposes a duty or confers a power on a particular branch of a State's government. This is one of them. Article II, §1, cl. 2, provides that "[e]ach State shall appoint, in such Manner as the *Legislature* thereof may direct," electors for President and Vice President. (Emphasis added.) Thus, the text of the election law itself, and not just its interpretation by the courts of the States, takes on independent significance.

In *McPherson v. Blacker* (1892), we explained that Art. II, §1, cl. 2, "convey[s] the broadest power of determination" and "leaves it to the legislature exclusively to define the method" of appointment. A significant departure from the legislative scheme for appointing Presidential electors presents a federal constitutional question. . . .

In Florida, the legislature has chosen to hold statewide elections to appoint the State's 25 electors. Importantly, the legislature has delegated the authority to run the elections and to oversee election disputes to the Secretary of State (Secretary) and to state circuit courts. Isolated sections of the code may well admit of more than one interpretation, but the general coherence of the legislative scheme may not be altered by judicial interpretation so as to wholly change the statutorily provided apportionment of responsibility among these various bodies. In any election but a Presidential election, the Florida Supreme Court can give as little or as much deference to Florida's executives as it chooses, so far as Article II is concerned, and this Court will have no cause to question the court's actions. But, with respect to a Presidential election, the court must be both mindful of the legislature's role under Article II in choosing the manner of appointing electors and deferential to those bodies expressly empowered by the legislature to carry out its constitutional mandate.

In order to determine whether a state court has infringed upon the legislature's authority, we necessarily must examine the law of the State as it existed prior to the action of the court. Though we generally defer to state courts on the interpretation of state law there are of course areas in which the Constitution requires this Court to undertake an independent, if still deferential, analysis of state law.

For example, in *NAACP v. Alabama ex rel. Patterson* (1958), it was argued that we were without jurisdiction because the petitioner had not pursued the correct appellate remedy in Alabama's state courts. Petitioners had sought a state-law writ of certiorari in the Alabama Supreme Court when a writ of mandamus, according to that court, was proper. We found this state-law ground inadequate to defeat our jurisdiction because we were "unable to reconcile the procedural holding of the Alabama Supreme Court" with prior Alabama precedent. The purported state-law ground was so novel, in our independent estimation, that "petitioner could not fairly be deemed to have been apprised of its existence."

Six years later we decided *Bouie v. City of Columbia* (1964), in which the state court had held, contrary to precedent, that the state trespass law applied to black sit-in demonstrators who had consent to enter private property but were then asked to leave. Relying upon *NAACP,* we concluded that the South Carolina Supreme Court's interpretation of a state penal statute had impermissibly broadened the scope of that statute beyond what a fair reading provided, in violation of due process. What we would do in the present case is precisely parallel: Hold that the Florida Supreme Court's interpretation of the Florida election laws impermissibly distorted them beyond what a fair reading required, in violation of Article II.

This inquiry does not imply a disrespect for state *courts* but rather a respect for the constitutionally prescribed role of state *legislatures.* To attach definitive weight to the pronouncement of a state court, when the very question at issue is whether the court has actually departed from the statutory meaning, would be to abdicate our responsibility to enforce the explicit requirements of Article II. . . .

JUSTICE STEVENS, with whom JUSTICE GINSBURG and JUSTICE BREYER join, dissenting.

The Constitution assigns to the States the primary responsibility for determining the manner of selecting the Presidential electors. When questions arise about the meaning of state laws, including election laws, it is our settled practice to accept the opinions of the highest courts of the States as providing the final answers. On rare occasions, however, either federal statutes or the Federal Constitution may require federal judicial intervention in state elections. This is not such an occasion.

The federal questions that ultimately emerged in this case are not substantial. Article II provides that "[e]ach *State* shall appoint, in such Manner as the Legislature *thereof* may direct, a Number of Electors." It does not create state legislatures out of whole cloth, but rather takes them as they come—as creatures born of, and constrained by, their state constitutions. Lest there be any doubt, we stated over 100 years ago in *McPherson v. Blacker* (1892), that "[w]hat is forbidden or required to be done by a State" in the Article II context "is forbidden or required of the legislative power under state constitutions as they exist." In the same vein, we also observed that "[t]he [State's] legislative power is the supreme authority except as limited by the constitution of the State." *Ibid.*; cf. *Smiley v. Holm* (1932). The legislative power in Florida is subject to judicial review pursuant to Article V of the Florida Constitution, and nothing in Article II of the Federal Constitution frees the state legislature from the constraints in the state constitution that created it. Moreover, the Florida Legislature's own decision to employ a unitary code for all elections indicates that it intended the Florida Supreme Court to play the same role in Presidential elections that it has historically played in resolving electoral disputes. The Florida Supreme Court's exercise of appellate jurisdiction therefore was wholly consistent with, and indeed contemplated by, the grant of authority in Article II.

It hardly needs stating that Congress, pursuant to 3 U.S.C. §5, did not impose any affirmative duties upon the States that their governmental branches could "violate." Rather, §5 provides a safe harbor for States to select electors in contested elections "by judicial or other methods" established by laws prior to the election day. Section 5, like Article II, assumes the involvement of the state judiciary in interpreting state election laws and resolving election disputes under those laws. Neither §5 nor Article II grants federal judges any special authority to substitute their views for those of the state judiciary on matters of state law. . . .

Admittedly, the use of differing substandards for determining voter intent in different counties employing similar voting systems may raise serious concerns. Those concerns are alleviated—if not eliminated—by the fact that a single impartial magistrate will ultimately adjudicate all objections arising from the recount process. Of course, as a general matter, "[t]he interpretation of constitutional principles must not be too literal. We must remember that the machinery of government would not work if it were not allowed a little play in its joints." *Bain Peanut Co. of Tex. v. Pinson* (1931) (Holmes, J.). If it were otherwise, Florida's decision to leave to each county the determination of what balloting system to employ—despite enormous differences in accuracy—might run afoul of equal protection. So, too, might the similar decisions of the vast majority of state legislatures to delegate to local authorities certain decisions with respect to voting systems and ballot design.

Even assuming that aspects of the remedial scheme might ultimately be found to violate the Equal Protection Clause, I could not subscribe to the majority's disposition of the case. As the majority explicitly holds, once a state legislature determines to select electors through a popular vote, the right to have one's vote counted is of constitutional stature. As the majority further acknowledges, Florida law holds that all ballots that reveal the intent of the voter constitute valid votes. Recognizing these principles, the majority nonetheless orders the termination of the contest proceeding before all such votes have been tabulated. Under their own reasoning, the appropriate course of action would be to remand to allow more specific procedures for implementing the legislature's uniform general standard to be established.

In the interest of finality, however, the majority effectively orders the disenfranchisement of an unknown number of voters whose ballots reveal their intent—and are therefore legal votes under state law—but were for some reason rejected by ballot-counting machines. It does so on the basis of the deadlines set forth in Title 3 of the United States Code. But . . . those provisions merely provide rules of decision for Congress to follow when selecting among conflicting slates of electors. They do not prohibit a State from counting what the majority concedes to be legal votes until a bona fide winner is determined. Indeed, in 1960, Hawaii appointed two slates of electors and Congress chose to count the one appointed on January 4, 1961, well after the Title 3 deadlines. Thus, nothing prevents the majority, even if it properly found an equal protection violation, from ordering relief appropriate to remedy that violation without depriving Florida voters of their right to have their votes counted. As the majority notes, "[a] desire for speed is not a general excuse for ignoring equal protection guarantees."

Finally, neither in this case, nor in its earlier opinion in *Palm Beach County Canvassing Bd. v. Harris* (Fla., Nov. 21, 2000), did the Florida Supreme Court make any substantive change in Florida electoral law. Its decisions were rooted in long-established precedent and were consistent with the relevant statutory provisions, taken as a whole. It did what courts do—it decided the case before it in light of the legislature's intent to leave no legally cast vote uncounted. In so doing, it relied on the sufficiency of the general "intent of the voter" standard articulated by the state legislature, coupled with a procedure for ultimate review by an impartial judge, to resolve the concern about disparate evaluations of contested ballots. If we assume—as I do—that the members of that court and the judges who would have carried out its mandate are impartial, its decision does not even raise a colorable federal question.

What must underlie petitioners' entire federal assault on the Florida election procedures is an unstated lack of confidence in the impartiality and capacity of the state judges who would make the critical decisions if the vote count were to proceed. Otherwise, their position is wholly without merit. The endorsement of that position by the majority of this Court can only lend credence to the most cynical appraisal of the work of judges throughout the land. It is confidence in the men and women who administer the judicial system that is the true backbone of the rule of law. Time will one day heal the wound to that confidence that will be inflicted by today's decision. One thing, however, is certain. Although we may never know with complete certainty the identity of the winner of this year's Presidential election, the identity of the loser is perfectly clear. It is the Nation's confidence in the judge as an impartial guardian of the rule of law.

I respectfully dissent.

JUSTICE SOUTER, with whom JUSTICE BREYER joins and with whom JUSTICE STEVENS and JUSTICE GINSBURG join with regard to all but [the paragraphs dealing with the third issue], dissenting.

The Court should not have reviewed either *Bush v. Palm Beach County Canvassing Bd.* or this case, and should not have stopped Florida's attempt to recount all undervote ballots by issuing a stay of the Florida Supreme Court's orders during the period of this review. If this Court had allowed the State to follow the course indicated by the opinions of its own Supreme Court, it is entirely possible that there would ultimately have been no issue requiring our review, and political tension could have worked itself out in the Congress. . . . The case being before us, however, its resolution by the majority is another erroneous decision. . . .

There are three issues: whether the State Supreme Court's interpretation of the statute providing for a contest of the state election results somehow violates 3 U.S.C. §5; whether that court's construction of the state statutory provisions governing contests impermissibly changes a state law from what the State's legislature has provided, in violation of Article II, §1, cl. 2, of the national Constitution; and whether the manner of interpreting markings on disputed ballots failing to cause machines to register votes for President (the undervote ballots) violates the equal protection or due process guaranteed by the Fourteenth Amendment. None of these issues is difficult to describe or to resolve.

The 3 U.S.C. §5 issue is not serious. That provision sets certain conditions for treating a State's certification of Presidential electors as conclusive in the event that a dispute over recognizing those electors must be resolved in the Congress under 3 U.S.C. §15. Conclusiveness requires selection under a legal scheme in place before the election, with results determined at least six days before the date set for casting electoral votes. But no State is required to conform to §5 if it cannot do that (for whatever reason); the sanction for failing to satisfy the conditions of §5 is simply loss of what has been called its "safe harbor." And even that determination is to be made, if made anywhere, in the Congress.

The second matter here goes to the State Supreme Court's interpretation of certain terms in the state statute governing election "contests.". . . The issue is whether the judgment of the state supreme court has displaced the state legislature's provisions for election contests: is the law as declared by the court different from the provisions made by the legislature, to which the national Constitution commits responsibility for determining how each State's Presidential electors are chosen? See U.S. Const., Art. II, §1, cl. 2. . . . What Bush . . . argue[s], as I understand the contention, is that the interpretation of [Florida law] was so unreasonable as to transcend the accepted bounds of statutory interpretation, to the point of being a nonjudicial act and producing new law untethered to the legislative act in question. . . .

. . . [T]he interpretations by the Florida court raise no substantial question under Article II. That court engaged in permissible construction in determining that Gore had instituted a contest authorized by the state statute, and it proceeded to direct the trial judge to deal with that contest in the exercise of the discretionary powers generously conferred by [Florida law], to "fashion such orders as he or she deems necessary to ensure that each allegation in the complaint is investigated, examined, or checked, to prevent or correct any alleged wrong, and to provide any relief appropriate under such circumstances.". . .

It is only on the third issue before us that there is a meritorious argument for relief, as this Court's *Per Curiam* opinion recognizes. It is an issue that might well have been dealt with adequately by the Florida courts if the state proceedings had not been interrupted, and if not disposed of at the state level it could have been considered by the Congress in any electoral vote dispute. But because the course of state proceedings has been interrupted, time is short, and the issue is before us, I think it sensible for the Court to address it.

Petitioners have raised an equal protection claim, in the charge that unjustifiably disparate standards are applied in different electoral jurisdictions to otherwise identical facts. It is true that the Equal Protection Clause does not forbid the use of a variety of voting mechanisms within a jurisdiction, even though different mechanisms will have different levels of effectiveness in recording voters' intentions; local variety can be justified by concerns about cost, the potential value of innovation, and so on. But evidence in the record here suggests that a different order of disparity obtains under rules for determining a voter's intent that have been applied (and could continue to be applied) to identical types of ballots used in identical brands of machines and exhibiting identical physical characteristics (such as "hanging" or "dimpled" chads). I can conceive of no legitimate state interest served by these differing treatments of the expressions of voters' fundamental rights. The differences appear wholly arbitrary.

In deciding what to do about this, we should take account of the fact that electoral votes are due to be cast in six days. I would therefore remand the case to the courts of Florida with instructions to establish uniform standards for evaluating the several types of ballots that have prompted differing treatments, to be applied within and among counties when passing on such identical ballots in any further recounting (or successive recounting) that the courts might order.

Unlike the majority, I see no warrant for this Court to assume that Florida could not possibly comply with this requirement before the date set for the meeting of electors, December 18. . . . To recount these [disputed votes] manually would be a tall order, but before this Court stayed the effort to do that the courts of Florida were ready to do their best to get that job done. There is no justification for denying the State the opportunity to try to count all disputed ballots now.

I respectfully dissent.

JUSTICE GINSBURG, with whom JUSTICE STEVENS joins, and with whom JUSTICE SOUTER and JUSTICE BREYER join [except as to the portion of the opinion dealing with the Equal Protection claim], dissenting.

THE CHIEF JUSTICE acknowledges that provisions of Florida's Election Code "may well admit of more than one interpretation." But instead of respecting the state high court's province to say what the State's Election Code means, THE CHIEF JUSTICE maintains that Florida's Su-

preme Court has veered so far from the ordinary practice of judicial review that what it did cannot properly be called judging. . . . I might join THE CHIEF JUSTICE were it my commission to interpret Florida law. But disagreement with the Florida court's interpretation of its own State's law does not warrant the conclusion that the justices of that court have legislated. There is no cause here to believe that the members of Florida's high court have done less than "their mortal best to discharge their oath of office," and no cause to upset their reasoned interpretation of Florida law. . . .

Rarely has this Court rejected outright an interpretation of state law by a state high court. *Fairfax's Devisee v. Hunter's Lessee* (1813), *NAACP v. Alabama ex rel. Patterson* (1958), and *Bouie v. City of Columbia* (1964), cited by THE CHIEF JUSTICE, are three such rare instances. But those cases are embedded in historical contexts hardly comparable to the situation here. . . .

THE CHIEF JUSTICE's casual citation of these cases might lead one to believe they are part of a larger collection of cases in which we said that the Constitution impelled us to train a skeptical eye on a state court's portrayal of state law. But one would be hard pressed, I think, to find additional cases that fit the mold. . . . [This] case involves nothing close to the kind of recalcitrance by a state high court that warrants extraordinary action by this Court. The Florida Supreme Court concluded that counting every legal vote was the overriding concern of the Florida Legislature when it enacted the State's Election Code. . . .

The extraordinary setting of this case has obscured the ordinary principle that dictates its proper resolution: Federal courts defer to state high courts' interpretations of their state's own law. This principle reflects the core of federalism, on which all agree. "The Framers split the atom of sovereignty. It was the genius of their idea that our citizens would have two political capacities, one state and one federal, each protected from incursion by the other." . . . Were the other members of this Court as mindful as they generally are of our system of dual sovereignty, they would affirm the judgment of the Florida Supreme Court.

I agree with JUSTICE STEVENS that petitioners have not presented a substantial equal protection claim. Ideally, perfection would be the appropriate standard for judging the recount. But we live in an imperfect world, one in which thousands of votes have not been counted. I cannot agree that the recount adopted by the Florida court, flawed as it may be, would yield a result any less fair or precise than the certification that preceded that recount.

Even if there were an equal protection violation, I would agree with JUSTICE STEVENS, JUSTICE SOUTER, and JUSTICE BREYER that the Court's concern about "the December 12 deadline," is misplaced. Time is short in part because of the Court's entry of a stay on December 9, several hours after an able circuit judge in Leon County had begun to superintend the recount process. More fundamentally, the Court's reluctance to let the recount go forward—despite its suggestion that "[t]he search for intent can be confined by specific rules designed to ensure uniform treatment,"—ultimately turns on its own judgment about the practical realities of implementing a recount, not the judgment of those much closer to the process.

Equally important . . . the December 12 "deadline" for bringing Florida's electoral votes into 3 U.S.C. §5's safe harbor lacks the significance the Court assigns it. Were that date to pass, Florida would still be entitled to deliver electoral votes Congress *must* count unless both Houses find that the votes "ha[d] not been . . . regularly given." 3 U.S.C. §15. The statute identifies other significant dates. But none of these dates has ultimate significance in light of Congress' detailed provisions for determining, on "the sixth day of January," the validity of electoral votes. §15.

The Court assumes that time will not permit "orderly judicial review of any disputed matters that might arise." But no one has doubted the good faith and diligence with which Florida election officials, attorneys for all sides of this controversy, and the courts of law have performed their duties. Notably, the Florida Supreme Court has produced two substantial opinions within 29 hours of oral argument. In sum, the Court's conclusion that a constitutionally adequate recount is impractical is a prophecy the Court's own judgment will not allow to be tested. Such an untested prophecy should not decide the Presidency of the United States.

JUSTICE BREYER, with whom JUSTICE STEVENS and JUSTICE GINSBURG join except as [paragraphs 3–4 below], and with whom JUSTICE SOUTER joins [except as to the final paragraph contained in this excerpt], dissenting.

The Court was wrong to take this case. It was wrong to grant a stay. It should now vacate that stay and permit the Florida Supreme Court to decide whether the recount should resume.

The political implications of this case for the country are momentous. But the federal legal questions presented, with one exception, are insubstantial.

The majority raises three Equal Protection problems with the Florida Supreme Court's recount order: first, the failure to include overvotes in the manual recount; second, the fact that *all* ballots, rather than simply the undervotes, were recounted in some, but not all, counties; and third, the absence of a uniform, specific standard to guide the recounts. As far as the first issue is concerned, petitioners presented no evidence, to this Court or to any Florida court, that a manual recount of overvotes would identify additional legal votes. The same is true of the second, and, in addition, the majority's reasoning would seem to invalidate any state provision for a manual recount of individual counties in a statewide election.

The majority's third concern does implicate principles of fundamental fairness. The majority concludes that the Equal Protection Clause requires that a manual recount be governed not only by the uniform general standard of the "clear intent of the voter," but also by uniform subsidiary standards (for example, a uniform determination whether indented, but not perforated, "undervotes" should count). The opinion points out that the Florida Supreme Court ordered the inclusion of Broward County's undercounted "legal votes" even though those votes included ballots that were not perforated but simply "dimpled," while newly recounted ballots from other counties will likely include only votes determined to be "legal" on the basis of a stricter standard. In light of our previous remand, the Florida Supreme Court may have been reluctant to adopt a more specific standard than that provided for by the legislature for fear of exceeding its authority under Article II. However, since the use of different standards could favor one or the other of the candidates, since time was, and is, too short to permit the lower courts to iron out significant differences through ordinary judicial review, and since the relevant distinction was embodied in the order of the State's highest court, I agree that, in these very special circumstances, basic principles of fairness may well have counseled the adoption of a uniform standard to address the problem. In light of the majority's disposition, I need not decide whether, or the extent to which, as a remedial matter, the Constitution would place limits upon the content of the uniform standard.

Nonetheless, there is no justification for the majority's remedy, which is simply to reverse the lower court and halt the recount entirely. An appropriate remedy would be, instead, to remand this case with instructions that, even at this late date, would permit the Florida Supreme Court to require recounting *all* undercounted votes in Florida, including those from Broward, Volusia, Palm Beach, and Miami-Dade Counties, whether or not previously recounted prior to the end of the protest period, and to do so in accordance with a single-uniform substandard.

The majority justifies stopping the recount entirely on the ground that there is no more time. In particular, the majority relies on the lack of time for the Secretary to review and approve equipment needed to separate undervotes. But the majority reaches this conclusion in the absence of *any* record evidence that the recount could not have been completed in the time allowed by the Florida Supreme Court. The majority finds facts outside of the record on matters that state courts are in a far better position to address. Of course, it is too late for any such recount to take place by December 12, the date by which election disputes must be decided if a State is to take advantage of the safe harbor provisions of 3 U.S.C. §5. Whether there is time to conduct a recount prior to December 18, when the electors are scheduled to meet, is a matter for the state courts to determine. And whether, under Florida law, Florida could or could not take further action is obviously a matter for Florida courts, not this Court, to decide.

By halting the manual recount, and thus ensuring that the uncounted legal votes will not be counted under any standard, this Court crafts a remedy out of proportion to the asserted harm. And that remedy harms the very fairness interests the Court is attempting to protect. The manual recount would itself redress a problem of unequal treatment of ballots. [I]n a system that allows counties to use different types of voting systems, voters already arrive at the polls with an unequal chance that their votes will be counted. I do not see how the fact that this results from counties' selection of different voting machines rather than a court order makes the outcome any more fair. Nor do I understand why the Florida Supreme Court's recount order, which helps to redress this inequity, must be entirely prohibited based on a deficiency that could easily be remedied.

The remainder of petitioners' claims, which are the focus of THE CHIEF JUSTICE's concurrence, raise no significant federal questions. I cannot agree that THE CHIEF JUSTICE's unusual review of state law in this case, is justified by reference either to Art. II, §1, or to 3 U.S.C. §5. Moreover, even were such review proper, the conclusion that the Florida Supreme Court's decision contravenes federal law is untenable. . . .

I fear that in order to bring this agonizingly long election process to a definitive conclusion, we have not adequately attended to that necessary "check upon our own exercise of power," "our own sense of self-restraint." *United States v. Butler* (1936) (Stone, J., dissenting). Justice Brandeis once said of the Court, "The most important thing we do is not doing." What it does today, the Court should have left undone. I would repair the damage done as best we now can, by permitting the Florida recount to continue under uniform standards.

I respectfully dissent.

The Court's decision in *Bush v. Gore* became the final chapter in the presidential election controversy of 2000. By stopping the Florida recount, the Court removed Vice President Gore's last hope of capturing the state's twenty-five electoral votes and guaranteed that Governor Bush would become the next president. While much of the nation was happy to see the election finally resolved, the Court's action caused intense debate in political and academic circles. Not only was there a question of whether the Supreme Court should have heard the case in the first place, many also believed, for the reasons we noted earlier, that the justices' votes were excessively influenced by their own partisan preferences. Do you agree?

Removal. Although the Framers hotly debated the subject of presidential selection, they apparently came to agreement rather quickly over removal. If an incumbent president (or vice president) abuses the office, the Constitution provides for impeachment as the method of removal. Impeachment is a two-stage process. First, the House of Representatives investigates the charges against the incumbent. The Constitution stipulates that impeachment can occur only upon charges of "Treason, Bribery, or other High Crimes and Misdemeanors." Once convinced that there is sufficient evidence of such misconduct, the House passes Articles of Impeachment specifying the crimes charged and authorizing a trial. The second

BOX 4-2   AFTERMATH . . .
BUSH V. GORE

THE ANNOUNCEMENT of the Supreme Court's decision in *Bush v. Gore* (2000) effectively ended the 2000 presidential election controversy. On December 13, 2000, the day after the justices ruled, Vice President Al Gore announced that he was ending his campaign: "I accept the finality of this outcome. . . . And tonight, for the sake of our unity as a people and the strength of our democracy, I offer my concession." Florida officials quickly certified the state's twenty-five electoral votes for Texas governor George W. Bush.

Florida's electoral votes gave Bush a total of 271, just one more than needed to become the forty-third president of the United States. Although Bush had won the Electoral College, he became only the fourth president in U.S. history to win office while losing the popular vote to his chief opponent. Vice President Gore captured 48.39 percent of the popular vote, as opposed to Governor Bush's 47.88 percent. Before Bush only John Quincy Adams in 1824, Rutherford B. Hayes in 1876, and Benjamin Harrison in 1888 had been elected president without leading in the popular vote count.

Because of the voting controversies in Florida, many states revised election laws and upgraded vote-counting equipment to avoid similar problems in future elections. The two Florida officials at the center of the controversy, Gov. Jeb Bush and Secretary of State Katherine Harris, continued their political careers. Jeb Bush was reelected governor of Florida in 2002 and Harris won a congressional seat that same year. Theodore Olson, the lawyer who successfully argued George Bush's case before the Supreme Court, was appointed solicitor general of the United States by the new president. Gore seriously considered a rematch against President Bush in the 2004 elections, but in late 2002 he announced that he would not be a candidate for his party's nomination.

Public opinion polls taken after the Court's ruling showed that a large majority of Americans accepted Bush as the legitimate president; and, contrary to many predictions, the polls failed to find any appreciable decline in public support for the Supreme Court due to its incursion into the 2000 presidential election.

SOURCE: Compiled by authors.

stage, the trial, takes place in the Senate, with the chief justice of the United States presiding. Conviction requires the agreement of two-thirds of the voting senators. Congress may impose no penalties on a convicted official other than removal from office. However, the officeholder may still be subject to a separate criminal prosecution in the courts.

Congress has never removed a president from office, although three barely escaped such a fate. Andrew Johnson was impeached by the House in 1868, but he survived his trial in the Senate by one vote. The House passed two articles of impeachment against Bill Clinton in 1998, but the Senate vote in February 1999 fell far short of the sixty-seven votes of guilt needed to convict. Richard Nixon was well on his way to being impeached in 1974 when he resigned from office. Since both the Clinton and Nixon episodes led to several important constitutional rulings on executive power, we have more to say about the circumstances surrounding their troubles in the coming pages.

Tenure and Succession. The Constitution sets the presidential term at four years. Originally, it placed no restriction on the number of terms a president could serve; George Washington began the tradition of a two-term limit when he announced at the end of his second administration that he would not run again. This tradition was honored by every president until Franklin Roosevelt sought election to a third term in 1940 and further violated the custom by running for a fourth term in 1944. In reaction, Congress proposed the Twenty-second Amendment, which held that no person could run for president after having served more than six years in that office. The states ratified the amendment in 1951.

In Article II the Framers provided a mechanism for the replacement of the president in the event of death, resignation, or disability:[3] the vice president assumes the powers and responsibilities of the office. The Constitution further authorizes Congress to determine presiden-

---

3. Eight sitting presidents failed to complete their terms. Four (William Henry Harrison, Zachary Taylor, Warren G. Harding, and Franklin Roosevelt) died of natural causes, and four (Abraham Lincoln, James A. Garfield, William McKinley, and John F. Kennedy) were assassinated.

Although presidential approval is not required for amendments to be proposed or ratified, President Lyndon B. Johnson, surrounded by congressional leaders, signed the Twenty-fifth Amendment on February 23, 1967. The amendment authorized the president to nominate a new vice president when a vacancy in that office occurred. If Johnson had died or become disabled before the 1964 election, seventy-four-year-old Speaker John McCormack (far right) would have assumed the presidency. Next in line of succession was president pro tempore of the Senate, eighty-eight-year-old Carl Hayden (third from left, standing).

tial succession if there is no sitting vice president when a vacancy occurs.

In 1965 Congress recommended additional changes in the Constitution to govern presidential succession. The need became apparent after Lyndon Johnson assumed the presidency following John F. Kennedy's assassination in 1963. Johnson's ascension left the vice presidency vacant. If anything had happened to Johnson, the federal succession law dictated that next in line was the Speaker of the House, followed by the president pro tempore of the Senate *(see Box 4-3)*. In 1965 the Speaker was John McCormack, D-Mass., who was seventy-four years old, and the president pro tempore was Carl Hayden, D-Ariz., who was eighty-eight. Neither was capable of handling the demands of the presidency. Congress proposed that the Constitution be amended to provide that when a vacancy occurs in the office of vice president, the president nominates a new vice president who takes office upon confirmation by majority vote in both houses of Con-

gress. The proposal also clarified procedures governing those times when a president is temporarily unable to carry out the duties of the office. The change was ratified by the states as the Twenty-fifth Amendment in 1967.

It was not long before the country used the procedures outlined in the Twenty-fifth Amendment. In 1973 Vice President Spiro Agnew resigned when he was charged with income tax evasion stemming from alleged corruption during his years as governor of Maryland. Nixon nominated, and Congress confirmed, Rep. Gerald R. Ford of Michigan to become vice president. Just one year later, Nixon resigned the presidency, and Ford became the nation's first unelected chief executive. Ford selected Nelson Rockefeller, former governor of New York, to fill the new vacancy in the vice presidency.

Constitutional Powers

The powers of the presidency are listed in Sections 2 and 3 of Article II, and, unlike presidential selection and

BOX 4-3   LINE OF SUCCESSION

ON MARCH 30, 1981, President Ronald Reagan was shot by would-be assassin John Hinckley outside a Washington hotel and rushed to an area hospital for surgery. Vice President George Bush was on a plane returning to Washington from Texas. Presidential aides and cabinet members gathered at the White House, where questions arose among them and the press corps about who was "in charge."[1] Secretary of State Alexander M. Haig Jr. rushed to the press briefing room and, before an audience of reporters and live television cameras, said, "As of now, I am in control here in the White House, pending the return of the vice president. . . . Constitutionally, gentlemen, you have the president, the vice president, and the secretary of state."

Haig was, as many gleeful critics subsequently pointed out, wrong. The Constitution says nothing about who follows the vice president in the line of succession. The Succession Act of 1947 (later modified to reflect the creation of new departments) establishes congressional leaders and the heads of the departments, in the order the departments were created, as filling the line of succession that follows the vice president.

The line of succession is:

vice president	secretary of commerce
Speaker of the House of Representatives	secretary of labor
president pro tempore of the Senate	secretary of health and human services
secretary of state	secretary of housing and urban development
secretary of the Treasury	secretary of transportation
secretary of defense	secretary of energy
attorney general	secretary of education
secretary of the interior	secretary of veterans affairs
secretary of agriculture	secretary of homeland security

A different "line"—not of succession to the presidency, but of National Command Authority in situations of wartime emergency—was created according to the National Security Act of 1947. The command rules are detailed in secret presidential orders that each new president signs at the outset of the term. Among other things, the orders authorize the secretary of defense to act as commander in chief in certain specific, limited situations in which neither the president nor the vice president is available. Presumably, such situations would follow a nuclear attack on Washington.

SOURCE: *Guide to the Presidency*, ed. Michael Nelson (Washington, D.C.: Congressional Quarterly, 1989), 339.

1. "Confusion over Who Was in Charge Arose Following Reagan Shooting," *Wall Street Journal*, April 1, 1981.

---

succession, they are the same today as when they were drafted by the Philadelphia convention. Some of these powers are quite specific. For example, the president has the power "to make treaties, provided two thirds of the Senators present concur." He also "shall nominate, and by and with the Advice and Consent of the Senate, shall appoint Ambassadors, other public Ministers and Consuls, Judges of the supreme Court, and all other Officers of the United States." But a good deal of the wording in Article II is quite vague, as exemplified by its "The Executive Power shall be vested in a President." What did the Framers mean by the term "Executive Power" in this sentence? There are two possibilities: (1) a mere designation of office, or (2) a general grant of power.

The "mere designation" view holds that the first sentence of Article II simply summarizes the powers listed later on. That is, the president is limited to those specific grants of power contained in Sections 2 and 3 of Article

II. This was a position James Madison implied in Federalist Paper No. 51 and that President William Howard Taft advocated:

The true view of the Executive function is, as I conceive it, that the President can exercise no power which cannot be fairly and reasonably traced to some specific grant of power or justly implied and included within such express grant as proper and necessary to its exercise. Such specific grant must be either in the Federal Constitution or in an act of Congress passed in pursuance thereof. There is no undefined residuum of power which he can exercise because it seems to him to be in the public interest.[4]

Is there any constitutional or historical basis for this position? A common response is based on pure logic: Why would the Framers bother with a list of specific powers, as they did in Article II, if they meant for the president to have more powers than those they enumerated?

Alexander Hamilton (see Federalist Paper No. 70) and other advocates of the "general grant of power" view (sometimes called the stewardship theory, or the prerogative or inherent powers approach, by modern-day scholars) take a much different position. On their account, the president has all the powers listed in Article II, plus those powers he needs to run the nation—regardless of whether the Constitution specifically authorizes their exercise. In other words, so long as neither the Constitution nor Congress has restricted the president from doing something for the common good, he may do it. Seen in this way, the term "Executive Power" in Article II is a general grant of power to the president, which he must exercise in ways that best serve the nation. Or, as President Theodore Roosevelt, a well-known adherent of this perspective, put it in his autobiography:

The most important factor in getting in the right spirit in my Administration . . . was my insistence upon the theory that the executive power was limited only by specific restrictions and prohibitions appearing in the Constitution or imposed by Congress under its constitutional powers. My view was that every Executive officer and above all every Executive officer in high position was *a steward of the people* bound actively and affirmatively to do all he could for the people and not to content him-

self with the negative merit of keeping his talents undamaged in a napkin. . . . My belief was that it was not only his right but his duty to do anything that the needs of the Nation demanded unless such action was forbidden by the Constitution or by the laws. (Emphasis added.)

On what bases did Roosevelt and others support this view? The first is what they considered to be common sense: because the president is the only national leader who is always available, twenty-four hours a day, he must be able to exercise his judgment. To do so he must have the latitude to deal with situations that the Framers never envisioned. The second relies on the Take Care Clause of Article II, Section 3, which states that the president shall be given the responsibility to "take Care that the Laws be faithfully executed." To carry out this command, adherents of the stewardship theory argue, the president must have powers that go beyond those Article II explicitly enumerates.

If the debate between these two camps reminds you of the controversy between Jefferson and Hamilton over the creation of the bank of the United States and, more generally, over congressional powers, you would not be wrong. Just as Jefferson argued that the Constitution limits Congress to enumerated powers, advocates of the "mere designation" approach suggest that the president can exercise only the powers listed in Article II. And, just as Hamilton asserted that the Necessary and Proper Clause of Article I provides Congress with some degree of flexibility, adherents of the stewardship theory argue that the Take Care Clause of Article II enables the president to exercise powers beyond those listed in Article II.

THE FAITHFUL EXECUTION OF THE LAWS: DEFINING THE CONTOURS OF PRESIDENTIAL POWER

Which view would the Court adopt? The justices provided one answer in the landmark case *In re Neagle* (1890). The appeal presenting this case was based on one of the more bizarre and twisted stories in constitutional history. The dispute began some three decades before the case reached the Supreme Court. When the trial court reviewed the essential facts, the story took more than five hundred pages. As you read this decision, consider the

---

4. *Our Chief Magistrate and His Powers* (New York: Columbia University, 1916), 139–140.

extent to which you think the Court's response was influenced by the fact that one of its own members had been threatened.

In re Neagle

135 U.S. 1 (1890)
http://laws.findlaw.com/US/135/1.html
Vote: 6 (Blatchford, Bradley, Brewer, Gray, Harlan, Miller)
*   2 (Fuller, Lamar)*
Opinion of the Court: Miller
Dissenting opinion: Lamar
Not participating: Field

Stephen J. Field and David S. Terry came to California during the 1849 gold rush, Field from New England and Terry from the South. Both became judges on the California Supreme Court, with Terry its chief justice.[5] In 1859 a bitter dispute erupted between Judge Terry and David Broderick, a U.S. senator. Terry resigned his position, challenged Broderick to a duel, and killed him. Field was a close friend of Broderick, and he vowed never to forget the killing. Field was then elevated to the chief justiceship of the state court, and four years later President Abraham Lincoln appointed him to the U.S. Supreme Court.

Terry went into private practice and eventually came to represent Sarah Althea Hill in a divorce action. Hill claimed to be the wife of William Sharon, a former U.S. senator from Nevada, who was a millionaire mine operator and hotel owner. Hill charged Sharon with adultery and sued for divorce, but Sharon denied ever having married her. Many believed that she was just another in a long series of mistresses Sharon had after his wife died. Sarah Hill claimed to have a document proving the marriage was valid, but during the divorce hearing the court ruled the document to be a forgery and dismissed her action.

In the meantime, William Sharon died, and his son Frederick took legal action to dismantle any claim Sarah Hill had to his father's estate. Attorney Terry by this time

Sarah Althea Hill Terry, wife of David Terry, and central figure in the dispute with Justice Stephen Field that led to the killing of her husband.

had fallen in love with his beautiful client (and perhaps also with her potentially large inheritance) and married her. As luck would have it, in September 1888 Justice Field was assigned to a three-judge circuit court to decide the suit brought by Frederick Sharon against Sarah Terry. When the judges announced their ruling in favor of Sharon, violence erupted in the courtroom. Sarah Terry shouted accusations that Field had been bribed to reach his decision. Field ordered the marshals to remove

5. For an account of the events surrounding this case, see Robert Kroninger, "The Justice and the Lady," in *1977 Yearbook of the Supreme Court Historical Society* (Washington, D.C.: Supreme Court Historical Society, 1977), 11–19.

David S. Terry, former California state supreme court judge.

Stephen J. Field, associate justice of the Supreme Court, 1863–1897.

her, and David Terry, defending his wife, struck a marshal and knocked out a tooth. He also brandished a bowie knife, and Sarah attempted to grab a revolver from her purse. The marshals subdued both of them. Sarah Terry was sentenced to one month in jail for contempt, and David Terry to six months in jail.

During his imprisonment, Terry's hatred of his former colleague festered. On several occasions and before numerous witnesses, he pledged to horsewhip and then kill Field if the justice ever returned to California. Sarah Terry also threatened to kill Field. In response, President Benjamin Harrison and the U.S. attorney general decided to provide protection for Justice Field on his next judicial visit to California. The administration authorized a federal marshal, David Neagle, to act as Field's bodyguard when the justice was assigned circuit court duty in California.

Field returned to California in the summer of 1889. Neagle was with him at all times. Traveling from Los Angeles to San Francisco by train, Field disembarked at Lathrop to eat breakfast in the station dining room. The Terrys, who had been on the same train, entered the din-

ing room and saw him. Sarah returned to the train to get her revolver, while David walked up behind Field, slapped him twice on the side of the face, and raised his fist for a third blow. Neagle immediately rose from his seat with his revolver drawn and ordered Terry to stop. Terry reached into his coat, and Neagle, fearing that he was going for a weapon, fired two shots, one to the chest and the other to the head. When Terry's body was searched, no weapons were found.

Sarah Terry, who was to spend her last forty-five years in a state mental institution, claimed that her husband had been murdered by Neagle in conspiracy with Field. She was sufficiently convincing that the bodyguard was arrested and charged with murder. Charges also were filed against Field as an accomplice, but they were later dropped.

A federal court granted a writ of habeas corpus ordering state authorities to release Neagle, and California appealed. The issue before the Supreme Court was Neagle's legal authority to act as he did. The central question was whether the president, without congressional action, could issue an executive order through the U.S. attorney

An illustration of U.S. Deputy Marshal David Neagle, assigned to protect Justice Stephen Field, shooting David Terry in a railroad station restaurant at Lathrop, California, in 1889.

general to authorize a bodyguard to protect Justice Field. The attorney general claimed that the president's constitutional obligation to take care that the laws be faithfully executed was sufficient ground for Neagle's appointment. The state contended that the president did not have such power, in which case Neagle could be tried for murder.

MR. JUSTICE MILLER delivered the opinion of the Court.

The justices of the Supreme Court have been members of the Circuit Courts of the United States ever since the organization of the government, and their attendance on the circuit and appearance at the places where the courts are held has always been thought to be a matter of importance. In order to enable him to perform this duty, Mr. Justice Field had to travel each year from Washington City, near the Atlantic coast, to San Francisco, on the Pacific coast. In doing this he was as much in the discharge of a duty imposed upon him by law as he was while sitting in court and trying cases. There are many duties which the judge performs outside of the court-room where he sits to pronounce judgment or to preside over a trial. The statutes of the United States, and the established practice of the courts, require that the judge perform a very large share of his judicial labors at what is called

"chambers." This chamber work is as important as necessary, as much a discharge of his official duty as that performed in the court-house. Important cases are often argued before the judge at any place convenient to the parties concerned, and a decision of the judge is arrived at by investigations made in his own room, wherever he may be, and it is idle to say that this is not as much the performance of judicial duty as the filing of the judgment with the clerk, and the announcement of the result in open court. . . .

Justice Field had not only left Washington and travelled the three thousand miles or more which were necessary to reach his circuit, but he had entered upon the duties of that circuit, had held the court at San Francisco for some time; and, taking a short leave of that court, had gone down to Los Angeles, another place where a court was to be held, and sat as a judge there for several days, hearing cases and rendering decisions. It was in the necessary act of returning from Los Angeles to San Francisco, by the usual mode of travel between the two places, where his court was still in session, and where he was required to be, that he was assaulted by Terry. . . .

The occurrence which we are called upon to consider was of so extraordinary a character that it is not to be expected that many cases can be found to cite as authority upon the subject. . . .

We have no doubt that Mr. Justice Field when attacked by Terry was engaged in the discharge of his duties as Circuit Justice of the Ninth Circuit, and was entitled to all the protection under those circumstances which the law could give him.

It is urged, however, that there exists no statute authorizing any such protection as that which Neagle was instructed to give Judge Field in the present case, and indeed no protection whatever against a vindictive or malicious assault growing out of the faithful discharge of his official duties; and that the language of section 753 of the Revised Statutes, that the party seeking the benefit of the writ of *habeas corpus* must in this connection show that he is "in custody for an act done or omitted in pursuance of a law of the United States," makes it necessary that upon this occasion it should be shown that the act for which Neagle is imprisoned was done by virtue of an act of Congress. It is not supposed that any special act of Congress exists which authorizes the marshals or deputy marshals of the United States in express terms to accompany the judges of the Supreme Court through their circuits, and act as a bodyguard to them, to defend them against malicious assaults against their persons. But we are of opinion that this view of the statute is an unwarranted restriction of the meaning of a law designed to extend in a liberal manner the benefit of the writ of *habeas corpus* to persons imprisoned for the performance of their duty. And we are satisfied that if it was the duty of Neagle, under the circumstances, a duty which could only arise under the laws of the United States, to defend Mr. Justice Field from a murderous attack upon him, he brings himself within the meaning of the section we have recited. This view of the subject is confirmed by the alternative provision, that he must be in custody "for an act done or omitted in pursuance of a law of the United States or of an order, process, or decree of a court or judge thereof, or is in custody in violation of the Constitution or of a law or treaty of the United States."

In the view we take of the Constitution of the United States, any obligation fairly and properly inferrible from that instrument, or any duty of the marshal to be derived from the general scope of his duties under the laws of the United States, is "a law" within the meaning of this phrase. It would be a great reproach to the system of government of the United States, declared to be within its sphere sovereign and supreme, if there is to be found within the domain of its

powers no means of protecting the judges, in the conscientious and faithful discharge of their duties, from the malice and hatred of those upon whom their judgments may operate unfavorably. . . .

Where, then, are we to look for the protection which we have shown Judge Field was entitled to when engaged in the discharge of his official duties? Not to the courts of the United States; because, as has been more than once said in this court, in the division of the powers of government between the three great departments, executive, legislative and judicial, the judicial is the weakest for the purposes of self-protection and for the enforcement of the powers which it exercises. The ministerial officers through whom its commands must be executed are marshals of the United States, and belong emphatically to the executive department of the government. They are appointed by the President, with the advice and consent of the Senate. They are removable from office at his pleasure. They are subjected by act of Congress to the supervision and control of the Department of Justice, in the hands of one of the cabinet officers of the President, and their compensation is provided by acts of Congress. The same may be said of the district attorneys of the United States, who prosecute and defend the claims of the government in the courts.

The legislative branch of the government can only protect the judicial officers by the enactment of laws for that purpose, and the argument we are now combating assumes that no such law has been passed by Congress.

If we turn to the executive department of the government, we find a very different condition of affairs. The Constitution, section 3, Article 2, declares that the President "shall take care that the laws be faithfully executed," and he is provided with the means of fulfilling this obligation by his authority to commission all the officers of the United States, and, by and with the advice and consent of the Senate, to appoint the most important of them and to fill vacancies. He is declared to be commander-in-chief of the army and navy of the United States. The duties which are thus imposed upon him he is further enabled to perform by the recognition in the Constitution, and the creation by acts of Congress, of executive departments, which have varied in number from four or five to seven or eight, the heads of which are familiarly called cabinet ministers. These aid him in the performance of the great duties of his office, and represent him in a thousand acts to which it can hardly be supposed his personal attention is called, and thus he is enabled to fulfill the duty of his great department, expressed in the phrase that "he shall take care that the laws be faithfully executed."

Is this duty limited to the enforcement of acts of Congress or of treaties of the United States according to their express terms, or does it include the rights, duties and obligations growing out of the Constitution itself, our international relations, and all the protection implied by the nature of the government under the Constitution? . . .

We cannot doubt the power of the President to take measures for the protection of a judge of one of the courts of the United States, who, while in the discharge of the duties of his office, is threatened with a personal attack which may probably result in his death, and we think it clear that where this protection is to be afforded through the civil power, the Department of Justice is the proper one to set in motion the necessary means of protection. The correspondence already recited in this opinion between the marshal of the Northern District of California, and the Attorney General, and the district attorney of the United States for that district, although prescribing no very specific mode of affording this protection by the Attorney General, is sufficient, we think, to warrant the marshal in taking the steps which he did take, in making the provisions which he did make, for the protection and defence of Mr. Justice Field. . . .

But all these questions being conceded, it is urged against the relief sought by this writ of habeas corpus, that the question of the guilt of the prisoner of the crime of murder is a question to be determined by the laws of California, and to be decided by its courts, and that there exists no power in the government of the United States to take away the prisoner from the custody of the proper authorities of the State of California and carry him before a judge of the court of the United States, and release him without a trial by jury according to the laws of the State of California. That the statute of the United States authorizes and directs such a proceeding and such a judgment in a case where the offence charged against the prisoner consists in an act done in pursuance of a law of the United States and by virtue of its authority, and where the imprisonment of the party is in violation of the Constitution and laws of the United States, is clear by its express language. . . .

It would seem as if the argument might close here. If the duty of the United States to protect its officers from vio-

lence, even to death, in discharge of the duties which its laws impose upon them, be established, and Congress has made the writ of habeas corpus one of the means by which this protection is made efficient, and if the facts of this case show that the prisoner was acting both under the authority of law, and the directions of his superior officers of the Department of Justice, we can see no reason why this writ should not be made to serve its purpose in the present case. . . .

The result at which we have arrived upon this examination is, that in the protection of the person and the life of Mr. Justice Field while in the discharge of his official duties, Neagle was authorized to resist the attack of Terry upon him; that Neagle was correct in the belief that without prompt action on his part the assault of Terry upon the judge would have ended in the death of the latter; that such being his well-founded belief, he was justified in taking the life of Terry, as the only means of preventing the death of the man who was intended to be his victim; that in taking the life of Terry, under the circumstances, he was acting under the authority of the law of the United States, and was justified in so doing; and that he is not liable to answer in the courts of California on account of his part in that transaction.

We therefore affirm the judgment of the Circuit Court authorizing his discharge from the custody of the sheriff of San Joaquin County.

In *Neagle*, the Court quite clearly adopted the "general grant" perspective of executive power. The justices held that the president has the constitutional power to take those actions necessary to enforce the laws of the nation, even if the Constitution did not provide an explicit authorization for doing so. Strong support from the Court for this view also came in the 1895 case *In re Debs*. In May 1894 President Grover Cleveland sent troops into Chicago to stop striking train workers from obstructing the movement of the mails, and he had his attorney general secure a court injunction against the striking workers. When the workers defied the injunction and violence erupted, their leader—Eugene Debs—was cited for contempt. Debs, in turn, challenged the injunction, claiming that the president could not obtain it in the absence of explicit congressional authorization. The justices disagreed: "Every government, entrusted, by the very terms of its being . . . has the right to its own courts for any proper assistance." Moreover, because the strike adversely affected the public, the president could forbid it.

Congressional Limitations on Executive Power

Debs and *Neagle* are examples of rulings that allow the president to take action without explicit approval from Congress or the Constitution—and, thus, that support the stewardship approach to the presidency. But the Court also has placed at least two types of limits on presidential prerogative.

The first—what we call the congressional limit—is best illustrated by *Youngstown Sheet & Tube Company v. Sawyer* (1952), also known as the Steel Seizure Case. The genesis of this case lay in a December 1951 announcement by the United Steelworkers Union that it would call a strike at the end of that month. Because the nation was engaged in a war in Korea, and steel was needed in the production of arms and other military equipment, President Harry S. Truman was not about to let a strike shut the mills down. Only hours before the strike was to begin, Truman issued an executive order commanding Secretary of Commerce Charles Sawyer to seize the nation's steel mills and keep them in operation. Sawyer in turn ordered the mill owners to continue to run their facilities as operators for the United States.

Truman's seizure order cited no statutory authority for his action because there was none. There were federal statutes permitting the seizure of industrial plants for certain specified reasons, but the settlement of a labor dispute was not one of them. In fact, the Taft-Hartley Act of 1947 rejected the idea that labor disputes could be resolved by such means. Instead, the act authorized the president to impose an eighty-day cooling-off period as a way to postpone any strike that seriously threatened the public interest. Truman, however, had little regard for the Taft-Hartley Act, which Congress had passed over his veto. The president ignored the cooling-off period alternative and took the direct action of seizing the mills. The inherent powers of the chief executive, he maintained, were enough to authorize the action.

A divided Supreme Court disagreed. Two members of the Court (Douglas and Black) adopted the "mere desig-

nation" or enumerated approach; they wrote, "The President's power, if any, to issue the order must stem either from an act of Congress or from the Constitution itself." Three justices (Vinson, Reed, and Minton) took the opposite position. In their opinion, the Take Care Clause provided the president with a sufficient constitutional basis for his actions: he was taking steps that were in the best interest of the country until Congress could act. Finally, a plurality of four (Burton, Clark, Frankfurter, and Jackson) settled somewhere between the two extremes. Unlike Black and Douglas, they asserted that the president has powers beyond those enumerated in Article II. But, in contrast to Vinson, Reed, and Minton, they argued that President Truman could not seize the mills because he had acted against the "implied" desires of Congress. As Jackson put it, "When the President takes measures incompatible with the expressed or implied will of Congress, his power is at the lowest ebb, for then he can rely only upon his own constitutional powers minus any constitutional powers of Congress over the matter." Despite these divisions, the lesson from *Youngstown Sheet and Tube* is clear: presidential powers may not be fixed, but the president cannot act against the will of Congress. (We have more to say about this case, including an excerpt, in Chapter 5, where we discuss the relative powers of the president and Congress in times of war and national emergencies.)

Another limit centers on the lack of enforcement of the laws. Simply put, the Constitution obliges the president to enforce all the laws, not just those the administration supports. Although a number of presidents have been criticized for failing to carry out certain laws with sufficient enthusiasm, it would be difficult to prove that the chief executive had not satisfied the constitutional mandate of faithful execution. On rare occasions, however, a president has openly refused to execute a law validly passed by Congress. In such cases court challenges are to be expected.

The Obligation to Enforce the Law

What happened when Congress passed the Federal Water Pollution Control Act Amendments of 1972 over

President Nixon's veto is a good illustration. The act made federal money available to local governments for sewers and clean water projects. After losing the legislative battle, the president instructed the appropriate officials of his administration not to allot to local governments the full funds authorized by Congress.

New York City, which expected to be a recipient of these funds, filed suit against Russell Train, head of the Environmental Protection Agency, to force the administration to release the impounded money. In interpreting the legislation, the Supreme Court in *Train v. City of New York* (1975) found no congressional grant of discretion to the president that would allow him to decide how much of the appropriated money to allocate. In the absence of such a grant, the president's obligation was to carry out the terms of the statute. The Court held that the funds must be distributed according to the intent of Congress. Faithful execution of the laws requires the executive branch to enforce and administer the policies enacted by the legislature even if the president opposes them.

DOMESTIC POWERS OF THE PRESIDENT

With this general discussion of executive power in mind, let us now turn to the specific powers of the president. In this section we examine domestic powers and in the next we consider powers over foreign affairs. Treating the powers separately reflects the perspective of political scientists, who suggest that there are actually two "presidencies": one for domestic affairs and one for foreign policy. There are differences between the two: the president is significantly more constrained—by the public, Congress, and even the Supreme Court—in domestic affairs than in the realm of foreign policy. As you read the material to come, consider whether this division makes sense. Has the Supreme Court given the president more latitude over foreign policy? More generally, what approaches have the justices taken to the specific powers of our nation's chief executive?

Veto Power

Section 7 of Article I of the Constitution contains what has become known as the Presentment Clause:

Every Bill which shall have passed the House of Representatives and the Senate, shall, before it become a Law, be presented to the President of the United States; If he approve he shall sign it, but if not he shall return it, with his Objections to that House in which it shall have originated, who shall enter the Objections at large on their Journal, and proceed to reconsider it. If after such Reconsideration two thirds of that House shall agree to pass the Bill, it shall be sent, together with the Objections, to the other House, by which it shall likewise be reconsidered, and if approved by two thirds of that House, it shall become a Law. But in all such Cases the Votes of both Houses shall be determined by yeas and Nays, and the Names of the Persons voting for and against the Bill shall be entered on the Journal of each House respectively. If any Bill shall not be returned by the President within ten Days (Sundays excepted) after it shall have been presented to him, the Same shall be a Law, in like Manner as if he had signed it, unless the Congress by their Adjournment prevent its Return, in which Case it shall not be a Law.

In other words, after Congress passes a piece of legislation, it is sent to the president. He, in turn, has three options: sign it, veto it, or do nothing. If he signs it, the bill becomes law. If he vetoes it, Congress can attempt to override him by the required two-thirds vote. If he does nothing, the bill becomes law after ten days, provided that Congress is in session; if Congress adjourns during the ten-day period, the bill is "pocket vetoed" and Congress cannot override the president's veto (but it can reintroduce the bill in its next session). Although presidents do not often invoke their pocket veto (since 1789, only about 1,070 times or about 5 times a year) or, for that matter, their regular veto (since 1789, around 1,500 times or about 7 times a year) power, they regard their option to do so as important.[6] At the very least, they can hold it out as a threat against a recalcitrant Congress.

For much of American history, the veto power generated few constitutional disputes, but that has changed in recent years. Two issues relating to the veto have been at the core of major controversies. The first, which we discuss in some detail in Chapter 5, is the legislative veto. The other is the line-item veto, which allowed the

---

6. Data are from Harold W. Stanley and Richard G. Niemi, *Vital Statistics on American Politics, 1999–2000* (Washington, D.C.: CQ Press, 2000), 256. These figures are quite small compared with the number of bills that come to the president for his signature.

president to cancel particular taxing and spending provisions after he has signed them into law. To understand why the line-item veto is controversial, think first about the way bills become laws: since the days of George Washington, Congress has passed laws and the president has been forced to decide whether to accept or reject them in their entirety. But this arrangement has not been wholly satisfactory to presidents. Beginning with Ulysses S. Grant, virtually all have sought the ability to veto parts of a bill and accept others.

Among the rationales presidents have offered for the line-item veto, a common one is this: because members of Congress must face periodic electoral checks, they often include in the federal budget "pork barrel" projects—those designed solely to appease constituents—even though such projects waste money. According to the Clinton administration, examples of such unnecessary expenditures in the 1995 budget include $70 million for a Pentagon housing facility, $58 million for university research facilities, and $1 billion for water resources. Because members of Congress are unwilling to take fiscal responsibility and omit such items from the budget, the argument goes, the president should take on this responsibility by being able to veto or "cancel" particular expenditures.

In 1996 Congress finally agreed, enacting the Line Item Veto Act, which allowed the president to cancel certain tax and spending benefits after they had been signed into law. In 1997 the Court heard a challenge to the act, *Raines v. Byrd*, but dismissed the case. The Court held that the members of Congress who brought suit had "not alleged a sufficiently concrete injury to have established Article III standing." In his concurring opinion, Justice David Souter expressed his belief that the day would eventually come when a party suffered a sufficient loss of federal funds to maintain a suit.

That day came the very next term. In *Clinton v. City of New York* (1998), the justices found that the litigants had standing to challenge the act, and the Court decided the case on its merits.[7] What did the majority decide? Does it make a compelling case for its position?

7. To hear oral arguments in this case, navigate to: *www.oyez.org/oyez/frontpage.*

Clinton v. City of New York

524 U.S. 417 (1998)
http://laws.findlaw.com/US/524/417.html
Vote: 6 (Ginsburg, Kennedy, Rehnquist, Souter, Stevens, Thomas)
  3 (Breyer, O'Connor, Scalia)
Opinion of the Court: Stevens
Concurring opinion: Kennedy
Opinion concurring in part and dissenting in part: Scalia
Dissenting opinion: Breyer

The Line Item Veto Act stated in part:

[T]he President may, with respect to any bill or joint resolution that has been signed into law pursuant to Article I, section 7, of the Constitution of the United States, cancel in whole—(1) any dollar amount of discretionary budget authority; (2) any item of new direct spending; or (3) any limited tax benefit; if the President—

(A) determines that such cancellation will—(i) reduce the Federal budget deficit; (ii) not impair any essential Government functions; and (iii) not harm the national interest; and

(B) notifies the Congress of such cancellation by transmitting a special message . . . within five calendar days (excluding Sundays) after the enactment of the law [to which the cancellation applies].

The act contained two other important provisions. First, although it gave the president the power to rescind various expenditures, it established a check on his ability to do so. Congress would consider "disapproval bills"—those that would render the president's cancellation "null and void." In other words, Congress could restore presidential cuts but, it is worth noting, new congressional legislation would be subject to a presidential veto. Second, the act stated, "Any Member of Congress or any individual adversely affected by [this act] may bring an action, in the United States District Court for the District of Columbia, for declaratory judgment and injunctive relief on the ground that any provision of this part violates the Constitution."

On January 2, 1997, just one day after the act went into effect, six members of Congress who voted against it took advantage of this provision and brought suit in federal court against Secretary of the Treasury Robert E. Rubin and Director of the Office of Management and

President Bill Clinton uses new power under the Line Item Veto Act to cancel two spending provisions and a special tax break on August 11, 1997. Groups challenging the law won a Supreme Court ruling declaring the act unconstitutional.

Budget Franklin D. Raines. These legislators argued that the act violated Article I of the Constitution (see, especially, Article I, Section 7). In their view, it "unconstitutionally expands the President's power," and "violates the requirements of bicameral passage and presentment by granting to the President, acting alone, the authority to 'cancel' and thus repeal provisions of federal law." They further asserted that the act injured them "directly and concretely . . . in their official capacities" by (1) altering the legal and practical effect of all votes they may cast on bills containing such separately vetoable items; (2) divesting them of their constitutional role in the repeal of legislation; and (3) altering the constitutional balance of powers between the legislative and executive branches.

Attorneys for the executive branch officials disagreed. They argued that the legislators lacked standing to sue and that their claim was not ripe, meaning that the president had not yet used the new veto authority.

The lower court agreed with the members of Congress, and executive branch officials appealed to the U.S. Supreme Court. Because the act directed the Court to hear as soon as possible any suit challenging its constitutionality, the justices established an expedited briefing schedule. They heard oral argument in the case of *Raines v. Byrd* on May 27, 1997, a little more than a month after the lower court's decision.

But, after all this, the Court dismissed the case. Writing for the majority, Chief Justice William H. Rehnquist held that the suit was not a real case or controversy because members of Congress were "not the right" litigants. After the Court's decision, President Clinton invoked the line item veto to cancel more than eighty items, including a provision of the Balanced Budget Act of 1997, which provided money for New York City hospitals, and a section of the Taxpayer Relief Act of 1997, which gave a tax break to potato growers in Idaho. These steps were immediately challenged by the affected parties. Those in the first case were the City of New York, two hospital associations, one hospital, and two unions representing health care employees. The parties in the second were a farmers' cooperative and one of its members.

A federal district court consolidated the cases, determined that at least one of the plaintiffs in each case had standing under Article III, and ruled that the Line Item Veto Act violated the Presentment Clause (Article I, Section 7, Clause 2).

JUSTICE STEVENS delivered the opinion of the Court.

Less than two months after our decision in [*Raines*], the President exercised his authority to cancel one provision in the Balanced Budget Act of 1997 and two provisions in the Taxpayer Relief Act of 1997. Appellees, claiming that they had been injured by two of those cancellations, filed these cases in the District Court. That Court again held the statute invalid and we again expedited our review. We now hold that these appellees have standing to challenge the constitutionality of the Act, and, reaching the merits, we agree that the cancellation procedures set forth in the Act violate the Presentment Clause, Art. I, Sec. 7, cl. 2, of the Constitution. . . .

In both legal and practical effect, the President has amended two Acts of Congress by repealing a portion of each. "[R]epeal of statutes, no less than enactment, must conform with Art. I." *INS v. Chadha* (1983). There is no provision in the Constitution that authorizes the President to enact, to amend, or to repeal statutes. Both Article I and Article II assign responsibilities to the President that directly relate to the lawmaking process, but neither addresses the issue presented by these cases. The President "shall from time to time give to the Congress Information on the State of the Union, and recommend to their Consideration such Measures as he shall judge necessary and expedient. . . ." Art. II, Sec. 3. Thus, he may initiate and influence legislative proposals. Moreover, after a bill has passed both Houses of Congress, but "before it become[s] a Law," it must be presented to the President. If he approves it, "he shall sign it, but if not he shall return it, with his Objections to that House in which it shall have originated, who shall enter the Objections at large on their Journal, and proceed to reconsider it." Art. I, Sec. 7, cl. 2. His "return" of a bill, which is usually described as a "veto," is subject to being overridden by a two-thirds vote in each House.

There are important differences between the President's "return" of a bill pursuant to Article I, Sec. 7, and the exercise of the President's cancellation authority pursuant to the Line Item Veto Act. The constitutional return takes place before the bill becomes law; the statutory cancellation occurs after the bill becomes law. The constitutional return is of the entire bill; the statutory cancellation is of only a part. Although the Constitution expressly authorizes the Presi-

dent to play a role in the process of enacting statutes, it is silent on the subject of unilateral Presidential action that either repeals or amends parts of duly enacted statutes.

There are powerful reasons for construing constitutional silence on this profoundly important issue as equivalent to an express prohibition. The procedures governing the enactment of statutes set forth in the text of Article I were the product of the great debates and compromises that produced the Constitution itself. Familiar historical materials provide abundant support for the conclusion that the power to enact statutes may only "be exercised in accord with a single, finely wrought and exhaustively considered, procedure." *Chadha.* Our first President understood the text of the Presentment Clause as requiring that he either "approve all the parts of a Bill, or reject it in toto." What has emerged in these cases from the President's exercise of his statutory cancellation powers, however, are truncated versions of two bills that passed both Houses of Congress. They are not the product of the "finely wrought" procedure that the Framers designed. . . .

. . . [O]ur decision rests on the narrow ground that the procedures authorized by the Line Item Veto Act are not authorized by the Constitution. The Balanced Budget Act of 1997 is a 500-page document that became "Public Law 105-33" after three procedural steps were taken: (1) a bill containing its exact text was approved by a majority of the Members of the House of Representatives; (2) the Senate approved precisely the same text; and (3) that text was signed into law by the President. The Constitution explicitly requires that each of those three steps be taken before a bill may "become a law." Art. I, Sec. 7. If one paragraph of that text had been omitted at any one of those three stages, Public Law 105-33 would not have been validly enacted. If the Line Item Veto Act were valid, it would authorize the President to create a different law—one whose text was not voted on by either House of Congress or presented to the President for signature. Something that might be known as "Public Law 105-33 as modified by the President" may or may not be desirable, but it is surely not a document that may "become a law" pursuant to the procedures designed by the Framers of Article I, Sec. 7, of the Constitution.

If there is to be a new procedure in which the President will play a different role in determining the final text of what may "become a law," such change must come not by legislation, but through the amendment procedures set forth in Article V of the Constitution. Cf. *U.S. Term Limits, Inc. v. Thornton* (1995).

The judgment of the District Court is

Affirmed.

JUSTICE KENNEDY, concurring.

A nation cannot plunder its own treasury without putting its Constitution and its survival in peril. The statute before us, then, is of first importance, for it seems undeniable the Act will tend to restrain persistent excessive spending. Nevertheless, for the reasons given by JUSTICE STEVENS in the opinion for the Court, the statute must be found invalid. Failure of political will does not justify unconstitutional remedies. . . .

The Constitution is not bereft of controls over improvident spending. Federalism is one safeguard, for political accountability is easier to enforce within the States than nationwide. The other principal mechanism, of course, is control of the political branches by an informed and responsible electorate. Whether or not federalism and control by the electorate are adequate for the problem at hand, they are two of the structures the Framers designed for the problem the statute strives to confront. The Framers of the Constitution could not command statesmanship. They could simply provide structures from which it might emerge. The fact that these mechanisms, plus the proper functioning of the separation of powers itself, are not employed, or that they prove insufficient, cannot validate an otherwise unconstitutional device. With these observations, I join the opinion of the Court.

JUSTICE SCALIA, with whom JUSTICE O'CONNOR joins, and with whom JUSTICE BREYER joins [in part], concurring in part and dissenting in part.

I turn . . . to the crux of the matter: whether Congress' authorizing the President to cancel an item of spending gives him a power that our history and traditions show must reside exclusively in the Legislative Branch. I may note, to begin with, that the Line Item Veto Act is not the first statute to authorize the President to "cancel" spending items. In *Bowsher v. Synar* we addressed the constitutionality of the Balanced Budget and Emergency Deficit Control Act

of 1985, which required the President, if the federal budget deficit exceeded a certain amount, to issue a "sequestration" order mandating spending reductions specified by the Comptroller General. The effect of sequestration was that "amounts sequestered . . . shall be permanently cancelled." We held that the Act was unconstitutional not because it impermissibly gave the Executive legislative power, but because it gave the Comptroller General, an officer of the Legislative Branch over whom Congress retained removal power, "the ultimate authority to determine the budget cuts to be made," "functions . . . plainly entailing execution of the law in constitutional terms." The President's discretion under the Line Item Veto Act is certainly broader than the Comptroller General's discretion was under the 1985 Act, but it is no broader than the discretion traditionally granted the President in his execution of spending laws.

Insofar as the degree of political, "lawmaking" power conferred upon the Executive is concerned, there is not a dime's worth of difference between Congress' authorizing the President to cancel a spending item, and Congress' authorizing money to be spent on a particular item at the President's discretion. And the latter has been done since the Founding of the Nation. From 1789–1791, the First Congress made lump-sum appropriations for the entire Government—"sum[s] not exceeding" specified amounts for broad purposes. From a very early date, Congress also made permissive individual appropriations, leaving the decision whether to spend the money to the President's unfettered discretion. . . .

The short of the matter is this: had the Line Item Veto Act authorized the President to "decline to spend" any item of spending contained in the Balanced Budget Act of 1997, there is not the slightest doubt that authorization would have been constitutional. What the Line Item Veto Act does instead—authorizing the President to "cancel" an item of spending—is technically different. But the technical difference does not relate to the technicalities of the Presentment Clause, which have been fully complied with; and the doctrine of unconstitutional delegation, which is at issue here, is preeminently not a doctrine of technicalities. The title of the Line Item Veto Act, which was perhaps designed to simplify for public comprehension, or perhaps merely to comply with the terms of a campaign pledge, has succeeded in faking out the Supreme Court. The President's action it authorizes in fact is not a line-item veto, and thus does not offend

Art. I, Sec. 7; and, insofar as the substance of that action is concerned, it is no different from what Congress has permitted the President to do since the formation of the Union.

JUSTICE BREYER, with whom JUSTICE O'CONNOR and JUSTICE SCALIA join [in part], dissenting.

I agree with the Court that the parties have standing, but I do not agree with its ultimate conclusion. In my view, the Line Item Veto Act does not violate any specific textual constitutional command, nor does it violate any implicit Separation of Powers principle. Consequently, I believe that the Act is constitutional. . . .

I recognize that the Act before us is novel. In a sense, it skirts a constitutional edge. But that edge has to do with means, not ends. The means chosen do not amount literally to the enactment, repeal, or amendment of a law. Nor, for that matter, do they amount literally to the "line item veto" that the Act's title announces. Those means do not violate any basic Separation of Powers principle. They do not improperly shift the constitutionally foreseen balance of power from Congress to the President. Nor, since they comply with Separation of Powers principles, do they threaten the liberties of individual citizens. They represent an experiment that may, or may not, help representative government work better. The Constitution, in my view, authorizes Congress and the President to try novel methods in this way. Consequently, with respect, I dissent.

In a statement issued after the Court handed down its decision, President Clinton expressed his displeasure: "I am deeply disappointed with today's Supreme Court decision striking down the line-item veto. The decision is a defeat for all Americans—it deprives the President of a valuable tool for eliminating waste in the Federal budget and for enlivening the public debate over how to make the best use of public funds." Given the views of the six-person majority, however, it is unlikely that the Court will reverse itself any time in the near future.

Power of Appointment and Removal

For presidents to carry out the executive duties of the government effectively, they must be able to staff the various departments and offices with administrators who share their views and in whom they have confidence. This duty implies the power to appoint and the power to remove. The Constitution is relatively clear on the president's appointment power, but it is silent on the right to remove.

Appointing Executive Officials. Article II, Section 2, contains what is known as the Appointments Clause. It details the president's authority to appoint major administrative and judicial officials, but it also allows Congress to allocate that authority to other bodies for minor administrative positions:

[The president] shall nominate, and by and with the Advice and Consent of the Senate, shall appoint Ambassadors, other public Ministers and Consuls, Judges of the supreme Court, and all other Officers of the United States, whose Appointments are not herein otherwise provided for, and which shall be established by Law: but the Congress may by Law vest the Appointment of such inferior Officers, as they think proper, in the President alone, in the Courts of Law, or in the Heads of Departments.

From time to time Congress has established government positions that, for various reasons, were to be filled by an appointing authority other than the president. When the executive has objected, legal disputes have arisen. In many cases the issue is whether the official holds a major position as an officer of the United States or is an inferior official. The former, according to the Appointments Clause, must be filled by presidential nomination and Senate confirmation, but the latter may be chosen by some other means as determined by Congress.

Buckley v. Valeo (1976) illustrates this point. The justices heard a challenge to the constitutionality of the 1974 amendments to the Federal Election Campaign Act. The appeal involved a complex set of issues regarding the regulation of federal election campaigns, including the question of who should enforce the law. The statute created the Federal Election Commission (FEC) to police the new regulations. Its powers included making available "for public inspection, preservation, and auditing and field investigations" campaign finance reports; serving "as a national clearinghouse for information in respect to the administration of elections"; making "rules and regulations to carry out" particular provisions of the act; formulating "general policy with respect to the administration of this Act"; and rendering "advisory opinions with respect to activities possibly violating the Act."

In light of the just-concluded Watergate controversy *(see pages 235–239)*, Congress did not want the eight members of the commission to be appointed exclusively by the president, so it devised a plan for choosing them. The secretary of the Senate and the clerk of the House were ex officio members without the right to vote. The president pro tempore of the Senate, the Speaker of the House, and the president each appointed two members, one Democrat and one Republican. The six voting members had to be confirmed by both houses of Congress.

This arrangement was challenged as a violation of the Appointments Clause. The argument was that the commissioners were officers of the United States who should be appointed by the president only and confirmed by the Senate, with no House involvement. Furthermore, the commission's appointment procedures were attacked because, as the body given responsibility to enforce the campaign laws (an executive function), the members should not be appointed by the legislature. To construct the commission this way was to violate the principle of separation of powers.

The Supreme Court, unanimously on this point, found the FEC to be unconstitutionally structured. The commissioners were not inferior officers; they were officers entrusted with major enforcement and administrative duties. As such, they belonged to the executive branch and should not be appointed by the legislature.

The Court reached a different conclusion in *Morrison v. Olson* (1988).[8] This decision involved the creation of the office of special prosecutor. Given the kinds of cases special prosecutors, or independent counsels, are appointed to investigate, are you convinced by the Court's analysis that this official is an "inferior officer" under the meaning of the Appointments Clause? Or is the Court taking a pragmatic approach, recognizing that it would be unworkable for an official prosecuting crime and corruption in the executive branch to be appointed by the president?

8. To hear oral arguments in this case, navigate to: *www.oyez.org/oyez/frontpage.*

In dissent, Justice Antonin Scalia accuses the majority of violating both the letter and the spirit of the separation of powers doctrine. Is his argument compelling?

Morrison v. Olson

487 U.S. 654 (1988)
http://laws.findlaw.com/US/487/654.html
Vote: 7 (Blackmun, Brennan, Marshall, O'Connor, Rehnquist, Stevens, White)
        1 (Scalia)
Opinion of the Court: Rehnquist
Dissenting opinion: Scalia
Not participating: Kennedy

Because of the problems encountered in prosecuting the Watergate case, Congress included a provision in the Ethics in Government Act of 1978 dealing with the position of special prosecutor. The law provided for an independent counsel to investigate and, when necessary, to prosecute high-ranking officials of the government for violations of federal criminal laws. The independent counsel was to be chosen by a group of three federal judges, who would be appointed by the chief justice for two years and known as the special division. The selection of independent counsels and the description of each counsel's jurisdiction are the special division's only functions. It carries out these responsibilities only after a preliminary investigation by the attorney general indicates that an independent counsel is necessary.

Once appointed, the independent counsel may exercise all of the powers of the Justice Department. A counsel appointed under the act may be removed by the attorney general, but only for cause or disabilities that substantially impair the counsel from completing the required duties. Such dismissals may be reviewed by the federal district court. The independent counsel's tenure otherwise ends when he or she declares the work to be completed, or the special division concludes that the independent counsel's assigned tasks have been accomplished.

In 1982 two House subcommittees investigated the activities of the Environmental Protection Agency and the Land and Natural Resources division of the Justice

Department. During that investigation the subcommittees asked the agencies to produce certain documents. A controversy flared up over whether the legislature could demand these documents from the executive branch, a dispute that was settled after contempt of Congress citations were made and lawsuits were filed. The following year the House Judiciary Committee began an investigation into the role of Justice Department officials in these events. Two years later, in 1985, the committee issued its report, which indicated that Theodore B. Olson, an assistant attorney general, had provided false and misleading statements when he testified before the committee. Two other Justice Department officials were implicated in obstructing the committee's investigation. The committee requested that the attorney general initiate action for the appointment of an independent counsel to pursue these cases.

The special division appointed James McKay as independent counsel, but when he resigned a month later, the judges selected Alexia Morrison. Olson and the other targets of the investigation refused to cooperate with orders to produce evidence on the ground that the independent counsel provision of the Ethics in Government Act violated the Constitution's Appointments Clause. They claimed that the independent counsel was not an "inferior officer" and therefore had to be appointed by the president, not by a group of three judges. The federal district court upheld the validity of the act, but the court of appeals reversed.

CHIEF JUSTICE REHNQUIST delivered the opinion of the Court.

The parties do not dispute that "[t]he Constitution for purposes of appointment . . . divides all its officers into two classes." As we stated in *Buckley v. Valeo* (1976), "[p]rincipal officers are selected by the President with the advice and consent of the Senate. Inferior officers Congress may allow to be appointed by the President alone, by the heads of departments, or by the Judiciary." The initial question is, accordingly, whether appellant is an "inferior" or a "principal" officer. If she is the latter, as the Court of Appeals concluded, then the Act is in violation of the Appointments Clause.

The line between "inferior" and "principal" officers is one that is far from clear, and the Framers provided little guidance into where it should be drawn. . . . We need not attempt here to decide exactly where the line falls between the two types of officers, because in our view appellant clearly falls on the "inferior officer" side of that line. Several factors lead to this conclusion.

First, appellant is subject to removal by a higher Executive Branch official. Although appellant may not be "subordinate" to the Attorney General (and the President) insofar as she possesses a degree of independent discretion to exercise the powers delegated to her under the Act, the fact that she can be removed by the Attorney General indicates that she is to some degree "inferior" in rank and authority. Second, appellant is empowered by the Act to perform only certain, limited duties. An independent counsel's role is restricted primarily to investigation and, if appropriate, prosecution for certain federal crimes. Admittedly, the Act delegates to appellant "full power and independent authority to exercise all investigative and prosecutorial functions and powers of the Department of Justice," but this grant of authority does not include any authority to formulate policy for the Government or the Executive Branch, nor does it give appellant any administrative duties outside of those necessary to operate her office. The Act specifically provides that in policy matters appellant is to comply to the extent possible with the policies of the Department.

Third, appellant's office is limited in jurisdiction. Not only is the Act itself restricted in applicability to certain federal officials suspected of certain serious federal crimes, but an independent counsel can only act within the scope of the jurisdiction that has been granted by the Special Division pursuant to a request by the Attorney General. Finally, appellant's office is limited in tenure. There is concededly no time limit on the appointment of a particular counsel. Nonetheless, the office of independent counsel is "temporary" in the sense that an independent counsel is appointed essentially to accomplish a single task, and when that task is over the office is terminated, either by the counsel herself or by action of the Special Division. Unlike other prosecutors, appellant has no ongoing responsibilities that extend beyond the accomplishment of the mission that she was appointed for and authorized by the Special Division to undertake. In our view, these factors relating to the "ideas of tenure, duration . . . and duties" of the independent counsel are sufficient to establish that appellant is an "inferior" officer in the constitutional sense. . . .

This does not, however, end our inquiry under the Appointments Clause. Appellees argue that even if appellant is an "inferior" officer, the Clause does not empower Congress to place the power to appoint such an officer outside the Executive Branch. They contend that the Clause does not contemplate congressional authorization of "interbranch appointments," in which an officer of one branch is appointed by officers of another branch. The relevant language of the Appointments Clause is worth repeating. It reads: ". . . but the Congress may by Law vest the Appointment of such inferior Officers, as they think proper, in the President alone, in the courts of Law, or in the Heads of Departments." On its face, the language of this "excepting clause" admits of no limitation on interbranch appointments. Indeed, the inclusion of "as they think proper" seems clearly to give Congress significant discretion to determine whether it is "proper" to vest the appointment of, for example, executive officials in the "courts of Law.". . .

We also note that the history of the clause provides no support for appellees' position. Throughout most of the process of drafting the Constitution, the Convention concentrated on the problem of who should have the authority to appoint judges. At the suggestion of James Madison, the Convention adopted a proposal that the Senate should have this authority, and several attempts to transfer the appointment power to the president were rejected. The August 6, 1787, draft of the Constitution reported by the Committee of Detail retained Senate appointment of Supreme Court Judges, provided also for Senate appointment of ambassadors, and vested in the president the authority to "appoint officers in all cases not otherwise provided for by this Constitution." This scheme was maintained until September 4, when the Committee of Eleven reported its suggestions to the Convention. This Committee suggested that the Constitution be amended to state that the president "shall nominate and by and with the advice and consent of the Senate shall appoint ambassadors, and other public Ministers, Judges of the Supreme Court, and all other Officers of the [United States], whose appointments are not otherwise herein provided for." After the addition of "Consuls" to the list, the Committee's proposal was adopted, and was subsequently reported to the Convention by the Committee of Style. It was at this point, on September 15, that Gouver-

neur Morris moved to add the Excepting Clause to Art. II, §2. The one comment made on this motion was by Madison, who felt that the Clause did not go far enough in that it did not allow Congress to vest appointment powers in "Superior Officers below Heads of Departments." The first vote on Morris's motion ended in a tie. It was then put forward a second time, with the urging that "some such provision [was] too necessary, to be omitted." This time the proposal was adopted. As this discussion shows, there was little or no debate on the question of whether the Clause empowers Congress to provide for interbranch appointments, and there is nothing to suggest that the Framers intended to prevent Congress from having that power.

We do not mean to say that Congress' power to provide for interbranch appointments of "inferior officers" is unlimited. In addition to separation of powers concerns, which would arise if such provisions for appointment had the potential to impair the constitutional functions assigned to one of the branches, . . . Congress' decision to vest the appointment power in the courts would be improper if there was some "incongruity" between the functions normally performed by the courts and the performance of their duty to appoint. In this case, however, we do not think it impermissible for Congress to vest the power to appoint independent counsels in a specially created federal court. We thus disagree with the Court of Appeals' conclusion that there is an inherent incongruity about a court having the power to appoint prosecutorial officers. . . . Congress of course was concerned when it created the office of independent counsel with the conflicts of interest that could arise in situations when the Executive Branch is called upon to investigate its own high-ranking officers. If it were to remove the appointing authority from the Executive Branch, the most logical place to put it was in the Judicial Branch. In the light of the Act's provision making the judges of the Special Division ineligible to participate in any matters relating to an independent counsel they have appointed, . . . we do not think that appointment of the independent counsels by the court runs afoul of the constitutional limitation on "incongruous" interbranch appointments.

Appellees next contend that the powers vested in the Special Division by the Act conflict with Article III of the Constitution. We have long recognized that by the express provision of Article III, the judicial power of the United States is limited to "Cases" and "Controversies." As a general rule, we have broadly stated that "executive or administrative duties of a nonjudicial nature may not be imposed on judges holding office under Art. III of the Constitution." The purpose of this limitation is to help ensure the independence of the Judicial Branch and to prevent the judiciary from encroaching into areas reserved for the other branches. With this in mind, we address in turn the various duties given to the Special Division by the Act.

Most importantly, the Act vests in the Special Division the power to choose who will serve as independent counsel and the power to define his or her jurisdiction. Clearly, once it is accepted that the Appointments Clause gives Congress the power to vest the appointment of officials such as the independent counsel in the "courts of Law," there can be no Article III objection to the Special Division's exercise of that power, as the power itself derives from the Appointments Clause, a source of authority for judicial action that is independent of Article III. . . .

We now turn to consider whether the Act is invalid under the constitutional principle of separation of powers. Two related issues must be addressed: The first is whether the provision of the Act restricting the Attorney General's power to remove the independent counsel to only those instances in which he can show "good cause," taken by itself, impermissibly interferes with the President's exercise of his constitutionally appointed functions. The second is whether, taken as a whole, the Act violates the separation of powers by reducing the President's ability to control the prosecutorial powers wielded by the independent counsel.

Two Terms ago we had occasion to consider whether it was consistent with the separation of powers for Congress to pass a statute that authorized a government official who is removable only by Congress to participate in what we found to be "executive powers." *Bowsher v. Synar* (1986). We held in *Bowsher* that "Congress cannot reserve for itself the power of removal of an officer charged with the execution of the laws except by impeachment." A primary antecedent for this ruling was our 1926 decision in *Myers v. United States*. *Myers* had considered the propriety of a federal statute by which certain postmasters of the United States could be removed by the President only "by and with the advice and consent of the Senate." There too, Congress' attempt to involve itself in the removal of an executive official was found to be sufficient grounds to render the statute invalid. As we observed in *Bowsher*, the essence of the decision in *Myers*

was the judgment that the Constitution prevents Congress from "draw[ing] to itself . . . the power to remove or the right to participate in the exercise of that power. To do this would be to go beyond the words and implications of the [Appointments Clause] and to infringe the constitutional principle of the separation of governmental powers."

Unlike both *Bowsher* and *Myers*, this case does not involve an attempt by Congress itself to gain a role in the removal of executive officials other than its established powers of impeachment and conviction. The Act instead puts the removal power squarely in the hands of the Executive Branch; an independent counsel may be removed from office, "only by the personal action of the Attorney General, and only for good cause." There is no requirement of congressional approval of the Attorney General's removal decision, though the decision is subject to judicial review. . . .

Considering for the moment the "good cause" removal provision in isolation from the other parts of the Act at issue in this case, we cannot say that the imposition of a "good cause" standard for removal by itself unduly trammels on executive authority. There is no real dispute that the functions performed by the independent counsel are "executive" in the sense that they are law enforcement functions that typically have been undertaken by officials within the Executive Branch. As we noted above, however, the independent counsel is an inferior officer under the Appointments Clause, with limited jurisdiction and tenure and lacking policymaking or significant administrative authority. Although the counsel exercises no small amount of discretion and judgment in deciding how to carry out her duties under the Act, we simply do not see how the President's need to control the exercise of that discretion is so central to the functioning of the Executive Branch as to require as a matter of constitutional law that the counsel be terminable at will by the President.

Nor do we think that the "good cause" removal provision at issue here impermissibly burdens the President's power to control or supervise the independent counsel, as an executive official, in the execution of her duties under the Act. This is not a case in which the power to remove an executive official has been completely stripped from the President, thus providing no means for the President to ensure the "faithful execution" of the laws. Rather, because the independent counsel may be terminated for "good cause," the Executive, through the Attorney General, retains ample authority to assure that the counsel is competently performing her statutory responsibilities in a manner that comports with the provisions of the Act. Although we need not decide in this case exactly what is encompassed within the term "good cause" under the Act, the legislative history of the removal provision also makes clear that the Attorney General may remove an independent counsel for "misconduct." Here, as with the provision of the Act conferring the appointment authority of the independent counsel on the special court, the congressional determination to limit the removal power of the Attorney General was essential, in the view of Congress, to establish the necessary independence of the office. We do not think that this limitation as it presently stands sufficiently deprives the President of control over the independent counsel to interfere impermissibly with his constitutional obligation to ensure the faithful execution of the laws.

The final question to be addressed is whether the Act, taken as a whole, violates the principle of separation of powers by unduly interfering with the role of the Executive Branch. Time and again we have reaffirmed the importance in our constitutional scheme of the separation of governmental powers into the three coordinate branches. As we stated in *Buckley v. Valeo* (1976), the system of separated powers and checks and balances established in the Constitution was regarded by the Framers as "a self-executing safeguard against the encroachment or aggrandizement of one branch at the expense of the other." We have not hesitated to invalidate provisions of law which violate this principle. On the other hand, we have never held that the Constitution requires that the three Branches of Government "operate with absolute independence.". . .

We observe first that this case does not involve an attempt by Congress to increase its own powers at the expense of the Executive Branch. Unlike some of our previous cases, most recently *Bowsher v. Synar*, this case simply does not pose a "dange[r] of congressional usurpation of Executive Branch functions." Indeed, with the exception of the power of impeachment—which applies to all officers of the United States—Congress retained for itself no powers of control or supervision over an independent counsel. The Act does empower certain members of Congress to request the Attorney General to apply for the appointment of an independent counsel, but the Attorney General has no duty to comply with the request, although he must respond within

a certain time limit. Other than that, Congress' role under the Act is limited to receiving reports or other information and oversight of the independent counsel's activities, functions that we have recognized generally as being incidental to the legislative functions of Congress.

Similarly, we do not think that the Act works any judicial usurpation of properly executive functions. As should be apparent from our discussion of the Appointments Clause above, the power to appoint inferior officers such as independent counsels is not in itself an "executive" function in the constitutional sense, at least when Congress has exercised its power to vest the appointment of an inferior office in the "courts of Law.". . .

Finally, we do not think that the Act "impermissibly undermine[s]" the powers of the Executive Branch, or "disrupts the proper balance between the coordinate branches [by] prevent[ing] the Executive Branch from accomplishing its constitutionally assigned functions." It is undeniable that the Act reduces the amount of control or supervision that the Attorney General and, through him, the President exercises over the investigation and prosecution of a certain class of alleged criminal activity. The Attorney General is not allowed to appoint the individual of his choice; he does not determine the counsel's jurisdiction; and his power to remove a counsel is limited. Nonetheless, the Act does give the Attorney General several means of supervising or controlling the prosecutorial powers that may be wielded by an independent counsel. Most importantly, the Attorney General retains the power to remove the counsel for "good cause," a power that we have already concluded provides the Executive with substantial ability to ensure that the laws are "faithfully executed" by an independent counsel. No independent counsel may be appointed without a specific request by the Attorney General, and the Attorney General's decision not to request appointment if he finds "no reasonable grounds to believe that further investigation is warranted" is committed to his unreviewable discretion. The Act thus gives the Executive a degree of control over the power to initiate an investigation by the independent counsel. In addition, the jurisdiction of the independent counsel is defined with reference to the facts submitted by the Attorney General, and once a counsel is appointed, the Act requires that the counsel abide by Justice Department policy unless it is not "possible" to do so. Notwithstanding the fact that the counsel is to some degree "independent" and free from Executive supervision to a greater extent than other federal prosecutors, in our view these features of the Act give the Executive Branch sufficient control over the independent counsel to ensure that the President is able to perform his constitutionally assigned duties.

In sum, we conclude today that it does not violate the Appointments Clause for Congress to vest the appointment of independent counsels in the Special Division; that the powers exercised by the Special Division under the Act do not violate Article III; and that the Act does not violate the separation of powers principle by impermissibly interfering with the functions of the Executive Branch. The decision of the Court of Appeals is therefore

Reversed.

JUSTICE SCALIA, dissenting.

The present case began when the Legislative and Executive Branches became "embroiled in a dispute concerning the scope of the congressional investigatory power," which—as is often the case with such interbranch conflicts—became quite acrimonious. . . .

. . . The Court devotes most of its attention to such relatively technical details as the Appointments Clause and the removal power, addressing briefly and only at the end of its opinion the separation of powers. . . . I think that has it backwards. . . .

. . . Article II, §1, cl. 1, of the Constitution provides: "The executive Power shall be vested in a President of the United States." . . . [T]his does not mean *some of* the executive power, but *all of* the executive power. It seems to me, therefore, that the decision of the Court of Appeals invalidating the present statute must be upheld on fundamental separation-of-powers principles if the following two questions are answered affirmatively: (1) Is the conduct of a criminal prosecution (and of an investigation to decide whether to prosecute) the exercise of purely executive power? (2) Does the statute deprive the President of the United States of exclusive control over the exercise of that power? Surprising to say, the Court appears to concede an affirmative answer to both questions, but seeks to avoid the inevitable conclusion that since the statute vests some purely executive power in a person who is not the President of the United States it is void.

The Court concedes that "[t]here is no real dispute that the functions performed by the independent counsel are 'executive,' " though it qualifies that concession by adding "in the sense that they are law enforcement functions that typically have been undertaken by officials within the Executive Branch." The qualifier adds nothing but atmosphere. In what *other* sense can one identify "the executive Power" that is supposed to be vested in the President (unless it includes everything the Executive Branch is given to do) *except* by reference to what has always and everywhere—if conducted by government at all—been conducted never by the legislature, never by the courts, and always by the executive. There is no possible doubt that the independent counsel's functions fit this description. She is vested with the "full power and independent authority to exercise all *investigative and prosecutorial* functions and powers of the Department of Justice [and] the Attorney General" (emphasis added). Governmental investigation and prosecution of crimes is a quintessentially executive function. See *Heckler v. Chaney* (1985); *Buckley v. Valeo* (1976); *United States v. Nixon* (1974).

As for the second question, whether the statute before us deprives the President of exclusive control over that quintessentially executive activity: The Court does not, and could not possibly, assert that it does not. That is indeed the whole object of the statute. Instead, the Court points out that the President, through his Attorney General, has at least *some* control. That concession is alone enough to invalidate the statute, but I cannot refrain from pointing out that the Court greatly exaggerates the extent of that "some" Presidential control. "Most importan[t]" among these controls, the Court asserts, is the Attorney General's "power to remove the counsel for 'good cause.' " This is somewhat like referring to shackles as an effective means of locomotion. . . .

. . . It effects a revolution in our constitutional jurisprudence for the Court, once it has determined that (1) purely executive functions are at issue here, and (2) those functions have been given to a person whose actions are not fully within the supervision and control of the President, nonetheless to proceed further to sit in judgment of whether "the President's need to control the exercise of [the independent counsel's] discretion is *so central* to the functioning of the Executive Branch" as to require complete control (emphasis added), whether the conferral of his powers upon someone else "*sufficiently* deprives the President of control over the independent counsel to interfere impermissibly with [his] constitutional obligation to ensure the faithful execution of the laws" (emphasis added), and whether "the Act give[s] the Executive Branch *sufficient* control over the independent counsel to ensure that the President is able to perform his constitutionally assigned duties" (emphasis added). It is not for us to determine, and we have never presumed to determine, how much of the purely executive powers of government must be within the full control of the President. The Constitution prescribes that they *all* are. . . .

Is it unthinkable that the President should have such exclusive power, even when alleged crimes by him or his close associates are at issue? No more so than that Congress should have the exclusive power of legislation, even when what is at issue is its own exemption from the burdens of certain laws. See Civil Rights Act of 1964, Title VII . . . (prohibiting "employers," not defined to include the United States, from discriminating on the basis of race, color, religion, sex, or national origin). No more so than that this Court should have the exclusive power to pronounce the final decision on justiciable cases and controversies, even those pertaining to the constitutionality of a statute reducing the salaries of the Justices. See *United States v. Will* (1980). A system of separate and coordinate powers necessarily involves an acceptance of exclusive power that can theoretically be abused. . . . While the separation of powers may prevent us from righting every wrong, it does so in order to ensure that we do not lose liberty. The checks against any branch's abuse of its exclusive powers are twofold: First, retaliation by one of the other branch's use of its exclusive powers: Congress, for example, can impeach the executive who willfully fails to enforce the laws; the executive can decline to prosecute under unconstitutional statutes; and the courts can dismiss malicious prosecutions. Second, and ultimately, there is the political check that the people will replace those in the political branches (the branches more "dangerous to the political rights of the Constitution," Federalist No. 78) who are guilty of abuse. Political pressures produced special prosecutors—for Teapot Dome and for Watergate, for example—long before this statute created the independent counsel.

. . . Once we depart from the text of the Constitution, just where short of that do we stop? The most amazing feature of the Court's opinion is that it does not even purport to give an answer. It simply *announces*, with no analysis, that the ability to control the decision whether to investigate and prosecute the President's closest advisers, and indeed the President himself, is not "so central to the functioning of the Executive Branch" as to be constitutionally required to be within the President's control. Apparently that is so because we say it is so. Having abandoned as the basis for our decisionmaking the text of Article II that "the executive Power" must be vested in the President, the Court does not even attempt to craft a *substitute* criterion—a "justiciable standard," however remote from the Constitution—that today governs, and in the future will govern, the decision of such questions. Evidently, the governing standard is to be what might be called the unfettered wisdom of a majority of this Court, revealed to an obedient people on a case-by-case basis. This is not only not the government of laws that the Constitution established; it is not a government of laws at all. . . .

In sum, this statute does deprive the President of substantial control over the prosecutory functions performed by the independent counsel, and it does substantially affect the balance of powers. That the Court could possibly conclude otherwise demonstrates both the wisdom of our former constitutional system, in which the degree of reduced control and political impairment were irrelevant, since *all* purely executive power had to be in the President; and the folly of the new system of standardless judicial allocation of powers we adopt today.

The independent counsel statute, upheld in *Morrison v. Olson*, expired at the end of 1992. It was not reenacted because of partisan differences over an investigation into the Iran-contra affair, a controversy involving members of the Reagan administration who allegedly offered to trade arms in return for Americans held hostage in Lebanon. The independent counsel, Lawrence E. Walsh, aggressively pursued the case, but he was regarded by Republicans as excessively partisan. In addition, investigations such as that headed by Walsh had no effective spending limitations and had become unreasonably expensive. President George H. W. Bush, a Republican, threatened to veto reauthorization legislation.

In June 1994, however, a new independent counsel statute became law. The act received bipartisan support in Congress and was endorsed by President Bill Clinton, the first chief executive to back independent counsel legislation. The new law imposed procedures modeled after the earlier statute: following a preliminary investigation by the Justice Department into alleged wrongdoing by top administration officials, the attorney general was to petition a special three-judge federal court to appoint an independent counsel to pursue the matter. The new law incorporated certain reform provisions, including effective spending guidelines. The new legislation was invoked almost immediately to appoint Kenneth Starr to continue the investigation of President Clinton's involvement in the Whitewater real estate business, which eventually led to his impeachment by the House in 1998.

The revised law received even more criticism than the earlier version. The special prosecutor's open-ended term of office, barely constrained use of prosecutorial power, and expensive operation doomed the prospects for renewing the statute without significant reform. In short, Scalia's dissent in *Morrison* proved prophetic indeed, and the legislation expired without reauthorization in 1999.

Dismissing Executive Officials. The president's need to have executive branch officials who support the administration's policy goals is only partially satisfied by the power to appoint. What is also required is the corollary— the discretionary right to remove administrative officials from office. This need may arise when a president's appointees do not carry out their duties the way the president wishes. It also applies when an official appointed by a previous administration will not voluntarily step aside to make way for a nominee of the new president's choosing.

Although an established removal procedure is obviously necessary, the Framers neglected to mention it in the Constitution. In the absence of constitutional guidelines, a lingering controversy has centered on whether administrative officials can be removed at the discretion of the president alone or whether Congress may play a role.

The argument supporting presidential discretion holds that the chief executive must be free to remove those subordinates who fail to meet the president's expectations or who are not loyal to the administration's policy objectives. It would be unreasonable to require the approval of Congress before such officials could be dis-

missed. Such a requirement might well paralyze the executive branch, particularly when the legislature and the presidency are under the control of different political parties.

The argument for legislative participation in the process holds that the Constitution anticipates Senate action. If the president can appoint major executive department officials only with senatorial approval, it is reasonable to infer that the chief executive can remove administrators only by going through the same process and obtaining the advice and consent of the Senate. This view was supported by Alexander Hamilton in *The Federalist Papers'* only reference to the removal powers. Hamilton flatly stated, "The consent of that body [the Senate] would be necessary to displace as well as to appoint." [9] Hamilton argued that if the president and the Senate agreed that an official should be removed, the decision would be much better accepted than if the president acted alone. Furthermore, Hamilton asserted that a new president should be restrained from removing an experienced official who had conducted his duties satisfactorily just because the president preferred to have a different person in the position.

Historical practice generally has rejected Hamilton's position. From the very beginning, Congress allowed the chief executive to remove administrative officials without Senate consent. In the First Congress James Madison proposed that three executive departments be created: Foreign Affairs, Treasury, and War. The creation of the Foreign Affairs (later State) Department received the most legislative attention. According to Madison's recommendation, the department was to have a secretary to be appointed by the president with the approval of the Senate who could be removed by the president alone. The House and the Senate held long comprehensive debates on the removal power at that time and passed legislation allowing the secretary of state to be removed at the president's discretion without Senate approval.

At times, however, the legislature has asserted a right to participate in the process. The most notable example

9. Alexander Hamilton, Federalist No. 77 in *The Federalist Papers*, by Alexander Hamilton, James Madison, and John Jay (New York: New American Library, 1961), 459.

occurred with the passage of the Tenure of Office Act in 1867. This statute was enacted to restrict the powers of President Andrew Johnson, who took office after Lincoln's assassination in 1865. Following the Civil War, the Radical Republicans dominated Congress and had little use for Johnson, a Democrat from Tennessee. Congress did not want Johnson to be able to remove Lincoln's appointees. The Tenure of Office Act stipulated that the president could not remove high-ranking executive department heads without first obtaining the approval of the Senate. Johnson blatantly defied the statute by dismissing Secretary of War Edwin M. Stanton in August 1867 and appointing Ulysses S. Grant as interim secretary. The Senate reacted by ordering Stanton reinstated. Grant left office and Stanton returned in January 1868. The next month Johnson fired Stanton again. The president's failure to comply with the Tenure of Office Act constituted one of the grounds upon which the House impeached him.

The Tenure of Office Act never had a judicial test. Once Johnson's term expired, the statute was weakened by amendment and then repealed in 1887. Consequently, as the nation entered the twentieth century there had yet to be an authoritative declaration of the constitutional parameters of the removal power, although some statutes remained on the books asserting a role for the Senate in the dismissal of administrative officials.

The Supreme Court finally faced this issue in 1926 when presented with an appeal from a fired postmaster. The Court's opinion was written by Chief Justice Taft, who compiled one of the nation's most spectacular résumés *(see Box 4-4)*. Among his positions were solicitor general, governor of the Philippines, secretary of war, president of the United States, and, finally, chief justice of the United States. Given Taft's rich experience in the executive branch and the fact that he had not served in the legislature, we would expect, correctly, that he would support a broad interpretation of the president's removal powers and reject the notion that the Senate had the right to limit that discretion. His long, detailed opinion in *Myers v. United States*, combined with the dissenting opinions it provoked, filled 243 pages.

Myers v. United States

272 u.s. 52 (1926)
http://laws.findlaw.com/US/272/52.html
Vote: 6 (Butler, Sanford, Stone, Sutherland, Taft, Van Devanter)
*　　3 (Brandeis, Holmes, McReynolds)*
Opinion of the Court: Taft
Dissenting opinions: Brandeis, Holmes, McReynolds

Prior to its replacement by the United States Postal Service in 1970, the post office department was considered a patronage agency. Postal officials, beginning with the postmaster general and continuing down to the local postmasters, were political appointees rewarded for loyal party service. In July 1917 President Woodrow Wilson, with the advice and consent of the Senate, appointed Frank Myers to be a first class postmaster in Portland, Oregon, for a four-year term.

In January 1920 Wilson asked for Myers's resignation. When Myers ignored tradition and refused Wilson's request, the president ordered the postmaster general to fire him, an act that was carried out in February. Myers complained that his removal was illegal. The basis for his argument was a law passed by Congress in 1876 stipulating that "Postmasters of the first, second and third classes shall be appointed and may be removed by the President by and with the advice and consent of the Senate and shall hold their offices for four years unless sooner removed or suspended according to law." Wilson strongly believed that his right to remove individuals from appointed office was not to be shared with Congress. In fact, Wilson had engaged in some bitter fights with Congress over this point.

Because Wilson had not received the approval of the Senate for the dismissal, Myers claimed to have been unlawfully fired. He sued for his unpaid salary from the date of his removal to the expiration of his four-year term, a claim of $8,838.71. During the period under question Myers accepted no other employment, and the Senate confirmed no other nominee for the position. After Myers died, his executor continued the legal action on behalf of his estate. The court of claims rejected Myers's suit, and an appeal was made to the Supreme Court.

BOX 4-4   WILLIAM HOWARD TAFT (1921–1930)

PUBLIC SERVICE was a tradition in the Taft family; William Howard Taft extended it to its limit during his lifetime. His grandfather, Peter Rawson Taft, was a judge on the probate and county courts in Windham County, Vermont; Alphonso Taft, William's father, served two terms on the Ohio Superior Court before he was named secretary of war in the last months of the Grant administration. He also briefly served President Ulysses S. Grant as attorney general, and later was ambassador to Austria-Hungary and Russia during the Arthur administration. William's brother, Charles Phelps Taft, R-Ohio, served a term in the U.S. House of Representatives, 1895–1897.

Born in Cincinnati September 15, 1857, Taft received an A.B. in 1878 from Yale University, where he was the salutatorian of his graduating class. He entered Cincinnati Law School and took a job as a law reporter for the Cincinnati Commercial. He continued to report for the newspaper through 1880, the year in which he received his LL.B. and was admitted to the bar.

On June 19, 1886, he married Helen Herron. They had one daughter and two sons, one of whom, Robert Alphonso Taft, R-Ohio, served in the U.S. Senate, 1939–1953. Taft's grandson, Robert Taft Jr., R-Ohio, served in the House of Representatives, 1963–1965, 1967–1971, and the Senate, 1971–1976.

IN 1881 TAFT PLUNGED into Republican politics and gave his support to a candidate for county prosecutor in Hamilton County, Ohio. After his candidate won, Taft was selected to be an assistant county prosecutor. He went back to private practice in 1883.

Taft was named to a two-year term as assistant county solicitor for Hamilton County in 1885 and, in 1887, when he was barely thirty years old, was appointed to the Ohio Superior Court.

He sat on the superior court bench until President Benjamin Harrison in 1890 named him U.S. solicitor general. In 1892, after Congress created additional judgeships for the federal circuit courts, Taft sought and received appointment to the Sixth Circuit.

Taft remained on the circuit court for eight years. He left reluctantly in 1900 when President William McKinley asked him to head a commission established to ensure the smooth transition from military to civilian government in the Philippines in the aftermath of the Spanish-American War. In 1901 he was made civilian governor of the Philippines, a position he held until President Theodore Roosevelt named him secretary of war to replace Elihu Root in 1904.

Once in the cabinet, Taft became one of Roosevelt's closest advisers; the president increasingly relied on Taft to handle important matters for the administration. As secretary of war, Taft was in command of the Panama Canal project

---

After a detailed discussion of the events surrounding Madison's proposals during the First Congress (the decision of 1789) and the controversy over the Tenure of Office Act, Chief Justice Taft explained the Court's decision in favor of presidential discretion in exercising the removal power.

MR. CHIEF JUSTICE TAFT delivered the opinion of the Court.

This case presents the question whether under the Constitution the President has the exclusive power of removing executive officers of the United States whom he has appointed by and with the advice and consent of the Senate. . . .

A veto by the Senate—a part of the legislative branch of the Government—upon removals is a much greater limitation upon the executive branch and a much more serious blending of the legislative with the executive than a rejection of a proposed appointment. It is not to be implied. The rejection of a nominee of the President for a particular office does not greatly embarrass him in the conscientious discharge of his high duties in the selection of those who are to aid him, because the President usually has an ample field

and made a goodwill tour of the site. He also was dispatched in 1906 to Cuba to investigate reports of revolutionary activity.

As Taft's prestige grew, so did his influence in the Republican Party. With Roosevelt's backing he won the party's nomination for president and the subsequent election in 1908. He was sworn in as the twenty-ninth president of the United States March 4, 1909.

The presidency was a post that Taft did not particularly covet—he would have preferred a seat on the Supreme Court as chief justice—but he sought the presidency at the urging of his wife and Republican Party regulars. His single term in office was not controversial. It saw the institution of the postal savings system and the Tariff Board, the intervention of American troops in the affairs of the Dominican Republic, the ratification of the Sixteenth Amendment to the Constitution, and a continuation of the trustbusting begun under Theodore Roosevelt.

Taft also named six men to the Supreme Court, including a chief justice, Edward D. White. The others were Horace H. Lurton, Charles Evans Hughes (who resigned from the Court to run for president in 1916, lost, and was named chief justice in 1930 by President Herbert Hoover to replace Taft), Willis Van Devanter, Joseph R. Lamar, and Mahlon Pitney. When Taft was named chief justice in 1921 only two of his appointees, Van Devanter and Pitney, were still on the bench.

Soon after he was elected president, Taft began to fall out of favor with former president Roosevelt. The two men came to represent opposing sides of a division within the Republican Party; when Taft was renominated in 1912, Roosevelt ran for president under the banner of his Bull Moose Party and effectively splintered the Republican vote. After the election, which was won by Democrat Woodrow Wilson, Taft described Roosevelt as "the most dangerous man that we have had in the country since its origin."

After leaving the White House, Taft taught constitutional law at Yale University, served a year as president of the American Bar Association, wrote magazine articles, and was a frequent participant on the lecture circuit. He was elected president of the League to Enforce Peace in 1915. In 1916 he and four other former presidents of the American Bar Association joined with current president Elihu Root in writing to the U.S. Senate to register their disapproval of President Wilson's nomination of Louis D. Brandeis to the Supreme Court. During this period Taft also continued discreetly to publicize his desire to be named to the Court, especially as chief justice.

Taft served as the joint chairman of the National War Labor Board, 1918–1919. An enthusiastic advocate of the League of Nations, he embarked on a fifteen-state tour in an attempt to rally support for it.

His greatest ambition was achieved when President Harding named him chief justice June 30, 1921, to replace Chief Justice White. The Senate confirmed him by voice vote the same day. Taft is the only person in U.S. history to hold both the presidency and the chief justiceship. He retired from the Court February 3, 1930, and died a month later on March 8 in Washington, D.C.

SOURCE: Joan Biskupic and Elder Witt, *Guide to the U.S. Supreme Court*, 3rd ed. (Washington, D.C.: Congressional Quarterly, 1997), 923–924.

from which to select for office, according to his preference, competent and capable men. The Senate has full power to reject newly proposed appointees whenever the President shall remove the incumbents. Such a check enables the Senate to prevent the filling of offices with bad or incompetent men or with those against whom there is tenable objection.

The power to prevent the removal of an officer who has served under the President is different from the authority to consent to or reject his appointment. When a nomination is made, it may be presumed that the Senate is, or may become, as well advised as to the fitness of the nominee as the President, but in the nature of things the defects in ability or intelligence or loyalty in the administration of the laws of one who has served as an officer under the President, are facts as to which the President, or his trusted subordinates, must be better informed than the Senate, and the power to remove him may, therefore, be regarded as confined, for very sound and practical reasons, to the governmental authority which has administrative control. The power of removal is incident to the power of appointment, not to the power of advising and consenting to appointment, and when the grant of the executive power is enforced by the express mandate to take care that the laws be faithfully executed, it emphasizes the necessity for including within the executive power as conferred the exclusive power of removal. . . .

Made responsible under the Constitution for the effective enforcement of the law, the President needs as an indispensable aid to meet it the disciplinary influence upon those who act under him of a reserve power of removal. But it is contended that executive officers appointed by the President with the consent of the Senate are bound by the statutory law and are not his servants to do his will, and that his obligation to care for the faithful execution of the laws does not authorize him to treat them as such. The degree of guidance in the discharge of their duties that the President may exercise over executive officers varies with the character of their service as prescribed in the law under which they act. The highest and most important duties which his subordinates perform are those in which they act for him. In such cases they are exercising not their own but his discretion. This field is a very large one. It is sometimes described as political. Each head of a department is and must be the President's alter ego in the matters of that department where the President is required by law to exercise authority. . . .

In all such cases, the discretion to be exercised is that of the President in determining the national public interest and in directing the action to be taken by his executive subordinates to protect it. In this field his cabinet officers must do his will. He must place in each member of his official family, and his chief executive subordinates, implicit faith. The moment that he loses confidence in the intelligence, ability, judgment or loyalty of any one of them, he must have the power to remove him without delay. To require him to file charges and submit them to the consideration of the Senate might make impossible that unity and coordination in executive administration essential to effective action.

The duties of the heads of departments and bureaus in which the discretion of the President is exercised and which we have described, are the most important in the whole field of executive action of the Government. There is nothing in the Constitution which permits a distinction between the removal of the head of a department or a bureau, when he discharges a political duty of the President or exercises his discretion, and the removal of executive officers engaged in the discharge of their other normal duties. The imperative reasons requiring an unrestricted power to remove the most important of his subordinates in their most important

duties must, therefore, control the interpretation of the Constitution as to all appointed by him.

But this is not to say that there are not strong reasons why the President should have a like power to remove his appointees charged with other duties than those above described. The ordinary duties of officers prescribed by statute come under the general administrative control of the President by virtue of the general grant to him of the executive power, and he may properly supervise and guide their construction of the statutes under which they act in order to secure that unitary and uniform execution of the laws which Article II of the Constitution evidently contemplated in vesting general executive power in the President alone. Laws are often passed with specific provision for the adoption of regulations by a department or bureau head to make the law workable and effective. The ability and judgment manifested by the official thus empowered, as well as his energy and stimulation of his subordinates, are subjects which the President must consider and supervise in his administrative control. Finding such officers to be negligent and inefficient, the President should have the power to remove them. Of course there may be duties so peculiarly and specifically committed to the discretion of a particular officer as to raise a question whether the President may overrule or revise the officer's interpretation of his statutory duty in a particular instance. Then there may be duties of a quasi-judicial character imposed on executive officers and members of executive tribunals whose decisions after hearing affect interests of individuals, the discharge of which the President can not in a particular case properly influence or control. But even in such a case he may consider the decision after its rendition as a reason for removing the officer, on the ground that the discretion regularly entrusted to that officer by statute has not been on the whole intelligently or wisely exercised. Otherwise he does not discharge his own constitutional duty of seeing that the laws be faithfully executed. . . .

We come now to consider an argument advanced and strongly pressed on behalf of the complainant, that this case concerns only the removal of a postmaster; that a postmaster is an inferior officer; that such an office was not included within the legislative decision of 1789, which related only to superior officers to be appointed by the President by and with the advice and consent of the Senate. . . .

The power to remove inferior executive officers, like that to remove superior executive officers, is an incident of the power to appoint them, and is in its nature an executive power. The authority of Congress given by the excepting clause to vest the appointment of such inferior officers in the heads of departments carries with it authority incidentally to invest the heads of departments with power to remove. It has been the practice of Congress to do so and this Court has recognized that power. . . . But the Court never has held, nor reasonably could hold, although it is argued to the contrary on behalf of the appellant, that the excepting clause enables Congress to draw to itself, or to either branch of it, the power to remove or the right to participate in the exercise of that power. To do this would be to go beyond the words and implications of that clause and to infringe the constitutional principle of the separation of governmental powers.

Assuming then the power of Congress to regulate removals as incidental to the exercise of its constitutional power to vest appointments of inferior officers in the heads of departments, certainly so long as Congress does not exercise that power, the power of removal must remain where the Constitution places it, with the President, as part of the executive power, in accordance with the legislative decision of 1789 which we have been considering. . . .

Our conclusion on the merits, sustained by the arguments before stated, is that Article II grants to the President the executive power of Government, i.e., the general administrative control of those executing the laws, including the power of appointment and removal of executive officers—a conclusion confirmed by his obligation to take care that the laws be faithfully executed; that Article II excludes the exercise of legislative power by Congress to provide for appointments and removals, except only as granted therein to Congress in the matter of inferior offices; that Congress is only given power to provide for appointments and removals of inferior officers after it has vested, and on condition that it does vest, their appointment in other authority than the President with the Senate's consent; that the provisions of the second section of Article II, which blend action by the legislative branch, or by part of it, in the work of the executive, are limitations to be strictly construed and not to be extended by implication; that the President's power of removal is further established as an incident to his specifically enumerated function of appointment by and with the advice of the Senate, but that such incident does not by implication extend to removals the Senate's power of checking

appointments; and finally that to hold otherwise would make it impossible for the President, in case of political or other differences with the Senate or Congress, to take care that the laws be faithfully executed. . . .

When, on the merits, we find our conclusion strongly favoring the view which prevailed in the First Congress, we have no hesitation in holding that conclusion to be correct; and it therefore follows that the Tenure of Office Act of 1867, in so far as it attempted to prevent the President from removing executive officers who had been appointed by him by and with the advice and consent of the Senate, was invalid, and that subsequent legislation of the same effect was equally so.

For the reasons given, we must therefore hold that the provision of the law of 1876, by which the unrestricted power of removal of first class postmasters is denied to the President, is in violation of the Constitution, and invalid. This leads to an affirmance of the judgment of the Court of Claims.

The separate opinion of MR. JUSTICE MCREYNOLDS.

Congress has long and vigorously asserted its right to restrict removals and there has been no common executive practice based upon a contrary view. The President has often removed, and it is admitted that he may remove, with either the express or implied assent of Congress; but the present theory is that he may override the declared will of the body. This goes far beyond any practice heretofore approved or followed; it conflicts with the history of the Constitution, with the ordinary rules of interpretation, and with the construction approved by Congress since the beginning and emphatically sanctioned by this court. To adopt it would be revolutionary. . . .

In any rational search for answer to the questions arising upon this record, it is important not to forget—

That this is a government of limited powers definitely enumerated and granted by a written Constitution.

That the Constitution must be interpreted by attributing to its words the meaning which they bore at the time of its adoption and in view of commonly-accepted canons of construction, its history, early and long-continued practices under it, and relevant opinions of this court.

That the Constitution endows Congress with plenary powers "to establish post offices and post roads."

That exercising this power during the years from 1789 to 1836, Congress provided for postmasters and vested the power to appoint and remove all of them at pleasure in the Postmaster General.

That the Constitution contains no words which specifically grant to the President power to remove duly appointed officers. And it is definitely settled that he cannot remove those whom he has not appointed—certainly they can be removed only as Congress may permit.

That postmasters are inferior officers within the meaning of Art. II, Sec. 2, of the Constitution.

That from its first session to the last one Congress has often asserted its right to restrict the President's power to remove inferior officers, although appointed by him with consent of the Senate.

That many Presidents have approved statutes limiting the power of the executive to remove, and that from the beginning such limitations have been respected in practice. . . .

That the proceedings in the Constitutional Convention of 1787, the political history of the times, contemporaneous opinion, common canons of construction, the action of Congress from the beginning and opinions of this court, all oppose the theory that by vesting "the executive power" in the President the Constitution gave him an illimitable right to remove inferior officers. . . .

That to declare the President vested with indefinite and illimitable executive powers would extend the field of his possible action far beyond the limits observed by his predecessors and would enlarge the powers of Congress to a degree incapable of fair appraisement.

Considering all these things, it is impossible for me to accept the view that the President may dismiss, as caprice may suggest, any inferior officer whom he has appointed with consent of the Senate, notwithstanding a positive inhibition by Congress. In the last analysis that view has no substantial support, unless it be the polemic opinions expressed by Mr. Madison (and eight others) during the debate of 1789, when he was discussing questions relating to a "superior officer" to be appointed for an indefinite term. Notwithstanding his justly exalted reputation as one of the creators and early expounders of the Constitution, sentiments expressed under such circumstances ought not now to outweigh the conclusion which Congress affirmed by deliberate action while he was leader in the House and has consistently maintained down to the present year, the opinion of this court solemnly announced through the great Chief Justice more than a century ago, and the canons of construction approved over and over again.

Judgment should go for the appellant.

MR. JUSTICE BRANDEIS, dissenting.

The practice of Congress to control the exercise of the executive power of removal from inferior offices is evidenced by many statutes which restrict it in many ways besides the removal clause here in question. Each of these restrictive statutes became law with the approval of the President. Every President who has held office since 1861, except President Garfield, approved one or more of such statutes. Some of these statutes, prescribing a fixed term, provide that removal shall be made only for one of several specified causes. Some provide a fixed term, subject generally to removal for cause. Some provide for removal only after hearing. Some provide a fixed term, subject to removal for reasons to be communicated by the President to the Senate. Some impose the restriction in still other ways. . . .

The historical data submitted present a legislative practice, established by concurrent affirmative action of Congress and the President, to make consent of the Senate a condition of removal from statutory inferior, civil, executive offices to which the appointment is made for a fixed term by the President with such consent. They show that the practice has existed, without interruption, continuously for the last fifty-eight years; that, throughout this period, it has governed a great majority of all such offices; that the legislation applying the removal clause specifically to the office of postmaster was enacted more than half a century ago; and that recently the practice has, with the President's approval, been extended to several newly created offices. The data show further, that the insertion of the removal clause in acts creating inferior civil offices with fixed tenures is part of the broader legislative practice, which has prevailed since the formation of our government, to restrict or regulate in many ways both removal from and nomination to such offices. A persistent legislative practice which involves a delimitation of the respective powers of Congress and the President, and which has been so established and maintained, should be deemed tantamount to judicial construction, in the absence of any decision by any court to the contrary.

The persuasive effect of this legislative practice is strengthened by the fact that no instance has been found,

even in the earlier period of our history, of concurrent affirmative action of Congress and the President which is inconsistent with the legislative practice of the last fifty-eight
years to impose the removal clause. Nor has any instance
been found of action by Congress which involves recognition in any other way of the alleged uncontrollable executive
power to remove an inferior civil officer. The action taken
by Congress in 1789 after the great debate does not present
such an instance. The vote then taken did not involve a decision that the President had uncontrollable power. It did
not involve a decision of the question whether Congress
could confer upon the Senate the right, and impose upon it
the duty, to participate in removals. It involved merely the
decision that the Senate does not, in the absence of legislative grant thereof, have the right to share in the removal of
an officer appointed with its consent; and that the President
has, in the absence of restrictive legislation, the constitutional power of removal without such consent. Moreover, as
Chief Justice Marshall recognized, the debate and the decision related to a high political office, not to inferior ones.

Nine years later the president's discretionary power to
remove administrators was challenged again. This time
the stakes were somewhat greater because the office involved had much more policy-making power than the
local postmaster position at issue in *Myers* had. Here the
fired officer was not a member of the regular executive
branch departments, but a member of the Federal Trade
Commission (FTC), an independent regulatory board.
Did these differences prompt the justices to rule differently on the president's removal power, or did the *Myers*
precedent apply here as well?

Humphrey's Executor v. United States

295 U.S. 602 (1935)
http://laws.findlaw.com/US/295/602.html
Vote: 9 (Brandeis, Butler, Cardozo, Hughes, McReynolds,
*   Roberts, Stone, Sutherland, Van Devanter)*
        0
Opinion of the Court: Sutherland

In 1914 Congress created the Federal Trade Commission as an independent regulatory agency to enforce antitrust laws and prevent unfair methods of commercial
competition. The statute called for the FTC to be staffed
by five commissioners appointed by the president and
confirmed by the Senate. Not more than three members
could be of the same political party, and members were
to serve staggered seven-year terms. These provisions
were intended to increase the independence of the board
and prevent its domination by the incumbent chief executive. The president could remove commissioners, but
only for inefficiency, neglect of duty, or malfeasance in
office. The commission had the powers of rule making,
investigation, and enforcement.

In 1931 President Herbert Hoover named FTC commissioner William E. Humphrey to a second seven-year
term, which would expire in 1938. Following his election
in 1932, Franklin Roosevelt made every effort to staff the
executive branch with people who were committed to his
New Deal programs for combating the Great Depression.
The president wrote to Humphrey July 25, 1933, asking
him to resign from his post on the ground that "the aims
and purposes of the Administration with respect to the
work of the Commission can be carried out most effectively with personnel of my own selection." When Humphrey did not reply, the president wrote to him August
31: "You will, I know, realize that I do not feel that your
mind and my mind go along together on either the policies or the administering of the Federal Trade Commission, and, frankly, I think it best for the people of this
country that I should have a full confidence." Humphrey
then told the president that he would not resign. In his
third letter, dated October 7, Roosevelt wrote to Humphrey: "Effective as of this date you are hereby removed
from the office of Commissioner of the Federal Trade
Commission." The president did not rest his action on
any of the statutory grounds for removing a commissioner; rather, he fired Humphrey because he did not approve of his positions on policy matters related to the jurisdiction of the FTC. Humphrey claimed he had been
illegally removed.

Humphrey died in February 1934. His executor filed
suit in the court of claims on behalf of Humphrey's estate
to recover the salary lost between the date of his dismissal and his death. The administration argued on the

basis of *Myers* that the president was free to remove executive officials at will. Humphrey's executor claimed that the law establishing the FTC placed constitutionally valid restraints on the president's discretion to remove officeholders. The court of claims asked the Supreme Court to answer two questions: Did the Federal Trade Commission Act restrict the president's removal power to those grounds cited in the statute? And, if so, is such a restriction constitutional?

MR. JUSTICE SUTHERLAND delivered the opinion of the Court.

First. The question first to be considered is whether, by the provisions of §1 of the Federal Trade Commission Act already quoted, the President's power is limited to removal for the specific causes enumerated therein. . . .

The commission is to be non-partisan; and it must, from the very nature of its duties, act with entire impartiality. It is charged with the enforcement of no policy except the policy of the law. Its duties are neither political nor executive, but predominantly quasi-judicial and quasi-legislative. Like the Interstate Commerce Commission, its members are called upon to exercise the trained judgment of a body of experts "appointed by law and informed by experience."

The legislative reports in both houses of Congress clearly reflect the view that a fixed term was necessary to the effective and fair administration of the law. In the report to the Senate the Senate Committee on Interstate Commerce, in support of the bill which afterwards became the act in question, after referring to the provision fixing the term of office at seven years, so arranged that the membership would not be subject to complete change at any one time. . . .

The debates in both houses demonstrate that the prevailing view was that the commission was not to be "subject to anybody in the government but . . . only to the people of the United States"; free from "political domination or control" or the "probability or possibility of such a thing"; to be "separate and apart from any existing department of the government—not subject to the orders of the President."

More to the same effect appears in the debates, which were long and thorough and contain nothing to the contrary. While the general rule precludes the use of these debates to explain the meaning of the words of the statute, they may be considered as reflecting light upon its general purposes and the evils which it sought to remedy.

Thus, the language of the act, the legislative reports, and the general purposes of the legislation as reflected by the debates, all combine to demonstrate the Congressional intent to create a body of experts who shall gain experience by length of service—a body which shall be independent of executive authority, *except in its selection*, and free to exercise its judgment without the leave or hindrance of any other official or department of the government. To the accomplishment of these purposes, it is clear that Congress was of opinion that length and certainty of tenure would vitally contribute. And to hold that, nevertheless, the members of the commission continue in office at the mere will of the President, might be to thwart, in large measure, the very ends which Congress sought to realize by definitely fixing the term of office.

We conclude that the intent of the act is to limit the executive power of removal to the causes enumerated, the existence of none of which is claimed here; and we pass to the second question.

Second. To support its contention that the removal provision of §1, as we have just construed it, is an unconstitutional interference with the executive power of the President, the government's chief reliance is *Myers v. United States*. That case has been so recently decided, and the prevailing and dissenting opinions so fully review the general subject of the power of executive removal, that further discussion would add little to the value of the wealth of material there collected. These opinions examine at length the historical, legislative and judicial data bearing upon the question, beginning with what is called "the decision of 1789" in the first Congress and coming down almost to the day when the opinions were delivered. . . . Nevertheless, the narrow point actually decided was only that the President had power to remove a postmaster of the first class, without the advice and consent of the Senate as required by act of Congress. In the course of the opinion of the court, expressions occur which tend to sustain the government's contention, but these are beyond the point involved and, therefore, do not come within the rule of *stare decisis*. In so far as they are out of harmony with the views here set forth, these expressions are disapproved. . . .

The office of a postmaster is so essentially unlike the office now involved that the decision in the *Myers* case cannot be accepted as controlling our decision here. A postmaster is an executive officer restricted to the performance of executive functions. He is charged with no duty at all related to either the legislative or judicial power. The actual decision in the *Myers* case finds support in the theory that such an officer is merely one of the units in the executive department and, hence, inherently subject to the exclusive and illimitable power of removal by the Chief Executive, whose subordinate and aid he is. Putting aside *dicta*, which may be followed if sufficiently persuasive but which are not controlling, the necessary reach of the decision goes far enough to include all purely executive officers. It goes no farther;— much less does it include an officer who occupies no place in the executive department and who exercises no part of the executive power vested by the Constitution in the President.

The Federal Trade Commission is an administrative body created by Congress to carry into effect legislative policies embodied in the statute in accordance with the legislative standard therein prescribed, and to perform other specified duties as a legislative or as a judicial aid. Such a body cannot in any proper sense be characterized as an arm or an eye of the executive. Its duties are performed without executive leave and, in the contemplation of the statute, must be free from executive control. In administering the provisions of the statute in respect of "unfair methods of competition"— that is to say in filling in and administering the details embodied by that general standard—the commission acts in part quasi-legislatively and in part quasi-judicially. In making investigations and reports thereon for the information of Congress under §6, in aid of the legislative power, it acts as a legislative agency. Under §7, which authorizes the commission to act as a master in chancery under rules prescribed by the court, it acts as an agency of the judiciary. To the extent that it exercises any executive function—as distinguished from executive power in the constitutional sense—it does so in the discharge and effectuation of its quasi-legislative or quasi-judicial powers, or as an agency of the legislative or judicial departments of the government. . . .

We think it plain under the Constitution that illimitable power of removal is not possessed by the President in respect of officers of the character of those just named. The authority of Congress, in creating quasi-legislative or quasi-judicial agencies, to require them to act in discharge of their duties independently of executive control cannot well be doubted; and that authority includes, as an appropriate incident, power to fix the period during which they shall continue in office, and to forbid their removal except for cause

in the meantime. For it is quite evident that one who holds his office only during the pleasure of another, cannot be depended upon to maintain an attitude of independence against the latter's will.

The fundamental necessity of maintaining each of the three general departments of government entirely free from the control or coercive influence, direct or indirect, of either of the others, has often been stressed and is hardly open to serious question. So much is implied in the very fact of the separation of the powers of these departments by the Constitution; and in the rule which recognizes their essential coequality. The sound application of a principle that makes one master in his own house precludes him from imposing his control in the house of another who is master there. . . .

The power of removal here claimed for the President falls within this principle, since its coercive influence threatens the independence of a commission, which is not only wholly disconnected from the executive department, but which, as already fully appears, was created by Congress as a means of carrying into operation legislative and judicial powers, and as an agency of the legislative and judicial departments. . . .

The result of what we now have said is this: Whether the power of the President to remove an officer shall prevail over the authority of Congress to condition the power by fixing a definite term and precluding a removal except for cause, will depend upon the character of the office; the *Myers* decision, affirming the power of the President alone to make the removal, is confined to purely executive officers; and as to officers of the kind here under consideration, we hold that no removal can be made during the prescribed term for which the officer is appointed, except for one or more of the causes named in the applicable statute.

To the extent that, between the decision in the *Myers* case, which sustains the unrestrictable power of the President to remove purely executive officers, and our present decision that such power does not extend to an office such as that here involved, there shall remain a field of doubt, we leave such cases as may fall within it for future consideration and determination as they may arise.

In *Humphrey's Executor* the Court distinguished between officials who exercise purely executive powers and those who carry out quasi-legislative and quasi-judicial functions. The former serve at the pleasure of the president and may be removed at his discretion. The latter may be removed only with procedures consistent with statutory conditions enacted by Congress. Would Chief Justice Taft have agreed with this distinction? Or did his opinion in *Myers* suggest that he would have opposed any constraints on the presidential power to remove officials?

No matter what Taft might have thought, the *Humphrey's Executor* scheme was reaffirmed in *Wiener v. United States* (1958). The case involved a member of the War Claims Commission, a body established by Congress in 1948 to receive and adjudicate claims for compensating certain parties who suffered damages at the hands of the enemy in World War II. The statute created a three-member commission appointed by the president and confirmed by the Senate. The commission was scheduled to go out of existence two years after the deadline for filing claims, but, after some legislative extensions, the expiration date was changed to 1954. The statute contained no provisions for terms of office or procedures for removal.

President Truman appointed Myron Wiener to the commission in 1950. President Dwight D. Eisenhower, elected in 1952, wanted to replace the commission members with Republicans, and he requested the resignations of the incumbents. Eisenhower wrote to Wiener, "I regard it as in the national interest to complete the administration of the War Claims Act of 1948, as amended, with personnel of my own selection." When the incumbents refused to resign, Eisenhower ordered them dismissed and appointed their replacements. The Eisenhower appointees served in office as recess appointments. The Senate had not yet confirmed them when the commission ceased to exist. Wiener sued for the salary denied him from the date of his removal to the expiration of the commission. The court of claims ruled in favor of the government, and Wiener appealed to the Supreme Court.

Justice Felix Frankfurter, writing for a unanimous bench, reversed. The justices concluded that Wiener had been fired illegally. The war claims commissioners exercised quasi-judicial functions, and therefore the position was governed by the decision in *Humphrey's Executor* rather than *Myers*. Because Wiener did not exercise purely executive powers, Eisenhower had no power under the Constitution or the statute creating the commission to remove

him. The *Wiener* decision is important because, by reaffirming *Humphrey's Executor*, it brought an authoritative end to questions regarding the extent of the president's power to remove officeholders at his discretion alone.

Executive Privilege: Protecting Presidential Confidentiality

Article II is silent on two potentially important and related questions pertaining to the president's roles as chief executive and commander in chief. The first, executive privilege, asks whether the president can refuse to supply the other branches of government with information about his activities. The second (covered in the next section), is immunity—whether and to what extent the president is protected from lawsuits while in office.

The executive privilege argument asserts that there are certain conversations, documents, and records that are so closely tied to the sensitive duties of the president that they should remain confidential. Neither the legislature nor the judiciary should be allowed access to these materials without presidential consent; nor should the other branches be empowered to compel the president to hand over such items. Matters concerning national security or foreign policy especially fall under this protection. Executive privilege, it is argued, is inherent to the office of the president.

Although infrequently invoked, the privilege doctrine has been part of American history since the beginning of the nation. In some early disputes between the president and Congress, chief executives refused to provide certain information to the legislature. George Washington balked at giving the House of Representatives certain documents pertaining to negotiations over the Jay Treaty. During the investigation and trial of Aaron Burr, Thomas Jefferson cooperated with congressional information requests, but only up to a point. He refused to produce some items and later declined to testify at the trial even though he was subpoenaed. Presidents through the years have refused to comply with congressional requests for testimony. It is generally accepted that Congress does not have the power to compel the president to come before it to answer questions. Other executive department officials are not usually covered by claims of privilege.

In most instances, disputes over executive privilege are handled through negotiation between the executive branch and the institution requesting information. Only rarely have such disputes blown up into major court cases. When pushed to the limit, executive privilege claims rarely prevail, but when sensitive military or diplomatic matters requiring secrecy are involved, a president can expect to be on relatively safe ground in asserting executive privilege.

No case involving executive privilege has been more important than *United States v. Nixon* (1974).[10] It occurred at a time of great constitutional stress, when all three branches were locked in a fight about fundamental separation of powers issues. The conflict ultimately was resolved when Nixon resigned. Much of the impetus for breaking the constitutional deadlock came from the unanimous decision of the justices in the *Nixon* case. Chief Justice Warren Burger's opinion for the Court reviewed the issues surrounding the executive privilege controversy and then rejected Nixon's invocation of the doctrine.

United States v. Nixon

418 U.S. 683 (1974)
http://laws.findlaw.com/US/418/683.html
Vote: 8 (Blackmun, Brennan, Burger, Douglas, Marshall,
   Powell, Stewart, White)
         0
Opinion of the Court: Burger
Not participating: Rehnquist

This case was one of many court actions spawned by the Watergate scandal. The controversy began on June 17, 1972, when seven men broke into the Democratic National Committee headquarters located in the Watergate complex in Washington, D.C. The men were apprehended and charged with criminal offenses. All had ties either to the White House or to the Committee to Reelect the President. Five of the seven pleaded guilty, and

two were convicted. At the end of the trial, one of the defendants, James McCord Jr., claimed that he had been pressured to plead guilty and that there were others involved in the break-in who had not been prosecuted. It was clear to many that the break-in was only the tip of a very large iceberg of shady dealings and cover-ups engaged in by influential persons closely tied to the Nixon administration.

In response to these events, the Senate began an investigation of the Watergate incident and the activities related to it. The star witness was John Dean III, special counsel to the president, who testified under a grant of immunity. Dean implicated high officials in the president's office, and he claimed that Nixon had known about the events and the subsequent cover-ups. As surprising as this testimony was, the most shocking revelation was made by Nixon adviser Alexander Butterfield, who testified that the president had installed a secret taping system that automatically recorded all conversations in the Oval Office. Obviously, the tape recordings held information that would settle the dispute between the witnesses claiming White House involvement in the Watergate affair and the administration officials who had denied involvement.

In addition to the Senate investigation, a special prosecutor was appointed to look into the Watergate affair. The first person to hold this position, Archibald Cox, asked Nixon to turn over the tapes. When Nixon declined, Cox went to court to get an order compelling him to deliver the materials. The district and appeals courts ruled in favor of Cox. Nixon then offered to release summaries of the recordings, but that did not satisfy Cox, who continued to pursue the tapes. In response, Nixon ordered that Cox be fired. When the two highest officials in the Justice Department resigned rather than comply with the order, Solicitor General Robert Bork became the acting attorney general and dismissed Cox. The firing, popularly known as the "Saturday Night Massacre," enraged the American people, and many began calling for the president's impeachment.

Leon Jaworski was appointed to take Cox's place. An attorney from Houston, Jaworski pursued the tapes with the same zeal as had Cox. Finally, Nixon relented and

---

10. To hear oral arguments in this case, navigate to: *www.oyez.org/oyez/ frontpage.*

GRAND JURY
Subpoena Duces Tecum

SUBPOENA DUCES TECUM

United States District Court

For the District of Columbia

Misc. #47-73

THE UNITED STATES
vs.

JOHN DOE

REPORT TO UNITED STATES DISTRICT
COURT HOUSE
Between 3d Street and John Marshall Place
and on Constitution Avenue NW.
~~ROOM~~ Grand Jury Room 3
Washington, D.C.

To: Richard M. Nixon, The White House, Washington, D. C., or any
subordinate officer, official, or employee with custody or
control of the documents or objects hereinafter described on
the attached schedule.

FILED ✓
JUL 24 1973

JAMES F. DAVEY, Clerk

You are hereby commanded to attend before the Grand Jury of said Court on ... **Thursday**
the **26th** day of **July**, 19 **73**, at **10** o'clock A. M., to testify
~~and there remain until discharged; and not depart the Court without leave of the Court or District Attorney.~~
and to bring with you the documents or objects listed on the attached sched- WITNESS: The Honorable **John J. Sirica** Chief Judge of said Court, this
ule.

23rd day of **July**, 19 **73**.

Archibald Cox

ARCHIBALD COX
Attorney for The United States

JAMES F. DAVEY, Clerk.

Robert L. Line

By   Deputy Clerk.

Form No. USA-9x-184 (Rev. 7-1-71)

34

This subpoena *duces tecum* was issued July 23, 1973. It ordered President Nixon or his representatives to appear before the federal grand jury on July 26 and to bring taped conversations relevant to the investigation of the Watergate affair.

This drawing illustrates Richard Nixon's attorney, James St. Clair, arguing the president's case before the Supreme Court in *United States v. Nixon* (1974). The four justices are (left to right): Chief Justice Warren Burger, William J. Brennan Jr., Byron R. White, and Harry A. Blackmun.

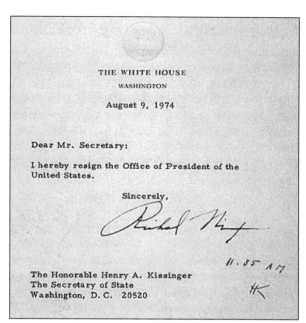

THE WHITE HOUSE
WASHINGTON

August 9, 1974

Dear Mr. Secretary:

I hereby resign the Office of President of the United States.

Sincerely,

Richard Nixon

11.35 A.M.

The Honorable Henry A. Kissinger
The Secretary of State
Washington, D.C. 20520

With this one-sentence letter Richard Nixon became the first American president to resign from office.

agreed to produce some of the materials. But when he did so, the prosecutor found that the tapes had been heavily edited. One contained eighteen and one-half minutes of mysterious buzzing at a crucial point, indicating that conversation had been erased.

Jaworski obtained criminal indictments against several Nixon aides. Although no criminal charges were brought against the president, he was named in the indictment as a co-conspirator. At about the same time, the House Judiciary Committee began an investigation into whether the president should be impeached.

Both the Judiciary Committee and Jaworski sought more of the tapes to review. Nixon steadfastly refused to comply, claiming that it was his right under executive privilege to decide what would be released and what would remain secret. The district court issued a final subpoena *duces tecum*, an order to produce the tapes and other documents. Both the United States and Nixon requested that the Supreme Court review the case, and the justices accepted the case on an expedited basis, bypassing the court of appeals.

MR. CHIEF JUSTICE BURGER delivered the opinion of the Court.

. . . [W]e turn to the claim that the subpoena should be quashed because it demands "confidential conversations between a President and his close advisors that it would be inconsistent with the public interest to produce." The first contention is a broad claim that the separation of powers doctrine precludes judicial review of a President's claim of privilege. The second contention is that if he does not prevail on the claim of absolute privilege, the court should hold as a matter of constitutional law that the privilege prevails over the subpoena *duces tecum*.

In the performance of assigned constitutional duties each branch of the Government must initially interpret the Constitution, and the interpretation of its powers by any branch is due great respect from the others. The President's counsel, as we have noted, reads the Constitution as providing an absolute privilege of confidentiality for all Presidential communications. Many decisions of this Court, however, have unequivocally reaffirmed the holding of *Marbury v. Madison* (1803) that "[i]t is emphatically the province and duty of the judicial department to say what the law is."

No holding of the Court has defined the scope of judicial power specifically relating to the enforcement of a subpoena for confidential Presidential communications for use in a criminal prosecution, but other exercises of power by the Executive Branch and the Legislative Branch have been found invalid as in conflict with the Constitution. *Powell v. McCormack* (1969); *Youngstown Sheet & Tube Co. v. Sawyer* (1952). . . .

Notwithstanding the deference each branch must accord the others, the "judicial Power of the United States" vested in the federal courts by Art. III, §1, of the Constitution can no more be shared with the Executive Branch than the Chief Executive, for example, can share with the Judiciary the veto power, or the Congress share with the Judiciary the power to override a Presidential veto. Any other conclusion would be contrary to the basic concept of separation of powers and the checks and balances that flow from the scheme of a tripartite government. We therefore reaffirm that it is the province and duty of this Court "to say what the law is" with respect to the claim of privilege presented in this case.

In support of his claim of absolute privilege, the President's counsel urges two grounds, one of which is common to all governments and one of which is peculiar to our system of separation of powers. The first ground is the valid need for protection of communications between high Government officials and those who advise and assist them in the performance of their manifold duties; the importance of this confidentiality is too plain to require further discussion. Human experience teaches that those who expect public dissemination of their remarks may well temper candor with a concern for appearances and for their own interests to the detriment of the decisionmaking process. Whatever the nature of the privilege of confidentiality of Presidential communications in the exercise of Art. II powers, the privilege can be said to derive from the supremacy of each branch within its own assigned area of constitutional duties. Certain powers and privileges flow from the nature of enumerated powers; the protection of the confidentiality of Presidential communications has similar constitutional underpinnings.

The second ground asserted by the President's counsel in support of the claim of absolute privilege rests on the doctrine of separation of powers. Here it is argued that the independence of the Executive Branch within its own sphere insulates a President from a judicial subpoena in an ongoing criminal prosecution, and thereby protects confidential Presidential communications.

However, neither the doctrine of separation of powers, nor the need for confidentiality of high-level communications, without more, can sustain an absolute, unqualified Presidential privilege of immunity from judicial process under all circumstances. The President's need for complete candor and objectivity from advisers calls for great deference from the courts. However, when the privilege depends solely on the broad, undifferentiated claim of public interest in the confidentiality of such conversations, a confrontation with other values arises. Absent a claim of need to protect military, diplomatic, or sensitive national security secrets, we find it difficult to accept the argument that even the very important interest in confidentiality of Presidential communications is significantly diminished by production of such material for *in camera* inspection with all the protection that a district court will be obliged to provide.

The impediment that an absolute, unqualified privilege would place in the way of the primary constitutional duty of the Judicial Branch to do justice in criminal prosecutions would plainly conflict with the function of the courts under

Art. III. In designing the structure of our Government and dividing and allocating the sovereign power among three co-equal branches, the Framers of the Constitution sought to provide a comprehensive system, but the separate powers were not intended to operate with absolute independence. . . . To read the Art. II powers of the President as providing an absolute privilege as against a subpoena essential to enforcement of criminal statutes on no more than a generalized claim of the public interest in confidentiality of nonmilitary and nondiplomatic discussions would upset the constitutional balance of "a workable government" and gravely impair the role of the courts under Art. III.

Since we conclude that the legitimate needs of the judicial process may outweigh Presidential privilege, it is necessary to resolve those competing interests in a manner that preserves the essential functions of each branch. The right and indeed the duty to resolve that question does not free the Judiciary from according high respect to the representations made on behalf of the President.

The expectation of a President to the confidentiality of his conversations and correspondence, like the claim of confidentiality of judicial deliberations, for example, has all the values to which we accord deference for the privacy of all citizens and, added to those values, is the necessity for protection of the public interest in candid, objective, and even blunt or harsh opinions in Presidential decisionmaking. A President and those who assist him must be free to explore alternatives in the process of shaping policies and making decisions and to do so in a way many would be unwilling to express except privately. These are the considerations justifying a presumptive privilege for Presidential communications. The privilege is fundamental to the operation of Government and inextricably rooted in the separation of powers under the Constitution. . . .

But this presumptive privilege must be considered in light of our historic commitment to the rule of law. This is nowhere more profoundly manifest than in our view that "the twofold aim [of criminal justice] is that guilt shall not escape or innocence suffer." We have elected to employ an adversary system of criminal justice in which the parties contest all issues before a court of law. The need to develop all relevant facts in the adversary system is both fundamental and comprehensive. The ends of criminal justice would be defeated if judgments were to be founded on a partial or speculative presentation of the facts. The very integrity of the judicial system and public confidence in the system depend on full disclosure of all the facts, within the framework of the rules of evidence. To ensure that justice is done, it is imperative to the function of courts that compulsory process be available for the production of evidence needed either by the prosecution or by the defense. . . .

In this case the President challenges a subpoena served on him as a third party requiring the production of materials for use in a criminal prosecution; he does so on the claim that he has a privilege against disclosure of confidential communications. He does not place his claim of privilege on the ground they are military or diplomatic secrets. As to these areas of Art. II duties the courts have traditionally shown the utmost deference to Presidential responsibilities. . . . No case of the Court, however, has extended this high degree of deference to a President's generalized interest in confidentiality. Nowhere in the Constitution, as we have noted earlier, is there any explicit reference to a privilege of confidentiality, yet to the extent this interest relates to the effective discharge of a President's powers, it is constitutionally based.

The right to the production of all evidence at a criminal trial similarly has constitutional dimensions. The Sixth Amendment explicitly confers upon every defendant in a criminal trial the right "to be confronted with the witnesses against him" and "to have compulsory process for obtaining witnesses in his favor." Moreover, the Fifth Amendment also guarantees that no person shall be deprived of liberty without due process of law. It is the manifest duty of the courts to vindicate those guarantees, and to accomplish that it is essential that all relevant and admissible evidence be produced.

In this case we must weigh the importance of the general privilege of confidentiality of Presidential communications in performance of the President's responsibilities against the inroads of such a privilege on the fair administration of criminal justice. The interest in preserving confidentiality is weighty indeed and entitled to great respect. However, we cannot conclude that advisers will be moved to temper the candor of their remarks by the infrequent occasions of disclosure because of the possibility that such conversations will be called for in the context of a criminal prosecution.

On the other hand, the allowance of the privilege to withhold evidence that is demonstrably relevant in a criminal trial would cut deeply into the guarantee of due process of law and gravely impair the basic function of the courts. A

President's acknowledged need for confidentiality in the communications of his office is general in nature, whereas the constitutional need for production of relevant evidence in a criminal proceeding is specific and central to the fair adjudication of a particular criminal case in the administration of justice. Without access to specific facts a criminal prosecution may be totally frustrated. The President's broad interest in confidentiality of communications will not be vitiated by disclosure of a limited number of conversations preliminarily shown to have some bearing on the pending criminal cases.

We conclude that when the ground for asserting privilege as to subpoenaed materials sought for use in a criminal trial is based only on the generalized interest in confidentiality, it cannot prevail over the fundamental demands of due process of law in the fair administration of criminal justice. The generalized assertion of privilege must yield to the demonstrated, specific need for evidence in a pending criminal trial.

The Court's ruling was clear. The peoples' interest in the fair administration of criminal justice outweighed the president's interest in confidentiality. Executive privilege was rejected as a justification for refusing to make the tapes available to the special prosecutor.

Nixon complied with the Court's ruling, knowing full well that it meant the end of his presidency. In obeying the Court order, he avoided provoking what many feared would be the most serious of all constitutional confrontations. What if Nixon had refused to comply? What if he had destroyed the tapes rather than turn them over? Who could have enforced sanctions on the president for doing so? Impeachment and conviction of the president probably would have been the only way to handle such a crisis. Whatever Nixon's culpability in Watergate and related matters, he spared the nation an unprecedented crisis by bowing to the Supreme Court's interpretation of the Constitution. The Nixon tapes revealed substantial wrongdoing. It was obvious to all that the House of Representatives would present articles of impeachment, and the Senate would vote to remove Nixon from office. Rather than put himself and the nation through such an ordeal, Nixon resigned.

Vice President Andrew Johnson, who had earlier served as a Democratic senator from Tennessee, assumed the presidency upon the assassination of Abraham Lincoln. Johnson's administration was characterized by fierce battles with the Radical Republicans in Congress. This conflict spawned several legal disputes, including *Mississippi v. Johnson,* and led to the president's near removal from office.

Immunity: Protecting the President from Lawsuit

Immunity is a variation on the notion of executive privilege. It deals with the extent to which the president is protected from lawsuits while in office, and the subject raises many interesting questions. May a president be ordered by a court to carry out certain executive actions, which are discretionary, or ministerial actions, which are performed as a matter of legal duty? Or, conversely, may a president be restrained by a court from taking such actions? May a private party sue the president for damages

that might have been suffered because of the president's actions or omissions? If so, may a court order the president to pay damages or provide some other restitution? If a doctrine of immunity exists, should it extend only to actions taken by presidents while in office? These questions place us in quandary. To grant the president immunity from such legal actions may remove needed accountability. But to allow the chief executive to be subject to suit could make the execution of presidential duties impossible.

The Supreme Court's first significant venture into the area of executive immunity came in the aftermath of the Civil War. In *Mississippi v. Johnson* (1867) the Court was asked to enjoin the president from executing laws passed by Congress on the ground that the laws were unconstitutional. The justices unanimously concluded that the president was immune from such suits. Is this conclusion reasonable? Does the Court's distinction between executive and ministerial acts make sense? To what degree do you think the Court was responding to the political conditions of the times? Following the *Scott v. Sandford* decision in 1857, the Court's prestige was at an all-time low, and congressional power was overwhelmingly dominant. Was the decision of the Court in *Mississippi v. Johnson* just a convenient way for the justices to avoid an unwinnable conflict with Congress?

Mississippi v. Johnson

4 WALL. (71 U.S.) 475 (1867)
http://laws.findlaw.com/US/71/475.html
Vote: 9 (Chase, Clifford, Davis, Field, Grier, Miller, Nelson,
   Swayne, Wayne)
   0
Opinion of the Court: Chase

Following the Civil War, Congress passed a number of laws "for the more efficient government of the rebel states." Commonly known as the Reconstruction Acts of 1867, they imposed military rule over the southern states until such time as loyal republican governments could be established. Andrew Johnson, a southerner from Tennessee, who had assumed the presidency after Lincoln's assassination, vetoed the legislation, but the Radical Republicans in Congress had sufficient votes to override him. Once the acts were part of federal law, the president had little choice but to enforce them, despite his belief that they were unconstitutional.

The state of Mississippi joined the fray. Applying directly to the Supreme Court, Mississippi sued Johnson, asking the justices to issue an order prohibiting him from enforcing the laws, which the state argued were unconstitutional.

THE CHIEF JUSTICE delivered the opinion of the court.

A motion was made, some days since, in behalf of the State of Mississippi, for leave to file a bill in the name of the State, praying this court perpetually to enjoin and restrain Andrew Johnson, President of the United States, and E. O. C. Ord, general commanding in the District of Mississippi and Arkansas, from executing, or in any manner carrying out, certain acts of Congress therein named.

The acts referred to are those of March 2d and March 23d, 1867, commonly known as the Reconstruction Acts.

The Attorney-General objected to the leave asked for, upon the ground that no bill which makes a President a defendant, and seeks an injunction against him to restrain the performance of his duties as President, should be allowed to be filed in this court.

This point has been fully argued, and we will now dispose of it.

We shall limit our inquiry to the question presented by the objection, without expressing any opinion on the broader issues discussed in argument, whether, in any case, the President of the United States may be required, by the process of this court, to perform a purely ministerial act under a positive law, or may be held amenable, in any case, otherwise than by impeachment for crime.

The single point which requires consideration is this: Can the President be restrained by injunction from carrying into effect an act of Congress alleged to be unconstitutional?

It is assumed by the counsel for the State of Mississippi, that the President, in the execution of the Reconstruction Acts, is required to perform a mere ministerial duty. In this assumption there is, we think, a confounding of the terms ministerial and executive, which are by no means equivalent in import.

A ministerial duty, the performance of which may, in proper cases, be required of the head of a department, by judicial process, is one in respect to which nothing is left to discretion. It is a simple, definite duty, arising under conditions admitted or proved to exist, and imposed by law.

The case of *Marbury v. Madison, Secretary of State*, furnishes an illustration. A citizen had been nominated, confirmed, and appointed a justice of the peace for the District of Columbia, and his commission had been made out, signed, and sealed. Nothing remained to be done except delivery, and the duty of delivery was imposed by law on the Secretary of State. It was held that the performance of this duty might be enforced by mandamus issuing from a court having jurisdiction.

So, in the case of *Kendall, Postmaster-General, v. Stockton & Stokes*, an act of Congress had directed the Postmaster-General to credit Stockton & Stokes with such sums as the Solicitor of the Treasury should find due to them; and that officer refused to credit them with certain sums, so found due. It was held that the crediting of this money was a mere ministerial duty, the performance of which might be judicially enforced.

In each of these cases nothing was left to discretion. There was no room for the exercise of judgment. The law required the performance of a single specific act; and that performance, it was held, might be required by mandamus.

Very different is the duty of the President in the exercise of the power to see that the laws are faithfully executed, and among these laws the acts named in the bill. By the first of these acts he is required to assign generals to command in the several military districts, and to detail sufficient military force to enable such officers to discharge their duties under the law. By the supplementary act, other duties are imposed on the several commanding generals, and these duties must necessarily be performed under the supervision of the President as commander-in-chief. The duty thus imposed on the President is in no just sense ministerial. It is purely executive and political.

An attempt on the part of the judicial department of the government to enforce the performance of such duties by the President might be justly characterized, in the language of Chief Justice Marshall, as "an absurd and excessive extravagance."

It is true that in the instance before us the interposition of the court is not sought to enforce action by the Executive under constitutional legislation, but to restrain such action under legislation alleged to be unconstitutional. But we are unable to perceive that this circumstance takes the case out of the general principles which forbid judicial interference with the exercise of Executive discretion.

It was admitted in the argument that the application now made to us is without a precedent; and this is of much weight against it. . . .

The fact that no such application was ever before made in any case indicates the general judgment of the profession that no such application should be entertained.

It will hardly be contended that Congress can interpose, in any case, to restrain the enactment of an unconstitutional law; and yet how can the right to judicial interposition to prevent such an enactment, when the purpose is evident and the execution of that purpose certain, be distinguished, in principle, from the right to such interposition against the execution of such a law by the President?

The Congress is the legislative department of the government; the President is the executive department. Neither can be restrained in its action by the judicial department; though the acts of both, when performed, are, in proper cases, subject to its cognizance.

The impropriety of such interference will be clearly seen upon consideration of its possible consequences.

Suppose the bill filed and the injunction prayed for be allowed. If the President refuse obedience, it is needless to observe that the court is without power to enforce its process. If, on the other hand, the President complies with the order of the court and refuses to execute the acts of Congress, is it not clear that a collision may occur between the executive and legislative departments of the government? May not the House of Representatives impeach the President for such refusal? And in that case could this court interfere, in behalf of the President, thus endangered by compliance with its mandate, and restrain by injunction the Senate of the United States from sitting as a court of impeachment? Would the strange spectacle be offered to the public world of an attempt by this court to arrest proceedings in that court?

These questions answer themselves.

It is true that a State may file an original bill in this court. And it may be true, in some cases, that such a bill may be filed against the United States. But we are fully satisfied that this court has no jurisdiction of a bill to enjoin the President in the performance of his official duties; and that no such bill ought to be received by us.

It has been suggested that the bill contains a prayer that, if the relief sought cannot be had against Andrew Johnson, as President, it may be granted against Andrew Johnson as a citizen of Tennessee. But it is plain that relief as against the execution of an act of Congress by Andrew Johnson, is relief against its execution by the President. A bill praying an injunction against the execution of an act of Congress by the incumbent of the presidential office cannot be received, whether it describes him as President or as a citizen of a State.

The motion for leave to file the bill is, therefore,

Denied.

The holding in this case is plain. The president of the United States cannot be sued to prevent the carrying out of executive responsibilities. But the Supreme Court has allowed suits against the actions of lower-ranking executive officials. The very next year, for example, the Supreme Court heard *Georgia v. Stanton* (1868), in which an injunction was sought to stop the secretary of war from enforcing the Reconstruction Acts.

This suit also was unsuccessful, but it was decided on entirely different grounds—that it was a political question. The Court found no bar to suing an executive branch administrator, even at the cabinet level. Only suits against the president are prohibited by the doctrine of executive immunity.

While the decision in *Johnson* settles the issue of whether the president may be personally sued with respect to executive functions, it does not answer the question of civil suits brought by private individuals who have been harmed by a president's actions. If an incumbent president engages in unlawful activities that cause damages to private individuals, can the president be held accountable in a court of law? Or is the president immune from such suits? President Nixon found himself the object of such a suit after he was involved in the dismissal of a federal employee. While reading this decision, consider the differences between the absolute immunity doctrine articulated by Justice Lewis F. Powell and the functional approach advocated in Justice Byron R. White's dissenting opinion.[11]

Nixon v. Fitzgerald

457 U.S. 731 (1982)
http:laws.findlaw.com/US/457/731.html
Vote: 5 (Burger, O'Connor, Powell, Rehnquist, Stevens)
*   4 (Blackmun, Brennan, Marshall, White)*
Opinion of the Court: Powell
Concurring opinion: Burger
Dissenting opinions: Blackmun, White

A. Ernest Fitzgerald was a civilian management analyst for the U.S. Air Force. In November 1968 Fitzgerald testified before a congressional committee chaired by Sen. William Proxmire, D-Wis. Fitzgerald reported that cost overruns for the C-5A transport plane might reach as high as $2 billion. In addition, he spoke about the technical problems the manufacturer had encountered in producing the aircraft. Needless to say, Fitzgerald's testimony was not well received by the Defense Department or military contractors.

Thirteen months later, in January 1970, Fitzgerald was removed from his job on the ground that a department reorganization had made a reduction in staff necessary. Fitzgerald believed he was fired in retaliation for his congressional appearance. The dismissal caused a great deal of concern among members of Congress, and Fitzgerald's story was widely reported in the media.

The question was whether the Nixon administration was trying to get rid of a trouble-making whistleblower. The president told a press conference that he would look into the matter, and there appeared to be some attempt to find Fitzgerald another government position. Those attempts failed, perhaps because of an internal memorandum circulated by presidential aide Alexander Butterfield concluding that "Fitzgerald is no doubt a topnotch

Ernest Fitzgerald sued President Richard Nixon after he was fired from his civilian job with the U.S. Air Force. Years later, the Supreme Court ruled against Fitzgerald.

cost expert, but he must be given very low marks in loyalty; and after all, loyalty is the name of the game . . . we should let him bleed, for a while at least."

Denied another government job, Fitzgerald began legal action, first complaining to the Civil Service Commission and then filing a suit for damages. When asked about the Fitzgerald matter, President Nixon responded, "I was totally aware that Mr. Fitzgerald would be fired or discharged or asked to resign. I approved it. . . . No, this was not a case of some person down the line deciding he should go. It was a decision that was submitted to me. I made it and I stick by it." The next day the president's

11. To hear oral arguments in this case, navigate to: *www.oyez.org/oyez/frontpage.*

office retracted his statements, explaining that Nixon had confused Fitzgerald with someone else. But, as revealed in the Watergate tapes, Nixon boasted privately that he gave the order to "get rid of that son of a bitch."

Fitzgerald's lawsuit was against a number of federal executive branch officials, including Nixon, who had resigned during the early stages of the lower court proceedings. The former president's lawyers asserted that he should be removed from the suit on the ground of absolute executive immunity from legal actions based on his official conduct as president. The lower courts rejected the absolute immunity claim, and Nixon appealed.

JUSTICE POWELL delivered the opinion of the Court.

This case now presents the claim that the President of the United States is shielded by absolute immunity from civil damages liability. In the case of the President the inquiries into history and policy, though mandated independently by our cases, tend to converge. Because the Presidency did not exist through most of the development of common law, any historical analysis must draw its evidence primarily from our constitutional heritage and structure. Historical inquiry thus merges almost at its inception with the kind of "public policy" analysis appropriately undertaken by a federal court. This inquiry involves policies and principles that may be considered implicit in the nature of the President's office in a system structured to achieve effective government under a constitutionally mandated separation of powers.

Here a former President asserts his immunity from civil damages claims of two kinds. He stands named as a defendant in a direct action under the Constitution and in two statutory actions under federal laws of general applicability. In neither case has Congress taken express legislative action to subject the President to civil liability for his official acts.

Applying the principles of our cases to claims of this kind, we hold that petitioner, as a former President of the United States, is entitled to absolute immunity from damages liability predicated on his official acts. We consider this immunity a functionally mandated incident of the President's unique office, rooted in the constitutional tradition of the separation of powers and supported by our history. . . .

The President occupies a unique position in the constitutional scheme. Article II, §1, of the Constitution provides that "[t]he executive Power shall be vested in a President of the United States. . . ." This grant of authority establishes the President as the chief constitutional officer of the Executive Branch, entrusted with supervisory and policy responsibilities of utmost discretion and sensitivity. These include the enforcement of federal law—it is the President who is charged constitutionally to "take Care that the Laws be faithfully executed"; the conduct of foreign affairs—a realm in which the Court has recognized that "[i]t would be intolerable that courts, without the relevant information, should review and perhaps nullify actions of the Executive taken on information properly held secret"; and management of the Executive Branch—a task for which "imperative reasons requir[e] an unrestricted power [in the President] to remove the most important of his subordinates in their most important duties."

In arguing that the President is entitled only to qualified immunity, the respondent relies on cases in which we have recognized immunity of this scope for governors and cabinet officers. We find these cases to be inapposite. The President's unique status under the Constitution distinguishes him from other executive officials.

Because of the singular importance of the President's duties, diversion of his energies by concern with private lawsuits would raise unique risks to the effective functioning of government. As is the case with prosecutors and judges—for whom absolute immunity now is established—a President must concern himself with matters likely to "arouse the most intense feelings." Yet, as our decisions have recognized, it is in precisely such cases that there exists the greatest public interest in providing an official "the maximum ability to deal fearlessly and impartially with" the duties of his office. This concern is compelling where the officeholder must make the most sensitive and far-reaching decisions entrusted to any official under our constitutional system. Nor can the sheer prominence of the President's office be ignored. In view of the visibility of his office and the effect of his actions on countless people, the President would be an easily identifiable target for suits for civil damages. Cognizance of this personal vulnerability frequently could distract a President from his public duties, to the detriment of not only the President and his office but also the Nation that the Presidency was designed to serve.

Courts traditionally have recognized the President's constitutional responsibilities and status as factors counseling judicial deference and restraint. For example, while courts generally have looked to the common law to determine the scope of an official's evidentiary privilege, we have recognized that the Presidential privilege is "rooted in the separation of powers under the Constitution." *United States v. Nixon* [1974]. It is settled law that the separation-of-powers doctrine does not bar every exercise of jurisdiction over the President of the United States. But our cases also have established that a court, before exercising jurisdiction, must balance the constitutional weight of the interest to be served against the dangers of intrusion on the authority and functions of the Executive Branch. When judicial action is needed to serve broad public interests—as when the Court acts, not in derogation of the separation of powers, but to maintain their proper balance, or to vindicate the public interest in an ongoing criminal prosecution—the exercise of jurisdiction has been held warranted. In the case of this merely private suit for damages based on a President's official acts, we hold it is not.

In defining the scope of an official's absolute privilege, this Court has recognized that the sphere of protected action must be related closely to the immunity's justifying purposes. Frequently our decisions have held that an official's absolute immunity should extend only to acts in performance of particular functions of his office. But the Court also has refused to draw functional lines finer than history and reason would support. In view of the special nature of the President's constitutional office and functions, we think it appropriate to recognize absolute Presidential immunity from damages liability for acts within the "outer perimeter" of his official responsibility.

Under the Constitution and laws of the United States the President has discretionary responsibilities in a broad variety of areas, many of them highly sensitive. In many cases it would be difficult to determine which of the President's innumerable "functions" encompassed a particular action. In this case, for example, respondent argues that he was dismissed in retaliation for his testimony to Congress—a violation of 5 U.S.C. §7211 (1976 ed., Supp. IV) and 18 U.S.C §1505. The Air Force, however, has claimed that the underlying reorganization was undertaken to promote efficiency. Assuming that petitioner Nixon ordered the reorganization in which respondent lost his job, an inquiry into the President's motives could not be avoided under the kind of "functional" theory asserted both by respondent and the dissent. Inquiries of this kind could be highly intrusive.

Here respondent argues that petitioner Nixon would have acted outside the outer perimeter of his duties by ordering the discharge of an employee who was lawfully entitled to retain his job in the absence of " 'such cause as will promote the efficiency of the service.' " Because Congress has granted this legislative protection, respondent argues, no federal official could, within the outer perimeter of his duties of office, cause Fitzgerald to be dismissed without satisfying this standard in prescribed statutory proceedings.

This construction would subject the President to trial on virtually every allegation that an action was unlawful, or was taken for a forbidden purpose. Adoption of this construction thus would deprive absolute immunity of its intended effect. It clearly is within the President's constitutional and statutory authority to prescribe the manner in which the Secretary will conduct the business of the Air Force. Because this mandate of office must include the authority to prescribe reorganizations and reductions in force, we conclude that petitioner's alleged wrongful acts lay well within the outer perimeter of his authority.

A rule of absolute immunity for the President will not leave the Nation without sufficient protection against misconduct on the part of the Chief Executive. There remains the constitutional remedy of impeachment. In addition, there are formal and informal checks on Presidential action that do not apply with equal force to other executive officials. The President is subjected to constant scrutiny by the press. Vigilant oversight by Congress also may serve to deter Presidential abuses of office, as well as to make credible the threat of impeachment. Other incentives to avoid misconduct may include a desire to earn reelection, the need to maintain prestige as an element of Presidential influence, and a President's traditional concern for his historical stature.

The existence of alternative remedies and deterrents establishes that absolute immunity will not place the President "above the law." For the President, as for judges and prosecutors, absolute immunity merely precludes a particular private remedy for alleged misconduct in order to advance compelling public ends.

For the reasons stated in this opinion, the decision of the Court of Appeals is reversed, and the case is remanded for action consistent with this opinion.

So ordered.

JUSTICE WHITE, with whom JUSTICE BRENNAN, JUSTICE MARSHALL, and JUSTICE BLACKMUN join, dissenting.

The four dissenting Members of the Court in *Butz v. Economou* (1978) argued that all federal officials are entitled to absolute immunity from suit for any action they take in connection with their official duties. That immunity would extend even to actions taken with express knowledge that the conduct was clearly contrary to the controlling statute or clearly violative of the Constitution. Fortunately, the majority of the Court rejected that approach: We held that although public officials perform certain functions that entitle them to absolute immunity, the immunity attaches to particular functions—not to particular offices. Officials performing functions for which immunity is not absolute enjoy qualified immunity; they are liable in damages only if their conduct violated well-established law and if they should have realized that their conduct was illegal.

The Court now applies the dissenting view in *Butz* to the Office of the President: A President, acting within the outer boundaries of what Presidents normally do, may, without liability, deliberately cause serious injury to any number of citizens even though he knows his conduct violates a statute or tramples on the constitutional rights of those who are injured. . . .

In declaring the President to be absolutely immune from suit for any deliberate and knowing violation of the Constitution or of a federal statute, the Court asserts that the immunity is "rooted in the constitutional tradition of the separation of powers and supported by our history." The decision thus has all the earmarks of a constitutional pronouncement—absolute immunity for the President's office is mandated by the Constitution. Although the Court appears to disclaim this, it is difficult to read the opinion coherently as standing for any narrower proposition: Attempts to subject the President to liability either by Congress through a statutory action or by the courts . . . would violate the separation of powers. Such a generalized absolute immunity cannot be sustained when examined in the traditional manner and in light of the traditional judicial sources. . . .

The functional approach to the separation-of-powers doctrine and the Court's more recent immunity decisions converge on the following principle: The scope of immunity is determined by function, not office. The wholesale claim that the President is entitled to absolute immunity in all of his actions stands on no firmer ground than did the claim that all Presidential communications are entitled to an absolute privilege, which was rejected in favor of a functional analysis, by a unanimous Court in *United States v. Nixon* (1974). Therefore, whatever may be true of the necessity of such a broad immunity in certain areas of executive responsibility, the only question that must be answered here is whether the dismissal of employees falls within a constitutionally assigned executive function, the performance of which would be substantially impaired by the possibility of a private action for damages. I believe it does not. . . .

Because of the importance of this case, it is appropriate to examine the reasoning of the majority opinion.

The opinion suffers from serious ambiguity even with respect to the most fundamental point: How broad is the immunity granted the President? The opinion suggests that its scope is limited by the fact that under none of the asserted causes of action "has Congress taken express legislative action to subject the President to civil liability for his official acts." We are never told, however, how or why congressional action could make a difference. It is not apparent that any of the propositions relied upon by the majority to immunize the President would not apply equally to such a statutory cause of action; nor does the majority indicate what new principles would operate to undercut those propositions.

. . . While the majority opinion recognizes that "[i]t is settled law that the separation-of-powers doctrine does not bar every exercise of jurisdiction over the President of the United States," it bases its conclusion, at least in part, on a suggestion that there is a special jurisprudence of the Presidency.

But in *United States v. Nixon* (1974), we upheld the power of a Federal District Court to issue a *subpoena duces tecum* against the President. In other cases we have enjoined executive officials from carrying out Presidential directives. See, *e.g., Youngstown Sheet & Tube Co. v. Sawyer* (1952). Not until this case has there ever been a suggestion that the mere formalism of the name appearing on the complaint was more important in resolving separation-of-powers problems than the substantive character of the judicial intrusion upon executive functions. . . .

Focusing on the actual arguments the majority offers for its holding of absolute immunity for the President, one finds surprisingly little. As I read the relevant section of the Court's opinion, I find just three contentions from which the majority draws this conclusion. Each of them is little more than a makeweight; together they hardly suffice to justify the wholesale disregard of our traditional approach to immunity questions.

First, the majority informs us that the President occupies a "unique position in the constitutional scheme," including responsibilities for the administration of justice, foreign affairs, and management of the Executive Branch. True as this may be, it says nothing about why a "unique" rule of immunity should apply to the President. . . .

Second, the majority contends that because the President's "visibility" makes him particularly vulnerable to suits for civil damages, a rule of absolute immunity is required. The force of this argument is surely undercut by the majority's admission that "there is no historical record of numerous suits against the President.". . .

Finally, the Court suggests that potential liability "frequently could distract a President from his public duties." Unless one assumes that the President himself makes the countless high-level executive decisions required in the administration of government, this rule will not do much to insulate such decisions from the threat of liability. The logic of the proposition cannot be limited to the President; its extension, however, has been uniformly rejected by this Court. . . . Furthermore, in no instance have we previously held legal accountability in itself to be an unjustifiable cost. The availability of the courts to vindicate constitutional and statutory wrongs has been perceived and protected as one of the virtues of our system of delegated and limited powers. . . .

The majority may be correct in its conclusion that "[a] rule of absolute immunity . . . will not leave the Nation without sufficient protection against misconduct on the part of the Chief Executive." Such a rule will, however, leave Mr. Fitzgerald without an adequate remedy for the harms that he may have suffered. More importantly, it will leave future plaintiffs without a remedy, regardless of the substantiality of their claims. The remedies in which the Court finds comfort were never designed to afford relief for individual harms. Rather, they were designed as political safety valves. Politics and history, however, are not the domain of the courts; the courts exist to assure each individual that he, as an individual, has enforceable rights that he may pursue to achieve a peaceful redress of his legitimate grievances.

I find it ironic, as well as tragic, that the Court would so casually discard its own role of assuring "the right of every individual to claim the protection of the laws," *Marbury v. Madison*, in the name of protecting the principle of separation of powers. Accordingly, I dissent.

In spite of the decisions in *Mississippi v. Johnson* and *Nixon v. Fitzgerald*, presidential immunity issues continue to appear—with *Clinton v. Jones* (1997) being the most recent example.[12]

Clinton was surrounded by political intrigue and scandal. Paula Jones, a former state employee, had sued President Clinton for making "abhorrent" sexual advances in a Little Rock hotel room while he was governor of Arkansas. There were heated public arguments over whether this was a case of inexcusable sexual harassment or a groundless, politically motivated lawsuit designed to undermine and embarrass the president. Political rhetoric aside, the case presented a major constitutional issue: Can a sitting president be required to stand trial on allegations concerning his unofficial conduct? Jones's supporters argued that the president is not immune from lawsuit and that Jones, like any other citizen, had the right to a prompt judicial determination on her claims of being unlawfully treated. Clinton supporters argued that the chief executive should not have to stand trial during his term of office. Allowing a trial to proceed would divert the president's attention from his official duties; the situation would be made worse by a potential rash of civil lawsuits following the trial. The Supreme Court settled the issue on May 27, 1997.

12. To hear oral arguments in this case, navigate to: *www.oyez.org/oyez/ frontpage*.

Clinton v. Jones

520 U.S. 681 (1997)
http://laws.findlaw.com/US/520/681.html
Vote: 9 (Breyer, Ginsburg, Kennedy, O'Connor, Rehnquist,
*   Scalia, Souter, Stevens, Thomas)*

        0

Opinion of the Court: Stevens
Concurring opinion: Breyer

Bill Clinton was elected to the presidency in 1992 and reelected in 1996. Prior to his elevation to the office of president, Clinton was the governor of Arkansas. In 1994 Paula Corbin Jones filed suit in federal district court in Arkansas against Clinton and Arkansas state trooper Danny Ferguson over an incident that was alleged to have occurred on May 8, 1991, at the Excelsior Hotel in Little Rock. On the day in question Jones, then an employee of the state Industrial Development Commission, was working at the registration desk for a management conference at which Governor Clinton had delivered a speech. According to her allegations, Trooper Ferguson approached Jones, indicating that the governor wanted to see her. Ferguson escorted her to Clinton's hotel suite. Jones and the governor were left alone in the room. The suit claimed that Clinton made "abhorrent" sexual advances to Jones, including exposing himself to her, touching her inappropriately, and making unwelcome sexual remarks. Jones said she rejected Clinton's suggestions, and the governor ceased his advances. As she was leaving the room, Jones alleged that the governor told her, "You are smart. Let's keep this between ourselves."

Jones's suit claimed that after she returned to her state job, her superiors began treating her rudely; she was ultimately transferred to another position that had little advancement potential. She attributed this harsh treatment to retaliation for her rejection of the governor. The suit asked for actual damages of $75,000 and punitive damages of $100,000 in compensation for Clinton's violations of state and federal civil rights and sexual harassment laws.

Clinton denied the allegations and claimed the lawsuit was politically motivated. He filed motions asking the district court to dismiss the case on the ground of presidential immunity and to prohibit Jones from refiling the suit until after the end of his presidency. The district judge rejected the presidential immunity argument. Although she allowed pretrial discovery activities to proceed, the judge ordered that no trial would take place until Clinton was no longer president. Both Jones and Clinton appealed. Holding that "the President, like all other government officials, is subject to the same laws that apply to all other members of society," the court of appeals ruled that the trial should not be postponed. Clinton asked the Supreme Court to reverse the decision.

JUSTICE STEVENS delivered the opinion of the Court.

This case raises a constitutional and a prudential question concerning the Office of the President of the United States. Respondent, a private citizen, seeks to recover damages from the current occupant of that office based on actions allegedly taken before his term began. The President submits that in all but the most exceptional cases the Constitution requires federal courts to defer such litigation until his term ends and that, in any event, respect for the office warrants such a stay. Despite the force of the arguments supporting the President's submissions, we conclude that they must be rejected. . . .

Only three sitting Presidents have been defendants in civil litigation involving their actions prior to taking office. Complaints against Theodore Roosevelt and Harry Truman had been dismissed before they took office; the dismissals were affirmed after their respective inaugurations. Two companion cases arising out of an automobile accident were filed against John F. Kennedy in 1960 during the Presidential campaign. After taking office, he unsuccessfully argued that his status as Commander in Chief gave him a right to a stay under the Soldiers' and Sailors' Civil Relief Act of 1940. The motion for a stay was denied by the District Court, and the matter was settled out of court. Thus, none of those cases sheds any light on the constitutional issue before us.

The principal rationale for affording certain public servants immunity from suits for money damages arising out of their official acts is inapplicable to unofficial conduct. In cases involving prosecutors, legislators, and judges we have repeatedly explained that the immunity serves the public interest in enabling such officials to perform their designated functions effectively without fear that a particular decision may give rise to personal liability. . . .

That rationale provided the principal basis for our holding that a former President of the United States was "entitled to absolute immunity from damages liability predicated on his official acts," [*Nixon v.*] *Fitzgerald* [1982]. Our central concern was to avoid rendering the President "unduly cautious in the discharge of his official duties."

This reasoning provides no support for an immunity for unofficial conduct. As we explained in *Fitzgerald*, "the sphere of protected action must be related closely to the immunity's justifying purposes." Because of the President's broad responsibilities, we recognized in that case an immunity from damages claims arising out of official acts extending to the "outer perimeter of his authority." But we have never suggested that the President, or any other official, has an immunity that extends beyond the scope of any action taken in an official capacity.

Moreover, when defining the scope of an immunity for acts clearly taken within an official capacity, we have applied a functional approach. "Frequently our decisions have held that an official's absolute immunity should extend only to acts in performance of particular functions of his office." Hence, for example, a judge's absolute immunity does not extend to actions performed in a purely administrative capacity. As our opinions have made clear, immunities are grounded in "the nature of the function performed, not the identity of the actor who performed it."

Petitioner's effort to construct an immunity from suit for unofficial acts grounded purely in the identity of his office is unsupported by precedent.

We are also unpersuaded by the evidence from the historical record to which petitioner has called our attention. . . .

Petitioner's strongest argument supporting his immunity claim is based on the text and structure of the Constitution. He does not contend that the occupant of the Office of the President is "above the law," in the sense that his conduct is entirely immune from judicial scrutiny. The President argues merely for a postponement of the judicial proceedings that will determine whether he violated any law. His argument is grounded in the character of the office that was created by Article II of the Constitution, and relies on separation of powers principles that have structured our constitutional arrangement since the founding.

As a starting premise, petitioner contends that he occupies a unique office with powers and responsibilities so vast and important that the public interest demands that he devote his undivided time and attention to his public duties. He submits that—given the nature of the office—the doctrine of separation of powers places limits on the authority of the Federal Judiciary to interfere with the Executive Branch that would be transgressed by allowing this action to proceed.

We have no dispute with the initial premise of the argument. Former presidents, from George Washington to George Bush, have consistently endorsed petitioner's characterization of the office. . . .

It does not follow, however, that separation of powers principles would be violated by allowing this action to proceed. The doctrine of separation of powers is concerned with the allocation of official power among the three coequal branches of our Government. . . .

Of course the lines between the powers of the three branches are not always neatly defined. But in this case there is no suggestion that the Federal Judiciary is being asked to perform any function that might in some way be described as "executive." Respondent is merely asking the courts to exercise their core Article III jurisdiction to decide cases and controversies. Whatever the outcome of this case, there is no possibility that the decision will curtail the scope of the official powers of the Executive Branch. The litigation of questions that relate entirely to the unofficial conduct of the individual who happens to be the President poses no perceptible risk of misallocation of either judicial power or executive power.

Rather than arguing that the decision of the case will produce either an aggrandizement of judicial power or a narrowing of executive power, petitioner contends that—as a by product of an otherwise traditional exercise of judicial power—burdens will be placed on the President that will hamper the performance of his official duties. . . . As a factual matter, petitioner contends that this particular case—as well as the potential additional litigation that an affirmance of the Court of Appeals judgment might spawn—may impose an unacceptable burden on the President's time and energy, and thereby impair the effective performance of his office.

Petitioner's predictive judgment finds little support in either history or the relatively narrow compass of the issues raised in this particular case. As we have already noted, in the more than 200 year history of the Republic, only three sitting Presidents have been subjected to suits for their private actions. If the past is any indicator, it seems unlikely that a deluge of such litigation will ever engulf the Presidency. As for the case at hand, if properly managed by the District Court, it appears to us highly unlikely to occupy any substantial amount of petitioner's time.

Of greater significance, petitioner errs by presuming that interactions between the Judicial Branch and the Executive, even quite burdensome interactions, necessarily rise to the level of constitutionally forbidden impairment of the Executive's ability to perform its constitutionally mandated functions. . . . The fact that a federal court's exercise of its traditional Article III jurisdiction may significantly burden the time and attention of the Chief Executive is not sufficient to establish a violation of the Constitution. Two long settled propositions, first announced by Chief Justice Marshall, support that conclusion.

First, we have long held that when the President takes official action, the Court has the authority to determine whether he has acted within the law. . . .

Second, it is also settled that the President is subject to judicial process in appropriate circumstances. Although Thomas Jefferson apparently thought otherwise, Chief Justice Marshall, when presiding in the treason trial of Aaron Burr, ruled that a subpoena *duces tecum* could be directed to the President. We unequivocally and emphatically endorsed Marshall's position when we held that President Nixon was obligated to comply with a subpoena commanding him to produce certain tape recordings of his conversations with his aides. *United States v. Nixon* (1974). As we explained, "neither the doctrine of separation of powers, nor the need for confidentiality of high level communications, without more, can sustain an absolute, unqualified Presidential privilege of immunity from judicial process under all circumstances."

Sitting Presidents have responded to court orders to provide testimony and other information with sufficient frequency that such interactions between the Judicial and Executive Branches can scarcely be thought a novelty. President Monroe responded to written interrogatories, President Nixon—as noted above—produced tapes in response to a subpoena *duces tecum*, President Ford complied with an order to give a deposition in a criminal trial, and President

Clinton has twice given videotaped testimony in criminal proceedings. Moreover, sitting Presidents have also voluntarily complied with judicial requests for testimony. . . .

In sum, "[i]t is settled law that the separation of powers doctrine does not bar every exercise of jurisdiction over the President of the United States." *Fitzgerald.* If the Judiciary may severely burden the Executive Branch by reviewing the legality of the President's official conduct, and if it may direct appropriate process to the President himself, it must follow that the federal courts have power to determine the legality of his unofficial conduct. The burden on the President's time and energy that is a mere by product of such review surely cannot be considered as onerous as the direct burden imposed by judicial review and the occasional invalidation of his official actions. We therefore hold that the doctrine of separation of powers does not require federal courts to stay all private actions against the President until he leaves office. . . .

. . . [W]e are persuaded that it was an abuse of discretion for the District Court to defer the trial until after the President leaves office. Such a lengthy and categorical stay takes no account whatever of the respondent's interest in bringing the case to trial. The complaint was filed within the statutory limitations period—albeit near the end of that period—and delaying trial would increase the danger of prejudice resulting from the loss of evidence, including the inability of witnesses to recall specific facts, or the possible death of a party.

The decision to postpone the trial was, furthermore, premature. The proponent of a stay bears the burden of establishing its need. . . . We think the District Court may have given undue weight to the concern that a trial might generate unrelated civil actions that could conceivably hamper the President in conducting the duties of his office. If and when that should occur, the court's discretion would permit it to manage those actions in such fashion (including deferral of trial) that interference with the President's duties would not occur. But no such impingement upon the President's conduct of his office was shown here.

We add a final comment on two matters that are discussed at length in the briefs: the risk that our decision will generate a large volume of politically motivated harassing and frivolous litigation, and the danger that national security concerns might prevent the President from explaining a legitimate need for a continuance.

We are not persuaded that either of these risks is serious. Most frivolous and vexatious litigation is terminated at the pleading stage or on summary judgment, with little if any personal involvement by the defendant. Moreover, the availability of sanctions provides a significant deterrent to litigation directed at the President in his unofficial capacity for purposes of political gain or harassment. History indicates that the likelihood that a significant number of such cases will be filed is remote. Although scheduling problems may arise, there is no reason to assume that the District Courts will be either unable to accommodate the President's needs or unfaithful to the tradition—especially in matters involving national security—of giving "the utmost deference to Presidential responsibilities." Several Presidents, including petitioner, have given testimony without jeopardizing the Nation's security. In short, we have confidence in the ability of our federal judges to deal with both of these concerns.

If Congress deems it appropriate to afford the President stronger protection, it may respond with appropriate legislation. . . . If the Constitution embodied the rule that the President advocates, Congress, of course, could not repeal it. But our holding today raises no barrier to a statutory response to these concerns.

The Federal District Court has jurisdiction to decide this case. Like every other citizen who properly invokes that jurisdiction, respondent has a right to an orderly disposition of her claims. Accordingly, the judgment of the Court of Appeals is affirmed.

It is so ordered.

JUSTICE BREYER, concurring in the judgment.

I agree with the majority that the Constitution does not automatically grant the President an immunity from civil lawsuits based upon his private conduct. Nor does the "doctrine of separation of powers . . . require federal courts to stay" virtually "all private actions against the President until he leaves office." Rather, as the Court of Appeals stated, the President cannot simply rest upon the claim that a private civil lawsuit for damages will "interfere with the constitutionally assigned duties of the Executive Branch . . . without detailing any specific responsibilities or explaining how or the degree to which they are affected by the suit." To obtain a postponement the President must "bea[r] the burden of establishing its need."

In my view, however, once the President sets forth and explains a conflict between judicial proceeding and public duties, the matter changes. At that point, the Constitution permits a judge to schedule a trial in an ordinary civil damages action (where postponement normally is possible without overwhelming damage to a plaintiff) only within the constraints of a constitutional principle—a principle that forbids a federal judge in such a case to interfere with the President's discharge of his public duties. I have no doubt that the Constitution contains such a principle applicable to civil suits, based upon Article II's vesting of the entire "executive Power" in a single individual, implemented through the Constitution's structural separation of powers, and revealed both by history and case precedent.

I recognize that this case does not require us now to apply the principle specifically, thereby delineating its contours; nor need we now decide whether lower courts are to apply it directly or categorically through the use of presumptions or rules of administration. Yet I fear that to disregard it now may appear to deny it. I also fear that the majority's description of the relevant precedents de-emphasizes the extent to which they support a principle of the President's independent authority to control his own time and energy. . . .

Case law, particularly, *Nixon v. Fitzgerald*, strongly supports the principle that judges hearing a private civil damages action against a sitting President may not issue orders that could significantly distract a President from his official duties. In *Fitzgerald*, the Court held that former President Nixon was absolutely immune from civil damage lawsuits based upon any conduct within the "outer perimeter" of his official responsibilities. . . .

The majority points to the fact that private plaintiffs have brought civil damage lawsuits against a sitting President only three times in our Nation's history; and it relies upon the threat of sanctions to discourage, and "the court's discretion" to manage, such actions so that "interference with the President's duties would not occur." I am less sanguine. Since 1960, when the last such suit was filed, the number of civil lawsuits filed annually in Federal District Courts has increased from under 60,000 to about 240,000; the number of federal district judges has increased from 233 to about 650; the time and expense associated with both discovery and trial have increased; an increasingly complex economy has led to increasingly complex sets of statutes, rules and regulations, that often create potential liability, with or without fault. And this Court has now made clear that such lawsuits may proceed against a sitting President. The consequence, as the Court warned in *Fitzgerald*, is that a sitting President, given "the visibility of his office," could well become "an easily identifiable target for suits for civil damages." The threat of sanctions could well discourage much unneeded litigation, but some lawsuits (including highly intricate and complicated ones) could resist ready evaluation and disposition; and individual district court procedural rulings could pose a significant threat to the President's official functions.

I concede the possibility that district courts, supervised by the Courts of Appeals and perhaps this Court, might prove able to manage private civil damage actions against sitting Presidents without significantly interfering with the discharge of Presidential duties—at least if they manage those actions with the constitutional problem in mind. Nonetheless, predicting the future is difficult, and I am skeptical. . . .

. . . The District Court in this case determined that the Constitution required the postponement of trial during the sitting President's term. It may well be that the trial of this case cannot take place without significantly interfering with the President's ability to carry out his official duties. Yet, I agree with the majority that there is no automatic temporary immunity and that the President should have to provide the District Court with a reasoned explanation of why the immunity is needed; and I also agree that, in the absence of that explanation, the court's postponement of the trial date was premature. For those reasons, I concur in the result.

The Court's conclusion that Jones's sexual harassment suit could proceed was a setback for President Clinton, who was by that time heavily involved in more serious controversies that ultimately led to his impeachment *(see Box 4-5)*. In the end, Clinton and Jones reached an out-of-court monetary settlement of the dispute. Although the Jones case never went to trial, the Supreme Court's ruling that presidents while in office may be sued for unofficial conduct is a significant addition to the law of presidential immunity. It also remains controversial, with many scholars suggesting that it will prove damaging to the presidency. Do you agree? Or do you believe that the Clinton episode was so anomalous that we are unlikely to see anyone taking advantage of the Court's ruling?

The Power to Pardon

Executive power historically has included the authority to reduce or rescind criminal punishments in individual cases. The executive stands as the last source of mercy, capable of sparing a person when extraordinary circumstances warrant such action. This power was exercised by monarchs in Europe long before the creation of the United States, so it was not surprising that the Constitutional Convention also gave it to the president. The wording of the Pardon Clause is straightforward: the president "shall have Power to grant Reprieves and Pardons for Offenses against the United States, except in Cases of Impeachment."

A pardon erases all penalties and other legal effects of a criminal conviction. It is, as described by Chief Justice John Marshall, an act of grace. A person receiving a complete pardon is released from serving any remaining sentence and has full civil rights restored. Legally, it is as if the individual had never committed the crime.[13] A reprieve, in contrast, is a presidential act that merely postpones the serving of a criminal penalty.

There are only a few limits on the president's power to grant pardons and reprieves. The words of Article II restrict the president's authority to crimes against the United States, which means that the president may pardon only individuals charged with federal offenses, not those in violation of state criminal laws. The governors of the various states have similar pardoning or clemency authority. Article II also prohibits the use of the pardoning power to nullify the effects of impeachment. And finally, the president may not impose a pardon on someone who refuses to accept it.[14]

---

13. See *Ex parte Garland* (1867).
14. See *United States v. Wilson* (1833) and *Burdick v. United States* (1915). Later, however, the Court held that acceptance was not required when the president commuted a death sentence to life in prison (*Biddle v. Perovich*, 1927).

BOX 4-5   AFTERMATH . . . PRESIDENT BILL CLINTON

IN *CLINTON V. JONES* (1997) the Supreme Court rejected President Clinton's request to postpone a trial on Paula Jones's sexual harassment charges until his presidency ended. Thus began two years of intense legal difficulties for the president. Clinton was already under investigation by Independent Counsel Kenneth Starr for possible financial improprieties in the Whitewater matter, an Arkansas land deal that occurred prior to his presidency. That investigation coupled with the Jones lawsuit subjected Clinton to more intense scrutiny than any previous president.

While preparing their case, Jones's attorneys were made aware of a possible illicit relationship between Clinton and a young White House intern, Monica Lewinsky. Attempting to establish a pattern of wrongdoing, Jones's lawyers subpoenaed Lewinsky and the president. Lewinsky initially denied any sexual relationship with Clinton. On January 17, 1998, President Clinton gave a sworn deposition claiming that he had not had a sexual relationship with Lewinsky. Nine days later he made the same denial to the American people on national television. Taped telephone conversations between Lewinsky and her friend Linda Tripp, who had given the tapes to the independent counsel's office, revealed that a sexual relationship between Lewinsky and Clinton had occurred. Starr expanded his investigation to include an inquiry into the Lewinsky matter.

After receiving immunity from prosecution, Lewinsky changed her testimony, acknowledging a past relationship with the president. In August Clinton admitted to "a critical lapse of judgment" that had led to his affair with Lewinsky. By this time, other women had come forward claiming that Clinton had acted inappropriately with them. In November the president settled his legal dispute with Jones for $850,000 with no apology or admission of guilt.

Settling the Jones case, however, did not end Clinton's troubles. In December the House of Representatives considered four articles of impeachment recommended by its Judiciary Committee. Two of the proposals passed: one charged Clinton with perjury, and the other alleged obstruction of justice. As a result, Bill Clinton became only the second president in U.S. history to be impeached.

In January 1999, with Chief Justice William Rehnquist presiding and the senators acting as a jury, the U.S. Senate tried Clinton on the two articles of impeachment. On February 12 Clinton was acquitted on both counts. The senators voted 55–45 to acquit on the perjury charge, and 50–50 on the obstruction of justice charge, both votes falling far short of the sixty-seven required to remove Clinton from office. Throughout the impeachment process, public opinion ran decidedly against removing Clinton from office.

Clinton's legal problems continued. U.S. judge Susan Webber Wright, who presided over the Jones lawsuit, found Clinton in contempt and fined him $90,000 for undermining "the integrity of the judicial system" by "false, misleading, and evasive answers that were designed to obstruct justice." In May 2000, the Arkansas Supreme Court initiated disbarment proceedings. But on January 19, 2001, his last full day in office, Clinton reached an agreement with the independent counsel in which he admitted wrongdoing and accepted a $25,000 fine and a five-year suspension of his license to practice law, thus settling the disbarment question.

Throughout all of these difficulties, Bill Clinton's presidency was surprisingly unaffected. Polls indicated that the public perceived Clinton as a man with serious personal character flaws, but gave him historically high approval ratings for the job he was doing as president.

SOURCES: *Los Angeles Times*, May 23, 2000; *Omaha World-Herald*, February 13, 1999; *New York Times*, February 13, 1999, July 30, 1999; *San Francisco Chronicle*, February 13, 1999.

Aside from these limits, the president is free to exercise the pardoning authority with full discretion, and some presidents have been quite generous in granting pardons. A pardon may completely void all criminal penalties for a crime or eliminate only a portion of the sentence. The president may place conditions on a pardon. For instance, in 1960 President Eisenhower spared army master sergeant Maurice Schick, a convicted murderer, from the death penalty on the condition that he be imprisoned for life without the possibility of parole.[15] A

15. See *Schick v. Reed* (1974).

president may pardon individuals before or after they are tried for an offense or even before the filing of formal criminal charges. Pardons may be granted to a single person or an entire class of individuals. For example, in 1795 George Washington granted amnesty to those who had participated in the Whiskey Rebellion, and in 1977 Jimmy Carter pardoned all Vietnam War draft evaders, an action that applied to an estimated one hundred thousand men.

For the most part, the Supreme Court has granted the chief executive great leeway in the exercise of the pardon power. *Ex parte Grossman* (1925) provides an example. The issue in this case was whether the president's pardon power extended to criminal contempt penalties imposed by a federal judge. Chief Justice Taft wrote the opinion of the Court. Taft, a former president, expressed strong support for a broad interpretation of the pardoning authority. In *Grossman,* note his use of history as a means of interpreting the Constitution.

Ex parte Grossman

267 U.S. 87 (1925)
http://laws.findlaw.com/US/267/87.html
Vote: 8 (Brandeis, Butler, Holmes, McReynolds, Sanford,
*   Sutherland, Taft, Van Devanter)*

0

Opinion of the Court: Taft

On November 24, 1920, legal action was taken against Philip Grossman in the District Court of the United States for the Northern District of Illinois. He was charged with selling liquor at his place of business in violation of the National Prohibition Act. Government attorneys requested that the court issue an injunction prohibiting Grossman from any further violations, and two days later a judge issued the injunction. On January 11, 1921, the government filed charges against Grossman for violating the judge's order, claiming that he had continued to sell alcoholic beverages at his establishment. The district court tried Grossman and found him guilty of criminal contempt of court for disobeying the order. The

judged sentenced him to one year in prison and a fine of $1,000, and the sentence was upheld by the court of appeals.

In December 1923 President Calvin Coolidge issued a pardon in which he reduced Grossman's sentence to payment of the fine. Grossman accepted the pardon, paid the fine, and was released from prison. The district judge, however, refused to acknowledge the pardon on the ground that the president had no authority to commute a sentence for criminal contempt of court. He ordered Grossman to serve the remainder of his sentence. Grossman objected and filed a habeas corpus action against prison superintendent Ritchie Graham, demanding to be released.

MR. CHIEF JUSTICE TAFT delivered the opinion of the Court.

The argument for the respondent is that the President's power extends only to offenses against the United States and a contempt of Court is not such an offense, that offenses against the United States are not common law offenses but can only be created by legislative act, that the President's pardoning power is more limited than that of the King of England at common law, which was a broad prerogative and included contempts against his courts chiefly because the judges thereof were his agents and acted in his name; that the context of the Constitution shows that the word "offences" is used in that instrument only to include crimes and misdemeanors triable by jury and not contempts of the dignity and authority of the federal courts, and that to construe the pardon clause to include contempts of court would be to violate the fundamental principle of the Constitution in the division of powers between the Legislative, Executive and Judicial branches, and to take from the federal courts their independence and the essential means of protecting their dignity and authority.

The language of the Constitution cannot be interpreted safely except by reference to the common law and to British institutions as they were when the instrument was framed and adopted. The statesmen and lawyers of the Convention who submitted it to the ratification of the Conventions of the thirteen States, were born and brought up in the atmosphere of the common law, and thought and spoke in its vocabulary. They were familiar with other forms of government, recent and ancient, and indicated in their discussions earnest study and consideration of many of them, but when they came to put their conclusions into the form of fundamental law in a compact draft, they expressed them in terms of the common law, confident that they could be shortly and easily understood. . . .

The King of England before our Revolution, in the exercise of his prerogative, had always exercised the power to pardon contempts of court, just as he did ordinary crimes and misdemeanors and as he has done to the present day. In the mind of a common law lawyer of the eighteenth century the word pardon included within its scope the ending by the King's grace of the punishment of such derelictions, whether it was imposed by the court without a jury or upon indictment, for both forms of trial for contempts were had. . . .

Nor is there any substance in the contention that there is any substantial difference in this matter between the executive power of pardon in our Government and the King's prerogative. The courts of Great Britain were called the King's Courts, as indeed they were; but for years before our Constitution they were as independent of the King's interference as they are today. The extent of the King's pardon was clearly circumscribed by law and the British Constitution, as the cases cited above show. The framers of our Constitution had in mind no necessity for curtailing this feature of the King's prerogative in transplanting it into the American governmental structures, save by excepting cases of impeachment; and even in that regard, as already pointed out, the common law forbade the pleading a pardon in bar to an impeachment. The suggestion that the President's power of pardon should be regarded as necessarily less than that of the King was pressed upon this Court . . . in *Ex parte William Wells*, [1855] but it did not prevail with the majority. . . .

Nothing in the ordinary meaning of the words "offences against the United States" excludes criminal contempts. That which violates the dignity and authority of federal courts such as an intentional effort to defeat their decrees justifying punishment violates a law of the United States, and so must be an offense against the United States. Moreover, this Court has held that the general statute of limitation which forbids prosecutions "for any offense unless instituted within three years next after such offense shall have been committed," applies to criminal contempts. . . .

. . . [C]riminal contempts of a federal court have been pardoned for eighty-five years. In that time the power has been exercised twenty-seven times. . . .

Executive clemency exists to afford relief from undue harshness or evident mistake in the operation or enforcement of the criminal law. The administration of justice by the courts is not necessarily always wise or certainly considerate of circumstances which may properly mitigate guilt. To afford a remedy, it has always been thought essential in popular governments, as well as in monarchies, to vest in some other authority than the courts power to ameliorate or avoid particular criminal judgments. It is a check entrusted to the executive for special cases. To exercise it to the extent of destroying the deterrent effect of judicial punishment would be to pervert it; but whoever is to make it useful must have full discretion to exercise it. Our Constitution confers this discretion on the highest officer in the nation in confidence that he will not abuse it. An abuse in pardoning contempts would certainly embarrass courts, but it is questionable how much more it would lessen their effectiveness than a wholesale pardon of other offenses. If we could conjure up in our minds a President willing to paralyze courts by pardoning all criminal contempts, why not a President ordering a general jail delivery? A pardon can only be granted for a contempt fully completed. Neither in this country nor in England can it interfere with the use of coercive measures to enforce a suitor's right. The detrimental effect of excessive pardons of completed contempts would be in the loss of the deterrent influence upon future contempts. It is of the same character as that of the excessive pardons of other offenses. The difference does not justify our reading criminal contempts out of the pardon clause by departing from its ordinary meaning confirmed by its common law origin and long years of practice and acquiescence.

If it be said that the President, by successive pardons of constantly recurring contempts in particular litigation, might deprive a court of power to enforce its orders in a recalcitrant neighborhood, it is enough to observe that such a course is so improbable as to furnish but little basis for argument. Exceptional cases like this, if to be imagined at all, would suggest a resort to impeachment rather than to a narrow and strained construction of the general powers of the President.

The power of a court to protect itself and its usefulness by punishing contemnors is of course necessary, but it is one exercised without the restraining influence of a jury and without many of the guaranties which the bill of rights offers to protect the individual against unjust conviction. Is it unreasonable to provide for the possibility that the personal element may sometimes enter into a summary judgment pronounced by a judge who thinks his authority is flouted or denied? May it not be fairly said that in order to avoid possible mistake, undue prejudice or needless severity, the chance of pardon should exist at least as much in favor of a person convicted by a judge without a jury as in favor of one convicted in a jury trial? The pardoning by the President of criminal contempts has been practiced more than three-quarters of a century, and no abuses during all that time developed sufficiently to invoke a test in the federal courts of its validity.

It goes without saying that nowhere is there a more earnest will to maintain the independence of federal courts and the preservation of every legitimate safeguard of their effectiveness afforded by the Constitution than in this Court. But the qualified independence which they fortunately enjoy is not likely to be permanently strengthened by ignoring precedent and practice and minimizing the importance of the coordinating checks and balances of the Constitution.

The rule is made absolute and the petitioner is discharged.

Undoubtedly, the most controversial exercise of the power was Ford's pardon of Nixon in 1974 *(see Box 4-6)*. By resigning, Nixon kept all of the benefits the nation provides its former chief executives, but the resignation did not make him immune from a trial for any crimes related to Watergate. The pardon covered any crimes Nixon may have committed during his entire tenure as chief executive, from January 20, 1969, through August 9, 1974. It was an extraordinary act: not only was Nixon the first president to be pardoned for possible wrongdoing, but also the pardon was a blanket one, covering almost six years and not restricted to any specific crimes or incidents. Furthermore, the pardon came before any formal criminal charges were brought against Nixon. Ford's stated intent was to begin to heal the nation by putting the Watergate scandal to rest.

Many people were appalled at the pardon, believing that if Nixon committed criminal acts he should be put on trial like any other citizen. They thought it was necessary for the former president to stand trial because his alleged wrongdoing compromised the very foundation of the American government and violated the sacred trust of the people. The granting of this blanket protection to Nixon was widely criticized, and some analysts cite it as one reason why Ford lost the 1976 election to Jimmy Carter.

Given the Supreme Court's interpretations of the pardon power, there was little doubt that Ford was acting constitutionally. Few legal scholars thought a court challenge had any chance of success. Prevailing legal opinion, however, did not deter a Michigan attorney from filing suit against Ford to have the pardon declared unconstitutional. The dispute did not reach the Supreme Court, but it was heard and decided in federal district court. As you read the opinion of the judge in *Murphy v. Ford*, notice how closely he ties his decision to the intention of the Framers and to the precedents handed down by the Supreme Court.

Murphy v. Ford

390 F. SUPP. 1372 (1975)
Decision of the U.S. District Court for the Western District of Michigan
Noel P. Fox, Chief Judge

F. Gregory Murphy, an attorney from Marquette, Michigan, filed suit against President Ford, asking the court to declare his unconditional pardon of Richard Nixon void. Murphy contended that a pardon cannot constitutionally be granted to a person who has not been indicted or convicted and who has not been formally charged with any crime against the United States. The suit was heard by Judge Noel Fox, a Democrat appointed to the district court by President Kennedy.

BOX 4-6 NIXON PARDON PROCLAMATION

Following is the text of the proclamation by which President Gerald R. Ford, September 8, 1974, pardoned former president Richard Nixon:

RICHARD NIXON became the thirty-seventh President of the United States on January 20, 1969, and was reelected in 1972 for a second term by the electors of forty-nine of the fifty states. His term in office continued until his resignation on August 9, 1974.

Pursuant to resolutions of the House of Representatives, its Committee on the Judiciary conducted an inquiry and investigation on the impeachment of the President extending over more than eight months. The hearings of the committee and its deliberations, which received wide national publicity over television, radio, and in printed media, resulted in votes adverse to Richard Nixon on recommended articles of impeachment.

As a result of certain acts or omissions occurring before his resignation from the office of President, Richard Nixon has become liable to possible indictment and trial for offenses against the United States. Whether or not he shall be so prosecuted depends on findings of the appropriate grand jury and on the discretion of the authorized prosecutor. Should an indictment ensue, the accused shall then be entitled to a fair trial by an impartial jury, as guaranteed to every individual by the Constitution.

It is believed that a trial of Richard Nixon, if it became necessary, could not fairly begin until a year or more has elapsed. In the meantime, the tranquility to which this nation has been restored by the events of recent weeks could be irreparably lost by the prospects of bringing to trial a former President of the United States. The prospects of such trial will cause prolonged and divisive debate over the propriety of exposing to further punishment and degradation a man who has already paid the unprecedented penalty of relinquishing the highest elective office in the United States.

Now, therefore, I, Gerald R. Ford, President of the United States, pursuant to the pardon power conferred upon me by Article II, Section 2, of the Constitution, have granted and by these presents do grant a full, free, and absolute pardon unto Richard Nixon for all offenses against the United States which he, Richard Nixon, has committed or may have committed or taken part in during the period from January 20, 1969, through August 9, 1974.

In witness whereof, I have hereunto set my hand this 8th day of September in the year of Our Lord Nineteen Hundred Seventy-Four, and of the Independence of the United States of America the 199th.

CHIEF JUDGE FOX delivered the opinion of the court.

The main issue is, did President Ford have the constitutional power to pardon former President Nixon for the latter's offenses against the United States?

In The Federalist No. 74, written in 1788 in support of the proposed Constitution, Alexander Hamilton explained why the Founding Fathers gave the President a discretionary power to pardon: "The principal argument for reposing the power of pardoning . . . [in] the Chief Magistrate," Hamilton wrote, "is this: in seasons of insurrection or rebellion, there are often critical moments, when a well-timed offer of pardon to the insurgents or rebels may restore the tranquillity of the commonwealth; and which, if suffered to pass unimproved, it may never be possible afterwards to recall."

Few would today deny that the period from the break-in at the Watergate in June 1972, until the resignation of President Nixon in August 1974, was a "season of insurrection or rebellion" by many actually in the Government. Since the end of 1970, various top officials of the Nixon Administration at times during this period deliberately and flagrantly violated the civil liberties of individual citizens and engaged in criminal violations of the campaign laws in order to preserve and expand their own and Nixon's personal power beyond constitutional limitations. When many illegal activities were threatened with exposure, some Nixon Administration officials formed and executed a criminal conspiracy to obstruct justice. Evidence now available suggests a strong probability that the Nixon Administration was conducting a covert assault on American liberty and an insurrection and rebellion against constitutional government itself, an insurrection and rebellion which might have succeeded but for timely intervention by a courageous free press, an enlightened Congress, and a diligent Judiciary dedicated to preserving the rule of law.

Certainly the summer and early fall of 1974 were a period of popular discontent, as the full extent of the Nixon Administration's misdeeds became known, and public trust in government virtually collapsed. After Mr. Nixon's resignation in August, the public clamor over the whole Watergate episode did not immediately subside; attention continued to focus on Mr. Nixon and his fate. When Mr. Ford became President, the executive branch was foundering in the wreckage of Watergate, and the country was in the grips of an apparently uncontrollable inflationary spiral and an energy crisis of unprecedented proportions.

Under these circumstances, President Ford concluded that the public interest required *positive steps to end the divisions caused by Watergate and to shift the focus of attention from the immediate problem of Mr. Nixon to the hard social and economic problems which were of more lasting significance.*

By pardoning Richard Nixon, who many believed was the leader of a conspiratorial insurrection and rebellion against American liberty and constitutional government, President Ford was taking steps, in the words of Alexander Hamilton in The Federalist, to *"restore the tranquillity of the commonwealth" by a "well-timed offer of pardon"* to the putative rebel leader. President Ford's pardon of Richard M. Nixon was thus within the letter and the spirit of the Presidential Pardoning Power granted by the Constitution. It was a prudent public policy judgment.

The fact that Mr. Nixon had been neither indicted nor convicted of an offense against the United States does not affect the validity of the pardon. *Ex parte Garland* (1867). In that case the Supreme Court considered the nature of the President's Pardoning Power, and the effect of a Presidential pardon. Mr. Justice Field, speaking for the court, said that the Pardoning Power is *"unlimited,"* except in cases of impeachment. "[The Power] extends to every offense known to the law, and may be exercised *at any time after its commission, either before legal proceedings are taken*, or during their pendency, or after conviction and judgment. . . . The be-

nign prerogative of mercy reposed in [the President] cannot be fettered by any legislative restrictions.

"Such being the case, the inquiry arises as to the effect and operation of a pardon, and on this point all the authorities concur. A pardon reaches both the punishment prescribed for the offense and the guilt of the offender; and when the pardon is full, it releases the punishment and blots out of existence the guilt. . . . If granted before conviction, it prevents any of the penalties and disabilities consequent from conviction from attaching. . . .

"There is only this limitation to its operation: it does not restore offices forfeited, or property or interests vested in others in consequence of the conviction and judgment.". . . However, ". . . as the very essence of a pardon is forgiveness or remission of penalty, a pardon implies guilt; *it does not obliterate the fact of the commission of the crime and the conviction thereof; it does not wash out the moral stain; as has been tersely said; it involves forgiveness and not forgetfulness."* *Page v. Watson* [Florida Supreme Court, 1938]. (Emphasis supplied.)

The . . . motion to dismiss this action is hereby granted.

The power to pardon continues to be an important executive prerogative. Often it is used to extend mercy where, because of special circumstances, strict application of the law would lead to unjust results. At times, however, its use is controversial because of political implications. For example, in December 1992, shortly after he had been defeated for reelection, President George H. W. Bush granted pardons to six former executive branch officials, including former secretary of defense Caspar Weinberger. Those pardoned faced criminal charges for alleged illegal dealings with Iran. President Bill Clinton also faced his share of criticism for his "11th hour" pardon of 140 individuals, including former housing secretary Henry Cisneros.

THE PRESIDENT AND FOREIGN POLICY

There can be no doubt that the Constitution confers on the president special authority over matters of foreign policy. A review of the powers granted to the chief executive by the Constitution demonstrates why this is the case.

First, Article II, Section 2, assigns to the president the role of commander in chief of the army and navy. The military capability of a nation clearly is tied to its foreign policy. Military power not only enables a nation to deter hostile actions from other countries, but also it can be used as a credible threat to persuade other nations to follow certain preferred courses of action. Armed interventions and full-scale wars can be major elements in executing a nation's foreign policy. Modern military actions, both small and large, taken by the United States in Grenada, Panama, and the Persian Gulf demonstrate the use of this power.

Second, Article II gives the president the sole authority to make treaties on behalf of the United States. These international agreements may cover almost any area of interaction among nations, including defense pacts, economic understandings, and human rights accords.

Third, the president selects the individuals to represent the United States in contacts with other nations. The power to appoint ambassadors and ministers influences U.S. relations with the leaders of other states.

Fourth, Article II, Section 3, provides that the president is the appropriate official to receive ambassadors and ministers from foreign nations. When the president accepts the credentials of foreign emissaries, the act confers U.S. recognition on the governments they represent. This provision also means that when foreign diplomats communicate with the United States they must do so through the president.

The Supreme Court has endorsed the notion that by the sum of these powers the Constitution has entrusted the president with the primary responsibility for creating and implementing foreign policy. For the most comprehensive statement of this position we need to refer once again to the Court's decision in *United States v. Curtiss-Wright Export Corp.* As you recall, this case is discussed in Chapter 3 in terms of the constitutional limits on the delegation of legislative power to the executive branch. But Justice George Sutherland's opinion for the Court also develops nicely the president's constitutional position in matters of foreign policy. A brief review of the essential facts appears here to remind you of the issues involved in the dispute.

United States v. Curtiss-Wright Export Corp.

299 U.S. 304 (1936)
http://laws.findlaw.com/US/299/304.html
Vote: 7 (Brandeis, Butler, Cardozo, Hughes, Roberts,
*   Sutherland, Van Devanter)*
*   1 (McReynolds)*
Opinion of the Court: Sutherland
Not participating: Stone

On May 28, 1934, Congress passed a joint resolution aimed at quelling the war between Bolivia and Paraguay over the Chaco region. The resolution gave the president the power to prohibit arms sales to the warring parties if that would help to reestablish peace. Once the president issued a proclamation to that effect, the sale of any arms and ammunition to the hostile nations would constitute a crime punishable by a fine and/or imprisonment. The day after passage of the joint resolution, President Roosevelt announced the arms sale prohibition, and the criminal sanctions immediately went into effect. On November 14, 1935, Roosevelt issued a second proclamation revoking the first.

On January 27, 1936, a grand jury returned an indictment against Curtiss-Wright Export Corporation charging that the company conspired to sell military equipment to Bolivia during the period covered by the first proclamation. Curtiss-Wright moved to quash the indictment and received a favorable ruling from the federal district court on one of the three points it asserted. The United States appealed to the Supreme Court. After explaining that Congress had not engaged in an unconstitutional delegation of powers to the executive branch, Justice Sutherland described the role the Constitution prescribes for the president in the area of foreign policy.

MR. JUSTICE SUTHERLAND delivered the opinion of the Court.

Not only, as we have shown, is the federal power over external affairs in origin and essential character different from that over internal affairs, but participation in the exercise of the power is significantly limited. In this vast external realm, with its important, complicated, delicate and manifold problems, the President alone has the power to speak or listen as a representative of the nation. He *makes* treaties with the advice and consent of the Senate; but he alone negotiates. Into the field of negotiation the Senate cannot intrude; and Congress itself is powerless to invade it. As Marshall said in his great argument of March 7, 1800, in the House of Representatives, "The President is the sole organ of the nation in its external relations, and its sole representative with foreign nations." The Senate Committee on Foreign Relations at a very early day in our history (February 15, 1816), reported to the Senate, among other things, as follows:

"The President is the constitutional representative of the United States with regard to foreign nations. He manages our concerns with foreign nations and must necessarily be most competent to determine when, how, and upon what subjects negotiation may be urged with the greatest prospect of success. For his conduct he is responsible to the Constitution. The committee consider this responsibility the surest pledge for the faithful discharge of his duty. They think the interference of the Senate in the direction of foreign negotiations calculated to diminish that responsibility and thereby to impair the best security for the national safety. The nature of transactions with foreign nations, moreover, requires caution and unity of design, and their success frequently depends on secrecy and dispatch."

It is important to bear in mind that we are here dealing not alone with an authority vested in the President by an exertion of legislative power, but with such an authority plus the very delicate, plenary and exclusive power of the President as the sole organ of the federal government in the field of international relations—a power which does not require as a basis for its exercise an act of Congress, but which, of course, like every other governmental power, must be exercised in subordination to the applicable provisions of the Constitution. It is quite apparent that if, in the maintenance of our international relations, embarrassment—perhaps serious embarrassment—is to be avoided and success for our aims achieved, congressional legislation which is to be made effective through negotiation and inquiry within the international field must often accord to the President a degree of discretion and freedom from statutory restriction which would not be admissible were domestic affairs alone involved. Moreover, he, not Congress, has the better opportunity of knowing the conditions which prevail in foreign countries, and especially is this true in time of war. He has his confidential sources of information. He has his agents in the form of diplomatic, consular and other officials. Secrecy

in respect of information gathered by them may be highly necessary, and the premature disclosure of it productive of harmful results. Indeed, so clearly is this true that the first President refused to accede to a request to lay before the House of Representatives the instructions, correspondence and documents relating to the negotiation of the Jay Treaty—a refusal the wisdom of which was recognized by the House itself and has never since been doubted. In his reply to the request, President Washington said:

"The nature of foreign negotiations requires caution, and their success must often depend on secrecy; and even when brought to a conclusion a full disclosure of all the measures, demands, or eventual concessions which may have been proposed or contemplated would be extremely impolitic: for this might have a pernicious influence on future negotiations, or produce immediate inconveniences, perhaps danger and mischief, in relation to other powers. The necessity of such caution and secrecy was one cogent reason for vesting the power of making treaties in the President, with the advice and consent of the Senate, the principle on which that body was formed confining it to a small number of members. To admit, then, a right in the House of Representatives to demand and to have as a matter of course all the papers respecting a negotiation with a foreign power would be to establish a dangerous precedent."

The marked difference between foreign affairs and domestic affairs in this respect is recognized by both houses of Congress in the very form of their requisitions for information from the executive departments. In the case of every department except the Department of State, the resolution *directs* the official to furnish the information. In the case of the State Department, dealing with foreign affairs, the President is *requested* to furnish the information "if not incompatible with the public interest." A statement that to furnish the information is not compatible with the public interest rarely, if ever, is questioned.

When the President is to be authorized by legislation to act in respect of a matter intended to affect a situation in foreign territory, the legislator properly bears in mind the important consideration that the form of the President's action—or, indeed, whether he shall act at all—may well depend, among other things, upon the nature of the confidential information which he has or may thereafter receive, or upon the effect which his action may have upon our foreign relations. This consideration, in connection with what we have already said on the subject, discloses the unwisdom of requiring Congress in this field of governmental power to lay down narrowly definite standards by which the President is to be governed. As this court said in *Mackenzie v. Hare* [1915], "As a government, the United States is invested with all the attributes of sovereignty. As it has the character of nationality it has the powers of nationality, especially those which concern its relations and intercourse with other countries. *We should hesitate long before limiting or embarrassing such powers.*" (Italics supplied.)

In the light of the foregoing observations, it is evident that this court should not be in haste to apply a general rule which will have the effect of condemning legislation like that under review as constituting an unlawful delegation of legislative power. The principles which justify such legislation find overwhelming support in the unbroken legislative practice which has prevailed almost from the inception of the national government to the present day.

This opinion provides strong statement of the president's power in foreign affairs. Note Justice Sutherland's words: the president is the "sole organ of the federal government in the field of international relations." These words may have particular resonance today, in the aftermath of September 11, 2001, and we explore their implications, as well as other Court decisions relating to presidential emergency power, in the next chapter. Still, and suffice it to note here, the Constitution does not leave the president completely unfettered in the pursuit of the nation's foreign policy. In fact, the Framers were sufficiently concerned about the distribution of these foreign policy prerogatives that they gave the legislative branch certain powers to counterbalance those of the executive.

Although the president is commander in chief of the military, Congress has the power to raise and support the army and the navy, to make rules for the military, and to call up the militia. According to Article I, only Congress may declare war. The president has the constitutional authority to make treaties, but a treaty cannot take effect unless the Senate ratifies it by a two-thirds vote. The president's appointments of ambassadors and other foreign policy ministers must be confirmed by the Senate.

But, as *Curtiss-Wright* indicates, the Supreme Court generally has been sympathetic to the executive branch when deciding disputes over the president's foreign policy role. For example, the justices have been quite lenient in the handling of the president's power to make treaties. In **Goldwater v. Carter** (1979) Sen. Barry Goldwater, R-Ariz., challenged President Carter's authority to terminate a defense treaty with Taiwan without the consent of the Senate. The justices were badly divided as to reasons, but seven refused to intervene on political question or justiciability grounds.

The Court also has supported the growing tendency of presidents to enter into executive agreements with other nations. Unlike treaties, these arrangements do not require Senate ratification. Consequently, they are often used when the president wants to avoid the time-consuming and very public ratification process. But executive agreements have their limitations: federal law requires that the president inform Congress whenever such agreements are made, and they can be nullified by acts of Congress. Moreover, executive agreements are not binding on future presidents without their consent.

As early as 1937, in **United States v. Belmont**, the Court not only endorsed the use of executive agreements but also blurred the distinction between such arrangements and fully ratified treaties. The Court held that the international agreements entered into by the president as part of the recognition of the Soviet Union had the force of law within the United States. The same set of agreements later was held to have sufficient force to supersede state law, just as treaties do.[16] Because of the advantages of executive agreements and their approval by the Court, presidents have grown to favor them over treaties. During its first century the United States entered into 275 treaties and 265 executive agreements, but between 1945 and 1998 the nation concluded 882 treaties and 14,350 executive agreements. President Ronald Reagan alone entered into 2,840 executive agreements, but only 125 treaties.[17]

In other areas, too, the justices have allowed the president to take actions in pursuit of American foreign policy that would be highly suspect in domestic affairs. *Haig v. Agee* (1981) provides illustration. Philip Agee was an American citizen living in what was then West Germany.

---

16. *United States v. Pink* (1942). See also *Dames & Moore v. Regan* (1981).
17. Stanley and Niemi, *Vital Statistics on American Politics*, 329.

Between 1957 and 1968 he worked for the Central Intelligence Agency (CIA) and was involved in covert intelligence-gathering in foreign countries. During this period he acquired a vast knowledge of CIA operations and of agents in the field. After he left government service, Agee called a press conference to declare a personal war against the CIA. He said he would do everything he could to expose CIA agents and drive them out of the countries where they worked. Agee pursued this goal by traveling to various countries, using his contacts to identify CIA agents, and then exposing them. He published two books that revealed secret information about the activities of the agency and made public the identities of undercover CIA operatives.

In reaction, President Carter, through his secretary of state, revoked Agee's passport, thereby making it impossible for him to travel abroad legally. Agee claimed that the executive branch did not have the authority to revoke his passport. The Supreme Court, however, interpreted the powers of the president quite broadly and by a 7–2 vote rejected Agee's objections. The Court essentially agreed that the executive branch could use its power to issue passports—or not issue them—as a way of protecting the nation's foreign policy efforts.

The creation of foreign policy is just one aspect of the dealings of the United States with other countries. Another involves the power to wage war—a power that has taken on particular relevance in post–September 11 America. We explore this issue in the next chapter, for, as we shall see, it presents something of an "invitation to struggle" between Congress and the president.

READINGS

Adler, David Gray, and Michael A. Genovese, eds. *The Presidency and the Law: The Clinton Legacy.* Lawrence: University Press of Kansas, 2002.

Adler, David Gray, and Larry N. George, eds. *The Constitution and the Conduct of American Foreign Policy.* Lawrence: University Press of Kansas, 1996.

Berger, Raoul. *Executive Privilege: A Constitutional Myth.* Cambridge: Harvard University Press, 1974.

Bessette, Joseph, and Jeffrey Tulis. *The Presidency in the Constitutional Order.* Baton Rouge: Louisiana State University Press, 1981.

Corwin, Edward S. *The President: Office and Powers,* 5th rev. ed. New York: New York University Press, 1984.

Crovitz, L. Gordon, and Jeremy A. Rabkin, eds. *The Fettered Presidency: Legal Constraints on the Executive Branch.* Washington, D.C.: American Enterprise Institute for Public Policy Research, 1989.

Dickinson, Matthew J. *Bitter Harvest: FDR, Presidential Power, and the Growth of the Presidential Branch.* Cambridge: Cambridge University Press, 1999.

Fisher, Louis. *Presidential War Power.* Lawrence: University Press of Kansas, 1995.

Gerhardt, Michael J. *The Federal Impeachment Process: A Constitutional and Historical Analysis.* Chicago: University of Chicago Press, 2000.

Gillman, Howard. *The Votes That Counted.* Chicago: University of Chicago Press, 2001.

Harriger, Katy J. *Independent Justice: The Federal Special Prosecutor in American Politics.* Lawrence: University Press of Kansas, 1992.

Henkin, Louis. *Foreign Affairs and the Constitution.* Mineola, N.Y.: Foundation Press, 1972.

McKenzie, G. Calvin. *The Politics of Presidential Appointments.* New York: Free Press, 1981.

McLoughlin, Merrill, ed. *The Impeachment and Trial of President Clinton.* New York: Random House, 1999.

Posner, Richard A. *An Affair of State: The Investigation, Impeachment, and Trial of President Clinton.* Cambridge: Harvard University Press, 1999.

———. *Breaking the Deadlock: The 2000 Election, the Constitution, and the Courts.* Princeton, N.J.: Princeton University Press, 2001.

Rehnquist, William H. *Grand Inquests: The Historic Impeachments of Justice Samuel Chase and President Andrew Johnson.* New York: William Morrow, 1999.

Rossiter, Clinton L. *Constitutional Dictatorship: Crisis Government in the Modern Democracies.* Princeton, N.J.: Princeton University Press, 1948.

Rozell, Mark J., and Clyde Wilcox. *The Clinton Scandal and the Future of American Government.* Washington, D.C.: Georgetown University Press, 2000.

Shapiro, Robert Y., Lawrence R. Jacobs, and Martha Joynt Kumar. *Presidential Power.* New York: Columbia University Press, 2000.

CHAPTER 5

THE SEPARATION OF POWERS SYSTEM IN ACTION

I N   T H E   L A S T three chapters we learned that the Constitution endows each branch of government with significant, though hardly unfettered, powers. But just how strong are the lines that divide the institutions? Consider just two examples:

• As part of its legislative responsibility, Congress must set penalties for crimes. But in 1984 the legislature created a special sentencing commission, with members appointed by the president, to establish sentencing guidelines for federal offenses. Could Congress turn over its legislative power to this commission?

• In the Immigration and Nationality Act, Congress gave the U.S. attorney general the power to make recommendations regarding the fate of aliens but kept for itself the power to veto decisions by the attorney general. Could Congress take for itself an executive power—the power of the veto?

As we shall see, the answer to the first is yes and to the second is no. Why? We take up this question in the first part of the chapter, in which we consider two aspects of the separation of powers problem: when Congress gives other branches legislative power and when it takes executive power for itself.

In the second part of the chapter, we turn to the subject of war and national emergencies. As we noted at the end of the last chapter, the power to wage war presents an "invitation to struggle" between the president and Congress because the Constitution provides each branch with significant and potentially overlapping powers. The

president may be the "Commander in Chief of the Army and Navy," but Article I enables Congress to:

• provide for the common Defence and general Welfare of the United States
• declare War
• raise and support armies
• provide and maintain a Navy
• make Rules for the Government and Regulation of the land and naval Forces
• provide for calling forth the Militia to execute the Laws of the Union, suppress Insurrections and repel Invasions
• provide for organising, arming, and disciplining the Militia

It is no wonder, then, that disputes have arisen between the president and Congress—and that the Court has occasionally been asked to resolve the controversies. As you read the cases and narrative about war and national emergencies, consider the justices' responses: Have they tended to side with one branch over another? What bearing do they have on current White House efforts to combat the terrorist threat confronting the nation? How far can the president go without obtaining approval from the legislature?

DOMESTIC POWERS

In our discussions so far, you may have noted a pattern in the Court's decisions dealing with the sources and scope of both congressional and executive powers. On the whole, with a few scattered exceptions, the Court has allowed Congress and the president a good deal of leeway in exercising enumerated and extraconstitutional power. But what happens when the Court is asked to decide disputes in which the branches take on powers not explicitly assigned to them in the Constitution? Have the justices taken a hard line on the separation of powers doctrine?

In what follows, we consider this question by exploring two types of activities that, at least at first blush, seem to cross institutional boundaries in ways that the Framers might not have anticipated: when Congress delegates some of its authority to another branch of government, and when Congress tries to assert powers assigned to the executive and judicial branches.

Although these sections deal with different substantive material, you may note some commonalities in Court rulings. Pay careful attention to how the Court delineates constitutional interactions from the unconstitutional. Has it acted in a consistent manner? Have the justices grounded their opinions in constitutional language or philosophy, or have other factors had a greater impact?

Delegation of Powers

Almost all discussions of the ability of Congress to delegate its lawmaking power begin with the old Latin maxim *delegata potestas non potest delegari*, which means "a power once delegated cannot be redelegated." We could apply this statement to Congress in the following way: because the Constitution delegates to that institution all legislative powers—lawmaking authority—it cannot give such power to another body or person.

Why not? To answer that question, suppose that after you take the final examination in this course, your instructor delegates the responsibility of grading the test papers to a teaching assistant. Being busy with other work, the TA then delegates that task to a roommate who has never taken a constitutional law course. Who would be responsible—the professor, the TA, or the roommate—if your final grade did not fairly reflect your work?[1] The same argu-

ment could be applied to delegations of lawmaking power to a president in charge of executing laws who in turn hands authority over to a bureaucrat.

However, no political institution has accepted fully the language of the Latin maxim. From the First Congress on, the legislature has delegated its power to other branches or even to nongovernmental entities. But why would Congress want to give away some of its power? One reason is that, like the professor in the example, Congress is often busy with other matters and must delegate some authority if it is to fulfill all of its responsibilities. Another is that Congress might be able to formulate general policies but lacks the expertise to fill in the details. As the job of governance grows increasingly technical and complex, this reason becomes even more valid. *United States v. Curtiss-Wright Export Co.* provides yet another reason: the need for flexibility. In *Curtiss-Wright* Congress had given the president authority to issue an arms embargo if such an action would help to bring peace to warring South American nations. Congress recognized that once it enacts legislation it may have difficulty amending it, but that the problems covered by the legislation, such as in the *Curtiss-Wright* example, may require sustained attention. Finally, there are political reasons why Congress might want to delegate. Sotirios A. Barber noted, "A Congress of buck passers is one of the results of the electorate's tendency to reward politicians who are responsive to its immediate wants, not [Congress's] considered constitutional duties."[2] In other words, to avoid dealing with certain "hot potato" issues, Congress might hand them off to others. The delegation of powers issue is tricky: although, in theory, Congress should not dole out its lawmaking authority, as a matter of practical and reasonable politics, it does so.

Not surprisingly, the Supreme Court has found itself enmeshed in this debate. As we saw in *Curtiss-Wright*, it has been asked to determine whether a particular delegation of power is appropriate, constitutionally speaking, and, as in that case, the Court generally has upheld such delegations, even if they involve domestic issues. *Wayman*

1. Craig R. Ducat, *Constitutional Interpretation*, 8th ed. (Belmont, Calif.: Wadsworth/Thomson, 2004), 129.

2. Sotirios A. Barber, *On What the Constitution Means* (Baltimore: Johns Hopkins University Press, 1984), 177.

v. Southard (1825) was the Court's first major ruling on the delegation of domestic powers. This dispute, unlike most in this area, involved a congressional grant of lawmaking authority to the courts, not to the executive. The case asked the justices to determine whether a section of the 1789 Judiciary Act, which gave the courts power to "make and establish all necessary laws" for the conduct of judicial business, constituted a violation of the separation of powers doctrine and, as such, an unconstitutional delegation of power.

Writing for the Court in *Wayman*, Chief Justice John Marshall responded pragmatically. He sought to balance the letter of the Constitution with the practical concerns facing Congress when he formulated the following standard: the legislature must itself "entirely" regulate "important subjects"; but for "those of less interest," it can enact a general provision and authorize "those who are to act under such general provisions to fill up the details." Put simply, Marshall established a different set of rules for the delegation of power, varying by the importance of the subject under regulation. Applying this standard to the delegation of power contained in the 1789 Judiciary Act, he found that Congress could grant courts authority to promulgate their own rules.

Wayman—in theory—created an important precedent for subsequent Courts to follow. We say "in theory" because, although for the next century or so the Supreme Court never struck down a congressional delegation of power, it did not quite follow Marshall's standard. Rather, it took an even broader approach to this kind of case. For example, in **Hampton & Co. v. United States** (1928) it let stand a grant of authority to the president that some suggest failed Marshall's standard. The Court examined the Fordney-McCumber Act of 1922, in which Congress established a tariff commission within the executive branch and permitted the president to increase or decrease tariffs on imported goods by as much as 50 percent. Because Congress gave the president (and the commission) virtually unlimited discretion to adjust rates, an import company challenged the act as a violation of the separation of powers doctrine. The company argued that Congress had provided the president with what was essentially lawmaking power. Writing for a unanimous

Court, Chief Justice William Howard Taft—a former president of the United States—disagreed: "In determining what [Congress] may do in seeking assistance from another branch, the extent and character of that assistance must be fixed according to common sense and the inherent necessities of the governmental coordination." So long as Congress "shall lay down by legislative act an intelligible principle to which the person or body authorized to [exercise the delegated authority] is directed to conform," according to Taft, "such legislative action is not a forbidden delegation of legislative power."

For nearly a decade, the Court seemed quite willing to accept the so-called "intelligible principle" approach to congressional delegations. But in 1935 the Court dealt Congress and the president major blows when it struck down provisions of the National Industrial Recovery Act of 1933 (NIRA) as excessive delegations of power. Box 5-1 describes the circumstances surrounding these cases—**Panama Refining Company v. Ryan** and *Schechter Poultry v. United States*—and the Court's rulings in them. *(For full details, see Chapter 7.)* The NIRA was a major piece of New Deal legislation designed to pull the nation out of the economic depression. In *Panama*, Congress had allowed the president to prohibit the shipment in interstate commerce of oil produced in excess of state quotas; in *Schechter*, Congress had authorized the president to approve fair competition codes and standards if representatives of a particular industry recommended he do so. In both instances, the Court struck down the delegations of power as unconstitutional.

Because Congress passed the NIRA under its power to regulate interstate commerce, we take up the Court's reasons for these decisions from a somewhat different angle in Chapter 7. For now, let us first consider it from a doctrinal perspective: Did earlier precedent, particularly *Wayman* and *Hampton*, necessarily lead to these outcomes? The Court undoubtedly thought so: by wide margins, it justified its opinions in *Panama* and *Schechter* as firmly grounded in past decisions. Eight of the nine justices agreed with the majority opinion in *Panama*, and the one dissenting justice, Benjamin Cardozo, joined the others in *Schechter*, noting that this law constituted "delegation running riot."

BOX 5-1   COURT'S DECISIONS IN *PANAMA* AND *SCHECHTER POULTRY*

	PANAMA REFINING CO. V. RYAN (January 7, 1935)	*SCHECHTER POULTRY V. UNITED STATES* (May 27, 1935)
Problem	The oil industry, as a result of overproduction to meet the demand for oil in the 1920s, began to ship "hot oil" (that which had been produced in excess of state quotas) across state lines as a way of dealing with falling prices.	The depression indicated the need for greater regulation of various industries, particularly prohibitions on certain kinds of "unfair" competition.
Congressional solution	A provision of the National Industrial Recovery Act (NIRA), which permitted the president to prohibit the shipment of hot oil in interstate commerce.	The NIRA, which allowed the president, at the request of industrial trade associations, to approve codes for the entire industry. The codes would regulate trade practices, wages, hours, and other business activities within the industry. Trade associations and other industry groups had responsibility for drafting the codes, which were submitted to the president for approval. In the absence of recommendations from the private sector, the president was authorized to draft the code himself. Once approved by the president, the codes had the force of law.
FDR's action	Issued an order prohibiting the shipment of oil produced in excess of state established quotas.	Approved industry codes.
The specific dispute	Small oil companies challenged the quota system, alleging that it hurt independent, small producers.	The Schechter brothers challenged the Live Poultry Code, which established industry standards and set work hours.
Delegation of powers question	Did challenged sections of the NIRA constitute overly broad (and thus unconstitutional) congressional delegations of power to the president?	
Majority opinion	Struck down challenged section of the NIRA: "In every case in which the question has been raised, the Court has recognized that there are limits of delegation which there is no constitutional authority to transcend. We think [the challenged section of the NIRA] goes beyond those limits. As to the transportation of oil production in excess of state permission the Congress has declared no policy, has established no standard, has laid down no rule."	Struck down parts of the NIRA: "In view of the scope of [the] broad declaration and of the nature of the restrictions that are imposed, the discretion of the President in approving or prescribing codes, and thus enacting laws for the government of trade and industry throughout the country, is virtually unfettered. We think that the code-making authority . . . is an unconstitutional delegation of legislative power."
Cardozo's opinion	In dissent: "My point of difference with the majority is narrow. I concede that to uphold the delegation there is a need to discover in the terms of the act a standard reasonably clear whereby discretion must be governed. I deny that such a standard is lacking in respect of the prohibitions permitted by this section when the act is considered as a whole."	Concurring: This is "delegation running riot."

TABLE 5-1   Powers Delegated to Select Agencies

Agency	Examples of Scope of Power
Food and Drug Administration	• Monitors the manufacture, import, transport, storage, and sale of $1 trillion worth of food, drugs, and cosmetics annually. • Oversees feed and drugs for pets and farm animals.
National Labor Relations Board	• Adjudicates charges of unfair labor practices on the part of employers or unions. • Enforces collective bargaining agreements.
Federal Energy Regulatory Commission	• Regulates the transmission of gas, electricity, and oil in interstate commerce. • Licenses and inspects private, municipal, and state hydroelectric projects.

Was the Court on firm legal ground? One way to think about this question is to compare the Court's rulings here with those in *Wayman* and *Hampton*. Were the NIRA delegations of power more onerous than that in *Hampton*? Or did they not meet Marshall's standard in *Wayman*? Another is to consider the briefs and arguments in the 1935 cases. Before the Supreme Court decided *Panama*, a federal court of appeals had upheld the law as a constitutional use of congressional commerce powers and, in so doing, gave "very casual treatment to the delegation issue," noting simply that it met previously set standards. When the oil company appealed the decision, U.S. attorneys responded with a 195-page brief filed with the Supreme Court. Apparently, "lulled . . . into a false sense of security" by the lower court ruling and believing that "precedent [was] uniformly on their side," the United States devoted only 3 of those 195 pages to the delegation of powers issue. Indeed, the matter probably would not have been seriously considered had it not been for oral arguments. There, the lawyers for the oil company hammered away at both issues, the delegation of powers and the Commerce Clause, arguing that Congress had "laid down no rule or criterion to guide or limit the President in the orders that he may promulgate." [3]

3. Peter H. Irons, *The New Deal Lawyers* (Princeton, N.J.: Princeton University Press, 1982), 69, 70, 71, 93.

Based on this sort of analysis, many scholars suggest that the justices were merely using the delegation of powers as an excuse to strike down New Deal legislation that they fundamentally and ideologically opposed. Whether this is true we leave for you to decide. More important for now is that the rulings in *Panama* and *Schechter* represent anomalies. For reasons we offer later, by 1937 the Court had begun to uphold New Deal legislation, and by the end of the decade it was allowing for all sorts of delegations of power by Congress to a diverse range of executive agencies, some of which are listed in Table 5-1.

What can we conclude about congressional delegations of power? Some analysts suggest that the Court's rulings in 1935 forced Congress to be more specific in the guidelines it sets out. Is that accurate? As noted in Table 5-1, some executive agencies wield power just as enormous as that which the Court struck in the mid-1930s, but since 1936 the Supreme Court has not overturned a law on such grounds (although a few of the most suspect never have reached the Court). Many have concluded that Congress can pretty much delegate as it sees fit.

An interesting example is *Mistretta v. United States* (1989), in which the Supreme Court scrutinized an act of Congress designed to minimize judicial discretion in sentencing. The Court's opinion takes us back to *Wayman v. Southard* and *Hampton & Co. v. United States*.

Mistretta v. United States

488 U.S. 361 (1989)
http://laws.findlaw.com/US/488/361.html
Vote: 8 (Blackmun, Brennan,[4] Kennedy, Marshall, O'Connor,
      Rehnquist, Stevens, White)
   1 (Scalia)
Opinion of the Court: Blackmun
Dissenting opinion: Scalia

Concerned about wide discrepancies in sentences imposed by federal court judges, Congress enacted the Sentencing Reform Act of 1984, which created the U.S. Sentencing Commission as "an independent commission in the judicial branch of government." The commission was empowered to create sentencing guidelines for all federal offenses, to which lower court judges generally would be bound. It was to have seven members, nominated by the president and confirmed by the Senate. Three of its members, at minimum, were to be federal court judges, and no more than four members could be of the same political party.

The commission fulfilled its charge, promulgating sentencing guidelines for federal offenses, but the federal courts were not in agreement over their constitutionality. More than 150 lower court judges found the guidelines constitutionally defective, while about 100 upheld them.

In *Mistretta v. United States* the lower federal court judge had upheld the plan, but the arguments of John Mistretta, who had been convicted of three counts of selling cocaine, were similar to those proffered by judges who did not approve of the guidelines. Of particular relevance here was Mistretta's charge that the act violated delegation of powers principles by giving the commission "excessive legislative authority."

JUSTICE BLACKMUN delivered the opinion of the Court.

Petitioner argues that in delegating the power to promulgate sentencing guidelines for every federal criminal offense to an independent Sentencing Commission, Congress has granted the Commission excessive legislative discretion

4. Brennan joined the majority in all but note 11 of its opinion, which dealt with the death penalty.

in violation of the constitutionally based nondelegation doctrine. We do not agree.

The nondelegation doctrine is rooted in the principle of separation of powers that underlies our tripartite system of government. The Constitution provides that "[a]ll legislative Powers herein granted shall be vested in a Congress of the United States," and we long have insisted that "the integrity and maintenance of the system of government ordained by the Constitution" mandate that Congress generally cannot delegate its legislative power to another Branch. We also have recognized, however, that the separation-of-powers principle, and the nondelegation doctrine in particular, do not prevent Congress from obtaining the assistance of its coordinate Branches. In a passage now enshrined in our jurisprudence, Chief Justice Taft, writing for the Court, explained our approach to such cooperative ventures: "In determining what [Congress] may do in seeking assistance from another branch, the extent and character of that assistance must be fixed according to common sense and the inherent necessities of the government co-ordination." *J. W. Hampton, Jr., & Co. v. United States* (1928). So long as Congress "shall lay down by legislative act an intelligible principle to which the person or body authorized to [exercise the delegated authority] is directed to conform, such legislative action is not a forbidden delegation of legislative power."

Applying this "intelligible principle" test to congressional delegations, our jurisprudence has been driven by a practical understanding that in our increasingly complex society, replete with ever changing and more technical problems, Congress simply cannot do its job absent an ability to delegate power under broad general directives....

Until 1935, this Court never struck down a challenged statute on delegation grounds.... After invalidating in 1935 two statutes as excessive delegations, see *Schechter Poultry Corp. v. United States* and *Panama Refining Co. v. Ryan*, we have upheld, again without deviation, Congress' ability to delegate power under broad standards.

In light of our approval of ... broad delegations, we harbor no doubt that Congress' delegation of authority to the Sentencing Commission is sufficiently specific and detailed to meet constitutional requirements. Congress charged the Commission with three goals: to "assure the meeting of the purposes of sentencing as set forth" in the Act; to "provide certainty and fairness in meeting the purposes of sentencing, avoiding unwarranted sentencing disparities among defendants with similar records . . . while maintaining sufficient flexibility to permit individualized sentences," where appropriate; and to "reflect to the extent practicable, advancement in knowledge of human behavior as it relates to the criminal justice process." Congress further specified four "purposes" of sentencing that the Commission must pursue in carrying out its mandate: "to reflect the seriousness of the offense, to promote respect for the law, and to provide just punishment for the offense"; "to afford adequate deterrence to criminal conduct"; "to protect the public from further crimes of the defendant"; and "to provide the defendant with needed . . . correctional treatment."

In addition, Congress prescribed the specific tool—the guidelines system—for the Commission to use in regulating sentencing. More particularly, Congress directed the Commission to develop a system of "sentencing ranges" applicable "for each category of offense involving each category of defendant.". . .

To guide the Commission in its formulation of offense categories, Congress directed it to consider seven factors: the grade of the offense; the aggravating and mitigating circumstances of the crime; the nature and degree of the harm caused by the crime; the community view of the gravity of the offense; the public concern generated by the crime; the deterrent effect that a particular sentence may have on others; and the current incidence of the offense. Congress set forth 11 factors for the Commission to consider in establishing categories of defendants. These include the offender's age, education, vocational skills, mental and emotional condition, physical condition (including drug dependence), previous employment record, family ties and responsibilities, community ties, role in the offense, criminal history, and degree of dependence upon crime for a livelihood. Congress also prohibited the Commission from considering the "race, sex, national origin, creed, and socio-economic status of offenders," and instructed that the guidelines should reflect the "general inappropriateness" of considering certain other factors, such as current unemployment, that might serve as proxies for forbidden factors.

In addition to these overarching constraints, Congress provided even more detailed guidance to the Commission about categories of offenses and offender characteristics. Congress directed that guidelines require a term of confinement at or near the statutory maximum for certain crimes of violence and for drug offenses, particularly when committed by recidivists. Congress further directed that the Commission assure a substantial term of imprisonment for an offense constituting a third felony conviction, for a career felon, for one convicted of a managerial role in a racketeering enterprise, for a crime of violence by an offender on release from a prior felony conviction, and for an offense involving a substantial quantity of narcotics. . . . In other words, although Congress granted the Commission substantial discretion in formulating guidelines, in actuality it legislated a full hierarchy of punishment—from near maximum imprisonment, to substantial imprisonment, to some imprisonment, to alternatives—and stipulated the most important offense and offender characteristics to place defendants within these categories.

We cannot dispute petitioner's contention that the Commission enjoys significant discretion in formulating guidelines. The Commission does have discretionary authority to determine the relative severity of federal crimes and to assess the relative weight of the offender characteristics that Congress listed for the Commission to consider. . . . The Commission also has significant discretion to determine which crimes have been punished too leniently, and which too severely. Congress has called upon the Commission to exercise its judgment about which types of crimes and which types of criminals are to be considered similar for the purposes of sentencing.

But our cases do not at all suggest that delegations of this type may not carry with them the need to exercise judgment on matters of policy. . . .

The Act sets forth more than merely an "intelligible principle" or minimal standards. One court has aptly put it: "The statute outlines the policies which prompted establishment of the Commission, explains what the Commission should do and how it should do it, and sets out specific directives to govern particular situations."

Developing proportionate penalties for hundreds of different crimes by a virtually limitless array of offenders is precisely the sort of intricate, labor-intensive task for which delegation to an expert body is especially appropriate. Although Congress has delegated significant discretion to the Commission to draw judgments from its analysis of existing sentencing practice and alternative sentencing models, "Congress is not confined to that method of executing its policy which involves the least possible delegation of discretion to administrative officers." We have no doubt that in the hands of the Commission "the criteria which Congress has supplied are wholly adequate for carrying out the general policy and purpose" of the Act.

Affirmed.

JUSTICE SCALIA, dissenting.

While the products of the Sentencing Commission's labors have been given the modest name "Guidelines," they have the force and effect of laws, prescribing the sentences criminal defendants are to receive. A judge who disregards them will be reversed. I dissent from today's decision because I can find no place within our constitutional system for an agency created by Congress to exercise no governmental power other than the making of laws. . . .

The focus of controversy, in the long line of our so-called excessive delegation cases, has been whether the degree of generality contained in the authorization for exercise of executive or judicial powers in a particular field is so unacceptably high as to amount to a delegation of legislative powers. I say "so-called excessive delegation" because although that convenient terminology is often used, what is really at issue is whether there has been any delegation of legislative power, which occurs (rarely) when Congress authorizes the exercise of executive or judicial power without adequate standards. Strictly speaking, there is no acceptable delegation of legislative power. As John Locke put it almost 300 years ago, "[t]he power of the legislative being derived from the people by a positive voluntary grant and institution, can be no other, than what the positive grant conveyed, which being only to make laws, and not to make legislators, the legislative can have no power to transfer their authority of making laws, and place it in other hands." Or as we have less epigrammatically said: "That Congress cannot delegate legislative power to the President is a principle universally recognized as vital to the integrity and maintenance of the system of government ordained by the Constitution." In the present case, however, a pure delegation of legislative power is precisely what we have before us. It is irrelevant whether the standards are adequate, because they are not standards related to the exercise of executive or judicial powers; they are, plainly and simply, standards for further legislation.

The lawmaking function of the Sentencing Commission is completely divorced from any responsibility for execution of the law or adjudication of private rights under the law. It is divorced from responsibility for execution of the law not only because the Commission is not said to be "located in the Executive Branch" . . . but, more importantly, because the Commission neither exercises any executive power on its own, nor is subject to the control of the President who does. The only functions it performs, apart from prescribing the law, conducting the investigations useful and necessary for prescribing the law, and clarifying the intended application of the law that it prescribes are data collection and intragovernmental advice giving and education. These latter activities—similar to functions performed by congressional agencies and even congressional staff—neither determine nor affect private rights, and do not constitute an exercise of governmental power. See *Humphrey's Executor v. United States*. And the Commission's lawmaking is completely divorced from the exercise of judicial powers since, not being a court, it has no judicial powers itself, nor is it subject to the control of any other body with judicial powers. The power to make law at issue here, in other words, is not ancillary but quite naked. The situation is no different in principle from what would exist if Congress gave the same power of writing sentencing laws to a congressional agency such as the General Accounting Office, or to members of its staff.

The delegation of lawmaking authority to the Commission is, in short, unsupported by any legitimating theory to explain why it is not a delegation of legislative power. To disregard structural legitimacy is wrong in itself—but since structure has purpose, the disregard also has adverse practical consequences. In this case . . . the consequence is to facilitate and encourage judicially uncontrollable delegation. . . .

By reason of today's decision, I anticipate that Congress will find delegation of its lawmaking powers much more attractive in the future. If rulemaking can be entirely unrelated to the exercise of judicial or executive powers, I foresee all manner of "expert" bodies, insulated from the political process, to which Congress will delegate various portions of its lawmaking responsibility. How tempting to create an expert Medical Commission (mostly M.D.'s, with perhaps a few Ph.D.'s in moral philosophy) to dispose of such thorny, "no-win" political issues as the withholding of life-support systems in federally funded hospitals, or the use of fetal tissue for research. This is an undemocratic precedent that we set—not because of the scope of the delegated power, but because its recipient is not one of the three Branches of Government. The only governmental power the Commission possesses is the power to make law; and it is not the Congress.

Despite Justice Antonin Scalia's vigorous dissent, *Mistretta* indicates that contemporary justices are no more willing to deviate from the delegation doctrine than their post–New Deal predecessors were. The case of **Loving v. United States** (1996) further underscores the point. Dwight Loving, an Army private stationed at Fort Hood, Texas, robbed and murdered two taxicab drivers from the nearby town of Killeen. He attempted to murder a third, but the driver disarmed him and escaped. Civilian and Army authorities arrested him the next afternoon, and he confessed. After a trial, an eight-member general court-martial found Loving guilty of premeditated murder and felony murder (a homicide committed during the commission of another serious crime). Section 1004 of the Rules for Courts-Martial requires that at least one aggravating factor be found (out of eleven possible categories) before the court can impose the death sentence in murder cases such as this one. In Loving's case, the tribunal found evidence of three aggravating factors: (1) that the premeditated murder of the second driver was committed during the course of a robbery; (2) that he acted as the triggerman in the felony murder of the first driver; and (3) that he committed a second murder. Having found these aggravating factors, the judges sentenced Loving to death. Loving appealed his sentence on the ground that the aggravating factors rules had been established by the president, when that authority belongs only to Congress. This argument was rejected by the United States Court of Appeals for the Armed Forces, and Loving asked the Supreme Court to review his case.

In a 9–0 vote, the justices ruled against Loving. In his majority opinion, Justice Anthony Kennedy noted: "There is no absolute rule . . . against Congress' delegation of authority to define criminal punishments." He went on to write:

It does not suffice to say that Congress announced its will to delegate certain authority. Congress as a general rule must also "lay down by legislative act an intelligible principle to which

the person or body authorized to [act] is directed to conform." *J. W. Hampton, Jr., & Co. v. United States* (1928). The intelligible-principle rule seeks to enforce the understanding that Congress may not delegate the power to make laws and so may delegate no more than the authority to make policies and rules that implement its statutes. Though in 1935 we struck down two delegations for lack of an intelligible principle, *A. L. A. Schechter Poultry Corp. v. United States* (1935), and *Panama Refining Co. v. Ryan*, we have since upheld, without exception, delegations under standards phrased in sweeping terms. Had the delegations here called for the exercise of judgment or discretion that lies beyond the traditional authority of the President, Loving's last argument that Congress failed to provide guiding principles to the President might have more weight. We find no fault, however, with the delegation in this case.

The Court's decision in *Loving*, while restricted to the military context, is consistent with a long line of decisions in which the Court has approved congressional delegation of power to the president or other executive officers. Moreover, the unanimous vote indicates that the justices are not likely to turn away from the delegation doctrine that has developed since the New Deal.

Congress and the Usurpation of Executive and Judicial Powers

The cases we discussed in the last section share a common thread: they involve cooperative relations between Congress and another branch of government, usually the executive. Congress was delegating some of its lawmaking authority—be it the establishment of tariff rates or the prohibition of the shipment of "hot oil"—to an executive desiring, perhaps even requesting, such authority. But Congress is not always so eager to give away its powers; indeed, on many occasions and through different devices, it has sought to exercise authority over both the judicial and executive branches.

In Chapters 2 and 4, we provided one example of a congressional attempt to take on judicial powers. Recall our discussion of the Religious Freedom Restoration Act of 1993 (RFRA), at issue in *City of Boerne v. Flores* (1997). Enacted to undercut the Court's 1990 decision in *Employment Division v. Smith*, the act directed the Court to use a particular standard of law to adjudicate First Amendment Free Exercise claims. But the justices would have none of it. Not only did the majority overturn RFRA, but also it rebuked the "political" branches for attempting to usurp judicial power:

Our national experience teaches that the Constitution is preserved best when each part of the government respects both the Constitution and the proper actions and determinations of the other branches. When the Court has interpreted the Constitution, it has acted within the province of the Judicial Branch, which embraces the duty to say what the law is. *Marbury v. Madison*. When the political branches of the Government act against the background of a judicial interpretation of the Constitution already issued, it must be understood that in later cases and controversies the Court will treat its precedents with the respect due them under settled principles, including stare decisis, and contrary expectations must be disappointed. RFRA was designed to control cases and controversies, such as the one before us; but as the provisions of the federal statute here invoked are beyond congressional authority, it is this Court's precedent, not RFRA, which must control.

Have the justices been equally protective of the executive branch? To address this question, let us consider an important device Congress developed to keep tabs on the executive: the so-called legislative veto. This kind of veto is a constitutional oddity because it flips the mandated lawmaking process. Rather than follow Article I procedures—both houses of Congress pass bills and the president signs or vetoes them—under this practice, the executive branch makes policies that Congress can veto by a vote of both houses, one house, or even a committee. It should come as no surprise that the legislative veto has been the source of contention between presidents and Congresses, with the former suggesting that they violate constitutional principles and the latter arguing that they represent a way to check all the lawmaking power Congress has delegated to the executive branch.

When it was first developed, the legislative veto was not all that contentious; to the contrary, it was part of a quid pro quo between Congress and President Herbert Hoover, who wanted "authority to reorganize the executive branch without having to submit a bill to Congress." The legislature agreed to go along, but only if either the Senate or the House could turn down a reorganization plan. When Congress passed the 1933 legislative appropriations bill with that condition attached to it, the legislative veto was born.

Although Hoover had agreed to the provision, he was less than pleased when Congress actually used it the following year to veto part of the reorganization plan. In fact, his attorney general, William D. Mitchell, decried the legislative veto as a violation of the separation of powers doctrine. That sort of sparring over the legislative veto continued through the early 1980s, but the patterns of debate were somewhat contradictory and confusing. On the one hand, until 1972 Congress had used the device rather sparingly, attaching it to only fifty-one laws *(see Box 5-2)*. Moreover, it did not seem to be a matter that either the president or Congress took very seriously. Dennis Simon, a political scientist, has suggested that presidents have rejected only a handful of laws solely because they contained legislative vetoes and that in those few instances Congress almost always repassed the bill without the veto provision.

On the other hand, presidents have complained about the practice. Dwight D. Eisenhower loathed the legislative veto, claiming that it violated "fundamental constitutional principles." Complaints grew louder after the Nixon presidency, when Congress sought to reassert itself over the executive, enacting sixty-two statutes with legislative vetoes between 1972 and 1979. In fact, in 1976 the House of Representatives came quite close to approving a proposal that would have made all rules enacted by all agencies subject to a legislative veto.

This issue came to a head during the Carter administration. Jimmy Carter, like Eisenhower, despised legislative vetoes. Suggesting that he did not consider them binding, he had the Justice Department join *Immigration and Naturalization Service v. Chadha*, as a test. The result was the first U.S. Supreme Court ruling centering specifically on the constitutionality of the legislative veto. On what grounds did the Court strike down the practice? Note, too, Justice Byron White's dissent. Why did he believe that the Court had committed a grave error?[5]

5. To hear oral arguments in this case, navigate to: *www.oyez.org/oyez/frontpage*.

BOX 5-2   EXAMPLES OF LAWS
CONTAINING LEGISLATIVE
VETOES

International Development and Food Assistance Act of 1975. Foreign assistance to countries not meeting human rights standards may be terminated by concurrent resolution.

Nuclear Non-Proliferation Act of 1978. Cooperative agreements concerning storage and disposition of spent nuclear fuel, proposed export of nuclear facilities, materials, or technology, and proposed agreements for international cooperation in nuclear reactor development may be disapproved by concurrent resolution.

Civil Rights of Institutionalized Persons. Attorney general's proposed standards for resolution of grievances of adults confined in correctional facilities may be disapproved by resolution of either House.

Full Employment and Balanced Growth Act of 1978. Presidential timetable for reducing unemployment may be superseded by concurrent resolution.

War Powers Resolution. Absent declaration of war, president may be directed by concurrent resolution to remove United States armed forces engaged in foreign hostilities.

Immigration and Naturalization Service v. Chadha

462 U.S. 919 (1983)
http://laws.findlaw.com/US/462/919.html
Vote: 7 (Blackmun, Brennan, Burger, Marshall, O'Connor, Powell, Stevens)
2 (Rehnquist, White)
Opinion of the Court: Burger
Concurring opinion: Powell
Dissenting opinions: Rehnquist, White

Jagdish Rai Chadha, an East Indian born in Kenya and holder of a British passport, was admitted into the United States in 1966 on a six-year student visa. More than a year after his visa expired, in October 1973, the Immigration and Naturalization Service ordered Chadha to attend a hearing and show cause why he should not be deported. After two such hearings, an immigration judge in June 1974 ordered a suspension of Chadha's deportation, which meant that Chadha could stay in the United States, because he was of "good moral character" and would "suffer extreme hardship" if deported.

Acting under a provision of the Immigration and Nationality Act, the U.S. attorney general recommended to Congress that Chadha be allowed to remain in the United States in accordance with the judge's opinion. The act states:

Upon application by any alien who is found by the Attorney General to meet the requirements of . . . this section the Attorney General may in his discretion suspend deportation of such alien. If the deportation of any alien is suspended . . . a complete and detailed statement of the facts and pertinent provisions of the law in the case shall be reported to the Congress with the reasons for such suspension. Such reports shall be submitted on the first day of each calendar month in which Congress is in session.

Congress, in turn, had the authority to veto—by a resolution passed in either house—the attorney general's decision. The act specifies:

[I]f during the session of the Congress at which a case is reported, or prior to the close of the session of the Congress next following the session at which a case is reported, either the Senate or the House of Representatives passes a resolution stating in substance that it does not favor the suspension of such deportation, the Attorney General shall thereupon deport such alien or authorize the alien's voluntary departure at his own expense under the order of deportation in the manner provided by law. If, within the time above specified, neither the Senate nor the House of Representatives shall pass such a resolution, the Attorney General shall cancel deportation proceedings.

For a while it appeared as if Chadha's suspension of deportation was secure, but at the last moment Congress asserted its veto power. Congress had until December 19, 1975, to take action, and on December 12 the chairman of a House committee introduced a resolution opposing the "granting of permanent residence in the United States to [six] aliens," including Chadha. Four days later the

House of Representatives passed the motion. No debate or recorded vote occurred; indeed, it was never really clear why the chamber took the action.

That vote set the stage for a major showdown between Congress and the executive branch. Chadha filed a suit, first with the immigration court and then with a federal court of appeals, asking that they declare the legislative veto unconstitutional. The Carter administration joined him to argue likewise. The president agreed with Chadha's basic position, and administration attorneys thought his suit provided a great test case because it aptly displayed the problems with the legislative veto: in this case, as apparently in others, there was no debate, no recorded vote, and no approval by the Senate. Given the importance of the dispute, the court of appeals asked both the House and the Senate to file amicus curiae briefs supporting the veto practice, but in 1980 it ruled against their position, finding that the device violated separation of powers principles.

By the time the case was first argued before the Supreme Court, in February 1982, the Carter administration was out and the Reagan administration was in. During his 1980 campaign, Ronald Reagan claimed to support the legislative veto, but, once in office, he instructed the attorney general to go forward with the *Chadha* case. The Justice Department presented the Court with several reasons why the legislative veto violated the Constitution:

The Constitution explicitly requires that all congressional actions constituting the exercise of legislative power receive the concurrence of both Houses and be presented to the President for his approval or disapproval.

[The veto] violated the constitutional principle of separation of powers because it authorizes one House of Congress to participate in the execution of a previously enacted law.

The House and Senate, which had become parties to the suit, responded this way:

The Constitution provides separately for each of the three Branches, and describes each Branch as vested with the respective functions of legislating, executing, and judging. But the Constitution does not say that the three great functions shall at all times be kept separate and independent of each other, or that the three functions can never be blended or mixed or delegated as among the three Branches. The notion of total separation of the powers "central or essential" to the operation of the

three great departments is an illogical and impractical formulation of the separation doctrine, not a constitutional command.

They also noted that the legislative veto was a "pragmatic" and necessary device reflecting the realities of modern government.

The Court apparently had some difficulty sorting through these claims. After the first round of oral arguments, on the last day of the term, it ordered new arguments, which were held on the first day of the following term. But it took the Court until June 23—almost the whole term—to issue its decision. One reason for the delay was the delicate nature of the problem confronting the justices; indeed, during their initial conference over the case, Lewis Powell recorded Warren Burger as saying the veto "issue is highly sensitive politically. Wish we could avoid the issue." After the Court voted to render legislative vetoes unconstitutional, a worried Chief Justice Burger circulated six drafts of his opinion, knowing that it was going to get "microscopic—and not always sympathetic!—scrutiny from across the park [that is, in Congress]."

CHIEF JUSTICE BURGER delivered the opinion of the Court.

We granted certiorari [to consider] the constitutionality of the provision in §244(c)(2) of the Immigration and Nationality Act, authorizing one House of Congress, by resolution, to invalidate the decision of the Executive Branch, pursuant to authority delegated by Congress to the Attorney General of the United States, to allow a particular deportable alien to remain in the United States. . . .

. . . We begin, of course, with the presumption that the challenged statute is valid. Its wisdom is not the concern of the courts; if a challenged action does not violate the Constitution, it must be sustained. . . .

By the same token, the fact that a given law or procedure is efficient, convenient, and useful in facilitating functions of government, standing alone, will not save it if it is contrary to the Constitution. Convenience and efficiency are not the primary objectives—the hallmarks—of democratic government and our inquiry is sharpened rather than blunted by the fact that congressional veto provisions are appearing with increasing frequency in statutes which delegate authority to executive and independent agencies. . . .

Justice White undertakes to make a case for the proposition that the one-House veto is a useful "political invention," and we need not challenge that assertion. . . . But policy arguments supporting even useful "political inventions" are subject to the demands of the Constitution which defines powers and . . . sets out just how those powers are to be exercised.

Explicit and unambiguous provisions of the Constitution prescribe and define the respective functions of the Congress and of the Executive in the legislative process. . . .

Just as we relied on the textual provision of Art II, §2, cl 2, to vindicate the principle of separation of powers in *Buckley* [v. *Valeo*, 1976], we see that the purposes underlying the Presentment Clauses, Art I, §7, cls 2, 3, and the bicameral requirement of Art I, §1, and §7, cl 2, guide our resolution of the important question present in these cases. . . .

The records of the Constitutional Convention reveal that the requirement that all legislation be presented to the President before becoming law was uniformly accepted by the Framers. Presentment to the President and the Presidential veto were considered so imperative that the draftsmen took special pains to assure that these requirements could not be circumvented. . . .

The decision to provide the President with a limited and qualified power to nullify proposed legislation by veto was based on the profound conviction of the Framers that the powers conferred on Congress were the powers to be most carefully circumscribed. It is beyond doubt that lawmaking was a power to be shared by both Houses and the President. . . .

The bicameral requirement of Art I, §§1, 7, was of scarcely less concern to the Framers than was the Presidential veto and indeed the two concepts are interdependent. By providing that no law could take effect without the concurrence of the prescribed majority of the Members of both Houses, the Framers reemphasized their belief . . . that legislation should not be enacted unless it has been carefully and fully considered by the Nation's elected officials. . . .

We see therefore that the Framers were acutely conscious that the bicameral requirement and the Presentment Clauses would serve essential constitutional functions. The President's participation in the legislative process was to protect the Executive Branch from Congress and to protect the whole people from improvident laws. The division of the Congress into two distinctive bodies assures that the legislative power would be exercised only after opportunity for full study and debate in separate settings. The President's unilateral veto power, in turn, was limited by the power of two-thirds of both Houses of Congress to overrule a veto thereby precluding final arbitrary action of one person. It emerges clearly that the prescription for legislative action in Art I, §§1, 7, represents the Framers' decision that the legislative power of the Federal Government be exercised in accord with a single, finely wrought and exhaustively considered, procedure. . . .

Examination of the action taken here by one House pursuant to §244(c)(2) reveals that it was essentially legislative in purpose and effect. In purporting to exercise power defined in Art I, §8, cl 4, to "establish an uniform Rule of Naturalization," the House took action that had the purpose and effect of altering the legal rights, duties, and relations of persons, including the Attorney General, Executive Branch officials and Chadha, all outside the Legislative Branch. . . .

The legislative character of the one-House veto in these cases is confirmed by the character of the congressional action it supplants. Neither the House of Representatives nor the Senate contends that, absent the veto provision in §244(c)(2), either one of them, or both of them acting together, could effectively require the Attorney General to deport an alien once the Attorney General, in the exercise of legislatively delegated authority, had determined the alien should remain in the United States. Without the challenged provision in §244(c)(2), this could have been achieved, if at all, only by legislation requiring deportation. Similarly, a veto by one House of Congress . . . cannot be justified as an attempt at amending the standards set out in §244(c)(2), or as a repeal of §244 as applied to Chadha. Amendment and repeal of statutes, no less than enactment, must conform with Art I.

The nature of the decision implemented by the one-House veto in these cases further manifests its legislative character. . . . Congress made a deliberate choice to delegate to the Executive Branch . . . the authority to allow deportable aliens to remain in this country in certain specified circumstances. Congress must abide by its delegation of authority until that delegation is legislatively altered or revoked. . . .

Since it is clear that the action by the House . . . was an exercise of legislative power, that action was subject to the standards prescribed in Art I. . . . To accomplish what has been attempted by one House of Congress in this case requires action in conformity with the express procedures of the Constitution's prescription for legislative action: passage by a majority of both Houses and presentment to the President.

The veto authorized by §244(c)(2) doubtless has been in many respects a convenient shortcut; the "sharing" with the Executive by Congress of its authority over aliens in this manner is, on its face, an appealing compromise. In purely practical terms, it is obviously easier for action to be taken by one House without submission to the President; but it is crystal clear from the records of the Convention, contemporaneous writings and debates, that the Framers ranked other values higher than efficiency. . . .

The choices we discern as having been made in the Constitutional Convention impose burdens on governmental processes that often seem clumsy, inefficient, even unworkable, but those hard choices were consciously made by men who had lived under a form of government that permitted arbitrary governmental acts to go unchecked. There is no support in the Constitution or decisions of this Court for the proposition that the cumbersomeness and delays often encountered in complying with explicit constitutional standards may be avoided, either by the Congress or by the President. With all the obvious flaws of delay, untidiness, and potential for abuse, we have not yet found a better way to preserve freedom than by making the exercise of power subject to the carefully crafted restraints spelled out in the Constitution.

We hold that the congressional veto provision . . . is severable from the Act and that it is unconstitutional.

Affirmed.

JUSTICE WHITE, dissenting.

Today the Court not only invalidates §244(c)(2) of the Immigration and Nationality Act, but also sounds the death knell for nearly 200 other statutory provisions in which Congress has reserved a "legislative veto." For this reason, the Court's decision is of surpassing importance. And it is for this reason that the Court would have been well advised to decide the cases, if possible, on the narrower grounds of separation of powers, leaving for full consideration the constitutionality of other congressional review statutes operating on such varied matters as war powers and agency rule-making, some of which concern the independent regulatory agencies.

The prominence of the legislative veto mechanism in our contemporary political system and its importance to Congress can hardly be overstated. It has become a central means by which Congress secures the accountability of executive and independent agencies. Without the legislative veto, Congress is faced with a Hobson's choice: either to refrain from delegating the necessary authority, leaving itself with a hopeless task of writing laws with the requisite specificity to cover endless special circumstances across the entire policy landscape, or in the alternative, to abdicate its lawmaking function to the Executive Branch and independent agencies. To choose the former leaves major national problems unresolved; to opt for the latter risks unaccountable policymaking by those not elected to fill that role. Accordingly, over the past five decades, the legislative veto has been placed in nearly 200 statutes. The device is known in every field of governmental concern: reorganization, budgets, foreign affairs, war powers, and regulation of trade, safety, energy, the environment, and the economy. . . .

I do not suggest that all legislative vetoes are necessarily consistent with separation-of-powers principles. A legislative check on an inherently executive function . . . poses an entirely different question. But the legislative veto device here—and in many other settings—is far from an instance of legislative tyranny over the Executive. It is a necessary check on the unavoidably expanding power of the agencies, both Executive and independent, as they engage in exercising authority delegated by Congress.

I regret that I am in disagreement with my colleagues on the fundamental questions that these cases present. But even more I regret the destructive scope of the Court's holding. It reflects a profoundly different conception of the Constitution than that held by the courts which sanctioned the modern administrative state. Today's decision strikes down in one fell swoop provisions in more laws enacted by Congress than the Court has cumulatively invalidated in its history. I fear it will now be more difficult to "insur[e] that the fundamental policy decisions in our society will be made not by an appointed official but by the body immediately responsible to the people," *Arizona v. California* (1963) (Harlan, J., dissenting in part). I must dissent.

In theory, the Court banished legislative vetoes from the government system because they undermined the spirit and letter of the Constitution. In practice, however, the chief justice was correct to be concerned: the Court's decision had a negligible effect on congressional-executive relations. Since *Chadha*, Congress has passed more than 200 new laws containing legislative vetoes. But even more important is that the practice continues even in the absence of specific legislation—agencies and departments still abide by congressional rejections of policy.[6]

Why has the Court's opinion resulted in such blatant noncompliance? More to the point, why do executive agencies and departments continue to respect the wishes of Congress, even though they need not? One reason is purely pragmatic: because departments and agencies depend on Congress for fiscal support, they relent, fearing retaliation on the part of Congress. Another reason was implied by Justice White in his dissenting opinion: *Chadha* "did not, and could not, eliminate the conditions that gave rise to the legislative veto: the desire of executive officials for broad delegations of power, and the insistence of Congress that it control those delegations without having to pass another public law."[7]

In this particular instance, then, the president may have won the battle but surely lost the war, as the legislative veto continues to operate. Perhaps the U.S. Supreme Court was the biggest loser: its decision offered a "solution" that was obviously "unacceptable to the political branches" and, as a result, will continue to "be eroded by open defiance and subtle evasion."[8]

Such a reaction has not prevented the Court from involving itself in reviewing other actions by or acts of Congress challenged on separation of powers grounds. As we saw in the previous chapter and as touched on in Box 5-3, in many other separation of powers cases the Court has authoritatively ruled for one of the political branches over the other.

An important example comes in *Bowsher v. Synar* (1986), in which Congress again sought to exercise a power given to the president—the responsibility and authority to enforce the laws. The suit involved a challenge to the constitutionality of certain provisions of the Balanced Budget and Emergency Deficit Control Act of 1985, better known as the Gramm-Rudman-Hollings Act. While reading this case, keep in mind the discussions of legislative power in Chapter 3. Did the Court make clear the distinction between legislative and executive functions? Was the Court's response to this statute reasonable, or was Justice White correct when he argued in dissent that the majority invalidated an important piece of legislation on the basis of a trivial objection, placing formalism above substance?[9]

Bowsher v. Synar

478 U.S. 714 (1986)
http://laws.findlaw.com/US/478/714.html
Vote: 7 (Brennan, Burger, Marshall, O'Connor, Powell,
    Rehnquist, Stevens)
    2 (Blackmun, White)
Opinion of the Court: Burger
Concurring opinion: Stevens
Dissenting opinions: Blackmun, White

President Reagan signed the Balanced Budget and Emergency Deficit Control Act, popularly known as the Gramm-Rudman-Hollings bill, into law December 12, 1985. The legislation attempted to control the federal budget deficit by imposing automatic budget cuts when members of Congress were unable or unwilling to exercise sufficient fiscal restraint. The law established maximum budget deficit levels for each year beginning in 1986. The size of the deficit was to decrease each year until fiscal 1991, when no deficit would be allowed. If the federal budget deficit in any year exceeded the maximum allowed, across-the-board budget cuts would automatically be imposed.

---

6. Louis Fisher, "The Legislative Veto: Invalidated, It Survives," *Law and Contemporary Problems* 56 (1993): 288.

7. Louis Fisher, *American Constitutional Law* (New York: McGraw-Hill, 1990), 231. For another perspective on this case, see William N. Eskridge Jr. and John Ferejohn, "The Article I, Section 7 Game," *Georgetown Law Journal* 80 (1992): 523–563.

8. Fisher, *American Constitutional Law*, 281.

9. To hear oral arguments in this case, navigate to: *www.oyez.org/oyez/frontpage.*

BOX 5-3   SEPARATION OF POWERS IN GLOBAL PERSPECTIVE

DURING THE 1970s and 1980s the Supreme Court found itself unusually busy reviewing acts of Congress that were challenged as infringing on the separation of powers implicit in the Constitution. More often than not, the Court agreed with the challenge and struck down the law as infringing too far on the sphere of the executive or the courts.

The Court's decisions in these cases include:

Buckley v. Valeo (1976). The 1974 Federal Election Campaign Act Amendments infringed executive power by giving Congress the power to appoint four of the five members of the Federal Election Commission, which would enforce the law.

Bowsher v. Synar (1986). Congress infringed on presidential prerogatives when it included in the 1985 Balanced Budget and Emergency Deficit Control Act a provision giving the comptroller general, an officer removable from office only by Congress, the power to tell the president where to cut federal spending.

Morrison v. Olson (1988). The 1978 Ethics in Government Act did not usurp executive power when it authorized a panel of judges to appoint independent prosecutors to investigate charges of misconduct by high government officials.

One explanation for the increase in this kind of litigation during this period is that it stemmed from divided government, meaning that the president and Congress were of different political parties. However, President Clinton found that relations could be contentious even with his party in control of Congress. Some of the squabbles were leftovers from previous administrations but had implications for the Clinton presidency. For example, in *Dalton v. Specter* (1994), the Court considered a challenge by Sen. Arlen Specter, R-Pa., to a 1991 decision, reached by an independent commission and finalized by the Bush administration, to close a Philadelphia naval base. By the time the case reached the Supreme Court, the battle pitted Specter against the Clinton administration, which supported the base-closing law. When the Court agreed with the administration's argument that congressional law had not contemplated judicial review of base-closing decisions, the press reported that President Clinton had won a major victory.

Dalton was not the only legislative-executive battle of the 1990s that made its way to the courts. In *Raines v. Byrd* (1997) members of Congress challenged the constitutionality of the Line Item Veto Act, allowing the president to veto specific spending provisions. The justices ruled that they could not decide the question because the suit was not brought by parties who suffered a direct injury as a consequence of such a veto. When President Clinton began using the line item veto, the conditions became ripe for a new lawsuit, *City of New York v. Clinton*, to settle this separation of powers issue *(see pages 212–216)*.

Surely these battles will continue during the next U.S. presidential administration. As George W. Bush took office, the Republicans had a razor thin majority in the House, and the Senate was split 50–50. But, as *Raines* indicates, it is difficult for U.S. legislators themselves to challenge the constitutionality of particular actions. Not so in many other countries, where legislators (or groups of legislators) can take their claims directly to their constitutional court *(see Box 1-2)*. There are no standing requirements that bar them from so doing. Quite the opposite: their constitutions specifically enable them and, in many instances, executives, to bring suits.

Over the past decade or so, such provisions have resulted in a number of interesting holdings. Here are two examples.

After Russian president Boris Yeltsin issued a series of decrees that had the effect of suspending the Communist Party and nationalizing its assets, a group of party deputies asked the country's constitutional court to determine whether the president's decrees were constitutional. In 1992 the court voted to uphold Yeltsin's ban on the Communist Party, but only as it pertained to national bodies; he could not bar local parties and regional party cells, nor could he confiscate property.

On May 26, 2000, the parliament of the Czech Republic adopted amendments to its electoral law that would have dramatic effects on the country's party and electoral systems—including, some argue, helping large political parties at the expense of smaller ones. President Vaclav Havel challenged the amendments in the Constitutional Court. He claimed that they violated Article 5 of the Czech Republic Constitution ("The political system is based on the free and voluntary foundation and free competition of political parties respecting fundamental democratic principles and rejecting force as a means for asserting their interests") and Article 18.1 ("Elections to the Chamber of Deputies shall be held on the basis of universal, equal, and direct suffrage by secret ballot, according to the principles of proportional representation").

SOURCES: Excerpted from Joan Biskupic and Elder Witt, *Guide to the U.S. Supreme Court*, 3rd ed. (Washington, D.C.: Congressional Quarterly, 1997), 74; and Holly Idelson and Pat Towell, "House and Supreme Court Take Hands-Off Stance," *Congressional Quarterly Weekly Report*, May 28, 1994, 1404; *East European Constitutional Review*, various issues (available at: *www.law.nyu.edu/eecr*).

Comptroller General Charles A. Bowsher (left), given enforcement authority under the Balanced Budget and Emergency Deficit Control Act of 1985, was sued by Rep. Mike Synar, D-Okla. (right), who challenged the constitutionality of the law.

Triggering the cuts involved steps to be taken by several government officials. First, the director of the Office of Management and Budget (OMB) and the director of the Congressional Budget Office (CBO) would independently estimate the projected deficit, with program-by-program calculations. Second, these estimates would be jointly reported to the comptroller general of the United States. Third, the comptroller general would review the reports submitted by OMB and CBO and issue a final report with recommendations. Fourth, the comptroller general would send the report to the president, who would issue an order mandating the automatic budget cuts recommended by the comptroller.

The statute's reliance on the comptroller general for the execution of this law presented a potential constitutional problem. The comptroller general heads the General Accounting Office (GAO), an agency created by Congress in 1921 to provide independent audits of the financial activities of executive agencies. The GAO is lo-

cated within the legislative branch, and the comptroller general, although appointed by the president, is an employee of Congress, not the White House. Under traditional views of the separation of powers, no legislative officer may exercise executive authority.

Just hours after the bill was signed, Rep. Mike Synar, D-Okla., who had voted against it, filed suit against Comptroller General Charles A. Bowsher to have the law declared unconstitutional. At the same time, the National Treasury Employees Union took legal action to have the statute declared void. A three-judge district court struck down the statutory provisions that permitted an enforcement role for the comptroller general. Bowsher, on behalf of Congress, appealed.

CHIEF JUSTICE BURGER delivered the opinion of the Court.

The question presented by these appeals is whether the assignment by Congress to the Comptroller General of the

United States of certain functions under the Balanced Budget and Emergency Deficit Control Act of 1985 violates the doctrine of separation of powers. . . .

Appellants urge that the Comptroller General performs his duties independently and is not subservient to Congress. We agree with the District Court that this contention does not bear close scrutiny.

The critical factor lies in the provisions of the statute defining the Comptroller General's office relating to removability. Although the Comptroller General is nominated by the President from a list of three individuals recommended by the Speaker of the House of Representatives and the President *pro tempore* of the Senate, and confirmed by the Senate, he is removable only at the initiative of Congress. He may be removed not only by impeachment but also by joint resolution of Congress "at any time" resting on any one of the following bases:

"(i) permanent disability;
"(ii) inefficiency;
"(iii) neglect of duty;
"(iv) malfeasance; or
"(v) a felony or conduct involving moral turpitude."

This provision was included, as one Congressman explained in urging passage of the Act, because Congress "felt that [the Comptroller General] should be brought under the sole control of Congress, so that Congress at any moment when it found he was inefficient and was not carrying on the duties of his office as he should and as the Congress expected, could remove him without the long, tedious process of a trial by impeachment.". . .

It is clear that Congress has consistently viewed the Comptroller General as an officer of the Legislative Branch. The Reorganization Acts of 1945 and 1949, for example, both stated that the Comptroller General and the GAO are "a part of the legislative branch of the Government." Similarly, in the Accounting and Auditing Act of 1950, Congress required the Comptroller General to conduct audits "as an agent of the Congress."

Over the years, the Comptrollers General have also viewed themselves as part of the Legislative Branch. In one of the early Annual Reports of Comptroller General, the official seal of his office was described as reflecting

"the independence of judgment to be exercised by the General Accounting Office, subject to the control of the legislative branch. . . . The combination represents an agency of the Congress independent of other authority auditing and checking the expenditures of the Government as required by law and subjecting any questions arising in that connection to quasi-judicial determination."

Later, Comptroller General Warren, who had been a Member of Congress for 15 years before being appointed Comptroller General, testified: "During most of my public life, . . . I have been a member of the legislative branch. Even now, although heading a great agency, it is an agency of the Congress, and *I am an agent of the Congress.*" (Emphasis added.) And, in one conflict during Comptroller General McCarl's tenure, he asserted his independence of the Executive Branch, stating:

"Congress . . . is . . . the only authority to which there lies an appeal from the decision of this office. . . ."

Against this background, we see no escape from the conclusion that, because Congress has retained removal authority over the Comptroller General, he may not be entrusted with executive powers. The remaining question is whether the Comptroller General has been assigned such powers in the Balanced Budget and Emergency Deficit Control Act of 1985.

The primary responsibility of the Comptroller General under the instant Act is the preparation of a "report." This report must contain detailed estimates of projected federal revenues and expenditures. The report must also specify the reductions, if any, necessary to reduce the deficit to the target for the appropriate fiscal year. The reductions must be set forth on a program-by-program basis.

In preparing the report, the Comptroller General is to have "due regard" for the estimates and reductions set forth in a joint report submitted to him by the Director of CBO and the Director of OMB, the President's fiscal and budgetary adviser. However, the Act plainly contemplates that the Comptroller General will exercise his independent judgment and evaluation with respect to those estimates. The Act also provides that the Comptroller General's report "shall explain fully any differences between the contents of such report and the report of the Directors."

Appellants suggest that the duties assigned to the Comptroller General in the Act are essentially ministerial and mechanical so that their performance does not constitute "execution of the law" in a meaningful sense. On the contrary, we view these functions as plainly entailing execution of the law in constitutional terms. Interpreting a law enacted by

Congress to implement the legislative mandate is the very essence of "execution" of the law. Under §251, the Comptroller General must exercise judgment concerning facts that affect the application of the Act. He must also interpret the provisions of the Act to determine precisely what budgetary calculations are required. Decisions of that kind are typically made by officers charged with executing a statute.

The executive nature of the Comptroller General's functions under the Act is revealed in §252(a)(3) which gives the Comptroller General the ultimate authority to determine the budget cuts to be made. Indeed, the Comptroller General commands the President himself to carry out, without the slightest variation (with exceptions not relevant to the constitutional issues presented), the directive of the Comptroller General as to the budget reductions:

"The [Presidential] order *must provide* for reductions in the manner specified in section 251(a)(3), *must incorporate* the provisions of the [Comptroller General's] report submitted under section 251(b), and *must be consistent with such report in all respects.* The President *may not modify or recalculate any of the estimates, determinations, specifications, bases, amounts, or percentages* set forth in the report submitted under section 251(b) in determining the reductions to be specified in the order with respect to programs, projects, and activities, or with respect to budget activities, within an account. . . ." (Emphasis added.)

Congress of course initially determined the content of the Balanced Budget and Emergency Deficit Control Act; and undoubtedly the content of the Act determines the nature of the executive duty. However, as [*INS v.*] *Chadha* [1983] makes clear, once Congress makes its choice in enacting legislation, its participation ends. Congress can thereafter control the execution of its enactment only indirectly—by passing new legislation. By placing the responsibility for execution of the Balanced Budget and Emergency Deficit Control Act in the hands of an officer who is subject to removal only by itself, Congress in effect has retained control over the execution of the Act and has intruded into the executive function. The Constitution does not permit such intrusion.

Affirmed.

JUSTICE WHITE, dissenting.

The Court, acting in the name of separation of powers, takes upon itself to strike down the Gramm-Rudman-Hollings Act, one of the most novel and far-reaching legislative responses to a national crisis since the New Deal. The basis of the Court's action is a solitary provision of another statute that was passed over 60 years ago and has lain dormant since that time. I cannot concur in the Court's action. Like the Court, I will not purport to speak to the wisdom of the policies incorporated in the legislation the Court invalidates; that is a matter for the Congress and the Executive, *both* of which expressed their assent to the statute barely half a year ago. I will, however, address the wisdom of the Court's willingness to interpose its distressingly formalistic view of separation of powers as a bar to the attainment of governmental objectives through the means chosen by the Congress and the President in the legislative process established by the Constitution. Twice in the past four years I have expressed my view that the Court's recent efforts to police the separation of powers have rested on untenable constitutional propositions leading to regrettable results. See *Northern Pipeline Construction Co. v. Marathon Pipe Line Co.* (1982) (WHITE, J., dissenting); *INS v. Chadha* (1983) (WHITE, J., dissenting). Today's result is even more misguided. . . . [T]he Court's decision rests on a feature of the legislative scheme that is of minimal practical significance and that presents no substantial threat to the basic scheme of separation of powers. In attaching dispositive significance to what should be regarded as a triviality, the Court neglects what has in the past been recognized as a fundamental principle governing consideration of disputes over separation of powers:

"The actual art of governing under our Constitution does not and cannot conform to judicial definitions of the power of any of its branches based on isolated clauses or even single Articles torn from context. While the Constitution diffuses power the better to secure liberty, it also contemplates that practice will integrate the dispersed powers into a workable government." *Youngstown Sheet & Tube Co. v. Sawyer* (1952) (Jackson, J., concurring).

Bowsher supplied a clear declaration of the boundaries between legislative and executive authority, but the decision had little impact on the legislation. Congress, anticipating the lawsuit, had written into the law certain "fallback" mechanisms to enforce the budget restrictions if any part of the original plan failed a constitutional challenge. This plan removed the comptroller general from any enforcement activity, which eliminated the constitutional violation.

PRESIDENTIAL POWER DURING WAR AND NATIONAL EMERGENCIES

The cases we have considered thus far all involve questions pertaining to the separation of powers in cases of domestic politics. But we should not take this to mean that such questions arise only in domestic disputes. Indeed, questions concerning the constitutional authority to make and wage war have plagued the nation from the very beginning. Even in post–September 11 America, many remain unresolved. Because war and conditions of national emergency customarily demand quick action, there is rarely sufficient time for the dispassionate consideration of legal questions. When national survival is at risk, the country is usually in an emotionally heightened state and may be willing to ignore the limitations on government power that would be insisted upon in peacetime.[10] Once the crisis has passed, the nation turns to other matters, and questions of war do not again capture its attention until the next threat occurs.

Constitutional War Powers

The constitutional authority to send troops into combat has always sparked controversy. As we noted at the beginning of this chapter, the root of the problem is that the legislative and the executive branches both have powers that can be interpreted as controlling the commitment of military forces to combat. The case for presidential control is based on the following passage: "The President shall be Commander in Chief of the Army and Navy of the United States, and of the Militia of the several States, when called into actual Service of the United States" (Article II, Section 2). Proponents of congressional dominance over the making of war rest their case on these words:

The Congress shall have Power . . . to declare War, grant Letters of Marque and Reprisal, and make Rules concerning Captures on Land and Water; To raise and support Armies, but no Appropriation of Money to that Use shall be for a longer Term than two Years; To provide and maintain a Navy; To make Rules for the Government and Regulation of the land and naval Forces; To provide for calling forth the Militia to execute the Laws of the Union, suppress Insurrections, and repel Invasions. (Article I, Section 8)

The distribution of war-making powers as determined by the Framers envisioned a situation in which Congress would raise and support military forces when necessary and provide the general rules governing them. By granting Congress the power to declare war, the Constitution anticipates that the legislature should determine when military force is to be used. Once the military is raised and war is declared, executive power becomes dominant, consistent with the philosophy that to wage war successfully requires that a single official be in charge.

This allocation of powers was more realistic at the end of the eighteenth century than it is today. At the time the Framers considered these issues, the United States was a remote nation far removed from the frequent wars in Europe. It took weeks for vessels to cross the Atlantic, allowing plenty of time for Congress to debate the question of initiating hostilities. Most delegates at the Constitutional Convention did not even anticipate the establishment of a standing military.

Today, with the rapid deployment of troops, air power, and intercontinental missiles, hostile conditions demand quick and decisive actions. The nation expects the president to act immediately to repel an attack and to worry about congressional approval later.

Hundreds of military actions have been initiated by the United States without a declaration of war. The first such action was taken by President John Adams when he authorized military strikes against French privateers. Most of these undeclared actions have been quick rather than prolonged conflicts. However, two major long-term military efforts, the Korean War and the Vietnam War, were conducted without the benefit of a declaration of war by Congress. In fact, Congress has taken the positive action of declaring a state of war only five times in the nation's history.[11]

1. The War of 1812 against Great Britain
2. The Mexican War in 1846

---

10. Clinton L. Rossiter, *Constitutional Dictatorship: Crisis Government in the Modern Democracies* (Princeton, N.J.: Princeton University Press, 1948).

11. Congress also declared a state of war during the Civil War, but this conflict is technically classified as an internal rebellion rather than a true war between independent nations.

3. The Spanish-American War in 1898
4. The First World War in 1917
5. The Second World War in 1941

Occasionally, military actions are begun and ended so quickly that the president's move allows no time for congressional approval; an example is President Reagan's air and sea strikes against Libya in 1986. When military actions extend over greater periods of time, Congress often has given approval through means other than a formal declaration of war. This approval may come in the form of a resolution authorizing the president to conduct some form of military action, such as the 1964 Tonkin Gulf Resolution that granted President Lyndon Johnson authority to use force to repel attacks on U.S. forces and to forestall future aggression. Similarly, on January 12, 1991, Congress passed a joint resolution authorizing President George H. W. Bush to use force against Iraq; Congress gave its approval to the Persian Gulf conflict in words just short of a formal declaration of war. Just days after September 11, 2001, the legislature passed a joint resolution authorizing President George W. Bush to use "United States Armed Forces against those responsible for the recent attacks launched against the United States." A little over a year later, in October 2002, it voted in favor of a similar resolution enabling Bush to use military force against Iraq *(see Box 5-4)*, though some suggest that the resolution did not authorize the war that later ensued. Finally, Congress can give indirect approval to the president in the form of continuing congressional appropriations to support the military action. For example, in the wake of September 11, Congress approved a bill authorizing $40 billion for various military operations and disaster relief.

But Congress has not abdicated its constitutional authority to approve war; in fact, the legislature has been adamant that the president consult it on all military actions. In 1973 Congress passed the War Powers Act over Nixon's veto. This legislation acknowledges the right of the president to undertake limited military action without first obtaining formal approval from Congress. However, the statute requires the president to file a formal report with Congress within forty-eight hours of initiating

hostilities. Military action under this act is limited to sixty days with a possible thirty-day extension. If the president wishes to pursue military activity beyond these limits, prior congressional consent is required. While the legislature intended to impose restrictions on the president with the passage of the War Powers Act, most experts believe the law actually expands the chief executive's right to employ military force. The authorization in Box 5-4 may provide an example. To be sure, it contains language requiring the president to submit to Congress "a report on matters relevant to this joint resolution" at least "once every 60 days." But note the broad wording of the grant of power to the chief executive: "The President is authorized to use the Armed Forces of the United States as he determines to be necessary and appropriate in order to—(1) defend the national security of the United States against the continuing threat posed by Iraq; and (2) enforce all relevant United Nations Security Council resolutions regarding Iraq."

What role does the Court play in times of war? Because it must wait for an appropriate case to be filed before it can act, and because of its slow, deliberative procedures, the judicial branch is least capable of taking a leading role in matters of war and national emergency. Furthermore, the Constitution gives the courts no specified authority in these areas. However, the judiciary is sometimes called upon to decide if government power is used legitimately and if constitutional limits have been exceeded. In times of war and national emergency the executive branch may find it necessary to take actions that would be unlawful at other times. The limits of the Constitution may be stretched to respond to the crisis. When legal disputes arise from such situations, the courts become active participants in determining the government's legitimate authority.

In what follows, we consider the Court's responses to litigation arising during four periods of threat: the Civil War, World War II, the Korean conflict, and the Iran hostage crisis. In the last section, we explain some of the steps President Bush and his administration have taken to combat terrorism. As you read the contemporary material, ask yourself whether, based on your reading of the existing case law, the Supreme Court will uphold any

BOX 5-4   JOINT AUTHORIZATION FOR USE OF MILITARY FORCE AGAINST IRAQ, OCTOBER 16, 2002

THREE days after the terrorist attacks of September 11, 2001, Congress enabled the president to take military action "against those responsible." That resolution received overwhelming support from the Senate (98–0) and the House (420–1).

About a year later, on October 16, 2002, it authorized President Bush to take action against Iraq.

PUBLIC LAW 107-243—OCT. 16, 2002 AUTHORIZATION FOR USE OF MILITARY FORCE AGAINST IRAQ RESOLUTION OF 2002

. . . WHEREAS IRAQ both poses a continuing threat to the national security of the United States and international peace and security in the Persian Gulf region and remains in material and unacceptable breach of its international obligations by, among other things, continuing to possess and develop a significant chemical and biological weapons capability, actively seeking a nuclear weapons capability, and supporting and harboring terrorist organizations;

Whereas Iraq persists in violating resolutions of the United Nations Security Council by continuing to engage in brutal repression of its civilian population thereby threatening international peace and security in the region, by refusing to release, repatriate, or account for non-Iraqi citizens wrongfully detained by Iraq, including an American serviceman, and by failing to return property wrongfully seized by Iraq from Kuwait;

Whereas the current Iraqi regime has demonstrated its capability and willingness to use weapons of mass destruction against other nations and its own people; . . .

Whereas members of al Qaida, an organization bearing responsibility for attacks on the United States, its citizens, and interests, including the attacks that occurred on September 11, 2001, are known to be in Iraq;

Whereas Iraq continues to aid and harbor other international terrorist organizations, including organizations that threaten the lives and safety of United States citizens;

Whereas the attacks on the United States of September 11, 2001, underscored the gravity of the threat posed by the acquisition of weapons of mass destruction by international terrorist organizations; . . .

Whereas on September 12, 2002, President Bush committed the United States to "work with the United Nations Security Council to meet our common challenge" posed by Iraq and to "work for the necessary resolutions," while also making clear that "the Security Council resolutions will be enforced, and the just demands of peace and security will be met, or action will be unavoidable";

Whereas the United States is determined to prosecute the war on terrorism and Iraq's ongoing support for international terrorist groups combined with its development of weapons of mass destruction in direct violation of its obligations under the 1991 cease-fire and other United Nations Security Council resolutions make clear that it is in the national security interests of the United States and in furtherance of the war on terrorism that all relevant United Nations Security Council resolutions be enforced, including through the use of force if necessary;

Whereas Congress has taken steps to pursue vigorously the war on terrorism through the provision of authorities and funding requested by the President to take the necessary actions against international terrorists and terrorist organizations, including those nations, organizations, or persons who planned, authorized, committed, or aided the terrorist attacks that occurred on September 11, 2001, or harbored such persons or organizations; . . .

Whereas the President has authority under the Constitution to take action in order to deter and prevent acts of international terrorism against the United States, as Congress recognized in the joint resolution on Authorization for Use of Military Force (Public Law 107-40); and

Whereas it is in the national security interests of the United States to restore international peace and security to the Persian Gulf region: Now, therefore, be it

Resolved by the Senate and House of Representatives of the United States of America in Congress assembled,

Section 1. Short Title.

This joint resolution may be cited as the "Authorization for Use of Military Force Against Iraq Resolution of 2002".

Section 2. Support for United States Diplomatic Efforts.

The Congress of the United States supports the efforts by the President to—

(1) strictly enforce through the United Nations Security Council all relevant Security Council resolutions regarding Iraq and encourages him in those efforts; and

(2) obtain prompt and decisive action by the Security Council to ensure that Iraq abandons its strategy of delay, evasion and noncompliance and promptly and strictly complies with all relevant Security Council resolutions regarding Iraq.

Section 3. Authorization for Use of United States Armed Forces.

(a) AUTHORIZATION.—The President is authorized to use the Armed Forces of the United States as he determines to be necessary and appropriate in order to—

(1) defend the national security of the United States against the continuing threat posed by Iraq; and

(2) enforce all relevant United Nations Security Council resolutions regarding Iraq.

(b) PRESIDENTIAL DETERMINATION.—In connection with the exercise of the authority granted in subsection (a) to use force the President shall, prior to such exercise or as soon thereafter as may be feasible, but no later than 48 hours after exercising such authority, make available to the Speaker of the House of Representatives and the President pro tempore of the Senate his determination that—

(1) reliance by the United States on further diplomatic or other peaceful means alone either (A) will not adequately protect the national security of the United States against the continuing threat posed by Iraq or (B) is not likely to lead to enforcement of all relevant United Nations Security Council resolutions regarding Iraq; and

(2) acting pursuant to this joint resolution is consistent with the United States and other countries continuing to take the necessary actions against international terrorists and terrorist organizations, including those nations, organizations, or persons who planned, authorized, committed or aided the terrorist attacks that occurred on September 11, 2001.

(c) WAR POWERS RESOLUTION REQUIREMENTS.—

(1) SPECIFIC STATUTORY AUTHORIZATION.—Consistent with section 8(a)(1) of the War Powers Resolution, the Congress declares that this section is intended to constitute specific statutory authorization within the meaning of section 5(b) of the War Powers Resolution.

(2) APPLICABILITY OF OTHER REQUIREMENTS.— Nothing in this joint resolution supersedes any requirement of the War Powers Resolution.

Section 4. Reports to Congress.

(a) REPORTS.—The President shall, at least once every 60 days, submit to the Congress a report on matters relevant to this joint resolution, including actions taken pursuant to the exercise of authority granted in section 3 and the status of planning for efforts that are expected to be required after such actions are completed, including those actions described in section 7 of the Iraq Liberation Act of 1998 (Public Law 105-338). . . .

Approved October 16, 2002.

SOURCE: U.S. Congress. *Congressional Record.* 107th Cong., 2nd sess., 2002. Vol. 148.

or all of these measures. This is an important question; although as of this writing none of President Bush's actions have reached the Court, the justices inevitably will have an opportunity to rule on them in the coming years. Will their decisions favor the administration, or does the answer to that question depend on whether the threat from terrorism continues to loom large, whether the president continues to have support from Congress, or other factors?

Civil War Disputes

If it is a generally recognized constitutional doctrine that government may exercise more power during times of war and national emergency than during times of peace and security, what is not evident from this rather vague statement is at what point the extraordinary powers of the government are activated. This question came to the Supreme Court in *The Prize Cases* in 1863. The disputes giving rise to these cases present the most fundamental questions of the constitutional allocation of the war powers. When does war begin? Who has power to initiate war? What war powers may the president pursue without a formal declaration from Congress?

The Prize Cases

22 BLACK (67 U.S.) 635 (1863)
http://laws.findlaw.com/US/67/635.html
Vote: 5 (Davis, Grier, Miller, Swayne, Wayne)
    4 (Catron, Clifford, Nelson, Taney)
Opinion of the Court: Grier
Dissenting opinion: Nelson

Abraham Lincoln was elected president in November 1860. Before his inauguration on March 4, 1861, seven southern states seceded from the Union, and Lincoln knew that he had to act quickly and decisively to preserve the nation. Beginning in mid-April, shortly after the first shots were fired at Fort Sumter, Lincoln imposed a naval blockade of southern ports. He took this action unilaterally without seeking the prior approval of Con-

gress, which did not enact a formal declaration of hostilities until July 13 and did not ratify Lincoln's blockade until August 6.

Prior to July 13, Union war vessels seized four ships trading with the Confederacy. The owners of the captured ships brought suit to recover their property, claiming that Lincoln had no authority to institute a blockade in the absence of a congressional declaration of war and that the seizures were illegal. Among other matters, the justices confronted this important constitutional issue: Did the president have the right to institute a blockade of ports under the control of persons in armed rebellion against the government before Congress had acted? Lincoln believed he did on the grounds that a state of insurrection existed as a result of the shots at Fort Sumter and he had the responsibility, under various constitutional provisions, to protect the country.

MR. JUSTICE GRIER delivered the opinion of the Court.

Neutrals have a right to challenge the existence of a blockade *de facto*, and also the authority of the party exercising the right to institute it. They have a right to enter the ports of a friendly nation for the purposes of trade and commerce, but are bound to recognize the rights of a belligerent engaged in actual war, to use this mode of coercion, for the purpose of subduing the enemy.

That a blockade *de facto* actually existed, and was formally declared and notified by the President on the 27th and 30th of April, 1861, is an admitted fact in these cases.

That the President, as the Executive Chief of the Government and Commander-in-chief of the Army and Navy, was the proper person to make such notification, has not been, and cannot be disputed.

The right of prize and capture has its origin in the *"jus belli,"* [laws of war] and is governed and adjudged under the law of nations. To legitimate the capture of a neutral vessel or property on the high seas, a war must exist *de facto*, and the neutral must have a knowledge or notice of the intention of one of the parties belligerent to use this mode of coercion against a port, city, or territory, in possession of the other.

Let us enquire whether, at the time this blockade was instituted, a state of war existed which would justify a resort to these means of subduing the hostile force.

War has been well defined to be, "That state in which a nation prosecutes its right by force."

The parties belligerent in a public war are independent nations. But it is not necessary to constitute war, that both parties should be acknowledged as independent nations or sovereign States. A war may exist where one of the belligerents claims sovereign rights as against the other.

Insurrection against a government may or may not culminate in an organized rebellion, but a civil war always begins by insurrection against the lawful authority of the Government. A civil war is never solemnly declared; it becomes such by its accidents—the number, power, and organization of the persons who originate and carry it on. When the party in rebellion occupy and hold in a hostile manner a certain portion of territory, have declared their independence, have cast off their allegiance, have organized armies, have commenced hostilities against their former sovereign, the world acknowledges them as belligerents, and the contest a *war. They* claim to be in arms to establish their liberty and independence, in order to become a sovereign State, while the sovereign party treats them as insurgents and rebels who owe allegiance, and who should be punished with death for their treason. . . .

As a civil war is never publicly proclaimed, *eo nomine* [under that name] against insurgents, its actual existence is a fact in our domestic history which the Court is bound to notice and to know.

The true test of its existence, as found in the writing of the sages of the common law, may be thus summarily stated: "When the regular course of justice is interrupted by revolt, rebellion, or insurrection, so that the Courts of Justice cannot be kept open, *civil war exists* and hostilities may be prosecuted on the same footing as if those opposing the Government were foreign enemies invading the land."

By the Constitution, Congress alone has the power to declare a national or foreign war. It cannot declare war against a State, or any number of States, by virtue of any clause in the Constitution. The Constitution confers on the President the whole Executive power. He is bound to take care that the laws be faithfully executed. He is Commander-in-chief of the Army and Navy of the United States, and of the militia of the several States when called into the actual service of the United States. He has no power to initiate or declare a war either against a foreign nation or a domestic State. But

by the Acts of Congress of February 28th, 1795, and 3d of March, 1807, he is authorized to call out the militia and use the military and naval forces of the United States in case of invasion by foreign nations, and to suppress insurrection against the government of a State or of the United States.

If a war be made by invasion of a foreign nation, the President is not only authorized but bound to resist force by force. He does not initiate the war, but is bound to accept the challenge without waiting for any special legislative authority. And whether the hostile party be a foreign invader, or States organized in rebellion, it is none the less a war, although the declaration of it be *"unilateral."* Lord Stowell observes, "It is not the less a war on *that account*, for war may exist without a declaration on either side. It is so laid down by the best writers on the law of nations. A declaration of war by one country only, is not a mere challenge to be accepted or refused at pleasure by the other.". . .

This greatest of civil wars was not gradually developed by popular commotion, tumultuous assemblies, or local unorganized insurrections. However long may have been its previous conception, it nevertheless sprung forth suddenly from the parent brain, a Minerva in the full panoply of *war*. The President was bound to meet it in the shape it presented itself, without waiting for Congress to baptize it with a name; and no name given to it by him or them could change the fact.

It is not the less a civil war, with belligerent parties in hostile array, because it may be called an "insurrection" by one side, and the insurgents be considered as rebels or traitors. It is not necessary that the independence of the revolted province or State be acknowledged in order to constitute it a party belligerent in a war according to the law of nations. Foreign nations acknowledge it as war by a declaration of neutrality. The condition of neutrality cannot exist unless there be two belligerent parties. . . .

The law of nations is also called the law of nature; it is founded on the common consent as well as the common sense of the world. It contains no such anomalous doctrine as that which this Court are now for the first time desired to pronounce, to wit: That insurgents who have risen in rebellion against their sovereign, expelled her Courts, established a revolutionary government, organized armies, and commenced hostilities, are not *enemies* because they are *traitors;* and a war levied on the Government by traitors, in order to dismember and destroy it, is not a *war* because it is an "insurrection."

Whether the President in fulfilling his duties, as Commander-in-chief, in suppressing an insurrection, has met with such armed hostile resistance, and a civil war of such alarming proportions as will compel him to accord to them the character of belligerents, is a question to be decided *by him*, and this Court must be governed by the decisions and acts of the political department of the Government to which this power was entrusted. "He must determine what degree of force the crisis demands." The proclamation of blockade is itself official and conclusive evidence to the Court that a state of war existed which demanded and authorized a recourse to such a measure, under the circumstances peculiar to the case. . . .

. . . [T]herefore we are of the opinion that the President had a right, *jure belli*, to institute a blockade of ports in possession of the States in rebellion, which neutrals are bound to regard.

MR. JUSTICE NELSON, dissenting.

Upon the whole, after the most careful consideration of this case which the pressure of other duties has admitted, I am compelled to the conclusion that no civil war existed between this Government and the States in insurrection till recognized by the Act of Congress 13th of July, 1861; that the President does not possess the power under the Constitution to declare war or recognize its existence within the meaning of the law of nations, which carries with it belligerent rights, and thus change the country and all its citizens from a state of peace to a state of war; that this power belongs exclusively to the Congress of the United States, and, consequently, that the President had no power to set on foot a blockade under the law of nations, and that the capture of the vessel and cargo in this case, and in all cases before us in which the capture occurred before the 13th of July, 1861, for breach of blockade, or as enemies' property, are illegal and void, and that the decrees of condemnation should be reversed and the vessel and cargo restored.

Lincoln's actions were supported by the barest of majorities. Three of the justices who voted to endorse the validity of the blockade were his own appointees, Samuel Miller, Noah Swayne, and David Davis. They were joined by two Democrats, Robert Grier of Pennsylvania and James Wayne, a Georgian who remained loyal to the Union. The decision is significant for expanding the right of the president to take military action without waiting for congressional approval. It further established that a state of war comes into existence when certain conditions are present, not when the legislature declares that it exists. The decision, however, did not fully settle the issue. The arguments raised in the majority and dissenting opinions in this case seem to reappear whenever a controversy over the power to conduct war arises.

The blockade was only the first of Lincoln's acts of questionable constitutionality. In *Ex parte Milligan* the justices addressed another, this one concerning Lincoln's actions suppressing civil liberties.[12] The ruling came after the president's death and the war's conclusion. Do you think the Court's decision would have been different had the case been heard when hostilities were at their peak and Confederate troops were scoring successes on the battlefield?

Ex parte Milligan

24 WALL. (71 U.S.) 2 (1866)
http://laws.findlaw.com/US/71/2.html
Vote: 9 (Chase, Clifford, Davis, Field, Grier, Miller, Nelson,
        Swayne, Wayne)
      0
Opinion of the Court: Davis
Concurring opinion: Chase

The Civil War was unlike other wars Americans had faced: the enemies were fellow Americans, not foreigners. The conflict touched every part of the nation, and Lincoln particularly worried about the presence of Confederate supporters in the northern and border states. These individuals were capable of aiding the southern forces without joining the Confederate Army. Of special

---

12. For a description of the events leading up to the Court's decision, see Allan Nevins, "The Case of the Copperhead Conspirator," in *Quarrels That Have Shaped the Constitution*, ed. John A. Garraty (New York: Harper Colophon Books, 1964).

The Union Army military commission that tried Lambdin P. Milligan and his fellow conspirators in October 1864.

concern were the large numbers of southern sympathizers, known as Copperheads, who were active in Indiana, Illinois, Ohio, and Missouri. Combating these civilian enemies posed a difficult problem for the president. He decided that the Union was more important than the procedural rights of individuals. Consequently, Lincoln gave his military commanders broad powers to arrest civilians suspected of engaging in traitorous activities. These suspects were to be tried in military courts.

In those areas of the country where hostilities were not occurring, however, the army had no legal authority to arrest and try civilians. State and federal courts were in full operation and were capable of trying civilians charged with treason or any other crime. To allow arrests and military trials for civilians a state of martial law had to be declared, and to do that, the right of habeas corpus had to be suspended. Habeas corpus is a legal procedure with roots extending far back into English legal history; it permits an arrested person to have a judge determine whether the detention is legal. If the court determines that there are no legal grounds for the arrest, it may order the release of the detained individual. Habeas corpus is essential to the doctrine of checks and balances because it gives the judiciary the right to intervene if the executive branch abuses the law enforcement power.

Article I, Section 9, of the Constitution provides for the suspension of habeas corpus in the following words: "The Privilege of the Writ of Habeas Corpus shall not be suspended, unless when in Cases of Rebellion or Invasion the public Safety may require it." This provision posed two problems for Lincoln: First, the suspension provision is found in Article I, which outlines legislative, not executive, powers. And second, if the civilian courts are in full operation and no armed hostilities are taking place in the area, the public safety probably does not demand a suspension of habeas corpus procedures.

These obstacles did not stop the president. Several times during the war he issued orders expanding military control over civilian areas, permitting military arrests and trials of civilians, and suspending habeas corpus. Congress later endorsed some of these actions. Arrests of suspected traitors and conspirators were common and often based on little evidence. Were such actions constitutional under the war powers doctrine? The Court addressed this question in *Ex parte Milligan* (1866), a decision of great importance in defining the wartime powers of the chief executive.

Lambdin P. Milligan was an attorney residing in southern Indiana. As a member of the Democratic Party, with strong states' rights beliefs, his sympathies lay with the Confederate cause during the war. He openly organized groups and gave speeches in support of the South. He also was involved in efforts to persuade men not to join the Union army. At one point Milligan and his fellow Copperheads were suspected of hatching a plan to raid prisoner of war camps in Illinois, Indiana, and Ohio and release the imprisoned Confederate soldiers, who would then take control of the three states. Federal military investigators followed Milligan closely and kept records of his activities and contacts.

On October 5, 1864, under orders from Gen. Alvin Hovey, commander of the Union armies in Indiana, federal agents arrested Milligan at his home. They also arrested four of Milligan's fellow Confederate sympathizers. Sixteen days later Hovey placed Milligan on trial before a military tribunal in Indianapolis. He was found guilty and sentenced to be hanged on May 19, 1865. On May 2, less than a month after the war ended with General Lee's surrender at Appomattox, President Andrew Johnson, who had succeeded Lincoln, sustained the order that Milligan be executed. In response, Milligan's attorneys filed for a writ of habeas corpus in federal circuit court, claiming that Milligan should not have been tried by a military tribunal and that the president should not have suspended the writ of habeas corpus. Uncertain of how to apply the law, the circuit judges requested that the Supreme Court resolve certain questions regarding the legal authority of a military commission to try and sentence Milligan.

Nine months later, in March 1866, the Court heard the *Milligan* case. Oral arguments took place at a time of heightened political tension. Relations were strained between Johnson, who supported a moderate position toward the reintroduction of the southern states into the Union, and the Radical Republicans in Congress, who demanded a more severe Reconstruction policy. A majority of the justices opposed the military trials at issue in *Milligan*, but there was concern about possible congressional retaliation if the justices struck a blow against military authority. The Court at this point was quite vulnerable, having suffered a decline in prestige because of the infamous decision in *Scott v. Sandford*. But the justices had a potential ally in Johnson. The president op-

posed the use of military tribunals, and the Radicals had not yet gained sufficient strength to override a veto of a congressional act. On April 3, 1866, the Court announced its decision in *Milligan*, but formal opinions were not issued until eight months later.

MR. JUSTICE DAVIS delivered the opinion of the Court.

Milligan insists that said military commission had no jurisdiction to try him upon the charges preferred, or upon any charges whatever; because he was a citizen of the United States and the State of Indiana, and had not been, since the commencement of the late Rebellion, a resident of any of the States whose citizens were arrayed against the government, and that the right of trial by jury was guaranteed to him by the Constitution of the United States. . . .

The importance of the main question presented by this record cannot be overstated; for it involves the very framework of the government and the fundamental principles of American liberty.

During the late wicked Rebellion, the temper of the times did not allow that calmness in deliberation and discussion so necessary to a correct conclusion of a purely judicial question. *Then*, considerations of safety were mingled with the exercise of power; and feelings and interests prevailed which are happily terminated. *Now* that the public safety is assured, this question, as well as all others, can be discussed and decided without passion or the admixture of any element not required to form a legal judgment. We approach the investigation of this case, fully sensible of the magnitude of the inquiry and the necessity of full and cautious deliberation. . . .

The controlling question in the case is this: Upon the *facts* stated in Milligan's petition, and the exhibits filed, had the military commission mentioned in it *jurisdiction*, legally, to try and sentence him? Milligan, not a resident of one of the rebellious states, or a prisoner of war, but a citizen of Indiana for twenty years past, and never in the military or naval service, is, while at his home, arrested by the military power of the United States, imprisoned, and, on certain criminal charges preferred against him, tried, convicted, and sentenced to be hanged by a military commission, organized under the direction of the military commander of the military district of Indiana. Had this tribunal the *legal* power and authority to try and punish this man?

No graver question was ever considered by this court, nor one which more nearly concerns the rights of the whole people, for it is the birthright of every American citizen when charged with crime, to be tried and punished according to law. The power of punishment is alone through the means which the laws have provided for that purpose, and, if they are ineffectual, there is an immunity from punishment, no matter how great an offender the individual may be, or how much his crimes may have shocked the sense of justice of the country, or endangered its safety. By the protection of the law human rights are secured; withdraw that protection, and they are at the mercy of wicked rulers, or the clamor of an excited people. If there was law to justify this military trial, it is not our province to interfere; if there was not, it is our duty to declare the nullity of the whole proceedings. The decision of this question does not depend on argument or judicial precedents, numerous and highly illustrative as they are. These precedents inform us of the extent of the struggle to preserve liberty and to relieve those in civil life from military trials. The founders of our government were familiar with the history of that struggle; and secured in a written constitution every right which the people had wrested from power during a contest of ages. By that Constitution and the laws authorized by it this question must be determined. The provisions of that instrument on the administration of criminal justice are too plain and direct, to leave room for misconstruction or doubt of their true meaning. Those applicable to this case are found in that clause of the original Constitution which says, "That the trial of all crimes, except in case of impeachment, shall be by jury;". . .

Time has proven the discernment of our ancestors; for even these provisions, expressed in such plain English words, that it would seem the ingenuity of man could not evade them, are now, after the lapse of more than seventy years, sought to be avoided. Those great and good men foresaw that troublous times would arise, when rulers and people would become restive under restraint, and seek by sharp and decisive measures to accomplish ends deemed just and proper; and that the principles of constitutional liberty would be in peril, unless established by irrepealable law. The history of the world had taught them that what was done in the past might be attempted in the future. The Constitution of the United States is a law for rulers and people, equally in war and in peace, and covers with the shield of its

Five southern sympathizers were charged with treason by military authorities. The question of the constitutionality of their arrests and trials before a military commission was settled by the Supreme Court in *Ex parte Milligan* (1866). Clockwise from top: William A. Bowles, Andrew Humphreys, Stephen Horsey, H. Heffren, and Lambdin P. Milligan.

protection all classes of men, at all times, and under all circumstances. No doctrine, involving more pernicious consequences, was ever invented by the wit of man than that any of its provisions can be suspended during any of the great exigencies of government. Such a doctrine leads directly to anarchy or despotism, but the theory of necessity on which it is based is false; for the government, within the Constitution, has all the powers granted to it, which are necessary to preserve its existence; as has been happily proved by the result of the great effort to throw off its just authority.

Have any of the rights guaranteed by the Constitution been violated in the case of Milligan? and if so, what are they?

Every trial involves the exercise of judicial power; and from what source did the military commission that tried him derive their authority? Certainly no part of the judicial power of the country was conferred on them; because the Constitution expressly vests it "in one supreme court and such inferior courts as the Congress may from time to time ordain and establish," and it is not pretended that the commission was a court ordained and established by Congress. They cannot justify on the mandate of the President; because he is controlled by law, and has his appropriate sphere of duty, which is to execute, not to make, the laws; and there is "no unwritten criminal code to which resort can be had as a source of jurisdiction."

But it is said that the jurisdiction is complete under the "laws and usages of war."

It can serve no useful purpose to inquire what those laws and usages are, whence they originated, where found, and on whom they operate; they can never be applied to citizens in states which have upheld the authority of the government, and where the courts are open and their process unobstructed. This court has judicial knowledge that in Indiana the Federal authority was always unopposed, and its courts always open to hear criminal accusations and redress grievances; and no usage of war could sanction a military trial there for any offence whatever of a citizen in civil life, in nowise connected with the military service. Congress could grant no such power; and to the honor of our national legislature be it said, it has never been provoked by the state of the country even to attempt its exercise. One of the plainest constitutional provisions was, therefore, infringed when Milligan was tried by a court not ordained and established by Congress, and not composed of judges appointed during good behavior.

Why was he not delivered to the Circuit Court of Indiana to be proceeded against according to law? No reason of necessity could be urged against it; because Congress had declared penalties against the offences charged, provided for their punishment, and directed that court to hear and determine them. And soon after this military tribunal was ended, the Circuit Court met, peacefully transacted its business, and adjourned. It needed no bayonets to protect it, and required no military aid to execute its judgments. It was held in a state, eminently distinguished for patriotism, by judges commissioned during the Rebellion, who were provided with juries, upright, intelligent, and selected by a marshal appointed by the President. The government had no right to conclude that Milligan, if guilty, would not receive in that court merited punishment; for its records disclose that it was constantly engaged in the trial of similar offences, and was never interrupted in its administration of criminal justice. If it was dangerous, in the distracted condition of affairs, to leave Milligan unrestrained of his liberty, because he "conspired against the government, afforded aid and comfort to rebels, and incited the people to insurrection," the law said arrest him, confine him closely, render him powerless to do further mischief; and then present his case to the grand jury of the district, with proofs of his guilt, and, if indicted, try him according to the course of the common law. If this had been done, the Constitution would have been vindicated, the law of 1863 enforced, and the securities for personal liberty preserved and defended. . . .

The discipline necessary to the efficiency of the army and navy, required other and swifter modes of trial than are furnished by the common law courts; and, in pursuance of the power conferred by the Constitution, Congress has declared the kinds of trial, and the manner in which they shall be conducted, for offences committed while the party is in the military or naval service. Every one connected with these branches of the public service is amenable to the jurisdiction which Congress has created for their government, and, while thus serving, surrenders his right to be tried by the civil courts. All other persons, citizens of states where the courts are open, if charged with crime, are guaranteed the inestimable privilege of trial by jury. This privilege is a vital principle, underlying the whole administration of criminal justice; it is not held by sufferance, and cannot be frittered away on any plea of state or political necessity. When peace prevails, and the authority of the government is undisputed, there is no difficulty of preserving the safeguards of liberty; for the ordinary modes of trial are never neglected, and no one wishes it otherwise; but if society is disturbed by civil commotion—if the passions of men are aroused and the restraints of law weakened, if not disregarded—these safeguards need, and should receive, the watchful care of those intrusted with the guardianship of the Constitution and laws. In no other way can we transmit to posterity unimpaired the blessings of liberty, consecrated by the sacrifices of the Revolution.

It is claimed that martial law covers with its broad mantle the proceedings of this military commission. The proposition is this: that in a time of war the commander of an armed force (if in his opinion the exigencies of the country demand it, and of which he is to judge), has the power, within the lines of his military district, to suspend all civil rights and their remedies, and subject citizens as well as soldiers to the rule of his will; and in the exercise of his lawful authority cannot be restrained, except by his superior officer or the President of the United States.

If this position is sound to the extent claimed, then when war exists, foreign or domestic, and the country is subdivided into military departments for mere convenience, the commander of one of them can, if he chooses, within his limits, on the plea of necessity, with the approval of the Executive, substitute military force for and to the exclusion of the laws, and punish all persons, as he thinks right and proper, without fixed or certain rules.

The statement of this proposition shows its importance; for, if true, republican government is a failure, and there is an end of liberty regulated by law. Martial law, established on such a basis, destroys every guarantee of the Constitution, and effectually renders the "military independent of and superior to the civil power"—the attempt to do which by the King of Great Britain was deemed by our fathers such an offence, that they assigned it to the world as one of the causes which impelled them to declare their independence. Civil liberty and this kind of martial law cannot endure together; the antagonism is irreconcilable; and, in the conflict, one or the other must perish.

This nation, as experience has proved, cannot always remain at peace, and has no right to expect that it will always have wise and humane rulers, sincerely attached to the principles of the Constitution. Wicked men, ambitious of power, with hatred of liberty and contempt of law, may fill the place once occupied by Washington and Lincoln; and if this right is conceded, and the calamities of war again befall us, the dangers to human liberty are frightful to contemplate. If our fathers had failed to provide for just such a contingency, they would have been false to the trust reposed in them. They knew—the history of the world told them—the nation they were founding, be its existence short or long, would be involved in war; how often or how long continued, human foresight could not tell; and that unlimited power, wherever lodged at such a time, was especially hazardous to freemen. For this, and other equally weighty reasons, they secured the inheritance they had fought to maintain, by incorporating in a written constitution the safeguards which time had proved were essential to its preservation. Not one of these safeguards can the President, or Congress, or the Judiciary disturb, except the one concerning the writ of habeas corpus.

It is essential to the safety of every government that, in a great crisis, like the one we have just passed through, there should be a power somewhere of suspending the writ of habeas corpus. In every war, there are men of previously good character, wicked enough to counsel their fellow-citizens to resist the measures deemed necessary by a good government to sustain its just authority and overthrow its enemies; and their influence may lead to dangerous combinations. In the emergency of the times, an immediate public investigation according to law may not be possible; and yet, the peril to the country may be too imminent to suffer such persons to go at large. Unquestionably, there is then an exigency which demands that the government, if it should see fit in the exercise of a proper discretion to make arrests, should not be required to produce the persons arrested in answer to a writ of habeas corpus. The Constitution goes no further. It does not say after a writ of habeas corpus is denied a citizen, that he shall be tried otherwise than by the course of the common law; if it had intended this result, it was easy by the use of direct words to have accomplished it. The illustrious men who framed that instrument were guarding the foundations of civil liberty against the abuses of unlimited power; they were full of wisdom, and the lessons of history informed them that a trial by an established court, assisted by an impartial jury, was the only sure way of protecting the citizen against oppression and wrong. Knowing this, they limited the suspension to one great right, and left the rest to remain forever inviolable. But, it is insisted that the safety of the country in time of war demands that this broad claim for martial law shall be sustained. If this were true, it could be well said that a country, preserved at the sacrifice of all the cardinal principles of liberty, is not worth the cost of preservation. Happily, it is not so.

It will be borne in mind that this is not a question of the power to proclaim martial law, when war exists in a community and the courts and civil authorities are overthrown. Nor is it a question what rule a military commander, at the head of his army, can impose on states in rebellion to cripple their resources and quell the insurrection. The jurisdiction claimed is much more extensive. The necessities of the service, during the late Rebellion, required that the loyal states should be placed within the limits of certain military districts and commanders appointed in them; and, it is urged, that this, in a military sense, constituted them the theatre of military operations; and, as in this case, Indiana had been and was again threatened with invasion by the enemy, the occasion was furnished to establish martial law. The conclusion does not follow from the premises. If armies were collected in Indiana, they were to be employed in another locality, where the laws were obstructed and the national authority disputed. On her soil there was no hostile foot; if once invaded, that invasion was at an end, and with it all pretext for martial law. Martial law cannot arise from a threatened invasion. The necessity must be actual and present; the invasion real, such as effectually closes the courts and deposes the civil administration.

It is difficult to see how the safety of the country required martial law in Indiana. If any of her citizens were plotting treason, the power of arrest could secure them, until the government was prepared for their trial, when the courts were open and ready to try them. It was as easy to protect witnesses before a civil as a military tribunal; and as there could be no wish to convict, except on sufficient legal evidence, surely an ordained and established court was better able to judge of this than a military tribunal composed of gentlemen not trained to the profession of the law.

THE CHIEF JUSTICE delivered the following opinion.

[T]he opinion . . . as we understand it, asserts not only that the military commission held in Indiana was not authorized by Congress, but that it was not in the power of Congress to authorize it, from which it may be thought to follow that Congress has no power to indemnify the officers who composed the commission against liability in civil courts for acting as members of it.

We cannot agree to this.

We agree in the proposition that no department of the government of the United States—neither President, nor Congress, nor the Courts—possesses any power not given by the Constitution.

We assent fully to all that is said in the opinion of the inestimable value of the trial by jury, and of the other constitutional safeguards of civil liberty. And we concur also in what is said of the writ of habeas corpus and of its suspension, with two reservations: (1) that, in our judgment, when the writ is suspended, the Executive is authorized to arrest, as well as to detain, and (2) that there are cases in which, the privilege of the writ being suspended, trial and punishment by military commission, in states where civil courts are open, may be authorized by Congress, as well as arrest and detention.

We think that Congress had power, though not exercised, to authorize the military commission which was held in Indiana.

We do not think it necessary to discuss at large the grounds of our conclusions. We will briefly indicate some of them.

The Constitution itself provides for military government, as well as for civil government. And we do not understand it to be claimed that the civil safeguards of the Constitution have application in cases within the proper sphere of the former.

What, then, is that proper sphere? Congress has power to raise and support armies, to provide and maintain a navy, to make rules for the government and regulation of the land and naval forces, and to provide for governing such part of the militia as may be in the service of the United States.

It is not denied that the power to make rules for the government of the army and navy is a power to provide for trial and punishment by military courts without a jury. It has been so understood and exercised from the adoption of the Constitution to the present time. . . .

We by no means assert that Congress can establish and apply the laws of war where no war has been declared or exists.

Where peace exists, the laws of peace must prevail. What we do maintain is that, when the nation is involved in war, and some portions of the country are invaded, and all are exposed to invasion, it is within the power of Congress to determine in what states or district such great and imminent public danger exists as justifies the authorization of military tribunals for the trial of crimes and offences against the discipline or security of the army or against the public safety. . . .

We cannot doubt that, in such a time of public danger, Congress had power under the Constitution to provide for the organization of a military commission and for trial by that commission of persons engaged in this conspiracy. The fact that the Federal courts were open was regarded by Congress as a sufficient reason for not exercising the power, but that fact could not deprive Congress of the right to exercise it. Those courts might be open and undisturbed in the execution of their functions, and yet wholly incompetent to avert threatened danger or to punish, with adequate promptitude and certainty, the guilty conspirators. . . .

Mr. Justice WAYNE, Mr. Justice SWAYNE, and Mr. Justice MILLER concur with me in these views.

Although the Court's decision was unanimous as to Milligan's claim of illegal imprisonment, the justices split on the power of the government to suspend habeas corpus under conditions presented in the case. A majority of five (Clifford, Davis, Field, Grier, and Nelson) held that neither the president nor Congress, acting separately or in agreement, could suspend the writ of habeas corpus as long as the civilian courts were in full operation and the area was not a combat zone. In a concurring opinion joined by Miller, Swayne, and Wayne, Chief Justice Chase argued that, although the president did not have the power to establish these military tribunals, Congress did.

Before the Court handed down its ruling in this case, President Johnson commuted Milligan's sentence to life in prison, a sentence he was serving under General Hovey in an Ohio prison when the case was decided. Milligan was released from custody in April 1866 *(see Box 5-5)*.

World War II

As we already have seen, the restriction of civil liberties during time of war is not uncommon. Nations pressed for their very survival may feel compelled to deny basic liberties to insure against the efforts of traitors and saboteurs. World War II was no exception. During that period, the government took many steps that amounted to suppressions of rights and liberties. The most infamous of such actions, which we shall discuss shortly, was the internment of Americans of Japanese descent.

Yet another action paralleled the one at issue in *Milligan:* the use of military tribunals. In *Ex parte Quirin* (1942), the Court considered the constitutionality of a presidential order authorizing the use of a military com-

---

BOX 5-5   AFTERMATH . . .
LAMBDIN P. MILLIGAN

BEGINNING with his October 1864 arrest for disloyal practices and continuing throughout the controversy over his activities, Lambdin Milligan claimed that the charges were a fantasy created by the Republicans for political gain. By the time the Supreme Court reversed his conviction and death sentence, Milligan had spent eighteen months in prison. Upon his release, he returned to his hometown of Huntington, Indiana, where he was received as a local hero. Two decades earlier Milligan had moved with his family to the Indiana town from Ohio to farm and practice law. He had also been active in local Democratic Party politics, unsuccessfully running for Congress and governor.

Milligan immediately sought revenge for the treatment he had received at the hands of the military. He filed suit for trespass and false imprisonment against James Slack, a local attorney who first urged that he be arrested; Gen. Alvin Hovey, who had ordered his arrest; and twenty-two others involved in his prosecution. The jury decided in favor of Milligan, but the law placed a $5 ceiling on damages awarded in such cases, limiting the satisfaction he received from his judicial victory.

Milligan ran a successful legal practice in Huntington for an additional thirty years. He retired in 1897 at the age of eighty-five. He died two years later, only three months after the death of his second wife.

SOURCE: *American National Biography*, vol. 15 (New York: Oxford University Press, 1999), 529–530.

---

mission to try eight saboteurs from Germany, with which the United States was at war at the time. While until recently this case has been the subject of somewhat less criticism and notoriety than litigation associated with the internment of Japanese Americans, it is worthy of our consideration. In light of President George W. Bush's order authorizing the use of military tribunals for foreign nationals suspected of terrorism *(see page 315)*, *Quirin,* coupled with *Milligan,* has taken on new relevance.

Ex parte Quirin

317 U.S. 1 (1942)
http://laws.findlaw.com/US/317/1.html
Opinion of the Court: Stone
Vote: 8 (Black, Byrnes, Douglas, Frankfurter, Jackson, Reed,
    Roberts, Stone)
    0
Not participating: Murphy

In his quest to demonstrate "America's vulnerability and the reach of Nazi power," Adolf Hitler commanded his military leaders to devise a sabotage plan.[13] They came up with a plot that would be run out of Chicago and lead, they hoped, to the destruction of railroads, bridges, and other parts of America's infrastructure.

The plan was to be executed by two four-men teams, both of which would set off from France in submarines headed for the United States. All eight men were born in Germany; all had lived in the United States and returned to Germany sometime between 1933 and 1941. Finally, all but one were citizens of the German Reich. (The one noncitizen, Herbert Hans Haupt, had come to the United States as a child but returned to Germany; there was some dispute as to whether he retained his U.S. citizenship.) One team was to land on Long Island, New York, the other in Jacksonville, Florida. The two were supposed to meet in Cincinnati on July 4, 1941.

George John Dasch, the leader of the Long Island team, and his three associates arrived at their destination on June 13, 1941. As the men began to change out of their military uniforms and bury the various explosive devices they had brought with them, John Cullen, a member of the U.S. Coast Guard, spotted Dasch. The German offered Cullen money to keep quiet, but Cullen reported the incident to the Coast Guard, which in turn informed the FBI. In the meantime, the "Nazi saboteurs" had left Long Island for New York City. Once in the city, Dasch told another member of the team, Ernest Peter Burger,

that he intended to tell the FBI about the plot, to which Burger agreed.

Dasch took a train to Washington, D.C., to meet with FBI agents, who he says were skeptical of his story until he opened a briefcase filled with money provided by the Germans. The $82,000 apparently convinced the FBI that it had "something real here." (FBI agents involved with the case refute this story, saying that they took Dasch seriously from the start.)

Dasch's 254-page confession, together with other evidence, enabled the FBI to capture the other seven men by June 27. They too signed confessions.

The arrests of the saboteurs led the FBI to question hundreds of German nationals on the East Coast, with action taken against some. For example, "when it emerged that three of the accused saboteurs had worked as waiters in the United States before the war, the Justice Department ordered the dismissal of all German and Italian waiters, barbers, busboys, housemen and maids from Washington's hotels, restaurants and clubs—on the theory that they might hear too much from loose-lipped customers."

In the meantime, the government had to determine what to do with the eight men they had arrested. President Franklin Roosevelt apparently favored a court-martial. But because the process would require a unanimous verdict and proof beyond a reasonable doubt, the president settled on a military commission that would invoke "lesser standards": for example, a two-thirds, rather than unanimous, vote would suffice for a conviction.

Accordingly, Roosevelt, in his capacity as president and commander in chief of the army and navy, issued an order on July 2, 1942, appointing a military commission to try the saboteurs for offenses against the law of war: Articles 81 (giving intelligence to the enemy) and 82 (spying) of the Articles of War. The order also prescribed regulations for how the trial would proceed.

On the same day, by proclamation, the president declared that "all persons who are subjects, citizens or residents of any nation at war with the United States or who give obedience to or act under the direction of any such nation, and who during time of war enter or attempt to enter the United States . . . through coastal or boundary

---

13. We derive this account from George Lardner Jr., "Nazi Saboteurs Captured!", *Washington Post*, January 13, 2002 (available at: www.law. uchicago.edu/tribunals/wp_011302.html). This article is based on research conducted by political scientist David J. Danelski.

   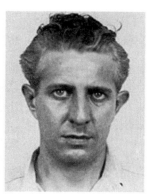

| Dasch | Burger | Heinck | Quirin |

The Long Island saboteurs—George John Dasch, Ernest Peter Burger, Heinrich Harm Heinck, and Richard Quirin—are seen in a series of photographs from the FBI.

defenses, and are charged with committing or attempting or preparing to commit sabotage, espionage, hostile or warlike acts, or violations of the law of war, shall be subject to the law of war and to the jurisdiction of military tribunals." The proclamation also stated that all such persons were denied access to the courts.

In accord with the order, the FBI handed the saboteurs over to the military, which kept them in custody for a trial before the commission.

On July 8, 1942, the commission met and proceeded with the trial, but defense lawyers, believing the deck was stacked against them, decided to challenge Roosevelt's authority to try their clients in a military tribunal. On July 28, after a federal district court denied their request for a writ of habeas corpus, they went to the U.S. Supreme Court, which heard their appeal the next day. By that time the commission had taken all the evidence for the prosecution and the defense and the case had been closed except for arguments of counsel.

On July 31, 1942, the Supreme Court issued a brief per curiam opinion, holding:

(1) That the charges preferred against petitioners on which they are being tried by military commission appointed by the order of the President of July 2, 1942, allege an offense or offenses which the President is authorized to order tried before a military commission.

(2) That the military commission was lawfully constituted.

(3) That petitioners are held in lawful custody for trial before the military commission, and have not shown cause for being discharged by writ of habeas corpus.

The motions for leave to file petitions for writs of habeas corpus are denied.

Apparently, some of the justices had reservations about this holding, but they nonetheless managed to reach a unanimous decision, which, in turn, paved the way for the eventual execution of six of the eight Nazi saboteurs on August 8. (Burger and Dasch were given long prison sentences for their help in securing the arrests of the others.)

But August 8 was not the end of the case for the U.S. Supreme Court. Three months after it had released its per curiam, it took the unusual step, on October 29, of issuing an opinion justifying its decision.

CHIEF JUSTICE STONE delivered the opinion of the Court.

It is conceded that ever since petitioners' arrest the state and federal courts in Florida, New York, and the District of Columbia, and in the states in which each of the petitioners was arrested or detained, have been open and functioning normally. . . .

Petitioners' main contention is that the President is without any statutory or constitutional authority to order the petitioners to be tried by military tribunal for offenses with which they are charged; that in consequence they are entitled to be tried in the civil courts with the safeguards, including trial by jury, which the Fifth and Sixth Amendments guarantee to all persons charged in such courts with criminal offenses. . . .

We are not here concerned with any question of the guilt or innocence of petitioners. . . . But the detention and trial of petitioners—ordered by the President in the declared exercise of his powers as Commander in Chief of the Army in time of war and of grave public danger—are not to be set aside by the courts without the clear conviction that they are in conflict with the Constitution or laws of Congress constitutionally enacted.

. . . The Constitution . . . invests the President as Commander in Chief with the power to wage war which Congress has declared, and to carry into effect all laws passed by Congress for the conduct of war and for the government and regulation of the Armed Forces, and all laws defining and punishing offences against the law of nations, including those which pertain to the conduct of war.

By the Articles of War, Congress has provided rules for the government of the Army. It has provided for the trial and punishment, by courts martial, of violations of the Articles by members of the armed forces and by specified classes of persons associated or serving with the Army. But the Articles also recognize the 'military commission' appointed by military command as an appropriate tribunal for the trial and punishment of offenses against the law of war not ordinarily tried by court martial. . . .

From the very beginning of its history this Court has recognized and applied the law of war as including that part of the law of nations which prescribes, for the conduct of war, the status, rights and duties of enemy nations as well as of enemy individuals. By the Articles of War, and especially Article 15, Congress has explicitly provided, so far as it may constitutionally do so, that military tribunals shall have jurisdiction to try offenders or offenses against the law of war in appropriate cases. Congress, in addition to making rules for the government of our Armed Forces, has thus exercised its authority to define and punish offenses against the law of nations by sanctioning, within constitutional limitations, the jurisdiction of military commissions to try persons for offenses which, according to the rules and precepts of the law of nations, and more particularly the law of war, are cognizable by such tribunals. And the President, as Commander in Chief, by his Proclamation in time of war h[a]s invoked that law. By his Order creating the present Commission he has undertaken to exercise the authority conferred upon him by Congress, and also such authority as the Constitution itself gives the Commander in Chief, to direct the performance of those functions which may constitutionally be performed by the military arm of the nation in time of war.

An important incident to the conduct of war is the adoption of measures by the military command not only to repel and defeat the enemy, but to seize and subject to disciplinary measures those enemies who in their attempt to thwart or impede our military effort have violated the law of war. It is unnecessary for present purposes to determine to what extent the President as Commander in Chief has constitutional power to create military commissions without the support of Congressional legislation. For here Congress has authorized trial of offenses against the law of war before such commissions. We are concerned only with the question whether it is within the constitutional power of the national government to place petitioners upon trial before a military commission for the offenses with which they are charged. We must therefore first inquire whether any of the acts charged is an offense against the law of war cognizable before a military tribunal, and if so whether the Constitution prohibits the trial. . . .

By universal agreement and practice the law of war draws a distinction between the armed forces and the peaceful populations of belligerent nations and also between those who are lawful and unlawful combatants. Lawful combatants are subject to capture and detention as prisoners of war by opposing military forces. Unlawful combatants are likewise subject to capture and detention, but in addition they are subject to trial and punishment by military tribunals for acts which render their belligerency unlawful. The spy who secretly and without uniform passes the military lines of a belligerent in time of war, seeking to gather military information and communicate it to the enemy, or an enemy combatant who without uniform comes secretly through the lines for the purpose of waging war by destruction of life or property, are familiar examples of belligerents who are generally deemed not to be entitled to the status of prisoners of war, but to be offenders against the law of war subject to trial and punishment by military tribunals.

Such was the practice of our own military authorities before the adoption of the Constitution, and during the Mexican and Civil Wars. . . .

By a long course of practical administrative construction by its military authorities, our Government has recognized that those who during time of war pass surreptitiously from enemy territory into our own, discarding their uniforms upon entry, for the commission of hostile acts involving destruction of life or property, have the status of unlawful combatants punishable as such by military commission. This precept of the law of war has been so recognized in practice both here and abroad, and has so generally been accepted as valid by authorities on international law that we think it must be regarded as a rule or principle of the law of war recognized by this Government by its enactment of the Fifteenth Article of War.

Specification 1 of the First charge is sufficient to charge all the petitioners with the offense of unlawful belligerency, trial of which is within the jurisdiction of the Commission, and the admitted facts affirmatively show that the charge is not merely colorable or without foundation.

Specification 1 states that petitioners 'being enemies of the United States and acting for . . . the German Reich, a belligerent enemy nation, secretly and covertly passed, in civilian dress, contrary to the law of war, through the military and naval lines and defenses of the United States . . . and went behind such lines, contrary to the law of war, in civilian dress . . . for the purpose of committing . . . hostile acts, and, in particular, to destroy certain war industries, war utilities and war materials within the United States'.

This specification so plainly alleges violation of the law of war as to require but brief discussion of petitioners' contentions. . . . [E]ntry upon our territory in time of war by enemy belligerents, including those acting under the direction of the armed forces of the enemy, for the purpose of destroying property used or useful in prosecuting the war, is a hostile and war-like act. It subjects those who participate in it without uniform to the punishment prescribed by the law of war for unlawful belligerents. It is without significance that petitioners were not alleged to have borne conventional weapons or that their proposed hostile acts did not necessarily contemplate collision with the Armed Forces of the United States. . . . The law of war cannot rightly treat those agents of enemy armies who enter our territory, armed with explosives intended for the destruction of war industries and supplies, as any the less belligerent enemies than are agent[s] similarly entering for the purpose of destroying fortified places or our Armed Forces. By passing our boundaries for such purposes without uniform or other emblem signifying their belligerent status, or by discarding that means of identification after entry, such enemies become unlawful belligerents subject to trial and punishment.

Citizenship in the United States of an enemy belligerent does not relieve him from the consequences of a belligerency which is unlawful because in violation of the law of war. Citizens who associate themselves with the military arm of the enemy government, and with its aid, guidance and direction enter this country bent on hostile acts are enemy belligerents within the meaning of the Hague Convention and the law of war. It is as an enemy belligerent that petitioner Haupt is charged with entering the United States, and unlawful belligerency is the gravamen of the offense of which he is accused.

Nor are petitioners any the less belligerents if, as they argue, they have not actually committed or attempted to commit any act of depredation or entered the theatre or zone of active military operations. The argument leaves out of account the nature of the offense which the Government charges and which the Act of Congress, by incorporating the law of war, punishes. It is that each petitioner, in circumstances which gave him the status of an enemy belligerent, passed our military and naval lines and defenses or went behind those lines, in civilian dress and with hostile purpose. The offense was complete when with that purpose they entered—or, having so entered, they remained upon—our territory in time of war without uniform or other appropriate means of identification. For that reason, even when committed by a citizen, the offense is distinct from the crime of treason defined in Article III, 3 of the Constitution, since the absence of uniform essential to one is irrelevant to the other.

But petitioners insist that even if the offenses with which they are charged are offenses against the law of war, their trial is subject to the requirement of the Fifth Amendment that no person shall be held to answer for a capital or otherwise infamous crime unless on a presentment or indictment of a grand jury, and that such trials must be by jury in a civil court. . . .

. . . In the light of this long-continued and consistent interpretation we must conclude that Section 2 of Article III and the Fifth and Sixth Amendments cannot be taken to have extended the right to demand a jury to trials by military commission, or to have required that offenses against the law of war not triable by jury at common law be tried only in the civil courts. . . .

. . . We conclude that the Fifth and Sixth Amendments did not restrict whatever authority was conferred by the Constitution to try offenses against the law of war by military commission, and that petitioners, charged with such an offense not required to be tried by jury at common law, were lawfully placed on trial by the Commission without a jury.

Petitioners, and especially petitioner Haupt, stress the pronouncement of this Court in the Milligan case that the law of war 'can never be applied to citizens in states which have upheld the authority of the government, and where the courts are open and their process unobstructed'. Elsewhere in its opinion, the Court was at pains to point out that Milligan, a citizen twenty years resident in Indiana, who had never been a resident of any of the states in rebellion, was not an enemy belligerent either entitled to the status of a prisoner of war or subject to the penalties imposed upon unlawful belligerents. We construe the Court's statement as to the inapplicability of the law of war to Milligan's case as having particular reference to the facts before it. From them the Court concluded that Milligan, not being a part of or associated with the armed forces of the enemy, was a non-belligerent, not subject to the law of war save as—in circumstances found not there to be present and not involved here—martial law might be constitutionally established.

The Court's opinion is inapplicable to the case presented by the present record. We have no occasion now to define with meticulous care the ultimate boundaries of the jurisdiction of military tribunals to try persons according to the law of war. It is enough that petitioners here, upon the conceded facts, were plainly within those boundaries, and were held in good faith for trial by military commission, charged with being enemies who, with the purpose of destroying war materials and utilities, entered or after entry remained in our territory without uniform—an offense against the law of war. We hold only that those particular acts constitute an offense against the law of war which the Constitution authorizes to be tried by military commission. . . .

While both in this case and *Ex parte Milligan* the Court dealt with the question of military tribunals, it reached two very different conclusions. Why? Some point to the difference in the defendants: Milligan was a U.S. citizen and not an "unlawful" combatant who had violated the "law of war"; the Nazi saboteurs, on the other hand, were belligerent enemies and (with the possible exception of Haupt) Germans at that. The *Quirin* Court itself differentiated *Milligan* on the ground that the earlier case did not cover the use of military tribunals to try violations of the "law of war." Other commentators suggest that the circumstances surrounding the cases help explain the different result: *Milligan* was decided after the war was over, and *Quirin* came down "during the darkest days of World War II," as Chief Justice William H. Rehnquist has written.[14]

We leave it to you to ponder these and other possibilities, such as the Court's statement in *Quirin* that "Congress has authorized trial of offenses against the law of war before such commissions." As you do so, you also might want to consider reactions to *Quirin*. At the time, public opinion was decidedly against the saboteurs; indeed, if anything Americans were "disappointed" that the Court even took the case, believing that the eight should be "shot on sight."[15] But subsequent responses have put the whole episode, including the Court's decision, in a different light. A decade or so after the Court decided *Quirin* Justice Felix Frankfurter deemed it "not a happy precedent," and his colleague Justice William O. Douglas once expressed his regret about the per curiam: "It is extremely undesirable to announce a decision on the merits without an opinion accompanying it." The legal scholar John Frank, who served as a clerk to Justice Hugo Black at the time the Court decided *Quirin*, said simply, "The Court allowed itself to be stampeded," presumably by the Roosevelt administration.[16] Still, and despite these reactions, *Quirin* remains good law; the Court

14. William H. Rehnquist, *All the Laws but One* (New York: Knopf, 1998).

15. Alpheus T. Mason, "Inter Arma Silent Leges." *Harvard Law Review* 69 (1955): 815.

16. The quotes in this paragraph come from Tony Mauro, "A Mixed Precedent for Military Tribunals," *Legal Times*, November 19, 2001.

has never overruled it. This is important to keep in mind when we return to the subject of military tribunals in the last section of this chapter.

However negatively history has treated *Quirin*, the reactions are relatively mild compared with those evoked by the Court's decision in *Korematsu v. United States* (1944), one of the Japanese-American internment cases. The origins of *Korematsu* lie in the Japanese bombing of Pearl Harbor on December 7, 1941, which touched off a wave of anti-Japanese hysteria. In the early weeks of the Pacific War the Japanese fleet showed remarkable strength and power, and the United States feared that Japanese forces were planning an invasion of the West Coast. The large numbers of people of Japanese ancestry living on the coast also became a matter of concern. Many thought that among the Japanese-American population were significant numbers of people sympathetic to the Japanese war effort, people who might aid the enemy in an invasion of the United States.

To prevent such an occurrence, on February 19, 1942, President Roosevelt issued the first of several orders affecting all people of Japanese background residing on the West Coast. His initial command placed all Japanese Americans under a tight curfew that required them to stay in their homes between 8:00 P.M. and 6:00 A.M. and to register for future relocation. This act was followed by the much harsher orders to evacuate Japanese Americans from the Pacific Coast area and move them to inland detention centers. Congress later enacted these orders into law. The program made no attempt to distinguish the loyal from the disloyal or the citizen from the noncitizen. The orders affected all persons of Japanese ancestry. The government interned an estimated 110,000 Japanese American citizens and resident aliens, some for as long as four years.[17] These programs spawned a number of important lawsuits.

In 1943 the Supreme Court heard a challenge to the curfew regulations that was brought by Gordon Hirabayashi, an American citizen of Japanese descent. He was a native of Washington State and a pacifist of the

17. See Peter H. Irons, *Justice at War: The Story of the Japanese-American Internment Cases* (New York: Oxford University Press, 1983).

Quaker faith. At the time he challenged the government actions, he was a senior at the University of Washington. In *Hirabayashi v. United States* (1943) the Supreme Court unanimously upheld the constitutionality of the curfew program. For the Court, Chief Justice Harlan Stone explained that the war powers doctrine gave the government ample authority to impose the restrictions. The grave and threatening conditions of war made the racially based program constitutionally acceptable.

The following year the Court heard *Korematsu v. United States* (1944), an appeal attacking the most serious denial of the civil liberties of Japanese Americans—the orders removing them to detention camps. Read Justice Black's decision carefully. Does he make a convincing case that the conditions of war stretch the Constitution to the point that exclusion orders based on race or national origin are permissible? How can you explain the fact that some of the justices who were the most sympathetic to civil liberties causes—Hugo Black, Harlan Stone, William O. Douglas, and Wiley Rutledge—voted to approve the military orders? Compare Black's opinion with the dissents of Justice Frank Murphy, who emphasizes the racial foundations of the policy, and of Justice Robert Jackson, who states the case for preserving guarantees of civil liberties even in times of war or national emergency.

Korematsu v. United States

323 U.S. 214 (1944)
http://laws.findlaw.com/US/323/214.html
Vote: 6 (Black, Douglas, Frankfurter, Reed, Rutledge, Stone)
*   3 (Jackson, Murphy, Roberts)*
Opinion of the Court: Black
Concurring opinion: Frankfurter
Dissenting opinions: Jackson, Murphy, Roberts

Fred Korematsu was arrested May 30, 1942, by San Leandro, California, police for being on the public streets in violation of the government's evacuation orders. Korematsu was a native-born American with Japanese American parents. He grew up in the San Francisco area.

Japanese Americans at the federal detention center in Owens Valley, California. In 1988, more than four decades after the war, Congress appropriated $20,000 in compensation for each of the 75,000 relocation camp survivors.

Rejected for military service for health reasons, he worked in the defense industry as a welder. When arrested, he tried to convince police that he was of Spanish-Hawaiian origin. He had undergone plastic surgery to make his racial characteristics less pronounced in an effort to avoid the anti-Japanese discrimination he feared because of his engagement to an Italian American woman.[18] After the arrest, representatives of the American Civil Liberties Union approached Korematsu and offered to defend him and challenge the validity of the evacuation program. The Japanese-American Citizens League also lent support.

MR. JUSTICE BLACK delivered the opinion of the Court.

It should be noted, to begin with, that all legal restrictions which curtail the civil rights of a single racial group are immediately suspect. That is not to say that all such restrictions are unconstitutional. It is to say that courts must subject them to the most rigid scrutiny. Pressing public necessity may sometimes justify the existence of such restrictions; racial antagonism never can. . . .

In the light of the principles we announced in the *Hirabayashi* case, we are unable to conclude that it was beyond the war power of Congress and the Executive to ex-

18. Ibid., 93–99.

clude those of Japanese ancestry from the West Coast war area at the time they did. True, exclusion from the area in which one's home is located is a far greater deprivation than constant confinement to the home from 8 P.M. to 6 A.M. Nothing short of apprehension by the proper military authorities of the gravest imminent danger to the public safety can constitutionally justify either. But exclusion from a threatened area, no less than curfew, has a definite and close relationship to the prevention of espionage and sabotage. The military authorities, charged with the primary responsibility of defending our shores, concluded that curfew provided inadequate protection and ordered exclusion. They did so, as pointed out in our *Hirabayashi* opinion, in accordance with Congressional authority to the military to say who should, and who should not, remain in the threatened areas.

In this case the petitioner challenges the assumptions upon which we rested our conclusions in the *Hirabayashi* case. He also urges that by May 1942, when Order No. 34 was promulgated, all danger of Japanese invasion of the West Coast had disappeared. After careful consideration of these contentions we are compelled to reject them.

Here, as in the *Hirabayashi* case, ". . . we cannot reject as unfounded the judgment of the military authorities and of Congress that there were disloyal members of that population, whose number and strength could not be precisely and quickly ascertained. We cannot say that the war-making branches of the Government did not have ground for believing that in a critical hour such persons could not readily be isolated and separately dealt with, and constituted a menace to the national defense and safety, which demanded that prompt and adequate measures be taken to guard against it."

Like curfew, exclusion of those of Japanese origin was deemed necessary because of the presence of an unascertained number of disloyal members of the group, most of whom we have no doubt were loyal to this country. It was because we could not reject the finding of the military authorities that it was impossible to bring about an immediate segregation of the disloyal from the loyal that we sustained the validity of the curfew order as applying to the whole group. In the instant case, temporary exclusion of the entire group was rested by the military on the same ground. The judgment that exclusion of the whole group was for the same reason a military imperative answers the contention that the exclusion was in the nature of group punishment based on antagonism to those of Japanese origin. That there were members of the group who retained loyalties to Japan has been confirmed by investigations made subsequent to the exclusion. Approximately five thousand American citizens of Japanese ancestry refused to swear unqualified allegiance to the United States and to renounce allegiance to the Japanese Emperor, and several thousand evacuees requested repatriation to Japan.

We uphold the exclusion order as of the time it was made and when the petitioner violated it. In doing so, we are not unmindful of the hardships imposed by it upon a large group of American citizens. But hardships are part of war, and war is an aggregation of hardships. All citizens alike, both in and out of uniform, feel the impact of war in greater or lesser measure. Citizenship has its responsibilities as well as its privileges, and in time of war the burden is always heavier. Compulsory exclusion of large groups of citizens from their homes, except under circumstances of direst emergency and peril, is inconsistent with our basic governmental institutions. But when under conditions of modern warfare our shores are threatened by hostile forces, the power to protect must be commensurate with the threatened danger. . . .

It is said that we are dealing here with the case of imprisonment of a citizen in a concentration camp solely because of his ancestry, without evidence or inquiry concerning his loyalty and good disposition towards the United States. Our task would be simple, our duty clear, were this a case involving the imprisonment of a loyal citizen in a concentration camp because of racial prejudice. Regardless of the true nature of the assembly and relocation centers—and we deem it unjustifiable to call them concentration camps with all the ugly connotations that term implies—we are dealing specifically with nothing but an exclusion order. To cast this case into outlines of racial prejudice, without reference to the real military dangers which were presented, merely confuses the issue. Korematsu was not excluded from the Military Area because of hostility to him or his race. He *was* excluded because we are at war with the Japanese Empire, because the properly constituted military authorities feared an invasion of our West Coast and felt constrained to take proper security measures, because they decided that the military urgency of the situation demanded that all citizens of Japanese ancestry be segregated from the West Coast temporarily, and finally, because Congress, reposing its confidence in this time of war in our military leaders—as inevitably it must—determined that they should have the power to do just this. There was evidence of disloyalty on the part of some, the military authorities considered that the need for action was great, and time was short. We cannot—by availing ourselves of the calm perspective of hindsight—now say that at that time these actions were unjustified.

Affirmed.

MR. JUSTICE MURPHY, dissenting.

This exclusion of "all persons of Japanese ancestry, both alien and non-alien," from the Pacific Coast area on a plea of military necessity in the absence of martial law ought not to be approved. Such exclusion goes over "the very brink of constitutional power" and falls into the ugly abyss of racism.

In dealing with matters relating to the prosecution and progress of a war, we must accord great respect and consideration to the judgments of the military authorities who are on the scene and who have full knowledge of the military facts. The scope of their discretion must, as a matter of necessity and common sense, be wide. And their judgments ought not to be overruled lightly by those whose training and duties ill-equip them to deal intelligently with matters so vital to the physical security of the nation.

At the same time, however, it is essential that there be definite limits to military discretion, especially where martial law has not been declared. Individuals must not be left impoverished of their constitutional rights on a plea of military necessity that has neither substance nor support. Thus, like other claims conflicting with the asserted constitutional rights of the individual, the military claim must subject itself to the judicial process of having its reasonableness determined and its conflicts with other interests reconciled. "What are the allowable limits of military discretion, and whether or not they have been overstepped in a particular case, are judicial questions." *Sterling v. Constantin* [1932].

The judicial test of whether the Government, on a plea of military necessity, can validly deprive an individual of any of his constitutional rights is whether the deprivation is reasonably related to a public danger that is so "immediate, imminent, and impending" as not to admit of delay and not to permit the intervention of ordinary constitutional processes to alleviate the danger. Civilian Exclusion Order No. 34, banishing from a prescribed area of the Pacific Coast "all persons of Japanese ancestry, both alien and non-alien," clearly does not meet that test. Being an obvious racial discrimination, the order deprives all those within its scope of the equal protection of the laws as guaranteed by the Fifth Amendment. It further deprives these individuals of their constitutional rights to live and work where they will, to establish a home where they choose and to move about freely. In excommunicating them without benefit of hearings, this order also deprives them of all their constitutional rights to procedural due process. Yet no reasonable relation to an "immediate, imminent, and impending" public danger is evident to support this racial restriction which is one of the most sweeping and complete deprivations of constitutional rights in the history of this nation in the absence of martial law.

It must be conceded that the military and naval situation in the spring of 1942 was such as to generate a very real fear of invasion of the Pacific Coast, accompanied by fears of sabotage and espionage in that area. The military command was therefore justified in adopting all reasonable means necessary to combat these dangers. In adjudging the military action taken in light of the then apparent dangers, we must not erect too high or too meticulous standards; it is necessary only that the action have some reasonable relation to the removal of the dangers of invasion, sabotage and espionage. But the exclusion, either temporarily or permanently, of all persons with Japanese blood in their veins has no such reasonable relation. And that relation is lacking because the exclusion order necessarily must rely for its reasonableness upon the assumption that *all* persons of Japanese ancestry may have a dangerous tendency to commit sabotage and espionage and to aid our Japanese enemy in other ways. It is difficult to believe that reason, logic or experience could be marshalled in support of such an assumption.

That this forced exclusion was the result in good measure of this erroneous assumption of racial guilt rather than bona fide military necessity is evidenced by the Commanding General's Final Report on the evacuation from the Pacific Coast area. In it he refers to all individuals of Japanese descent as "subversive," as belonging to "an enemy race" whose "racial strains are undiluted," and as constituting "over 112,000 potential enemies . . . at large today" along the Pacific Coast. . . .

The main reasons relied upon by those responsible for the forced evacuation, therefore, do not prove a reasonable relation between the group characteristics of Japanese Americans and the dangers of invasion, sabotage and espionage. The reasons appear, instead, to be largely an accumulation of much of the misinformation, half-truths and insinuations that for years have been directed against Japanese Americans by people with racial and economic prejudices—the same people who have been among the foremost advocates of the evacuation. A military judgment based upon such racial and sociological considerations is not entitled to the great weight ordinarily given the judgments based upon strictly military considerations. Especially is this so when every charge relative to race, religion, culture, geographical location, and legal and economic status has been substantially discredited by independent studies made by experts in these matters.

The military necessity which is essential to the validity of the evacuation order thus resolves itself into a few intimations that certain individuals actively aided the enemy, from which it is inferred that the entire group of Japanese Americans could not be trusted to be or remain loyal to the United States. . . . To give constitutional sanction to that inference in this case, however well-intentioned may have been the military command on the Pacific Coast, is to adopt one of the cruelest of the rationales used by our enemies to destroy the dignity of the individual and to encourage and open the door to discriminatory actions against other minority groups in the passions of tomorrow. . . .

I dissent, therefore, from this legalization of racism. Racial discrimination in any form and in any degree has no justifiable part whatever in our democratic way of life. It is unattractive in any setting but it is utterly revolting among a free people who have embraced the principles set forth in the Constitution of the United States. All residents of this nation are kin in some way by blood or culture to a foreign land. Yet they are primarily and necessarily a part of the new and distinct civilization of the United States. They must accordingly be treated at all times as the heirs of the American experiment and as entitled to all the rights and freedoms guaranteed by the Constitution.

MR. JUSTICE JACKSON, dissenting.

Korematsu was born on our soil, of parents born in Japan. The Constitution makes him a citizen of the United States by nativity and a citizen of California by residence. No claim is made that he is not loyal to this country. There is no suggestion that apart from the matter involved here he is not law-abiding and well disposed. Korematsu, however, has been convicted of an act not commonly a crime. It consists merely of being present in the state whereof he is a citizen, near the place where he was born, and where all his life he has lived.

Even more unusual is the series of military orders which made this conduct a crime. They forbid such a one to remain, and they also forbid him to leave. They were so drawn that the only way Korematsu could avoid violation was to give himself up to the military authority. This meant submission to custody, examination, and transportation out of the territory, to be followed by indeterminate confinement in detention camps.

A citizen's presence in the locality, however, was made a crime only if his parents were of Japanese birth. Had Korematsu been one of four—the others being, say, a German alien enemy, an Italian alien enemy, and a citizen of American-born ancestors, convicted of treason but out on parole—only Korematsu's presence would have violated the order. The difference between their innocence and his crime would result, not from anything he did, said, or thought, different than they, but only in that he was born of different racial stock.

Now, if any fundamental assumption underlies our system, it is that guilt is personal and not inheritable. Even if all of one's antecedents had been convicted of treason, the Constitution forbids its penalties to be visited upon him, for it provides that "no attainder of treason shall work corruption of blood, or forfeiture except during the life of the person attainted." But here is an attempt to make an otherwise innocent act a crime merely because this prisoner is the son of parents as to whom he had no choice, and belongs to a race from which there is no way to resign. If Congress in peace-time legislation should enact such a criminal law, I should suppose this Court would refuse to enforce it.

But the "law" which this prisoner is convicted of disregarding is not found in an act of Congress, but in a military order. Neither the Act of Congress nor the Executive Order of the President, nor both together, would afford a basis for this conviction. It rests on the orders of General DeWitt. And it is said that if the military commander had reasonable military grounds for promulgating the orders, they are constitutional and become law, and the Court is required to enforce them. There are several reasons why I cannot subscribe to this doctrine. . . .

Much is said of the danger to liberty from the Army program for deporting and detaining these citizens of Japanese extraction. But a judicial construction of the due process clause that will sustain this order is a far more subtle blow to liberty than the promulgation of the order itself. A military order, however unconstitutional, is not apt to last longer than the military emergency. Even during that period a succeeding commander may revoke it all. But once a judicial opinion rationalizes such an order to show that it conforms to the Constitution, or rather rationalizes the Constitution to show that the Constitution sanctions such an order, the Court for all time has validated the principle of racial discrimination in criminal procedure and of transplanting American citizens. The principle then lies about like a loaded weapon ready for the hand of any authority that can bring forward a plausible claim of an urgent need. . . .

I should hold that a civil court cannot be made to enforce an order which violates constitutional limitations even

BOX 5-6   AFTERMATH . . . FRED KOREMATSU

FOLLOWING his arrest and conviction in 1942 for refusing to leave his Northern California home in compliance with President Roosevelt's evacuation orders, Fred T. Korematsu was sentenced to five years' probation. He was also sent with other Japanese Americans to an isolated internment camp in Topaz, Utah. After the war, he returned to his home in San Leandro, California, married, and continued his work as a welder.

Almost forty years later, documents were discovered providing evidence that officials of the navy and the Justice Department had intentionally deceived the Supreme Court by suppressing information showing that Japanese Americans posed no threat during World War II. Based on this new evidence, lawyers representing Korematsu filed a legal action to clear his name. In November 1983, a federal district court in San Francisco overturned Korematsu's conviction. Charges

President Bill Clinton stands with Fred Korematsu after awarding him the Presidential Medal of Freedom, January 15, 1998.

against Gordon Hirabayashi for violating a curfew imposed on Japanese Americans, upheld by the Supreme Court in 1942, were similarly reversed by a Seattle federal court in 1986. These legal actions helped fuel a movement that led Congress in 1988 to approve $20,000 in reparations for every living Japanese American who was interned during the war.

In 1998 President Clinton awarded Korematsu, then seventy-eight years old, the Presidential Medal of Freedom, the nation's highest civilian award. "In the long history of our country's constant search for justice," Clinton said, "some names of ordinary citizens stand for millions of souls. Plessy, Brown, Parks. To that distinguished list, today we add the name of Fred Korematsu."

SOURCES: *New York Times,* January 31, 1983, November 11, 1983, August 11, 1988, February 19, 1992; *San Francisco Chronicle,* January 16, 1998.

---

if it is a reasonable exercise of military authority. The courts can exercise only the judicial power, can apply only law, and must abide by the Constitution, or they cease to be civil courts and become instruments of military policy. . . .

My duties as a justice as I see them do not require me to make a military judgment as to whether General DeWitt's evacuation and detention program was a reasonable military necessity. I do not suggest that the courts should have attempted to interfere with the Army in carrying out its task. But I do not think they may be asked to execute a military expedient that has no place in law under the Constitution. I would reverse the judgment and discharge the prisoner.

The *Korematsu* decision was softened, but only slightly, by *Ex parte Endo* (1944), handed down the same day. In this case Mitsuye Endo had been caught escaping from a detention center. However, she had gone through the ap-

propriate government procedures and had been classified as loyal to the United States. The justices ruled in her favor, holding that the government does not have the authority to detain persons whose loyalty has been established. The *Korematsu* decision has been severely criticized, and in 1988 Congress approved $20,000 in reparations for every living Japanese American who was interned during the war *(see Box 5-6)*.

The Korean Conflict

During the Korean conflict the justices were called upon to decide the constitutional validity of yet another executive action taken in the name of the war powers doctrine, but this case involved property rights rather than civil liberties. As you read Justice Black's opinion for the Court in *Youngstown Sheet & Tube Company v. Sawyer* (1952), compare it to his opinion in *Korematsu*. Both involved actions taken by the president to strengthen war efforts. Does it make sense to you that the Court approved the detention of more than 110,000 individuals on the basis of national origin but ruled that the government could not take nominal possession of the steel mills? Note the analysis provided in Justice Jackson's concurring opinion, in which he lays out a formula for deciding questions of presidential power in relation to congressional action. Consider, too, the dissenting opinion of Chief Justice Frederick Vinson, who concludes that the national emergency justified the president's actions.

Youngstown Sheet & Tube Company v. Sawyer

343 U.S. 579 (1952)
http://laws.findlaw.com/US/343/579.html
Vote: 6 (Black, Burton, Clark, Douglas, Frankfurter, Jackson)
*   3 (Minton, Reed, Vinson)*
Opinion of the Court: Black
Concurring opinions: Burton, Clark, Douglas, Frankfurter,
*   Jackson*
Dissenting opinion: Vinson

John W. Davis (left) arriving at the Supreme Court May 13, 1952, with acting attorney general Philip B. Perlman

In 1951 a labor dispute began in the steel industry. In December the United Steelworkers Union announced that it would call a strike at the end of that month, when its contract with the steel companies expired. For the next several months the Federal Mediation and Conciliation Service and the Federal Wage Stabilization Board tried to work out a settlement, but the efforts were unsuccessful. On April 4, 1952, the union said that its strike would begin on April 9.

President Harry S. Truman was not about to let a strike hit the steel industry. The nation was engaged in a war in Korea, and steel was needed to produce arms and other military equipment. Only hours before the strike was to begin, Truman issued an executive order commanding Secretary of Commerce Charles Sawyer to seize the nation's steel mills and keep them in operation. Sawyer in turn ordered the mill owners to continue to run their facilities as operators for the United States.

Truman's seizure order cited no statutory authority for his action because there was none. There were federal statutes permitting the seizure of industrial plants for certain specified reasons, but the settlement of a labor dispute was not one of them. In fact, the Taft-Hartley Act of 1947 rejected the idea that labor disputes could be resolved by such means. Instead, the act authorized the president to impose an eighty-day cooling-off period as a way to postpone any strike that seriously threatened the public interest. Truman, however, had little regard for the Taft-Hartley Act, which Congress had passed over his veto. The president ignored the cooling-off period alternative and took the direct action of seizing the mills. The inherent powers of the chief executive, he maintained, were enough to authorize the action.

Congress might have improved the president's legal ground by immediately passing legislation authorizing such seizures retroactively, but it did not. The mill owners complied with the seizure orders under protest and filed suit in federal court to have Truman's action declared unconstitutional. The district court ruled in favor of the steel industry, enjoining the secretary from seizing the plants, but the same day the court of appeals stayed the injunction.

MR. JUSTICE BLACK delivered the opinion of the Court.

We are asked to decide whether the President was acting within his constitutional power when he issued an order directing the Secretary of Commerce to take possession of and operate most of the Nation's steel mills. The mill owners argue that the President's order amounts to lawmaking, a legislative function which the Constitution has expressly confided to the Congress and not to the President. The Government's position is that the order was made on findings of the President that his action was necessary to avert a national catastrophe which would inevitably result from a stoppage of steel production, and that in meeting this grave emergency the President was acting within the aggregate of his constitutional powers as the Nation's Chief Executive and the Commander in Chief of the Armed Forces of the United States. . . .

The President's power, if any, to issue the order must stem either from an act of Congress or from the Constitution itself. There is no statute that expressly authorizes the President to take possession of property as he did here. Nor is there any act of Congress to which our attention has been directed from which such a power can fairly be implied. Indeed, we do not understand the Government to rely on statutory authorization for this seizure. . . .

It is clear that if the President had authority to issue the order he did, it must be found in some provision of the Constitution. And it is not claimed that express constitutional language grants this power to the President. The contention is that presidential power should be implied from the aggregate of his powers under the Constitution. Particular reliance is placed on provisions in Article II which say that "The executive Power shall be vested in a President . . ."; that "he shall take Care that the Laws be faithfully executed"; and that he "shall be Commander in Chief of the Army and Navy of the United States."

The order cannot properly be sustained as an exercise of the President's military power as Commander in Chief of the Armed Forces. The Government attempts to do so by citing a number of cases upholding broad powers in military commanders engaged in day-to-day fighting in a theater of war. Such cases need not concern us here. Even though "theater of war" be an expanding concept, we cannot with faithfulness to our constitutional system hold that the Commander in Chief of the Armed Forces has the ultimate power as such to take possession of private property in order to keep labor disputes from stopping production. This is a job for the Nation's lawmakers, not for its military authorities.

Nor can the seizure order be sustained because of the several constitutional provisions that grant executive power to the President. In the framework of our Constitution, the President's power to see that the laws are faithfully executed refutes the idea that he is to be a lawmaker. The Constitution limits his functions in the lawmaking process to the recommending of laws he thinks wise and the vetoing of laws he thinks bad. And the Constitution is neither silent nor equivocal about who shall make laws which the President is to execute. The first section of the first article says that "All legislative Powers herein granted shall be vested in a Congress of the United States. . . ." After granting many powers to the Congress, Article I goes on to provide that Congress may "make all Laws which shall be necessary and proper for carrying into Execution the foregoing Powers, and all other Powers vested by this Constitution in the Government of the United States, or in any Department or Officer thereof."

The President's order does not direct that a congressional policy be executed in a manner prescribed by Congress—it directs that a presidential policy be executed in a manner prescribed by the President. The preamble of the order itself, like that of many statutes, sets out reasons why the President believes certain policies should be adopted, proclaims these policies as rules of conduct to be followed, and again, like a statute, authorizes a government official to promulgate additional rules and regulations consistent with the policy proclaimed and needed to carry that policy into execution. The power of Congress to adopt such public policies as those proclaimed by the order is beyond question. It can authorize the taking of private property for public use. It can make laws regulating the relationships between employers and employees, prescribing rules designed to settle labor disputes, and fixing wages and working conditions in certain fields of our economy. The Constitution does not subject this lawmaking power of Congress to presidential or military supervision or control.

It is said that other Presidents without congressional authority have taken possession of private business enterprises in order to settle labor disputes. But even if this be true, Congress has not thereby lost its exclusive constitutional authority to make laws necessary and proper to carry out the powers vested by the Constitution "in the Government of the United States, or any Department or Officer thereof."

The Founders of this Nation entrusted the lawmaking power to the Congress alone in both good and bad times. It would do no good to recall the historical events, the fears of power and the hopes for freedom that lay behind their choice. Such a review would but confirm our holding that this seizure order cannot stand.

The judgment of the District Court is

Affirmed.

MR. JUSTICE JACKSON, concurring in the judgment and opinion of the Court.

A judge, like an executive adviser, may be surprised at the poverty of really useful and unambiguous authority applicable to concrete problems of executive power as they actually present themselves. Just what our forefathers did envision, or would have envisioned had they foreseen modern conditions, must be divined from materials almost as enigmatic as the dreams Joseph was called upon to interpret for Pharaoh. A century and a half of partisan debate and scholarly speculation yields no net result but only supplies more or less apt quotations from respected sources on each side of any question. They largely cancel each other. And court decisions are indecisive because of the judicial practice of dealing with the largest questions in the most narrow way.

. . . We may well begin by a somewhat over-simplified grouping of practical situations in which a President may doubt, or others may challenge, his powers, and by distinguishing roughly the legal consequences of this factor of relativity.

1. When the President acts pursuant to an express or implied authorization of Congress, his authority is at its maximum, for it includes all that he possesses in his own right plus all that Congress can delegate. . . .

2. When the President acts in absence of either a congressional grant or denial of authority, he can only rely upon his own independent powers, but there is a zone of twilight in which he and Congress may have concurrent authority, or in which its distribution is uncertain. Therefore, congressional inertia, indifference or quiescence may sometimes, at least as a practical matter, enable, if not invite, measures on independent presidential responsibility. In this area, any actual test of power is likely to depend on the imperatives of events and contemporary imponderables rather than on abstract theories of law.

3. When the President takes measures incompatible with the expressed or implied will of Congress, his power is at its lowest ebb, for then he can rely only upon his own constitutional powers minus any constitutional powers of Congress over the matter. . . .

Into which of these classifications does this executive seizure of the steel industry fit? It is eliminated from the first by admission, for it is conceded that no congressional authorization exists for this seizure. That takes away also the support of the many precedents and declarations which were made in relation, and must be confined, to this category.

Can it then be defended under flexible tests available to the second category? It seems clearly eliminated from that class because Congress has not left seizure of private property an open field but has covered it by three statutory policies inconsistent with this seizure. . . .

This leaves the current seizure to be justified only by the severe tests under the third grouping, where it can be supported only by any remainder of executive power after subtraction of such powers as Congress may have over the subject. In short, we can sustain the President only by holding that seizure of such strike-bound industries is within his domain and beyond control by Congress. Thus, this Court's first review of such seizures occurs under circumstances which leave presidential power most vulnerable to attack and in the least favorable of possible constitutional postures. . . .

The Solicitor General, acknowledging that Congress has never authorized the seizure here, says practice of prior Presidents has authorized it. He seeks color of legality from claimed executive precedents, chief of which is President Roosevelt's seizure on June 9, 1941, of the California plant of the North American Aviation Company. Its superficial similarities with the present case, upon analysis, yield to distinctions so decisive that it cannot be regarded as even a precedent, much less an authority for the present seizure.

The appeal, however, that we declare the existence of inherent powers *ex necessitate* to meet an emergency asks us to do what many think would be wise, although it is something the forefathers omitted. They knew what emergencies were, knew the pressures they engender for authoritative action, knew, too, how they afford a ready pretext for usurpation. We may also suspect that they suspected that emergency powers would tend to kindle emergencies. Aside from suspension of the privilege of the writ of habeas corpus in time of rebellion or invasion, when the public safety may require it, they made no express provision for exercise of extraordinary authority because of a crisis. I do not think we rightfully may so amend their work, and, if we could, I am not convinced it would be wise to do so, although many modern nations have forthrightly recognized that war and economic crises may upset the normal balance between liberty and authority. . . .

The essence of our free Government is "leave to live by no man's leave, underneath the law"—to be governed by those impersonal forces which we call law. Our Government is fashioned to fulfill this concept so far as humanly possible. The Executive, except for recommendation and veto, has no legislative power. The executive action we have here originates in the individual will of the President and represents an exercise of authority without law. No one, perhaps not even the President, knows the limits of the power he may seek to exert in this instance and the parties affected cannot learn the limit of their rights. We do not know today what powers over labor or property would be claimed to flow from Government possession if we should legalize it, what rights to compensation would be claimed or recognized, or on what contingency it would end. With all its defects, delays and inconveniences, men have discovered no technique for long preserving free government except that the Executive be under the law, and that the law be made by parliamentary deliberations.

Such institutions may be destined to pass away. But it is the duty of the Court to be last, not first, to give them up.

MR. CHIEF JUSTICE VINSON, with whom MR. JUSTICE REED and MR. JUSTICE MINTON join, dissenting.

The President of the United States directed the Secretary of Commerce to take temporary possession of the Nation's steel mills during the existing emergency because "a work stoppage would immediately jeopardize and imperil our national defense and the defense of those joined with us in resisting aggression, and would add to the continuing danger of our soldiers, sailors, and airmen engaged in combat in the field.". . .

In passing upon the question of Presidential powers in this case, we must first consider the context in which those powers were exercised.

Those who suggest that this is a case involving extraordinary powers should be mindful that these are extraordinary times. A world not yet recovered from the devastation of World War II has been forced to face the threat of another and more terrifying global conflict.

Accepting in full measure its responsibility in the world community, the United States was instrumental in securing adoption of the United Nations Charter, approved by the Senate by a vote of 89 to 2. The first purpose of the United Nations is to "maintain international peace and security, and to that end: to take effective collective measures for the prevention and removal of threats to the peace, and for the suppression of acts of aggression or other breaches of the peace. . . ." In 1950, when the United Nations called upon member nations "to render every assistance" to repel aggression in Korea, the United States furnished its vigorous support. For almost two full years, our armed forces have been fighting in Korea, suffering casualties of over 108,000 men. Hostilities have not abated. The "determination of the United Nations to continue its action in Korea to meet the aggression" has been reaffirmed. Congressional support of the action in Korea has been manifested by provisions for increased military manpower and equipment and for economic stabilization. . . .

Congress recognized the impact of these defense programs upon the economy. Following the attack in Korea, the President asked for authority to requisition property and to allocate and fix priorities for scarce goods. In the Defense Production Act of 1950, Congress granted the powers requested and, *in addition*, granted power to stabilize prices and wages and to provide for settlement of labor disputes arising in the defense program. The Defense Production Act was extended in 1951, a Senate Committee noting that in the dislocation caused by the programs for purchase of military equipment "lies the seed of an economic disaster that might well destroy the military might we are straining to build." Significantly, the Committee examined the problem "in terms of just one commodity, steel," and found "a graphic picture of the over-all inflationary danger growing out of re-duced civilian supplies and rising incomes." Even before Korea, steel production at levels above theoretical 100% capacity was not capable of supplying civilian needs alone. Since Korea, the tremendous military demand for steel has far exceeded the increases in productive capacity. This Committee emphasized that the shortage of steel, even with the mills operating at full capacity, coupled with increased civilian purchasing power, presented grave danger of disastrous inflation. . . .

A review of executive action demonstrates that our Presidents have on many occasions exhibited the leadership contemplated by the Framers when they made the President Commander in Chief, and imposed upon him the trust to "take Care that the Laws be faithfully executed." With or without explicit statutory authorization, Presidents have at such times dealt with national emergencies by acting promptly and resolutely to enforce legislative programs, at least to save those programs until Congress could act. Congress and the courts have responded to such executive initiative with consistent approval. . . .

The broad executive power granted by Article II to an officer on duty 365 days a year cannot, it is said, be invoked to avert disaster. Instead, the President must confine himself to sending a message to Congress recommending action. Under this messenger-boy concept of the Office, the President cannot even act to preserve legislative programs from destruction so that Congress will have something left to act upon. There is no judicial finding that the executive action was unwarranted because there was in fact no basis for the President's finding of the existence of an emergency for, under this view, the gravity of the emergency and the immediacy of the threatened disaster are considered irrelevant as a matter of law.

Seizure of plaintiffs' property is not a pleasant undertaking. Similarly unpleasant to a free country are the draft which disrupts the home and military procurement which causes economic dislocation and compels adoption of price controls, wage stabilization and allocation of materials. The President informed Congress that even a temporary Government operation of plaintiffs' properties was "thoroughly distasteful" to him, but was necessary to prevent immediate paralysis of the mobilization program. Presidents have been in the past, and any man worthy of the Office should be in the future, free to take at least interim action necessary to execute legislative programs essential to survival of the Nation. A sturdy judiciary should not be swayed by the unpleasantness or unpopularity of necessary executive action, but must independently determine for itself whether the President was acting, as required by the Constitution, to "take Care that the Laws be faithfully executed."

Youngstown is interesting in at least two regards. First, as we noted in Chapter 4, the justices were sharply divided over the nature of executive power. Two members of the Court (Douglas and Black) adopted the "mere designation" or enumerated approach, writing that "The President's power, if any, to issue the order must stem either from an act of Congress or from the Constitution itself." Three justices (Vinson, Reed, and Minton) took the opposite position. In their opinion, the Take Care clause of Article II provided the president with a sufficient constitutional basis for his actions: he was taking steps that were in the best interest of the country until Congress could act. Finally, a plurality of four (Burton, Clark, Frankfurter, and Jackson) settled somewhere between the two extremes. Unlike Black and Douglas, they asserted that the president has powers beyond those enumerated in Article II. But, in contrast to Vinson, Reed, and Minton, they argued that President Truman could not seize the mills because he had acted against the "implied" desires of Congress. As Jackson put it, "When the President takes measures incompatible with the expressed or implied will of Congress, his power is at its lowest ebb, for then he can rely only upon his own constitutional powers minus any constitutional powers of Congress over the matter."

A second interesting point is this: while it is typically the majority opinion that establishes precedent for the nation, in *Youngstown* legal analysts regard Jackson's concurrence as the most important statement coming out of the case. The explanation, it seems, is that Jackson provided a useful framework for dealing with presidential power vis-à-vis Congress.

The Iran Hostage Crisis

Would the Court adopt the Jackson framework in similar cases in times of national emergency? *Dames &*

Moore v. Regan (1981) provides one answer.[19] Here the justices considered an appeal based on one of the more serious foreign policy problems the United States has faced in recent decades—the Iran hostage crisis. *Dames & Moore* involved the power of the president to seize Iranian assets and use them as a bargaining chip to help resolve an international stalemate. To preserve the assets under his control, the president disallowed any lawsuits by U.S. citizens and corporations, requesting that the assets be used to pay off judgments against Iran. Was the president acting within his legitimate foreign policy powers? Or was Dames & Moore Company correct in arguing that he had gone too far? As you read the opinion, compare it with the views expressed in *Youngstown*. See how closely Rehnquist—a former law clerk to Justice Jackson—ties his opinion to both Black's majority views and Jackson's concurrence in *Youngstown*.

Dames & Moore v. Regan

453 U.S. 654 (1981)
http://laws.findlaw.com/US/453/654.html
Vote: 9 (Blackmun, Brennan, Burger, Marshall, Powell,
    Rehnquist, Stevens, Stewart, White)
        0
Opinion of the Court: Rehnquist
Opinion concurring in part: Stevens
Opinion concurring in part and dissenting in part: Powell

On November 4, 1979, Iranians seized the American Embassy in Tehran, captured its diplomatic personnel, and held them hostage. In response, President Carter invoked the International Economic Emergency Powers Act (IEEPA) and froze all assets of the Iranian government or its agencies within the jurisdiction of the United States. As part of the regulations enforcing that order, the Treasury Department ruled that, unless otherwise stipulated, the seized Iranian assets were protected against judgments, decrees, or attachments by U.S. courts.

On December 19 Dames & Moore Company filed suit in federal district court against the government of Iran,

19. To hear oral arguments in this case, navigate to: *www.oyez.org/oyez/frontpage.*

the Atomic Energy Organization of Iran, and a number of Iranian banks. The suit claimed that the company had been under contract with the Iranian Atomic Energy Organization to conduct site inspections for a proposed nuclear power facility and had not been fully paid for its services. Dames & Moore contended that the Iranians still owed the company almost $3.5 million and asked the court to grant it the back payments plus interest. Furthermore, Dames & Moore wanted the district court to attach Iranian assets in the United States to ensure payment of the judgment.

The crisis ended in January 1981 when the United States and Iran reached an agreement and the hostages were released. As part of the settlement the United States agreed to terminate all American lawsuits involving the frozen Iranian assets. A special Iran–United States Claims Tribunal was established to settle disputes over the Iranian assets; the tribunal's judgments were to be final and enforceable in the courts of any nation. To implement these arrangements, the day before he left office, President Carter ordered that all frozen Iranian assets be moved to the Federal Reserve Bank in New York for ultimate transfer back to Iran, with a portion set aside for payment of Claims Tribunal judgments. In February 1981 President Reagan issued executive orders reaffirming Carter's actions.

With these orders in effect, the district court denied attachments against the Iranian assets to pay Dames & Moore. The company then filed a suit against Secretary of the Treasury Donald Regan, arguing that the president had exceeded his constitutional and statutory power by removing Iranian assets from possible attachment by the federal courts. Furthermore, the company protested that the president did not have authority to impose claims settlement procedures by executive agreement. The district court ruled in favor of the government, and the Supreme Court accepted the company's appeal using expedited procedures to bring the case immediately before the justices.

JUSTICE REHNQUIST delivered the opinion of the Court.

[W]e freely confess that we are obviously deciding only one more episode in the never-ending tension between the President exercising the executive authority in a world that presents each day some new challenge with which he must deal and the Constitution under which we all live and which no one disputes embodies some sort of system of checks and balances. . . .

The parties and the lower courts . . . have all agreed that much relevant analysis is contained in *Youngstown Sheet & Tube Co. v. Sawyer* (1952). Justice Black's opinion for the Court in that case, involving the validity of President Truman's effort to seize the country's steel mills in the wake of a nationwide strike, recognized that "[t]he President's power, if any, to issue the order must stem either from an act of Congress or from the Constitution itself." Justice Jackson's concurring opinion elaborated in a general way the consequences of different types of interaction between the two democratic branches in assessing Presidential authority to act in any given case. When the President acts pursuant to an express or implied authorization from Congress, he exercises not only his powers but also those delegated by Congress. In such a case the executive action "would be supported by the strongest of presumptions and the widest latitude of judicial interpretation, and the burden of persuasion would rest heavily upon any who might attack it." When the President acts in the absence of congressional authorization he may enter "a zone of twilight in which he and Congress may have concurrent authority, or in which its distribution is uncertain." In such a case the analysis becomes more complicated, and the validity of the President's action, at least so far as separation-of-powers principles are concerned, hinges on a consideration of all the circumstances which might shed light on the views of the Legislative Branch toward such action, including "congressional inertia, indifference or quiescence." Finally, when the President acts in contravention of the will of Congress, "his power is at its lowest ebb," and the Court can sustain his actions "only by disabling the Congress from acting upon the subject."

Although we have in the past found and do today find Justice Jackson's classification of executive actions into three general categories analytically useful, we should be mindful of Justice Holmes' admonition . . . that "[t]he great ordinances of the Constitution do not establish and divide fields of black and white." *Springer v. Philippine Islands* (1928) (dissenting opinion). Justice Jackson himself recognized that his three categories represented "a somewhat over-simplified grouping," and it is doubtless the case that executive action in any particular instance falls, not neatly in one of three pi-

geonholes, but rather at some point along a spectrum running from explicit congressional authorization to explicit congressional prohibition. This is particularly true as respects cases such as the one before us, involving responses to international crises the nature of which Congress can hardly have been expected to anticipate in any detail. . . .

This Court has previously recognized that the congressional purpose in authorizing blocking orders is "to put control of foreign assets in the hands of the President. . . ." *Propper v. Clark* (1949). Such orders permit the President to maintain the foreign assets at his disposal for use in negotiating the resolution of a declared national emergency. The frozen assets serve as a "bargaining chip" to be used by the President when dealing with a hostile country. Accordingly, it is difficult to accept petitioner's argument because the practical effect of it is to allow individual claimants throughout the country to minimize or wholly eliminate this "bargaining chip" through attachments, garnishments, or similar encumbrances on property. Neither the purpose the statute was enacted to serve nor its plain language supports such a result.

Because the President's action in nullifying the attachments and ordering the transfer of the assets was taken pursuant to specific congressional authorization, it is "supported by the strongest of presumptions and the widest latitude of judicial interpretation, and the burden of persuasion would rest heavily upon any who might attack it." *Youngstown* (Jackson, J., concurring). Under the circumstances of this case, we cannot say that petitioner has sustained that heavy burden. A contrary ruling would mean that the Federal Government as a whole lacked the power exercised by the President, and that we are not prepared to say. . . .

Although we have declined to conclude that the IEEPA or the Hostage Act directly authorizes the President's suspension of claims for the reasons noted, we cannot ignore the general tenor of Congress' legislation in this area in trying to determine whether the President is acting alone or at least with the acceptance of Congress. As we have noted, Congress cannot anticipate and legislate with regard to every possible action the President may find it necessary to take or every possible situation in which he might act. Such failure of Congress specifically to delegate authority does not, "especially . . . in the areas of foreign policy and national security," imply "congressional disapproval" of action taken by the Executive. On the contrary, the enactment of legislation closely related to the question of the President's authority in a particular case which evinces legislative intent to accord the President broad discretion may be considered to "invite" "measures on independent presidential responsibility," *Youngstown* (Jackson, J., concurring). At least this is so where there is no contrary indication of legislative intent and when, as here, there is a history of congressional acquiescence in conduct of the sort engaged in by the President. It is to that history which we now turn.

Not infrequently in affairs between nations, outstanding claims by nationals of one country against the government of another country are "sources of friction" between the two sovereigns. *United States v. Pink* (1942). To resolve these difficulties, nations have often entered into agreements settling the claims of their respective nationals. . . . Consistent with that principle, the United States has repeatedly exercised its sovereign authority to settle the claims of its nationals against foreign countries. Though those settlements have sometimes been made by treaty, there has also been a longstanding practice of settling such claims by executive agreement without the advice and consent of the Senate. Under such agreements, the President has agreed to renounce or extinguish claims of United States nationals against foreign governments in return for lump-sum payments or the establishment of arbitration procedures. To be sure, many of these settlements were encouraged by the United States claimants themselves, since a claimant's only hope of obtaining any payment at all might lie in having his Government negotiate a diplomatic settlement on his behalf. . . . Since 1952, the President has entered into at least 10 binding settlements with foreign nations, including an $80 million settlement with the People's Republic of China.

Crucial to our decision today is the conclusion that Congress has implicitly approved the practice of claim settlement by executive agreement. This is best demonstrated by Congress' enactment of the International Claims Settlement Act of 1949. The Act had two purposes: (1) to allocate to United States nationals funds received in the course of an executive claims settlement with Yugoslavia, and (2) to provide a procedure whereby funds resulting from future settlements could be distributed. To achieve these ends Congress created the International Claims Commission, now the Foreign Claims Settlement Commission, and gave it jurisdiction to make final and binding decisions with respect to claims by United States nationals against settlement funds. By creating a procedure to implement future settlement agreements, Congress placed its stamp of approval on such agreements. Indeed, the legislative history of the Act observed that the United States was seeking settlements with countries other than Yugoslavia and that the bill contemplated settlements of a similar nature in the future. . . .

In addition to congressional acquiescence in the President's power to settle claims, prior cases of this Court have also recognized that the President does have some measure of power to enter into executive agreements without obtaining the advice and consent of the Senate. In *United States v. Pink*, for example, the Court upheld the validity of the Litvinov Assignment, which was part of an Executive Agreement whereby the Soviet Union assigned to the United States amounts owed to it by American nationals so that outstanding claims of other American nationals could be paid. . . .

In light of all the foregoing—the inferences to be drawn from the character of the legislation Congress has enacted in the area, such as the IEEPA and the Hostage Act, and from the history of acquiescence in executive claims settlement—we conclude that the President was authorized to suspend pending claims pursuant to Executive Order No. 12294. . . .

Just as importantly, Congress has not disapproved of the action taken here. Though Congress has held hearings on the Iranian Agreement itself, Congress has not enacted legislation or even passed a resolution, indicating its displeasure with the Agreement. Quite the contrary, the relevant Senate Committee has stated that the establishment of the Tribunal is "of vital importance to the United States." We are thus clearly not confronted with a situation in which Congress has in some way resisted the exercise of Presidential authority.

Finally, we re-emphasize the narrowness of our decision. We do not decide that the President possesses plenary power to settle claims, even as against foreign governmental entities. . . . But where, as here, the settlement of claims has been determined to be a necessary incident to the resolution of a major foreign policy dispute between our country and another, and where, as here, we can conclude that Congress acquiesced in the President's action, we are not prepared to say that the President lacks the power to settle such claims.

Affirmed.

The *Dames & Moore* decision underscores the same principle that the Court articulated almost a half-century earlier in *Curtiss-Wright*—the president is the primary government authority over matters of foreign policy. The decision also recognizes that in times of emergency the president's powers expand. Yet those powers are not unlimited, and undoubtedly, as we emphasize in the next section, the Court will continue to be faced with claims that the president has exceeded his constitutional authority. As emphasized in *Youngstown* as well as in *Dames & Moore*, the president stands on much firmer constitutional ground when acting with the assent of Congress.

September 11 and Beyond

These lessons may have particular relevance today, in post–September 11 America. In the process of waging a "war on terrorism"—a battle that may endure far longer than any others Americans have experienced—the Bush administration sent military forces into two countries, Afghanistan and Iraq. The president, following in the footsteps of so many of his predecessors confronted with threats to the nation's security, also took steps that amounted to restrictions on the rights and liberties of Americans and foreigners alike.

Some of these measures seem to have had the full and explicit support of Congress. For example, as we already have mentioned, the legislature authorized the president to use the military "to defend the national security of the United States against the continuing threat posed by Iraq." It also enacted, and President Bush signed, the USA Patriot Act of 2001. Under this act government officials can, among other things, detain suspected terrorists for up to seven days before charging them with a crime; monitor international students in the United States; subpoena Internet providers to force them to turn over e-mails sent by terrorist suspects; and obtain court orders to install "roving wiretaps," which would allow them to tap any telephones a suspected foreign terrorist might use. These are only a few examples of the act's many expansions of law enforcement authority, especially in the area of searches and seizures.[20]

The Bush administration also has taken steps that have lacked explicit endorsement from the legislature. Many, intriguingly enough, seem designed to maneuver around the federal courts or even to remove them from adjudicating cases related to the war on terrorism, such as enabling the government to monitor communications between lawyers and September 11 detainees in the absence of a federal court order, detaining foreign nationals suspected of terrorism at a U.S. Navy base in Cuba to avoid challenges in the federal courts, issuing regulations to stay any order by an immigration judge that authorizes the release of aliens until the Board of Immigration Appeals reaches a decision on the order, and detaining material witnesses without allowing them access to their attorneys. Finally, just as Presidents Lincoln and Roosevelt authorized military tribunals under certain circumstances, so too did President Bush. In his capacity as commander in chief, he issued a military order on November 13, 2001, that permits non-U.S. citizens determined to be members of al Qaeda, or persons involved in acts of international terrorism against the United States or who knowingly harbor such terrorists, to be tried by military commissions. These bodies consist of three to seven members each, chosen by the secretary of defense, and have the power to impose the death penalty.

While some of these steps have lacked explicit legislative approval, they certainly enjoyed public support. For example, when asked whether they approved of the "U.S. decision to try Al Qaeda prisoners before military tribunals rather than in the U.S. civilian courts," 61 percent of Americans reacted positively (24 percent disapproved of the decision and 15 percent did not know or refused to answer).[21]

But public support does not necessarily mean that the government's actions are constitutional. Lawyers already have challenged many of the Bush administration's orders, including those enabling the detention of alleged terrorists in Cuba and government monitoring of conversations of lawyers and inmates in federal prisons.

---

20. The full text of the USA Patriot Act is available on many Web sites. Search under the act's formal name: Uniting and Strengthening America by Providing Appropriate Tools Required to Intercept and Obstruct Terrorism.

21. Poll conducted by Princeton Survey Research Associates for the Pew Research Center for the People & the Press on April 3–8, 2002.

At this writing it is the lower federal courts that have considered these and other measures. Without doubt, though, they will reach the Supreme Court soon enough. Based on all you have learned in this chapter—be it about the doctrine the justices have promulgated or the political pressures that come to bear on them during times of crisis—how do you think the Court will rule?

READINGS

Barber, Sotirios A. *The Constitution and the Delegation of Congressional Power*. Chicago: University of Chicago Press, 1975.

Craig, Barbara H. *Chadha: The Story of an Epic Constitutional Struggle*. New York: Oxford University Press, 1988.

Edwards, Harry T. "The Judicial Function and the Elusive Goal of Principled Decisionmaking." *Wisconsin Law Review* 1991 (1991): 837–865.

Ely, John Hart. *War and Responsibility: Constitutional Lessons of Vietnam and Its Aftermath*. Princeton, N.J.: Princeton University Press, 1993.

Eskridge, William N., Jr., and John Ferejohn. "The Article I, Section 7 Game." *Georgetown Law Journal* 80 (1992): 523–563.

Fisher, Louis. *Constitutional Conflicts Between Congress and the President*. Lawrence: University Press of Kansas, 1997.

———. *Nazi Saboteurs on Trial: A Military Tribunal and American Law*. Lawrence: University Press of Kansas, 2003.

———. *Presidential War Power*. Lawrence: University Press of Kansas, 1995.

Grossman, Joel B. "The Japanese American Cases and the Vagaries of Constitutional Adjudication in Wartime: An Institutional Perspective." *Hawaii Law Review* 19 (1997): 649–695.

Henkin, Louis. *Foreign Affairs and the Constitution*. New York: Oxford University Press, 1996.

Irons, Peter. *Justice at War: The Story of the Japanese-American Internment Cases*. New York: Oxford University Press, 1983.

Koenig, Louis. *The Chief Executive*, 3rd ed. New York: Harcourt Brace Jovanovich, 1975.

Korn, Jessica. *The Power of Separation: American Constitutionalism and the Myth of Legislative Veto*. Princeton, N.J.: Princeton University Press, 1998.

Marcus, Maeva. *Truman and the Steel Seizure Case: The Limits of Presidential Power*. Durham: Duke University Press, 1994.

Mason, Alpheus Thomas. "Inter Arma Silent Leges." *Harvard Law Review* 69 (1955): 806–838.

May, Christopher. *In the Name of War: Judicial Review and the War Powers Since 1918*. Cambridge: Harvard University Press, 1989.

Randall, James. *Constitutional Problems under Lincoln*. Urbana: University of Illinois Press, 1964.

Rehnquist, William H. *All the Laws but One: Civil Liberties in Wartime*. New York: Knopf, 1998.

Reveley, W. Taylor, III. *War Powers of the President and Congress*. Charlottesville: University Press of Virginia, 1981.

Sheffer, Martin S. *The Judicial Development of Presidential War Powers*. Westport, Conn.: Praeger, 1999.

Silverstein, Gordon. *Imbalance of Powers: Constitutional Interpretation and the Making of American Foreign Policy*. New York: Oxford University Press, 1996.

Westin, Alan F. *Anatomy of a Constitutional Law Case*. Morningside ed. New York: Columbia University Press, 1990.

Whittington, Keith E. *Constitutional Construction: Divided Powers and Constitutional Meaning*. Cambridge: Harvard University Press, 1999.

Yoo, John C. "The Continuation of Politics by Other Means: The Original Understanding of War Powers." *California Law Review* 84 (1996): 167–305.

ALLOCATING GOVERNMENT POWER

IF WE catalogued the types of governments that exist in the world today, we would have a fairly diverse list. Some are unitary systems in which power is located in a central authority that may or may not mete out power to its subdivisions. Others are virtually the opposite: authority rests largely with local governments, and only certain powers are reserved to national authority. When the Framers drafted the Constitution, they had to make some basic decisions about the allocation of government power between the states and the national government they were creating. Their choice, generally speaking, was federalism: a system in which "a constitution divides governmental power between a central government and one or more subdivisional governments, giving each substantial functions." [1]

That decision turned out to be a good one, and we reap the advantages of it today. For example, because the government is multilayered, Americans have many points of access to influence the system. If your state enacts legislation you do not like, you might be able to challenge it in federal court or lobby your representative in Congress. Moreover, the system provides for further checks on the exercise of government power because federal, state, and even local systems are all involved in policy making. Finally, it encourages experimentation and provides for flexibility. Justice Louis Brandeis once wrote,

"It is one of the happy incidents of the federal system that a single courageous State may, if its citizens choose, serve as a laboratory; and try novel social and economic experiments without risk to the rest of the country." [2] Because of their proximity to many problems, state and local governments may be better positioned to fashion effective public policy than is the federal government. If successful, such policy innovations may be copied in other states or even adopted nationwide. The states were first to implement tougher drinking and driving laws, policies protecting workers' rights, welfare reforms, and so forth. However, other problems, such as those associated with foreign policy, are better left to the national government, which can act on behalf of the entire country.

But federalism is not perfect. For example, it adds considerable inefficiency to government operations. The implementation of certain kinds of policies might require the coordination of the national government, fifty states, and numerous subdivisions, which inevitably slows down the process.

For our purposes, the most relevant concern about federalism is its complexity. It is quite difficult for citizens to keep abreast of such a decentralized system. People may not understand which level of government makes specific policies, and some citizens may have so little interest that they do not know the names of their representatives. At the other end of the spectrum, governments sometimes do not well understand the boundaries of

1. J. W. Peltason, *Corwin and Peltason's Understanding the Constitution*, 14th ed. (Fort Worth, Texas: Harcourt Brace, 1997), 17. See also J. W. Peltason and Sue Davis, *Corwin and Peltason's Understanding the Constitution*, 15th ed. (Fort Worth, Texas: Harcourt Brace, 2000) ch. 1.

2. Dissent in *New State Ice Co. v. Liebmann*, 285 U.S. 262 at 311 (1932).

their own power. American history is full of examples of allegations by states that the federal government has gone too far in regulating "their" business; indeed, this was one issue over which the Civil War, the most extreme disagreement, was fought.

Yet, in most circumstances, it is neither war that has resolved these disputes nor the entities themselves that have shed light on their complexities. Rather, since the nation's founding, the U.S. Supreme Court has played the major role in delineating and defining the contours of American federalism. Why and how it has done so are the subjects of the chapters that follow. Chapter 6 focuses on the various and general theories of federal-state relations with which the Court has dealt. Chapters 7 and 8 consider the exercise of government power over the most contentious of issues: the regulation of commerce and the taxing and spending powers.

But first, let us explore several issues emanating from our discussion so far: the kind of system the Framers adopted, the amending of that system, and its complexity, which often leads to the involvement of "neutral" arbiters—judges and Supreme Court justices.

THE FRAMERS AND FEDERALISM

We have already mentioned that the Framers selected federalism from among several alternative forms of government, although the word *federalism* does not appear in the Constitution. The Founders had some general vision of the sort of government they wanted or, more aptly, of those they did not want. They rejected a unitary system as wholly incompatible with basic values and traditions already existing within the states. They also rejected a confederation in which power would reside with the states; after all, that is what they had under the Articles of Confederation, the charter they came to Philadelphia to revise.

How to divide power, then, became the delegates' central concern. In the end, they wrote into the document a rather elaborate "pattern of allocation." Nevertheless, ambiguity resulted.[3] One source of this confusion was the question of constitutional relationships; that is, in

the parlance of the eighteenth century, the Framers looked at the Constitution as a contract, but a contract between whom? Some commentators argue that it specifies the relationship between the people and the national government and that the former empower the latter. Justice Joseph Story wrote:

The constitution of the United States was ordained and established, not by the states in their sovereign capacities, but emphatically, as the preamble of the constitution declares, by "the people of the United States.". . . The constitution was not, therefore, necessarily carved out of existing state sovereignties, nor a surrender of powers already existing in state institutions.[4]

Others suggest that the contract is between the states and the nation. In a 1798 resolution of the Virginia Assembly, James Madison wrote:

That this Assembly doth explicitly and peremptorily declare that it views the powers of the Federal Government as resulting from the compact, to which the States are parties, as limited by the plain sense and intention of the instrument constituting that compact; as no further valid than they are authorized by the grants enumerated in that compact; and that in case of deliberate, palpable, and dangerous exercise of other powers not granted by the said compact, the States, who are the parties thereto, have the right, and are in duty bound, to interpose for arresting the progress of the evil, and for maintaining within their respective limits, the authorities, rights, and liberties appertaining to them.[5]

This debate is not abstract: it has real consequences. In its most violent incarnation, the Civil War, southern leaders took Madison's logic to its limit. They argued that the Constitution represented a contract between the states and the federal government, with the states creating the national government. When the federal government—controlled by the northern states—abrogated its end of the agreement, the contract was no longer valid. The Civil War ended that particular dispute, but the principle continued to flare up in less extreme, but no less important, forms. The refusal of some southern states to abide by federal civil rights laws is one example.

This problem continues to manifest itself largely because the Constitution supports both sides and therefore

---

3. C. Herman Pritchett, *Constitutional Law of the Federal System* (Englewood Cliffs, N.J.: Prentice Hall, 1984), 58.

4. *Martin v. Hunter's Lessee*, 1 Wheat. (14 U.S.) 304 at 324–325 (1816).
5. Reprinted in *Documents of American Constitutional and Legal History*, vol. 1, ed. Melvin I. Urofsky (New York: Knopf, 1989), 159.

neither. Those who favor the national government–people approach point to the document's preamble: *"We the people of the United States . . . do ordain and establish this Constitution."* To support the national government–state argument, proponents turn to the language of Article VII, that the ratification of nine states "shall be sufficient for the Establishment of this Constitution *between the States* so ratifying." When the issue of the contractual nature of the Constitution arises, therefore, many look to the Supreme Court to resolve it. As we shall see in the next chapter, different Courts have approached this debate in varying ways, adopting one view over the other at distinct points in American history.

THE TENTH AND ELEVENTH AMENDMENTS

Arguments over who are the parties to the constitutional contract may never be fully resolved, but another point of ambiguity was thought so onerous that it could not be left to interpretation. That area is the balance of power between the states and the federal government. The original charter, in the view of many, placed too much authority with the federal government. In particular, states' rights advocates pointed to two sections of the Constitution as working against their interests.

The first section is the Necessary and Proper Clause: Congress has the power "To make all Laws which shall be necessary and proper for carrying into Execution [its] Powers, and all other Powers vested by this Constitution in the Government of the United States, or in any Department or Officer thereof."

The other section is the Supremacy Clause: "This Constitution, and the Laws of the United States which shall be made in Pursuance thereof; and all Treaties made, or which shall be made, under the Authority of the United States, shall be the supreme Law of the Land; and the Judges in every state shall be bound thereby, any Thing in the Constitution or Laws of any State to the Contrary notwithstanding." These clauses seem to allocate a great deal of power to the national government.

Yet, as Madison wrote in Federalist Paper No. 45:

The powers delegated by the proposed Constitution to the Federal Government, are few and defined. Those which are to remain in the State Governments are numerous and indefinite.

The former will be exercised principally on external objects, as war, peace, negotiation, and foreign commerce; with which last the power of taxation will for the most part be connected. The powers reserved to the several States will extend to all the objects, which, in the ordinary course of affairs, concern the lives, liberties and properties of the people; and the internal order, improvement, and prosperity of the State.

Nevertheless, states remained concerned that the national government would attempt to cut into their power and sovereignty, and the language of the Constitution did little to allay their fears. At worst, it suggested that the federal institutions would always be supreme; at best, it was highly ambiguous. Even Madison recognized its lack of clarity when he wrote in Federalist Paper No. 39:

The proposed Constitution therefore . . . is in strictness neither a national nor a federal Constitution; but a composition of both. In its foundation it is federal, not national; in the sources from which the ordinary powers of the Government are drawn, it is partly federal, and partly national: in the operation of these powers, it is national, not federal. In the extent of them, again, it is federal; not national: And finally in the authoritative mode of introducing amendments, it is neither wholly federal, nor wholly national.

Madison clearly thought this ambiguity was an asset of the new system of government, an advantage that made it fit compatibly into the overall philosophies of separation of powers and checks and balances. But this argument proved insufficient; when the perceived unfair balance of power proved to be an obstacle to the ratification of the Constitution, those favoring its adoption promised to remedy it.

This remedy took the form of the Tenth Amendment, which—in terms of the rest of the Bill of Rights—is a constitutional oddity. While the first nine amendments deal mainly with the rights of the people vis-à-vis the federal government (for example, the First Amendment: "Congress shall make no law respecting an establishment of religion"), the Tenth Amendment states: "The powers not delegated to the United States by the Constitution, nor prohibited by it to the States, are reserved to the States respectively, or to the people." With these words in place, states' rights advocates were mollified, at least temporarily, and the American system of government— that unique brand of federalism—was established. The

TABLE III-1   The Constitutional Allocation of Government Power

Powers Specified Within the Constitution or by Court Interpretation		
Powers Exclusive to the National Government	Powers Exclusive to State Governments	Concurrent Powers to Both Federal and State Governments
Coin money	Run elections	Tax
Regulate interstate and foreign commerce	Regulate intrastate commerce	Borrow money
Tax imports and exports	Establish republican forms of state and local governments	Establish courts
Make treaties	Protect public health, safety, and morals	Charter banks and corporations
Make all laws "necessary and proper"	All powers not delegated to the national government or denied to the states by the Constitution	Make and enforce laws
Make war		Take property (power of eminent domain)
Regulate postal system		

Powers Denied by the Constitution or by Court Interpretation		
Expressly Prohibited to the National Government	Expressly Prohibited to State Government	Expressly Prohibited to Both
Tax state exports	Tax imports and exports	Pass bills of attainder
Change state boundaries	Coin money	Pass ex post facto laws
	Enter into treaties	Grant titles of nobility
	Impair obligation of contracts	Impose religious tests
		Pass laws in conflict with the Bill of Rights and subsequent amendments

SOURCES: Adapted from Paul E. Johnson et al., *American Government* (Boston: Houghton Mifflin, 1990), 84; J. W. Peltason, *Corwin & Peltason's Understanding the Constitution*, 14th ed. (Fort Worth, Texas, Harcourt Brace, 1997), 20–22; and C. Herman Pritchett, *Constitutional Law of the Federal System* (Englewood Cliffs, N.J.: Prentice-Hall, 1984), 58.

Tenth Amendment appeared to be a constitutional affirmation that the states retained significant powers.

Supporters of state authority quickly learned, however, that the Tenth Amendment did not offer the states adequate protection against federal encroachment. Just three years after the amendment was ratified, the Supreme Court in *Chisholm v. Georgia* (1793) upheld the authority of the federal courts to hear cases brought against a state by citizens of another state. The idea that the fortunes of a state could be decided by a federal tribunal was unacceptable to state power advocates. They demanded constitutional protection against such intrusions. The result was the Eleventh Amendment, ratified in 1795, which restricted the power of the federal courts to hear disputes brought against a state by the citizens of another state or by citizens of other nations. As history would quickly show, however, neither the Tenth nor the Eleventh Amendment settled the perennial question of the proper distribution of political power between the federal government and the various states.

In the final analysis, what does the system look like? In other words, who gets what? Table III-1 depicts the allocation of powers emanating from the Constitution. As we can see, the different levels of government have some exclusive and some concurrent powers, but also they are prohibited from operating in certain spheres.

The elaborate system of American federalism depicted in Table III-1 seems to belie what we noted at the beginning of this essay. At this point, you may be wondering how such a well-articulated division of power could be the center of so much controversy. In part, the answer takes us back to the contractual nature of the Constitution. As we shall see in the following chapter, which explores general theoretical approaches to federalism, the Court has had some difficulty determining the parties to the contract, and its confusion encouraged litigation. In more concrete terms, no matter how elaborate the design, it does not (and perhaps cannot) address the range of real disputes that arise between nation and state.

Indeed, the irony here is that the complexity of the system coupled with the language of the Constitution is what fosters the need for interpretation. We often must ask, where do state powers begin and federal powers end and vice versa? For example, states have the authority to regulate intrastate commerce, and the federal government regulates interstate commerce, but is it so easy to delineate those boundaries? Which entity controls the manufacturing of goods in one state that are shipped to another? And, more to the point, what happens when the state and federal governments have different ideas over how to regulate the manufacturing?

If that problem is not enough, compare the constitutional language of the Tenth Amendment with that of the Necessary and Proper and Supremacy Clauses. The latter prohibits states from passing laws that directly conflict with the Constitution, federal laws, and so forth. But so often the issues are not that clear. For example, is the federal authority supreme only in its sphere of operations (those activities where it has clear constitutional mandates), as some argue the Tenth Amendment dictates? Or is it the case that every time the federal government enters into a particular realm, it automatically preempts the actions of states? Or does the answer depend on the intent of Congress—that is, whether it intended to preempt state action?

It should be clear that American federalism is something of a two-edged sword. On the one hand, the balance of power it created pacified those who were opposed to ratifying the Constitution, and this balance continues to define the contours of the U.S. system of government. On the other hand, the complexity of federalism has given rise to tensions between the levels of government, often leading to disputes that require settlement by the courts. It may be that the system has been so resilient because it constantly requires fresh interpretation. But we will leave that up to you to decide as we now turn to the way the Supreme Court has formulated theories and specific rulings in response to two distinct but interrelated issues: the general contours of state-federal relations and the important powers of commerce and taxing and spending.

READINGS

Berger, Raoul. *Federalism: The Founders' Design*. Norman: University of Oklahoma Press, 1987.

Davis, S. R. *The Federal Principle*. Berkeley: University of California Press, 1978.

Killenbeck, Mark R., ed. *The Tenth Amendment and State Sovereignty*. Lanham, Md.: Rowman & Littlefield, 2002.

Mason, Alpheus. *The States Rights Debate: Anti-Federalism and the Constitution*. Englewood Cliffs, N.J.: Prentice Hall, 1964.

Orth, John V. *The Judicial Power of the United States: The Eleventh Amendment in American History*. New York: Oxford University Press, 1987.

Peltason, J. W., and Sue Davis. *Corwin and Peltason's Understanding the Constitution*, 15th ed. Fort Worth, Texas: Harcourt Brace, 2000.

Rutland, Robert. *The Ordeal of the Constitution: The Antifederalists and the Ratification Struggle of 1787–1788*. Norman: University of Oklahoma Press, 1966.

Schmidhauser, John R. *The Supreme Court as Final Arbiter in Federal-State Relations, 1789–1957*. Chapel Hill: University of North Carolina Press, 1958.

Sprague, John D. *Voting Patterns of the U.S. Supreme Court: Cases in Federalism, 1889–1959*. Indianapolis: Bobbs-Merrill, 1968.

Vile, M. J. C. *The Structure of American Federalism*. London: Oxford University Press, 1961.

CHAPTER 6
FEDERALISM

D URING THE 1960s Congress amended a labor standards act and required state governments to pay virtually all their employees a specified minimum wage and to compensate them for overtime work. Were these amendments constitutional, or did they interfere with state authority and autonomy? The answer depends on how we view the letter and spirit of the Constitution. We would reach very different conclusions depending on whether we subscribed to the dual approach or to the cooperative approach to nation-state relations *(see Table 6-1)*.

Proponents of dual federalism would want the Court to strike down the law. As advocates of states' rights, they would argue that the Constitution represents an agreement between the states and the federal government in which the states empower the central government; states, therefore, are not subservient to the federal government. In other words, because each state is supreme within its own sphere, the federal government could no more impose minimum wage requirements on states than the states could on the federal government. To back their theory, dual federalists invoke the Tenth Amendment, arguing that Congress cannot "invade" power reserved to the states; they contend that if Congress does enact legislation that encroaches on traditional state functions, the courts should void it.

Cooperative federalism takes precisely the opposite view. Proponents argue that the people, not the states, created and animated the federal government. This view holds that the Supremacy Clause and the Necessary and Proper Clause, not the Tenth Amendment, would control the balance of power between the federal government and the states. That amendment, according to cooperative federalism, grants no express power to the states. As a result, the law regulating wages would pass constitutional muster.

The history of nation-state relations issues before the Supreme Court has been characterized by swings back and forth between cooperative federalism and dual federalism. The amendments to the labor standards act were, in fact, struck down by the Court in 1976 in *National League of Cities v. Usery*, only to be upheld in 1985 in *Garcia v. San Antonio Metropolitan Transit Authority*, which effectively overruled the 1976 decision. But just fourteen years after *Garcia*, in *Alden v. Maine* (2000), the Court held that state employees could not bring a federal suit against their nonconsenting state for alleged violations of the overtime pay provisions of the labor act. This decision may not have overruled *Garcia*, but it certainly made it difficult for employees to take advantage of the act.

NATION-STATE RELATIONS: THE DOCTRINAL CYCLE

The Court's about-face from *National League of Cities* to *Garcia* to *Alden* is not an anomaly in this area of the law; rather, it is a symptom of the general confusion that has surrounded American federalism since the eighteenth century. As depicted in Table 6-2, throughout U.S. history different Courts have subscribed to dual federalism, cooperative federalism, or one of their variants. Even

TABLE 6-1   A Comparison of Dual and Cooperative Federalism

	Dual Federalism	Cooperative Federalism
General View	Operates under the assumption that the two levels of government are co-equal sovereigns, each supreme within its own sphere.	Operates under the assumption that the national government is supreme even if its actions touch state functions. States and the federal government are "partners," but the latter largely sets policy for the nation.
View of the Constitution	It is a compact among the states and a contract between the states and the federal government.	Rejects view of it as a "compact"; the people, not the states, empower the national government.
Constitutional Support	Tenth Amendment reserves certain powers to the states and thus limits the national government to those powers specifically delegated to it.	Tenth Amendment does not provide additional powers to the states.
	Necessary and Proper Clause is to be read literally and narrowly.	Necessary and Proper Clause is to be read expansively and loosely.
		Supremacy Clause means that the national government is supreme within its own sphere, even if its actions touch on state functions.

TABLE 6-2   Doctrinal Cycles of Nation-State Relations

Court Era	General Approach Adopted
Marshall Court (1801–1835)	Cooperative federalism (National supremacy)
Taney Court (1835–1864)	Dual federalism
Civil War/Reconstruction Courts (1865–1895)	Cooperative federalism (National supremacy)
Laissez-faire Courts (1896–1936)	Dual federalism (grounded in laissez-faire philosophy)
Post–New Deal Courts (1937–1975)	Cooperative federalism
Burger Court: *National League of Cities v. Usery* (1976)	Dual federalism (Traditional state functions)
Burger Court: *Garcia v. SAMTA* (1985)	Cooperative federalism
Burger and Rehnquist Courts	New *judicial* federalism
Rehnquist Court	Dual federalism (States cannot be treated as administrative units of the federal government)

more intriguing is that something of a doctrinal cycle has developed as the justices have moved between states' rights and national supremacy positions over time. This chapter examines the components of the cycle. As you read the cases, consider not only which doctrine governed each decision, but also why the philosophies have grown stronger or weaker. What forces—legal, political, and historical—have influenced the justices to choose one approach over the other?

What is more, since the Burger Court, the justices have revitalized state courts as important policy makers. In a series of opinions since the 1970s the Court (or, at least, some of its members) has given impetus to a doctrine called "new judicial federalism." In a narrow sense, this doctrine refers to the renewed willingness of state courts to rely only on state law, especially state constitutional law, when deciding cases involving individual rights.[1] In a broader sense, it suggests a role of increased importance for state courts in the American government system. The Supreme Court encouraged this trend by chipping away at the various and traditional mechanisms for federal judicial

1. See Shirley S. Abrahamson and Diane S. Gutman, "The New Judicial Federalism: State Constitutions and State Courts," *Judicature* 71 (1987): 90.

supervision of states and their courts. In the second part of this chapter, we examine new judicial federalism and its implications for the balance of power between the states and the federal government. We also ask you to consider how much *Bush v. Gore* (2000), in which the U.S. Supreme Court reversed a decision of the Florida Supreme Court and effectively decided the outcome of the 2000 presidential election, may change perceptions about the Court's commitment to new judicial federalism.

The Marshall Court and the Rise of National Supremacy

An ardent Federalist, Chief Justice John Marshall was true to his party's tenets over the course of his long career on the Court. In case after case (in particular, *Cohens v. Virginia*), he was more than willing to elevate the powers of the federal government above those of the states—even when he knew that some states were questioning the authority of the Court or failing to respect its decisions.

Such behavior may not be unusual in new democracies, as our discussion of the problems of the Russian Constitutional Court demonstrates *(see Box 6-1)*. But that did not deter Marshall from making a number of important statements on national supremacy—with perhaps the most significant coming in *McCulloch v. Maryland* (1819). In Chapter 3 we saw how he used this case to assert that Congress has implied powers. Here, we shall see that *McCulloch* also served as Marshall's vehicle to expound the notion of national supremacy. We offer a brief review of the essential facts to remind you of the issues in this case.

McCulloch v. Maryland

4 WHEAT. (17 U.S.) 316 (1819)
http://supct.law.cornell.edu/supct/cases/name.htm
Vote: 6 (Duvall, Johnson, Livingston, Marshall, Story, Washington)

o

Opinion of the Court: Marshall
Not participating: Todd

Congress established the second Bank of the United States in 1816. Because of inefficiency and corruption, the bank was very unpopular, and many blamed it for the nation's economic problems. To show its displeasure, the Maryland legislature passed a law saying that banks operating in the state that were not chartered by the state—in other words, the national bank—could issue bank notes only on special paper, which the state taxed. When James McCulloch, the cashier of the Baltimore branch of the Bank of the United States, refused to pay the tax, Maryland took legal action to enforce its law. The United States challenged the constitutionality of the Maryland tax, and in return Maryland disputed the constitutionality of the bank.[2]

MR. CHIEF JUSTICE MARSHALL delivered the opinion of the Court.

The constitution of our country, in its most interesting and vital parts, is to be considered; the conflicting powers of the government of the Union and of its members, as marked in that constitution, are to be discussed; and an opinion given, which may essentially influence the great operations of the government. . . .

In discussing this . . . the counsel for the state of Maryland have deemed it of some importance, in the construction of the constitution, to consider that instrument not as emanating from the people, but as the act of sovereign and independent states. The powers of the general government, it has been said, are delegated by the states, who alone are truly sovereign; and must be exercised in subordination to the states, who alone possess supreme dominion.

It would be difficult to sustain this proposition. The convention which framed the constitution was indeed elected by the state legislatures. But the instrument, when it came from their hands, was a mere proposal, without obligation, or pretensions to it. It was reported to the then existing Congress of the United States, with a request that it might "be submitted to a convention of delegates, chosen in each state by the people thereof, under the recommendation of its legislature, for their assent and ratification." This mode

2. The first part of the opinion deals with the question of whether Congress had the power to create the bank. See the excerpt in Chapter 3. The second part deals with the constitutionality of the Maryland tax. Marshall clearly delineates this division in his opinion.

BOX 6-1 FEDERALISM IN GLOBAL PERSPECTIVE

As our discussion of *McCulloch v. Maryland* in this chapter and judicial review of state court decisions in Chapter 2 (pages 78–85) illustrates, the states of the United States zealously guarded their power from federal encroachment during Chief Justice Marshall's tenure. The justices were well aware of the possibility that at least some states would disregard its decisions—as, in fact, some did.

As it turns out, the U.S. Supreme Court has not been the only judicial tribunal to face such challenges. Quite early in its history, the Russian Constitutional Court confronted a similar lack of respect from republics in its country.

Created in 1991, the Russian court was given substantial powers, including the ability to review the constitutionality of all state actions (in the absence of a concrete dispute) at the request of various executive and legislative bodies. In other words, if a member of Russia's parliament or even the president believed that a republic was violating constitutional mandates, he or she could bring the claim directly to the court, which could then issue a ruling.

In March 1992 a group of Russian legislators took advantage of this right to challenge an action of Tatarstan, a republic within the Russian Federation. Specifically, they argued that a referendum Tatarstan hoped to put to its citizens was unconstitutional. The referendum asked whether the citizens agreed or disagreed "that the Tatarstan Republic is a sovereign state and a party to international law, basing its relations with the Russian Federation as partners."

The justices accepted the case and scheduled hearings, which Tatarstan officials refused to attend. After hearing the arguments, the justices held that, in fact, the referendum violated several constitutional provisions, especially those establishing national supremacy: "The denial of the supremacy of federal laws over the laws of members of the federation is contrary to the constitutional status of the republics in a federated state and precludes the establishment of a law-governed state."

When the Tatar government decided to ignore the ruling, the justices requested that their chair (chief justice), Valerii Zor'kin, persuade parliament to seek compliance with their decision. Parliament acceded, issuing a resolution that supported the court's ruling and requesting the president to enforce it. That was insufficient, however, to deter Tatarstan from going ahead with its referendum about a week later.

To be sure, the U.S. Supreme Court continues to confront challenges from the states. But blatant disregard for its decisions is unusual today. Whether the Russian Constitutional Court will be able to attain a similar status is a question only time can answer.

SOURCES: Herman Schwartz, *The Struggle for Constitutional Justice in Post-Communist Europe* (Chicago: University of Chicago Press, 2000); Robert Sharlet, "The Russian Constitutional Court: The First Term," *Post-Soviet Affairs* 9 (1993): 1–39; Julia Wishnevsky, "Russian Constitutional Court: A Third Branch of Government?" *RFE/RL Research Report* 2 (1993): 1.

---

of proceeding was adopted; and by the convention, by Congress, and by the state legislatures, the instrument was submitted to the people. They acted upon it in the only manner in which they can act safely, effectively, and wisely, on such a subject, by assembling in convention. It is true, they assembled in their several states—and where else should they have assembled? No political dreamer was ever wild enough to think of breaking down the lines which separate the states, and of compounding the American people into one common mass. Of consequence, when they act, they act in their states. But the measures they adopt do not, on that account, cease to be the measures of the people themselves, or become the measures of the state governments. . . .

The government of the Union, then . . . is, emphatically, and truly, a government of the people. . . .

It is the government of all; its powers are delegated by all; it represents all, and acts for all. Though any one state may be willing to control its operations, no state is willing to allow others to control them. The nation, on those subjects on which it can act, must necessarily bind its component parts. But this question is not left to mere reason; the people have, in express terms, decided it by saying, "this constitution, and the laws of the United States, which shall be made in pursuance thereof," "shall be the supreme law of the land," and by requiring that the members of the state legislatures, and the officers of the executive and judicial departments of the states shall take the oath of fidelity to it. The government of the United States, then, though limited in its powers, is supreme; and its laws, when made in pursuance of the constitution, form the supreme law of the land, "anything in the constitution or laws of any State to the contrary notwithstanding."

Among the enumerated powers, we do not find that of establishing a bank or creating a corporation. But there is no phrase in the instrument which, like the articles of confederation, excludes incidental or implied powers; and which requires that everything granted shall be expressly and minutely described. Even the 10th amendment, which was framed for the purpose of quieting the excessive jealousies which had been excited, omits the word "expressly," and declares only that the powers "not delegated to the United States, nor prohibited to the states, are reserved to the states or to the people;" thus leaving the question, whether the particular power which may become the subject of contest has been delegated to the one government, or prohibited to the other, to depend on a fair construction of the whole instrument. The men who drew and adopted this amendment had experienced the embarrassments resulting from the insertion of this word in the articles of confederation, and probably omitted it to avoid those embarrassments. A constitution, to contain an accurate detail of all the subdivisions of which its great powers will admit, and of all the means by which they may be carried into execution, would partake of a prolixity of a legal code, and could scarcely be embraced by the human mind. It would probably never be understood by the public. Its nature, therefore, requires, that only its great outlines should be marked, its important objects designated, and the minor ingredients which compose those objects be deduced from the nature of the objects themselves. That this idea was entertained by the framers of the American constitution, is not only to be inferred from the nature of the instrument, but from the language. . . .

After this declaration, it can scarcely be necessary to say that the existence of state banks can have no possible influence on the question. No trace is to be found in the constitution of an intention to create a dependence of the government of the Union on those of the states, for the execution of the great powers assigned to it. Its means are adequate to its ends; and on those means alone was it expected to rely for the accomplishment of its ends. To impose on it the necessity of resorting to means which it cannot control, which another government may furnish or withhold, would render its course precarious; the result of its measures uncertain, and create a dependence on other governments, which might disappoint its most important designs and is incompatible with the language of the constitution. But were it otherwise, the choice of means implies a right to choose a national bank in preference to state banks, and Congress alone can make the election.

After the most deliberate consideration, it is the unanimous and decided opinion of this court that the act to incorporate the bank of the United States is a law made in pursuance of the constitution, and is part of the supreme law of the land. . . .

It being the opinion of the court, that the act incorporating the bank is constitutional; and that the power of establishing a branch in the State of Maryland might be properly exercised by the bank itself, we proceed to inquire . . . whether the State of Maryland may, without violating the constitution, tax that branch? . . .

The argument on the part of the State of Maryland, is, not that the States may directly resist a law of Congress, but that they may exercise their acknowledged powers upon it, and that the constitution leaves them this right in the confidence that they will not abuse it.

That the power to tax involves the power to destroy; that the power to destroy may defeat and render useless the power to create; that there is a plain repugnance, in conferring on one government a power to control the constitutional measures of another, which other, with respect to those very measures, is declared to be supreme over that which exerts the control, are propositions not to be denied. But all inconsistencies are to be reconciled by the magic of the word CONFIDENCE Taxation, it is said, does not necessarily and unavoidably destroy. To carry it to the excess of destruction would be an abuse, to presume which, would banish that confidence which is essential to all government.

But is this a case of confidence? Would the people of any one State trust those of another with a power to control the most insignificant operations of their State government? We know they would not. Why, then, should we suppose that the people of any one State should be willing to trust those of another with a power to control the operations of a government to which they have confided their most important and most valuable interests? In the legislature of the Union alone, are all represented. The legislature of the Union alone, therefore, can be trusted by the people with the power of controlling measures which concern all, in the confidence that it will not be abused. This, then, is not a case of confidence, and we must consider it as it really is.

If we apply the principle for which the State of Maryland contends, to the constitution generally, we shall find it capable of changing totally the character of that instrument. We shall find it capable of arresting all the measures of the government, and of prostrating it at the foot of the States. The American people have declared their constitution, and the laws made in pursuance thereof, to be supreme; but this principle would transfer the supremacy, in fact, to the States.

If the States may tax one instrument, employed by the government in the execution of its powers, they may tax any and every other instrument. They may tax the mail; they may tax the mint; they may tax patent rights; they may tax the papers of the custom-house; they may tax judicial process; they may tax all the means employed by the government, to an excess which would defeat all the ends of government. This was not intended by the American people. They did not design to make their government dependent on the States. . . .

It has also been insisted, that, as the power of taxation in the general and State governments is acknowledged to be concurrent, every argument which would sustain the right of the general government to tax banks chartered by the States, will equally sustain the right of the States to tax banks chartered by the general government.

But the two cases are not on the same reason. The people of all the States have created the general government, and have conferred upon it the general power of taxation. The people of all the States, and the States themselves, are represented in Congress, and, by their representatives, exercise this power. When they tax the chartered institutions of the States, they tax their constituents; and these taxes must be uniform. But, when a State taxes the operations of the government of the United States, it acts upon institutions created, not by their own constituents, but by people over whom they claim no control. It acts upon the measures of a government created by others as well as themselves, for the benefit of others in common with themselves. The difference is that which always exists, and always must exist, between the action of the whole on a part, and the action of a part on the whole—between the laws of a government declared to be supreme, and those of a government which, when in opposition to those laws, is not supreme.

But if the full application of this argument could be admitted, it might bring into question the right of Congress to tax the State banks, and could not prove the right of the States to tax the Bank of the United States.

The court has bestowed on this subject its most deliberate consideration. The result is a conviction that the states have no power, by taxation or otherwise, to retard, impede, burden, or in any manner control the operations of the constitutional laws enacted by Congress to carry into execution the powers vested in the general government. This is, we think, the unavoidable consequence of that supremacy which the constitution has declared.

We are unanimously of opinion that the law passed by the legislature of Maryland, imposing a tax on the Bank of the United States, is unconstitutional and void.

Constitutional scholars regard *McCulloch* as an unequivocal statement of national power over the states. Its strength lies in Marshall's treatment of the three relevant constitutional provisions: the Necessary and Proper Clause, the Tenth Amendment, and the Supremacy Clause.

First, according to *McCulloch*, the Necessary and Proper Clause permits Congress to pass legislation implied by its enumerated functions, bounded only in this way: "Let the end be legitimate, let it be within the scope of the constitution, and all means which are appropriate, which are plainly adapted to that end, which are not prohibited, but consist with the letter and spirit of the constitution, are constitutional."

Second, because the Tenth Amendment reserves to the states or to the people only power that has not been delegated (expressly or otherwise) to Congress, it stands as no significant bar to Congress's exercise of its powers, including those that are implied. Given Marshall's treatment of the Necessary and Proper Clause, implied powers are quite broad.

Third, the Supremacy Clause places the national government at the top within its sphere of operation, a sphere that again, according to Marshall's interpretation

TABLE 6-3   Selected Events Leading to the Civil War

Date	Event	Significance
November 1832	South Carolina passes ordinance of nullification.	Suggests that states can nullify acts of the federal government and, if necessary, secede from the Union.
December 1832	Jackson issues proclamation warning South Carolina against secession.	Temporarily halts secession crisis, as no state follows South Carolina's lead.
December 1835	Jackson nominates Taney to be chief justice of the U.S. Supreme Court.	The Senate delays confirming Taney, a former slaveholder, until 1836.
May 1854	Congress repeals the Missouri Compromise.	Allows territories to enter the Union with or without slavery.
March 1857	*Scott v. Sandford.*	Increases tension between the North and South, as the former loudly denounces the decision.
November 1860	Lincoln is elected president.	South proclaims that secession is inevitable.
December 1860	South Carolina passes ordinance of secession.	South Carolina votes to secede from the Union. Within a few weeks, six other states follow suit.

of the Necessary and Proper Clause, is expansive. If the Supremacy Clause means anything, it means that no state may "retard, impede, burden, or in any manner control, the operations of the constitutional laws enacted by Congress." Note, too, Marshall's view of the constitutional arrangement; as one would expect, he fully endorsed the position that the charter represents a contract between the people—not the states—and the federal government.

McCulloch's holdings—supporting congressional creation of the bank and negating state taxation of it—were not particularly surprising. Most observers thought the Marshall Court would rule the way it did. It was the chief justice's language and the constitutional theories he offered that sparked a serious debate in a states' rights newspaper, the *Richmond Enquirer*. The debate began just weeks after *McCulloch* was decided, as a barrage of state rights' advocates wrote in to condemn the ruling. Apparently concerned that, if their views took hold, the Union would revert back to its form under the Articles of Confederation, Marshall took an unusual step for a Supreme Court justice: he responded to his critics. Initially, he wrote two articles, carried by a Philadelphia newspaper,

defending *McCulloch*. But when an old enemy, Spencer Roane, the Virginia Supreme Court judge who was the target of the Court's decision in *Martin v. Hunter's Lessee*, launched an unbridled attack, Marshall responded with nine essays published under the pseudonym "A Friend of the Constitution." [3]

The Taney Court and the (Re) Emergence of States' Rights

While Marshall was chief justice of the United States, it was his view of nation-state relations, not Roane's, that prevailed. But their argument foreshadowed a series of events that took place between the 1830s and 1860s, events that would change the country forever *(see Table 6-3)*. The first occurred in November 1832. After Congress passed a tariff act that the South thought unfairly burdensome, South Carolina adopted an ordinance that nullified the federal law. Several days later, the state said it was prepared to enforce its nullification by military force and, if necessary, secession from the Union. It is not

3. For records of these essays, see Gerald Gunther, ed., *John Marshall's Defense of McCulloch v. Maryland* (Stanford: Stanford University Press, 1969).

surprising that South Carolina took the lead in the battle for state sovereignty. The state was the home of John C. Calhoun, a former vice president of the United States and an outspoken proponent of slavery and states' rights. Indeed, Calhoun is best remembered as an advocate of the doctrine of concurrent majorities, a view that would provide states with a veto over federal policies. This doctrine was the underpinning for South Carolina's ordinance of nullification.

The president, Andrew Jackson, was no great nationalist; rather, he believed that states' rights were not incompatible with those of the federal government. But even he took issue with South Carolina's ordinance. Just a month after the state acted, as Table 6-3 illustrates, Jackson issued a proclamation, warning the state that it could not secede from the Union. The president's action infuriated South Carolina, but it temporarily averted a major crisis, as no other state attempted to act on the nullification doctrine.

Another event that would have major implications was Chief Justice Marshall's death in 1835 and Roger Taney's ascension to the chief justiceship *(see Box 6-2, page 333)*. In some ways, Marshall and Taney were alike. Both had begun their political careers in their respective states—Virginia and Maryland—and then held major positions within the executive branch of the national government. Both were committed partisan activists. The difference was that they were committed to completely opposite conceptions of government structure, particularly of nation-state relations. In contrast to Marshall's Federalist sentiments, Taney was a Jacksonian Democrat, a full believer in those ideas espoused by President Jackson, under whom he had served as attorney general, secretary of war, and secretary of the Treasury, and who had appointed him chief justice. The two chief justices' views on the Bank of the United States provide a clear example of their political ideas in action. In *McCulloch* Marshall lent his full support to the bank; in 1832 Taney helped write President Jackson's veto message, in which he said:

It is maintained by the advocates of the bank that its constitutionality in all its features ought to be considered as settled by precedent and by the decision of the Supreme Court. To this

TABLE 6-4 From the Marshall Court to the Taney Court

Marshall Court (1819)	Taney Court (1841)
Marshall	Taney
Livingston	Thompson
Story	Story
Washington	Baldwin
Duval	Daniel
Johnson	Wayne
Todd	McLean
	Catron
	McKinley

conclusion I can not assent. Mere precedent is a dangerous source of authority, and should not be regarded as deciding questions of constitutional power except where the acquiescence of the people and the States can be considered as well settled.

Jackson refused to recharter the bank.

Had Taney been Jackson's only appointment to the Court, the course of federalism might not have been altered. But that was not the case. Table 6-4 shows that by 1841 Joseph Story was the only justice remaining from the Marshall Court that decided *McCulloch*. The others, like Taney, were schooled in Jacksonian democracy. It was, R. Kent Newmyer noted, no longer "the Marshall Court. But, then again it was not the age of Marshall." [4] This observation holds on two levels: doctrinally and politically. The Taney Court ushered in substantial legal changes, especially in federal-state relations. Although there is no true Taney corollary to Marshall's opinion in *McCulloch*, examples of his views abound: in many opinions he explicated the doctrine of dual federalism, that national and state governments are equivalent sovereigns within their own spheres of operation. Unlike Marshall, he read the Tenth Amendment in a broad sense: that it did, in fact, reserve to the states certain powers and limited the power of the federal government over them. In the *License Cases* (1847), Taney wrote: "Every power delegated to the federal government must be in

4. R. Kent Newmyer, *The Supreme Court Under Marshall and Taney* (New York: Crowell, 1968), 94.

BOX 6-2   ROGER BROOKE TANEY (1836–1864)

ROGER TANEY WAS descended on both sides from prominent Maryland families. His mother's family, named Brooke, first arrived in the state in 1650, complete with fox hounds and other trappings of aristocracy. The first Taney arrived about 1660 as an indentured servant but was able to acquire a large amount of property and became a member of the landed Maryland tidewater gentry.

Taney was born March 17, 1777, on his father's tobacco plantation in Calvert County. He was educated in local rural schools and privately tutored by a Princeton student. In 1795, at the age of eighteen, he graduated first in his class from Dickinson College in Pennsylvania.

As his father's second son, Taney was not in line to inherit the family property and so decided on a career in law and politics. For three years, he was an apprentice lawyer in the office of Judge Jeremiah Chase of the Maryland General Court in Annapolis. He was admitted to the bar in 1799.

Taney married Anne Key, daughter of a prominent farmer and the sister of Francis Scott Key, on January 7, 1806. Since Taney was a devout Roman Catholic and his wife an Episcopalian, they agreed to raise their sons as Catholics and their daughters as Episcopalians. The couple had six daughters and a son who died in infancy. Shortly before *Scott v. Sandford* came to the Supreme Court, Taney's wife and youngest daughter died of yellow fever.

TANEY BEGAN his political career as a member of the Federalist Party, serving one term in the Maryland legislature from 1799 to 1800. After being defeated for reelection, he moved from Calvert County to Frederick, where he began to develop a profitable law practice. In 1803 Taney was beaten again in an attempt to return to the House of Delegates. Despite this setback, he began to achieve prominence in the Frederick community as a lawyer and politician. He lived there for twenty years.

In supporting the War of 1812, Taney split with the majority of Maryland Federalists. But in 1816, as a result of shifting political loyalties, he was elected to the state senate and became a dominant figure in party politics. Taney's term expired in 1821. In 1823 he settled in Baltimore, where he continued his successful law practice and political activities. By this time, the Federalist Party had virtually disintegrated, and Taney threw his support to Andrew Jackson's Democrats. He led Jackson's 1828 presidential campaign in Maryland and served as the state's attorney general from 1827 until 1831. At that time, he was named U.S. attorney general for the Jackson administration and left Baltimore for Washington.

It was at this stage in his career that Taney played a leading role in the controversy over the second Bank of the United States, helping to write President Jackson's message in 1832 vetoing the bank's recharter. The next year, when Treasury Secretary William Duane refused to withdraw federal deposits from the national bank, Duane was dismissed and replaced by Taney, who promptly carried out the action.

Taney held the Treasury job for nine months, presiding over a new system of state bank depositories called "pet banks." Jackson, who had delayed as long as he could, was eventually forced to submit Taney's nomination as Treasury secretary to the Senate, which rejected it. Taney was forced to resign.

In 1835 Jackson named Taney to replace aging Supreme Court justice Gabriel Duvall, but the nomination was indefinitely postponed by a close Senate vote. Ten months later, on December 28, Jackson proposed Taney's name again, this time to fill the seat left vacant by the death of Chief Justice John Marshall. To the horror of the Whigs, who considered him much too radical, Taney was confirmed as chief justice on March 15, 1836. He served until his death in Washington, October 12, 1864.

SOURCE: Joan Biskupic and Elder Witt, *Guide to the U.S. Supreme Court*, 3rd ed. (Washington, D.C.: Congressional Quarterly, 1997), 879–880.

coincidence with a perfect right in the states to all that they have not been delegated; in coincidence, too, with the possessing of every power and right necessary for their existence and preservation."

Early Taney Court decisions, such as the *License Cases*, were not controversial. They may have represented a break from previous doctrine, but they matched the tenor of the times. Although Jackson had his feuds with the states (as his battle with South Carolina illustrated), his general philosophical approach to federalism and governance aligned with popular opinion. The issue of slavery was another matter. It had been the cause of acrimony at the Philadelphia convention in 1787, and animosity between the North and the South had continued. The country remained united only through compromises, such as the "three-fifths" plan in the U.S. Constitution, by which a slave was counted as three-fifths of a person for purposes of determining state populations, and the Missouri Compromise of 1820, which provided a plan for slavery in newly admitted states and the territories. By the 1850s old battles began heating up; for example, after California was admitted as a free state, South Carolina once again issued a secession call.

Slavery, therefore, represented the most immediate concern of the day, splitting the nation into two ideological camps. On a different level, however, it was a symptom of a larger problem: the growing resistance of southern states to federal supremacy. As the North's criticism of slavery became more vocal, calls for secession or, at the very least, for adoption of Calhoun's "concurrent majority" doctrine became more widespread in the South.

It was at this critical moment that the Taney-led Supreme Court interceded in both issues—slavery and federal supremacy—by planting its feet firmly in the states' rights camp. With its decision in the infamous case of *Scott v. Sandford*, the Court may have contributed to the collapse of the Union. Also, as you read Taney's opinion, note his theory of the nature of the constitutional contract. How do his views differ from Marshall's in *McCulloch*?

Scott v. Sandford

19 HOW. (60 U.S.) 393 (1857)
http://laws.findlaw.com/US/60/393.html
Vote: 7 (Campbell, Catron, Daniel, Grier, Nelson, Taney, Wayne)
 2 (Curtis, McLean)
Opinion of the Court: Taney
Concurring opinions: Campbell, Catron, Daniel, Grier, Nelson, Wayne
Dissenting opinions: Curtis, McLean

Dred Scott was born into slavery in Virginia about 1795.[5] His original owner was Peter Blow, a plantation owner. Although the title to Scott would be transferred several times, Blow's family remained connected to Scott throughout his life.

Blow moved to St. Louis with his family and slaves in 1827. In 1833, after Blow's death, Scott was sold to John Emerson, a surgeon in the U.S. Army. In 1834 Emerson took Scott to the free state of Illinois, and in 1836 to the Upper Louisiana territory, which was to remain free of slavery under the Missouri Compromise of 1820. While in the Wisconsin territory, Scott married Harriet Robinson, also a slave. They had two daughters.

Eventually, Scott and Emerson returned to Missouri, but the doctor died shortly thereafter. Upon Emerson's death, title to Scott transferred to his widow, E. Irene Sanford Emerson.[6] She had little need for a slave and hired him out to other families in St. Louis. Scott, however, was a poor worker and produced little income. Irene Emerson then moved to Massachusetts, leaving Scott and his family behind. She married Calvin Clifford Chaffee, a New England abolitionist, without telling him that she held title to a slave in St. Louis.[7]

---

5. Sources for the facts of this case are: *National Cyclopaedia of American Biography*, vol. II (New York: James T. White, 1892), 306–307; *Dictionary of American Biography*, vol. VIII (New York: Charles Scribner's Sons, 1935), 488–489; *American National Biography*, vol. 19 (New York: Oxford University Press, 1999), 487–489.

6. The name Sanford was misspelled Sandford in the official records.

7. Just prior to the Court's decision in *Scott v. Sandford*, an embarrassed Calvin Chaffee discovered his wife's previous ownership of the slave. When the justices ruled against Scott, Chaffee and Sanford transferred title to

Dred Scott

In 1846 Henry T. Blow, wealthy son of Scott's original owner, initiated a lawsuit in Missouri state courts to gain Scott's freedom. Blow and Scott believed that Scott no longer had slave status because he had lived on free soil. While the courts considered this petition, Scott remained in the custody of the St. Louis sheriff, and was hired out at $5 per month.

Scott received a favorable decision at the trial court level, but lost in the Missouri Supreme Court. When state courts rejected Scott's bid for emancipation, Blow arranged for ownership of the slave to be transferred to Irene Chaffee's brother, John Sanford of New York. This sale allowed Scott to take his case to federal court under diversity of citizenship jurisdiction—Scott was a citizen

Scott to Taylor Blow, another son of his original owner. They did so to facilitate Scott's emancipation. Under state law, a Missouri slave could be freed only if the owner was a Missouri citizen. Blow emancipated Dred Scott and his family on May 26, 1857, just two and a half months after the Supreme Court's ruling. By this time, Scott had become a local celebrity in St. Louis. He spent the rest of his life as a porter at the Barum Hotel. He lived slightly more than a year as a free man and died of tuberculosis on September 17, 1858. Henry Blow paid for his funeral and burial in St. Louis.

of Missouri and Sanford of New York. Sanford argued that the suit should be dismissed because blacks could not be citizens. The lower federal courts seemed perplexed by the issue. In the end, they ruled in favor of Sanford but suggested that for legal purposes Scott may be a citizen. From 1854 to 1857, while the federal courts considered his cause, Scott lived in St. Louis with virtually no restraints on his freedom.

By the time the case arrived at the U.S. Supreme Court for final judgment in 1856, the facts and the political situation had grown increasingly complex. In 1854, under mounting pressure, Congress had repealed the Missouri Compromise, replacing it with legislation declaring congressional neutrality on the issue of slavery. Given this new law and the growing tensions between the North and the South and the free and slave states, some observers speculated that the Court would decline to decide the case: it had become so controversial and political.

For at least a year, the Court chose that route. Historians, in fact, have suggested that after hearing the case the justices wanted simply to affirm the state court's decision, thereby evading the issue of slavery and citizenship for blacks. But when Justice James Wayne, a Jackson appointee from Georgia, insisted that the Court deal with these concerns, the majority of the others—including Chief Justice Taney, a former slaveholder—went along. Waiting until after the presidential election, a very divided Court (nine separate opinions were written) announced its decision.

MR. CHIEF JUSTICE TANEY delivered the opinion of the Court.

The question is simply this: can a negro whose ancestors were imported into this country and sold as slaves, become a member of the political community formed and brought into existence by the Constitution of the United States, and as such become entitled to all the rights, and privileges, and immunities, guaranteed by that instrument to the citizen. One of these rights is the privilege of suing in a court of the United States in the cases specified in the Constitution.

It will be observed, that the plea applies to that class of persons only whose ancestors were negroes of the African race, and imported into this country, and sold and held as slaves. The only matter in issue before the court, therefore, is, whether the descendants of such slaves, when they shall be emancipated, or who are born of parents who had become free before their birth, are citizens of a state, in the sense in which the word "citizen" is used in the Constitution of the United States. And this being the only matter in dispute on the pleadings, the court must be understood as speaking in this opinion of that class only; that is, of those persons who are the descendants of Africans who were imported into this country and sold as slaves. . . .

The words "people of the United States" and "citizens" are synonymous terms, and mean the same thing. They both describe the political body, who, according to our republican institutions, form the sovereignty, and who hold the power and conduct the government through their representatives. They are what we familiarly call the "sovereign people," and every citizen is one of this people, and a constituent member of this sovereignty. The question before us is, whether the class of persons described in the plea in abatement compose a portion of this people, and are constituent members of this sovereignty. We think they are not, and that they are not included, and were not intended to be included, under the word "citizens" in the Constitution, and can, therefore, claim none of the rights and privileges which that instrument provides for and secures to citizens of the United States. On the contrary, they were at that time considered as a subordinate and inferior class of beings, who had been subjugated by the dominant race, and whether emancipated or not, yet remained subject to their authority, and had no rights or privileges but such as those who held the power and the government might choose to grant them.

It is not the province of the court to decide upon the justice or injustice, the policy or impolicy of these laws. The decision of that question belonged to the political or lawmaking power; to those who formed the sovereignty and framed the Constitution. The duty of the court is to interpret the instrument they have framed, with the best lights we can obtain on the subject, and to administer it as we find it, according to its true intent and meaning when it was adopted.

In discussing this question, we must not confound the rights of citizenship which a state may confer within its own limits, and the rights of citizenship as a member of the Union. It does not by any means follow, because he has all the rights and privileges of a citizen of a State, that he must

be a citizen of the United States. He may have all the rights and privileges of the citizen of a State, and yet not be entitled to the rights and privileges of a citizen in any other State. For, previous to the adoption of the Constitution of the United States, every State had the undoubted right to confer on whomsoever it pleased the character of a citizen, and to endow him with all its rights. But this character, of course, was confined to the boundaries of the State, and gave him no rights or privileges in other States beyond those secured to him by the laws of nations and the comity of States. Nor have the several States surrendered the power of conferring these rights and privileges by adopting the Constitution of the United States. Each State may still confer them upon an alien, or any one it thinks proper, or upon any class or description of persons; yet he would not be a citizen in the sense in which that word is used in the Constitution of the United States, nor entitled to sue as such in one of its courts, nor to the privileges and immunities of a citizen in the other States. The rights which he would acquire would be restricted to the State which gave them. The Constitution has conferred on Congress the right to establish an uniform rule of naturalization, and this right is evidently exclusive, and has always been held by this court to be so. Consequently, no State, since the adoption of the Constitution, can, by naturalizing an alien, invest him with the rights and privileges secured to a citizen of a State under the federal government, although, so far as the State alone was concerned, he would undoubtedly be entitled to the rights of a citizen, and clothed with all the rights and immunities which the Constitution and laws of the State attached to that character.

It is very clear, therefore, that no State can, by any Act or law of its own, passed, since the adoption of the Constitution, introduce a new member into the political community created by the Constitution of the United States. It cannot make him a member of this community by making him a member of its own. And for the same reason it cannot introduce any person, or description of persons, who were not intended to be embraced in this new political family, which the Constitution brought into existence, but were intended to be excluded from it. . . .

It is true, every person, and every class and description of persons, who were at the time of the adoption of the Constitution recognized as citizens in the several States, became also citizens of this new political body; but none other; it was formed by them, and for them and their posterity, but for no one else. And the personal rights and privileges guarantied to citizens of this new sovereignty were intended to embrace those only who were then members of the several state communities, or who should afterwards, by birthright or otherwise, become members, according to the provisions of the Constitution and the principles on which it was founded. It was the union of those who were at that time members of distinct and separate political communities into one political family, whose power, for certain specified purposes, was to extend over the whole territory of the United States. And it gave to each citizen rights and privileges outside of his State which he did not before possess, and placed him in every other State upon a perfect equality with its own citizens as to rights of person and rights of property; it made him a citizen of the United States.

It becomes necessary, therefore, to determine who were citizens of the several States when the Constitution was adopted. . . .

In the opinion of the court, the legislation and histories of the times, and the language used in the Declaration of Independence, show, that neither the class of persons who had been imported as slaves, nor their descendants, whether they had become free or not, were then acknowledged as a part of the people, nor intended to be included in the general words used in that memorable instrument.

It is difficult at this day to realize the state of public opinion in relation to that unfortunate race, which prevailed in the civilized and enlightened portions of the world at the time of the Declaration of Independence, and when the Constitution of the United States was framed and adopted. But the public history of every European nation displays it in a manner too plain to be mistaken.

They had for more than a century before been regarded as beings of an inferior order, and altogether unfit to associate with the white race, either in social or political relations; and so far inferior, that they had no rights which the white man was bound to respect; and that the negro might justly and lawfully be reduced to slavery for his benefit. He was bought and sold, and treated as an ordinary article of merchandise and traffic, whenever a profit could be made by it. This opinion was at that time fixed and universal in the civilized portion of the white race. It was regarded as an axiom in morals as well as in politics, which no one thought of disputing, or supposed to be open to dispute; and men in

every grade and position in society daily and habitually acted upon it in their private pursuits, as well as in matters of public concern, without doubting for a moment the correctness of this opinion. . . .

The legislation of the States . . . shows, in a manner not to be mistaken, the inferior and subject condition of that race at the time the Constitution was adopted, and long afterwards, throughout the thirteen States by which that instrument was framed; and it is hardly consistent with the respect due to these States, to suppose that they regarded at that time, as fellow citizens and members of the sovereignty, a class of beings whom they had thus stigmatized; whom, as we are bound, out of respect to the State sovereignties, to assume they had deemed it just and necessary thus to stigmatize, and upon whom they had impressed such deep and enduring marks of inferiority and degradation; or that when they met in convention to form the Constitution, they looked upon them as a portion of their constituents, or designed to include them in the provisions so carefully inserted for the security and protection of the liberties and rights of their citizens. It cannot be supposed that they intended to secure to them rights, and privileges, and rank, in the new political body throughout the Union, which every one of them denied within the limits of its own dominion. More especially, it cannot be believed that the large slaveholding States regarded them as included in the word "citizens," or would have consented to a constitution which might compel them to receive them in that character from another State. For if they were so received, and entitled to the privileges and immunities of citizens, it would exempt them from the operation of the special laws and from the police regulations which they considered to be necessary for their own safety. It would give to persons of the negro race, who were recognized as citizens in any one State of the Union, the right to enter every other State whenever they pleased, singly or in companies, without pass or passport, and without obstruction, to sojourn there as long as they pleased, to go where they pleased at every hour of the day or night without molestation, unless they committed some violation of law for which a white man would be punished; and it would give them the full liberty of speech in public and in private upon all subjects upon which its own citizens might speak; to hold public meetings upon political affairs, and to keep and carry arms wherever they went. And all of this would be done in the face of the subject race of the same color, both free and slaves, inevitably producing discontent and insubordination among them, and endangering the peace and safety of the State.

It is impossible, it would seem, to believe that the great men of the slaveholding States, who took so large a share in framing the Constitution of the United States, and exercised so much influence in procuring its adoption, could have been so forgetful or regardless of their own safety and the safety of those who trusted and confided in them. . . .

What the construction was at that time, we think can hardly admit of doubt. We have the language of the Declaration of Independence and of the Articles of Confederation, in addition to the plain words of the Constitution itself; we have the legislation of the different States, before, about the time, and since the Constitution was adopted; we have the legislation of Congress, from the time of its adoption to a recent period; and we have the constant and uniform action of the Executive Department, all concurring together, and leading to the same result. And if anything in relation to the construction of the Constitution can be regarded as settled, it is that which we now give to the word "citizen" and the word "people."

And upon a full and careful consideration of the subject, the court is of opinion that, upon the facts stated in the plea in abatement, Dred Scott was not a citizen of Missouri within the meaning of the Constitution of the United States, and not entitled as such to sue in its courts; and, consequently, that the Circuit Court had no jurisdiction of the case, and that the judgment on the plea in abatement is erroneous. . . .

We proceed, therefore, to inquire whether the facts relied on by the plaintiff entitled him to his freedom. . . .

The counsel for the plaintiff has laid much stress upon that article in the Constitution which confers on Congress the power "to dispose of and make all needful rules and regulations respecting the territory or other property belonging to the United States;" but, in the judgment of the court, that provision has no bearing on the present controversy, and the power there given, whatever it may be, is confined, and was intended to be confined, to the territory which at that time belonged to, or was claimed by, the United States, and was within their boundaries as settled by the Treaty with Great Britain, and can have no influence upon a territory afterwards acquired from a foreign government. It was a special provision for a known and particular Territory, and to meet a present emergency, and nothing more. . . .

This brings us to examine by what provision of the Constitution the present Federal Government under its delegated and restricted powers, is authorized to acquire territory outside of the original limits of the United States, and what powers it may exercise therein over the person or property of a citizen of the United States, while it remains a territory, and until it shall be admitted as one of the States of the Union.

There is certainly no power given by the Constitution to the Federal Government to establish or maintain Colonies bordering on the United States or at a distance, to be ruled and governed at its own pleasure; nor to enlarge its territorial limits in any way, except by the admission of new States. That power is plainly given; and if a new State is admitted it needs no further legislation by Congress, because the Constitution itself defines the relative rights and powers and duties of the State, and the citizens of the State, and the Federal Government. But no power is given to acquire a Territory to be held and governed permanently in that character. . . .

We do not mean, however, to question the power of Congress in this respect. The power to expand the territory of the United States by the admission of new States is plainly given; and in the construction of this power by all the departments of the government, it has been held to authorize the acquisition of territory, not fit for admission at the time, but to be admitted as soon as its population and situation would entitle it to admission. It is acquired to become a State, and not to be held as a colony and governed by Congress with absolute authority; and as the propriety of admitting a new State is committed to the sound discretion of Congress, the power to acquire territory for that purpose, to be held by the United States until it is in a suitable condition to become a state upon an equal footing with the other States, must rest upon the same discretion. . . . All we mean to say on this point is, that, as there is no express regulation in the Constitution defining the power which the general government may exercise over the person or property of a citizen in a territory thus acquired, the court must necessarily look to the provisions and principles of the Constitution, and its distribution of powers, for the rules and principles by which its decision must be governed.

Taking this rule to guide us, it may be safely assumed that citizens of the United States who migrate to a territory belonging to the people of the United States, cannot be ruled as mere colonists, dependent upon the will of the general government, and to be governed by any laws it may think proper to impose. The principle upon which our governments rest, and upon which alone they continue to exist, is the union of States, sovereign and independent within their own limits in their internal and domestic concerns, and bound together as one people by a general government, possessing certain enumerated and restricted powers, delegated to it by the people of the several States, and exercising supreme authority within the scope of the powers granted to it, throughout the dominion of the United States. A power, therefore, in the general government to obtain and hold Colonies and dependent Territories, over which they might legislate without restriction, would be inconsistent with its own existence in its present form. Whatever it acquires, it acquires for the benefit of the people of the several States who created it. It is their trustee acting for them, and charged with the duty of promoting the interests of the whole people of the Union in the exercise of the powers specifically granted. . . .

. . . The powers of the government and the rights and privileges of the citizen are regulated and plainly defined by the Constitution itself. And when the territory becomes a part of the United States, the Federal Government enters into possession in the character impressed upon it by those who created it. It enters upon it with its powers over the citizen strictly defined, and limited by the Constitution, from which it derives its own existence, and by virtue of which alone it continues to exist and act as a government and sovereignty. It has no power of any kind beyond it; and it cannot, when it enters a territory of the United States, put off its character, and assume discretionary or despotic powers which the Constitution has denied to it. It cannot create for itself a new character separated from the citizens of the United States, and the duties it owes them under the provisions of the Constitution. The territory being a part of the United States, the government and the citizen both enter it under the authority of the Constitution, with their respective rights defined and marked out; and the Federal Government can exercise no power over his person or property, beyond what that instrument confers, nor lawfully deny any right which it has reserved. . . .

Now, as we have already said in an earlier part of this opinion, upon a different point, the right of property in a slave is distinctly and expressly affirmed in the Constitution. The right to traffic in it, like an ordinary article of mer-

chandise and property, was guaranteed to the citizens of the United States, in every State that might desire it, for twenty years. And the government in express terms is pledged to protect it in all future time, if the slave escapes from his owner. This is done in plain words—too plain to be misunderstood. And no word can be found in the Constitution which gives Congress a greater power over slave property, or which entitles property of that kind to less protection than property of any other description. The only power conferred is the power coupled with the duty of guarding and protecting the owner in his rights.

Upon these considerations, it is the opinion of the court that the Act of Congress which prohibited a citizen from holding and owning property of this kind in the territory of the United States north of the line therein mentioned, is not warranted by the Constitution, and is therefore void; and that neither Dred Scott himself, nor any of his family, were made free by being carried into this territory; even if they had been carried there by the owner, with the intention of becoming a permanent resident.

But there is another point in the case which depends on state power and state law. And it's contended, on that part of the plaintiff, that he is made free by being taken to . . . Illinois, independently of his residence in the territory of the United States; and being so made free he was not again reduced to a state of slavery by being brought back to Missouri.

Our notice of this part of the case will be very brief; for the principle on which it depends was decided in this court, upon much consideration, in the case of *Strader v. Graham*. In that case, the slaves had been taken from Kentucky to Ohio with the consent of the owner, and afterwards brought back to Kentucky. And this court held that their status or condition, as free or slave, depended upon the laws of Kentucky, when they were brought back into that State, and not of Ohio; and that this court had no jurisdiction to revise the judgment of a state court upon its laws. This was the point directly before the court, and the decision that this court had no jurisdiction, turned upon it. . . .

So in this case: as Scott was a slave when taken into the State of Illinois by his owner, and was there held as such, and brought back in that character, his status, as free or slave, depended on the laws of Missouri, and not of Illinois. . . . We are satisfied, upon careful examination of all the cases decided in the State courts of Missouri that it is now firmly settled by the decisions of the highest court in the

State, that Scott and his family upon their return were not free, but were, by the laws of Missouri the property of the defendant; and that the Circuit Court of the United States had no jurisdiction, when, by the laws of the State, the plaintiff was a slave not a citizen. . . .

Upon the whole, therefore, it is the judgment of this court, that it appears by the record before us that the plaintiff in error is not a citizen of Missouri, in the sense in which that word is used in the Constitution; and that the Circuit Court of the United States, for that reason, had no jurisdiction in the case, and could give no judgment in it.

Its judgment for the defendant must, consequently, be reversed, and a mandate issued directing the suit to be dismissed for want of jurisdiction.

Taney's opinion held that Scott was still a slave for the following reasons.[8] First, although Scott could become a citizen of a state, he could not be considered, in a legal sense, to be a citizen of the United States; the nation's history and the words of the Constitution and other documents foreclosed that possibility. As a result, Scott could not sue in federal courts. Second, Congress had no constitutional power to regulate slavery in the territories (in reaching this result, the Court struck down the Missouri Compromise, which already had been repealed by Congress), and the Constitution protects the right to property, a category into which slaves, according to Taney, fell. Third, the status of slaves depends on the law of the state to which they voluntarily returned, regardless of where they had been. Because the Missouri Supreme Court ruled that Scott was a slave, the U.S. Supreme Court would follow suit.

Scott was decided as the nation was on the verge of collapse (*see Table 6-3, page 331*). Taney's holding, coupled with his vision of the nature of the federal-state relationship, rather than calming matters, probably added fuel to the fire. From the perspective of northerners and abolitionists, the opinion was among the most evil and heinous ever issued by the Court. Opponents of slavery

used the ruling to rally support for their position; they took aim at Taney and the Court, claiming that the institution was so pro-South that it could not be taken seriously. Northern newspapers aroused anti-Court sentiment around the country, with stories about the decision. As one wrote:

The whole slavery agitation was reopened by the proceedings in the Supreme Court today, and that tribunal voluntarily introduced itself into the political arena. . . . Much feeling is excited by this decree, and the opinion is freely expressed that a new element of sectional strife has been wantonly imposed upon the country.[9]

Members of Congress lambasted the Court for the raw and unnecessary display of judicial power it had exercised in striking down the Missouri Compromise. A leading history on the period asserted, "Never has the Supreme Court been treated with such ineffable contempt, and never has that tribunal so often cringed before the clamor of the mob." [10] As for the chief justice, his reputation was forever tarnished. Even after his death, Congress resisted commissioning a bust of him to sit beside those of other chief justices in the Capitol's Supreme Court room. At the time, Sen. Charles Sumner said: "I object that an emancipated country should make a bust to the author of the Dred Scott decision," because "the name of Taney is to be hooted down the page of history." [11]

To southerners, *Scott* was a cause for celebration. Indeed, Taney's notions of slavery and dual federalism appeared in a more energized form just a few years later when South Carolina issued its Declaration of the Causes of Secession. President Abraham Lincoln presented precisely the opposite view—the Marshall approach—in his 1861 inaugural address, but his words could not prevent the outbreak of war.

Thus, at its core the Civil War was about not only slavery but also the supremacy of the national government over the states. It was the culmination of the debates be-

---

8. See Melvin I. Urofsky, *A March of Liberty* (New York: Knopf, 1988), 387; and Walter Ehrlich, "*Scott v. Sandford*," *The Oxford Companion to the Supreme Court*, ed. Kermit L. Hall (New York: Oxford University Press, 1992), 759–761.

9. Quoted by Charles Warren in *The Supreme Court in United States History*, vol. 2 (Boston: Little, Brown, 1926), 304.

10. Quoted by Bernard Schwartz in *A History of the Supreme Court* (New York: Oxford University Press, 1993), 154.

11. It was not until 1874 that busts of Samuel Chase and Roger Taney were approved "without debate." See Warren, *The Supreme Court in United States History*, 393–394.

Young girls working in a clothing factory. Congressional attempts to curb child labor by taxing the items produced were repeatedly rebuffed by the Supreme Court.

tween the Federalists and Anti-Federalists, between Marshall and Roane, and so forth. When the Union won the war, it seemed to have also won the debate over the nature of federal-state relations. In the immediate aftermath of the battle, the Court acceded, though not willingly, to congressional power over the defeated region.

Dual Federalism and Laissez-Faire Economics

Did the end of the Civil War and the rise of national supremacy mean that Taney's dual federalism had seen its last days? Indeed, it remained under wraps for several decades but then resurfaced in a somewhat different form in the courts from the 1890s to the 1930s. The most vivid example of its revival came in *Hammer v. Dagenhart* (1918). Some analysts think that this Court's version of dual federalism differed from Taney's in *Scott*. Do you see the distinction? Or do the words of the *Hammer* Court echo its predecessor's sentiment?

Hammer v. Dagenhart

247 U.S. 251 (1918)
http://laws.findlaw.com/US/247/251.html
Vote: 5 (Day, McReynolds, Pitney, Van Devanter, White)
*   4 (Brandeis, Clarke, Holmes, McKenna)*
Opinion of the Court: Day
Dissenting opinion: Holmes

In the 1880s America entered the industrial age, which was characterized by the unfettered growth of the private-sector economy. The Industrial Revolution changed the United States for the better in countless ways, but it also had a downside. Lacking any significant government controls, many businesses had less than benevolent relations with their workers. Some forced employees to work more than fourteen hours a day at absurdly low wages and under dreadful conditions. They also had no qualms about employing children under the age of sixteen.

Americans were divided over these practices. On one side were the entrepreneurs, stockholders, and others who gained from worker exploitation. By employing children, paying low wages, and providing no benefits, they were able to minimize expenses and maximize profits. On the other side were the Progressives, reformist groups, and individuals who sought to persuade the states and the federal government to enact laws to protect workers. These two camps repeatedly clashed in their struggle to attain diametrically opposed policy ends.[12]

One of the first battles came in 1915 when Congress was considering the Federal Child Labor Act. The bill prohibited shipment in interstate commerce of factory products made by children under the age of fourteen or by children aged fourteen to sixteen who worked more than eight hours a day. Supported by numerous progressive groups, the legislation faced substantial opposition from employer associations, including the Executive Committee of Southern Cotton Manufacturers. The committee was made up of militant mill owners who organized in 1915 solely to defeat federal child labor legislation. Its first attempt failed, and in 1916 Congress passed the child labor law. The committee's leader, David Clark, vowed that his group would challenge the constitutionality of the act in court. He retained the services of a corporate law firm that held a laissez-faire philosophy and had successfully placed this argument before the Supreme Court. He then sought the right test case to challenge the law. Eventually, he decided on a suit against the Fidelity Manufacturing Company.

The case he brought was perfect for the committee's needs. Roland Dagenhart and his two minor sons were employed by Fidelity, a cotton mill in North Carolina. Under state law, both of Dagenhart's sons were permitted to work up to eleven hours a day. Under the new federal act, however, the older boy could work only eight

hours, and the younger one could not work at all. Not only were the facts relating to the Dagenharts advantageous, but Clark also secured the cooperation of the company, which had equal disdain for the law, in planning the litigation. One month before the effective date of the law, the company posted the new federal regulations on its door and "explained" to affected employees that they would be unable to continue to work. A week later, having already secured the consent of the Dagenharts and the factory, the committee's attorneys filed an injunction against the company and William C. Hammer, a U.S. attorney, to prevent enforcement of the law.

Within a month, the district court heard arguments and ruled the act unconstitutional. The judge did not write an opinion, but when he handed down his decision, he fully agreed with the committee's arguments, suggesting that the federal government had usurped state power.

Once the district court stayed enforcement of the act, both the committee and the U.S. Justice Department began to plan the strategies they would use before the U.S. Supreme Court. The committee argued that Congress had no authority to impose its policies on the states. The government's defense was led by Solicitor General John W. Davis. One of the great attorneys of the day, he made a strong case for the law, although he probably opposed it. Not only did he argue that the regulation of child labor fell squarely within Congress's purview, but he also supplied the Court with data indicating that the states themselves had sought to eliminate such practices. His brief pointed out that only three states placed no age limit on factory employees, and only ten allowed those between the ages of fourteen and sixteen to work.

MR. JUSTICE DAY delivered the opinion of the Court.

It is . . . contended that the authority of Congress may be exerted to control interstate commerce in the shipment of child-made goods because of the effect of the circulation of such goods in other states where the evil of this class of labor has been recognized by local legislation, and the right to thus employ child labor has been more rigorously restrained than in the state of production. In other words, that

---

12. We derive what follows from Lee Epstein, *Conservatives in Court* (Knoxville: University of Tennessee Press, 1985); and Stephen B. Wood, *Constitutional Politics in the Progressive Era* (Chicago: University of Chicago Press, 1968).

the unfair competition thus engendered may be controlled by closing the channels of interstate commerce to manufacturers in those states where the local laws do not meet what Congress deems to be the more just standard of other states.

There is no power vested in Congress to require the states to exercise their police power so as to prevent possible unfair competition. Many causes may co-operate to give one state, by reason of local laws or conditions, an economic advantage over others. The commerce clause was not intended to give to Congress a general authority to equalize such conditions. In some of the states laws have been passed fixing minimum wages for women; in others the local law regulates the hours of labor of women in various employments. Business done in such states may be at an economic disadvantage when compared with states which have no such regulations; surely, this fact does not give Congress the power to deny transportation in interstate commerce to those who carry on business where the hours of labor and the rate of compensation for women have not been fixed by a standard in the use in other states and approved by Congress.

The grant of power to Congress over the subject of interstate commerce was to enable it to regulate such commerce, and not to give it authority to control the states in their exercise of the police power over local trade and manufacture.

The grant of authority over a purely Federal matter was not intended to destroy the local power always existing and carefully reserved to the states in the 10th Amendment to the Constitution. . . .

That there should be limitations upon the right to employ children in mines and factories in the interest of their own and the public welfare, all will admit. That such employment is generally deemed to require regulation is shown by the fact that the brief of counsel states that every state in the Union has a law upon the subject, limiting the right to thus employ children. In North Carolina, the state wherein is located the factory in which the employment was had in the present case, no child under twelve years of age is permitted to work.

. . . The maintenance of the authority of the states over matters purely local is as essential to the preservation of our institutions as is the conservation of the supremacy of the Federal power in all matters intrusted to the nation by the Federal Constitution.

In interpreting the Constitution it must never be forgotten that the nation is made up of states, to which are intrusted the powers of local government. And to them and to the people the powers not expressly delegated to the national government are reserved. The power of the states to regulate their purely internal affairs by such laws as seem wise to the local authority is inherent, and has never been surrendered to the general government. To sustain this statute would not be, in our judgment, a recognition of the lawful exertion of congressional authority over interstate commerce, but would sanction an invasion by the Federal power of the control of a matter purely local in its character, and over which no authority has been delegated to Congress in conferring the power to regulate commerce among the states.

We have neither authority nor disposition to question the motives of Congress in enacting this legislation. The purposes intended must be attained consistently with constitutional limitations, and not by an invasion of the powers of the states. This court has no more important function than that which devolves upon it the obligation to preserve inviolate the constitutional limitations upon the exercise of authority, Federal and state, to the end that each may continue to discharge, harmoniously with the other, the duties intrusted to it by the Constitution.

In our view the necessary effect of this act is, by means of a prohibition against the movement in interstate commerce of ordinary commercial commodities, to regulate the hours of labor of children in factories and mines within the states,—a purely state authority. Thus the act in a twofold sense is repugnant to the Constitution. It not only transcends the authority delegated to Congress over commerce, but also exerts a power as to a purely local matter to which the Federal authority does not extend. The far-reaching result of upholding the act cannot be more plainly indicated than by pointing out that if Congress can thus regulate matters intrusted to local authority by prohibition of the movement of commodities in interstate commerce, all freedom of commerce will be at an end, and the power of the states over local matters may be eliminated, and thus our system of government be practically destroyed.

For these reasons we hold that this law exceeds the constitutional authority of Congress. It follows that the decree of the District Court must be affirmed.

BOX 6-3   AFTERMATH . . . REUBEN DAGENHART

FIVE YEARS after the Supreme Court's decision in *Hammer v. Dagenhart* striking down the child labor law, a journalist interviewed Reuben Dagenhart, whose father had sued to prevent Congress from interfering with his sons' jobs in a North Carolina cotton mill. Reuben was twenty when he was interviewed. Excerpts follow:

"What benefit . . . did you get out of the suit which you won in the United States Supreme Court?"

"I don't see that I got any benefit. I guess I'd be a lot better off if they hadn't won it.

"Look at me! A hundred and five pounds, a grown man, and no education. I may be mistaken, but I think the years I've put in the cotton mills have stunted my growth. They kept me from getting any schooling. I had to stop school after the third grade and now I need the education I didn't get."

"Just what did you and John get out of that suit then?" he was asked.

"Why, we got some automobile rides when them big lawyers from the North was down here. Oh yes, and they bought both of us a Coca-Cola! That's all we got out of it."

"What did you tell the judge when you were in court?"

"Oh, John and me was never in court. Just Paw was there. John and me was just little kids in short pants. I guess we wouldn't have looked like much in court. . . . We were working in the mill while the case was going on."

Reuben hasn't been to school in years, but his mind has not been idle.

"It would have been a good thing for all the kids in this state if that law they passed had been kept. Of course, they do better now than they used to. You don't see so many babies working in the factories, but you see a lot of them that ought to be going to school."

SOURCE: *Labor*, November 17, 1923, 3, quoted in *The Supreme Court in American Life*, 2nd ed., by Leonard F. James (Glenview, Ill.: Scott, Foresman, 1971), 74.

MR. JUSTICE HOLMES, dissenting.

The act does not meddle with anything belonging to the states. They may regulate their internal affairs and their domestic commerce as they like. But when they seek to send their products across the state line they are no longer within their rights. If there were no Constitution and no Congress their power to cross the line would depend upon their neighbors. Under the Constitution such commerce belongs not to the states, but to Congress to regulate. It may carry out its views of public policy whatever indirect effect they may have upon the activities of the states. Instead of being encountered by a prohibitive tariff at her boundaries, the state encounters the public policy of the United States which it is for Congress to express. The public policy of the United States is shaped with a view to the benefit of the nation as a whole. . . . The national welfare as understood by Congress may require a different attitude within its sphere from that of some self-seeking state. It seems to me entirely constitutional for Congress to enforce its understanding by all the means at its command.

William Day's opinion was a total victory for the Executive Committee, but it meant little to the Dagenharts *(see Box 6-3)*. However, the opinion—a clear endorsement of dual federalism—rested on tenuous grounds. C. Herman Pritchett points out that Justice Day misquoted the Tenth Amendment: it does not contain the word *expressly*. In so doing, he ignored Marshall's reasoning in *McCulloch*. It was critical to Marshall's interpretation of congressional powers that the word *expressly* did not appear. When Congress considered the Tenth Amendment, one representative proposed to "add the word 'expressly' so as to read 'the powers not expressly delegated by this Constitution.' " James Madison and others objected and the motion was defeated.[13] So Day assumed "a position that was historically inaccurate." [14]

Although this error seemed to undermine Day's logic, a more important question may be this: Was Day's expli-

13. Daniel A. Farber and Suzanna Sherry, *A History of the American Constitution* (St. Paul: West Publishing, 1990), 239.
14. C. Herman Pritchett, *Constitutional Law of the Federal System* (Englewood Cliffs, N.J.: Prentice Hall, 1984), 60–61.

cation of dual federalism the same as Taney's? Many scholars think not; in fact, they argue that *Hammer*— taken in conjunction with other opinions of that Court era—diverges from Taney's philosophy. While Taney viewed dual federalism as a way to equalize state and federal power, it may be that the Supreme Court between 1890 and 1930 was not concerned with the rights of states as states. Rather, the justices were bent on prohibiting any state *or* federal interference with the growth of the nation's booming private-sector economy. They used dual federalism as a vehicle to strike down federal regulation of the sort at issue in *Hammer*. At the same time, the Court limited the ability of states to pass similar legislation because that would restrict individual liberties *(see Chapter 10)*. The Court's approach was quite distinct from Taney's. For the Courts from the 1890s through the 1930s, dual federalism and the Tenth Amendment were masks to hide their laissez-faire philosophy.

The justices' frame of reference, their wholehearted support of business, was as well suited to their day as Taney's ideology was to his, or so some have argued. At the very least, the Court's willingness to embrace a free enterprise philosophy reflected the general mood of Americans, some of whom were benefiting financially from the growth of the economy. When the economic boom of the 1920s turned into the Great Depression of the 1930s, however, citizens and their newly elected leaders clamored for the sort of regulation struck down in *Hammer*. Yet, as we saw in the delegation of powers section of Chapter 3, the Court was still set in a 1920s mold. It struck down one New Deal program after another on various grounds, including the unconstitutional delegation of power and the impermissible congressional use of its authority to regulate commerce *(see Chapter 7)*. The Court also invoked the Tenth Amendment. In *Schechter Poultry Corporation v. United States* (1935), which examined the constitutionality of the National Industrial Recovery Act of 1933—a major piece of New Deal legislation—the Court noted:

Extraordinary conditions do not create or enlarge constitutional power. The Constitution established a national government with powers deemed to be adequate, as they have proved to be both in war and peace, but these powers of the national government are limited by the constitutional grants. Those who act under these grants are not at liberty to transcend the imposed limits because they believe that more or different power is necessary. *Such assertions of extra-constitutional authority were anticipated and precluded by the explicit terms of the Tenth Amendment.* (Emphasis added.)

The (Re)Emergence of National Supremacy: Cooperative Federalism

Despite the Court's language, the days of dual federalism were numbered. Amid increasing pressure for change, including President Franklin Roosevelt's Court-packing scheme, came the famous "switch-in-time-that-saved-nine" and with it the demise of broad interpretations of the Tenth Amendment *(see Chapter 7)*. Although this process began in 1937, the death knell rang most loudly with the decision in *United States v. Darby Lumber* (1941).[15] As you read Chief Justice Harlan Stone's opinion, think about Marshall's in *McCulloch*. Are they making similar claims, or can you detect differences?

United States v. Darby Lumber

312 U.S. 100 (1941)
http://laws.findlaw.com/US/312/100.html
Vote: 8 (Black, Douglas, Frankfurter, Hughes, Murphy, Reed, Roberts, Stone)
   0
Opinion of the Court: Stone

In 1938 Congress, under its power to regulate interstate commerce, enacted an important piece of New Deal legislation, the Fair Labor Standards Act (FLSA). It provided that all employers "engaged in interstate commerce, or in the production of goods for that commerce" must pay all their employees a minimum wage of twenty-five cents per hour and not permit employees to work longer than forty-four hours per week without paying them one and one-half times their regular pay. In November 1939 the federal government sought and obtained an indictment against Fred W. Darby for violating

---

15. See Joseph F. Kobylka, "The Court, Justice Blackmun, and Federalism," *Creighton Law Review* 19 (1985–1986): 21.

the FLSA. The indictment alleged that Darby, the owner of a lumber company, was engaged in the production and manufacturing of goods shipped out of state, but that he had not abided by either of the FLSA's major pay requirements.

Darby did not dispute the charges. Rather, invoking the logic of *Hammer,* his brief argued:

The Fair Labor Standards Act . . . is an unconstitutional attempt to regulate conditions in production of goods and commodities and it can not be sustained as a regulation of interstate commerce within the delegated power of Congress under the commerce clause. It violated the Tenth Amendment.

The government responded more pragmatically than legally, stating:

State legislators, Congressional committees, federal commissions, and businessmen over a period of time have realized that no state, acting alone, could require labor standards substantially higher than those obtained in other states whose producers and manufacturers competed in the interstate market.

The reiterated conclusion that the individual states were helpless gained added force during the prolonged economic depression of the 1930's. The . . . National Industrial Recovery Act . . . and the Fair Labor Standards Act itself each reflect a great volume of testimony adduced at congressional hearings and elsewhere to the effect that employers with lower labor standards possess an unfair advantage in interstate competition, and that only the national government could deal with the problem.

The lumber industry, the government asserted, well illustrated "the inability of the particular states to ensure adequate labor standards; over 57 percent of the lumber produced enters into interstate or foreign commerce from 45 of the states."

MR. JUSTICE STONE delivered the opinion of the Court.

The motive and purpose of the present regulation are plainly to make effective the Congressional conception of public policy that interstate commerce should not be made the instrument of competition in the distribution of goods produced under substandard labor conditions, which competition is injurious to the commerce and to the states from and to which the commerce flows. The motive and purpose of a regulation of interstate commerce are matters for the legislative judgment upon the exercise of which the Consti-

tution places no restriction and over which the courts are given no control. . . . Whatever their motive and purpose, regulations of commerce which do not infringe some constitutional prohibition are within the plenary power conferred on Congress by the Commerce Clause. Subject only to that limitation, presently to be considered, we conclude that the prohibition of the shipment interstate of goods produced under the forbidden substandard labor conditions is within the constitutional authority of Congress. . . .

Our conclusion is unaffected by the Tenth Amendment which provides: "The powers not delegated to the United States by the Constitution nor prohibited by it to the states are reserved to the states respectively or to the people." The amendment states but a truism that all is retained which has not been surrendered. There is nothing in the history of its adoption to suggest that it was more than declaratory of the relationship between the national and state governments as it had been established by the Constitution before the amendment or that its purpose was other than to allay fears that the new national government might seek to exercise powers not granted, and that the states might not be able to exercise fully their reserved powers.

From the beginning and for many years the amendment has been construed as not depriving the national government of authority to resort to all means for the exercise of a granted power which are appropriate and plainly adapted to the permitted end. . . .

Reversed.

Justice Stone's opinion in *Darby Lumber* brought the Court full circle, from Marshall's nationalism to Taney's dual federalism and back. Not only did *Darby Lumber* explicitly overrule *Hammer* and uphold the FLSA, but also it gutted the Tenth Amendment: it denied that the amendment constituted a tool that litigants could wield to build up state authority that they could then use to challenge the exercise of enumerated and implied powers by the federal government. According to Justice Stone, and supported by a surprisingly unanimous Court, the Tenth Amendment was "but a truism."

For the next thirty-five years dual federalism was out, and Stone's cooperative federalism was in. Under this doctrine, at least theoretically, the various levels of government shared policy-making responsibilities. In practice, it meant, as Stone's opinion implies, that the national government took the lead in formulating policy goals, which it expected state and local officials to implement. Tremendous changes in government followed, not the least of which was that a huge shift occurred in the balance between national and state spending. As the federal government took advantage of its new constitutional freedom—creating more and more programs and projects covering all aspects of American life—it began to account for greater and greater percentages of government spending. By the 1960s the federal government reigned supreme.

Although federal supremacy was a fact of American life, it was not universally applauded or even accepted. Some opposition came from familiar sources: politicians in southern states, who vehemently opposed congressional (and Court) efforts to force integration of schools and other public facilities. Governors, like Alabama's George Wallace, simply refused to relent, making similar kinds of arguments their counterparts had made in the 1860s. He and others even formed their own political party to advocate states' rights.

Other opposition was more national in scope. President Richard Nixon lamented the tremendous growth of the federal government and the concomitant demise of states' authority over their own affairs. To restore some balance he proposed a "new federalism" plan. Under it, states and localities would have increased authority to determine how they spent their money by participating in a revenue-sharing arrangement with the federal government, which would allocate money to them to spend as they saw fit. New federalism, however, was not dual federalism. Nixon may have wanted to give the states and localities greater authority in certain policy arenas, but he was not one to argue that the federal government, particularly the executive branch, and the states were "co-equal sovereigns." Moreover, issues of federalism were never the most important items on the president's agenda, particularly when it came to nominations to the Supreme Court. Nixon looked for jurists who would be inclined toward judicial restraint generally and to a law-and-order posture, in particular.

When "Nixon's" Supreme Court handed down its decision in *National League of Cities v. Usery* (1976), there-

fore, it took many legal scholars by surprise. A greater concern with states' rights was certainly within the realm of the politics of the day, but the Court took that concern to a rather extreme level. What did the justices rule in *National League of Cities,* and why was their ruling so controversial?[16]

National League of Cities v. Usery

426 U.S. 833 (1976)
http://laws.findlaw.com/US/426/833.html
Vote: 5 (Blackmun, Burger, Powell, Rehnquist, Stewart)
  4 (Brennan, Marshall, Stevens, White)
Opinion of the Court: Rehnquist
Concurring opinion: Blackmun
Dissenting opinions: Brennan, Stevens

At issue in this case was the Fair Labor Standards Act, which the Court had upheld in *United States v. Darby Lumber.* Since the decision in 1941, Congress had amended the act to cover public employees, and those amendments, along with other attempts to regulate state employment, were themselves the subjects of several major Supreme Court rulings. As noted in Box 6-4, the Court had upheld those regulations.

This case crystallized when Congress in 1974 once again expanded the scope of the FLSA, this time bringing virtually all state public employees, who were excluded in the original legislation, under its reach. As a result, various cities and states and two organizations representing their collective interests, the National League of Cities and the National Governors' Conference, challenged the constitutionality of the new amendments. In particular, they argued that the amendments represented a "collision" between federal expansion and states' rights in violation of the Tenth Amendment. As one litigant claimed, the Tenth Amendment should protect the powers states already possessed, including authority over public workers. It is interesting to note that in representing the federal government Solicitor General Robert Bork did not

---

16. To hear oral arguments in this case, navigate to: *www.oyez.org/oyez/frontpage.*

BOX 6-4   HISTORY OF WAGE REGULATION LEADING TO
NATIONAL LEAGUE OF CITIES V. USERY

CONGRESSIONAL ACTION	COURT RESPONSE
Fair Labor Standards Act of 1938 (FLSA): requires employers to pay employees a minimum wage and one and one-half times their regular pay for overtime work. States and localities are excluded from the act.	Upheld in *United States v. Darby Lumber* (1941).
1966 Extension of the FLSA: extended the law to workers in publicly operated schools, hospitals, and institutions. The extension covered employees of transit companies insofar as their public employers had to pay them minimum wage. But the 1966 extension did not provide overtime pay protection.	Upheld in *Maryland v. Wirtz* (1968). Congress can prescribe wage regulations for employees, even if their employer is a state.
Economic Stabilization Act of 1970: limited wage increases for state employees.	Upheld in *Fry v. United States* (1975). This decision falls under Congress's commerce power. However, Congress cannot use its "power in a fashion that impairs the States' integrity or their ability to function effectively in a federal system."

SOURCE: Adapted from Joseph F. Kobylka, "The Court, Justice Blackmun, and Federalism," *Creighton Law Review* 19 (1985–1986): 22–23. Reprinted with permission. Copyright © 1986 by Creighton University.

---

take issue with this analysis. Rather, he argued that the Tenth Amendment was inapplicable because Congress had passed the 1974 amendments under its power to regulate commerce.

MR. JUSTICE REHNQUIST delivered the opinion of the Court.

Appellants' essential contention is that the 1974 amendments to the Act, while undoubtedly within the scope of the Commerce Clause, encounter a similar constitutional barrier because they are to be applied directly to the States and subdivisions of States as employers. . . .

Appellee Secretary argues that the cases in which this Court has upheld sweeping exercises of authority by Congress, even though those exercises pre-empted state regulation of the private sector, have already curtailed the sovereignty of the States quite as much as the 1974 amendments to the Fair Labor Standards Act. We do not agree. It is one thing to recognize the authority of Congress to enact laws regulating individual businesses necessarily subject to the dual sovereignty of the government of the Nation and of the

State in which they reside. It is quite another to uphold a similar exercise of congressional authority directed, not to private citizens, but to the States as States. We have repeatedly recognized that there are attributes of sovereignty attaching to every state government which may not be impaired by Congress, not because Congress may lack an affirmative grant of legislative authority to reach the matter, but because the Constitution prohibits it from exercising the authority in that manner. . . .

One undoubted attribute of state sovereignty is the States' power to determine the wages which shall be paid to those whom they employ in order to carry out their governmental functions, what hours those persons will work, and what compensation will be provided where these employees may be called upon to work overtime. The question we must resolve here, then, is whether these determinations are " 'functions essential to separate and independent existence' " so that Congress may not abrogate the States' otherwise plenary authority to make them.

In their complaint appellants advanced estimates of substantial costs which will be imposed upon them by the 1974 amendments. Since the District Court dismissed their complaint, we take its well-pleaded allegations as true, although it appears from appellee's submissions in the District Court and in this Court that resolution of the factual disputes as to the effect of the amendments is not critical to our disposition of the case.

Judged solely in terms of increased costs in dollars, these allegations show a significant impact on the functioning of the governmental bodies involved. The Metropolitan Government of Nashville and Davidson County, Tenn., for example, asserted that the Act will increase its costs of providing essential police and fire protection, without any increase in service or in current salary levels, by \$938,000 per year. . . .

Increased costs are not, of course, the only adverse effects which compliance with the Act will visit upon state and local governments, and in turn upon the citizens who depend upon those governments. In its complaint in intervention, for example, California asserted that it could not comply with the overtime costs (approximately \$750,000 per year) which the Act required to be paid to California Highway Patrol cadets during their academy training program. California reported that it had thus been forced to reduce its academy training program from 2,080 hours to only 960 hours, a compromise undoubtedly of substantial importance to those whose safety and welfare may depend upon the preparedness of the California Highway Patrol. . . .

Quite apart from the substantial costs imposed upon the States and their political subdivisions, the Act displaces state policies regarding the manner in which they will structure delivery of those governmental services which their citizens require. The Act, speaking directly to the States *qua* States, requires that they shall pay all but an extremely limited minority of their employees the minimum wage rates currently chosen by Congress. It may well be that as a matter of economic policy it would be desirable that States, just as private employers, comply with these minimum wage requirements. But it cannot be gainsaid that the federal requirement directly supplants the considered policy choices of the States' elected officials and administrators as to how they wish to structure pay scales in state employment. The State might wish to employ persons with little or no training, or those who wish to work on a casual basis, or those who for some other reason do not possess minimum employment requirements, and pay them less than the federally prescribed minimum wage. It may wish to offer part-time or summer employment to teenagers at a figure less than the minimum wage, and if unable to do so may decline to offer such employment at all. But the Act would forbid such choices by the States. The only "discretion" left to them under the Act is either to attempt to increase their revenue to meet the additional financial burden imposed upon them by paying congressionally prescribed wages to their existing complement of employees, or to reduce that complement to a number which can be paid the federal minimum wage without increasing revenue.

This dilemma presented by the minimum wage restrictions may seem not immediately different from that faced by private employers, who have long been covered by the Act and who must find ways to increase their gross income if they are to pay higher wages while maintaining current earnings. The difference, however, is that a State is not merely a factor in the "shifting economic arrangements" of the private sector of the economy, but is itself a coordinate element in the system established by the Framers for governing our Federal Union.

The degree to which FLSA amendments would interfere with traditional aspects of state sovereignty can be seen even more clearly upon examining the overtime requirements of the Act. The general effect of these provisions is to require the States to pay their employees at premium rates whenever their work exceeds a specified number of hours in a given period. . . . [T]he vice of the Act as sought to be applied here is that it directly penalizes the States for choosing to hire governmental employees on terms different from those which Congress has sought to impose.

This congressionally imposed displacement of state decisions may substantially restructure traditional ways in which the local governments have arranged their affairs. Although at this point many of the actual effects under the proposed amendments remain a matter of some dispute among the parties, enough can be satisfactorily anticipated for an outline discussion of their general import. The requirement imposing premium rates upon any employment in excess of what Congress has decided is appropriate for a governmental employee's workweek, for example, appears likely to have the effect of coercing the States to structure work periods in some employment areas, such as police and fire protection, in a manner substantially different from practices which have long been commonly accepted among local governments of this Nation. In addition, appellee represents that the Act will require that the premium compensation for overtime worked must be paid in cash, rather than with compensatory time off, unless such compensatory time is taken in the same pay period. This too appears likely to be highly disruptive of accepted employment practices in many governmental areas where the demand for a number of employees to perform important jobs for extended periods on short notice can be both unpredictable and critical. . . .

Our examination of the effect of the 1974 amendments, as sought to be extended to the States and their political subdivisions, satisfies us that both the minimum wage and the maximum hour provisions will impermissibly interfere with the integral governmental functions of these bodies. We earlier noted some disagreement between the parties regarding the precise effect the amendments will have in application. We do not believe particularized assessments of actual impact are crucial to resolution of the issue presented, however. For even if we accept appellee's assessments concerning the impact of the amendments, their application will nonetheless significantly alter or displace the States' abilities to structure employer-employee relationships in such areas as fire prevention, police protection, sanitation, public health, and parks and recreation. These activities are typical of those performed by state and local governments in discharging their dual functions of administering the public law and furnishing public services. Indeed, it is functions such as these which governments are created to provide, services such as these which the States have traditionally afforded their citizens. If Congress may withdraw from the States the authority to make those fundamental employment decisions upon which their systems for performance of these functions must rest, we think there would be little left of the States' " 'separate and independent existence.' " Thus, even if appellants may have overestimated the effect which the Act will have upon their current levels and patterns of governmental activity, the dispositive factor is that Congress has attempted to exercise its Commerce Clause authority to prescribe minimum wages and maximum hours to be paid by the States in their capacities as sovereign governments. In so doing, Congress has sought to wield its power in a fashion that would impair the States' "ability to function effectively in a federal system." This exercise of congressional authority does not comport with the federal system of government embodied in the Constitution. We hold that insofar as the challenged amendments operate to directly displace the States' freedom to structure integral operations in areas of traditional governmental functions, they are not within the authority granted Congress by Art I, §8, cl 3.

One final matter requires our attention. Appellee has vigorously urged that we cannot, consistently with the Court's decisions in *Maryland v. Wirtz* (1968) and *Fry [v. United States*, 1975], rule against him here. It is important to examine this contention so that it will be clear what we hold today, and what we do not. . . .

We think our holding today quite consistent with *Fry*. The enactment at issue there was occasioned by an extremely serious problem which endangered the well-being of all the component parts of our federal system and which only collective action by the National Government might forestall. The means selected were carefully drafted so as not to interfere with the States' freedom beyond a very limited, specific period of time. . . .

With respect to the Court's decision in *Wirtz*, we reach a different conclusion. Both appellee and the District Court thought that decision required rejection of appellants' claims. Appellants, in turn, advance several arguments by which they seek to distinguish the facts before the Court in *Wirtz* from those presented by the 1974 amendments to the Act. There are undoubtedly factual distinctions between the two situations, but in view of the conclusions expressed earlier in this opinion we do not believe the reasoning in *Wirtz* may any longer be regarded as authoritative. . . .

. . . [W]e have reaffirmed today that the States as States stand on a quite different footing from an individual or a corporation when challenging the exercise of Congress' power to regulate commerce. . . . Congress may not exercise that power so as to force directly upon the States its choices as to how essential decisions regarding the conduct of integral governmental functions are to be made. We agree that such assertions of power, if unchecked, would indeed, as Mr. Justice Douglas cautioned in his dissent in *Wirtz*, allow "the National Government [to] devour the essentials of state sovereignty," and would therefore transgress the bounds of the authority granted Congress under the Commerce Clause. While there are obvious differences between the schools and hospitals involved in *Wirtz*, and the fire and police departments affected here, each provides an integral portion of those governmental services which the States and their political subdivisions have traditionally afforded their citizens. We are therefore persuaded that *Wirtz* must be overruled.

MR. JUSTICE BLACKMUN, concurring.

The Court's opinion and the dissents indicate the importance and significance of this litigation as it bears upon the relationship between the Federal Government and our States. Although I am not untroubled by certain possible implications of the Court's opinion—some of them suggested by the dissents—I do not read the opinion so despairingly as does my Brother BRENNAN. In my view, the result with respect to the statute under challenge here is necessarily correct. I may misinterpret the Court's opinion, but it seems to me that it adopts a balancing approach, and does not outlaw federal power in areas such as environmental protection, where the federal interest is demonstrably greater and where state facility compliance with imposed federal standards would be essential. With this understanding on my part of the Court's opinion, I join it.

MR. JUSTICE BRENNAN, with whom MR. JUSTICE WHITE and MR. JUSTICE MARSHALL join, dissenting.

The Court concedes, as of course it must, that Congress enacted the 1974 amendments pursuant to its exclusive power under Art. I, §8, cl. 3, of the Constitution "[t]o regulate Commerce . . . among the several States." It must therefore be surprising that my Brethren should choose this bicentennial year of our independence to repudiate principles governing judicial interpretation of our Constitution settled since the time of Mr. Chief Justice John Marshall, discarding his postulate that the Constitution contemplates that restraints upon exercise by Congress of its plenary commerce power lie in the political process and not in the judicial process. . . .

My Brethren do not successfully obscure today's patent usurpation of the role reserved for the political process by their purported discovery in the Constitution of a restraint derived from sovereignty of the States on Congress' exercise of the commerce power. Mr. Chief Justice Marshall recognized that limitations "prescribed in the constitution," *Gibbons v. Ogden*, restrain Congress' exercise of the power. . . . But there is no restraint based on state sovereignty requiring or permitting judicial enforcement anywhere expressed in the Constitution; our decisions over the last century and

a half have explicitly rejected the existence of any such restraint on the commerce power. . . .

The reliance of my Brethren upon the Tenth Amendment as "an express declaration of [a state sovereignty] limitation," not only suggests that they overrule governing decisions of this Court that address this question but must astound scholars of the Constitution. For not only early decisions, . . . *McCulloch v. Maryland*, and *Martin v. Hunter's Lessee* hold that nothing in the Tenth Amendment constitutes a limitation on congressional exercise of powers delegated by the Constitution to Congress. Rather, as the Tenth Amendment's significance was more recently summarized:

"The amendment states but a truism that all is retained which has not been surrendered. *There is nothing in the history of its adoption to suggest that it was more than declaratory of the relationship between the national and state governments as it had been established by the Constitution before the amendment* or that its purpose was other than to allay fears that the new national government might seek to exercise powers not granted, and that the states might not be able to exercise fully their reserved powers. . . .

"From the beginning and for many years the amendment has been construed as not depriving the national government of authority to resort to all means for the exercise of a granted power which are appropriate and plainly adapted to the permitted end." *United States v. Darby* (emphasis added).

. . . Today's repudiation of this unbroken line of precedents that firmly reject my Brethren's ill-conceived abstraction can only be regarded as a transparent cover for invalidating a congressional judgment with which they disagree. The only analysis even remotely resembling that adopted today is found in a line of opinions dealing with the Commerce Clause and the Tenth Amendment that ultimately provoked a constitutional crisis for the Court in the 1930's. *E.g., Carter v. Carter Coal Co.* (1936); . . . *Hammer v. Dagenhart* (1918). We tend to forget that the Court invalidated legislation during the Great Depression, not solely under the Due Process Clause, but also and primarily under the Commerce Clause and the Tenth Amendment. It may have been the eventual abandonment of that overly restrictive construction of the commerce power that spelled defeat for the Court-packing plan, and preserved the integrity of this institution see, *e.g., United States v. Darby* (1941), . . . but my Brethren today are transparently trying to cut back on that recognition of the scope of the commerce power. My Brethren's approach to this case is not far different from the dissenting opinions in the cases that averted the crisis. . . .

My Brethren do more than turn aside longstanding constitutional jurisprudence that emphatically rejects today's conclusion. More alarming is the startling restructuring of our federal system, and the role they create therein for the federal judiciary. This Court is simply not at liberty to erect a mirror of its own conception of a desirable governmental structure. If the 1974 amendments have any "vice," . . . it represents "merely . . . a policy issue which has been firmly resolved by the branches of government having power to decide such questions." It bears repeating "that effective restraints on . . . exercise [of the commerce power] must proceed from political rather than from judicial processes."

It is unacceptable that the judicial process should be thought superior to the political process in this area. Under the Constitution the Judiciary has no role to play beyond finding that Congress has not made an unreasonable legislative judgment respecting what is "commerce." My Brother BLACKMUN suggests that controlling judicial supervision of the relationship between the States and our National Government by use of a balancing approach diminishes the ominous implications of today's decision. Such an approach, however, is a thinly veiled rationalization for judicial supervision of a policy judgment that our system of government reserves to Congress.

Judicial restraint in this area merely recognizes that the political branches of our Government are structured to protect the interests of the States, as well as the Nation as a whole, and that the States are fully able to protect their own interests in the premises. Congress is constituted of representatives in both the Senate and House *elected from the States*. Decisions upon the extent of federal intervention under the Commerce Clause into the affairs of the States are in that sense decisions of the States themselves. Judicial redistribution of powers granted the National Government by the terms of the Constitution violates the fundamental tenet of our federalism that the extent of federal intervention into the States' affairs in the exercise of delegated powers shall be determined by States' exercise of political power through their representatives in Congress. There is no reason whatever to suppose that in enacting the 1974 amendments Congress, even if it might extensively obliterate state sovereignty by fully exercising its plenary power respecting commerce, had any purpose to do so. Surely the presumption must be to the contrary. Any realistic assessment of our federal political system, dominated as it is by representatives of the people *elected from the States*, yields the conclusion that it is highly unlikely that those representatives will ever be motivated to disregard totally the concerns of these States. Certainly this was the premise upon which the Constitution . . . was founded. Indeed, though the States are represented in the National Government, national interests are not similarly represented in the States' political processes. Perhaps my Brethren's concern with the Judiciary's role in preserving federalism might better focus on whether Congress, not the States, is in greater need of this Court's protection. . . .

My Brethren's disregard for precedents recognizing these long-settled constitutional principles is painfully obvious in their cavalier treatment of *Maryland v. Wirtz*. Without even a passing reference to the doctrine of *stare decisis*, *Wirtz*—regarded as controlling only last Term, *Fry v. United States* . . . is by exercise of raw judicial power overruled.

No effort is made to distinguish the FLSA amendments sustained in *Wirtz* from the 1974 amendments. We are told at the outset that "the 'far-reaching implications' of *Wirtz* should be overruled," later it is said that the "reasoning in *Wirtz*" is no longer "authoritative." My Brethren then merely restate their essential-function test and say that *Wirtz* must "therefore" be overruled. There is no analysis whether *Wirtz* reached the correct result, apart from any flaws in reasoning, even though we are told that "there are obvious differences" between this case and *Wirtz*. Are state and federal interests being silently balanced, as in the discussion of *Fry*? The best I can make of it is that the 1966 FLSA amendments are struck down and *Wirtz* is overruled on the basis of the conceptually unworkable essential-function test; and that the test is unworkable is demonstrated by my Brethren's inability to articulate any meaningful distinctions among state-operated railroads, state-operated schools and hospitals, and state-operated police and fire departments.

We are left then with a catastrophic judicial body blow at Congress' power under the Commerce Clause. Even if Congress may nevertheless accomplish its objectives—for example, by conditioning grants of federal funds upon compliance with federal minimum wage and overtime standards—there is an ominous portent of disruption of our constitutional structure implicit in today's mischievous decision. I dissent.

In their scrutiny of the FLSA, the Nixon appointees plus Justice Potter Stewart provided an undeniable signal that dual federalism was far from dead. As you undoubtedly noted, the decision echoed the underlying federalism logic seen in cases like *Scott* and *Hammer,* when it suggested that the Court had

repeatedly recognized that there are attributes of sovereignty attaching to every state government which may not be impaired by Congress, not because Congress may lack an affirmative grant of legislative authority to reach the matter, but because the Constitution prohibits it from exercising the authority in that manner.

Where is the line separating constitutional from unconstitutional federal intrusions into state business? William Rehnquist provided one answer when he wrote in *National League of Cities:* "Congress may not exercise that power so as to force directly upon the States its choices as to how essential decisions regarding the conduct of integral governmental functions are to be made." "While clearly not delineating these functions," Joseph Kobylka wrote, "the Court did say that they must be 'essential to [the] separate and independent existence of the states.' " [17] Examples of activities outside congressional authority and "well within the area of traditional operations of state and local governments" included firefighting, police protection, sanitation, public health, and parks and recreation.

In his concurrence, Justice Harry Blackmun argued that the Court was adopting a "balancing approach" to federal-state relations. But others saw it quite differently. *National League of Cities,* in fact, provoked numerous scholarly articles, many of which agreed with points raised by Justice William Brennan. Like the dissenters, some scholars criticized the Court for elevating the Tenth Amendment and for reasserting the "discredited" doctrine of dual federalism. Others focused on the vagueness of some of the terms the Court invoked. In particular, what would the justices define as "essential to the separate and independent existence of the state"? *(See Table 6-5.)* This was not a question of mere academic interest:

between 1976 and 1978 litigants filed some forty-five cases asking the Court to address it.

As noted in Table 6-5, the Court issued several decisions designed to clarify its 1976 ruling. But almost from the start the justices began to chip away at its core. In *Hodel v. Virginia Surface Mining & Reclamation Assn.* (1981) and *United Transportation Union v. Long Island Rail Road* (1982) a unanimous Court rejected invitations to apply and thus expand the 1976 ruling. Major breaks with the decision, however, came in 1982 and 1983, when sharply divided Courts so whittled down *National League of Cities* as to make it almost invisible. In theory, *National League of Cities* remained on the books as good law until 1985, when the Court overruled it in *Garcia v. San Antonio Metropolitan Transit Authority.*[18]

Garcia v. San Antonio Metropolitan Transit Authority

469 U.S. 528 (1985)
http://laws.findlaw.com/US/469/528.html
Vote: 5 (Blackmun, Brennan, Marshall, Stevens, White)
    4 (Burger, O'Connor, Powell, Rehnquist)
Opinion of the Court: Blackmun
Dissenting opinions: Powell, O'Connor, Rehnquist

Garcia was virtually a carbon copy of *National League of Cities.* Once again litigation centered on amendments to the FLSA that required states to pay almost all public employees minimum wages and overtime. The facts, however, were a bit more complicated.

The San Antonio Transit System (SATS) began operation in 1959. For almost a decade the mass transit system was a moneymaking venture, but by 1969 it was operating at a loss and turned to the federal government for assistance. The federal Urban Mass Transit Administration (UMTA) provided it with a $4 million grant. In 1978 the city replaced SATS with SAMTA (San Antonio Metropolitan Transit Authority), and federal grants continued to

---

17. Kobylka, "The Court, Justice Blackmun, and Federalism," 21.

18. To hear oral arguments in this case, navigate to: *www.oyez.org/oyez/frontpage.*

TABLE 6-5 Supreme Court Cases between *National League of Cities* and *Garcia*

Case	Question	Holding (Vote)
Hodel v. Virginia Surface Mining & Reclamation Assn. (1981)	Is the Surface Mining Control and Reclamation Act of 1977, which sets minimum federal standards with which states had to comply and imposed federal standards on those that did not, an impermissible regulation of interstate commerce under *National League of Cities?*	No. (9–0) Marshall, for the majority, read *National League of Cities* to provide a three-prong test (now the *Hodel* test): "First, there must be a showing that the challenged statute regulates the 'States as States.' ... Second, the federal regulation must address matters that are indisputably 'attribute[s] of state sovereignty.' ... And third, it must be apparent that the States' compliance with the federal law would directly impair their ability 'to structure integral operations in areas of traditional governmental functions.' " Since this act fails to meet the first prong, it is a permissible regulation.
United Transportation Union v. Long Island Rail Road (1982)	Does the Federal Railway Act, as applied to employees of a state-operated railroad, transgress the limitations of national power?	No. (9–0) The Court held that the act did not "directly impair [the state's] ability 'to structure integral operations in areas of traditional governmental functions' " and therefore was within the bounds of national power.
Federal Energy Regulatory Commission v. Mississippi (1982)	Is the Public Utility Regulatory Policies Act, which provided for the guidance and regulation of state utility regulatory commissions by FERC and the states, beyond the limits of federal power enunciated in *National League of Cities?*	No. (5–4) Since *National League of Cities* did not hold that "all aspects of a State's sovereign authority are immune from federal control," the nature of the federal interest can overcome state sovereignty, and the interest here does not act to "impair the ability of the States."
Equal Employment Opportunity Commission v. Wyoming (1983)	Under *National League of Cities,* may Congress extend the Age Discrimination Act to prevent a state from setting a mandatory retirement age of fifty-five for game wardens?	Yes. (5–4) Although the act did regulate the "States as States," it did not " 'directly impair' the State's ability to 'structure integral operations in areas of traditional governmental functions.' "

SOURCE: Adapted from Joseph F. Kobylka, "The Court, Justice Blackmun, and Federalism," *Creighton Law Review* 19 (1985–1986); 26–31. Reprinted with permission. Copyright © 1986 by Creighton University.

subsidize it. Between 1970 and 1980, the transit system received more than $51 million or 40 percent of its costs from the federal government. The case started in 1979, when, "in response to a specific inquiry about the applicability of the FLSA to employees of SAMTA," the Department of Labor issued an opinion holding that SAMTA must abide by the act's wage provisions. SAMTA filed a challenge to the department's holding, and Joe G. Garcia and other SAMTA employees, in turn, initiated a suit against their employer for overtime pay.

When this case and a companion, *Donovan v. San Antonio Metropolitan Transit Authority,* reached the U.S. Supreme Court, SAMTA relied heavily on *National League of*

Cities. It argued, for example, that "transit is a traditional [city] function" and that, as the operator of that function, it was not covered by FLSA amendments. The U.S. government and Garcia countered by arguing that *National League of Cities* was not necessarily applicable. In their view, application of the FLSA to public transit did not violate the Tenth Amendment because (1) operation of a transit system is not a traditional government function, and (2) operation of a transit system is not a core government function that must be exempted from federal commerce power legislation to preserve the states' independence. To demonstrate these points, attorneys emphasized the fact that SAMTA received significant funding from the federal government. This, in their view, indicated that "the growth of public transit service reflects cooperative federalism, not independent state initiatives."

JUSTICE BLACKMUN delivered the opinion of the Court.

We revisit in these cases an issue raised in *National League of Cities v. Usery* (1976). In that litigation, this Court, by a sharply divided vote, ruled that the Commerce Clause does not empower Congress to enforce the minimum-wage and overtime provisions of the Fair Labor Standards Act (FLSA) against the States "in areas of traditional government functions." Although *National League of Cities* supplied some examples of "traditional governmental functions," it did not offer a general explanation of how a "traditional" function is to be distinguished from a "nontraditional" one. Since then, federal and state courts have struggled with the task, thus imposed, of identifying a traditional function for purposes of state immunity under the Commerce Clause.

In the present cases, a Federal District Court concluded that municipal ownership and operation of a mass-transit system is a traditional governmental function and thus, under *National League of Cities,* is exempt from the obligations imposed by the FLSA. Faced with the identical question, three Federal Courts of Appeals and one state appellate court have reached the opposite conclusion.

Our examination of this "function" standard applied in these and other cases over the last eight years now persuades us that the attempt to draw the boundaries of state regulatory immunity in terms of "traditional governmental function" is not only unworkable but is also inconsistent with established principles of federalism and, indeed, with those very federalism principles on which *National League of Cities* purported to rest. That case, accordingly, is overruled. . . .

The central theme of *National League of Cities* was that the States occupy a special position in our constitutional system and that the scope of Congress' authority under the Commerce Clause must reflect that position. Of course, the Commerce Clause by its specific language does not provide any special limitation on Congress' actions with respect to the States. It is equally true, however, that the text of the Constitution provides the beginning rather than the final answer to every inquiry into questions of federalism, for "[b]ehind the words of the constitutional provisions are

postulates which limit and control." *National League of Cities* reflected the general conviction that the Constitution precludes "the National Government [from] devour[ing] the essentials of state sovereignty." In order to be faithful to the underlying federal premises of the Constitution, courts must look for the "postulates which limit and control."

What has proved problematic is not the perception that the Constitution's federal structure imposes limitations on the Commerce Clause, but rather the nature and content of those limitations. One approach to defining the limits on Congress' authority to regulate the States under the Commerce Clause is to identify certain underlying elements of political sovereignty that are deemed essential to the States' "separate and independent existence." This approach obviously underlay the Court's use of the "traditional governmental function" concept in *National League of Cities*. It also has led to the separate requirement that the challenged federal statute "address matters that are indisputably 'attribute[s] of state sovereignty.' " In *National League of Cities* itself, for example, the Court concluded that decisions by a State concerning the wages and hours of its employees are an "undoubted attribute of state sovereignty." The opinion did not explain what aspects of such decisions made them such an "undoubted attribute," and the Court since then has remarked on the uncertain scope of the concept. The point of the inquiry, however, has remained to single out particular features of a State's internal governance that are deemed to be intrinsic parts of state sovereignty.

We doubt that courts ultimately can identify principled constitutional limitations on the scope of Congress' Commerce Clause powers over the States merely by relying on a priori definitions of state sovereignty. In part, this is because of the elusiveness of objective criteria for "fundamental" elements of state sovereignty, a problem we have witnessed in the search for "traditional governmental functions." There is, however, a more fundamental reason: the sovereignty of the States is limited by the Constitution itself. A variety of sovereign powers, for example, are withdrawn from the States by Article I, §10. Section 8 of the same Article works an equally sharp contraction of state sovereignty by authorizing Congress to exercise a wide range of legislative powers and (in conjunction with the Supremacy Clause of Article VI) to displace contrary state legislation. . . .

The States unquestionably do "retai[n] a significant measure of sovereign authority." They do so, however, only to the extent that the Constitution has not divested them of their original powers and transferred those powers to the Federal Government. In the words of James Madison to the Members of the First Congress: "Interference with the power of the States was no constitutional criterion of the power of Congress. If the power was not given, Congress could not exercise it; if given, they might exercise it, although it should interfere with the laws, or even the Constitution of the states.". . .

As a result, to say that the Constitution assumes the continued role of the States is to say little about the nature of that role. Only recently, this Court recognized that the purpose of the constitutional immunity recognized in *National League of Cities* is not to preserve "a sacred province of state autonomy." With rare exceptions, like the guarantee, in Article IV, §3, of state territorial integrity, the Constitution does not carve out express elements of state sovereignty that Congress may not employ its delegated powers to displace. . . . The power of the Federal Government is a "power to be respected" as well, and the fact that the States remain sovereign as to all powers not vested in Congress or denied them by the Constitution offers no guidance about where the frontier between state and federal power lies. In short, we have no license to employ freestanding conceptions of state sovereignty when measuring congressional authority under the Commerce Clause. . . .

Insofar as the present cases are concerned, then, we need go no further than to state that we perceive nothing in the overtime and minimum-wage requirements of the FLSA, as applied to SAMTA, that is destructive of state sovereignty or violative of any constitutional provision. SAMTA faces nothing more than the same minimum-wage and overtime obligations that hundreds of thousands of other employers, public as well as private, have to meet.

In these cases, the status of public mass transit simply underscores the extent to which the structural protections of the Constitution insulate the States from federally imposed burdens. When Congress first subjected state mass-transit systems to FLSA obligations in 1966, and when it expanded those obligations in 1974, it simultaneously provided extensive funding for state and local mass transit through UMTA. In the two decades since its enactment, UMTA has provided over $22 billion in mass-transit aid to States and localities. In 1983 alone, UMTA funding amounted to $3.7 billion. . . . In short, Congress has not simply placed a financial burden on the shoulders of States and localities that operate mass-transit systems, but has provided substantial countervailing financial assistance as well, assistance that may leave individual mass-transit systems better off than they would have been had Congress never intervened at all in the area. Congress' treatment of public mass transit reinforces our conviction that the national political process systematically protects States from the risk of having their functions in that area handicapped by Commerce Clause regulation.

This analysis makes clear that Congress' action in affording SAMTA employees the protections of the wage and hour provisions of the FLSA contravened no affirmative limit on Congress' power under the Commerce Clause. The judgment of the District Court therefore must be reversed.

Of course, we continue to recognize that the States occupy a special and specific position in our constitutional system and that the scope of Congress' authority under the Commerce Clause must reflect that position. But the principal and basic limit on the federal commerce power is that inherent in all congressional action—the built-in restraints that our system provides through state participation in federal governmental action. The political process ensures that laws that unduly burden the States will not be promulgated. In the factual setting of these cases the internal safeguards of the political process have performed as intended.

These cases do not require us to identify or define what affirmative limits the constitutional structure might impose on federal action affecting the States under the Commerce Clause. . . .

Though the separate concurrence providing the fifth vote in *National League of Cities* was "not untroubled by certain possible implications" of the decision, the Court in that case attempted to articulate affirmative limits on the Commerce Clause power in terms of core governmental functions and fundamental attributes of state sovereignty. But the model of democratic decisionmaking the Court there identified underestimated, in our view, the solicitude of the national political process for the continued vitality of the States. Attempts by other courts since then to draw guidance from this model have proved it both impracticable and doctrinally barren. In sum, in *National League of Cities* the Court tried to repair what did not need repair.

We do not lightly overrule recent precedent. We have not hesitated, however, when it has become apparent that a prior decision has departed from a proper understanding of congressional power under the Commerce Clause. Due respect for the reach of congressional power within the federal system mandates that we do so now.

National League of Cities v. Usery (1976) is overruled. The judgment of the District Court is reversed, and these cases are remanded to that court for further proceedings consistent with this opinion.

It is so ordered.

JUSTICE POWELL, with whom THE CHIEF JUSTICE, JUSTICE REHNQUIST, and JUSTICE O'CONNOR join, dissenting.

The Court today, in its 5–4 decision, overrules *National League of Cities v. Usery*, a case in which we held that Congress lacked authority to impose the requirements of the Fair Labor Standards Act on state and local governments. Because I believe this decision substantially alters the federal system embodied in the Constitution, I dissent. . . .

Whatever effect the Court's decision may have in weakening the application of stare decisis, it is likely to be less important than what the Court has done to the Constitution itself. A unique feature of the United States is the federal system of government guaranteed by the Constitution and implicit in the very name of our country. Despite some genuflecting in the Court's opinion to the concept of federalism, today's decision effectively reduces the Tenth Amendment to meaningless rhetoric when Congress acts pursuant to the Commerce Clause. . . .

Thus, the harm to the States that results from federal overreaching under the Commerce Clause is not simply a matter of dollars and cents. *National League of Cities.* Nor is it a matter of the wisdom or folly of certain policy choices. Rather, by usurping functions traditionally performed by the States, federal overreaching under the Commerce Clause undermines the constitutionally mandated balance of power between the States and the Federal Government, a balance designed to protect our fundamental liberties. . . .

As I view the Court's decision today as rejecting the basic precepts of our federal system and limiting the constitutional role of judicial review, I dissent.

JUSTICE O'CONNOR, with whom JUSTICE POWELL and JUSTICE REHNQUIST join, dissenting.

The Court today surveys the battle scene of federalism and sounds a retreat. . . . I would prefer to hold the field and, at the very least, render a little aid to the wounded. . . . I . . . write separately to note my fundamental disagreement with the majority's views of federalism and the duty of this Court.

The Court overrules *National League of Cities v. Usery* (1976) on the grounds that it is not "faithful to the role of federalism in a democratic society." *National League of Cities* is held to be inconsistent with this narrow view of federalism because it attempts to protect only those fundamental aspects of state sovereignty that are essential to the States' separate and independent existence, rather than protecting all state activities "equally."

In my view, federalism cannot be reduced to the weak "essence" distilled by the majority today. There is more to federalism than the nature of the constraints that can be imposed on the States in "the realm of authority left open to them by the Constitution." The central issue of federalism, of course, is whether any realm is left open to the States by the Constitution—whether any area remains in which a State may act free of federal interference. "The issue . . . is whether the federal system has any *legal* substance, any core of constitutional right that courts will enforce." The true "essence" of federalism is that the States *as* States have legitimate interests which the National Government is bound to respect even though its laws are supreme. If federalism so conceived and so carefully cultivated by the Framers of our Constitution is to remain meaningful, this Court cannot abdicate its constitutional responsibility to oversee the Federal Government's compliance with its duty to respect the legitimate interests of the States.

Due to the emergence of an integrated and industrialized national economy, this Court has been required to examine and review a breathtaking expansion of the powers of Congress. In doing so the Court correctly perceived that the Framers of our Constitution intended Congress to have sufficient power to address national problems. . . .

It would be erroneous, however, to conclude that the Supreme Court was blind to the threat to federalism when it expanded the commerce power. The Court based the expansion on the authority of Congress, through the Necessary and Proper Clause, "to resort to all means for the exercise of a granted power which are appropriate and plainly adapted to the permitted end." It is through this reasoning that an interstate activity "affecting" interstate commerce can be reached through the commerce power. . . .

It is worth recalling the cited passage in *McCulloch v. Maryland* (1819) that lies at the source of the recent expansion of the commerce power. "Let the end be legitimate, let it be within the scope of the constitution," Chief Justice Marshall said, "and all means which are appropriate, which are plainly adapted to that end, which are not prohibited, but consist with the letter *and spirit* of the constitution, are constitutional" (emphasis added). The *spirit* of the Tenth Amendment, of course, is that the States will retain their integrity in a system in which the laws of the United States are nevertheless supreme.

It is not enough that the "end be legitimate"; the means to that end chosen by Congress must not contravene the spirit of the Constitution. Thus many of this Court's decisions acknowledge that the means by which national power is exercised must take into account concerns for state autonomy. . . . The operative language of these cases varies, but the underlying principle is consistent: state autonomy is a relevant factor in assessing the means by which Congress exercises its powers.

This principle requires the Court to enforce affirmative limits on federal regulation of the States to complement the judicially crafted expansion of the interstate commerce power. *National League of Cities v. Usery* represented an attempt to define such limits. The Court today rejects *National League of Cities* and washes its hands of all efforts to protect the States. In the process, the Court opines that unwarranted federal encroachments on state authority are and will remain " 'horrible possibilities that never happen in the real world.' " There is ample reason to believe to the contrary.

The last two decades have seen an unprecedented growth of federal regulatory activity, as the majority itself acknowledges. . . . Today, as federal legislation and coercive grant programs have expanded to embrace innumerable activities that were once viewed as local, the burden of persuasion has surely shifted, and the extraordinary has become ordinary. For example, recently the Federal Government has, with this Court's blessing, undertaken to tell the States the age at which they can retire their law enforcement officers, and the regulatory standards, procedures, and even

the agenda which their utilities commissions must consider and follow. See *EEOC v. Wyoming*. The political process has not protected against these encroachments on state activities, even though they directly impinge on a State's ability to make and enforce its laws. With the abandonment of *National League of Cities*, all that stands between the remaining essentials of state sovereignty and Congress is the latter's underdeveloped capacity for self-restraint.

The problems of federalism in an integrated national economy are capable of more responsible resolution than holding that the States as States retain no status apart from that which Congress chooses to let them retain. The proper resolution, I suggest, lies in weighing state autonomy as a factor in the balance when interpreting the means by which Congress can exercise its authority on the States as States. It is insufficient, in assessing the validity of congressional regulation of a State pursuant to the commerce power, to ask only whether the same regulation would be valid if enforced against a private party. That reasoning, embodied in the majority opinion, is inconsistent with the spirit of our Constitution. It remains relevant that a State is being regulated, as *National League of Cities* and every recent case have recognized. . . .

It has been difficult for this Court to craft bright lines defining the scope of the state autonomy protected by *National League of Cities*. Such difficulty is to be expected whenever constitutional concerns as important as federalism and the effectiveness of the commerce power come into conflict. Regardless of the difficulty, it is and will remain the duty of this Court to reconcile these concerns in the final instance. That the Court shuns the task today by appealing to the "essence of federalism" can provide scant comfort to those who believe our federal system requires something more than a unitary, centralized government. I would not shirk the duty acknowledged by *National League of Cities* and its progeny, and I share JUSTICE REHNQUIST's belief that this Court will in time again assume its constitutional responsibility.

I respectfully dissent.

With his opinion in *Garcia*, Justice Blackmun once again buried dual federalism and returned the Court to its posture in *Darby Lumber*. The timing of the decision also was interesting. Stephen L. Wasby wrote:

If *National League of Cities* came at the end of eight years of a Republican administration that made some efforts to return matters to the states, *Garcia* came during a subsequent Republican administration far more committed not merely to limiting, but to reducing the national government's power. By sustaining national authority, Blackmun helped lead the Court's majority on a path counter to the thrust of contemporary political developments.[19]

President Ronald Reagan was, in fact, far more determined to return power to the states than any of his immediate predecessors; *Garcia* put a damper on his plans.[20] But, as we shall soon see, he would have been pleased indeed with the current Court's use of the Eleventh Amendment to clamp down on the ability of litigants to bring challenges under the FLSA.

Return of Dual Federalism

Given the cyclical history of debates over the proper form of American federalism, it should not be surprising that *Garcia* did not settle the issue. Justice Sandra Day O'Connor's prediction in *Garcia* that the principles of *National League of Cities* would return one day "to command the support of a majority of the Court" proved to be accurate. In the early 1990s, five justices left the Court, including William Brennan and Thurgood Marshall, two members of the five-justice *Garcia* majority. In addition, William Rehnquist, a strong supporter of state authority, became chief justice. New members, appointed by Presidents Reagan and George H. W. Bush, sufficiently changed the makeup of the Court to prompt observers to look for a rekindling of the federalism debate. The first indication that the balance of power had shifted occurred in *New York v. United States* (1992).[21] This decision involved one of the most important federalism questions of the 1990s: May the federal government constitutionally command the states to carry out federal policy? The Court's position was announced by Justice O'Connor, an ardent supporter of state interests.

19. Stephen L. Wasby, "Justice Harry A. Blackmun in the Burger Court," *Hamline Law Review* 11 (1988): 214.

20. Congress softened its impact by enacting legislation in 1985 that allowed states to provide employees with compensation time instead of pay.

21. To hear oral arguments in this case, navigate to: *www.oyez.org/oyez/frontpage.*

New York v. United States

505 U.S. 144 (1992)
http://laws.findlaw.com/US/505/144.html
Vote: 6 (Kennedy, O'Connor, Rehnquist, Scalia, Souter, Thomas)
   3 (Blackmun, Stevens, White)
Opinion of the Court: O'Connor
Dissenting opinions: Stevens, White

In 1980 Congress passed the Low-Level Radioactive Waste Policy Act. The law was a response to the growing problem of the disposal of radioactive waste generated by private industry, government, hospitals, and research institutions. When the act was passed, disposal sites existed only in South Carolina, Washington, and Nevada. These states were increasingly uncomfortable accepting radioactive waste from the other forty-seven states. Moreover, the existing sites were approaching capacity. The 1980 statute and its subsequent 1985 amendments declared each state responsible for radioactive waste within its borders and encouraged states to develop disposal sites or enter into interstate compacts to develop regional disposal programs. The three existing sites were required to continue accepting out-of-state waste until 1992, allowing the other states sufficient time to develop alternatives. The law allowed the South Carolina, Washington, and Nevada sites to impose a surcharge when accepting waste that originated in states that had not yet complied with the act.

Congress imposed three types of incentives to encourage the states to comply with the law. First, 25 percent of the surcharges collected at the three existing disposal sites would be transferred to the secretary of energy, who would distribute the moneys to states that were complying with the statute. Second, the longer a state failed to comply with the law, the higher the surcharge that would be imposed on that state's waste brought to the existing sites. Ultimately, the operational sites could deny access to noncomplying states altogether. Third, after 1996 any state that had not developed an in-state disposal site or had not entered into a regional compact for that purpose would be required to "take title" of radioactive waste generated inside the state and be fully responsible for it.

In 1990 New York filed suit challenging the constitutionality of the waste disposal law. The state claimed that the incentive provisions violated, among other provisions, the Tenth Amendment. The federal government defended the law and was supported by a group of states that were already participating in the program. Lower courts upheld the law.

JUSTICE O'CONNOR delivered the opinion of the Court.

This case implicates one of our Nation's newest problems of public policy and perhaps our oldest question of constitutional law. The public policy issue involves the disposal of radioactive waste: In this case, we address the constitutionality of three provisions of the Low-Level Radioactive Waste Policy Amendments Act of 1985. The constitutional question is as old as the Constitution: It consists of discerning the proper division of authority between the Federal Government and the States. We conclude that while Congress has substantial power under the Constitution to encourage the States to provide for the disposal of the radioactive waste generated within their borders, the Constitution does not confer upon Congress the ability simply to compel the States to do so. We therefore find that only two of the Act's three provisions at issue are consistent with the Constitution's allocation of power to the Federal Government. . . .

This case . . . concerns the circumstances under which Congress may use the States as implements of regulation; that is, whether Congress may direct or otherwise motivate the States to regulate in a particular field or a particular way. Our cases have established a few principles that guide our resolution of the issue.

As an initial matter, Congress may not simply "commandee[r] the legislative processes of the States by directly compelling them to enact and enforce a federal regulatory program." *Hodel v. Virginia Surface Mining & Reclamation Assn., Inc.* (1981). In *Hodel*, the Court upheld the Surface Mining Control and Reclamation Act of 1977 precisely because it did *not* "commandeer" the States into regulating mining. . . .

The Court reached the same conclusion the following year in *FERC v. Mississippi*. At issue in *FERC* was the Public Utility Regulatory Policies Act of 1978, a federal statute encouraging the States in various ways to develop programs to combat the Nation's energy crisis. We observed that "this Court never has sanctioned explicitly a federal command to the States to promulgate and enforce laws and regulations.". . .

This is not to say that Congress lacks the ability to encourage a State to regulate in a particular way, or that Congress may not hold out incentives to the States as a method of influencing a State's policy choices. Our cases have identified a variety of methods, short of outright coercion, by which Congress may urge a State to adopt a legislative program consistent with federal interests. Two of these methods are of particular relevance here.

First, under Congress' spending power, "Congress may attach conditions on the receipt of federal funds." *South Dakota v. Dole* [1987]. . . .

Second, where Congress has the authority to regulate private activity under the Commerce Clause, we have recognized Congress' power to offer States the choice of regulating that activity according to federal standards or having state law pre-empted by federal regulation. This arrangement, which has been termed "a program of cooperative federalism" is replicated in numerous federal statutory schemes. . . .

By either of these two methods, as by any other permissible method of encouraging a State to conform to federal policy choices, the residents of the State retain the ultimate decision as to whether or not the State will comply. If a State's citizens view federal policy as sufficiently contrary to local interests, they may elect to decline a federal grant. If state residents would prefer their government to devote its attention and resources to problems other than those deemed important by Congress, they may choose to have the Federal Government rather than the State bear the expense of a federally mandated regulatory program, and they may continue to supplement that program to the extent state law is not pre-empted. Where Congress encourages state regulation rather than compelling it, state governments remain responsive to the local electorate's preferences; state officials remain accountable to the people.

By contrast, where the Federal Government compels States to regulate, the accountability of both state and federal officials is diminished. If the citizens of New York, for example, do not consider that making provision for the disposal of radioactive waste is in their best interest, they may elect state officials who share their view. That view can always be pre-empted under the Supremacy Clause if it is contrary to the national view, but in such a case it is the Federal Government that makes the decision in full view of the public, and it will be federal officials that suffer the consequences if the decision turns out to be detrimental or unpopular. But where the Federal Government directs the States to regulate, it may be state officials who will bear the brunt of public disapproval, while the federal officials who devised the regulatory program may remain insulated from the electoral ramifications of their decision. Accountability is thus diminished when, due to federal coercion, elected state officials cannot regulate in accordance with the views of the local electorate in matters not pre-empted by federal regulation.

With these principles in mind, we turn to the three challenged provisions of the Low-Level Radioactive Waste Policy Amendments Act of 1985. . . .

The first set of incentives works in three steps. First, Congress has authorized States with disposal sites to impose a surcharge on radioactive waste received from other States. Second, the Secretary of Energy collects a portion of this surcharge and places the money in an escrow account. Third, States achieving a series of milestones receive portions of this fund. . . .

The Act's first set of incentives, in which Congress has conditioned grants to the States upon the States' attainment of a series of milestones, is . . . well within the authority of Congress under the Commerce and Spending Clauses. Because the first set of incentives is supported by affirmative constitutional grants of power to Congress, it is not inconsistent with the Tenth Amendment.

In the second set of incentives, Congress has authorized States and regional compacts with disposal sites gradually to increase the cost of access to the sites, and then to deny access altogether, to radioactive waste generated in States that do meet federal deadlines. As a simple regulation, this provision would be within the power of Congress to authorize the States to discriminate against interstate commerce. Where federal regulation of private activity is within the scope of the Commerce Clause, we have recognized the ability of Congress to offer states the choice of regulating that activity according to federal standards or having state law pre-empted by federal regulation.

This is the choice presented to nonsited States by the Act's second set of incentives: States may either regulate the disposal of radioactive waste according to federal standards by attaining local or regional self-sufficiency, or their residents who produce radioactive waste will be subject to federal regulation authorizing sited States and regions to deny access to their disposal sites. The affected States are not compelled by Congress to regulate, because any burden caused by a State's refusal to regulate will fall on those who generate waste and find no outlet for its disposal, rather than on the State as a sovereign. A State whose citizens do not wish it to attain the Act's milestones may devote its attention and its resources to issues its citizens deem more worthy; the choice remains at all times with the residents of the State, not with Congress. The State need not expend any funds, or participate in any federal program, if local residents do not view such expenditures or participation as worthwhile. Nor must the State abandon the field if it does not accede to federal direction; the State may continue to regulate the generation and disposal of radioactive waste in any manner its citizens see fit.

The Act's second set of incentives thus represents a conditional exercise of Congress' commerce power, along the lines of those we have held to be within Congress' authority. As a result, the second set of incentives does not intrude on the sovereignty reserved to the States by the Tenth Amendment.

The take title provision is of a different character. This third so-called "incentive" offers States, as an alternative to regulating pursuant to Congress' direction, the option of taking title to and possession of the low level radioactive waste generated within their borders and becoming liable for all damages waste generators suffer as a result of the States' failure to do so promptly. In this provision, Congress has crossed the line distinguishing encouragement from coercion. . . .

The take title provision appears to be unique. No other federal statute has been cited which offers a state government no option other than that of implementing legislation enacted by Congress. Whether one views the take title provision as lying outside Congress' enumerated powers, or as infringing upon the core of state sovereignty reserved by the Tenth Amendment, the provision is inconsistent with the federal structure of our Government established by the Constitution.

Respondents raise a number of objections to this understanding of the limits of Congress' power.

The United States proposes three alternative views of the constitutional line separating state and federal authority.

While each view concedes that Congress *generally* may not compel state governments to regulate pursuant to federal direction, each purports to find a limited domain in which such coercion is permitted by the Constitution.

First, the United States argues that the Constitution's prohibition of congressional directives to state governments can be overcome where the federal interest is sufficiently important to justify state submission. . . . But whether or not a particularly strong federal interest enables Congress to bring state governments within the orbit of generally applicable *federal* regulation, no Member of the Court has ever suggested that such a federal interest would enable Congress to command a state government to enact *state* regulation. No matter how powerful the federal interest involved, the Constitution simply does not give Congress the authority to require the States to regulate. The Constitution instead gives Congress the authority to regulate matters directly and to pre-empt contrary state regulation. Where a federal interest is sufficiently strong to cause Congress to legislate, it must do so directly; it may not conscript state governments as its agents.

Second, the United States argues that the Constitution does, in some circumstances, permit federal directives to state governments. Various cases are cited for this proposition, but none support it. . . .

Third, the United States, supported by the three sited regional compacts as *amici*, argues that the Constitution envisions a role for Congress as an arbiter of interstate disputes. . . .

While the Framers no doubt endowed Congress with the power to regulate interstate commerce in order to avoid further instances of the interstate trade disputes that were common under the Articles of Confederation, the Framers did not intend that Congress should exercise that power through the mechanism of mandating state regulation. The Constitution established Congress as "a superintending authority over the reciprocal trade" among the States, by empowering Congress to regulate that trade directly, not by authorizing Congress to issue trade related orders to state governments. . . .

The sited State respondents focus their attention on the process by which the Act was formulated. They correctly observe that public officials representing the State of New York lent their support to the Act's enactment. A Deputy Commissioner of the State's Energy Office testified in favor of the Act. Senator Moynihan of New York spoke in support of the Act on the floor of the Senate. Respondents note that the Act embodies a bargain among the sited and unsited States, a compromise to which New York was a willing participant and from which New York has reaped much benefit. Respondents then pose what appears at first to be a troubling question: How can a federal statute be found an unconstitutional infringement of State sovereignty when state officials consented to the statute's enactment?

The answer follows from an understanding of the fundamental purpose served by our Government's federal structure. The Constitution does not protect the sovereignty of States for the benefit of the States or state governments as abstract political entities, or even for the benefit of the public officials governing the States. To the contrary, the Constitution divides authority between federal and state governments for the protection of individuals. . . .

Where Congress exceeds its authority relative to the States, therefore, the departure from the constitutional plan cannot be ratified by the "consent" of state officials. . . .

State officials thus cannot consent to the enlargement of the powers of Congress beyond those enumerated in the Constitution. Indeed, the facts of this case raise the possibility that powerful incentives might lead both federal and state officials to view departures from the federal structure to be in their personal interests. Most citizens recognize the need for radioactive waste disposal sites, but few want sites near their homes. As a result, while it would be well within the authority of either federal or state officials to choose where the disposal sites will be, it is likely to be in the political interest of each individual official to avoid being held accountable to the voters for the choice of location. If a federal official is faced with the alternatives of choosing a location or directing the States to do it, the official may well prefer the latter, as a means of shifting responsibility for the eventual decision. If a state official is faced with the same set of alternatives—choosing a location or having Congress direct the choice of a location—the state official may also prefer the latter, as it may permit the avoidance of personal responsibility. The interests of public officials thus may not coincide with the Constitution's intergovernmental allocation of authority. Where state officials purport to submit to the direction of Congress in this manner, federalism is hardly being advanced. . . .

Some truths are so basic that, like the air around us, they are easily overlooked. Much of the Constitution is concerned with setting forth the form of our government, and the courts have traditionally invalidated measures deviating from that form. The result may appear "formalistic" in a given case to partisans of the measure at issue, because such measures are typically the product of the era's perceived necessity. But the Constitution protects us from our own best intentions: It divides power among sovereigns and among branches of government precisely so that we may resist the temptation to concentrate power in one location as an expedient solution to the crisis of the day. The shortage of disposal sites for radioactive waste is a pressing national problem, but a judiciary that licensed extra-constitutional government with each issue of comparable gravity would, in the long run, be far worse.

States are not mere political subdivisions of the United States. State governments are neither regional offices nor administrative agencies of the Federal Government. The positions occupied by state officials appear nowhere on the Federal Government's most detailed organizational chart. The Constitution instead "leaves to the several States a residuary and inviolable sovereignty," The Federalist No. 39, reserved explicitly to the States by the Tenth Amendment.

Whatever the outer limits of that sovereignty may be, one thing is clear: The Federal Government may not compel the States to enact or administer a federal regulatory program. The Constitution permits both the Federal Government and the States to enact legislation regarding the disposal of low level radioactive waste. The Constitution enables the Federal Government to pre-empt state regulation contrary to federal interests, and it permits the Federal Government to hold out incentives to the States as a means of encouraging them to adopt suggested regulatory schemes. It does not, however, authorize Congress simply to direct the States to provide for the disposal of the radioactive waste generated within their borders. While there may be many constitutional methods of achieving regional self-sufficiency in radioactive waste disposal, the method Congress has chosen is not one of them. The judgment of the Court of Appeals is accordingly

Affirmed in part and reversed in part.

JUSTICE WHITE, with whom JUSTICE BLACKMUN and JUSTICE STEVENS join, concurring in part and dissenting in part.

The ultimate irony of the decision today is that in its formalistically rigid obeisance to "federalism," the Court gives Congress fewer incentives to defer to the wishes of state officials in achieving local solutions to local problems. This legislation was a classic example of Congress acting as an arbiter among the States in their attempts to accept responsibility for managing a problem of grave import. The States urged the National Legislature not to impose from Washington a solution to the country's low-level radioactive waste management problems. Instead, they sought a reasonable level of local and regional autonomy consistent with Art. I, §10, cl. 3, of the Constitution. By invalidating the measure designed to ensure compliance for recalcitrant States, such as New York, the Court upsets the delicate compromise achieved among the States and forces Congress to erect several additional formalistic hurdles to clear before achieving exactly the same objective. Because the Court's justifications for undertaking this step are unpersuasive to me, I respectfully dissent.

In *New York v. United States* the Supreme Court once again explicated the delicate relationship between the federal government and the states, a relationship that becomes more complex with the growth of problems as serious as the disposal of nuclear waste. The majority stated clearly that the Constitution does not allow the federal government to command the states to pass legislation to implement federal policy. The federal government may provide incentives for the states to act, but the constitutional division of authority between the general government and the various states is offended when the states are compelled to act. The decision also indicated the presence of a majority concerned with preserving the traditional role of the states.

A similar issue concerning the proper relationship between the central government and the states was argued in *Printz v. United States* (1997). The lawsuit involved the Brady Act, a gun control act that Congress passed in 1993. A provision in that statute commanded that local law enforcement officials play a role in the law's implementation.

The case raised this question: Can Congress compel local political officials to carry out federal legislation?

Printz v. United States

521 U.S. 898 (1997)
http://laws.findlaw.com/US/521/898.html
Vote: 5 (Kennedy, O'Connor, Rehnquist, Scalia, Thomas)
*   4 (Breyer, Ginsburg, Souter, Stevens)*
Opinion of the Court: Scalia
Concurring opinions: O'Connor, Thomas
Dissenting opinions: Breyer, Souter, Stevens

The Gun Control Act of 1968 forbids firearms dealers to transfer firearms to convicted felons, unlawful users of controlled substances, fugitives from justice, persons judged to be mentally defective, persons dishonorably discharged from the military, persons who have renounced their citizenship, and persons who have committed certain acts of domestic violence. In 1993 Congress amended the Gun Control Act with the Brady Handgun Violence Prevention Act. This act required the attorney general to establish by November 30, 1998, a national database allowing for instant background checks of those attempting to buy handguns. In the interim, the Brady Act allowed gun dealers to sell a firearm to buyers who already possessed a state handgun permit or who lived in states with existing instant background check systems.

In states where these two alternatives were not possible, the act required certain actions by the local chief law enforcement officer (CLEO). It mandated that CLEOs receive firearm purchase forms from gun dealers and make a reasonable effort within five business days to verify that the proposed sale was not to a person unqualified under the law. Essentially this required local CLEOs to conduct a background check of all potential gun purchasers. When CLEOs determined that proposed sales would violate the law, they were required upon request to submit a written report to the proposed purchasers stating the reasons for that determination. If CLEOs found no reason for objecting to a sale, they were required to destroy all records pertaining to it. These mandated responsibilities were to terminate in 1998 once the federal instant background check program became operative.

James S. Brady, former press secretary for President Reagan, who was wounded during an assassination attempt on the president, listens as President Clinton speaks before signing the Brady Bill gun control legislation in 1993.

Jay Printz, sheriff of Ravalli County, Montana, and Richard Mack, sheriff of Graham County, Arizona, filed separate suits challenging the constitutionality of the Brady Act's interim provisions. They argued that the federal government had no authority to command state or local officials to administer a federal program. In each case the district court declared the act unconstitutional to the extent that it forced state officers to carry out federal policies. Other provisions of the law were left untouched. The court of appeals disagreed, finding no provisions of the law to violate the Constitution. The

Supreme Court accepted the cases for review. Although the decision immediately affected only a temporary provision that was scheduled to become operative in 1998, the constitutional issue involved is a significant one.

JUSTICE SCALIA delivered the opinion of the Court.

The question presented in these cases is whether certain interim provisions of the Brady Handgun Violence Prevention Act, commanding state and local law enforcement officers to conduct background checks on prospective handgun purchasers and to perform certain related tasks, violate the Constitution. . . .

. . . [I]t is apparent that the Brady Act purports to direct state law enforcement officers to participate, albeit only temporarily, in the administration of a federally enacted regulatory scheme. Regulated firearms dealers are required to forward Brady Forms not to a federal officer or employee, but to the CLEOs, whose obligation to accept those forms is implicit in the duty imposed upon them to make "reasonable efforts" within five days to determine whether the sales reflected in the forms are lawful. While the CLEOs are subjected to no federal requirement that they prevent the sales determined to be unlawful (it is perhaps assumed that their state law duties will require prevention or apprehension), they are empowered to grant, in effect, waivers of the federally prescribed 5 day waiting period for handgun purchases by notifying the gun dealers that they have no reason to believe the transactions would be illegal.

The petitioners here object to being pressed into federal service, and contend that congressional action compelling state officers to execute federal laws is unconstitutional. Because there is no constitutional text speaking to this precise question, the answer to the CLEOs' challenge must be sought in historical understanding and practice, in the structure of the Constitution, and in the jurisprudence of this Court. . . .

Petitioners contend that compelled enlistment of state executive officers for the administration of federal programs is, until very recent years at least, unprecedented. The Government contends, to the contrary, that "the earliest Congresses enacted statutes that required the participation of state officials in the implementation of federal laws." The Government's contention demands our careful consideration, since early congressional enactments "provid[e] 'contemporaneous and weighty evidence' of the Constitution's meaning.". . . Conversely if, as petitioners contend, earlier Congresses avoided use of this highly attractive power, we would have reason to believe that the power was thought not to exist.

The Government observes that statutes enacted by the first Congresses required state courts to record applications for citizenship, to transmit abstracts of citizenship applications and other naturalization records to the Secretary of State, and to register aliens seeking naturalization and issue certificates of registry. It may well be, however, that these requirements applied only in States that authorized their courts to conduct naturalization proceedings. Other statutes of that era apparently or at least arguably required state

Richard Mack, sheriff of Graham County, Arizona, who, along with Sheriff Jay Printz of Ravalli County, Montana, challenged the constitutionality of those provisions of the Brady Bill that required local law enforcement officials to conduct background checks of prospective handgun purchasers.

courts to perform functions unrelated to naturalization, such as resolving controversies between a captain and the crew of his ship concerning the seaworthiness of the vessel, hearing the claims of slave owners who had apprehended fugitive slaves and issuing certificates authorizing the slave's forced removal to the State from which he had fled, taking proof of the claims of Canadian refugees who had assisted the United States during the Revolutionary War, and ordering the deportation of alien enemies in times of war.

These early laws establish, at most, that the Constitution was originally understood to permit imposition of an obligation on state *judges* to enforce federal prescriptions, insofar as those prescriptions related to matters appropriate for the judicial power. That assumption was perhaps implicit in one of the provisions of the Constitution, and was explicit in another. In accord with the so called Madisonian Compromise, Article III, §1, established only a Supreme Court, and made the creation of lower federal courts optional with the Congress—even though it was obvious that the Supreme Court alone could not hear all federal cases throughout the United States. And the Supremacy Clause, Art. VI, cl. 2, announced that "the Laws of the United States . . . shall be the supreme Law of the Land; and the Judges in every State shall be bound thereby." It is understandable why courts should have been viewed distinctively in this regard; unlike legislatures and executives, they applied the law of other sovereigns all the time. . . .

For these reasons, we do not think the early statutes imposing obligations on state courts imply a power of Congress to impress the state executive into its service. Indeed, it can be argued that the numerousness of these statutes, contrasted with the utter lack of statutes imposing obligations on the States' executive (notwithstanding the attractiveness of that course to Congress), suggests an assumed absence of such power. The only early federal law the Government has brought to our attention that imposed duties on state executive officers is the Extradition Act of 1793, which required the "executive authority" of a State to cause the arrest and delivery of a fugitive from justice upon the request of the executive authority of the State from which the fugitive had fled. That was in direct implementation, however, of the Extradition Clause of the Constitution itself. . . .

To complete the historical record, we must note that there is not only an absence of executive commandeering statutes in the early Congresses, but there is an absence of

them in our later history as well, at least until very recent years. The Government points to the Act of August 3, 1882, which enlisted state officials "to take charge of the local affairs of immigration in the ports within such State, and to provide for the support and relief of such immigrants therein landing as may fall into distress or need of public aid"; to inspect arriving immigrants and exclude any person found to be a "convict, lunatic, idiot," or indigent; and to send convicts back to their country of origin "without compensation." The statute did not, however, mandate those duties, but merely empowered the Secretary of the Treasury "to *enter into contracts* with such State . . . officers as may be designated for that purpose by the governor of any State." (Emphasis added.) . . .

The Government points to a number of federal statutes enacted within the past few decades that require the participation of state or local officials in implementing federal regulatory schemes. Some of these are connected to federal funding measures, and can perhaps be more accurately described as conditions upon the grant of federal funding than as mandates to the States; others, which require only the provision of information to the Federal Government, do not involve the precise issue before us here, which is the forced participation of the States' executive in the actual administration of a federal program. . . .

The constitutional practice we have examined above tends to negate the existence of the congressional power asserted here, but is not conclusive. We turn next to consideration of the structure of the Constitution, to see if we can discern among its "essential postulate[s]" a principle that controls the present cases.

It is incontestible that the Constitution established a system of "dual sovereignty." Although the States surrendered many of their powers to the new Federal Government, they retained "a residuary and inviolable sovereignty," The Federalist No. 39 (J. Madison). . . . Residual state sovereignty was also implicit, of course, in the Constitution's conferral upon Congress of not all governmental powers, but only discrete, enumerated ones, which implication was rendered express by the Tenth Amendment's assertion that "[t]he powers not delegated to the United States by the Constitution, nor prohibited by it to the States, are reserved to the States respectively, or to the people."

The Framers' experience under the Articles of Confederation had persuaded them that using the States as the instruments of federal governance was both ineffectual and provocative of federal-state conflict. . . . [T]he Framers rejected the concept of a central government that would act upon and through the States, and instead designed a system in which the state and federal governments would exercise concurrent authority over the people—who were, in Hamilton's words, "the only proper objects of government," The Federalist No. 15. We have set forth the historical record in more detail elsewhere, see *New York v. United States* [1992] and need not repeat it here. It suffices to repeat the conclusion: "The Framers explicitly chose a Constitution that confers upon Congress the power to regulate individuals, not States.". . .

We have thus far discussed the effect that federal control of state officers would have upon the first element of the "double security" alluded to by Madison: the division of power between State and Federal Governments. It would also have an effect upon the second element: the separation and equilibration of powers between the three branches of the Federal Government itself. The Constitution does not leave to speculation who is to administer the laws enacted by Congress; the President, it says, "shall take Care that the Laws be faithfully executed," personally and through officers whom he appoints (save for such inferior officers as Congress may authorize to be appointed by the "Courts of Law" or by "the Heads of Departments" who are themselves presidential appointees). The Brady Act effectively transfers this responsibility to thousands of CLEOs in the 50 States, who are left to implement the program without meaningful Presidential control (if indeed meaningful Presidential control is possible without the power to appoint and remove). The insistence of the Framers upon unity in the Federal Executive—to insure both vigor and accountability—is well known. That unity would be shattered, and the power of the President would be subject to reduction, if Congress could act as effectively without the President as with him, by simply requiring state officers to execute its laws.

The dissent of course resorts to the last, best hope of those who defend *ultra vires* congressional action, the Necessary and Proper Clause. It reasons that the power to regulate the sale of handguns under the Commerce Clause, coupled with the power to "make all Laws which shall be necessary and proper for carrying into Execution the foregoing Powers," Art. I, §8, conclusively establishes the Brady Act's constitutional validity, because the Tenth Amendment imposes no limitations on the exercise of delegated powers but merely prohibits the exercise of powers "not delegated to the United States." What destroys the dissent's Necessary and Proper Clause argument, however, is not the Tenth Amendment but the Necessary and Proper Clause itself. When a "La[w] . . . for carrying into Execution" the Commerce Clause violates the principle of state sovereignty reflected in the various constitutional provisions we mentioned earlier, it is not a "La[w] . . . proper for carrying into Execution the Commerce Clause," and is thus, in the words of The Federalist, "merely [an] ac[t] of usurpation" which "deserve[s] to be treated as such." The Federalist No. 33 (A. Hamilton). We in fact answered the dissent's Necessary and Proper Clause argument in *New York:* "[E]ven where Congress has the authority under the Constitution to pass laws requiring or prohibiting certain acts, it lacks the power directly to compel the States to require or prohibit those acts. . . . [T]he Commerce Clause, for example, authorizes Congress to regulate interstate commerce directly; it does not authorize Congress to regulate state governments' regulation of interstate commerce.". . .

Finally, and most conclusively in the present litigation, we turn to the prior jurisprudence of this Court. . . .

When we were at last confronted squarely with a federal statute that unambiguously required the States to enact or administer a federal regulatory program, our decision should have come as no surprise. At issue in *New York v. United States* (1992) were the so called "take title" provisions of the Low Level Radioactive Waste Policy Amendments Act of 1985, which required States either to enact legislation providing for the disposal of radioactive waste generated within their borders, or to take title to, and possession of the waste—effectively requiring the States either to legislate pursuant to Congress's directions, or to implement an administrative solution. We concluded that Congress could constitutionally require the States to do neither. "The Federal Government," we held, "may not compel the States to enact or administer a federal regulatory program.". . .

. . . It is an essential attribute of the States' retained sovereignty that they remain independent and autonomous within their proper sphere of authority. See *Texas v. White* [1869]. It is no more compatible with this independence and autonomy that their officers be "dragooned" (as Judge Fernandez put it in his dissent below) into administering federal law, than it would be compatible with the independence and autonomy of the United States that its officers be impressed into service for the execution of state laws. . . .

Finally, the Government puts forward a cluster of arguments that can be grouped under the heading: "The Brady Act serves very important purposes, is most efficiently administered by CLEOs during the interim period, and places a minimal and only temporary burden upon state officers." There is considerable disagreement over the extent of the burden, but we need not pause over that detail. Assuming all the mentioned factors were true, they might be relevant if we were evaluating whether the incidental application to the States of a federal law of general applicability excessively interfered with the functioning of state governments. But where, as here, it is the whole object of the law to direct the functioning of the state executive, and hence to compromise the structural framework of dual sovereignty, such a "balancing" analysis is inappropriate. It is the very principle of separate state sovereignty that such a law offends, and no comparative assessment of the various interests can overcome that fundamental defect. We expressly rejected such an approach in *New York*, and what we said bears repeating:

"Much of the Constitution is concerned with setting forth the form of our government, and the courts have traditionally invalidated measures deviating from that form. The result may appear 'formalistic' in a given case to partisans of the measure at issue, because such measures are typically the product of the era's perceived necessity. But the Constitution protects us from our own best intentions: It divides power among sovereigns and among branches of government precisely so that we may resist the temptation to concentrate power in one location as an expedient solution to the crisis of the day."

We adhere to that principle today, and conclude categorically, as we concluded categorically in *New York:* "The Federal Government may not compel the States to enact or administer a federal regulatory program." The mandatory obligation imposed on CLEOs to perform background checks on prospective handgun purchasers plainly runs afoul of that rule. . . .

We held in *New York* that Congress cannot compel the States to enact or enforce a federal regulatory program. Today we hold that Congress cannot circumvent that prohibition by conscripting the State's officers directly. The Federal Government may neither issue directives requiring the States to address particular problems, nor command the States' officers, or those of their political subdivisions, to administer or enforce a federal regulatory program. It

matters not whether policymaking is involved, and no case by case weighing of the burdens or benefits is necessary; such commands are fundamentally incompatible with our constitutional system of dual sovereignty. Accordingly, the judgment of the Court of Appeals for the Ninth Circuit is reversed.

It is so ordered.

JUSTICE THOMAS, concurring.

In my "revisionist" view, the Federal Government's authority under the Commerce Clause, which merely allocates to Congress the power "to regulate Commerce . . . among the several states," does not extend to the regulation of wholly intrastate, point of sale transactions. Absent the underlying authority to regulate the intrastate transfer of firearms, Congress surely lacks the corollary power to impress state law enforcement officers into administering and enforcing such regulations. . . . Even if we construe Congress' authority to regulate interstate commerce to encompass those intrastate transactions that "substantially affect" interstate commerce, I question whether Congress can regulate the particular transactions at issue here. The Constitution, in addition to delegating certain enumerated powers to Congress, places whole areas outside the reach of Congress' regulatory authority. The First Amendment, for example, is fittingly celebrated for preventing Congress from "prohibiting the free exercise" of religion or "abridging the freedom of speech." The Second Amendment similarly appears to contain an express limitation on the government's authority. . . . This Court has not had recent occasion to consider the nature of the substantive right safeguarded by the Second Amendment. If, however, the Second Amendment is read to confer a personal right to "keep and bear arms," a colorable argument exists that the Federal Government's regulatory scheme, at least as it pertains to the purely intrastate sale or possession of firearms, runs afoul of that Amendment's protections.

JUSTICE STEVENS, with whom JUSTICE SOUTER, JUSTICE GINSBURG, and JUSTICE BREYER join, dissenting.

When Congress exercises the powers delegated to it by the Constitution, it may impose affirmative obligations on executive and judicial officers of state and local governments as well as ordinary citizens. This conclusion is firmly supported by the text of the Constitution, the early history of the Nation, decisions of this Court, and a correct understanding of the basic structure of the Federal Government.

These cases do not implicate the more difficult questions associated with congressional coercion of state legislatures addressed in *New York v. United States* (1992). Nor need we consider the wisdom of relying on local officials rather than federal agents to carry out aspects of a federal program, or even the question whether such officials may be required to perform a federal function on a permanent basis. The question is whether Congress, acting on behalf of the people of the entire Nation, may require local law enforcement officers to perform certain duties during the interim needed for the development of a federal gun control program. . . .

The text of the Constitution provides a sufficient basis for a correct disposition of this case.

Article I, §8, grants the Congress the power to regulate commerce among the States. Putting to one side the revisionist views expressed by Justice Thomas in his concurring opinion in *United States v. Lopez* (1995), there can be no question that that provision adequately supports the regulation of commerce in handguns effected by the Brady Act. Moreover, the additional grant of authority in that section of the Constitution "[t]o make all Laws which shall be necessary and proper for carrying into Execution the foregoing Powers" is surely adequate to support the temporary enlistment of local police officers in the process of identifying persons who should not be entrusted with the possession of handguns. In short, the affirmative delegation of power in Article I provides ample authority for the congressional enactment.

Unlike the First Amendment, which prohibits the enactment of a category of laws that would otherwise be authorized by Article I, the Tenth Amendment imposes no restriction on the exercise of delegated powers. . . .

The Amendment confirms the principle that the powers of the Federal Government are limited to those affirmatively granted by the Constitution, but it does not purport to limit the scope or the effectiveness of the exercise of powers that are delegated to Congress. Thus, the Amendment provides no support for a rule that immunizes local officials from obligations that might be imposed on ordinary citizens. . . .

There is not a clause, sentence, or paragraph in the entire text of the Constitution of the United States that sup-ports the proposition that a local police officer can ignore a command contained in a statute enacted by Congress pursuant to an express delegation of power enumerated in Article I. . . .

With colorful hyperbole, the Court suggests that the unity in the Executive Branch of the Federal Government "would be shattered, and the power of the President would be subject to reduction, if Congress could . . . require . . . state officers to execute its laws." Putting to one side the obvious tension between the majority's claim that impressing state police officers will unduly tip the balance of power in favor of the federal sovereign and this suggestion that it will emasculate the Presidency, the Court's reasoning contradicts *New York v. United States*.

That decision squarely approved of cooperative federalism programs, designed at the national level but implemented principally by state governments. *New York* disapproved of a particular *method* of putting such programs into place, not the *existence* of federal programs implemented locally. . . .

The provision of the Brady Act that crosses the Court's newly defined constitutional threshold is more comparable to a statute requiring local police officers to report the identity of missing children to the Crime Control Center of the Department of Justice than to an offensive federal command to a sovereign state. If Congress believes that such a statute will benefit the people of the Nation, and serve the interests of cooperative federalism better than an enlarged federal bureaucracy, we should respect both its policy judgment and its appraisal of its constitutional power.

Accordingly, I respectfully dissent.

JUSTICE SOUTER, dissenting.

In deciding these cases, which I have found closer than I had anticipated, it is The Federalist that finally determines my position. I believe that the most straightforward reading of No. 27 is authority for the Government's position here, and that this reading is both supported by No. 44 and consistent with Nos. 36 and 45.

Hamilton in No. 27 first notes that because the new Constitution would authorize the National Government to bind individuals directly through national law, it could "employ the ordinary magistracy of each [State] in the execution of its laws." Were he to stop here, he would not necessarily be speaking of anything beyond the possibility of cooperative arrangements by agreement. But he then addresses the combined effect of the proposed Supremacy Clause, and state officers' oath requirement, and he states that "the Legislatures, Courts and Magistrates of the respective members will be incorporated into the operations of the national government, as far as its just and constitutional authority extends; and will be rendered auxiliary to the enforcement of its laws." The natural reading of this language is not merely that the officers of the various branches of state governments may be employed in the performance of national functions; Hamilton says that the state governmental machinery "will be incorporated" into the Nation's operation, and because the "auxiliary" status of the state officials will occur because they are "bound by the sanctity of an oath," I take him to mean that their auxiliary functions will be the products of their obligations thus undertaken to support federal law, not of their own, or the States', unfettered choices.

Madison in No. 44 supports this reading in his commentary on the oath requirement. He asks why state magistrates should have to swear to support the National Constitution, when national officials will not be required to oblige themselves to support the state counterparts. His answer is that national officials "will have no agency in carrying the State Constitutions into effect. The members and officers of the State Governments, on the contrary, will have an essential agency in giving effect to the Federal Constitution.". . . .

In the light of all these passages, I cannot persuade myself that the statements from No. 27 speak of anything less than the authority of the National Government, when exercising an otherwise legitimate power (the commerce power, say), to require state "auxiliaries" to take appropriate action.

The *Printz* decision had little impact on gun control. After all, the challenged mandates to local law enforcement officers were scheduled to be phased out no later than November 1998, when the national instant background check system became operative. However, *Printz* gives a clear indication of the Rehnquist Court's position on federalism. Five justices, all appointees of Republican presidents Ronald Reagan and George H. W. Bush, are committed to maintaining traditional views of federalism: that the national government can exercise only the powers delegated to it and that the states are not merely administrative units of the federal government. Justice

Antonin Scalia, for the majority, repeatedly invoked the term "dual sovereignty" to describe the constitutionally mandated division of power between the central government and the states. Justice John Paul Stevens, writing for the four justices in dissent, explicitly endorsed "cooperative federalism." The same pattern emerged in the Rehnquist Court's interpretation of the Eleventh Amendment.

The Court's explicit shift back toward dual federalism should not be interpreted as a return to the pre–Civil War days of Roger Taney or to the laissez-faire philosophies that were popular prior to the New Deal. Rather, in cases such as *New York* and *Printz*, the majority seemed to be reminding us that under our constitutional system the states retain significant independent sovereignty. Congress may achieve its goals by cooperating with the states or by providing incentives to encourage states to participate in the administration of federally established policies. But the federal government may not commandeer the states and order them to carry out federal directives. This seems to be the message of cases such as *Printz* that invoke the Tenth Amendment, as well as those, discussed in the next section, such as *Alden v. Maine* (1999) *(pages 372–379)*, in which the current Court has breathed new life into the Eleventh Amendment.

THE ELEVENTH AMENDMENT

The swing of the pendulum back toward the dual federalism position is closely associated with changes in the Court's membership. Table 6-6 illustrates how the makeup of the Court has changed from *National League of Cities* to *Alden*. In subsequent chapters we shall see federal and state interests clash over issues such as commerce and taxation. For now it is important to realize that in addition to the Burger and Rehnquist Courts backing away from the previously established doctrines of cooperative federalism and handing down decisions that favored the authority of the states, the Court has also worked to limit exceptions to the Eleventh Amendment and to advance a doctrine called "new judicial federalism," to which we turn in the next section.

But first, we look at the Eleventh Amendment and the notion of sovereign immunity. When the states were considering whether to ratify the new U.S. Constitution,

TABLE 6-6 Changes in Court Personnel and Voting in Selected Federalism Cases

Justice	Vote in *National League of Cities* (1976)	Vote in *Garcia* (1985)	Vote in *New York* (1992)	Vote in *Printz* (1997)	Vote in *Alden* (1999)
Blackmun	STATE	FED	FED	—	—
Brennan	FED	FED	—	—	—
Breyer	—	—	—	FED	FED
Burger	STATE	STATE	—	—	—
Ginsburg	—	—	—	FED	FED
Kennedy	—	—	STATE	STATE	STATE
Marshall	FED	FED	—	—	—
O'Connor	—	STATE	STATE	STATE	STATE
Powell	STATE	STATE	—	—	—
Rehnquist	STATE	STATE	STATE	STATE	STATE
Scalia	—	—	STATE	STATE	STATE
Souter	—	—	STATE	FED	FED
Stevens	FED	FED	FED	FED	FED
Stewart	STATE	—	—	—	—
Thomas	—	—	STATE	STATE	STATE
White	FED	FED	FED	—	—

FED = Federal authority
STATE = State sovereignty
NOTE: Each of the cases in this table involved a clash between the authority of the federal government to act and the opposing interests of the states. The table reflects which interests the individual justices supported in each case.

some concern was expressed that federal judicial power would extend to suits brought against them by citizens of other states or even foreign countries. In Federalist Paper No. 81 Alexander Hamilton tried to put such fears to rest: "It is inherent in the nature of sovereignty not to be amenable to the suit of an individual without its consent." In other words, a principle often called sovereign immunity would protect a state from suits to which it did not consent. This principle, it is worth noting, had its origins in English common law, which held that a king was immune from suits from his subjects on the ground that he had established the law and, therefore, could not be held accountable in courts he created.

Quite early on, however, it appeared that the United States would not adhere to this principle. As we noted in Chapter 2, in 1793 the Supreme Court accepted original jurisdiction in **Chisholm v. Georgia**, a suit brought against the state of Georgia by two citizens of South Carolina trying to collect a debt. This action was based on Article III's authorization for federal courts to adjudicate controversies "between a State and citizens of another State." Congress and the states reacted quickly by adopting the Eleventh Amendment, which gives states immunity from being sued, without their consent, in federal courts by "Citizens of another State, or by Citizens or Subjects of any Foreign State."

Soon afterwards, however, the Supreme Court gave the Eleventh Amendment a "stingy" reading. In **Cohens v. Virginia** (1821) Chief Justice Marshall held that the Eleventh Amendment did not preclude the Supreme Court's exercising jurisdiction over a federal question raised on appeal by citizens of their own states, in accord with Section 25 of the 1789 Judiciary Act. This trend continued into the 1980s. In case after case, the Court allowed Congress to make exceptions to the sovereign immunity established in the Eleventh Amendment. For example, in *Fitzpatrick v. Bitzer* (1976) the Court held that, because the Fourteenth Amendment expressly authorizes Congress to enforce the amendment "by appropriate legislation," Congress could, when exercising that authority, abrogate

In *Alden v. Maine* the U.S. Supreme Court ruled that state workers like Julio Martinez, left, Linda Maher, and Joe DeFilipp of Maine could not sue the state for federal labor law violations.

the states' immunity from suit under the Eleventh Amendment. Similarly, in *Pennsylvania v. Union Gas Co.* (1989) a divided Court ruled that the Commerce Clause (Article I, Section 8) permitted Congress to make an exception to the Eleventh Amendment's grant of immunity, holding that the power to regulate commerce "among the several States" would be "incomplete without the authority to render States liable in damages."

But the Court soon overruled *Union Gas* in *Seminole Tribe of Florida v. Florida* (1996), a case involving the Indian Gaming Regulatory Act. This act requires that states negotiate in good faith with tribes over gambling activities. If a tribe thinks a state is not doing so, the act permits the tribe to bring suit in a federal court to compel the state to negotiate in good faith. Writing for the Court, Chief Justice Rehnquist said, "Even when the Constitution vests in Congress complete law-making authority over a particular area, the Eleventh Amendment prevents congressional authorization of suits by private parties against unconsenting States." In other words, the Court asserted that the specific terms of Article I of the constitutional text do not permit Congress to abrogate the states' immunity from suits commenced or prosecuted in the federal courts.

Would the Court push *Seminole Tribe* even further, holding that Congress cannot subject nonconsenting

states to private suits for damages even in their own courts? This question was at the heart of *Alden v. Maine* (1999).[22]

Alden v. Maine

527 U.S.706 (1999)
http://laws.findlaw.com/US/527/706.html
Vote: 5 (Kennedy, O'Connor, Rehnquist, Scalia, Thomas)
   4 (Breyer, Ginsburg, Souter, Stevens)
Opinion of the Court: Kennedy
Dissenting opinion: Souter

The Eleventh Amendment states: "The Judicial power of the United States shall not be construed to extend to any suit in law or equity, commenced or prosecuted against one of the United States by Citizens of another State, or by Citizens or Subjects of any Foreign State." In other words, the amendment bars states from being sued in federal court without their express consent. For some years, however, the Supreme Court allowed Congress to make exceptions to the general rule. Congress took advantage of these decisions, occasionally abrogating the

22. To hear oral arguments in this case, navigate to: *www.oyez.org/oyez/ frontpage.*

Eleventh Amendment immunity from suit. The Fair Labor Standards Act (FLSA), for example, enables state employees to bring federal suits against their state.

In 1992, sixty-five probation officers took advantage of this provision and sued their employer, the state of Maine, in federal district court for violating overtime pay provisions of the FLSA. But, while the suit was pending, the Supreme Court reversed course. In *Seminole Tribe of Florida* it held that Article I does not permit Congress to abrogate the states' sovereign immunity from suits commenced or prosecuted in the federal courts. This decision, in turn, led the district court to dismiss the probation officers' suit.

Not willing to give up the battle, the officers took their claim to a Maine state court. Despite the fact that the FLSA enables employees to bring suit against their states in state courts, the trial court dismissed the suit on the basis of sovereign immunity, and the Maine Supreme Judicial Court affirmed.

When the officers appealed to the Supreme Court, the justices were confronted with the following question: Do the powers delegated to Congress under Article I include the power to subject nonconsenting states to private suits for damages in state courts? After reviewing the history surrounding the adoption of the Eleventh Amendment, which itself was a response to the Supreme Court's decision in *Chisholm v. Georgia* (1793), the majority opinion turned to "history, practice, precedent, and the structure of the Constitution."

JUSTICE KENNEDY delivered the opinion of the Court.

In this case we must determine whether Congress has the power, under Article I, to subject nonconsenting States to private suits in their own courts. [T]he fact that the Eleventh Amendment by its terms limits only "[t]he Judicial power of the United States" does not resolve the question. . . .

In determining whether there is "compelling evidence" that this derogation of the States' sovereignty is "inherent in the constitutional compact," we [discuss] history, practice, precedent, and the structure of the Constitution.

We look first to evidence of the original understanding of the Constitution. Petitioners contend that because the ratification debates and the events surrounding the adoption of the Eleventh Amendment focused on the States' immunity from suit in federal courts, the historical record gives no instruction as to the founding generation's intent to preserve the States' immunity from suit in their own courts.

We believe, however, that the founders' silence is best explained by the simple fact that no one, not even the Constitution's most ardent opponents, suggested the document might strip the States of the immunity. In light of the overriding concern regarding the States' war-time debts, together with the well known creativity, foresight, and vivid imagination of the Constitution's opponents, the silence is most instructive. It suggests the sovereign's right to assert immunity from suit in its own courts was a principle so well established that no one conceived it would be altered by the new Constitution.

The arguments raised against the Constitution confirm this strong inference. In England, the rule was well established that "no lord could be sued by a vassal in his own court, but each petty lord was subject to suit in the courts of a higher lord." It was argued that, by analogy, the States could be sued without consent in federal court. The point of the argument was that federal jurisdiction under Article III would circumvent the States' immunity from suit in their own courts. The argument would have made little sense if the States were understood to have relinquished the immunity in all events.

The response the Constitution's advocates gave to the argument is also telling. Relying on custom and practice—and, in particular, on the States' immunity from suit in their own courts—they contended that no individual could sue a sovereign without its consent. It is true the point was directed toward the power of the Federal Judiciary, for that was the only question at issue. The logic of the argument, however, applies with even greater force in the context of a suit prosecuted against a sovereign in its own courts, for in this setting, more than any other, sovereign immunity was long established and unquestioned.

Similarly, while the Eleventh Amendment by its terms addresses only "the Judicial power of the United States," nothing in *Chisholm*, the catalyst for the Amendment, suggested the States were not immune from suits in their own courts. . . . The language of the Eleventh Amendment, furthermore, was directed toward the only provisions of the constitutional text believed to call the States' immunity from private suits into question. Although Article III expressly contemplated jurisdiction over suits between States and individuals, nothing in the Article or in any other part of the Constitution suggested the States could not assert immunity from private suit in their own courts or that Congress had the power to abrogate sovereign immunity there.

Finally, the Congress which endorsed the Eleventh Amendment rejected language limiting the Amendment's scope to cases where the States had made available a remedy in their own courts. Implicit in the proposal, it is evident, was the premise that the States retained their immunity and the concomitant authority to decide whether to allow private suits against the sovereign in their own courts.

In light of the language of the Constitution and the historical context, it is quite apparent why neither the ratification debates nor the language of the Eleventh Amendment addressed the States' immunity from suit in their own courts. [T]he furor raised by *Chisholm*, and the speed and unanimity with which the Amendment was adopted, moreover, underscore the jealous care with which the founding generation sought to preserve the sovereign immunity of the States. To read this history as permitting the inference that the Constitution stripped the States of immunity in their own courts and allowed Congress to subject them to suit there would turn on its head the concern of the founding generation—that Article III might be used to circumvent state-court immunity. In light of the historical record it is difficult to conceive that the Constitution would have been adopted if it had been understood to strip the States of immunity from suit in their own courts and cede to the Federal Government a power to subject nonconsenting States to private suits in these fora.

Our historical analysis is supported by early congressional practice, which provides "contemporaneous and weighty evidence of the Constitution's meaning." Although early Congresses enacted various statutes authorizing federal suits in state court, we have discovered no instance in which they purported to authorize suits against nonconsenting States in these fora. The "numerousness of these statutes [authorizing suit in state court], contrasted with the utter lack of statutes" subjecting States to suit, "suggests an assumed *absence* of such power." It thus appears early Congresses did not believe they had the power to authorize private suits against the States in their own courts.

Not only were statutes purporting to authorize private suits against nonconsenting States in state courts not en-

acted by early Congresses, statutes purporting to authorize such suits in any forum are all but absent from our historical experience. The first statute we confronted that even arguably purported to subject the States to private actions was the FELA [Federal Employers' Liability Act]. As we later recognized, however, even this statute did not clearly create a cause of action against the States. The provisions of the FLSA at issue here are among the first statutory enactments purporting in express terms to subject nonconsenting States to private suits. Although similar statutes have multiplied in the last generation, "they are of such recent vintage that they are no more probative than the [FLSA] of a constitutional tradition that lends meaning to the text. Their persuasive force is far outweighed by almost two centuries of apparent congressional avoidance of the practice." Even the recent statutes, moreover, do not provide evidence of an understanding that Congress has a greater power to subject States to suit in their own courts than in federal courts. On the contrary, the statutes purport to create causes of actions against the States which are enforceable in federal, as well as state, court. To the extent recent practice thus departs from longstanding tradition, it reflects not so much an understanding that the States have surrendered their immunity from suit in their own courts as the erroneous view, perhaps inspired by . . . [earlier decisions of this Court] that Congress may subject nonconsenting States to private suits in any forum.

The theory and reasoning of our earlier cases suggest the States do retain a constitutional immunity from suit in their own courts. We have often described the States' immunity in sweeping terms, without reference to whether the suit was prosecuted in state or federal court.

We have said on many occasions, furthermore, that the States retain their immunity from private suits prosecuted in their own courts. We have also relied on the States' immunity in their own courts as a premise in our Eleventh Amendment rulings. . . .

Our final consideration is whether a congressional power to subject nonconsenting States to private suits in their own courts is consistent with the structure of the Constitution. We look both to the essential principles of federalism and to the special role of the state courts in the constitutional design.

Although the Constitution grants broad powers to Congress, our federalism requires that Congress treat the States in a manner consistent with their status as residuary sovereigns and joint participants in the governance of the Nation. See, *e.g., United States v. Lopez* [1995]; *Printz* [*v. United States*, 1997]; *New York* [*v. United States*, 1992]. The founding generation thought it "neither becoming nor convenient that the several States of the Union, invested with that large residuum of sovereignty which had not been delegated to the United States, should be summoned as defendants to answer the complaints of private persons." The principle of sovereign immunity preserved by constitutional design "thus accords the States the respect owed them as members of the federation." Petitioners contend that immunity from suit in federal court suffices to preserve the dignity of the States. Private suits against nonconsenting States, however, present "the indignity of subjecting a State to the coercive process of judicial tribunals at the instance of private parties," regardless of the forum. Not only must a State defend or default but also it must face the prospect of being thrust, by federal fiat and against its will, into the disfavored status of a debtor, subject to the power of private citizens to levy on its treasury or perhaps even government buildings or property which the State administers on the public's behalf.

In some ways, of course, a congressional power to authorize private suits against nonconsenting States in their own courts would be even more offensive to state sovereignty than a power to authorize the suits in a federal forum. Although the immunity of one sovereign in the courts of another has often depended in part on comity or agreement, the immunity of a sovereign in its own courts has always been understood to be within the sole control of the sovereign itself. A power to press a State's own courts into federal service to coerce the other branches of the State, furthermore, is the power first to turn the State against itself and ultimately to commandeer the entire political machinery of the State against its will and at the behest of individuals. Such plenary federal control of state governmental processes denigrates the separate sovereignty of the States.

It is unquestioned that the Federal Government retains its own immunity from suit not only in state tribunals but also in its own courts. In light of our constitutional system recognizing the essential sovereignty of the States, we are reluctant to conclude that the States are not entitled to a reciprocal privilege.

Underlying constitutional form are considerations of great substance. Private suits against nonconsenting States—especially suits for money damages—may threaten the financial integrity of the States. It is indisputable that, at the time of the founding, many of the States could have been forced into insolvency but for their immunity from private suits for money damages. Even today, an unlimited congressional power to authorize suits in state court to levy upon the treasuries of the States for compensatory damages, attorney's fees, and even punitive damages could create staggering burdens, giving Congress a power and a leverage over the States that is not contemplated by our constitutional design. The potential national power would pose a severe and notorious danger to the States and their resources. . . .

Congress cannot abrogate the States' sovereign immunity in federal court; were the rule to be different here, the National Government would wield greater power in the state courts than in its own judicial instrumentalities. . . .

The constitutional privilege of a State to assert its sovereign immunity in its own courts does not confer upon the State a concomitant right to disregard the Constitution or valid federal law. The States and their officers are bound by obligations imposed by the Constitution and by federal statutes that comport with the constitutional design. We are unwilling to assume the States will refuse to honor the Constitution or obey the binding laws of the United States. The good faith of the States thus provides an important assurance that "[t]his Constitution, and the Laws of the United States which shall be made in Pursuance thereof . . . shall be the supreme Law of the Land." U.S. Const., Art. VI.

Sovereign immunity, moreover, does not bar all judicial review of state compliance with the Constitution and valid federal law. Rather, certain limits are implicit in the constitutional principle of state sovereign immunity.

The first of these limits is that sovereign immunity bars suits only in the absence of consent. Many States, on their own initiative, have enacted statutes consenting to a wide variety of suits. The rigors of sovereign immunity are thus "mitigated by a sense of justice which has continually expanded by consent the suability of the sovereign." Nor, subject to constitutional limitations, does the Federal Government lack the authority or means to seek the States' voluntary consent to private suits.

The States have consented, moreover, to some suits pursuant to the plan of the Convention or to subsequent constitutional amendments. In ratifying the Constitution, the States consented to suits brought by other States or by the Federal Government. A suit which is commenced and prosecuted against a State in the name of the United States by those who are entrusted with the constitutional duty to "take Care that the Laws be faithfully executed," U.S. Const., Art. II, §3, differs in kind from the suit of an individual: While the Constitution contemplates suits among the members of the federal system as an alternative to extralegal measures, the fear of private suits against nonconsenting States was the central reason given by the founders who chose to preserve the States' sovereign immunity. Suits brought by the United States itself require the exercise of political responsibility for each suit prosecuted against a State, a control which is absent from a broad delegation to private persons to sue nonconsenting States.

We have held also that in adopting the Fourteenth Amendment, the people required the States to surrender a portion of the sovereignty that had been preserved to them by the original Constitution, so that Congress may authorize private suits against nonconsenting States pursuant to its §5 enforcement power. By imposing explicit limits on the powers of the States and granting Congress the power to enforce them, the Amendment "fundamentally altered the balance of state and federal power struck by the Constitution." When Congress enacts appropriate legislation to enforce this Amendment, federal interests are paramount, and Congress may assert an authority over the States which would be otherwise unauthorized by the Constitution. *Fitzpatrick* [*v. Bitzer*, 1976]. . . .

The second important limit to the principle of sovereign immunity is that it bars suits against States but not lesser entities. The immunity does not extend to suits prosecuted against a municipal corporation or other governmental entity which is not an arm of the State. The principle of sovereign immunity as reflected in our jurisprudence strikes the proper balance between the supremacy of federal law and the separate sovereignty of the States. Established rules provide ample means to correct ongoing violations of law and to vindicate the interests which animate the Supremacy Clause. That we have, during the first 210 years of our constitutional history, found it unnecessary to decide the question presented here suggests a federal power to subject nonconsenting States to private suits in their own courts is unnecessary to uphold the Constitution and valid federal statutes as the supreme law.

The sole remaining question is whether Maine has waived its immunity. The State of Maine "regards the im-

munity from suit as 'one of the highest attributes inherent in the nature of sovereignty,' " and adheres to the general rule that "a specific authority conferred by an enactment of the legislature is requisite if the sovereign is to be taken as having shed the protective mantle of immunity." Petitioners have not attempted to establish a waiver of immunity under this standard. Although petitioners contend the State has discriminated against federal rights by claiming sovereign immunity from this FLSA suit, there is no evidence that the State has manipulated its immunity in a systematic fashion to discriminate against federal causes of action. To the extent Maine has chosen to consent to certain classes of suits while maintaining its immunity from others, it has done no more than exercise a privilege of sovereignty concomitant to its constitutional immunity from suit. The State, we conclude, has not consented to suit.

This case at one level concerns the formal structure of federalism, but in a Constitution as resilient as ours form mirrors substance. Congress has vast power but not all power. When Congress legislates in matters affecting the States, it may not treat these sovereign entities as mere prefectures or corporations. Congress must accord States the esteem due to them as joint participants in a federal system, one beginning with the premise of sovereignty in both the central Government and the separate States. Congress has ample means to ensure compliance with valid federal laws, but it must respect the sovereignty of the States.

In apparent attempt to disparage a conclusion with which it disagrees, the dissent attributes our reasoning to natural law. We seek to discover, however, only what the Framers and those who ratified the Constitution sought to accomplish when they created a federal system. We appeal to no higher authority than the Charter which they wrote and adopted. Theirs was the unique insight that freedom is enhanced by the creation of two governments, not one. We need not attach a label to our dissenting colleagues' insistence that the constitutional structure adopted by the founders must yield to the politics of the moment. Although the Constitution begins with the principle that sovereignty rests with the people, it does not follow that the National Government becomes the ultimate, preferred mechanism for expressing the people's will. The States exist as a refutation of that concept. In choosing to ordain and establish the Constitution, the people insisted upon a federal structure for the very purpose of rejecting the idea that the will of the people in all instances is expressed by the central power, the one most remote from their control. The Framers of the Constitution did not share our dissenting colleagues' belief that the Congress may circumvent the federal design by regulating the States directly when it pleases to do so, including by a proxy in which individual citizens are authorized to levy upon the state treasuries absent the States' consent to jurisdiction. . . .

The judgment of the Supreme Judicial Court of Maine is

Affirmed.

JUSTICE SOUTER, with whom JUSTICE STEVENS, JUSTICE GINSBURG, and JUSTICE BREYER join, dissenting.

The Court's rationale for today's holding based on a conception of sovereign immunity as somehow fundamental to sovereignty or inherent in statehood fails for the lack of any substantial support for such a conception in the thinking of the founding era. The Court cannot be counted out yet, however, for it has a second line of argument looking not to a clause-based reception of the natural law conception or even to its recognition as a "background principle," but to a structural basis in the Constitution's creation of a federal system. Immunity, the Court says, "inheres in the system of federalism established by the Constitution," its "contours [being] determined by the founders' understanding, not by the principles or limitations derived from natural law." Again, "[w]e look both to the essential principles of federalism and to the special role of the state courts in the constitutional design." That is, the Court believes that the federal constitutional structure itself necessitates recognition of some degree of state autonomy broad enough to include sovereign immunity from suit in a State's own courts, regardless of the federal source of the claim asserted against the State. If one were to read the Court's federal structure rationale in isolation from the preceding portions of the opinion, it would appear that the Court's position on state sovereign immunity might have been rested entirely on federalism alone. If it had been, however, I would still be in dissent, for the Court's argument that state court sovereign immunity on federal questions is inherent in the very concept of federal structure is demonstrably mistaken.

The National Constitution formally and finally repudiated the received political wisdom that a system of multiple sovereignties constituted the "great solecism of an imperium in imperio." Once "the atom of sovereignty" had been split,

the general scheme of delegated sovereignty as between the two component governments of the federal system was clear, and was succinctly stated by Chief Justice Marshall: "In America, the powers of sovereignty are divided between the government of the Union, and those of the States. They are each sovereign, with respect to the objects committed to it, and neither sovereign with respect to the objects committed to the other." *McCulloch v. Maryland* (1819).

Hence the flaw in the Court's appeal to federalism. The State of Maine is not sovereign with respect to the national objective of the FLSA. It is not the authority that promulgated the FLSA, on which the right of action in this case depends. That authority is the United States acting through the Congress, whose legislative power under Article I of the Constitution to extend FLSA coverage to state employees has already been decided, see *Garcia v. San Antonio Metropolitan Transit Authority* (1985), and is not contested here. . . .

If today's decision occasions regret at its anomalous versions of history and federal theory, it is the more regrettable in being the second time the Court has suddenly changed the course of prior decision in order to limit the exercise of authority over a subject now concededly within the Article I jurisdiction of the Congress. The FLSA, which requires employers to pay a minimum wage, was first enacted in 1938, with an exemption for States acting as employers. See *Maryland v. Wirtz* (1968). In 1966, it was amended to remove the state employer exemption so far as it concerned workers in hospitals, institutions, and schools. In *Wirtz*, the Court upheld the amendment over the dissent's argument that extending the FLSA to these state employees was "such a serious invasion of state sovereignty protected by the Tenth Amendment that it is . . . not consistent with our constitutional federalism."

In 1974, Congress again amended the FLSA, this time "extend[ing] the minimum wage and maximum hour provisions to almost all public employees employed by the States and by their various political subdivisions." *National League of Cities*. This time the Court went the other way: in *National League of Cities*, the Court held the extension of the Act to these employees an unconstitutional infringement of state sovereignty; for good measure, the Court overturned *Wirtz*, dismissing its reasoning as no longer authoritative.

But *National League of Cities* was not the last word. In *Garcia*, decided some nine years later, the Court addressed the question whether a municipally owned mass-transit system was exempt from the FLSA. In holding that it was not, the Court overruled *National League of Cities*, this time taking the position that Congress was not barred by the Constitution from binding the States as employers under the Commerce Clause. [T]he Court held that whatever protection the Constitution afforded to the States' sovereignty lay in the constitutional structure, not in some substantive guarantee. *Garcia* remains good law, its reasoning has not been repudiated, and it has not been challenged here.

The FLSA has not, however, fared as well in practice as it has in theory. The Court in *Seminole Tribe* created a significant impediment to the statute's practical application by rendering its damages provisions unenforceable against the States by private suit in federal court. Today's decision blocking private actions in state courts makes the barrier to individual enforcement a total one.

The Court might respond to the charge that in practice it has vitiated *Garcia* by insisting, as counsel for Maine argued, that the United States may bring suit in federal court against a State for damages under the FLSA. It is true, of course, that the FLSA does authorize the Secretary of Labor to file suit seeking damages, but unless Congress plans a significant expansion of the National Government's litigating forces to provide a lawyer whenever private litigation is barred by today's decision and *Seminole Tribe*, the allusion to enforcement of private rights by the National Government is probably not much more than whimsy. Facing reality, Congress specifically found, as long ago as 1974, "that the enforcement capability of the Secretary of Labor is not alone sufficient to provide redress in all or even a substantial portion of the situations where compliance is not forthcoming voluntarily." One hopes that such voluntary compliance will prove more popular than it has in Maine, for there is no reason today to suspect that enforcement by the Secretary of Labor alone would likely prove adequate to assure compliance with this federal law in the multifarious circumstances of some 4.7 million employees of the 50 States of the Union.

The point is not that the difficulties of enforcement should drive the Court's decision, but simply that where Congress has created a private right to damages, it is implausible to claim that enforcement by a public authority without any incentive beyond its general enforcement power will ever afford the private right a traditionally adequate remedy. No one would think the remedy adequate if private tort claims against a State could only be brought by the National

Government: the tradition of private enforcement, as old as the common law itself, is the benchmark. But wage claims have a lineage of private enforcement just as ancient, and a claim under the FLSA is a claim for wages due on work performed. Denying private enforcement of an FLSA claim is thus on par with closing the courthouse door to state tort victims unaccompanied by a lawyer from Washington.

So there is much irony in the Court's profession that it grounds its opinion on a deeply rooted historical tradition of sovereign immunity, when the Court abandons a principle nearly as inveterate, and much closer to the hearts of the Framers: that where there is a right, there must be a remedy. ... The generation of the Framers thought the principle so crucial that several States put it into their constitutions. And when Chief Justice Marshall asked about Marbury, "If he has a right, and that right has been violated, do the laws of his country afford him a remedy?" *Marbury v. Madison* (1803), the question was rhetorical, and the answer clear:

"The very essence of civil liberty certainly consists in the right of every individual to claim the protection of the laws, whenever he receives an injury. One of the first duties of government is to afford that protection. In Great Britain the king himself is sued in the respectful form of a petition, and he never fails to comply with the judgment of his court."

Yet today the Court has no qualms about saying frankly that the federal right to damages afforded by Congress under the FLSA cannot create a concomitant private remedy. The right was "made for the benefit of" petitioners; they have been "hindered by another of that benefit"; but despite what has long been understood as the "necessary consequence of law," they have no action. It will not do for the Court to respond that a remedy was never available where the right in question was against the sovereign. A State is not the sovereign when a federal claim is pressed against it, and even the English sovereign opened itself to recovery and, unlike Maine, provided the remedy to complement the right. To the Americans of the founding generation it would have been clear (as it was to Chief Justice Marshall) that if the King would do right, the democratically chosen Government of the United States could do no less. The Chief Justice's contemporaries might well have reacted to the Court's decision today in the words spoken by Edmund Randolph when responding to the objection to jurisdiction in *Chisholm*: "[The Framers] must have viewed human rights in their essence, not in their mere form."

The Court has swung back and forth with regrettable disruption on the enforceability of the FLSA against the States, but if the present majority had a defensible position one could at least accept its decision with an expectation of stability ahead. As it is, any such expectation would be naive. The resemblance of today's state sovereign immunity to the *Lochner* era's industrial due process is striking. The Court began this century by imputing immutable constitutional status to a conception of economic self-reliance that was never true to industrial life and grew insistently fictional with the years, and the Court has chosen to close the century by conferring like status on a conception of state sovereign immunity that is true neither to history nor to the structure of the Constitution. I expect the Court's late essay into immunity doctrine will prove the equal of its earlier experiment in laissez-faire, the one being as unrealistic as the other, as indefensible, and probably as fleeting.

To answer the question we posed at the beginning of this case, in *Alden* the justices did indeed push *Seminole Tribe* further, ruling that Congress cannot subject nonconsenting states to private suits for damages even in their own courts. What is more, since *Alden* the Court has *generally* reinforced the logic of *Seminole Tribe* and *Alden*. For example, in **Kimel v. Florida Board of Regents** (2000), the five justices in the majority in *Alden* held that Congress could not makes states liable for suits brought under the federal Age Discrimination in Employment Act. In **Board of Trustees of the University of Alabama v. Garrett** (2001) the same five justices ruled that state employees cannot sue their employers for violations of the Americans with Disabilities Act of 1990, which prohibits certain employers, including state governments, from "discriminat[ing] against a qualified individual with a disability because of the disability of such individual in regard to job application procedures, the hiring, advancement, or discharge of employees, employee compensation, job training, and other terms, conditions, and privileges of employment."

Whether this trend will continue is an interesting question in light of the rather slim five-person majority that has been largely responsible for it. What we do know for now is that the Court bucked it in its most recent statement on the Eleventh Amendment. In **Nevada Department of Human Resources v. Hibbs** (2003), the justices surprised observers when they held that states are not immune from suits brought by their employees under the federal Family and Medical Leave Act (FMLA) of 1993, which provides employees with up to twelve workweeks of unpaid leave annually for the onset of a "serious health condition" in the employee's spouse and for other reasons. One purpose of the act, according to Congress, was "to minimize the potential for employment discrimination on the basis of sex by ensuring generally that leave is available on a gender-neutral basis and to promote the goal of equal employment opportunity for women and men." Congress believed this was necessary because "due to the nature of the roles of men and women in our society, the primary responsibility for family caretaking often falls on women, and such responsibility affects the working lives of women more than it affects the working lives of men."

In an opinion joined by the *Alden* dissenters and Justice O'Connor, Chief Justice Rehnquist explained why the Court rejected the state's claim of immunity from suit in this case but not in *Kimel* and *Garrett*. Specifically, he noted that discrimination based on age and disability receive a lower level of scrutiny than classifications based on gender, and this law—unlike the ones at issue in *Kimel* and *Garrett*—is aimed at minimizing gender discrimination. In Rehnquist's words:

The FMLA aims to protect the right to be free from gender-based discrimination in the workplace. We have held that statutory classifications that distinguish between males and females are subject to heightened scrutiny. For a gender-based classification to withstand such scrutiny, it must "serv[e] important governmental objectives," and "the discriminatory means employed [must be] substantially related to the achievement of those objectives." The State's justification for such a classification "must not rely on overbroad generalizations about the different talents, capacities, or preferences of males and females."

Accordingly, the Court inquired whether Congress had uncovered evidence of a pattern of constitutional violations on the part of the States in this area. It found that indeed the legislature had: "The States' record of unconstitutional participation in, and fostering of, gender-based discrimination in the administration of leave benefits is weighty enough to justify the enactment of [the law]." This was not the case in *Garrett* and *Kimel*, as Rehnquist emphasized:

We reached the opposite conclusion in *Garrett* and *Kimel*. In those cases, the legislation under review responded to a purported tendency of state officials to make age- or disability-based distinctions. Under our equal protection case law, discrimination on the basis of such characteristics is not judged under a heightened review standard, and passes muster if there is "a rational basis for doing so at a class-based level, even if it 'is probably not true' that those reasons are valid in the majority of cases." Thus, in order to impugn the constitutionality of state discrimination against the disabled or the elderly, Congress must identify, not just the existence of age- or disability-based state decisions, but a "widespread pattern" of irrational reliance on such criteria. We found no such showing with respect to the Age Discrimination Act and the Americans with Disabilities Act.

Whether *Hibbs* represents an aberration or the start of a new trend, again it is hard to say—though, in light of the lengths Rehnquist went to differentiate *Hibbs* from *Kimel* and other recent Eleventh Amendment rulings, the former characterization seems more apt. Then again, the slim majorities that produced *Alden*, *Kimel*, and *Garrett* suggest that even one membership change on the Court could produce many more opinions in the *Hibbs* mold.

NEW JUDICIAL FEDERALISM

Another tool recent Courts have used to advance state interests is the doctrine of new judicial federalism. In the narrow sense, this doctrine refers to the renewed willingness of state courts to rely solely on state law, especially state constitutional law, when deciding questions of individual rights.[23] In a broader sense, it suggests that state courts will assume greater importance in the American government system. Either way, it is clear that the U.S. Supreme Court has encouraged this trend, first, by rearticulating standards for reviewing state decisions and, second, by restricting the scope of habeas corpus review.

23. See Abrahamson and Gutman, "The New Judicial Federalism," 90.

Reviewing the Decisions of State Supreme Courts

The principles of federalism, says Laurence H. Tribe, require that federal courts further "the twin policies of preserving the integrity of state law and respecting the institutional autonomy of state judicial systems."[24] Potential conflicts between federal and state courts are limited by the principle of comity: the respect that the two court systems owe to each other requires federal judges to follow state interpretations of state law and to respect, but not necessarily to defer to, state judges' interpretations of federal statutes and the Constitution.

Following that principle, the Court in *Murdock v. City of Memphis* (1875) said that it would not review state decisions unless the state court's interpretation implicated issues of federal law. This traditional view is called the "adequate and independent state grounds test": so long as a state court decision rests on adequate and independent state grounds, the Supreme Court will not resolve either the state or the federal issues in the case. Consequently, state courts are entitled to interpret their own statutes and constitutional provisions, and if their reasoning rests on "independent and adequate" state grounds, their decisions are not subject to review by federal courts.[25]

Until the 1970s the adequate and independent doctrine caused little concern among litigants and interest groups seeking expansive interpretations of constitutional rights. For the two previous decades, the U.S. Supreme Court, under the leadership of Earl Warren, was, as we noted in Chapter 1, among the most liberal in contemporary American history. In decision after decision, it sought to protect the disadvantaged in society against the tyranny of the majority. During the heyday of that era (1962–1968 terms), when the justices were ruling for disadvantaged societal interests in more than 75 per-

24. Laurence H. Tribe, *American Constitutional Law*, 2nd ed. (New York: Foundation Press, 1988), 196–197.

25. As Abrahamson and Gutman explain in "The New Judicial Federalism," the Court had two justifications for promulgating this doctrine: a respect for the independence of state judiciaries and a desire to avoid "issuing . . . opinions that discuss and answer legal questions unnecessary to the resolution of the case," otherwise known as advisory opinions. See *Herb v. Pitcairn* (1945), in which the Court discusses its rationale for the "adequate and independent state grounds test."

cent of their cases, "the notion of a state court [being] more liberal than the Supreme Court was oxymoronic."[26]

This situation changed dramatically when President Richard Nixon had the opportunity to replace some of the most liberal members of the Warren Court. His choice of Warren Burger for chief justice was particularly effective: Earl Warren supported the claims of criminal defendants and other societal "underdogs" in more than 75 percent of the Court's cases, but Burger supported such claims in only about 30 percent of cases.

It is not surprising that commentators perceived that the Burger Court had reduced protection of certain constitutional rights. This perception was shared by Warren Court holdovers, particularly Justices Brennan and Marshall, who were disappointed with the Burger Court's drift toward conservatism. They took a number of steps to offset this trend.

First, in a dissenting opinion in *Michigan v. Mosley* (1975), a case involving the Miranda right, Brennan and Marshall argued that state courts should turn to their own, not federal, constitutions and laws to protect civil rights and liberties. In their estimation, as Harold Spaeth explains, the use of state constitutional provisions and statutory law "for this purpose [was] unobjectionable . . . because federal law sets a floor on rights, rather than a ceiling." In other words, Brennan and Marshall argued that states may permissibly invoke their own constitutional guarantees and laws to extend the protection of liberties and rights beyond the level provided by the federal Constitution as interpreted by the more conservative Burger Court. That Brennan and Marshall would offer this argument makes sense in light of the existing state of doctrine governing the Court's responsibility to review state court decisions interpreting state statutory and constitutional provisions—the adequate and independent state grounds test.

In Brennan and Marshall's thinking, state court judges could use their constitutions and laws to reach liberal decisions—or, at least, decisions more liberal than

those of the Burger Court—and, under the adequate and independent standard test, the Supreme Court would refrain from reviewing (overturning) them. By relying more on state courts, litigants representing liberal civil liberties interests would also avoid having their cases heard by the lower federal courts, which were increasingly staffed by conservative Nixon appointees.

Second, two years after the *Mosley* dissent, Brennan presented an extended version of it directly to the legal community. In an influential *Harvard Law Review* article, he implied that the Supreme Court, as it was then composed, had brought to a halt the expansion of rights ushered in by the Warren Court. He urged attorneys to consider taking their cases into state courts and state jurists to view their constitutions as sources for the expansion of rights, rather than to follow blindly the dictates of the federal bench. Brennan wrote:

> The essential point I am making . . . is not that the United States Supreme Court is necessarily wrong in its interpretation of the federal constitution . . . it is simply that decisions of the Court are not, and should not be, dispositive of questions regarding rights guaranteed by counterpart provisions of state law. Accordingly, such decisions are not mechanically applicable to state law issues, and state court judges, and the members of the bar seriously err if they so treat them.[27]

Just as Brennan and Marshall's arguments were beginning to take hold in the legal community, their more conservative colleagues stepped directly into the debate. As you read the excerpts from *Michigan v. Long* (1983), consider whether the Burger Court's approach to the adequate and independent grounds test contributed to new judicial federalism, as some scholars argue, or compromised it, as others assert.[28]

---

26. Harold J. Spaeth, "Burger Court Review of State Court Civil Liberties Decisions," *Judicature* 68 (1985): 285.

27. William J. Brennan Jr., "State Constitutions and the Protection of Individual Rights," *Harvard Law Review* 90 (1977): 502.

28. To hear oral arguments in this case, navigate to: *www.oyez.org/oyez/frontpage.*

Michigan v. Long

463 U.S. 1032 (1983)
http://laws.findlaw.com/US/463/1032.html
Vote: 6 (Blackmun, Burger, O'Connor, Powell, Rehnquist, White)
    3 (Brennan, Marshall, Stevens)
Opinion of the Court: O'Connor
Concurring opinion: Blackmun
Dissenting opinions: Brennan, Stevens

Under the adequate and independent state grounds test, the Supreme Court refrains from reviewing state court interpretations of state constitutions and laws unless those decisions involve issues of federal law. This test is not as clear as it might seem because, occasionally, state court opinions rely on both federal and state law. So the question often emerges as to whether these kinds of "ambiguous" decisions do or do not rest on adequate and independent state grounds.

Addressing it proved to be a vexing task for the justices, and the results have been inconsistent. Prior to *Long,* the Court had used several methods of responding to appeals about which there was ambiguity as to whether the state court decided the case on adequate and independent grounds: dismiss the case; vacate the decision and send it back to the state court for clarification of the grounds on which the decision rested; direct the litigant to obtain such clarification from the state; or make an independent determination whether the state court relied on federal or state laws/constitutions.

In *Long* the Supreme Court tried to clarify its approach to the adequate and independent state grounds test. The case involved the constitutionality of a police search of David Long's car, which resulted in the seizure of a substantial amount of marijuana. A lower state court found Long guilty of possessing controlled substances, but the Michigan Supreme Court reversed his conviction. The state high court held that the officers' search of the car violated both the Fourth Amendment of the U.S. Constitution and Article I, §11, of the Michigan Constitution.

That the Michigan Supreme Court used the state constitution to reach a liberal decision—one that favored the criminally accused—was just the kind of action Brennan

and Marshall had wanted. However, there was a glitch. Because the Michigan Supreme Court rested its decision on both the federal and state constitutions, the ruling fell into the "ambiguous" zone. Did it rest on sufficiently independent and adequate state grounds so that the U.S. Supreme Court should not examine it? Or was the invocation of the U.S. Constitution grounds enough for Supreme Court review? In what follows, we excerpt those parts of the opinions that deal with these questions.

JUSTICE O'CONNOR delivered the opinion of the Court.

In *Terry v. Ohio* (1968), we upheld the validity of a protective search for weapons in the absence of probable cause to arrest because it is unreasonable to deny a police officer the right "to neutralize the threat of physical harm," when he possesses an articulable suspicion that an individual is armed and dangerous. We did not, however, expressly address whether such a protective search for weapons could extend to an area beyond the person in the absence of probable cause to arrest. In the present case, respondent David Long was convicted for possession of marihuana found by police in the passenger compartment and trunk of the automobile that he was driving. The police searched the passenger compartment because they had reason to believe that the vehicle contained weapons potentially dangerous to the officers. We hold that the protective search of the passenger compartment was reasonable under the principles articulated in *Terry* and other decisions of this Court. We also examine Long's argument that the decision below rests upon an adequate and independent state ground, and we decide in favor of our jurisdiction. . . .

. . . [W]e must consider Long's argument that we are without jurisdiction to decide this case because the decision below rests on an adequate and independent state ground. The court below referred twice to the State Constitution in its opinion, but otherwise relied exclusively on federal law. Long argues that the Michigan courts have provided greater protection from searches and seizures under the State Constitution than is afforded under the Fourth Amendment, and the references to the State Constitution therefore establish an adequate and independent ground for the decision below.

It is, of course, "incumbent upon this Court . . . to ascertain for itself . . . whether the asserted non-federal ground independently and adequately supports the judgment." Although we have announced a number of principles in order to help us determine whether various forms of references to state law constitute adequate and independent state grounds, we openly admit that we have thus far not developed a satisfying and consistent approach for resolving this vexing issue. . . . In some instances, we have taken the strict view that if the ground of decision was at all unclear, we would dismiss the case. In other instances, we have vacated, or continued a case in order to obtain clarification about the nature of a state court decision. In more recent cases, we have ourselves examined state law to determine whether state courts have used federal law to guide their application of state law or to provide the actual basis for the decision that was reached. . . .

This ad hoc method of dealing with cases that involve possible adequate and independent state grounds is antithetical to the doctrinal consistency that is required when sensitive issues of federal-state relations are involved. Moreover none of the various methods of disposition that we have employed thus far recommends itself as the preferred method that we should apply to the exclusion of others, and we therefore determine that it is appropriate to reexamine our treatment of this jurisdictional issue in order to achieve the consistency that is necessary. . . .

Respect for the independence of state courts, as well as avoidance of rendering advisory opinions, have been the cornerstones of this Court's refusal to decide cases where there is an adequate and independent state ground. It is precisely because of this respect for state courts, and this desire to avoid advisory opinions, that we do not wish to continue to decide issues of state law that go beyond the opinion that we review, or to require state courts to reconsider cases to clarify the grounds of their decisions. Accordingly, when, as in this case, a state court decision fairly appears to rest primarily on federal law, or to be interwoven with the federal law, and when the adequacy and independence of any possible state law ground is not clear from the face of the opinion, we will accept as the most reasonable explanation that the state court decided the case the way it did because it believed that federal law required it to do so. If a state court chooses merely to rely on federal precedents as it would on the precedents of all other jurisdictions, then it need only make clear by a plain statement in its judgment or opinion that the federal cases are being used only for the purpose of guidance, and do not themselves compel the result that the court has reached. In this way, both justice and judicial administration will be greatly improved. If the state court decision indicates clearly and expressly that it is alternatively based on bona fide separate, adequate, and independent grounds, we, of course, will not undertake to review the decision.

This approach obviates in most instances the need to examine state law in order to decide the nature of the state court decision, and will at the same time avoid the danger of our rendering advisory opinions. It also avoids the unsatisfactory and intrusive practice of requiring state courts to clarify their decisions to the satisfaction of this Court. We believe that such an approach will provide state judges with a clearer opportunity to develop state jurisprudence unimpeded by federal interference, and yet will preserve the integrity of federal law. . . .

Our review of the decision below under this framework leaves us unconvinced that it rests upon an independent state ground. Apart from its two citations to the State Constitution, the court below relied *exclusively* on its understanding of *Terry* and other federal cases. Not a single state case was cited to support the state court's holding that the search of the passenger compartment was unconstitutional. Indeed, the court declared that the search in this case was unconstitutional because "[the] Court of Appeals erroneously applied the principles of *Terry v. Ohio* . . . to the search of the interior of the vehicle in this case." The references to the State Constitution in no way indicate that the decision below rested on grounds in any way *independent* from the state court's interpretation of federal law. Even if we accept that the Michigan Constitution has been interpreted to provide independent protection for certain rights also secured under the Fourth Amendment, it fairly appears in this case that the Michigan Supreme Court rested its decision primarily on federal law.

Rather than dismissing the case, or requiring that the state court reconsider its decision on our behalf solely because of a mere possibility that an adequate and independent ground supports the judgment, we find that we have jurisdiction in the absence of a plain statement that the decision below rested on an adequate and independent state ground. It appears to us that the state court "felt compelled by what it understood to be federal constitutional considerations to construe . . . its own law in the manner it did.". . .

The judgment of the Michigan Supreme Court is reversed and the case is remanded for further proceedings not inconsistent with this opinion.

It is so ordered.

JUSTICE STEVENS, dissenting.

The jurisprudential questions presented in this case are far more important than the question whether the Michigan police officer's search of respondent's car violated the Fourth Amendment. The case raises profoundly significant questions concerning the relationship between two sovereigns— the State of Michigan and the United States of America.

The Supreme Court of the State of Michigan expressly held "that the deputies' search of the vehicle was proscribed by the Fourth Amendment to the United States Constitution and *art 1, §11 of the Michigan Constitution*" (emphasis added). The state law ground is clearly adequate to support the judgment, but the question whether it is independent of the Michigan Supreme Court's understanding of federal law is more difficult. Four possible ways of resolving that question present themselves: (1) asking the Michigan Supreme Court directly, (2) attempting to infer from all possible sources of state law what the Michigan Supreme Court meant, (3) presuming that adequate state grounds are independent unless it clearly appears otherwise, or (4) presuming that adequate state grounds are not independent unless it clearly appears otherwise. This Court has, on different occasions, employed each of the first three approaches; never until today has it even hinted at the fourth. In order to "achieve the consistency that is necessary," the Court today undertakes a reexamination of all the possibilities. It rejects the first approach as inefficient and unduly burdensome for state courts, and rejects the second approach as an inappropriate expenditure of our resources. Although I find both of those decisions defensible in themselves, I cannot accept the Court's decision to choose the fourth approach over the third—to presume that adequate state grounds are intended to be dependent on federal law unless the record plainly shows otherwise. I must therefore dissent.

If we reject the intermediate approaches, we are left with a choice between two presumptions: one in favor of our taking jurisdiction, and one against it. Historically, the latter presumption has always prevailed.... The Court today points out that in several cases we have weakened the tradi-

tional presumption by using the other two intermediate approaches identified above. Since those two approaches are now to be rejected, however, I would think that *stare decisis* would call for a return to historical principle. Instead, the Court seems to conclude that because some precedents are to be rejected, we must overrule them all.

Even if I agreed with the Court that we are free to consider as a fresh proposition whether we may take presumptive jurisdiction over the decisions of sovereign States, I could not agree that an expansive attitude makes good sense. It appears to be common ground that any rule we adopt should show "respect for state courts, and [a] desire to avoid advisory opinions." And I am confident that all Members of this Court agree that there is a vital interest in the sound management of scarce federal judicial resources. All of those policies counsel against the exercise of federal jurisdiction. They are fortified by my belief that a policy of judicial restraint—one that allows other decisional bodies to have the last word in legal interpretation until it is truly necessary for this Court to intervene—enables this Court to make its most effective contribution to our federal system of government. . . .

The Court offers only one reason for asserting authority over cases such as the one presented today: "an important need for uniformity in federal law [that] goes unsatisfied when we fail to review an opinion that rests primarily upon federal grounds and where the independence of an alleged state ground is not apparent from the four corners of the opinion." Of course, the supposed need to "review an opinion" clashes directly with our oft-repeated reminder that "our power is to correct wrong judgments, not to revise opinions." The clash is not merely one of form: the "need for uniformity in federal law" is truly an ungovernable engine. That same need is no less present when it is perfectly clear that a state ground is both independent and adequate. In fact, it is equally present if a state prosecutor announces that he believes a certain policy of nonenforcement is commanded by federal law. Yet we have never claimed jurisdiction to correct such errors, no matter how egregious they may be, and no matter how much they may thwart the desires of the state electorate. We do not sit to expound our understanding of the Constitution to interested listeners in the legal community; we sit to resolve disputes. If it is not apparent that our views would affect the outcome of a particular case, we cannot presume to interfere.

Finally, I am thoroughly baffled by the Court's suggestion that it must stretch its jurisdiction and reverse the judgment of the Michigan Supreme Court in order to show "[respect] for the independence of state courts.". . .

I respectfully dissent.

Writing for the Court in *Long*, Justice O'Connor—a former state court judge—offered a new approach for applying the adequate and independent state grounds standard to ambiguous state court decisions. In her words, the justices would "accept as the most reasonable explanation that the state court decided the case the way it did because it believed that Federal law required it to do so." To put it another way, as Shirley S. Abrahamson and Diane S. Gutman explain, "the Court set forth a presumption that the state decision rested on federal grounds." [29] Should state judges desire to avoid this presumption, O'Connor writes, they "need only make clear by a plain statement in [their] judgment that the federal cases are being used only for the purpose of guidance, and do not themselves compel the result the court has reached." For, if they indicate "clearly and expressly" that their decisions are "based on bona fide separate, adequate, and independent state grounds," then the Court will "not undertake to review the decision."

Naturally, the majority justified this new approach to the adequate and independent state grounds test as a reasonable way to resolve "the vexing issue" of ambiguous state decisions. Even Justice Stevens, in his dissent, did not take issue with the notion that a clear approach to this area of the law was needed. He simply disliked the one O'Connor fashioned, as did many other commentators, who asserted that the majority's solution was ideologically grounded, designed to provide the conservative justices with a way to oppose the liberal state courts' new course. The decision in *Long* shores up this point: by invoking this new approach—the presumption that a state court decision rested on federal grounds—to the independent and adequate state grounds standard, the Court was able to review and overturn a liberal (here, prodefendant) state court decision.

Some scholars have suggested that "the availability of state law as a basis for expanded protection of civil rights and liberties appears to have been compromised" by *Long*.[30] Support for this claim comes from various studies suggesting that many state jurists do not and, more pointedly, cannot rely exclusively on their own constitutional texts to reach decisions in many areas, including criminal law. Most criminal cases arising under state law deal with issues on which the U.S. Supreme Court has spoken. Moreover, many state criminal constitutional guarantees are worded in much the same language as is the U.S. constitutional document. Therefore, it is possible that state jurists now tend to read state provisions and their federal counterparts in similar ways. From the perspective of those who want state judges to defend minorities and protect the rights of criminally accused, the result has been a resounding defeat. The fear is that state jurists will routinely apply doctrines established by the law-and-order-minded Burger and Rehnquist Courts.

Other scholars, however, take a quite different perspective. In their view, *Long* "seeks to protect the integrity of the state. If a state court plainly says that it is relying on state law, the Supreme Court will not review its decision. The Court reaffirms the state court's opportunity to be the final arbiter of its own law and to divest the U.S. Supreme Court of jurisdiction to review." [31] To support this position, analysts point to the willingness of state judges to reconsider their functions and roles, as this telling comment reveals:

During the years I have been a Montana Supreme Court Justice, I have become more interested in developing the area of law known as "independent state grounds." The new Montana Constitution adopted in 1972 is a rather unique document and provides a basis for considerable departure from federal precedent. This has been particularly true in the civil rights area where we have developed a new equal protection law relying upon the implication of fundamental rights declared in our State Constitution and requiring a showing of a compelling state interest to justify legislative discrimination.[32]

---

29. Abrahamson and Gutman, "The New Judicial Federalism," 97.

30. Spaeth, "Burger Court Review," 286.
31. Abrahamson and Gutman, "The New Judicial Federalism," 96.
32. Quoted by Ronald K. L. Collins, Peter J. Galie, and John Kincaid in "State High Courts, State Constitutions, and Individual Rights Litigation Since 1980," *Hastings Constitutional Law Quarterly* 13 (1986): 704.

At the end of the day, the evidence on whether Brennan and Marshall accomplished their particular (ideological) end is quite mixed. And, yet, at the very least, there does exist a perception among certain segments of the legal community that the Rehnquist Court has encouraged state courts to become more active (if not more liberal) policy makers. One indication may be the growing use of state courts by interest group litigators. As Figure 6-1 shows, the number of state court cases containing amicus curiae briefs increased threefold between 1965 and 1990.

But we wonder how much that perception may change in response to the Court's decision in *Bush v. Gore* (2000). There, the Court reversed a decision of the Florida Supreme Court, which, among other things, had ordered manual recounts in all counties in the state where "undervotes" had not been recounted by hand. The U.S. Supreme Court's reversal rested largely on equal protection grounds; the majority of the justices believed that the Florida court did not provide the guidance necessary to carry out its command—that manual recounts take into account "the intent of the voter"—and, thus, to ensure the equal application of its order. But the dissenters were quick to take on aspects of the suit implicating federalism. For example, Justice Stevens, in a dissent joined by Justices Ginsburg and Breyer, opened his opinion with the following:

The Constitution assigns to the States the primary responsibility for determining the manner of selecting the Presidential electors. See Art. I, §1, cl. 2. When questions arise about the meaning of state laws, including election laws, it is our settled practice to accept the opinions of the highest courts of the States as providing the final answers. On rare occasions, however, either federal statutes or the Federal Constitution may require federal judicial intervention in state elections. This is not such an occasion.

The federal questions that ultimately emerged in this case are not substantial.

He concluded with a paragraph that, at least some suggest, was designed to taunt those justices who agreed with the Court's decision to reverse—Kennedy, O'Connor, Rehnquist, Scalia, and Thomas—the very same justices who have attempted to limit access to the federal courts and enhance the role of state forums:

What must underlie petitioners' entire federal assault on the Florida election procedures is an unstated lack of confidence in the impartiality and capacity of the state judges who would make the critical decisions if the vote count were to proceed. Otherwise, their position is wholly without merit. The endorsement of that position by the majority of this Court can only lend credence to the most cynical appraisal of the work of judges throughout the land. It is confidence in the men and women who administer the judicial system that is the true backbone of the rule of law. Time will one day heal the wound to that confidence that will be inflicted by today's decision. One thing, however, is certain. Although we may never know with complete certainty the identity of the winner of this year's Presidential election, the identity of the loser is perfectly clear. It is the Nation's confidence in the judge as an impartial guardian of the rule of law.

Does *Bush v. Gore* signal a retreat from new judicial federalism? We will not know the answer with certainty until the Court issues new decisions on the subject, but we suspect not; the justices supporting the doctrine have expressed their commitment to it in case after case. Their departure from it—if that is what it was—in *Bush* was, in all likelihood, an anomaly, and not the beginning of the end. Nonetheless, we cannot help but wonder what effect it will have on perceptions, especially among state supreme court justices, of the Court's willingness to allow state courts to have the final say on a range of issues—to say nothing of the Court's motives. Indeed, some scholars (and, perhaps, Justice Stevens as well) suggest that *Bush v. Gore* points up the ideological nature of the Court's support for new judicial federalism; that at least five of the justices, the five who supported the disposition in *Bush*, are willing to accept state court decisions only if those decisions comport with their right-of-center values, but not if they are "liberal." Inasmuch as *Bush* effectively decided the election in favor of the Republican candidate, they may have some justification for this belief.

Restricting Habeas Corpus

It is clear that scholars disagree over whether Burger Court examinations of the adequate and independent state grounds test, such as *Michigan v. Long*, enhanced or limited new judicial federalism. Less open for debate is

FIGURE 6-1 Median Amicus Curiae Participation in Sixteen State Courts of Last Resort, 1965–1990

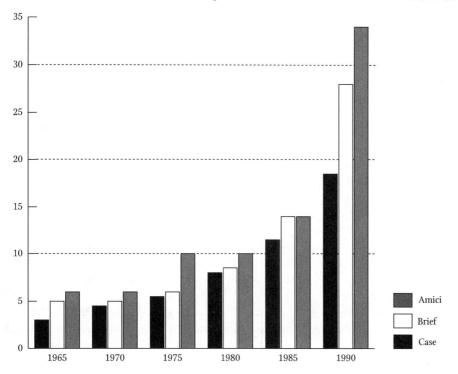

SOURCE: Lee Epstein, "Exploring the Participation of Organized Interests in State Court Litigation," *Political Research Quarterly* 47 (1993): 342.

NOTE: The sixteen states are: Alabama, California, Idaho, Illinois, Kansas, Maine, Michigan, Minnesota, Nevada, New Jersey, North Carolina, Oregon, Rhode Island, South Dakota, Tennessee, and West Virginia. Amici indicate the median number of amici curiae participating in the cases; briefs indicate the median number of briefs filed in the cases; cases indicate the median number of cases containing at least one amicus curiae brief.

that the Burger and Rehnquist Courts increased the importance of state courts with decisions constraining access to federal courts. One of the mechanisms for doing so is the justices' institution of limits on federal habeas corpus relief.

Generally speaking, habeas corpus (translated from Latin as "you have the body") petitions are filed by people held in custody to challenge their detention and to request a court to release them. Until 1867 the writ was not available against any sentence imposed by a court of competent jurisdiction. But that year Congress, anticipating southern resistance to new civil rights legislation

and constitutional guaranties, conferred on federal courts broad authority to issue writs of habeas corpus for prisoners in custody "in violation of the Constitution or of any treaty or law of the United States." As Justice Brennan commented in *Fay v. Noia* (1963): "A remedy almost in the nature of removal from the state to the federal courts of state prisoners' constitutional contentions seems to have been envisaged."

The result was that defendants convicted in state criminal proceedings had two separate channels for seeking federal judicial redress. First, they could petition for direct review by the U.S. Supreme Court of an adverse decision by the highest state court. If this route failed, prisoners could attack their convictions collaterally by seeking habeas corpus from the federal court for the district in which they were held, with appeal to the court of appeals and finally to the Supreme Court once again. The major accommodation between the two systems required by the Supreme Court in *Fay v. Noia* was that the defendants exhaust their state remedies before seeking habeas corpus in a federal court.

Applications from convicted state prisoners for habeas corpus from federal courts increased rapidly as the Supreme Court became more sensitive to the rights of accused persons. In the 1940s federal judges received about 130 such petitions per year; in recent years, that figure exceeded 10,000 *(see Figure 6-2)*.[33] The most common allegation was that evidence used to convict had been secured by unreasonable searches in violation of the Fourth and Fourteenth Amendments.

Scholars, judges, and other public officials differ over the virtue of this upward trend. Those who want to restrict federal habeas corpus review of convictions in state courts argue that these petitions create tension between state and federal judges because they provide one federal district judge with the opportunity to revisit the judgments of state supreme courts—not to mention all the state tribunals below them. As a result, they dramatically diminish the authority of state judges. Opponents also suggest that petitions for habeas corpus generate long and unnecessary procedural delays, an argument particularly telling in death penalty cases, in which those convicted of state capital offenses "typically file several successive writ of *habeas corpus* petitions, raising different constitutional claims, in their efforts to overturn their convictions and sentences."[34] These delays may undermine the deterrent effect of criminal law. Supporters of expansive habeas corpus policies marshal equally impressive arguments. They assert that the procedure is "essential to safeguard Federal constitutional rights in

general, ensure national uniformity in the enforcement of rights; overcome the errors of ineffective counsel in state trials; and avoid improper incarceration or, worse, execution of individual defendants."[35] The fact that state courts often wrongly impose death sentences does nothing to weaken claims for postconviction review by federal courts.

Despite these differences, supporters and opponents alike agree that the Rehnquist Court has attempted to reduce the scope of federal habeas corpus and, accordingly, the role of federal courts as a check on state courts. Indeed, as Table 6-7 shows, with the exception of only one recent case, *Withrow v. Williams* (1993), the justices have time and again restricted the ability of state prisoners to obtain relief in federal courts.

To date, however, these rulings, coupled with congressional legislation limiting the availability of habeas corpus for certain crimes, do not seem to be having much effect on the efforts of state prisoners. While U.S. courts of appeals saw a 4.8 percent decline in the number of habeas corpus petitions received between 1996 and 1997, U.S. district courts experienced an increase of 33 percent. Whether decreases will occur in the future is a matter of speculation. Still, it seems reasonably clear that by placing stricter limits on the ability of losers in state courts to raise claims in federal courts, the justices have advanced the cause of a new judicial federalism. At the very least, rulings of the Rehnquist Court have increased the probability that decisions of state courts will be the final word in many disputes about criminal justice.

NATIONAL PREEMPTION OF STATE LAWS

One of the more important recurring issues of federalism arises when both state and federal governments lay claim to regulate the same activity. The Supremacy Clause seems to offer an easy answer to such conflicts: if Congress passes legislation with the intent of occupying a certain issue area and precluding state involvement in that area, then any state legislation that "stands as an obstacle" must fall. The federal statute preempts state in-

33. Victor E. Flango, *Habeas Corpus in State and Federal Courts* (Williamsburg, Va.: National Center for State Courts, 1994), 14.

34. David M. O'Brien, *Supreme Court Watch—1993* (New York: Norton, 1993), 220.

35. Flango, *Habeas Corpus,* 3.

FIGURE 6-2 State Prisoner Habeas Corpus Filings in U.S. District Court, 1961–1996

Number of Filings

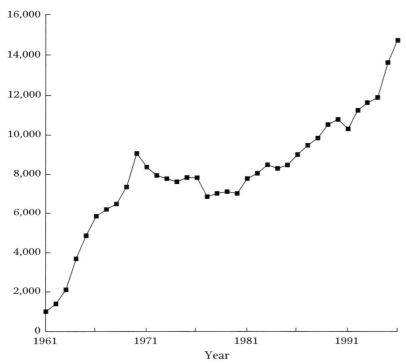

SOURCE: Data provided by Administrative Office of the U.S. Courts. See Victor E. Flango, *Habeas Corpus in State and Federal Courts* (Williamsburg, Va.: National Center for State Courts, 1994), 14; John Scalia, *Prisoner Petitions in the Federal Courts, 1980–96* (Washington, D.C.: U.S. Justice Department, 1997), 4.

volvement, even if Congress and the states exercise concurrent authority over the subject in question. The problem is that federal laws usually do not specify whether they are intended to preclude state action. In such instances, it is up to the Supreme Court to determine whether Congress desires to exercise exclusive or concurrent jurisdiction.

For certain subjects, the Court has found the task easy. There is little question, in the Court's view, that when Congress acts in the area of foreign affairs, it does so exclusively even if its actions touch on areas over which states have some authority. The Court made this point quite clear in *State of Missouri v. Holland*.

State of Missouri v. Holland

252 U.S. 416 (1920)

http://laws.findlaw.com/US/252/416.html

Vote: 7 (Brandeis, Clark, Day, Holmes, McKenna, McReynolds, White)

2 (Pitney, Van Devanter)

Opinion of the Court: Holmes

In 1913 Congress enacted legislation to protect certain species of migratory birds in danger of extinction, but the act was struck down as an unconstitutional use of congressional commerce power. Three years later, the

TABLE 6-7 Selected Rehnquist Court Decisions Limiting the Scope of Federal Habeas Corpus

Case	Holding
Teague v. Lane (1989)	Court holds that "new rules" of constitutional law are not generally applicable to pending habeas corpus petitions.
McCleskey v. Zant (1991)	Court makes it very difficult for lower federal court judges to accept second petitions in all but the rarest of circumstances.
Coleman v. Thompson (1991)	Court rules that federal court judges should dismiss prisoners' petitions if prisoners have not exhausted all available state remedies to *any* of their federal claims.
Withrow v. Williams (1993)	Court rules that prisoners may continue to file federal petitions raising claims of violations of *Miranda v. Arizona* (1966), which held that police must inform suspects of certain constitutional rights prior to custodial interrogation.
Brecht v. Abrahamson (1993)	Court holds that in assessing prisoners' petitions based on alleged violations of *Miranda,* federal courts should reverse convictions only if the error had a "substantial" effect on the jury's verdict.
Felker v. Turpin (1996)	Court rules the Antiterrorism and Effective Death Penalty Act of 1996 to be constitutional. The law directed courts to dismiss habeas corpus petitions presenting issues that had been presented in previous petitions. The law also commanded that second and subsequent habeas petitions be dismissed unless they raised issues based on changes in the law or on facts that could not have been known at the time of the first petition.

SOURCE: Adapted from Victor E. Flango, *Habeas Corpus in State and Federal Courts* (Williamsburg, Va.: National Center for State Courts, 1994), 6–7; updated by the authors.

United States and Great Britain entered into a treaty that addressed a similar concern. The treaty noted that many species of migratory birds "traversed certain parts of the United States and of Canada, that they were of great value as a source of food and in destroying insects injurious to vegetation, but were in danger of extermination through lack of adequate protection." Britain and the United States agreed that their "law-making bodies" should take steps to prevent the extinction of these birds. To give effect to this agreement, Congress in 1918 enacted another law, the Migratory Bird Treaty Act, which prohibited anyone from "killing, capturing, or selling" any species of birds cited in the treaty.

Missouri challenged the act, bringing suit against a U.S. game warden to prevent him from enforcing it. The state alleged, in accord with dual federalism, that the act was just like the earlier law that had been struck down; Congress was merely using its treaty power as a vehicle to interfere with rights reserved to the states under the Tenth Amendment. In other words, Missouri argued that the law infringed on states' rights regardless of whether it is based in congressional commerce power or in treaty-making authority.

MR. JUSTICE HOLMES delivered the opinion of the Court.

[T]he question raised is the general one whether the treaty and statute are void as an interference with the rights reserved to the states.

To answer this question it is not enough to refer to the 10th Amendment, reserving the powers not delegated to the United States, because by article 2, §2, the power to make treaties is delegated expressly, and by article 6, treaties made under the authority of the United States, along with the Constitution and laws of the United States, made in pursuance thereof, are declared the supreme law of the land. If the treaty is valid, there can be no dispute about the validity of the statute under article 1, §8, as a necessary and proper means to execute the powers of the government. The language of the Constitution as to the supremacy of treaties being general, the question before us is narrowed to an inquiry into the ground upon which the present supposed exception is placed.

It is said that a treaty cannot be valid if it infringes the Constitution; that there are limits, therefore, to the treaty-making power; and that one such limit is that what an act of Congress could not do unaided, in derogation of the powers reserved to the states, a treaty cannot do. An earlier act of Congress that attempted by itself, and not in pursuance of a treaty, to regulate the killing of migratory birds within the states, had been held bad in the district court. *United States v. Shauver; United States v. McCullagh*. Those decisions were supported by arguments that migratory birds were owned by the states in their sovereign capacity, for the benefit of their people, and that . . . this control was one that Congress had no power to displace. The same argument is supposed to apply now with equal force.

Whether the two cases cited were decided rightly or not, they cannot be accepted as a test of the treaty power. Acts of Congress are the supreme law of the land only when made in pursuance of the Constitution, while treaties are declared to be so when made under the authority of the United States. It is open to question whether the authority of the United States means more than the formal acts prescribed to make the convention. We do not mean to imply that there are no qualifications to the treaty-making power; but they must be ascertained in a different way. It is obvious that there may be matters of the sharpest exigency for the national well-being that an act of Congress could not deal with, but that a treaty followed by such an act could, and it is not lightly to be assumed that, in matters requiring national action, "a power which must belong to and somewhere reside in every civilized government" is not to be found. What was said in that case with regard to the powers of the states applies with equal force to the powers of the nation in cases where the states individually are incompetent to act. We are not yet discussing the particular case before us, but only are considering the validity of the test proposed. With regard to that, we may add that when we are dealing with words that also are a constituent act, like the Constitution of the United States, we must realize that they have called into life a being the development of which could not have been foreseen completely by the most gifted of its

begetters. It was enough for them to realize or to hope that they had created an organism; it has taken a century and has cost their successors much sweat and blood to prove that they created a nation. The case before us must be considered in the light of our whole experience, and not merely in that of what was said a hundred years ago. The treaty in question does not contravene any prohibitory words to be found in the Constitution. The only question is whether it is forbidden by some invisible radiation from the general terms of the 10th Amendment. We must consider what this country has become in deciding what that amendment has reserved.

The state, as we have intimated, founds its claim of exclusive authority upon an assertion of title to migratory birds,—an assertion that is embodied in statute. No doubt it is true that, as between a state and its inhabitants, the state may regulate the killing and sale of such birds, but it does not follow that its authority is exclusive of paramount powers. To put the claim of the state upon title is to lean upon a slender reed. Wild birds are not in the possession of anyone; and possession is the beginning of ownership. The whole foundation of the state's rights is the presence within their jurisdiction of birds that yesterday had not arrived, tomorrow may be in another state, and in a week a thousand miles away. If we are to be accurate, we cannot put the case of the state upon higher ground than that the treaty deals with creatures that for the moment are within the state borders, that it must be carried out by officers of the United States within the same territory, and that, but for the treaty, the state would be free to regulate this subject itself.

As most of the laws of the United States are carried out within the states, and as many of them deal with matters which, in the silence of such laws, the state might regulate, such general grounds are not enough to support Missouri's claim. Valid treaties, of course, "are as binding within the territorial limits of the states as they are effective throughout the dominion of the United States." No doubt the great body of private relations usually falls within the control of the state, but a treaty may override its power. . . .

Here a national interest of very nearly the first magnitude is involved. It can be protected only by national action in concert with that of another power. The subject-matter is only transitorily within the state, and has no permanent habitat therein. But for the treaty and the statute, there soon might be no birds for any powers to deal with. We see nothing in the Constitution that compels the government to sit by while a food supply is cut off and the protectors of our forests and of our crops are destroyed. It is not sufficient to rely upon the states. The reliance is vain, and were it otherwise, the question is whether the United States is forbidden to act. We are of opinion that the treaty and statute must be upheld.

Decree affirmed.

Justice Holmes's opinion was narrowly drawn; he focused on the matter at hand. Even so, his message was clear: when Congress acts in the area of foreign affairs, it does so exclusively even if its actions touch on areas over which states have some authority. The Rehnquist Court reiterated this basic message in a case dealing with trade with Burma.[36]

Crosby v. National Foreign Trade Council

530 U.S.363 (2000)
http://laws.findlaw.com/US/530/363.html
Vote: 9 (Breyer, Ginsburg, Kennedy, O'Connor, Rehnquist,
Scalia, Souter, Stevens, Thomas)

o

Opinion of the Court: Souter
Opinion concurring in judgment: Scalia

In June 1996 Massachusetts passed a law barring state entities from buying goods or services from companies doing business with Burma. The law defines "doing business with Burma" to cover any person (including a business):

(a) having a principal place of business, place of incorporation or its corporate headquarters in Burma (Myanmar) or having any operations, leases, franchises, majority-owned subsidiaries, distribution agreements, or any other similar agreements in Burma (Myanmar), or being the majority-owned subsidiary, licensee or franchise of such a person;
(b) providing financial services to the government of Burma (Myanmar), including providing direct loans, underwriting government securities, providing any consulting advice or assis-

tance, providing brokerage services, acting as a trustee or escrow agent, or otherwise acting as an agent pursuant to a contractual agreement;
(c) promoting the importation or sale of gems, timber, oil, gas or other related products, commerce in which is largely controlled by the government of Burma (Myanmar), from Burma (Myanmar);
(d) providing any goods or services to the government of Burma (Myanmar).

In September, three months after the Massachusetts law was enacted, Congress passed a statute imposing a set of mandatory and conditional sanctions on Burma. The federal act has five basic parts, three substantive and two procedural. First, it imposes three sanctions directly on Burma. It bans all aid to the Burmese government except for humanitarian assistance, counternarcotics efforts, and promotion of human rights and democracy. These restrictions are to remain in effect "until such time as the President determines and certifies to Congress that Burma has made measurable and substantial progress in improving human rights practices and implementing democratic government." Second, the federal act authorizes the president to impose further sanctions subject to certain conditions. He may prohibit "United States persons" from "new investment" in Burma, and shall do so if he determines and certifies to Congress that the Burmese Government has physically harmed, rearrested, or exiled Daw Aung San Suu Kyi (the opposition leader selected to receive the Nobel Peace Prize), or has committed "large-scale repression of or violence against the Democratic opposition" §570(b). Third, the statute directs the president to work to develop "a comprehensive, multilateral strategy to bring democracy to and improve human rights practices and the quality of life in Burma" §570(c). As for the procedural provisions of the federal statute, the fourth section requires the president to report periodically to certain congressional committee chairmen on the progress toward democratization and better living conditions in Burma as well as on the development of the required strategy. The fifth part of the federal act authorizes the president "to waive, temporarily or permanently, any sanction [under the federal act] . . . if he determines and certifies to Congress

---

36. To hear oral arguments in this case, navigate to: *www.oyez.org/oyez/frontpage.*

Three Burmese monks stand in front of the U.S. Supreme Court March 22, 2000, to demonstrate their support for Massachusetts's "selective purchasing" law. The law, which condemns Burma's human rights record and all but prohibits state government purchases from companies operating there, was overturned by the Court in 2000.

that the application of such sanction would be contrary to the national security interests of the United States."

On May 20, 1997, the president issued Executive Order No. 13047. He certified that the Government of Burma had "committed large-scale repression of the democratic opposition in Burma" and found that the Burmese government's actions and policies constituted "an unusual and extraordinary threat to the national security and foreign policy of the United States," a threat characterized as a national emergency. The president

then prohibited new investment in Burma "by United States persons," any approval or facilitation by a United States person of such new investment by foreign persons and any transaction meant to evade or avoid the ban. Subsequently, Congress imposed mandatory and conditional sanctions on Burma.

Because several members of the National Foreign Trade Council, a nonprofit corporation representing companies engaged in foreign commerce, were affected by the state act, the council brought a federal suit against Massachusetts, claiming that the state act unconstitutionally infringes on the federal foreign affairs power, violates the Commerce Clause, and is preempted by the federal act. The district court held that the state law "unconstitutionally impinged on the federal government's exclusive authority to regulate foreign affairs," and the First Circuit Court of Appeals affirmed.

JUSTICE SOUTER delivered the opinion of the Court.

The issue is whether the Burma law of the Commonwealth of Massachusetts, restricting the authority of its agencies to purchase goods or services from companies doing business with Burma, is invalid under the Supremacy Clause of the National Constitution owing to its threat of frustrating federal statutory objectives. We hold that it is. . . .

A fundamental principle of the Constitution is that Congress has the power to preempt state law. Art. VI, cl. 2. Even without an express provision for preemption, we have found that state law must yield to a congressional Act in at least two circumstances. When Congress intends federal law to "occupy the field," state law in that area is preempted. And even if Congress has not occupied the field, state law is naturally preempted to the extent of any conflict with a federal statute. We will find preemption where it is impossible for a private party to comply with both state and federal law and where "under the circumstances of [a] particular case, [the challenged state law] stands as an obstacle to the accomplishment and execution of the full purposes and objectives of Congress." What is a sufficient obstacle is a matter of judgment, to be informed by examining the federal statute as a whole and identifying its purpose and intended effects:

"For when the question is whether a Federal act overrides a state law, the entire scheme of the statute must of course be considered and that which needs must be implied is of no less force than that which is expressed. If the purpose of the act cannot otherwise be accomplished—if its operation within its chosen field else must be frustrated and its provisions be refused their natural effect— the state law must yield to the regulation of Congress within the sphere of its delegated power." [*Savage v. Jones*, 1912.]

Applying this standard, we see the state Burma law as an obstacle to the accomplishment of Congress's full objectives under the federal Act. We find that the state law undermines the intended purpose and "natural effect" of at least three provisions of the federal Act, that is, its delegation of effective discretion to the President to control economic sanctions against Burma, its limitation of sanctions solely to United States persons and new investment, and its directive to the President to proceed diplomatically in developing a comprehensive, multilateral strategy towards Burma.

First, Congress clearly intended the federal act to provide the President with flexible and effective authority over economic sanctions against Burma. Although Congress immediately put in place a set of initial sanctions, it authorized the President to terminate any and all of those measures upon determining and certifying that there had been progress in human rights and democracy in Burma. It invested the President with the further power to ban new investment by United States persons, dependent only on specific Presidential findings of repression in Burma. And, most significantly, Congress empowered the President "to waive, temporarily or permanently, any sanction [under the federal act] . . . if he determines and certifies to Congress that the application of such sanction would be contrary to the national security interests of the United States."

This express investiture of the President with statutory authority to act for the United States in imposing sanctions with respect to the government of Burma, augmented by the flexibility* to respond to change by suspending sanc-

tions in the interest of national security, recalls Justice Jackson's observation in *Youngstown Sheet & Tube Co. v. Sawyer* (1952): "When the President acts pursuant to an express or implied authorization of Congress, his authority is at its maximum, for it includes all that he possesses in his own right plus all that Congress can delegate." Within the sphere defined by Congress, then, the statute has placed the President in a position with as much discretion to exercise economic leverage against Burma, with an eye toward national security, as our law will admit. And it is just this plenitude of Executive authority that we think controls the issue of preemption here. The President has been given this authority not merely to make a political statement but to achieve a political result, and the fullness of his authority shows the importance in the congressional mind of reaching that result. It is simply implausible that Congress would have gone to such lengths to empower the President if it had been willing to compromise his effectiveness by deference to every provision of state statute or local ordinance that might, if enforced, blunt the consequences of discretionary Presidential action.

And that is just what the Massachusetts Burma law would do in imposing a different, state system of economic pressure against the Burmese political regime. As will be seen, the state statute penalizes some private action that the federal Act (as administered by the President) may allow, and pulls levers of influence that the federal Act does not reach. But the point here is that the state sanctions are immediate. This unyielding application undermines the President's intended statutory authority by making it impossible for him to restrain fully the coercive power of the national economy when he may choose to take the discretionary action open to him, whether he believes that the national interest requires sanctions to be lifted, or believes that the promise of lifting sanctions would move the Burmese regime in the democratic direction. Quite simply, if the Massachusetts law is enforceable the President has less to offer and less economic and diplomatic leverage as a conse-

---

* [Footnote 9] Statements by the sponsors of the federal Act underscore the statute's clarity in providing the President with flexibility in implementing its Burma sanctions policy. See 142 Cong. Rec. 19212 (1996) (emphasizing importance of providing "the administration flexibility in reacting to changes, both positive and negative, with respect to the behavior of the [Burmese regime]) (statement of principal sponsor Sen. Cohen); *id.*, at 19213; *id.*, at 19221 (describing the federal act as "giv[ing] the President, who, whether Democrat or Republican, is charged with conducting our Nation's foreign policy, some flexibility") (statement of cosponsor Sen. McCain); *id.*, at 19220 ("We need to be able to have the flexibility to remove sanctions and provide support for Burma if it reaches a transition stage that is moving toward the restoration of democracy, which all of us support") (statement of cosponsor Sen. Feinstein). These sponsors chose a

pliant policy with the explicit support of the Executive. See, *e.g.*, *id.*, at 19219 (letter from Barbara Larkin, Assistant Secretary, Legislative Affairs, U.S. Department of State to Sen. Cohen) (admitted by unanimous consent) ("We believe the current and conditional sanctions which your language proposes are consistent with Administration policy. As we have stated on several occasions in the past, we need to maintain our flexibility to respond to events in Burma and to consult with Congress on appropriate responses to ongoing and future development there").

quence. In *Dames & Moore v. Regan* (1981), we used the metaphor of the bargaining chip to describe the President's control of funds valuable to a hostile country; here, the state Act reduces the value of the chips created by the federal statute. It thus "stands as an obstacle to the accomplishment and execution of the full purposes and objectives of Congress."

Congress manifestly intended to limit economic pressure against the Burmese Government to a specific range. The federal Act confines its reach to United States persons, imposes limited immediate sanctions, places only a conditional ban on a carefully defined area of "new investment," and pointedly exempts contracts to sell or purchase goods, services, or technology. These detailed provisions show that Congress's calibrated Burma policy is a deliberate effort "to steer a middle path."

The State has set a different course, and its statute conflicts with federal law at a number of points by penalizing individuals and conduct that Congress has explicitly exempted or excluded from sanctions. While the state Act differs from the federal in relying entirely on indirect economic leverage through third parties with Burmese connections, it otherwise stands in clear contrast to the congressional scheme in the scope of subject matter addressed. It restricts all contracts between the State and companies doing business in Burma. . . . It is specific in targeting contracts to provide financial services, and general goods and services, to the Government of Burma, and thus prohibits contracts between the State and United States persons for goods, services, or technology, even though those transactions are explicitly exempted from the ambit of new investment prohibition when the President exercises his discretionary authority to impose sanctions under the federal Act.

As with the subject of business meant to be affected, so with the class of companies doing it: the state Act's generality stands at odds with the federal discreteness. The Massachusetts law directly and indirectly imposes costs on all companies that do any business in Burma. It sanctions companies promoting the importation of natural resources controlled by the government of Burma, or having any operations or affiliates in Burma. The state Act thus penalizes companies with pre-existing affiliates or investments, all of which lie beyond the reach of the federal act's restrictions on "new investment" in Burmese economic development.

The state Act, moreover, imposes restrictions on foreign companies as well as domestic, whereas the federal Act limits its reach to United States persons. . . .

Finally, the state Act is at odds with the President's intended authority to speak for the United States among the world's nations in developing a "comprehensive, multilateral strategy to bring democracy to and improve human rights practices and the quality of life in Burma." Congress called for Presidential cooperation with . . . other countries in developing such a strategy, directed the President to encourage a dialogue between the government of Burma and the democratic opposition, and required him to report to the Congress on the progress of his diplomatic efforts. As with Congress's explicit delegation to the President of power over economic sanctions, Congress's express command to the President to take the initiative for the United States among the international community invested him with the maximum authority of the National Government, cf. *Youngstown Sheet & Tube Co.* in harmony with the President's own constitutional powers, U.S. Const., Art. II, §2, cl. 2 ("[The President] shall have Power, by and with the Advice and Consent of the Senate, to make Treaties" and "shall appoint Ambassadors, other public Ministers and Consuls"); §3 ("[The President] shall receive Ambassadors and other public Ministers"). This clear mandate and invocation of exclusively national power belies any suggestion that Congress intended the President's effective voice to be obscured by state or local action.

Again, the state Act undermines the President's capacity, in this instance for effective diplomacy. It is not merely that the differences between the state and federal Acts in scope and type of sanctions threaten to complicate discussions; they compromise the very capacity of the President to speak for the Nation with one voice in dealing with other governments. We need not get into any general consideration of limits of state action affecting foreign affairs to realize that the President's maximum power to persuade rests on his capacity to bargain for the benefits of access to the entire national economy without exception for enclaves fenced off willy-nilly by inconsistent political tactics. When such exceptions do qualify his capacity to present a coherent position on behalf of the national economy, he is weakened, of course, not only in dealing with the Burmese regime, but in working together with other nations in hopes of reaching common policy and "comprehensive" strategy. . . .

[The state] contends that the failure of Congress to preempt the state Act demonstrates implicit permission. The State points out that Congress has repeatedly declined to enact express preemption provisions aimed at state and local sanctions, and it calls our attention to the large number of such measures passed against South Africa in the 1980s, which various authorities cited have thought were not preempted. The State stresses that Congress was aware of the state Act in 1996, but did not preempt it explicitly when it adopted its own Burma statute. The State would have us conclude that Congress's continuing failure to enact express preemption implies approval, particularly in light of occasional instances of express preemption of state sanctions in the past.

The argument is unconvincing on more than one level. A failure to provide for preemption expressly may reflect nothing more than the settled character of implied preemption doctrine that courts will dependably apply, and in any event, the existence of conflict cognizable under the Supremacy Clause does not depend on express congressional recognition that federal and state law may conflict. The State's inference of congressional intent is unwarranted here, therefore, simply because the silence of Congress is ambiguous. Since we never ruled on whether state and local sanctions against South Africa in the 1980s were preempted or otherwise invalid, arguable parallels between the two sets of federal and state Acts do not tell us much about the validity of the latter.

Because the state Act's provisions conflict with Congress's specific delegation to the President of flexible discretion, with limitation of sanctions to a limited scope of actions and actors, and with direction to develop a comprehensive, multilateral strategy under the federal Act, it is preempted, and its application is unconstitutional, under the Supremacy Clause.

The judgment of the Court of Appeals for the First Circuit is affirmed.

It is so ordered.

JUSTICE SCALIA, with whom JUSTICE THOMAS joins, concurring in the judgment.

It is perfectly obvious on the face of this statute that Congress, with the concurrence of the President, intended to "provid[e] the President with flexibility in implementing its Burma sanctions policy." I therefore see no point in devoting a footnote [footnote 9] to the interesting (albeit unsurprising) proposition that "[s]tatements by the sponsors of the federal Act" show that they shared this intent and that a statement in a letter from a State Department officer shows that flexibility had "the explicit support of the Executive." This excursus is especially pointless since the immediately succeeding footnote must rely upon the statute itself (devoid of any support in statements by "sponsors" or the "Executive") to refute the quite telling argument that the statements were addressed only to flexibility in administering the sanctions of the *federal* Act, and said nothing at all about state sanctions.

It is perfectly obvious on the face of the statute that Congress expected the President to use his discretionary authority over sanctions to "move the Burmese regime in the democratic direction." I therefore see no point in devoting a footnote to the interesting (albeit unsurprising) proposition that "the sponsors of the federal Act" shared this expectation.

It is perfectly obvious on the face of the statute that Congress's Burma policy was a "calibrated" one, which "limit[ed] economic pressure against the Burmese Government to a specific range." I therefore see no point in devoting a footnote to the interesting (albeit unsurprising) proposition that bills imposing greater sanctions were introduced but not adopted and to the (even less surprising) proposition that the sponsors of the legislation made clear that its "limits were deliberate.". . .

It is perfectly obvious on the face of the statute that Congress intended the President to develop a "multilateral strategy" in cooperation with other countries. In fact, the statute says that in so many words. I therefore see no point in devoting two footnotes to the interesting (albeit unsurprising) proposition that three Senators *also* favored a multilateral approach.

It is perfectly obvious from the record, as the Court discusses, that the inflexibility produced by the Massachusetts statute has in fact caused difficulties with our allies and has in fact impeded a "multilateral strategy." And as the Court later says in another context, "the existence of conflict cognizable under the Supremacy Clause does not depend on express congressional recognition that federal and state law may conflict." I therefore see no point in devoting a footnote to the interesting (albeit unsurprising) fact that the "congressional sponsors" of the Act and "the Executive" actually *predicted* that inflexibility would have the effect of causing difficulties with our allies and impeding a "multilateral strategy."

Of course even if all of the Court's invocations of legislative history were not utterly irrelevant, I would still object to them, since neither the statements of individual Members of Congress (ordinarily addressed to a virtually empty floor), nor Executive statements and letters addressed to congressional committees, nor the nonenactment of other proposed legislation, is a reliable indication of what a majority of both Houses of Congress intended when they voted for the statute before us. The *only* reliable indication of *that* intent—the only thing we know for sure can be attributed to *all* of them—is the words of the bill that they voted to make law. In a way, using unreliable legislative history to confirm what the statute plainly says anyway (or what the record plainly shows) is less objectionable since, after all, it has absolutely no effect upon the outcome. But in a way, this utter lack of necessity makes it even worse. . . .

In any case, the portion of the Court's opinion that I consider irrelevant is quite extensive, comprising, in total, about one-tenth of the opinion's size and (since it is in footnote type) even more of the opinion's content. I consider that to be not just wasteful (it was not preordained, after all, that this was to be a 25-page essay) but harmful, since it tells future litigants that, even when a statute is clear on its face, and its effects clear upon the record, statements from the legislative history may help (and presumably harm) the case. If so, they must be researched and discussed by counsel—which makes appellate litigation considerably more time consuming, and hence considerably more expensive, than it need be. This to my mind outweighs the arguable good that may come of such persistent irrelevancy, at least when it is indulged in the margins: that it may encourage readers to ignore our footnotes.

For this reason, I join only the judgment of the Court.

Crosby is an interesting case for several reasons, among them Scalia's concurring opinion. Scalia demonstrates his interest in reaching decisions based on the clear language in laws without delving into the intent of their framers or legislative history.

Further, as in *Holland*, the justices held that states were preempted from taking action in the areas of foreign affairs. And, if this holding needed even more reinforcement, the Court gave it such in the recent dispute of ***American Insurance Association v. Garamendi*** (2003), in which the Court considered a California law that required any insurer doing business in the State to disclose information about all policies sold in Europe between 1920 and 1945 by the company itself or any one "related" to it. The aim of the law was to ensure that Holocaust victims or their heirs could take direct action on their own behalf to receive payment on their insurance policies. The American Insurance Association, joined by the United States as an amicus curiae, challenged the law on the ground that it interfered with the federal government's conduct of foreign relations and thus is preempted.

Writing for the majority, Justice David Souter agreed with this argument. He noted that the federal government's position, "expressed unmistakably in the executive agreements signed by the President with Germany and Austria, has been to encourage European insurers to work . . . to develop acceptable claim procedures," rather than to encourage lawsuits. "California," Souter noted, "has taken a different tack of providing regulatory sanctions to compel disclosure and payment, supplemented by a new cause of action for Holocaust survivors if the other sanctions should fail." He continued:

The situation created by the California legislation calls to mind the impact of the Massachusetts Burma law on the effective exercise of the President's power, as recounted in the statutory preemption case, *Crosby v. National Foreign Trade Council* (2000). [The California law's] economic compulsion to make public disclosure employs "a different, state system of economic pressure," and in doing so undercuts the President's diplomatic discretion and the choice he has made exercising it. . . . The law thus "compromise[s] the very capacity of the President to speak for the Nation with one voice in dealing with other governments" to resolve claims against European companies arising out of World War II.

Clearly, in the cases of *Holland, Crosby,* and *Garamendi,* the Court has delivered a singular message to the states. Where the Court has had greater difficulty explicating a coherent preemption doctrine is in cases involving domestic power—but not for lack of effort. In *Pennsylvania v. Nelson*, the justices sought to lay out a standard for adjudicating these sorts of disputes.[37] What was that test? Is it sufficiently specific, or does it leave room for interpretation?

Pennsylvania v. Nelson

350 U.S. 497 (1956)
http://laws.findlaw.com/US/350/497.html
Vote: 6 (Black, Clark, Douglas, Frankfurter, Harlan, Warren)
   3 (Burton, Minton, Reed)
Opinion of the Court: Warren
Dissenting opinion: Reed

During the 1940s and 1950s Congress passed a host of legislation designed to combat subversive activities in the United States. Among these was the Smith Act of 1940, which prohibited the willful advocacy of the overthrow of the United States by force and violence. Those found guilty could face a maximum penalty of a $10,000 fine and/or a ten-year prison sentence.

Congress, however, was not the only legislature concerned with subversive activities. Forty-two states, including Pennsylvania, enacted laws similar to the Smith Act. They made it a crime to advocate the violent overthrow of both state and federal governments, and some carried harsher penalties than the federal statute. Under Pennsylvania's law, for example, violators could receive twenty or more years in jail.

Steve Nelson, a Communist Party member convicted of violating Pennsylvania's law, challenged the constitutionality of the act. In his view, the federal law preempted the state's: Congress had passed antisubversive legislation, and it now occupied that field. Had Congress wanted state action as well, it would have said so in the Smith Act. The state's response was not surprising: because the law represented a perfectly legitimate exercise of its police powers—states have a paramount interest in their self-preservation—and because it was compatible

37. To hear oral arguments in this case, navigate to: *www.oyez.org/oyez/frontpage.*

with Congress's law, the "dual form of government" would be devastated by such a reading of the Smith Act.

MR. CHIEF JUSTICE WARREN delivered the opinion of the Court.

Many State Attorneys General and the Solicitor General of the United States appeared as amici curiae for petitioner, and several briefs were filed on behalf of the respondent. Because of the important question of federal-state relationship involved, we granted certiorari.

It should be said at the outset that the decision in this case does not affect the right of States to enforce their sedition laws at times when the Federal Government has not occupied the field and is not protecting the entire country from seditious conduct. The distinction between the two situations was clearly recognized by the court below. Nor does it limit the jurisdiction of the States where the Constitution and Congress have specifically given them concurrent jurisdiction. . . . Neither does it limit the right of the State to protect itself at any time against sabotage or attempted violence of all kinds. Nor does it prevent the State from prosecuting where the same act constitutes both a federal offense and a state offense under the police power. . . .

Where, as in the instant case, Congress has not stated specifically whether a federal statute has occupied a field in which the States are otherwise free to legislate, different criteria have furnished touchstones for decision. Thus,

"[t]his Court, in considering the validity of state laws in the light of . . . federal laws touching the same subject, has made use of the following expressions: conflicting; contrary to; occupying the field; repugnance; difference; irreconcilability; inconsistency; violation; curtailment; and interference. But none of these expressions provides an infallible constitutional test or an exclusive constitutional yardstick. In the final analysis, there can be no one crystal clear distinctly marked formula."

In this case, we think that each of several tests of supersession is met.

First, "[t]he scheme of federal regulation [is] so pervasive as to make reasonable the inference that Congress left no room for the States to supplement it." The Congress determined in 1940 that it was necessary for it to re-enter the field of antisubversive legislation, which had been abandoned by it in 1921. In that year, it enacted the Smith Act which proscribes advocacy of the overthrow of any government—federal, state or local—by force and violence and organization of and knowing membership in a group which so advocates. . . . The Internal Security Act of 1950 is aimed more directly at Communist organizations. . . . The Communist Control Act of 1954 declares "that the Communist Party of the United States, although purportedly a political party, is in fact an instrumentality of a conspiracy to overthrow the Government of the United States" and that "its role as the agency of a hostile foreign power renders its existence a clear present and continuing danger to the security of the United States.". . .

We examine these Acts only to determine the congressional plan. Looking to all of them in the aggregate, the conclusion is inescapable that Congress has intended to occupy the field of sedition. Taken as a whole, they evince a congressional plan which makes it reasonable to determine that no room has been left for the States to supplement it. Therefore, a state sedition statute is superseded regardless of whether it purports to supplement the federal law. . . .

Second, the federal statutes "touch a field in which the federal interest is so dominant that the federal system [must] be assumed to preclude enforcement of state laws on the same subject." Congress has devised an all-embracing program for resistance to the various forms of totalitarian aggression. Our external defenses have been strengthened, and a plan to protect against internal subversion has been made by it. It has appropriated vast sums, not only for our own protection, but also to strengthen freedom throughout the world. It has charged the Federal Bureau of Investigation and the Central Intelligence Agency with responsibility for intelligence concerning Communist seditious activities against our Government, and has denominated such activities as part of a world conspiracy. It accordingly proscribed sedition against all government in the nation—national, state and local. . . . Congress having thus treated seditious conduct as a matter of vital national concern, it is in no sense a local enforcement problem. . . .

Third, enforcement of state sedition acts presents a serious danger of conflict with the administration of the federal program. Since 1939, in order to avoid a hampering of uniform enforcement of its program by sporadic local prosecutions, the Federal Government has urged local authorities not to intervene in such matters, but to turn over to the federal authorities immediately and unevaluated all information concerning subversive activities. . . .

Steve Nelson challenged his conviction under Pennsylvania state antisubversive laws, arguing that federal regulation of subversive activities preempted state statutes.

Since we find that Congress has occupied the field to the exclusion of parallel state legislation, that the dominant interest of the Federal Government precludes state intervention, and that administration of state Acts would conflict with the operation of the federal plan, we are convinced that the decision of the Supreme Court of Pennsylvania is unassailable.

We are not unmindful of the risk of compounding punishments which would be created by finding concurrent state power. In our view of the case, we do not reach the question whether double or multiple punishment for the same overt acts directed against the United States has constitutional sanction. Without compelling indication to the contrary, we will not assume that Congress intended to permit the possibility of double punishment.

The judgment of the Supreme Court of Pennsylvania is

Affirmed.

MR. JUSTICE REED, with whom MR. JUSTICE BURTON, and MR. JUSTICE MINTON join, dissenting.

The problems of governmental power may be approached in this case free from the varied viewpoints that focus on the problems of national security. This is a jurisdictional problem of general importance because it involves an asserted limitation on the police power of the States when it is applied to a crime that is punishable also by the Federal Government. As this is a recurring problem, it is appropriate to explain our dissent.

Congress has not, in any of its statutes relating to sedition, specifically barred the exercise of state power to punish the same Acts under state law. And, we read the majority opinion to assume for this case that, absent federal legislation, there is no constitutional bar to punishment of sedition against the United States by both a State and the Nation. The majority limits to the federal courts the power to try charges of sedition against the Federal Government.

First, the Court relies upon the pervasiveness of the antisubversive legislation embodied in the Smith Act of 1940, the Internal Security Act of 1950, and the Communist Control Act of 1954. It asserts that these Acts in the aggregate mean that Congress has occupied the "field of sedition" to the exclusion of the States. . . .

But the federal sedition laws are distinct criminal statutes that punish willful advocacy of the use of force against "the government of the United States or the government of any State." These criminal laws proscribe certain local activity without creating any statutory or administrative regulation. There is, consequently, no question as to whether some general congressional regulatory scheme might be upset by a coinciding state plan. In these circumstances the conflict should be clear and direct before this Court reads a congressional intent to void state legislation into the federal sedition acts. . . .

Secondly, the Court states that the federal sedition statutes touch a field "in which the federal interest is so dominant" they must preclude state laws on the same subject. . . .

We look upon the Smith Act as a provision for controlling incitements to overthrow by force and violence the Nation, or any State, or any political subdivision of either. Such an exercise of federal police power carries, we think, no such dominancy over similar state powers as might be attributed to continuing federal regulations concerning foreign affairs or coinage, for example. In the responsibility of national and local governments to protect themselves against sedition, there is no "dominant interest."

We are citizens of the United States and of the State wherein we reside and are dependent upon the strength of both to preserve our rights and liberties. Both may enact criminal statutes for mutual protection unless Congress has otherwise provided. . . .

Thirdly, the Court finds ground for abrogating Pennsylvania's antisedition statute because, in the Court's view, the State's administration of the Act may hamper the enforcement of the federal law. . . . We find no suggestion from any official source that state officials should be less alert to ferret out or punish subversion. The Court's attitude as to interference seems to us quite contrary to that of the Legislative and Executive Departments. Congress was advised of the existing state sedition legislation when the Smith Act was enacted and has been kept current with its spread. No declaration of exclusiveness followed. In this very case the Executive appears by brief of the Department of Justice, amicus curiae. The brief summarizes this point:

"The administration of the various state laws has not, in the course of the fifteen years that the federal and state sedition laws have existed side by side, in fact interfered with, embarrassed, or impeded the enforcement of the Smith Act. The significance of this absence of conflict in administration or enforcement of the federal and state sedition laws will be appreciated when it is realized that this period has included the stress of wartime security requirements and the federal investigation and prosecution under the Smith Act of the principal national and regional Communist leaders."

Mere fear by courts of possible difficulties does not seem to us in these circumstances a valid reason for ousting a State from exercise of its police power. Those are matters for legislative determination.

Finally, and this one point seems in and of itself decisive, there is an independent reason for reversing the Pennsylvania Supreme Court. The Smith Act appears in Title 18 of the United States Code, which Title codifies the federal criminal laws. Section 3231 of that Title provides:

"Nothing in this title shall be held to take away or impair the jurisdiction of the courts of the several States under the laws thereof."

That declaration springs from the federal character of our Nation. It recognizes the fact that maintenance of order and fairness rests primarily with the States. The section was first enacted in 1825 and has appeared successively in the federal criminal laws since that time. This Court has interpreted the section to mean that States may provide concurrent legislation in the absence of explicit congressional intent to the contrary. The majority's position in this case cannot be reconciled with that clear authorization of Congress.

The law stands against any advocacy of violence to change established governments. Freedom of speech allows full play to the processes of reason. The state and national legislative bodies have legislated within constitutional limits so as to allow the widest participation by the law enforcement officers of the respective governments. The individual States were not told that they are powerless to punish local acts of sedition, nominally directed against the United States. Courts should not interfere. We would reverse the judgment of the Supreme Court of Pennsylvania.

Although the Court clearly sets out a preemption standard, many argue that it has led to an ad hoc balancing of state-federal interests, turning more or less on the particular facts of disputes. As noted in Table 6-8, which lists some of the Court's preemption rulings, this observation may be true. Given Warren's opinion in *Nelson*, is that not to be expected? Consider that question as you read the next case.

===

Pacific Gas and Electric Company v. State Energy Resources Conservation and Development Commission

461 U.S. 190 (1983)
http://laws.findlaw.com/US/461/190.html
Vote: 9 (Blackmun, Brennan, Burger, Marshall, O'Connor, Powell, Rehnquist, Stevens, White)
    0
Opinion of the Court: White
Concurring opinion: Blackmun

In 1954 Congress passed the Atomic Energy Act, which it has amended several times subsequently. The act was designed to promote the safe development of nuclear energy. Over time the public has become increasingly concerned with nuclear safety issues. Opposition to nuclear power prompted several states to pass laws placing restrictions on future nuclear power development.

In 1974 California passed the Warren-Alquist State Energy Resources Conservation and Development Act, which was amended in 1976. Section 25524.2 of the amendments dealt with long-term solutions to the nuclear waste problem. It imposed a moratorium on all new nuclear power plants until technology for the effective disposal of high-level nuclear waste was developed and approved. The Pacific Gas and Electric Company, along with the Southern California Edison Company, filed suit to have the moratorium declared unconstitutional. The companies argued that the California law was preempted by the federal Atomic Energy Act. The Court of Appeals for the Ninth Circuit rejected the companies' preemption argument, and they appealed to the U.S. Supreme Court.

JUSTICE WHITE delivered the opinion of the Court.

The turning of swords into plowshares has symbolized the transformation of atomic power into a source of energy in American society. To facilitate this development the Federal Government relaxed its monopoly over fissionable materials and nuclear technology, and in its place, erected a complex scheme to promote the civilian development of nuclear energy, while seeking to safeguard the public and the environment from the unpredictable risks of a new technology. Early on, it was decided that the States would continue their traditional role in the regulation of electricity production. The interrelationship of federal and state authority in the nuclear energy field has not been simple; the federal regulatory structure has been frequently amended to optimize the partnership. . . .

It is well established that within constitutional limits Congress may pre-empt state authority by so stating in express terms. Absent explicit pre-emptive language, Congress' intent to supersede state law altogether may be found from a " 'scheme of federal regulation . . . so pervasive as to make reasonable the inference that Congress left no room for the States to supplement it,' because 'the Act of Congress may touch a field in which the federal interest is so dominant that the federal system will be assumed to preclude enforcement of state laws on the same subject,' or because 'the object sought to be obtained by the federal law and the character of obligations imposed by it may reveal the same purpose.' " *Fidelity Federal Savings & Loan Assn. v.*

TABLE 6-8   Preemption Cases after *Pennsylvania v. Nelson*

Case	Question	Holding (Vote)
Campbell v. Hussey (1961)	Is Georgia's Tobacco Identification Act, which requires that a certain type of tobacco be marked with a white tag, barred by the 1935 Federal Tobacco Inspection Act?	Yes. (6–3) Douglas, for a plurality, held that "[w]e do not have here the question whether Georgia's law conflicts with the federal law. Rather we have the question of preemption. . . . Congress, in legislating concerning types of tobacco . . . preempted the field."
Florida Lime & Avocado Growers, Inc. v. Paul (1963)	Is California's requirement of minimum oil content for avocados preempted by federal regulations that certify as mature avocados that have lower levels of oil?	No. (5–4) Brennan, for the majority, concluded that "there is neither such actual conflict between the two schemes of regulation that both cannot stand in the same area, nor evidence of a congressional design to pre-empt the field."
City of Burbank v. Lockheed Air Terminal (1973)	Is a City of Burbank ordinance that prohibits the take-off of aircraft between 11 p.m. and 7 a.m. preempted by federal laws regulating the aviation industry?	Yes. (5–4) The pervasively national nature of the airline industry requires preemption of local regulations by federal law.
Pacific Gas & Electric Co. v. Energy Resources Commission (1983)	Does the federal Atomic Energy Act preempt a California law imposing a statewide moratorium on the certification of nuclear energy plants for reasons other than safety?	No. (9–0) While "the Federal Government has occupied the entire field of nuclear safety concerns," such preemption would only prevent state moratoriums that had as their rationale safety concerns. Since California provided other, nonsafety reasons for its action, the law is valid.
Silkwood v. Kerr-McGee (1984)	Does the Atomic Energy Act preempt a state tort law system that allows for the award of punitive damages for harm caused by the escape of plutonium from a federally licensed nuclear facility?	No. (5–4) Although such awards may influence the safety decisions that are at the heart of the AEA, there is no evidence that Congress intended to preempt state tort law remedies. Absent such a congressional intent, the state tort remedy is valid.
Wisconsin Public Intervenor v. Mortier (1991)	Does the Federal Insecticide, Fungicide, and Rodenticide Act, a comprehensive regulatory law enforced by the Environmental Protection Agency, preempt regulation of pesticides by local governments?	No. (9–0) The states' historic powers are not superseded by federal law unless that is the clear and manifest purpose of Congress. Compliance with both local and federal regulations is not a physical impossibility.
Cipollone v. Liggett Group (1992)	Do the federally required warnings on cigarette packages preempt states from allowing lawsuits filed by individuals for damages arising from cigarette-related illnesses?	No. (7–2) Federal warning requirements preempt state warning laws. Damage suits under state law may not be filed based on a failure of manufacturers to warn adequately. However, suits may be filed against manufacturers on grounds other than adequate warning.
Lorillard Tobacco Co. v. Reilly (2000)	Does a federal cigarette advertising act that prescribes mandatory health warnings for cigarette packaging and advertising preempt the attorney general of Massachusetts from promulgating regulations on cigarette advertising and sales?	Yes. (5–4) According to the Court, "Congress pre-empted state cigarette advertising regulations like the Attorney General's because they would upset federal legislative choices to require specific warnings and to impose the ban on cigarette advertising in electronic media in order to address concerns about smoking and health."

De la Cuesta (1982). Even where Congress has not entirely displaced state regulation in a specific area. state law is preempted to the extent that it actually conflicts with federal law. Such a conflict arises when "compliance with both federal and state regulations is a physical impossibility," *Florida Lime & Avocado Growers, Inc. v. Paul* (1963), or where state law "stands as an obstacle to the accomplishment and execution of the full purposes and objectives of Congress." *Hines v. Davidowitz* (1941).

Petitioners, the United States, and supporting amici, present three major lines of argument as to why 25524.2 is pre-empted. First, they submit that the statute—because it regulates construction of nuclear plants and because it is allegedly predicated on safety concerns—ignores the division between federal and state authority created by the Atomic Energy Act, and falls within the field that the Federal Government has preserved for its own exclusive control. Second, the statute, and the judgments that underlie it, conflict with decisions concerning the nuclear waste disposal issue made by Congress and the Nuclear Regulatory Commission. Third, the California statute frustrates the federal goal of developing nuclear technology as a source of energy. We consider each of these contentions in turn.

Even a brief perusal of the Atomic Energy Act reveals that, despite its comprehensiveness, it does not at any point expressly require the States to construct or authorize nuclear powerplants or prohibit the States from deciding, as an absolute or conditional matter, not to permit the construction of any further reactors. . . .

. . . [F]rom the passage of the Atomic Energy Act in 1954, through several revisions, and to the present day, Congress has preserved the dual regulation of nuclear-powered electricity generation: the Federal Government maintains complete control of the safety and "nuclear" aspects of energy generation; the States exercise their traditional authority over the need for additional generating capacity, the type of generating facilities to be licensed, land use, ratemaking, and the like.

The above is not particularly controversial. But deciding how 25524.2 is to be construed and classified is a more difficult proposition. At the outset, we emphasize that the statute does not seek to regulate the construction or operation of a nuclear powerplant. It would clearly be impermissible for California to attempt to do so, for such regulation, even if enacted out of nonsafety concerns, would neverthe-

less directly conflict with the NRC's [Nuclear Regulatory Commission] exclusive authority over plant construction and operation. Respondents appear to concede as much. Respondents do broadly argue, however, that although safety regulation of nuclear plants by States is forbidden, a State may completely prohibit new construction until its safety concerns are satisfied by the Federal Government. We reject this line of reasoning. State safety regulation is not pre-empted only when it conflicts with federal law. Rather, the Federal Government has occupied the entire field of nuclear safety concerns, except the limited powers expressly ceded to the States. When the Federal Government completely occupies a given field or an identifiable portion of it, as it has done here, the test of pre-emption is whether "the matter on which the State asserts the right to act is in any way regulated by the Federal Act." A state moratorium on nuclear construction grounded in safety concerns falls squarely within the prohibited field. Moreover, a state judgment that nuclear power is not safe enough to be further developed would conflict directly with the countervailing judgment of the NRC, that nuclear construction may proceed notwithstanding extant uncertainties as to waste disposal. A state prohibition on nuclear construction for safety reasons would also be in the teeth of the Atomic Energy Act's objective to insure that nuclear technology be safe enough for widespread development and use—and would be pre-empted for that reason.

That being the case, it is necessary to determine whether there is a nonsafety rationale for 25524.2. California has maintained, and the Court of Appeals agreed, that 25524.2 was aimed at economic problems, not radiation hazards. . . .

Although [the] specific indicia of California's intent in enacting 25524.2 are subject to varying interpretation, there are two further reasons why we should not become embroiled in attempting to ascertain California's true motive. First, inquiry into legislative motive is often an unsatisfactory venture. What motivates one legislator to vote for a statute is not necessarily what motivates scores of others to enact it. Second, it would be particularly pointless for us to engage in such inquiry here when it is clear that the States have been allowed to retain authority over the need for electrical generating facilities easily sufficient to permit a State so inclined to halt the construction of new nuclear plants by refusing on economic grounds to issue certificates of public convenience in individual proceedings. In these circumstances, it should be up to Congress to determine whether a State has misused the authority left in its hands.

Therefore, we accept California's avowed economic purpose as the rationale for enacting 25524.2. Accordingly, the statute lies outside the occupied field of nuclear safety regulation.

Petitioners' second major argument concerns federal regulation aimed at the nuclear waste disposal problem itself. It is contended that 25524.2 conflicts with federal regulation of nuclear waste disposal, with the NRC's decision that it is permissible to continue to license reactors, notwithstanding uncertainty surrounding the waste disposal problem, and with Congress' recent passage of legislation directed at that problem.

The NRC's imprimatur, however, indicates only that it is safe to proceed with such plants, not that it is economically wise to do so. Because the NRC order does not and could not compel a utility to develop a nuclear plant, compliance with both it and 25524.2 is possible. Moreover, because the NRC's regulations are aimed at insuring that plants are safe, not necessarily that they are economical, 25524.2 does not interfere with the objective of the federal regulation.

Nor has California sought through 25524.2 to impose its own standards on nuclear waste disposal. The statute accepts that it is the federal responsibility to develop and license such technology. As there is no attempt on California's part to enter this field, one which is occupied by the Federal Government, we do not find 25524.2 pre-empted any more by the NRC's obligations in the waste disposal field than by its licensing power over the plants themselves. . . .

Finally, it is strongly contended that 25524.2 frustrates the Atomic Energy Act's purpose to develop the commercial use of nuclear power. It is well established that state law is pre-empted if it "stands as an obstacle to the accomplishment and execution of the full purposes and objectives of Congress."

There is little doubt that a primary purpose of the Atomic Energy Act was, and continues to be, the promotion of nuclear power. The Act itself states that it is a program "to encourage widespread participation in the development and utilization of atomic energy for peaceful purposes to the maximum extent consistent with the common defense and security and with the health and safety of the public.". . .

The Court of Appeals is right, however, that the promotion of nuclear power is not to be accomplished "at all costs." The elaborate licensing and safety provisions and the continued preservation of state regulation in traditional areas belie that. Moreover, Congress has allowed the States to determine—as a matter of economics—whether a nuclear plant vis-à-vis a fossil fuel plant should be built. The decision of California to exercise that authority does not, in itself, constitute a basis for pre-emption. Therefore, while the argument of petitioners and the United States has considerable force, the legal reality remains that Congress has left sufficient authority in the States to allow the development of nuclear power to be slowed or even stopped for economic reasons. Given this statutory scheme, it is for Congress to rethink the division of regulatory authority in light of its possible exercise by the States to undercut a federal objective. The courts should not assume the role which our system assigns to Congress.

The judgment of the Court of Appeals is

Affirmed.

JUSTICE BLACKMUN, with whom JUSTICE STEVENS joins, concurring in part and concurring in the judgment.

I join the Court's opinion, except to the extent it suggests that a State may not prohibit the construction of nuclear power plants if the State is motivated by concerns about the safety of such plants. . . .

Congress has not required States to "go nuclear," in whole or in part. The Atomic Energy Act's twin goals were to promote the development of a technology and to ensure the safety of that technology. Although that Act reserves to the NRC decisions about how to build and operate nuclear plants, the Court reads too much into the Act in suggesting that it also limits the States' traditional power to decide what types of electric power to utilize. Congress simply has made the nuclear option available, and a State may decline that option for any reason. Rather than rest on the elusive test of legislative motive, therefore, I would conclude that the decision whether to build nuclear plants remains with the States. In my view, a ban on construction of nuclear powerplants would be valid even if its authors were motivated by fear of a core meltdown or other nuclear catastrophe.

In *Pacific Gas* the Court applied the preemption doctrine in a somewhat narrow way. By enacting safety regulations and promoting the development of safe nuclear energy, Congress did not automatically supersede all state regulations with respect to nuclear power. Such an act, as we have seen throughout this chapter, sits comfortably with the current Court's general approach to nation-state relations.

READINGS

Brennan, William J., Jr. "State Constitutions and the Protection of Individual Rights." *Harvard Law Review* 90 (1977): 489–504.

Bright, Stephen B. "Is Fairness Irrelevant? The Evisceration of Federal Habeas Corpus Review and Limits on the Ability of State Courts to Protect Fundamental Rights." *Washington and Lee Law Review* 54 (1997): 1–30.

Corwin, Edward S. "The Passing of Dual Federalism." *Virginia Law Review* 36 (1950): 1–24.

Farole, Donald J. *Interest Groups and Judicial Federalism: Organizational Litigation in State Judiciaries.* Westport, Conn.: Praeger, 1998.

Fino, Susan P. *The Role of State Supreme Courts in New Judicial Federalism.* Westport, Conn.: Greenwood Press, 1987.

Flango, Victor E. *Habeas Corpus in State and Federal Courts.* Williamsburg, Va.: National Center for State Courts, 1994.

Gunther, Gerald, ed. *John Marshall's Defense of McCulloch v. Maryland.* Stanford: Stanford University Press, 1969.

Hartman, Marshall J., and Jeanette Nyden. "Habeas Corpus and the New Federalism after the Anti-Terrorism and Effective Death Penalty Act of 1996." *John Marshall Law Review* 30 (1997): 337–387.

Howard, A. E. Dick. "The States and the Supreme Court." *Catholic University Law Review* 31 (1982): 375–438.

Kagan, Robert A., Bliss Cartwright, Lawrence M. Friedman, and Stanton Wheeler. "The Evolution of State Supreme Courts." *Michigan Law Review* 76 (1978): 961–1005.

Killenbeck, Mark R., ed. *The Tenth Amendment and State Sovereignty.* Lanham, Md.: Rowman & Littlefield, 2002.

Kobylka, Joseph F. "The Court, Justice Blackmun, and Federalism." *Creighton Law Review* 19 (1985–1986): 9–49.

Langer, Laura. *Judicial Review in State Supreme Courts: A Comparative Study.* Albany, N.Y.: State University Press of America, 2002.

Latzer, Barry. *State Constitutions and Criminal Justice.* Westport, Conn.: Greenwood Press, 1991.

Mason, Alpheus. *The States' Rights Debate: Anti-Federalism and the Constitution.* New York: Oxford University Press, 1972.

Nagel, Robert F. *The Implosion of American Federalism.* Oxford: Oxford University Press, 2002.

Newmyer, R. Kent. *The Supreme Court Under Marshall and Taney.* New York: Crowell, 1968.

Porter, Mary Cornelia, and G. Alan Tarr, eds. *State Supreme Courts: Policymakers in the Federal System.* Westport, Conn.: Greenwood Press, 1982.

Schecter, Stephen. "The State of American Federalism." *Publius* 10 (1980): 3–11.

Schmidhauser, John R. *The Supreme Court as Final Arbiter in Federal-State Relations, 1789–1957.* Chapel Hill: University of North Carolina Press, 1958.

Semonche, John E. *Charting the Future: The Supreme Court Responds to a Changing Society, 1890–1920.* Westport, Conn.: Greenwood Press, 1978.

Spaeth, Harold J. "Burger Court Review of State Court Civil Liberties Decisions." *Judicature* 68 (1985): 285–291.

Stahlkopf, Deborah L. "A Dark Day for Habeas Corpus: Successive Petitions Under the Anti-Terrorism and Effective Death Penalty Act of 1996." *Arizona Law Review* 40 (1998): 1115–1136.

Stumpf, Harry P., and John H. Culver. *The Politics of State Courts.* New York: Longman, 1992.

Tarr, G. Alan, and Mary C. Porter. *State Supreme Courts in State and Nation.* New Haven: Yale University Press, 1988.

Waltenburg, Eric N., and Bill Swinford. *Litigating Federalism: The States Before the U.S. Supreme Court.* Westport, Conn.: Greenwood Press, 1999.

Wasby, Stephen L. "Justice Harry Blackmun in the Burger Court." *Hamline Law Review* 11 (1988): 183–245.

Wood, Stephen B. *Constitutional Politics in the Progressive Era: Child Labor and the Law.* Chicago: University of Chicago Press, 1968.

CHAPTER 7
THE COMMERCE POWER

O F ALL THE POWERS granted to government, perhaps none has resulted in more controversies and litigation than the power to regulate commerce. Concern over the exercise of this power was present at the Constitution's birth and continues today. At each stage of the nation's development, from a former colony isolated from the world's commercial centers to a country wielding vast economic power, legal disputes of great significance tested the powers of government to regulate the economy. During certain periods, such as John Marshall's chief justiceship, the decisions of the Supreme Court enhanced the role of the federal government in promoting economic development. At other times, however, such as the period immediately following the Great Depression, the Court's interpretations thwarted the government's attempts to overcome economic collapse. From the earliest days of the nation, battles over the commerce power have raised basic questions: What is commerce? What is interstate commerce? What powers of commercial regulation did the Constitution grant to the federal government, and what role remains to be played by the states?

CONSTITUTIONAL FOUNDATIONS
OF THE COMMERCE POWER

A primary reason for calling the Constitutional Convention was the inability of the government under the Articles of Confederation to control the country's commercial activity effectively. Economic conditions following the Revolutionary War were dismal. The national

and state governments were deeply in debt. The tax base of the newly independent nation was minimal, and commerce was undeveloped, leaving property taxes and customs duties as the primary sources of government funds.

The states were almost exclusively in charge of economic regulation. To raise enough revenue to pay their debts, the states imposed substantial taxes on land, placing farmers in an economically precarious condition. The states also erected trade barriers and imposed duties on the importation of foreign goods. While such policies were enacted in part to promote the states' domestic businesses, the result was a general strangulation of commercial activity. Several states printed their own money and passed statutes canceling debts. With each of the states working independently, the national economy continued to slide into stagnation, and, for all practical purposes, the central government was powerless to respond effectively.

When agrarian interests reached their economic breaking point—culminating in the 1787 march on the Massachusetts state capital by a makeshift army of farmers led by Daniel Shays—it was clear that something had to be done. Congress called for a convention to reconsider the status of the Articles of Confederation, a convention that ultimately resulted in the drafting of the United States Constitution.

Commerce and the Constitutional Convention

The delegates to the Constitutional Convention recognized the necessity of giving the power to regulate the economy to the central government. The state of the nation could no longer tolerate the individual states pursuing independent policies, each having a different impact on the country's economic health. To that end, Article I of the Constitution removed certain powers from the states and gave the federal government powers it did not have under the articles. States were stripped of the ability to print money, to impair the obligation of contracts, or to levy import duties. The federal government obtained the authority necessary to impose uniform regulations for the national economy. Among the powers granted to the central government were the authority to tax and impose customs duties, to spend and borrow, to develop and protect a single monetary system, and to regulate bankruptcies. Most important was the authority to regulate interstate and foreign commerce. Article I, Section 8, states: "The Congress shall have the power . . . to regulate Commerce with foreign Nations, and among the several States, and with the Indian Tribes."

The need for Congress to speak for the nation with a single voice on these matters was clear to the Framers. Even Alexander Hamilton and James Madison, who disagreed on many questions of federalism, were in accord on the necessity of the central government to control interstate and foreign commerce. Hamilton wrote in *The Federalist Papers*:

In addition to the defects already enumerated in the existing federal system, there are others of not less importance which concur in rendering it altogether unfit for the administration of the affairs of the Union. The want of a power to regulate commerce is by all parties allowed to be of the number.[1]

Madison took a similar position, arguing that the experience under the articles, as well as that of the European nations, demonstrated that a central government without broad powers over the nation's commerce was destined to fail.[2]

Congress quickly seized upon the authority to regulate commerce with other nations. Almost immediately, it imposed import duties as a means of raising revenue. The constitutional grant in this area was clear: the power

to regulate foreign commerce, as well as other matters of foreign policy, was given unambiguously to the national government, and the role of the states was eliminated. Since ratification, the states have challenged congressional supremacy over foreign commerce only on rare occasions.

The power to regulate interstate commerce, however, was a different story. Congress was slow in responding to this grant of authority. For the first several decades, federal officials continued to view business as an activity occurring within the borders of the individual states. In fact, Congress did not pass comprehensive legislation governing commerce among the states until the Interstate Commerce Act of 1887.

Marshall Defines Commerce

The history of the Commerce Clause is replete with disputes over definitions. For example, how do we distinguish between commercial activities and noncommercial activities? More important, what is the difference between *inter*state commerce, authority over which the Constitution gave to the federal government, and *intra*state commerce, over which the states retain regulatory power? Problems associated with such distinctions were difficult enough in the early years, but they became even more complex as the economy grew and the country changed from agrarian to industrialized. As many constitutional law cases illustrate, disputes over commercial regulatory authority often involve power struggles between the national government and the states.

Disputes over the meaning of the Commerce Clause came to the Supreme Court even during the early years of nationhood. The justices probed the constitutional definition of commerce and the proper division of federal and state power to regulate it. Of the commerce cases decided by the Supreme Court in those early decades, none was more important than *Gibbons v. Ogden* (1824). This dispute involved some of the nation's most prominent and powerful businessmen and attorneys. A great deal was at stake both economically and politically. In his opinion for the Court, Chief Justice Marshall responded to the fundamental problems of defining commerce and allocating the power to control it. His answers to the

---

1. Alexander Hamilton, Federalist No. 22, in *The Federalist Papers*, ed. Clinton Rossiter (New York: New American Library, 1961).
2. James Madison, Federalist No. 42, in ibid.

Aaron Ogden

Thomas Gibbons

questions presented in this case are still very much a part of our constitutional fabric.

Gibbons v. Ogden

9 WHEAT. (22 U.S.) 1 (1824)
http://laws.findlaw.com/US/22/1.html
Vote: 6 (Duvall, Johnson, Marshall, Story, Todd, Washington)
*   0*
Opinion of the Court: Marshall
Concurring opinion: Johnson
Not participating: Thompson

This complicated litigation can be traced back to 1798, when the New York legislature granted the wealthy and prominent Robert R. Livingston a monopoly to operate steamboats on all waters within the state, including the two most important commercial waterways, New York Harbor and the Hudson River. New York officials did not see the monopoly grant as particularly important because no one had yet developed a steamship that could operate reliably and profitably. Livingston, however, joined forces with Robert Fulton, and together they produced a commercially viable steamship. This mode of transportation became extremely popular and very profitable for the partners. When they obtained a similar monopoly over the port of New Orleans in 1811, they had significant control over the nation's two most important harbors.

The rapid westward expansion taking place at that time fueled the need for modern transportation systems. The Livingston-Fulton monopoly, however, put a damper on the use of steam in the evolution of such a system. The New York monopoly was so strong and so vigorously enforced that retaliatory laws were enacted by other states, which refused to let steam-powered vessels from New York use their waters. Especially hostile relations developed between New York and New Jersey, and violence between the crews of rival companies became common. Livingston died in 1813, followed two years later by Fulton, but their monopoly lived on.

Daniel Webster's 1821 handwritten note to Cornelius Vanderbilt acknowledging receipt of a $500 retainer to represent Thomas Gibbons in the case of *Gibbons v. Ogden.*

Aaron Ogden, a former governor of New Jersey, and Thomas Gibbons, a successful Georgia lawyer, entered into a partnership to carry passengers between New York City and Elizabethtown, New Jersey. Ogden had purchased the right to operate in New York waters from the Livingston-Fulton monopoly, and Gibbons had a federal permit issued under the 1793 Coastal Licensing Act to operate steamships along the coast. With these grants of authority the two partners could carry passengers between New York and New Jersey. The New York monopoly, however, pressured Ogden to terminate his relationship with Gibbons. As a result the partnership dissolved.

Gibbons then joined forces with Cornelius Vanderbilt, and they began a fierce competition with Ogden and the New York monopoly interests. Gibbons and Vanderbilt entered New York waters in violation of the monopoly whenever they could, picking up as much New York business as possible. In response, Ogden successfully convinced the New York courts to enjoin Gibbons from entering New York waters. Gibbons appealed this ruling to the U.S. Supreme Court.

To press their case, Gibbons and Vanderbilt acquired the services of two of the best lawyers of the day, William Wirt and Daniel Webster. Wirt, who later served as attorney general of the United States, argued that the federal permit issued to Gibbons took precedence over any state-issued monopoly and therefore Gibbons had the right to enter New York waters. Webster took a more radical position, explicitly stating that the Commerce Clause of the Constitution gave Congress exclusive power over commerce and that the state-granted monopoly was a violation of that clause. Ogden's lawyer responded that navigation was not commerce under the meaning of the Constitution but instead was an intrastate enterprise left to the states to regulate. The arguments in the case lasted four and a half days.

MR. CHIEF JUSTICE MARSHALL delivered the opinion of the Court.

The appellant contends that this decree is erroneous, because the laws which purport to give the exclusive privilege it sustains, are repugnant to the constitution and laws of the United States.

They are said to be repugnant—

To that clause in the constitution which authorizes Congress to regulate commerce. . . .

The words are, "Congress shall have power to regulate commerce with foreign nations, and among the several States, and with the Indian tribes."

The subject to be regulated is commerce; and our constitution being . . . one of enumeration, and not of definition, to ascertain the extent of the power, it becomes necessary to settle the meaning of the word. The counsel for the appellee would limit it to traffic, to buying and selling, or the interchange of commodities, and not admit that it comprehends navigation. This would restrict a general term, applicable to many objects, to one of its significations. Commerce, undoubtedly, is traffic, but it is something more: it is intercourse. It describes the commercial intercourse between nations, and parts of nations, in all its branches, and is regulated by prescribing rules for carrying on that intercourse. The mind can scarcely conceive a system for regulating commerce between nations, which shall exclude all laws concerning navigation, which shall be silent on the admission of the vessels of the one nation into the ports of the other, and be confined to prescribing rules for the conduct of individuals, in the actual employment of buying and selling, or of barter.

If commerce does not include navigation, the government of the Union has no direct power over that subject, and can make no law prescribing what shall constitute American vessels, or requiring that they shall be navigated by American seamen. Yet this power has been exercised from the commencement of the government, has been exercised with the consent of all, and has been understood by all to be a commercial regulation. All America understands, and has uniformly understood, the word "commerce," to comprehend navigation. It was so understood, and must have been so understood, when the constitution was framed. The power over commerce, including navigation, was one of the primary objects for which the people of America adopted their government, and must have been contemplated in forming it. The convention must have used the word in that sense, because all have understood it in that sense; and the attempt to restrict it comes too late. . . .

The word used in the constitution, then, comprehends, and has been always understood to comprehend, navigation within its meaning; and a power to regulate navigation, is as expressly granted, as if that term had been added to the word "commerce."

To what commerce does this power extend? The constitution informs us, to commerce "with foreign nations, and among the several States, and with the Indian tribes."

It has, we believe, been universally admitted, that these words comprehend every species of commercial intercourse between the United States and foreign nations. No sort of trade can be carried on between this country and any other, to which this power does not extend. It has been truly said, that commerce, as the word is used in the constitution, is a unit, every part of which is indicated by the term.

If this be the admitted meaning of the word, in its application to foreign nations, it must carry the same meaning throughout the sentence, and remain a unit, unless there be some plain intelligible cause which alters it.

The subject to which the power is next applied, is to commerce "among the several States." The word "among" means intermingled with. A thing which is among others, is intermingled with them. Commerce among the States, cannot stop at the external boundary line of each State, but may be introduced into the interior.

It is not intended to say that these words comprehend that commerce, which is completely internal, which is carried on between man and man in a State, or between different parts of the same State, and which does not extend to or affect other States. Such a power would be inconvenient, and is certainly unnecessary.

Comprehensive as the word "among" is, it may very properly be restricted to that commerce which concerns more States than one. The phrase is not one which would probably have been selected to indicate the completely interior traffic of a State, because it is not an apt phrase for that purpose; and the enumeration of the particular classes of commerce, to which the power was to be extended, would not have been made, had the intention been to extend the power to every description. The enumeration presupposes something not enumerated; and that something, if we regard the language or the subject of the sentence, must be the exclusively internal commerce of a State. The genius and character of the whole government seem to be, that its action is to be applied to all the external concerns of the nation, and to those internal concerns which affect the States generally; but not to those which are completely within a particular State, which do not affect other States, and with which it is not necessary to interfere, for the purpose of executing some of the general powers of the government. The completely internal commerce of a State, then, may be considered as reserved for the State itself.

But, in regulating commerce with foreign nations, the power of Congress does not stop at the jurisdictional lines of the several States. It would be a very useless power, if it could not pass those lines. The commerce of the United States with foreign nations, is that of the whole United States. Every district has a right to participate in it. The deep streams which penetrate our country in every direction, pass through the interior of almost every State in the Union, and furnish the means of exercising this right. If Congress has the power to regulate it, that power must be exercised whenever the subject exists. If it exists within the States, if a foreign voyage may commence or terminate at a port within a State, then the power of Congress may be exercised within a State.

This principle is, if possible, still more clear, when applied to commerce "among the several States." They either join each other, in which case they are separated by a mathematical line, or they are remote from each other, in which case other States lie between them. What is commerce "among" them; and how is it to be conducted? Can a trading expedition between two adjoining States, commence and terminate outside of each? And if the trading intercourse be between two States remote from each other, must it not commence in one, terminate in the other, and probably pass through a third? Commerce among the States must, of necessity, be commerce with the States. . . .

We are now arrived at the inquiry—What is this power?

It is the power to regulate; that is, to prescribe the rule by which commerce is to be governed. This power, like all others vested in Congress, is complete in itself, may be exercised to its utmost extent, and acknowledges no limitations, other than are prescribed in the constitution. . . . If, as has always been understood, the sovereignty of Congress, though limited to specified objects, is plenary as to those objects, the power over commerce with foreign nations, and among the several States, is vested in Congress as absolutely as it would be in a single government, having in its constitution the same restrictions on the exercise of the power as are found in the constitution of the United States. The wisdom and the discretion of Congress, their identity with the people, and the influence which their constituents possess at elections, are, in this, as in many other instances, as that, for example, of declaring war, the sole restraints on which they have relied, to secure them from its abuse. They are the restraints on which the people must often rely solely, in all representative governments.

The power of Congress, then, comprehends navigation, within the limits of every State in the Union; so far as that navigation may be, in any manner, connected with "commerce with foreign nations, or among the several States, or with the Indian tribes." It may, of consequence, pass the jurisdictional line of New York, and act upon the very waters to which the prohibition now under consideration applies.

But it has been urged with great earnestness, that, although the power of Congress to regulate commerce with foreign nations, and among the several States, be co-extensive with the subject itself, and have no other limits than are prescribed in the constitution, yet the States may severally exercise the same power, within their respective jurisdictions. In support of this argument, it is said, that they possessed it as an inseparable attribute of sovereignty, before the formation of the constitution, and still retain it, except so far as they have surrendered it by that instrument; that

this principle results from the nature of the government, and is secured by the tenth amendment; that an affirmative grant of power is not exclusive, unless in its own nature it be such that the continued exercise of it by the former possessor is inconsistent with the grant, and that this is not of that description.

The appellant, conceding these postulates, except the last, contends, that full power to regulate a particular subject, implies the whole power, and leaves no residuum; that a grant of the whole is incompatible with the existence of a right in another to any part of it. . . .

In discussing the question, whether this power is still in the States, in the case under consideration, we may dismiss from it the inquiry, whether it is surrendered by the mere grant to Congress, or is retained until Congress shall exercise the power. We may dismiss that inquiry, because it has been exercised, and the regulations which Congress deemed it proper to make, are now in full operation. The sole question is, can a State regulate commerce with foreign nations and among the States, while Congress is regulating it?

The counsel for the respondent answer this question in the affirmative, and rely very much on the restrictions in the 10th section, as supporting their opinion. . . .

It has been contended by the general counsel for the appellant, that, as the word "to regulate" implies in its nature, full power over the thing to be regulated, it excludes, necessarily, the action of all others that would perform the same operation on the same thing. That regulation is designed for the entire result, applying to those parts which remain as they were, as well as to those which are altered. It produces a uniform whole, which is as much disturbed and deranged by changing what the regulating power designs to leave untouched, as that on which it has operated.

There is great force in this argument, and the Court is not satisfied that it has been refuted.

Since, however, in exercising the power of regulating their own purely internal affairs, whether of trading or police, the States may sometimes enact laws, the validity of which depends on their interfering with, and being contrary to, an act of Congress passed in pursuance of the constitution, the Court will enter upon the inquiry, whether the laws of New York, as expounded by the highest tribunal of that State, have, in their application to this case, come into collision with an act of Congress, and deprived a citizen of a right to which that act entitles him. Should this collision exist, it will be immaterial whether those laws were passed in virtue of a concurrent power "to regulate commerce with foreign nations and among the several States," or, in virtue of a power to regulate their domestic trade and police. In one case and the other, the acts of New York must yield to the law of Congress; and the decision sustaining the privilege they confer, against a right given by a law of the Union, must be erroneous. . . .

But the framers of our constitution foresaw this state of things, and provided for it, by declaring the supremacy not only of itself, but of the laws made in pursuance of it. The nullity of any act, inconsistent with the constitution, is produced by the declaration, that the constitution is the supreme law. The appropriate application of that part of the clause which confers the same supremacy on laws and treaties, is to such acts of the State Legislatures as do not transcend their powers, but, though enacted in the execution of acknowledged State powers, interfere with, or are contrary to the laws of Congress, made in pursuance of the constitution, or some treaty made under the authority of the United States. In every such case, the act of Congress, or the treaty, is supreme; and the law of the State, though enacted in the exercise of powers not controverted, must yield to it. . . .

But all inquiry into this subject seems to the Court to be put completely at rest, by the act already mentioned, entitled, "An act for the enrolling and licensing of steam boats."

This act authorizes a steam boat employed, or intended to be employed, only in a river or bay of the United States, owned wholly or in part by an alien, resident within the United States, to be enrolled and licensed as if the same belonged to a citizen of the United States.

This act demonstrates the opinion of Congress, that steam boats may be enrolled and licensed, in common with vessels using sails. They are, of course, entitled to the same privileges, and can no more be restrained from navigating waters, and entering ports which are free to such vessels, than if they were wafted on their voyage by the winds, instead of being propelled by the agency of fire. The one element may be as legitimately used as the other, for every commercial purpose authorized by the laws of the Union; and the act of a State inhibiting the use of either to any vessel having a license under the act of Congress, comes, we think, in direct collision with that act.

Like his opinions in *Marbury* and *McCulloch*, Marshall's opinion in *Gibbons* laid a constitutional foundation that remains in place today. The decision made several important points. First, commerce involves more than buying and selling. It includes the commercial intercourse between nations and states, and therefore transportation and navigation clearly fall within the definition of commerce. Second, the power to regulate commerce that occurs completely within the boundaries of a single state, and does not extend to or affect other states, is reserved for the states. Third, commerce among the states begins in one state and ends in another; it does not stop when the act of crossing a state border is completed. Consequently, commerce that occurs within a state may be part of a larger interstate process. Fourth, once an act is considered part of interstate commerce, Congress is empowered by the Constitution to regulate it. The power to regulate interstate commerce is complete and has no limitation other than what may be found in other constitutional provisions.

Gibbons v. Ogden was a substantial victory for national power. It broadly construed the definitions of both commerce and interstate commerce. But Marshall did not go as far as Daniel Webster had urged. The opinion asserts only that Congress has complete power to regulate interstate commerce and that federal regulations are superior to any state laws. The decision does not answer the question of the legitimacy of states regulating interstate commerce in the absence of federal action. That controversy was left for future justices to decide.

DEFINING INTERSTATE COMMERCE

The regulation of commerce by the federal government did not become a major item on the Supreme Court's agenda until the latter half of the nineteenth century. By this time, small intrastate businesses were giving way to large interstate corporations. Industrial expansion blossomed, and the interstate railroad and pipeline systems were well under way. The infamous captains of industry were creating large monopolistic trusts that dominated huge segments of the national economy, squeezing out small businesses and discouraging new entrepreneurs. The industrial combines that controlled the railroads also, in effect, ruled agriculture and other interests that relied on the rails to transport goods to market. This commercial growth brought great prosperity to some, but it also caused horrendous social problems. Unsafe working conditions, sweat shops, child labor, and low wages plagued employees, who eventually formed labor unions.

In light of these developments, Congress decided to exert control over interstate commerce. As the nineteenth century drew to a close, the legislature passed two major laws based on the commerce power. The first was the Interstate Commerce Act of 1887, which established a mechanism for regulating the nation's interstate railroads. The second was the Sherman Anti-Trust Act of 1890, which was designed to break up monopolies that restrained trade. Critics immediately attacked Congress for exceeding its constitutional authority. While the Commerce Clause and Marshall's interpretation of it clearly established congressional power, discriminating between inter- and intrastate commerce was not easy. The Supreme Court faced a significant number of appeals that asked the justices to clarify whether the national legislature had overstepped its bounds and regulated commerce that was purely intrastate. To say that the Court had difficulty developing a coherent doctrine is an understatement.

The regulation of the railroads provides a case in point. The first railroads were small local operations regulated by the states, but, as the interstate systems developed, the justices held that their regulation was rightfully a federal responsibility.[3] Congress responded with the Interstate Commerce Act, which established the Interstate Commerce Commission (ICC) to regulate the railroads and set rates. The Supreme Court approved the constitutionality of the commission but later stripped it of its rate-setting powers.[4] In 1906 Congress revised the au-

thority and procedures of the commission and reestablished its power to set rates. The Court generally supported this amended version of the regulatory plan.[5]

The Court's decision in **Houston, E. & W. Texas Railway Co. v. United States** (1914), better known as the *Shreveport Rate Case*, firmly established congressional power over the nation's rails. This dispute arose from competition among three railroad companies to serve various cities in Texas. Two were based in Texas, one in Houston and the other in Dallas, and the third competitor operated out of Shreveport, Louisiana. The Texas Railroad Commission regulated the Texas companies because their operations were exclusively intrastate, but the Shreveport company came under the jurisdiction of the ICC. Difficulties arose when the Texas regulators set rates substantially lower than did the ICC. The motive behind these lower rates was clear: the Texas commission wanted to encourage intrastate trade and to discourage companies from taking their business to Shreveport. The rates placed the Shreveport railroad at a distinct disadvantage in competing for the Texas market. In response, the ICC ordered the intrastate Texas rates to be raised to the interstate levels. When the commission's authority to set intrastate rail rates was challenged, the Supreme Court ruled in favor of the ICC, articulating what became known as the "Shreveport Doctrine." The Court held that the federal government had the power to regulate intrastate commerce when a failure to regulate would cripple, retard, or destroy interstate commerce. According to Justice Charles Evans Hughes's opinion for the Court, whenever interstate and intrastate commercial activities are entwined so that the regulation of one controls the other, "it is Congress, and not the State, that is entitled to prescribe the final and dominant rule."

Manufacturing and Direct Effects on Interstate Commerce

The Court's endorsement of the federal power to regulate interstate transportation and distribution did not

---

3. *Wabash, St. Louis & Pacific Railway Co. v. Illinois* (1886).

4. *Interstate Commerce Commission v. Brimson* (1894); *Interstate Commerce Commission v. Cincinnati, New Orleans & Texas Pacific Railway Co.* (1897); *Interstate Commerce Commission v. Alabama-Midland Railway Co.* (1897).

5. See *Illinois Central Railroad Co. v. Interstate Commerce Commission* (1907).

extend initially to the attempts by Congress to impose effective antitrust legislation. The targets of the antitrust statutes were the monopolies that controlled basic industries and choked out all competition. During the late 1800s these trusts grew to capture and exercise dominance over many industries, including oil, meat packing, sugar, and steel. The Sherman Act was Congress's first attempt to break up these anticompetitive combines. It outlawed all contracts and combinations of companies that had the effect of restraining trade and commerce or eliminating competition.

For the antitrust law to be fully effective, however, its provisions had to cover the manufacturing and processing stages of commercial activity, which raised a serious constitutional problem. In earlier cases the Court had ruled that manufacturing was essentially a local activity and not part of interstate commerce. For example, in *Veazie v. Moor* (1853) the Court had labeled it a far-reaching "pretension" to suggest that the federal power over interstate commerce extended to manufacturing. Later, in **Kidd v. Pearson** (1888), the Court took an even stronger stand. At issue was an Iowa statute that outlawed the production of alcoholic beverages. The law was challenged on the ground that the liquor being manufactured was intended for interstate shipment and sale; and consequently, the state was unconstitutionally regulating interstate commerce. Speaking for the Court, Justice Lucius Q. C. Lamar rejected the attack, arguing:

No distinction is more popular to the common mind, or more clearly expressed in economic and political literature, than that between manufactures and commerce. Manufacture is transformation—the fashioning of raw materials into a change of form for use. The functions of commerce are different. The buying and selling and the transportation incident thereto constitute commerce.

Could the new antitrust law be applied to manufacturing? Or had Congress exceeded its constitutional authority in regulating production? These questions were answered in *United States v. E. C. Knight Co.* (1895), a battle over the federal government's attempts to break up the sugar trust.

United States v. E. C. Knight Co.

156 U.S. 1 (1895)
http://laws.findlaw.com/US/156/1.html
Vote: 8 (Brewer, Brown, Field, Fuller, Gray, Jackson, Shiras, White)
  1 (Harlan)
Opinion of the Court: Fuller
Dissenting opinion: Harlan

At the end of the nineteenth century six companies dominated the American sugar refining industry. The American Sugar Refining Company was the largest, with control of about 65 percent of the nation's refining capacity. Four Pennsylvania refiners shared 33 percent of the market, and a Boston company had a scant 2 percent. In March 1892 American Sugar entered into agreements that allowed it to acquire the four Pennsylvania refineries, including the E. C. Knight Company, giving it absolute control over 98 percent of the sugar refining business in the United States.

The federal government sued to have the acquisition agreements canceled. According to Justice Department attorneys, the sugar trust operated as a monopoly in restraint of trade in violation of the Sherman Anti-Trust Act. Attorneys for American Sugar and the acquired companies held that the law did not apply to sugar refining because that activity is manufacturing subject to state, not federal, control.

E. C. Knight was the Court's first antitrust case. The outcome was crucial to the government's attempts to break up powerful monopolies. Some observers have charged that Attorney General Richard Olney failed to provide the best prosecution of the case. Olney was not a dedicated trustbuster; he had opposed the passage of the antitrust act and later worked for its repeal.[6]

MR. CHIEF JUSTICE FULLER delivered the opinion of the Court.

The fundamental question is, whether conceding that the existence of a monopoly in manufacture is established by the

6. Joan Biskupic and Elder Witt, *Guide to the U.S. Supreme Court*, 3rd ed. (Washington, D.C.: Congressional Quarterly, 1997), 98.

evidence, that monopoly can be directly suppressed under the act of Congress in the mode attempted by this bill.

It cannot be denied that the power of a State to protect the lives, health, and property of its citizens, and to preserve good order and the public morals, "the power to govern men and things within the limits of its dominion," is a power originally and always belonging to the States, not surrendered by them to the general government, not directly restrained by the Constitution of the United States, and essentially exclusive. The relief of the citizens of each State from the burden of monopoly and the evils resulting from the restraint of trade among such citizens was left with the States to deal with, and this court has recognized their possession of that power even to the extent of holding that an employment or business carried on by private individuals, when it becomes a matter of such public interest and importance as to create a common charge or burden upon the citizen; in other words, when it becomes a practical monopoly, to which the citizen is compelled to resort and by means of which a tribute can be exacted from the community, is subject to regulation by state legislative power. On the other hand, the power of Congress to regulate commerce among the several States is also exclusive. The Constitution does not provide that interstate commerce shall be free, but, by the grant of this exclusive power to regulate it, it was left free except as Congress might impose restraints. Therefore it has been determined that the failure of Congress to exercise this exclusive power in any case is an expression of its will that the subject shall be free from restrictions or impositions upon it by the several States, and if a law passed by a State in the exercise of its acknowledged powers comes into conflict with that will, the Congress and the State cannot occupy the position of equal opposing sovereignties, because the Constitution declares its supremacy and that of the laws passed in pursuance thereof; and that which is not supreme must yield to that which is supreme. "Commerce, undoubtedly, is traffic," said Chief Justice Marshall, "but it is something more; it is intercourse. It describes the commercial intercourse between nations and parts of nations in all its branches, and is regulated by prescribing rules for carrying on that intercourse." That which belongs to commerce is within the jurisdiction of the United States, but that which does not belong to commerce is within the jurisdiction of the police power of the State.

The argument is that the power to control the manufacture of refined sugar is a monopoly over a necessary of life, to the enjoyment of which by a large part of the population of the United States interstate commerce is indispensable, and that, therefore, the general government in the exercise of the power to regulate commerce may repress such monopoly directly and set aside the instruments which have created it. But this argument cannot be confined to necessaries of life merely, and must include all articles of general consumption. Doubtless the power to control the manufacture of a given thing involves in a certain sense the control of its disposition, but this is a secondary and not the primary sense; and although the exercise of that power may result in bringing the operation of commerce into play, it does not control it, and affects it only incidentally and indirectly. Commerce succeeds to manufacture, and is not a part of it. The power to regulate commerce is the power to prescribe the rule by which commerce shall be governed, and is a power independent of the power to suppress monopoly. But it may operate in repression of monopoly whenever that comes within the rules by which commerce is governed or whenever the transaction is itself a monopoly of commerce.

It is vital that the independence of the commercial power and of the police power, and the delimitation between them, however sometimes perplexing, should always be recognized and observed, for while the one furnishes the strongest bond of union, the other is essential to the preservation of the autonomy of the States as required by our dual form of government; and acknowledged evils, however grave and urgent they may appear to be, had better be borne, than the risk be run, in the effort to suppress them, of more serious consequences by resort to expedients of even doubtful constitutionality.

It will be perceived how far-reaching the proposition is that the power of dealing with a monopoly directly may be exercised by the general government whenever interstate or international commerce may be ultimately affected. The regulation of commerce applies to the subjects of commerce and not to matters of internal police. Contracts to buy, sell, or exchange goods to be transported among the several States, the transportation and its instrumentalities, and articles bought, sold, or exchanged for the purposes of such transit among the States, or put in the way of transit, may be regulated, but this is because they form part of interstate trade or commerce. The fact that an article is manufactured for export to another State does not of itself make it an article of interstate commerce, and the intent of the manufacturer does not determine the time when the article or product passes from the control of the States and belongs to commerce. This was so ruled in *Coe v. Errol*, in which the question before the court was whether certain logs cut at a place in New Hampshire and hauled to a river town for the purpose of transportation to the State of Maine were liable to be taxed like other property in the State of New Hampshire. Mr. Justice Bradley, delivering the opinion of the court, said: "Does the owner's state of mind in relation to the goods, that is, his intent to export them, and his partial preparation to do so, exempt them from taxation? This is the precise question for solution. . . . There must be a point of time when they cease to be governed exclusively by the domestic law and begin to be governed and protected by the national law of commercial regulation, and that moment seems to us to be a legitimate one for this purpose, in which they commence their final movement from the State of their origin to that of their destination."

And again, in *Kidd v. Pearson*, where the question was discussed whether the right of a State to enact a statute prohibiting within its limits the manufacture of intoxicating liquors, except for certain purposes, could be overthrown by the fact that the manufacturer intended to export the liquors when made, it was held that the intent of the manufacturer did not determine the time when the article or product passed from the control of the State and belonged to commerce, and that, therefore, the statute, in omitting to except from its operation the manufacture of intoxicating liquors within the limits of the State for export, did not constitute an unauthorized interference with the right of Congress to regulate commerce. . . .

Contracts, combinations, or conspiracies to control domestic enterprise in manufacture, agriculture, mining, production in all its forms, or to raise or lower prices or wages, might unquestionably tend to restrain external as well as domestic trade, but the restraint would be an indirect result, however inevitable and whatever its extent, and such result would not necessarily determine the object of the contract, combination, or conspiracy.

Again, all the authorities agree that in order to vitiate a contract or combination it is not essential that its result should be a complete monopoly; it is sufficient if it really tends to that end and to deprive the public of the advantages which flow from free competition. Slight reflection will show that if the national power extends to all contracts and combinations in manufacture, agriculture, mining, and other productive industries, whose ultimate result may affect external commerce, comparatively little of business operations and affairs would be left for state control.

It was in the light of well-settled principles that the act of July 2, 1890, was framed. Congress did not attempt thereby to assert the power to deal with monopoly directly as such; or to limit and restrict the rights of corporations created by the States or the citizens of the States in the acquisition, control, or disposition of property; or to regulate or prescribe the price or prices at which such property or the products thereof should be sold; or to make criminal the acts of persons in the acquisition and control of property which the States of their residence or creation sanctioned or permitted. Aside from the provisions applicable where Congress might exercise municipal power, what the law struck at was combinations, contracts, and conspiracies to monopolize trade and commerce among the several States or with foreign nations; but the contracts and acts of the defendants related exclusively to the acquisition of the Philadelphia refineries and the business of sugar refining in Pennsylvania, and bore no direct relation to commerce between the States or with foreign nations. The object was manifestly private gain in the manufacture of the commodity, but not through the control of interstate or foreign commerce. It is true that the bill alleged that the products of these refineries were sold and distributed among the several States, and that all the companies were engaged in trade or commerce with the several States and with foreign nations; but this was no more than to say that trade and commerce served manufacture to fulfill its function. Sugar was refined for sale, and sales were probably made at Philadelphia for consumption, and undoubtedly for resale by the first purchasers throughout Pennsylvania and other States, and refined sugar was also forwarded by the companies to other States for sale. Nevertheless it does not follow that an attempt to monopolize, or the actual monopoly of, the manufacture was an attempt, whether executory or consummated, to monopolize commerce, even though, in order to dispose of the product, the instrumentality of commerce was necessarily invoked. There was nothing in the proofs to indicate any intention to put a restraint upon trade or commerce, and the fact, as we have seen, that trade or commerce might be indirectly affected was not enough to entitle complainants to a decree. . . .

Decree affirmed.

MR. JUSTICE HARLAN, dissenting.

In my judgment, the citizens of the several States composing the Union are entitled, of right, to buy goods in the State where they are manufactured, or in any other State, without being confronted by an illegal combination whose business extends throughout the whole country, which by the law everywhere is an enemy to the public interests, and which prevents such buying, except at prices arbitrarily fixed by it. I insist that the free course of trade among the States cannot coexist with such combinations. When I speak of trade I mean the buying and selling of articles of every kind that are recognized articles of interstate commerce. Whatever improperly obstructs the free course of interstate intercourse and trade, as involved in the buying and selling of articles to be carried from one State to another, may be reached by Congress, under its authority to regulate commerce among the States. The exercise of that authority so as to make trade among the States, in all recognized articles of commerce, absolutely free from unreasonable or illegal restrictions imposed by combinations, is justified by an express grant of power to Congress and would redound to the welfare of the whole country. I am unable to perceive that any such result would imperil the autonomy of the States, especially as that result cannot be attained through the action of any one State.

Undue restrictions or burdens upon the purchasing of goods, in the market for sale, to be transported to other States, cannot be imposed even by a State without violating the freedom of commercial intercourse guaranteed by the Constitution. But if a *State* within whose limits the business of refining sugar is exclusively carried on may not constitutionally impose burdens upon purchases of sugar *to be transported to other States*, how comes it that combinations of corporations or individuals, within the same State, may not be prevented by the national government from putting unlawful restraints upon the purchasing of that article *to be carried from the State in which such purchases are made?* If the national power is competent to repress State action in restraint of interstate trade as it may be involved in purchases of refined sugar to be transported from one State to another

State, surely it ought to be deemed sufficient to prevent unlawful restraints attempted to be imposed by combinations of corporations or individuals upon those identical purchases; otherwise, illegal combinations of corporations or individuals may—so far as national power and interstate commerce are concerned—do, with impunity, what no State can do. . . .

To the general government has been committed the control of commercial intercourse among the States, to the end that it may be free at all times from any restraints except such as Congress may impose or permit for the benefit of the whole country. The common government of all the people is the only one that can adequately deal with a matter which directly and injuriously affects the entire commerce of the country, which concerns equally all the people of the Union, and which, it must be confessed, cannot be adequately controlled by any one State. Its authority should not be so weakened by construction that it cannot reach and eradicate evils that, beyond all question, tend to defeat an object which that government is entitled, by the Constitution, to accomplish.

Chief Justice Melville W. Fuller's opinion shows the initial development of the Court's concern with the effects of various economic activities on interstate commerce. Proponents of federal regulation often argued that if an intrastate economic activity had an effect—any effect—on interstate commerce, it could be regulated by Congress. The Supreme Court rejected this position in *E. C. Knight,* holding that federal authority is not activated unless the intrastate activity has a *direct* effect on interstate commerce. In the sugar trust case, Fuller concluded that the challenged monopoly of refining facilities had only an indirect effect on interstate commerce and therefore was not subject to federal regulation. The distinction between direct and indirect effects is not very clear and can be interpreted various ways. In the hands of the Court's conservative majority, the direct effects test would later be used to strike down other federal regulatory attempts.

Although this decision removed manufacturing from the authority of the Sherman Act, the decision did not doom federal antitrust efforts. In fact, when the monopolistic activity was not manufacturing, the Court was quite willing to apply the law. For example, the Court held that companies engaged in production and interstate sale of pipe came under the sections of the Sherman Act.[7] In 1904 the Court went even further, ruling in *Northern Securities Company v. United States* that stock transactions creating a holding company (the result of an effective merger between the Northern Pacific and the Great Northern Railroad companies) were subject to Sherman Act scrutiny. In spite of these applications of the antitrust law, *E. C. Knight* set an important precedent, declaring manufacturing to be outside the definition of interstate commerce. This ruling later would be extended, with serious repercussions, to bar many of the New Deal programs passed to combat the Great Depression. It was only at such a time of economic collapse that the wisdom expressed in Justice John Marshall Harlan's dissent in *E. C. Knight* became apparent: the federal government must be empowered to regulate economic evils that are injurious to the nation's commerce and that a single state is incapable of eradicating.

The Stream of Commerce Doctrine

Government efforts to break up the meat-packing trust presented a different constitutional challenge. The corporations that dominated the meat industry, such as Armour, Cudahy, and Swift, ruled the nation's stockyards, which stood at the throat of the meat-distribution process. Western ranchers sent their livestock to the stockyards to be sold, butchered, and packed for shipment to consumers in the East. Livestock brokers, known as commission men, received the animals at the stockyards and sold them to the meat-packing companies for the ranchers. Consequently, when the meat-packing trust acquired control of the stockyards and the commission men who worked there, it was in a position to direct where the ranchers sent their stock, fix meat prices, demand unreasonably low rates for transporting stock, and decide when to withhold meat from the market. The government believed these actions constituted a restraint of trade in violation of the Sherman Act. The meat packers argued that their control over the stockyards was an in-

7. *Addystone Pipe and Steel Co. v. United States* (1899).

trastate matter to be regulated by the states. The Court settled the dispute in *Swift & Company v. United States* (1905), in which Justice Oliver Wendell Holmes for a unanimous Court held that the Sherman Act applied to the stockyards. The commercial sale of beef, the justice reasoned, began when the cattle left the range and did not terminate until final sale. The fact that the cattle stopped at the stockyards, midpoint in this commercial enterprise, did not mean that they were removed from interstate commerce. Holmes's opinion develops what has become known as the "stream of commerce doctrine," which allows federal regulation of interstate commerce from the point of its origin to the point of its termination. Interruptions in the course of that interstate commerce do not suspend the right of Congress to regulate. *Stafford v. Wallace*, an appeal based on another federal assault on the meat-packing combines, develops the doctrine more fully.

Stafford v. Wallace

258 U.S. 495 (1922)
http://laws.findlaw.com/US/258/495.html
Vote: 7 (Brandeis, Clarke, Holmes, McKenna, Pitney, Taft, Van Devanter)
1 (McReynolds)
Opinion of the Court: Taft
Not participating: Day

Armed with the *Swift & Company* precedent, Congress in 1921 passed the Packers and Stockyard Act. This legislation attempted to go beyond antitrust considerations in regulating the meat-packing industry. In addition to making it unlawful for the packers to fix prices or engage in monopolistic practices, the law forbade packers in interstate commerce to engage in any unfair, discriminatory, or deceptive practices. It required all stockyard dealers and commission men to register with the secretary of agriculture. The transactions at the stockyards had to conform to a schedule of charges open for public inspection. Fees and charges could be changed only after ten days' notice to the secretary. The Agriculture Department had the authority delegated by Congress to make rules and regulations to carry out the act, set stockyard rates, and prescribe record-keeping procedures for stockyard officials.

Stafford and Company, a corporation engaged in commercial transactions of cattle, sued Secretary of Agriculture Henry Wallace asking the courts to enjoin his enforcement of the act. The lower court refused to issue the requested injunction, and the company appealed.

MR. CHIEF JUSTICE TAFT delivered the opinion of the Court.

The object to be secured by the act is the free and unburdened flow of live stock from the ranges and farms of the West and the Southwest through the great stockyards and slaughtering centers on the borders of that region, and thence in the form of meat products to the consuming cities of the country in the Middle West and East, or, still as live stock, to the feeding places and fattening farms in the Middle West or East for further preparation for the market.

The chief evil feared is the monopoly of the packers, enabling them unduly and arbitrarily to lower prices to the shipper who sells, and unduly and arbitrarily to increase the price to the consumer who buys. Congress thought that the power to maintain this monopoly was aided by control of the stockyards. Another evil which it sought to provide against by the act, was exorbitant charges, duplication of commissions, deceptive practices in respect of prices, in the passage of the live stock through the stockyards, all made possible by collusion between the stockyards management and the commission men, on the one hand, and the packers and dealers on the other. Expenses incurred in the passage through the stockyards necessarily reduce the price received by the shipper, and increase the price to be paid by the consumer. If they be exorbitant or unreasonable, they are an undue burden on the commerce which the stockyards are intended to facilitate. Any unjust or deceptive practice or combination that unduly and directly enhances them is an unjust obstruction to that commerce. . . .

The stockyards are not a place of rest or final destination. Thousands of head of live stock arrive daily by carload and trainload lots, and must be promptly sold and disposed of and moved out to give place to the constantly flowing traffic that presses behind. The stockyards are but a throat through which the current flows, and the transactions which occur therein are only incident to this current from the West to the East, and from one State to another. Such transactions can not be separated from the movement to which they contribute and necessarily take on its character. The commission men are essential in making the sales without which the flow of the current would be obstructed, and this, whether they are made to packers or dealers. The dealers are essential to the sales to the stock farmers and feeders. The sales are not in this aspect merely local transactions. They create a local change of title, it is true, but they do not stop the flow; they merely change the private interests in the subject of the current, not interfering with, but, on the contrary, being indispensable to its continuity. The origin of the live stock is in the West, its ultimate destination known to, and intended by, all engaged in the business is in the Middle West and East either as meat products or stock for feeding and fattening. This is the definite and well-understood course of business. The stockyards and the sales are necessary factors in the middle of this current of commerce.

The act, therefore, treats the various stockyards of the country as great national public utilities to promote the flow of commerce from the ranges and farms of the West to the consumers in the East. It assumes that they conduct a business affected by a public use of a national character and subject to national regulation. That it is a business within the power of regulation by legislative action needs no discussion. . . . Nor is there any doubt that in the receipt of live stock by rail and in their delivery by rail the stockyards are an interstate commerce agency. The only question here is whether the business done in the stockyards between the receipt of the live stock in the yards and the shipment of them therefrom is a part of interstate commerce, or is so associated with it as to bring it within the power of national regulation. A similar question has been before this court and had great consideration in *Swift & Co. v. United States.* The judgment in that case gives a clear and comprehensive exposition which leaves to us in this case little but the obvious application of the principles there declared. . . .

The application of the commerce clause of the Constitution in the *Swift Case* was the result of the natural development of interstate commerce under modern conditions. It was the inevitable recognition of the great central fact that such streams of commerce from one part of the country to another which are ever flowing are in their very essence the commerce among the States and with foreign nations which historically it was one of the chief purposes of the Constitution to bring under national protection and control. This court declined to defeat this purpose in respect of such a stream and take it out of complete national regulation by a nice and technical inquiry into the non-interstate character of some of its necessary incidents and facilities when considered alone and without reference to their association with the movement of which they were an essential but subordinate part.

The principles of the *Swift Case* have become a fixed rule of this court in the construction and application of the commerce clause. . . .

Of course, what we are considering here is not a bill in equity or an indictment charging conspiracy to obstruct interstate commerce, but a law. The language of the law shows that what Congress had in mind primarily was to prevent such conspiracies by supervision of the agencies which would be likely to be employed in it. If Congress could provide for punishment or restraint of such conspiracies after their formation through the Anti-Trust Law as in the *Swift Case*, certainly it may provide regulation to prevent their formation. . . .

As already noted, the word "commerce" when used in the act is defined to be interstate and foreign commerce. Its provisions are carefully drawn to apply only to those practices and obstructions which in the judgment of Congress are likely to affect interstate commerce prejudicially. Thus construed and applied, we think the act clearly within congressional power and valid.

Other objections are made to the act and its provisions as violative of other limitations of the Constitution, but the only one seriously pressed was that based on the Commerce Clause and we do not deem it necessary to discuss the others.

The orders of the District Court refusing the interlocutory injunctions are

Affirmed.

The "stream of commerce" precedents set in the *Swift* and *Stafford* stockyards cases were applied later to other regulatory schemes. Most notable was *Chicago Board of Trade v. Olsen* (1923), which brought the grain exchanges under the rubric of interstate commerce. Such decisions broadened the power of the federal government to control the economy. But the Court still found that certain commercial activities exerted too little direct impact on interstate commerce to justify congressional control. The most prominent among these were manufacturing and processing. The 1895 sugar trust case of *E. C. Knight* established this principle, and it was reinforced in 1918 by *Hammer v. Dagenhart*, the child labor case discussed in Chapter 6.

Still, during the 1920s the federal government had more power to regulate the economy than ever before, but not enough to cope effectively with a full-scale economic collapse. When the stock market crashed, the central government did not have the constitutional authority to impose adequate corrective measures, and the justices of the Supreme Court, at least initially, were unwilling to provide the political branches with that authority. This situation touched off history's most dramatic confrontation between the Court and the president, which permanently altered the distribution of government powers.

THE SUPREME COURT AND THE NEW DEAL

The New York Stock Exchange crash on October 29, 1929, set in motion a series of events that shook the American economy and drove the nation into a deep depression. For the next two years, the stock market continued to tumble, with the Standard and Poor's Industrial Average falling 75 percent. The gross national product declined 27 percent over three years, and the unemployment rate rose from a healthy 3.2 percent in 1929 to a catastrophic 24.9 percent in 1933.

The Republican Party, which had been victorious in the November 1928 elections, controlled the White House and both houses of Congress. The party attempted to cope with the Depression by following philosophies of government that had been successful during the previous years of prosperity, with dismal results. The economic forces against which the Republicans fought were enormous. A different political approach was necessary to battle the collapse, and the American people were demanding such a change.

TABLE 7-1 The Great Depression and Political Change

	1929	1931	1933	1935	1937
House of Representatives					
No. of Democratic seats	163	216	313	332	333
No. of Republican seats	267	218	117	103	89
Senate					
No. of Democratic senators	39	47	59	69	75
No. of Republican senators	56	48	36	25	17
Presidency					
Incumbent	Hoover (R)	—	Roosevelt (D)	—	Roosevelt (D)
% of popular vote	58.2	—	57.4	—	60.8
Electoral vote margin	444–87	—	472–59	—	523–8
Supreme Court					
Republican justices	6	6	5	5	5
Number of new appointments over previous two years	0	2	1	0	0

NOTES: Data depict the change in political representation in the three branches of the federal government following the 1929 stock market crash and the deepening depression that continued over the next several years.

Members of the House and one-third of the senators were elected the previous November. Data on presidential election margins are based on previous November's elections. Supreme Court information is as of January of the designated years.

The Depression and Political Change

In the 1932 presidential election, voters rejected incumbent Herbert Hoover and swept Democratic candidate Franklin Roosevelt into office by a huge margin. With new Democratic majorities in the House and Senate, the president began combating the Depression with policies he called the New Deal. The overwhelming Democratic margins in Congress gave Roosevelt all the political clout he needed to gain approval of his radical new approach to boosting the economy. His programs were so popular with the American people that in 1936 they reelected Roosevelt by an even greater margin and provided him with even larger Democratic majorities in Congress, reducing the Republicans almost to minor party status. Clearly, the severe economic events following the 1929 crash triggered substantial political change, with the legislative and executive branches experiencing wholesale partisan shifts *(see Table 7-1)*.

The U.S. Supreme Court, however, did not change. In 1929, just before the stock market crashed, the Court membership was six Republicans and three Democrats. The economic conservatives (Taft, Van Devanter, McReynolds, Butler, Sutherland, and Sanford) were in control, clearly outnumbering the justices more sympathetic to political and economic change (Holmes, Brandeis, and Stone). By 1932 the Court had three new justices. Hughes, who had resigned his seat in 1916 to seek the presidency, succeeded William Howard Taft as chief justice; Benjamin Cardozo took Holmes's seat; and Owen Roberts replaced Edward Sanford. Although these changes reduced the Republican majority to five, there was no appreciable change in the ideological balance of the Court. Hoover had filled all three of these vacancies, which occurred before Roosevelt took office. Inaugurated in March 1933, Roosevelt had no opportunity to name a Supreme Court justice until Willis Van Devanter retired in June 1937. Roosevelt's first appointment, Hugo Black, assumed his seat in August of that year. Not until 1940 did the Court have a majority appointed from the period after Roosevelt's first election.

In the executive branch, Roosevelt assembled a cadre of young, creative people to devise novel ways of approaching the ailing economy, and these New Deal Democrats quickly set out to develop, enact, and implement their programs. Congress passed the first legislation, the Emergency Banking Act of 1933, just five days after Roosevelt's inauguration, and a string of statutes designed to control all major sectors of the nation's economy followed *(see Box 7-1)*. In adopting these programs, Congress relied on a number of constitutional powers, including the powers to tax, spend, and regulate interstate and foreign commerce.

The new political majority that dominated the legislative and executive branches called for the government to take a significantly more active role in economic regulation. The Supreme Court remained firmly in the control of representatives of the old order, with views on the relationship of government and the economy at odds with the political branches. A clash between the president and the Court was inevitable.

The Court Attacks the New Deal

As soon as the New Deal programs came into being, conservative business interests began to challenge their constitutional validity. In just two years the appeals started to reach the Court's doorstep. Beginning in 1935 and lasting for two long, tense years, the Court and the New Deal Democrats fought over the constitutionality of an expanded federal role in managing the economy.

During this period, the justices struck down a number of important New Deal statutes. Of ten major programs, the Supreme Court approved only two—the Tennessee Valley Authority and the emergency monetary laws. Four hard-line conservative justices—Willis Van Devanter, James McReynolds, George Sutherland, and Pierce Butler—formed the heart of the Court's opposition. Many thought their obstruction of New Deal initiatives would bring about the nation's ruin. As a consequence, they became known as the Four Horsemen of the Apocalypse, a biblical reference to the end of the world in Revelation. Two of the four, McReynolds and Butler, were Democrats *(see Box 7-2)*.

Naturally, these four justices by themselves could not declare void any act of Congress. They needed the vote of at least one other justice. As Box 7-3 indicates, they had little trouble attracting others to their cause. Of the eight major 1935–1936 decisions in which they were able to

---

BOX 7-1   NEW DEAL LEGISLATION

THE Roosevelt Democrats moved on the nation's economic problems with great speed. Roosevelt took the oath of office on March 4, 1933. Listed below are the major economic actions passed during his first term. Note how many were enacted within the first one hundred days of the new administration.

March 9, 1933	Emergency Banking Act
March 31, 1933	Civilian Conservation Corps created
May 12, 1933	Agricultural Adjustment Act
May 12, 1933	Federal Emergency Relief Act
May 18, 1933	Tennessee Valley Authority created
June 5, 1933	Nation taken off gold standard
June 13, 1933	Home Owners Loan Corporation created
June 16, 1933	Federal Deposit Insurance Corporation created
June 16, 1933	Farm Credit Administration created
June 16, 1933	National Industrial Recovery Act
January 30, 1934	Dollar devalued
June 6, 1934	Securities and Exchange Commission authorized
June 12, 1934	Reciprocal Tariff Act
June 19, 1934	Federal Communications Commission created
June 27, 1934	Railroad Retirement Act
June 28, 1934	Federal Housing Administration authorized
April 8, 1935	Works Progress Administration created
July 5, 1935	National Labor Relations Act
August 14, 1935	Social Security Act
August 26, 1935	Federal Power Commission created
August 30, 1935	National Bituminous Coal Conservation Act
February 19, 1936	Soil Conservation and Domestic Allotment Act

strike down congressional policies, three were by 5–4 votes in which Justice Roberts joined the four conservatives. In one additional case, both Roberts and Chief Justice Hughes voted with them. But in three of these significant decisions, the Court was unanimous, with even the more liberal Brandeis, Cardozo, and Stone voting to strike down the challenged legislation.

The first salvo in the war between the two branches occurred on January 7, 1935, when the Supreme Court by an 8–1 vote in *Panama Refining Company v. Ryan* struck down a section of the National Industrial Recovery Act of 1933 (NIRA) as an improper delegation of congressional power to the executive branch. The section in question was a major New Deal weapon in regulating the oil industry. It gave the president the power to prohibit interstate shipment of oil and petroleum products that were produced or stored in a manner illegal under state law. The justices found fault with the act because it did not provide sufficiently clear standards to guide the executive branch; rather, it gave the president almost unlimited discretion in applying the prohibitions. *Panama Refining* was the first case in which the Court struck down legislation because it was an improper delegation of power.

Although the decision in *Panama Refining* was restricted to the delegation question and did not focus on Congress's interstate commerce authority, it promised bad days ahead for the administration. Not only was the decision a disappointment for the president, but also the vote was lopsided. Only Justice Cardozo voted to approve the law.

The Supreme Court dropped its biggest bomb on the New Deal four months later, in May 1935. The justices voted 5–4 on May 6 to declare the Railroad Retirement Act of 1934 an unconstitutional violation of the Commerce Clause and the Due Process Clause of the Fifth Amendment.[8] Then, on May 27—a date that became known as Black Monday—the justices announced three significant blows to the administration's efforts to fight the Depression—all by unanimous votes. First, in *Humphrey's Executor v. United States*, the Court declared that the president did not have the power to remove a

8. *Railroad Retirement Board v. Alton Railroad Co.* (1935).

BOX 7-2 THE FOUR HORSEMEN

Willis Van Devanter
(1910–1937)

Republican from Wyoming. Born 1859. University of Cincinnati Law School. Wyoming state legislator and state supreme court judge. Federal appeals court judge. Appointed by William Howard Taft.

James Clark McReynolds
(1914–1941)

Democrat from Tennessee. Born 1862. University of Virginia Law School. United States Attorney General. Appointed by Woodrow Wilson.

George Sutherland
(1922–1938)

Republican from Utah. Born 1862. University of Michigan Law School. State legislator, U.S. Representative, U.S. Senator. Appointed by Warren G. Harding.

Pierce Butler
(1922–1939)

Democrat from Minnesota. Born 1866. No law school, studied privately. Corporate attorney. Appointed by Warren G. Harding.

BOX 7-3   THE SUPREME COURT AND THE NEW DEAL

Listed below are eight major decisions handed down by the Supreme Court in 1935 and 1936 declaring parts of the New Deal legislative program unconstitutional.

Case/Decision Date	Acts Ruled Unconstitutional/Grounds	Majority	Dissent
Panama Refining Co. v. Ryan (January 7, 1935)	Portions of the National Industrial Recovery Act. (Improper delegation of congressional powers)	Brandeis, Butler, Hughes, McReynolds, Roberts, Stone, Sutherland, Van Devanter	Cardozo
Railroad Retirement Board v. Alton Railroad Co. (May 6, 1935)	Railroad Retirement Act of 1934. (Exceeded Commerce Clause powers; Fifth Amendment due process violations)	Butler, McReynolds, Roberts, Sutherland, Van Devanter	Brandeis, Cardozo, Hughes, Stone
Schechter Poultry Corp. v. United States (May 27, 1935)	Portions of the National Industrial Recovery Act. (A regulation of intrastate commerce and improper delegation of congressional power)	Brandeis, Butler, Cardozo, Hughes, McReynolds, Roberts, Stone, Sutherland, Van Devanter	
Louisville Bank v. Radford (May 27, 1935)	Frazier-Lemke Act of 1934 extending bankruptcy relief. (Fifth Amendment property rights)	Brandeis, Butler, Cardozo, Hughes, McReynolds, Roberts, Stone, Sutherland, Van Devanter	
Hopkins Savings Association v. Cleary (December 12, 1935)	Home Owners Loan Act of 1933. (Tenth Amendment)	Brandeis, Butler, Cardozo, Hughes, McReynolds, Roberts, Stone, Sutherland, Van Devanter	
United States v. Butler (January 6, 1936)	Agricultural Adjustment Act. (Taxing and spending power violations)	Butler, Hughes, McReynolds, Roberts, Sutherland, Van Devanter	Brandeis, Cardozo, Stone
Carter v. Carter Coal Co. (May 18, 1936)	Bituminous Coal Conservation Act. (A regulation of intrastate commerce; improper delegation of congressional power)	Butler, McReynolds, Roberts, Sutherland, Van Devanter	Brandeis, Cardozo, Hughes, Stone
Ashton v. Cameron County District Court (May 25, 1936)	Municipal Bankruptcy Act. (Tenth Amendment; Fifth Amendment property rights)	Butler, McReynolds, Roberts, Sutherland, Van Devanter	Brandeis, Cardozo, Hughes, Stone

member of the Federal Trade Commission. Second, the justices invalidated the 1934 Frazier-Lemke Act, which had provided mortgage relief, especially to farmers.[9] Finally, in *Schechter Poultry Corp. v. United States* the Court handed the president his most stinging defeat by declaring major portions of the National Industrial Recovery Act unconstitutional as an improper delegation of legislative power and a violation of the Commerce Clause.

A. L. A. Schechter Poultry Corp. v. United States

295 U.S. 495 (1935)
http://laws.findlaw.com/US/295/495.html
Vote: 9 (Brandeis, Butler, Cardozo, Hughes, McReynolds,
        Roberts, Stone, Sutherland, Van Devanter)

        0

Opinion of the Court: Hughes
Concurring opinion: Cardozo

Congress passed the National Industrial Recovery Act, the most far-reaching and comprehensive of all the New Deal legislation, on June 16, 1933. Applying to every sector of American industry, the NIRA called for the creation of codes of fair competition for business. The codes would regulate trade practices, wages, hours, and other business activities within various industries. Trade associations and other industry groups had the responsibility for drafting the codes, which were submitted to the president for approval. In the absence of the private sector's recommendations, the president was authorized to draft codes himself. Once approved by the president, the codes had the force of law, and violators faced fines and even jail.

The NIRA was vulnerable to constitutional challenge on two grounds. First, it set virtually no standards for the president in approving or drafting the codes. Congress had handed Roosevelt a blank check to bring all of American industry into line with his views of what was best for the recovery of the economy. Second, the law regulated what at that time was considered intrastate commerce.

The *Schechter* case involved a challenge to the NIRA poultry codes, focusing on the industry in New York, the nation's largest chicken market.[10] This market clearly was operating in interstate commerce; 96 percent of the poultry sold in New York came from out-of-state suppliers. The industry was riddled with graft and plagued by deplorable health and sanitary conditions. The Live Poultry Code approved by President Roosevelt set a maximum workweek of forty hours and a minimum hourly wage of fifty cents. In addition, the code established a health inspection system, regulations to govern slaughtering procedures, and compulsory record keeping.

The A. L. A. Schechter Poultry Corporation, owned by Joseph, Martin, Aaron, and Alex Schechter, was a poultry slaughtering business in Brooklyn. Slaughterhouse operators, such as the Schechters, purchased large numbers of live chickens from local poultry dealers who imported the fowl from out of state to be killed and dressed for sale.

Government officials found the Schechters in violation of the Poultry Code on numerous counts. They ignored the code's wage and hour provisions, failed to comply with government record-keeping requirements, and did not conform to the slaughter regulations. Their worst offense, however, was selling unsanitary poultry that the government found unfit for human consumption. For this reason, *Schechter Poultry* was known as the Sick Chicken case.

The government obtained indictments against the Schechter Poultry Corporation and the four brothers on sixty counts of violating the code, and the jury found them guilty of nineteen. Each of the brothers was sentenced to a short jail term. They appealed unsuccessfully to the court of appeals and then pressed their case to the U.S. Supreme Court, asserting that the NIRA was unconstitutional on improper delegation and Commerce Clause grounds.

---

9. *Louisville Bank v. Radford* (1935).

10. For a good discussion of the *Schechter* case, see Chapter 5 in *The New Deal Lawyers,* by Peter H. Irons (Princeton, N.J.: Princeton University Press, 1982).

A. L. A. Schechter (center) of Schechter Poultry Corporation with his attorneys Joseph Heller (left) and Frederick Wood, May 2, 1935.

MR. CHIEF JUSTICE HUGHES delivered the opinion of the Court.

The question of the delegation of legislative power. We recently had occasion to review the pertinent decisions and the general principles which govern the determination of this question. The Constitution provides that "All legislative powers herein granted shall be vested in a Congress of the United States, which shall consist of a Senate and House of Representatives." Art. I, §1. And the Congress is authorized "To make all laws which shall be necessary and proper for carrying into execution" its general powers. Art. I, §8, par. 18. The Congress is not permitted to abdicate or to transfer to others the essential legislative functions with which it is thus vested. . . .

Section 3 of the Recovery Act is without precedent. It supplies no standards for any trade, industry or activity. It does not undertake to prescribe rules of conduct to be applied to particular states of fact determined by appropriate administrative procedure. Instead of prescribing rules of conduct, it authorizes the making of codes to prescribe them. For that legislative undertaking, §3 sets up no standards, aside from the statement of the general aims of rehabilitation, correction and expansion described in section one. In view of the scope of that broad declaration, and of the nature of the few restrictions that are imposed, the discretion of the President in approving or prescribing codes, and thus enacting laws for the government of trade and industry throughout the country, is virtually unfettered. We think that the code-making authority thus conferred is an unconstitutional delegation of legislative power.

. . . *The question of the application of the provisions of the Live Poultry Code to intrastate transactions.* . . . This aspect of the case presents the question whether the particular provisions of the Live Poultry Code, which the defendants were convicted for violating and for having conspired to violate, were within the regulating power of Congress.

These provisions relate to the hours and wages of those employed by defendants in their slaughterhouses in Brooklyn and to the sales there made to retail dealers and butchers.

(1) Were these transactions *"in"* interstate commerce? Much is made of the fact that almost all the poultry coming to New York is sent there from other States. But the code provisions, as here applied, do not concern the transportation of the poultry from other States to New York, or the transactions of the commission men or others to whom it is consigned, or the sales made by such consignees to defendants. When defendants had made their purchases, whether at the West Washington Market in New York City or at the railroad terminals serving the City, or elsewhere, the poultry was trucked to their slaughterhouses in Brooklyn for local disposition. The interstate transactions in relation to that poultry then ended. Defendants held the poultry at their slaughterhouse markets for slaughter and local sale to retail dealers and butchers who in turn sold directly to consumers. Neither the slaughtering nor the sales by defendants were transactions in interstate commerce.

The undisputed facts thus afford no warrant for the argument that the poultry handled by defendants at their slaughterhouse markets was in a *"current"* or *"flow"* of interstate commerce and was thus subject to congressional regulation. The mere fact that there may be a constant flow of commodities into a State does not mean that the flow continues after the property has arrived and has become commingled with the mass of property within the State and is there held solely for local disposition and use. So far as the poultry here in question is concerned; the flow in interstate commerce had ceased. The poultry had come to a permanent rest within the State. It was not held, used, or sold by defendants in relation to any further transactions in interstate commerce and was not destined for transportation to other States. Hence, decisions which deal with a stream of interstate commerce—where goods come to rest within a State temporarily and are later to go forward in interstate commerce—and with the regulations of transactions involved in that practical continuity of movement, are not applicable here.

(2) Did the defendants' transactions directly *"affect"* interstate commerce so as to be subject to federal regulation? The power of Congress extends not only to the regulation of transactions which are part of interstate commerce, but to the protection of that commerce from injury. It matters not that the injury may be due to the conduct of those engaged in intrastate operations. Thus, Congress may protect the safety of those employed in interstate transportation "no matter what may be the source of the dangers which threaten it." We said in *Second Employers' Liability Cases*, that it is the "effect upon interstate commerce," not "the source of the injury," which is "the criterion of congressional power." We have held that, in dealing with common carriers engaged in both interstate and intrastate commerce, the dominant authority of Congress necessarily embraces the right to control their intrastate operations in all matters having such a close and substantial relation to interstate traffic that the control is essential or appropriate to secure the freedom of that traffic from interference or unjust discrimination and to promote the efficiency of the interstate service. And combinations and conspiracies to restrain interstate commerce, or to monopolize any part of it, are none the less within the reach of the Anti-Trust Act because the conspirators seek to attain their end by means of intrastate activities. . . .

In determining how far the federal government may go in controlling intrastate transactions upon the ground that they "affect" interstate commerce, there is a necessary and well-established distinction between direct and indirect effects. The precise line can be drawn only as individual cases arise, but the distinction is clear in principle. Direct effects are illustrated by the railroad cases we have cited, as, *e.g.*, the effect of failure to use prescribed safety appliances on railroads which are the highways of both interstate and intrastate commerce, injury to an employee engaged in interstate transportation by the negligence of an employee engaged in an intrastate movement, the fixing of rates for intrastate transportation which unjustly discriminate against interstate commerce. But where the effect of intrastate transactions upon interstate commerce is merely indirect, such transactions remain within the domain of state power. If the commerce clause were construed to reach all enterprises and transactions which could be said to have an indirect effect upon interstate commerce, the federal authority would embrace practically all the activities of the people and the authority of the State over its domestic concerns would exist only by sufferance of the federal government. Indeed, on such a theory, even the development of the State's commercial facilities would be subject to federal control. As we said in the *Minnesota Rate Cases:* "In the intimacy of commercial relations, much that is done in the superintendence of local matters may have an indirect bearing upon interstate commerce. The development of local resources and the extension of local facilities may have a very important effect upon communities less favored and to an appreciable degree alter the course of trade. The freedom of local trade may stimulate interstate commerce, while restrictive measures within the police power of the State enacted exclusively with respect to internal business, as distinguished from interstate traffic, may in their reflex or indirect influence diminish the latter and reduce the volume of articles transported into or out of the State."

The distinction between direct and indirect effects has been clearly recognized in the application of the Anti-Trust Act. Where a combination or conspiracy is formed, with the intent to restrain interstate commerce or to monopolize any part of it, the violation of the statute is clear. But where that intent is absent, and the objectives are limited to intrastate activities, the fact that there may be an indirect effect upon interstate commerce does not subject the parties to the federal statute, notwithstanding its broad provisions. . . .

. . . [T]he distinction between direct and indirect effects of intrastate transactions upon interstate commerce must be recognized as a fundamental one, essential to the maintenance of our constitutional system. Otherwise, as we have said, there would be virtually no limit to the federal power and for all practical purposes we should have a completely centralized government. We must consider the provisions here in question in the light of this distinction.

The question of chief importance relates to the provisions of the Code as to the hours and wages of those employed in defendants' slaughterhouse markets. It is plain that these requirements are imposed in order to govern the details of defendants' management of their local business. The persons employed in slaughtering and selling in local trade are not employed in interstate commerce. Their hours and wages have no direct relation to interstate commerce. The question of how many hours these employees should work and what they should be paid differs in no essential respect from similar questions in other local businesses which handle commodities brought into a State and there dealt in as a part of its internal commerce. This appears from an examination of the considerations urged by the Government with respect to conditions in the poultry trade. Thus, the Government argues that hours and wages affect prices; that slaughterhouse men sell at a small margin above operating costs; that a slaughterhouse operator paying lower wages or reducing his cost by exacting long hours of work, translates his saving into lower prices; that this results in demands for a cheaper grade of goods; and that the cutting of prices brings about a demoralization of the price structure. Similar conditions may be adduced in relation to other businesses. The argument of the Government proves too much. If the federal government may determine the wages and hours of employees in the internal commerce of a State, because of their relation to cost and prices and their indirect effect upon interstate commerce, it would seem that a similar control might be exerted over other elements of cost, also affecting prices, such as the number of employees, rents, advertising, methods of doing business, etc. All the processes of production and distribution that enter into cost could likewise be controlled. If the cost of doing an intrastate business is in itself the permitted object of federal control, the extent of the regulation of cost would be a question of discretion and not of power.

The Government also makes the point that efforts to enact state legislation establishing high labor standards have been impeded by the belief that unless similar action is taken generally, commerce will be diverted from the States adopting such standards, and that this fear of diversion has led to demands for federal legislation on the subject of wages and hours. The apparent implication is that the federal authority under the commerce clause should be deemed to extend to the establishment of rules to govern wages and hours in intrastate trade and industry generally throughout the country, thus overriding the authority of the States to deal with domestic problems arising from labor conditions in their internal commerce.

It is not the province of the Court to consider the economic advantages or disadvantages of such a centralized system. It is sufficient to say that the Federal Constitution does not provide for it. Our growth and development have called for wide use of the commerce power of the federal government in its control over the expanded activities of interstate commerce, and in protecting that commerce from burdens, interferences, and conspiracies to restrain and monopolize it. But the authority of the federal government may not be pushed to such an extreme as to destroy the distinction, which the commerce clause itself establishes, between commerce "among the several States" and the internal concerns of a State. The same answer must be made to the contention that is based upon the serious economic situation which led to the passage of the Recovery Act—the fall in prices, the decline in wages and employment, and the curtailment of the market for commodities. Stress is laid upon the great importance of maintaining wage distributions which would provide the necessary stimulus in starting "the cumulative forces making for expanding commercial activity." Without in any way disparaging this motive, it is enough to say that the recuperative efforts of the federal government must be made in a manner consistent with the authority granted by the Constitution.

We are of the opinion that the attempt through the provisions of the Code to fix the hours and wages of employees of defendants in their intrastate business was not a valid exercise of federal power.

The other violations for which defendants were convicted related to the making of local sales. Ten counts, for violation of the provision as to "straight killing," were for permitting customers to make "selections of individual chickens taken from particular coops and half coops." Whether or not this practice is good or bad for the local trade, its effect, if any, upon interstate commerce was only indirect. The same may be said of violations of the Code by intrastate transactions consisting of the sale "of an unfit chicken" and of sales which were not in accord with the ordinances of the City of New York. The requirement of reports as to prices and volumes of defendants' sales was incident to the effort to control their intrastate business. . . .

On both the grounds we have discussed, the attempted delegation of legislative power, and the attempted regulation of intrastate transactions which affect interstate commerce only indirectly, we hold the code provisions here in question to be invalid and that the judgment of conviction must be reversed.

MR. JUSTICE CARDOZO, concurring.

The delegated power of legislation which has found expression in this code is not canalized within banks that keep it from overflowing. It is unconfined and vagrant. . . .

This is delegation running riot. . . .

The code does not confine itself to the suppression of methods of competition that would be classified as unfair according to accepted business standards or accepted norms of ethics. It sets up a comprehensive body of rules to promote the welfare of the industry, if not the welfare of the nation, without reference to standards, ethical or commercial, that could be known or predicted in advance of its

adoption. . . . Even if the statute itself had fixed the meaning of fair competition by way of contrast with practices that are oppressive or unfair, the code outruns the bounds of the authority conferred. What is excessive is not sporadic or superficial. It is deep-seated and pervasive. The licit and illicit sections are so combined and welded as to be incapable of severance without destructive mutilation.

But there is another objection, far-reaching and incurable, aside from any defect of unlawful delegation.

If this code had been adopted by Congress itself, and not by the President on the advice of an industrial association, it would even then be void, unless authority to adopt it is included in the grant of power "to regulate commerce with foreign nations, and among the several States." United States Constitution, art. 1, 8, cl. 3.

I find no authority in that grant for the regulation of wages and hours of labor in the intrastate transactions that make up the defendants' business. As to this feature of the case, little can be added to the opinion of the court. There is a view of causation that would obliterate the distinction between what is national and what is local in the activities of commerce. . . .

I am authorized to state that MR. JUSTICE STONE joins in this opinion.

The decision in *Schechter* closely paralleled the *E. C. Knight* ruling and rejected the application of the stream of commerce doctrine. In *E. C. Knight* the Court held that sugar refining was a manufacturing stage not part of interstate commerce and, therefore, the federal government could not regulate it. Similarly, in *Schechter* the Court classified the slaughtering and local sale of chickens as intrastate commerce. The stream of commerce evident in the stockyards decisions did not apply. In *Schechter* the interstate movement of the poultry had ceased. Once the distributor had sold to local processors like the Schechter company, the chickens had reached their state of final destination and became a part of intrastate commerce. Also consistent with *E. C. Knight*, the justices concluded that the poultry slaughter business had only an indirect effect on interstate commerce.

Through the remaining months of 1935 and into 1936, the Court continued to strike down federal legislation designed to cope with the Depression. In some cases the

Court found the statutes defective for violating the federal taxing and spending power or for depriving individuals of their right to property without due process of law, topics covered in later chapters. No matter what the reason for the decision, the Court throughout this period was concerned with congressional actions that went beyond constitutional authority to regulate interstate commerce. Congress could not constitutionally legislate local business activity, such as manufacturing, processing, or refining, unless it had a direct effect on interstate commerce. The Court supported congressional regulation when the commerce was in movement from one state to another, but, as demonstrated in *Schechter*, the justices were unwilling to allow Congress to act on commerce after it had completed its interstate journey. *Schechter* examined when interstate commerce ends; in May 1936 the Court taught the administration a lesson in when interstate commerce begins.

Carter v. Carter Coal Company

298 U.S. 238 (1936)
http://laws.findlaw.com/US/298/238.html
Vote: 5 (Butler, McReynolds, Roberts, Sutherland, Van Devanter)
  4 (Brandeis, Cardozo, Hughes, Stone)
Opinion of the Court: Sutherland
Opinion dissenting in part: Hughes
Dissenting opinion: Cardozo

Congress passed the Bituminous Coal Conservation Act in August 1935, following the *Schechter* decision. This law replaced the NIRA coal codes, which had been reasonably effective in bringing some stability to the depressed coal industry. The new act called for the establishment of a commission empowered to develop regulations regarding fair competition, production, wages, hours, and labor relations. The commission included representatives from the coal producers, coal miners, and the public. To fund the program, Congress imposed a tax at the mines of 15 percent of the value of the coal produced. Unlike the NIRA codes, compliance with the new code regulations was voluntary. There was, however, an incentive for joining the program. Companies who

participated were given a rebate of 90 percent of the taxes levied by the act.

James W. Carter and other shareholders urged their company not to participate in the program. The board of directors did not want to join but believed that the company could not afford to pay the 15 percent tax and forgo the participation rebate. The stockholders sued to prevent the company from joining the program on the ground that the Coal Act was unconstitutional. Of Carter's several attacks on the law, the most deadly was the charge that coal mining was not in interstate commerce.

MR. JUSTICE SUTHERLAND delivered the opinion of the Court.

Since the validity of the act depends upon whether it is a regulation of interstate commerce, the nature and extent of the power conferred upon Congress by the commerce clause becomes the determinative question in this branch of the case. The commerce clause vests in Congress the power— "To regulate Commerce with foreign Nations, and among the several States, and with the Indian Tribes." The function to be exercised is that of regulation. The thing to be regulated is the commerce described. In exercising the authority conferred by this clause of the Constitution, Congress is powerless to regulate anything which is not commerce, as it is powerless to do anything about commerce which is not regulation. We first inquire, then—What is commerce? . . .

As used in the Constitution, the word "commerce" is the equivalent of the phrase "intercourse for the purposes of trade," and includes transportation, purchase, sale, and exchange of commodities between the citizens of the different states. And the power to regulate commerce embraces the instruments by which commerce is carried on. In *Adair v. United States* the phrase "Commerce among the several States" was defined as comprehending "traffic, intercourse, trade, navigation, communication, the transit of persons and the transmission of messages by telegraph—indeed, every species of commercial intercourse among the several States.". . .

That commodities produced or manufactured within a state are intended to be sold or transported outside the state does not render their production or manufacture subject to federal regulation under the commerce clause. . . .

In *Heisler v. Thomas Colliery Co.* we held that the possibility, or even certainty of exportation of a product or article from a state did not determine it to be in interstate commerce before the commencement of its movement from the state. To hold otherwise "would nationalize all industries, it would nationalize and withdraw from state jurisdiction and deliver to federal commercial control the fruits of California and the South, the wheat of the West and its meats, the cotton of the South, the shoes of Massachusetts and the woolen industries of other States, at the very inception of their production or growth, that is, the fruits unpicked, the cotton and wheat ungathered, hides and flesh of cattle yet 'on the hoof,' wool yet unshorn, and coal yet unmined, because they are in varying percentages destined for and surely to be exported to States other than those of their production."

In *Oliver Iron [Mining] Co. v. Lord* [1923] we said on the authority of numerous cited cases: "Mining is not interstate commerce, but, like manufacturing, is a local business subject to local regulation and taxation. . . . Its character in this regard is intrinsic, is not affected by the intended use or disposal of the product, is not controlled by contractual engagements, and persists even though the business be conducted in close connection with interstate commerce."

The same rule applies to the production of oil. "Such production is essentially a mining operation and therefore is not a part of interstate commerce even though the product obtained is intended to be and in fact is immediately shipped in such commerce." One who produces or manufactures a commodity, subsequently sold and shipped by him in interstate commerce, whether such sale and shipment were originally intended or not, has engaged in two distinct and separate activities. So far as he produces or manufactures a commodity, his business is purely local. So far as he sells and ships, or contracts to sell and ship, the commodity to customers in another state, he engages in interstate commerce. In respect of the former, he is subject only to regulation by the state; in respect of the latter, to regulation only by the federal government. Production is not commerce; but a step in preparation for commerce.

We have seen that the word "commerce" is the equivalent of the phrase "intercourse for the purposes of trade." Plainly, the incidents leading up to and culminating in the mining of coal do not constitute such intercourse. The employment of men, the fixing of their wages, hours of labor and working conditions, the bargaining in respect of these things—whether carried on separately or collectively—each and all constitute intercourse for the purposes of production, not of trade. The latter is a thing apart from the relation of employer and employee, which in all producing occupations is purely local in character. Extraction of coal from the mine is the aim and the completed result of local activities. Commerce in the coal mined is not brought into being by force of these activities, but by negotiations, agreements, and circumstances entirely apart from production. Mining brings the subject matter of commerce into existence. Commerce disposes of it.

A consideration of the foregoing, and of many cases which might be added to those already cited, renders inescapable the conclusion that the effect of the labor provisions of the act, including those in respect of minimum wages, wage agreements, collective bargaining, and the Labor Board and its powers, primarily falls upon production and not upon commerce; and confirms the further resulting conclusion that production is a purely local activity. It follows that none of these essential antecedents of production constitutes a transaction in or forms any part of interstate commerce. Everything which moves in interstate commerce has had a local origin. Without local production somewhere, interstate commerce, as now carried on, would practically disappear. Nevertheless, the local character of mining, of manufacturing and of crop growing is a fact, and remains a fact, whatever may be done with the products. . . .

Another group of cases, of which *Swift & Co. v. United States* is an example, rest upon the circumstance that the acts in question constituted direct interferences with the "flow" of commerce among the states. In the *Swift* case, livestock was consigned and delivered to the stockyards—not as a place of final destination, but, as the court said in *Stafford v. Wallace*, "a throat through which the current flows." The sales which ensued merely changed the private interest in the subject of the current without interfering with its continuity. It was nowhere suggested in these cases that the interstate commerce power extended to the growth or production of the things which, after production, entered the flow. If the court had held that the raising of the cattle, which were involved in the *Swift* case, including the wages paid to and working conditions of the herders and others employed in the business, could be regulated by Congress, that decision and decisions holding similarly would be in point; for it is that situation, and not the one with which the court actually dealt, which here concerns us. . . .

The restricted field covered by the *Swift* and kindred cases is illustrated by the *Schechter* case. There the commodity in question, although shipped from another state, had come to rest in the state of its destination, and, as the court pointed out, was no longer in a current or flow of interstate commerce. The *Swift* doctrine was rejected as inapposite. In the *Schechter* case the flow had ceased. Here it had not begun. The difference is one of substance. The applicable principle is the same. . . .

Whether the effect of a given activity or condition is direct or indirect is not always easy to determine. The word "direct" implies that the activity or condition invoked or blamed shall operate proximately—not mediately, remotely, or collaterally—to produce the effect. It connotes the absence of an efficient intervening agency or condition. And the extent of the effect bears no logical relation to its character. The distinction between a direct and an indirect effect turns, not upon the magnitude of either the cause or the effect, but entirely upon the manner in which the effect has been brought about. If the production by one man of a single ton of coal intended for interstate sale and shipment, and actually so sold and shipped, affects interstate commerce indirectly, the effect does not become direct by multiplying the tonnage, or increasing the number of men employed, or adding to the expense or complexities of the business, or by all combined. It is quite true that rules of law are sometimes qualified by considerations of degree, as the government argues. But the matter of degree has no bearing upon the question here, since that question is not— What is the *extent* of the local activity or condition, or the *extent* of the effect produced upon interstate commerce? but—What is the *relation* between the activity or condition and the effect?

Much stress is put upon the evils which come from the struggle between employers and employees over the matter of wages, working conditions, the right of collective bargaining, etc., and the resulting strikes, curtailment and irregularity of production and effect on prices; and it is insisted that interstate commerce is *greatly* affected thereby. But, in addition to what has just been said, the conclusive answer is that the evils are all local evils over which the federal government has no legislative control. The relation of employer and employee is a local relation. At common law, it is one of the domestic relations. The wages are paid for the doing of local work. Working conditions are obviously local conditions. The employees are not engaged in or about commerce, but exclusively in producing a commodity. And the controversies and evils, which it is the object of the act to regulate and minimize, are local controversies and evils affecting local work undertaken to accomplish that local result. Such effect as they may have upon commerce, however extensive it may be, is secondary and indirect. An increase in the greatness of the effect adds to its importance. It does not alter its character.

The government's contentions in defense of the labor provisions are really disposed of adversely by our decision in the *Schechter* case. The only perceptible difference between that case and this is that in the *Schechter* case the federal power was asserted with respect to commodities which had come to rest after their interstate transportation; while here, the case deals with commodities at rest before interstate commerce has begun. That difference is without significance. The federal regulatory power ceases when interstate commercial intercourse ends; and, correlatively, the power does not attach until interstate commercial intercourse begins. There is no basis in law or reason for applying different rules to the two situations. No such distinction can be found in anything said in the *Schechter* case. . . . A reading of the entire opinion makes clear, what we now declare, that the want of power on the part of the federal government is the same whether the wages, hours of service, and working conditions, and the bargaining about them, are related to production before interstate commerce has begun, or to sale and distribution after it has ended.

MR. JUSTICE CARDOZO (dissenting . . .).

I am satisfied that the act is within the power of the central government in so far as it provides for minimum and maximum prices upon sales of bituminous coal in the transactions of interstate commerce and in those of intrastate commerce where interstate commerce is directly or intimately affected. Whether it is valid also in other provisions that have been considered and condemned in the opinion of the Court, I do not find it necessary to determine at this time. . . .

My vote is for affirmance.

I am authorized to state that MR. JUSTICE BRANDEIS and MR. JUSTICE STONE join in this opinion.

In *Carter* the five-justice majority held that coal mining was not interstate commerce because the activity occurred within a single state. The stream of commerce doctrine was inapplicable because the movement of the coal to other states had not yet begun. Furthermore, the justices concluded that the production of coal did not have a direct effect on interstate commerce. For these reasons, the Court invalidated federal regulation of coal mining, but *Carter v. Carter Coal* was Roosevelt's last major defeat at the hands of the Four Horsemen and their allies.

Court-Packing Plan

The Court entered its summer recess in 1936 having completed a year and a half of dealing with Roosevelt's legislative program and striking down several of the New Deal's most significant programs. The Four Horsemen constituted a solid block, and in important cases these justices could count on the support of at least one of the other members—usually Owen Roberts. Roosevelt was understandably frustrated with what he viewed as the Court's obstructionism; he was also impatient that no vacancies had occurred that he might fill with appointees sympathetic to the New Deal.

The national elections took center stage during the fall of 1936. There was little doubt that Roosevelt would be reelected and that the Democrats would continue to control Congress.[11] The only question was how big the margin was going to be. Roosevelt won by a landslide, capturing 98 percent of the electoral votes. His Republican opponent, Alf Landon of Kansas, carried only Maine and Vermont. The congressional elections were also a triumph for the Democrats. When the legislature reconvened in early 1937, they controlled approximately 80

11. Not everyone predicted a Roosevelt victory. The *Literary Digest* published a famous poll during that election year forecasting a Roosevelt defeat. The poll has become universally regarded as a classic case of defective research procedures. Within months after the election, the *Literary Digest* was defunct.

Editorial cartoon on President Roosevelt's Court-packing plan, *Washington Post*, February 6, 1937.

percent of the seats in both houses. With such an impressive mandate from the people and such strong party support in Congress, Roosevelt was willing to proceed with his planned attack on the Court. If no vacancies on the Supreme Court occurred naturally, Roosevelt would try to create some.

On February 5, 1937, the president announced his plan to reorganize the federal court system. His proposed legislation was predicated, at least formally, on the argument that the judiciary was too overworked and understaffed to carry out its duties effectively. His idea was to expand the number of lower court judgeships; streamline federal jurisdiction, especially with respect to cases having constitutional significance; and adopt a flexible method of temporarily moving lower court judges from their normal duties to districts with case backlogs.

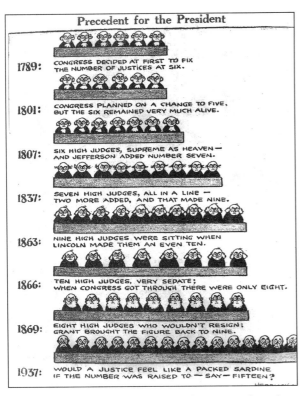

Precedent for the President

1789: CONGRESS DECIDED AT FIRST TO FIX THE NUMBER OF JUSTICES AT SIX.

1801: CONGRESS PLANNED ON A CHANGE TO FIVE, BUT THE SIX REMAINED VERY MUCH ALIVE.

1807: SIX HIGH JUDGES, SUPREME AS HEAVEN — AND JEFFERSON ADDED NUMBER SEVEN.

1837: SEVEN HIGH JUDGES, ALL IN A LINE — TWO MORE ADDED, AND THAT MADE NINE.

1863: NINE HIGH JUDGES WERE SITTING WHEN LINCOLN MADE THEM AN EVEN TEN.

1866: TEN HIGH JUDGES, VERY SEDATE; WHEN CONGRESS GOT THROUGH THERE WERE ONLY EIGHT.

1869: EIGHT HIGH JUDGES WHO WOULDN'T RESIGN; GRANT BROUGHT THE FIGURE BACK TO NINE.

1937: WOULD A JUSTICE FEEL LIKE A PACKED SARDINE IF THE NUMBER WAS RAISED TO — SAY — FIFTEEN?

A *Washington Post* Herblock cartoon on the Court-packing plan, February 22, 1937.

To many observers these administrative reforms were little more than a smoke screen for Roosevelt's Supreme Court proposals. The president asked Congress to authorize the creation of one new seat on the Supreme Court for every justice who had attained the age of seventy but remained in active service. These expanded positions would have an upper limit of six, bringing the potential size of the Court to a maximum of fifteen. At the time of his proposal, six sitting justices were older than seventy. If Roosevelt could appoint six New Deal advocates to the Court, they probably could attract the votes of at least two others and form a majority that would give constitutional approval to the president's programs. Although Roosevelt attempted to justify his Supreme Court proposal on the ground that the advanced age of several sitting justices called for the addition of younger, more

vigorous colleagues, everyone saw the plan for what it was—an attempt to pack the Court.

Reaction was not favorable.[12] Public opinion polls taken during the course of the debate over the plan revealed that at no time did a majority of Americans support Roosevelt's proposal *(see Figure 7-1)*. Members of the organized bar were overwhelmingly opposed. Even with large Democratic majorities in both houses of Congress, Roosevelt had difficulty selling his proposal to the legislature. Chief Justice Hughes wrote a public letter criticizing the proposal to Sen. Burton Wheeler of Montana, a leader of Democrats opposing the president.[13] The press expressed sharp disapproval. In spite of the general support the people gave Roosevelt and the New Deal, they did not appreciate his tampering with the structure of government to get his way. Roosevelt's response to this unexpected criticism was to go directly to the people to press his case, and in doing so he became a little more open about his objectives. In his radio broadcast *(see Box 7-4 for excerpts)* the president explained his proposal and urged the American public to support it.

The Switch in Time

The battle in Congress over the president's plan was closely fought.[14] A continuation of the confrontation, however, was averted in large measure by the actions of the Supreme Court itself. On March 29, 1937, just twenty days after the president's broadcast, the Court signaled that changes were in the making. The first indication was the 5–4 decision in *West Coast Hotel v. Parrish* (1937), which upheld the validity of a Washington State law regulating wages and working conditions for women and children.

Although this case involved a state law rather than a federal statute and concerned issues of substantive due process rather than the Commerce Clause, it had great

12. See Gregory A. Caldeira, "Public Opinion and the U.S. Supreme Court: FDR's Court-Packing Plan," *American Political Science Review* 81 (December 1987): 1139–1153.

13. The letter from Hughes to Wheeler, dated March 21, 1937, is reprinted in *Guide to the U.S. Supreme Court*, 1039–1040.

14. See William E. Leuchtenburg, "The Origins of Franklin D. Roosevelt's 'Court-Packing' Plan," *Supreme Court Review 1966* (Chicago: University of Chicago Press, 1966), 347–400; Leuchtenburg, *Franklin D. Roosevelt and the New Deal, 1932–1940* (New York: Harper & Row, 1963).

FIGURE 7-1 Public Support for Roosevelt's 1937 Court-Packing Plan

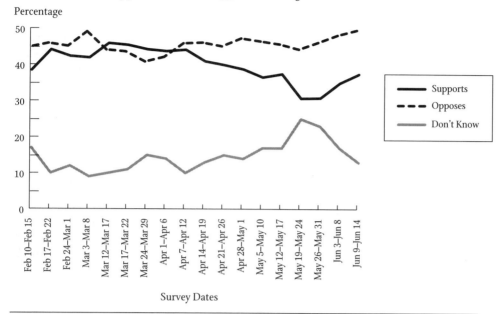

DATA SOURCE: Lee Epstein, Jeffrey A. Segal, Harold Spaeth, and Thomas G. Walker, *The Supreme Court Compendium: Data, Decisions, and Developments*, 3rd ed. (Washington, D.C.: CQ Press, 2003), Table 8-28.

significance. Aside from the doctrinal importance of the case, discussed in Chapter 10, the voting coalitions on the Court had changed. Justice Roberts, so long an ally of the Four Horsemen, deserted the conservatives and voted with the liberal bloc to approve the legislation. Just months earlier Roberts had voted with the conservatives in a 5–4 decision striking down a New York law that was nearly a carbon copy of the one he now approved.[15]

Two weeks later Roberts proved that his *West Coast Hotel* vote was not an aberration. On April 12 the Court issued its ruling in *National Labor Relations Board v. Jones & Laughlin Steel Corporation*. Once again Roberts joined Hughes, Brandeis, Cardozo, and Stone to form a majority, this time upholding a major piece of New Deal legislation. The decision may be the most significant economic ruling of the twentieth century. In it the Court announced a break from the past and ushered in a new

15. *Morehead v. New York ex rel. Tipaldo* (1936).

era in the constitutional relationship between the government and the economy.

National Labor Relations Board v. Jones & Laughlin Steel Corporation

301 U.S. 1 (1937)
http://laws.findlaw.com/US/301/1.html
Vote: 5 (Brandeis, Cardozo, Hughes, Roberts, Stone)
    4 (Butler, McReynolds, Sutherland, Van Devanter)
Opinion for the Court: Hughes
Dissenting opinion: McReynolds

In 1935 Congress passed the National Labor Relations Act, more commonly known as the Wagner Act. The purpose of the legislation was to help workers achieve gains in wages and working conditions through the collective bargaining process. The act's primary aim was to protect the rights of employees to organize and join labor unions

BOX 7-4   EXCERPTS FROM THE WHITE HOUSE BROADCAST, MARCH 9, 1937

TONIGHT, sitting at my desk in the White House, I make my first radio report to the people in my second term of office. . . .

Last Thursday I described the American form of Government as a three horse team provided by the Constitution to the American people so that their field might be plowed. The three horses are, of course, the three branches of government—the Congress, the Executive and the Courts. Two of the horses are pulling in unison today; the third is not. Those who have intimated that the President of the United States is trying to drive that team overlook the simple fact that the President, as Chief Executive, is himself one of the three horses.

It is the American people themselves who are in the driver's seat.

It is the American people themselves who want the furrow plowed.

It is the American people themselves who expect the third horse to pull in unison with the other two. . . .

When the Congress has sought to stabilize national agriculture, to improve the conditions of labor, to safeguard business against unfair competition, to protect our national resources, and in many other ways, to serve our clearly national needs, the majority of the Court has been assuming the power to pass on the wisdom of these Acts of the Congress—and to approve or disapprove the public policy written into these laws. . . .

The Court . . . has improperly set itself up as a third House of the Congress—a super-legislature, as one of the Justices has called it—reading into the Constitution words and implications which are not there, and which were never intended to be there.

We have, therefore, reached the point as a Nation where we must take action to save the Constitution from the Court and the Court from itself. We must find a way to take an appeal from the Supreme Court to the Constitution itself. We want a Supreme Court which will do justice under the Constitution—not over it. In our Courts we want a government of laws and not of men.

I want—as all Americans want—an independent judiciary as proposed by the framers of the Constitution. That means a Supreme Court that will enforce the Constitution as written—that will refuse to amend the Constitution by the arbitrary exercise of judicial power—amendment by judicial say-so. It does not mean a judiciary so independent that it can deny the existence of facts universally recognized. . . .

What is my proposal? It is simply this: whenever a Judge or Justice of any Federal Court has reached the age of seventy and does not avail himself of the opportunity to retire on a pension, a new member shall be appointed by the President then in office, with the approval, as required by the Constitution, of the Senate of the United States.

That plan has two chief purposes. By bringing into the Judicial system a steady and continuing stream of new and younger blood, I hope, first, to make the administration of all Federal justice speedier and, therefore, less costly; secondly, to bring to the decision of social and economic problems younger men who have had personal experience and contact with modern facts and circumstances under which average men have to live and work. This plan will save our national Constitution from hardening of the judicial arteries.

The number of Judges to be appointed would depend wholly on the decision of present Judges now over seventy, or those who would subsequently reach the age of seventy.

If, for instance, any one of the six Justices of the Supreme Court now over the age of seventy should retire as provided under the plan, no additional place would be created. Consequently, although there never can be more than fifteen, there may be only fourteen, or thirteen, or twelve. And there may be only nine.

There is nothing novel or radical about this idea. It seeks to maintain the Federal bench in full vigor. It has been discussed and approved by many persons of high authority ever since a similar proposal passed the House of Representatives in 1869. . . .

The statute would apply to all the Courts in the Federal system. There is general approval so far as the lower Federal courts are concerned. The plan has met opposition only so far as the Supreme Court of the United States itself is concerned. If such a plan is good for the lower courts it certainly ought to be equally good for the highest Court from which there is no appeal.

Those opposing this plan have sought to arouse prejudice and fear by crying that I am seeking to "pack" the Supreme Court and that a baneful precedent will be established.

What do they mean by the words "packing the Court"?

Let me answer this question with a bluntness that will end all honest misunderstanding of my purposes.

If by that phrase "packing the Court" it is charged that I wish to place on the bench spineless puppets who would disregard the law and would decide specific cases as I wished them to be decided, I make this answer—that no President fit for his office would appoint, and no Senate of honorable men fit for their office would confirm, that kind of appointees to the Supreme Court.

But if by that phrase the charge is made that I would appoint and the Senate would confirm Justices worthy to sit beside present members of the Court who understand those modern conditions—that I will appoint Justices who will not undertake to override the judgment of the Congress on legislative policy—that I will appoint Justices who will act as Justices and not as legislators—if the appointment of such Justices can be called "packing the Courts," then I say that I and with me the vast majority of the American people favor doing just that thing—now.

Is it a dangerous precedent for the Congress to change the number of the Justices? The Congress has always had, and will have, that power. The number of Justices has been changed several times before—in the Administrations of John Adams and Thomas Jefferson—both signers of the Declaration of Independence—Andrew Jackson, Abraham Lincoln and Ulysses S. Grant. . . .

We think it so much in the public interest to maintain a vigorous judiciary that we encourage the retirement of elderly Judges by offering them a life pension at full salary. Why then should we leave the fulfillment of this public policy to chance or make it dependent upon the desire or prejudice of any individual Justice?

It is the clear intention of our public policy to provide for a constant flow of new and younger blood into the Judiciary. Normally every President appoints a large number of District and Circuit Judges and a few members of the Supreme Court. Until my first term practically every President of the United States had appointed at least one member of the Supreme Court. President Taft appointed five members and named a Chief Justice—President Wilson three—President Harding four including a Chief Justice—President Coolidge one—President Hoover three including a Chief Justice.

Such a succession of appointments should have provided a Court well-balanced as to age. But chance and the disinclination of individuals to leave the Supreme bench have now given us a Court in which five Justices will be over seventy-five years of age before next June and one over seventy. Thus a sound public policy has been defeated.

I now propose that we establish by law an assurance against any such ill-balanced Court in the future. I propose that hereafter, when a Judge reaches the age of seventy, a new and younger Judge shall be added to the Court automatically. In this way I propose to enforce a sound public policy by law instead of leaving the composition of our Federal Courts, including the highest, to be determined by chance or the personal decision of individuals.

If such a law as I propose is regarded as establishing a new precedent—is it not a most desirable precedent?

Like all lawyers, like all Americans, I regret the necessity of this controversy. But the welfare of the United States, and indeed of the Constitution itself, is what we all must think about first. Our difficulty with the Court today rises not from the Court as an institution but from human beings within it. But we cannot yield our constitutional destiny to the personal judgment of a few men who, being fearful of the future, would deny us the necessary means of dealing with the present.

This plan of mine is no attack on the Court; it seeks to restore the Court to its rightful and historic place in our system of Constitutional Government and to have it resume its high task of building anew on the Constitution "a system of living law.". . .

During the past half century the balance of power between the three great branches of the Federal Government has been tipped out of balance by the Courts in direct contradiction of the high purposes of the framers of the Constitution. It is my purpose to restore that balance. You who know me will accept my solemn assurance that in a world in which democracy is under attack, I seek to make American democracy succeed.

and to provide a means for the enforcement of those rights. The law authorized the creation of the National Labor Relations Board (NLRB), which was empowered to hear complaints of unfair labor practices and impose certain corrective measures. The act was based on the power of Congress to regulate interstate commerce and upon the assertion that labor unrest and strikes caused an interruption in such commerce that Congress had the right to prevent.

Jones & Laughlin was one of the nation's largest steel producers. Its operations were fully integrated, extending into many states and involving every aspect of steel production from mining through production and distribution. Complaints were filed against the company for engaging in unfair labor practices at its plant in Aliquippa, Pennsylvania. The charges included discriminating against workers who wanted to join a labor union. The NLRB ruled against the company and ordered it to reinstate ten workers who had been dismissed because of their union activities. The company refused, claiming that the National Labor Relations Act was unconstitutional. Steel production facilities, according to the company, were engaged in a manufacturing activity that had been declared by the Supreme Court to be intrastate commerce outside the regulatory authority of Congress. The lower courts, applying existing Supreme Court precedent, ruled in favor of the company, and the NLRB appealed.

MR. CHIEF JUSTICE HUGHES delivered the opinion of the Court.

First. The Scope of the Act.—The Act is challenged in its entirety as an attempt to regulate all industry, thus invading the reserved powers of the States over their local concerns. It is asserted that the references in the Act to interstate and foreign commerce are colorable at best; that the Act is not a true regulation of such commerce or of matters which directly affect it but on the contrary has the fundamental object of placing under the compulsory supervision of the federal government all industrial labor relations within the nation. . . .

If this conception of terms, intent and consequent inseparability were sound, the Act would necessarily fall by reason of the limitation upon the federal power which inheres in the constitutional grant, as well as because of the explicit reservation of the Tenth Amendment. The authority of the federal government may not be pushed to such an extreme as to destroy the distinction, which the commerce clause itself establishes, between commerce "among the several States" and the internal concerns of a State. That distinction between what is national and what is local in the activities of commerce is vital to the maintenance of our federal system. . . .

We think it clear that the National Labor Relations Act may be construed so as to operate within the sphere of constitutional authority. The jurisdiction conferred upon the Board, and invoked in this instance, is found in §10 (a), which provides:

"Sec. 10 (a). The Board is empowered, as hereinafter provided, to prevent any person from engaging in any unfair labor practice (listed in section 8 . . .) affecting commerce. The critical words of this provision, prescribing the limits of the Board's authority in dealing with the labor practices, are 'affecting commerce.' The Act specifically defines the 'commerce' to which it refers (§2 (6) . . .):

"The term 'commerce' means trade, traffic, commerce, transportation, or communication among the several States, or between the District of Columbia or any Territory of the United States and any State or other Territory, or between any foreign country and any State, Territory, or the District of Columbia, or within the District of Columbia or any Territory, or between points in the same State but through any other State or any Territory or the District of Columbia or any foreign country."

There can be no question that the commerce thus contemplated by the Act (aside from that within a Territory or the District of Columbia) is interstate and foreign commerce in the constitutional sense. The Act also defines the term "affecting commerce" (§2 (7) . . .):

"The term 'affecting commerce' means in commerce, or burdening or obstructing commerce or the free flow of commerce or having led or tending to lead to a labor dispute burdening or obstructing commerce or the free flow of commerce."

This definition is one of exclusion as well as inclusion. The grant of authority to the Board does not purport to extend to the relationship between all industrial employees and employers. Its terms do not impose collective bargaining upon all industry regardless of effects upon interstate and foreign commerce. It purports to reach only what may be deemed to burden or obstruct that commerce and, thus qualified, it must be construed as contemplating the exercise of control within constitutional bounds. It is a familiar principle that acts which directly burden or obstruct interstate or foreign commerce, or its free flow, are within the reach of the congressional power. Acts having that effect are not rendered immune because they grow out of labor disputes. It is the effect upon commerce, not the source of the injury, which is the criterion. Whether or not particular action does affect commerce in such a close and intimate fashion as to be subject to federal control, and hence to lie within the authority conferred upon the Board, is left by the statute to be determined as individual cases arise. We are thus to inquire whether in the instant case the constitutional boundary has been passed.

Second. The Unfair Labor Practices in Question.— . . . [T]he statute goes no further than to safeguard the right of employees to self-organization and to select representatives of their own choosing for collective bargaining or other mutual protection without restraint or coercion by their employer.

That is a fundamental right. Employees have as clear a right to organize and select their representatives for lawful purposes as the respondent has to organize its business and select its own officers and agents. Discrimination and coercion to prevent the free exercise of the right of employees to self-organization and representation is a proper subject for condemnation by competent legislative authority. Long ago we stated the reason for labor organizations. We said that they were organized out of the necessities of the situation; that a single employee was helpless in dealing with an employer; that he was dependent ordinarily on his daily wage for the maintenance of himself and family; that if the employer refused to pay him the wages that he thought fair, he was nevertheless unable to leave the employ and resist arbitrary and unfair treatment; that union was essential to give laborers opportunity to deal on an equality with their employer. We reiterated these views when we had under consideration the Railway Labor Act of 1926. Fully recognizing the legality of collective action on the part of employees in order to safeguard their proper interests, we said that Congress was not required to ignore this right but could safeguard it. Congress could seek to make appropriate collective action of employees an instrument of peace rather than of strife. We said that such collective action would be a mockery if representation were made futile by interference with freedom of choice. Hence the prohibition by Congress of interference with the selection of representatives for the purpose of negotiation and conference between employers and employees, "instead of being an invasion of the constitutional right of either, was based on the recognition of the rights of both." We have reasserted the same principle in sustaining the application of the Railway Labor Act as amended in 1934.

Third. The Application of the Act to Employees Engaged in Production.—The Principle Involved.—Respondent says that whatever may be said of employees engaged in interstate commerce, the industrial relations and activities in the manufacturing department of respondent's enterprise are not subject to federal regulation. The argument rests upon the proposition that manufacturing in itself is not commerce.

The Government distinguishes these cases. The various parts of respondent's enterprise are described as interdependent and as thus involving "a great movement of iron ore, coal and limestone along well-defined paths to the steel mills, thence through them, and thence in the form of steel products into the consuming centers of the country—a definite and well-understood course of business." It is urged that these activities constitute a "stream" or "flow" of commerce, of which the Aliquippa manufacturing plant is the focal point, and that industrial strife at that point would cripple the entire government. Reference is made to our decision sustaining the Packers and Stockyards Act. . . .

We do not find it necessary to determine whether these features of defendant's business dispose of the asserted analogy to the "stream of commerce" cases. The instances in which that metaphor has been used are but particular, and not exclusive, illustrations of the protective power which the Government invokes in support of the present Act. The congressional authority to protect interstate commerce from burdens and obstructions is not limited to transactions which can be deemed to be an essential part of a "flow" of interstate or foreign commerce. Burdens and obstructions may be due to injurious action springing from other sources. The fundamental principle is that the power to regulate commerce is the power to enact "all appropriate legislation" for "its protection and advancement"; to adopt measures "to promote its growth and insure its safety"; "to foster, protect, control and restrain." That power is plenary and may be exerted to protect interstate commerce "no matter what the source of the dangers which threaten it."

Although activities may be intrastate in character when separately considered, if they have such a close and substantial relation to interstate commerce that their control is essential or appropriate to protect that commerce from burdens and obstructions, Congress cannot be denied the power to exercise that control. . . .

It is thus apparent that the fact that the employees here concerned were engaged in production is not determinative. The question remains as to the effect upon interstate commerce of the labor practice involved. . . .

Fourth. Effects of the Unfair Labor Practice in Respondent's Enterprise.—Giving full weight to respondent's contention with respect to a break in the complete continuity of the "stream of commerce" by reason of respondent's manufacturing operations, the fact remains that the stoppage of those operations by industrial strife would have a most serious effect upon interstate commerce. In view of respondent's far-flung activities, it is idle to say that the effect would be indirect or remote. It is obvious that it would be immediate and might be catastrophic. We are asked to shut our eyes to the plainest facts of our national life and to deal with the question of direct and indirect effects in an intellectual vacuum. Because there may be but indirect and remote effects upon interstate commerce in connection with a host of local enterprises throughout the country, it does not follow that other industrial activities do not have such a close and intimate relation to interstate commerce as to make the presence of industrial strife a matter of the most urgent national concern. When industries organize themselves on a national scale, making their relation to interstate commerce the dominant factor in their activities, how can it be maintained that their industrial labor relations constitute a forbidden field into which Congress may not enter when it is necessary to protect interstate commerce from the paralyzing consequences of industrial war? We have often said that interstate commerce itself is a practical conception. It is equally true that interferences with that commerce must be appraised by a judgment that does not ignore actual experience.

Experience has abundantly demonstrated that the recognition of the right of employees to self-organization and to have representatives of their own choosing for the purpose of collective bargaining is often an essential condition of industrial peace. Refusal to confer and negotiate has been one of the most prolific causes of strife. This is such an out-

standing fact in the history of labor disturbances that it is a proper subject of judicial notice and requires no citation of instances. . . . These questions have frequently engaged the attention of Congress and have been the subject of many inquiries. The steel industry is one of the great basic industries of the United States, with ramifying activities affecting interstate commerce at every point. The Government aptly refers to the steel strike of 1919–1920 with its far-reaching consequences. The fact that there appears to have been no major disturbance in that industry in the more recent period did not dispose of the possibilities of future and like dangers to interstate commerce which Congress was entitled to foresee and to exercise its protective power to forestall. It is not necessary again to detail the facts as to respondent's enterprise. Instead of being beyond the pale, we think that it presents in a most striking way the close and intimate relation which a manufacturing industry may have to interstate commerce and we have no doubt that Congress had constitutional authority to safeguard the right of respondent's employees to self-organization and freedom in the choice of representatives for collective bargaining. . . .

Reversed.

MR. JUSTICE MCREYNOLDS delivered the following dissenting opinion in the cases preceding:

MR. JUSTICE VAN DEVANTER, MR. JUSTICE SUTHERLAND, MR. JUSTICE BUTLER and I are unable to agree with the decisions just announced. . . .

Considering the far-reaching import of these decisions, the departure from what we understand has been consistently ruled here, and the extraordinary power confirmed to a Board of three [the NLRB], the obligation to present our views becomes plain. . . .

The precise question for us to determine is whether in the circumstances disclosed Congress has power to authorize what the Labor Board commanded the respondents to do. Stated otherwise, in the circumstances here existing could Congress by statute direct what the Board has ordered? . . .

The argument in support of the Board affirms: "Thus the validity of any specific application of the preventive measures of this Act depends upon whether industrial strife resulting from the practices in the particular enterprise under consideration would be of the character which Federal power could control if it occurred. If strife in that enterprise could be controlled, certainly it could be prevented."

Manifestly that view of Congressional power would extend it into almost every field of human industry. With striking lucidity, fifty years ago, *Kidd v. Pearson* declared: "If it be held that the term [commerce with foreign nations and among the several states] includes the regulation of all such manufactures as are intended to be the subject of commercial transactions in the future, it is impossible to deny that it would also include all productive industries that contemplate the same thing. The result would be that Congress would be invested, to the exclusion of the States, with the power to regulate, not only manufactures, but also agriculture, horticulture, stock raising, domestic fisheries, mining—in short, every branch of human activity." This doctrine found full approval in *United States v. E. C. Knight Co.*, *Schechter Poultry Corp. v. United States*, and *Carter v. Carter Coal Co.*, where the authorities are collected and principles applicable here are discussed. . . .

The Constitution still recognizes the existence of states with indestructible powers; the Tenth Amendment was supposed to put them beyond controversy.

We are told that Congress may protect the "stream of commerce" and that one who buys raw material without the state, manufactures it therein, and ships the output to another state is in that stream. Therefore it is said he may be prevented from doing anything which may interfere with its flow.

This, too, goes beyond the constitutional limitations heretofore enforced. If a man raises cattle and regularly delivers them to a carrier for interstate shipment, may Congress prescribe the conditions under which he may employ or discharge helpers on the ranch? The products of a mine pass daily into interstate commerce; many things are brought to it from other states. Are the owners and miners within the power of Congress in respect of the miners' tenure and discharge? May a mill owner be prohibited from closing his factory or discontinuing his business because so to do would stop the flow of products to and from his plant in interstate commerce? May employees in a factory be restrained from quitting work in a body because this will close the factory and thereby stop the flow of commerce? May arson of a factory be made a Federal offense whenever this would interfere with such flow? If the business cannot continue with the existing

wage scale, may Congress command a reduction? If the ruling of the Court just announced is adhered to these questions suggest some of the problems certain to arise. . . .

There is no ground on which reasonably to hold that refusal by a manufacturer, whose raw materials come from states other than that of his factory and whose products are regularly carried to other states, to bargain collectively with employees in his manufacturing plant, directly affects interstate commerce. In such business, there is not one but two distinct movements or streams in interstate transportation. The first brings in raw material and there ends. Then follows manufacture, a separate and local activity. Upon completion of this, and not before, the second distinct movement or stream in interstate commerce begins and the products go to other states. Such is the common course for small as well as large industries. It is unreasonable and unprecedented to say the commerce clause confers upon Congress power to govern the relations between employers and employees in these local activities. In *Schechter*'s case we condemned as unauthorized by the commerce clause assertion of federal power in respect of commodities which had come to rest after interstate transportation. And, in *Carter*'s case, we held Congress lacked the power to regulate labor relations in respect of commodities before interstate commerce has begun.

It is gravely stated that experience teaches that if an employer discourages membership in "any organization of any kind" "in which employees participate, and which exists for the purpose in whole or in part of dealing with employers concerning grievances, labor disputes, wages, rates of pay, hours of employment or conditions of work," discontent may follow and this in turn may lead to a strike, and as the outcome of the strike there may be a block in the stream of interstate commerce. Therefore Congress may inhibit the discharge! Whatever effect any cause of discontent may ultimately have upon commerce is far too indirect to justify Congressional regulation. Almost anything—marriage, birth, death—may in some fashion affect commerce.

That Congress has power by appropriate means, not prohibited by the Constitution, to prevent direct and material interference with the conduct of interstate commerce is settled doctrine. But the interference struck at must be direct and material, not some mere possibility contingent on wholly uncertain events; and there must be no impairment of rights guaranteed. . . .

The things inhibited by the Labor Act relate to the management of a manufacturing plant—something distinct from commerce and subject to the authority of the state. And this may not be abridged because of some vague possibility of distant interference with commerce. . . .

The right to contract is fundamental and includes the privilege of selecting those with whom one is willing to assume contractual relations. This right is unduly abridged by the Act now upheld. A private owner is deprived of power to manage his own property by freely selecting those to whom his manufacturing operations are to be entrusted. We think this cannot lawfully be done in circumstances like those here disclosed.

It seems clear to us that Congress has transcended the powers granted.

The decisions in *West Coast Hotel v. Parrish* and *NLRB v. Jones & Laughlin Steel* took the energy out of Roosevelt's drive to pack the Court. It no longer appeared necessary, as the Court now was looking with greater approval at state and federal legislation to correct the failing economy. In addition, on May 18 Justice Van Devanter, a consistent foe of Roosevelt's New Deal programs, announced that he would retire from the Court at the end of the term. At long last the president would have an opportunity to put a justice of his own choosing on the Court.

On June 7 the Senate Judiciary Committee recommended that the Court-packing bill not be passed. To the president's great displeasure, seven of the ten senators signing the report were Democrats. Majority Leader Joseph Robinson, D-Ark., mounted a last-ditch effort on behalf of the president, advocating a compromise plan that would have raised the threshold age for replacing the justices from seventy to seventy-five years. He made considerable progress in forging a coalition to pass this modified plan, but the effort stalled when Robinson died from a heart attack on July 14.[16]

Much has been said and written about Justice Roberts's change in position. At the time, it was described as "the switch in time that saved nine," because his move from the conservative to the liberal wing of the Court was largely responsible for killing the Court-packing plan and preserving the Court as a nine-justice institution. Such a characterization is not flattering for a judge, who is not supposed to make decisions on the basis of external political pressures. Nevertheless, it would certainly be understandable for a justice to rethink his views if the future of the Court as an institution were at stake.

More contemporary analyses of Roberts's switch point out that the notion that he caved in to the pressures of the president's plan is overly simplistic. Although the decision in *West Coast Hotel* was announced after Roosevelt sent his proposal to Congress, it was argued and initially voted upon weeks before the president made his plans public. Roosevelt had kept the Court-packing proposal carefully under wraps before he announced it, and there is little likelihood that the justices had advance knowledge of it. Furthermore, Roberts was not a doctrinaire conservative. Although he joined the Court's right wing in several important decisions, he did not have the laissez-faire zeal of the Four Horsemen. In fact, Roberts had voted on a number of occasions in support of state efforts to combat economic problems.[17] Some observers now conclude that Roberts's change of position was primarily a matter of his growing disenchantment with the hard-line conservative view and that he followed "his sound judicial intuition to a well-reasoned position in keeping with the public interest." [18] As for Roberts's own explanation, he maintained traditional judicial silence. When asked in a 1946 interview why he had altered his position, he deflected the question by responding, "Who knows what causes a judge to decide as he does? Maybe the breakfast he had has something to do with it." [19] Whatever the reasons for his switch, it broke the conservatives' domination of the Court.

---

16. For a full account of the events surrounding this compromise plan, see William E. Leuchtenburg, "FDR's Court Packing Plan: A Second Life, a Second Death," *Duke Law Journal* (June–September 1985): 673–689.

17. See, for example, his opinion for the Court in *Nebbia v. New York* (1934).

18. Merlo J. Pusey, "Justice Roberts' 1937 Turnaround," *Yearbook of the Supreme Court Historical Society* (Washington, D.C.: Supreme Court Historical Society, 1983), 107.

19. Ibid., 106.

Justice Owens Roberts. He cast critical votes in 1937 Supreme Court cases that expanded the authority of the federal government to regulate the economy.

Consolidating the New Interpretation of the Commerce Power

Van Devanter's retirement was followed over the next four years by the retirements of Justices Sutherland and Brandeis and the deaths of Justices Cardozo and Butler. By 1940 Franklin Roosevelt had appointed a majority of the sitting justices. And in 1941 Justice McReynolds, the last of the Four Horsemen, also retired.

With *NLRB v. Jones & Laughlin Steel* showing the way, the increasingly liberal Court upheld a number of New Deal programs. It also continued to expand the concept of interstate commerce. Gone were the old notions that production, manufacturing, mining, and processing were exclusively intrastate affairs with insufficient direct effects on interstate commerce to activate federal commerce powers. Precedents such as *E. C. Knight, Hammer,*

Panama Refining, Schechter Poultry, and *Carter Coal* were substantially overruled, discredited, or severely limited *(see Box 7-5).*

Wickard v. Filburn (1942) illustrates how far the Court had moved from its pre-1937 idea of interstate commerce. As you compare this decision to earlier rulings, recall that in *E. C. Knight* a sugar trust controlling 98 percent of the nation's sugar refining was considered to be operating in intrastate commerce. And in *Carter v. Carter Coal* the entire coal mining industry was said to be outside the power of Congress to regulate interstate commerce. How do these industries compare with Roscoe Filburn's farm?

Wickard v. Filburn

317 U.S. 111 (1942)
http://laws.findlaw.com/US/317/111.html
Vote: 9 (Black, Byrnes, Douglas, Frankfurter, Jackson, Murphy,
    Reed, Roberts, Stone)
    0
Opinion of the Court: Jackson

The 1938 Agricultural Adjustment Act, as amended, allowed the secretary of agriculture to establish production limits for various grains. Under these limits, acreage allotments were assigned to the individual farmer. The purpose of the law was to stop the wild swings in grain prices by eliminating both surpluses and shortfalls.

Roscoe Filburn owned a small farm in Montgomery County, Ohio. For many years he raised dairy cattle and chickens, selling the milk, poultry, and eggs the farm produced. He also raised winter wheat on a small portion of his farm. He sold some wheat and used the rest to feed his cattle and chickens, make flour for home consumption, and produce seeds for the next planting.

In July 1940 Secretary of Agriculture Claude R. Wickard set the wheat production limits for the 1941 crop. Filburn was allotted 11.1 acres to be planted in wheat with a yield of 20.1 bushels per acre. He planted not only his allotted acres but also some other land to produce the wheat for home consumption. In total Filburn planted 23 acres in wheat, from which he harvested 239 bushels

BOX 7-5   SUPREME COURT EXPANSION OF THE COMMERCE
POWERS, 1937–1941

DECISION	RULING
NLRB v. Friedman-Harry Marks Clothing Company (1937)	The National Labor Relations Act applies to a company engaged in the manufacturing of clothing.
NLRB v. Fruehauf Trailer Company (1937)	The National Labor Relations Act applies to a company engaged in the manufacturing of trailers.
Steward Machine v. Davis (1937)	Unemployment provisions of the Social Security Act are constitutional.
Helvering v. Davis (1937)	Old-age benefits provisions of the Social Security Act are constitutional.
Santa Cruz Fruit Packing v. NLRB (1938)	The National Labor Relations Act applies to a fruit packing company although only 37 percent of its product is sold in interstate commerce.
Consolidated Edison Company v. NLRB (1938)	The National Labor Relations Act applies to a power company although all of its power is sold in state.
NLRB v. Fainblatt (1939)	The National Labor Relations Act applies to a small garment manufacturer even though all of its goods are sold in state.
United States v. Rock Royal Cooperative (1939)	Legislation allowing the secretary of agriculture to set milk prices paid to farmers is constitutional.
Mulford v. Smith (1939)	Tobacco production quotas set by secretary of agriculture under Agricultural Adjustment Act of 1938 are constitutional.
United States v. Darby Lumber Company (1941)	Congressional action prohibiting shipment in interstate commerce of goods in violation of federal wage and hour laws is constitutional.

more than the government allowed him. For this excess planting Filburn was fined $117.11. He refused to pay the fine, claiming that Congress had exceeded its powers under the Commerce Clause by regulating the planting by an individual of wheat on his own property for on-farm consumption. The lower court ruled in Filburn's favor, and Secretary Wickard appealed.

MR. JUSTICE JACKSON delivered the opinion of the Court.

It is urged that under the Commerce Clause of the Constitution, Article I, §8, clause 3, Congress does not possess the power it has in this instance sought to exercise. The question would merit little consideration since our decision in *United States v. Darby* sustaining the federal power to regulate production of goods for commerce, except for the fact that this Act extends federal regulation to production not intended in any part for commerce but wholly for consumption on the farm. The Act includes a definition of "market" and its derivatives, so that as related to wheat, in addition to its conventional meaning, it also means to dispose of "by feeding (in any form) to poultry or livestock which, or the products of which, are sold, bartered, or exchanged, or to be so disposed of." Hence, marketing quotas not only embrace all that may be sold without penalty but also what may be consumed on the premises. Wheat produced on excess acreage is designated as "available for marketing" as so defined, and the penalty is imposed thereon. Penalties do not depend upon whether any part of the wheat, either within or without the quota, is sold or intended to be sold. The sum of this is that the Federal Government fixes a quota including all that the farmer may harvest for sale or for his own farm needs, and declares that wheat produced on excess acreage may neither be disposed of nor used except upon payment of the penalty, or except it is stored as required by the Act or delivered to the Secretary of Agriculture.

Appellee says that this is a regulation of production and consumption of wheat. Such activities are, he urges, beyond the reach of Congressional power under the Commerce Clause, since they are local in character, and their effects upon interstate commerce are at most "indirect." In answer the Government argues that the statute regulates neither production nor consumption, but only marketing; and, in the alternative, that if the Act does go beyond the regulation of marketing it is sustainable as a "necessary and proper" implementation of the power of Congress over interstate commerce.

The Government's concern lest the Act be held to be a regulation of production or consumption, rather than of marketing, is attributable to a few dicta and decisions of this Court which might be understood to lay it down that activities such as "production," "manufacturing," and "mining" are strictly "local" and, except in special circumstances which are not present here, cannot be regulated under the commerce power because their effects upon interstate commerce are, as matter of law, only "indirect." Even today, when this power has been held to have great latitude, there is no decision of this Court that such activities may be regulated where no part of the product is intended for interstate commerce or intermingled with the subjects thereof. We believe that a review of the course of decision under the Commerce Clause will make plain, however, that questions of the power of Congress are not to be decided by reference to any formula which would give controlling force to nomenclature such as "production" and "indirect" and foreclose consideration of the actual effects of the activity in question upon interstate commerce.

At the beginning Chief Justice Marshall described the federal commerce power with a breadth never yet exceeded. *Gibbons v. Ogden*. He made emphatic the embracing and penetrating nature of this power by warning that effective restraints on its exercise must proceed from political rather than from judicial processes.

For nearly a century, however, decisions of this Court under the Commerce Clause dealt rarely with questions of what Congress might do in the exercise of its granted power under the Clause, and almost entirely with the permissibility of state activity which it was claimed discriminated against or burdened interstate commerce. During this period there was perhaps little occasion for the affirmative exercise of the commerce power, and the influence of the Clause on American life and law was a negative one, resulting almost wholly from its operation as a restraint upon the powers of the states. In discussion and decision the point of reference, instead of being what was "necessary and proper" to the exercise by Congress of its granted power, was often some concept of sovereignty thought to be implicit in the status of statehood. Certain activities such as "production," "manufacturing," and "mining" were occasionally said to be within the province of state governments and beyond the power of Congress under the Commerce Clause.

It was not until 1887, with the enactment of the Interstate Commerce Act, that the interstate commerce power began to exert positive influence in American law and life. This first important federal resort to the commerce power was followed in 1890 by the Sherman Anti-Trust Act and, thereafter, mainly after 1903, by many others. These statutes ushered in new phases of adjudication, which required the Court to approach the interpretation of the Commerce Clause in the light of an actual exercise by Congress of its power thereunder.

When it first dealt with this new legislation, the Court adhered to its earlier pronouncements, and allowed but little scope to the power of Congress. *United States v. Knight Co.* These earlier pronouncements also played an important part in several of the five cases in which this Court later held that Acts of Congress under the Commerce Clause were in excess of its power.

Even while important opinions in this line of restrictive authority were being written, however, other cases called forth broader interpretations of the Commerce Clause destined to supersede the earlier ones, and to bring about a return to the principles first enunciated by Chief Justice Marshall in *Gibbons v. Ogden*. . . .

Whether the subject of the regulation in question was "production," "consumption," or "marketing" is . . . not material for purposes of deciding the question of federal power before us. That an activity is of local character may help in a doubtful case to determine whether Congress intended to reach it. The same consideration might help in determining whether in the absence of Congressional action it would be permissible for the state to exert its power on the subject matter, even though in so doing it to some degree affected interstate commerce. But even if appellee's activity be local and though it may not be regarded as commerce, it may still, whatever its nature, be reached by Congress if it exerts a substantial economic effect on interstate commerce, and this irrespective of whether such effect is what might at some earlier time have been defined as "direct" or "indirect.". . . .

The effect of consumption of home-grown wheat on interstate commerce is due to the fact that it constitutes the most variable factor in the disappearance of the wheat crop. Consumption on the farm where grown appears to vary in an amount greater than 20 per cent of average production. The total amount of wheat consumed as food varies but relatively little, and use as seed is relatively constant.

The maintenance by government regulation of a price for wheat undoubtedly can be accomplished as effectively by sustaining or increasing the demand as by limiting the supply. The effect of the statute before us is to restrict the amount which may be produced for market and the extent as well to which one may forestall resort to the market by producing to meet his own needs. That appellee's own contribution to the demand for wheat may be trivial by itself is not enough to remove him from the scope of federal regulation where, as here, his contribution, taken together with that of many others similarly situated, is far from trivial.

It is well established by decisions of this Court that the power to regulate commerce includes the power to regulate the prices at which commodities in that commerce are dealt in and practices affecting such prices. One of the primary purposes of the Act in question was to increase the market price of wheat, and to that end to limit the volume thereof that could affect the market. It can hardly be denied that a factor of such volume and variability as home-consumed wheat would have a substantial influence on price and market conditions. This may arise because being in marketable condition such wheat overhangs the market and, if induced

by rising prices, tends to flow into the market and check price increases. But if we assume that it is never marketed, it supplies a need of the man who grew it which would otherwise be reflected by purchases in the open market. Homegrown wheat in this sense competes with wheat in commerce. The stimulation of commerce is a use of the regulatory function quite as definitely as prohibitions or restrictions thereon. This record leaves us in no doubt that Congress may properly have considered that wheat consumed on the farm where grown, if wholly outside the scheme of regulation, would have a substantial effect in defeating and obstructing its purpose to stimulate trade therein at increased prices. . . .

Reversed.

With decisions such as *NLRB v. Jones & Laughlin Steel* and *Wickard v. Filburn*, the Court had entered a new era of Commerce Clause interpretation. No longer would the justices grapple with issues such as direct versus indirect effects or stream of commerce concerns. Under the modern interpretations very little commercial activity could be defined as purely intrastate. The legislature has taken great advantage of this discretion by regulating a vast number of activities that previous generations of justices might have considered outside the definition of "interstate commerce." This approach became firmly established in Commerce Clause jurisprudence.

Modern Limitations on the Commerce Power

Occasionally, individual justices have expressed doubts about the expansiveness of the modern definitions of interstate commerce. An example is Hugo Black's reaction to the Court's decision in **Daniel v. Paul** (1969). At issue was the application of federal regulations to the Lake Nixon Club, a small recreational facility located in a rural area of Arkansas, on county roads far from any interstate highway. To avoid desegregation laws, owner Euell Paul operated it as a private club, charging a nominal twenty-five cent membership fee for activities such as swimming, dancing, picnicking, and boating. The club served a local clientele: there was no evidence that any interstate traveler had ever used it. The Court ruled that the club operated in interstate commerce for the following reasons: (1) it advertised for business in publications known to be read by some interstate travelers; (2) it leased fifteen paddle boats from an Oklahoma company; (3) it owned a juke box and records that, while purchased from an Arkansas company, had been manufactured out of state; and (4) three out of the four items sold at the snack bar (for example, bread and soft drinks) contained ingredients from out of state.

This reasoning was too much for Justice Black. Although he opposed the racial policies of the club, Black nonetheless refused to accept the conclusion that this "sleepy hollow" was engaged in interstate commerce. The Court's decision, he argued, was "stretching the Commerce Clause so as to give the Federal Government complete control over every little remote country place of recreation in every nook and cranny of every precinct and county in every one of the 50 states. This goes too far for me." His dissent was ironic because Black was the first of the ardent New Deal justices.

In spite of such occasional protests that the Court has erased the distinction between inter- and intrastate commerce, the justices remained wedded to a broad interpretation of the congressional commerce power. The post–New Deal approach approximates Justice Cardozo's dissent in *Carter v. Carter Coal Co.*, in which he stated that the commerce power is "as broad as the need that evokes it."

That the Court remained loyal to this modern interpretation of the commerce power for six decades led constitutional scholars to conclude that it was "settled law." Perhaps that is why the Court's decision in *United States v. Lopez* (1995) was so shocking.[20] For the first time since the battles over the New Deal, the justices struck down a federal statute for falling outside the authority granted to Congress by the Commerce Clause.

20. To hear oral arguments in this case navigate to: *www.oyez.org/oyez/frontpage.*

United States v. Lopez

514 U.S. 549 (1995)
http://laws.findlaw.com/US/514/549.html
Vote: 5 (Kennedy, O'Connor, Rehnquist, Scalia, Thomas)
    4 (Breyer, Ginsburg, Souter, Stevens)
Opinion of the Court: Rehnquist
Concurring opinions: Kennedy, Thomas
Dissenting opinions: Breyer, Souter, Stevens

On March 10, 1992, Alfonso Lopez Jr. came to Edison High School carrying a concealed .38 caliber handgun and five rounds of ammunition. Acting on an anonymous tip, officials at the San Antonio school confronted the twelfth-grade student, and he admitted having the weapon. Lopez claimed that he had been given the gun by a person who instructed him to deliver it to another individual. The gun was to be used in gang-related activities. Lopez was arrested for violating the federal Gun-Free School Zones Act of 1990.

Lopez, who had no record of previous criminal activity, was convicted in federal district court and sentenced to six months in prison, two years of supervised release, and a fifty dollar fine. His attorneys appealed to the Fifth Circuit Court of Appeals, claiming that Congress had no constitutional authority to pass the Gun-Free School Zones Act. Attorneys for the United States countered by arguing that the law was an appropriate exercise of congressional power to regulate interstate commerce. The appeals court held in favor of Lopez, and the government asked the Supreme Court to review that ruling.

Congress passed the Gun-Free School Zones Act—section 922(q) of chapter 18 of the United States Code—in 1990. In passing the act, Congress did not issue any findings showing a relationship between gun possession on school property and commerce. The federal government argued that such findings should not be required, that it would be sufficient if Congress could reasonably conclude that gun-related violence in schools affects interstate commerce directly or indirectly. Lopez argued that the simple possession of a weapon on school grounds is not a commercial activity that reasonably falls under Commerce Clause jurisdiction. Furthermore, the regulation of crime and education are traditional areas of state, not federal, jurisdiction.

CHIEF JUSTICE REHNQUIST delivered the opinion of the Court.

In the Gun-Free School Zones Act of 1990, Congress made it a federal offense "for any individual knowingly to possess a firearm at a place that the individual knows, or has reasonable cause to believe, is a school zone." The Act neither regulates a commercial activity nor contains a requirement that the possession be connected in any way to interstate commerce. We hold that the Act exceeds the authority of Congress "[t]o regulate Commerce . . . among the several States.". . .

We start with first principles. The Constitution creates a Federal Government of enumerated powers. As James Madison wrote, "[t]he powers delegated by the proposed Constitution to the federal government are few and defined. Those which are to remain in the State governments are numerous and indefinite." This constitutionally mandated division of authority "was adopted by the Framers to ensure protection of our fundamental liberties." *Gregory v. Ashcroft*, (1991). . . .

. . . The Court, through Chief Justice Marshall, first defined the nature of Congress' commerce power in *Gibbons v. Ogden* (1824):

"Commerce, undoubtedly, is traffic, but it is something more: it is intercourse. It describes the commercial intercourse between nations, and parts of nations, in all its branches, and is regulated by prescribing rules for carrying on that intercourse."

The commerce power "is the power to regulate; that is, to prescribe the rule by which commerce is to be governed. This power, like all others vested in Congress, is complete in itself, may be exercised to its utmost extent, and acknowledges no limitations, other than are prescribed in the constitution." Id. . . .

For nearly a century thereafter, the Court's Commerce Clause decisions dealt but rarely with the extent of Congress' power, and almost entirely with the Commerce Clause as a limit on state legislation that discriminated against interstate commerce. . . . Under this line of precedent, the Court held that certain categories of activity such as "production," "manufacturing," and "mining" were within the province of state governments, and thus were beyond the power of Congress under the Commerce Clause. See *Wickard v. Filburn* (1942).

In 1887, Congress enacted the Interstate Commerce Act, and in 1890, Congress enacted the Sherman Antitrust Act. These laws ushered in a new era of federal regulation under the commerce power. When cases involving these laws first reached this Court, we imported from our negative Commerce Clause cases the approach that Congress could not regulate activities such as "production," "manufacturing," and "mining." See, e.g., *United States v. E. C. Knight Co.* (1895); *Carter v. Carter Coal Co.* (1936). Simultaneously, however, the Court held that, where the interstate and intrastate aspects of commerce were so mingled together that full regulation of interstate commerce required incidental regulation of intrastate commerce, the Commerce Clause authorized such regulation. See, e.g., *Houston, E. & W. T. R. Co. v. United States* (1914) (Shreveport Rate Cases).

In *A. L. A. Schechter Poultry Corp. v. United States* (1935), the Court struck down regulations that fixed the hours and wages of individuals employed by an intrastate business because the activity being regulated related to interstate commerce only indirectly. In doing so, the Court characterized the distinction between direct and indirect effects of intrastate transactions upon interstate commerce as "a fundamental one, essential to the maintenance of our constitutional system." Activities that affected interstate commerce directly were within Congress' power; activities that affected interstate commerce indirectly were beyond Congress' reach. The justification for this formal distinction was rooted in the fear that otherwise "there would be virtually no limit to the federal power and for all practical purposes we should have a completely centralized government."

Two years later, in the watershed case of *NLRB v. Jones & Laughlin Steel Corp.* (1937), the Court upheld the National Labor Relations Act against a Commerce Clause challenge, and in the process, departed from the distinction between "direct" and "indirect" effects on interstate commerce. The Court held that intrastate activities that "have such a close and substantial relation to interstate commerce that their control is essential or appropriate to protect that commerce from burdens and obstructions" are within Congress' power to regulate.

In *United States v. Darby* (1941), the Court upheld the Fair Labor Standards Act, stating:

"The power of Congress over interstate commerce is not confined to the regulation of commerce among the states. It extends to those activities intrastate which so affect interstate commerce or the exercise of the power of Congress over it as to make regulation of them appropriate means to the attainment of a legitimate end, the exercise of the granted power of Congress to regulate interstate commerce."

In *Wickard v. Filburn*, the Court upheld the application of amendments to the Agricultural Adjustment Act of 1938 to the production and consumption of homegrown wheat. The *Wickard* Court explicitly rejected earlier distinctions between direct and indirect effects on interstate commerce, stating:

"[E]ven if appellee's activity be local and though it may not be regarded as commerce, it may still, whatever its nature, be reached by Congress if it exerts a substantial economic effect on interstate commerce, and this irrespective of whether such effect is what might at some earlier time have been defined as 'direct' or 'indirect.'"

The *Wickard* Court emphasized that although Filburn's own contribution to the demand for wheat may have been trivial by itself, that was not "enough to remove him from the scope of federal regulation where, as here, his contribution, taken together with that of many others similarly situated, is far from trivial."

Jones & Laughlin Steel, Darby, and *Wickard* ushered in an era of Commerce Clause jurisprudence that greatly expanded the previously defined authority of Congress under that Clause. In part, this was a recognition of the great changes that had occurred in the way business was carried on in this country. Enterprises that had once been local or at most regional in nature had become national in scope. But the doctrinal change also reflected a view that earlier Commerce Clause cases artificially had constrained the authority of Congress to regulate interstate commerce.

But even these modern era precedents which have expanded congressional power under the Commerce Clause confirm that this power is subject to outer limits. In *Jones & Laughlin Steel,* the Court warned that the scope of the interstate commerce power "must be considered in the light of our dual system of government and may not be extended so as to embrace effects upon interstate commerce so indirect and remote that to embrace them, in view of our complex society, would effectually obliterate the distinction between what is national and what is local and create a completely centralized government." See also *Darby* (Congress may regulate intrastate activity that has a "substantial effect" on interstate commerce); *Wickard* (Congress may regulate activity that "exerts a substantial economic effect on interstate commerce"). Since that time, the Court has heeded that warning and undertaken to decide whether a rational basis existed for concluding that a regulated activity sufficiently affected interstate commerce. . . .

Consistent with this structure, we have identified three broad categories of activity that Congress may regulate under its commerce power. First, Congress may regulate the use of the channels of interstate commerce. Second, Congress is empowered to regulate and protect the instrumentalities of interstate commerce, or persons or things in interstate commerce, even though the threat may come only from intrastate activities. Finally, Congress' commerce authority includes the power to regulate those activities having a substantial relation to interstate commerce.

Within this final category, admittedly, our case law has not been clear whether an activity must "affect" or "substantially affect" interstate commerce in order to be within Congress' power to regulate it under the Commerce Clause. We conclude, consistent with the great weight of our case law, that the proper test requires an analysis of whether the regulated activity "substantially affects" interstate commerce.

We now turn to consider the power of Congress, in the light of this framework, to enact 922(q). The first two categories of authority may be quickly disposed of: 922(q) is not a regulation of the use of the channels of interstate commerce, nor is it an attempt to prohibit the interstate transportation of a commodity through the channels of commerce; nor can 922(q) be justified as a regulation by which Congress has sought to protect an instrumentality of interstate commerce or a thing in interstate commerce. Thus, if 922(q) is to be sustained, it must be under the third category as a regulation of an activity that substantially affects interstate commerce.

First, we have upheld a wide variety of congressional Acts regulating intrastate economic activity where we have concluded that the activity substantially affected interstate commerce. Examples include the regulation of intrastate coal mining, intrastate extortionate credit transactions, restaurants utilizing substantial interstate supplies, inns and hotels catering to interstate guests, and production and consumption of home-grown wheat. These examples are by no means exhaustive, but the pattern is clear. Where economic activity substantially affects interstate commerce, legislation regulating that activity will be sustained. . . .

Section 922(q) is a criminal statute that by its terms has nothing to do with "commerce" or any sort of economic enterprise, however broadly one might define those terms. Section 922(q) is not an essential part of a larger regulation of economic activity, in which the regulatory scheme could be undercut unless the intrastate activity were regulated. It cannot, therefore, be sustained under our cases upholding regulations of activities that arise out of or are connected with a commercial transaction, which viewed in the aggregate, substantially affects interstate commerce.

Second, 922(q) contains no jurisdictional element which would ensure, through case-by-case inquiry, that the firearm possession in question affects interstate commerce. For example, in *United States v. Bass* (1971), the Court interpreted former 18 U.S.C. 1202(a), which made it a crime for a felon to "receiv[e], posses[s], or transpor[t] in commerce or affecting commerce . . . any firearm." The Court interpreted the possession component of 1202(a) to require an additional nexus to interstate commerce both because the statute was ambiguous and because "unless Congress conveys its purpose clearly, it will not be deemed to have significantly changed the federal-state balance.". . . Unlike the statute in *Bass*, 922(q) has no express jurisdictional element which might limit its reach to a discrete set of firearm possessions that additionally have an explicit connection with or effect on interstate commerce.

Although as part of our independent evaluation of constitutionality under the Commerce Clause we of course consider legislative findings, and indeed even congressional committee findings, regarding effect on interstate commerce, the Government concedes that "[n]either the statute nor its legislative history contain[s] express congressional findings regarding the effects upon interstate commerce of gun possession in a school zone." We agree with the Government that Congress normally is not required to make formal findings as to the substantial burdens that an activity has on interstate commerce. But to the extent that congressional findings would enable us to evaluate the legislative judgment that the activity in question substantially affected interstate commerce, even though no such substantial effect was visible to the naked eye, they are lacking here. . . .

The Government's essential contention, *in fine*, is that we may determine here that 922(q) is valid because possession of a firearm in a local school zone does indeed substan-

tially affect interstate commerce. The Government argues that possession of a firearm in a school zone may result in violent crime and that violent crime can be expected to affect the functioning of the national economy in two ways. First, the costs of violent crime are substantial, and, through the mechanism of insurance, those costs are spread throughout the population. Second, violent crime reduces the willingness of individuals to travel to areas within the country that are perceived to be unsafe. The Government also argues that the presence of guns in schools poses a substantial threat to the educational process by threatening the learning environment. A handicapped educational process, in turn, will result in a less productive citizenry. That, in turn, would have an adverse effect on the Nation's economic well-being. As a result, the Government argues that Congress could rationally have concluded that 922(q) substantially affects interstate commerce.

We pause to consider the implications of the Government's arguments. The Government admits, under its "costs of crime" reasoning, that Congress could regulate not only all violent crime, but all activities that might lead to violent crime, regardless of how tenuously they relate to interstate commerce. Similarly, under the Government's "national productivity" reasoning, Congress could regulate any activity that it found was related to the economic productivity of individual citizens: family law (including marriage, divorce, and child custody), for example. Under the theories that the Government presents in support of 922(q), it is difficult to perceive any limitation on federal power, even in areas such as criminal law enforcement or education where States historically have been sovereign. Thus, if we were to accept the Government's arguments, we are hard-pressed to posit any activity by an individual that Congress is without power to regulate. . . .

Admittedly, a determination whether an intrastate activity is commercial or noncommercial may in some cases result in legal uncertainty. But, so long as Congress' authority is limited to those powers enumerated in the Constitution, and so long as those enumerated powers are interpreted as having judicially enforceable outer limits, congressional legislation under the Commerce Clause always will engender "legal uncertainty.". . .

These are not precise formulations, and in the nature of things they cannot be. But we think they point the way to a correct decision of this case. The possession of a gun in a local school zone is in no sense an economic activity that might, through repetition elsewhere, substantially affect any sort of interstate commerce. Respondent was a local student at a local school; there is no indication that he had recently moved in interstate commerce, and there is no requirement that his possession of the firearm have any concrete tie to interstate commerce.

To uphold the Government's contentions here, we would have to pile inference upon inference in a manner that would bid fair to convert congressional authority under the Commerce Clause to a general police power of the sort retained by the States. Admittedly, some of our prior cases have taken long steps down that road, giving great deference to congressional action. The broad language in these opinions has suggested the possibility of additional expansion, but we decline here to proceed any further. To do so would require us to conclude that the Constitution's enumeration of powers does not presuppose something not enumerated, and that there never will be a distinction between what is truly national and what is truly local. This we are unwilling to do. For the foregoing reasons the judgment of the Court of Appeals is

Affirmed.

JUSTICE BREYER, with whom JUSTICE STEVENS, JUSTICE SOUTER, and JUSTICE GINSBURG join, dissenting.

The issue in this case is whether the Commerce Clause authorizes Congress to enact a statute that makes it a crime to possess a gun in, or near, a school. In my view, the statute falls well within the scope of the commerce power as this Court has understood that power over the last half-century.

In reaching this conclusion, I apply three basic principles of Commerce Clause interpretation. First, the power to "regulate Commerce . . . among the several States" encompasses the power to regulate local activities insofar as they significantly affect interstate commerce. . . . I use the word "significant" because the word "substantial" implies a somewhat narrower power than recent precedent suggests. But, to speak of "substantial effect" rather than "significant effect" would make no difference in this case.

Second, in determining whether a local activity will likely have a significant effect upon interstate commerce,

a court must consider, not the effect of an individual act (a single instance of gun possession), but rather the cumulative effect of all similar instances (i.e., the effect of all guns possessed in or near schools).

Third, the Constitution requires us to judge the connection between a regulated activity and interstate commerce, not directly, but at one remove. Courts must give Congress a degree of leeway in determining the existence of a significant factual connection between the regulated activity and interstate commerce—both because the Constitution delegates the commerce power directly to Congress and because the determination requires an empirical judgment of a kind that a legislature is more likely than a court to make with accuracy. The traditional words "rational basis" capture this leeway. Thus, the specific question before us, as the Court recognizes, is not whether the "regulated activity sufficiently affected interstate commerce," but, rather, whether Congress could have had "a rational basis" for so concluding.

I recognize that we must judge this matter independently. "[S]imply because Congress may conclude that a particular activity substantially affects interstate commerce does not necessarily make it so." And, I also recognize that Congress did not write specific "interstate commerce" findings into the law under which Lopez was convicted. Nonetheless, as I have already noted, the matter that we review independently (i.e., whether there is a "rational basis") already has considerable leeway built into it. And, the absence of findings, at most, deprives a statute of the benefit of some extra leeway. This extra deference, in principle, might change the result in a close case, though, in practice, it has not made a critical legal difference. . . .

Applying these principles to the case at hand, we must ask whether Congress could have had a rational basis for finding a significant (or substantial) connection between gun-related school violence and interstate commerce. . . . As long as one views the commerce connection, not as a "technical legal conception," but as "a practical one," *Swift & Co. v. United States* (1905), the answer to this question must be yes. . . .

For one thing, reports, hearings, and other readily available literature make clear that the problem of guns in and around schools is widespread and extremely serious. . . . Congress obviously could have thought that guns and learning are mutually exclusive. And, Congress could therefore have found a substantial educational problem—teachers unable to teach, students unable to learn—and concluded that guns near schools contribute substantially to the size and scope of that problem.

Having found that guns in schools significantly undermine the quality of education in our Nation's classrooms, Congress could also have found, given the effect of education upon interstate and foreign commerce, that gun-related violence in and around schools is a commercial, as well as a human, problem. Education, although far more than a matter of economics, has long been inextricably intertwined with the Nation's economy. . . .

In recent years the link between secondary education and business has strengthened, becoming both more direct and more important. Scholars on the subject report that technological changes and innovations in management techniques have altered the nature of the workplace so that more jobs now demand greater educational skills. . . .

Increasing global competition also has made primary and secondary education economically more important. . . . Indeed, Congress has said, when writing other statutes, that "functionally or technologically illiterate" Americans in the work force "erod[e]" our economic "standing in the international marketplace," and that "our Nation is . . . paying the price of scientific and technological illiteracy, with our productivity declining, our industrial base ailing, and our global competitiveness dwindling."

Finally, there is evidence that, today more than ever, many firms base their location decisions upon the presence, or absence, of a work force with a basic education. . . .

The economic links I have just sketched seem fairly obvious. Why then is it not equally obvious, in light of those links, that a widespread, serious, and substantial physical threat to teaching and learning also substantially threatens the commerce to which that teaching and learning is inextricably tied? That is to say, guns in the hands of six percent of inner-city high school students and gun-related violence throughout a city's schools must threaten the trade and commerce that those schools support. The only question, then, is whether the latter threat is (to use the majority's terminology) "substantial." And, the evidence of (1) the extent of the gun-related violence problem, (2) the extent of the resulting negative effect on classroom learning, and (3) the extent of the consequent negative commercial effects, when taken together, indicate a threat to trade and commerce that is "substantial." At the very least, Congress could rationally have concluded that the links are "substantial."

Specifically, Congress could have found that gun-related violence near the classroom poses a serious economic threat (1) to consequently inadequately educated workers who must endure low paying jobs, and (2) to communities and businesses that might (in today's "information society") otherwise gain, from a well-educated work force, an important commercial advantage, of a kind that location near a railhead or harbor provided in the past. . . . The violence related facts, the educational facts, and the economic facts, taken together, make this conclusion rational. And, because under our case law, the sufficiency of the constitutionally necessary Commerce Clause link between a crime of violence and interstate commerce turns simply upon size or degree, those same facts make the statute constitutional.

The majority's holding—that 922 falls outside the scope of the Commerce Clause—creates three serious legal problems. First, the majority's holding runs contrary to modern Supreme Court cases that have upheld congressional actions despite connections to interstate or foreign commerce that are less significant than the effect of school violence. . . .

The second legal problem the Court creates comes from its apparent belief that it can reconcile its holding with earlier cases by making a critical distinction between "commercial" and noncommercial "transaction[s]." That is to say, the Court believes the Constitution would distinguish between two local activities, each of which has an identical effect upon interstate commerce, if one, but not the other, is "commercial" in nature. . . .

The third legal problem created by the Court's holding is that it threatens legal uncertainty in an area of law that, until this case, seemed reasonably well settled. . . .

In sum, to find this legislation within the scope of the Commerce Clause would permit "Congress . . . to act in terms of economic . . . realities." . . . Upholding this legislation would do no more than simply recognize that Congress had a "rational basis" for finding a significant connection between guns in or near schools and (through their effect on education) the interstate and foreign commerce they threaten. For these reasons, I would reverse the judgment of the Court of Appeals. Respectfully, I dissent.

Just how significant was *United States v. Lopez*? How did it fit into the Court's evolving Commerce Clause jurisprudence? Some interpreted it quite narrowly, as a simple warning to Congress that it must justify its legislation by showing the relationship between the activities regulated and interstate commerce. Had Congress explicitly demonstrated that it was responding to the negative impact school violence has on commerce, it is likely that the Court would have found no fault with the law. In any event, the decision was a relatively narrow one, with no indication that it represented a full-scale retreat from the body of Commerce Clause jurisprudence that flows almost seamlessly from *NLRB v. Jones & Laughlin Steel Corporation* onward.

Others viewed the decision as much more significant, a signal that the Court would no longer allow Congress to regulate whatever it wished on the ground that all activities somehow affect interstate commerce. These critics concluded that *Lopez* was not an isolated ruling, but that it should be considered in conjunction with *New York v. United States* (1992) and *Printz v. United States* (1997), other decisions in which a majority of the Rehnquist Court ruled against federal action that was seen as encroaching on the states.

The justices themselves seemed divided on what the case represented. In their concurring opinions, Justice Anthony Kennedy called *Lopez* a "limited holding," but Justice Clarence Thomas declared that it was time "to modify our Commerce Clause jurisprudence." The Court's 5–4 vote contributed additional uncertainty. Whether *Lopez* was an aberration or a signal that the Court was following Thomas's advice became more clear five years later, when the Court issued its decision in *United States v. Morrison*.[21]

21. To hear oral arguments in this case navigate to: *www.oyez.org/oyez/frontpage*.

United States v. Morrison

529 U.S. 598 (2000)
http://laws.findlaw.com/US/529/598.html
Vote: 5 (Kennedy, O'Connor, Rehnquist, Scalia, Thomas)
     4 (Breyer, Ginsburg, Souter, Stevens)
Opinion of the Court: Rehnquist
Concurring opinion: Thomas
Dissenting opinions: Breyer, Souter

Not long after Christy Brzonkala enrolled at Virginia Polytechnic Institute (Virginia Tech) in the fall of 1994, she met Antonio Morrison and James Crawford, members of the varsity football team. Brzonkala alleged that within thirty minutes of meeting Morrison and Crawford, they assaulted and repeatedly raped her. Brzonkala claimed that the attack caused her to become severely emotionally disturbed and depressed. In early 1995 she filed a complaint under the university's Sexual Assault Policy. At the subsequent hearing Morrison admitted having sexual contact with Brzonkala. Despite the fact that she had twice told him no, he claimed that the sexual activity was ultimately consensual. The Judicial Committee found insufficient evidence against Crawford, but it found Morrison guilty of sexual assault and sentenced him to an immediate suspension from the university for two semesters. Morrison appealed his conviction, and, because of procedural technicalities, the university retried Morrison under its Abusive Conduct Policy. This time Morrison was found guilty of "using abusive language" and sentenced once more to a two-semester suspension. Morrison again appealed. The university provost set aside Morrison's punishment. She concluded that it was "excessive" when compared with other convictions under the Abusive Conduct Policy. Morrison's final punishment was probation and minimal counseling.

Brzonkala then filed suit in federal district court against Morrison, Crawford, and Virginia Tech under 42 U.S.C. 13981, the Violence Against Women Act of 1994, which provided a federal civil remedy for the victims of gender-motivated violence. The district court held that Congress lacked the authority to pass this particular provision under either the Commerce Clause or the Fourteenth

Amendment. A divided court of appeals affirmed that conclusion. The United States intervened in the suit to defend the validity of the statute. Because of the importance of the case, the Supreme Court granted certiorari.

The justices concluded that Congress did not have the power to enact the challenged statute under the Fourteenth Amendment. In the portion of the decision excerpted here, the Court addresses Congress's authority to enact this legislation under the Commerce Clause.

CHIEF JUSTICE REHNQUIST delivered the opinion of the Court.

Due respect for the decisions of a coordinate branch of Government demands that we invalidate a congressional enactment only upon a plain showing that Congress has exceeded its constitutional bounds. With this presumption of constitutionality in mind, we turn to the question whether §13981 falls within Congress' power under Article I, §8, of the Constitution. Brzonkala and the United States rely upon the third clause of the Article, which gives Congress power "[t]o regulate Commerce with foreign Nations, and among the several States, and with the Indian Tribes."

As we discussed at length in *[United States v.] Lopez* [1995], our interpretation of the Commerce Clause has changed as our Nation has developed. We need not repeat that detailed review of the Commerce Clause's history here; it suffices to say that, in the years since *NLRB v. Jones & Laughlin Steel Corp.* (1937), Congress has had considerably greater latitude in regulating conduct and transactions under the Commerce Clause than our previous case law permitted.

Lopez emphasized, however, that even under our modern, expansive interpretation of the Commerce Clause, Congress' regulatory authority is not without effective bounds.

"[E]ven [our] modern-era precedents which have expanded congressional power under the Commerce Clause confirm that this power is subject to outer limits. In *Jones & Laughlin Steel*, the Court warned that the scope of the interstate commerce power 'must be considered in the light of our dual system of government and may not be extended so as to embrace effects upon interstate commerce so indirect and remote that to embrace them, in view of our complex society, would effectually obliterate the distinction between what is national and what is local and create a completely centralized government.' "

As we observed in *Lopez*, modern Commerce Clause jurisprudence has "identified three broad categories of activity that Congress may regulate under its commerce power." "First, Congress may regulate the use of the channels of interstate commerce." "Second, Congress is empowered to regulate and protect the instrumentalities of interstate commerce, or persons or things in interstate commerce, even though the threat may come only from intrastate activities." "Finally, Congress' commerce authority includes the power to regulate those activities having a substantial relation to interstate commerce, . . . i.e., those activities that substantially affect interstate commerce."

Petitioners do not contend that these cases fall within either of the first two of these categories of Commerce Clause regulation. They seek to sustain §13981 as a regulation of activity that substantially affects interstate commerce. . . .

Since *Lopez* most recently canvassed and clarified our case law governing this third category of Commerce Clause regulation, it provides the proper framework for conducting the required analysis of §13981. In *Lopez*, we held that the Gun-Free School Zones Act of 1990, which made it a federal crime to knowingly possess a firearm in a school zone, exceeded Congress' authority under the Commerce Clause. Several significant considerations contributed to our decision.

First, we observed that [the Gun-Free School Zones Act] was "a criminal statute that by its terms has nothing to do with 'commerce' or any sort of economic enterprise, however broadly one might define those terms.". . .

. . . *Lopez*'s review of Commerce Clause case law demonstrates that in those cases where we have sustained federal regulation of intrastate activity based upon the activity's substantial effects on interstate commerce, the activity in question has been some sort of economic endeavor.

The second consideration that we found important . . . was that the statute contained "no express jurisdictional element which might limit its reach to a discrete set of firearm possessions that additionally have an explicit connection with or effect on interstate commerce.". . .

Third, we noted that neither [the Gun-Free School Zones Act] " 'nor its legislative history contain[s] express congressional findings regarding the effects upon interstate commerce of gun possession in a school zone.' " While "Congress normally is not required to make formal findings as to the substantial burdens that an activity has on interstate commerce," the existence of such findings may "enable us to evaluate the legislative judgment that the activity in question substantially affect[s] interstate commerce, even though no such substantial effect [is] visible to the naked eye."

Finally, our decision in *Lopez* rested in part on the fact that the link between gun possession and a substantial effect on interstate commerce was attenuated. The United States argued that the possession of guns may lead to violent crime, and that violent crime "can be expected to affect the functioning of the national economy in two ways. First, the costs of violent crime are substantial, and, through the mechanism of insurance, those costs are spread throughout the population. Second, violent crime reduces the willingness of individuals to travel to areas within the country that are perceived to be unsafe." The Government also argued that the presence of guns at schools poses a threat to the educational process, which in turn threatens to produce a less efficient and productive workforce, which will negatively affect national productivity and thus interstate commerce.

We rejected these "costs of crime" and "national productivity" arguments because they would permit Congress to "regulate not only all violent crime, but all activities that might lead to violent crime, regardless of how tenuously they relate to interstate commerce.". . .

". . . Thus, if we were to accept the Government's arguments, we are hard pressed to posit any activity by an individual that Congress is without power to regulate." [*Lopez.*]

With these principles underlying our Commerce Clause jurisprudence as reference points, the proper resolution of the present cases is clear. Gender-motivated crimes of violence are not, in any sense of the phrase, economic activity. While we need not adopt a categorical rule against aggregating the effects of any noneconomic activity in order to decide these cases, thus far in our Nation's history our cases have upheld Commerce Clause regulation of intrastate activity only where that activity is economic in nature.

Like the Gun-Free School Zones Act at issue in *Lopez*, §13981 contains no jurisdictional element establishing that the federal cause of action is in pursuance of Congress' power to regulate interstate commerce. . . .

In contrast with the lack of congressional findings that we faced in *Lopez*, §13981 is supported by numerous findings regarding the serious impact that gender-motivated violence has on victims and their families. But the existence of congressional findings is not sufficient, by itself, to sustain the constitutionality of Commerce Clause legislation. As we stated in *Lopez*, " '[S]imply because Congress may conclude that a particular activity substantially affects interstate commerce does not necessarily make it so.' " Rather, " '[w]hether particular operations affect interstate commerce sufficiently to come under the constitutional power of Congress to regulate them is ultimately a judicial rather than a legislative question, and can be settled finally only by this Court.' "

. . . Congress' findings are substantially weakened by the fact that they rely so heavily on a method of reasoning that we have already rejected as unworkable if we are to maintain the Constitution's enumeration of powers. Congress found that gender-motivated violence affects interstate commerce

"by deterring potential victims from traveling interstate, from engaging in employment in interstate business, and from transacting with business, and in places involved in interstate commerce; . . . by diminishing national productivity, increasing medical and other costs, and decreasing the supply of and the demand for interstate products."

Given these findings and petitioners' arguments, the concern that we expressed in *Lopez* that Congress might use the Commerce Clause to completely obliterate the Constitution's distinction between national and local authority seems well founded. . . . If accepted, petitioners' reasoning would allow Congress to regulate any crime as long as the nationwide, aggregated impact of that crime has substantial effects on employment, production, transit, or consumption. Indeed, if Congress may regulate gender-motivated violence, it would be able to regulate murder or any other type of violence since gender-motivated violence, as a subset of all violent crime, is certain to have lesser economic impacts than the larger class of which it is a part.

Petitioners' reasoning, moreover, will not limit Congress to regulating violence but may, as we suggested in *Lopez*, be applied equally as well to family law and other areas of traditional state regulation since the aggregate effect of marriage, divorce, and childrearing on the national economy is undoubtedly significant. Congress may have recognized this specter when it expressly precluded §13981 from being used in the family law context. Under our written Constitution, however, the limitation of congressional authority is not solely a matter of legislative grace.

We accordingly reject the argument that Congress may regulate noneconomic, violent criminal conduct based solely on that conduct's aggregate effect on interstate commerce. The Constitution requires a distinction between what is truly national and what is truly local. In recognizing this fact we preserve one of the few principles that has been consistent since the Clause was adopted. The regulation and punishment of intrastate violence that is not directed at the instrumentalities, channels, or goods involved in interstate commerce has always been the province of the States. Indeed, we can think of no better example of the police power, which the Founders denied the National Government and reposed in the States, than the suppression of violent crime and vindication of its victims. . . .

Petitioner Brzonkala's complaint alleges that she was the victim of a brutal assault. . . . If the allegations here are true, no civilized system of justice could fail to provide her a remedy for the conduct of respondent Morrison. But under our federal system that remedy must be provided by the Commonwealth of Virginia, and not by the United States. The judgment of the Court of Appeals is

Affirmed.

JUSTICE SOUTER, with whom JUSTICE STEVENS, JUSTICE GINSBURG, and JUSTICE BREYER join, dissenting.

The Court says both that it leaves Commerce Clause precedent undisturbed and that the Civil Rights Remedy of the Violence Against Women Act of 1994 exceeds Congress's power under that Clause. I find the claims irreconcilable and respectfully dissent.

Our cases, which remain at least nominally undisturbed, stand for the following propositions. Congress has the power to legislate with regard to activity that, in the aggregate, has a substantial effect on interstate commerce. The fact of such a substantial effect is not an issue for the courts in the first instance, but for the Congress, whose institutional capacity for gathering evidence and taking testimony far exceeds ours. By passing legislation, Congress indicates its conclusion, whether explicitly or not, that facts support its exercise of the commerce power. The business of the courts is to review the congressional assessment, not for soundness but simply for the rationality of concluding that a jurisdictional basis exists in fact. Any explicit findings that Congress chooses to make, though not dispositive of the question of rationality, may advance judicial review by identifying fac-

tual authority on which Congress relied. Applying those propositions in these cases can lead to only one conclusion.

One obvious difference from *United States v. Lopez* (1995) is the mountain of data assembled by Congress, here showing the effects of violence against women on interstate commerce. Passage of the Act in 1994 was preceded by four years of hearings, which included testimony from physicians and law professors; from survivors of rape and domestic violence; and from representatives of state law enforcement and private business. The record includes reports on gender bias from task forces in 21 States, and we have the benefit of specific factual findings in the eight separate Reports issued by Congress and its committees over the long course leading to enactment. . . .

Congress thereby explicitly stated the predicate for the exercise of its Commerce Clause power. Is its conclusion irrational in view of the data amassed? True, the methodology of particular studies may be challenged, and some of the figures arrived at may be disputed. But the sufficiency of the evidence before Congress to provide a rational basis for the finding cannot seriously be questioned. . . .

The Act would have passed muster at any time between *Wickard* [v. *Filburn*] in 1942 and *Lopez* in 1995, a period in which the law enjoyed a stable understanding that congressional power under the Commerce Clause, complemented by the authority of the Necessary and Proper Clause, extended to all activity that, when aggregated, has a substantial effect on interstate commerce. . . .

The fact that the Act does not pass muster before the Court today is therefore proof, to a degree that *Lopez* was not, that the Court's nominal adherence to the substantial effects test is merely that. Although a new jurisprudence has not emerged with any distinctness, it is clear that some congressional conclusions about obviously substantial, cumulative effects on commerce are being assigned lesser values than the once-stable doctrine would assign them. These devaluations are accomplished not by any express repudiation of the substantial effects test or its application through the aggregation of individual conduct, but by supplanting rational basis scrutiny with a new criterion of review. . . .

All of this convinces me that today's ebb of the commerce power rests on error, and at the same time leads me to doubt that the majority's view will prove to be enduring law. There is yet one more reason for doubt. Although we sense the presence of [*Carter v.*] *Carter Coal* [1936], *Schechter*

BOX 7-6   AFTERMATH . . . *UNITED STATES V. MORRISON*

CHRISTY BRZONKALA arrived at Virginia Tech in 1994 with the goal of becoming a sports nutritionist. Antonio Morrison and James Crawford were members of the highly ranked Virginia Tech football team. They had dreams of careers in athletics, perhaps even in professional football. The ambitions of all three were shattered as the result of an incident in a dormitory room on a September evening just one month after the school year began. Brzonkala claimed that she was gang-raped by Morrison and Crawford. What followed was a tangled legal battle ending in the Supreme Court's decision in *United States v. Morrison* (2000). By the time the Supreme Court issued its opinion, the case had evolved into a federalism controversy over the extent to which Congress can regulate under its interstate commerce powers. Left behind were the lives of the three principals in the case.

Christy Brzonkala, with one of her attorneys, Kathryn Rodgers of the NOW Legal Defense Fund.

Brzonkala initially failed to tell anyone about the alleged assault. After several months of rarely leaving her room, performing poorly in her courses, and abusing thyroid medication, she finally came forward with her story. When the university refused to expel Morrison and Crawford, she dropped out of college and moved back to her home in Fairfax County, Virginia. Brzonkala resumed her academic career at George Mason University, but remained there only briefly. She then moved to Washington, D.C., and worked as a waitress. Brzonkala's suit against the university for sex discrimination was settled out of court. Virginia Tech agreed to pay her $75,000, but admitted no wrongdoing.

The football players argued that they were unfairly charged. Morrison claimed that his sexual encounter with Brzonkala was consensual, and Crawford said that he left the room before any sexual activity occurred. Although police investigated the incident, neither Morrison nor Crawford was charged with any criminal offense.

Morrison was placed on probation by the university, but was allowed to remain in school. Not long thereafter he was suspended from the football team, following his arrest during a bar brawl. He transferred to Hampton University, but returned to Virginia Tech a semester later. He did not play football again. He ultimately received a degree in human nutrition, foods, and exercise. After graduating, Morrison found it difficult to find work as an athletic trainer. He claimed that racial factors were partially responsible for the unfair treatment he received and the damage his reputation suffered.

James Crawford was later convicted of an unrelated sexual assault and disorderly conduct after an altercation in a parking lot. He was stripped of his football scholarship and left the university. He returned to his home state of Florida and began work in retail.

Although the Supreme Court held that the federal government had acted unconstitutionally in passing the Violence Against Women Act, Brzonkala was free to take her suit against Morrison and Crawford to state court. However, Brzonkala and her attorneys said there was little chance that they would do so. Such a suit would be for monetary damages, and, even if it were successful, Morrison and Crawford had little means of satisfying any judgment against them.

SOURCES: *Baltimore Sun*, January 8, 2000; *Washington Post*, May 20, 2000.

[*Poultry v. United States*, 1935], and [*National League of Cities v.*] *Usery* [1976] once again, the majority embraces them only at arm's-length. Where such decisions once stood for rules, today's opinion points to considerations by which substantial effects are discounted. Cases standing for the sufficiency of substantial effects are not overruled; cases overruled since 1937 are not quite revived. The Court's thinking betokens less clearly a return to the conceptual straitjackets of *Schechter* and *Carter Coal* and *Usery* than to something like the unsteady state of obscenity law between

Redrup v. New York (1967) and *Miller v. California* (1973), a period in which the failure to provide a workable definition left this Court to review each case ad hoc. As our predecessors learned then, the practice of such ad hoc review cannot preserve the distinction between the judicial and the legislative, and this Court, in any event, lacks the institutional capacity to maintain such a regime for very long. This one will end when the majority realizes that the conception of the commerce power for which it entertains hopes would inevitably fail the test expressed in Justice Holmes's statement that "[t]he first call of a theory of law is that it should fit the facts." The facts that cannot be ignored today are the facts of integrated national commerce and a political relationship between States and Nation much affected by their respective treasuries and constitutional modifications adopted by the people. The federalism of some earlier time is no more adequate to account for those facts today than the theory of laissez-faire was able to govern the national economy 70 years ago.

By the same 5–4 vote as occurred in *Lopez* and using the same reasoning, the Supreme Court struck down the Violence Against Women Act. Four months later the justices in *Jones v. United States* (2000) held that a federal criminal statute against arson, passed pursuant to the interstate commerce power, could not be applied to a man who tossed a Molotov cocktail into his cousin's house. Because the target of the arson was a private residence not used in any commercial activity, the Court concluded that Congress under the Commerce Clause had no authority to regulate.

The Court reinforced this revised view of the federal commerce power in *Solid Waste Agency of Northern Cook County v. United States Army Corps of Engineers* (2001), a case presenting a very different factual story than those challenging the authority of Congress to regulate gun possession, rape, or arson. At issue was an application of the federal Clean Water Act. A consortium of twenty-three Chicago-area cities attempted to develop a solid waste facility on a 533-acre parcel that previously had been used as a sand and gravel pit operation. The site included a series of small ponds, some permanent and others seasonal. The Army Corps of Engineers claimed that

federal approval was necessary before development could take place because the ponds were used as habitats by migratory birds that cross state lines. The Court, in another 5–4 ruling, held that the Corps action impinged on the states' traditional power over land and water use, and that there was no evidence that Congress's regulation of navigable waters extended to abandoned gravel pits.

The *Lopez, Morrison, Jones,* and *Solid Waste* cases, taken together with other Rehnquist Court federalism and taxation decisions, clearly demonstrate that the justices have modified their Commerce Clause jurisprudence *(see Box 7-7)*. Following the New Deal revolution, the federal government was given wide latitude to regulate in the name of interstate commerce. But in recent decisions the Court has cautioned that the Commerce Clause does not give Congress a blank check. How important this evolution in doctrine is remains to be seen. Thus far, the Court has not nullified any major federal programs because Congress has overstepped its power to regulate under the Commerce Clause, and the states are fully competent to legislate in those areas where the Court has declared federal action impermissible. In addition, the most significant decisions in this line of cases have been decided by 5–4 votes, leaving the Court's modified position vulnerable to change as new justices are appointed.

REGULATING COMMERCE AS A FEDERAL POLICE POWER

"Police power" refers to the general authority of a government to regulate for the health, safety, morals, and general welfare of its citizens. The states possessed general police powers prior to the adoption of the federal Constitution and retained them when the national government was created. Consequently, states may pass laws for the general welfare without any specific grant of power to do so. As long as the legislation does not run afoul of specific constitutional limitations (such as the Bill of Rights), the state is free to act.

The federal government, on the other hand, is a government of delegated powers. It does not possess any general police power. For a piece of federal legislation to be valid, it must rest on a specific grant of authority—an enumerated, implied, or inherent power. Madison

BOX 7-7   THE EVOLUTION OF INTERSTATE COMMERCE DOCTRINE

MARSHALL INTERPRETATION

Gibbons v. Ogden (1824)
Marshall opinion for 6–0 Court

Commerce begins in one state and ends in another. It does not stop when the act of crossing a state border is completed. Commerce occurring within a state may be part of a larger interstate process.

SHREVEPORT DOCTRINE

Shreveport Rate Case (1914)
Hughes opinion for a 7–2 Court

Congress may regulate intrastate commerce when it is intertwined with interstate commerce and a failure to regulate intrastate commerce would injure interstate commerce.

STREAM OF COMMERCE DOCTRINE

Swift and Company v. United States (1905)
Holmes opinion for 9–0 Court

Stafford v. Wallace (1922)
Taft opinion for a 7–1 Court

An article in interstate commerce does not lose its status until it reaches its final destination. Stopping along the way to its terminal sale does not remove an article from the stream of interstate commerce.

MANUFACTURING EXCLUDED FROM INTERSTATE COMMERCE

United States v. E. C. Knight Co. (1895)
Fuller opinion for an 8–1 Court

Schechter Poultry v. United States (1935)
Hughes opinion for a 9–0 Court

Carter v. Carter Coal Co. (1936)
Sutherland opinion for a 5–4 Court

Manufacturing, processing, and mining activities are local by nature and not a part of interstate commerce. Their effect on interstate commerce is indirect. That an article is intended for interstate commerce does not make its manufacture part of interstate commerce. Commerce succeeds to manufacture and is not a part of it.

MODERN INTERPRETATION OF INTERSTATE COMMERCE

NLRB v. Jones & Laughlin Steel Corp. (1937)
Hughes opinion for a 5–4 Court

Congress may enact all appropriate legislation to protect, advance, promote, and insure interstate commerce. Although activities may be intrastate in character when separately considered, if they have such a close and substantial relation to interstate commerce that their control is essential or appropriate to protect that commerce from burdens and obstructions, Congress cannot be denied the power to exercise that control.

COMMERCE POWER LIMITATIONS

United States v. Lopez (1995)
Rehnquist opinion for a 5–4 Court

United States v. Morrison (2000)
Rehnquist opinion for a 5–4 Court

Federal legislation is constitutionally suspect if it does not regulate an economic activity that, in the aggregate, substantially affects interstate commerce.

described the situation aptly in Federalist Paper No. 45: the "powers delegated by the proposed Constitution to the federal government are few and defined. Those which are to remain in the State governments are numerous and indefinite."

Take, for example, the problem of violence in schools that we discussed in the previous section. Based on its police powers, a state could pass legislation making it a crime to carry a firearm onto school grounds without any justification necessary. The federal government, however, could pass such a law only if Congress could justify it as an exercise of a delegated power. Consequently, we have the dispute in *United States v. Lopez* over whether the federal Gun-Free School Zones Act was a valid exercise of the power to regulate interstate commerce.

Historically, battles over the meaning of interstate commerce have been almost exclusively economic. The regulation of commerce, however, can be structured in a way that affects matters of health, safety, and morals. This poses an exceptionally important question: May Congress legitimately use the Commerce Clause as means of exercising an authority at the national level similar to the states' police powers? If so, then federal power expands far beyond that envisioned by the Framers.

Initial Rulings on Federal Police Powers

In 1903 the Court issued its first significant ruling on this question. At issue in *Champion v. Ames* was a federal law prohibiting the movement of lottery tickets in interstate commerce. The case demonstrates how Congress can use the regulation of commerce to depress certain activities. This goal is much different from those that are present when Congress regulates commerce for economic reasons. In reading Justice John Marshall Harlan's opinion for the Court, notice the expansive terms he uses to describe the commerce power. Does he convince you that the Commerce Clause can be stretched to include the power to prohibit what Congress thought was an immoral trade? The four dissenters did not think so. They argued that Congress was not regulating commerce at all but was really trying to prohibit lotteries, a matter for the police powers of the state to address.

Champion v. Ames

188 U.S. 321 (1903)
http://laws.findlaw.com/US/188/321.html
Vote: 5 (Brown, Harlan, Holmes, McKenna, White)
     4 (Brewer, Fuller, Peckham, Shiras)
Opinion of the Court: Harlan
Dissenting opinion: Fuller

In 1895 Congress passed a statute prohibiting lottery tickets from interstate or foreign commerce and from being sent through the mail. Federal authorities charged Charles Champion with violating this act. Champion had arranged for a shipment of lottery tickets, supposedly printed in Paraguay, to be transported from Texas to California by the Wells Fargo Company. He challenged his arrest on several grounds, arguing that he was not engaged in interstate commerce, that the power to regulate interstate commerce did not include the authority to prohibit items from such commerce, and that lotteries should be regulated only through the police powers of the states.

MR. JUSTICE HARLAN delivered the opinion of the Court.

What is the import of the word "commerce" as used in the Constitution? It is not defined by that instrument. Undoubtedly, the carrying from one State to another by independent carriers of things or commodities that are ordinary subjects of traffic, and which have in themselves a recognized value in money, constitutes interstate commerce. But does not commerce among the several States include something more? Does not the carrying from one State to another, by independent carriers, of lottery tickets that entitle the holder to the payment of a certain amount of money therein specified also constitute commerce among the States? . . .

The leading case under the commerce clause of the Constitution is *Gibbons v. Ogden*. Referring to that clause, Chief Justice Marshall said: ". . . This power, like all others vested in Congress, is *complete in itself*, may be exercised *to its utmost extent*, and acknowledges *no limitations, other than are prescribed in the Constitution*. These are expressed in plain terms, and do not affect the questions which arise in this case or which have been discussed at the bar. If, as has always been understood, the sovereignty of Congress, though limited to specified objects, is plenary as to those objects, the power over commerce with foreign nations, and among the several States, is vested in Congress *as absolutely as it would be in a single government, having in its constitution the same restrictions on the exercise of the power as are found in the Constitution of the United States.".* . . .

. . . [P]rior adjudications . . . sufficiently indicate the grounds upon which this court has proceeded when determining the meaning and scope of the commerce clause. They show that commerce among the States embraces navigation, intercourse, communication, traffic, the transit of persons, and the transmission of messages by telegraph. They also show that the power to regulate commerce among the several States is vested in Congress as absolutely as it would be in a single government, having in its constitution the same restrictions on the exercise of the power as are found in the Constitution of the United States; that such power is plenary, complete in itself, and may be exerted by Congress to its utmost extent, subject *only* to such limitations as the Constitution imposes upon the exercise of the powers granted by it; and that in determining the character of the regulations to be adopted Congress has a large discretion which is not to be controlled by the courts, simply because, in their opinion, such regulations may not be the best or most effective that could be employed.

We come then to inquire whether there is any solid foundation upon which to rest the contention that Congress may not regulate the carrying of lottery tickets from one State to another, at least by corporations or companies whose business it is, for hire, to carry tangible property from one State to another. . . .

We are of opinion that lottery tickets are subjects of traffic and therefore are subjects of commerce, and the regulation of the carriage of such tickets from State to State, at least by independent carriers, is a regulation of commerce among the several States. . . .

It is to be remarked that the Constitution does not define what is to be deemed a legitimate regulation of interstate commerce. In *Gibbons v. Ogden* it was said that the power to regulate such commerce is the power to prescribe the rule by which it is to be governed. But this general ob-

servation leaves it to be determined, when the question comes before the court, whether Congress in prescribing a particular rule has exceeded its power under the Constitution. While our Government must be acknowledged by all to be one of enumerated powers, the Constitution does not attempt to set forth all the means by which such powers may be carried into execution. It leaves to Congress a large discretion as to the means that may be employed in executing a given power. . . .

If a State, when considering legislation for the suppression of lotteries within its own limits, may properly take into view the evils that inhere in the raising of money, in that mode, why may not Congress, invested with the power to regulate commerce among the several States, provide that such commerce shall not be polluted by the carrying of lottery tickets from one State to another? In this connection it must not be forgotten that the power of Congress to regulate commerce among the States is plenary, is complete in itself, and is subject to no limitations except such as may be found in the Constitution. What provision in that instrument can be regarded as limiting the exercise of the power granted? What clause can be cited which, in any degree, countenances the suggestion that one may, of right, carry or cause to be carried from one State to another that which will harm the public morals? We cannot think of any clause of that instrument that could possibly be invoked by those who assert their right to send lottery tickets from State to State except the one providing that no person shall be deprived of his liberty without the due process of law. We have said that the liberty protected by the Constitution embraces the right to be free in the enjoyment of one's faculties; "to be free to use them in all lawful ways; to live and work where he will; to earn his livelihood by any lawful calling; to pursue any livelihood or avocation, and for that purpose to enter into all contracts that may be proper." But surely it will not be said to be a part of any one's liberty, as recognized by the supreme law of the land, that he shall be allowed to introduce into commerce among the States an element that will be confessedly injurious to the public morals. . . .

Besides, Congress, by that act, does not assume to interfere with traffic or commerce in lottery tickets carried on exclusively within the limits of any State, but has in view only commerce of that kind among the several States. It has not assumed to interfere with the completely internal affairs of any State, and has only legislated in respect of a matter which concerns the people of the United States. As a State may, for the purpose of guarding the morals of its own people, forbid all sales of lottery tickets within its limits, so Congress, for the purpose of guarding the people of the United States against the "widespread pestilence of lotteries" and to protect the commerce which concerns all the States, may prohibit the carrying of lottery tickets from one State to another. . . .

The whole subject is too important, and the questions suggested by its consideration are too difficult of solution to justify any attempt to lay down a rule for determining in advance the validity of every statute that may be enacted under the commerce clause. We decide nothing more in the present case than that lottery tickets are subjects of traffic among those who choose to sell or buy them; that the carriage of such tickets by independent carriers from one State to another is therefore interstate commerce; that under its power to regulate commerce among the several States Congress—subject to the limitations imposed by the Constitution upon the exercise of the powers granted—has plenary authority over such commerce, and may prohibit the carriage of such tickets from State to State; and that legislation to that end, and of that character, is not inconsistent with any limitation or restriction imposed upon the exercise of the powers granted to Congress.

The judgment is

Affirmed.

MR. CHIEF JUSTICE FULLER, with whom concur MR. JUSTICE BREWER, MR. JUSTICE SHIRAS, and MR. JUSTICE PECKHAM, dissenting.

The naked question is whether the prohibition by Congress of the carriage of lottery tickets from one State to another by means other than the mails is within the powers vested in that body by the Constitution of the United States. That the purpose of Congress in this enactment was the suppression of lotteries cannot reasonably be denied. That purpose is avowed in the title of the act, and is its natural and reasonable effect, and by that its validity must be tested.

The power of the State to impose restraints and burdens on persons and property in conservation and promotion of the public health, good order and prosperity is a power originally and always belonging to the States, not surren-

dered by them to the General Government nor directly restrained by the Constitution of the United States, and essentially exclusive, and the suppression of lotteries as a harmful business falls within this power, commonly called of police.

It is urged, however, that because Congress is empowered to regulate commerce between the several States, it, therefore, may suppress lotteries by prohibiting the carriage of lottery matter. Congress may indeed make all laws necessary and proper for carrying the powers granted to it into execution, and doubtless an act prohibiting the carriage of lottery matter would be necessary and proper to the execution of a power to suppress lotteries; but that power belongs to the States and not to Congress. To hold that Congress has general police power would be to hold that it may accomplish objects not entrusted to the General Government, and to defeat the operation of the Tenth Amendment, declaring that: "The powers not delegated to the United States by the Constitution, nor prohibited by it to the States, are reversed to the States respectively, or to the people."

The *Champion* case set the precedent that Congress may indeed use the Commerce Clause in much the same manner as states use their police powers. In the years following *Champion*, the legislature passed a number of laws designed to accomplish social, not economic, goals through the exercise of the commerce power. For example, in 1906 Congress approved the Meat Inspection Act and the Pure Food and Drug Act, which prohibited contaminated foods from interstate commerce. Five years later the Supreme Court upheld the food and drug act as a proper exercise of the commerce power.[22] In 1910, as a method of curtailing interstate prostitution rings, Congress passed the Mann Act, making it a criminal violation to take "any woman or girl" across state lines "for the purpose of prostitution or debauchery, or for any other immoral purpose." The Supreme Court unanimously ruled that the federal government has the authority under the Commerce Clause to prohibit such movement among the states.[23] In addition, Congress passed various laws that federalized criminal activity that extends beyond the boundaries of a single state. Kidnap-

22. See *Hipolite Egg Company v. United States* (1911).
23. *Hoke v. United States* (1913).

ping that crosses state lines, interstate transportation of stolen property, or even interstate flight to avoid prosecution are all federal crimes because of Congress's power to regulate commerce among the states.

In the matter of child labor, however, the Court dealt a significant blow to the development of police powers. In *Hammer v. Dagenhart*, discussed in Chapter 6, the Court struck down the Keating-Owen Act of 1916, which barred from interstate commerce any goods produced by child labor. In the Court's thinking at that time, the manufacture of goods was intrastate commerce and therefore to be regulated only by the states. The justices saw the law as a regulation of the manufacturing stage rather than a regulation of interstate commerce. The decision was not so much a rejection of the power of Congress to regulate social matters as it was a reminder that the social problems must be a part of interstate commerce before Congress can use the Commerce Clause to justify action against them.

Modern Uses of the Commerce Power to Regulate Social Evils

With each expansion of the definition of interstate commerce that occurred after 1936, there was a commensurate expansion of the federal police powers. These changes gave Congress sufficient power to combat social problems that it otherwise would be unable to fight effectively. Modern civil rights laws provide a good example. The constitutional protections against discrimination are found primarily in the Equal Protection Clause of the Fourteenth Amendment and the Due Process Clause of the Fifth, which have erected powerful barriers against invidious discrimination. But their exclusive target is discrimination perpetuated by the government. The words of the Fourteenth Amendment, for example, are clear: "Nor shall any state . . . deny to any person within its jurisdiction the equal protection of the laws." Nothing in the Fifth or Fourteenth Amendments prohibits discrimination by private parties. These amendments were not intended to prohibit a private citizen from being discriminatory, but only to bar discriminatory government action. Although the Fourteenth Amendment includes a clause giving Congress the authority to enforce the pro-

vision with appropriate legislation, the Supreme Court has ruled that such enforcement legislation may not extend beyond the scope of the amendment itself. Consequently, the amendment does not empower Congress to regulate private discriminatory behavior.

When the civil rights movement of the 1950s and 1960s campaigned for the elimination of discriminatory conditions, high on its list was the eradication of discrimination by private parties who operated public accommodations. Targeted were the owners of hotels, restaurants, movie theaters, recreation areas, and transportation systems. In the aftermath of *Brown v. Board of Education* (1954), governments could not maintain laws mandating segregation of such facilities, but private operators could still impose discrimination on their own. In the South, where segregation was the way of life, no one expected the states to pass civil rights statutes prohibiting private parties from discriminating. Therefore, civil rights advocates pressured Congress to do something about the situation.

Congress responded with passage of the Civil Rights Act of 1964, the most comprehensive legislation of its type ever passed. The act, as amended, is still the nation's most significant statute aimed at eliminating discrimination. However, the primary authority for passing this groundbreaking legislation was not a clause in the Bill of Rights or one of the Civil War amendments, but the Commerce Clause. Because the Court had treated Commerce Clause legislation favorably since 1937, members of Congress had confidence that the Civil Rights Act would withstand a legal challenge. Opponents of the legislation argued that Congress had misused its power to regulate commerce by invoking it as justifying a civil rights law. Obviously, they said, the Framers, many of whom owned slaves, did not intend the power to regulate commerce among the states to be used to enact civil rights legislation.

Was Congress on solid ground in doing so? The primary test of the law's constitutionality was *Heart of Atlanta Motel v. United States* (1964).[24] As you read this case,

---

24. To hear oral arguments in this case navigate to: *www.oyez.org/oyez/frontpage*.

Moreton Rolleston Jr., owner of the Heart of Atlanta Motel, who challenged the constitutionality of the Civil Rights Act of 1964.

note Justice Tom C. Clark's description of how racial discrimination has a negative impact on interstate commerce. Also note the Court's expansive view of interstate commerce and its conclusion that the Commerce Clause can be used to combat moral wrongs.

Heart of Atlanta Motel v. United States

379 U.S. 241 (1964)
http://laws.findlaw.com/US/379/241.html
Vote: 9 (Black, Brennan, Clark, Douglas, Goldberg, Harlan,
*   Stewart, Warren, White)*
          0
Opinion of the Court: Clark
Concurring opinions: Black, Douglas, Goldberg

Title II of the 1964 Civil Rights Act in its original form prohibited discrimination on the basis of race, color, religion, or national origin by certain public accommodations that operated in or affected interstate commerce. The accommodations specifically included were:

1. Inns, hotels, motels, or other lodging facilities of five rooms or more. Because they served the traveling public, these facilities were considered part of interstate commerce by definition.

2. Restaurants and cafeterias, if they served interstate travelers or if a substantial portion of their food or other products had moved in interstate commerce.

3. Motion picture houses, if they presented films that had moved in interstate commerce.

4. Any facility physically located within any of the other covered accommodations, which included operations such as hotel shops and theater snack bars.

The Heart of Atlanta Motel was a 216-room facility in Atlanta, Georgia. Located near the commercial center of the city, it had easy access to two interstate highways and two major state roads. The motel advertised for business in national publications and maintained more than fifty billboards and highway signs around the state. Both the government and the motel agreed that the facility met the act's definition of a public accommodation in interstate commerce.

The motel admitted that prior to the enactment of the civil rights law it practiced a policy of racial discrimination. Furthermore, it acknowledged that it intended to continue its policy of not serving blacks. To secure its right to do so, the motel filed suit to have the 1964 Civil Rights Act declared unconstitutional.

MR. JUSTICE CLARK delivered the opinion of the Court.

The Basis of Congressional Action.

While the Act as adopted carried no congressional findings the record of its passage through each house is replete with evidence of the burdens that discrimination by race or color places upon interstate commerce. This testimony included the fact that our people have become increasingly mobile with millions of people of all races traveling from State to State; that Negroes in particular have been the subject of discrimination in transient accommodations, having to travel great distances to secure the same; that often they have been unable to obtain accommodations and have had to call upon friends to put them up overnight; and that these conditions had become so acute as to require the listing of available lodging for Negroes in a special guidebook which was itself "dramatic testimony to the difficulties" Negroes encounter in travel. These exclusionary practices were found to be nationwide, the Under Secretary of Commerce testifying that there is "no question that this discrimination in the North still exists to a large degree" and in the West and Midwest as well. This testimony indicated a qualitative as well as a quantitative effect on interstate travel by Negroes. The former was the obvious impairment of the Negro traveler's pleasure and convenience that resulted when he continually was uncertain of finding lodging. As for the latter, there was evidence that this uncertainty stemming from racial discrimination had the effect of discouraging travel on the part of a substantial portion of the Negro community. This was the conclusion not only of the Under Secretary of Commerce but also of the Administrator of the Federal Aviation Agency who wrote the Chairman of the Senate Commerce Committee that it was his "belief that air commerce is adversely affected by the denial to a substantial segment of the traveling public of adequate and desegregated public accommodations." We shall not burden this opinion with further details since the voluminous testimony presents overwhelming evidence that discrimination by hotels and motels impedes interstate travel.

The Power of Congress Over Interstate Travel.

The power of Congress to deal with these obstructions depends on the meaning of the Commerce Clause. Its meaning was first enunciated 140 years ago by the great Chief Justice John Marshall in *Gibbons v. Ogden* (1824), in these words:

"The subject to be regulated is commerce; and . . . to ascertain the extent of the power, it becomes necessary to settle the meaning of the word. The counsel for the appellee would limit it to traffic, to buying and selling, or the interchange of commodities . . . but it is something more: it is intercourse . . . between nations, and parts of nations, in all its branches, and is regulated by prescribing rules for carrying on that intercourse.

"To what commerce does this power extend? The constitution informs us, to commerce 'with foreign nations and among the several States, and with the Indian tribes.'

"It has, we believe, been universally admitted, that these words comprehend every species of commercial intercourse. . . . No sort of trade can be carried on . . . to which this power does not extend.

"The subject to which the power is next applied, is to commerce 'among the several States,' The word 'among' means intermingled.". . .

In short, the determinative test of the exercise of power by the Congress under the Commerce Clause is simply whether the activity sought to be regulated is "commerce which concerns more States than one" and has a real and substantial relation to the national interest. Let us now turn to this facet of the problem.

That the "intercourse" of which the Chief Justice spoke included the movement of persons through more States than one was settled as early as 1849, in the *Passenger Cases*, where Mr. Justice McLean stated: "That the transportation of passengers is a part of commerce is not now an open question." Again in 1913 Mr. Justice McKenna, speaking for the Court, said: "Commerce among the States, we have said, consists of intercourse and traffic between their citizens, and includes the transportation of persons and property. . . . Nor does it make any difference whether the transportation is commercial in character.". . .

The same interest in protecting interstate commerce which led Congress to deal with segregation in interstate carriers and the white-slave traffic has prompted it to extend the exercise of its power to gambling; to criminal enterprises; to deceptive practices in the sale of products; to fraudulent security transactions; to misbranding of drugs; to wages and hours; to members of labor unions; to crop control; to discrimination against shippers; to the protection of small business from injurious price cutting; to resale price maintenance; to professional football; and to racial discrimination by owners and managers of terminal restaurants.

That Congress was legislating against moral wrongs in many of these areas rendered its enactments no less valid.

In framing Title II of this Act Congress was also dealing with what it considered a moral problem. But that fact does not detract from the overwhelming evidence of the disruptive effect that racial discrimination has had on commercial intercourse. It was this burden which empowered Congress to enact appropriate legislation, and, given this basis for the exercise of its power, Congress was not restricted by the fact that the particular obstruction to interstate commerce with which it was dealing was also deemed a moral and social wrong.

It is said that the operation of the motel here is of a purely local character. But . . . the power of Congress to promote interstate commerce also includes the power to regulate the local incidents thereof, including local activities in both the States of origin and destination, which might have a substantial and harmful effect upon that commerce. One need only examine the evidence which we have discussed above to see that Congress may—as it has—prohibit racial discrimination by motels serving travelers, however "local" their operations may appear. . . .

We, therefore, conclude that the action of the Congress in the adoption of the Act as applied here to a motel which concededly serves interstate travelers is within the power granted it by the Commerce Clause of the Constitution, as interpreted by this Court for 140 years. It may be argued that Congress could have pursued other methods to eliminate the obstructions it found in interstate commerce caused by racial discrimination. But this is a matter of policy that rests entirely with the Congress not with the courts. How obstructions in commerce may be removed—what means are to be employed—is within the sound and exclusive discretion of the Congress. It is subject only to one caveat—that the means chosen by it must be reasonably adapted to the end permitted by the Constitution. We cannot say that its choice here was not so adapted. The Constitution requires no more.

Affirmed.

Employing the same sweeping language as the Court used in *Wickard v. Filburn* to declare wheat grown for home consumption to be in interstate commerce, Justice Clark's opinion gives Congress broad powers to use the Commerce Clause as authority to regulate moral wrongs that occur in interstate commerce. In this way, the Commerce Clause became one of the most powerful weapons in the federal government's arsenal not only to regulate the economy but also to use as a police power.

While a broad interpretation of Congress's regulatory powers under the Commerce Clause has become generally accepted, the Court's recent restrictions on the commerce power must not be forgotten. In decisions such as *Lopez* and *Morrison,* the justices found that the congressional regulation of firearms in school yards and sexual assaults intruded on areas reserved for state legislation. It is clear that the modern Court is demanding that congressional regulation of social evils under the Commerce Clause must be justified by showing that the target of the regulation has a substantial effect on interstate commerce.

THE COMMERCE POWER OF THE STATES

Resolving the question of federal power over interstate and foreign commerce leaves unsettled the question of state commercial regulation. Marshall wrote in *Gibbons* that commerce completely internal to the state that does not extend to or affect other states is reserved for state regulation. This grant of power was substantial prior to the Civil War when most commercial activity was distinctly local and subject to state regulation. But with the Industrial Revolution and improved transportation systems, business became increasingly interstate in nature. Finally, the Supreme Court's 1937 redefinition of interstate commerce left little that met Marshall's notion of commerce that is "completely internal."

If the regulation of any business activity that affects interstate commerce were the exclusive preserve of the federal government, the role of the states would be minimal indeed. But this is not the case. The decisions of the Supreme Court have left a substantial sphere of authority for the states to regulate commerce. The dividing line between federal and state power, however, has varied over time as the Supreme Court has struggled in building an appropriate doctrine to govern this difficult area of federal-state relations.

The Doctrine of Selected Exclusiveness

Constructing the parameters of state power began in 1829 with the decision in **Willson v. Black-Bird Creek Marsh**

Company.[25] The dispute involved a Delaware law that authorized the building of a dam on a creek to stop water from entering a local marsh. Thompson Willson owned and operated a vessel that was federally licensed under the Coastal Licensing Act of 1793, the same legislation under which Thomas Gibbons had operated his steamboats. Willson objected to the dam as an impediment to commerce on a navigable stream. His ship purposefully rammed the dam, causing it considerable damage. The company that owned the dam took legal action against Willson, and the state courts ruled in favor of the company. Willson appealed, claiming that the Delaware law authorizing the dam was in conflict with the federal constitution. He argued that only Congress had the power to pass a law permitting the construction of an impediment to commerce on a navigable stream.

Chief Justice Marshall, speaking for the Court, rejected Willson's position. The justices concluded that, in the absence of federal laws to the contrary, the police powers of the state to regulate for the health and general welfare of its citizens were sufficient to authorize the construction of the dam. Indeed, Congress had not enacted any legislation dealing with commercial streams and the problems associated with marshland. "If congress had passed any act . . . the object of which was to control state legislation over those small navigable creeks into which the tide flows," Marshall's opinion stated, "we should feel not much difficulty in saying that a state law coming in conflict with such act would be void." The Court's decision in *Willson* began to carve out an area of state authority over commerce that is not purely intrastate, but the boundaries of that authority were not yet well developed.

With Marshall's death in 1835, his successor, Chief Justice Roger Taney, was left with the task of more sharply defining the commerce powers of the states. Taney was far more sympathetic to the states than Marshall had been, and it is not surprising that the rulings of

the Taney era strike a balance between federal and state authority. The Taney Court first grappled with the problem in *Mayor of New York v. Miln* (1837), a case that had been carried over from the last Marshall term.

The dispute arose over the validity of New York's Passenger Act of 1824, which was designed to curb the flow of foreign indigents into the state. The law required the masters of incoming ships to supply the mayor of New York with comprehensive information on all passengers. This material was necessary for the city to enforce a regulation that allowed it to keep out people likely to require public assistance. Ship captains who did not comply were liable for fines and penalties of $75 per passenger. In addition, the law required that passengers refused entry be returned to their point of origin at the shipowner's expense. George Miln, who had a financial interest in a ship called *The Emily*, was fined when the ship's master refused to comply with the law. Miln protested the stiff $7,500 penalty on the ground that regulating foreign commerce was the exclusive jurisdiction of Congress, leaving no room for state action.

The Supreme Court upheld the New York law. In doing so, the justices did everything possible to avoid the complicated commerce issues the case presented. Instead, the Court followed the lead taken by Marshall in *Willson* and focused on the state's police powers. According to Justice Philip Barbour's majority opinion, the states have the sovereign power to regulate for the well-being of their residents. That power is complete and unqualified. In the absence of federal commercial legislation to the contrary, there is nothing to bar the state from using its police authority, even if it affects foreign commerce as in the matter here. In fact, Barbour argued that it was the duty of the state to protect its citizens from the financial obligations inevitably resulting from admitting "multitudes of poor persons, who come from foreign countries without possessing the means of supporting themselves." As a consequence, a state may use its police powers to ward off the "moral pestilence of paupers, vagabonds, and possibly convicts."

While the Court has long since abandoned this attitude toward the poor, the *Miln* decision revealed the

---

25. Disputes over the power of the states to impose taxes on interstate and foreign commerce actually began two years earlier in *Brown v. Maryland* (1827). The taxation issues will be discussed in the next chapter, where the fiscal authority to tax and spend is our focus.

Taney Court's readiness to support state regulations in the absence of federal action.[26] This thinking was consistent with the dual-federalism philosophy of that day (see Chapter 6). But, because the Court relied so heavily on the police powers, it failed to develop a complete doctrine of state commercial authority.

The License Cases of 1847 further revealed the difficulty the Taney Court had in crafting an adequate policy for the commerce powers of the states. These appeals came from New Hampshire, Rhode Island, and Massachusetts, where the legislatures had passed statutes licensing and taxing alcoholic beverages.[27] The regulations applied to domestic liquors as well as imported alcoholic beverages. Once again the Supreme Court upheld the laws as exercises of state police power, but the Court was badly divided as to rationale. No majority opinion was reached, an unusual occurrence for that time. In fact, six justices wrote opinions. All supported the state laws, but the highly fractionalized opinions provided no authoritative guidance for the states.

Two years later the Court heard arguments in Smith v. Turner and Norris v. Boston, which are known as the Passenger Cases (1849). These appeals tested the constitutionality of laws passed by New York and Massachusetts to regulate foreigners coming into the United States. The legislation was intended to discourage indigent immigrants and to provide for the treatment of individuals who arrived for entry in a diseased condition. The laws included provisions for taxes, bonding, and record keeping. The New York law taxed each incoming ship $1.00–$1.50 per passenger. These fees were used to fund a hospital to treat arriving immigrants. The Massachusetts law prohibited the importation of passengers who were indigent or had physical or mental disabilities. In addition, Massachusetts charged arriving ships $2.00 for each passenger, with the proceeds going to a fund for immigrants

who later required public assistance. George Smith and James Norris were British shipmasters. Smith landed in New York City with 290 immigrant passengers, and Norris docked in Boston with 19. Both protested the constitutionality of the taxes on Commerce Clause grounds.

The justices found these cases difficult to resolve. In fact, they were argued three times, and still the justices had trouble reaching a majority decision. Finally, by a 5–4 vote, the Court struck down the laws as being in conflict with the authority of Congress to regulate foreign commerce. The five justices in the majority each wrote separate opinions. The four dissenters, led by Taney, adhered to the view that such regulations to protect a state's citizens from indigent and ill immigrants were within the states' police powers.

The Passenger Cases left the law unsettled. Not only was the decision in conflict with previous rulings, but also the Court had failed to produce an opinion supported by a majority of the justices. This situation demanded a ruling that would authoritatively explain the constitutional division between federal and state commerce powers, but instead many questions remained unanswered. Did Congress have the exclusive power to regulate interstate and foreign commerce, leaving no authority for the states? Could the states regulate such commerce only if Congress had failed to enact any relevant legislation? Was the commerce power concurrent? Could Congress delegate its regulatory power to the states? Three years after the Passenger Cases, in Cooley v. Board of Wardens (1852), the justices issued a ruling that resolved some of the confusion.

Cooley v. Board of Wardens

12 HOW. (53 U.S.) 299 (1852)

http://laws.findlaw.com/US/53/299.html

Vote: 7 (Catron, Curtis, Daniel, Grier, McKinley, Nelson, Taney)
    2 (McLean, Wayne)

Opinion of the Court: Curtis
Concurring opinion: Daniel
Dissenting opinion: McLean

Based on its power over interstate and foreign commerce, Congress passed a statute in 1789 pertaining to

---

26. Edwards v. California (1941) effectively overruled Miln. In Edwards the justices struck down an "anti-Okie" law passed to discourage large numbers of people from Oklahoma and neighboring states from moving into California in an effort to escape the economic depression caused by the dust-bowl conditions in the central states. The Court found the law violated the right of citizens to travel freely among the various states.

27. Peirce v. New Hampshire, Fletcher v. Rhode Island, and Thurlow v. Massachusetts (The License Cases) (1847).

Philadelphia's ordinance regulating the use of pilots in the city's harbor was challenged as an infringement on the commerce power of the federal government. The Supreme Court upheld the ordinance in *Cooley v. Board of Wardens,* stating that some aspects of interstate and foreign commerce are essentially local and can be regulated locally if Congress has not already passed laws to the contrary.

the regulation of ports. The legislation said that until Congress acted otherwise, state and local authorities would continue to control the nation's ports and harbors. In 1803 Pennsylvania passed a port regulation law requiring that all vessels hire a local pilot to guide ships in and out of the Port of Philadelphia. Ship owners who did not comply were fined. The money from these fines was placed in a "charitable fund for the distressed or decayed pilots, their widows and children."

Aaron Cooley owned a vessel that sailed into Philadelphia without hiring a local pilot. The port's Board of Wardens took legal action against him, and Cooley was fined. He responded by claiming that the Pennsylvania law was unconstitutional; only Congress, he asserted, could regulate the port because the harbor was an integral part of interstate and foreign commerce, and the states had no constitutional authority to set regulations for such commerce. By implication, Cooley also was challenging the 1789 act of Congress that had delegated the powers to the states. The Pennsylvania Supreme Court upheld the law and the fine, and Cooley pressed his case to the U.S. Supreme Court.

MR. JUSTICE CURTIS delivered the opinion of the Court.

That the power to regulate commerce includes the regulation of navigation, we consider settled. And when we look to the nature of the service performed by pilots, to the relations which that service and its compensations bear to navigation between the several States, and between the ports of the United States and foreign countries, we are brought to the conclusion, that the regulation of the qualifications of pilots, of the modes and times of offering and rendering their services, of the responsibilities which shall rest upon them, of the powers they shall possess, of the compensation they may demand, and of the penalties by which their rights and duties may be enforced, do constitute regulations of navigation, and consequently of commerce, within the just meaning of this clause of the Constitution. . . .

Nor should it be lost sight of, that this subject of the regulation of pilots and pilotage has an intimate connection with, and an important relation to the general subject of commerce with foreign nations and among the several States, over which it was one main object of the Constitution to create a national control. Conflicts between the laws of neighboring States, and discriminations favorable or adverse to commerce with particular foreign nations, might be created by State laws regulating pilotage, deeply affecting that equality of commercial rights, and that freedom from State interference, which those who formed the Constitution were so anxious to secure, and which the experience of more than half a century has taught us to value so highly. . . .

It becomes necessary, therefore, to consider whether this law of Pennsylvania, being a regulation of commerce, is valid.

The act of Congress of the 7th of August, 1789, sect. 4, is as follows:

"That all pilots in the bays, inlets, rivers, harbors, and ports of the United States shall continue to be regulated in conformity with the existing laws of the States, respectively, wherein such pilots may be, or with such laws as the States may respectively hereafter enact for the purpose, until further legislative provision shall be made by Congress."

If the law of Pennsylvania, now in question, had been in existence at the date of this act of Congress, we might hold it to have been adopted by Congress, and thus made a law of the United States, and so valid. Because this act does, in effect, give the force of an act of Congress, to the then existing State laws on this subject, so long as they should continue unrepealed by the State which enacted them.

But the law on which these actions are founded was not enacted till 1803. What effect then can be attributed to so much of the act of 1789, as declares, that pilots shall continue to be regulated in conformity, "with such laws as the States may respectively hereafter enact for the purpose, until further legislative provision shall be made by Congress"?

If the States were divested of the power to legislate on this subject by the grant of the commercial power to Congress, it is plain this act could not confer upon them power thus to legislate. If the Constitution excluded the States from making any law regulating commerce, certainly Congress cannot regrant, or in any manner reconvey to the States that power. And yet this act of 1789 gives its sanction only to laws enacted by the States. This necessarily implies a constitutional power to legislate; for only a rule created by the sovereign power of a State acting in its legislative capacity, can be deemed a law, enacted by a State; and if the State has so limited its sovereign power that it no longer extends to a particular subject, manifestly it cannot, in any proper sense, be said to enact laws thereon. Entertaining these views we are brought directly and unavoidably to the consideration of the question, whether the grant of the commercial power to Congress, did *per se* deprive the States of all power to regulate pilots. This question has never been

decided by this court, nor, in our judgment, has any case depending upon all the considerations which must govern this one, come before this court. The grant of commercial power to Congress does not contain any terms which expressly exclude the States from exercising an authority over its subject matter. If they are excluded it must be because of the nature of the power, thus granted to Congress, requires that a similar authority should not exist in the States. If it were conceded on the one side, that the nature of this power, like that to legislate for the District of Columbia, is absolutely and totally repugnant to the existence of similar power in the States, probably no one would deny that the grant of the power to Congress, as effectually and perfectly excludes the States from all future legislation on the subject, as if express words had been used to exclude them. And on the other hand, if it were admitted that the existence of this power in Congress, like the power of taxation, is compatible with the existence of a similar power in the States, then it would be in conformity with the contemporary exposition of the Constitution, (Federalist, No. 32) and with the judicial construction, given from time to time by this court, after the most deliberate consideration, to hold that the mere grant of such a power to Congress, did not imply a prohibition on the States to exercise the same power; that it is not the mere existence of such a power, but its exercise by Congress, which may be incompatible with the exercise of the same power by the States, and that the States may legislate in the absence of congressional regulations.

The diversities of opinion, therefore, which have existed on this subject, have arisen from the different views taken of the nature of this power. But when the nature of a power like this is spoken of, when it is said that the nature of the power requires that it should be exercised exclusively by Congress, it must be intended to refer to the subjects of that power, and to say they are of such a nature as to require exclusive legislation by Congress. Now the power to regulate commerce, embraces a vast field, containing not only many, but exceedingly various subjects, quite unlike in their nature; some imperatively demanding a single uniform rule, operating equally on the commerce of the United States in every port; and some, like the subject now in question, as imperatively demanding that diversity, which alone can meet the local necessities of navigation.

Either absolutely to affirm, or deny that the nature of this power requires exclusive legislation by Congress, is to lose sight of the nature of the subjects of this power, and to assert concerning all of them, what is really applicable but to a part. Whatever subjects of this power are in their nature national, or admit only of one uniform system, or plan of regulation, may justly be said to be of such a nature as to require exclusive legislation by Congress. That this cannot be affirmed of laws for the regulation of pilots and pilotage is plain. The act of 1789 contains a clear and authoritative declaration by the first Congress, that the nature of this subject is such, that until Congress should find it necessary to exert its power, it should be left to the legislation of the States; that it is local and not national; that it is likely to be the best provided for, not by one system, or plan of regulations, but by as many as the legislative discretion of the several States should deem applicable to the local peculiarities of the ports within their limits.

Viewed in this light, so much of this act of 1789 as declares that pilots shall continue to be regulated "by such laws as the States may respectively hereafter enact for that purpose," instead of being held to be inoperative, as an attempt to confer on the States a power to legislate, of which the Constitution had deprived them, is allowed an appropriate and important signification. It manifests the understanding of Congress, at the outset of the government, that the nature of this subject is not such as to require its exclusive legislation. The practice of the States, and of the national government, has been in conformity with this declaration, from the origin of the national government to this time; and the nature of the subject when examined, is such as to leave no doubt of the superior fitness and propriety, not to say the absolute necessity, of different systems of regulation, drawn from local knowledge and experience, and conformed to local wants. How then can we say, that by the mere grant of power to regulate commerce, the States are deprived of all the power to legislate on this subject, because from the nature of the power the legislation of Congress must be exclusive. . . .

It is the opinion of a majority of the court that the mere grant to Congress of the power to regulate commerce, did not deprive the States of power to regulate pilots, and that although Congress has legislated on this subject, its legislation manifests an intention, with a single exception, not to regulate this subject, but to leave its regulation to the several States. To these precise questions, which are all we are called on to decide, this opinion must be understood to be confined. It does not extend to the question what other subjects, under the commercial power, are within the exclusive control of Congress, or may be regulated by the States in the absence of all congressional legislation; nor to the general question how far any regulation of a subject by Congress, may be deemed to operate as an exclusion of all legislation by the States upon the same subject. We decide the precise questions before us, upon what we deem sound principles, applicable to this particular subject in the state in which the legislation of Congress has left it. We go no further. . . .

We are of opinion that this State law was enacted by virtue of a power, residing in the State to legislate; that it is not in conflict with any law of Congress; that it does not interfere with any system which Congress has established by making regulations, or by intentionally leaving individuals to their own unrestricted action; that this law is therefore valid, and the judgment of the Supreme Court of Pennsylvania in each case must be affirmed.

Justice Benjamin Curtis's opinion in *Cooley* nicely outlines the basic constitutional principles governing the state's power to regulate commerce. From this decision and those that preceded it, we can begin to build some understanding of how far the states may go in regulating commercial enterprise:

1. The states retain the power to regulate purely intrastate commerce.

2. Congress has the power to regulate interstate and foreign commerce. When it exercises this power any contrary state laws are preempted.

3. The power of Congress to regulate interstate and foreign commerce is exclusive over those elements of commercial activity that are national in scope or require uniform regulation.

4. Those elements of interstate and foreign commerce that are not national in scope or do not require uniformity, and which have not been regulated by Congress, may be subject to state authority including the state's police powers.

This division of authority is known as the doctrine of selected exclusiveness. It designates certain aspects of interstate and foreign commerce over which the powers of

Congress are exclusive, allowing no state action. This exclusiveness, however, is not complete; in the absence of federal legislation, states may regulate some business activity affecting interstate commerce. The regulation of the Philadelphia port is an obvious part of interstate and foreign commerce where local harbor conditions require state supervision.

State Burdens on Interstate Commerce: The Dormant Commerce Clause

The problem with the selected exclusiveness approach is that it leaves a great deal to interpretation. Those aspects of interstate commerce that require uniformity are not clear, nor are the essentially local aspects of interstate commerce. These and other issues of similar importance have been left to the judiciary to settle, a formidable task given the complexity of the nation's economy. The basic principles articulated in *Cooley* often cannot be neatly applied to contemporary conditions.

Among the essentially local aspects of interstate commerce are matters of public safety. Interstate trucking provides a good illustration. The use of trucks for the transportation of goods is an integral part of interstate commerce, but trucks use local roads that are the state's concern. One of the primary elements of a state's police powers is regulation to ensure the safety of its citizens, and safety regulations may impose a burden on interstate commerce.

The Supreme Court addressed this conflict in 1938 in **South Carolina State Highway Department v. Barnwell Brothers**. For purposes of public safety and to prevent damage to its highways, the South Carolina legislature passed a statute prohibiting certain trucks from using its highways. No truck with a gross weight in excess of twenty thousand pounds or a width greater than ninety inches was permitted. The Barnwell Brothers Trucking Company challenged the regulation as an unreasonable burden on interstate commerce. Evidence presented at trial showed that between 85 percent and 90 percent of all interstate trucks were ninety-six inches wide and weighed more than the prescribed limit. Only four other states had weight limits as low as that imposed by South

Carolina, and none had width restrictions as severe. Based on this information, the trial court ruled that South Carolina's law was an unconstitutional burden on the flow of interstate commerce.

The Supreme Court reversed. Justice Harlan Stone's opinion for the Court stressed that there were some state regulations affecting interstate commerce that were clearly unconstitutional. For example, states are prohibited from giving a preference to intrastate businesses at the expense of interstate commerce or placing unreasonable burdens on out-of-state businesses. However, "there are matters of local concern, the regulation of which unavoidably involves some regulation of interstate commerce but which, because of their local character and their number and diversity, may never be fully dealt with by Congress." The regulation of such matters, in the absence of federal legislation, is left to the states. Congress has recognized this situation by not regulating parts of commerce such as the use of highways, ports, harbors, rivers, and docks. Congress also has not prohibited certain quarantine laws imposed by the states. Naturally, Congress may act in any of these areas when it determines that uniform national legislation is required. In their 7–0 decision, the justices held that South Carolina's regulation of trucks using the state highways fell into this category. Because of an absence of federal legislation over highway safety and because the state regulations applied to vehicles in intra- and interstate commerce equally, the state law was not in violation of the Constitution.

Still, *Barnwell Brothers* left a number of issues unresolved: How far may a state go in regulating interstate commerce for safety purposes? How much of a burden may be imposed on the free flow of commerce among the states to achieve greater safety? Were the highways, which were built, owned, and maintained by the states, a special case, or did state authority similarly extend to other areas of interstate commerce? The justices took a second look at these issues in *Southern Pacific Co. v. Arizona* (1945). Once again Stone wrote the opinion for the Court, but this time the outcome was different. Was *Southern Pacific* consistent with *Barnwell Brothers*, or did the Court modify its position?

Southern Pacific Company v. Arizona

325 U.S. 761 (1945)
http://laws.findlaw.com/US/325/761.html
Vote: 7 (Frankfurter, Jackson, Murphy, Reed, Roberts, Rutledge,
   Stone)
   2 (Black, Douglas)
Opinion for the Court: Stone
Dissenting opinions: Black, Douglas

On May 16, 1912, the Arizona legislature passed the Train Limit Law, making it unlawful for any individual or corporation to operate a train with more than fourteen passenger cars or seventy freight cars within the state. Violators were subject to fines. In 1940 the state brought a legal action against Southern Pacific Company, which acknowledged operating passenger and freight trains in excess of the state limits. The company argued that the state law was unconstitutional because it conflicted with the Commerce Clause.

The jury returned a verdict for the company, but the state supreme court reversed, holding that Arizona was free to enact such regulations because Congress had not legislated the length of railroad trains. The Arizona law was a safety measure that could be justified as an exercise of the state's police powers to act in the interests of local health, safety, and well-being. The railroad appealed the ruling to the U.S. Supreme Court, arguing that the state law placed an undue burden on the flow of interstate commerce. In presenting its case, Southern Pacific enjoyed the support of some powerful allies: the U.S. government and the Association of American Railroads submitted amicus curiae briefs attacking the constitutionality of the state law.

MR. CHIEF JUSTICE STONE delivered the opinion of the Court.

Although the commerce clause conferred on the national government power to regulate commerce, its possession of the power does not exclude all state power of regulation. Ever since *Willson v. Black-Bird Creek Marsh Co.* and *Cooley v. Board of Wardens*, it has been recognized that, in the absence of conflicting legislation by Congress, there is a residuum of power in the state to make laws governing matters of local concern which nevertheless in some measure affect interstate commerce or even, to some extent, regulate it. Thus the states may regulate matters which, because of their number and diversity, may never be adequately dealt with by Congress. *Cooley v. Board of Wardens, South Carolina Highway Dept. v. Barnwell Bros.* When the regulation of matters of local concern is local in character and effect, and its impact on the national commerce does not seriously interfere with its operation, and the consequent incentive to deal with them nationally is slight, such regulation has been generally held to be within state authority.

But ever since *Gibbons v. Ogden*, the states have not been deemed to have authority to impede substantially the free flow of commerce from state to state, or to regulate those phases of the national commerce which, because of the need of national uniformity, demand that their regulation, if any, be prescribed by a single authority. Whether or not this long-recognized distribution of power between the national and the state governments is predicated upon the implications of the commerce clause itself, or upon the presumed intention of Congress, where Congress has not spoken, the result is the same.

In the application of these principles some enactments may be found to be plainly within and others plainly without state power. But between these extremes lies the infinite variety of cases, in which regulation of local matters may also operate as a regulation of commerce, in which reconciliation of the conflicting claims of state and national power is to be attained only by some appraisal and accommodation of the competing demands of the state and national interests involved.

For a hundred years it has been accepted constitutional doctrine that the commerce clause, without the aid of Congressional legislation, thus affords some protection from state legislation inimical to the national commerce and that in such cases, where Congress has not acted, this Court, and not the state legislature, is under the commerce clause the final arbiter of the competing demands of state and national interests.

Congress has undoubted power to redefine the distribution of power over interstate commerce. It may either permit the states to regulate the commerce in a manner which would otherwise not be permissible, or exclude state regulation even of matters of peculiarly local concern which nevertheless affect interstate commerce.

But in general Congress has left it to the courts to formulate the rules thus interpreting the commerce clause in its application, doubtless because it has appreciated the destructive consequences to the commerce of the nation if their protection were withdrawn, and has been aware that in their application state laws will not be invalidated without the support of relevant factual material which will "afford a sure basis" for an informed judgment. Meanwhile, Congress has accommodated its legislation, as have the states, to these rules as an established feature of our constitutional system. There has thus been left to the states wide scope for the regulation of matters of local state concern, even though it in some measure affects the commerce, provided it does not materially restrict the free flow of commerce across state lines, or interfere with it in matters with respect to which uniformity of regulation is of predominant national concern.

Hence the matters for ultimate determination here are the nature and extent of the burden which the state regulation of interstate trains, adopted as a safety measure, imposes on interstate commerce, and whether the relative weights of the state and national interests involved are such as to make inapplicable the rule, generally observed, that the free flow of interstate commerce and its freedom from local restraints in matters requiring uniformity of regulation are interests safeguarded by the commerce clause from state interference. . . .

The findings show that the operation of long trains, that is trains of more than fourteen passenger and more than seventy freight cars, is standard practice over the main lines of the railroads of the United States, and that, if the length of trains is to be regulated at all, national uniformity in the regulation adopted, such as only Congress can prescribe, is practically indispensable to the operation of an efficient and economical national railway system. On many railroads passenger trains of more than fourteen cars and freight trains of more than seventy cars are operated, and on some systems freight trains are run ranging from one hundred and twenty-five to one hundred and sixty cars in length. Outside of Arizona, where the length of trains is not restricted, appellant runs a substantial proportion of long trains. In 1939 on its comparable route for through traffic through Utah

and Nevada from 66 to 85% of its freight trains were over seventy cars in length and over 43% of its passenger trains included more than fourteen passenger cars.

In Arizona, approximately 93% of the freight traffic and 95% of the passenger traffic is interstate. Because of the Train Limit Law appellant is required to haul over 30% more trains in Arizona than would otherwise have been necessary. The record shows a definite relationship between operating costs and the length of trains, the increase in length resulting in a reduction of operating costs per car. The additional cost of operation of trains complying with the Train Limit Law in Arizona amounts for the two railroads traversing that state to about $1,000,000 a year. The reduction in train lengths also impedes efficient operation. More locomotives and more manpower are required; the necessary conversion and reconversion of train lengths at terminals and the delay caused by breaking up and remaking long trains upon entering and leaving the state in order to comply with the law, delays the traffic and diminishes its volume moved in a given time, especially when traffic is heavy. . . .

The unchallenged findings leave no doubt that the Arizona Train Limit Law imposes a serious burden on the interstate commerce conducted by appellant. It materially impedes the movement of appellant's interstate trains through that state and interposes a substantial obstruction to the national policy proclaimed by Congress, to promote adequate, economical and efficient railway transportation service. Enforcement of the law in Arizona, while train lengths remain unregulated or are regulated by varying standards in other states, must inevitably result in an impairment of uniformity of efficient railroad operation because the railroads are subjected to regulation which is not uniform in its application. Compliance with a state statute limiting train lengths requires interstate trains of a length lawful in other states to be broken up and reconstituted as they enter each state according as it may impose varying limitations upon train lengths. The alternative is for the carrier to conform to the lowest train limit restriction of any of the states through which its trains pass, whose laws thus control the carriers' operations both within and without the regulating state.

Although the seventy car maximum for freight trains is the limitation which has been commonly proposed, various bills introduced in the state legislatures provided for maximum freight train lengths of from fifty to one hundred and twenty-five cars, and maximum passenger train lengths of from ten to eighteen cars. With such laws in force in states which are interspersed with those having no limit on train lengths, the confusion and difficulty with which interstate operations would be burdened under the varied system of state regulation and the unsatisfied need for uniformity in such regulation, if any, are evident. . . .

We think, as the trial court found, that the Arizona Train Limit Law, viewed as a safety measure, affords at most slight and dubious advantage, if any, over unregulated train lengths, because it results in an increase in the number of trains and train operations and the consequent increase in train accidents of a character generally more severe than those due to slack action. Its undoubted effect on the commerce is the regulation, without securing uniformity, of the length of trains operated in interstate commerce, which lack is itself a primary cause of preventing the free flow of commerce by delaying it and by substantially increasing its cost and impairing its efficiency. In these respects the case differs from those where a state, by regulatory measures affecting the commerce, has removed or reduced safety hazards without substantial interference with the interstate movement of trains. Such are measures abolishing the car stove, requiring locomotives to be supplied with electric headlights, providing for full train crews, and for the equipment of freight trains with cabooses. . . .

Here we conclude that the state does go too far. Its regulation of train lengths, admittedly obstructive to interstate train operation, and having a seriously adverse effect on transportation efficiency and economy, passes beyond what is plainly essential for safety since it does not appear that it will lessen rather than increase the danger of accident. Its attempted regulation of the operation of interstate trains cannot establish nationwide control such as is essential to the maintenance of an efficient transportation system, which Congress alone can prescribe. The state interest cannot be preserved at the expense of the national interest by an enactment which regulates interstate train lengths without securing such control, which is a matter of national concern. To this the interest of the state here asserted is subordinate. . . .

Reversed.

MR. JUSTICE BLACK, dissenting.

. . . [T]he determination of whether it is in the interest of society for the length of trains to be governmentally reg-

ulated is a matter of public policy. Someone must fix that policy—either the Congress, or the state, or the courts. A century and a half of constitutional history and government admonishes this Court to leave that choice to the elected legislative representatives of the people themselves, where it properly belongs both on democratic principles and the requirements of efficient government. . . .

Representatives elected by the people to make their laws, rather than judges appointed to interpret those laws, can best determine the policies which govern the people. That at least is the basic principle on which our democratic society rests. I would affirm the judgment of the Supreme Court of Arizona.

MR. JUSTICE DOUGLAS, dissenting.

I have expressed my doubts whether the courts should intervene in situations like the present and strike down state legislation on the grounds that it burdens interstate commerce. My view has been that the courts should intervene only where the state legislation discriminated against interstate commerce or was out of harmony with laws which Congress had enacted. It seems to me particularly appropriate that that course be followed here. For Congress has given the Interstate Commerce Commission broad powers of regulation over interstate carriers. The Commission is the national agency which has been entrusted with the task of promoting a safe, adequate, efficient, and economical transportation service. It is the expert on this subject. It is in a position to police the field. And if its powers prove inadequate for the task, Congress, which has paramount authority in this field, can implement them.

Stone's opinion in *Southern Pacific* is a strong declaration of how state requirements affect the flow of interstate traffic and commerce. The Commerce Clause leaves no room for state legislation that is inimical to national commerce, even if the subject of that regulation has not been touched by federal legislation. A state law that obstructs interstate commerce, going beyond what is clearly necessary for safety regulation, cannot stand in the face of the Commerce Clause.

The justices often refer to this as an application of the dormant Commerce Clause or the negative Commerce

Clause. This jurisprudence recognizes that although the Commerce Clause is a positive grant of power to the federal government, it carries with it a negative command as well: states may not unreasonably discriminate against or burden interstate or foreign commerce.

This judicially created rule is based on the essential purposes of the Commerce Clause. The authority to regulate interstate and foreign commerce was given to Congress by the Framers to ensure free and robust commercial activity among the states. Under the Articles of Confederation the states often imposed protective barriers that obstructed interstate business activity and impeded the growth of the national economy. To make sure that such state barriers were no longer erected, power over interstate commerce was given to Congress.

In 1803 John Marshall, writing in *Marbury v. Madison*, declared, "Affirmative words are often, in their operation, negative of other objects than those affirmed." Over the years the justices have often applied this principle to state regulations of the economy: the affirmative grant of power to the federal government to regulate interstate and foreign commerce means that the states are prohibited from regulating in ways that discriminate or burden interstate commerce—even if Congress does not explicitly bar them from doing so. Thus, the Court creates a balancing situation. In the absence of federal laws to the contrary, states may regulate local activities that affect interstate commerce for valid reasons, such as safety concerns. However, when such regulations unreasonably burden or discriminate against interstate commerce, the "dormant" or "negative" Commerce Clause prohibits them.

Discriminating against Interstate Commerce

Even though the Court's decisions in *Barnwell Brothers* and *Southern Pacific* deal with transportation and distribution activities, the principles set down in those cases also apply to state regulations that place burdens on other aspects of interstate commerce, especially a state's attempt to protect local businesses by discriminating against interstate commerce. In *Hunt v. Washington State Apple Advertising Commission* the justices confronted a state regulation that restricted the kind of information that could be displayed on containers of out-of-state agricultural products.[28] The state claimed that the rule was an exercise of the police powers to protect its citizens from fraud and deception. Does the state make a convincing case, or is the regulation nothing more than a way to prevent interstate commerce from having a negative impact on local producers?

Hunt v. Washington State Apple Advertising Commission

432 U.S. 333 (1977)
http://laws.findlaw.com/US/432/333.html
Vote: 8 (Blackmun, Brennan, Burger, Marshall, Powell, Stevens, Stewart, White)
    0
Opinion of the Court: Burger
Not participating: Rehnquist

In 1972 the North Carolina Board of Agriculture adopted a regulation that required all closed containers of apples shipped into the state to display either the U.S. Department of Agriculture (USDA) grade or nothing at all. It barred information based on the grading systems of the states in which the apples were grown. The reason for the regulation, according to North Carolina, which has a significant apple industry, was to ensure that all apples coming into the state used the same grading systems, thereby removing the danger that multiple systems would confuse purchasers and lead to deception and fraud in the market. No other state had such a regulation.

Through their industry advertising commission, apple growers in Washington State challenged the North Carolina regulations. Washington grows approximately 30 percent of the nation's apples and is responsible for roughly half of all apples shipped in interstate commerce. Because the industry is so important to that state, it has taken steps to enhance its reputation by imposing a strict mandatory inspection and grading system. Washington's

---

28. To hear oral arguments in this case navigate to: *www.oyez.org/oyez/frontpage*.

standards are higher than the USDA's, and the grading system has widespread acceptance in the apple trade.

The Washington commission asked North Carolina to alter its regulation or to allow certain exceptions. When North Carolina refused, the commission sued to have the regulation declared unconstitutional. It asserted that interstate commerce was being unreasonably burdened in three ways. First, the law clearly discriminated against interstate commerce in favor of local growers. Second, denying Washington growers the ability to use the widely accepted quality grading system diminished the marketing advantage the state's industry had earned. Third, the unique North Carolina regulation increased the cost of interstate commerce by requiring out-of-state growers to package their North Carolina–bound products differently from those being sent to the other states. The federal trial court found that the regulation violated the Commerce Clause, and North Carolina governor James Hunt, on behalf of the state, appealed to the U.S. Supreme Court.

MR. CHIEF JUSTICE BURGER delivered the opinion of the Court.

We turn ... to the appellant's claim that the District Court erred in holding that the North Carolina statute violated the Commerce Clause insofar as it prohibited the display of Washington State grades on closed containers of apples shipped into the State. Appellants do not really contest the District Court's determination that the challenged statute burdened the Washington apple industry by increasing its costs of doing business in the North Carolina market and causing it to lose accounts there. Rather, they maintain that any such burdens on the interstate sale of Washington apples were far outweighed by the local benefits flowing from what they contend was a valid exercise of North Carolina's inherent police powers designed to protect its citizenry from fraud and deception in the marketing of apples.

Prior to the statute's enactment, appellants point out, apples from 13 different States were shipped into North Carolina for sale. Seven of those States, including the State of Washington, had their own grading system which, while differing in their standards, used similar descriptive labels (*e.g.*, fancy, extra fancy, etc.). This multiplicity of inconsistent grades, as the District Court itself found, posed dangers of deception and confusion not only in the North Carolina market, but in the Nation as a whole. The North Carolina statute, appellants claim, was enacted to eliminate this source of deception and confusion by replacing the numerous state grades with a single uniform standard. Moreover, it is contended that North Carolina sought to accomplish this goal of uniformity in an evenhanded manner as evidenced by the fact that its statute applies to all apples sold in closed containers in the State without regard to their point of origin. Nonetheless, appellants argue that the District Court gave "scant attention" to the obvious benefits flowing from the challenged legislation and to the long line of decisions from this Court holding that the State possesses "broad powers" to protect local purchasers from fraud and deception in the marketing of foodstuffs.

As the appellants properly point out, not every exercise of state authority imposing some burden on the free flow of commerce is invalid. Although the Commerce Clause acts as a limitation upon state power even without congressional implementation, our opinions have long recognized that,

"in the absence of conflicting legislation by Congress, there is a residuum of power in the state to make laws governing matters of local concern which nevertheless in some measure affect interstate commerce or even, to some extent, regulate it." *Southern Pacific Co. v. Arizona* (1945).

Moreover, as appellants correctly note, that "residuum" is particularly strong when the State acts to protect its citizenry in matters pertaining to the sale of foodstuffs. By the same token, however, a finding that state legislation furthers matters of legitimate local concern, even in the health and consumer protection areas, does not end the inquiry. Such a view, we have noted, "would mean that the Commerce Clause of itself imposes no limitations on state action ... save for the rare instance where a state artlessly discloses an avowed purpose to discriminate against interstate goods." *Dean Milk Co. v. Madison* (1951). Rather, when such state legislation comes into conflict with the Commerce Clause's overriding requirement of a national "common market," we are confronted with the task of effecting an accommodation of the competing national and local interests. We turn to that task.

As the District Court correctly found, the challenged statute has the practical effect of not only burdening interstate sales of Washington apples, but also discriminating against them. This discrimination takes various forms. The first, and most obvious, is the statute's consequence of raising the costs of doing business in the North Carolina market for Washington apple growers and dealers, while leaving those of their North Carolina counterparts unaffected. As previously noted, this disparate effect results from the fact that North Carolina apple producers, unlike their Washington competitors, were not forced to alter their marketing practices in order to comply with the statute. They were still free to market their wares under the USDA grade or none at all as they had done prior to the statute's enactment. Obviously, the increased costs imposed by the statute would tend to shield the local apple industry from the competition of Washington apple growers and dealers who are already at a competitive disadvantage because of their great distance from the North Carolina market.

Second, the statute has the effect of stripping away from the Washington apple industry the competitive and economic advantages it has earned for itself through its expensive inspection and grading system. The record demonstrates that the Washington apple-grading system has gained nationwide acceptance in the apple trade. Indeed, it contains numerous affidavits from apple brokers and dealers located both inside and outside of North Carolina who state their preference, and that of their customers, for apples graded under the Washington, as opposed to the USDA, system because of the former's greater consistency, its emphasis on color, and its supporting mandatory inspections. Once again, the statute had no similar impact on the North Carolina apple industry and thus operated to its benefit.

Third, by prohibiting Washington growers and dealers from marketing apples under their State's grades, the statute has a leveling effect which insidiously operates to the advantage of local apple producers. As noted earlier, the Washington State grades are equal or superior to the USDA grades in all corresponding categories. Hence, with free market forces at work, Washington sellers would normally enjoy a distinct market advantage vis-à-vis local producers in those categories where the Washington grade is superior. However, because of the statute's operation, Washington apples which would otherwise qualify for and be sold under the superior Washington grades will now have to be marketed under their inferior USDA counterparts. Such "downgrading" offers the North Carolina apple industry the very sort of protection against competing out-of-state products that the Commerce Clause was designed to prohibit. At

worst, it will have the effect of an embargo against those Washington apples in the superior grades as Washington dealers withhold them from the North Carolina market. At best, it will deprive Washington sellers of the market premium that such apples would otherwise command.

Despite the statute's facial neutrality, the Commission suggests that its discriminatory impact on interstate commerce was not an unintended byproduct and there are some indications in the record to that effect. The most glaring is the response of the North Carolina Agriculture Commissioner to the Commission's request for an exemption following the statute's passage in which he indicated that before he could support such an exemption, he would "want to have the sentiment from our apple producers *since they were mainly responsible for this legislation being passed . . .*" (emphasis added). Moreover, we find it somewhat suspect that North Carolina singled out only closed containers of apples, the very means by which apples are transported in commerce, to effectuate the statute's ostensible consumer protection purpose when apples are not generally sold at retail in their shipping containers. However, we need not ascribe an economic protection motive to the North Carolina Legislature to resolve this case; we conclude that the challenged statute cannot stand insofar as it prohibits the display of Washington State grades even if enacted for the declared purpose of protecting consumers from deception and fraud in the marketplace.

When discrimination against commerce of the type we have found is demonstrated, the burden falls on the State to justify it both in terms of the local benefits flowing from the statute and the unavailability of nondiscriminatory alternatives adequate to preserve the local interests at stake. North Carolina has failed to sustain that burden on both scores.

The several States unquestionably possess a substantial interest in protecting their citizens from confusion and deception in the marketing of foodstuffs, but the challenged statute does remarkably little to further that laudable goal at least with respect to Washington apples and grades. The statute, as already noted, permits the marketing of closed containers of apples under *no* grades at all. Such a result can hardly be thought to eliminate the problems of deception and confusion created by the multiplicity of differing state grades; indeed, it magnifies them by depriving purchasers of all information concerning the quality of the contents of closed apple containers. Moreover, although the statute is ostensibly a consumer protection measure, it directs its primary efforts, not at the consuming public at large, but at apple wholesalers and brokers who are the principal purchasers of closed containers of apples. And those individuals are presumably the most knowledgeable individuals in this area. Since the statute does nothing at all to purify the flow of information at the retail level, it does little to protect consumers against the problems it was designed to eliminate. Finally, we note that any potential for confusion and deception created by the Washington grades was not of the type that led to the statute's enactment. Since Washington grades are in all cases equal or superior to their USDA counterparts, they could only "deceive" or "confuse" a consumer to his benefit, hardly a harmful result.

In addition, it appears that nondiscriminatory alternatives to the outright ban of Washington State grades are readily available. For example, North Carolina could effectuate its goal by permitting out-of-state growers to utilize state grades only if they also marked their shipments with the applicable USDA label. In that case, the USDA grade would serve as a benchmark against which the consumer could evaluate the quality of the various state grades. If this alternative was for some reason inadequate to eradicate problems caused by state grades inferior to those adopted by the USDA, North Carolina might consider banning those state grades which, unlike Washington's, could not be demonstrated to be equal or superior to the corresponding USDA categories. Concededly, even in this latter instance, some potential for "confusion" might persist. However, it is the type of "confusion" that the national interest in the free flow of goods between the States demands be tolerated.

The judgment of the District Court is

Affirmed.

The *Southern Pacific* and *Hunt* cases are but two examples from a long line of decisions in which the Court has cast a disapproving eye on state laws that discriminate against interstate commerce or place an unreasonable burden on it. Other examples are summarized in Box 7-8.

It would be a mistake to conclude, however, that all state regulations that discriminate against interstate products are unconstitutional. In fact, the Court on occasion has ruled that states may ban certain products altogether. There is little problem with such regulations if

the ban applies equally to goods produced inside the state as well as outside, and if the prohibition is reasonable, such as a ban against fireworks. These devices can be prohibited as a safety matter, but a state would be hard pressed to defend a law that prohibited only fireworks produced out of state.

But are there circumstances under which a state may constitutionally prohibit the importation of articles manufactured out of state but allow similar goods produced within its borders to be commercially traded? According to the state's arguments in *Maine v. Taylor*, such circumstances do exist.[29] Does Maine offer a sufficiently strong case that its trade barrier is not offensive to the Constitution, or is the state using the police power as a means of protecting a domestic industry against interstate competition?

Maine v. Taylor

477 U.S. 131 (1986)
http://laws.findlaw.com/US/477/131.html
Vote: 8 (Blackmun, Brennan, Burger, Marshall, O'Connor,
  Powell, Rehnquist, White)
  1 (Stevens)
Opinion of the Court: Blackmun
Dissenting opinion: Stevens

Maine passed a law prohibiting the importation of any live fish to be used as bait in any of the state's inland waters. The state said the law was to protect indigenous fish from parasites and diseases that are common among imported baitfish and to prevent the introduction of fish that might be detrimental to the state's ecology. Coupled with this state law was a federal statute (the Lacey Act) that, among other things, made it a crime to transport any fish or wildlife in violation of state laws.

Robert J. Taylor, operator of a bait business in Maine, imported 158,000 live golden shiners, a species of minnow commonly used as bait in freshwater fishing. This act was in clear violation of the state statute. The fish were intercepted at the state border, and the federal

---

29. To hear oral arguments in this case navigate to: *www.oyez.org/oyez/ frontpage.*

BOX 7-8   SUPREME COURT DECISIONS STRIKING DOWN STATE AND LOCAL RESTRICTIONS ON INTERSTATE COMMERCE

CASE	LAW DECLARED UNCONSTITUTIONAL
Edwards v. California (1941)	California law making it a crime knowingly to bring an indigent into the state.
Dean Milk Company v. Madison (1951)	City ordinance discriminating against milk produced out of state.
Bibb v. Navajo Freight Lines (1959)	Illinois statute requiring a particular mudflap on all trucks and outlawing a conventional mudflap legal in forty-five other states.
Pike v. Bruce Church (1970)	Arizona law commanding that all Arizona-grown cantaloupes be packaged inside the state.
Great Atlantic and Pacific Tea Company v. Cottrell (1976)	Mississippi law banning milk produced in Louisiana in response to Louisiana's refusal to sign a reciprocity agreement.
Raymond Motor Transit v. Rice (1978)	Wisconsin regulation prohibiting from the state's highways double trucks exceeding sixty-five feet in length.
Philadelphia v. New Jersey (1978)	New Jersey ban on the importation and dumping of out-of-state garbage.
Hughes v. Oklahoma (1979)	Law outlawing the transportation of Oklahoma-grown minnows for out-of-state sale.
Kassell v. Consolidated Freightways (1981)	Iowa law banning sixty-five-foot double trucks.
New England Power Company v. New Hampshire (1982)	New Hampshire prohibition against selling domestically produced power to out-of-state interests.
Healy v. Beer Institute (1989)	Connecticut law requiring out-of-state beer distributors to show that the prices charged inside Connecticut are not higher than prices charged in bordering states.
State of Wyoming v. State of Oklahoma (1992)	Oklahoma law mandating that electrical utility companies purchase at least 10 percent of their coal from Oklahoma mining operations.
C & A Carbone, Inc. v. Town of Clarkstown, New York (1994)	City ordinance requiring that all nonhazardous solid waste within the town be sent to a local transfer station, forbidding such waste to be shipped to out-of-state facilities.
Camps Newfound/Owatoona v. Town of Harrison (1997)	Maine statute singling out institutions that served mostly state residents for beneficial tax treatment and penalizing those institutions that did primarily interstate business.

government indicted Taylor for violating the Lacey Act. In his defense, Taylor attacked the constitutionality of the Maine law. He claimed that the ban on the interstate shipment of baitfish was a direct violation of the Commerce Clause. Maine intervened to defend its statute. The federal district court upheld the constitutionality of the law, but the court of appeals reversed. The state of Maine and the United States petitioned the U.S. Supreme Court to review the case.

JUSTICE BLACKMUN delivered the opinion of the Court.

Once again, a little fish has caused a commotion. See *Hughes v. Oklahoma* (1979); *TVA v. Hill* (1978); *Cappaert v. United States* (1976). The fish in this case is the golden shiner, a species of minnow commonly used as live bait in sport fishing. . . .

The Commerce Clause of the Constitution grants Congress the power "[t]o regulate Commerce with foreign Nations, and among the several States, and with the Indian Tribes." Art. I, §8, cl. 3. "Although the Clause thus speaks in terms of powers bestowed upon Congress, the Court long has recognized that it also limits the power of the States to erect barriers against interstate trade." Maine's statute restricts interstate trade in the most direct manner possible, blocking all inward shipments of live baitfish at the State's border. Still, as both the District Court and the Court of Appeals recognized, this fact alone does not render the law unconstitutional. The limitation imposed by the Commerce Clause on state regulatory power "is by no means absolute," and "the States retain authority under their general police powers to regulate matters of 'legitimate local concern,' even though interstate commerce may be affected."

In determining whether a State has overstepped its role in regulating interstate commerce, this Court has distinguished between state statutes that burden interstate transactions only incidentally, and those that affirmatively discriminate against such transactions. While statutes in the first group violate the Commerce Clause only if the burdens they impose on interstate trade are "clearly excessive in relation to the putative local benefits," statutes in the second group are subject to more demanding scrutiny. The Court explained in *Hughes v. Oklahoma* that once a state law is shown to discriminate against interstate commerce "either on its face or in practical effect," the burden falls on the State to demonstrate both that the statute "serves a legitimate local purpose," and that this purpose could not be served as well by available nondiscriminatory means. . . .

No matter how one describes the abstract issue whether "alternative means could promote this local purpose as well without discriminating against interstate commerce," *Hughes v. Oklahoma*, the more specific question whether scientifically accepted techniques exist for the sampling and inspection of live baitfish is one of fact, and the District Court's finding that such techniques have not been devised cannot be characterized as clearly erroneous. Indeed, the record probably could not support a contrary finding. Two prosecution witnesses testified to the lack of such procedures, and appellee's expert conceded the point, although he disagreed about the need for such tests. That Maine has allowed the importation of other freshwater fish after inspection hardly demonstrates that the District Court clearly erred in crediting the corroborated and uncontradicted expert testimony that standardized inspection techniques had not yet been developed for baitfish. . . .

After reviewing the expert testimony . . . we cannot say that the District Court clearly erred in finding that substantial scientific uncertainty surrounds the effect that baitfish parasites and nonnative species could have on Maine's fisheries. Moreover, we agree with the District Court that Maine has a legitimate interest in guarding against imperfectly understood environmental risks, despite the possibility that they may ultimately prove to be negligible. "[T]he constitutional principles underlying the commerce clause cannot be read as requiring the State of Maine to sit idly by and wait until potentially irreversible environmental damage has occurred or until the scientific community agrees on what disease organisms are or are not dangerous before it acts to avoid such consequences."

Nor do we think that much doubt is cast on the legitimacy of Maine's purposes by what the Court of Appeals took to be signs of protectionist intent. Shielding in-state industries from out-of-state competition is almost never a legitimate local purpose, and state laws that amount to "simple economic protectionism" consequently have been subject to a "virtually *per se* rule of invalidity." But there is little reason in this case to believe that the legitimate justifications the State has put forward for its statute are merely a sham or a "*post hoc* rationalization.". . .

The Commerce Clause significantly limits the ability of States and localities to regulate or otherwise burden the flow of interstate commerce, but it does not elevate free trade above all other values. As long as a State does not needlessly obstruct interstate trade or attempt to "place itself in a position of economic isolation," it retains broad regulatory authority to protect the health and safety of its citizens and the integrity of its natural resources. The evidence in this case amply supports the District Court's findings that Maine's ban on the importation of live baitfish serves legitimate local purposes that could not adequately be served by available nondiscriminatory alternatives. This is not a case of arbitrary discrimination against interstate commerce; the record suggests that Maine has legitimate reasons "apart from their origin, to treat [out-of-state baitfish] differently." The judgment of the Court of Appeals setting aside appellee's conviction is therefore reversed.

JUSTICE STEVENS, dissenting.

There is something fishy about this case. Maine is the only State in the Union that blatantly discriminates against out-of-state baitfish by flatly prohibiting their importation. Although golden shiners are already present and thriving in Maine (and, perhaps not coincidentally, the subject of a flourishing domestic industry), Maine excludes golden shiners grown and harvested (and, perhaps not coincidentally, sold) in other States. This kind of stark discrimination against out-of-state articles of commerce requires rigorous justification by the discriminating State. "When discrimination against commerce of the type we have found is demonstrated, the burden falls on the State to justify it both in terms of the local benefits flowing from the statute and the unavailability of nondiscriminatory alternatives adequate to preserve the local interests at stake." *Hunt v. Washington State Apple Advertising Comm'n* (1977).

. . . [T]he Court concludes that uncertainty about possible ecological effects from the possible presence of parasites and nonnative species in shipments of out-of-state shiners suffices to carry the State's burden of proving a legitimate public purpose. The Court similarly concludes that the State has no obligation to develop feasible inspection procedures that would make a total ban unnecessary. It seems clear, however, that the presumption should run the other way. Since the State engages in obvious discrimination against out-of-state commerce, it should be put to its proof. Ambiguity about dangers and alternatives should actually defeat, rather than sustain, the discriminatory measure.

This is not to derogate the State's interest in ecological purity. But the invocation of environmental protection or public health has never been thought to confer some kind of special dispensation from the general principle of nondiscrimination in interstate commerce. "A different view, that the ordinance is valid simply because it professes to be a health measure, would mean that the Commerce Clause of itself imposes no restraints on state action other than those laid down by the Due Process Clause, save for the rare instance where a state artlessly discloses an avowed purpose to discriminate against interstate goods." If Maine wishes to rely on its interest in ecological preservation, it must show that interest, and the infeasibility of other alternatives, with far greater specificity. Otherwise, it must further that asserted interest in a manner far less offensive to the notions of comity and cooperation that underlie the Commerce Clause.

Significantly, the Court of Appeals, which is more familiar with Maine's natural resources and with its legislation than we are, was concerned by the uniqueness of Maine's ban. That court felt, as I do, that Maine's unquestionable natural splendor notwithstanding, the State has not carried its substantial burden of proving why it cannot meet its environmental concerns in the same manner as other States with the same interest in the health of their fish and ecology.

I respectfully dissent.

The authority of the states to regulate interstate commerce remains consistent with the principles set out in *Cooley v. Board of Wardens* (1852). The Constitution without doubt gives supremacy in this area to the national government. If Congress elects to regulate such commerce, the power of the state is preempted. But where Congress does not regulate, the states may have a role. When national uniformity is not necessary, states may pass reasonable forms of regulation to meet legitimate local needs. If these ordinances place unreasonable burdens on interstate commerce or discriminate against interstate commerce in favor of domestic business, the Court will view them with suspicion, requiring the state to meet a heavy obligation of proving their legitimacy. *Maine v. Taylor*, however, serves as an example that gaining Supreme Court approval for such statutes is not impossible.

READINGS

Baker, Leonard. *Back to Back: The Duel Between FDR and the Supreme Court*. New York: Macmillan, 1967.

Baxter, Maurice G. *The Steamboat Monopoly: Gibbons v. Ogden*. New York: Knopf, 1972.

Benson, Paul R., Jr. *The Supreme Court and the Commerce Clause, 1937–1970*. New York: Dunellen, 1970.

Cortner, Richard. *Civil Rights and Public Accommodations: The Heart of Atlanta Motel and McClung Cases*. Lawrence: University Press of Kansas, 2001.

———. *The Wagner Act Cases*. Knoxville: University of Tennessee Press, 1964.

Corwin, Edward S. *The Commerce Power versus States' Rights*. Princeton, N.J.: Princeton University Press, 1936.

Cushman, Barry. *Rethinking the New Deal Court: The Structure of a Constitutional Revolution*. New York: Oxford University Press, 1998.

Dawson, Nelson. *Louis D. Brandeis, Felix Frankfurter, and the New Deal*. Hamden, Conn.: Archon Books, 1980.

Frankfurter, Felix. *The Commerce Clause under Marshall, Taney, and Waite*. Chapel Hill: University of North Carolina Press, 1937.

Himmelberg, Robert. *The Origins of the National Recovery Administration*. New York: Fordham University Press, 1976.

Irons, Peter H. *New Deal Lawyers*. Princeton, N.J.: Princeton University Press, 1982.

Leuchtenburg, William E. *The Supreme Court Reborn: The Constitutional Revolution in the Age of Roosevelt*. New York: Oxford University Press, 1995.

McClosky, Robert. *American Conservatism in the Age of Enterprise, 1865–1910*. Cambridge: Harvard University Press, 1951.

Pearson, Drew, and Robert S. Allen. *The Nine Old Men*. Garden City, N.Y.: Doubleday, 1936.

Pritchett, C. Herman. *The Roosevelt Court: A Study in Judicial Politics and Values*. New York: Macmillan, 1948.

Whalen, Charles W., and Barbara Whalen. *The Longest Debate: A Legislative History of the 1964 Civil Rights Act*. Washington, D.C.: Seven Locks Press, 1985.

Wood, Stephen B. *Constitutional Politics in the Progressive Era: Child Labor and the Law*. Chicago: University of Chicago Press, 1968.

CHAPTER 8
THE POWER TO TAX AND SPEND

ERHAPS no government power affects Americans more directly than the authority to tax and spend. Each year federal, state, and local governments collect billions of dollars in taxes imposed on a wide variety of activities, transactions, and goods. The federal government reminds us of its power to tax when we receive our paychecks, to say nothing of every April 15, the deadline for filing tax returns. Many state governments lay taxes on our incomes as well, and a majority of them also impose a levy each time we make a retail purchase. If we own a house, we must annually pay a tax on its value. We pay state and/or federal excise taxes whenever we make a long distance telephone call or put gas in the car. When we buy goods from abroad, the price includes a duty imposed on imports.

Americans have strong opinions about the government's taxing and spending activities. Many people think they pay too much and receive too few of the government's services in return. The battles over spending priorities are never ending, especially when choices must be made between defense and social programs. In addition, there are constant complaints about inefficient and ineffective government agencies that waste tax dollars. The mere mention of the Internal Revenue Service (IRS) strikes fear in the hearts of many. Minor tax revolts at the state and local level are not unusual. In spite of this general dissatisfaction, however, most Americans pay their taxes honestly and on time and accept the reality that taxation is a fact of modern life.

Today the government's power to tax and spend is firmly established, with reasonably well-defined contours, but this was not always the case. Some of the country's greatest constitutional battles were fought over the fiscal powers. The results of these legal disputes have significantly shaped the powers and constraints of American political institutions. In this chapter, we examine the Supreme Court's interpretations of the twin fiscal powers of taxation and spending.

THE CONSTITUTIONAL POWER TO TAX AND SPEND

The power to tax was a fundamental issue at the Constitutional Convention. The government under the Articles of Confederation was ineffective in part because it had no authority to levy taxes. It could only request funds from the states and had no power to collect payments if the states refused to cooperate. The taxing authority resided solely with the states, which left the national government unable to execute public policies unless the states overwhelmingly supported them, a situation that did not occur with any regularity. It was clear that the central government would have to gain some revenue-gathering powers under the new constitution, while the states retained concurrent authority to impose taxes.

Article I, Section 8, of the Constitution enumerates the powers of the federal government, and the first of those listed is the power to tax and spend: "The Congress shall have the Power to lay and collect Taxes,

Duties, Imposts and Excises, to pay the Debts and provide for the common Defence and general Welfare of the United States."

The wording of this grant of authority is quite broad. The revenue function breaks into three categories. The first is the general grant of taxation power. Second is the authority to collect duties and imposts, both of which are taxes levied on imports, the primary source of revenue at that time. The third is the power to impose excises, which are taxes on the manufacture, sale, or use of goods, or on occupational or other activities.

The power to spend is also broadly constructed. The revenues gathered through the various taxing mechanisms may be used to pay government debts, to fund the nation's defense, and to provide for the general welfare. Although James Madison (and others) argued that the Framers intended the spending power to be limited to funding those government activities explicitly authorized in the Constitution, the wording of Article I, Section 8, does not impose any such restriction. As we shall see later in this chapter, the fact that Congress may spend federal funds to provide for the *general welfare* is indeed a broad grant of authority.

This is not to say that the federal power to tax and spend is without limits. The Framers were wary enough of the dangers of a strong central government to impose some restrictions.

First, Article I, Section 8, stipulates that "all Duties, Imposts and Excises shall be uniform throughout the United States." The purpose of this provision was to prevent Congress from imposing different tax rates on various regions or requiring the citizens of one state to pay a tax rate higher than the citizens of other states. Geographical uniformity is the only stated constitutional requirement for excise taxes and taxes on imports. If this standard is met, the tax is likely to be valid.

Second, Article I, Section 9, holds that "No capitation, or other direct, Tax shall be laid, unless in Proportion to the Census or Enumeration herein before directed to be taken." This same admonition is found in Article I, Section 2, where the Framers wrote "direct Taxes shall be apportioned among the several States . . . according to

their respective Numbers" as determined by the national census. The term *direct tax* is not defined in the Constitution and is a difficult concept to understand. When the Framers referred to direct taxes, they most likely meant a head tax—a tax imposed on each person—or a tax on land. As we shall see in the next section of this chapter, the requirement that direct taxes be apportioned on the basis of population has proved troublesome, and Congress has generally avoided such levies.

Third, Article I, Section 9, also dictates that "No Tax or Duty shall be laid on Articles exported from any State." Consistent with the prevailing philosophy of increased commerce and trade, the Framers wanted to ensure that the products of the states would move freely without the burden of federal taxes being placed on them.

The Framers generally allowed the states to retain their taxing authority as it existed prior to the ratification of the Constitution. Consequently, state and local governments today tax a wide array of activities and goods, including individual and corporate incomes, personal property, real estate, retail sales, investment holdings, and inheritances. But the Constitution imposed some new restraints on state taxing authority. These limitations specifically removed from the states any power to place a tax on certain forms of commerce. Article I, Section 10, prohibits them from imposing any duty on imports or exports, as well as any tax on the cargo capacity of vessels using the nation's ports. The Framers were interested in the promotion of commerce, and these provisions precluded states from retarding commerce by using foreign trade as a source of tax revenue.

In addition to these specific restrictions, state and federal taxation must be consistent with the other provisions of the Constitution. It would be a violation of the Constitution, for example, if a state or the federal government taxed the exercise of a constitutional right, such as the freedom of speech or the exercise of religion. By the same token, if the government imposed varying tax rates based on a person's sex or race, such levies would be in violation of the constitutional rights of due process and equal protection of the laws.

BOX 8-1   DIRECT AND INDIRECT TAXES: APPORTIONMENT V. GEOGRAPHICAL UNIFORMITY

THIS EXAMPLE demonstrates the difference between direct and indirect taxing methods. The facts and figures used are purely hypothetical.

Assume that Congress decides to raise $1 million through a tax on the nation's 100,000 thoroughbred horses. If this tax is considered an excise tax, it must conform to the constitutional requirement of geographical uniformity. Congress would have to require that all thoroughbred horse owners pay a tax of ten dollars per horse. The rate would be the same in Maine as in Oregon. If, however, the tax on thoroughbred horses is classified as a direct tax, a different set of calculations would have to be made to meet the constitutionally required apportionment standard. Three factors would need to be known. First, the amount of money Congress intends to raise. Second, the proportion of the national population residing in each state. Third, the number of thoroughbred horses in each state. Apportionment means that the proportion of the revenue obtained from a state must equal the proportion of the country's population living there.

The impact of apportionment can be seen by the following calculations in applying the $1 million horse tax to three states. State A is a densely populated, urban state with few horses. State B is a moderately populated state with some ranching areas. And State C is a sparsely populated,

primarily agricultural state, with a relatively large number of thoroughbreds.

State	Percentage of National Population	Taxes Due from State	Number of Horses in State	Tax Rate per Horse
State A	10	$100,000	100	$1,000
State B	5	$50,000	1,000	$50
State C	1	$10,000	10,000	$1

Obviously, the horse owners in State A would be greatly disadvantaged if the horse tax were classified as a direct tax and apportioned among the states on the basis of population. State C, on the other hand, would be greatly benefited. Because State C has only 1 percent of the nation's population, it would be responsible for raising only 1 percent of the tax revenues. Furthermore, that smaller tax obligation would be distributed over a disproportionately large number of horses.

Horse owners in State A clearly would prefer the tax on thoroughbreds to be defined as an excise tax with its required geographical uniformity. State C's thoroughbred owners obviously would argue for the horse tax to be considered a direct tax and be apportioned among the states on the basis of population.

DIRECT TAXES AND THE POWER TO TAX INCOME

The Constitution stipulates two standards for assessing federal taxes. The first is geographical uniformity. Duties, imposts, and excise taxes all must be applied according to this standard. If Congress taxes a particular product entering the ports of the United States, the tax rate on the article must be the same regardless of the point of entry. Excise taxes also must be applied uniformly throughout the nation. If an excise is placed on automobiles, for example, the amount assessed must be the same in California as it is in Tennessee.

The second standard for imposing taxes is population distribution. The Constitution says that all direct

taxes must be apportioned among the states on the basis of population. The delegates from the sparsely populated states supported this provision because they feared that the larger states, with greater representation in the House of Representatives, would craft tax measures in such a way that the burden would fall disproportionately upon the citizens of the smaller states. Unfortunately, the Framers did not explain what they meant by a direct tax. As Box 8-1 illustrates, whether a tax is levied uniformly or is apportioned on the basis of population makes a great deal of difference as to who pays how much. In *The Federalist Papers*, Alexander Hamilton claimed that direct taxes were only those imposed on land and buildings, but Hamilton's opinion did not settle the issue.[1] It required a Supreme Court decision to do that.

Defining Direct Taxation

In one of the Court's earliest cases, **Hylton v. United States** (1796), the justices defined the term *direct tax*. The dispute stemmed from a tax on carriages Congress had passed June 5, 1794. The statute classified the tax as an excise and, therefore, applied the same rate on carriages nationwide. The Federalist majorities in Congress passed the statute over Anti-Federalist opposition, and the tax was completely partisan. The Federalists generally represented the states in the Northeast with large populations but relatively few carriages; the Anti-Federalist strongholds were the less densely populated and more agricultural states with larger numbers of carriages. Because the carriage tax was deemed an excise, the Anti-Federalist areas would pay a much greater share of it than would the residents of the Northeast. The Anti-Federalists would have preferred to classify the measure as a direct tax and apportion it on the basis of population.

Daniel Hylton, a resident of Virginia, challenged the constitutionality of the assessment, claiming that it was a direct tax, not an excise, and should have been apportioned on the basis of population. The government took the position that, as a tax on an article, the carriage tax was an excise.

By almost every rule of judicial authority developed since that time, the Court should have refused to hear the dispute.[2] The evidence showed that the case did not involve adverse parties. In fact, the suit appeared to be little more than a ploy by the government to obtain Court approval of its interpretation of the taxation provisions of the Constitution. Both sides to the dispute agreed that Hylton owned 125 carriages exclusively for his private use. In reality, he owned only 1, but the tax due on a single carriage was insufficient to meet the threshold for federal court jurisdiction. If Hylton owned 125 carriages,

the taxes and penalties due would reach $2,000, enough for federal court action. This jurisdictional point was important because Federalist judges dominated the federal courts, and they were likely to give the law a sympathetic hearing. Administration officials also agreed that if the tax were found valid they would demand that Hylton pay only $16. Perhaps an even greater indication of collusion was that the government paid the fees of the attorneys for both sides.

Former secretary of the Treasury Alexander Hamilton presented the government's case. Hamilton was one of the most vigorous supporters of a strong national government and of broad federal taxation powers. He understood the problems associated with apportioning taxes on the basis of population and consequently wanted the Court to set down a very narrow definition of direct taxes.

Hamilton's side was victorious. The three justices who participated in the decision each voted in favor of the statute and in agreement with Congress's determination that the carriage tax was an excise tax.[3] As was the custom in the years before John Marshall became chief justice, each justice wrote a separate opinion explaining his vote.[4] The opinions of James Iredell and Samuel Chase stressed the inappropriateness of attempting to apportion a tax on carriages and the inevitable inequities that would result. William Paterson's opinion emphasized the intention of the Framers. His opinion had particular credibility because Paterson, having been a New Jersey delegate to the Constitutional Convention, was one of the Framers.[5] All three agreed that only two kinds of

---

1. Alexander Hamilton, Federalist No. 21, in *The Federalist Papers*, ed. Clinton Rossiter (New York: New American Library, 1961).

2. See Melvin I. Urofsky, *A March of Liberty: A Constitutional History of the United States* (New York: Knopf, 1988), 146–148. See also Robert F. Cushman, *Cases in Constitutional Law*, 7th ed. (Englewood Cliffs, N.J.: Prentice Hall, 1989), 177–178.

3. The other three members of the Court were absent for various reasons. Oliver Ellsworth had just been sworn in as chief justice and, because he had missed some of the arguments, did not participate in the decision. Justice James Wilson heard arguments but did not vote in the case because he had participated in the lower court decision upholding the tax. Justice William Cushing was not present for the arguments and therefore did not vote on the merits.

4. The practice of each justice writing a separate opinion explaining individual views was borrowed from the British courts. When Marshall became chief justice, he moved away from the use of these seriatim opinions to the current practice of a single opinion explaining the views of the majority. Marshall believed that the use of a single opinion increased the Court's status and effectiveness.

5. Justice Wilson was also a delegate at the Constitutional Convention and, therefore, one of the Framers. Although he did not participate at the Supreme Court level, Wilson earlier voted to uphold the tax as an excise in the lower court.

taxes fell into the direct tax category: capitation (or head) taxes and taxes on land.

Apportioning taxes on the basis of population is very cumbersome and almost inevitably leads to unjust tax burdens. The *Hylton* decision, by limiting the kinds of taxes that fell into the direct taxation category, significantly strengthened federal taxation powers. It freed Congress from having to apply unpopular apportionment standards to most taxes. So difficult is the apportionment problem that Congress only rarely has attempted to use a direct tax, and such efforts generally have been unsatisfactory.

Hylton was the first case in which the Supreme Court heard a challenge to the constitutionality of a federal statute; the decision predated *Marbury v. Madison* by seven years. It is clear from the arguments before the Court and the justices' opinions that the law was tested for its constitutionality. *Hylton* has not received the notoriety of *Marbury* because the act of Congress was found to be valid.

The Constitutionality of the Income Tax

From *Hylton* in 1796 to the 1860s federal taxing authority remained generally unchanged. The government financed its activities largely through import duties and excise taxes. The Civil War, however, placed an incredible financial strain on the federal government. Between 1858 and the end of the war, it ran unusually high budget deficits and needed to find new sources of revenue to fund the war effort. In response, Congress in 1862 and 1864 imposed the first taxes on individual incomes. The 1881 case of **Springer v. United States** involved a challenge to the validity of that tax. William M. Springer, an attorney, claimed that the income tax was a direct tax and should have been apportioned on the basis of population. The justices unanimously rejected this position, once again holding that only capitation taxes and taxes on land were direct taxes. Although the challenged tax was a levy on the income of individuals, it could not be considered a capitation tax within the normal meaning of that term. *Springer*, then, set precedent that the federal government had the power to tax incomes.

As the government reduced its war debts, Congress in 1872 was able to repeal the income tax law.[6] But the issue of taxing incomes did not go away. The Populist movement favored the use of the income tax as the primary method of raising federal revenues. In addition, labor groups and farm organizations began arguing that new revenue sources should be developed to shift the burden away from reliance on import duties. Members of the Democratic Party criticized the regressive aspects of the tax structure of that time. In response to these demands, Congress enacted an income tax law in 1894. The statute, which was passed as part of the Wilson-Gorman Tariff Act, imposed a 2 percent tax on all corporate profits and on individual incomes. Income derived from salaries and wages, gifts, inheritances, dividends, rents, and interest, including interest from state and municipal bonds, all were subject to this tax. People with annual incomes under $4,000 paid no tax. This exemption, set at a level much higher than the average worker earned, meant that most of the burden fell upon the wealthy. For this reason, the tax received overwhelming support from rank-and-file citizens and bitter opposition from businesses and those individuals enjoying high incomes. The wealthy classes, in fact, claimed that the income tax would destroy the very fabric of the nation, replacing our historical principles of private property with communism and socialism.

The income tax law was promptly challenged in Court in an 1895 appeal, *Pollock v. Farmers' Loan & Trust Co.* One of the primary arguments of the law's opponents was that the income tax was a direct tax, and since Congress had not apportioned it, the law was unconstitutional. Given precedents such as *Hylton* and *Springer,* would you anticipate that this position would be successful?

---

6. For an excellent review of the history of the income tax in the United States, see John F. Witte, *The Politics and Development of the Federal Income Tax* (Madison: University of Wisconsin Press, 1985).

Pollock v. Farmers' Loan & Trust Co.

158 U.S. 601 (1895)
http://laws.findlaw.com/US/158/601.html
Vote: 5 (Brewer, Field, Fuller, Gray, Shiras)
*   4 (Brown, Harlan, Jackson, White)*
Opinion of the Court: Fuller
Dissenting opinions: Brown, Harlan, Jackson, White

Charles Pollock, a shareholder in the Farmers' Loan & Trust Company of New York, filed suit on behalf of himself and his fellow stockholders to block the company from paying the national income tax on the ground that the tax was unconstitutional. The lawsuit was obviously collusive: the company no more wanted to pay the tax than did its shareholders. Opponents of the law claimed (1) that taxing income from state and city bonds was an unconstitutional encroachment on the state's power to borrow money; (2) that a tax on income from real property was a direct tax and must be apportioned on the basis of population; and (3) that these taxes were so integral to the entire tax act that the whole law should be declared unconstitutional.

The Court heard arguments on the *Pollock* case twice. In its first decision, the majority declared the tax on state and municipal bonds unconstitutional.[7] It further ruled that a tax on income from land was essentially the same as taxing land itself. Because a tax on land is a direct tax, so too is a tax on the income from land. Therefore, such taxes must be apportioned on the basis of population. But the Court was unable to reach a decision on whether the entire law should be declared unconstitutional. On this question the justices divided 4–4 because Justice Howell Jackson, ill with tuberculosis, was absent.

Pollock filed a petition for a second hearing, and Jackson made it known that he would be present for it. The second decision reviewed much of what the Court concluded in the first, but this time the Court went on to rule on the question of the general constitutionality of the income tax act.

The *Pollock* decision was one of the most controversial and important of its day. It contained all the elements of high drama. The case pitted the interests of business and wealthy individuals against those supporting social and fiscal reform. Both sides believed that a victory for their opponents would have disastrous consequences for the nation. Newspapers editorialized with enthusiasm. With the first decision ending in a tie, the suspense surrounding the second hearing grew tremendously. The human interest factor was heightened when Justice Jackson was transported to Washington to cast what he thought would be the deciding vote in favor of the tax. (He died three months later.) Oral arguments took place from May 6 to May 8. The justices did not act in a manner consistent with detached objectivity. Loren P. Beth reports that "Harlan wrote privately that Justice Stephen J. Field acted like a 'madman' throughout the case, but the dissenters' own opinions were similarly emotional."[8] In the end the opponents of the tax were victorious. Although Jackson, as expected, voted to uphold the law, Justice George Shiras, who had supported the tax in the first hearing, changed positions and became the crucial fifth vote to strike it down.

MR. CHIEF JUSTICE FULLER delivered the opinion of the court.

Whenever this court is required to pass upon the validity of an act of Congress as tested by the fundamental law enacted by the people, the duty imposed demands in its discharge the utmost deliberation and care, and invokes the deepest sense of responsibility. And this is especially so when the question involves the exercise of a great governmental power, and brings into consideration, as vitally affected by the decision, that complex system of government, so sagaciously framed to secure and perpetuate "an indestructible Union, composed of indestructible States.". . .

As heretofore stated, the Constitution divided Federal taxation into two great classes, the class of direct taxes, and

7. *Pollock v. Farmers' Loan & Trust Co.*, 157 U.S. 429 (1895).

8. Loren P. Beth, "*Pollock v. Farmers' Loan & Trust Co.*," in *The Oxford Companion to the Supreme Court*, ed. Kermit L. Hall (New York: Oxford University Press, 1992), 655.

the class of duties, imposts and excises; and prescribed two rules which qualified the grant of power as to each class.

The power to lay direct taxes apportioned among the several States in proportion to their representation in the popular branch of Congress, a representation based on population as ascertained by the census, was plenary and absolute; but to lay direct taxes without apportionment was forbidden. The power to lay duties, imposts, and excises was subject to the qualification that the imposition must be uniform throughout the United States.

Our previous decision was confined to the consideration of the validity of the tax on the income from real estate, and on the income from municipal bonds. The question thus limited was whether such taxation was direct or not, in the meaning of the Constitution; and the court went no farther, as to the tax on the income from real estate, than to hold that it fell within the same class as the source whence the income was derived, that is, that a tax upon the realty and a tax upon the receipts therefrom were alike direct; while as to the income from municipal bonds, that could not be taxed because of want of power to tax the source, and no reference was made to the nature of the tax as being direct or indirect.

We are now permitted to broaden the field of inquiry, and to determine to which of the two great classes a tax upon a person's entire income, whether derived from rents, or products, or otherwise, of real estate, or from bonds, stocks, or other forms of personal property, belongs; and we are unable to conclude that the enforced subtraction from the yield of all the owner's real or personal property, in the manner prescribed, is so different from a tax upon the property itself, that it is not a direct, but an indirect tax, in the meaning of the Constitution. . . .

The reasons for the clauses of the Constitution in respect of direct taxation are not far to seek. The States, respectively, possessed plenary powers of taxation. They could tax the property of their citizens in such manner and to such extent as they saw fit; they had unrestricted powers to impose duties or imposts on imports from abroad, and excises on manufactures, consumable commodities, or otherwise. They gave up the great sources of revenue derived from commerce; they retained the concurrent power o[f] levying excises, and duties if covering anything other than excises; but in respect of them the range of taxation was narrowed by the power granted over interstate commerce, and by the danger of being put at disadvantage in dealing with excises

on manufactures. They retained the power of direct taxation, and to that they looked as their chief resource; but even in respect of that, they granted the concurrent power, and if the tax were placed by both governments on the same subject, the claim of the United States had preference. Therefore, they did not grant the power of direct taxation without regard to their own condition and resources as States; but they granted the power of apportioned direct taxation, a power just as efficacious to serve the needs of the general government, but securing to the States the opportunity to pay the amount apportioned, and to recoup from their own citizens in the most feasible way, and in harmony with their systems of local self-government. If, in the changes of wealth and population in particular States, apportionment produced inequality, it was an inequality stipulated for, just as the equal representation of the States, however small, in the Senate, was stipulated for. The Constitution ordains affirmatively that each State shall have two members of that body, and negatively that no State shall by amendment be deprived of its equal suffrage in the Senate without its consent. The Constitution ordains affirmatively that representatives and direct taxes shall be apportioned among the several States according to numbers, and negatively that no direct tax shall be laid unless in proportion to the enumeration.

The founders anticipated that the expenditures of the States, their counties, cities, and towns, would chiefly be met by direct taxation on accumulated property, while they expected that those of the Federal government would be for the most part met by indirect taxes. And in order that the power of direct taxation by the general government should not be exercised, except on necessity; and, when the necessity arouse, should be so exercised as to leave the States at liberty to discharge their respective obligations, and should not be so exercised, unfairly and discriminatingly, as to particular States or otherwise, by a mere majority vote, possibly of those whose constituents were intentionally not subjected to any part of the burden, the qualified grant was made. . . .

It is said that a tax on the whole income of property is not a direct tax in the meaning of the Constitution, but a duty, and, as a duty, leviable without apportionment, whether direct or indirect. We do not think so. Direct taxation was not restricted in one breath, and the restriction blown to the winds in another. . . .

We have unanimously held in this case that, so far as this law operates on the receipts from municipal bonds, it cannot be sustained, because it is a tax on the power of the States, and on their instrumentalities to borrow money, and consequently repugnant to the Constitution. But if, as contended, the interest when received has become merely money in the recipient's pocket, and taxable as such without reference to the source from which it came, the question is immaterial whether it could have been originally taxed at all or not. This was admitted by the Attorney General with characteristic candor; and it follows that, if the revenue derived from municipal bonds cannot be taxed because the source cannot be, the same rule applies to revenue from any other source not subject to the tax; and the lack of power to levy any but an apportioned tax on real and personal property equally exists as to the revenue therefrom.

Admitting that this act taxes the income of property irrespective of its source, still we cannot doubt that such a tax is necessarily a direct tax in the meaning of the Constitution. . . .

We are not here concerned with the question whether an income tax be or be not desirable, nor whether such a tax would enable the government to diminish taxes on consumption and duties on imports, and to enter upon what may be believed to be a reform of its fiscal and commercial system. Questions of that character belong to the controversies of political parties, and cannot be settled by judicial decision. In these cases our province is to determine whether this income tax on the revenue from property does or does not belong to the class of direct taxes. If it does, it is, being unapportioned, in violation of the Constitution, and we must so declare. . . .

We have considered the act only in respect of the tax on income derived from real estate, and from invested personal property, and have not commented on so much of it as bears on gains or profits from business, privileges, or employments, in view of the instances in which taxation on business, privileges, or employments has assumed the guise of an excise tax and been sustained as such.

Being of opinion that so much of the sections of this law as lays a tax on income from real and personal property is invalid, we are brought to the question of the effect of that conclusion upon these sections as a whole.

It is elementary that the same statute may be in part constitutional and in part unconstitutional, and if the parts are wholly independent of each other, that which is consti-tutional may stand while that which is unconstitutional will be rejected. And in the case before us there is no question as to the validity of this act, except sections twenty-seven to thirty-seven, inclusive, which relate to the subject which has been under discussion; and as to them we think . . . that if the different parts "are so mutually connected with and dependent on each other, as to warrant a belief that the legislature intended them as a whole, and that, if all could not be carried into effect, the legislature would not pass the residue independently, and some parts are unconstitutional, all the provisions which are thus dependent, conditional or connected, must fall with them.". . .

According to the census, the true valuation of real and personal property in the United States in 1890 was $65,037,091,197, of which real estate with improvements thereon made up $39,544,544,333. Of course, from the latter must be deducted, in applying these sections, all unproductive property and all property whose net yield does not exceed four thousand dollars; but, even with such deductions, it is evident that the income from realty formed a vital part of the scheme for taxation embodied therein. If that be stricken out, and also the income from all invested personal property, bonds, stocks, investments of all kinds, it is obvious that by far the largest part of the anticipated revenue would be eliminated, and this would leave the burden of the tax to be borne by professions, trades, employments, or vocations; and in that way what was intended as a tax on capital would remain in substance a tax on occupations and labor. We cannot believe that such was the intention of Congress. We do not mean to say that an act laying by apportionment a direct tax on all real estate and personal property, or the income thereof, might not also lay excise taxes on business, privileges, employments, and vocations. But this is not such an act; and the scheme must be considered as a whole. Being invalid as to the greater part, and falling, as the tax would, if any part were held valid, in a direction which could not have been contemplated except in connection with the taxation considered as an entirety, we are constrained to conclude that sections twenty-seven to thirty-seven, inclusive, of the act, which became a law without the signature of the President on August 28, 1894, are wholly inoperative and void.

Our conclusions may, therefore, be summed up as follows:

First. We adhere to the opinion already announced, that, taxes on real estate being indisputably direct taxes, taxes on the rents or income of real estate are equally direct taxes.

Second. We are of opinion that taxes on personal property, or on the income of personal property, are likewise direct taxes.

Third. The tax imposed by sections twenty-seven to thirty-seven, inclusive, of the act of 1894, so far as it falls on the income of real estate and of personal property, being a direct tax within the meaning of the Constitution, and, therefore, unconstitutional and void because not apportioned according to representation, all those sections, constituting one entire scheme of taxation, are necessarily invalid.

MR. JUSTICE HARLAN, dissenting.

Assuming it to be the settled construction of the constitution that the general government cannot tax lands, . . . except by apportioning the tax among the states according to their respective numbers, does it follow that a tax on incomes derived from rents is a direct tax on the real estate from which such rents arise?

In my judgment, a tax on income derived from real property ought not to be, and until now has never been, regarded by any court as a direct tax on such property, within the meaning of the constitution. As the great mass of lands in most of the states do not bring any rents, and as incomes from rents vary in the different states, such a tax cannot possibly be apportioned among the states, on the basis merely of numbers, with any approach to equality of right among taxpayers, any more than a tax on carriages or other personal property could be so apportioned. And in view of former adjudications, beginning with the *Hylton Case,* and ending with the *Springer Case,* a decision now that a tax on income from real property can be laid and collected only by apportioning the same among the states on the basis of numbers may not improperly be regarded as a judicial revolution that may sow the seeds of hate and distrust among the people of different sections of our common country. . . .

While a tax on the land itself, whether at a fixed rate applicable to all lands, without regard to their value, or by the acre, or according to their market value, might be deemed a direct tax, within the meaning of the constitution, as interpreted in the *Hylton Case,* a duty on rents is a duty on something distinct and entirely separate from, although issuing out of, the land. . . .

But the court, by its judgment just rendered, goes far in advance, not only of its former decisions, but of any decision heretofore rendered by an American court. . . .

This 1895 editorial cartoon, published after the Supreme Court's decision in *Pollock v. Farmers' Loan and Trust,* illustrates the defeat of the federal income tax law of 1894. In 1913, however, the situation reversed itself when the states ratified the Sixteenth Amendment, which gave the federal government the power to tax incomes regardless of source.

In my judgment,—to say nothing of the disregard of the former adjudications of this court, and of the settled practice of the government,—this decision may well excite the gravest apprehensions. It strikes at the very foundations of national authority, in that it denies to the general government a power which is or may become vital to the very existence and preservation of the Union in a national emergency, such as that of war with a great commercial nation, during which the collection of all duties upon imports will cease or be materially diminished. It tends to re-establish that condition of helplessness in which congress found itself during the period of the Articles of Confederation, when it was without authority, by laws operating directly upon individuals, to lay and collect, through its own agents, taxes sufficient to pay the debts and defray the expenses of government, but was dependent in all such matters upon the good will of the states, and their promptness in meeting requisitions made upon them by congress.

Why do I say that the decision just rendered impairs or menaces the national authority? The reason is so apparent that it need only be stated. In its practical operation this decision withdraws from national taxation not only all incomes derived from real estate, but tangible personal property, "invested personal property, bonds, stocks, investments of all kinds," and the income that may be derived from such property. This results from the fact that, by the decision of the court, all such personal property and all incomes from real estate and personal property are placed beyond national taxation otherwise than by apportionment among the states on the basis simply of population. No such apportionment can possibly be made without doing gross injustice to the many for the benefit of the favored few in particular states. Any attempt upon the part of congress to apportion among the states, upon the basis simply of their population, taxation of personal property or of incomes, would tend to arouse such indignation among the freemen of America that it would never be repeated. When, therefore, this court adjudges, as it does now adjudge, that congress cannot impose a duty or tax upon personal property, or upon income arising either from rents of real estate or from personal property, including invested personal property, bonds, stocks, and investments of all kinds, except by apportioning the sum to be so raised among the states according to population, it practically decides that, without an amendment of the constitution,—two-thirds of both houses of congress and three-fourths of the states concurring,—such property and incomes can never be made to contribute to the support of the national government. . . .

I dissent from the opinion and judgment of the court.

The Sixteenth Amendment

The decision to invalidate the entire income tax act was quite unpopular. Because that statute had placed a greater obligation on the wealthy, the ruling convinced the middle and working classes that the Supreme Court was little more than the defender of the rich. Various political groups immediately began working to reverse the impact of the Court's decision by means of either a constitutional amendment or revised federal legislation. Labor and farming interests supported a new income tax, as did Progressive Republicans and Democratic Populists. Opposition came primarily from conservative Republicans in the Northeast.

Finally, in 1909 Congress began serious work on an income tax measure. There were sufficient votes in the legislature to reform the tax structure, moving the federal government away from excessive reliance on regressive tariffs and excise taxes. The major question was whether to pass another income tax bill or to propose a constitutional amendment. Finding themselves in a minority, conservative Republicans threw their support to an amendment. They hoped the state legislatures would not ratify it, but, even if they did, the process would take several years to complete.

Congress proposed a constitutional amendment to authorize a federal income tax in July 1909 by overwhelming votes of 77 to 0 in the Senate and 318 to 14 in the House. The amendment received the required number of approvals from the state legislatures in February 1913 and became the Sixteenth Amendment to the United States Constitution: "The Congress shall have power to lay and collect taxes on incomes, from whatever source derived, without apportionment among the several States, and without regard to any census or enumeration."

The amendment, which effectively ended the debate over direct taxation, is one of only four designed to overturn a Supreme Court precedent. It gave Congress sufficient taxing authority to fund the federal government without having to resort to direct taxes. The Constitution now made all sources of income subject to Congress's taxing power and removed any requirement that a tax on income be apportioned on the basis of population.

Congress wasted no time. In 1913 the legislature imposed a 1 percent tax rate on individual incomes in excess of $3,000 and on incomes of married couples over $4,000. Not surprisingly, the statute's constitutionality was challenged in Court, but the justices upheld the law three years later in *Brushaber v. Union Pacific Railroad*

TABLE 8-1 Federal Tax Revenues: The Impact of the Sixteenth Amendment

Source	1800	1850	1900	1950	2000	2001
Customs duties	83.7	91.0	41.1	1.0	1.0	0.9
Excises	7.5	—	50.1	18.4	3.4	3.3
Gifts and inheritances	—	—	—	1.7	1.4	1.4
Individual incomes	—	—	—	38.5	49.6	47.3
Corporate incomes	—	—	—	25.5	10.2	10.0
Insurance trust (Social Security, etc.)	—	—	—	10.7	32.2	35.3
Other income	8.8	9.0	8.8	4.2	2.2	1.8

SOURCES: *Historical Statistics of the United States: Colonial Times to 1970* (Washington, D.C.: U.S. Bureau of the Census, 1975); *World Almanac and Book of Facts 2003* (New York: World Almanac Books, 2003), 116.
NOTE: The data represent the proportion of total federal revenues for each of seven sources of taxation. The data prior to ratification of the Sixteenth Amendment in 1913 demonstrate the federal government's reliance on customs duties and excise taxes. Data from the period after 1913 illustrate the shift to income taxes as the primary sources for federal tax dollars.

(1916) by a 7–2 vote. As shown in Table 8-1, the income tax is now the primary source of federal revenue.

TAXATION OF EXPORTS

Article I, Section 9, of the Constitution contains a prohibition against the taxation of exports: "No Tax or Duty shall be laid on Articles exported from any State." The purpose of this provision was to promote trade by removing impediments to the sale of American goods to other nations. In spite of the absolute language of the ban, Congress on occasion has passed assessments that have been attacked as taxes on exports. Such was the issue under consideration in *United States v. United States Shoe Corporation* (1998).

United States v. United States Shoe Corporation

523 U.S. 360 (1998)
http://laws.findlaw.com/US/523/360.html
Vote: 9 (Breyer, Ginsburg, Kennedy, O'Connor, Rehnquist, Scalia, Souter, Stevens, Thomas)
  0
Opinion of the Court: Ginsburg

As part of the Water Resources Development Act of 1986, Congress imposed the Harbor Maintenance Tax (HMT). This legislation assessed a uniform charge on shipments of commercial cargo through the nation's ports. The charge was set at 0.125 percent of the cargo's value. Exporters, importers, and domestic shippers were liable for the HMT, which was imposed at the time of loading for exports and unloading for other shipments. The HMT was collected by the Customs Service and deposited in the Harbor Maintenance Trust Fund. Congress could appropriate amounts from the fund to pay for harbor maintenance and development projects, including costs associated with the St. Lawrence Seaway, or related expenses.

United States Shoe Corporation paid the HMT for articles the company exported during the period April to June 1994 and then filed a protest with the Customs Service alleging that the toll was unconstitutional to the extent it applied to exports. The Customs Service responded with a form letter stating that the HMT was a statutorily mandated user fee, not an unconstitutional tax on exports. U.S. Shoe filed suit in the Court of International Trade challenging the constitutionality of the tax. The federal government defended the HMT, claiming that it was a legitimate user fee. The Court of International Trade held that the tax was not a user fee but a tax prohibited by the Export Clause. A divided court of appeals agreed, and the United States took its case to the Supreme Court.

JUSTICE GINSBURG delivered the opinion of the Court.

The Export Clause of the Constitution states: "No Tax or Duty shall be laid on Articles exported from any State." We held in *United States v. International Business Machines Corp.* (1996) (*IBM*), that the Export Clause categorically bars Congress from imposing any tax on exports. The Clause, however, does not rule out a "user fee," provided that the fee lacks the attributes of a generally applicable tax or duty and is, instead, a charge designed as compensation for government-supplied services, facilities, or benefits. This case presents the question whether the Harbor Maintenance Tax (HMT), as applied to goods loaded at United States ports for export, is an impermissible tax on exports or, instead, a legitimate user fee. We hold, in accord with the Federal Circuit, that the tax, which is imposed on an ad valorem basis, is not a fair approximation of services, facilities, or benefits furnished to the exporters, and therefore does not qualify as a permissible user fee.

Two Terms ago, in *IBM,* this Court considered the question whether a tax on insurance premiums paid to protect exports against loss violated the Export Clause. Distinguishing case law developed under the Commerce Clause and the Import-Export Clause, the Court held that the Export Clause allows no room for any federal tax, however generally applicable or nondiscriminatory, on goods in export transit. Before this Court's decision in *IBM,* the Government argued that the HMT, even if characterized as a "tax" rather than a "user fee," should survive constitutional review "because it applies without discrimination to exports, imports and domestic commerce alike." Recognizing that *IBM* "rejected an indistinguishable contention," the Government now asserts only that HMT is " 'a permissible user fee,' " a toll within the tolerance of Export Clause precedent. Adhering to the Court's reasoning in *IBM,* we reject the Government's current position.

The HMT bears the indicia of a tax. Congress expressly described it as "a tax on any port use," and codified the HMT as part of the Internal Revenue Code. In like vein, Congress provided that, for administrative, enforcement, and jurisdictional purposes, the HMT should be treated "as if [it] were a customs duty." However, "we must regard things rather than names," in determining whether an imposition on exports ranks as a tax. The crucial question is whether the HMT is a tax on exports in operation as well as nomenclature or whether, despite the label Congress has put on it, the exaction is instead a bona fide user fee.

In arguing that the HMT constitutes a user fee, the Government relies on our decisions in *United States v. Sperry Corp.* (1989), *Massachusetts v. United States* (1978), and *Evansville-Vanderburgh Airport Authority Dist. v. Delta Airlines, Inc.* (1972). In those cases, this Court upheld flat and ad valorem charges as valid user fees. . . . Those decisions involved constitutional provisions other than the Export Clause, however, and thus do not govern here. *IBM* plainly stated that the Export Clause's simple, direct, unqualified prohibition on any taxes or duties distinguishes it from other constitutional limitations on governmental taxing authority. The Court there emphasized that the "text of the Export Clause . . . expressly prohibits Congress from laying any tax or duty on exports." Accordingly, the Court reasoned in *IBM* "[o]ur decades-long struggle over the meaning of the nontextual negative command of the dormant Commerce Clause does not lead to the conclusion that our interpretation of the textual command of the Export Clause is equally fluid.". . .

The guiding precedent for determining what constitutes a bona fide user fee in the Export Clause context remains our time-tested decision in *Pace* [*v. Burgess,* 1876]. *Pace* involved a federal excise tax on tobacco. Congress provided that the tax would not apply to tobacco intended for export. To prevent fraud, however, Congress required that tobacco the manufacturer planned to export carry a stamp indicating that intention. Each stamp cost 25 cents (later 10 cents) per package of tobacco. Congress did not limit the quantity or value of the tobacco packaged for export or the size of the stamped package; "[t]hese were unlimited, except by the description of the exporter or the convenience of handling."

The Court upheld the charge, concluding that it was "in no sense a duty on exportation," but rather "compensation given for services [in fact] rendered." In so ruling, the Court emphasized two characteristics of the charge: It "bore no proportion whatever to the quantity or value of the package on which [the stamp] was affixed"; and the fee was not excessive, taking into account the cost of arrangements needed both "to give to the exporter the benefit of exemption from taxation, and . . . to secure . . . against the perpetration of fraud." *Pace* establishes that, under the Export

Clause, the connection between a service the Government renders and the compensation it receives for that service must be closer than is present here. Unlike the stamp charge in *Pace*, the HMT is determined entirely on an ad valorem basis. The value of export cargo, however, does not correlate reliably with the federal harbor services used or usable by the exporter. As the Federal Circuit noted, the extent and manner of port use depend on factors such as the size and tonnage of a vessel, the length of time it spends in port, and the services it requires, for instance, harbor dredging.

In sum, if we are "to guard against . . . the imposition of a [tax] under the pretext of fixing a fee," *Pace v. Burgess*, and resist erosion of the Court's decision in *IBM*, we must hold that the HMT violates the Export Clause as applied to exports. This does not mean that exporters are exempt from any and all user fees designed to defray the cost of harbor development and maintenance. It does mean, however, that such a fee must fairly match the exporters' use of port services and facilities.

For the foregoing reasons, the judgment of the Court of Appeals for the Federal Circuit is

Affirmed.

INTERGOVERNMENTAL TAX IMMUNITY

The operation of a federal system carries within it inherent risks of conflict between the national government and the states. When both levels of government are authorized to tax, one government can use the power as a weapon against the other. No specific provision of the Constitution prohibits the federal government from taxing state governments or vice versa, but for the federal system to operate effectively, the entities need to avoid such conflicts.

Establishing the Tax Immunity Doctrine

The issue of intergovernmental tax immunity was first raised in *McCulloch v. Maryland* (1819), which tested the constitutional validity of the national bank. The Supreme Court's decision in *McCulloch* was tremendously important in a number of ways. We have already discussed its significance for the development of congressional power and the concept of federalism, but *McCul-loch* also is relevant to the constitutional limitations on the power to tax.

McCulloch involved a challenge to a tax imposed by the state of Maryland on the national bank, a creation of the federal government. Supporters of federal power argued that the union could not be maintained if the states were permitted to place debilitating taxes on those operations of the federal government they did not approve of. States' rights advocates claimed that the power of the states to tax within their own borders was absolute and that there was no constitutional bar to such taxes. The Supreme Court ruled in favor of the federal government, declaring the state tax unconstitutional. Chief Justice Marshall's hard-hitting opinion for a unanimous Court put an immediate stop to a conflict that would have desperately weakened the union if allowed to continue.

In doing so, Marshall created the doctrine of intergovernmental tax immunity. He wrote, "[T]he power to tax involves the power to destroy; . . . the power to destroy may defeat and render useless the power to create; . . . there is plain repugnance, in conferring on one government a power to control the constitutional measures of another." The ability of the states to tax the legitimate operations of the federal government is simply incompatible with the Framers' intent of creating viable government units at both the national and state levels.

Marshall's decision in *McCulloch* was consistent with his general philosophy of favoring a strong national government. But was the doctrine of intergovernmental tax immunity a two-way street? Marshall's opinion fell short of proclaiming that the national government was prohibited from taxing the legitimate operations of the states. He was more concerned in this case with reinforcing principles of federal supremacy. Yet a strong case can be made that it would also violate the principles of the Constitution for the federal government to be permitted to destroy the states through its taxing power.

The first case that tested whether the states enjoyed immunity from federal taxation was **Collector v. Day** (1871), which stemmed from an application of the Civil War federal income tax law. Judge J. M. Day of the probate court in Massachusetts objected to paying a federal tax on his income on intergovernmental tax immunity grounds. Three decades earlier the Supreme Court had ruled that the state governments could not tax the income of federal officeholders, and now Day was asking the Court to adopt the converse of that.[9] The Supreme Court, 8–1, held that Day's judicial income was immune from federal taxation. The Court reasoned that the Constitution protects the legitimate functions of the state. The federal government cannot use its taxation powers to curtail or destroy the operations or instruments of the state, and the probate court system is a legitimate and necessary agency of state government. To allow the federal government to tax the income of state judges would be to open the door for Congress to tax all state government functions.

For several decades the justices vigorously maintained the doctrine that the Constitution did not allow one government to tax the essential functions of another. In the *Pollock* income tax decisions, as we have already seen, the court struck down a federal tax on interest income from state and municipal bonds as an unconstitutional burden on the state's authority to borrow. The Court struck down state taxes on income from federal land leases and federally granted patents and copyrights, and on the sales of petroleum products to the federal government.[10] It also invalidated a federal tax on revenues derived from the sales of goods to state agencies.[11] The only significant standard imposed by the Court in this line of cases was that immunity covered only essential government functions. Consequently, the justices upheld a federal tax on the profits of South Carolina's state-run liquor stores.[12] As a merchant of alcoholic beverages, the state was acting as a private business, not exercising a government function, and therefore was not immune from federal taxation.

Erosion of the Tax Immunity Doctrine

The Court's general support for the tax immunity doctrine was closely related to its conservatism; it opposed both big government and comprehensive regulation of the economy. When the more activist New Deal justices took control of the Court, however, support for the tax immunity doctrine began to wane. A series of Supreme Court decisions modified or reversed the earlier rulings that had established an almost impenetrable barrier against one government taxing the instruments or operations of another.

For example, in **Helvering v. Gerhardt** (1938) the Court overruled *Dobbins v. Commissioners of Erie County* (1842) and permitted states to tax the income of federal officials. The very next year the justices overruled *Collector v. Day* in **Graves v. New York ex rel. O'Keefe** (1939), holding that there was no constitutional bar to the federal government taxing the income of state employees. "The theory," said the Court, "that a tax on income is legally or economically a tax on its source, is no longer tenable." Also falling were bans on taxing profits from doing business with state or federal government agencies. The Supreme Court went so far as to allow a state to impose taxes on a federal contractor even when those taxes were passed on to the federal government through a cost-plus contract.[13]

Although these rulings seriously weakened the doctrine of intergovernmental tax immunity, the principle still has some vitality. It would be unconstitutional for a state to place a tax on cases filed in the federal courts operating within its boundaries, or for the federal government to impose an excise tax on the tickets issued by a state highway patrol. But aside from these obvious examples, where is the line between permissible and impermissible taxation? The Supreme Court helped answer that question in *South Carolina v. Baker* (1988), which involved a challenge to a federal law taxing the income from long-term state and city bonds.[14] To uphold the federal tax would require the Court to overrule that portion of the *Pollock* decision that conferred immunity on such debt instruments of the state. The opinion by Justice William Brennan not only answered the specific question presented to the Court but also provided an informative review of the status of the intergovernmental tax

9. *Dobbins v. Commissioners of Erie County* (1842).

10. *Gillespie v. Oklahoma* (1922) and *Long v. Rockwood* (1928) concerned patents and copyrights; *Panhandle Oil Co. v. Mississippi* (1928) dealt with petroleum sales.

11. *Indian Motorcycle Co. v. United States* (1931).

12. *South Carolina v. United States* (1905).

13. *Alabama v. King and Boozer* (1941).

14. To hear oral arguments in this case, navigate to: *www.oyez.org/oyez/ frontpage.*

immunity doctrine. Also instructive is the dissenting opinion of Justice Sandra Day O'Connor, who vigorously defended the immunity position.

South Carolina v. Baker

485 U.S. 505 (1988)
http://laws.findlaw.com/US/485/505.html
Vote: 7 (Blackmun, Brennan, Marshall, Rehnquist, Scalia,
*   Stevens, White)*
*   1 (O'Connor)*
Opinion of the Court: Brennan
Concurring opinions: Rehnquist, Scalia, Stevens
Dissenting opinion: O'Connor
Not participating: Kennedy

Municipal and state bonds traditionally have been issued either as bearer bonds or as registered bonds. Interest from bearer bonds is presumed to belong to the person who owns the bonds, and the interest is paid when the owner redeems coupons attached to the bond. Owners of registered bonds are recorded on a central list, and if a bond is sold the transaction must be recorded. The owner of record automatically receives interest payments by check or electronic transfer of funds. State and municipal bonds of both types have been free from federal taxation on interest earned since the Supreme Court's decision in *Pollock*.

In 1982 Congress passed the Tax Equity and Fiscal Responsibility Act (TEFRA). Section 310(b)(1) of that statute removed the federal income tax exemption for interest earned on publicly offered long-term bonds issued by state and local governments unless the bonds were issued in registered form. The primary purpose of Section 310 was to increase compliance with federal tax laws and thereby increase federal revenues. Congress estimated that income of $97 billion was going unreported. Bearer bonds became a target of reform efforts because of the ease with which they could be bought and sold. If the ownership transfer was not registered, the bondholder could evade income tax on capital gains. Unregistered bonds also were used to evade estate taxes. Other provisions in this law encouraged the federal govern-

ment and private corporations to stop issuing nonregistered long-term bonds.

The state of South Carolina sued the United States, in the name of Secretary of the Treasury James Baker, to have the law declared unconstitutional as a violation of the Tenth Amendment and the intergovernmental tax immunity doctrine. The federal government responded that the law did not violate the Constitution or the immunity doctrine because it did not eliminate the state's power to issue bonds exempt from federal taxation. The law required only that for such bonds to be tax exempt, they must be issued in a particular format. The case was heard on original jurisdiction. A special master appointed by the Court to give preliminary consideration to the case recommended that the justices uphold the validity of the law.

JUSTICE BRENNAN delivered the opinion of the Court.

South Carolina contends that even if a statute banning state bearer bonds entirely would be constitutional, §310 unconstitutionally violates the doctrine of intergovernmental tax immunity because it imposes a tax on the interest earned on a state bond. We agree with South Carolina that §310 is inconsistent with *Pollock v. Farmers' Loan & Trust Co.* (1895), which held that any interest earned on a state bond was immune from federal taxation. . . .

Under the intergovernmental tax immunity jurisprudence prevailing at the time, *Pollock* did not represent a unique immunity limited to income derived from state bonds. Rather, *Pollock* merely represented one application of the more general rule that neither the federal nor the state governments could tax income an individual directly derived from *any* contract with another government. Not only was it unconstitutional for the Federal Government to tax a bondowner on the interest she received on any state bond, but it was also unconstitutional to tax a state employee on the income earned from his employment contract, to tax a lessee on income derived from lands leased from a State, or to impose a sales tax on proceeds a vendor derived from selling a product to a state agency. Income derived from the same kinds of contracts with the Federal Government were likewise immune from taxation by the States. . . .

This general rule was based on the rationale that any tax on income a party received under a contract with the government was a tax on the contract and thus a tax "on" the government because it burdened the government's power to enter into the contract. . . . Thus, although a tax was collected from an independent private party, the tax was considered to be "on" the government because the tax burden might be passed on to it through the contract. This reasoning was used to define the basic scope of both federal and state tax immunities with respect to all types of government contracts. . . .

The rationale underlying *Pollock* and the general immunity for government contract income has been thoroughly repudiated by modern intergovernmental immunity case-law. . . .

With the rationale for conferring a tax immunity on parties dealing with another government rejected, the government contract immunities recognized under prior doctrine were, one by one, eliminated. . . .

In sum, then, under current intergovernmental tax immunity doctrine the States can never tax the United States directly but can tax any private parties with whom it does business, even though the financial burden falls on the United States, as long as the tax does not discriminate against the United States or those with whom it deals. A tax is considered to be directly on the Federal Government only "when the levy falls on the United States itself, or on an agency or instrumentality so closely connected to the Government that the two cannot realistically be viewed as separate entities." The rule with respect to state tax immunity is essentially the same, except that at least some nondiscriminatory federal taxes can be collected directly from the States even though a parallel state tax could not be collected directly from the Federal Government.

We thus confirm that subsequent case law has overruled the holding in *Pollock* that state bond interest is immune from a nondiscriminatory federal tax. We see no constitutional reason for treating persons who receive interest on government bonds differently than persons who receive income from other types of contracts with the government, and no tenable rationale for distinguishing the costs imposed on States by a tax on state bond interest from the costs imposed by a tax on the income from any other state contract. . . . Likewise, the owners of state bonds have no constitutional entitlement not to pay taxes on income they earn from state bonds, and States have no constitutional entitlement to issue bonds paying lower interest rates than other issuers. . . .

TEFRA §310 thus clearly imposes no direct tax on the States. The tax is imposed on and collected from bondholders, not States, and any increased administrative costs incurred by States in implementing the registration system are not "taxes" within the meaning of the tax immunity doctrine. . . . Nor does §310 discriminate against States. The provisions of §310 seek to assure that *all* publicly offered long-term bonds are issued in registered form, whether issued by state or local governments, the Federal Government, or private corporations. Accordingly, the Federal Government has directly imposed the same registration requirement on itself that it has effectively imposed on States. The incentives States have to switch to registered bonds are necessarily different than those of corporate bond issuers because only state bonds enjoy any exemption from the federal tax on bond interest, but the sanctions for issuing unregistered corporate bonds are comparably severe. Removing the tax exemption for interest earned on state bonds would not, moreover, create a discrimination between state and corporate bonds since corporate bond interest is already subject to federal tax.

Because the federal imposition of a bond registration requirement on States does not violate the Tenth Amendment and because a nondiscriminatory federal tax on the interest earned on state bonds does not violate the intergovernmental tax immunity doctrine, we uphold the constitutionality of §310. . . .

It is so ordered.

JUSTICE O'CONNOR, dissenting.

The Court today overrules a precedent that it has honored for nearly a hundred years and expresses a willingness to cancel the constitutional immunity that traditionally has shielded the interest paid on state and local bonds from federal taxation. Henceforth the ability of state and local governments to finance their activities will depend in part on whether Congress voluntarily abstains from tapping this permissible source of additional income tax revenue. I believe that state autonomy is an important factor to be considered in reviewing the National Government's exercise of its enumerated powers. I dissent from the decision to overrule *Pollock v. Farmers' Loan & Trust Co.* (1895), and I would invalidate Congress' attempt to regulate the sovereign States by threatening to deprive them of this tax immunity, which would increase their dependence on the National Government. . . .

Long-term debt obligations are an essential source of funding for state and local governments. In 1974, state and local governments issued approximately $23 billion of new municipal bonds; in 1984, they issued $102 billion of new bonds. State and local governments rely heavily on borrowed funds to finance education, road construction, and utilities, among other purposes. As the Court recognizes, States will have to increase the interest rates they pay on bonds by 28–35% if the interest is subject to the federal income tax. Governmental operations will be hindered severely if the cost of capital rises by one-third. If Congress may tax the interest paid on state and local bonds, it may strike at the very heart of state and local government activities. . . .

Federal taxation of state activities is inherently a threat to state sovereignty. As Chief Justice Marshall observed long ago, "the power to tax involves the power to destroy." Justice Holmes later qualified this principle, observing that "[t]he power to tax is not the power to destroy while this Court sits." If this Court is the States' sole protector against the threat of crushing taxation, it must take seriously its responsibility to sit in judgment of federal tax initiatives. I do not think that the Court has lived up to its constitutional role in this case. The Court has failed to enforce the constitutional safeguards of state autonomy and self-sufficiency that may be found in the Tenth Amendment and the Guarantee Clause, as well as in the principles of federalism implicit in the Constitution. I respectfully dissent.

South Carolina v. Baker continued a long-standing trend of the Court to erode the doctrine of intergovernmental tax immunity. A statement of the contemporary status of the doctrine, in Justice Brennan's words, is that "the States can never tax the United States directly but can tax any private parties with whom it does business, even though the financial burden falls on the United States, as long as the tax does not discriminate against the United States or those with whom it deals." A similar, although not quite as rigid, prohibition applies to federal taxes on the states.

Even in those cases, such as *South Carolina v. Baker*, that have limited intergovernmental tax immunity, the Court repeatedly has stressed the principle that taxes must be nondiscriminatory. If a state wishes to tax a company's profits from a business transaction with the federal government, for example, the tax obligation must be the same as that imposed on profits from business with nongovernment parties. This bar against discriminatory taxation was tested in *Davis v. Michigan Department of Treasury* (1989). At issue was a Michigan tax exemption given to state government retirees but not to federal government retirees. Justice Anthony Kennedy's opinion for the Court provides an informative review of the immunity doctrine's development as well as an answer to the challenge presented by the case.

Davis v. Michigan Department of Treasury

489 U.S. 803 (1989)
http://laws.findlaw.com/US/489/803.html
Vote: 8 (Blackmun, Brennan, Kennedy, Marshall, O'Connor,
    Rehnquist, Scalia, White)
    1 (Stevens)
Opinion of the Court: Kennedy
Dissenting opinion: Stevens

Michigan's revenue code provided that retirement benefits paid to individuals by the state or any of its political subdivisions were exempt from state income taxes. Retirement benefits from any other source, including federal retirement income, were subject to the tax. Paul S. Davis spent his career in federal service, as a lawyer for the Securities and Exchange Commission and then as an administrative law judge. As a Michigan resident, he paid state income taxes on his federal retirement benefits. In 1984, however, Davis petitioned the state for a refund of taxes paid on his federal benefits for the 1979–1984 tax years.

He based his case on a federal statute (4 U.S.C. §111) passed in 1939 to clarify the doctrine of intergovernmental tax immunity. The law provided:

The United States consents to the taxation of pay or compensation for personal service as an officer or employee of the United States . . . by a duly constituted taxing authority having jurisdiction, if the taxation does not discriminate against the officer or employee because of the source of the pay or compensation.

Davis's claim was rejected by state revenue authorities and in the state courts. The state argued that Davis was not covered by the act because he was no longer an "employee" of the federal government but simply a receiver of annuity benefits. Further, Michigan claimed that the state law did not discriminate against federal employees but only provided a special exemption for state retirees, a reasonable incentive to attract and keep qualified people in state government service.

Davis appealed to the U.S. Supreme Court, and, in fact, personally argued his case before the justices. He enjoyed the help of a powerful ally, however, when the U.S. government supported his claim as a friend of the court.

JUSTICE KENNEDY delivered the opinion of the Court.

Section 111 was enacted as part of the Public Salary Tax Act of 1939, the primary purpose of which was to impose federal income tax on the salaries of all state and local government employees. Prior to the adoption of the Act, salaries of most government employees, both state and federal, generally were thought to be exempt from taxation by another sovereign under the doctrine of intergovernmental tax immunity. This doctrine had its genesis in *McCulloch v. Maryland* (1819), which held that the State of Maryland could not impose a discriminatory tax on the Bank of the United States. Chief Justice Marshall's opinion for the Court reasoned that the Bank was an instrumentality of the Federal Government used to carry into effect the Government's delegated powers, and taxation by the State would unconstitutionally interfere with the exercise of those powers.

For a time, *McCulloch* was read broadly to bar most taxation by one sovereign of the employees of another. See *Collector v. Day* (1871) (invalidating federal income tax on salary of state judge); *Dobbins v. Commissioners of Erie County* (1842) (invalidating state tax on federal officer). This rule "was based on the rationale that any tax on income a party received under a contract with the government was a tax on the contract and thus a tax 'on' the government because it burdened the government's power to enter into the contract." *South Carolina v. Baker* (1988).

In subsequent cases, however, the Court began to turn away from its more expansive applications of the immunity doctrine. Thus, in *Helvering v. Gerhardt* (1938), the Court held that the Federal Government could levy nondiscriminatory taxes on the incomes of most state employees. The following year, *Graves v. New York ex rel. O'Keefe* (1939) over-

ruled the *Day-Dobbins* line of cases that had exempted government employees from nondiscriminatory taxation. After *Graves*, therefore, intergovernmental tax immunity barred only those taxes that were imposed directly on one sovereign by the other or that discriminated against a sovereign or those with whom it dealt.

It was in the midst of this judicial revision of the immunity doctrine that Congress decided to extend the federal income tax to state and local government employees. The Public Salary Tax Act was enacted after *Helvering v. Gerhardt* had upheld the imposition of federal income taxes on state civil servants, and Congress relied on that decision as support for its broad assertion of federal taxing authority. However, the Act was drafted, considered in Committee, and passed by the House of Representatives before the announcement of the decision in *Graves v. New York ex rel. O'Keefe*, which for the first time permitted state taxation of federal employees. As a result, during most of the legislative process leading to adoption of the Act it was unclear whether state taxation of federal employees was still barred by intergovernmental tax immunity despite the abrogation of state employees' immunity from federal taxation. . . .

Dissatisfied with this uncertain state of affairs, and concerned that considerations of fairness demanded equal tax treatment for state and federal employees, Congress decided to ensure that federal employees would not remain immune from state taxation at the same time that state government employees were being required to pay federal income taxes. Accordingly, section 4 of the proposed Act (now section 111) expressly waived whatever immunity would have otherwise shielded federal employees from nondiscriminatory state taxes. . . .

Section 111 did not waive all aspects of intergovernmental tax immunity, however. The final clause of the section contains an exception for state taxes that discriminate against federal employees on the basis of the source of their compensation. This nondiscrimination clause closely parallels the nondiscrimination component of the constitutional immunity doctrine which has, from the time of *McCulloch v. Maryland*, barred taxes that "operat[e] so as to discriminate against the Government of those with whom it deals."

. . . When Congress codifies a judicially defined concept, it is presumed, absent an express statement to the contrary, that Congress intended to adopt the interpretation placed on that concept by the courts. Hence, we conclude that the retention of immunity in section 111 is coextensive with the prohibition against discriminatory taxes embodied in the modern constitutional doctrine of intergovernmental tax immunity.

. . . Thus, the dispositive question in this case is whether the tax imposed on appellant is barred by the doctrine of intergovernmental tax immunity.

It is undisputed that Michigan's tax system discriminates in favor of retired state employees and against retired federal employees. The State argues, however, that appellant is not entitled to claim the protection of the immunity doctrine, and that in any event the State's inconsistent treatment of Federal and State Government retirees is justified by meaningful differences between the two classes.

In support of its first contention, the State points out that the purpose of the immunity doctrine is to protect the governments and not private entities or individuals. As a result, so long as the challenged tax does not interfere with the Federal Government's ability to perform its governmental functions, the constitutional doctrine has not been violated.

It is true that intergovernmental tax immunity is based on the need to protect each sovereign's governmental operations from undue interference by the other. But it does not follow that private entities or individuals who are subjected to discriminatory taxation on account of their dealings with a sovereign cannot themselves receive the protection of the constitutional doctrine. Indeed, all precedent is to the contrary. . . .

Under our precedents, "[t]he imposition of a heavier tax burden on [those who deal with one sovereign] than is imposed on [those who deal with the other] must be justified by significant differences between the two classes." *Phillips Chemical Co. v. Dumas Independent School District* [1960]. . . .

The State points to two allegedly significant differences between federal and state retirees. First, the State suggests that its interest in hiring and retaining qualified civil servants through the inducement of a tax exemption for retirement benefits is sufficient to justify the preferential treatment of its retired employees. This argument is wholly beside the point, however, for it does nothing to demonstrate that there are "significant differences between the two classes" themselves; rather, it merely demonstrates that the State has a rational reason for discriminating between two similar groups of retirees. The State's interest in adopting the discriminatory tax, no matter how substantial, is simply

irrelevant to an inquiry into the nature of the two classes receiving inconsistent treatment.

Second, the State argues that its retirement benefits are significantly less munificent than those offered by the Federal Government, in terms of vesting requirements, rate of accrual, and computation of benefit amounts. The substantial differences in the value of the retirement benefits paid the two classes should, in the State's view, justify the inconsistent tax treatment.

Even assuming the State's estimate of the relative value of state and federal retirement benefits is generally correct, we do not believe this difference suffices to justify the type of blanket exemption at issue in this case. While the average retired federal civil servant receives a larger pension than his state counterpart, there are undoubtedly many individual instances in which the opposite holds true. A tax exemption truly intended to account for differences in retirement benefits would not discriminate on the basis of the source of those benefits, as Michigan's statute does; rather, it would discriminate on the basis of the amount of benefits received by individual retirees. . . .

For these reasons, we conclude that the Michigan Income Tax Act violates principles of intergovernmental tax immunity by favoring retired state and local government employees over retired federal employees. . . .

. . . The judgment of the Court of Appeals is reversed, and the case is remanded for further proceedings not inconsistent with this opinion.

JUSTICE STEVENS, dissenting.

The Court today strikes down a state tax that applies equally to the vast majority of Michigan residents, including federal employees, because it treats retired state employees differently from retired federal employees. The Court's holding is not supported by the rationale for the intergovernmental immunity doctrine and is not compelled by our previous decisions. I cannot join the unjustified, court-imposed restriction on a State's power to administer its own affairs. . . .

If Michigan were to tax the income of federal employees without imposing a like tax on others, the tax would be plainly unconstitutional. Cf. *McCulloch v. Maryland* (1819). On the other hand, if the State taxes the income of all its residents equally, federal employees must pay the tax. *Graves v.*

New York ex rel. O'Keefe (1939). The Michigan tax here applies to approximately 4 1/2 million individual taxpayers in the State, including the 24,000 retired federal employees. It exempts only the 130,000 retired state employees. Once one understands the underlying reason for the *McCulloch* holding [the immunity doctrine is a check against the abusive use of the taxing power by one sovereign against the other], it is plain that this tax does not unconstitutionally discriminate against federal employees. . . .

Today, it is not the great Chief Justice's dictum about how the power to tax includes the power to destroy that obscures the issue in a web of unreality; it is the virtually automatic rejection of anything that can be labeled "discriminatory." The question in this case deserves more careful consideration than is provided by the mere use of that label. It should be answered by considering whether the *ratio decidendi* of our holding in *McCulloch v. Maryland* is applicable to this quite different case. It is not. I, therefore, respectfully dissent.

As a result of this decision, Paul Davis received tax refunds of $4,299. But the impact of the decision extended far beyond Davis. Fourteen other states had similar discriminatory tax provisions. As a consequence, this ruling cost these states hundreds of millions of dollars in tax refunds to federal retirees and lost future revenues. The states were required to revise their laws, making a choice between extending the tax exemptions to retired federal employees or eliminating the exemption granted to state and local retirees. The Court's decision in *Davis* reminds us that the tax immunity doctrine remains viable in spite of decisions that have imposed limitations on it.

TAXATION AS A REGULATORY POWER

Normally, we think of taxation as a method of funding the government. Yet Marshall's well-known statement that the "power to tax involves the power to destroy" was an early recognition that taxes can be used for purposes other than raising revenue. Excessive taxation can make the targeted activities so unprofitable that it is no longer feasible to engage in them. The converse also is true. Favorable tax status, including tax exemptions, can encourage a preferred activity. These observations lead

us to several important constitutional questions regarding the taxation powers of the federal government: Is it proper for the United States to impose taxes for reasons other than revenue raising? Is it constitutional for the government to use taxation as a method of regulation? Is it valid for Congress to enact tax laws as means of controlling activities not otherwise within the jurisdiction of the federal government? Here we are confronting a question similar to one we examined relative to the Commerce Clause: May the federal government use the power to tax as the equivalent of a state's police power?

Taxation for Nonrevenue Purposes

From the beginning, Congress has used its authority to tax for purposes other than raising revenue. Before the ratification of the Sixteenth Amendment, the federal government relied heavily on customs duties. In deciding what imported products to tax and at what level, the legislators clearly were guided by their policy preferences. Certain industries received protection from imports and were able to grow with little foreign competition. The practice of combining revenue gathering with other policy objectives continues to this day.

The only serious challenge to the use of import taxes as a regulatory mechanism came in *J. W. Hampton, Jr. & Co. v. United States* (1928). Hampton Company imported into New York a quantity of barium dioxide that was assessed a duty of six cents per pound, two cents higher than the rate set by Congress. However, Congress had authorized the president to raise or lower tariff duties up to 50 percent of the amount set by Congress whenever the chief executive found that such adjustments were necessary for equitable foreign trade. In this case President Calvin Coolidge had concluded that an increased tariff was necessary to equalize the barium dioxide production costs between Germany and the United States. Hampton objected to the tax, claiming that the flexible tariff was an improper delegation of legislative power to the executive branch and that Congress violated the Constitution by using the taxation powers for reasons other than revenue gathering. As we saw in Chapter 5, the Supreme Court ruled that the delegation was proper.

The justices also held in *Hampton* that Congress did not have to rely exclusively on revenue needs in constructing tariff laws. In reaching this conclusion, the Court showed a deference to history. Chief Justice William Howard Taft, writing for the majority, noted that the very first revenue act in 1789 imposed import duties with an eye toward encouraging growth of domestic industry and protecting it from foreign competition. The Court was not likely to rule unconstitutional a practice that had been followed uninterrupted for almost a century and a half. "So long as the motive of Congress and the effect of its legislative action are to secure revenue for the benefit of the general government," Taft wrote, "the existence of other motives in the selection of the subjects of taxes cannot invalidate Congressional action."

Deciding that Congress may impose import duties with regulatory purposes does not necessarily answer a similar question with respect to excise taxes. Customs duties, after all, have a limited range. They can be applied only to those goods that are brought into the country from abroad. Excise taxes can be applied to the broad spectrum of domestic goods, services, and activities. The only restriction on such taxes explicitly mentioned in the Constitution is that they be geographically uniform. But is there an implied requirement that excise taxes can be generated only by revenue objectives, or can Congress regulate through the use of the excise? If Congress is allowed to regulate domestic activities through the power to tax, does that not give the federal government the equivalent of a police power that the Framers reserved to the states?

Shortly after the Civil War, the Court heard **Veazie Bank v. Fenno** (1869), which presented a challenge to a federal excise tax that was imposed far more to regulate the economy than to raise revenue. In 1866 Congress passed a law placing a 10 percent tax on notes issued by state banks. The law was intended to protect the newly chartered national bank from state competition by making these notes far too costly for state banks to issue. Veazie Bank paid the tax under protest, claiming that Congress had no authority to issue such an excise. But in a 5–2 decision, the Court held that the tax was proper given the constitutional power of Congress to regulate the monetary system.

Did the *Veazie Bank* decision mean that Congress may impose excise taxes for any regulatory purpose or only as a means of promoting a power already granted to the federal government? The first major case to confront this question focused on a federal excise tax placed on margarine.

McCray v. United States

195 U.S. 27 (1904)
http://laws.findlaw.com/US/195/27.html
Vote: 6 (Brewer, Day, Harlan, Holmes, McKenna, White)
3 (Brown, Fuller, Peckham)
Opinion of the Court: White

In the latter half of the nineteenth century, food producers developed a commercially marketable oleomargarine. The product was made of oleo oil, lard, milk, cream, and salt. It had a taste and consistency similar to butter but was less expensive. Especially successful was a margarine that was artificially colored to make the naturally white product look like butter. As margarine grew in popularity, the dairy industry became concerned and demanded protection. In response, Congress passed the Oleomargarine Act of 1886 and amended it in 1902. In addition to licensing producers and retailers of margarine, the statute imposed an excise tax of one-quarter cent per pound on uncolored margarine, and a tax of ten cents per pound on artificially colored margarine. The manufacturers of the product were responsible for payment of the tax. Although the act raised revenue, its central purpose was to protect the dairy industry by raising the price of margarine and discouraging the sale of the artificially colored product.

Leo McCray, a licensed retail seller of margarine, was assessed a $50 penalty for knowingly purchasing from the Ohio Butterine Company a fifty-pound package of margarine for resale upon which sufficient taxes had not been paid. The package bore the one-quarter cent tax stamps, but the margarine was artificially colored and subject to the higher tax. McCray challenged his fine, claiming that the federal tax was unconstitutional. Its defect, according to McCray, was that the law was a regulation on the intrastate manufacture of margarine, a sphere of authority reserved for the states. The federal government countered with the argument that the margarine tax was an excise tax, and as such the Constitution required only that it meet the standard of geographical uniformity. The lower courts upheld the validity of the tax.

MR. JUSTICE WHITE delivered the opinion of the Court.

Did Congress in passing the acts which are assailed, exert a power not conferred by the Constitution?

That the acts in question on their face impose excise taxes which Congress had the power to levy is so completely established as to require only statement. . . .

It is, however, argued if a lawful power may be exerted for an unlawful purpose, and thus by abusing the power it may be made to accomplish a result not intended by the Constitution, all limitations of power must disappear, and the grave function lodged in the judiciary, to confine all the departments within the authority conferred by the Constitution, will be of no avail. This, when reduced to its last analysis, comes to this, that, because a particular department of the government may exert its lawful powers with the object or motive of reaching an end not justified, therefore it becomes the duty of the judiciary to restrain the exercise of a lawful power wherever it seems to the judicial mind that such lawful power has been abused. But this reduces itself to the contention that, under our constitutional system, the abuse by one department of the government of its lawful powers is to be corrected by the abuse of its powers by another department.

The proposition, if sustained, would destroy all distinction between the powers of the respective departments of the government, would put an end to that confidence and respect for each other which it was the purpose of the Constitution to uphold, and would thus be full of danger to the permanence of our institutions. . . .

It is, of course, true, as suggested, that if there be no authority in the judiciary to restrain a lawful exercise of power by another department of the government, where a wrong motive or purpose has impelled to the exertion of the power, that abuses of a power conferred may be temporarily effectual. The remedy for this, however, lies, not in the abuse by the judicial authority of its functions, but in the people, upon whom, after all, under our institutions, reliance must be placed for the correction of abuses committed in the exercise of a lawful power. . . .

The decisions of this court from the beginning lend no support whatever to the assumption that the judiciary may restrain the exercise of lawful power on the assumption that a wrongful purpose or motive has caused the power to be exerted. As we have previously said, from the beginning no case can be found announcing such a doctrine, and on the contrary the doctrine of a number of cases is inconsistent with its existence. As quite recently pointed out by this court in *Knowlton v. Moore* (1900), the often quoted statement of Chief Justice Marshall in *McCulloch v. Maryland*, that the power to tax is the power to destroy, affords no support whatever to the proposition that where there is a lawful power to impose a tax its imposition may be treated as without the power because of the destructive effect of the exertion of the authority. . . .

It being thus demonstrated that the motive or purpose of Congress in adopting the acts in question may not be inquired into, we are brought to consider the contentions relied upon to show that the acts assailed were beyond the power of Congress, putting entirely out of view all considerations based upon purpose or motive.

1. Undoubtedly, in determining whether a particular act is within a granted power, its scope and effect are to be considered. Applying this rule to the acts assailed, it is self-evident that on their face they levy an excise tax. That being their necessary scope and operation, it follows that the acts are within the grant of power. The argument to the contrary rests on the proposition that, although the tax be within the power, as enforcing it will destroy or restrict the manufacture of artificially colored oleomargarine, therefore the power to levy the tax did not obtain. This, however, is but to say that the question of power depends, not upon the authority conferred by the Constitution but upon what may be the consequence arising from the exercise of the lawful authority.

Since, as pointed out in all the decisions referred to, the taxing power conferred by the Constitution knows no limits except those expressly stated in that instrument, it must follow, if a tax be within the lawful power, the exertion of that power may not be judicially restrained because of the results to arise from its exercise. . . .

2. The proposition that where a tax is imposed which is within the grant of powers, and which does not conflict

with any express constitutional limitation, the courts may hold the tax to be void because it is deemed that the tax is too high, is absolutely disposed of by the opinions in the cases hitherto cited, and which expressly hold . . . that "The judicial department cannot prescribe to the legislative department limitations upon the exercise of its acknowledged powers. The power to tax may be exercised oppressively upon persons; but the responsibility of the legislature is not to the courts, but to the people by whom its members are elected."

3. Whilst undoubtedly both the Fifth and Tenth Amendments qualify, in so far as they are applicable, all the provisions of the Constitution, nothing in those amendments operates to take away the grant of power to tax conferred by the Constitution upon Congress. The contention on this subject rests upon the theory that the purpose and motive of Congress in exercising its undoubted powers may be inquired into by the courts, and the proposition is therefore disposed of by what has been said on that subject.

The right of Congress to tax within its delegated power being unrestrained, except as limited by the Constitution, it was within the authority conferred on Congress to select the objects upon which an excise should be laid. It therefore follows that, in exerting its power, no want of due process of law could possibly result, because that body chose to impose an excise on artificially colored oleomargarine and not upon natural butter artificially colored. . . .

4. Lastly we come to consider the argument that, even though as a general rule a tax of the nature of the one in question would be within the power of Congress, in this case the tax should be held not to be within such power, because of its effect. This is based on the contention that, as the tax is so large as to destroy the business of manufacturing oleomargarine artificially colored, to look like butter, it thus deprives the manufacturers of that article of their freedom to engage in a lawful pursuit, and hence, irrespective of the distribution of powers made by the Constitution, the taxing laws are void, because they violate those fundamental rights which it is the duty of every free government to safeguard, and which, therefore, should be held to be embraced by implied though none the less potential guaranties, or in any event to be within the protection of the due process clause of the Fifth Amendment.

Let us concede, for the sake of argument only, the premise of fact upon which the proposition is based. Moreover,

concede for the sake of argument only, that even although a particular exertion of power by Congress was not restrained by any express limitation of the Constitution, if by the perverted exercise of such power so great an abuse was manifested as to destroy fundamental rights which no free government could consistently violate, that it would be the duty of the judiciary to hold such acts to be void upon the assumption that the Constitution by necessary implication forbade them.

Such concession, however, is not controlling in this case. This follows when the nature of oleomargarine, artificially colored to look like butter, is recalled. As we have said, it has been conclusively settled by this court that the tendency of that article to deceive the public into buying it for butter is such that the States may, in the exertion of their police powers, without violating the due process clause of the Fourteenth Amendment, absolutely prohibit the manufacture of the article. It hence results, that even though it be true that the effect of the tax in question is to repress the manufacture of artificially colored oleomargarine, it cannot be said that such repression destroys rights which no free government could destroy, and, therefore, no ground exists to sustain the proposition that the judiciary may invoke an implied prohibition, upon the theory that to do so is essential to save such rights from destruction. And the same considerations dispose of the contention based upon the due process clause of the Fifth Amendment. That provision, as we have previously said, does not withdraw or expressly limit the grant of power to tax conferred upon Congress by the Constitution. From this it follows, as we have also previously declared, that the judiciary is without authority to avoid an act of Congress exerting the taxing power, even in a case where to the judicial mind it seems that Congress had in putting such power in motion abused its lawful authority by levying a tax which was unwise or oppressive, or the result of the enforcement of which might be to indirectly affect subjects not within the powers delegated to Congress.

Let us concede that if a case was presented where the abuse of the taxing power was so extreme as to be beyond the principles which we have previously stated, and where it was plain to the judicial mind that the power had been called into play not for revenue but solely for the purpose of destroying rights which could not be rightfully destroyed consistently with the principles of freedom and justice upon which the Constitution rests, that it would be the duty of the courts to say that such an arbitrary act was not merely an abuse of a delegated power, but was the exercise of an authority not conferred. This concession, however, like the one previously made, must be without influence upon the decision of this cause for the reasons previously stated; that is, that the manufacture of artificially colored oleomargarine may be prohibited by a free government without a violation of fundamental rights.

Affirmed.

With decisions such as *Veazie, McCray,* and others, Congress reasonably concluded that the power to tax could be used as a regulatory weapon. The legislators were encouraged by statements such as that written by Justice White in *McCray:* "The decisions of this court from the beginning lend no support whatever to the assumption that the judiciary may restrain the exercise of lawful power on the assumption that a wrongful purpose or motive has caused the power to be exerted." The Court seemed committed to a policy of approving legislation that took the proper form of an excise tax and met the geographical uniformity requirement regardless of the congressional motives behind it. If motives were not to be probed by the judiciary, the legislative branch would have a free hand in using taxation to regulate or even destroy certain activities considered by Congress to be detrimental to the nation.

Rejection and Reestablishment of Regulatory Taxation

Among Congress's targets was child labor. As we saw in our discussions of federalism and the Commerce Clause, Congress first attempted to regulate child labor in the 1916 Keating-Owen Act, which prohibited articles produced by child labor from being shipped in interstate and foreign commerce. Just two years after that law was enacted, the Supreme Court in *Hammer v. Dagenhart* struck it down on the ground that Congress, under the guise of interstate commerce regulation, was actually controlling manufacturing and mining, considered at that time to be intrastate activities the regulation of which was reserved to the states.

After suffering this defeat at the hands of the Supreme Court, Congress drafted a second statute to attack child labor, this time using the power to tax. Could the national legislature constitutionally use the excise tax as a means of eliminating child labor? Would the justices once again refuse to examine congressional motives? The answer to these questions came in *Bailey v. Drexel Furniture Co.* (1922). As you read Chief Justice Taft's opinion, note his distinction between a tax and a penalty. Does he make a compelling argument? And does it surprise you that progressive members of the Court, such as Oliver Wendell Holmes and Louis Brandeis, voted to strike down the law?

Bailey v. Drexel Furniture Co.

259 U.S. 20 (1922)
http://laws.findlaw.com/US/259/20.html
Vote: 8 (Brandeis, Day, Holmes, McKenna, McReynolds,
            Pitney, Taft, Van Devanter)
        1 (Clarke)
Opinion of the Court: Taft

Congress passed the Child Labor Tax Law on February 24, 1919. The statute imposed an excise tax of 10 percent on the net profits of any company hiring child labor. Under the law, child labor was defined as the employment of children under the age of sixteen in any mine or quarry, or under the age of fourteen in any mill, cannery, workshop, factory, or manufacturing establishment. The definition also included the use of children between the ages of fourteen and sixteen who worked more than eight hours a day or more than six days a week, or who worked between the hours of 7:00 P.M. and 6:00 A.M.

Drexel was a furniture manufacturing company in North Carolina. On September 20, 1921, it received from J. W. Bailey, the IRS collector for the Western District of North Carolina, a notice that it had been assessed $6,312.79 in excise taxes for having employed a boy under the age of fourteen during the 1919 tax year. The company paid the tax under protest and sued for a refund. Drexel argued that the tax was nothing more than an unconstitutional attempt to regulate manufacturing. The United States defended the statute as an excise tax that need meet no standard but geographical uniformity. The lower court ruled in favor of the company.

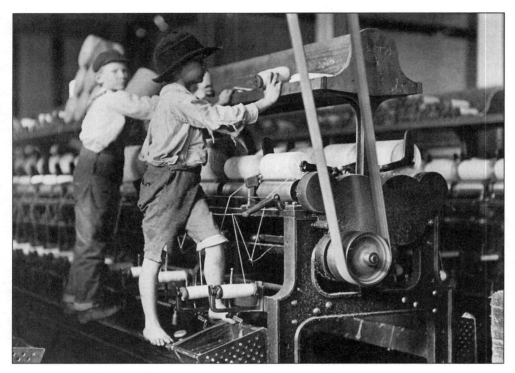

Young boys working a loom in Macon, Georgia, circa 1910. Conditions such as these were the target of reform legislation passed by Congress and declared unconstitutional by the Supreme Court in *Hammer v. Dagenhart* (1918) and *Bailey v. Drexel Furniture Company* (1922).

MR. CHIEF JUSTICE TAFT delivered the opinion of the Court.

The law is attacked on the ground that it is a regulation of the employment of child labor in the States—an exclusively state function under the Federal Constitution and within the reservations of the Tenth Amendment. It is defended on the ground that it is a mere excise tax levied by the Congress of the United States under its broad power of taxation conferred by §8, Article I, of the Federal Constitution. We must construe the law and interpret the intent and meaning of Congress from the language of the act. The words are to be given their ordinary meaning unless the context shows that they are differently used. Does this law impose a tax with only that incidental restraint and regulation which a tax must inevitably involve? Or does it regu-

late by the use of the so-called tax as a penalty? If a tax, it is clearly an excise. If it were an excise on a commodity or other thing of value we might not be permitted under previous decisions of this court to infer solely from its heavy burden that the act intends a prohibition instead of a tax. But this act is more. It provides a heavy exaction for a departure from a detailed and specified course of conduct in business. That course of business is that employers shall employ in mines and quarries, children of an age greater than sixteen years; in mills and factories, children of an age greater than fourteen years, and shall prevent children of less than sixteen years in mills and factories from working more than eight hours a day or six days in the week. If an employer departs from this prescribed course of business, he is to pay to the Government one-tenth of his entire net income in the business for a full year. The amount is not to be proportioned in any degree to the extent or frequency of the departures, but is to be paid by the employer in full measure whether he employs five hundred children for a year, or employs only one for a day. Moreover, if he does not know the child is within the named age limit, he is not to pay; that is to say, it is only where he knowingly departs from the prescribed course that payment is to be exacted. Scienter is associated with penalties, not with taxes. The employer's factory is to be subject to inspection at any time not only by the taxing officers of the Treasury, the Department normally charged with the collection of taxes, but also by the Secretary of Labor and his subordinates, whose normal function is the advancement and protection of the welfare of the workers. In the light of these features of the act, a court must be blind not to see that the so-called tax is imposed to stop the employment of children within the age limits prescribed. Its prohibitory and regulatory effect and purpose are palpable. All others can see and understand this. How can we properly shut our minds to it?

It is the high duty and function of this court in cases regularly brought to its bar to decline to recognize or enforce seeming laws of Congress, dealing with subjects not entrusted to Congress but left or committed by the supreme law of the land to the control of the States. We cannot avoid the duty, even though it require us to refuse to give effect to legislation designed to promote the highest good. The good sought in unconstitutional legislation is an insidious feature because it leads citizens and legislators of good purpose to promote it without thought of the serious breach it will make in the ark of our covenant or the harm which will come from breaking down recognized standards. In the maintenance of local self-government, on the one hand, and the national power, on the other, our country has been able to endure and prosper for near a century and a half.

Out of a proper respect for the acts of a co-ordinate branch of the Government, this court has gone far to sustain taxing acts as such, even though there has been ground for suspecting from the weight of the tax it was intended to destroy its subject. But, in the act before us, the presumption of validity cannot prevail, because the proof of the contrary is found on the very face of its provisions. Grant the validity of this law, and all that Congress would need to do, hereafter, in seeking to take over to its control any one of the great number of subjects of public interest, jurisdiction

of which the States have never parted with, and which are reserved to them by the Tenth Amendment, would be to enact a detailed measure of complete regulation of the subject and enforce it by a so-called tax upon departures from it. To give such magic to the word "tax" would be to break down all constitutional limitation of the powers of Congress and completely wipe out the sovereignty of the States.

The difference between a tax and a penalty is sometimes difficult to define and yet the consequences of the distinction in the required method of their collection often are important. Where the sovereign enacting the law has power to impose both tax and penalty, the difference between revenue production and mere regulation may be immaterial, but not so when one sovereign can impose a tax only, and the power of regulation rests in another. Taxes are occasionally imposed in the discretion of the legislature on proper subjects with the primary motive of obtaining revenue from them and with the incidental motive of discouraging them by making their continuance onerous. They do not lose their character as taxes because of the incidental motive. But there comes a time in the extension of the penalizing features of the so-called tax when it loses its character as such and becomes a mere penalty with the characteristics of regulation and punishment. Such is the case in the law before us. Although Congress does not invalidate the contract of employment or expressly declare that the employment within the mentioned ages is illegal, it does exhibit its intent practically to achieve the latter result by adopting the criteria of wrongdoing and imposing its principal consequence on those who transgress its standard. The case before us cannot be distinguished from that of *Hammer v. Dagenhart*. Congress there enacted a law to prohibit transportation in interstate commerce of goods made at a factory in which there was employment of children within the same ages and for the same number of hours a day and days in a week as are penalized by the act in this case. This court held the law in that case to be void. It said:

"In our view the necessary effect of this act is, by means of a prohibition against the movement in interstate commerce of ordinary commercial commodities, to regulate the hours of labor of children in factories and mines within the States, a purely state authority."

In the case at the bar, Congress in the name of a tax which on the face of the act is a penalty seeks to do the same thing, and the effort must be equally futile.

The analogy of the *Dagenhart Case* is clear. The congressional power over interstate commerce is, within its proper scope, just as complete and unlimited as the congressional power to tax, and the legislative motive in its exercise is just as free from judicial suspicion and inquiry. Yet when Congress threatened to stop interstate commerce in ordinary and necessary commodities, unobjectionable as subjects of transportation, and to deny the same to the people of a State in order to coerce them into compliance with Congress's regulation of state concerns, the court said this was not in fact regulation of interstate commerce, but rather that of State concerns and was invalid. So here the so-called tax is a penalty to coerce people of a State to act as Congress wishes them to act in respect of a matter completely the business of the state government under the Federal Constitution. . . .

. . . For the reasons given, we must hold the Child Labor Tax Law invalid and the judgment of the District Court is

Affirmed.

With the Court's rejection of both its attempts to regulate child labor through the commerce and taxation powers, Congress pursued yet another alternative. In 1924, two years after *Drexel*, Congress proposed a constitutional amendment that gave the national government power to regulate and prohibit child labor. Unlike most proposed amendments, this one had no congressionally determined deadline on the states for ratification. Slightly more than half of the state legislatures endorsed the amendment before support for it began to decline. In the end, the amendment was unnecessary. Many states responded to decisions such as *Hammer* and *Drexel* by passing their own child labor laws. In addition, the 1937 constitutional revolution that redefined the concept of interstate commerce, along with subsequent employment regulation decisions such as *United States v. Darby Lumber* (1941), gave the federal government ample authority to control child labor.

The decision in *Drexel* was a reversal of the position on excise taxes the Court had held since the early 1800s. It proved to be out of line with Supreme Court rulings both before and after. The Court repeatedly has faced the question of taxation and regulation and generally has ruled in favor of the federal power to tax; the Court has even acknowledged that to some degree all taxes have regulatory effects. For example, in *United States v. Doremus* (1919) and *Nigro v. United States* (1928) the Court upheld federal excise taxes on narcotics, and in *United States v. Sanchez* (1950) it upheld a tax on marijuana. Similarly, an excise tax on objectionable firearms was declared valid in *Sonzinsky v. United States* (1937), even though the Court admitted that the law had an unmistakable "legislative purpose to regulate rather than to tax." In **United States v. Kahriger** (1953) the justices found no constitutional defects with an excise levied on professional gamblers. These taxes expand federal regulatory powers. If Congress has the power to impose the tax, then the federal government also has the power to enforce the tax laws, creating, to an extent, "police powers" within the federal government that originally resided with the states.

The authority to use the excise tax as a regulatory power is not unlimited. Such taxes cannot be levied or enforced in a manner that violates other provisions of the Constitution. *Kahriger* provides an illustration. The tax imposed required those engaged in accepting bets to pay an annual excise of $50 and to register with the collector of internal revenue. Although it is constitutionally valid for Congress to impose an occupational excise tax, the law cannot compel a person to admit to criminal activity. To do so would be a violation of the Fifth Amendment's Self-Incrimination Clause. Joseph Kahriger raised these objections in his appeal, but the majority upheld the statute's requirements that gamblers register with the government. Fifteen years later, however, the Court reexamined this position in **Marchetti v. United States** (1968). Here the Court held that no laws, including tax laws, can constitutionally require a person to admit to criminal activities. To the extent that the *Kahriger* decision permitted such procedures, it was overruled.

TAXING AND SPENDING FOR THE GENERAL WELFARE

The Constitution authorizes Congress to tax and spend for the general welfare. Whether the term *general welfare* was intended to expand the powers of Congress beyond those explicitly stated in the Constitution is subject to debate. James Madison, for example, argued that general welfare was only a reference to the other enumerated powers. Because the United States is a government of limited and specified powers, he asserted, the authority to tax and spend must be confined to those spheres of authority the Constitution explicitly granted. Alexander Hamilton took the opposite position. He interpreted the power to tax and spend for the general welfare to be a separate power altogether. For Hamilton taxing and spending authority was given in addition to the other granted powers, not limited by them. The conflict between these two opposing interpretations was the subject of legal disputes throughout much of the nation's history. During the constitutional crisis over legislation passed during the New Deal, however, the final battle between the two was waged.

A Restricted View of Taxing and Spending

Many of the programs recommended by Franklin Roosevelt to reestablish the nation's economic strength involved regulatory activity far more extensive than ever before proposed. Several depended on the power of the federal government to tax and spend for the general welfare. Opponents of the New Deal claimed that these programs, while ostensibly based upon the taxing and spending authority, in reality were regulations of matters the Constitution reserved for the states.

One of the most important objectives of the Roosevelt administration was to restore stability to the agricultural markets and to impose conditions that would make farms profitable. To accomplish these goals, Congress passed the Agricultural Adjustment Act of 1933, which was challenged in *United States v. Butler* (1936). Although the issues were crucial both to the economic welfare of the nation and to the constitutional future of federalism, Justice Owen Roberts, writing for the majority, presented an uncomplicated formula for deciding the case: "Lay the article of the Constitution which is invoked beside the statute which is challenged and . . . decide whether the latter squares with the former." Do you believe the process of judicial review is that simple—especially when so much is riding on the outcome of the Court's deliberations?

United States v. Butler

297 U.S. 1 (1936)
http://laws.findlaw.com/US/297/1.html
Vote: 6 (Butler, Hughes, McReynolds, Roberts, Sutherland,
*   Van Devanter)*
*   3 (Brandeis, Cardozo, Stone)*
Opinion of the Court: Roberts
Dissenting opinion: Stone

During the Great Depression, agriculture was one of the hardest-hit sectors of the economy. The nation's farmers were overproducing, which caused prices for farm products to drop. In many cases the cost of production was higher than the income from crop sales, leaving farmers in desperate straits. Most had their farms mortgaged, and all owed taxes on their lands. The more the farmers got behind economically, the more they attempted to produce to improve their situation. This strategy further increased production, making matters even worse. At that time agriculture was responsible for a much larger proportion of the nation's economy than it is today, and conditions in the farming sector had dire effects on the general welfare of the entire country.

In response, Roosevelt proposed and Congress passed the Agricultural Adjustment Act (AAA), a statute that combined the taxing and spending powers to combat the agricultural crisis. The central purpose of the plan was to reduce the amount of acreage being farmed. To accomplish this goal, the federal government would "rent" a percentage of the nation's farmland and leave this acreage unplanted. In effect, the government would pay the farmers not to farm. If the plan succeeded, production would drop, prices would rise, and the farmers would have a sufficient income. Making payments to the nation's farmers was an expensive proposition, and to fund these expenditures the AAA imposed an excise tax on the processing of agricultural products.

The program was a success until William M. Butler challenged the constitutionality of the law. Butler was the bankruptcy receiver for Hoosac Mills Corporation, a cotton processor. When the government imposed the

William M. Butler, receiver for Hoosac Mills, objected to paying the federal tax on processing cotton. His lawsuit successfully challenged the constitutionality of the Agricultural Adjustment Act of 1933.

processing tax on Hoosac, Butler took legal action to avoid payment, claiming that the AAA exceeded the taxing and spending powers granted to the federal government. The district court upheld the law, but the court of appeals reversed. The United States appealed to the Supreme Court.

A number of amicus curiae briefs were filed by groups having a direct interest in the outcome of the case. Supporting the validity of the act were groups of farmers and other agricultural producers, such as the American Farm Bureau Federation. Arguing to strike down the AAA were agricultural processing interests, such as the National Association of Cotton Manufacturers, the National Biscuit Company, P. Lorillard Co., and General Mills.

MR. JUSTICE ROBERTS delivered the opinion of the Court.

The Government asserts that even if the respondents may question the propriety of the appropriation embodied in the statute their attack must fail because Article I, §8 of the Constitution authorizes the contemplated expenditure of the funds raised by the tax. This contention presents the great and the controlling question in the case. We approach its decision with a sense of our grave responsibility to render judgment in accordance with the principles established for the government of all three branches of the Government.

There should be no misunderstanding as to the function of this court in such a case. It is sometimes said that the court assumes a power to overrule or control the action of the people's representatives. This is a misconception. The Constitution is the supreme law of the land ordained and established by the people. All legislation must conform to the principles it lays down. When an act of Congress is appropriately challenged in the courts as not conforming to the constitutional mandate the judicial branch of the Government has only one duty,—to lay the article of the Constitution which is invoked beside the statute which is challenged and to decide whether the latter squares with the former. All the court does, or can do, is to announce its considered judgment upon the question. The only power it has, if such it may be called, is the power of judgment. This court neither approves nor condemns any legislative policy. Its delicate and difficult office is to ascertain and declare whether the legislation is in accordance with, or in contravention of, the provisions of the Constitution; and, having done that, its duty ends.

The question is not what power the Federal Government ought to have but what powers in fact have been given by the people. It hardly seems necessary to reiterate that ours is a dual form of government; that in every state there are two governments,—the state and the United States. Each State has all governmental powers save such as the people, by their Constitution, have conferred upon the United States, denied to the States, or reserved to themselves. The federal union is a government of delegated powers. It has only such as are expressly conferred upon it and such as are reasonably to be implied from those granted. In this respect we differ radically from nations where all legislative power, without restriction or limitation, is vested in a parliament or other legislative body subject to no restrictions except the discretion of its members.

Article I, §8, of the Constitution vests sundry powers in the Congress. But two of its clauses have any bearing upon the validity of the statute under review.

The third clause endows the Congress with power "to regulate Commerce . . . among the several States." Despite a reference in its first section to a burden upon, and an obstruction of the normal currents of commerce, the act under review does not purport to regulate transactions in interstate or foreign commerce. Its stated purpose is the control of agricultural production, a purely local activity, in an effort to raise the prices paid the farmer. Indeed, the Government does not attempt to uphold the validity of the act on the basis of the commerce clause, which, for the purpose of the present case, may be put aside as irrelevant.

The clause thought to authorize the legislation,—the first,—confers upon the Congress power "to lay and collect Taxes, Duties, Imposts and Excises, to pay the Debts and provide for the common Defence and general Welfare of the United States. . . ." It is not contended that this provision grants power to regulate agricultural production upon the theory that such legislation would promote the general welfare. The Government concedes that the phrase "to provide for the general welfare" qualifies the power "to lay and collect taxes." The view that the clause grants power to provide for the general welfare, independently of the taxing power, has never been authoritatively accepted. . . . The true construction undoubtedly is that the only thing granted is the power to tax for the purpose of providing funds for payment of the nation's debts and making provision for the general welfare.

Nevertheless the Government asserts that warrant is found in this clause for the adoption of the Agricultural Adjustment Act. The argument is that Congress may appropriate and authorize the spending of moneys for the "general welfare"; that the phrase should be liberally construed to cover anything conducive to national welfare; that decision as to what will promote such welfare rests with Congress alone, and the courts may not review its determination; and finally that the appropriation under attack was in fact for the general welfare of the United States.

The Congress is expressly empowered to lay taxes to provide for the general welfare. Funds in the Treasury as a result of taxation may be expended only through appropria-

tion. (Art. I, §9, cl. 7.) They can never accomplish the objects for which they were collected unless the power to appropriate is as broad as the power to tax. The necessary implication from the terms of the grant is that the public funds may be appropriated "to provide for the general welfare of the United States." These words cannot be meaningless, else they would not have been used. The conclusion must be that they were intended to limit and define the granted power to raise and to spend money. How shall they be construed to effectuate the intent of the instrument?

Since the foundation of the Nation sharp differences of opinion have persisted as to the true interpretation of the phrase. Madison asserted it amounted to no more than a reference to the other powers enumerated in the subsequent clauses of the same section; that, as the United States is a government of limited and enumerated powers, the grant of power to tax and spend for the general national welfare must be confined to the enumerated legislative fields committed to the Congress. In this view the phrase is mere tautology, for taxation and appropriation are or may be necessary incidents of the exercise of any of the enumerated legislative powers. Hamilton, on the other hand, maintained the clause confers a power separate and distinct from those later enumerated, is not restricted in meaning by the grant of them, and Congress consequently has a substantive power to tax and to appropriate, limited only by the requirement that it shall be exercised to provide for the general welfare of the United States. Each contention has had the support of those whose views are entitled to weight. This court has noticed the question, but has never found it necessary to decide which is the true construction. Mr. Justice Story, in his Commentaries, espouses the Hamiltonian position. We shall not review the writings of public men and commentators or discuss the legislative practice. Study of all these leads us to conclude that the reading advocated by Mr. Justice Story is the correct one. While, therefore, the power to tax is not unlimited, its confines are set in the clause which confers it, and not in those of §8 which bestow and define the legislative powers of the Congress. It results that the power of Congress to authorize expenditure of public moneys for public purposes is not limited by the direct grants of legislative power found in the Constitution. . . .

We are not now required to ascertain the scope of the phrase "general welfare of the United States" or to determine whether an appropriation in aid of agriculture falls within it. Wholly apart from that question, another principle embedded in our Constitution prohibits the enforcement of the Agricultural Adjustment Act. The act invades the reserved rights of the states. It is a statutory plan to regulate and control agricultural production, a matter beyond the powers delegated to the federal government. The tax, the appropriation of the funds raised, and the direction for their disbursement, are but parts of the plan. They are but means to an unconstitutional end.

From the accepted doctrine that the United States is a government of delegated powers, it follows that those not expressly granted, or reasonably to be implied from such as are conferred, are reserved to the states or to the people. To forestall any suggestion to the contrary, the Tenth Amendment was adopted. The same proposition, otherwise stated, is that powers not granted are prohibited. None to regulate agricultural production is given, and therefore legislation by Congress for that purpose is forbidden.

It is an established principle that the attainment of a prohibited end may not be accomplished under the pretext of the exertion of powers which are granted. . . .

The power of taxation, which is expressly granted, may, of course, be adopted as a means to carry into operation another power also expressly granted. But resort to the taxing power to effectuate an end which is not legitimate, not within the scope of the Constitution, is obviously inadmissible. . . .

. . . If the taxing power may not be used as the instrument to enforce a regulation of matters of state concern with respect to which the Congress has no authority to interfere, may it, as in the present case, be employed to raise the money necessary to purchase a compliance which the Congress is powerless to command? The Government asserts that whatever might be said against the validity of the plan if compulsory, it is constitutionally sound because the end is accomplished by voluntary cooperation. There are two sufficient answers to the contention. The regulation is not in fact voluntary. The farmer, of course, may refuse to comply, but the price of such refusal is the loss of benefits. The amount offered is intended to be sufficient to exert pressure on him to agree to the proposed regulation. The power to confer or withhold unlimited benefits is the power to coerce or destroy. If the cotton grower elects not to accept the benefits, he will receive less for his crops; those who receive payments will be able to undersell him. The result will

be financial ruin. The coercive purpose and intent of the statute is not obscured by the fact that it has not been perfectly successful. It is pointed out that, because there still remained a minority whom the rental and benefit payments were insufficient to induce to surrender their independence of action, the Congress has gone further and, in the Bankhead Cotton Act, used the taxing power in a more directly minatory fashion to compel submission. This progression only serves more fully to expose the coercive purpose of the so-called tax imposed by the present act. It is clear that the Department of Agriculture has properly described the plan as one to keep a non-cooperating minority in line. This is coercion by economic pressure. The asserted power of choice is illusory. . . .

But if the plan were one for purely voluntary cooperation it would stand no better so far as federal power is concerned. At best it is a scheme for purchasing with federal funds submission to federal regulation of a subject reserved to the states. . . .

Congress has no power to enforce its commands on the farmer to the ends sought by the Agricultural Adjustment Act. It must follow that it may not indirectly accomplish those ends by taxing and spending to purchase compliance. The Constitution and the entire plan of our government negative any such use of the power to tax and to spend as the act undertakes to authorize. It does not help to declare that local conditions throughout the nation have created a situation of national concern; for this is but to say that whenever there is a widespread similarity of local conditions, Congress may ignore constitutional limitations upon its own powers and usurp those reserved to the states. If, in lieu of compulsory regulation of subjects within the states' reserved jurisdiction, which is prohibited, the Congress could invoke the taxing and spending power as a means to accomplish the same end, clause 1 of §8 of Article I would become the instrument for total subversion of the governmental powers reserved to the individual states.

If the act before us is a proper exercise of the federal taxing power, evidently the regulation of all industry throughout the United States may be accomplished by similar exercises of the same power. It would be possible to exact money from one branch of an industry and pay it to another branch in every field of activity which lies within the province of the states. The mere threat of such a procedure might well induce the surrender of rights and the compliance with federal regulation as the price of continuance in business. . . .

The judgment is

Affirmed.

MR. JUSTICE STONE, dissenting.

I think the judgment should be reversed.

The present stress of widely held and strongly expressed differences of opinion of the wisdom of the Agricultural Adjustment Act makes it important, in the interest of clear thinking and sound result, to emphasize at the outset certain propositions which should have controlling influence in determining the validity of the Act. They are:

1. The power of the courts to declare a statute unconstitutional is subject to two guiding principles of decision which ought never to be absent from judicial consciousness. One is that courts are concerned only with the power to enact statutes, not with their wisdom. The other is that while unconstitutional exercise of power by the legislative and executive branches of the government is subject to judicial restraint, the only check upon our own exercise of power is our own sense of self-restraint. For the removal of unwise laws from the statute books appeal lies not to the courts but to the ballot and to the processes of democratic government.

2. The constitutional power of Congress to levy an excise tax upon the processing of agricultural products is not questioned. The present levy is held invalid, not for any want of power in Congress to lay such a tax to defray public expenditures, including those for the general welfare, but because the use to which its proceeds are put is disapproved.

3. As the present depressed state of agriculture is nation wide in its extent and effects, there is no basis for saying that the expenditure of public money in aid of farmers is not within the specifically granted power of Congress to levy taxes to "provide for the . . . general welfare." The opinion of the Court does not declare otherwise.

4. No question of a variable tax fixed from time to time by fiat of the Secretary of Agriculture, or of unauthorized delegation of legislative power, is now presented. The schedule of rates imposed by the Secretary in accordance with the original command of Congress has since been specifically adopted and confirmed by Act of Congress, which has declared that it shall be the lawful tax. That is the tax which the government now seeks to collect. Any defects there may have been in the manner of laying the tax by the Secretary have now been removed by the exercise of the power of Congress to pass a curative statute validating an intended, though defective, tax. The Agricultural Adjustment Act as thus amended declares that none of its provisions shall fail because others are pronounced invalid.

It is with these preliminary and hardly controverted matters in mind that we should direct our attention to the pivot on which the decision of the Court is made to turn. It is that a levy unquestionably within the taxing power of Congress may be treated as invalid because it is a step in a plan to regulate agricultural production and is thus a forbidden infringement of state power. The levy is not any less an exercise of taxing power because it is intended to defray an expenditure for the general welfare rather than for some other support of government. Nor is the levy and collection of the tax pointed to as effecting the regulation. While all federal taxes inevitably have some influence on the internal economy of the states, it is not contended that the levy of a processing tax upon manufacturers using agricultural products as raw material has any perceptible regulatory effect upon either their production or manufacture. . . . Here regulation, if any there be, is accomplished not by the tax but by the method by which its proceeds are expended, and would equally be accomplished by any like use of public funds, regardless of their source.

. . . [T]he power to tax and spend includes the power to relieve a nationwide economic maladjustment by conditional gifts of money.

Butler had a mixed outcome. The Court concluded that the federal government had broad powers to tax and spend for the general welfare. The justices decided, consistent with the position previously articulated by Alexander Hamilton, that Congress's fiscal authority was not limited to those subjects specifically enumerated in Article I. However, this philosophy did not mean that congressional powers had no limits. The majority in *Butler* concluded that the law was unconstitutional because what it imposed was not truly a tax. Instead, the government was taking money from one group (the processors) to give to another (the farmers), and doing this to regulate farm production, a matter of intrastate commerce reserved for state regulation.

Expanding the Powers to Tax and Spend

The impact of the *Butler* case was short-lived. Following the Court's dramatic change in position after Roosevelt's threat to add new members, the justices ruled that agriculture could be regulated under the commerce power.[15] As for the power to tax and spend for the general welfare, the position taken in *Butler* was reevaluated the very next year in *Steward Machine Co. v. Davis* (1937), a challenge to the constitutionality of the newly formed Social Security system. The Social Security Act of 1935 (SSA) shared several characteristics with the Agricultural Adjustment Act the Court had condemned in *Butler*. Both used the taxing and spending powers to combat the effects of the Depression; both took money from one group of people to give to another; and both regulated areas previously thought to be reserved to the states. But in *Steward Machine* the justices upheld the validity of the act. Note that in this case Hughes and Roberts desert the *Butler* majority and join with the liberal wing of the Court to forge new constitutional interpretations.

Steward Machine Co. v. Davis

301 U.S. 548 (1937)
http://laws.findlaw.com/US/301/548.html
Vote: 5 (Brandeis, Cardozo, Hughes, Roberts, Stone)
        4 (Butler, McReynolds, Sutherland, Van Devanter)
Opinion of the Court: Cardozo
Dissenting opinions: Butler, McReynolds, Sutherland

On August 14, 1935, Congress passed the Social Security Act, a comprehensive law designed to provide economic security to groups of individuals who were particularly in need. Its three most important programs were the creation of an old age and survivors benefits program; the implementation of benefits for dependent children,

---

15. See *Mulford v. Smith* (1939) and *Wickard v. Filburn* (1942).

the handicapped, and the sight-impaired; and the development of a cooperative federal-state unemployment compensation system. The unemployment provisions were the focus of the constitutional challenge in this case.

The act, as originally passed, imposed an excise tax on employers who hired more than eight workers. The tax was based on the total amount of wages paid. However, employers could receive a tax credit, not to exceed 90 percent of their unemployment tax obligations, for contributions made to an approved state unemployment compensation program.

The state programs had to meet federal specifications. The money employers contributed to these state funds was deposited with the secretary of the U.S. Treasury. The secretary would pay funds back to the states for their unemployment compensation programs. Congress also authorized additional federal funds to be used to assist the states in administering their compensation systems.

The Steward Machine Company, an Alabama corporation, paid the taxes due under the program and then sued the collector of internal revenue for a refund, claiming that the SSA violated the Constitution on a number of grounds. The amount of the contested refund was $46.14. The district court and the court of appeals upheld the validity of the act.

MR. JUSTICE CARDOZO delivered the opinion of the Court.

The assault on the statute proceeds on an extended front. Its assailants take the ground that the tax is not an excise; that it is not uniform throughout the United States as excises are required to be; that its exceptions are so many and arbitrary as to violate the Fifth Amendment; that its purpose was not revenue, but an unlawful invasion of the reserved powers of the states; and that the states in submitting to it have yielded to coercion and have abandoned governmental functions which they are not permitted to surrender.

The objections will be considered seriatim with such further explanation as may be necessary to make their meaning clear.

First. The tax, which is described in the statute as an excise, is laid with uniformity throughout the United States as a duty, an impost or an excise upon the relation of employment. . . .

The subject matter of taxation open to the power of the Congress is as comprehensive as that open to the power lof the states, though the method of apportionment may at times be different. . . . The statute books of the states are strewn with illustrations of taxes laid on occupations pursued of common right. We find no basis for a holding that the power in that regard which belongs by accepted practice to the legislatures of the states, has been denied by the Constitution to the Congress of the nation.

The tax being an excise, its imposition must conform to the canon of uniformity. There has been no departure from this requirement. According to the settled doctrine the uniformity exacted is geographical, not intrinsic.

Second. The excise is not invalid under the provisions of the Fifth Amendment by force of its exemptions.

The statute does not apply, as we have seen, to employers of less than eight. It does not apply to agricultural labor, or domestic service in a private home or to some other classes of less importance. Petitioner contends that the effect of these restrictions is an arbitrary discrimination vitiating the tax. . . .

The classifications and exemptions directed by the statute now in controversy have support in considerations of policy and practical convenience that cannot be condemned as arbitrary. . . . The act of Congress is therefore valid, so far at least as its system of exemptions is concerned, and this though we assume that discrimination, if gross enough, is equivalent to confiscation and subject under the Fifth Amendment to challenge and annulment.

Third. The excise is not void as involving the coercion of the States in contravention of the Tenth Amendment or of restrictions implicit in our federal form of government.

The proceeds of the excise when collected are paid into the Treasury at Washington, and thereafter are subject to appropriation like public moneys generally. No presumption can be indulged that they will be misapplied or wasted. Even if they were collected in the hope or expectation that some other and collateral good would be furthered as an incident, that without more would not make the act invalid. This indeed is hardly questioned. The case for the petitioner is built on the contention that here an ulterior aim is wrought into the very structure of the act, and what is even more important that the aim is not only ulterior, but essentially unlawful. In particular, the 90 per cent credit is relied upon as supporting that conclusion. But before the statute

succumbs to an assault upon these lines, two propositions must be made out by the assailant. There must be a showing in the first place that separated from the credit the revenue provisions are incapable of standing by themselves. There must be a showing in the second place that the tax and the credit in combination are weapons of coercion, destroying or impairing the autonomy of the states. The truth of each proposition being essential to the success of the assault, we pass for convenience to a consideration of the second, without pausing to inquire whether there has been a demonstration of the first.

To draw the line intelligently between duress and inducement there is need to remind ourselves of facts as to the problem of unemployment that are now matters of common knowledge. The relevant statistics are gathered in the brief of counsel for the Government. Of the many available figures a few only will be mentioned. During the years 1929 to 1936, when the country was passing through a cyclical depression, the number of the unemployed mounted to unprecedented heights. Often the average was more than 10 million; at times a peak was attained of 16 million or more. Disaster to the breadwinner meant disaster to dependents. Accordingly the roll of the unemployed, itself formidable enough, was only a partial roll of the destitute or needy. The fact developed quickly that the states were unable to give the requisite relief. The problem had become national in area and dimensions. There was need of help from the nation if the people were not to starve. It is too late today for the argument to be heard with tolerance that in a crisis so extreme the use of the moneys of the nation to relieve the unemployed and their dependents is a use for any purpose narrower than the promotion of the general welfare. . . .

In the presence of this urgent need for some remedial expedient, the question is to be answered whether the expedient adopted has overleapt the bounds of power. The assailants of the statute say that its dominant end and aim is to drive the state legislatures under the whip of economic pressure into the enactment of unemployment compensation laws at the bidding of the central government. Supporters of the statute say that its operation is not constraint, but the creation of a larger freedom, the states and the nation joining in a co-operative endeavor to avert a common evil. . . .

The Social Security Act is an attempt to find a method by which all these public agencies may work together to a common end. Every dollar of the new taxes will continue in all likelihood to be used and needed by the nation as long as states are unwilling, whether through timidity or for other motives, to do what can be done at home. At least the inference is permissible that Congress so believed, though retaining undiminished freedom to spend the money as it pleased. On the other hand fulfillment of the home duty will be lightened and encouraged by crediting the taxpayer upon his account with the Treasury of the nation to the extent that his contributions under the laws of the locality have simplified or diminished the problem of relief and the probable demand upon the resources of the fisc. Duplicated taxes, or burdens that approach them, are recognized hardships that government, state or national, may properly avoid. If Congress believed that the general welfare would better be promoted by relief through local units than by the system then in vogue, the cooperating localities ought not in all fairness to pay a second time.

Who then is coerced through the operation of this statute? Not the taxpayer. He pays in fulfillment of the mandate of the local legislature. Not the state. Even now she does not offer a suggestion that in passing the unemployment law she was affected by duress. For all that appears she is satisfied with her choice, and would be sorely disappointed if it were now to be annulled. The difficulty with the petitioner's contention is that it confuses motive with coercion. "Every tax is in some measure regulatory. To some extent it interposes an economic impediment to the activity taxed as compared with others not taxed." In like manner every rebate from a tax when conditioned upon conduct is in some measure a temptation. But to hold that motive or temptation is equivalent to coercion is to plunge the law in endless difficulties. The outcome of such a doctrine is the acceptance of a philosophical determinism by which choice becomes impossible. Till now the law has been guided by a robust common sense which assumes the freedom of the will as a working hypothesis in the solution of its problems. . . .

United States v. Butler is cited by petitioner as a decision to the contrary. There a tax was imposed on processors of farm products, the proceeds to be paid to farmers who would reduce their acreage and crops under agreements with the Secretary of Agriculture, the plan of the act being to increase the prices of certain farm products by decreasing the quantities produced. The court held (1) that the so-called tax was not a true one, the proceeds being earmarked

for the benefit of farmers complying with the prescribed conditions, (2) that there was an attempt to regulate production without the consent of the state in which production was affected, and (3) that the payments to farmers were coupled with coercive contracts, unlawful in their aim and oppressive in their consequences. The decision was by a divided court, a minority taking the view that the objections were untenable. None of them is applicable to the situation here developed.

(a) The proceeds of the tax in controversy are not earmarked for a special group.

(b) The unemployment compensation law which is a condition of the credit has had the approval of the state and could not be a law without it.

(c) The condition is not linked to an irrevocable agreement, for the state at its pleasure may repeal its unemployment law, terminate the credit, and place itself where it was before the credit was accepted.

(d) The condition is not directed to the attainment of an unlawful end, but to an end, the relief of unemployment, for which nation and state may lawfully cooperate.

Fourth. The statute does not call for a surrender by the states of powers essential to their quasi-sovereign existence. . . .

The judgment is

Affirmed.

Separate opinion of MR. JUSTICE MCREYNOLDS.

That portion of the Social Security legislation here under consideration, I think, exceeds the power granted to Congress. It unduly interferes with the orderly government of the state by her own people and otherwise offends the Federal Constitution.

In *Texas v. White* (1869), a cause of momentous importance, this Court, through Chief Justice Chase, declared—"But the perpetuity and indissolubility of the Union, by no means implies the loss of distinct and individual existence, or of the right of self-government by the States. . . ."

The doctrine thus announced and often repeated, I had supposed was firmly established. Apparently the states remained really free to exercise governmental powers, not delegated or prohibited, without interference by the federal government through threats of punitive measures or offers of seductive favors. Unfortunately, the decision just announced opens the way for practical annihilation of this theory; and no cloud of words or ostentatious parade of irrelevant statistics should be permitted to obscure that fact.

Separate opinion of MR. JUSTICE SUTHERLAND.

With most of what is said in the opinion just handed down, I concur. . . .

But the question with which I have difficulty is whether the administrative provisions of the act invade the governmental administrative powers of the several states reserved by the Tenth Amendment. . . .

The precise question, therefore, which we are required to answer by an application of these principles is whether the congressional act contemplates a surrender by the state to the federal government, in whole or in part, of any state governmental power to administer its own unemployment law or the state pay roll-tax funds which it has collected for the purposes of that law. An affirmative answer to this question, I think, must be made. . . .

If we are to survive as the United States, the balance between the powers of the nation and those of the states must be maintained. There is grave danger in permitting it to dip in either direction, danger—if there were no other—in the precedent thereby set for further departures from the equipoise. The threat implicit in the present encroachment upon the administrative functions of the states is that greater encroachments, and encroachments upon other functions, will follow.

For the foregoing reasons, I think the judgment below should be reversed.

MR. JUSTICE VAN DEVANTER joins in this opinion.

MR. JUSTICE BUTLER, dissenting.

I think that the objections to the challenged enactment expressed in the separate opinions of MR. JUSTICE MC-REYNOLDS and MR. JUSTICE SUTHERLAND are well taken. I am also of opinion that, in principle and as applied to bring about and to gain control over state unemployment compensation, the statutory scheme is repugnant to the Tenth Amendment. . . . The Constitution grants to the United States no power to pay unemployed persons or to require the states to enact laws or to raise or disburse money for that purpose. The provisions in question, if not amounting to coercion in a legal sense, are manifestly designed and intended directly to affect state action in the respects specified. And, if valid as so employed, this 'tax and credit' device may be made effective to enable federal authorities to induce, if not indeed to compel, state enactments for any purpose within the realm of state power and generally to control state administration of state laws. . . .

The terms of the measure make it clear that the tax and credit device was intended to enable federal officers virtually to control the exertion of powers of the states in a field in which they alone have jurisdiction and from which the United States is by the Constitution excluded.

I am of opinion that the judgment of the Circuit Court of Appeals should be reversed.

In a second case decided the same day, the Court upheld the old age benefits provisions of the Social Security Act.[16] From that point on, the Social Security program became a permanent fixture in the lives of American workers. The Social Security cases also firmly established that the taxing and spending powers are to be broadly construed. If Congress decides that the general welfare of the United States demands a program requiring the use of these fiscal powers, the Supreme Court likely will find it constitutionally valid unless parts of the law violate specific provisions of the Constitution. In fact, *United States v. Butler* was the last case in which the Supreme Court ruled that Congress had exceeded its spending powers. Since these 1937 decisions, Congress has used the spending authority to expand greatly the role of the federal government.

Federal-State Fiscal Tensions

Serious challenges to a federal spending program are now unusual. Yet a battle over federal and state authority with respect to spending programs does occasionally flare up. One such case was *South Dakota v. Dole* (1987).[17] This dispute involved a conflict over federal spending power and the state's authority to regulate highway safety and alcoholic beverages. The use of federal funds to coerce the states into taking particular policy positions was criticized in much the same manner as arguments in *Steward*

16. *Helvering v. Davis* (1937).
17. To hear oral arguments in this case navigate to: *www.oyez.org/oyez/frontpage.*

Machine attacked the establishment of state unemployment compensation programs. It is interesting to note that Chief Justice William Rehnquist, normally considered a strong defender of states' rights, wrote the majority opinion upholding the exercise of federal authority over the states. A dissenting vote was cast by Justice Brennan, another surprise because Brennan usually could be counted on to support federal power. Not surprising was the stinging dissent registered by Justice O'Connor on behalf of state interests.

South Dakota v. Dole

483 U.S. 203 (1987)
http://laws.findlaw.com/US/483/203.html
Vote: 7 (Blackmun, Marshall, Powell, Rehnquist, Scalia,
        Stevens, White)
    2 (Brennan, O'Connor)
Opinion of the Court: Rehnquist
Dissenting opinions: Brennan, O'Connor

In 1984 Congress passed a statute, 23 U.S.C. 158, directing the secretary of transportation to withhold a portion of federal highway funds from any state that did not establish a minimum drinking age of twenty-one years. Many states at that time had a lower minimum drinking age. The purpose of the law was to decrease the number of serious automobile accidents among a group that statistics showed had a high percentage of accidents. The legislators correctly believed that withholding federal dollars would be an effective way of encouraging the states to comply with the federal program.

South Dakota, which allowed the purchase of beer containing 3.2 percent alcohol by persons nineteen years or older, objected to the statute, arguing that Congress was infringing on the rights of the states. The Twenty-first Amendment, which repealed prohibition in 1933, gave full authority to the states to regulate alcoholic beverages; therefore, South Dakota claimed that Congress had no authority to set minimum drinking ages. According to the state, the federal government was using its considerable spending power to coerce the states into enacting laws that were otherwise outside congressional authority.

The state sued Secretary of Transportation Elizabeth Dole, asking the courts to declare the law unconstitutional. Both the district court and the court of appeals ruled against the state and upheld the law.

CHIEF JUSTICE REHNQUIST delivered the opinion of the Court.

The Constitution empowers Congress to "lay and collect Taxes, Duties, Imposts, and Excises, to pay the Debts and provide for the common Defence and general Welfare of the United States." Art. I, §8, cl. 1. Incident to this power, Congress may attach conditions on the receipt of federal funds, and has repeatedly employed the power "to further broad policy objectives by conditioning receipt of federal moneys upon compliance by the recipient with federal statutory and administrative directives." The breadth of this power was made clear in *United States v. Butler* (1936), where the Court, resolving a longstanding debate over the scope of the Spending Clause, determined that "the power of Congress to authorize expenditure of public moneys for public purposes is not limited by the direct grants of legislative power found in the Constitution." Thus, objectives not thought to be within Article I's "enumerated legislative fields" may nevertheless be attained through the use of the spending power and the conditional grant of federal funds.

The spending power is of course not unlimited, but is instead subject to several general restrictions articulated in our cases. The first of these limitations is derived from the language of the Constitution itself: the exercise of the spending power must be in pursuit of "the general welfare." In considering whether a particular expenditure is intended to serve general public purposes, courts should defer substantially to the judgment of Congress. Second, we have required that if Congress desires to condition the States' receipt of federal funds, it "must do so unambiguously . . . , enabl[ing] the States to exercise their choice knowingly, cognizant of the consequences of their participation." Third, our cases have suggested (without significant elaboration) that conditions on federal grants might be illegitimate if they are unrelated "to the federal interest in particular national projects or programs." Finally, we have noted that other constitutional provisions may provide an independent bar to the conditional grant of federal funds.

South Dakota does not seriously claim that §158 is inconsistent with any of the first three restrictions mentioned above. We can readily conclude that the provision is designed to serve the general welfare, especially in light of the fact that "the concept of welfare or the opposite is shaped by Congress. . . ." Congress found that the differing drinking ages in the States created particular incentives for young persons to combine their desire to drink with their ability to drive, and that this interstate problem required a national solution. The means it chose to address this dangerous situation were reasonably calculated to advance the general welfare. The conditions upon which States receive the funds, moreover, could not be more clearly stated by Congress. And the State itself, rather than challenging the germaneness of the condition to federal purposes, admits that it "has never contended that the congressional action was . . . unrelated to a national concern in the absence of the Twenty-first Amendment." Indeed, the condition imposed by Congress is directly related to one of the main purposes for which highway funds are expended—safe interstate travel. This goal of the interstate highway system had been frustrated by varying drinking ages among the States. . . . By enacting §158, Congress conditioned the receipt of federal funds in a way reasonably calculated to address this particular impediment to a purpose for which the funds are expended.

The remaining question about the validity of §158—and the basic point of disagreement between the parties—is whether the Twenty-first Amendment constitutes an "independent constitutional bar" to the conditional grant of federal funds. Petitioner, relying on its view that the Twenty-first Amendment prohibits *direct* regulation of drinking ages by Congress, asserts that "Congress may not use the spending power to regulate that which it is prohibited from regulating directly under the Twenty-first Amendment." But our cases show that this "independent constitutional bar" limitation on the spending power is not of the kind petitioner suggests. *United States v. Butler*, for example, established that the constitutional limitations on Congress when exercising its spending power are less exacting than those on its authority to regulate directly. . . .

. . . [T]he "independent constitutional bar" limitation on the spending power is not, as petitioner suggests, a prohibition on the indirect achievement of objectives which Congress is not empowered to achieve directly. Instead, we think that the language in our earlier opinions stands for the unexceptionable proposition that the power may not be used to induce the States to engage in activities that would themselves be unconstitutional. Thus, for example, a grant of federal funds conditioned on invidiously discriminatory state action or the infliction of cruel and unusual punishment would be an illegitimate exercise of the Congress' broad spending power. But no such claim can be or is made here. Were South Dakota to succumb to the blandishments offered by Congress and raise its drinking age to 21, the State's action in so doing would not violate the constitutional rights of anyone.

Our decisions have recognized that in some circumstances the financial inducement offered by Congress might be so coercive as to pass the point at which "pressure turns into compulsion." Here, however, Congress has directed only that a State desiring to establish a minimum drinking age lower than 21 lose a relatively small percentage of certain federal highway funds. Petitioner contends that the coercive nature of this program is evident from the degree of success it has achieved. We cannot conclude, however, that a conditional grant of federal money of this sort is unconstitutional simply by reason of its success in achieving the congressional objective.

When we consider, for a moment, that all South Dakota would lose if she adheres to her chosen course as to a suitable minimum drinking age is 5% of the funds otherwise obtainable under specified highway grant programs, the argument as to coercion is shown to be more rhetoric than fact. . . .

Here Congress has offered relatively mild encouragement to the States to enact higher minimum drinking ages than they would otherwise choose. But the enactment of such laws remains the prerogative of the States not merely in theory but in fact. Even if Congress might lack the power to impose a national minimum drinking age directly, we conclude that encouragement to state action found in §158 is a valid use of the spending power. Accordingly, the judgment of the Court of Appeals is

Affirmed.

JUSTICE O'CONNOR, dissenting.

The Court today upholds the National Minimum Drinking Age Amendment, 23 U.S.C. §158, as a valid exercise of the spending power conferred by Article I, §8. But §158 is not a condition on spending reasonably related to the expenditure of federal funds and cannot be justified on that ground. Rather, it is an attempt to regulate the sale of liquor, an attempt that lies outside Congress' power to regulate commerce because it falls within the ambit of §2 of the Twenty-first Amendment. . . .

When Congress appropriates money to build a highway, it is entitled to insist that the highway be a safe one. But it is not entitled to insist as a condition of the use of highway funds that the State impose or change regulations in other areas of the State's social and economic life because of an attenuated or tangential relationship to highway use or safety. Indeed, if the rule were otherwise, the Congress could effectively regulate almost any area of a State's social, political, or economic life on the theory that use of the interstate transportation system is somehow enhanced. If, for example, the United States were to condition highway moneys upon moving the state capital, I suppose it might argue that interstate transportation is facilitated by locating local governments in places easily accessible to interstate highways—or, conversely, that highways might become overburdened if they had to carry traffic to and from the state capital. In my mind, such a relationship is hardly more attenuated than the one which the Court finds supports §158.

There is a clear place at which the Court can draw the line between permissible and impermissible conditions on federal grants. It is the line identified in the Brief for the National Conference of State Legislatures et al. as *Amici Curiae:*

"Congress has the power to *spend* for the general welfare, it has the power to *legislate* only for the delegated purposes.". . .

This approach harks back to *United States v. Butler* (1936), the last case in which this Court struck down an Act of Congress as beyond the authority granted by the Spending Clause. . . .

While *Butler*'s authority is questionable insofar as it assumes that Congress has no regulatory power over farm production, its discussion of the spending power and its description of both the power's breadth and its limitations remain sound. The Court's decision in *Butler* also properly recognizes the gravity of the task of appropriately limiting the spending power. If the spending power is to be limited only by Congress' notion of the general welfare, the reality, given the vast financial resources of the Federal Government, is that the Spending Clause gives "power to the Congress to tear down the barriers, to invade the states' jurisdiction, and to become a parliament of the whole people, subject to no restrictions save such as are self-imposed." This, of course, as *Butler* held, was not the Framers' plan and it is not the meaning of the Spending Clause. . . .

The immense size and power of the Government of the United States ought not obscure its fundamental character. It remains a Government of enumerated powers. Because 23 U.S.C. §158 cannot be justified as an exercise of any power delegated to the Congress, it is not authorized by the Constitution. The Court errs in holding it to be the law of the land, and I respectfully dissent.

Rehnquist's opinion gave strong support to the federal spending power. The majority held that there are only four basic requirements that must be met for a federal spending statute to be valid: (1) the expenditure must be for the general welfare; (2) any conditions imposed on the expenditure must be unambiguous; (3) the conditions must be reasonably related to the purpose of the expenditure; and (4) the legislation must not violate any independent constitutional provision. These are minimal requirements indeed, especially since the Court acknowledged a policy of deferring to the legislature as to determinations of what promotes the general welfare. O'Connor's dissent, which praised much of what the Court concluded in *Butler,* is not likely to find a great deal of support today; rather, since 1937 the Court repeatedly has given approval to an expansive interpretation of the powers of the federal government to tax and spend for the general welfare.

Decisions such as *South Dakota v. Dole* give wide latitude to Congress in using the power to tax and spend to "encourage" states' compliance with federal policy preferences. If Congress uses this power effectively, it can extend its policy influence well beyond the customary limits. Congress simply enlists the states to regulate areas where the federal government may not constitutionally act on its own. States may resent what they consider to be "coercive" federal action, and, as exemplified by South Dakota's opposition to the federal government's intrusion into alcohol regulation, it is not uncommon for states to challenge these federal incentive programs.

However, as long as Congress uses the spending power to encourage the states to cooperate with federal policies, the Court is likely to approve. It is only when the federal government orders the states to carry out public policy that the justices find violations of the Constitution's federalism principles. Recall the decisions in *New York v. United States* (1992) and *Printz v. United States* (1997), which we discussed in previous chapters. In those decisions the Court concluded that the national government had stepped over the line and had treated the states as administrative units of the federal government.

RESTRICTIONS ON THE REVENUE POWERS OF THE STATES

Taxation is a concurrent power: the states exercised the power to tax prior to the ratification of the Constitution and retain that authority today. The powers of the states to tax are very broad, limited primarily by provisions in their own constitutions and laws. Taxes on property, income, and sales provide the bulk of funds for state government activities.

The federal Constitution, however, removed certain sources of revenue from the states. Article I, Section 10, explicitly prohibits the states from taxing imports. In addition, the Commerce Clause blocks the states from imposing taxes that place an unreasonable burden on interstate or foreign commerce. Aside from these limitations, the states remain free to develop their own tax structures and sources of revenue.

State Taxes on Foreign Commerce

In *Brown v. Maryland* (1827) the Supreme Court first faced a question of the validity of state taxes on imports. The dispute centered on a Maryland law that required importers of foreign goods to pay a license fee. The Supreme Court struck down the statute as a tax on imports

and as infringing on the authority of the federal government to regulate foreign commerce. An important part of the Court's opinion, however, dealt with the following question: When does an imported article cease to be an import and become part of the taxable goods within a state? The Court's answer to this question was the "original package" doctrine. For the majority, John Marshall wrote, "While [the imported article remains] the property of the importer, in his warehouse, in the original form or package in which it was imported, a tax upon it is too plainly a duty on imports to escape the prohibition in the constitution."

The original package doctrine meant that goods flowing into the United States remained within the federal government's taxing and regulating power until they were sold, processed, or broken out of their original packaging. Once any of those events took place, the articles became normal property within the state and subject to state taxation. The impact of this interpretation was that large warehouses filled with imported goods ready for shipment to other parts of the United States were free from state taxation as long as no sale took place and the materials remained in their original packages. The states balked at this rule, arguing that they should be able to levy property taxes on such goods as long as the tax was nondiscriminatory—that is, if imported articles stored in warehouses were taxed on exactly the same basis as other property within the state. In *Low v. Austin* (1872) the Court rejected the constitutionality of such nondiscriminatory taxes, adhering to Marshall's rationale in *Brown*.

Although attacked by legal scholars and those promoting the interests of the states, the original package doctrine survived until 1976, when the justices accepted an appeal from a decision by the Georgia Supreme Court that approved certain nondiscriminatory taxes on warehoused imports. After reanalyzing the issues involved, the Court altered a rule of law that had been in effect for more than a century.[18]

---

18. To hear oral arguments in this case navigate to: *www.oyez.org/oyez/frontpage.*

Michelin Tire Corp. v. Wages

423 U.S. 276 (1976)

http://laws.findlaw.com/US/423/276.html

Vote: 8 (Blackmun, Brennan, Burger, Marshall, Powell,
    Rehnquist, Stewart, White)

        0

Opinion of the Court: Brennan
Concurring opinion: White
Not participating: Stevens

Michelin Tire Corporation operated a warehouse in Gwinnett County, Georgia, just outside of Atlanta. The company imported tires and tire products into the United States from France and Nova Scotia and stored them in the Georgia warehouse for later distribution to retail outlets. When the county tax assessors levied a nondiscriminatory ad valorem property tax on the inventory, the company sued W. L. Wages, the county tax commissioner, for relief, claiming that, except for some tire tubes that had been removed from their original containers, the warehouse contents were constitutionally free from state taxation.

The local court granted the relief requested, and the Georgia Supreme Court heard the county's appeal. The state high court ruled that the tires were subject to tax because, after being imported in bulk, they had been sorted and arranged for sale. Michelin sought a reversal by the U.S. Supreme Court, which ignored subtle questions regarding the application of the original package doctrine and instead focused on the fundamental issue of whether any warehoused imports are subject to state taxation.

MR. JUSTICE BRENNAN delivered the opinion of the Court.

Low v. Austin [1872] is the leading decision of this Court holding that the States are prohibited by the Import-Export Clause from imposing a nondiscriminatory ad valorem property tax on imported goods until they lose their character as imports and become incorporated into the mass of property in the State. The Court there reviewed a decision of the California Supreme Court that had sustained the con-

stitutionality of California's nondiscriminatory ad valorem tax on the ground that the Import-Export Clause only prohibited taxes upon the character of the goods as imports and therefore did not prohibit nondiscriminatory taxes upon the goods as property. This Court reversed on its reading of the seminal opinion construing the Import-Export Clause, *Brown v. Maryland* (1827), as holding that "[w]hilst retaining their character as imports, a tax upon them, in any shape, is within the constitutional prohibition."

Scholarly analysis has been uniformly critical of *Low v. Austin*. It is true that Mr. Chief Justice Marshall, speaking for the Court in *Brown v. Maryland,* said that "while [the thing imported remains] the property of the importer, in his warehouse, in the original form or package in which it was imported, a tax upon it is too plainly a duty on imports to escape the prohibition in the constitution." Commentators have uniformly agreed that *Low v. Austin* misread this dictum in holding that the Court in *Brown* included nondiscriminatory ad valorem property taxes among prohibited "imposts" or "duties," for the contrary conclusion is plainly to be inferred from consideration of the specific abuses which led the Framers to include the Import-Export Clause in the Constitution.

Our independent study persuades us that a nondiscriminatory ad valorem property tax is not the type of state exaction which the Framers of the Constitution or the Court in *Brown* had in mind as being an "impost" or "duty" and that *Low v. Austin*'s reliance upon the *Brown* dictum to reach the contrary conclusion was misplaced.

One of the major defects of the Articles of Confederation, and a compelling reason for the calling of the Constitutional Convention of 1787, was the fact that the Articles essentially left the individual States free to burden commerce both among themselves and with foreign countries very much as they pleased. Before 1787 it was commonplace for seaboard States with port facilities to derive revenue to defray the costs of state and local government by imposing taxes on imported goods destined for customers in other States. At the same time, there was no secure source of revenue for the central government. . . .

The Framers of the Constitution thus sought to alleviate three main concerns by committing sole power to lay imposts and duties on imports in the Federal Government, with no concurrent state power: the Federal Government must speak with one voice when regulating commercial relations with foreign governments, and tariffs, which might affect foreign relations, could not be implemented by the States consistently with that exclusive power; import revenues were to be the major source of revenue of the Federal Government and should not be diverted to the States; and harmony among the States might be disturbed unless seaboard States, with their crucial ports of entry, were prohibited from levying taxes on citizens of other States by taxing goods merely flowing through their ports to the other States not situated as favorably geographically.

Nothing in the history of the Import-Export Clause even remotely suggests that a nondiscriminatory ad valorem property tax which is also imposed on imported goods that are no longer in import transit was the type of exaction that was regarded as objectionable by the Framers of the Constitution. For such an exaction, unlike discriminatory state taxation against imported goods as imports, was not regarded as an impediment that severely hampered commerce or constituted a form of tribute by seaboard States to the disadvantage of the other States.

It is obvious that such nondiscriminatory property taxation can have no impact whatsoever on the Federal Government's exclusive regulation of foreign commerce, probably the most important purpose of the Clause's prohibition. By definition, such a tax does not fall on imports as such because of their place of origin. It cannot be used to create special protective tariffs or particular preferences for certain domestic goods, and it cannot be applied selectively to encourage or discourage any importation in a manner inconsistent with federal regulation.

Nor will such taxation deprive the Federal Government of the exclusive right to all revenues from imposts and duties on imports and exports, since that right by definition only extends to revenues from exactions of a particular category; if nondiscriminatory ad valorem taxation is not in that category, it deprives the Federal Government of nothing to which it is entitled. Unlike imposts and duties, which are essentially taxes on the commercial privilege of bringing goods into a country, such property taxes are taxes by which a State apportions the cost of such services as police and fire protection among the beneficiaries according to their respective wealth; there is no reason why an importer should not bear his share of these costs along with his competitors handling only domestic goods. The Import-Export Clause clearly prohibits state taxation based on the foreign origin

of the imported goods, but it cannot be read to accord imported goods preferential treatment that permits escape from uniform taxes imposed without regard to foreign origin for services which the State supplies. . . .

Finally, nondiscriminatory ad valorem property taxes do not interfere with the free flow of imported goods among the States, as did the exactions by States under the Articles of Confederation directed solely at imported goods. . . .

Since prohibition of nondiscriminatory ad valorem property taxation would not further the objectives of the Import-Export Clause, only the clearest constitutional mandate should lead us to condemn such taxation. . . .

The Court in *Low v. Austin* nevertheless expanded the prohibition of the Clause to include nondiscriminatory ad valorem property taxes, and did so with no analysis, but with only the statement that *Brown v. Maryland* had marked the line "where the power of Congress over the goods imported ends, and that of the State begins, with as much precision as the subject admits." But the opinion in *Brown v. Maryland* cannot properly be read to propose such a broad definition of "imposts" or "duties." The tax there held to be prohibited by the Import-Export Clause was imposed under a Maryland statute that required importers of foreign goods, and wholesalers selling the same by bale or package, to obtain a license and pay a $50 fee therefor, subject to certain forfeitures and penalties for noncompliance. The importers contested the validity of the statute, arguing that the license was a "palpable evasion" of the Import-Export Clause because it was essentially equivalent to a duty on imports. Since the power to impose a license on importers would also entail a power to price them out of the market or prohibit them entirely, the importers concluded that such a power must be repugnant to the exclusive federal power to regulate foreign commerce.

The Attorney General of Maryland, Roger Taney, later Chief Justice, defended the constitutionality of Maryland's law. He argued that the fee was not a prohibited "impost" or "duty" because the license fee was not a tax upon the imported goods, but on the importers, a tax upon the occupation and nothing more, and the Import-Export Clause prohibited only exactions on the right of importation and not an exaction upon the occupation of importers. . . .

The Court in *Brown* refused to define "imposts" or "duties" comprehensively, since the Maryland statute presented only the question "whether the legislature of a State can constitutionally require the importer of foreign articles to take out a license from the State, before he shall be permitted to sell a bale or package so imported." However, in holding that the Maryland license fee was within prohibited "imposts, or duties on imports . . ." the Court significantly characterized an impost or duty as "a custom or a tax levied on articles brought into a country," although also holding that, while normally levied before the articles are permitted to enter, the exactions are no less within the prohibition if levied upon the goods as imports after entry; since "imports" are the goods imported, the prohibition of imposts or duties on "imports" was more than a prohibition of a tax on the act of importation; it "extends to a duty levied after [the thing imported] has entered the country." And since the power to prohibit sale of an article is the power to prohibit its introduction into the country, the privilege of sale must be a concomitant of the privilege of importation, and licenses on the right to sell must therefore also fall within the constitutional prohibition.

Taney's argument was persuasive, however, to the extent that the Court "was prompted to declare that the words of the prohibition ought not to be pressed to their utmost extent; . . . in our complex system, the object of the powers conferred on the government of the Union, and the nature of the often conflicting powers which remain in the States, must always be taken into view. . . . [T]here must be a point of time when the prohibition ceases, and the power of the State to tax commences. . . ."

Despite the language and objectives of the Import-Export Clause, and despite the limited nature of the holding in *Brown v. Maryland*, the Court in *Low v. Austin* ignored the warning that the boundary between the power of States to tax persons and property within their jurisdictions and the limitations on the power of the States to impose imposts or duties with respect to "imports" was a subtle and difficult line which must be drawn as the cases arise. *Low v. Austin* also ignored the cautionary remark that, for those reasons, it "might be premature to state any rule as being universal in its application." Although it was "sufficient" in the context of Maryland's license tax on the right to sell imported goods to note that a tax imposed directly on imported goods which have not been acted upon in any way would clearly fall within the constitutional prohibition, that observation did not apply, as the foregoing analysis indi-

cates, to a state tax which treated those same goods without regard to the fact of their foreign origin. . . .

It follows from the foregoing that *Low v. Austin* was wrongly decided. That decision must be, and is, overruled.

Petitioner's tires in this case were no longer in transit. They were stored in a distribution warehouse from which petitioner conducted a wholesale operation, taking orders from franchised dealers and filling them from a constantly replenished inventory. The warehouse was operated no differently than would be a distribution warehouse utilized by a wholesaler dealing solely in domestic goods, and we therefore hold that the nondiscriminatory property tax levied on petitioner's inventory of imported tires was not interdicted by the Import-Export Clause of the Constitution. The judgment of the Supreme Court of Georgia is accordingly

Affirmed.

State Taxes on Interstate Commerce

State taxes on interstate commerce have provided another source of constitutional disputes. A state has the right to tax commerce that occurs within its borders, but it cannot impose taxes that discriminate against or place an undue burden on interstate commerce. In the nation's formative years this rule of constitutional interpretation was relatively easy to apply, but, given the changes in economic realities and the significant alterations in the definition of interstate commerce, the situation is now much more complex.

Today, relatively little commercial activity is purely intrastate. Consequently, whenever a state imposes a tax on business activity, it can be charged that the state is placing a burden on interstate commerce. The Supreme Court has attempted to fashion a rule that copes with modern economic conditions and yet is mindful of three important considerations. First, if the states are to remain viable entities, they must retain the ability to tax commercial activities. Second, true burdens on interstate commerce, as well as taxes that discriminate against it, must be avoided. Third, simply engaging in an interstate commercial activity should not suffice to exempt a company from paying its fair share in state taxes. Naturally, these principles are far easier to state than to apply to real situations.

In *Complete Auto Transit v. Brady* (1977) the justices concluded that their previous decisions were inconsistent with contemporary conditions and that a new statement on the authority of states to tax activities affecting interstate commerce was required.[19] In his opinion for the Court, Justice Harry Blackmun found fault with some leading precedents and replaced them with a four-pronged test to determine the validity of state taxation.

Complete Auto Transit v. Brady

430 U.S. 274 (1977)
http://laws.findlaw.com/US/430/274.html
Vote: 9 (Blackmun, Brennan, Burger, Marshall, Powell,
        Rehnquist, Stevens, Stewart, White)
        0
Opinion of the Court: Blackmun

Complete Auto Transit was a Michigan corporation doing business in Mississippi. Under its contract with General Motors (GM), Complete transported new vehicles manufactured out of state and brought into Mississippi by rail. The automobiles were loaded onto Complete's trucks in the Jackson, Mississippi, rail yards and delivered to GM dealerships around the state. There is no doubt that Complete's business was interstate commerce. The company provided the last segment in the transportation of goods manufactured out of state to their retail destinations within the state.

Mississippi imposed a tax on transportation companies for the privilege of doing business in the state at a rate of 5 percent of gross income from state business. The state applied the tax to businesses operating in intra- and interstate commerce. In 1971 the Mississippi Tax Commission informed Complete that it owed $122,160.59 in taxes from a three-year period beginning in 1968. In 1972 Complete received a second bill for $42,990.89 for taxes due over the previous year. Complete paid the taxes under protest and sued for a refund.

19. To hear oral arguments in this case navigate to: *www.oyez.org/oyez/frontpage.*

Complete based its case on a 1951 Supreme Court precedent, ***Spector Motor Service v. O'Connor,*** which held that a state tax on the privilege of doing business is unconstitutional if imposed on any activity that is part of interstate commerce. The Mississippi Supreme Court upheld the tax, holding that Complete enjoyed the various services of the state and should be obliged to pay its fair share of state taxes. Because the tax did not discriminate against interstate commerce and was based exclusively on income derived from Mississippi sources, it was not constitutionally defective. Complete appealed to the U.S. Supreme Court, asking it to strike down the tax on the basis of the *Spector* precedent.

MR. JUSTICE BLACKMUN delivered the opinion of the Court.

Once again we are presented with " 'the perennial problem of the validity of a state tax for the privilege of carrying on within a state, certain activities' related to a corporation's operation of an interstate business." The issue in this case is whether Mississippi runs afoul of the Commerce Clause when it applies the tax it imposes on "the privilege of . . . doing business" within the State to appellant's activity in interstate commerce. The Supreme Court of Mississippi unanimously sustained the tax against appellant's constitutional challenge. We noted probable jurisdiction in order to consider anew the applicable principles in this troublesome area. . . .

Appellant's attack is based solely on decisions of this Court holding that a tax on the "privilege" of engaging in an activity in the State may not be applied to an activity that is part of interstate commerce. See, *e.g., Spector Motor Service v. O'Connor* (1951); *Freeman v. Hewit* (1946). This rule looks only to the fact that the incidence of the tax is the "privilege of doing business"; it deems irrelevant any consideration of the practical effect of the tax. The rule reflects an underlying philosophy that interstate commerce should enjoy a sort of "free trade" immunity from state taxation.

Appellee, in its turn, relies on decisions of this Court stating that "[i]t was not the purpose of the commerce clause to relieve those engaged in interstate commerce from their just share of state tax burden even though it increases the cost of doing the business," *Western Live Stock v. Bureau of Revenue* (1938). These decisions have considered not the formal language of the tax statute but rather its practical effect, and have sustained a tax against Commerce Clause challenge when the tax is applied to an activity with a substantial nexus with the taxing State, is fairly apportioned, does not discriminate against interstate commerce, and is fairly related to the services provided by the State.

Over the years, the Court has applied this practical analysis in approving many types of tax that avoided running afoul of the prohibition against taxing the "privilege of doing business," but in each instance it has refused to overrule the prohibition. Under the present state of the law, the *Spector* rule, as it has come to be known, has no relationship to economic realities. Rather it stands only as a trap for the unwary draftsman.

The modern origin of the *Spector* rule may be found in *Freeman v. Hewit*. . . .

Mr. Justice Frankfurter, speaking for five Members of the Court, announced a blanket prohibition against any state taxation imposed directly on an interstate transaction. He explicitly deemed unnecessary to the decision of the case any showing of discrimination against interstate commerce or error in apportionment of the tax. He recognized that a State could constitutionally tax local manufacture, impose license taxes on corporations doing business in the State, tax property within the State, and tax the privilege of residence in the State and measure the privilege by net income, including that derived from interstate commerce. Nevertheless, a direct tax on interstate sales, even if fairly apportioned and nondiscriminatory, was held to be unconstitutional *per se*. . . .

The rule announced in *Freeman* was viewed in the commentary as a triumph of formalism over substance, providing little guidance even as to formal requirements. . . .

The prohibition against state taxation of the "privilege" of engaging in commerce that is interstate was reaffirmed in *Spector Motor Service v. O'Connor* (1951), a case similar on its facts to the instant case. The taxpayer there was a Missouri corporation engaged exclusively in interstate trucking. Some of its shipments originated or terminated in Connecticut. Connecticut imposed on a corporation a "tax or excise upon its franchise for the privilege of carrying on or doing business within the state," measured by apportioned net income. Spector brought suit in federal court to enjoin collection of the tax as applied to its activities. The District Court issued the injunction. The Second Circuit reversed. This Court, with three Justices in dissent, in turn reversed the Court of Appeals and held the tax unconstitutional as applied. . . .

In this case, of course, we are confronted with a situation like that presented in *Spector*. The tax is labeled a privilege tax "for the privilege of . . . doing business" in Mississippi, and the activity taxed is, or has been assumed to be, interstate commerce. We note again that no claim is made that the activity is not sufficiently connected to the State to justify a tax, or that the tax is not fairly related to benefits provided the taxpayer, or that the tax discriminates against interstate commerce, or that the tax is not fairly apportioned.

The view of the Commerce Clause that gave rise to the rule of *Spector* perhaps was not without some substance. Nonetheless, the possibility of defending it in the abstract does not alter the fact that the Court has rejected the proposition that interstate commerce is immune from state taxation:

"It is a truism that the mere act of carrying on business in interstate commerce does not exempt a corporation from state taxation. 'It was not the purpose of the commerce clause to relieve those engaged in interstate commerce from their just share of state tax burden even though it increases the cost of doing business.' " *Western Live Stock v. Bureau of Revenue* (1938).

Not only has the philosophy underlying the rule been rejected, but the rule itself has been stripped of any practical significance. If Mississippi had called its tax one on "net income" or on the "going concern value" of appellant's business, the *Spector* rule could not invalidate it. There is no economic consequence that follows necessarily from the use of the particular words, "privilege of doing business," and a focus on that formalism merely obscures the question whether the tax produces a forbidden effect. Simply put, the *Spector* rule does not address the problems with which the Commerce Clause is concerned. Accordingly, we now reject the rule of *Spector Motor Service, Inc. v. O'Connor*, that a state tax on the "privilege of doing business" is *per se* unconstitutional when it is applied to interstate commerce, and that case is overruled.

There being no objection to Mississippi's tax on appellant except that it was imposed on nothing other than the "privilege of doing business" that is interstate, the judgment of the Supreme Court of Mississippi is affirmed.

It is so ordered.

The *Complete Auto Transit* decision established four criteria that must be met for a state tax on interstate commerce to be valid: (1) the targeted activity must be sufficiently connected to the state to justify a tax; (2) the tax must be fairly apportioned so that the levy is based on intrastate activity or income not subject to taxation by other states; (3) the tax must not discriminate against interstate commerce; and (4) the tax must be fairly related to the services provided by the state. These criteria assume that Congress has not preempted the state tax by imposing conflicting regulations on the interstate commerce activities involved.

In an unusual occurrence by today's standards, the entire Court supported Justice Blackmun's opinion in *Complete Auto Transit*. There were no concurring or dissenting views. Given this unanimity, it is not surprising that the Court has applied the precedent to subsequent disputes over the validity of state taxes on activities affecting interstate and foreign commerce. In *Wardair Canada v. Florida Department of Revenue* (1986) the justices ruled that a state tax on the sale of aviation fuel to an airline engaged in foreign commerce satisfied the four requirements. Similarly, in *Goldberg v. Sweet* (1989) the justices upheld an Illinois excise tax on interstate telephone calls; and in *Oklahoma Tax Commission v. Jefferson Lines* (1995) the Court concluded that a state tax on tickets for interstate bus travel did not violate the constitutional principles established in *Complete Auto Transit*. Therefore, the four-pronged test established in 1977 constitutes the Court's current policy on state taxation of interstate activities. It appears to provide a workable compromise between the needs of the states to secure revenue and the Constitution's mandate that interstate commerce not be unreasonably burdened.

Complete Auto Transit v. Brady dealt with a state's attempt to tax the intrastate portion of a larger interstate enterprise. Because the company used its trucks to transport GM cars from the railroad station to dealers across the state, it was clear that the company had both an economic and a physical presence in Mississippi. But what if a company does business within a state and yet has no physical presence there—in other words, no offices, warehouses, stores, or employees? For example, a company might easily do business exclusively by interstate mail, the Internet, or telephone. May the state impose a tax on that economic activity? Or would this be an unconstitutional tax on interstate commerce? Traditionally, the position of the Court has been that if a company has no physical presence in a state, the state has no authority to tax the company—no matter how much business the company does with state residents. *Quill Corp. v. North Dakota* (1992) asked the Court to reconsider this position.

Quill Corp. v. North Dakota

504 U.S. 298 (1992)
http://laws.findlaw.com/US/504/298.html
Vote: 8 (Blackmun, Kennedy, O'Connor, Rehnquist, Scalia,
        Souter, Stevens, Thomas)
    1 (White)
Opinion for the Court: Stevens
Opinion concurring in part: Scalia
Opinion concurring in part and dissenting in part: White

Quill was an office supply company with offices and warehouses in Illinois, California, and Georgia. None of its employees worked in North Dakota, and the company had no tangible property in that state. Quill sold its products nationwide via catalog, direct mail, and telephone sales. Its goods were delivered by mail or shipped by truck or rail. The company had annual sales of about $1 million to some three thousand North Dakota customers, making Quill the sixth largest vendor of office supplies in the state. In 1987 North Dakota amended its tax code to impose a use tax (similar to a sales tax) on sales made by companies who regularly or systematically solicit customers in the state. The law, therefore, required mail order operators, like Quill, to collect a tax on all sales made to North Dakota residents. Quill refused to pay such taxes, claiming that North Dakota had no taxation authority over corporations that did not have a physical presence in the state.

North Dakota filed a legal action to compel Quill to comply with the law. Quill relied on a 1967 precedent,

National Bellas Hess, Inc. v. Department of Revenue of Illinois. That decision held that a state violates due process of law and imposes an unconstitutional burden on interstate commerce when it taxes a corporation that has no physical presence within its boundaries. The North Dakota Supreme Court upheld the law, concluding that the enormous growth in the mail order industry and changes in the U.S. Supreme Court's interpretation of the law (for example, *Complete Auto Transit v. Brady*) made it inappropriate to follow the *Bellas Hess* precedent. The state court concluded that Quill had a sufficient economic presence in the state to justify the North Dakota tax. Quill appealed.

JUSTICE STEVENS delivered the opinion of the Court.

As in a number of other cases involving the application of state taxing statutes to out-of-state sellers, our holding in [*National*] *Bellas Hess* [*v. Department of Revenue of Illinois*, 1967] relied on both the Due Process Clause and the Commerce Clause. Although the "two claims are closely related," the clauses pose distinct limits on the taxing powers of the States. Accordingly, while a State may, consistent with the Due Process Clause, have the authority to tax a particular taxpayer, imposition of the tax may nonetheless violate the Commerce Clause.

The two constitutional requirements differ fundamentally, in several ways. . . . [T]he Due Process Clause and the Commerce Clause reflect different constitutional concerns. Moreover, while Congress has plenary power to regulate commerce among the States and thus may authorize state actions that burden interstate commerce, it does not similarly have the power to authorize violations of the Due Process Clause.

Thus, although we have not always been precise in distinguishing between the two, the Due Process Clause and the Commerce Clause are analytically distinct. . . .

The Due Process Clause "requires some definite link, some minimum connection, between a state and the person, property or transaction it seeks to tax" and that the "income attributed to the State for tax purposes must be rationally related to 'values connected with the taxing State.' ". . .

Applying these principles, we have held that if a foreign corporation purposefully avails itself of the benefits of an economic market in the forum State, it may subject itself to the State's *in personam* jurisdiction even if it has no physical presence in the State. . . .

. . . Thus, to the extent that our decisions have indicated that the Due Process Clause requires physical presence in a State for the imposition of duty to collect a use tax, we overrule those holdings as superseded by developments in the law of due process.

In this case, there is no question that Quill has purposefully directed its activities at North Dakota residents, that the magnitude of those contacts are more than sufficient for due process purposes, and that the use tax is related to the benefits Quill receives from access to the State. We therefore agree with the North Dakota Supreme Court's conclusion that the Due Process Clause does not bar enforcement of that State's use tax against Quill.

Article I, §8, cl. 3 of the Constitution expressly authorizes Congress to "regulate Commerce with foreign Nations, and among the several States." It says nothing about the protection of interstate commerce in the absence of any action by Congress. Nevertheless, as Justice Johnson suggested in his concurring opinion in *Gibbons v. Ogden* (1824), the Commerce Clause is more than an affirmative grant of power; it has a negative sweep as well. The clause, in Justice Stone's phrasing, "by its own force" prohibits certain state actions that interfere with interstate commerce. *South Carolina State Highway Dept. v. Barnwell Bros., Inc.* (1938).

Our interpretation of the "negative" or "dormant" Commerce Clause has evolved substantially over the years, particularly as that clause concerns limitations on state taxation powers. . . .

While contemporary Commerce Clause jurisprudence might not dictate the same result were the issue to arise for the first time today, *Bellas Hess* is not inconsistent with *Complete Auto* and our recent cases. Under *Complete Auto*'s four-part test, we will sustain a tax against a Commerce Clause challenge so long as the "tax 1. is applied to an activity with a substantial nexus with the taxing State, 2. is fairly apportioned, 3. does not discriminate against interstate commerce, and 4. is fairly related to the services provided by the State." *Bellas Hess* concerns the first of these tests and stands for the proposition that a vendor whose only contacts with the taxing State are by mail or common carrier lacks the "substantial nexus" required by the Commerce Clause.

Thus, three weeks after *Complete Auto* was handed down, we cited *Bellas Hess* for this proposition and discussed the case at some length. In *National Geographic Society v. California Bd. of Equalization* (1977) we affirmed the continuing vitality of *Bellas Hess'* "sharp distinction . . . between mail-order sellers with [a physical presence in the taxing] State and those . . . who do no more than communicate with customers in the State by mail or common carrier as part of a general interstate business." We have continued to cite *Bellas Hess* with approval ever since. . . . For these reasons, we disagree with the State Supreme Court's conclusion that our decision in *Complete Auto* undercut the *Bellas Hess* rule.

The State of North Dakota relies less on *Complete Auto* and more on the evolution of our due process jurisprudence. The State contends that the nexus requirements imposed by the Due Process and Commerce Clauses are equivalent and that if, as we concluded above, a mail-order house that lacks a physical presence in the taxing State nonetheless satisfies the due process "minimum contacts" test, then that corporation also meets the Commerce Clause "substantial nexus" test. We disagree. Despite the similarity in phrasing, the nexus requirements of the Due Process and Commerce Clauses are not identical. The two standards are animated by different constitutional concerns and policies.

Due process centrally concerns the fundamental fairness of governmental activity. Thus, at the most general level, the due process nexus analysis requires that we ask whether an individual's connections with a State are substantial enough to legitimate the State's exercise of power over him. . . . In contrast, the Commerce Clause, and its nexus requirement, are informed not so much by concerns about fairness for the individual defendant as by structural concerns about the effects of state regulation on the national economy. Under the Articles of Confederation, State taxes and duties hindered and suppressed interstate commerce; the Framers intended the Commerce Clause as a cure for these structural ills. It is in this light that we have interpreted the negative implication of the Commerce Clause. Accordingly, we have ruled that that Clause prohibits discrimination against interstate commerce and bars state regulations that unduly burden interstate commerce.

The *Complete Auto* analysis reflects these concerns about the national economy. The second and third parts of that analysis, which require fair apportionment and non-discrimination, prohibit taxes that pass an unfair share of the tax burden onto interstate commerce. The first and fourth prongs, which require a substantial nexus and a relationship between the tax and State-provided services, limit the reach of State taxing authority so as to ensure that State taxation does not unduly burden interstate commerce. Thus, the "substantial-nexus" requirement is . . . a means for limiting state burdens on interstate commerce. Accordingly, contrary to the State's suggestion, a corporation may have the "minimum contacts" with a taxing State as required by the Due Process Clause, and yet lack the "substantial nexus" with that State as required by the Commerce Clause.

The State Supreme Court reviewed our recent Commerce Clause decisions and concluded that those rulings signaled a "retreat from the formalistic constrictions of a stringent physical presence test in favor of a more flexible substantive approach" and thus supported its decision not to apply *Bellas Hess*. Although we agree with the State Court's assessment of the evolution of our cases, we do not share its conclusion that this evolution indicates that the Commerce Clause ruling of *Bellas Hess* is no longer good law. . . .

Like other bright-line tests, the *Bellas Hess* rule appears artificial at its edges: whether or not a State may compel a vendor to collect a sales or use tax may turn on the presence in the taxing State of a small sales force, plant, or office. This artificiality, however, is more than offset by the benefits of a clear rule. Such a rule firmly establishes the boundaries of legitimate state authority to impose a duty to collect sales and use taxes and reduces litigation concerning those taxes. This benefit is important, for as we have so frequently noted, our law in this area is something of a "quagmire" and the "application of constitutional principles to specific state statutes leaves much room for controversy and confusion and little in the way of precise guides to the States in the exercise of their indispensable power of taxation."

Moreover, a bright-line rule in the area of sales and use taxes also encourages settled expectations and, in doing so, fosters investment by businesses and individuals. Indeed, it is not unlikely that the mail-order industry's dramatic growth over the last quarter-century is due in part to the bright-line exemption from state taxation created in *Bellas Hess*. . . .

In sum, although in our cases subsequent to *Bellas Hess* and concerning other types of taxes we have not adopted a similar bright-line, physical-presence requirement, our reasoning in those cases does not compel that we now reject the rule that *Bellas Hess* established in the area of sales and use taxes. To the contrary, the continuing value of a bright-line rule in this area and the doctrine and principles of *stare decisis* indicate that the *Bellas Hess* rule remains good law. . . .

This aspect of our decision is made easier by the fact that the underlying issue is not only one that Congress may be better qualified to resolve, but also one that Congress has the ultimate power to resolve. No matter how we evaluate the burdens that use taxes impose on interstate commerce, Congress remains free to disagree with our conclusions. Indeed, in recent years Congress has considered legislation that would "overrule" the *Bellas Hess* rule. Its decision not to take action in this direction may, of course, have been dictated by respect for our holding in *Bellas Hess* that the Due Process Clause prohibits States from imposing such taxes, but today we have put that problem to rest. Accordingly, Congress is now free to decide whether, when, and to what extent the States may burden interstate mail-order concerns with a duty to collect use taxes. . . .

The judgment of the Supreme Court of North Dakota is reversed and the case is remanded for further proceedings not inconsistent with this opinion.

It is so ordered.

The *Quill* decision backed away from the position that due process of law is violated when a state taxes the sales of out-of-state businesses that have no physical presence in the taxing jurisdiction. Yet the Court remained committed to the proposition that such taxes violate the Commerce Clause. Because Congress has expansive powers over interstate commerce, it could pass legislation allowing the states to tax mail order operations such as Quill. At stake are billions of dollars in potential state revenues each year.

Even more significant is the growing volume of commerce transacted over the Internet. Most companies that engage in sales over the Internet operate nationally with a physical presence in no more than a few states. As such, under current legal interpretations these retailers may conduct most of their transactions free from the obligation of collecting state sales taxes. The value of goods traded over the Internet provides an enormously lucrative source of potential tax revenues for the state. But according to the principles set in *National Bellas Hess* and

Quill, state taxes on Internet business may run afoul of the Commerce Clause.

However, as we learned from the Court's opinion in *Quill*, Congress's power over interstate commerce allows it to decide if the states will be allowed to tax Internet sales. Thus far, Congress has blocked the imposition of new state and local taxes on Internet transactions. In 1998 Congress passed the Internet Tax Freedom Act, which placed a three-year moratorium on such taxes, and in 2001 it extended the act for an additional two years. The legislators took these actions believing that the initial development of Internet commerce is best encouraged by shielding electronic transactions from state taxation. The states, however, have pressured Congress to remove the prohibition. The Internet has developed beyond its embryonic stage, they argue, and no longer needs special protection. There is little doubt, however, that the states will increasingly push Congress to allow them to tax Internet sales as electronic commerce replaces more traditional transactions and thus reduces state sales tax revenues.

Taxing and Spending for the Protection of Intrastate Interests

In decisions such as *Complete Auto Transit* and *Quill Corp.* states attempted to tax interstate commerce activities that occurred within their boundaries or involved their residents. The goal was simply to gather revenue. States are continually searching for new revenue sources. Imposing taxes on out-of-state corporations is a politically appealing strategy because revenue can be raised without directly affecting the state's residents (or upsetting its voters).

Sometimes the goal of a state taxation policy is not just to raise revenue. States can create tax policies to protect intrastate businesses or to promote intrastate development. When such policies place a burden on interstate commerce and give an advantage to intrastate enterprises, constitutional challenges are common. Tax policies that discriminate against interstate commerce often meet the same fate as we saw discriminatory commerce regulation suffer in Chapter 7. The Court takes a dim view of state laws that place a financial obligation on interstate commerce that is not equally placed on intrastate business—no matter if those obligations take the form of taxes, fees, tariffs, duties, or similar assessments.

Today the states share a zeal to raise their revenues, improve their economic climates, increase jobs for their citizens, and protect their resources from encroachment by other states. In attempting to achieve these goals, legislatures on occasion use their taxing powers in a way that invites legal challenge. One example is *Oregon Waste Systems v. Department of Environmental Quality of the State of Oregon* (1994). In this case Oregon attempted to increase revenues and to protect its own environmental resources by imposing fees on solid waste generated in other states and transported to Oregon for disposal. The majority struck down the state's plan. The two dissenters, Rehnquist and Blackmun, unsuccessfully argued that the Court unnecessarily restricted the state's taxation power and in doing so made it difficult for Oregon to deal effectively with the growing problem of solid waste disposal. That these two justices would be found dissenting together against the rest of the Court was somewhat unusual. Rehnquist and Blackmun had very different ideological positions and usually found themselves on opposite sides of controversial issues.

Oregon Waste Systems v. Department of Environmental Quality of the State of Oregon

511 U.S. 93 (1994)
http://laws.findlaw.com/US/511/93.html
Vote: 7 (Ginsburg, Kennedy, O'Connor, Scalia, Souter, Stevens,
Thomas)
2 (Blackmun, Rehnquist)
Opinion of the Court: Thomas
Dissenting opinion: Rehnquist

The Oregon Department of Environmental Quality is in charge of administering the state's comprehensive policy for the management, reduction, and recycling of solid waste. To fund these activities the state levied various fees on landfill operators. In 1989 the state legislature decided to assess an additional surcharge for disposing of any solid waste generated out of state and authorized the

department to set the surcharge rate based on the costs to the state of disposing of the materials. After studying the problem, the department set the surcharge on out-of-state waste at $2.25 per ton. The charge for the disposal of solid waste generated in state was $.85.

Oregon Waste Systems was in the business of transporting solid waste from Washington State by barge to landfills in Oregon. The company filed suit over the surcharge, claiming that the assessment discriminated against interstate commerce in violation of the Commerce Clause. State courts upheld the Oregon law, concluding that the surcharge was not a discriminatory tax but a compensatory fee that was reasonably related to the cost of the services rendered. Oregon Waste Systems asked the Supreme Court to review that decision.

JUSTICE THOMAS delivered the opinion of the Court.

Two Terms ago, in *Chemical Waste Management, Inc. v. Hunt* (1992), we held that the negative Commerce Clause prohibited Alabama from imposing a higher fee on the disposal in Alabama landfills of hazardous waste from other States than on the disposal of identical waste from Alabama. In reaching that conclusion, however, we left open the possibility that such a differential surcharge might be valid if based on the costs of disposing of waste from other States. Today, we must decide whether Oregon's purportedly cost-based surcharge on the in-state disposal of solid waste generated in other States violates the Commerce Clause. . . .

The Commerce Clause provides that "[t]he Congress shall have Power . . . [t]o regulate Commerce . . . among the several States." Though phrased as a grant of regulatory power to Congress, the Clause has long been understood to have a "negative" aspect that denies the States the power unjustifiably to discriminate against or burden the interstate flow of articles of commerce. The Framers granted Congress plenary authority over interstate commerce in "the conviction that in order to succeed, the new Union would have to avoid the tendencies toward economic Balkanization that had plagued relations among the Colonies and later among the States under the Articles of Confederation." *Hughes v. Oklahoma* (1979). "This principle that our economic unit is the Nation, which alone has the gamut of powers necessary to control of the economy, . . . has as its corollary that the states are not separable economic units." *H. P. Hood & Sons, Inc. v. Du Mond* (1949).

Consistent with these principles, we have held that the first step in analyzing any law subject to judicial scrutiny under the negative Commerce Clause is to determine whether it "regulates evenhandedly with only 'incidental' effects on interstate commerce, or discriminates against interstate commerce." *Hughes*. See also *Chemical Waste*. As we use the term here, "discrimination" simply means differential treatment of in-state and out-of-state economic interests that benefits the former and burdens the latter. If a restriction on commerce is discriminatory, it is virtually *per se* invalid. . . .

In *Chemical Waste*, we easily found Alabama's surcharge on hazardous waste from other States to be facially discriminatory because it imposed a higher fee on the disposal of out-of-state waste than on the disposal of identical in-state waste. We deem it equally obvious here that Oregon's $2.25 per ton surcharge is discriminatory on its face. The surcharge subjects waste from other States to a fee almost three times greater than the $0.85 per ton charge imposed on solid in-state waste. The statutory determinant for which fee applies to any particular shipment of solid waste to an Oregon landfill is whether or not the waste was "generated out-of-state." It is well-established, however, that a law is discriminatory if it " 'tax[es] a transaction or incident more heavily when it crosses state lines than when it occurs entirely within the State.' " *Chemical Waste*.

Respondents argue, and the Oregon Supreme Court held, that the statutory nexus between the surcharge and "the [otherwise uncompensated] costs to the State of Oregon and its political subdivisions of disposing of solid waste generated out-of-state," necessarily precludes a finding that the surcharge is discriminatory. We find respondents' narrow focus on Oregon's compensatory aim to be foreclosed by our precedents. As we reiterated in *Chemical Waste*, the purpose of, or justification for, a law has no bearing on whether it is facially discriminatory. Consequently, even if the surcharge merely recoups the costs of disposing of out-of-state waste in Oregon, the fact remains that the differential charge favors shippers of Oregon waste over their counterparts handling waste generated in other States. In making that geographic distinction, the surcharge patently discriminates against interstate commerce.

Because the Oregon surcharge is discriminatory, the virtually *per se* rule of invalidity provides the proper legal standard here. . . . As a result, the surcharge must be invalidated unless respondents can "sho[w] that it advances a legiti-

mate local purpose that cannot be adequately served by reasonable nondiscriminatory alternatives." *New Energy Co. of Indiana v. Limbach* (1988). Our cases require that justifications for discriminatory restrictions on commerce pass the "strictest scrutiny." *Hughes*. The State's burden of justification is so heavy that "facial discrimination by itself may be a fatal defect." *Ibid*.

At the outset, we note two justifications that respondents have *not* presented. No claim has been made that the disposal of waste from other States imposes higher costs on Oregon and its political subdivisions than the disposal of in-state waste. Also, respondents have not offered any safety or health reason unique to nonhazardous waste from other States for discouraging the flow of such waste into Oregon. Consequently, respondents must come forward with other legitimate reasons to subject waste from other States to a higher charge than is levied against waste from Oregon. . . .

Respondents' principal defense of the higher surcharge on out-of-state waste is that it is a "compensatory tax" necessary to make shippers of such waste pay their "fair share" of the costs imposed on Oregon by the disposal of their waste in the State. In *Chemical Waste* we noted the possibility that such an argument might justify a discriminatory surcharge or tax on out-of-state waste. In making that observation, we implicitly recognized the settled principle that interstate commerce may be made to " 'pay its way.' " *Complete Auto Transit, Inc. v. Brady* (1977). See also *Maryland* [*v. Louisiana*, 1981]. . . .

To justify a charge on interstate commerce as a compensatory tax, a State must, as a threshold matter, "identif[y] . . . the [intrastate tax] burden for which the State is attempting to compensate." *Maryland*. Once that burden has been identified, the tax on interstate commerce must be shown roughly to approximate—but not exceed—the amount of the tax on intrastate commerce. Finally, the events on which the interstate and intrastate taxes are imposed must be "substantially equivalent"; that is, they must be sufficiently similar in substance to serve as mutually exclusive "prox[ies]" for each other. . . .

Although it is often no mean feat to determine whether a challenged tax is a compensatory tax, we have little difficulty concluding that the Oregon surcharge is not such a tax. Oregon does not impose a specific charge of at least $2.25 per ton on shippers of waste generated in Oregon, for which the out-of-state surcharge might be considered compensatory. In fact, the only analogous charge on the disposal of Oregon waste is $0.85 per ton, approximately one-third of the amount imposed on waste from other States. Respondents' failure to identify a specific charge on intrastate commerce equal to or exceeding the surcharge is fatal to their claim. . . .

Respondents' final argument is that Oregon has an interest in spreading the costs of the in-state disposal of Oregon waste to all Oregonians. That is, because all citizens of Oregon benefit from the proper in-state disposal of waste from Oregon, respondents claim it is only proper for Oregon to require them to bear more of the costs of disposing of such waste in the State through a higher general tax burden. At the same time, however, Oregon citizens should not be required to bear the costs of disposing of out-of-state waste, respondents claim. The necessary result of that limited cost-shifting is to require shippers of out-of-state waste to bear the full costs of in-state disposal, but to permit shippers of Oregon waste to bear less than the full cost.

We fail to perceive any distinction between respondents' contention and a claim that the State has an interest in reducing the costs of handling in-state waste. Our cases condemn as illegitimate, however, any governmental interest that is not "unrelated to economic protectionism," and regulating interstate commerce in such a way as to give those who handle domestic articles of commerce a cost advantage over their competitors handling similar items produced elsewhere constitutes such protectionism. To give controlling effect to respondents' characterization of Oregon's tax scheme as seemingly benign cost-spreading would require us to overlook the fact that the scheme necessarily incorporates a protectionist objective as well. . . .

Respondents counter that if Oregon is engaged in any form of protectionism, it is "resource protectionism," not economic protectionism. It is true that by discouraging the flow of out-of-state waste into Oregon landfills, the higher surcharge on waste from other States conserves more space in those landfills for waste generated in Oregon. Recharacterizing the surcharge as resource protectionism hardly advances respondents' cause, however. . . . As we held more than a century ago, "if the State, under the guise of exerting its police powers, should [impose a burden] . . . applicable solely to articles [of commerce] . . . produced or manufactured in other States, the courts would find no difficulty in holding such legislation to be in conflict with the Constitution of the United States." *Guy v. Baltimore* (1880). . . .

We recognize that the States have broad discretion to configure their systems of taxation as they deem appropriate. All we intimate here is that their discretion in this regard, as in all others, is bounded by any relevant limitations of the Federal Constitution, in this case the negative Commerce Clause. Because respondents have offered no legitimate reason to subject waste generated in other States to a discriminatory surcharge approximately three times as high as that imposed on waste generated in Oregon, the surcharge is facially invalid under the negative Commerce Clause. Accordingly, the judgment of the Oregon Supreme Court is reversed, and the cases are remanded for further proceedings not inconsistent with this opinion.

It is so ordered.

CHIEF JUSTICE REHNQUIST, with whom JUSTICE BLACKMUN joins, dissenting.

Landfill space evaporates as solid waste accumulates. State and local governments expend financial and political capital to develop trash control systems that are efficient, lawful, and protective of the environment. The State of Oregon responsibly attempted to address its solid waste disposal problem through enactment of a comprehensive regulatory scheme for the management, disposal, reduction, and recycling of solid waste. For this Oregon should be applauded. The regulatory scheme included a fee charged on out-of-state solid waste. The Oregon Legislature directed the Commission to determine the appropriate surcharge "based on the costs . . . of disposing of solid waste generated out-of-state." The Commission arrived at a surcharge of $2.25 per ton, compared to the $0.85 per ton charged on in-state solid waste. The surcharge works out to an increase of about $0.14 per week for the typical out-of-state solid waste producer. This seems a small price to pay for the right to deposit your "garbage, rubbish, refuse . . . ; sewage sludge, septic tank and cesspool pumpings or other sludge; . . . manure, . . . dead animals, [and] infectious waste" on your neighbors.

Nearly 20 years ago, we held that a State cannot ban all out-of-state waste disposal in protecting themselves from hazardous or noxious materials brought across the State's borders. *Philadelphia v. New Jersey* (1978). Two Terms ago in *Chemical Waste Management, Inc. v. Hunt* (1992), in striking down the State of Alabama's $72 per ton fee on the disposal of out-of-state hazardous waste, the Court left open the possibility that such a fee could be valid if based on the costs of disposing of waste from other States. Once again, however, as in *Philadelphia* and *Chemical Waste Management*, the Court further cranks the dormant Commerce Clause ratchet against the States by striking down such cost-based fees, and by so doing ties the hands of the States in addressing the vexing national problem of solid waste disposal. . . .

The State of Oregon is not prohibiting the export of solid waste from neighboring States; it is only asking that those neighbors pay their fair share for the use of Oregon landfill sites. I see nothing in the Commerce Clause that compels less densely populated States to serve as the low-cost dumping grounds for their neighbors, suffering the attendant risks that solid waste landfills present. The Court, deciding otherwise, further limits the dwindling options available to States as they contend with the environmental, health, safety, and political challenges posed by the problem of solid waste disposal in modern society.

For the foregoing reasons, I respectfully dissent.

Despite the Court's position that discriminatory taxation is unconstitutional, states continue to search for systems that might survive legal challenge. In **West Lynn Creamery v. Healy** (1994), for example, the Court reviewed a Massachusetts law that required a "premium" to be paid on all sales of milk products. The assessment was imposed equally on milk produced in Massachusetts and on milk produced out of state. The state used these revenues to provide subsidies for Massachusetts farmers. Here the goal of the state was not to gather general revenues; rather, the goal was to promote the interests of Massachusetts dairy farmers.

The Court's majority, again with Rehnquist and Blackmun in dissent, struck down the Massachusetts plan as using the power to tax and spend in a manner that discriminated against interstate commerce. In effect, this was an old-fashioned protective tariff presented in a newly designed package. The purpose of the plan was to give in-state producers a significant edge over non-Massachusetts farmers. As such, the plan violated the Constitution's prohibition against state policies that advantage intrastate commerce and discriminate against interstate concerns.

Similarly, in **South Central Bell Telephone v. Alabama** (1999) the justices struck down an Alabama law that imposed a franchise tax on each corporation doing business in the state. The tax was based on the company's capital. However, in-state businesses and out-of-state corporations were made to use different formulas to calculate this figure, which, not surprisingly, led to higher taxes on out-of-state businesses.

Although the Court has developed relatively clear guidelines on federal and state taxing and spending powers, each term brings new disputes for resolution. It is not likely that this tendency will change in the near future. Policies that impose taxes and distribute funds are among the most politically and emotionally charged of all government programs. They not only give rise to questions of constitutional philosophy, but also they affect people's pocketbooks. It is not surprising, therefore, that when government uses its powers to tax and spend, legal challenges are common.

READINGS

Carson, Gerald. "The Income Tax and How It Grew." *American Heritage*, December 1973, 4–7, 79–88.

Corwin, Edward S. "The Spending Power of Congress—Apropos the Maternity Act." *Harvard Law Review* 36 (1923): 548–582.

Dakin, Melvin G. "The Protective Cloak of the Export-Import Clause: Immunity for the Goods or Immunity for the Process?" *Louisiana Law Review* 19 (1959): 747–776.

Dunne, Gerald T. *Monetary Decisions of the Supreme Court.* New Brunswick, N.J.: Rutgers University Press, 1960.

Early, Alexander R., and Robert G. Weitzman. "A Century of Dissent: The Immunity of Goods Imported for Resale from Nondiscriminatory State Personal Property Taxes." *Southwestern University Law Review* 7 (1975): 247–272.

Hurst, James Willard. *A Legal History of Money in the United States, 1774–1970.* Lincoln: University of Nebraska Press, 1973.

Lund, Nelson. "Congressional Power over Taxation and Commerce: The Supreme Court's Lost Chance to Devise a Consistent Doctrine." *Texas Tech Law Review* 18 (1987): 729–760.

McCoy, Thomas R., and Barry Friedman. "Conditional Spending: Federalism's Trojan Horse." *Supreme Court Review* (1988): 85–127.

Powell, Thomas Reed. "State Taxation of Imports—When Does an Import Cease to Be an Import?" *Harvard Law Review* 58 (1945): 858–876.

Weisman, Steven R. *The Great Tax Wars: Lincoln to Wilson—The Fierce Battles over Money and Power.* New York: Simon & Schuster, 2001.

Witte, John F. *The Politics and Development of the Federal Income Tax.* Madison: University of Wisconsin Press, 1985.

ECONOMIC LIBERTIES AND INDIVIDUAL RIGHTS

I F ASKED what we Americans admire about the United States, many of us would answer that citizens are guaranteed the freedoms of speech, press, and religion. But when asked to make political decisions—to choose elected officials, for example—we may put other considerations ahead of cherished freedoms. As is often remarked, people tend to vote their pocketbooks. Americans might not admit that the state of the economy drives their behavior, but it is perhaps the single most important determinant in choosing the nation's leaders.

That we hold economic well-being as a priority is not surprising. In Part III we saw that economic issues—commerce, taxing, and spending—were major sources of friction between the federal government and the states virtually from the beginning of U.S. history.

Economic questions, however, are not the exclusive domain of federalism cases. Quite the contrary. The Supreme Court often has heard constitutional challenges in which individuals claim that their personal economic liberties have been violated by government actions. In such cases the justices must determine how much power federal and state governments have to seize private property, to alter freely made contracts, and to restrict private employment agreements as to wages and hours. Seen in this way, there is a strong relationship between civil liberties, such as the freedom of speech, and economic liberties, such as the right to private property. Indeed, both provoke the same fundamental question: To what extent can government enact legislation that infringes on per-

sonal rights? Both also involve the same perennial conflict between the interests of the individual and those of the society.

Even so, most people, including elected officials and even Supreme Court justices, tend to separate economic liberties from other civil liberties. We consider the right to express our views as significantly different from the right to conduct business. The Framers, however, viewed both as vested rights, those so fundamental to an individual that they cannot be infringed upon by government control, and they were very much on the minds of the men who gathered to write the Constitution in 1787. According to James Madison, one of the most important objectives of the Framers was to provide "more effectively for the security of private rights and the steady dispensement of justice within the states. Interference with these were the evils which had, more perhaps than anything else, produced this convention."

But, as Madison's comment implies, the Framers' conception of liberties and what interfered with their exercise was somewhat different from ours. They equated liberty with the protection of private property, and in their view the states, not the new government, posed the greater threat. Given the economic chaos under the Articles of Confederation, we can easily understand the Founders' concerns. They believed that the states had "crippled" both the government and the economy, and they wanted to create a national government strong enough to protect economic liberty from aggressive state governments. We must also keep in mind that many who attended the convention were wealthy men who wanted to keep the property they had accumulated. In short, the Framers were concerned about the nonpropertied masses taking control of state legislatures and using their numerical advantage to promote legislation that would place excessive taxes on business, abrogate contracts, and so forth. Indeed, in an important (albeit controversial) work, *An Economic Interpretation of the Constitution*, historian Charles A. Beard depicted the Founders as self-serving, even greedy, men who viewed the Constitution as a vehicle for the protection of their property interests.

Other analysts have taken issue with Beard's interpretation. Some contend that we cannot necessarily equate modern definitions of property with those used by the Framers; that is, the property interests they sought to protect were probably more encompassing than those we envision today. We might consider property as something tangible or of clear monetary value; but to at least some of the Framers, property was "shorthand for an expanse of personal freedoms that need[ed] only be tangentially related, if at all, to economic activity."[1]

To protect these paramount property rights, however conceptualized, the Framers inserted several provisions into the Constitution. An important provision, which we examine in Chapter 9, is the Contract Clause. Under Article I, Section 10, "No State shall . . . pass any . . . Law impairing the Obligation of Contracts." To understand the meaning of the clause, we must consider its language within the context of the day. As one book suggests:

For the generation of 1787–91, property was probably a natural right, though the constitutional text did not so label it. And, because the right to property included rights to use and increase property, that basic right included a cognate right to contract with other property holders. Thus did the right to contract borrow a measure of moral status from the broader right in which it originated: the obligation to keep one's contracts was a duty flowing from the natural right to property.[2]

If the Contract Clause was one of the ways the Framers sought to protect property interests against the "evils" of

government interference, it worked, at least initially. For the Marshall Court the Contract Clause, in particular, was an effective vehicle for promoting federal supremacy and economic growth. That Court read Article I, Section 10, to prohibit state action that infringed on property rights and impeded economic development.

But this interpretation did not endure. With the end of the Marshall Court and the ascendancy of the Taney Court in the mid-1830s, use of the Contract Clause as a vehicle to protect property interests waned. Why that occurred is considered fully in Chapter 9; for now, it is important to note that the "death" of the Contract Clause did not mean that courts were no longer interested in protecting economic liberties. They simply turned to another section of the Constitution to do so. The Fourteenth Amendment's Due Process Clause says no state shall "deprive any person of life, liberty, or property, without due process of law." Under a doctrine called substantive due process, which is reviewed in Chapter 10, between the 1890s and 1930s, the Supreme Court used the Fourteenth Amendment to prohibit states from interfering with "liberty" interests. For example, the Court struck down legislation mandating maximum work hours on the ground that such legislation interfered with the rights of employers to enter into contracts with their employees. Like the Court's interpretation of the Contract Clause, this treatment of the Fourteenth Amendment eventually fell into disuse. In Chapter 10 we examine the reasons for its decline.

More recently, the Court has taken a serious look at yet another provision of the Constitution designed to protect property interests—the Takings Clause of the Fifth Amendment. While in the Contract Clause the Framers sought to prevent state governments from infringing on contractual agreements, in the Takings Clause they tried to protect private property from government seizure: "nor shall private property be taken for public use without just compensation." The Founders recognized that the government could confiscate property, for example, to construct roads or erect government buildings, but that property owners should have some form of protection from abusive government practices.

---

1. Walter F. Murphy, James E. Fleming, and William Harris II, *American Constitutional Interpretation*, 2nd ed. (Mineola, N.Y.: Foundation Press, 1995), 1071.
   2. Ibid., 1073.

As described in Chapter 11, the Court's interpretation of the Takings Clause has undergone more twists and turns than has its reading of the Contract Clause or even of its application of the Due Process Clause to economic issues. While the heyday of the Contract Clause and economic substantive due process has long since passed, the Takings Clause is enjoying a renaissance. Some members of the Rehnquist Court, particularly Antonin Scalia, have sought to revitalize the Takings Clause as a significant vehicle for protecting property rights.

Whether the Court will continue to move in the direction advocated by Scalia and others and increase protection for private property interests is one of many questions we consider in Chapter 11. Here, we simply note that the current Court seems to be taking a greater interest in all kinds of economic issues than did its immediate predecessors. As the Court entered the twenty-first century, almost one-fifth of its docket involved economic issues of various kinds. This figure, of course, pales in comparison to those of the 1930s, a period during which the majority of the cases the Court accepted for review had an economic dimension, or even from the 1800s, when fully one-third of the business of the Court involved economic issues. Nevertheless, the proportion of the current Court's docket devoted to economic questions is substantial and at odds with the popular notion that the contemporary Court is almost exclusively focused on the resolution of civil liberties and criminal justice disputes.

The number of economic cases on the Court's agenda is important as an indicator of the role it plays in American society.[3] When the justices were deciding large numbers of economic cases, as they did for the first 150 years of the Court's history, it is not surprising that they exerted great influence in that area, and not in civil liberties, rights, or criminal justice. Moreover, if today's Court is seeking to play a greater role in the economic realm, it will be forced to confront the same fundamental issue that bedeviled its predecessors: the complex relationship between "vested rights" and "community interests." While—as we suggested—many of the Founders were concerned about individual liberty (such as the protection of private property), we now know that in a mature democratic society the pursuit of such individual interests may impinge on those of the collective good. For example, if a state enacts a law setting a minimum wage, that statute affects the individual liberty of employers: it would be in their best interest, economically speaking, to pay their employees as little as possible. As a result, they may argue that minimum wage laws violate their constitutional guarantees. But is there another interest at stake? What are the results of paying workers a substandard wage? Does the state have a responsibility to enact legislation for the "health, safety, and welfare" of all its citizens?

It is the clash between these two interests—individual liberty (vested rights) and the state (community interests)—that has been a primary cause of the Court's involvement in this area. Because that conflict is unlikely to change, our discussion of these issues will center on the approaches different Courts have taken to balance them. As we shall see, some Courts exalted liberty interests above those of the community; others took precisely the opposite approach. What political, legal, and historical factors contributed to these varying approaches to economic liberties are things to think about as you read the chapters that follow.

READINGS

Ackerman, Bruce A. *Private Property and the Constitution.* New Haven, Conn.: Yale University Press, 1977.

Beard, Charles A. *An Economic Interpretation of the Constitution.* New York: Macmillan, 1935.

Brown, Robert E. *Charles Beard and the Constitution.* Princeton, N.J.: Princeton University Press, 1956.

Dorn, James, and Henry G. Manne, eds. *Economic Liberties and the Judiciary.* Fairfax, Va.: George Mason University Press, 1987.

McDonald, Forrest. *We the People: The Economic Origins of the Constitution.* Chicago: University of Chicago Press, 1958.

Miller, Arthur Selwyn. *The Supreme Court and American Capitalism.* New York: Free Press, 1968.

Semonche, John E. *Charting the Future: The Supreme Court Responds to a Changing Society, 1890–1920.* Westport, Conn.: Greenwood Press, 1978.

---

3. See Richard Pacelle Jr., *The Transformation of the Supreme Court's Agenda* (Boulder, Colo: Westview Press, 1991); and Pacelle, "The Dynamics and Determinants of Agenda Change in the Rehnquist Court," in *Contemplating Courts,* ed. Lee Epstein (Washington, D.C.: CQ Press, 1995).

CHAPTER 9
THE CONTRACT CLAUSE

SUPPOSE that some years ago a friend of yours accepted a position with a large corporation. One of the reasons she took this particular job was that the company offered an attractive savings plan as a fringe benefit. Under the terms of the savings plan contract, she regularly placed a portion of her income into the fund, and the company matched her contributions. Money deposited in the fund belonged to the individual savers, and the company had no authority to use the funds for any corporate purpose. Over the years her savings account grew steadily. Then, in a national recession, the company's fortunes reversed, and it, along with many others, faced bankruptcy. The state rushed to relieve the troubled businesses by passing a law that allowed them unilaterally to use the assets in employee savings plans to finance operations until the economy regained its strength. The company took advantage of this statute, but, after it spent all of the savings plan funds, the company still went under.

This story raises some basic questions: How can the state pass a law that releases a company from its contractual obligations? The company's employees were cheated out of their money, and the state was involved. How can one participate in any investment or commercial activity without some assurance that a state will not grant similar special considerations to corporations or other parties?

If you were angered by your friend's fate, your reaction would be understandable. One of the hallmarks of a society that values commercial activity is the right to enter into legally binding contracts. It would be hard to imagine a market-based economy that did not recognize and protect such agreements. In most instances, we would expect the government to enforce contracts and not encourage parties who wish to break them.

The individuals who drafted the Constitution felt much the same way. Disturbed by the actions of state governments in the economic upheaval that followed the Revolution, the delegates to the Constitutional Convention moved to block state interference with contractual obligations. They did this by drafting the Contract Clause, one of the most important provisions of the Constitution during the nation's formative years.

THE FRAMERS AND THE CONTRACT CLAUSE

It might be difficult to find a group of people more supportive of the right to enter into binding agreements than the delegates to the convention. For the most part, these individuals represented the propertied classes, and they assembled in Philadelphia at a time of economic turmoil. Many of them feared that as the states coped with their economic problems they might suspend the obligation to honor contracts.

Following the Revolutionary War the economy was very unstable, and the government under the Articles of Confederation was powerless to correct the situation. Hardest hit were small farmers, many of whom had taken out large loans they could not repay. When creditors started foreclosing on real estate and debtors were jailed for failing to pay, farmers and others faced with unmanageable obligations began to agitate for relief. Several states responded by passing laws to help them. Among these acts were bankruptcy laws that erased certain debt obligations or extended the time to pay—legal obstacles that blocked creditors from asserting their contractual rights against their debtors. Also, state currencies of dubious value were declared legal tender to satisfy debt obligations.

These policies hurt the creditors, many of whom were wealthy landowners. They called for a strengthening of the national government to deal with economic problems and a ban on the state governments' practice of nullifying contractual obligations. In response, Congress authorized a convention to propose changes in the Articles of Confederation. Once assembled, the delegates, as we know, went much further than originally authorized and created the Constitution of the United States.

The document drafted in Philadelphia clearly reflected the economic interests of the delegates. Among the provisions they wrote was a protection of contracts against state government infringement. Article I, Section 10, declares: "No State shall . . . pass any . . . Law impairing the Obligation of Contracts."

The eighteenth century's understanding of the term *contract* was little different from today's. A contract is an agreement voluntarily entered into by two or more parties in which a promise is made and something of value is given or pledged. Contractual agreements are made in almost every commercial transaction, such as a mining company's promise to deliver a quantity of iron ore to a steel mill in return for a particular fee, or a lawyer's promise to represent a client at a specified rate of compensation.

For the Framers, the right to enter into contracts was an important freedom closely tied to the right of private property. The ownership of private property implies the right to buy, sell, divide, occupy, lease, and use it; but one cannot effectively exercise these various property rights without the ability to enter into legally binding arrangements with others. In commercial transactions the parties rely on each other to carry out the contractual provisions. During the nation's formative years, those who failed to live up to contractual promises were dealt with harshly. In the minds of the propertied classes of the eighteenth century, this was how it should be, and the government should not be allowed to intervene in such private arrangements.

Evidence from the convention indicates that the Framers adopted the Contract Clause as a means of protecting agreements between private parties from state interference. However, at that time contracts also were a means of carrying out public policy. Because governments then were much more limited than they are today, the states regularly entered into contracts with individuals or corporations to carry out government policy or to distribute government benefits. These state actions included land grants, commercial monopolies, and licenses to construct roads and bridges. Individuals who entered into a contractual agreement with the state expected it to live up to its obligations and not abrogate the arrangement or unilaterally change the terms. In spite of what the Framers might have intended, the Contract Clause is generally worded and therefore offers protection both to contracts among private parties and to agreements made between private parties and the government.

The Contract Clause was not a major point of controversy at the convention; rather, the records show that the delegates accepted its wisdom with little debate. The clause was one of several prohibitions the Framers imposed on state economic regulation. For example, states could no longer coin money, issue bills of credit, create tender for payment of debts, or tax and regulate certain forms of interstate or foreign commerce.

The debates over ratification of the Constitution also made little reference to the Contract Clause. In *The Federalist Papers,* Alexander Hamilton justified the prohibition against state impairment of contract obligations by claiming, "Laws in violation of private contracts . . . may be considered as another probable source of hostility." [1] James Madison declared that "laws impairing the obligation of contracts are contrary to the first principles of the social compact and to every principle of sound legislation." [2]

In spite of this lack of attention at the drafting and ratification stages, the Contract Clause became an important legal force in the early years of the nation's devel-

---

1. Alexander Hamilton, Federalist No. 7, in *The Federalist Papers,* ed. Clinton Rossiter (New York: New American Library, 1961).
2. James Madison, Federalist No. 44, in *The Federalist Papers.*

opment. As political majorities changed from election to election, it was not unusual for state legislatures to enter into contracts with private parties only to break or change those agreements in subsequent legislative sessions. In addition, state governments often would adopt policies that ran contrary to contracts among private individuals. When such actions occurred, injured parties would challenge the state in court. Because the states were not obliged to follow principles of due process of law until after ratification of the Fourteenth Amendment in 1868, the Contract Clause was the primary constitutional ground to challenge state policies. As a result, it was one of the most litigated constitutional provisions in the first decades of U.S. history. One study concluded that roughly 40 percent of all Supreme Court cases prior to 1889 that attacked the validity of state legislation did so on the basis of Contract Clause arguments.[3]

JOHN MARSHALL AND THE CONTRACT CLAUSE

The significance of the Contract Clause increased dramatically through the Marshall Court's interpretations of its meaning. Chief Justice Marshall had strong views on private property, economic development, and the role of the federal government. He consistently supported aggressive policies that would result in vigorous economic expansion. Underlying this position was a philosophy that elevated private property to the level of a natural right that government had little authority to limit. Furthermore, Marshall firmly believed that the nation's interests could be served best if the federal government, rather than the states, became the primary agent for economic policymaking. As we have seen in the areas of federalism and commerce, Marshall could be counted on to uphold actions taken by the federal government and to favor it over competing state interests. Marshall's ideology predisposed him to champion the Contract Clause, which he viewed as essential to the right to private property. Moreover, the clause's restriction of the regulatory powers of the states appealed to his views on federalism.

3. Benjamin F. Wright, *The Contract Clause of the Constitution* (Cambridge: Harvard University Press, 1938).

Given Marshall's domination of the Court for more than three decades, it is not surprising that the Contract Clause achieved an elevated status during those years.

Establishing the Importance of the Contract Clause

The first major Supreme Court decision to consider the Contract Clause was *Fletcher v. Peck* (1810), which concerned whether a state could nullify a public contract. The suit flowed from one of the most notorious incidents of corruption and bribery in the nation's early history—the Yazoo River land fraud. In this litigation the beneficiaries of the scheme sought to use the Contract Clause to protect their gains.

Chief Justice Marshall was caught in a bind. To give force to the Contract Clause would be to rule in favor of those who profited from state government corruption. To rule against the unpopular fraudulent transactions would be to hand down a precedent significantly curtailing the meaning of the provision. Which option did Marshall choose?

Fletcher v. Peck

6 CRANCH (10 U.S.) 87 (1810)
http://laws.findlaw.com/US/10/87.html
Vote: 5 (Johnson, Livingston, Marshall, Todd, Washington)
    0

Opinion of the Court: Marshall
Concurring opinion: Johnson
Not participating: Chase, Cushing

This dispute had its roots in the 1795 session of the Georgia legislature. Clearly motivated by wholesale bribery, the legislators sold about 35 million acres of public lands to several land companies at ridiculously low prices. The territory in question, known as the "Yazoo lands" after one of its major rivers, encompassed most of what is now Mississippi and Alabama. Some of the nation's most prominent public figures, including a number of members of Congress, supported this transaction or invested in it. The citizens of Georgia were outraged by the sale and turned out most of the legislators in the next election. In 1796 the newly elected legislature promptly rescinded the sales contract and moved to re-possess the land. Unfortunately, by this time the land companies had sold numerous parcels to third-party investors and settlers. A massive and complicated set of legal actions ensued to determine ownership of the disputed lands. Attempts to negotiate a settlement proved unsuccessful. Even the president, Thomas Jefferson, was drawn into the controversy as he tried to work out a compromise settlement that would satisfy the state of Georgia as well as the investors.

Fletcher v. Peck was a lawsuit filed to obtain a judicial determination of the ownership question. John Peck acquired 600,000 acres of Yazoo land, purchased from James Gunn, one of the original buyers in the Georgia land sales. Peck in turn sold 15,000 acres to land speculator Robert Fletcher. The sale was part of a carefully designed strategy between Peck and Fletcher to test the constitutionality of the Georgia repeal statute. After the sale was completed, Fletcher sued Peck for return of the purchase price, claiming that Peck had sold Fletcher a parcel of land for which he did not hold valid title. The real issue, however, rested squarely on the meaning of the Contract Clause: May a state that has entered into a valid contract later rescind that contract?

Joseph Story, who was later to become the youngest man appointed to the Supreme Court, represented those who had purchased the land and wanted clear title to it. He argued that the Contract Clause barred the state from rescinding the original sales agreements. Attorneys supporting Georgia's repudiation of the land sale held that the state was empowered to declare it void because the original transaction was based on fraud. Furthermore, they contended that the Contract Clause was intended to protect against the abrogation of private contracts, not those made by the states.

MARSHALL, CH. J., delivered the opinion of the court as follows:

The importance and the difficulty of the questions, presented by these pleadings, are deeply felt by the court.

The lands in controversy vested absolutely in James Gunn and others, the original grantees, by the conveyance of the governor, made in pursuance of an act of assembly to which the legislature was fully competent. Being thus in full possession of the legal estate, they, for a valuable consideration, conveyed portions of the land to those who were willing to purchase. If the original transaction was infected with fraud, these purchasers did not participate in it, and had no notice of it. They were innocent. Yet the legislature of Georgia has involved them in the fate of the first parties to the transaction, and, if the act be valid, has annihilated their rights also. . . .

If a suit be brought to set aside a conveyance obtained by fraud, and the fraud be clearly proved, the conveyance will be set aside, as between the parties; but the rights of third persons, who are purchasers without notice, for a valuable consideration, cannot be disregarded. Titles, which according to every legal test, are perfect, are acquired with that confidence which is inspired by the opinion that the purchaser is safe. If there be any concealed defect, arising from the conduct of those who had held the property long before he acquired it, of which he had no notice, that concealed defect cannot be set up against him. He has paid the money for a title good at law, he is innocent, whatever may be the guilt of others, and equity will not subject him to the penalties attached to that guilt. All titles would be insecure, and the intercourse between man and man would be very seriously obstructed if this principle be overturned. . . .

If the legislature felt itself absolved from those rules of property which are common to all the citizens of the United States, and from those principles of equity which are acknowledged in all our courts, its act is to be supported by its power alone, and the same power may devest any other individual of his lands, if it shall be the will of the legislature so to exert it. . . .

Is the power of the legislature competent to the annihilation of such title, and to a resumption of the property thus held?

The principle asserted is, that one legislature is competent to repeal any act which a former legislature was competent to pass; and that one legislature cannot abridge the powers of a succeeding legislature.

The correctness of this principle, so far as respects general legislation, can never be controverted. But, if an act be done under a law, a succeeding legislature cannot undo it. The past cannot be recalled by the most absolute power. Conveyances have been made, those conveyances have vested legal estates, and, if those estates may be seized by the sovereign authority, still, that they originally vested is a fact, and cannot cease to be a fact.

When, then, a law is in its nature a contract, when absolute rights have vested under that contract, a repeal of the law cannot devest those rights; and the act of annulling them, if legitimate, is rendered so by a power applicable to the case of every individual in the community.

It may well be doubted whether the nature of society and of government does not prescribe some limits to the legislative power; and, if any be prescribed, where are they to be found, if the property of an individual, fairly and honestly acquired, may be seized without compensation.

To the legislature all legislative power is granted; but the question, whether the act of transferring the property of an individual to the public, be in the nature of the legislative power, is well worthy of serious reflection.

It is the peculiar province of the legislature to prescribe general rules for the government of society; the application of those rules to individuals in society would seem to be the duty of other departments. How far the power of giving the law may involve every other power, in cases where the constitution is silent, never has been, and perhaps never can be, definitely stated.

The validity of this rescinding act, then, might well be doubted, were Georgia a single sovereign power. But Georgia cannot be viewed as a single, unconnected, sovereign power, on whose legislature no other restrictions are imposed than may be found in its own constitution. She is a part of a large empire; she is a member of the American union; and that union has a constitution the supremacy of which all acknowledge, and which imposes limits to the legislature of the several states, which none claim a right to pass. The constitution of the United States declares that no state shall pass any bill of attainder, *ex post facto* law, or law impairing the obligation of contracts.

Does the case now under consideration come within this prohibitory section of the constitution?

In considering this very interesting question, we immediately ask ourselves what is a contract? Is a grant a contract?

A contract is a compact between two or more parties, and is either executory or executed. An executory contract is one in which a party binds himself to do, or not to do, a particular thing; such was the law under which the conveyance was made by the governor. A contract executed is

one in which the object of contract is performed; and this, says Blackstone, differs in nothing from a grant. The contract between Georgia and the purchasers was executed by the grant. A contract executed, as well as one which is executory, contains obligations binding on the parties. A grant, in its own nature, amounts to an extinguishment of the right of the grantor, and implies a contract not to reassert that right. A party is, therefore, always estopped by his own grant.

Since, then, in fact, a grant is a contract executed, the obligation of which still continues, and since the constitution uses the general term contract, without distinguishing between those which are executory and those which are executed, it must be construed to comprehend the latter as well as the former. A law annulling conveyances between individuals, and declaring that the grantors should stand seised of their former estates, notwithstanding those grants, would be as repugnant to the constitution as a law discharging the vendors of property from the obligation of executing their contracts by conveyances. It would be strange if a contract to convey was secured by the constitution, while an absolute conveyance remained unprotected.

If, under a fair construction [of] the constitution, grants are comprehended under the term contracts, is a grant from the state excluded from the operation of the provision? Is the clause to be considered as inhibiting the state from impairing the obligation of contracts between two individuals, but as excluding from that inhibition contracts made with itself?

The words themselves contain no such distinction. They are general, and are applicable to contracts of every description. If contracts made with the state are to be exempted from their operation, the exception must arise from the character of the contracting party, not from the words which are employed.

Whatever respect might have been felt for the state sovereignties, it is not to be disguised that the framers of the constitution viewed, with some apprehension, the violent acts which might grow out of the feelings of the moment; and that the people of the United States, in adopting that instrument, have manifested a determination to shield themselves and their property from the effects of those sudden and strong passions to which men are exposed. The restrictions on the legislative power of the states are obviously founded in this sentiment; and the constitution of the

United States contains what may be deemed a bill of rights for the people of each state.

No state shall pass any bill of attainder, *ex post facto* law, or law impairing the obligation of contracts.

A bill of attainder may affect the life of an individual, or may confiscate his property, or may do both.

In this form the power of the legislature over the lives and fortunes of individuals is expressly restrained. What motive, then, for implying, in words which import a general prohibition to impair the obligation of contracts, an exception in favour of the right to impair the obligation of those contracts into which the state may enter?

The state legislatures can pass no *ex post facto* law. An *ex post facto* law is one which renders an act punishable in a manner in which it was not punishable when it was committed. Such a law may inflict penalties on the person, or may inflict pecuniary penalties which swell the public treasury. The legislature is then prohibited from passing a law by which a man's estate, or any part of it, shall be seized for a crime which was not declared, by some previous law, to render him liable to that punishment. Why, then, should violence be done to the natural meaning of words for the purpose of leaving to the legislature the power of seizing, for public use, the estate of an individual in the form of a law annulling the title by which he holds that estate? The court can perceive no sufficient grounds for making this distinction. This rescinding act would have the effect of an *ex post facto* law. It forfeits the estate of Fletcher for a crime not committed by himself, but by those from whom he purchased. This cannot be effected in the form of an *ex post facto* law, or bill of attainder; why, then, is it allowable in the form of a law annulling the original grant?

The argument in favour of presuming an intention to except a case, not excepted by the words of the constitution, is susceptible of some illustration from a principle originally ingrafted in that instrument, though no longer a part of it. The constitution, as passed, gave the courts of the United States jurisdiction in suits brought against individual states. A state, then, which violated its own contract was suable in the courts of the United States for that violation. Would it have been a defence in such a suit to say that the state had passed a law absolving itself from the contract? It is scarcely to be conceived that such a defence could be set up. And yet, if a state is neither restrained by the general principles of our political institutions, nor by the words of the consti-

tution, from impairing the obligation of its own contracts, such a defence would be a valid one. This feature is no longer found in the constitution; but it aids in the construction of those clauses with which it was originally associated.

It is, then, the unanimous opinion of the court, that, in this case, the estate having passed into the hands of a purchaser for a valuable consideration, without notice, the state of Georgia was restrained, either by general principles which are common to our free institutions, or by the particular provisions of the constitution of the United States, from passing a law whereby the estate of the plaintiff in the premises so purchased could be constitutionally and legally impaired and rendered null and void.

Although *Fletcher v. Peck* did not fully settle the Yazoo land controversy *(see Box 9-1)*, Marshall's opinion breathed considerable life into the Contract Clause. While acknowledging that the original transactions were based on bribery and corruption, Marshall concluded that such matters are beyond the power of the courts to control. He concentrated instead on whether a state could lawfully rescind a previously passed, binding agreement. According to the Court's holding in this case, the Constitution prohibits the states from impairing the obligation of any contract, even those contrary to the public good. In striking down the 1796 Georgia statute, the Supreme Court for the first time nullified a state law on constitutional grounds. *Fletcher v. Peck* established the Contract Clause as an important provision of the new Constitution and encouraged its use in challenging economic regulations of the states.

Marshall's initial interpretation of the Contract Clause was reinforced just two years later in *New Jersey v. Wilson* (1812). This dispute can be traced back to 1758, when the remnants of the Delaware Indian tribe settled its land claims with the state of New Jersey. The Delawares consented to give up their claim to the disputed lands if the state would purchase a tract for the tribe to inhabit. The agreement also freed the tribe from state taxation on the land. In 1801 members of the tribe decided to move to New York, and New Jersey allowed them to sell their land. Three years later the state passed a law subjecting the property to state taxes. The new owners objected, claiming that the repeal of tax-exempt

---

BOX 9-1 AFTERMATH . . . THE YAZOO LANDS CONTROVERSY

THE SUPREME COURT'S decision in *Fletcher v. Peck* (1810) provided a landmark ruling on the meaning of the Contract Clause, but it did not fully resolve the issues surrounding the Yazoo land claims. In the period between the original land sale by the Georgia legislature in 1795 and the state's voiding of the sale in 1796, parcels were bought and sold in a climate of feverish land speculation. About 60 percent of the purchasers were New England residents eager to participate in western land investments. After Georgia repealed the original sale, titles to the Yazoo lands were in considerable doubt. Not only did the actions by the Georgia legislature thoroughly confuse the issue, but also claims by Indian tribes, old Spanish interests, squatters, and those who had been granted lands by Georgia governors over the years clouded the issue. Bogus titles and sales of nonexistent land further complicated matters.

When purchasers learned that Georgia had passed legislation canceling the original sale, they pressured Congress to provide compensation if their titles proved to be invalid. Northern representatives favored a compensation program to provide relief to constituents who had purchased property, but southerners, especially representatives from Georgia, opposed any compensation as rewarding those who sought to benefit from the original acts of bribery and fraud. *Fletcher v. Peck* was first filed in federal circuit court in Massachusetts in 1803 in an attempt to have the judiciary settle the matter. Action on the lawsuit and subsequent appeals was delayed, with the parties hoping that Congress would settle the issue by passing a compensation act. When legisla-

tion failed in 1804, 1805, and 1806, it appeared that the courts would have to answer the lingering questions. By the time the Supreme Court decided *Fletcher v. Peck*, fifteen years had elapsed since the original sales. By that time determining valid title to each parcel of land was impossible.

The decision in *Fletcher v. Peck* was unpopular in many circles. Some thought the Court should not uphold contracts based on wholesale corruption. Thomas Jefferson used the decision as an opportunity to renew his attacks on Marshall. He claimed the chief justice's opinion was filled with "twistifications," "cunning," and "sophistry." According to Jefferson, it illustrated once again "how dexterously [Marshall] can reconcile law to his personal biases."

The decision, however, put pressure on Congress to bring closure to the controversy. Northerners again demanded a compensation program, but southerners still resisted. In 1814 Congress appropriated $5 million from federal land sales to compensate those who held title to the Yazoo lands. Investors released their land claims in return for monetary compensation. It took four years for the claims to be settled. Northern representatives had obtained relief for their constituents, but southern interests also benefited. Resolving the confusion over the Yazoo lands cleared the way for organizing the Mississippi territory, which was admitted as a slave-holding state in 1817.

SOURCE: Peter Magrath, *Yazoo* (Providence: Brown University Press, 1966).

---

status was an impairment of the 1758 contract. Chief Justice Marshall, for a unanimous Court, ruled in favor of the landowners. The legislature had granted the tax exemption to the land as part of a legally binding contract. That contractual obligation could not later be impaired by the state. The tax status conferred in 1758 remained with the land even though the original parties to the agreement had sold it.

In 1819 the Court heard *Sturges v. Crowninshield*, an appeal that presented issues hitting squarely on the concerns expressed by the delegates at the Constitutional Conven-

tion. Richard Crowninshield, whose business enterprises had suffered hard times, received two loans from Josiah Sturges totaling approximately $1,500. The loans were secured by promissory notes. When Crowninshield became insolvent, he sought relief from his debts by invoking New York's recently passed bankruptcy law. Sturges objected, claiming that the New York law was a state impairment of the obligation of contracts in violation of the Constitution. The New York bankruptcy law was an example of just what the Framers had intended to prohibit—states interfering with debtor-creditor agreements.

The case presented two issues to the Supreme Court. The first was whether a state may enact a bankruptcy law at all. Article I, Section 8, Clause 4, of the Constitution expressly gave the federal government power to enact such legislation. Did this power preclude the states from acting? A unanimous Court, again through an opinion written by Chief Justice Marshall, held that in the absence of any federal action the states were free to enact bankruptcy laws. The second issue was whether the New York law was invalid as an impairment of contracts. Here the Court found the law defective. The New York law discharged Crowninshield's contractual indebtedness entered into prior to the passage of the statute, which, according to the Court, was beyond the power of the state.[4]

Corporate Charters as Contracts

The same year the Court decided *Sturges,* the justices announced their decision in *Trustees of Dartmouth College v. Woodward* (1819), perhaps the most famous of the Marshall-era Contract Clause cases. The Dartmouth College case presented a question of particular significance to the business community: Is a corporation charter a contract protected against state impairment? The case had added intrigue because it involved a bitter partisan battle between the Republicans and the Federalists.

Trustees of Dartmouth College v. Woodward

4 WHEAT. (17 U.S.) 518 (1819)
http://laws.findlaw.com/US/17/518.html
Vote: 5 (Johnson, Livingston, Marshall, Story, Washington)
   1 (Duvall)
Opinion of the Court: Marshall
Concurring opinions: Story, Washington
Not participating: Todd

In 1769 King George III issued a corporate charter establishing Dartmouth College in New Hampshire. The charter designated a board of trustees as the ultimate governing body, and the board's authority extended to

---

4. Eight years later, however, the Court held in *Ogden v. Saunders* (1827) that state bankruptcy laws did not violate the Contract Clause if the contract was entered into after the enactment of the bankruptcy statute.

the college president. The board was self-perpetuating, with the power to fill its own vacancies. The founder and first president of Dartmouth was Eleazar Wheelock, who also had authority to designate his own successor. He chose his son, John Wheelock, who assumed the presidency upon Eleazar's death. John Wheelock was ill suited for the position, and for years friction existed between him and the board.

To shore up his position, Wheelock made political alliances with the Jeffersonian Republicans who had gained control of the state legislature in 1816. The Republicans gladly took his side in the dispute with the Federalist-dominated board of trustees and passed a law radically changing the governing structure of the college. The law called for an expansion of the board from twelve to twenty-one members to be appointed by the governor, and it created a supervisory panel with veto power over the actions of the trustees. The new officials removed the old trustees from office. In effect, the legislature had converted Dartmouth College, renamed Dartmouth University under the new law, from a private to a public institution. The result was chaos. The students and faculty for the most part remained loyal to the old trustees, but the state essentially took over the buildings and records of the college. As might be expected, the college soon found itself on the edge of fiscal collapse.

To resolve the situation, the old trustees hired Daniel Webster to represent them. Webster, an 1801 Dartmouth graduate, agreed to take the case for a fee of $1,000, a considerable sum of money in those days. The old trustees sued William Woodward, the secretary of the college, who had in his possession the college charter, records, and seal. Webster and the old trustees lost in the state courts and then appealed to the U.S. Supreme Court. When the case was argued in March 1818, Webster engaged in four hours of brilliant oratory before the justices. At times his argument was quite emotional; he is said to have brought tears to the eyes of those present when he spoke his often-quoted line, "It is, sir, as I have said, a small college, and yet there are those that love it." The justices, however, did not act in the heat of emotion. Almost a full year went by before the Court decided. By the time the opinion was released, both John Wheelock and William Woodward had died.

Rev. Eleazar Wheelock (left) was the founder and first president of Dartmouth College; John Wheelock (middle), son of Eleazar, was the second president, and his dispute with the college board of trustees led to the famed litigation. William H. Woodward (right) was the secretary-treasurer of the college and the defendant in the Contract Clause case of *Dartmouth College v. Woodward.*

The opinion of the Court was delivered by MR. CHIEF JUSTICE MARSHALL.

This Court can be insensible neither to the magnitude nor delicacy of this question. The validity of a legislative act is to be examined; and the opinion of the highest law tribunal of a State is to be revised: an opinion which carries with it intrinsic evidence of the diligence, of the ability, and the integrity, with which it was formed. On more than one occasion, this Court has expressed the cautious circumspection with which it approaches the consideration of such questions; and has declared, that, in no doubtful case, would it pronounce a legislative act to be contrary to the constitution. But the American people have said, in the constitution of the United States, that "no State shall pass any bill of attainder, *ex post facto* law, or law impairing the obligation of contracts." In the same instrument they have also said, "that the judicial power shall extend to all cases in law and equity arising under the constitution." On the judges of this Court, then, is imposed the high and solemn duty of protecting, from even legislative violation, those contracts which the constitution of our country has placed beyond

legislative control; and, however irksome the task may be, this is a duty from which we dare not shrink. . . .

It can require no argument to prove, that the circumstances of this case constitute a contract. An application is made to the crown for a charter to incorporate a religious and literary institution. In the application, it is stated that large contributions have been made for the object, which will be conferred on the corporation, as soon as it shall be created. The charter is granted, and on its faith the property is conveyed. Surely in this transaction every ingredient of a complete and legitimate contract is to be found.

The points for consideration are,

1. Is this contract protected by the constitution of the United States?

2. Is it impaired by the acts under which the defendant holds? . . .

1. . . . [T]he term *"contract"* must be understood in a . . . limited sense. . . . [I]t must be understood as intended to guard against a power of at least doubtful utility, the abuse of which had been extensively felt; and to restrain the legislature in future from violating the right to property. That anterior to the formation of the constitution, a course of legislation had

Drawing of Dartmouth College, 1793.

prevailed in many, if not in all, of the States, which weakened the confidence of man in man, and embarrassed all transactions between individuals, by dispensing with a faithful performance of engagements. To correct this mischief, by restraining the power which produced it, the State legislatures were forbidden "to pass any law impairing the obligation of contracts," that is, of contracts respecting property, under which some individual could claim a right to something beneficial to himself; and that since the clause in the constitution must in construction receive some limitation, it may be confined, and ought to be confined, to cases of this description; to cases within the mischief it was intended to remedy. . . .

The parties in this case differ less on general principles, less on the true construction of the constitution in the abstract, than on the application of those principles to this case, and on the true construction of the charter of 1769. This is the point on which the cause essentially depends. If the act of incorporation be a grant of political power, if it create a civil institution to be employed in the administration of the government, or if the funds of the college be public property, or if the State of New Hampshire, as a government, be alone interested in its transactions, the subject is one in which the legislature of the State may act according to its own judgment, unrestrained by any limitation of its power imposed by the constitution of the United States.

But if this be a private eleemosynary institution, endowed with a capacity to take property for objects unconnected with government, whose funds are bestowed by individuals on the faith of the charter; if the donors have stipulated for the future disposition and management of those funds in the manner prescribed by themselves; there may be more difficulty in the case. . . .

It becomes then the duty of the Court most seriously to examine this charter, and to ascertain its true character. . . .

Whence, then, can be derived the idea, that Dartmouth College has become a public institution, and its trustees public officers, exercising powers conferred by the public for public objects? Not from the source whence its funds were drawn; for its foundation is purely private and eleemosynary—Not from the application of those funds; for money may be given for education, and the persons receiving it do not, by being employed in the education of youth, become members of the civil government. Is it from the act of incorporation? Let this subject be considered.

A corporation is an artificial being, invisible, intangible, and existing only in contemplation of law. Being the mere creature of law, it possesses only those properties which the charter of its creation confers upon it, either expressly, or as incidental to its very existence. These are such as are supposed best calculated to effect the object for which it was created. Among the most important are immortality, and, if the expression may be allowed, individuality; properties, by which a perpetual succession of many persons are considered as the same, and may act as a single individual. They enable a corporation to manage its own affairs, and to hold property without the perplexing intricacies, the hazardous and endless necessity of perpetual conveyances for the purpose of transmitting it from hand to hand. It is chiefly for the purpose of clothing bodies of men, in succession, with these qualities and capacities, that corporations were invented, and are in use. By these means, a perpetual succession of individuals are capable of acting for the promotion of the particular object, like one immortal being. But this being does not share in the civil government of the country, unless that be the purpose for which it was created. Its immortality no more confers on it political power, or a political character, than immortality would confer such power or character on a natural person. It is no more a State instrument, than a natural person exercising the same powers would be. If, then, a natural person, employed by individuals in the education of youth, or for the government of a seminary in which youth is educated, would not become a public officer, or be considered as a member of the civil government, how is it, that this artificial being, created by law, for the purpose of being employed by the same individuals for the same purposes, should become a part of the civil government of the country? Is it because its existence, its capacities, its powers, are given by law? Because the government has given it the power to take and to hold property in a particular form, and for particular purposes, has the government a consequent right substantially to change that form, or to vary the purposes to which the property is to be applied? This principle has never been asserted or recognized, and is supported by no authority. Can it derive aid from reason? . . .

From the fact, then, that a charter of incorporation has been granted, nothing can be inferred which changes the character of the institution, or transfers to the government any new power over it. The character of civil institutions does not grow out of their incorporation, but out of the manner in which they are formed, and the objects for which

they are created. The right to change them is not founded on their being incorporated, but on their being the instruments of government, created for its purposes. The same institutions, created for the same objects, though not incorporated, would be public institutions, and, of course, be controllable by the legislature. The incorporating act neither gives nor prevents this control. Neither, in reason, can the incorporating act change the character of a private eleemosynary institution. . . .

From this review of the charter, it appears, that Dartmouth College is an eleemosynary institution, incorporated for the purpose of perpetuating the application of the bounty of the donors, to the specified objects of that bounty; that its trustees or governors were originally named by the founder, and invested with the power of perpetuating themselves; that they are not public officers, nor is it a civil institution, participating in the administration of government; but a charity school, or a seminary of education, incorporated for the preservation of its property, and the perpetual application of that property to the objects of its creation. . . .

This is plainly a contract to which the donors, the trustees, and the crown, (to whose rights and obligations New Hampshire succeeds,) were the original parties. It is a contract made on a valuable consideration. It is a contract for the security and disposition of property. It is a contract, on the faith of which, real and personal estate has been conveyed to the corporation. It is then a contract within the letter of the constitution, and within its spirit also. . . .

The opinion of the Court, after mature deliberation, is, that this is a contract, the obligation of which cannot be impaired, without violating the constitution of the United States. This opinion appears to us to be equally supported by reason, and by the former decisions of this Court.

2. We next proceed to the inquiry, whether its obligation has been impaired by those acts of the legislature of New Hampshire. . . .

From the review of this charter, which has been taken, it appears, that the whole power of governing the college, of appointing and removing tutors, of fixing their salaries, of directing the course of study to be pursued by the students, and of filling up vacancies created in their own body, was vested in the trustees. On the part of the crown it was expressly stipulated, that this corporation, thus constituted, should continue forever; and that the number of trustees should forever consist of twelve, and no more. By this contract the crown was bound, and could have made no violent alteration in its essential terms, without impairing its obligation.

By the revolution, the duties, as well as the powers, of government devolved on the people of New Hampshire.... It is too clear to require the support of argument, that all contracts, and rights, respecting property, remained unchanged by the revolution. The obligations then, which were created by the charter to Dartmouth College, were the same in the new, that they had been in the old government. The power of the government was also the same. A repeal of this charter at any time prior to the adoption of the present constitution of the United States, would have been an extraordinary and unprecedented act of power, but one which could have been contested only by the restrictions upon the legislature, to be found in the constitution of the State. But the constitution of the United States has imposed this additional limitation, that the legislature of a State shall pass no act "impairing the obligation of contracts."...

The whole power of governing the college is transferred from trustees appointed according to the will of the founder, expressed in the charter, to the executive of New Hampshire. The management and application of the funds of this eleemosynary institution, which are placed by the donors in the hands of trustees named in the charter, and empowered to perpetuate themselves, are placed by this act under the control of the government of the State. The will of the State is substituted for the will of the donors, in every essential operation of the college. This is not an immaterial change. The founders of the college contracted, not merely for the perpetual application of the funds which they gave, to the objects for which those funds were given; they contracted also, to secure that application by the constitution of the corporation. They contracted for a system, which should, as far as human foresight can provide, retain forever the government of the literary institution they had formed, in the hands of persons approved by themselves. This system is totally changed. The charter of 1769 exists no longer. It is reorganized; and reorganized in such a manner, as to convert a literary institution, moulded according to the will of its founders, and placed under the control of private literary men, into a machine entirely subservient to the will of the government. This may be for the advantage of this college in particular, and may be for the advantage of literature in general; but it is not according to the will of the donors,

and is subversive of that contract, on the faith of which their property was given. . . .

It results from this opinion, that the acts of the legislature of New Hampshire . . . are repugnant to the constitution of the United States. . . . The judgment of the State Court must, therefore, be reversed.

MR. JUSTICE STORY, [concurring].

In my judgment, it is perfectly clear that any act of a legislature which takes away any powers or franchises vested by its charter in a private corporation, or its corporate officers, or which restrains or controls the legitimate exercise of them, or transfers them to other persons without its assent is a violation of the obligations of that charter. If the legislature mean to claim such an authority, it must be reserved in the grant. The charter of Dartmouth College contains no such reservation, and I am therefore bound to declare that the acts of the Legislature of New Hampshire now in question do impair the obligations of that charter, and are consequently unconstitutional and void.

In pronouncing this judgment, it has not for one moment escaped me how delicate, difficult, and ungracious is the task devolved upon us. The predicament in which this Court stands in relation to the nation at large is full of perplexities and embarrassments. It is called to decide on causes between citizens of different States, between a State and its citizens, and between different States. It stands, therefore in the midst of jealousies and rivalries of conflicting parties with the most momentous interests confided to its care. Under such circumstances, it never can have a motive to do more than its duty, and I trust it will always be found to possess firmness enough to do that.

Under these impressions, I have pondered on the case before us with the most anxious deliberation. I entertain great respect for the Legislature whose acts are in question. I entertain no less respect for the enlightened tribunal whose decision we are called upon to review. In the examination, I have endeavored to keep . . . under the guidance of authority and principle. It is not for judges to listen to the voice of persuasive eloquence or popular appeal. We have nothing to do, but to pronounce the law as we find it, and, having done this, our justification must be left to the impartial judgment of our country.

The Dartmouth College case was a clear victory for Webster and the board. The old trustees regained control of the college, and Webster's reputation as one of the nation's leading legal advocates was firmly established. The decision was also a victory for business interests. By holding that corporate charters were contracts under the meaning of Article I, Section 10, the Court gave businesses considerable protection against state regulation. The decision, however, was not totally one-sided. Marshall acknowledged the power of the state to include within its contracts and charters provisions reserving the right to make future changes.

The importance of the Contract Clause reached its zenith under the Marshall Court. These early decisions protecting contractual agreements helped spur economic development and expansion. But an inevitable battle was on the horizon, a battle between the constitutional sanctity of contracts and a state's authority to regulate for the public good.

DECLINE OF THE CONTRACT CLAUSE: FROM THE TANEY COURT TO THE NEW DEAL

The Marshall years ended when the chief justice died July 6, 1835, at the age of seventy-nine. Marshall had been appointed in 1801 in one of the last acts of the once-dominant Federalist Party, and he had imposed his political philosophy on the Court's constitutional interpretations for more than three decades. His decisions in Contract Clause disputes, as well as in other areas of federalism and economic regulation, encouraged economic development and fostered entrepreneurial activity.

Importance of the Public Good

The days of the Federalist philosophy sympathetic to the interests of business and the economic elite had passed. Andrew Jackson now occupied the White House. Jackson came from the American frontier and was committed to policies beneficial to ordinary citizens; he had little sympathy for the moneyed classes of the Northeast. Within a short period, Jackson had the opportunity to change the course of the Supreme Court. He filled not only the center chair left vacant by Marshall's death but

also those of five associate justices during his presidency.[5] The new appointees all held ideologies consistent with principles of Jacksonian democracy, especially the new chief justice, Roger Brooke Taney, a Maryland Democrat who had served in a number of posts in the Jackson administration (see Box 6-2, page 333). Changes in constitutional interpretation were inevitable, although in the final analysis the Taney Court did not veer as far from Marshall precedents as many had predicted.

Given the differences between Federalist and Jacksonian values, however, the Court was likely to reevaluate the Contract Clause. The Taney Court's first opportunity to do so came in *Proprietors of Charles River Bridge v. Proprietors of Warren Bridge* (1837). As you read the Court's opinion, compare it with the positions Marshall stated in the *Fletcher* and *Dartmouth College* cases. Although Taney did not repudiate Marshall's rulings, his opinion in *Charles River Bridge* struck a new balance between the inviolability of contracts and the power of the state to legislate for the public good. The Court also held that contracts should be strictly construed, a position at odds with Marshall's rather expansive interpretations of contractual obligations. Justice Story, who had appeared as an attorney in *Fletcher* and had supported Marshall's views of the Contract Clause since he joined the Court in 1811, disagreed with this change in doctrine.

═══════════════════════════════

Proprietors of Charles River Bridge v. Proprietors of Warren Bridge

11 PET. (36 U.S.) 420 (1837)
http://laws.findlaw.com/US/36/420.html
Vote: 5 (Baldwin, Barbour, McLean, Taney, Wayne)
    2 (Story, Thompson)
Opinion of the Court: Taney
Concurring opinion: McLean
Dissenting opinions: Story, Thompson

In 1785 the Massachusetts legislature created by charter the Charles River Bridge Company. The charter gave

5. This number includes Associate Justice John Catron, who was nominated on Jackson's last day in office and whose appointment is often credited to Jackson's successor, Martin Van Buren.

The Charles River Bridge ran from Prince Street in Boston to Charlestown. The bridge, considered a very advanced design at the time of its construction, was built on seventy-five oak piers and was more than 1,500 feet long.

the company the right to construct a bridge between Boston and Charlestown and to collect tolls for its use. This agreement replaced a ferry franchise between the two cities that the colonial legislature had granted to Harvard College in 1650. In 1792 the legislature extended the charter. Because of the population growth in the Boston area, the bridge received heavy use, and its investors prospered. In 1828, when traffic congestion on the bridge became a significant problem, the legislature decided that a second bridge was necessary. Consequently, the state incorporated the Warren Bridge Company and authorized it to construct a bridge to be located about a hundred yards from the first. The Warren Bridge investors had authority to collect tolls to pay for the expense of construction plus an agreed-upon profit. However, in no more than six years the state was to assume ownership of the Warren Bridge and then operate it on a toll-free basis.

The Charles River Bridge Company opposed the construction of a second bridge. It claimed that its charter conferred the exclusive right to build and operate a bridge between Boston and Charlestown. A second bridge, eventually to be operated without tolls, would deprive the company of the profits from its investment.

The second charter, the company claimed, was a violation of the Contract Clause. To represent it, the Charles River Bridge Company hired Daniel Webster, who had won the Dartmouth College case two decades earlier *(see Box 9-2)*. When the Massachusetts courts failed to grant relief, Charles River Bridge took its case to the U.S. Supreme Court.

The case was first argued in March 1831. John Marshall still led the Court at that time, and Webster understandably felt confident of victory. However, the justices could not agree on a decision, and the case was scheduled for reargument in 1833. Once again, no decision was reached. Before a third hearing could be scheduled, deaths and resignations had changed the ideological complexion of the Court. When Jackson announced Taney as his choice for chief justice, Webster is said to have proclaimed, "The Constitution is gone." From Webster's perspective perhaps that was true. The Taney justices scheduled the bridge case to be reargued in 1837, and Webster no longer had a sympathetic audience for his strong Contract Clause position.

MR. CHIEF JUSTICE TANEY delivered the opinion of the Court.

The plaintiffs in error insist . . . [t]hat . . . the acts of the legislature of Massachusetts . . . by their true construction, necessarily implied that the legislature would not authorize

---

BOX 9-2   DANIEL WEBSTER (1782–1852)

DANIEL WEBSTER played an influential role in the development of American law and politics during a public career that spanned almost fifty years. He was born in Salisbury, New Hampshire, January 18, 1782, and educated at Phillips Exeter Academy and Dartmouth College. He was admitted to the bar in 1805 and immediately began the practice of law in his home state.

In 1813 Webster was first elected to Congress as a Federalist representative from New Hampshire. This office was only the beginning of an illustrious series of important positions:

United States representative, New Hampshire,
   1813–1817

Monroe delegate to electoral college, 1820

United States representative, Massachusetts,
   1823–1827

United States senator, Massachusetts,
   1827–1841

Presidential candidate, 1836

Secretary of state (Harrison-Tyler administrations),
   1841–1843

United States senator, Massachusetts,
   1845–1850

Secretary of state (Fillmore administration), 1850–1852

WEBSTER was perhaps best known for his role as an advocate before the Supreme Court and the brilliant oratorical skills he displayed in both Congress and the courts. Webster appeared before the Supreme Court in 168 cases, winning about half of them. In twenty-four of his appearances he was an advocate in a major constitutional dispute. Among his most celebrated cases were:

McCulloch v. Maryland (1819)
Dartmouth College v. Woodward (1819)
Cohens v. Virginia (1821)
Gibbons v. Ogden (1824)
Osborn v. Bank of the United States (1824)
Ogden v. Saunders (1827)
Wheaton v. Peters (1834)
Charles River Bridge v. Warren Bridge (1837)
Swift v. Tyson (1842)
West River Bridge v. Dix (1848)
Luther v. Borden (1849)

NOTE: For a review of Webster's legal career, see Maurice G. Baxter, *Daniel Webster and the Supreme Court* (Amherst: University of Massachusetts Press, 1966).

---

another bridge, and especially a free one, by the side of this, and placed in the same line of travel, whereby the franchise granted to the "proprietors of the Charles River Bridge" should be rendered of no value; and the plaintiffs in error contend, that the grant of the ferry to the college, and of the charter to the proprietors of the bridge, are both contracts on the part of the state; and that the law authorizing the erection of the Warren Bridge in 1828, impairs the obligation of one or both of these contracts. . . .

. . . [W]e are not now left to determine, for the first time, the rules by which public grants are to be construed in this

country. The subject has already been considered in this Court . . . and the principle recognized, that in grants by the public, nothing passes by implication. . . .

. . . [T]he object and end of all government is to promote the happiness and prosperity of the community by which it is established; and it can never be assumed, that the government intended to diminish its power of accomplishing the end for which it was created. And in a country like ours, free, active, and enterprising, continually advancing in numbers and wealth; new channels of communication are daily found necessary, both for travel and trade; and are essential to the comfort, convenience, and prosperity of the people. A state ought never to be presumed to surrender this power, because, like the taxing power, the whole community have an interest in preserving it undiminished. And when a corporation alleges, that a state has surrendered for seventy years, its power of improvement, and public accommodation, in a great and important line of travel, along which a vast number of its citizens must daily pass; the community have a right to insist, in the language of this Court above quoted, "that its abandonment ought not to be presumed, in a case, in which the deliberate purpose of the state to abandon it does not appear." The continued existence of a government would be of no great value, if by implications and presumptions, it was disarmed of the powers necessary to accomplish the ends of its creation; and the functions it was designed to perform, transferred to the hands of privileged corporations. The rule of construction announced by the Court, was not confined to the taxing power; nor is it so limited in the opinion delivered. On the contrary, it was distinctly placed on the ground that the interests of the community were concerned in preserving, undiminished, the power then in question; and whenever any power of the state is said to be surrendered or diminished, whether it be the taxing power or any other affecting the public interest, the same principle applies, and the rule of construction must be the same. No one will question that the interests of the great body of the people of the state, would, in this instance, be affected by the surrender of this great line of travel to a single corporation, with the right to exact toll, and exclude competition for seventy years. While the rights of private property are sacredly guarded, we must not forget that the community also have rights, and that the happiness and well being of every citizen depends on their faithful preservation.

Adopting the rule of construction above stated as the settled one, we proceed to apply it to the charter of 1785, to the proprietors of the Charles River Bridge. This act of incorporation is in the usual form, and the privileges such as are commonly given to corporations of that kind. It confers on them the ordinary faculties of a corporation, for the purpose of building the bridge; and establishes certain rates of toll, which the company are authorized to take. This is the whole grant. There is no exclusive privilege given to them over the waters of Charles river, above or below their bridge. No right to erect another bridge themselves, nor to prevent other persons from erecting one. No engagement from the state, that another shall not be erected; and no undertaking not to sanction competition, nor to make improvements that may diminish the amount of its income. Upon all these subjects the charter is silent; and nothing is said in it about a line of travel, so much insisted on in the argument, in which they are to have exclusive privileges. No words are used, from which an intention to grant any of these rights can be inferred. If the plaintiff is entitled to them, it must be implied, simply, from the nature of the grant; and cannot be inferred from the words by which the grant is made.

The relative position of the Warren Bridge has already been described. It does not interrupt the passage over the Charles River Bridge, nor make the way to it or from it less convenient. None of the faculties or franchises granted to that corporation, have been revoked by the legislature; and its right to take the tolls granted by the charter remains unaltered. In short, all the franchises and rights of property enumerated in the charter, and there mentioned to have been granted to it, remain unimpaired. But its income is destroyed by the Warren Bridge; which, being free, draws off the passengers and property which would have gone over it, and renders their franchise of no value. This is the gist of the complaint. For it is not pretended, that the erection of the Warren Bridge would have done them any injury, or in any degree affected their right of property; if it had not diminished the amount of their tolls. In order then to entitle themselves to relief, it is necessary to show, that the legislature contracted not to do the act of which they complain; and that they impaired, or in other words, violated that contract by the erection of the Warren Bridge.

The inquiry then is, does the charter contain such a contract on the part of the state? Is there any such stipulation to be found in that instrument? It must be admitted on all hands, that there is none—no words that even relate to another bridge or to the diminution of their tolls, or to the line of travel. If a contract on that subject can be gathered from the charter, it must be by implication; and cannot be found in the words used. Can such an agreement be implied? The rule of construction before stated is an answer to the question. In charters of this description, no rights are taken from the public, or given to the corporation, beyond those which the words of the charter, by their natural and proper construction, purport to convey. There are no words which import such a contract as the plaintiffs in error contend for, and none can be implied. . . .

Indeed, the practice and usage of almost every state in the Union, old enough to have commenced the work of internal improvement, is opposed to the doctrine contended for on the part of the plaintiffs in error. Turnpike roads have been made in succession, on the same line of travel; the later ones interfering materially with the profits of the first. These corporations have, in some instances, been utterly ruined by the introduction of newer and better modes of transportation, and travelling. In some cases, rail roads have rendered the turnpike roads on the same line of travel so entirely useless, that the franchise of the turnpike corporation is not worth preserving. Yet in none of these cases have the corporations supposed that their privileges were invaded, or any contract violated on the part of the state. Amid the multitude of cases which have occurred, and have been daily occurring for the last forty or fifty years, this is the first instance in which such an implied contract has been contended for, and this Court called upon to infer it from an ordinary act of incorporation, containing nothing more than the usual stipulations and provisions to be found in every such law. The absence of any such controversy, when there must have been so many occasions to give rise to it, proves that neither states, nor individuals, nor corporations, ever imagined that such a contract could be implied from such charters. It shows that the men who voted for these laws, never imagined that they were forming such a contract; and if we maintain that they have made it, we must create it by a legal fiction, in opposition to the truth of the fact, and the obvious intention of the party. We cannot deal thus with the rights reserved to the states; and by legal intendments and mere technical reasoning, take away from them any portion of that power over their own internal police and improvement, which is so necessary to their well being and prosperity. . . .

The judgment of the supreme judicial court of the commonwealth of Massachusetts, dismissing the plaintiff's bill, must, therefore, be affirmed, with costs.

MR. JUSTICE STORY, dissenting.

I maintain, that, upon the principles of common reason and legal interpretation, the present grant carries with it a necessary implication that the legislature shall do no act to destroy or essentially to impair the franchise; that, (as one of the learned judges of the state court expressed it,) there is an implied agreement that the state will not grant another bridge between Boston and Charlestown, so near as to draw away the custom from the old one; and, (as another learned judge expressed it,) that there is an implied agreement of the state to grant the undisturbed use of the bridge and its tolls so far as respects any acts of its own, or of any persons acting under its authority. In other words, the state, impliedly, contracts not to resume its grant, or to do any act to the prejudice or destruction of its grant. I maintain, that there is no authority or principle established in relation to the construction of crown grants, or legislative grants; which does not concede and justify this doctrine. Where the thing is given, the incidents, without which it cannot be enjoyed, are also given. . . . I maintain that a different doctrine is utterly repugnant to all the principles of the common law, applicable to all franchises of a like nature; and that we must overturn some of the best securities of the rights of property, before it can be established. I maintain, that the common law is the birthright of every citizen of Massachusetts, and that he holds the title deeds of his property, corporeal, and incorporeal, under it. I maintain, that under the principles of the common law, there exists no more right in the legislature of Massachusetts, to erect the Warren Bridge, to the ruin of the franchise of the Charles River Bridge than exists to transfer the latter to the former, or to authorize the former to demolish the latter. If the legislature does not mean in its grant to give any exclusive rights, let it say so, expressly; directly; and in terms admitting of no misconstruction. The grantees will then take at their peril, and must abide the results of their overweening confidence, indiscretion, and zeal.

My judgment is formed upon the terms of the grant, its nature and objects, its design and duties; and, in its interpretation, I seek for no new principles, but I apply such as are as old as the very rudiments of the common law.

In spite of Justice Story's protest that the majority had rendered the Contract Clause meaningless, the Taney Court continued to allow the states more leeway in regulating for the public good. As Taney noted in *Charles River Bridge*, "While the rights of private property are sacredly guarded, we must not forget that the community also have rights, and that the happiness and well being of every citizen depends on their faithful preservation." For example, in *West River Bridge Company v. Dix* (1848) the Court upheld the state's right to exercise eminent domain authority even when it conflicted with existing contracts. In that case Vermont had previously granted to a private company a charter to construct a bridge and collect tolls. When the state later decided to build a public highway to be used without tolls, it canceled the company's charter. The state offered to compensate the company for its loss, but the owners were not satisfied with the amount. In an opinion by Justice Peter V. Daniel, the Court rejected the bridge company's claim that the state had violated the Constitution, holding that the Contract Clause did not restrict the state's right to regulate for the public good under the power of eminent domain.

The Taney justices, however, did not totally abandon the Marshall Court's posture favoring business, nor did they repeal the Contract Clause by judicial fiat; instead, the Court took a more balanced position. In a number of cases, especially when the contractual provisions were clear, the Taney Court struck down state regulations on Contract Clause grounds. For example, in *Bronson v. Kinzie* (1843) the Court invalidated Illinois laws that expanded the rights of debtors. The challenged statutes placed certain limits on mortgage debt, including protecting the rights of owners to repurchase properties lost to foreclosure. To the extent that these laws were applied to contracts in existence before their passage, the laws were unconstitutional. In *Piqua Branch of the State Bank of Ohio v. Knoop* (1854) the justices declared void the assessment of state taxes on a bank because, in calculating the taxes, Ohio had used a basis different from that specified under the state charter establishing the bank.

Post–Civil War Period

After the Taney years, the Court continued to move away from strong enforcement of the Contract Clause and to accord the states increased freedom to exercise their police powers. *Fertilizing Company v. Hyde Park* (1878) provides a good illustration. The Illinois state legislature passed a statute March 8, 1867, creating the Northwestern Fertilizing Company. The charter authorized the company within a designated territory to operate a facility that converted dead animals to fertilizer and other products. The charter also gave the company the right to transport dead animals and animal parts (offal) through the territory. Based on this authority, the company operated its plant in a sparsely populated, swampy area.

The facility was located within the boundaries of the village of Hyde Park, which was beginning to experience considerable population growth. In 1869 the legislature upgraded the village charter, giving it full powers of local government including the authority to "define or abate nuisances which are, or may be, injurious to the public health." Recognizing its charter with Northwestern, the legislature stipulated that no village regulations could be applied to the company for at least two years. At the end of the two years, the village passed an ordinance that said, "No person shall transfer, carry, haul, or convey any offal, dead animals, or other offensive or unwholesome matter or material, into or through the village of Hyde Park." Parties in violation of the law were subject to fines. In 1873, following the arrest and conviction of railroad workers hauling dead animals to its plant, Northwestern filed suit claiming that their original charter was a contract that could not be abrogated by the state or its local governments. The company was unsuccessful in the state courts and appealed to the U.S. Supreme Court.

Justice Noah Swayne's opinion made clear at the outset that the company faced a difficult task in its attempt to convince the justices:

The rule of construction in this class of cases is that it shall be most strongly against the corporation. Every reasonable doubt is to be resolved adversely. Nothing is to be taken as conceded but what is given in unmistakable terms, or by an implication equally clear. The affirmative must be shown. Silence is negation, and doubt is fatal to the claim. This doctrine is vital to the public welfare.

The Court then went on to rule against the Contract Clause arguments of the company. The justices had no doubt that the transportation of offal was a public nuisance. Nor was there any doubt that the state had ample police power to combat such an offensive practice. According to Swayne, "That power belonged to the States when the Federal Constitution was adopted. They did not surrender it, and they all have it now. . . . It rests upon the fundamental principle that every one shall so use his own as not to wrong and injure another. To regulate and abate nuisances is one of its ordinary functions." The states, the Court was implying, could not contract away their inherent powers to regulate for their citizens' health, safety, and welfare.

Two years after the Northwestern Fertilizing Company case, the justices addressed a similar appeal, this time dealing with questions of public morality. *Stone v. Mississippi* focused on the use of the state's police power to combat lotteries, a form of gambling that large portions of the population considered evil at that time. As you read Chief Justice Morrison Waite's opinion for the Court, compare it with the decisions written during the Marshall era. Note how much the Court's interpretation of the Contract Clause had changed.

Stone v. Mississippi

101 U.S. 814 (1880)
http://laws.findlaw.com/US/101/814.html
Vote: 9 (Bradley, Clifford, Field, Harlan, Hunt, Miller, Strong, Swayne, Waite)

o

Opinion of the Court: Waite

In 1867 the post–Civil War provisional state legislature chartered the Mississippi Agricultural, Educational, and Manufacturing Aid Society. In spite of its name, the society's only purpose was to operate a lottery. The charter gave the society authority to run a lottery in Mississippi for twenty-five years, and, in return, the society paid an initial sum of cash to the state, an additional annual payment for each year of operation, plus a percentage of the lottery receipts. In 1868, however, a state convention drafted a new constitution, which the people ratified the next year. This constitution contained provisions explicitly outlawing lotteries. On July 16, 1870, the legislature passed a statute providing for enforcement of the antilottery provisions, and four years later, on March 17, 1874, the state attorney general filed charges against John B. Stone and others associated with the Mississippi Agricultural, Educational, and Manufacturing Aid Society for being in violation of state law. The state admitted that the company was operating within the provisions of

its 1867 charter but contended that the new constitution and subsequent enforcement legislation effectively repealed that grant. Stone countered that the federal Contract Clause explicitly prohibits the state from negating the provisions of the charter.

MR. CHIEF JUSTICE WAITE delivered the opinion of the Court.

It is now too late to contend that any contract which a State actually enters into when granting a charter to a private corporation is not within the protection of the clause in the Constitution of the United States that prohibits States from passing laws impairing the obligation of contracts. Art. 1, SECT. 10. The doctrines of *Trustees of Dartmouth College v. Woodward* [1819], announced by this court more than sixty years ago, have become so imbedded in the jurisprudence of the United States as to make them to all intents and purposes a part of the Constitution itself. In this connection, however, it is to be kept in mind that it is not the charter which is protected, but only any contract the charter may contain. If there is no contract, there is nothing in the grant on which the Constitution can act. Consequently, the first inquiry in this class of cases always is, whether a contract has in fact been entered into, and if so, what its obligations are.

In the present case the question is whether the State of Mississippi, in its sovereign capacity, did by the charter now under consideration bind itself irrevocably by a contract to permit "the Mississippi Agricultural, Educational, and Manufacturing Aid Society," for twenty-five years, "to receive subscriptions, and sell and dispose of certificates of subscription which shall entitle the holders thereof to" "any lands, books, paintings, antiques, scientific instruments or apparatus, or any other property or thing that may be ornamental, valuable, or useful," "awarded to them" "by casting of lots, or by lot, chance, or otherwise." There can be no dispute but that under this form of words the legislature of the State chartered a lottery company, having all the powers incident to such a corporation, for twenty-five years, and that in consideration thereof the company paid into the State treasury $5,000 for the use of a university, and agreed to pay, and until the commencement of this suit did pay, an annual tax of $1,000 and "one-half of one per cent on the amount of receipts derived from the sale of certificates or tickets." If the legislature that granted this charter had the power to bind the people of the State and all succeeding legislatures to allow the corporation to continue its corporate business during the whole term of its authorized existence, there is no doubt about the sufficiency of the language employed to effect that object, although there was an evident purpose to conceal the vice of the transaction by the phrases that were used. Whether the alleged contract exists, therefore, or not, depends on the authority of the legislature to bind the State and the people of the State in that way.

All agree that the legislature cannot bargain away the police power of a State. "Irrevocable grants of property and franchises may be made if they do not impair the supreme authority to make laws for the right government of the State; but no legislature can curtail the power of its successors to make such laws as they may deem proper in matters of police." Many attempts have been made in this court and elsewhere to define the police power, but never with entire success. It is always easier to determine whether a particular case comes within the general scope of the power, than to give an abstract definition of the power itself which will be in all respects accurate. No one denies, however, that it extends to all matters affecting the public health or the public morals. Neither can it be denied that lotteries are proper subjects for the exercise of this power. We are aware that formerly, when the sources of public revenue were fewer than now, they were used in some or all of the States, and even in the District of Columbia, to raise money for the erection of public buildings, making public improvements, and not infrequently for educational and religious purposes; but this court said, more than thirty years ago, speaking through Mr. Justice Grier, that "experience has shown that the common forms of gambling are comparatively innocuous when placed in contrast with the wide-spread pestilence of lotteries. The former are confined to a few persons and places, but the latter infests the whole community; it enters every dwelling; it reaches every class; it preys upon the hard earnings of the poor; and it plunders the ignorant and simple." Happily, under the influence of restrictive legislation, the evils are not so apparent now; but we very much fear that with the same opportunities of indulgence the same results would be manifested.

If lotteries are to be tolerated at all, it is no doubt better that they should be regulated by law, so that the people may be protected as far as possible against the inherent vices of the system; but that they are demoralizing in their effects, no matter how carefully regulated, cannot admit of a doubt. When the government is untrammelled by any claim of vested rights or chartered privileges, no one has ever supposed that lotteries could not lawfully be suppressed, and those who manage them punished severely as violators of the rules of social morality. From 1822 to 1867, without any constitutional requirement, they were prohibited by law in Mississippi, and those who conducted them punished as a kind of gambler. During the provisional government of that State, in 1867, at the close of the late civil war, the present act of incorporation, with more of like character, was passed. The next year, 1868, the people, in adopting a new constitution with a view to the resumption of their political rights as one of the United States, provided that "the legislature shall never authorize any lottery, nor shall the sale of lottery-tickets be allowed, nor shall any lottery heretofore authorized be permitted to be drawn, or tickets therein to be sold.". . .

The question is therefore directly presented, whether, in view of these facts, the legislature of a State can, by the charter of a lottery company, defeat the will of the people, authoritatively expressed, in relation to the further continuance of such business in their midst. We think it cannot. No legislature can bargain away the public health or the public morals. The people themselves cannot do it, much less their servants. The supervision of both these subjects of governmental power is continuing in its nature, and they are to be dealt with as the special exigencies of the moment may require. Government is organized with a view to their preservation, and cannot divest itself of the power to provide for them. For this purpose the largest legislative discretion is allowed, and the discretion cannot be parted with any more than the power itself. . . .

. . . [T]he power of governing is a trust committed by the people to the government, no part of which can be granted away. The people, in their sovereign capacity, have established their agencies for the preservation of the public health and the public morals, and the protection of public and private rights. These several agencies can govern according to their discretion, if within the scope of their general authority, while in power; but they cannot give away nor sell the discretion of those that are to come after them, in respect to matters the government of which, from the very nature of things, must "vary with varying circumstances." They may create corporations, and give them, so to speak, a limited citizenship; but as citizens, limited in their privileges, or otherwise, these creatures of the government creation are subject to such rules and regulations as may from time to time be ordained and established for the preservation of health and morality.

The contracts which the Constitution protects are those that relate to property rights, not governmental. It is not always easy to tell on which side of the line which separates governmental from property rights a particular case is to be put; but in respect to lotteries there can be no difficulties. They are not, in the legal acceptation of the term, *mala in se,* [wrong by its very nature] but, as we have just seen, may properly be made *mala prohibita* [wrong by government declaration]. They are a species of gambling, and wrong in their influences. They disturb the checks and balances of a well-ordered community. Society built on such a foundation would almost of necessity bring forth a population of speculators and gamblers, living on the expectation of what, "by the casting of lots, or by lot, chance, or otherwise," might be "awarded" to them from the accumulations of others. Certainly the right to suppress them is governmental, to be exercised at all times by those in power, at their discretion. Any one, therefore, who accepts a lottery charter does so with the implied understanding that the people, in their sovereign capacity, and through their properly constituted agencies, may resume it at any time when the public good shall require, whether it be paid for or not. All that one can get by such a charter is a suspension of certain governmental rights in his favor, subject to withdrawal at will. He has in legal effect nothing more than a license to enjoy the privilege on the terms named for the specified time, unless it be sooner abrogated by the sovereign power of the State. It is a permit, good as against existing laws, but subject to future legislative and constitutional control or withdrawal.

On the whole, we find no error in the record.

Judgment affirmed.

Following *Stone v. Mississippi* it was clear that the Court would no longer be sympathetic to Contract Clause attacks on state regulatory statutes. With Contract Clause avenues closing, opponents of state regulation of business and commercial activities turned to another provision of the Constitution, the Due Process Clause of the Fourteenth Amendment. From the late 1880s to the 1930s, the Court heard and often responded favorably to these substantive due process arguments, a period of Court history discussed in Chapter 10.

National Emergencies

The Contract Clause reached its lowest status during the Great Depression of the 1930s. With the stock market crash of 1929, the nation entered its worst economic crisis; most Americans were placed in serious financial jeopardy. The 1932 election of Franklin Roosevelt ushered in the New Deal, and the federal government began innovative economic programs to combat the Depression. At the same time, various states were developing their own programs to protect their citizens against the economic ravages the country was experiencing.

What people feared the most during the Depression was losing the family home. Homeowners did what they could to meet their mortgage obligations, but, because so many were out of work, they were unable to make their payments. Financial institutions had little choice but to foreclose on these properties as stipulated in the mortgage contracts. To provide relief, several states passed statutes to increase homeowners' chances of saving their houses. Banks and other creditors opposed these assistance measures. For them, intervention by the state was a direct violation of the constitutional ban against impairment of contracts.

The showdown between the Contract Clause and the government's authority to cope with economic crisis occurred in *Home Building and Loan Association v. Blaisdell* (1934). As you read Chief Justice Charles Evans Hughes's opinion for the Court, think about the Constitutional Convention and the concerns that led the Framers to adopt the Contract Clause. Would they agree with the Court that the Constitution should bend in the face of national crises, or would they side with Justice George Sutherland's position that the provisions of the Constitution should be interpreted the same way regardless of the conditions of the times?

Home Building and Loan Association v. Blaisdell

290 U.S. 398 (1934)
http://laws.findlaw.com/US/290/398.html
Vote: 5 (Brandeis, Cardozo, Hughes, Roberts, Stone)
    4 (Butler, McReynolds, Sutherland, Van Devanter)
Opinion of the Court: Hughes
Dissenting opinion: Sutherland

During the Great Depression, the nation experienced high unemployment, low prices for agricultural and manufactured products, a stagnation of business, and a scarcity of credit. In response to these conditions, the Minnesota legislature declared that a state of economic emergency existed that demanded the use of extraordinary police powers for the protection of the people. One of the legislature's actions was passage of the Minnesota Mortgage Moratorium Act of 1933, which was designed to prevent homeowners from losing their houses when they could not make their mortgage payments. The act allowed homeowners who were behind in their payments to petition a state court for an extension of time to meet their mortgage obligations. During the period of the extension, the homeowners would not make normal mortgage payments but instead would pay a reasonable rental amount to the mortgage holder. The maximum extension was two years. The act was to be in effect only as long as the economic emergency continued. Its provisions applied to all mortgages, including those signed prior to the passage of the statute.

John and Rosella Blaisdell owned a house in Minneapolis that was mortgaged to the Home Building and Loan Association. They lived in one part of the house and rented out the other part. When the Blaisdells were unable to keep their payments current or to obtain additional credit, they requested an extension in accordance with the moratorium law. After initially denying the request and then being reversed by the state supreme court, the trial court granted the Blaisdells a two-year moratorium on mortgage payments. During this period the Blaisdells were ordered to pay forty dollars a month, which would be applied to taxes, insurance, interest, and mortgage principal.

The Home Building and Loan Association opposed the extension and appealed to the Minnesota Supreme Court on the ground that the law was an impairment of contracts in violation of the Contract Clause of the federal Constitution. The Minnesota court conceded that the law impaired the obligation of contracts, but it concluded that the statute was within the police powers of the state because of the severe economic emergency. Home Building and Loan appealed to the U.S. Supreme Court.

MR. CHIEF JUSTICE HUGHES delivered the opinion of the Court.

In determining whether the provision for this temporary and conditional relief exceeds the power of the State by reason of the clause in the Federal Constitution prohibiting impairment of the obligations of contracts, we must consider the relation of emergency to constitutional power, the historical setting of the contract clause, the development of the jurisprudence of this Court in the construction of that clause, and the principles of construction which we may consider to be established.

Emergency does not create power. Emergency does not increase granted power or remove or diminish the restrictions imposed upon power granted or reserved. The Constitution was adopted in a period of grave emergency. Its grants of power to the Federal Government and its limitations of the power of the States were determined in the light of emergency and they are not altered by emergency. What power was thus granted and what limitations were thus imposed are questions which have always been, and always will be, the subject of close examination under our constitutional system.

While emergency does not create power, emergency may furnish the occasion for the exercise of power. "Although an emergency may not call into life a power which has never lived, nevertheless emergency may afford a reason for the exertion of a living power already enjoyed." The constitutional question presented in the light of an emergency is whether the power possessed embraces the particular exercise of it in response to particular conditions. Thus, the war power of the Federal Government is not created by the emergency of war, but it is a power given to meet that emergency. It is a power to wage war successfully, and thus it permits the harnessing of the entire energies of the people in a supreme cooperative effort to preserve the nation. But even the war power does not remove constitutional limitations safeguarding essential liberties. When the provisions of the Constitution, in grant or restriction, are specific, so particularized as not to admit of construction, no question is presented. Thus, emergency would not permit a State to have more than two Senators in the Congress, or permit the election of President by a general popular vote without regard to the number of electors to which the States are respectively entitled, or permit the States to "coin money" or to "make anything but gold and silver coin a tender in payment of debts." But where constitutional grants and limitations of power are set forth in general clauses, which afford a broad outline, the process of construction is essential to fill in the details. That is true of the contract clause. The necessity of construction is not obviated by the fact that the contract clause is associated in the same section with other and more specific prohibitions. Even the grouping of subjects in the same clause may not require the same application to each of the subjects, regardless of differences in their nature.

In the construction of the contract clause, the debates in the Constitutional Convention are of little aid. But the reasons which led to the adoption of that clause, and of the other prohibitions of Section 10 of Article I, are not left in doubt and have frequently been described with eloquent emphasis. The widespread distress following the revolutionary period, and the plight of debtors, had called forth in the States an ignoble array of legislative schemes for the defeat of creditors and the invasion of contractual obligations. Legislative interferences had been so numerous and extreme that the confidence essential to prosperous trade had been undermined and the utter destruction of credit was threatened. "The sober people of America" were convinced that some "thorough reform" was needed which would "inspire a general prudence and industry, and give a regular course to the business of society." *The Federalist*, No. 44. It was necessary to impose the restraining power of a central authority in order to secure the foundations even of "private faith.". . .

But full recognition of the occasion and general purpose of the clause does not suffice to fix its precise scope. Nor does an examination of the details of prior legislation in the States yield criteria which can be considered controlling. To ascertain the scope of the constitutional prohibition we ex-amine the course of judicial decisions in its application. These put it beyond question that the prohibition is not an absolute one and is not to be read with literal exactness like a mathematical formula. . . .

The legislature cannot "bargain away the public health or the public morals." Thus, the constitutional provision against the impairment of contracts was held not to be violated by an amendment of the state constitution which put an end to a lottery theretofore authorized by the legislature. *Stone v. Mississippi* [1880]. The lottery was a valid enterprise when established under express state authority, but the legislature in the public interest could put a stop to it. A similar rule has been applied to the control by the State of the sale of intoxicating liquors. *Boston Beer Company v. Massachusetts* [1877]. The States retain adequate power to protect the public health against the maintenance of nuisances despite insistence upon existing contracts. *Northwestern Fertilizing Company v. Hyde Park* [1878]. Legislation to protect the public safety comes within the same category of reserved power. This principle has had recent and noteworthy application to the regulation of the use of public highways by common carriers and "contract carriers," where the assertion of interference with existing contract rights has been without avail, *Sproles v. Binford* [1932]. . . .

It is manifest from this review of our decisions that there has been a growing appreciation of public needs and of the necessity of finding ground for a rational compromise between individual rights and public welfare. The settlement and consequent contraction of the public domain, the pressure of a constantly increasing density of population, the interrelation of the activities of our people and the complexity of our economic interests, have inevitably led to an increased use of the organization of society in order to protect the very bases of individual opportunity. Where, in earlier days, it was thought that only the concerns of individuals or of classes were involved, and that those of the State itself were touched only remotely, it has later been found that the fundamental interests of the State are directly affected; and that the question is no longer merely that of one party to a contract as against another, but of the use of reasonable means to safeguard the economic structure upon which the good of all depends.

It is no answer to say that this public need was not apprehended a century ago, or to insist that what the provision of the Constitution meant to the vision of that day it must mean to the vision of our time. If by the statement that what the Constitution meant at the time of its adoption it means today, it is intended to say that the great clauses of the Constitution must be confined to the interpretation which the framers, with the conditions and outlook of their time, would have placed upon them, the statement carries its own refutation. It was to guard against such a narrow conception that Chief Justice Marshall uttered the memorable warning—"We must never forget that it is *a constitution* we are expounding": (*McCulloch v. Maryland*)—"a constitution intended to endure for ages to come, and consequently, to be adapted to the various *crises* of human affairs." When we are dealing with the words of the Constitution, said this Court in *Missouri v. Holland* [1920], "we must realize that they have called into life a being the development of which could not have been foreseen completely by the most gifted of its begetters. . . . The case before us must be considered in the light of our whole experience and not merely in that of what was said a hundred years ago."

Nor is it helpful to attempt to draw a fine distinction between the intended meaning of the words of the Constitution and their intended application. When we consider the contract clause and the decisions which have expounded it in harmony with the essential reserved power of the States to protect the security of their peoples, we find no warrant for the conclusion that the clause has been warped by these decisions from its proper significance or that the founders of our Government would have interpreted the clause differently had they had occasion to assume that responsibility in the conditions of the later day. The vast body of law which has been developed was unknown to the fathers, but it is believed to have preserved the essential content and the spirit of the Constitution. With a growing recognition of public needs and the relation of individual right to public security, the court has sought to prevent the perversion of the clause through its use as an instrument to throttle the capacity of the States to protect their fundamental interests. This development is a growth from the seeds which the fathers planted. . . . The principle of this development is . . . that the reservation of the reasonable exercise of the protective power of the State is read into all contracts and there is no greater reason for refusing to apply this principle to Minnesota mortgages than to New York leases.

Applying the criteria established by our decisions we conclude:

1. An emergency existed in Minnesota which furnished a proper occasion for the exercise of the reserved power of the State to protect the vital interests of the community. . . .

2. The legislation was addressed to a legitimate end, that is, the legislation was not for the mere advantage of particular individuals but for the protection of a basic interest of society.

3. In view of the nature of the contracts in question—mortgages of unquestionable validity—the relief afforded and justified by the emergency, in order not to contravene the constitutional provision, could only be of a character appropriate to that emergency and could be granted only upon reasonable conditions.

4. The conditions upon which the period of redemption is extended do not appear to be unreasonable. . . .

5. The legislation is temporary in operation. It is limited to the exigency which called it forth. . . .

We are of the opinion that the Minnesota statute as here applied does not violate the contract clause of the Federal Constitution. Whether the legislation is wise or unwise as a matter of policy is a question with which we are not concerned. . . .

The judgment of the Supreme Court of Minnesota is affirmed.

MR. JUSTICE SUTHERLAND, dissenting.

Few questions of greater moment than that just decided have been submitted for judicial inquiry during this generation. He simply closes his eyes to the necessary implications of the decision who fails to see in it the potentiality of future gradual but ever-advancing encroachments upon the sanctity of private and public contracts. The effect of the Minnesota legislation, though serious enough in itself, is of trivial significance compared with the far more serious and dangerous inroads upon the limitations of the Constitution which are almost certain to ensue as a consequence naturally following any step beyond the boundaries fixed by that instrument. And those of us who are thus apprehensive of the effect of this decision would, in a matter so important, be neglectful of our duty should we fail to spread upon the permanent records of the court the reasons which move us to the opposite view.

A provision of the Constitution, it is hardly necessary to say, does not admit of two distinctly opposite interpretations. It does not mean one thing at one time and an entirely different thing at another time. If the contract impairment clause, when framed and adopted, meant that the terms of a contract for the payment of money could not be altered . . . by a state statute enacted for the relief of hardly pressed debtors to the end and with the effect of postponing payment or enforcement during and because of an economic or financial emergency, it is but to state the obvious to say that it means the same now. This view, at once so rational in its application to the written word, and so necessary to the stability of constitutional principles, though from time to time challenged, has never, unless recently, been put within the realm of doubt by the decisions of this court. . . .

The provisions of the Federal Constitution, undoubtedly, are pliable in the sense that in appropriate cases they have the capacity of bringing within their grasp every new condition which falls within their meaning. But, their *meaning* is changeless; it is only their *application* which is extensible. . . .

A statute which materially delays enforcement of the mortgagee's contractual right of ownership and possession does not modify the remedy merely; it destroys, for the period of delay, *all* remedy so far as the enforcement of that right is concerned. The phrase, "obligation of a contract," in the constitutional sense imports a legal duty to perform the specified obligation of *that* contract, not to substitute and perform, against the will of one of the parties, a different, albeit equally valuable, obligation. And a state, under the contract impairment clause, has no more power to accomplish such a substitution than has one of the parties to the contract against the will of the other. It cannot do so either by acting directly upon the contract, or by bringing about the result under the guise of a statute in form acting only upon the remedy. If it could, the efficacy of the constitutional restriction would, in large measure, be made to disappear. . . .

I quite agree with the opinion of the court that whether the legislation under review is wise or unwise is a matter with which we have nothing to do. Whether it is likely to work well or work ill presents a question entirely irrelevant to the issue. The only legitimate inquiry we can make is whether it is constitutional. If it is not, its virtues, if it have any, cannot save it; if it is, its faults cannot be invoked to accomplish its destruction. If the provisions of the Constitution be not upheld when they pinch as well as when they comfort, they may as well be abandoned. Being unable to reach any other conclusion than that the Minnesota statute infringes the constitutional restriction under review, I have no choice but to say so.

The Court upheld the Minnesota statute because the majority concluded that the economic emergency justified the state's use of extensive police powers. Does the Contract Clause retain any vitality under such an interpretation? Or did the *Home Building and Loan Association* decision render it virtually meaningless? After all, there would be little reason to pass such a statute in good economic times.

MODERN APPLICATIONS OF THE CONTRACT CLAUSE

For four decades following the Minnesota Mortgage Moratorium Act decision, parties challenging state laws rarely rested their arguments on the Contract Clause. It made little practical sense to do so when the justices were reluctant to use the provision to strike down state legislation designed to promote the economic welfare of the citizens. Litigants who attempted to invoke the clause usually were unsuccessful. For example, in *El Paso v. Simmons* (1965) the Contract Clause was used to attack a Texas statute governing defaults on land sales agreements with the state. Consistent with the trend that began with *Charles River Bridge* more than a century earlier, the justices turned a deaf ear to the Contract Clause claims and upheld the challenged legislation. The justices made it quite clear that they were not eager to interfere with the sovereign right of the state to protect the general welfare of the people and would give the state legislatures wide discretion in determining proper public policy over economic matters. The Contract Clause, once one of the most litigated constitutional provisions, had lost much of its relevance.

To conclude, however, that the Contract Clause had been effectively and forever erased from the Constitution would be incorrect. In the decades following the New Deal, the Court was dominated by justices who took generally liberal positions on economic matters. They were philosophically opposed to allowing business interests to use the clause as a weapon to strike down legislation benefiting the people at large. But the Court's liberal majority began to unravel following the retirement of Chief

Justice Earl Warren and President Richard Nixon's appointment of Warren Burger to replace him in 1969. As succeeding appointments brought more conservative and business-oriented justices to the Court, the prospects for a revitalized Contract Clause grew. This fact was not lost on enterprising lawyers, who began to consider raising Contract Clause issues once again.

In 1977 and 1978 the Court handed down two Contract Clause decisions: *United States Trust Co. v. New Jersey*[6] and *Allied Structural Steel Co. v. Spannaus.* In both cases the justices struck down state legislation intended to promote the general welfare because the statutes were found to impair the obligation of contracts. Each time the Court's liberal justices voiced strong objections. As you read the opinions in these cases, try to determine if they represent a sharp break from the position the Court had taken over the preceding century or if they possibly can be reconciled with decisions such as *Home Building and Loan Association v. Blaisdell.*

United States Trust Co. v. New Jersey

431 U.S. 1 (1977)
http://laws.findlaw.com/US/431/1.html
Vote: 4 (Blackmun, Burger, Rehnquist, Stevens)
    3 (Brennan, Marshall, White)

Opinion of the Court: Blackmun
Concurring opinion: Burger
Dissenting opinion: Brennan
Not participating: Powell, Stewart

In 1921 the states of New York and New Jersey entered into a compact to establish the Port Authority of New York, a body responsible for developing and coordinating transportation and commerce. The Port Authority was financially independent, with funds primarily derived from private investors. It had the power to mortgage its facilities and to pledge its revenues as payment for bonds issued to its investors. In 1962, in response to increased interest in mass transit, the Port Authority took control of the financially ailing Hudson & Manhat-

tan Railroad. As part of the acquisition, the states agreed that none of the authority's revenues pledged as security for existing bonds would be used for any additional railroad expenditures.

Between 1972 and 1974, with the nation in the midst of an energy crisis and under intense pressure to develop mass transit, New York and New Jersey moved to expand their system. Because money was difficult to raise, the states decided that they would use revenues previously pledged as security for existing bonds. To free such funds both state legislatures passed statutes in 1974 retroactively repealing their pledge not to use these moneys for increased mass transit expenditures. United States Trust Company, a holder of the affected bonds, sued to invalidate the repeal as an unconstitutional impairment of the obligation of contracts. The New Jersey courts ruled against the company on the ground that the repeal was a proper exercise of state police powers. The company sought U.S. Supreme Court review.

MR. JUSTICE BLACKMUN delivered the opinion of the Court.

At the time the Constitution was adopted, and for nearly a century thereafter, the Contract Clause was one of the few express limitations on state power. The many decisions of this Court involving the Contract Clause are evidence of its important place in our constitutional jurisprudence. Over the last century, however, the Fourteenth Amendment has assumed a far larger place in constitutional adjudication concerning the States. We feel that the present role of the Contract Clause is largely illuminated by two of this Court's decisions. In each, legislation was sustained despite a claim that it had impaired the obligations of contracts.

Home Building & Loan Assn. v. Blaisdell (1934) is regarded as the leading case in the modern era of Contract Clause interpretation. At issue was the Minnesota Mortgage Moratorium Law, enacted in 1933, during the depth of the Depression and when that State was under severe economic stress, and appeared to have no effective alternative. . . . A closely divided Court, in an opinion by Mr. Chief Justice Hughes, observed that "emergency may furnish the occasion for the exercise of power" and that the "constitutional question presented in the light of an emergency is whether the power possessed embraces the particular exercise of it in response to particular conditions.". . .

This Court's most recent Contract Clause decision is *El Paso v. Simmons* (1965). That case concerned a 1941 Texas statute that limited to a 5-year period the reinstatement rights of an interest-defaulting purchaser of land from the State. . . . This Court held that "it is not every modification of a contractual promise that impairs the obligation of contract under federal law." It observed that the State "has the 'sovereign right . . . to protect the . . . general welfare of the people' " and " 'we must respect the "wide discretion on the part of the legislature in determining what is and what is not necessary." ' ". . .

Both of these cases eschewed a rigid application of the Contract Clause to invalidate state legislation. Yet neither indicated that the Contract Clause was without meaning in modern constitutional jurisprudence, or that its limitation on state power was illusory. Whether or not the protection of contract rights comports with current views of wise public policy, the Contract Clause remains a part of our written Constitution. We therefore must attempt to apply that constitutional provision to the instant case with due respect for its purpose and the prior decisions of the Court. . . .

Although the Contract Clause appears literally to proscribe "any" impairment, this Court observed in *Blaisdell* that "the prohibition is not an absolute one and is not to be read with literal exactness like a mathematical formula." Thus, a finding that there has been a technical impairment is merely a preliminary step in resolving the more difficult question whether that impairment is permitted under the Constitution. In the instant case, as in *Blaisdell*, we must attempt to reconcile the strictures of the Contract Clause with the "essential attributes of sovereign power" necessarily reserved by the States to safeguard the welfare of their citizens.

The trial court concluded that repeal of the 1962 covenant was a valid exercise of New Jersey's police power because repeal served important public interests in mass transportation, energy conservation, and environmental protection. Yet the Contract Clause limits otherwise legitimate exercises of state legislative authority, and the existence of an important public interest is not always sufficient to overcome that limitation. "Undoubtedly, whatever is reserved of state power must be consistent with the fair intent of the constitutional limitation of that power." Moreover,

the scope of the State's reserved power depends on the nature of the contractual relationship with which the challenged law conflicts.

The States must possess broad power to adopt general regulatory measures without being concerned that private contracts will be impaired, or even destroyed, as a result. Otherwise, one would be able to obtain immunity from state regulation by making private contractual arrangements. This principle is summarized in Mr. Justice Holmes' well-known dictum: "One whose rights, such as they are, are subject to state restriction, cannot remove them from the power of the State by making a contract about them." *Hudson Water Co. v. McCarter* (1908).

Yet private contracts are not subject to unlimited modification under the police power. The Court in *Blaisdell* recognized that laws intended to regulate existing contractual relationships must serve a legitimate public purpose. A State could not "adopt as its policy the repudiation of debts or the destruction of contracts or the denial of means to enforce them." Legislation adjusting the rights and responsibilities of contracting parties must be upon reasonable conditions and of a character appropriate to the public purpose justifying its adoption. As is customary in reviewing economic and social regulation, however, courts properly defer to legislative judgment as to the necessity and reasonableness of a particular measure.

When a State impairs the obligation of its own contract, the reserved-powers doctrine has a different basis. The initial inquiry concerns the ability of the State to enter into an agreement that limits its power to act in the future. As early as *Fletcher v. Peck* [1810], the Court considered the argument that "one legislature cannot abridge the powers of a succeeding legislature." It is often stated that "the legislature cannot bargain away the police power of a State." *Stone v. Mississippi* (1880). This doctrine requires a determination of the State's power to create irrevocable contract rights in the first place, rather than an inquiry into the purpose or reasonableness of the subsequent impairment. In short, the Contract Clause does not require a State to adhere to a contract that surrenders an essential attribute of its sovereignty. . . .

In applying this standard, however, complete deference to a legislative assessment of reasonableness and necessity is not appropriate because the State's self-interest is at stake. A governmental entity can always find a use for extra money, especially when taxes do not have to be raised. If a State could reduce its financial obligations whenever it wanted to spend the money for what it regarded as an important public purpose, the Contract Clause would provide no protection at all. . . .

Mass transportation, energy conservation, and environmental protection are goals that are important and of legitimate public concern. Appellees contend that these goals are so important that any harm to bondholders from repeal of the 1962 covenant is greatly outweighed by the public benefit. We do not accept this invitation to engage in a utilitarian comparison of public benefit and private loss. . . . [A] State cannot refuse to meet its legitimate financial obligations simply because it would prefer to spend the money to promote the public good rather than the private welfare of its creditors. We can only sustain the repeal of the 1962 covenant if that impairment was both reasonable and necessary to serve the admittedly important purposes claimed by the State.

The more specific justification offered for the repeal of the 1962 covenant was the States' plan for encouraging users of private automobiles to shift to public transportation. The States intended to discourage private automobile use by raising bridge and tunnel tolls and to use the extra revenue from those tolls to subsidize improved commuter railroad service. Appellees contend that repeal of the 1962 covenant was necessary to implement this plan because the new mass transit facilities could not possibly be self-supporting and the covenant's "permitted deficits" level had already been exceeded. We reject this justification because the repeal was neither necessary to achievement of the plan nor reasonable in light of the circumstances.

The determination of necessity can be considered on two levels. First, it cannot be said that total repeal of the covenant was essential; a less drastic modification would have permitted the contemplated plan without entirely removing the covenant's limitations on the use of Port Authority revenues and reserves to subsidize commuter railroads. Second, without modifying the covenant at all, the States could have adopted alternative means of achieving their twin goals of discouraging automobile use and improving mass transit. Appellees contend, however, that choosing among these alternatives is a matter for legislative discretion. But a State is not completely free to consider impairing the obligations of its own contract on a par with

other policy alternatives. Similarly, a State is not free to impose a drastic impairment when an evident and more moderate course would serve its purposes equally well. . . .

. . . [T]he need for mass transportation in the New York metropolitan area was not a new development, and the likelihood that publicly owned commuter railroads would produce substantial deficits was well known. As early as 1922, over a half century ago, there were pressures to involve the Port Authority in mass transit. It was with full knowledge of these concerns that the 1962 covenant was adopted. Indeed, the covenant was specifically intended to protect the pledged revenues and reserves against the possibility that such concerns would lead the Port Authority into greater involvement in deficit mass transit.

During the 12-year period between adoption of the covenant and its repeal, public perception of the importance of mass transit undoubtedly grew because of increased general concern with environmental protection and energy conservation. But these concerns were not unknown in 1962, and the subsequent changes were of degree and not of kind. We cannot say that these changes caused the covenant to have a substantially different impact in 1974 than when it was adopted in 1962. And we cannot conclude that the repeal was reasonable in the light of changed circumstances.

We therefore hold that the Contract Clause of the United States Constitution prohibits the retroactive repeal of the 1962 covenant. The judgment of the Supreme Court of New Jersey is reversed.

MR. JUSTICE BRENNAN, with whom MR. JUSTICE WHITE and MR. JUSTICE MARSHALL join, dissenting.

Decisions of this Court for at least a century have construed the Contract Clause largely to be powerless in binding a State to contracts limiting the authority of successor legislatures to enact laws in furtherance of the health, safety, and similar collective interests of the polity. In short, those decisions established the principle that lawful exercises of a State's police powers stand paramount to private rights held under contract. Today's decision, in invalidating the New Jersey Legislature's 1974 repeal of its predecessor's 1962 covenant, rejects this previous understanding and remolds the Contract Clause into a potent instrument for overseeing important policy determinations of the state legislature. At the same time, by creating a constitutional safe haven for property rights embodied in a contract, the decision substantially distorts modern constitutional jurisprudence governing regulation of private economic interests. I might understand, though I do not accept, this revival of the Contract Clause were it in accordance with some coherent and constructive view of public policy. But elevation of the Clause to the status of regulator of the municipal bond market at the heavy price of frustration of sound legislative policymaking is as demonstrably unwise as it is unnecessary. The justification for today's decision, therefore, remains a mystery to me, and I respectfully dissent.

The legislation challenged in *United States Trust* was passed for the general welfare of the people of New York and New Jersey and in large measure was a response to a national energy crisis. These factors seemed similar to the conditions prompting the Court to approve the Minnesota Mortgage Moratorium Act. Therefore, many were surprised by the Court's resurrection of the Contract Clause, and there was considerable interest in what the case meant for the future. Although the decision used the Contract Clause to invalidate state laws, the opinion was a moderate one without the absolutist tones of the Marshall era. Did the Court's decision signal a change in policy or was it an aberration?

A case can be made that *United States Trust* breathed new life into the Contract Clause—at least with respect to a limited class of contractual agreements. In its opinion the Court drew a distinction between a state's passing legislation that affects private contracts and a state's taking action to abrogate contracts to which the state itself was a party. In the latter case, Blackmun's opinion called for a higher standard of judicial scrutiny: the Court will uphold laws that impair state contractual obligations only "if that impairment was both reasonable and necessary to serve the admittedly important purposes claimed by the State." The justices made it more difficult for states to defend the abrogation of contracts they had made, reducing the level of deference the Court had shown to state legislatures since *Home Building and Loan Association v. Blaisdell.*

How solid was this newly expressed support for the Contract Clause? After all, only seven justices participated in the decision, and the majority consisted of just four. Would the outcome have been different had the full Court voted? The justices provided some answers to these questions the very next year in *Allied Structural Steel Co. v. Spannaus.*[7]

Allied Structural Steel Co. v. Spannaus

438 U.S. 234 (1978)
http://laws.findlaw.com/US/438/234.html
Vote: 5 (Burger, Powell, Rehnquist, Stevens, Stewart)
  3 (Brennan, Marshall, White)
Opinion of the Court: Stewart
Dissenting opinion: Brennan
Not participating: Blackmun

Although its principal place of business was Illinois, Allied Structural Steel Company maintained an office with thirty employees in Minnesota. In 1963 the company adopted a general pension plan, in which employees became vested after working the required number of years and reaching the specified age. Employees who quit or were terminated before meeting these requirements did not acquire any pension rights. The company, which made annual payments to a pension trust fund, was the sole contributor to the plan. The company retained a virtually unrestricted right to modify the plan or to terminate it at any time.

On April 9, 1974, Minnesota enacted the Private Pension Benefits Protection Act. Under the provisions of that law, a company that terminated a pension plan or closed down its Minnesota operations would be subject to a charge to the extent that its retirement funds did not assure full pensions to all workers employed by the company for ten or more years. During the summer of 1974, Allied began closing its Minnesota office and discharged a number of its employees. Nine of the terminated workers had been with the company longer than ten years, but they did not qualify for a pension under Allied's plan. The state invoked the Private Pension Benefits Protection Act and assessed Allied $185,000 for the employees' pensions. Claiming that the Minnesota law impaired

---

7. To hear oral arguments, navigate to: *www.oyez.org/oyez/frontpage.*

the obligation of its pension contract with its employees, Allied filed suit in federal district court against Warren Spannaus, the state attorney general. The court ruled in favor of the state, and Allied continued its attack on the statute in the U.S. Supreme Court.

MR. JUSTICE STEWART delivered the opinion of the Court.

There can be no question of the impact of the Minnesota Private Pension Benefits Protection Act upon the company's contractual relationships with its employees. The Act substantially altered those relationships by superimposing pension obligations upon the company conspicuously beyond those that it had voluntarily agreed to undertake. But it does not inexorably follow that the Act as applied to the company, violates the Contract Clause of the Constitution.

The language of the Contract Clause appears unambiguously absolute: "No State shall . . . pass any . . . Law impairing the Obligation of Contracts." U.S. Const., Art. I, §10. The Clause is not, however, the Draconian provision that its words might seem to imply. As the Court has recognized, "literalism in the construction of the contract clause . . . would make it destructive of the public interest by depriving the State of its prerogative of self-protection."

Although it was perhaps the strongest single constitutional check on state legislation during our early years as a Nation, the Contract Clause receded into comparative desuetude with the adoption of the Fourteenth Amendment, and particularly with the development of the large body of jurisprudence under the Due Process Clause of that Amendment in modern constitutional history. Nonetheless, the Contract Clause remains part of the Constitution. It is not a dead letter. . . .

If the Contract Clause is to retain any meaning at all . . . it must be understood to impose *some* limits upon the power of a State to abridge existing contractual relationships, even in the exercise of its otherwise legitimate police power. The existence and nature of those limits were clearly indicated in a series of cases in this Court arising from the efforts of the States to deal with the unprecedented emergencies brought on by the severe economic depression of the early 1930's.

In *Home Building & Loan Assn. v. Blaisdell* [1934] the Court upheld against a Contract Clause attack a mortgage

moratorium law that Minnesota had enacted to provide relief for homeowners threatened with foreclosure. Although the legislation conflicted directly with lenders' contractual foreclosure rights, the Court there acknowledged that, despite the Contract Clause, the States retain residual authority to enact laws "to safeguard the vital interests of [their] people." In upholding the state mortgage moratorium law, the Court found five factors significant. First, the state legislature had declared in the Act itself that an emergency need for the protection of homeowners existed. Second, the state law was enacted to protect a basic societal interest, not a favored group. Third, the relief was appropriately tailored to the emergency that it was designed to meet. Fourth, the imposed conditions were reasonable. And, finally, the legislation was limited to the duration of the emergency.

The *Blaisdell* opinion thus clearly implied that if the Minnesota moratorium legislation had not possessed the characteristics attributed to it by the Court, it would have been invalid under the Contract Clause of the Constitution. . . .

In applying these principles to the present case, the first inquiry must be whether the state law has, in fact, operated as a substantial impairment of a contractual relationship. The severity of the impairment measures the height of the hurdle the state legislation must clear. Minimal alteration of contractual obligations may end the inquiry at its first stage. Severe impairment, on the other hand, will push the inquiry to a careful examination of the nature and purpose of the state legislation.

The severity of an impairment of contractual obligations can be measured by the factors that reflect the high value the Framers placed on the protection of private contracts. Contracts enable individuals to order their personal and business affairs according to their particular needs and interests. Once arranged, those rights and obligations are binding under the law, and the parties are entitled to rely on them.

Here, the company's contracts of employment with its employees included as a fringe benefit or additional form of compensation, the pension plan. The company's maximum obligation was to set aside each year an amount based on the plan's requirements for vesting. The plan satisfied the current federal income tax code and was subject to no other legislative requirements. And, of course, the company was free to amend or terminate the pension plan at any time. The company thus had no reason to anticipate that its employees' pension rights could become vested except in accordance with the terms of the plan. It relied heavily, and reasonably, on this legitimate contractual expectation in calculating its annual contributions to the pension fund.

The effect of Minnesota's Private Pension Benefits Protection Act on this contractual obligation was severe. The company was required in 1974 to have made its contributions throughout the pre-1974 life of its plan as if employees' pension rights had vested after 10 years, instead of vesting in accord with the terms of the plan. Thus a basic term of the pension contract—one on which the company had relied for 10 years—was substantially modified. The result was that, although the company's past contributions were adequate when made, they were not adequate when computed under the 10-year statutory vesting requirement. The Act thus forced a current recalculation of the past 10 years' contributions based on the new, unanticipated 10-year vesting requirement.

Not only did the state law thus retroactively modify the compensation that the company had agreed to pay its employees from 1963 to 1974, but also it did so by changing the company's obligations in an area where the element of reliance was vital—the funding of a pension plan. . . .

Moreover, the retroactive state-imposed vesting requirement was applied only to those employers who terminated their pension plans or who, like the company, closed their Minnesota offices. The company was thus forced to make all the retroactive changes in its contractual obligations at one time. By simply proceeding to close its office in Minnesota, a move that had been planned before the passage of the Act, the company was assessed an immediate pension funding charge of approximately $185,000.

Thus, the statute in question here nullifies express terms of the company's contractual obligations and imposes a completely unexpected liability in potentially disabling amounts. . . . Yet there is no showing in the record before us that this severe disruption of contractual expectations was necessary to meet an important general social problem. The presumption favoring "legislative judgment as to the necessity and reasonableness of a particular measure" simply cannot stand in this case. . . .

Moreover, in at least one other important respect the Act does not resemble the mortgage moratorium legislation whose constitutionality was upheld in the *Blaisdell* case. This legislation, imposing a sudden, totally unanticipated, and substantial retroactive obligation upon the company to

its employees, was not enacted to deal with a situation remotely approaching the broad and desperate emergency economic conditions of the early 1930's—conditions of which the Court in *Blaisdell* took judicial notice.

Entering a field it had never before sought to regulate, the Minnesota Legislature grossly distorted the company's existing contractual relationships with its employees by superimposing retroactive obligations upon the company substantially beyond the terms of its employment contracts. And that burden was imposed upon the company only because it closed its office in the State.

This Minnesota law simply does not possess the attributes of those state laws that in the past have survived challenge under the Contract Clause of the Constitution. The law was not even purportedly enacted to deal with a broad, generalized economic or social problem. It did not operate in an area already subject to state regulation at the time the company's contractual obligations were originally undertaken, but invaded an area never before subject to regulation by the State. It did not effect simply a temporary alteration of the contractual relationships of those within its coverage, but worked a severe, permanent, and immediate change in those relationships—irrevocably and retroactively. And its narrow aim was leveled, not at every Minnesota employer, not even at every Minnesota employer who left the State, but only at those who had in the past been sufficiently enlightened as voluntarily to agree to establish pension plans for their employees.

. . . [I]f the Contract Clause means anything at all, it means that Minnesota could not constitutionally do what it tried to do to the company in this case.

The judgment of the District Court is reversed.

MR. JUSTICE BRENNAN, with whom MR. JUSTICE WHITE and MR. JUSTICE MARSHALL join, dissenting.

In cases involving state legislation affecting private contracts, this Court's decisions over the past half century, consistently with both the constitutional text and its original understanding, have interpreted the Contract Clause as prohibiting state legislative Acts which, "[w]ith studied indifference to the interests of the [contracting party] or to his appropriate protection," effectively diminished or nullified the obligation due him under the terms of a contract. But the Contract Clause has not, during this period, been applied to state legislation that, while creating new duties, in nowise diminished the efficacy of any contractual obligation owed the constitutional claimant. . . .

Today's decision greatly expands the reach of the Clause. The Minnesota Private Pension Benefits Protection Act (Act) does not abrogate or dilute any obligation due a party to a private contract; rather, like all positive social legislation, the Act imposes new, additional obligations on a particular class of persons. . . .

The Act does not relieve either the employer or his employees of any existing contract obligation. Rather, the Act simply creates an additional, supplemental duty of the employer, no different in kind from myriad duties created by a wide variety of legislative measures which defeat settled expectations but which have nonetheless been sustained by this Court. For this reason, the Minnesota Act, in my view, does not implicate the Contract Clause in any way. The basic fallacy of today's decision is its mistaken view that the Contract Clause protects all contract-based expectations, including that of an employer that his obligations to his employees will not be legislatively enlarged beyond those explicitly provided in his pension plan. . . .

. . . [I]n my view, the Contract Clause has no applicability whatsoever to the Act. . . . I would affirm the judgment of the District Court.

Justice Potter Stewart's opinion provides insight into the meaning of the Contract Clause in the contemporary era. First, although the Court invalidated the charges assessed against Allied Steel, the Court did not restore the Contract Clause to the prominence it had during the Marshall era. Second, the Contract Clause places some limits on the exercise of the state's police powers, but it does not obliterate those powers. Third, the Contract Clause applies to laws that either increase or decrease the duties of a party to a contract. Fourth, the clause is not limited to creditor-debtor contracts. Fifth, in applying the Contract Clause, the Court will first necessarily examine the extent of the impairment of contractual obligations, and "the severity of the impairment measures the height of the hurdle the state legislation must clear." If there has been substantial impairment of a contractual relationship, the Court will consider with care the nature and purpose of the legislation. In short, the majority assumed a position that balanced the importance of contractual relationships against the need of the state to exercise its police powers for the public welfare. Such a position neither returns the Contract Clause to the preferred position it enjoyed during the Marshall era nor substantially strips it of its meaning as occurred in later years.

In the years following *Allied Structural Steel* the Court has continued to take a moderate approach. In Stewart's terms, it has not interpreted the Contract Clause as a "dead letter," but it has also not applied the clause in an absolute, "Draconian," fashion. The justices have generally expressed a sensitivity to the need of the states to use their police powers to combat social problems. For example, in *Energy Reserves Group, Inc. v. Kansas Power and Light Company* (1983) the justices unanimously upheld a Kansas act that dictated an energy pricing system in conflict with existing contracts. The Court held that the Contract Clause prohibits only state actions that "substantially impair the contractual arrangement." And even such a substantial impairment can be justified if there is a significant and legitimate public purpose behind the regulation, such as remedying a broad and general social or economic problem.[8] In 1987 the justices upheld a Pennsylvania law that required coalmine operators to leave 50 percent of the coal in the ground beneath certain structures to provide surface support.[9] This provision was at odds with contracts between the mining companies and the landowners that allowed the companies to extract a much higher proportion of the coal. The justices, however, upheld the right of the state, pursuant to its police powers, to impose such a regulation, explaining that the Contract Clause "is not to be read literally."

Decisions such as these have signaled potential litigants that successfully challenging state laws on Contract Clause grounds, although more likely today than in the years immediately following the New Deal, remains a difficult task. As a consequence, parties wishing to defend private property rights against state regulation have begun to turn to other constitutional provisions for possible relief. Most often, the Fifth Amendment Takings Clause has served as a vehicle for such challenges. This subject is addressed in Chapter 11.

8. See also *Exxon Corporation v. Eagerton* (1983).
9. *Keystone Bituminous Coal Association v. DeBenedictis* (1987).

READINGS

Ackerman, Bruce. *Private Property and the Constitution*. New Haven: Yale University Press, 1977.

Dowd, Morgan D. "Justice Story, the Supreme Court, and the Obligation of Contract." *Case Western Reserve Law Review* 19 (1968): 493–527.

Hagin, Horace H. "Fletcher vs. Peck." *Georgetown Law Journal* 16 (November 1927): 1–40.

Hall, Kermit L., ed. *Law, Economy, and the Power of Contract: Major Historical Interpretations*. New York: Garland, 1987.

Horowitz, Morton J. *The Transformation of American Law, 1780–1860*. Cambridge: Harvard University Press, 1977.

Hunting, Warren B. *The Obligation of Contracts Clause of the United States Constitution*. Baltimore: Johns Hopkins University Press, 1919.

Isaacs, Nathan. "John Marshall on Contracts: A Study in Early American Juristic Theory." *Virginia Law Review* 7 (March 1921): 413–428.

Kutler, Stanley I. *Privilege and Creative Destruction: The Charles River Bridge Case*. Philadelphia: J. B. Lippincott, 1971.

Magrath, C. Peter. *Yazoo: Law and Politics in the New Republic*. Providence: Brown University Press, 1966.

Scheiber, Harry N., ed. *The State and Freedom of Contract*. Stanford: Stanford University Press, 1999.

Schulz, Ernst B. *Effect of the Contract Clause and the Fourteenth Amendment upon the Powers of the States to Control Municipal Corporations*. Bethlehem, Pa.: Lehigh University Press, 1938.

Schwartz, Bernard. "Old Wine in New Bottles? The Renaissance of the Contract Clause." *Supreme Court Review* 1979 (1980): 95–121.

Stites, Francis N. *Private Interest and Public Gain: The Dartmouth College Case*. Amherst: University of Massachusetts Press, 1972.

Trimble, Bruce. "Chief Justice Waite and the Limitations on the Dartmouth College Decision." *University of Cincinnati Law Review* 9 (January 1935): 41–66.

Wright, Benjamin F. *The Contract Clause of the Constitution*. Cambridge: Harvard University Press, 1938.

ECONOMIC SUBSTANTIVE DUE PROCESS

SUPPOSE that federal and state agents receive a tip that the owners of a factory are violating the federal law that prohibits the employment of children younger than fourteen. Without stopping to obtain a warrant, the agents enter the factory and observe that underage employees are indeed working there. The agents arrest the owners, and a court convicts them. But the factory owners challenge their conviction on two similarly named, but distinct, grounds—procedural due process and substantive due process.

Citing the first ground, the factory owners allege that the procedure the agents used—entering the factory without a warrant—violated guarantees in the Constitution, including sections of the Fifth and Fourteenth Amendments that prohibit government from depriving persons of "life, liberty, or property, without due process of law." For many, the term *due process* is synonymous with fairness. The American system of justice is based on the idea that even people guilty of violating the law deserve fair treatment. What fair treatment means is often in dispute, but what is not is this particular characterization of due process. Known as *procedural due process*, it is the most traditional and widely accepted use of the term. It suggests that governments must proceed in fair ways, but it does not bar their action completely. If the government had proceeded fairly against the factory owners, their conviction was justified.

What is the second ground on which the factory owners base their appeal? None other than due process. Under this approach to the Due Process Clauses, the owners

argue that the law prohibiting the employment of minors violated due process guarantees because, in an unreasonable way, it took away their "liberty," their right to do business. In their appeal, the owners say that due process implies something more than procedural fairness; they seek to inject into it some substantive meaning. In other words, in their view, the term not only covers the way government operates, it also provides a concrete right that government cannot violate. Under this interpretation, often called *substantive due process*, the guarantee places a limit on government activity: it suggests, using the factory example, that the federal law cannot stand because it is inherently not just and not fair when the Constitution requires that the substance of the law must be just and must not unfairly deprive persons of their life, liberty, or property. *(See Box 10-1.)*

This chapter examines whether this is a reasonable reading of the Due Process Clauses. We shall see that modern Supreme Courts, for the most part, have rejected substantive due process as it applies to laws governing economic relationships. However, for approximately forty years between the 1890s and the 1930s, the Court read due process in substantive terms and used the principle to strike down many laws that allegedly infringed on economic rights. In our example, even if the agents had obtained a search warrant, these earlier Courts might have ruled in favor of the factory owners.

If economic substantive due process is now a generally discredited doctrine, why should we devote an entire chapter to it? There are several reasons. First, its rise and

BOX 10-1   PROCEDURAL AND SUBSTANTIVE DUE PROCESS

THE U.S. CONSTITUTION contains two clauses—in the Fifth and Fourteenth Amendments—prohibiting the federal government and the states from depriving any person of life, liberty, or property without due process of law. When James Madison included the clause in the Fifth Amendment—part of the Bill of Rights—the meaning of the words "due process" was considered in its literal sense as guaranteeing only that government would follow fair and proper procedure in its dealings with private individuals. This became known in law as procedural due process—essentially a requirement that those who were adversely affected by particular government action had to be given fair notice, as well as proper opportunity to be heard, before the government could take action against them. Observance of procedural due process, or fair procedure, was actually as old as Magna Carta, if not older. As an English judge noted in 1723: "Even God himself did not pass sentence upon Adam, before he [Adam] was called upon to make his defence. Adam [says God] where art thou? Has thou not eaten of the tree, whereof I commanded thee that thou shouldst not eat?"

In the years prior to the Civil War, state courts also began to interpret due process as a protection against arbitrary or unjust laws. In other words, even where the fairest procedure was followed, legislation could deprive a person of life, liberty, or property unless he were protected by limitations imposed by due process on the substance of that legislation. As Supreme Court Justice John Marshall Harlan defined this aspect of due process at a later time, substantive due process "includes a freedom from all substantial arbitrary impositions."

Since arbitrary action is synonymous with unreasonable action, due process requires a determination of reasonableness. Substantive due process thus allowed courts to decide on the reasonableness of challenged government action in

Justice Stephen J. Field

relation to the ends which may be legitimately furthered by government, a procedure that permitted judges to substitute their own opinions for those of legislatures on the question of what constituted reasonable government acts. This, in fact, is what occurred toward the close of the nineteenth century when the Supreme Court, at the urging of Justices Stephen J. Field and Joseph P. Bradley, adopted the substantive due process approach in its decisions. Particularly after the turn of the century, in cases following that of *Lochner v. New York* in 1905, the Court relied on its independent judgment to determine the reasonableness of challenged statutes. In those cases, the Court came close to exercising the functions of what dissenting Justice Louis D. Brandeis called a "superlegislature," setting itself up as virtual supreme censor of the wisdom of legislation.

Under the *Lochner* approach, substantive due process became the great instrument of judicially imposed laissez faire and was employed to invalidate a host of laws, particularly those seeking to regulate economic abuses. As the twentieth century went on, the justices themselves came to see that *Lochner* went too far and that due process was not intended to make them judges of the wisdom or desirability of government measures. Eventually, they adopted a view urged by Justice Oliver Wendell Holmes on the proper judicial role in due process cases. The Holmes test was whether a reasonable legislator—the legislative version of the "reasonable man"—could have adopted the law at issue. The legislative judgment might well be debatable. But that was the whole point about the Holmes approach. Under it, the courts left debatable issues, as respects business, economic, and social affairs, to legislative decision.

SOURCE: Bernard Schwartz, *The Law in America* (New York: McGraw-Hill, 1974), 137.

TABLE 10-1   The Legal Tools of the Laissez-Faire Courts, 1890s to 1930s: Some Examples

	1890–1899	1900–1909	1910–1919	1920–1929	1930–1939
Used to Strike State Laws					
Substantive Due Process	*Allgeyer v. Louisiana* (1897)	*Lochner v. New York* (1905)			*Morehead v. Tipaldo* (1936)
Used to Strike Federal Laws					
Delegation of Powers					*Panama Refining Co. v. Ryan* (1935)
					Schechter Poultry v. United States (1935)
Commerce Clause			*Hammer v. Dagenhart* (1918)		*Panama Refining Co. v. Ryan* (1935)
					Schechter Poultry v. United States (1935)
					Carter v. Carter Coal (1936)
Taxing and Spending				*Bailey v. Drexel Furniture* (1922)	*United States v. Butler* (1936)
Tenth Amendment			*Hammer v. Dagenhart* (1918)		

fall from the Court's grace is an intriguing part of legal history. The adoption of substantive due process came about gradually and resulted from the push and pull of the legal and political environment of the day. Second, it provides us with an opportunity to revisit the concept of judicial activism. For most of the latter half of the twentieth century, that term was most often associated with liberalism, with Courts that overturned restrictive government laws and practices, such as those requiring segregation of public facilities or prohibiting seditious speech. But, as we pointed out in Chapter 1, activism does not always mean liberalism. Indeed, the Courts of the 1890s–1930s were activist in overturning many laws, but that activism was conservative, not liberal.

Third, substantive due process is a way to reexamine the cycles of history we have already discussed. As depicted in Table 10-1, substantive due process was another weapon in the Court's laissez-faire arsenal. While it was using delegation of power doctrines (Chapter 5), the

Tenth Amendment (Chapter 6), the Commerce Clause (Chapter 7), and taxing and spending provisions (Chapter 8) to strike down federal regulations of business, the Court also invoked substantive due process to hold against similar legislation passed by the states. This use was particularly ironic because, at the time, the Court was espousing notions of dual federalism and invoking the Tenth Amendment. In other words, the Court found ways to strike down all sorts of economic regulation, even though, in so doing, it often took contradictory stances. Therefore, substantive due process provides a way to tie together much of what has been covered in this book.

Finally, the doctrine of substantive due process has relevance today. The Court continues to apply due process guarantees to certain noneconomic relations, especially to legislation that allegedly infringes on privacy rights. In addition, the justices recently have turned to principles of substantive due process to evaluate court-awarded civil damages that are attacked as being "unfair" and "excessive."

We shall consider the modern uses of substantive due process at the end of this chapter, but first let us review the doctrine's development chronologically—how it came to be, why the Court embraced it, and what led to its decline.

THE DEVELOPMENT OF SUBSTANTIVE DUE PROCESS

In general terms, prior to the adoption of the Fourteenth Amendment, judges interpreted due process guarantees contained in the Fifth Amendment and in state constitutions as procedural in intent and nature. Historian Kermit L. Hall wrote, "Before the Civil War [due process] had essentially one meaning," that people were "entitled" to fair and orderly proceedings, particularly criminal proceedings.[1]

There were some exceptions. Writing in *Scott v. Sandford (see Chapter 6, pages 334–340)*, Chief Justice Roger B. Taney invoked the specter of due process to strike government interference in "property rights":

An act of Congress which deprives a citizen of the United States of his liberty or property [a slave], merely because he came himself or brought his property into a particular Territory . . . could hardly be dignified with the name of due process of law.

Around the same time, a New York court in *Wynehamer v. People* (1856) invoked a substantive interpretation of the state's due process requirement in striking down an alcohol prohibition law. It asserted that due process guarantees "prohibit, regardless of the matter of procedure, a certain kind or degree of exertion of legislative power altogether" and that the "substantive content of legislation" is covered, not simply protecting the "mode of procedure."

But decisions like *Wynehamer* represented the exception, not the rule. Neither state court judges interpreting their due process clauses, nor their federal court counterparts treating the Fifth Amendment, read them to possess a substantive right and, therefore, a bar on interventionist government legislation. Rather, they viewed them through a procedural lens, and for good reason: it was simply unclear whether the due process clauses were meant to have substance. More to the point, some argue that the country needed the kinds of regulations that substantive due process would find so offensive. As the United States changed from an agrarian to an industrial society, economic abuses called for limits. In Chapter 9 we saw that this perceived need provided one explanation of why the Contract Clause—as a mechanism for protecting economic interests—vanished from the legal scene.

Initial Interpretation of the Fourteenth Amendment's Due Process Clause

The federal and state governments' recognition of the need for limits on individual liberties, especially economic liberties, caused at least one sector of American life, business, intense displeasure. As the Court weakened its major source of protection—the Contract Clause—business was subjected to increasing regulation by the states, and these regulations decreased profits. Not surprisingly, business interests looked to other parts of the Constitution for protection.

As *The Slaughterhouse Cases* (1873) reveal, business thought it had found an answer in the newly ratified Fourteenth Amendment. Although the Court's majority did not see it their way, some of the dissenters surely did. As you read *Slaughterhouse*, pay careful attention to the Court's opinion and the dissents. Justice Joseph P. Bradley's dissent sets the tone for many majority opinions that follow.

═══════════════════════════════════════

The Slaughterhouse Cases (Butchers' Benevolent Association v. Crescent City Livestock Landing & Slaughter House Company)

16 WALL. (83 U.S.) 36 (1873)
http://laws.findlaw.com/US/83/36.html
Vote: 5 (Clifford, Davis, Hunt, Miller, Strong)
      4 (Bradley, Chase, Field, Swayne)
Opinion of the Court: Miller
Dissenting opinions: Bradley, Field, Swayne

After the Civil War, the United States experienced an industrial revolution, an economic diversification that

---

1. Kermit L. Hall, *The Magic Mirror* (New York: Oxford University Press, 1989), 232.

touched the entire country. Along with the benefits of industrialization came some negative side effects. For example, the Louisiana state legislature claimed that the Mississippi River had become polluted because New Orleans butchers dumped garbage into it. To remedy this problem (or, as some have suggested, to use it as an excuse to create a monopolistic enterprise), the legislature created a company—the Crescent City Livestock Landing & Slaughter House Company—to receive and slaughter all city livestock for twenty-five years.

Because the butchers were forced to use the company facilities and to pay top dollar for the privilege, they formed their own organization, the Butchers' Benevolent Association, and hired an attorney, former U.S. Supreme Court justice John A. Campbell, to sue the corporation. In his arguments, Campbell sought to apply the Fourteenth Amendment to the butchers' cause. In general terms, he asserted that the amendment, although passed in the wake of the Civil War, was not meant solely to protect blacks. Rather, its language was broad enough to encompass all citizens. He used that point as a base from which to launch his more specific argument, that Louisiana's law deprived his clients of their right to pursue their business, a basic guarantee granted by the Fourteenth Amendment's Privileges and Immunities Clause: "No State shall make or enforce any law which shall abridge the privileges or immunities of citizens of the United States." For good measure, he noted that the Louisiana law also violated the amendment's two other central guarantees, due process and equal protection, and that it was involuntary servitude outlawed by the Thirteenth Amendment.

MR. JUSTICE MILLER, now, April 14th, 1873, delivered the opinion of the court.

The plaintiffs in error . . . allege that the statute is a violation of the Constitution of the United States in these several particulars:

That it creates an involuntary servitude forbidden by the 13th article of amendment;

That it abridges the privileges and immunities of citizens of the United States;

That it denies to the plaintiffs the equal protection of the laws; and,

That it deprives them of their property without due process of law; contrary to the provisions of the 1st section of the 14th article of amendment.

This court is thus called upon for the first time to give construction to these articles.

We do not conceal from ourselves the great responsibility which this duty devolves upon us. No questions so far reaching and pervading in their consequences, so profoundly interesting to the people of this country, and so important in their bearing upon the relations of the United States and of the several states to each other, and to the citizens of the states, and of the United States, have been before this court during the official life of any of its present members. We have given every opportunity for a full hearing at the bar; we have discussed it freely and compared views among ourselves; we have taken ample time for careful deliberation, and we now propose to announce the judgments which we have formed in the construction of those articles, so far as we have found them necessary to the decision of the cases before us, and beyond that we have neither the inclination nor the right to go. . . .

The most cursory glance at these articles [Amendments 13–15] discloses a unity of purpose, when taken in connection with the history of the times, which cannot fail to have an important bearing on any question of doubt concerning their true meaning. Nor can such doubts, when any reasonably exist, be safely and rationally solved without a reference to that history; for in it is found the occasion and the necessity for recurring again to the great source of power in this country, the people of the states, for additional guaranties of human rights; additional powers to the Federal government; additional restraints upon those of the states. Fortunately that history is fresh within the memory of us all, and its leading features, as they bear upon the matter before us, free from doubt.

The institution of African slavery, as it existed in about half the states of the Union, and the contests pervading the public mind for many years, between those who desired its curtailment and ultimate extinction and those who desired additional safeguards for its security and perpetuation, culminated in the effort, on the part of most of the states in which slavery existed, to separate from the Federal government, and to resist its authority. This constituted the War of the Rebellion, and whatever auxiliary causes may have contributed to bring about this war, undoubtedly the overshadowing and efficient cause was African slavery. . . .

. . . [I]n the light of this recapitulation of events, almost too recent to be called history, but which are familiar to us all, and on the most casual examination of the language of these amendments, no one can fail to be impressed with the one pervading purpose found in them all, lying at the foundation of each, and without which none of them would have been even suggested; we mean the freedom of the slave race, the security and firm establishment of that freedom, and the protection of the newly made freeman and citizen from the oppressions of those who had formerly exercised unlimited dominion over him. It is true that only the fifteenth amendment, in terms, mentions the negro by speaking of his color and his slavery. But it is just as true that each of the other articles was addressed to the grievances of that race, and designed to remedy them as the fifteenth.

We do not say that no one else but the negro can share in this protection. Both the language and spirit of these articles are to have their fair and just weight in any question of construction. Undoubtedly while negro slavery alone was in the mind of the Congress which proposed the thirteenth article, it forbids any other kind of slavery, now or hereafter. . . . But what we do say, and what we wish to be understood, is that, in any fair and just construction of any section or phrase of these amendments, it is necessary to look to the purpose which we have said was the pervading spirit of them all, the evil which they were designed to remedy, and the process of continued addition to the Constitution, until that purpose was supposed to be accomplished as far as constitutional law can accomplish it. . . .

The language is: "No state shall make or enforce any law which shall abridge the privileges or immunities of citizens of the United States.". . .

Fortunately, we are not without judicial construction of this clause of the Constitution. The first and the leading case on the subject is that of *Corfield v. Coryell*, decided by Mr. Justice Washington in the Circuit Court for the District of Pennsylvania in 1823.

"The inquiry," he says, "is, what are the privileges and immunities of citizens of the several states? We feel no hesitation in confining these expressions to those privileges and immunities which are fundamental; which belong of right to the citizens of all free governments, and which have at all times been enjoyed by citizens of the several states which compose this Union, from the time of their becoming free, independent, and sovereign. What these fundamental principles are, it would be more tedious than difficult to enumerate. They may all, however, be comprehended under the following general heads: protection by the government, with the right to acquire and possess property of every kind, and to pursue and obtain happiness and safety, subject, nevertheless, to such restraints as the government may prescribe for the general good of the whole.". . .

In the case of *Paul v. Virginia* [1869], the court, in expounding this clause of the Constitution, says that the privileges and immunities secured to citizens of each State in the several States by the provision in question are those privileges and immunities which are common to the citizens in the latter States under the constitution and laws by virtue of their being citizens. . . .

. . . [W]e may hold ourselves excused from defining the privileges and immunities of citizens of the United States which no State can abridge until some case involving those privileges may make it necessary to do so.

But lest it should be said that no such privileges and immunities are to be found if those we have been considering are excluded, we venture to suggest some which owe their existence to the Federal government, its national character, its Constitution, or its laws.

One of these is well described in the case of *Crandall v. Nevada* [1868]. It is said to be the right of the citizen of this great country, protected by implied guarantees of its Constitution, to come to the seat of government to assert any claim he may have upon that government, to transact any business he may have with it, to seek its protection, to share its offices, to engage in administering its functions. He has the right of free access to its seaports, through which operations of foreign commerce are conducted, to the subtreasuries, land offices, and courts of justice in the several States. . . .

Another privilege of a citizen of the United States is to demand the care and protection of the Federal government over his life, liberty, and property when on the high seas or within the jurisdiction of a foreign government. Of this there can be no doubt, nor that the right depends upon his character as a citizen of the United States. The right to peaceably assemble and petition for redress of grievances, the privilege of the writ of habeas corpus, are rights of the citizen guaranteed by the Federal Constitution. The right to use the navigable waters of the United States, however they may penetrate the territory of the several States, all rights secured to our citizens by treaties with foreign nations, are dependent upon citizenship of the United States, and not citizenship of a State. One of these privileges is conferred by the very article under consideration. It is that a citizen of the United States can, of his own volition, become a citizen of any State of the Union by a bona fide residence therein, with the same rights as other citizens of that State. To these may be added the rights secured by the thirteenth and fifteenth articles of amendment, and by the other clause of the fourteenth, next to be considered.

But it is useless to pursue this branch of the inquiry, since we are of opinion that the rights claimed by these plaintiffs in error, if they have any existence, are not privileges and immunities of citizens of the United States within the meaning of the clause of the thirteenth amendment under consideration.

"All persons born or naturalized in the United States, and subject to the jurisdiction thereof, are citizens of the United States and of the state, wherein they reside. No state shall make or enforce any law which shall abridge the privileges or immunities of citizens of the United States, nor shall any state deprive any person of life, liberty or property without due process of law, nor deny to any person within its jurisdiction the equal protection of the laws."

The argument has not been much pressed in these cases that the defendant's charter deprives the plaintiffs of their property without due process of law, or that it denies to them the equal protection of the law. The first of these paragraphs has been in the Constitution since the adoption of the 5th Amendment, as a restraint upon the Federal power. It is also to be found in some form of expression in the constitutions of nearly all the states, as a restraint upon the power of the states. This law, then, has practically been the same as it now is during the existence of the government, except so far as the present Amendment may place the restraining power over the states in this matter in the hands of the Federal government.

We are not without judicial interpretation, therefore, both state and national, of the meaning of this clause. And it is sufficient to say that under no construction of that provision that we have ever seen, or any that we deem admissible, can the restraint imposed by the state of Louisiana upon the exercise of their trade by the butchers of New Orleans be held to be a deprivation of property within the meaning of that provision.

"Nor shall any state deny to any person within its jurisdiction the equal protection of the laws."

In the light of the history of these amendments, and the pervading purpose of them, . . . it is not difficult to give a meaning to this clause. The existence of laws in the states where the newly emancipated negroes resided, which discriminated with gross injustice and hardship against them as a class, was the evil to be remedied by this clause, and by it such laws are forbidden.

If, however, the states did not conform their laws to its requirements, then by the 5th section of the article of amendment Congress was authorized to enforce it by suitable legislation. We doubt very much whether any action of a state not directed by way of discrimination against the negroes as a class, or on account of their race, will ever be held to come within the purview of this provision. It is so clearly a provision for that race and that emergency, that a strong case would be necessary for its application to any other. But as it is a state that is to be dealt with, and not alone the validity of its laws, we may safely leave that matter until Congress shall have exercised its power, or some case of state oppression, by denial of equal justice in its courts, shall have claimed a decision at our hands. We find no such case in the one before us, and we do not deem it necessary to go over the argument again, as it may have relation to this particular clause of the Amendment.

In the early history of the organization of the government, its statesmen seem to have divided on the line which should separate the powers of the national government from those of the state governments, and though this line has never been very well defined in public opinion, such a division has continued from that day to this.

The adoption of the first eleven amendments to the Constitution so soon after the original instrument was accepted shows a prevailing sense of danger at that time from the Federal power and it cannot be denied that such a jealousy continued to exist with many patriotic men until the breaking out of the late Civil War. It was then discovered that the true danger to the perpetuity of the Union was in the capacity of the state organizations to combine and concentrate all the powers of the state, and of contiguous states, for a determined resistance to the general government.

Unquestionably this has given great force to the argument, and added largely to the number of those who believe in the necessity of a strong national government.

But, however pervading this sentiment, and however it may have contributed to the adoption of the Amendments we have been considering, we do not see in those Amendments any purpose to destroy the main features of the general system. Under the pressure of all the excited feeling growing out of the war, our statesmen have still believed that the existence of the states with powers for domestic and local government, including the regulation of civil rights, the rights of person and of property, was essential to the perfect working of our complex form of government, though they have thought proper to impose additional limitations on the states, and to confer additional power on that of the nation.

But whatever fluctuations may be seen in the history of public opinion on this subject during the period of our national existence, we think it will be found that this court, so far as its functions required, has always held, with a steady and an even hand, the balance between state and Federal power, and we trust that such may continue to be the history of its relation to that subject so long as it shall have duties to perform which demand of it a construction of the Constitution, or of any of its parts.

The judgments of the Supreme Court of Louisiana in these cases are affirmed.

MR. JUSTICE FIELD, dissenting.

The question presented is . . . one of the gravest importance, not merely to the parties here, but to the whole country. It is nothing less than the question whether the recent Amendments to the Federal Constitution protect the citizens of the United States against the deprivation of their common rights by state legislation. In my judgment the 14th Amendment does afford such protection, and was so intended by the Congress which framed and the states which adopted it. . . .

The provisions of the Fourteenth Amendment, which is properly a supplement to the thirteenth, cover, in my judgment, the case before us, and inhibit any legislation which confers special and exclusive privileges like these under consideration. The Amendment was adopted to obviate objections which had been raised and pressed with great force to the validity of the civil rights act, and to place the common rights of the American citizens under the protection of the National government. It first declares that "all persons born or naturalized in the United States, and subject to the jurisdiction thereof, are citizens of the United States and of the state wherein they reside." It then declares that "No state shall make or enforce any law which shall abridge the privileges or immunity of citizens of the United States, nor shall any state deprive any person of life, liberty or property, without due process of law, nor deny to any person within its jurisdiction the equal protection of the laws.". . .

The first clause of the fourteenth Amendment . . . removes it from the region of discussion and doubt. It recognizes in express terms, if it does not create, citizens of the United States, and it makes their citizenship dependent upon the place of their birth, or the fact of their adoption, and not upon the Constitution or laws of any state or the condition of their ancestry. A citizen of a state is now only a citizen of the United States residing in that state. The fundamental rights, privileges, and immunities which belong to him as a free man and a free citizen, now belong to him as a citizen of the United States, and are not dependent upon his citizenship of any state. The exercise of these rights and privileges, and the degree of enjoyment received from such exercise, are always more or less affected by the condition and the local institutions of the state, or city, or town where he resides. They are thus affected in a state by the wisdom of its laws, the ability of its officers, the efficiency of its magistrates, the education and morals of its people, and by many other considerations. This is a result which follows from the constitution of society, and can never be avoided, but in no other way can they be affected by the action of the state, or by the residence of the citizen therein. They do not derive their existence from its legislation, and cannot be destroyed by its power. . . .

. . . [G]rants of exclusive privileges, such as is made by the act in question, are opposed to the whole theory of free government, and it requires no aid from any bill of rights to render them void. That only is a free government, in the American sense of the term, under which the inalienable right of every citizen to pursue his happiness is unrestrained, except by just, equal, and impartial laws.

MR. JUSTICE BRADLEY, dissenting.

The [Fourteenth] Amendment . . . prohibits any state from depriving any person (citizen or otherwise) of life, liberty or property, without due process of law.

In my view, a law which prohibits a large class of citizens from adopting a lawful employment, or from following a lawful employment previously adopted, does deprive them of liberty as well as property, without due process of law. Their right of choice is a portion of their liberty; their occupation is their property. Such a law also deprives those citizens of the equal protection of the laws, contrary to the last clause of the section.

The constitutional question is distinctly raised in these cases; the constitutional right is expressly claimed; it was violated by state law, which was sustained by the state court, and we are called upon in a legitimate and proper way to afford redress. Our jurisdiction and our duty are plain and imperative.

It is futile to argue that none but persons of the African race are intended to be benefited by this Amendment. They may have been the primary cause of the Amendment, but its language is general, embracing all citizens, and I think it was purposely so expressed.

The mischief to be remedied was not merely slavery and its incidents and consequences; but that spirit of insubordination and disloyalty to the national government which had troubled the country for so many years in some of the states, and that intolerance of free speech and free discussion which often rendered life and property insecure, and led to much unequal legislation. The Amendment was an attempt to give voice to the strong national yearning for that time and that condition of things, in which American citizenship should be a sure guaranty of safety, and in which every citizen of the United States might stand erect in every portion of its soil, in the full enjoyment of every right and privilege belonging to a freeman, without fear of violence or molestation.

But great fears are expressed that this construction of the Amendment will lead to enactments by Congress interfering with the internal affairs of the states, and establishing therein civil and criminal codes of law for the government of the citizens, and thus abolishing the state governments in everything but name; or else, that it will lead the Federal courts to draw to their cognizance the supervision of state tribunals on every subject of judicial inquiry, on the plea of ascertaining whether the privileges and immunities of citizens have not been abridged.

In my judgment no such practical inconveniences would arise. Very little, if any, legislation on the part of Congress would be required to carry the Amendment into effect. Like the prohibition against passing a law impairing the obligation of a contract, it would execute itself. The point would be regularly raised in a suit at law, and settled by final reference to the Federal Court. As the privileges and immunities protected are only those fundamental ones which belong to every citizen, they would soon become so far defined as to cause but a slight accumulation of business in the Federal Courts. Besides, the recognized existence of the law would prevent its frequent violation. But even if the business of the national courts should be increased, Congress could easily supply the remedy by increasing their number and efficiency. The great question is: what is the true construction of the Amendment? When once we find that, we shall find the means of giving it effect. The argument from inconvenience ought not to have a very controlling influence in questions of this sort. The national will and national interest are of far greater importance.

In my opinion the judgment of the Supreme Court of Louisiana ought to be reversed.

The *Slaughterhouse* opinions are significant for several reasons. First, it was ironic that the first major case asking the Court to interpret the Fourteenth Amendment was brought by whites, not blacks. This irony did not escape Justice Samuel Miller, who relied on history to stress the true purpose of the amendment—to protect blacks and to refute Campbell's basic position. Next, he demolished the attorney's application of the specific guarantees to the dispute at hand. He spent the most energy on the primary claim of privileges and immunities (truly emasculating the clause), but he also rejected the Due Process Clause claim. Why did Miller take such a hard-line position? In large measure, he did so because he did not want to see the Court become a "superlegislature," a censor on what states could and could not do.

The Beginning of Substantive Due Process: The Court Opens a Window

Miller's opinion in *Slaughterhouse*, taken in conjunction with Bradley's and Field's dissents, are clear statements of the initial positions taken by members of the Court on the substantive due process question. Indeed, the Miller and Bradley-Field opinions are considered to represent the epitome of opposing views on the subject *(see Box 10-1, page 577)*.

It was Miller's view, however, that for the moment carried the day—there was no substance in due process. Given the terse language of the opinion, we might suspect that it closed the book on the subject forever. But that was not the case. Miller observed just five years later:

It is not a little remarkable, that while [due process] has been in the Constitution . . . as a restraint upon the authority of the Federal government, for nearly a century . . . its powers ha[d] rarely been invoked in the judicial forum or the more enlarged theatre of public discussion. But while it has been a part of the Constitution, as a restraint upon the power of the States, only a very few years, the docket of this court is crowded with cases in which we are asked to hold that State courts and State legislatures have deprived their own citizens of life, liberty, or property without due process of law. There is here abundant evidence that there exists some strange misconception of the scope of this provision as found in the fourteenth amendment.[2]

Why was it necessary for Miller to write this? Had not *Slaughterhouse* eradicated the notion of the Fourteenth Amendment's Due Process Clause as a prohibition of state economic regulation?

It had, but that did not prevent attorneys, representing increasingly desperate business interests, from continuing to make substantive due process arguments. From their perspective, the current environment held promise for the eventual adoption of such arguments. Within legal circles, for example, there was much discussion of several theories that lent themselves to Bradley's dissenting position in *Slaughterhouse*. One was expressed in Thomas M. Cooley's influential *Constitutional Limita-*

tions, which elevated the word *liberty* within the Due Process Clause to the status of an important constitutional right. The protection of this right, in Cooley's eyes, required a substantive reading of the Fourteenth Amendment, which, in turn, would serve as a mechanism for protecting property rights and for restricting government regulation. While Cooley's theory was specific, Herbert Spencer offered a more general view. Called Social Darwinism, it treated social evolution in the same terms that Charles Darwin used to explain biological evolution: If government simply maintained order and protected property rights and otherwise left people alone, the "fittest" would survive and make good; but if government attempted to intrude in other ways, then those other than "the fittest" also would survive, which would have a detrimental effect on society in the long term. This proposition had a natural compatibility with laissez-faire economic theories: if government leaves business alone, the best will prosper. Applying substantive due process would persuade government to leave business alone.

But perhaps the most important factor contributing to the vitality of substantive due process was the Court. Social Darwinism may have influenced some scholars, the social elite, and business, but most Americans did not buy its tenets. If they had, states would not have kept on trying to regulate businesses; the public would have demanded policies of noninterference. But they did continue. To a large extent, the crowded docket to which Miller referred was the Court's own doing.

An important, and certainly vivid, example of how the Court encouraged substantive due process arguments came in *Munn v. Illinois*. This decision cut both ways: the Court upheld the state's regulation but provided enough of a loophole for clever attorneys to exploit later. What was that loophole? One way to answer this question is to reconsider Miller's opinion in *Slaughterhouse* as you read *Munn*. Do you spot any differences?

---

2. *Davidson v. New Orleans* (1878).

Munn v. Illinois

94 U.S. 113 (1877)

http://laws.findlaw.com/US/94/113.html

Vote: 7 (Bradley, Clifford, Davis, Hunt, Miller, Swayne, Waite)
      2 (Field, Strong)

Opinion of the Court: Waite

Dissenting opinion: Field

The Industrial Revolution affected much of the nation, but its impact on the city of Chicago was monumental. Because of its status as an important trading post, particularly for the grain market, Chicago was becoming the "New York of the West." [3] Grain produced by farmers in the Midwest would flow into Chicago to be shipped to merchants throughout the United States. As a result, grain storage developed as a lucrative industry in Chicago. Typically, until grain was sold and shipped, companies stored it in warehouses that looked like huge skyscrapers. These warehouses were called grain elevators because of the way the grain "was mechanically loaded by dump baskets fastened to conveyor belts."

A dozen or more grain storage companies sprang up in Chicago. Among the most successful was Munn & Scott, co-owned by Ira Munn. He started with one warehouse with a capacity of 8,000 bushels of grain, but within a few short years, Munn was overseeing an enterprise with four elevators and a storage capacity of 2,700,000 bushels. He was, in short, a very successful entrepreneur.

Despite his success, Munn (along with many others) engaged in fraudulent business practices. He charged exorbitantly high fees, mixed inferior with superior grain, and engaged in price fixing with other companies. As these abuses became more obvious, farmers and merchants pleaded with city officials to regulate the industry. After several ineffective attempts by a local board to do so, the state—under continued pressure from farmers' organizations (known as the Granger movement)—in

3. We adapt this discussion largely from C. Peter Magrath's "The Case of the Unscrupulous Warehouseman," in *Quarrels That Have Shaped the Constitution*, ed. John A. Garraty (New York: Harper and Row, 1987).

1871 enacted a law that included provisions establishing boards to regulate, among other aspects of the business, the maximum rates grain elevators could charge. The state justified the law as compatible with its constitution, which specified that public warehouses were subject to regulation. Shortly after the act took effect, Munn went into bankruptcy, amid allegations of ethical and professional violations. The company that took over his warehouses also refused to comply with the act and challenged it as a violation of the Fourteenth Amendment's Due Process Clause.

MR. CHIEF JUSTICE WAITE delivered the opinion of the court.

The question to be determined in this case is whether the General Assembly of Illinois can, under the limitations upon the legislative power of the States imposed by the Constitution of the United States, fix by law the maximum of charges for the storage of grain in warehouses at Chicago and other places in the State having not less than one hundred thousand inhabitants, "in which grain is stored in bulk, and in which the grain of different owners is mixed together, or in which grain is stored in such a manner that the identity of different lots or parcels cannot be accurately preserved."

It is claimed that such a law is repugnant. . . .

To that part of amendment 14, which ordains that no State shall "Deprive any person of life, liberty or property, without due process of law, nor deny to any person within its jurisdiction the equal protection of the laws.". . .

The Constitution contains no definition of the word "deprive," as used in the Fourteenth Amendment. To determine its signification, therefore, it is necessary to ascertain the effect which usage has given it, when employed in the same or a like connection.

While this provision of the Amendment is new in the Constitution of the United States as a limitation upon the powers of the States, it is old as a principle of civilized government. It is found in Magna Charta, and, in substance if not in form, in nearly or quite all the constitutions that have been from time to time adopted by the several States of the Union. By the 5th Amendment, it was introduced into the Constitution of the United States as a limitation upon the powers of the National Government, and by the Fourteenth, as a guar-

In the late nineteenth century, grain elevators, used to store grain until it was sold, were a common sight on the Chicago River. Ira Munn and George Scott's grain elevators (at right) were among the most successful, until Munn's corrupt business practices brought the industry under government scrutiny.

anty against any encroachment upon an acknowledged right of citizenship by the Legislatures of the States. . . .

When one becomes a member of society, he necessarily parts with some rights or privileges which, as an individual not affected by his relations to others, he might retain. "A body politic," as aptly defined in the preamble of the Constitution of Massachusetts, is a social compact by which the whole people covenants with each citizen, and each citizen with the whole people, that all shall be governed by certain laws for the common good. This does not confer power upon the whole people to control rights which are purely and exclusively private; but it does authorize the establishment of laws requiring each citizen to so conduct himself, and so use his own property, as not unnecessarily to injure another. This is the very essence of government. . . . From this source come the police powers, which, as was said by Mr. Chief Justice Taney in the License Cases, are nothing

more or less than the powers of government inherent in every sovereignty, . . . that is to say, . . . the power to govern men and things. Under these powers, the government regulates the conduct of its citizens one towards another, and the manner in which each shall use his own property, when such regulation becomes necessary for the public good. In their exercise, it has been customary in England from time immemorial, and in this country from its first colonization, to regulate ferries, common carriers, hackmen, bakers, millers, wharfingers, innkeepers, &c., and, in so doing, to fix a maximum of charge to be made for services rendered, accommodations furnished, and articles sold. To this day, statutes are to be found in many of the States upon some or all these subjects; and we think it has never yet been successfully contended that such legislation came within any of the constitutional prohibitions against interference with private property. . . .

From this it is apparent that, down to the time of the adoption of the Fourteenth Amendment, it was not supposed that statutes regulating the use, or even the price of the use, of private property necessarily deprived an owner of his property without due process of law. Under some circumstances they may, but not under all. The Amendment does not change the law in this particular; it simply prevents the States from doing that which will operate as such a deprivation.

This brings us to inquire as to the principles upon which this power of regulation rests, in order that we may determine what is within and what without its operative effect. Looking, then, to the common law, from whence came the right which the Constitution protects, we find that when private property is "affected with a public interest, it ceases to be juris privati only.". . . Property does become clothed with a public interest when used in a manner to make it of public consequence, and affect the community at large. When, therefore, one devotes his property to a use in which the public has an interest, he, in effect, grants to the public an interest in that use, and must submit to be controlled by the public for the common good, to the extent of the interest he has thus created. He may withdraw his grant by discontinuing the use; but, so long as he maintains the use, he must submit to the control. . . .

. . . [W]hen private property is devoted to a public use, it is subject to public regulation. It remains only to ascertain whether the warehouses of these plaintiffs in error, and the business which is carried on there, come within the operation of this principle.

For this purpose, we accept as true the statements of fact contained in the elaborate brief of one of the counsel of the plaintiffs in error. From this it appears that ". . . the trade in grain is carried on by the inhabitants of seven or eight of the great States of the West with four or five of the States lying on the seashore, and forms the largest part of interstate commerce in these States. The grain warehouses or elevators in Chicago are immense structures, holding from 300,000 to 1,000,000 bushels at one time, according to size. They are divided into bins of large capacity and great strength. . . . They are located with the river harbor on one side and the railway tracks on the other; and the grain is run through them from car to vessel, or boat to car, as may be demanded in the course of business. It has been found impossible to preserve each owner's grain separate, and this has given rise to a system of inspection and grading, by which the grain of different owners is mixed, and receipts issued for the number of bushels which are negotiable, and redeemable in like kind, upon demand. This mode of conducting the business was inaugurated more than twenty years ago, and has grown to immense proportions. The railways have found it impracticable to own such elevators, and public policy forbids the transaction of such business by the carrier; the ownership has, therefore, been by private individuals, who have embarked their capital and devoted their industry to such business as a private pursuit.". . .

Under such circumstances it is difficult to see why, if the common carrier, or the miller, or the ferryman, or the innkeeper, or the wharfinger, or the baker, or the cartman, or the hackney-coachman, pursues a public employment and exercises "a sort of public office," these plaintiffs in error do not. They stand, to use again the language of their counsel, in the very "gateway of commerce," and take toll from all who pass. Their business most certainly "tends to a common charge, and is become a thing of public interest and use." Every bushel of grain for its passage "pays a toll, which is a common charge," and, therefore . . . every such warehouseman "ought to be under public regulation, viz.: that he . . . take but reasonable toll." Certainly, if any business can be clothed "with a public interest, and cease to be juris privati only," this has been. It may not be made so by the operation of the Constitution of Illinois or this statute, but it is by the facts. . . .

We conclude, therefore, that the statute in question is not repugnant to the Constitution of the United States, and that there is no error in the judgment. In passing upon this case we have not been unmindful of the vast importance of the questions involved. This and cases of a kindred character were argued before us more than a year ago by the most eminent counsel, and in a manner worthy of their well earned reputations. We have kept the cases long under advisement, in order that their decision might be the result of our mature deliberations.

The judgment is affirmed.

MR. JUSTICE FIELD . . . dissented.

I am compelled to dissent from the decision of the court in this case, and from the reasons upon which that decision is founded. The principle upon which the opinion of the majority proceeds is, in my judgment, subversive of the rights of private property, heretofore believed to be protected by constitutional guaranties against legislative interference, and is in conflict with the authorities cited in its support. . . .

By the term "liberty," as used in the [Fourteenth Amendment to the Constitution], something more is meant than mere freedom from physical restraint or the bounds of a prison. It means freedom to go where one may choose, and to act in such manner, not inconsistent with the equal rights of others, as his judgment may dictate for the promotion of his happiness; that is, to pursue such callings and avocations as may be most suitable to develop his capacities, and give to them their highest enjoyment.

The same liberal construction which is required for the protection of . . . liberty . . . should be applied to the protection of private property. If the legislature of a State, under pretense of providing for the public good, or for any other reason, can determine, against the consent of the owner, the uses to which private property shall be devoted, or the prices which the owner shall receive for its uses, it can deprive him of the property as completely as by a special act for its confiscation or destruction. If, for instance, the owner is prohibited from using his building for the purposes for which it was designed, it is of little consequence that he is permitted to retain the title and possession; or, if he is compelled to take as compensation for its use less than the expenses to which he is subjected by its ownership, he is, for all practical purposes, deprived of the property, as effectually as if the legislature had ordered his forcible dispossession. If it be admitted that the legislature has any control over the compensation, the extent of that compensation becomes a mere matter of legislative discretion. The amount fixed will operate as a partial destruction of the value of the property, if it fall below the amount which the owner would obtain by contract, and, practically, as a complete destruction, if it be less than the cost of retaining its possession. There is, indeed, no protection of any value under the constitutional provision, which does not extend to the use and income of the property, as well as to its title and possession. . . .

There is nothing in the character of the business of the defendants as warehousemen which called for the interference complained of in this case. Their buildings are not nuisances; their occupation of receiving and storing grain infringes upon no rights of others, disturbs no neighborhood, infects not the air, and in no respect prevents others from using and enjoy-

ing their property as to them may seem best. The legislation in question is nothing less than a bold assertion of absolute power by the State to control at its discretion the property and business of the citizen, and fix the compensation he shall receive. The will of the legislature is made the condition upon which the owner shall receive the fruits of his property and the just reward of his labor, industry, and enterprise. "That government," says Story, "can scarcely be deemed to be free where the rights of property are left solely dependent upon the will of a legislative body without any restraint. The fundamental maxims of a free government seem to require that the rights of personal liberty and private property should be held sacred." The decision of the court in this case gives unrestrained license to legislative will.

To return to our question, what was the loophole in Chief Justice Morrison Waite's opinion? Like Miller, he seemed to reject substantive due process completely, asserting that most regulatory legislation should be presumed valid; indeed, the American Bar Association, which was then a newly formed organization and full of business-oriented attorneys, denounced the ruling as "barbarous" and vowed to see it overturned.[4] Also consider the statement in Justice Field's acrimonious dissent, which largely reflected Bradley's in *Slaughterhouse*: the law was "nothing less than a bold assertion of absolute power by the state to control at its discretion the property and business of the citizen." So it is not surprising that Waite's majority opinion "has generally been regarded as a great victory for liberalism and a judicial refusal to recognize due process as a limit on the substance of legislative regulatory power."[5]

But is that description precise? Not exactly. Although Waite could have taken the same approach as Miller in *Slaughterhouse*—the complete rejection of the due process claim—he did not. Instead, Waite qualified his opinion, asserting first that state regulations of private property were "not supposed" to deprive owners of their right to due process, but that "under some circumstances they may." What differentiated "some circumstances" from

4. C. Herman Pritchett, *The American Constitution* (New York: McGraw-Hill, 1959), 558.
5. Ibid., 557.

others? In Waite's opinion, the answer lay in the nature of the subject of the regulation: "We find that when private property is 'affected with a public interest it ceases to be [of private right] only.'" Waite used this doctrine, often called the business-affected-with-a-public-interest doctrine (BAPI), to find against Munn's claim.

In dissent, Justice Field charged that the BAPI test provided businesses inadequate protection against government regulation: "There is hardly an enterprise or business engaging the attention and labor of any considerable portion of the community, in which the public has not an interest in the sense in which that term is used by the court." Yet Waite's opinion, perhaps unwittingly, provided a loophole for lawyers representing business clients who were unhappy with state regulation. The opinion implied that businesses not affected with the public interest could raise a due process defense against unreasonable state regulation. By avoiding a hard-line stance of the sort taken by Miller in *Slaughterhouse*, Waite's "maybe yes, maybe no" approach in the end provided some elbowroom for the concept of substantive due process.

In two cases, coming a decade or so after *Munn*, the Court moved closer to the concession only implied by Waite. In the first, **Mugler v. Kansas** (1887), the Court considered a state law that prohibited the manufacture and sale of liquor. Although the majority upheld the regulation against a substantive due process challenge, the Court's opinion represented something of a break from *Munn*. First, it articulated the view that not "every statute enacted ostensibly for the promotion of [the public interest] is to be accepted as a legitimate exertion of police powers of the state." This opinion was far more explicit than Waite's: there were clear limits of state regulatory power. Second, and more important, it took precisely the opposite position from the majority in *Slaughterhouse*. Recall that Justice Miller wanted to avoid the Court being placed in the position of a "superlegislature," scrutinizing and perhaps censoring state action. But in *Mugler*, that is precisely what the Court said it would do:

There are . . . limits beyond which legislation cannot rightfully go. . . . If, therefore, a statute purporting to have been enacted to protect the public health, the public morals, or the public safety, has no real or substantial relation to those objects, or is a palpable invasion of rights secured by the fundamental law, *it is the duty of the courts to so adjudge*, and thereby give effect to the Constitution. (Emphasis added.)

In *Mugler* the Court did not fully adopt the doctrine of substantive due process; it even upheld the state regulation on liquor. It also established its intent to review legislation to determine whether it was a "reasonable" exercise of state power. In essence, the Court would balance the interests of the state against those of individual due process guarantees.

The legislation tested in *Mugler* was deemed reasonable, but in **Chicago, Milwaukee & St. Paul Railway v. Minnesota** (1890), decided three years after *Mugler*, the Court went the other way: the justices struck down a state regulation on the ground that it interfered with due process guarantees. At first glance, *Chicago, Milwaukee & St. Paul Railway* bears a distinct resemblance to *Munn v. Illinois*. Strong lobbying efforts by farm groups led Minnesota in 1887 to establish a commission to set "equal and reasonable" rates for railroad transportation of goods and for warehouse storage. The commission received a complaint that the Chicago, Milwaukee, and St. Paul Railway Company was charging dairy farmers unreasonable rates to ship their milk. It held hearings to investigate the claim and ruled against the railroad. When the company refused to abide by the ruling and reduce its rates, the commission went to the state supreme court. In the opinion of that tribunal, the commission's enabling legislation intended that the rates it "recommended and published" were to be "not simply advisory . . . but final and conclusive as to what are equal and reasonable charges." The railroad took its case to the U.S. Supreme Court, where it argued that the commission had interfered with "its property" without providing it with due process of law.

Writing for the majority, Justice Samuel Blatchford held for the railroad on two grounds, both centering on the Fourteenth Amendment's Due Process Clause. Procedurally, he found the law—at least as construed by the state supreme court—defective. Because courts could not review the rates the commission set, the law deprived the railroad of a certain degree of fairness. On this point, the Court took a "traditional" approach to due process, asserting that "procedural safeguards" must be "attached to public expropriations of private property." [6] But Blatchford did not stop there; rather, he examined the law in terms of the reasonableness standard promulgated in *Mugler:* "The question of the reasonableness of a rate of charge for transportation by a railroad company . . . is eminently a question for judicial investigation, requiring due process of law for its determination."

Blatchford found the law deprived the company of its property in an unfair way:

If the company is deprived of the power of charging reasonable rates . . . and such deprivation takes place in the absence of an investigation by judicial machinery, it is deprived of the lawful use of its property, and thus, in substance and effect, of the property itself, without due process of law.

The *Chicago, Milwaukee & St. Paul Railway* case was not all that extraordinary: it merely applied the standard articulated in *Mugler,* a standard that obviously cut both ways. Sometimes the Court, in its attempt to inquire (balance interests), would find a law a "reasonable" use of state power (*Mugler*), and sometimes it would find it violative of substantive due process guarantees, as it did here. But this case and, to a lesser extent, *Mugler,* were remarkable if we consider how different they were from *Slaughterhouse.* Over a seventeen-year period, the Court had moved from a refusal to inject substance into due process to a near affirmation of the doctrine of substantive due process; it had moved from the assertion that it would become a censor to one arguing that judicial inquiry was necessary, if not mandated, by the Constitution. And although, as we shall see, it did not fully endorse Thomas Cooley's position defining due process "liberty" in economic terms until seven years later, Blatchford's ruling laid the groundwork for exactly that.

This change in position prompts us to ask why the Court did such a turnabout over two decades. The most obvious answer is personnel changes. As Table 10-2 shows, by the time the Court decided *Mugler,* only one member of the *Slaughterhouse* majority, Miller, remained. By 1890 Miller also was gone, as was Chief Justice Waite, who, despite the loophole in the *Munn* opinion, generally favored

TABLE 10-2 The U.S. Supreme Court: From *Slaughterhouse* to *Mugler*

The *Slaughterhouse* Court (1873)	The *Mugler* Court (1887)
Chase[1]	Waite
Hunt	Blatchford
Clifford	Gray
Strong	Woods
Miller	Miller
Bradley[1]	Bradley
Swayne[1]	Matthews
Davis	Harlan
Field[1]	Field

1. In minority in *Slaughterhouse.*

state regulatory power. Their replacements were quite different. Some had been corporate attorneys schooled in the philosophies of Cooley and Spencer and quite willing to borrow from the briefs of their former colleagues who argued against state regulation. Justice David J. Brewer, who replaced Stanley Matthews, a moderate-conservative states' rights advocate, had refused to follow *Munn* as a court of appeals judge. It is not surprising that many eagerly awaited the *Chicago, Milwaukee & St. Paul Railway* decision to see how membership changes might affect the direction of this area of the law.[7] Given the backgrounds of the new appointees, it also is not surprising to find that the views of the *Slaughterhouse* dissenters—especially Field and Bradley—went on to rule the day.

But there may have been more to it. By asserting the standard it did, the Court was engaging in extreme judicial activism. Peter Woll wrote:

By substituting its judgment for that of state legislators in determining the fairness of regulations of property and liberty under the due process clause of the Fourteenth Amendment, the Court was acting contrary to the public opinion that spurred state regulation. Political pressures upon state legislatures throughout the country had resulted in laws regulating business which courts were unwilling to sustain.[8]

6. Hall, *The Magic Mirror,* 236.

7. See Arnold M. Paul, *Conservative Crisis and the Rule of Law* (Ithaca, N.Y.: Cornell University Press, 1960), 42.

8. Peter Woll, *Constitutional Law* (Englewood Cliffs, N.J.: Prentice Hall, 1981), 486.

It seems fair to say that the justices did not see it this way. Rather, they viewed these "political pressures" as just that—as particularized, radical, "socialistic" elements that did not reflect majority interests. If this was their perception, it had a solid foundation. Some legislation had resulted from the lobbying efforts of farm and labor movements and later, as we shall see, of the Progressives and New Dealers. In the minds of many conservatives of the day, including some of the justices, such pressures were illegitimate because they sought to subvert the free enterprise system. In short, while the Populists, Progressives, and New Dealers, in the opinion of conservatives, tried to put the brakes on businesses and inculcate the government with socialistic legislation, the conservatives strongly believed that the best interests of the country lay with "an utterly free market, unfettered by governmental regulation." This, not the plans of radicals, would be more advantageous to society in the long run because in the end all would benefit financially.

A fundamental change was in the wind, and many point to the Court's decision in *Allgeyer v. Louisiana* (1897) as the turning point. What did the Court say here that it had not fully articulated in cases like *Mugler* and *Chicago, Milwaukee & St. Paul Railway?*

Allgeyer v. Louisiana

165 U.S. 578 (1897)
http://laws.findlaw.com/US/165/578.html
Vote: 9 (Brewer, Brown, Field, Fuller, Gray, Harlan, Peckham,
*   Shiras, White)*
    0
Opinion of the Court: Peckham

With the alleged purpose of protecting against fraud, Louisiana enacted a law that barred its citizens and corporations from doing business with out-of-state insurance companies, unless they complied with a specified set of requirements. State attorneys alleged that E. Allgeyer & Company had violated the law when it entered into an agreement by mail with the Atlantic Mutual Insurance Company of New York to purchase marine insurance covering one hundred bales of cotton being shipped to foreign ports.

Rather than argue its innocence, the company challenged the constitutionality of the law on Fourteenth Amendment due process grounds. In its view, the term *liberty* included the right to use and enjoy all "endowments" without constraint, and the term *property* included the right to acquire it and engage in business. Here, Allgeyer's attorney alleged, the law acts as a significant and unconstitutional curtailment of the business activity of the company.

MR. JUSTICE PECKHAM, after stating the case, delivered the opinion of the Court.

The question presented is the simple proposition whether under the act a party while in the state can insure property in Louisiana in a foreign insurance company, which has not complied with the laws of the state, under an open policy, the special contract or insurance and the open policy being contracts made and entered into beyond the limits of the state. . . .

It is natural that the state court should have remarked that there is in this "statute an apparent interference with the liberty of defendants in restricting their rights to place insurance on property of their own whenever and in what company they desired." Such interference is not only apparent, but it is real, and we do not think that it is justified for the purpose of upholding what the state says is its policy with regard to foreign insurance companies which had not complied with the laws of the state for doing business within its limits. In this case the company did no business within the state, and the contracts were not therein made.

The supreme court of Louisiana says that the act of writing, within that state, the letter of notification, was an act therein done to effect an insurance on property then in the state, in a marine insurance company which had not complied with its laws, and such act was therefore prohibited by the statute. As so construed we think the statute is a violation of the 14th Amendment of the Federal Constitution, in that it deprives the defendants of their liberty without due process of law. The statute which forbids such act does not become due process of law, because it is inconsistent with the provisions of the Constitution of the Union. The liberty mentioned in that amendment means, not only the right of the citizen to be free from the mere physical restraint of his person, as by incarceration, but the term is deemed to embrace the right of the citizen to be free in the enjoyment of all his faculties; to be free to use them in all lawful ways; to live and work where he will; to earn his livelihood by any lawful calling; to pursue any livelihood or avocation, and for that purpose to enter into all contracts which may be proper, necessary, and essential to his carrying out to a successful conclusion the purposes above mentioned.

It was said by Mr. Justice Bradley in *Butchers' Union S. H. & L. S. L. Co. v. Crescent City L. S. L. & S. H. Co.* [*Slaughterhouse Cases*], in the course of his concurring opinion in that case, that "the right to follow any of the common occupations of life is an inalienable right. It was formulated as such under the phrase 'pursuit of happiness' in the Declaration of Independence, which commenced with the fundamental proposition that 'all men are created equal, that they are endowed by their Creator with certain inalienable rights; and among these are life, liberty, and the pursuit of happiness.' This right is a large ingredient in the civil liberty of the citizen." Again, the learned justice said: "I hold that the liberty of pursuit—the right to follow any of the ordinary callings of life—is one of the privileges of a citizen of the United States." And again, "But if it does not abridge the privileges and immunities of a citizen of the United States to prohibit him from pursuing his chosen calling, and giving to others the exclusive right of pursuing it, it certainly does deprive him, to a certain extent, of his liberty; for it takes from him the freedom of adopting and following the pursuit which he prefers; which, as already intimated, is a material part of the liberty of the citizen." It is true that these remarks were made in regard to questions of monopoly, but they well describe the rights which are covered by the word "liberty" as contained in the 14th Amendment. . . .

The foregoing extracts have been made for the purpose of showing what general definitions have been given in regard to the meaning of the word "liberty" as used in the amendment, but we do not intend to hold that in no such case can the state exercise its police power. When and how far such power may be legitimately exercised with regard to these subjects may be left for determination to each case as it arises.

Has not a citizen of a state, under the provisions of the Federal Constitution above mentioned, a right to contract outside of the state for insurance on his property—a right of which state legislation cannot deprive him? We are not alluding to acts done within the state by an insurance company or its agents doing business therein, which are in violation of the state statutes . . . and would be controlled by it. When we speak of the liberty to contract for insurance or to do an act to effectuate such a contract already existing, we refer to and have in mind the facts of this case, where the contract was made outside the state, and as such was a valid and proper contract. The act done within the limits of the state under the circumstances of this case and for the purpose therein mentioned, we hold a proper act, one which the defendants were at liberty to perform and which the state legislature had no right to prevent, at least with reference to the Federal Constitution. To deprive the citizen of such a right as herein described without due process of law is illegal. Such a statute as this in question is not due process of law, because it prohibits an act which under the Federal Constitution the defendants had a right to perform. This does not interfere in any way with the acknowledged right of the state to enact such legislation in the legitimate exercise of its police or other powers as to it may seem proper. In the exercise of such right, however, care must be taken not to infringe upon those other rights of the citizen which are protected by the Federal Constitution.

In the privilege of pursuing an ordinary calling or trade and of acquiring, holding, and selling property must be embraced the right to make all proper contracts in relation thereto, and although it may be conceded that this right to contract in relation to persons or property or to do business within the jurisdiction of the state may be regulated and sometimes prohibited when the contracts or business conflict with the policy of the state as contained in the statutes, yet the power does not and cannot extend to prohibiting the citizen from making contracts of the nature involved in this case outside of the limits and jurisdiction of the state, and which are also to be performed outside of such jurisdiction; nor can the state legally prohibit its citizens from doing such an act as writing this letter of notification, even though the property which is the subject of the insurance may at the time when such insurance attaches be within the limits of the state. The mere fact that a citizen may be within the limits of a particular state does not prevent his making a contract outside its limits while he himself remains within it. The contract in this case was thus made. It was a valid contract, made outside of the state, to be performed outside of the state, although the subject was property temporarily within the state. As the contract was valid in the place where made and where it was to be performed, the party to the contract upon whom is devolved the right or duty to send the notification in order that the insurance provided for by the contract may attach to the property specified in the shipment mentioned in the notice, must have the liberty to do that act and to give that notification within the limits of the state, any prohibition of the state statute to the contrary notwithstanding.

Justice Rufus Peckham's opinion is not so different from the majority's opinion in *Chicago, Milwaukee & St. Paul Railway*. He struck down the state law in part on the ground that it was not reasonable. But he went much further. By merging substantive due process with freedom of contract, by reading the term *liberty* to mean economic liberty, encompassing the right to "enter into all contracts," Peckham's opinion was strong, to say the least. He adopted the position that businesses had been pressing since the demise of the Contract Clause as a source of protection. Now their right to do business, to set their own rates and enter into contracts with other businesses and perhaps even with employees, had the highest level of legal protection. In just under twenty-five years, business interests had pushed the Court from *Slaughterhouse*, in which it refused to review state legislation for its compatibility with due process guarantees, to *Munn*, in which legislation was presumed valid *generally*, but was open to judicial inquiry into its "reasonableness." The Court then moved from a balancing of state versus individual interests (*Chicago, Milwaukee & St. Paul Railway*) to placing state regulations in a less-exalted position than the fundamental liberty of contract (*Allgeyer*).

THE ROLLER-COASTER RIDE OF SUBSTANTIVE DUE PROCESS: 1898–1923

However explicit *Allgeyer* was, the true test of its importance would come in its application. Some read it to mean that the Court would not uphold legislation that infringed on economic "liberty," but **Holden v. Hardy**, decided the very next year, dispelled this notion. In this case, the Court examined a Utah law prohibiting companies engaged in the excavation of mines from working their employees more than eight hours a day, except in emergency situations. Attorneys challenging the law claimed:

It is . . . not within the power of the legislature to prevent persons who are . . . perfectly competent to contract, from entering into employment and voluntarily making contracts in relation thereto merely because the employment . . . may be considered by the legislature to be dangerous or injurious to the health of the employee; and if such right to contract cannot be prevented, it certainly cannot be restricted by the legislature to suit its own ideas of the ability of the employee to stand the physical and mental strain incident to the work.

The state asserted that the challenged statute was a "health regulation" and within the state's power because it was aimed at "preserving to a citizen his ability to work and support himself."

In *Holden* the Court reiterated its *Mugler* position: "The question in each case is whether the legislature has adopted the statute in exercise of a reasonable discretion or whether its actions be a mere excuse for an unjust discrimination." The Supreme Court, now acting as the nation's "superlegislature," deemed the legislation "reasonable"; that is, it did not impinge on the liberty of contract because the state had well justified its interest in protecting the unique health problems caused by working in mines.

Holden was a victory for the still-forming Progressive Movement and emerging labor groups, which were vigorously lobbying state legislatures to pass laws protecting workers. As the industrial revolution wore on, they argued, the need for such laws was becoming increasingly critical because corporations were even more profit oriented and, as a result, more likely to exploit employees. Although they succeeded in convincing many state legislatures to enact laws like Utah's, the possibility that courts would strike them down remained a threat. *Holden* had proven otherwise.

That ruling, however, took on a different gloss once the Court decided *Lochner v. New York* (1905). Although the law at issue varied only slightly from Utah's, the justices reached a wholly different conclusion. Why? Does the case fit compatibly with the logic of *Holden*, as Justice Peckham implies, or does it reveal the true reach of his ruling in *Allgeyer*?

After Joseph Lochner, the owner of a bakery located in Utica, New York, was convicted of violating a state maximum hour work law, he asked the U.S. Supreme Court to strike it down as violative of his constitutional rights. In *Lochner v. New York* (1905), the justices agreed. The majority found that the law impermissibly interfered with the right of employers to enter into contracts with their employees.

Lochner v. New York

198 U.S. 45 (1905)
http://laws.findlaw.com/US/198/45.html
Vote: 5 (Brewer, Brown, Fuller, McKenna, Peckham)
      4 (Day, Harlan, Holmes, White)
Opinion of the Court: Peckham
Dissenting opinions: Harlan, Holmes

In 1897 New York enacted a law that prohibited employees of bakeries from working more than ten hours per day and sixty hours per week. The state justified the law on the following grounds:

1. Police power is necessarily invoked to control work conditions in a "great commercial and manufacturing State" like New York. The police power here reflects community standards and is properly exercised by an elected body that is aware of unique local conditions.

2. New York, through its use of the police power, protects both consumers and workers from bad health and sickness; therefore, this law is a health measure.

After he was convicted of violating the law, Joseph Lochner, the owner of a New York bakery, challenged it on Fourteenth Amendment due process grounds. In part, he alleged:

1. Employees and employer have the right to agree upon hours and wages, and the use of the police power by New York to interfere with such agreements is so "paternal" as to violate the Fourteenth Amendment.

2. Regardless of the state's asserted interests, the "most cherished rights of American citizenship"—freedom of contract and property rights—"should be most closely and jealously scrutinized by this court." Since the interests here are not sufficiently "clear and apparent," the Court should strike the law.

MR. JUSTICE PECKHAM . . . delivered the opinion of the Court.

The mandate of the statute, that "no employee shall be required or permitted to work," is the substantial equivalent of an enactment that "no employee shall contract or agree to work," more than ten hours per day; and, as there is no provision for special emergencies, the statute is mandatory in all cases. It is not an act merely fixing the number of hours which shall constitute a legal day's work, but an absolute prohibition upon the employer permitting, under any circumstances, more than ten hours' work to be done in his establishment. The employee may desire to earn the extra money which would arise from his working more than the prescribed time, but this statute forbids the employer from permitting the employee to earn it.

The statute necessarily interferes with the right of contract between the employer and employees, concerning the number of hours in which the latter may labor in the bakery of the employer. The general right to make a contract in relation to his business is part of the liberty of the individual protected by the 14th Amendment of the Federal Constitution. *Allgeyer v. Louisiana*. Under that provision no state can deprive any person of life, liberty, or property without due process of law. The right to purchase or to sell labor is part of the liberty protected by this amendment, unless there are circumstances which exclude the right. There are, however, certain powers, existing in the sovereignty of each state in the Union, somewhat vaguely termed police powers, the exact description and limitation of which have not been attempted by the courts. Those powers, broadly stated, and without, at present, any attempt at a more specific limitation, relate to the safety, health, morals, and general welfare of the public. Both property and liberty are held on such reasonable conditions as may be imposed by the governing power of the state in the exercise of those powers, and with such conditions the 14th Amendment was not designed to interfere.

The state, therefore, has power to prevent the individual from making certain kinds of contracts, and in regard to them the Federal Constitution offers no protection. If the contract be one which the state, in the legitimate exercise of its police power, has the right to prohibit, it is not prevented from prohibiting it by the 14th Amendment. Contracts in violation of a statute, either of the Federal or state government, or a contract to let one's property for immoral purposes, or to do any other unlawful act, could obtain no protection from the Federal Constitution, as coming under the liberty of person or of free contract. Therefore, when the state, by its legislature, in the assumed exercise of its police powers, has passed an act which seriously limits the right to labor or the right of contract in regard to their means of livelihood between persons who are *sui juris* (both employer

and employee), it becomes of great importance to determine which shall prevail,—the right of the individual to labor for such time as he may choose, or the right of the state to prevent the individual from laboring, or from entering into any contract to labor, beyond a certain time prescribed by the state.

This court has recognized the existence and upheld the exercise of the police powers of the states in many cases which might fairly be considered as border ones, and it has, in the course of its determination of questions regarding the asserted invalidity of such statutes, on the ground of their violation of the rights secured by the Federal Constitution, been guided by rules of a very liberal nature, the application of which has resulted, in numerous instances, in upholding the validity of state statutes thus assailed. Among the later cases where the state law has been upheld by this court is that of *Holden v. Hardy*. A provision in the act of the legislature of Utah was there under consideration, the act limiting the employment of workmen in all underground mines or workings, to eight hours per day, "except in cases of emergency, where life or property is in imminent danger." It also limited the hours of labor in smelting and other institutions for the reduction or refining of ores or metals to eight hours per day, except in like cases of emergency. The act was held to be a valid exercise of the police powers of the state . . . [because the] law applies only to the classes subjected by their employment to the peculiar conditions and effects attending underground mining and work in smelters, and other works for the reduction and refining of ores. Therefore it is not necessary to discuss or decide whether the legislature can fix the hours of labor in other employments. . . .

It must, of course, be conceded that there is a limit to the valid exercise of the police power by the state. There is no dispute concerning this general proposition. Otherwise the 14th Amendment would have no efficacy and the legislatures of the states would have unbounded power, and it would be enough to say that any piece of legislation was enacted to conserve the morals, the health, or the safety of the people; such legislation would be valid, no matter how absolutely without foundation the claim might be. The claim of the police power would be a mere pretext,—become another and delusive name for the supreme sovereignty of the state to be exercised free from constitutional restraint. This is not contended for. In every case that comes before this court, therefore, where legislation of this character is concerned, and where the protection of the Federal Constitution is sought, the question necessarily arises: Is this a fair, reasonable, and appropriate exercise of the police power of the state, or is it an unreasonable, unnecessary, and arbitrary interference with the right of the individual to his personal liberty, or to enter into those contracts in relation to labor which may seem to him appropriate or necessary for the support of himself and his family? Of course the liberty of contract relating to labor includes both parties to it. The one has as much right to purchase as the other to sell labor.

This is not a question of substituting the judgment of the court for that of the legislature. If the act be within the power of the state it is valid, although the judgment of the court might be totally opposed to the enactment of such a law. But the question would still remain: Is it within the police power of the state? and that question must be answered by the court.

The question whether this act is valid as a labor law, pure and simple, may be dismissed in a few words. There is no reasonable ground for interfering with the liberty of person or the right of free contract, by determining the hours of labor, in the occupation of a baker. There is no contention that bakers as a class are not equal in intelligence and capacity to men in other trades or manual occupations, or that they are not able to assert their rights and care for themselves without the protecting arm of the state, interfering with their independence of judgment and of action. They are in no sense wards of the state. Viewed in the light of a purely labor law, with no reference whatever to the question of health, we think that a law like the one before us involves neither the safety, the morals, nor the welfare, of the public, and that the interest of the public is not in the slightest degree affected by such an act. The law must be upheld, if at all, as a law pertaining to the health of the individual engaged in the occupation of a baker. It does not affect any other portion of the public than those who are engaged in that occupation. Clean and wholesome bread does not depend upon whether the baker works but ten hours per day or only sixty hours a week. The limitation of the hours of labor does not come within the police power on that ground.

It is a question of which of two powers or rights shall prevail—the power of the state to legislate or the right of the individual to liberty of person and freedom of contract. The mere assertion that the subject relates, though but in a remote degree, to the public health, does not necessarily render the enactment valid. The act must have a more direct relation, as a means to an end, and the end itself must be appropriate and legitimate, before an act can be held to be valid which interferes with the general right of an individual to be free in his person and in his power to contract in relation to his own labor. . . .

We think the limit of the police power has been reached and passed in this case. There is, in our judgment, no reasonable foundation for holding this to be necessary or appropriate as a health law to safeguard the public health, or the health of the individuals who are following the trade of a baker. If this statute be valid, and if, therefore, a proper case is made out in which to deny the right of an individual, *sui juris*, as employer or employee, to make contracts for the labor of the latter under the protection of the provisions of the Federal Constitution, there would seem to be no length to which legislation of this nature might not go. The case differs widely, as we have already stated, from the expressions of this court in regard to laws of this nature, as stated in *Holden v. Hardy*. . . .

We think that there can be no fair doubt that the trade of a baker, in and of itself, is not an unhealthy one to that degree which would authorize the legislature to interfere with the right to labor, and with the right of free contract on the part of the individual, either as employer or employee. In looking through statistics regarding all trades and occupations, it may be true that the trade of a baker does not appear to be as healthy as some other trades, and is also vastly more healthy than still others. To the common understanding the trade of a baker has never been regarded as an unhealthy one. Very likely physicians would not recommend the exercise of that or of any other trade as a remedy for ill health. Some occupations are more healthy than others, but we think there are none which might not come under the power of the legislature to supervise and control the hours of working therein, if the mere fact that the occupation is not absolutely and perfectly healthy is to confer that right upon the legislative department of the government. It might be safely affirmed that almost all occupations more or less affect the health. There must be more than the mere fact of the possible existence of some small amount of unhealthiness to warrant legislative interference with liberty. It is unfortunately true that labor, even in any department, may possibly carry with it the seeds of unhealthiness. But are we all, on that account, at the mercy of legislative majorities? A printer, a tinsmith, a locksmith, a carpenter, a cabinetmaker, a dry goods clerk, a bank's, a lawyer's, or a physician's clerk, or a clerk in almost any kind of business, would all come under the power of the legislature, on this assumption. No trade, no occupation, no mode of earning one's living, could escape this all-pervading power, and the acts of the legislature in limiting the hours of labor in all employments would be valid, although such limitation might seriously cripple the ability of the laborer to support himself and his family. In our large cities there are many buildings into which the sun penetrates for but a short time in each day, and these buildings are occupied by people carrying on the business of bankers, brokers, lawyers, real estate, and many other kinds of business, aided by many clerks, messengers, and other employees. Upon the assumption of the validity of this act under review, it is not possible to say that an act, prohibiting lawyers' or bank clerks, or others, from contracting to labor for their employers more than eight hours a day would be invalid. It might be said that it is unhealthy to work more than that number of hours in an apartment lighted by artificial light during the working hours of the day; that the occupation of the bank clerk, the lawyer's clerk, the real-estate clerk, or the broker's clerk, in such offices is therefore unhealthy, and the legislature, in its paternal wisdom, must, therefore, have the right to legislate on the subject of, and to limit, the hours for such labor; and, if it exercises that power, and its validity be questioned, it is sufficient to say, it has reference to the public health; it has reference to the health of the employees condemned to labor day after day in buildings where the sun never shines; it is a health law, and therefore it is valid, and cannot be questioned by the courts.

It is also urged, pursuing the same line of argument, that it is to the interest of the state that its population should be strong and robust, and therefore any legislation which may be said to tend to make people healthy must be valid as health laws, enacted under the police power. If this be a valid argument and a justification for this kind of legislation, it follows that the protection of the Federal Constitution from undue interference with liberty of person and freedom of contract is visionary, wherever the law is sought to be justified as a valid exercise of the police power. Scarcely any law but might find shelter under such assumptions, and conduct, properly so called, as well as contract,

would come under the restrictive sway of the legislature. Not only the hours of employees, but the hours of employers, could be regulated, and doctors, lawyers, scientists, all professional men, as well as athletes and artisans, could be forbidden to fatigue their brains and bodies by prolonged hours of exercise, lest the fighting strength of the state be impaired. We mention these extreme cases because the contention is extreme. We do not believe in the soundness of the views which uphold this law. On the contrary, we think that such a law as this, although passed in the assumed exercise of the police power, and as relating to the public health, or the health of the employees named, is not within that power, and is invalid. The act is not, within any fair meaning of the term, a health law, but is an illegal interference with the rights of individuals, both employers and employees, to make contracts regarding labor upon such terms as they may think best, or which they may agree upon with the other parties to such contracts. Statutes of the nature of that under review, limiting the hours in which grown and intelligent men may labor to earn their living, are mere meddlesome interferences with the rights of the individual and they are not saved from condemnation by the claim that they are passed in the exercise of the police power and upon the subject of the health of the individual whose rights are interfered with, unless there be some fair ground, reasonable in and of itself, to say that there is material danger to the public health, or to the health of the employees, if the hours of labor are not curtailed. If this be not clearly the case, the individuals whose rights are thus made the subject of legislative interference are under the protection of the Federal Constitution regarding their liberty of contract as well as of person; and the legislature of the state has no power to limit their right as proposed in this statute. All that it could properly do has been done by it with regard to the conduct of bakeries, as provided for in the other sections of the act, above set forth. These several sections provide for the inspection of the premises where the bakery is carried on, with regard to furnishing proper wash rooms and waterclosets, apart from the bake room, also with regard to providing proper drainage, plumbing, and painting; the sections, in addition, provide for the height of the ceiling, the cementing or tiling of floors, where necessary in the opinion of the factory inspector, and for other things of that nature; alterations are also provided for and are to be made where necessary in the opinion of the inspector, in order to comply with the provisions of the statute. These various sections may be wise and valid regulations, and they certainly go to the full extent of providing for the cleanliness and the healthiness, so far as possible, of the quarters in which bakeries are to be conducted. Adding to all these requirements a prohibition to enter into any contract of labor in a bakery for more than a certain number of hours a week is, in our judgment, so wholly beside the matter of a proper, reasonable, and fair provision as to run counter to that liberty of person and of free contract provided for in the Federal Constitution.

It was further urged on the argument that restricting the hours of labor in the case of bakers was valid because it tended to cleanliness on the part of the workers, as a man was more apt to be cleanly when not overworked, and if cleanly then his "output" was also more likely to be so. What has already been said applies with equal force to this contention. We do not admit the reasoning to be sufficient to justify the claimed right of such interference. The state in that case would assume the position of a supervisor, or *pater familias*, over every act of the individual, and its right of governmental interference with his hours of labor, his hours of exercise, the character thereof, and the extent to which it shall be carried would be recognized and upheld. In our judgment it is not possible in fact to discover the connection between the number of hours a baker may work in the bakery and the healthful quality of the bread made by the workman. The connection, if any exist, is too shadowy and thin to build any argument for the interference of the legislature. If the man works ten hours a day it is all right, but if ten and a half or eleven his health is in danger and his bread may be unhealthy, and, therefore, he shall not be permitted to do it. This, we think, is unreasonable and entirely arbitrary. When assertions such as we have adverted to become necessary in order to give, if possible, a plausible foundation for the contention that the law is a "health law," it gives rise to at least a suspicion that there was some other motive dominating the legislature than the purpose to subserve the public health or welfare.

This interference on the part of the legislatures of the several states with the ordinary trades and occupations of the people seems to be on the increase. . . .

It is impossible for us to shut our eyes to the fact that many of the laws of this character, while passed under what is claimed to be the police power for the purpose of protecting the public health or welfare, are, in reality, passed from other motives. We are justified in saying so when, from the character of the law and the subject upon which it legislates, it is apparent that the public health or welfare bears but the most remote relation to the law. The purpose of a statute must be determined from the natural and legal effect of the language employed; and whether it is or is not repugnant to the Constitution of the United States must be determined from the natural effect of such statutes when put into operation, and not from their proclaimed purpose.

It is manifest to us that the limitation of the hours of labor provided for in this section of the statute under which the indictment was found, and the plaintiff in error convicted, has no such direct relation to, and no such substantial effect upon, the health of the employee, as to justify us in regarding the section as really a health law. It seems to us that the real object and purpose were simply to regulate the hours of labor between the master and his employees (all being men, *sui juris*), in a private business, not dangerous in any degree to morals, or in any real and substantial degree to the health of the employees. Under such circumstances the freedom of master and employee to contract with each other in relation to their employment, and in defining the same, cannot be prohibited or interfered with, without violating the Federal Constitution.

The judgment of the Court of Appeals of New York, as well as that of the Supreme Court and the County Court of Oneida County, must be reversed and the case remanded to the County Court for further proceedings not inconsistent with this opinion.

Reversed.

MR. JUSTICE HOLMES, dissenting.

This case is decided upon an economic theory which a large part of the country does not entertain. If it were a question whether I agreed with that theory I should desire to study it further and long before making up my mind. But I do not conceive that to be my duty, because I strongly believe that my agreement or disagreement has nothing to do with the right of a majority to embody their opinions in law. It is settled by various decisions of this court that state constitutions and state laws may regulate life in many ways which we as legislators might think as injudicious or if you like as tyrannical as this, and which equally with this interfere with the liberty to contract. Sunday laws and usury laws are ancient examples. A more modern one is the prohibition of lotteries. The liberty of the citizen to do as he likes so long as he does not interfere with the liberty of others to do the same, which has been a shibboleth for some well-known writers, is interfered with by school laws, by the Post Office, by every state or municipal institution which takes his money for purposes thought desirable, whether he likes it or not. The Fourteenth Amendment does not enact Mr. Herbert Spencer's Social Statics. . . . United States and state statutes and decisions cutting down the liberty to contract by way of combination are familiar to this court. Two years ago we upheld the prohibition of sales of stock on margins or for future delivery in the constitution of California. *Otis v. Parker*. The decision sustaining an eight hour law for miners is still recent. *Holden v. Hardy*. Some of these laws embody convictions or prejudices which judges are likely to share. Some may not. But a constitution is not intended to embody a particular economic theory, whether of paternalism and the organic relation of the citizen to the State or of *laissez faire*. It is made for people of fundamentally differing views, and the accident of our finding certain opinions natural and familiar or novel and even shocking ought not to conclude our judgment upon the question whether statutes embodying them conflict with the Constitution of the United States.

General propositions do not decide concrete cases. The decision will depend on a judgment or intuition more subtle than any articulate major premise. But I think that the proposition just stated, if it is accepted, will carry us far toward the end. Every opinion tends to become a law. I think that the word liberty in the Fourteenth Amendment is perverted when it is held to prevent the natural outcome of a dominant opinion, unless it can be said that a rational and fair man necessarily would admit that the statute proposed would infringe fundamental principles as they have been understood by the traditions of our people and our law. It does not need research to show that no such sweeping condemnation can be passed upon the statute before us. A reasonable man might think it a proper measure on the score of health. Men whom I certainly could not pronounce unreasonable would uphold it as a first installment of a general regulation of the hours of work. Whether in the latter aspect it would be open to the charge of inequality I think it unnecessary to discuss.

Many scholars have called *Lochner* the Court's strongest expression of economic substantive due process. Although the Court said the question to be asked in this case is the same one it had been addressing since *Mugler*— Is the law a fair, reasonable, and appropriate exercise of police power?—its answer is quite different. By distinguishing *Holden* to the point of nonexistence and by narrowing the definition of what constitutes reasonable state regulations, the Court moved away from a strict "reasonableness" approach to one that reflected *Allgeyer*: an employer's right "to make a contract" with employees is virtually sacrosanct.

That the Court, although divided 5–4, accomplished this feat not by changing the legal question but by changing the answer creates something of a puzzle, particularly with regard to the immediate subject of the dispute—maximum work hours. Think about it this way: it upheld the Utah law at issue in *Holden* on the ground that the "kind of employment . . . and the character of the employees . . . were such as to make [the state law] reasonable and proper"; it struck the *Lochner* law because bakers can "care for themselves" (despite evidence to the contrary) and that the production of "clean and wholesome bread" is not affected. Was this distinction significant? Or was it merely a way to mask what the Court wanted to do: narrow the grounds on which states could reasonably regulate and, thereby, strike protective legislation as a violation of the right to contract? Justice Oliver Wendell Holmes's dissent certainly implies the latter. He goes so far as to accuse the Court of using the Fourteenth Amendment to "enact Mr. Herbert Spencer's Social Statics." Many scholars agree with Holmes's assessment and argue that the justices in the *Lochner* majority were "motivated by their own policy preferences favoring laissez faire economics and Social Darwinism." [9] Other analysts present a somewhat different picture.[10] They suggest that the Court was seeking to remain faithful to "a long-standing constitutional ideology that dis-

9. C. Ian Anderson, "Courts and the Constitution," *Michigan Law Review* 92 (1994): 1438.
10. See, especially, Howard Gillman, *The Constitution Besieged: The Rise and Demise of Lochner Era Police Powers Jurisprudence* (Durham, N.C.: Duke University Press, 1993).

tinguished between valid economic regulation and invalid 'class,' or factional legislation." [11] In other words, *Lochner* represented a "principled effort" on the part of the justices to keep this area of the law consistent and coherent, and not merely a statement of their ideological predilections.

Regardless of who is right, these issues moved to the fore in *Muller v. Oregon* (1908). As you read this most interesting case, think about the following. Some scholars argue that the Court's decision in *Muller* merely echoed the logic of *Holden* and *Lochner;* that is, the Court followed the "reasonableness" approach. Others suggest that there were extralegal factors at work that had a great influence on the Court. With which view do you agree?

Muller v. Oregon

208 U.S. 412 (1908)
http://laws.findlaw.com/US/208/412.html
Vote: 9 (Brewer, Day, Fuller, Harlan, Holmes, McKenna,
     Moody, Peckham, White)

     0

Opinion of the Court: Brewer

At the forefront of the Progressive Movement was an organization called the National Consumers' League (NCL). Through the efforts of the NCL and others, the drive for maximum hour legislation had succeeded in many states, which, by the early 1900s, had imposed some type of restriction. After *Lochner,* however, all of their efforts were threatened by employers who sought to use that ruling to challenge state regulations.

This case began when the state of Oregon brought charges against Curt Muller for working his female laundry workers longer than the state maximum of ten hours per day. After his conviction, Muller decided to challenge the law. In the view of his attorneys, Oregon's regulation, which prohibited women, but not men, from working in laundries more than ten hours violated his right to enter into a contract with his employees.

Recognizing that in light of *Lochner,* Muller's argument rested on strong grounds, the NCL grew concerned. It was reluctant to see its hard work to attain passage of the Oregon law nullified by the Supreme Court. To defend the law, the NCL contacted Louis Brandeis, a well-known attorney of the day and a future U.S. Supreme Court justice. Because his philosophical position was very much akin to the NCL's, he agreed to help the organization with the Muller case, but only if it could convince Oregon's attorneys to give him complete control over its course.

When NCL leaders managed to accomplish this, Brandeis got down to work. Because of the decision in *Lochner* and the stability of the Court's membership, he decided that bold action was necessary. Instead of filling his brief with legal arguments, he would provide the Court with "*facts,* published by anyone with expert knowledge of industry in its relation to women's hours of labor," which indicated the evils of Muller's actions. In particular, the brief pointed out that forcing women to work long hours affected their health and their reproductive systems.[12] It was full of statements such as the following:

Report of the Massachusetts State Board of Health, 1873.

All additions to the physical, moral, or intellectual power of individuals—in any individual are, to that extent, additions to the energy and the productive force—the effectiveness of the State; and on the contrary, all deductions from these forces, whether of mind or body—every sickness, and injury or disability, every, impairment of energy—take so much from the mental force, the safe administration of the body politic.

The State thus has an interest not only in the prosperity, but also in the health and strength and effective power of each one of its members.

The first and largest interest of the State lies in the great agency of human power—the health of the people.

Report of the Massachusetts Bureau of Labor Statistics, 1871.

It is claimed that legislation on this subject is an interference between labor and capital. But legislation has interfered with capital and labor both, in the demand for public safety and the public good. Now public safety and public good, the wealth of the commonwealth, centered, as such wealth is, in the well-being of

---

11. Anderson, "Courts and the Constitution," 1439.

12. Clement E. Vose, *Constitutional Change* (Lexington, Mass.: Lexington Books, 1972), 172.

Curt Muller (with arms folded) made constitutional history when he asked the U.S. Supreme Court to strike down as violative of his rights an Oregon law regulating the number of hours his laundresses could work at his cleaning establishment. In *Muller v. Oregon* (1908), however, the Court held that states may constitutionally enact maximum hour work laws for women.

its common people, demands that the State should interfere by special act in favor of working-women, and working children, by enacting a ten-hour law, to be enforced by a system of efficient inspection.

International Conference in Relation to Labor Legislation. Berlin, 1890.

It is the idea of the German Emperor that the industrial question demands the attention of all the civilized nations.

The quest of a solution becomes not only a humanitarian duty, but it is exacted also by governmental wisdom, which should at once look out for the well-being of all its citizens and the preservation of the inestimable benefits of civilization.[13]

In the end, with the help of the NCL, Brandeis produced an incredible document. Known in legal history as

the Brandeis Brief, it contained 113 pages of sociological data culled from various secondary sources and only 2 pages of legal argument *(see Box 10-2)*.

MR. JUSTICE BREWER delivered the opinion of the Court.

We held in *Lochner v. New York* that a law providing that no laborer shall be required or permitted to work in bakeries more than sixty hours in a week or ten hours in a day was not, as to men, a legitimate exercise of the police power of the state, but an unreasonable, unnecessary and arbitrary interference with the right and liberty of the individual to contract in relation to his labor, and as such was in conflict with, and void under, the Federal Constitution. That decision is invoked by plaintiff in error as decisive of the question before us. But this assumes that the difference between the sexes does not justify a different rule respecting a restriction of the hours of labor.

13. For more excerpts, see John Monahan and Laurens Walker, *Social Science in Law* (Westbury, N.Y.: Foundation Press, 1998), 4–7.

In patent cases counsel are apt to open the argument with a discussion of the state of the art. It may not be amiss, in the present case, before examining the constitutional question, to notice the course of legislation, as well as expressions of opinion from other than judicial sources. In the brief filed by Mr. Louis D. Brandeis for the defendant in error is a very copious collection of all these matters, an epitome of which is found in the margin.

The legislation and opinions referred to in the margin may not be, technically speaking, authorities, and in them is little or no discussion of the constitutional question presented to us for determination, yet they are significant of a widespread belief that woman's physical structure, and the functions she performs in consequence thereof, justify special legislation restricting or qualifying the conditions under which she should be permitted to toil. Constitutional questions, it is true, are not settled by even a consensus of present public opinion, for it is the peculiar value of a written constitution that it places in unchanging form limitations upon legislative action, and thus gives a permanence and stability to popular government which otherwise would be lacking. At the same time, when a question of fact is debated and debatable, and the extent to which a special constitutional limitation goes is affected by the truth in respect to that fact, a widespread and long-continued belief concerning it is worthy of consideration. We take judicial cognizance of all matters of general knowledge.

It is undoubtedly true, as more than once declared by this court, that the general right to contract in relation to one's business is part of the liberty of the individual, protected by the 14th Amendment to the Federal Constitution; yet it is equally well settled that this liberty is not absolute and extending to all contracts, and that a state may, without conflicting with the provisions of the 14th Amendment, restrict in many respects the individual's power of contract. Without stopping to discuss at length the extent to which a state may act in this respect, we refer to the following cases in which the question has been considered: *Allgeyer v. Louisiana*; *Holden v. Hardy*; *Lochner v. New York*.

That woman's physical structure and the performance of maternal functions place her at a disadvantage in the struggle for subsistence is obvious. This is especially true when the burdens of motherhood are upon her. Even when they are not, by abundant testimony of the medical fraternity continuance for a long time on her feet at work, repeating this from day to day, tends to injurious effects upon the body, and, as healthy mothers are essential to vigorous offspring, the physical well-being of woman becomes an object of public interest and care in order to preserve the strength and vigor of the race.

Still again, history discloses the fact that woman has always been dependent upon man. He established his control at the outset by superior physical strength, and this control in various forms, with diminishing intensity, has continued to the present. As minors, though not to the same extent, she has been looked upon in the courts as needing especial care that her rights may be preserved. Education was long denied her, and while now the doors of the schoolroom are opened and her opportunities for acquiring knowledge are great, yet even with that and the consequent increase of capacity for business affairs it is still true that in the struggle for subsistence she is not an equal competitor with her brother. Though limitations upon personal and contractual rights may be removed by legislation, there is that in her disposition and habits of life which will operate against a full assertion of those rights. She will still be where some legislation to protect her seems necessary to secure a real equality of right. Doubtless there are individual exceptions, and there are many respects in which she has an advantage over him; but looking at it from the viewpoint of the effort to maintain an independent position in life, she is not upon an equality. Differentiated by these matters from the other sex, she is properly placed in a class by herself, and legislation designed for her protection may be sustained, even when like legislation is not necessary for men, and could not be sustained. It is impossible to close one's eyes to the fact that she still looks to her brother and depends upon him. Even though all restrictions on political, personal, and contractual rights were taken away, and she stood, so far as statutes are concerned, upon an absolutely equal plane with him, it would still be true that she is so constituted that she will rest upon and look to him for protection; that her physical structure and a proper discharge of her maternal functions—having in view not merely her own health, but the well-being of the race—justify legislation to protect her from the greed as well as the passion of man. The limitations which this statute places upon her contractual powers, upon her right to agree with her employer as to the time she shall labor, are not imposed solely for her benefit, but also largely for the benefit of all. Many words cannot make

BOX 10-2   THE BRANDEIS BRIEF

AT THE TURN OF THE CENTURY the function of interpreting the law was largely regarded as a matter of logic. The Court had accepted the theories of *laissez faire* economics and the doctrine of evolution expounded by Herbert Spencer to such an extent that any kind of regulation of private business was considered a violation of "liberty." Only exceptional circumstances that forced the attention of the members of the Court on matters other than the logic of the law would suffice to cause them to alter this view.

When it was recognized that political, economic, and social considerations ought to be included in the process of determining the law, the legal tradition offered little means of placing such factual data before the judges. Thus decisions regarding matters of contract, in regard to labor or business regulation, were shaped by the personal philosophies of Court members and the rigid pattern of law unleavened by knowledge of its relationship to society. Consequently the use of logic alone "resulted in proscribing any realistic test of legislative-judicial conclusions." The questions that needed to be asked, and answered, dealt with the social consequences of the law at issue and the consequences which could be expected to follow the judicial decision.

In reference to the first question regarding social consequences of the law, by what means were the judges to obtain the background of facts which led to its enactment? Many justices felt this was the responsibility of the legislature, that law should be passed after legislative inquiry as to its needs had been made. Suppose, however, the Court would not accept the legislative decisions that the law was needed; how could the Court obtain sufficient data to discuss the law? In a sense this was the dilemma in *Lochner v. New York,* for the use of logic produced the rule that the restriction of employer-employee rights to contract over hours of labor violated due process. Justice Peckham refused to acknowledge that the health and welfare of employees provided any basis whatever for restricting business. It was clear that the Court would not uphold such legislation, *unless* it could be convinced that there was a reasonable relationship between such regulation and the public welfare.

It is at this crucial point in the history of constitutional development that Brandeis introduced his brief as "authoritative extralegal data" to provide the Court with information as to the reasonable relation of the law to the object to be regulated. He differed from the other liberals of the day in the method he used. Rather than deal in invective and generalities, he examined the social ills in detail and offered concrete plans for social legislation. In effect, Brandeis was doing no more than taking cognizance of the facts of modern industrial life.

THE TECHNIQUE OF THE BRIEF: *MULLER V. OREGON, 1908.*

As has been stated previously, the key to the Brandeis Brief was the *factual data* be submitted to show the *reasonableness* of the specific law at issue and the *relationship* of the regulation to the *needs* of society. In the briefs he presented, as a lawyer defending social legislation in four states, there is a definite pattern that he followed to prove his point. An analysis of these briefs and the data they include can be compiled into a single "brief" outline to illustrate Brandeis's methodology. The following construct represents the general pattern, omitting details and using the hours of labor for women as the subject.

Part First
    I. Legal Argument
      (Varying from two to forty pages, citing rules from
      supporting cases).
Part Second
    II. Legislation Restricting Hours of Work for Women
      A. American Legislation
        1. List of States having such legislation
      B. Foreign Legislation
        1. List of countries having such legislation
      C. Summary Combined Experience of Above
        Legislation
    III. The World's Experience upon which the Legislation Limiting the Hours of Work for Women Is
       Based

A. The Dangers of Long Hours
 1. Causes
  a. physical difference between men and women
  b. nature of industrial work
B. Bad Effect of Long Hours on Health
 1. General injuries
 2. Problem of fatigue
 3. Specific evil effects on childbirth
C. Bad Effect of Long Hours on Safety
D. Bad Effect of Long Hours on Morals
E. Bad Effect of Long Hours on General Welfare
IV. Shorter Hours the Only Possible Protection
V. Benefits of Shorter Hours
A. Good Effect on Individual
 1. Health
 2. Morals
 3. Home Life
B. Good Effect on General Welfare
VI. Economic Aspects of Short Hours
A. Effect on Output
 1. Increases efficiency
 2. Improves product
B. Aids Regularity of Employment
C. Widens Job Opportunities for Women
VII. Uniformity of Restriction Necessary
A. Overtime Dangerous to Health
B. Essential to Enforcement
C. Necessary for Just Application
VIII. Reasonableness of Short Hours
A. Opinions of Physicians
B. Opinions of Employers
C. Opinions of Employees
IX. Conclusion

The outline of the brief indicates the wealth of the material Brandeis presented to the Court to support his very brief legal argument. The evidence he produced relied, as Jerome Frank described it, on facts that "do not involve witnesses' credibility." It reveals a concern for why legislation was passed, what it is intended to do, and the benefits, including a dollars and cents consideration, that will accrue to business and labor alike. Thus, it was an intellectual inquiry whose ends were social justice. It is so persuasive in content that the burden of proof placed on the opposing party in the suit is almost impossible to overcome. The simplicity and clarity of the organized evidence is an invitation to apply a pragmatic test to the reasonableness of the law, and in the final analysis it becomes an irresistible force. . . .

The first successful use of the brief before the Supreme Court of the United States came in 1908, when Brandeis argued in *Muller v. Oregon* to sustain an Oregon law establishing a ten-hour day for women employed in "any mechanical establishment, or factory or laundry." The argument consisted of two pages of the legal rules applicable to the case, and was followed by 102 pages of evidence. . . .

The most interesting aspect of the case is that Brandeis relied on the rule of *Lochner v. New York* to prove his point. He began by agreeing that "the right to purchase or sell labor is a part of the 'liberty' protected by the fourteenth amendment" *but*, he pointed out, "such 'liberty' is subject to *reasonable restraint* by the police power of the state *if* there is a relationship to public 'health, safety or welfare.'" Brandeis concluded that the statute was "obviously enacted for the purpose of protecting the public health, safety and welfare" and submitted "the facts of common knowledge of which the Court may take judicial notice" as proof of his argument.

The supporting evidence which followed the argument deeply impressed the Court, and Justice Brewer, who delivered the opinion, quoted extensively from it. . . . Thus, for the first time in the history of the Court, due process was determined, not just by consideration of abstract legal concepts, but also on the basis of the social and economic implications of the law at issue.

SOURCES: Marion E. Doro, "The Brandeis Brief," *Vanderbilt Law Review* 11 (1958): 784. Reprinted in *Social Research in the Judicial Process* by Wallace D. Loh (New York: Russell Sage, 1984), 88–90.

this plainer. The two sexes differ in structure of body, in the functions to be performed by each, in the amount of physical strength, in the capacity for long-continued labor, particularly when done standing, the influence of vigorous health upon the future well-being of the race, the self-reliance which enables one to assert full rights, and in the capacity to maintain the struggle for subsistence. This difference justifies a difference in legislation, and upholds that which is designed to compensate for some of the burdens which rest upon her.

We have not referred in this discussion to the denial of the elective franchise in the state of Oregon, for while that may disclose a lack of political equality in all things with her brother, that is not of itself decisive. The reason runs deeper, and rests in the inherent difference between the two sexes, and in the different functions in life which they perform.

For these reasons, and without questioning in any respect the decision in *Lochner v. New York*, we are of the opinion that it cannot be adjudged that the act in question is in conflict with the Federal Constitution, so far as it respects the work of a female in a laundry, and the judgment of the Supreme Court of Oregon is affirmed.

Why did the justices affirm the Oregon law? One answer is that the Court did not depart from *Lochner*: it merely found that Oregon's regulations, unlike New York's, were a reasonable use of the state's power. But the Court applied the reasonableness approach both in *Lochner* and *Holden* and came to completely different conclusions. So, despite the Court's attempt to distinguish *Lochner*, how much can the application of that standard possibly explain about *Muller*'s outcome? Another possibility is that Brandeis forced the Court to see the reasonableness of the Oregon regulation. By presenting such a mass of statistical data, he kept the justices riveted on the law and diverted their attention from a substantive due process approach. The strategy worked. The Court even commended Brandeis's brief.

Winning *Muller* gave a big boost to the Progressive Movement. Some worried, however, that the decision depended on the fact that the law covered only women and that, when the Court had an opportunity to review a law covering all workers, it would apply *Lochner*. This fear in-

creased when the Court agreed to review **Bunting v. Oregon** (1917), which involved another Oregon law providing that "no person shall be employed in any mill, factory, or manufacturing establishment in this state more than ten hours in any one day." Compounding the NCL's concern was that Brandeis now sat on the Supreme Court and, since he had participated in oral argument, would almost certainly disqualify himself from the case.

In 1917, however, the Supreme Court dispelled their concerns. In a 5–3 decision, with Brandeis not participating, the majority upheld the Oregon law. Writing for the Court, Justice Joseph McKenna explained that, although Bunting contended that "the law . . . is not either necessary or useful 'for the preservation of the health of employees,' " no evidence was provided to support that contention. Moreover, the judgment of the Oregon legislature and supreme court was that " 'it cannot be held, as a matter of law, that the legislative requirement is unreasonable or arbitrary.' " McKenna concluded, therefore, that no further discussion was "necessary" and upheld the law.

The Court failed even to mention *Lochner*. But, given its holding, many predicted the death of that decision; after all, it was wholly incompatible with *Bunting*. Perhaps the demise of substantive due process would follow. Indeed, throughout the period between *Mugler* (1887) and up to about *Bunting*, it appeared that *Lochner* was more the exception than the rule. Between 1887 and 1910, the Court decided 558 cases involving due process claims challenging state regulations and upheld 83 percent of the laws. It now seemed that *Lochner*, not *Muller*, was the unusual case.[14]

THE HEYDAY OF SUBSTANTIVE DUE PROCESS: 1923–1936

The *Bunting* funeral for *Lochner* proved to be premature. Within six years, not only did the Court virtually overrule *Bunting*, but also it seemed to be more committed to the *Lochner* version of due process than ever before. *Adkins v. Children's Hospital* (1923) provides an excel-

---

14. Alfred H. Kelly, Winfred A. Harbison, and Herman Belz, *The American Constitution*, 7th ed. (New York: W. W. Norton, 1991), 405.

lent illustration of the magnitude of this resurgence. As you read the Court's ruling, compare it with *Muller*. Is there any way, legally speaking, to distinguish the two decisions? Or do you suspect that other, extralegal factors came into play?

Adkins v. Children's Hospital

261 U.S. 525 (1923)
http://laws.findlaw.com/US/261/525.html
Vote: 5 (Butler, McKenna, McReynolds, Sutherland,
    Van Devanter)
    3 (Holmes, Sanford, Taft)
Opinion of the Court: Sutherland
Dissenting opinions: Holmes, Taft
Not participating: Brandeis

In 1918 Congress, with the support of the progressive-oriented president, Woodrow Wilson, enacted a law that fixed minimum wages for women and children in the District of Columbia.[15] The act authorized the establishment of the Minimum Wage Board to set pay rates. The board, staffed by progressives, ordered that restaurants and hospitals pay women workers a minimum wage of 34.5 cents per hour, $16.50 per week, or $71.50 per month. According to the board, these rates would "supply the necessary cost of living to . . . women workers to maintain them in good health and morals."

Children's Hospital of the District of Columbia, which employed many women, refused to comply. In its opinion, the law violated the Due Process Clause of the Fifth Amendment encompassing the liberty to enter into salary contracts with employees.[16]

Because of delay at the lower court level, the case did not reach the Supreme Court until 1923. An attorney for the wage board, assisted by NCL attorney (and future Supreme Court justice) Felix Frankfurter and other NCL staffers, sought to defend the 1918 law on grounds similar to Brandeis's in *Muller*. They offered the Court "im-

pressive documentation on the cost of living and the desirability of good wages."

MR. JUSTICE SUTHERLAND delivered the opinion of the Court.

The statute now under consideration is attacked upon the ground that it authorizes an unconstitutional interference with the freedom of contract included within the guaranties of the due process clause of the 5th Amendment. That the right to contract about one's affairs is a part of the liberty of the individual protected by this clause is settled by the decisions of this court, and is no longer open to question. . . .

There is, of course, no such thing as absolute freedom of contract. It is subject to a great variety of restraints. But freedom of contract is, nevertheless, the general rule and restraint the exception; and the exercise of legislative authority to abridge it can be justified only by the existence of exceptional circumstances. . . .

[The statute under consideration] is simply and exclusively a price-fixing law, confined to adult women . . . who are legally as capable of contracting for themselves as men. It forbids two parties having lawful capacity—under penalties as to the employer—to freely contract with one another in respect of the price for which one shall render service to the other in a purely private employment. . . .

The feature of this statute which, perhaps more than any other, puts upon it the stamp of invalidity is that it exacts from the employer an arbitrary payment for a purpose and upon a basis having no causal connection with his business, or the contract, or the work the employee engages to do. The declared basis . . . is not the value of the service rendered, but the extraneous circumstance that the employee needs to get a prescribed sum of money to insure her subsistence, health, and morals. . . . The moral requirement, implicit in every contract of employment, viz., that the amount to be paid and the service to be rendered shall bear to each other some relation of just equivalence, is completely ignored. The necessities of the employee are alone considered, and these arise outside of the employment, are the same when there is no employment, and as great in one occupation as in another. Certainly the employer, by paying a fair equivalent for the service rendered, though not sufficient to support the employee, has neither caused nor contributed to her poverty. . . . A statute requiring an employer

---

15. We derive this account from Vose, *Constitutional Change*, 190–196.

16. Because the District of Columbia is not a state, the Due Process Clause of the Fourteenth Amendment did not apply.

to pay in money, to pay at prescribed and regular intervals, to pay the value of the services rendered, even to pay with fair relation to the extent of the benefit obtained from the service, would be understandable. But a statute which prescribes payment without regard to any of these things, and solely with relation to circumstances apart from the contract of employment, the business affected by it, and the work done under it, is so clearly the product of a naked, arbitrary exercise of power, that it cannot be allowed to stand under the Constitution of the United States. . . .

It has been said that legislation of the kind now under review is required in the interest of social justice, for whose ends freedom of contract may lawfully be subjected to restraint. The liberty of the individual to do as he pleases, even in innocent matters, is not absolute. It must frequently yield to the common good, and the line beyond which the power of interference may not be pressed is neither definite nor unalterable, but may be made to move, within limits not well defined, with changing need and circumstance. Any attempt to fix a rigid boundary would be unwise as well as futile. But, nevertheless, there are limits to the power, and when these have been passed, it becomes the plain duty of the courts, in the proper exercise of their authority, to so declare. To sustain the individual freedom of action contemplated by the Constitution is not to strike down the common good, but to exalt it; for surely the good of society as a whole cannot be better served than by the preservation against arbitrary restraint of the liberties of its constituent members.

It follows from what has been said that the act in question passes the limit prescribed by the Constitution, and, accordingly, the decrees of the court below are affirmed.

MR. CHIEF JUSTICE TAFT, dissenting.

I regret much to differ from the court in these cases.

The boundary of the police power beyond which its exercise becomes an invasion of the guaranty of liberty under the Fifth and Fourteenth Amendments to the Constitutions is not easy to mark. Our court has been laboriously engaged in pricking out a line in successive cases. We must be careful, it seems to me, to follow that line as well as we can, and not to depart from it by suggesting a distinction that is formal rather than real.

Legislatures in limiting freedom of contract between employee and employer by a minimum wage proceed on the assumption that employees, in the class receiving least pay, are not upon a full level of equality of choice with their employer and in their necessitous circumstances are prone to accept pretty much anything that is offered. They are peculiarly subject to the overreaching of the harsh and greedy employer. The evils of the sweating system and of the long hours and low wages which are characteristic of it are well known. Now, I agree that it is a disputable question in the field of political economy how far a statutory requirement of maximum hours or minimum wages may be a useful remedy for these evils, and whether it may not make the case of the oppressed employee worse than it was before. But it is not the function of this court to hold congressional acts invalid simply because they are passed to carry out economic views which the court believes to be unwise or unsound. . . .

The right of the Legislature under the Fifth and Fourteenth Amendments to limit the hours of employment on the score of the health of the employee, it seems to me, has been firmly established. As to that, one would think, the line had been pricked out so that it has become a well formulated rule. In *Holden v. Hardy* it was applied to miners and rested on the unfavorable environment of employment in mining and smelting. In *Lochner v. New York* it was held that restricting those employed in bakeries to 10 hours a day was an arbitrary and invalid interference with the liberty of contract secured by the Fourteenth Amendment. Then followed a number of cases beginning with *Muller v. Oregon,* sustaining the validity of a limit on maximum hours of labor for women to which I shall hereafter allude, and following these cases came *Bunting v. Oregon.* In that case, this court sustained a law limiting the hours of labor of any person, whether man or woman, working in any mill, factory, or manufacturing establishment to 10 hours a day with a proviso as to further hours to which I shall hereafter advert. The law covered the whole field of industrial employment and certainly covered the case of persons employed in bakeries. Yet the opinion in the *Bunting* Case does not mention the *Lochner* Case. No one can suggest any constitutional distinction between employment in a bakery and one in any other kind of a manufacturing establishment which should make a limit of hours in the one invalid, and the same limit in the other permissible. It is impossible for me to reconcile the *Bunting* Case and the *Lochner* Case, and I have always supposed that the *Lochner* Case was thus overruled *sub silentio.* . . .

I am authorized to say that Mr. Justice SANFORD concurs in this opinion.

MR. JUSTICE HOLMES, dissenting.

The question in this case is the broad one, whether Congress can establish minimum rates of wages for women in the District of Columbia, with due provision for special circumstances, or whether we must say that Congress has no power to meddle with the matter at all. To me, notwithstanding the deference due to the prevailing judgment of the court, the power of Congress seems absolutely free from doubt. The end—to remove conditions leading to ill health, immorality, and the deterioration of the race—no one would deny to be within the scope of constitutional legislation. The means are means that have the approval of Congress, of many states, and of those governments from which we have learned our greatest lessons. When so many intelligent persons, who have studied the matter more than any of us can, have thought that the means are effective and are worth the price, it seems to me impossible to deny that the belief reasonably may be held by reasonable men. . . . [T]he only objection that can be urged is found within the vague contours of the 5th Amendment, prohibiting the depriving any person of liberty or property without due process of law. To that I turn.

The earlier decisions upon the same words in the 14th Amendment began within our memory, and went no farther than an unpretentious assertion of the liberty to follow the ordinary callings. Later that innocuous generality was expanded into the dogma, Liberty of Contract. Contract is not specially mentioned in the text that we have to construe. It is merely an example of doing what you want to do, embodied in the word "liberty." But pretty much all law consists in forbidding men to do some things that they want to do, and contract is no more exempt from law than other acts. . . .

I confess that I do not understand the principle on which the power to fix a minimum for the wages of women can be denied by those who admit the power to fix a maximum for their hours of work. I fully assent to the proposition that here, as elsewhere, the distinctions of the law are distinctions of degree; but I perceive no difference in the kind or degree of interference with liberty, the only matter with which we have any concern, between the one case and the other. The bargain is equally affected whichever half you regulate. . . .

I am of opinion that the statute is valid.

Adkins represented the return of substantive due process; indeed, it made clear that *Muller* and *Bunting* had not nullified that doctrine. If anything, as Justice Holmes's dissent noted, it had come back stronger than ever with the term "due process of law" evolving into the "dogma, Liberty of Contract."

Why the change? In large measure, it can be traced back to the political climate of the day. Following World War I, the U.S. economy boomed, and voters elected one president after another who was committed to a free market economy. These presidents, in turn, appointed justices, at least some of whom shared those beliefs. As Table 10-3 indicates, one president, Warren Harding, made the first four of these new Supreme Court appointments. Clement E. Vose notes that "the most important single fact about the Harding appointments was that he named two ardent conservatives of the old school— Sutherland and Butler—to serve along with two justices similarly committed who were already sitting—Van Devanter and McReynolds." [17] Thus, by 1922 the Four Horsemen were all in place.

The entrenchment of substantive due process, as we mentioned at the beginning of this chapter, was but one manifestation of the impact of Republican appointments to the Court. With their stronger commitment to an unfettered market, these conservative justices also invoked creative theories of the limits of national power, especially dual federalism, to strike down federal regulatory efforts. Collectively, the doctrines of dual federalism and substantive due process became effective weapons in nullifying meaningful social legislation.

THE DEPRESSION, THE NEW DEAL, AND THE DECLINE OF SUBSTANTIVE DUE PROCESS

The laissez-faire approach of the Court through the 1920s was in keeping with the times. The nation continued to boom and to elect politicians—President Herbert Hoover, for example—who were committed to a private sector–based economy that they were convinced would remain successful if left free from regulation. The Great

17. Vose, *Constitutional Change*, 194.

TABLE 10-3 From *Bunting* to *Adkins*

Justice	*Bunting* Vote (1917)	Harding Appointments (1921–1922)	*Adkins* Vote (1923)
McKenna	Upheld law	No change	Struck law
Holmes	Upheld law	No change	Upheld law
Day	Upheld law	Replaced by Butler	Struck law
Pitney	Upheld law	Replaced by Sanford	Upheld law
Clarke	Upheld law	Replaced by Sutherland	Struck law
White	Struck law	Replaced by Taft	Upheld law
Van Devanter	Struck law	No change	Struck law
McReynolds	Struck law	No change	Struck law
Brandeis	No participation	No change	No participation

Depression, triggered by the stock market crash of 1929, and the subsequent election of Franklin Roosevelt demonstrate just how quickly that perception changed. The Depression undermined the faith of many who believed that an unregulated economy is capable of successfully adjusting itself to changing economic conditions. Roosevelt's election indicated the desire of the citizenry for greater regulation to get the nation back on its feet.

At first, it appeared as if the Court, although dominated by Republican-appointed justices, might go along with the Depression-fighting regulatory efforts of the new administration and of the states, which in part required that it repudiate substantive due process. How could states exercise any control on employers if the Court continued to strike down the legislatures' efforts on "liberty of contracts" grounds? This was a central question confronting the Court in *Nebbia v. New York*.

Nebbia v. New York

291 U.S. 502 (1934)
http://laws.findlaw.com/US/291/502.html
Vote: 5 (Brandeis, Cardozo, Hughes, Roberts, Stone)
    4 (Butler, McReynolds, Sutherland, Van Devanter)
Opinion of the Court: Roberts
Dissenting opinion: McReynolds

In 1933 the New York State legislature created the Milk Control Board, with the power to fix minimum and maximum prices stores could charge consumers for milk. The board set the price of a quart of milk at nine cents, but Leo Nebbia, the owner of a grocery store in Rochester, sold two quarts of milk and a five-cent loaf of bread for eighteen cents. He was convicted of violating the board's order.

In arguing against the law, Nebbia invoked the Fourteenth Amendment's Due Process Clause: the establishment of fixed milk prices interfered with his ability to conduct his business. Attorneys for the state countered that the law authorizing the board to set prices was a valid exercise of state police power. New York had reached this position, the attorneys claimed, after conducting an "exhaustive investigation of conditions in the milk industry in the States." Among the findings of the investigation:

• Milk is an essential item of the diet. It cannot long be stored. It is an excellent medium for growth of bacteria. These facts necessitate safeguards in its production and handling for human consumption which greatly increase the cost of the business. Failure of producers to receive a reasonable return for their labor and investment over an extended period threaten a relaxation of vigilance against contamination.

• The production and distribution of milk is a paramount industry of the state, and largely affects the health and prosperity of its people. Dairying yields fully one-half of the total income from all farm products. Dairy farm investment amounts to approximately

To help stabilize the market, the New York Milk Control Board fixed the price of a quart of milk at nine cents. When Leo Nebbia, pictured above, the owner of a grocery store, sold two quarts of milk and a loaf of bread for eighteen cents, the state convicted him of violating the board's order. In 1934 the Supreme Court rejected Nebbia's claim that the order violated his constitutional rights, ruling that it was a valid exercise of state power.

$1,000,000,000. Curtailment or destruction of the dairy industry would cause a serious economic loss to the people of the state.

• In addition to the general price decline, other causes for the low price of milk include: a periodic increase in the number of cows and in milk production; the prevalence of unfair and destructive trade practices in the distribution of milk, leading to a demoralization of prices in the metropolitan area and other markets; and the failure of transportation and distribution charges to be reduced in proportion to the reduction in retail prices for milk and cream.

MR. JUSTICE ROBERTS delivered the opinion of the Court.

The . . . question is whether . . . the enforcement of [New York's law] denied the appellant the due process secured to him by the Fourteenth Amendment. . . .

Under our form of government the use of property and the making of contracts are normally matters of private and not of public concern. The general rule is that both shall be free of governmental interference. But neither property rights nor contract rights are absolute; for government cannot exist if the citizen may at will use his property to the detriment of his fellows, or exercise his freedom of contract to work them harm. Equally fundamental with the private right is that of the public to regulate it in the common interest. As Chief Justice Marshall said, speaking specifically of inspection laws, such laws form "a portion of that immense mass of legislation, which embraces every thing within the territory of a State . . . all which can be most advantageously exercised by the States themselves. Inspection laws, quarantine laws, health laws of every description, as well as laws for regulating the internal commerce of a State, . . . are component parts of this mass.". . .

Thus has this court from the early days affirmed that the power to promote the general welfare is inherent in government. Touching the matters committed to it by the Constitution, the United States possesses the power, as do the states in their sovereign capacity touching all subjects jurisdiction of which is not surrendered to the federal government. . . . These correlative rights, that of the citizen to

exercise exclusive dominion over property and freely to contract about his affairs, and that of the state to regulate the
use of property and the conduct of business, are always in
collision. No exercise of the private right can be imagined
which will not in some respect, however slight, affect the
public; no exercise of the legislative prerogative to regulate
the conduct of the citizen which will not to some extent
abridge his liberty or affect his property. But subject only to
constitutional restraint the private right must yield to the
public need. . . .

The milk industry in New York has been the subject of
long-standing and drastic regulation in the public interest.
The legislative investigation of 1932 was persuasive of the
fact that for this and other reasons unrestricted competition
aggravated existing evils, and the normal law of supply and
demand was insufficient to correct maladjustments detrimental to the community. The inquiry disclosed destructive
and demoralizing competitive conditions and unfair trade
practices which resulted in retail price-cutting and reduced
the income of the farmer below the cost of production. We
do not understand the appellant to deny that in these circumstances the legislature might reasonably consider further regulation and control desirable for protection of the
industry and the consuming public. That body believed
conditions could be improved by preventing destructive
price-cutting by stores which, due to the flood of surplus
milk, were able to buy at much lower prices than the larger
distributors and to sell without incurring the delivery costs
of the latter. In the order of which complaint is made the
Milk Control Board fixed a price of ten cents per quart for
sales by a distributor to a consumer, and nine cents by a
store to a consumer, thus recognizing the lower costs of the
store, and endeavoring to establish a differential which
would be just to both. In the light of the facts the order appears not to be unreasonable or arbitrary, or without relation to the purpose to prevent ruthless competition from
destroying the wholesale price structure on which the
farmer depends for his livelihood, and the community for
an assured supply of milk.

But we are told that because the law essays to control
prices it denies due process. Notwithstanding the admitted
power to correct existing economic ills by appropriate regulation of business, even though an indirect result may be a
restriction of the freedom of contract or a modification of
charges for services or the price of commodities, the appel-

lant urges that direct fixation of prices is a type of regulation
absolutely forbidden. His position is that the Fourteenth
Amendment requires us to hold the challenged statute void
for this reason alone. The argument runs that the public
control of rates or prices is *per se* unreasonable and unconstitutional, save as applied to businesses affected with a public
interest; that a business so affected is one in which property
is devoted to an enterprise of a sort which the public itself
might appropriately undertake, or one whose owner relies
on a public grant or franchise for the right to conduct the
business, or in which he is bound to serve all who apply; in
short, such as is commonly called a public utility; or a business in its nature a monopoly. The milk industry, it is said,
possesses none of these characteristics, and, therefore, not
being affected with a public interest, its charges may not be
controlled by the state. Upon the soundness of this contention the appellant's case against the statute depends.

We may as well say at once that the dairy industry is not,
in the accepted sense of the phrase, a public utility. . . . But if,
as must be conceded, the industry is subject to regulation
in the public interest, what constitutional principle bars the
state from correcting existing maladjustments by legislation
touching prices? We think there is no such principle. The due
process clause makes no mention of sales or of prices any
more than it speaks of business or contracts or buildings or
other incidents of property. The thought seems nevertheless
to have persisted that there is something peculiarly sacrosanct about the price one may charge for what he makes or
sells, and that, however able to regulate other elements of
manufacture or trade, with incidental effect upon price, the
state is incapable of directly controlling the price itself. This
view was negatived many years ago. *Munn v. Illinois.* . . .

It is clear that there is no closed class or category of businesses affected with a public interest, and the function of
courts in the application of the Fifth and Fourteenth
Amendments is to determine in each case whether circumstances vindicate the challenged regulation as a reasonable
exertion of governmental authority or condemn it as arbitrary or discriminatory. The phrase "affected with a public
interest" can, in the nature of things, mean no more than
that an industry, for adequate reason, is subject to control
for the public good. In several of the decisions of this court
wherein the expressions "affected with a public interest,"
and "clothed with a public use," have been brought forward
as the criteria of the validity of price control, it has been ad-

mitted that they are not susceptible of definition and form an unsatisfactory test of the constitutionality of legislation directed at business practices or prices. These decisions must rest, finally, upon the basis that the requirements of due process were not met because the laws were found arbitrary in their operation and effect. But there can be no doubt that upon proper occasion and by appropriate measures the state may regulate a business in any of its aspects, including the prices to be charged for the products or commodities it sells.

So far as the requirement of due process is concerned, and in the absence of other constitutional restriction, a state is free to adopt whatever economic policy may reasonably be deemed to promote public welfare, and to enforce that policy by legislation adapted to its purpose. The courts are without authority either to declare such policy, or, when it is declared by the legislature, to override it. If the laws passed are seen to have a reasonable relation to a proper legislative purpose, and are neither arbitrary nor discriminatory, the requirements of due process are satisfied, and judicial determination to that effect renders a court *functus officio* [a task performed]. . . . And it is equally clear that if the legislative policy be to curb unrestrained and harmful competition by measures which are not arbitrary or discriminatory it does not lie with the courts to determine that the rule is unwise. With the wisdom of the policy adopted, the adequacy or practicability of the law enacted to forward it, the courts are both incompetent and unauthorized to deal. The course of decision in this court exhibits a firm adherence to these principles. Times without number we have said that the legislature is primarily the judge of the necessity of such an enactment, that every possible presumption is in favor of its validity, and that though the court may hold views inconsistent with the wisdom of the law, it may not be annulled unless palpably in excess of legislative power. . . .

Tested by these considerations we find no basis in the due process clause of the Fourteenth Amendment for condemning the provisions of the . . . Law here drawn into question.

The judgment is affirmed.

Separate opinion of MR. JUSTICE MCREYNOLDS.

Regulation to prevent recognized evils in business has long been upheld as permissible legislative action. But fixa-

tion of the price at which A, engaged in an ordinary business, may sell, in order to enable B, a producer, to improve his condition, has not been regarded as within legislative power. This is not regulation, but management, control, dictation—it amounts to the deprivation of the fundamental right which one has to conduct his own affairs honestly and along customary lines. The argument advanced here would support general prescription of prices for farm products, groceries, shoes, clothing, all the necessities of modern civilization, as well as labor, when some Legislature finds and declares such action advisable and for the public good. This Court has declared that a state may not by legislative fiat convert a private business into a public utility. And if it be now ruled that one dedicates his property to public use whenever he embarks on an enterprise which the Legislature may think it desirable to bring under control, this is but to declare that rights guaranteed by the Constitution exist only so long as supposed public interest does not require their extinction. To adopt such a view, of course, would put an end to liberty under the Constitution. . . .

Not only does the statute interfere arbitrarily with the rights of the little grocer to conduct his business according to standards long accepted—complete destruction may follow; but it takes away the liberty of 12,000,000 consumers to buy a necessity of life in an open market. It imposes direct and arbitrary burdens upon those already seriously impoverished with the alleged immediate design of affording special benefits to others. To him with less than 9 cents it says: You cannot procure a quart of milk from the grocer although he is anxious to accept what you can pay and the demands of your household are urgent! A superabundance; but no child can purchase from a willing storekeeper below the figure appointed by three men at headquarters! And this is true although the storekeeper himself may have bought from a willing producer at half that rate and must sell quickly or lose his stock through deterioration. The fanciful scheme is to protect the farmer against undue exactions by prescribing the price at which milk disposed of by him at will may be resold! . . .

The judgment of the court below should be reversed.

Mr. Justice VAN DEVANTER, Mr. Justice SUTHERLAND, and Mr. Justice BUTLER authorize me to say that they concur in this opinion.

Although *Nebbia*, in retrospect, was a sign that the heyday of substantive due process was drawing to a close, that was hardly the case in the context of the day. As you will recall from the chapters on federalism (6) and the Commerce Clause (7), for the next two years the Court generally continued along its laissez-faire path of the 1920s—seemingly in ignorance of the political, economic, and social events transpiring around it. In particular, it refused to let go of the doctrine of substantive due process.

Just two years after *Nebbia*, it decided another New York case, but in a quite different way. At issue in ***Morehead v. New York ex rel. Tipaldo*** (1936) was a 1933 minimum wage law that "declared it to be against public policy for any employer to employ any woman at an oppressive and unreasonable wage." It defined as unreasonable a wage that was "both less than the fair and reasonable value of the services rendered and less than sufficient to meet the minimum cost of living necessary for health." If a woman thought that her employer was paying her inadequate wages, she could file a complaint with a state board. Women employees of a laundry invoked this procedure against Joseph Tipaldo, the manager of the operation. In 1934 Tipaldo was found guilty: he paid his employees only seven to ten dollars per week, when the board had set $12.40 as a minimum wage.

When the case reached the Supreme Court, Tipaldo received some support from an unexpected source: the feminist National Woman's Party (NWP). Although it did not agree with his substantive due process claim, the NWP argued that the New York law violated the Constitution on the ground that it treated the sexes differently and fostered inequality. As NWP leaders explained:

The Woman's Party stands for equality between men and women in all laws. This includes laws affecting the position of women in industry as well as all other laws. The Woman's Party does not take any position with regard to the merits of minimum wage legislation, but it does demand that such legislation, if passed, shall be for both sexes. It is opposed to all legislation having a sex basis and applying to one sex alone.[18]

Attorneys defending the state's action, including National Consumers' League representatives, therefore, faced a difficult challenge. The constituency benefiting from the law—women—was divided over the issue, but more important, the attorneys had to deal with the *Adkins* precedent. In part, they did so by trying to distinguish this law from the one at issue in *Adkins;* they also tried to demonstrate that economic conditions had changed considerably since 1923 and required this kind of regulation. Moreover, they had the *Nebbia* ruling in hand. It was just possible that the Court might go along with the state. But it was not to be. In keeping with their rulings on federal New Deal legislation and as a result of Justice Owen Roberts's defection from the *Nebbia* majority, the Court struck the New York law. Writing for a majority of five, Justice Pierce Butler was just as emphatic on the subject of substantive due process as the *Adkins* Court had been: "Freedom of contract is the general rule and restraint the exception."

West Coast Hotel v. Parrish:
The End of Substantive Due Process

The Court's refusal to uphold federal New Deal legislation, as you recall from Chapter 7, angered President Roosevelt. Its ruling in *Morehead* cut even deeper. Peter Irons wrote, "More than any other decision by the Court during the New Deal period, *Morehead* unleashed a barrage of criticism from conservatives as well as from liberals," who sympathized with the plight of women and children workers.[19] Even the Republican Party's 1936 platform included a plank supporting the adoption of minimum wage and maximum hour laws of the sort struck in *Morehead*.

Amid all this pressure, including Roosevelt's Court-packing scheme, the Court did a major about-face on the constitutionality of New Deal programs (see Chapter 7). Prominent among the decisions ushering in the Court's new jurisprudence was *West Coast Hotel v. Parrish*, a ruling that would mean the demise of substantive due process.

---

18. Quoted in Vose, *Constitutional Change*, 212.

19. Peter H. Irons, *The New Deal Lawyers* (Princeton, N.J.: Princeton University Press, 1982), 278.

West Coast Hotel v. Parrish

300 U.S. 379 (1937)
http://laws.findlaw.com/US/300/379.html
Vote: 5 *(Brandeis, Cardozo, Hughes, Roberts, Stone)*
    4 *(Butler, McReynolds, Sutherland, Van Devanter)*
Opinion of the Court: Hughes
Dissenting opinion: Sutherland

Elsie Parrish had worked as a chambermaid in a Washington State hotel for a wage of twenty-two cents to twenty-five cents per hour.[20] When she was discharged in 1935, she asked the management for back pay of $216.19, "the difference between what she had received and what she would have gotten" if the hotel had abided by the Washington wage board's minimum wage rate of $14.30 per week.

The hotel offered her $17, but Parrish refused to settle and brought suit against it. She found an attorney willing to represent her, but the attorney could not generate much interest in her case among outside organizations. Even the National Consumers' League declined to participate, viewing such efforts as a waste of time in light of *Morehead*.

MR. CHIEF JUSTICE HUGHES delivered the opinion of the Court.

This case presents the question of the constitutional validity of the minimum wage law of the State of Washington. . . .

The appellant relies upon the decision of this Court in *Adkins v. Children's Hospital*, which held invalid the District of Columbia Minimum Wage Act which was attacked under the due process clause of the Fifth Amendment. On the argument at bar, counsel for the appellees attempted to distinguish the *Adkins* Case upon the ground that the appellee was employed in a hotel and that the business of an innkeeper was affected with a public interest. That effort at distinction is obviously futile, as it appears that in one of the cases ruled by the *Adkins* opinion the employee was a woman employed as an elevator operator in a hotel.

The recent case of *Morehead v. New York* came here on certiorari to the New York court which had held the New York minimum wage act for women to be invalid. A minority of this Court thought that the New York statute was distinguishable in a material feature from that involved in the *Adkins* Case and that for that and other reasons the New York statute should be sustained. But the Court of Appeals of New York had said that it found no material difference between the two statutes and this Court held that the "meaning of the statute" as fixed by the decisions of the state court "must be accepted here as if the meaning had been specifically expressed in the enactment." That view led to the affirmance by this Court of the judgment in the *Morehead* Case, as the Court considered that the only question before it was whether the *Adkins* Case was distinguishable and that reconsideration of that decision had not been sought. Upon that point the Court said: "The petition for the writ sought review upon the ground that this case [*Morehead*] is distinguishable from that one [*Adkins*]. No application has been made for reconsideration of the constitutional question there decided. The validity of the principles upon which that decision rests is not challenged. This court confines itself to the ground upon which the writ was asked or granted. . . . Here the review granted was no broader than that sought by the petitioner. . . . He is not entitled and does not ask to be heard upon the question whether the *Adkins* Case should be overruled. He maintains that it may be distinguished on the ground that the statutes are vitally dissimilar."

We think that the question which was not deemed to be open in the *Morehead* Case is open and is necessarily presented here. The Supreme Court of Washington has upheld the minimum wage statute of that State. It has decided that the statute is a reasonable exercise of the police power of the State. In reaching that conclusion the state court has invoked principles long established by this Court in the application of the Fourteenth Amendment. The state court has refused to regard the decision in the *Adkins* Case as determinative and has pointed to our decisions both before and since that case as justifying its position. We are of the opinion that this ruling of the state court demands on our part a reexamination of the *Adkins* Case. The importance of the

---

20. We derive this account from William E. Leuchtenburg, "The Case of the Wenatchee Chambermaid," in *Quarrels That Have Shaped the Constitution*.

question, in which many States having similar laws are concerned, the close division by which the decision in the *Adkins* Case was reached, and the economic conditions which have supervened, and in the light of which the reasonableness of the exercise of the protective power of the State must be considered, make it not only appropriate, but we think imperative, that in deciding the present case the subject should receive fresh consideration. . . .

The principle which must control our decision is not in doubt. The constitutional provision invoked is the due process clause of the Fourteenth Amendment governing the States, as the due process clause invoked in the *Adkins* Case governed Congress. In each case the violation alleged by those attacking minimum wage regulation for women is deprivation of freedom of contract. What is this freedom? The Constitution does not speak of freedom of contract. It speaks of liberty and prohibits the deprivation of liberty without due process of law. In prohibiting that deprivation the Constitution does not recognize an absolute and uncontrollable liberty. Liberty in each of its phases has its history and connotation. But the liberty safeguarded is liberty in a social organization which requires the protection of law against the evils which menace the health, safety, morals and welfare of the people. Liberty under the Constitution is thus necessarily subject to the restraints of due process, and regulation which is reasonable in relation to its subject and is adopted in the interests of the community is due process.

This essential limitation of liberty in general governs freedom of contract in particular. More than twenty-five years ago we set forth the applicable principle in these words after referring to the cases where the liberty guaranteed by the Fourteenth Amendment had been broadly described:

"But it was recognized in the cases cited, as in many others, that freedom of contract is a qualified and not an absolute right. There is no absolute freedom to do as one wills or to contract as one chooses. The guaranty of liberty does not withdraw from legislative supervision that wide department of activity which consists of the making of contracts, or deny to government the power to provide restrictive safeguards. Liberty implies the absence of arbitrary restraint, not immunity from reasonable regulations and prohibitions imposed in the interests of the community." *Chicago, Burlington & Quincy R. Co. v. McGuire* [1911].

This power under the Constitution to restrict freedom of contract has had many illustrations. That it may be exercised in the public interest with respect to contracts between employer and employee is undeniable. . . . In dealing with the relation of employer and employed, the legislature has necessarily a wide field of discretion in order that there may be suitable protection of health and safety, and that peace and good order may be promoted through regulations designed to insure wholesome conditions of work and freedom from oppression.

The point that has been strongly stressed that adult employees should be deemed competent to make their own contracts was decisively met nearly forty years ago in *Holden v. Hardy*, where we pointed out the inequality in the footing of the parties. . . .

It is manifest that this established principle is peculiarly applicable in relation to the employment of women in whose protection the State has a special interest. That phase of the subject received elaborate consideration in *Muller v. Oregon* (1908). . . . In later rulings this Court sustained the regulation of hours of work of women employees.

This array of precedents and the principles they applied were thought by the dissenting Justices in the *Adkins* Case to demand that the minimum wage statute be sustained. The validity of the distinction made by the Court between a minimum wage and a maximum of hours in limiting liberty of contract was especially challenged. That challenge persists and is without any satisfactory answer. . . .

One of the points which was pressed by the Court in supporting its ruling in the *Adkins* Case was that the standard set up by the District of Columbia Act did not take appropriate account of the value of the services rendered. In the *Morehead* Case, the minority thought that the New York statute had met that point in its definition of a "fair wage" and that it accordingly presented a distinguishable feature which the Court could recognize within the limits which the *Morehead* petition for certiorari was deemed to present. The Court, however, did not take that view and the New York Act was held to be essentially the same as that for the District of Columbia. The statute now before us is like the latter, but we are unable to conclude that in its minimum wage requirement the State has passed beyond the boundary of its broad protective power.

The minimum wage to be paid under the Washington statute is fixed after full consideration by representatives of employers, employees and the public. It may be assumed that the minimum wage is fixed in consideration of the services that are performed in the particular occupations under normal conditions. Provision is made for special licenses at less wages in the case of women who are incapable of full service. The statement of Mr. Justice Holmes in the *Adkins* Case is pertinent: "This statute does not compel anybody to pay anything. It simply forbids employment at rates below those fixed as the minimum requirement of health and right living. It is safe to assume that women will not be employed at even the lowest wages allowed unless they earn them, or unless the employer's business can sustain the burden. In short the law in its character and operation is like hundreds of so-called police laws that have been upheld.". . .

We think that the views thus expressed are sound and that the decision in the *Adkins* Case was a departure from the true application of the principles governing the regulation by the State of the relation of employer and employed. Those principles have been reenforced by our subsequent decisions. . . .

With full recognition of the earnestness and vigor which characterize the prevailing opinion in the *Adkins* Case, we find it impossible to reconcile that ruling with these well-considered declarations. What can be closer to the public interest than the health of women and their protection from unscrupulous and overreaching employers? And if the protection of women is a legitimate end of the exercise of state power, how can it be said that the requirement of the payment of a minimum wage fairly fixed in order to meet the very necessities of existence is not an admissible means to that end? The legislature of the State was clearly entitled to consider the situation of women in employment, the fact that they are in the class receiving the least pay, that their bargaining power is relatively weak, and that they are the ready victims of those who would take advantage of their necessitous circumstances. The legislature was entitled to adopt measures to reduce the evils of the "sweating system," the exploiting of workers at wages so low as to be insufficient to meet the bare cost of living, thus making their very helplessness the occasion of a most injurious competition. The legislature had the right to consider that its minimum wage requirements would be an important aid in carrying out its policy of protection. The adoption of similar requirements by many States evidences a deep-seated conviction both as to the presence of the evil and as to the means adapted to check it. Legislative response to the conviction cannot be regarded as arbitrary or capricious and that is all we have to decide. Even if the wisdom of the policy be re-

garded as debatable and its effects uncertain, still the legislature is entitled to its judgment.

There is an additional and compelling consideration which recent economic experience has brought into a strong light. The exploitation of a class of workers who are in an unequal position with respect to bargaining power and are thus relatively defenceless against the denial of a living wage is not only detrimental to their health and well-being but casts a direct burden for their support upon the community. What these workers lose in wages the taxpayers are called upon to pay. The bare cost of living must be met. We may take judicial notice of the unparalleled demands for relief which arose during the recent period of depression and still continue to an alarming extent despite the degree of economic recovery which has been achieved. It is unnecessary to cite official statistics to establish what is of common knowledge through the length and breadth of the land. While in the instant case no factual brief has been presented, there is no reason to doubt that the State of Washington has encountered the same social problem that is present elsewhere. The community is not bound to provide what is in effect a subsidy for unconscionable employers. The community may direct its law-making power to correct the abuse which springs from their selfish disregard of the public interest. The argument that the legislation in question constitutes an arbitrary discrimination, because it does not extend to men, is unavailing. This Court has frequently held that the legislative authority, acting within its proper field, is not bound to extend its regulation to all cases which it might possibly reach. The legislature "is free to recognize degrees of harm and it may confine its restrictions to those classes of cases where the need is deemed to be clearest.". . .

Our conclusion is that the case of *Adkins v. Children's Hospital* should be, and it is, overruled. The judgment of the Supreme Court of the State of Washington is affirmed.

MR. JUSTICE SUTHERLAND, dissenting.

The principles and authorities relied upon to sustain the judgment, were considered in *Adkins v. Children's Hospital* and *Morehead v. New York ex rel. Tipaldo*, and their lack of application to cases like the one in hand was pointed out. A sufficient answer to all that is now said will be found in the opinions of the court in those cases. Nevertheless, in the circumstances, it seems well to restate our reasons and conclusions.

Under our form of government, where the written Constitution, by its own terms, is the supreme law, some agency, of necessity, must have the power to say the final word as to the validity of a statute assailed as unconstitutional. The Constitution makes it clear that the power has been intrusted to this court when the question arises in a controversy within its jurisdiction; and so long as the power remains there, its exercise cannot be avoided without betrayal of the trust.

It has been pointed out many times, as in the *Adkins* case, that this judicial duty is one of gravity and delicacy, and that rational doubts must be resolved in favor of the constitutionality of the statute. But whose doubts, and by whom resolved? Undoubtedly it is the duty of a member of the court, in the process of reaching a right conclusion, to give due weight to the opposing views of his associates; but in the end, the question which he must answer is not whether such views seem sound to those who entertain them, but whether they convince him that the statute is constitutional or engender in his mind a rational doubt upon that issue. The oath which he takes as a judge is not a composite oath, but an individual one. And in passing upon the validity of a statute, he discharges a duty imposed upon *him*, which cannot be consummated justly by an automatic acceptance of the views of others which have neither convinced, nor created a reasonable doubt in, his mind. If upon a question so important he thus surrender his deliberate judgment, he stands forsworn. He cannot subordinate his convictions to that extent and keep faith with his oath or retain his judicial and moral independence.

The suggestion that the only check upon the exercise of the judicial power, when properly invoked, to declare a constitutional right superior to an unconstitutional statute is the judge's own faculty of self-restraint, is both ill considered and mischievous. Self-restraint belongs in the domain of will and not of judgment. The check upon the judge is that imposed by his oath of office, by the Constitution and by his own conscientious and informed convictions; and since he has the duty to make up his own mind and adjudge accordingly, it is hard to see how there could be any other restraint. This court acts as a unit. It cannot act in any other way; and the majority (whether a bare majority or a majority of all but one of its members), therefore, establishes the controlling rule as the decision of the court, binding, so long as it remains unchanged, equally upon those who disagree and upon those who subscribe to it. Otherwise, orderly administration of justice would cease. But it is the right of those in the minority to disagree, and sometimes, in matters of grave importance, their imperative duty to voice their disagreement at such length as the occasion demands—always, of course, in terms which, however forceful, do not offend the proprieties or impugn the good faith of those who think otherwise.

It is urged that the question involved should now receive fresh consideration, among other reasons, because of "the economic conditions which have supervened"; but the meaning of the Constitution does not change with the ebb and flow of economic events. We frequently are told in more general words that the Constitution must be construed in the light of the present. If by that it is meant that the Constitution is made up of living words that apply to every new condition which they include, the statement is quite true. But to say, if that be intended, that the words of the Constitution mean today what they did not mean when written—that is, that they do not apply to a situation now to which they would have applied then—is to rob that instrument of the essential element which continues it in force as the people have made it until they, and not their official agents, have made it otherwise. . . .

The judicial function is that of interpretation; it does not include the power of amendment under the guise of interpretation. To miss the point of difference between the two is to miss all that the phrase "supreme law of the land" stands for and to convert what was intended as inescapable and enduring mandates into mere moral reflections.

If the Constitution, intelligently and reasonably construed in the light of these principles, stands in the way of desirable legislation, the blame must rest upon that instrument, and not upon the court for enforcing it according to its terms. The remedy in that situation—and the only true remedy—is to amend the Constitution.

The Aftermath of West Coast Hotel

West Coast Hotel was an explicit repudiation of economic substantive due process. In one fell swoop, the justices overruled *Adkins* and changed the way the Court viewed state regulatory efforts. But the period stretching from 1890 through 1936 continues to have an impact on

Supreme Court rulings. Following the New Deal's revolution in constitutional interpretation, however, the Court has adopted a rational basis test that presumes the constitutionality of legislation; the burden is on the law's challengers to show that no rational relationship exists between the law and a legitimate government function. As such, it is similar to the position expressed by Chief Justice Waite in *Munn v. Illinois.* The difference between Waite's standard in *Munn* and that of today's Court generally lies in application. The Waite Court and its successors allowed incursions into their standard, and we should remember that the standard was amenable to exceptions; modern Courts have not done so. Indeed, in the post–New Deal period, the Court has generally rejected challenges to state economic regulatory efforts. One reason for these decisions is the nature of the current legal test: it is extremely difficult for attorneys to demonstrate no conceivable rational relationship between the legislation and a legitimate government interest. Additionally, the modern Court has been averse to conducting its own inquiry into what is and is not in the public interest or what is rational and what is not.

Williamson v. Lee Optical Company (1955) provides a good example of how the modern Court has treated Fourteenth Amendment economic claims. This case can be compared with the classic statements for and against a substantive interpretation of the Due Process Clause: Miller's in *Slaughterhouse,* Waite's in *Munn,* Peckham's in *Lochner,* and so forth.

Williamson v. Lee Optical Company

348 U.S. 483 (1955)
http://laws.findlaw.com/US/348/483.html
Vote: 8 (Black, Burton, Clark, Douglas, Frankfurter, Minton,
    Reed, Warren)

        o

Opinion of the Court: Douglas
Not participating: Harlan

In 1953 Oklahoma passed a law that made it "unlawful for any person . . . to fit, adjust, adapt, or to apply . . . lenses, frames . . . or any other optical appliances to the face," unless that person was a licensed ophthalmologist, "a physician who specializes in the care of eyes," or an optometrist, "one who examines eyes for refractory error . . . and fills prescriptions." An optician, an "artisan qualified to grind lenses to fill prescriptions," could do so only from a written prescription from an ophthalmologist or optometrist.

Lee Optical Company challenged the law. The state argued that it was a constitutional exercise of state police power; the company maintained that the statute bore no reasonable relation to a public health and welfare interest and unconstitutionally deprived opticians of their right to perform their craft.

MR. JUSTICE DOUGLAS delivered the opinion of the Court.

The effect of [the act] is to forbid the optician from fitting or duplicating lenses without a prescription from an ophthalmologist or optometrist. In practical effect, it means that no optician can fit old glasses into new frames or supply a lens, whether it be a new lens or one to duplicate a lost or broken lens, without a prescription. The District Court conceded that it was in the competence of the police power of a State to regulate the examination of the eyes. But it rebelled at the notion that a State could require a prescription from an optometrist or ophthalmologist "to take old lenses and place them in new frames and then fit the completed spectacles to the *face* of the eyeglass wearer.". . . It was, accordingly, the opinion of the court that this provision of the law violated the Due Process Clause by arbitrarily interfering with the optician's right to do business. . . .

The Oklahoma law may exact a needless, wasteful requirement in many cases. But it is for the legislature, not the courts, to balance the advantages and disadvantages of the new requirement. It appears that in many cases the optician can easily supply the new frames or new lenses without reference to the old written prescription. It also appears that many written prescriptions contain no directive data in regard to fitting spectacles to the face. But in some cases the directions contained in the prescription are essential, if the glasses are to be fitted so as to correct the particular defects of vision or alleviate the eye condition. The legislature might have concluded that the frequency of occasions when a prescription is necessary was sufficient to justify this regulation of the fitting of eyeglasses. Likewise, when it is necessary to duplicate a lens, a written prescription may or may not be necessary. But the legislature might have concluded that one was needed often enough to require one in every case. Or the legislature may have concluded that eye examinations were so critical, not only for correction of vision but also for detection of latent ailments or diseases, that every change in frames and every duplication of a lens should be accompanied by a prescription from a medical expert. To be sure, the present law does not require a new examination of the eyes every time the frames are changed or the lenses duplicated. For if the old prescription is on file with the optician, he can go ahead and make the new fitting or duplicate the lenses. But the law need not be in every respect logically consistent with its aims to be constitutional. It is enough that there is an evil at hand for correction, and that it might be thought that the particular legislative measure was a rational way to correct it.

The day is gone when this Court uses the Due Process Clause of the Fourteenth Amendment to strike down state laws, regulatory of business and industrial conditions, because they may be unwise, improvident, or out of harmony with a particular school of thought. . . . We emphasize again what Chief Justice Waite said in *Munn v. Illinois*, . . . "For protection against abuses by legislatures the people must resort to the polls, not to the courts."

THE CONTEMPORARY RELEVANCE OF SUBSTANTIVE DUE PROCESS

Although *Williamson* was decided in 1955, it has continued to characterize the Court's thinking on substantive due process. In *Pennell v. City of San Jose* (1988), the Court rejected the claims of a landlord who sought to invalidate a city rent-control scheme on substantive due process grounds. In applying a rational basis standard, Chief Justice William Rehnquist concluded, "We have long recognized that a legitimate and rational goal of price or rate regulation is the protection of consumer welfare." And in *City of Cuyahoga Falls, Ohio v. Buckeye Community Hope Foundation* (2003), the justices rejected a claim that a city ordinance allowing a popular referendum to overturn a housing policy decision was so arbitrary as to violate a developer's substantive due process rights.

In spite of these decisions, which generally rebuffed substantive due process challenges to state regulatory matters, the doctrine has seen somewhat of a resurgence in at least one other economic area: court-ordered monetary damages in civil cases. The first such case of note, *BMW of North America v. Gore* (1996), began when an Alabama doctor became dissatisfied with the condition of the paint on his newly acquired automobile.[21]

BMW of North America v. Gore (1996)

517 U.S. 559 (1996)
http://laws.findlaw.com/US/517/559.html
Vote: 5 (Breyer, Kennedy, O'Connor, Souter, Stevens)
     4 (Ginsburg, Rehnquist, Scalia, Thomas)
Opinion of the Court: Stevens
Concurring opinion: Breyer
Dissenting opinions: Ginsburg, Scalia

In January 1990 Dr. Ira Gore Jr. purchased a black BMW sports sedan for $40,750.88 from an authorized dealer in Birmingham, Alabama. Nine months later he took the car to an independent detailer for some appearance enhancements. The detailer informed Gore that he believed the car had been repainted. Gore, convinced that he had been wronged, filed suit against BMW of North America for failure to disclose that his new car had undergone repainting prior to purchase. He asked the court to award him compensatory and punitive damages.[22]

At trial, BMW acknowledged a policy, adopted in 1983, concerning automobiles damaged in manufacture or transport. If repairing the damage cost more than 3 percent of the vehicle's retail value, the car was placed in company service and later sold as used. If the damages amounted to less than 3 percent of the car's value, the vehicle would be fixed and sold as new without disclosing the repair history either to the dealer or the purchaser. Because the cost to refinish the automobile purchased

---

21. To hear oral arguments in this case navigate to *www.oyez.org/oyez/frontpage*.
22. The purpose of compensatory damages is to reimburse wronged parties for actual damages suffered. The purpose of punitive damages is to punish wrongdoers for their unlawful acts.

by Gore amounted to only 1.5 percent of the car's value, it was sold as new.

In support of his claim for compensatory damages, Gore presented evidence that a refinished BMW would fetch $4,000 less on the open market than an identical model that had not been repainted. To justify his claim for punitive damages, Gore presented documentation that during the previous decade BMW of North America sold approximately one thousand refinished automobiles as new. BMW replied that the new paint on Gore's automobile was every bit as good as the original factory finish, and therefore the company was under no obligation to disclose the refinishing.

The jury found in favor of Gore, awarding him $4,000 in compensatory damages and $4,000,000 in punitive damages. The justification for the punitive damage award was the jury's conclusion that BMW's nondisclosure policy amounted to "gross, oppressive, or malicious" fraud. BMW asked that the award be set aside or reduced because it was excessive. The trial court denied the request. The state supreme court reduced the punitive damage award to $2,000,000, not because the original award was excessive, but because it found fault with the jury's method of arriving at that figure. The jury erred, according to the state's high court, by considering BMW's wrongdoing in other states when it should have focused only on the company's behavior in Alabama. BMW, still convinced that the revised award was excessive, requested review by the United States Supreme Court.

JUSTICE STEVENS delivered the opinion of the Court.

Punitive damages may properly be imposed to further a State's legitimate interests in punishing unlawful conduct and deterring its repetition. *Gertz v. Robert Welch, Inc.* (1974); *Newport v. Fact Concerts, Inc.* (1981); [*Pacific Mutual Life Ins. Co. v.*] *Haslip* (1991). In our federal system, States necessarily have considerable flexibility in determining the level of punitive damages that they will allow in different classes of cases and in any particular case. Most States that authorize exemplary damages afford the jury similar latitude, requiring only that the damages awarded be reasonably necessary to vindicate the State's legitimate interests in punishment and deterrence. See *TXO* [*Production Corp. v. Alliance Resources Corp.*

(1993)]; *Haslip.* Only when an award can fairly be categorized as "grossly excessive" in relation to these interests does it enter the zone of arbitrariness that violates the Due Process Clause of the Fourteenth Amendment....

No one doubts that a State may protect its citizens by prohibiting deceptive trade practices and by requiring automobile distributors to disclose presale repairs that affect the value of a new car. But the States need not, and in fact do not, provide such protection in a uniform manner. Some States rely on the judicial process to formulate and enforce an appropriate disclosure requirement by applying principles of contract and tort law. Other States have enacted various forms of legislation that define the disclosure obligations of automobile manufacturers, distributors, and dealers. The result is a patchwork of rules representing the diverse policy judgments of lawmakers in 50 States.

That diversity demonstrates that reasonable people may disagree about the value of a full disclosure requirement....

We think it follows from these principles of state sovereignty and comity that a State may not impose economic sanctions on violators of its laws with the intent of changing the tortfeasors' lawful conduct in other States. Before this Court Dr. Gore argued that the large punitive damages award was necessary to induce BMW to change the nationwide policy that it adopted in 1983. But by attempting to alter BMW's nationwide policy, Alabama would be infringing on the policy choices of other States. To avoid such encroachment, the economic penalties that a State such as Alabama inflicts on those who transgress its laws, whether the penalties take the form of legislatively authorized fines or judicially imposed punitive damages, must be supported by the State's interest in protecting its own consumers and its own economy. Alabama may insist that BMW adhere to a particular disclosure policy in that State. Alabama does not have the power, however, to punish BMW for conduct that was lawful where it occurred and that had no impact on Alabama or its residents. Nor may Alabama impose sanctions on BMW in order to deter conduct that is lawful in other jurisdictions.

... [This] award must be analyzed ... with consideration given only to the interests of Alabama consumers, rather than those of the entire Nation. When the scope of the interest in punishment and deterrence that an Alabama court may appropriately consider is properly limited, it is apparent—for reasons that we shall now address—that this award is grossly excessive.

Elementary notions of fairness enshrined in our constitutional jurisprudence dictate that a person receive fair notice not only of the conduct that will subject him to punishment but also of the severity of the penalty that a State may impose. Three guideposts, each of which indicates that BMW did not receive adequate notice of the magnitude of the sanction that Alabama might impose for adhering to the nondisclosure policy adopted in 1983, lead us to the conclusion that the $2 million award against BMW is grossly excessive: the degree of reprehensibility of the nondisclosure; the disparity between the harm or potential harm suffered by Dr. Gore and his punitive damages award; and the difference between this remedy and the civil penalties authorized or imposed in comparable cases. We discuss these considerations in turn.

Degree of Reprehensibility

Perhaps the most important indicium of the reasonableness of a punitive damages award is the degree of reprehensibility of the defendant's conduct. . . . This principle reflects the accepted view that some wrongs are more blameworthy than others. . . . In *TXO*, both the West Virginia Supreme Court and the Justices of this Court placed special emphasis on the principle that punitive damages may not be "grossly out of proportion to the severity of the offense.". . .

In this case, none of the aggravating factors associated with particularly reprehensible conduct is present. The harm BMW inflicted on Dr. Gore was purely economic in nature. The presale refinishing of the car had no effect on its performance or safety features, or even its appearance for at least nine months after his purchase. BMW's conduct evinced no indifference to or reckless disregard for the health and safety of others. To be sure, infliction of economic injury, especially when done intentionally through affirmative acts of misconduct, or when the target is financially vulnerable, can warrant a substantial penalty. But this observation does not convert all acts that cause economic harm into torts that are sufficiently reprehensible to justify a significant sanction in addition to compensatory damages. . . .

Finally, the record in this case discloses no deliberate false statements, acts of affirmative misconduct, or concealment of evidence of improper motive, such as were present in *Haslip* and *TXO*. We accept, of course, the jury's finding that BMW suppressed a material fact which Alabama law obligated it to communicate to prospective purchasers of repainted cars in that State. But the omission of a material fact may be less reprehensible than a deliberate false statement, particularly when there is a good-faith basis for believing that no duty to disclose exists.

. . . Because this case exhibits none of the circumstances ordinarily associated with egregiously improper conduct, we are persuaded that BMW's conduct was not sufficiently reprehensible to warrant imposition of a $2 million exemplary damages award.

Ratio

The second and perhaps most commonly cited indicium of an unreasonable or excessive punitive damages award is its ratio to the actual harm inflicted on the plaintiff. The principle that exemplary damages must bear a "reasonable relationship" to compensatory damages has a long pedigree. . . . Our decisions in both *Haslip* and *TXO* endorsed the proposition that a comparison between the compensatory award and the punitive award is significant.

In *Haslip* we concluded that even though a punitive damages award of "more than 4 times the amount of compensatory damages," might be "close to the line," it did not "cross the line into the area of constitutional impropriety." *TXO*, following dicta in *Haslip*, refined this analysis by confirming that the proper inquiry is " 'whether there is a reasonable relationship between the punitive damage award and the harm likely to result from the defendant's conduct as well as the harm that actually has occurred.' " Thus, in upholding the $10 million award in *TXO*, we relied on the difference between that figure and the harm to the victim that would have ensued if the tortious plan had succeeded. That difference suggested that the relevant ratio was not more than 10 to 1.

The $2 million in punitive damages awarded to Dr. Gore by the Alabama Supreme Court is 500 times the amount of his actual harm as determined by the jury. . . .

Of course, we have consistently rejected the notion that the constitutional line is marked by a simple mathematical formula, even one that compares actual and potential damages to the punitive award. . . . When the ratio is a breathtaking 500 to 1, however, the award must surely "raise a suspicious judicial eyebrow." *TXO* (O'CONNOR, J., dissenting).

Sanctions for Comparable Misconduct

Comparing the punitive damages award and the civil or criminal penalties that could be imposed for comparable misconduct provides a third indicium of excessiveness. . . . In this case the $2 million economic sanction imposed on BMW is substantially greater than the statutory fines available in Alabama and elsewhere for similar malfeasance.

The maximum civil penalty authorized by the Alabama Legislature for a violation of its Deceptive Trade Practices Act is $2,000; other States authorize more severe sanctions, with the maxima ranging from $5,000 to $10,000. . . .

The sanction imposed in this case cannot be justified on the ground that it was necessary to deter future misconduct without considering whether less drastic remedies could be expected to achieve that goal. . . .

We assume, as the juries in this case . . . found, that the undisclosed damage to the new BMW's affected their actual value. Notwithstanding the evidence adduced by BMW in an effort to prove that the repainted cars conformed to the same quality standards as its other cars, we also assume that it knew, or should have known, that as time passed the repainted cars would lose their attractive appearance more rapidly than other BMW's. Moreover, we of course accept the Alabama courts' view that the state interest in protecting its citizens from deceptive trade practices justifies a sanction in addition to the recovery of compensatory damages. We cannot, however, accept the conclusion of the Alabama Supreme Court that BMW's conduct was sufficiently egregious to justify a punitive sanction that is tantamount to a severe criminal penalty. . . .

. . . [W]e are fully convinced that the grossly excessive award imposed in this case transcends the constitutional limit. . . .

The judgment is reversed, and the case is remanded for further proceedings not inconsistent with this opinion.

It is so ordered.

JUSTICE BREYER, with whom JUSTICE O'CONNOR and JUSTICE SOUTER join, concurring.

The Alabama state courts have assessed the defendant $2 million in "punitive damages" for having knowingly failed to tell a BMW automobile buyer that, at a cost of $600, it had repainted portions of his new $40,000 car, thereby lowering its potential resale value by about 10%.

The Court's opinion, which I join, explains why we have concluded that this award, in this case, was "grossly excessive" in relation to legitimate punitive damages objectives, and hence an arbitrary deprivation of life, liberty, or property in violation of the Due Process Clause. . . .

The . . . severe disproportionality between the award and the legitimate punitive damages objectives . . . reflects a judgment about a matter of degree. I recognize that it is often difficult to determine just when a punitive award exceeds an amount reasonably related to a State's legitimate interests, or when that excess is so great as to amount to a matter of constitutional concern. Yet whatever the difficulties of drawing a precise line, once we examine the award in this case, it is not difficult to say that this award lies on the line's far side. The severe lack of proportionality between the size of the award and the underlying punitive damages objectives shows that the award falls into the category of "gross excessiveness" set forth in this Court's prior cases.

. . . I conclude that the award in this unusual case violates the basic guarantee of nonarbitrary governmental behavior that the Due Process Clause provides.

JUSTICE SCALIA, with whom JUSTICE THOMAS joins, dissenting.

Today we see the latest manifestation of this Court's recent and increasingly insistent "concern about punitive damages that 'run wild.'" *Pacific Mut. Life Ins. Co. v. Haslip* (1991). Since the Constitution does not make that concern any of our business, the Court's activities in this area are an unjustified incursion into the province of state governments.

In earlier cases that were the prelude to this decision, I set forth my view that a state trial procedure that commits the decision whether to impose punitive damages, and the amount, to the discretion of the jury, subject to some judicial review for "reasonableness," furnishes a defendant with all the process that is "due." I do not regard the Fourteenth Amendment's Due Process Clause as a secret repository of substantive guarantees against "unfairness"—neither the unfairness of an excessive civil compensatory award, nor the unfairness of an "unreasonable" punitive award. What the Fourteenth Amendment's procedural guarantee assures is an opportunity to contest the reasonableness of a damages judgment in state court; but there is no federal guarantee a damages award actually be reasonable. . . .

The most significant aspects of today's decision—the identification of a "substantive due process" right against a "grossly excessive" award, and the concomitant assumption of ultimate authority to decide anew a matter of "reasonableness" resolved in lower court proceedings—are of course not new. *Haslip* and *TXO* revived the notion, moribund since its appearance in the first years of this century, that the measure of civil punishment poses a question of constitutional dimension to be answered by this Court. Neither of those cases, however, nor any of the precedents upon which they relied, actually took the step of declaring a punitive award unconstitutional simply because it was "too big." At the time of adoption of the Fourteenth Amendment, it was well understood that punitive damages represent the assessment by the jury, as the voice of the community, of the measure of punishment the defendant deserved. Today's decision, though dressed up as a legal opinion, is really no more than a disagreement with the community's sense of indignation or outrage expressed in the punitive award of the Alabama jury, as reduced by the State Supreme Court. It reflects not merely, as the concurrence candidly acknowledges, "a judgment about a matter of degree"; but a judgment about the appropriate degree of indignation or outrage, which is hardly an analytical determination.

There is no precedential warrant for giving our judgment priority over the judgment of state courts and juries on this matter. The only support for the Court's position is to be found in a handful of errant federal cases, bunched within a few years of one other, which invented the notion that an unfairly severe civil sanction amounts to a violation of constitutional liberties. These were the decisions upon which the *TXO* plurality relied in pronouncing that the Due Process Clause "imposes substantive limits 'beyond which penalties may not go,' " Although they are our precedents, they are themselves too shallowly rooted to justify the Court's recent undertaking. . . .

More importantly, this latter group of cases—which again are the sole precedential foundation put forward for the rule of constitutional law espoused by today's Court—simply fabricated the "substantive due process" right at issue. . . .

. . . [T]he Court identifies "[t]hree guideposts" that lead it to the conclusion that the award in this case is excessive: degree of reprehensibility, ratio between punitive award and plaintiff's actual harm, and legislative sanctions pro-

vided for comparable misconduct. The legal significance of these "guideposts" is nowhere explored, but their necessary effect is to establish federal standards governing the hitherto exclusively state law of damages. . . .

Of course it will not be easy for the States to comply with this new federal law of damages, no matter how willing they are to do so. In truth, the "guideposts" mark a road to nowhere; they provide no real guidance at all. As to "degree of reprehensibility" of the defendant's conduct, we learn that " 'nonviolent crimes are less serious than crimes marked by violence or the threat of violence,' " and that " 'trickery and deceit' " are "more reprehensible than negligence." As to the ratio of punitive to compensatory damages, we are told that a " 'general concer[n] of reasonableness . . . enter[s] into the constitutional calculus,' "—though even "a breathtaking 500 to 1" will not necessarily do anything more than " 'raise a suspicious judicial eyebrow.' " And as to legislative sanctions provided for comparable misconduct, they should be accorded " 'substantial deference.' " One expects the Court to conclude: "To thine own self be true."

These criss-crossing platitudes yield no real answers in no real cases. . . .

For the foregoing reasons, I respectfully dissent.

JUSTICE GINSBURG, with whom THE CHIEF JUSTICE joins, dissenting.

The Court, I am convinced, unnecessarily and unwisely ventures into territory traditionally within the States' domain, and does so in the face of reform measures recently adopted or currently under consideration in legislative arenas. . . .

. . . [T]he Alabama Supreme Court left standing the jury's decision that the facts warranted an award of punitive damages—a determination not contested in this Court—and the state court concluded that, considering only acts in Alabama, $2 million was "a constitutionally reasonable punitive damages award."

The Court finds Alabama's $2 million award not simply excessive, but grossly so, and therefore unconstitutional. The decision leads us further into territory traditionally within the States' domain, and commits the Court, now and again, to correct "misapplication of a properly stated rule of law." The Court is not well equipped for this mission. Tellingly, the Court repeats that it brings to the task no "mathematical formula," no "categorical approach," no "bright line." It has only a vague concept of substantive due process, a "raised eyebrow" test, as its ultimate guide. . . .

For the reasons stated, I dissent from this Court's disturbance of the judgment the Alabama Supreme Court has made.

In *BMW v. Gore* the justices directly applied concepts of substantive due process to jury awards. Grossly excessive awards violate the essential fairness guarantees of the Fourteenth Amendment. The dissenters, especially Justice Antonin Scalia, chastised the majority for reverting back to the doctrines popular in the early twentieth century. Scalia charged the Court with establishing imprecise guidelines that allow the justices to impose their own views of what constitutes an award that is "too big." This criticism resembles those of an earlier era that charged the Court with setting itself up as a "superlegislature."

The Court has continued to apply the substantive due process reasoning in subsequent challenges to large punitive damage awards. For example, in *Cooper Industries v. Leatherman Tool Group* (2001), a dispute between two companies over a false advertising claim, the justices required lower courts to reconsider a $4.5 million punitive damage award when only $50,000 was awarded in compensatory damages. Similarly, in **State Farm Mutual Automobile Insurance Co. v. Campbell** (2003), the Court considered awards of $1 million in compensatory damages and $145 million in punitive damages against an insurance company charged with improperly dealing with a policyholder following a fatal auto accident. The justices concluded that the 145 to 1 ratio of punitive to compensatory damages was grossly excessive and in conflict with due process guarantees. The Court once again rejected any firm mathematical criteria but suggested that award ratios in excess of 10 to 1 begin to lose their presumption of validity.

Clearly, the Court's damage award decisions are confined to a single area and do not represent a return to the era of *Lochner* and *Adkins*. Yet they indicate that the doctrine of substantive due process has not lost all of its relevance to contemporary constitutional law.

In addition, substantive due process guarantees play a role in the Court's interpretation of privacy rights. Indeed, at least some of the justices in the majority of **Griswold v. Connecticut** (1965), in which the Court struck a Connecticut law prohibiting the disbursement of birth control and established a right to privacy, did so on substantive due process grounds. Justice John Marshall Harlan wrote in a concurring opinion:

In my view, the proper constitutional inquiry in this case is whether this Connecticut statute infringes the Due Process Clause of the Fourteenth Amendment because the enactment violates basic values "implicit in the concept of ordered liberty.". . . The Due Process Clause of the Fourteenth Amendment stands, in my opinion, on its own bottom.

Furthermore, Justice Harry Blackmun's 1973 opinion in **Roe v. Wade** legalizing abortion during the first two trimesters of pregnancy also invoked the Due Process Clause:

[The] right of privacy, whether it be founded in the Fourteenth Amendment's concept of personal liberty and restrictions upon state action, as we feel it is, or [another clause] . . . is broad enough to encompass a woman's decision whether or not to terminate her pregnancy.

That the *Roe* right rests, in part, on the Due Process Clause has been a source of contention among legal scholars. There are those, like John Hart Ely, who accuse Blackmun of "*Lochner*-ing," of returning to a discredited theory of individual rights as the peg on which to hang abortion rights. Others point out the difference between *Lochner* and *Roe* in the nature of the rights at issue.

Either way, it is true that the doctrine—so exalted as the nation entered the twentieth century and so despised following the New Deal—has had a significant effect on the course of the law. What could have simply faded out of existence with Miller's *Slaughterhouse* opinion became the source of one of the most interesting episodes in constitutional law.

READINGS

Berger, Raoul. *Government by Judiciary*. Cambridge: Harvard University Press, 1977.

Cortner, Richard C. *The Iron Horse and the Constitution: The Railroads and the Transformation of the Fourteenth Amendment*. Westport, Conn.: Greenwood Press, 1993.

Gillman, Howard. *The Constitution Besieged: The Rise and Demise of Lochner-Era Police Powers Jurisprudence*. Durham, N.C.: Duke University Press, 1993.

Hovenkamp, Herbert. *Enterprise and American Law, 1836–1937*. Cambridge: Harvard University Press, 1991.

Jacobs, Clyde E. *Law Writers and the Courts*. Berkeley: University of California Press, 1954.

Keller, Morton. *Affairs of State*. Cambridge: Harvard University Press, 1977.

Kens, Paul. *Judicial Power and Reform Politics: The Anatomy of Lochner v. New York*. Lawrence: University Press of Kansas, 1990.

Keynes, Edward. *Liberty, Property, and Privacy: Toward a Jurisprudence of Substantive Due Process*. University Park: Pennsylvania State University Press, 1996.

Paul, Arnold M. *Conservative Crisis and the Rule of Law*. Ithaca, N.Y.: Cornell University Press, 1960.

Phillips, Michael J. *The Lochner Court, Myth and Reality: Substantive Due Process from the 1890s to the 1930s*. Westport, Conn.: Praeger, 2001.

Strong, Frank R. *Substantive Due Process of Law: A Dichotomy of Sense and Nonsense*. Durham, N.C.: Carolina Academic Press, 1986.

Swindler, William F. *Court and Constitution in the Twentieth Century*. 3 vols. Indianapolis: Bobbs-Merrill, 1970.

Vose, Clement E. *Constitutional Change*. Lexington, Mass.: Lexington Books, 1972.

Wolfe, Christopher. *The Rise of Modern Judicial Review*. New York: Basic Books, 1986.

CHAPTER 11
THE TAKINGS CLAUSE

ONE DAY a certified letter arrives at your house informing you that the government has decided to construct a new highway, and your property lies directly in its path. The letter further states that in return for your property the government will pay you $100,000, an amount it considers "fair market value" for your home. Finally, the letter instructs you to vacate the house within six months.

Does the government have the right to seize your property in this fashion? What if this house has been in your family for five generations and you do not want to sell? What if this is your dream house, just completed after years of saving and sacrificing? If you consider the government's offer to be much less than the property is worth, can you challenge the amount offered? What about your rights to private property? Don't they mean anything?

The general answer to these questions is that the government indeed has the right to seize private property for a public purpose, such as a new roadway. This authority is referred to as the power of eminent domain. When federal, state, or local governments embark on new construction projects for roads, schools, military bases, or government offices, they usually must acquire private property. Sometimes the projects need only a parcel or two, but at other times the government requires large-scale property condemnation. Although the property owner may feel mistreated when the government seizes the land, such government power is generally regarded as necessary. Moreover, property owners have an

important protection. The Constitution contains a provision, known as the Takings Clause, that checks the authority of the government against the individual's right to property.

PROTECTING PRIVATE PROPERTY FROM GOVERNMENT SEIZURE

We normally associate the Bill of Rights with important civil liberties, such as the freedoms of speech, press, and religion. But when the members of the First Congress proposed a listing of those rights considered important enough to merit constitutional protection, they included in the Fifth Amendment a significant private property guarantee—the Takings Clause—which states: "nor shall private property be taken for public use, without just compensation."

That the Framers would have protected private property in this way is not surprising. The men who fashioned the U.S. Constitution were firm believers in private property rights, but they also supported a national government that would be stronger than it was under the Articles of Confederation. The Takings Clause acknowledges that government projects sometimes require the seizure of private property. Without the power of eminent domain, individuals could block government programs, such as the interstate highway system, by refusing to sell property to the government or by demanding unreasonable compensation, holding the government project for ransom. But James Madison, the primary author of the Bill of Rights, rejected the notion that government should have the absolute power to confiscate private property.[1] The Takings Clause was intended to moderate that authority by ensuring that property owners would not be unduly disadvantaged when the government seized their land. It guarantees that property owners will be fairly compensated for their loss. As Justice Hugo Black explained, the Takings Clause "was designed to bar Government from forcing some people to bear public burdens which, in all fairness and justice, should be borne by the public as a whole." [2]

Provisions similar to the Takings Clause were already in effect in several states at the time the Bill of Rights was drafted. Vermont's Constitution of 1777 and the Massachusetts Constitution of 1780 were among the first to protect owners from absolute government seizures. Other states, while not elevating the right to constitutional status, passed just-compensation statutes. States commonly imposed such protections when chartering companies to build roads, dams, and other projects. In 1785 Virginia required compensation to be paid for unimproved land seized for the building of roadways. South Carolina in the 1780s incorporated several companies to build canals, granting them the power of eminent domain on the condition that they compensate owners for their property losses. Similar provisions were incorporated into Virginia's charter creating the Dismal Swamp Canal Company in 1787.[3] With the states routinely adopting such provisions, it could be expected that the Framers would see the need to restrain federal property-seizure authority in much the same way. In fact, the Takings Clause proposal was uncontroversial, spurring little debate in Congress or during the ratification process.

Because many states already protected private property against state government seizures, the Takings Clause was intended to apply only to federal government confiscations. This interpretation was endorsed by the Supreme Court in the case of **Barron v. Baltimore** in 1833.[4] The dispute arose when the city of Baltimore initiated a series of street improvements, which also necessitated the alteration of several small streams. As a result, large amounts of sand and dirt were swept downstream into Baltimore Harbor, causing serious problems for the owners of wharves operating in the harbor. John Barron and John Craig were particularly damaged. Their wharf had been very profitable because it was located in deep water and was capable of servicing large ships. The accumulation of silt and waste near their wharf was so great that the water became too shallow for large vessels, and Barron and Craig lost considerable business. They demanded compensation from the city for their loss. When the city refused, they sued, asking for $20,000 in damages. The local court awarded them $4,500, but a state appellate court reversed, and Barron and Craig appealed to the U.S. Supreme Court.

They claimed that the city's construction caused their loss of profitability. That constituted a "taking" under the meaning of the Fifth Amendment, and they deserved "just compensation." The justices, however, were not concerned with questions of whether a taking had occurred or what constituted just compensation. Instead, the Court focused on a more fundamental issue: Did the Fifth Amendment apply to state actions at all? The Court concluded that it did not. In the words of Chief Justice John Marshall:

We are of opinion that the provision in the fifth amendment to the constitution, declaring that private property shall not be taken for public use without just compensation, is intended solely as a limitation on the exercise of power by the government of the United States, and is not applicable to the legislation of the states.[5]

For the next half century this interpretation remained the law of the land. The Takings Clause applied only to

---

1. James W. Ely Jr., *The Guardian of Every Other Right: A Constitutional History of Property Rights* (New York: Oxford University Press, 1992), 55.

2. *Armstrong v. United States* (1960).

3. For a discussion of these early provisions, see Ely, *The Guardian of Every Other Right*, chap. 2.

4. For a discussion of this case, see Lee Epstein and Thomas G. Walker, *Constitutional Law for a Changing America: Rights, Liberties, and Justice*, 5th ed. (Washington, D.C.: CQ Press, 2004), 76–78.

5. The implications of this decision went far beyond the Takings Clause issue. In ruling as it did, the Supreme Court held that the states did not have to abide by any of the provisions of the Bill of Rights, that those sections of the Constitution limited federal government actions only. The states were governed only by their own bills of rights. Over time, the Court incrementally changed its position, but it took more than 130 years for it to conclude that the states were bound by almost all the provisions of the Bill of Rights. For a discussion of this history, see Epstein and Walker, *Constitutional Law for a Changing America: Rights, Liberties, and Justice*, chap. 3.

the federal government. If states did not impose similar restraints on themselves, they were free to exercise the power of eminent domain without providing adequate compensation to landowners whose property had been seized.

In the late 1800s, prompted by the ratification of the Fourteenth Amendment, the Court began to reconsider this position. The Fourteenth Amendment contains a provision, known as the Due Process Clause, that says: "nor shall any state deprive any person of life, liberty, or property, without due process of law." Lawyers began arguing that when states confiscated private property without giving the owners adequate compensation they were depriving the owners of property without due process of law, a violation of the Fourteenth Amendment. If adopted by the Court, this interpretation would make the Takings Clause binding on the states and nullify the immediate impact of *Barron v. Baltimore*.

The test case for this proposition was ***Chicago, Burlington, and Quincy Railroad Company v. Chicago*** (1897). The controversy began in 1880 when the Chicago City Council passed an ordinance to open and widen certain city streets. The project required the condemnation of various parcels of land. Some of this property was owned by individuals, but other sections were part of a right-of-way belonging to the Chicago, Burlington, and Quincy Railroad. A condemnation trial was held in the circuit court for Cook County. The court agreed to condemn the land, and the jury set the amounts of compensation to be paid to the landowners. While the individuals whose property was confiscated received considerable compensation for their losses, the jury awarded the railroad only $1. When the railroad company's demand for a new trial was rejected and the Illinois Supreme Court offered no relief, the company appealed to the U.S. Supreme Court.

The justices, by a 7–1 vote, ruled in favor of the railroad. The opinion of the Court, written by Justice John Marshall Harlan, held:

The conclusion of this Court on the question is, that since the adoption of the 14th Amendment compensation for private property taken for public uses constitutes an essential element in "due process of law," and that without such compensation the appropriation of private property to public uses, no matter under what form of procedure it is taken, would violate the provisions of the Federal Constitution.

The Court held that the Takings Clause of the U.S. Constitution was binding not only upon the federal government but also upon state and local governments. It affirmed the government's power of eminent domain but required the payment of adequate compensation whenever that power was exercised.[6] With this ruling, the Takings Clause became the first provision of the Bill of Rights to be made binding on the states.

The authority of government to take private property when needed to carry out legitimate projects is now well established. The most common issue that flows from government takings cases is the question of what constitutes "just compensation." In the normal course of events, the government attempts to buy the necessary land from the owners. If negotiations fail, the government may declare the power of eminent domain and take the property, giving the owners what it thinks is a fair price. Usually fair market value is the appropriate standard. It is not uncommon, however, for the owners to argue that the government's offer is inadequate. In such situations the owners may go to court to challenge the amount. Questions of just compensation normally are settled through negotiation or trial court action and rarely involve issues of significance beyond the specific land under dispute.[7] Although legal battles may be fought over whether the offered compensation is just, there is no doubt about the power of the government to seize the property.

Of greater importance are two questions of more general significance in understanding the meaning of the Fifth Amendment Takings Clause: What is a taking and

6. See David A. Schultz, *Property, Power, and American Democracy* (New Brunswick, N.J.: Transaction Books, 1992).

7. Although disputes over compensation levels normally are settled at the trial court level, occasionally such controversies involve significant issues and large amounts of money. For example, in *United States v. Sioux Nation of Indians* (1980), the Supreme Court settled a long-standing dispute over the abrogation of the Fort Laramie Treaty of 1868. The treaty had established the right of the Sioux nation to the Black Hills, but an 1877 act of Congress essentially took back those lands. The Court ruled that the treaty abrogation was governed by the Takings Clause and that the Sioux were entitled to the value of the land in 1877 plus 5 percent annual interest since that year, amounting to a total claim of some $100 million.

what constitutes a public use? Both questions have required authoritative answers by the Supreme Court.

WHAT CONSTITUTES A TAKING?

In many cases it is relatively easy to determine that a taking has occurred. If the federal government decides to build a new post office and must acquire a piece of privately owned property upon which to build, a taking is necessary if a voluntary sale is not negotiated. Similarly, a taking occurs when, in designing a water control project, the government finds it necessary to dam certain streams and cause privately owned land to become permanently flooded. In these situations private land is totally taken by the government and is used for a public purpose. There is no question that the individual has been deprived of ownership rights over the property and is entitled to compensation.

Courts are much more likely to conclude that a taking has occurred if the government has in some fashion physically invaded the owner's property. The physical invasion does not have to be complete, as in the instance of a government-constructed dam permanently flooding a piece of property, nor does it have to result in the owner's total loss of the right to use the property. In *Loretto v. Teleprompter Manhattan CATV Corp.* (1982), for example, the Court held that a New York law requiring landlords to allow a cable television company to install cable facilities on their property constituted a taking. The law required landlords to accept the direct physical attachment of plates, boxes, wires, cables, bolts, and screws on their properties. As a permanent physical occupation of the owner's property, the requirement amounted to a taking that constitutionally required just compensation.

Although a physical invasion meets the traditional definition of a taking, is such an intrusion a necessary requirement? What happens when a government activity so severely curtails the possible uses of a piece of property that its value almost disappears? *United States v. Causby* (1946), a case involving a North Carolina couple whose modest chicken farm was ruined by the U.S. military, answered these questions. Did a taking occur even though the Causbys retained title to their property? The majority held that it did. But pay attention to the dissent

by Justice Black, which is interesting on two counts. First, it reflects Black's generally sympathetic attitude toward federal government programs, and second, it demonstrates the importance he placed on applying the words as written. Here he attempts to apply the word "taking" as he believes the Framers intended it to be used.

United States v. Causby

328 U.S. 256 (1946)
http://laws.findlaw.com/US/328/256.html
Vote: 5 (Douglas, Frankfurter, Murphy, Reed, Rutledge)
      2 (Black, Burton)
Opinion of the Court: Douglas
Dissenting opinion: Black
Not participating: Jackson

The Causbys owned 2.8 acres outside Greensboro, North Carolina. On this land were their house and the various outbuildings they needed for their chicken business. In 1942 the federal government leased a local airfield for use by army and navy aircraft. Bombers, fighters, and transport planes regularly flew in and out of this facility at all hours of the day and night. Planes often flew in close formation and in considerable numbers. The end of the airport runway was only 2,220 feet from the Causbys' property. The authorized flight patterns allowed planes to fly at an altitude of 83 feet over the Causbys' land, just 67 feet over their house, and within 18 feet of the highest tree on their property.

This activity caused the couple considerable discomfort as well as economic loss. The noise was described as startling, and the Causbys found it difficult to sleep at night. Although there were no aircraft accidents on their property, there had been several near the airport, which made the Causbys fearful and nervous. In addition, the productivity of their chickens decreased. Significant numbers of them died when they flew into the walls of their coops out of fear and panic when the planes flew particularly close. The property could no longer be used as a commercial chicken farm.

The Causbys filed suit in the federal court of claims arguing that the government had taken their land without just compensation in violation of the Takings Clause. The court agreed and ordered the government to pay them $2,000 for their loss. The federal government appealed to the Supreme Court, claiming that there had been no taking because there had been no physical violation of the landowners' property.

MR. JUSTICE DOUGLAS delivered the opinion of the Court.

It is ancient doctrine that at common law ownership of the land extended to the periphery of the universe. . . . But that doctrine has no place in the modern world. The air is a public highway, as Congress has declared. Were that not true, every transcontinental flight would subject the operator to countless trespass suits. Common sense revolts at the idea. To recognize such private claims to the airspace would clog these highways, seriously interfere with their control and development in the public interest, and transfer into private ownership that to which only the public has a just claim.

But that general principle does not control the present case. For the United States conceded on oral argument that if the flights over respondents' property rendered it uninhabitable, there would be a taking compensable under the Fifth Amendment. It is the owner's loss, not the taker's gain, which is the measure of the value of the property taken. Market value fairly determined is the normal measure of the recovery. And that value may reflect the use to which the land could readily be converted, as well as the existing use. If, by reason of the frequency and altitude of the flights, respondents could not use this land for any purpose, their loss would be complete. It would be as complete as if the United States had entered upon the surface of the land and taken exclusive possession of it.

. . . The owner's right to possess and exploit the land— that is to say, his beneficial ownership of it—would be destroyed. It would not be a case of incidental damages arising from a legalized nuisance. . . .

There is no material difference between the supposed case and the present one, except that here enjoyment and use of the land are not completely destroyed. But that does not seem to us to be controlling. The path of glide for airplanes might reduce a valuable factory site to grazing land, an orchard to a vegetable patch, a residential section to a wheat field. Some value would remain. But the use of the airspace immediately above the land would limit the utility of the land and cause a diminution in its value. . . .

We have said that the airspace is a public highway. Yet it is obvious that if the landowner is to have full enjoyment of the land, he must have exclusive control of the immediate reaches of the enveloping atmosphere. Otherwise buildings could not be erected, trees could not be planted, and even fences could not be run. The principle is recognized when the law gives a remedy in case overhanging structures are erected on adjoining land. The landowner owns at least as much of the space above the ground as he can occupy or use in connection with the land. The fact that he does not occupy it in a physical sense—by the erection of buildings and the like—is not material. As we have said, the flight of airplanes, which skim the surface but do not touch it, is as much an appropriation of the use of the land as a more conventional entry upon it. We would not doubt that, if the United States erected an elevated railway over respondents' land at the precise altitude where its planes now fly, there would be a partial taking, even though none of the supports of the structure rested on the land. The reason is that there would be an intrusion so immediate and direct as to subtract from the owner's full enjoyment of the property and to limit his exploitation of it. While the owner does not in any physical manner occupy that stratum of airspace or make use of it in the conventional sense, he does use it in somewhat the same sense that space left between buildings for the purpose of light and air is used. The superadjacent airspace at this low altitude is so close to the land that continuous invasions of it affect the use of the surface of the land itself. We think that the landowner, as an incident to his ownership, has a claim to it and that invasions of it are in the same category as invasions of the surface. . . .

The airplane is part of the modern environment of life, and the inconveniences which it causes are normally not compensable under the Fifth Amendment. The airspace, apart from the immediate reaches above the land, is part of the public domain. We need not determine at this time what those precise limits are. Flights over private land are not a taking, unless they are so low and so frequent as to be a direct and immediate interference with the enjoyment and use of the land. We need not speculate on that phase of the present case. For the findings of the Court of Claims plainly establish that there was a diminution in value of the property and that the frequent, low-level flights were the direct and immediate cause. We agree with the Court of Claims that a servitude has been imposed upon the land. . . .

The judgment is reversed and the cause is remanded to the Court of Claims so that it may make the necessary findings in conformity with this opinion.

Reversed.

MR. JUSTICE BLACK, dissenting.

The Fifth Amendment provides that "private property" shall not "be taken for public use without just compensation." The Court holds today that the Government has "taken" respondents' property by repeatedly flying Army bombers directly above respondents' land at a height of eighty-three feet where the light and noise from these planes caused respondents to lose sleep and their chickens to be killed. Since the effect of the Court's decision is to limit, by the imposition of relatively absolute constitutional barriers, possible future adjustments through legislation and regulation which might become necessary with the growth of air transportation, and since in my view the Constitution does not contain such barriers, I dissent. . . .

The Court's opinion seems to indicate that the mere flying of planes through the column of air directly above respondents' land does not constitute a "taking." Consequently, it appears to be noise and glare, to the extent and under the circumstances shown here, which make the Government a seizer of private property. . . . The concept of taking property as used in the Constitution has heretofore never been given so sweeping a meaning. The Court's opinion presents no case where a man who makes noise or shines light onto his neighbor's property has been ejected from that property for wrongfully taking possession of it. Nor would anyone take seriously a claim that noisy automobiles passing on a highway are taking wrongful possession of the homes located thereon, or that a city elevated train which greatly interferes with the sleep of those who live next to it wrongfully takes their property. . . . I am not willing, nor do I think the Constitution and the decisions authorize me, to extend that phrase so as to guarantee an absolute constitutional right to relief not subject to legislative change, which is based on averments that at best show mere torts committed by government agents while flying over land. The future adjustment of the rights and remedies of property owners, which might be found necessary because

of the flight of planes at safe altitudes, should, especially in view of the imminent expansion of air navigation, be left where I think the Constitution left it, with Congress. . . .

No greater confusion could be brought about in the coming age of air transportation than that which would result were courts by constitutional interpretation to hamper Congress in its efforts to keep the air free. Old concepts of private ownership of land should not be introduced into the field of air regulation. I have no doubt that Congress will, if not handicapped by judicial interpretations of the Constitution, preserve the freedom of the air, and at the same time, satisfy the just claims of aggrieved persons. The noise of newer, larger, and more powerful planes may grow louder and louder and disturb people more and more. But the solution of the problems precipitated by these technological advances and new ways of living cannot come about through the application of rigid constitutional restraints formulated and enforced by the courts. What adjustments may have to be made, only the future can reveal. It seems certain, however, that courts do not possess the techniques or the personnel to consider and act upon the complex combinations of factors entering into the problems. . . . Today's opinion is, I fear, an opening wedge for an unwarranted judicial interference with the power of Congress to develop solutions for new and vital national problems. In my opinion this case should be reversed on the ground that there has been no "taking" in the constitutional sense.

Mr. Justice BURTON joins in this dissent.

How far can the definition of a taking be legitimately extended? After all, every time the government passes a law regulating the use of property, the rights of owners are diminished. Does regulation constitute a taking? Justice Oliver Wendell Holmes addressed this question in ***Pennsylvania Coal Co. v. Mahon*** (1922). For Holmes, the answer depended upon the extent of the regulation: "The general rule at least is, that while property may be regulated to a certain extent, if regulation goes too far it will be recognized as a taking." Holmes feared that given too much discretion the government might regulate "until the last private property disappears." [8]

8. See Ely, *The Guardian of Every Other Right*, chap. 6.

Generally, government regulation that only incidentally infringes on the owner's use of property is not considered a taking; nor is regulation that outlaws noxious or dangerous use of property. Obvious examples are zoning laws or other regulatory ordinances that make certain uses unlawful.[9] Owners may be distressed that they can no longer use their property in particular ways, but the Supreme Court has held that such statutes do not constitute a Fifth Amendment taking that deserves compensation. For example, the justices ruled that takings did not occur when a state ordered property owners to cut down standing cedar trees because a disease they carried threatened nearby apple orchards, when a local government passed an ordinance removing an individual's right to use his land as a brickyard seen as inconsistent with the surrounding neighborhood, and when for safety reasons a city prohibited a person from mining sand and gravel on his land.[10] In these and numerous similar cases the government's action significantly reduced the way the land could be used and decreased its commercial value; yet the Court held that a taking had not occurred. Instead, these government policies had been formulated in response to social, economic, or environmental problems that could be addressed through the use of the government's police powers.

The questions of how far such regulation may go and for what reasons were addressed in *Penn Central Transportation Company v. City of New York* in 1978.[11] The issue is important. If the government imposes regulations that seriously curtail the economic use of the property, has a taking occurred? Although Justice William Brennan's opinion acknowledges that this area of the law has proved to be one of "considerable difficulty," it presents a good review of the principles the Court has developed to determine when a taking has occurred.

---

9. See *Agins v. City of Tiburon* (1980).

10. *Miller v. Schoene* (1928); *Hadacheck v. Los Angeles* (1915); *Goldblatt v. Hempstead* (1962), respectively.

11. To hear oral arguments, navigate to: *www.oyez.org/oyez/frontpage.*

Penn Central Transportation Company v. City of New York

438 U.S. 104 (1978)
http://laws.findlaw.com/US/438/104.html
Vote: 6 (Blackmun, Brennan, Marshall, Powell, Stewart, White)
    3 (Burger, Rehnquist, Stevens)
Opinion of the Court: Brennan
Dissenting opinion: Rehnquist

New York City passed the Landmarks Preservation Law in 1965 as part of an effort to protect historic buildings and districts. Each of the fifty states and more than five hundred cities had similar statutes. The law was administered by the Landmarks Preservation Commission. The task of the commission was to identify buildings and areas that held special historic or aesthetic value. The buildings were then discussed in hearings to determine whether landmark status should be conferred. If a building or area was designated historic, the owner was restricted as to what could be done to the property. For example, owners of landmark buildings were required to keep the exterior in good repair and not alter the building without securing approval from the commission. Owners of such buildings received no direct compensation, but they were accorded enhanced development rights for other properties.

This case involved the application of the preservation law to the Grand Central Terminal, owned by the Penn Central Transportation Company. The station opened in 1913 and is widely regarded as an example of ingenious engineering in response to problems presented by modern urban rail stations. It is also cited as a magnificent example of French beaux arts style. The terminal was designated a historic landmark in 1967, although Penn Central initially opposed the action.

In 1968, to increase revenue, Penn Central entered into an agreement with UGP Properties to build a multistory office building above the terminal. UGP and Penn Central presented two separate plans to the commission for its approval. One of the plans proposed a change in the existing facade of the building and construction of a fifty-three-story office tower above it. The other envisioned a fifty-five-story office building cantilevered above the existing facade and resting on the roof of the terminal. The commission rejected both proposals.

In response, Penn Central and UGP filed suit claiming that the application of the Landmarks Preservation Law to the terminal constituted a taking of their property without just compensation. The New York courts denied their claims, with the state's highest court rejecting the notion that the property had been "taken" under the meaning of the Fifth Amendment.

MR. JUSTICE BRENNAN delivered the opinion of the Court.

Before considering appellants' specific contentions, it will be useful to review the factors that have shaped the jurisprudence of the Fifth Amendment injunction "nor shall private property be taken for public use, without just compensation." The question of what constitutes a "taking" for purposes of the Fifth Amendment has proved to be a problem of considerable difficulty. . . . [T]his Court, quite simply, has been unable to develop any "set formula" for determining when "justice and fairness" require that economic injuries caused by public action be compensated by the government, rather than remain disproportionately concentrated on a few persons. Indeed, we have frequently observed that whether a particular restriction will be rendered invalid by the government's failure to pay for any losses proximately caused by it depends largely "upon the particular circumstances [in that] case."

In engaging in these essentially ad hoc, factual inquiries, the Court's decisions have identified several factors that have particular significance. The economic impact of the regulation on the claimant and, particularly, the extent to which the regulation has interfered with distinct investment-backed expectations are, of course, relevant considerations. So, too, is the character of the government action. A "taking" may more readily be found when the interference with property can be characterized as a physical invasion by the government than when interference arises from some public program adjusting the benefits and burdens of economic life to promote the common good.

"Government hardly could go on if to some extent values incident to property could not be diminished without paying for every such change in the general law," *Pennsylva-*

Artist's conception of a fifty-five-story office building to be "floated" over the waiting room of New York's Grand Central Terminal, which had been designated a historic landmark. Plans for this building, and several others, were rejected by the Landmarks Preservation Commission, and the Supreme Court ruled that such a rejection did not constitute a taking.

nia Coal Co. v. Mahon (1922), and this Court has accordingly recognized, in a wide variety of contexts, that government may execute laws or programs that adversely affect recognized economic values. Exercises of the taxing power are one obvious example. A second are the decisions in which this Court has dismissed "taking" challenges on the ground that, while the challenged government action caused economic harm, it did not interfere with interests that were sufficiently bound up with the reasonable expectations of the claimant to constitute "property" for Fifth Amendment purposes.

More importantly for the present case, in instances in which a state tribunal reasonably concluded that "the health, safety, morals, or general welfare" would be promoted by prohibiting particular contemplated uses of land, this Court has upheld land-use regulations that destroyed or adversely affected recognized real property interests. Zoning laws are, of course, the classic example. . . .

Zoning laws generally do not affect existing uses of real property, but "taking" challenges have also been held to be without merit in a wide variety of situations when the challenged governmental actions prohibited a beneficial use to which individual parcels had previously been devoted and thus caused substantial individualized harm. . . .

Pennsylvania Coal Co. v. Mahon (1922) is the leading case for the proposition that a state statute that substantially furthers important public policies may so frustrate distinct investment-backed expectations as to amount to a "taking." There the claimant had sold the surface rights to particular parcels of property, but expressly reserved the right to remove the coal thereunder. A Pennsylvania statute, enacted after the transactions, forbade any mining of coal that caused the subsidence of any house, unless the house was the property of the owner of the underlying coal and was more than 150 feet from the improved property of another. Because the statute made it commercially impracticable to mine the coal, and thus had nearly the same effect as the complete destruction of rights claimant had reserved from the owners of the surface land, the Court held that the statute was invalid as effecting a "taking" without just compensation. . . .

In contending that the New York City law has "taken" their property in violation of the Fifth and Fourteenth Amendments, appellants make a series of arguments, which, while tailored to the facts of this case, essentially urge that any substantial restriction imposed pursuant to a landmark law must be accompanied by just compensation if it is to be constitutional. Before considering these, we emphasize what is not in dispute. Because this Court has recognized in a number of settings, that States and cities may enact land-use restrictions or controls to enhance the quality of life by preserving the character and desirable aesthetic features of a city, appellants do not contest that New York City's objective of preserving structures and areas with special historic, architectural, or cultural significance is an entirely permissible governmental goal. They also do not dispute that the restrictions imposed on its parcel are appropriate means of securing the purposes of the New York City law. Finally, appellants do not challenge any of the specific factual premises of the decision below. They accept for present purposes both that the parcel of land occupied by Grand Central Terminal must, in its present state, be regarded as capable of earning a reasonable return, and that the transferable development rights afforded the appellants by virtue of the Terminal's designation as a landmark are valuable, even if not as valuable as the rights to construct above the Terminal. In appellants' view none of these factors derogate from their claim that New York City's law has effected a "taking."

They first observe that the airspace above the Terminal is a valuable property interest, citing *United States v. Causby*. They urge that the Landmarks Law has deprived them of any gainful use of their "air rights" above the Terminal and that, irrespective of the value of the remainder of their parcel, the city has "taken" their right to this superadjacent airspace, thus entitling them to "just compensation" measured by the fair market value of these air rights.

Apart from our own disagreement with appellants' characterization of the effect of the New York City law, the submission that appellants may establish a "taking" simply by showing that they have been denied the ability to exploit a property interest that they heretofore had believed was available for development is quite simply untenable. . . . "Taking" jurisprudence does not divide a single parcel into discrete segments and attempt to determine whether rights in a particular segment have been entirely abrogated. In deciding whether a particular governmental action has effected a taking, this Court focuses rather both on the character of the action and on the nature and extent of the interference with rights in the parcel as a whole—here, the city tax block designated as the "landmark site."

Secondly, appellants, focusing on the character and impact of the New York City law, argue that it effects a "taking" because its operation has significantly diminished the value of the Terminal site. Appellants concede that the decisions sustaining other land-use regulations, which, like the New York City law, are reasonably related to the promotion of the general welfare, uniformly reject the proposition that diminution in property value, standing alone, can establish a "taking.". . . [B]ut appellants argue that New York City's regulation of individual landmarks is fundamentally different from zoning or from historic-district legislation because the controls imposed by New York City's law apply only to individuals who own selected properties.

Stated baldly, appellants' position appears to be that the only means of ensuring that selected owners are not singled out to endure financial hardship for no reason is to hold that any restriction imposed on individual landmarks pursuant to the New York City scheme is a "taking" requiring the payment of "just compensation." Agreement with this argument would, of course, invalidate not just New York City's law, but all comparable landmark legislation in the Nation. We find no merit in it. . . .

Equally without merit is the related argument that the decision to designate a structure as a landmark "is inevitably arbitrary or at least subjective, because it is basically a matter of taste," thus unavoidably singling out individual landowners for disparate and unfair treatment. The argument has a particularly hollow ring in this case. . . . [A] landmark owner has a right to judicial review of any Commission decision, and, quite simply, there is no basis whatsoever for a conclusion that courts will have any greater difficulty identifying arbitrary or discriminatory action in the context of landmark regulation than in the context of classic zoning or indeed in any other context. . . .

In any event, appellants' repeated suggestions that they are solely burdened and unbenefited is factually inaccurate. This contention overlooks the fact that the New York City law applies to vast numbers of structures in the city in addition to the Terminal—all the structures contained in the 31 historic districts and over 400 individual landmarks, many of which are close to the Terminal. Unless we are to reject the judgment of the New York City Council that the preservation of landmarks benefits all New York citizens and all structures, both economically and by improving the quality of life in the city as a whole—which we are unwilling to

do—we cannot conclude that the owners of the Terminal have in no sense been benefited by the Landmarks Law. . . .

. . . [T]he New York City law does not interfere in any way with the present uses of the Terminal. Its designation as a landmark not only permits but contemplates that appellants may continue to use the property precisely as it has been used for the past 65 years: as a railroad terminal containing office space and concessions. So the law does not interfere with what must be regarded as Penn Central's primary expectation concerning the use of the parcel. More importantly, on this record, we must regard the New York City law as permitting Penn Central not only to profit from the Terminal but also to obtain a "reasonable" return on its investment. . . .

On this record, we conclude that the application of New York City's Landmarks Law has not effected a "taking" of appellants' property. The restrictions imposed are substantially related to the promotion of the general welfare and not only permit reasonable beneficial use of the landmark site but also afford appellants opportunities further to enhance not only the Terminal site proper but also other properties.

Affirmed.

MR. JUSTICE REHNQUIST, with whom THE CHIEF JUSTICE, and MR. JUSTICE STEVENS join, dissenting.

Of the over one million buildings and structures in the city of New York, appellees have singled out 400 for designation as official landmarks. The owner of a building might initially be pleased that his property has been chosen by a distinguished committee of architects, historians, and city planners for such a singular distinction. But he may well discover, as appellant Penn Central Transportation Co. did here, that the landmark designation imposes upon him a substantial cost, with little or no offsetting benefit except for the honor of the designation. The question in this case is whether the cost associated with the city of New York's desire to preserve a limited number of "landmarks" within its borders must be borne by all of its taxpayers or whether it can instead be imposed entirely on the owners of the individual properties. . . .

The Fifth Amendment provides in part: "nor shall private property be taken for public use, without just compensation." In a very literal sense, the actions of appellees violated this constitutional prohibition. Before the city of New York declared Grand Central Terminal to be a landmark, Penn Central could have used its "air rights" over the Terminal to build a multistory office building, at an apparent value of several million dollars per year. Today, the Terminal cannot be modified in any form, including the erection of additional stories, without the permission of the Landmark Preservation Commission, a permission which appellants, despite good-faith attempts, have so far been unable to obtain. . . .

As Mr. Justice Holmes pointed out in *Pennsylvania Coal Co. v. Mahon*, "the question at bottom" in an eminent domain case "is upon whom the loss of the changes desired should fall." The benefits that appellees believe will flow from preservation of the Grand Central Terminal will accrue to all the citizens of New York City. There is no reason to believe that appellants will enjoy a substantially greater share of these benefits. If the cost of preserving Grand Central Terminal were spread evenly across the entire population of the city of New York, the burden per person would be in cents per year—a minor cost appellees would surely concede for the benefit accrued. Instead, however, appellees would impose the entire cost of several million dollars per year on Penn Central. But it is precisely this sort of discrimination that the Fifth Amendment prohibits. . . .

Over 50 years ago, Mr. Justice Holmes, speaking for the Court, warned that the courts were "in danger of forgetting that a strong public desire to improve the public condition is not enough to warrant achieving the desire by a shorter cut than the constitutional way of paying for the change." The Court's opinion in this case demonstrates that the danger thus foreseen has not abated. The city of New York is in a precarious financial state, and some may believe that the costs of landmark preservation will be more easily borne by corporations such as Penn Central than the overburdened individual taxpayers of New York. But these concerns do not allow us to ignore past precedents construing the Eminent Domain Clause to the end that the desire to improve the public condition is, indeed, achieved by a shorter cut than the constitutional way of paying for the change.

PUBLIC USE REQUIREMENT

Although the Fifth Amendment recognizes the government's power to take private property, it does not allow all such seizures. Quite explicitly, the Takings Clause stipulates that the government may take private property only for a "public use." Even if the government provides adequate compensation, it may not take property against the owner's will for the sole benefit of a private individual or organization. When the government plans to build a new courthouse, road, or park, the public use is clear, but it would be of doubtful constitutionality, for example, if a state seized a piece of private property under the power of eminent domain and gave it to a fraternal organization to construct a new lodge.

Throughout most of the nation's history, the justices were relatively insistent about the public use requirement.[12] The Court commented on this subject as early as 1884 in *Cole v. LaGrange*. In this dispute the city of LaGrange, Missouri, had issued twenty-five bonds to the LaGrange Iron and Steel Company to help finance the operation of a mill. This act was attacked on the ground that the bonds were being used for a private, not public use. For the Court, Justice Horace Gray agreed:

The general grant of legislative power in the Constitution of a state does not enable the legislature, in the exercise either of the right of eminent domain, or the right of taxation, to take private property, without the owner's consent, for any but a public object.

Later, in *Missouri Pacific Railway Company v. Nebraska* (1896), the Court ruled that the taking of private property, without the owner's consent, for the private use of another, violates due process of law.

Even in the early twentieth century the Court remained wedded to a strict enforcement of the requirement. *Cincinnati v. Vester* (1930) illustrates this point. The city of Cincinnati had confiscated private property to carry out a road-widening project. The amount of property seized, however, was in excess of what was needed. The surplus property was later sold at a profit or otherwise transferred to another private party. The Court ruled this taking to be unlawful for its failure to meet the public use requirement.

After the New Deal, however, the Court's position began to change. In **United States ex rel. Tennessee Valley Authority v. Welch** (1946) the justices upheld the authority of the federal government to condemn private land

---

12. See Schultz, *Property, Power, and American Democracy*.

that would be flooded as a consequence of the Tennessee Valley Authority's flood control programs. In doing so, the Court deferred to Congress's authority to determine what constitutes a public use. That same position was articulated in the Court's unanimous decision in *Berman v. Parker* (1954). Here the Court failed to provide relief to a landowner whose property was being taken from him as part of an urban renewal project only later to be transferred to another private party. Is this decision consistent with the letter and spirit of the Takings Clause?

Berman v. Parker

348 U.S. 26 (1954)
http://laws.findlaw.com/US/348/26.html
Vote: 8 (Black, Burton, Clark, Douglas, Frankfurter, Minton,
  Reed, Warren)
  o
Opinion of the Court: Douglas

Concerned about growing slums and urban blight in Washington, D.C., Congress passed the District of Columbia Redevelopment Act of 1945. This law authorized the National Capital Planning Commission to develop comprehensive land use plans to improve the District's "housing, business, industry, recreation, education, public buildings, public reservations, and other general categories of public and private uses of the land" for the public health, safety, morals, and welfare of its citizens. The law required public hearings on any proposals, and the plans were subject to the approval of the District's commissioners. Once the urban renewal plans were approved, the District of Columbia Redevelopment Land Agency was empowered to acquire, through eminent domain if necessary, the land needed to improve the blighted conditions. After acquisition, the agency would transfer title to government agencies as necessary for public purposes such as streets, utilities, recreational facilities, and schools. The remainder would be leased or sold to private concerns for redevelopment consistent with the land use plan.

Berman v. Parker arose over a comprehensive plan for a section known as Project Area B in Southwest Washing-

ton. The Planning Commission reported the following facts about the area: 64.3 percent of the dwellings were beyond repair, 18.4 percent needed major repairs, only 17.3 percent were satisfactory; 57.8 percent of the dwellings had outside toilets, 60.3 percent had no baths, 29.3 percent lacked electricity, 82.2 percent had no wash basins or laundry tubs, and 83.8 percent lacked central heating. About five thousand people lived in Area B, of whom 97.5 percent were black. The commission concluded that the area required redevelopment in the interests of public health.

Max R. Morris owned a piece of property in Area B, on which was located a department store. He objected to the government's acquisition of his property on the ground that it was not slum housing. Under the comprehensive plan, Morris's property would be sold or leased to other private owners for redevelopment. Following Morris's death his executors, Samuel Berman and Solomon Feldman, pursued legal action, arguing that contrary to the Fifth Amendment's Takings and Due Process Clauses, the government was seizing the property for private, not public, use. Ridding the area of slum housing, they argued, was one thing, but here the government was taking the Morris property and transferring it to other owners only to develop a better balanced, more attractive community. Although it expressed reservations, the district court upheld the constitutionality of the government's actions. Berman and Feldman appealed.

MR. JUSTICE DOUGLAS delivered the opinion of the Court.

The power of Congress over the District of Columbia includes all the legislative powers which a state may exercise over its affairs. We deal, in other words, with what traditionally has been known as the police power. An attempt to define its reach or trace its outer limits is fruitless, for each case must turn on its own facts. The definition is essentially the product of legislative determinations addressed to the purposes of government, purposes neither abstractly nor historically capable of complete definition. Subject to specific constitutional limitations, when the legislature has spoken, the public interest has been declared in terms well-nigh conclusive. In such cases, the legislature, not the judiciary, is the main guardian of the public needs to be served by social legislation, whether it be Congress legislating concerning the District of Columbia or the States legislating concerning local affairs. This principle admits of no exception merely because the power of eminent domain is involved. The role of the judiciary in determining whether that power is being exercised for a public purpose is an extremely narrow one.

Public safety, public health, morality, peace and quiet, law and order—these are some of the more conspicuous examples of the traditional application of the police power to municipal affairs. Yet they merely illustrate the scope of the power and do not delimit it. Miserable and disreputable housing conditions may do more than spread disease and crime and immorality. They may also suffocate the spirit by reducing the people who live there to the status of cattle. They may indeed make living an almost insufferable burden. They may also be an ugly sore, a blight on the community which robs it of charm, which makes it a place from which men turn. The misery of housing may despoil a community as an open sewer may ruin a river.

We do not sit to determine whether a particular housing project is or is not desirable. The concept of public welfare is broad and inclusive. The values it represents are spiritual as well as physical, aesthetic as well as monetary. It is within the power of the legislature to determine that the community should be beautiful as well as healthy, spacious as well as clean, well-balanced as well as carefully patrolled. In the present case, the Congress and its authorized agencies have made determinations that take into account a wide variety of values. It is not for us to reappraise them. If those who govern the District of Columbia decide that the Nation's Capital should be beautiful as well as sanitary, there is nothing in the Fifth Amendment that stands in its way.

Once the object is within the authority of Congress, the right to realize it through the exercise of eminent domain is clear. For the power of eminent domain is merely the means to an end. Once the object is within the authority of Congress, the means by which it will be attained is also for Congress to determine. Here one of the means chosen is the use of private enterprise for redevelopment of the area. Appellants argue that this makes the project a taking from one businessman for the benefit of another businessman. But the means of executing the project are for Congress and Congress alone to determine, once the public purpose

has been established. The public end may be as well or better served through an agency of private enterprise than through a department of government—or so the Congress might conclude. We cannot say that public ownership is the sole method of promoting the public purposes of community redevelopment projects. What we have said also disposes of any contention concerning the fact that certain property owners in the area may be permitted to repurchase their properties for redevelopment in harmony with the over-all plan. That, too, is a legitimate means which Congress and its agencies may adopt, if they choose.

In the present case, Congress and its authorized agencies attack the problem of the blighted parts of the community on an area rather than on a structure-by-structure basis. That, too, is opposed by the appellants. They maintain that since their building does not imperil health or safety nor contribute to the making of a slum or a blighted area, it cannot be swept into a redevelopment plan by the mere dictum of the Planning Commission or the Commissioners. The particular uses to be made of the land in the project were determined with regard to the needs of the particular community. The experts concluded that if the community were to be healthy, if it were not to revert again to a blighted or slum area, as though possessed of a congenital disease, the area must be planned as a whole. It was not enough, they believed, to remove existing buildings that were insanitary or unsightly. It was important to redesign the whole area so as to eliminate the conditions that cause slums—the overcrowding of dwellings, the lack of parks, the lack of adequate streets and alleys, the absence of recreational areas, the lack of light and air, the presence of outmoded street patterns. It was believed that the piecemeal approach, the removal of individual structures that were offensive, would only be a palliative. The entire area needed redesigning so that a balanced, integrated plan could be developed for the region, including not only new homes but also schools, churches, parks, streets, and shopping centers. In this way it was hoped that the cycle of decay of the area could be controlled and the birth of future slums prevented. Such diversification in future use is plainly relevant to the maintenance of the desired housing standards and therefore within congressional power.

The District Court below suggested that, if such a broad scope were intended for the statute, the standards contained in the Act would not be sufficiently definite to sustain the delegation of authority. We do not agree. We think the standards prescribed were adequate for executing the plan to eliminate not only slums as narrowly defined by the District Court but also the blighted areas that tend to produce slums. Property may of course be taken for this redevelopment which, standing by itself, is innocuous and unoffending. But we have said enough to indicate that it is the need of the area as a whole which Congress and its agencies are evaluating. If owner after owner were permitted to resist these redevelopment programs on the ground that his particular property was not being used against the public interest, integrated plans for redevelopment would suffer greatly. The argument pressed on us is, indeed, a plea to substitute the landowner's standard of the public need for the standard prescribed by Congress. But as we have already stated, community redevelopment programs need not, by force of the Constitution, be on a piecemeal basis—lot by lot, building by building.

It is not for the courts to oversee the choice of the boundary line nor to sit in review on the size of a particular project area. Once the question of the public purpose has been decided, the amount and character of land to be taken for the project and the need for a particular tract to complete the integrated plan rests in the discretion of the legislative branch.

The District Court indicated grave doubts concerning the Agency's right to take full title to the land as distinguished from the objectionable buildings located on it. We do not share those doubts. If the Agency considers it necessary in carrying out the redevelopment project to take full title to the real property involved, it may do so. It is not for the courts to determine whether it is necessary for successful consummation of the project that unsafe, unsightly, or insanitary buildings alone be taken or whether title to the land be included, any more than it is the function of the courts to sort and choose among the various parcels selected for condemnation.

The rights of these property owners are satisfied when they receive that just compensation which the Fifth Amendment exacts as the price of the taking.

The judgment of the District Court, as modified by this opinion, is

Affirmed.

The Court's deference to the legislature on questions of what constitutes a public purpose was extended to the state level in *Hawaii Housing Authority v. Midkiff*.[13] Challenged here was Hawaii's plan to redistribute land, using the power of eminent domain to force large landowners to sell their properties to the people who leased them. The transfer of land was clearly from one private owner to another. Was this program a benefit to the public generally, or did it serve only the private interests of those who now were able to become landowners?

Hawaii Housing Authority v. Midkiff

467 U.S. 229 (1984)
http://laws.findlaw.com/US/467/229.html
*Vote: 8 (Blackmun, Brennan, Burger, O'Connor, Powell,
        Rehnquist, Stevens, White)*
        0
Opinion of the Court: O'Connor
Not participating: Marshall

The Hawaiian Islands were settled by Polynesians who developed an economic system based upon principles of feudalism. Ownership and control of the land rested with the islands' high chief, who distributed parcels to various lower-ranking chiefs. At the end of the chain, tenant farmers and their families lived on the land and worked it. Private ownership of real property was not permitted. Ultimate ownership of all lands rested with the royal family.

The monarchy was overthrown in 1893, and, after a brief period as a republic, the islands were annexed by the United States in 1898. When Hawaii became the fiftieth state in 1959, the land still remained in the hands of a few. In the mid-1960s the federal government owned 49 percent of the land in the Hawaiian Islands, and just seventy-two private landowners held another 47 percent. On Oahu, the most commercially developed island, twenty-two landowners controlled more than 72 percent of the private real estate. The Hawaiian legislature deter-

---

13. For oral arguments, navigate to: *www.oyez.org/oyez/frontpage.*

mined that this land concentration condition was detrimental to the state's economy and general welfare.

The legislature first decided to compel landowners to sell a large portion of their holdings to those individuals who leased the land from them. The landowners opposed this plan because it would result in exceedingly high capital gains that would be subject to significant federal taxation. The legislature then revised its plans and enacted the Land Reform Act of 1967. This legislation allowed the state to condemn tracts of residential real estate. The Hawaii Housing Authority (HHA) would then seize the condemned property, compensate the landowners for their loss, and resell the parcels to the private individuals who had been leasing the land. Compensation for land seized by the government enjoyed a more favorable tax status than did profits from outright sales, making the legislation more acceptable to the landowners.

Frank Midkiff and others owned a large tract of land that was condemned under the land reform program, but Midkiff and the HHA could not agree on a fair price. He and his co-owners filed suit in federal district court to have the Land Reform Act declared unconstitutional as a violation of the Takings Clause. Among the arguments presented was the claim that redistributing land ownership was not an appropriate "public use" under the meaning of the Fifth Amendment. The district court rejected this argument, but the Court of Appeals for the Ninth Circuit reversed. The housing authority appealed to the Supreme Court.

JUSTICE O'CONNOR delivered the opinion of the Court.

The Fifth Amendment of the United States Constitution provides, in pertinent part, that "private property [shall not] be taken for public use, without just compensation." These cases present the question whether the Public Use Clause of that Amendment, made applicable to the States through the Fourteenth Amendment, prohibits the State of Hawaii from taking, with just compensation, title in real property from lessors and transferring it to lessees in order to reduce the concentration of ownership of fees simple in the State. We conclude that it does not. . . .

The majority of the Court of Appeals . . . determined that the Act violates the "public use" requirement of the Fifth and Fourteenth Amendments. On this argument, however, we find ourselves in agreement with the dissenting judge in the Court of Appeals.

The starting point for our analysis of the Act's constitutionality is the Court's decision in *Berman v. Parker* (1954). In *Berman,* the Court held constitutional the District of Columbia Redevelopment Act of 1945. That Act provided both for the comprehensive use of the eminent domain power to redevelop slum areas and for the possible sale or lease of the condemned lands to private interests. In discussing whether the takings authorized by that Act were for a "public use," the Court stated:

"We deal . . . with what traditionally has been known as the police power. An attempt to define its reach or trace its outer limits is fruitless, for each case must turn on its own facts. The definition is essentially the product of legislative determinations addressed to the purposes of government, purposes neither abstractly nor historically capable of complete definition. Subject to specific constitutional limitations, when the legislature has spoken, the public interest has been declared in terms well-nigh conclusive. In such cases the legislature, not the judiciary, is the main guardian of the public needs to be served by social legislation, whether it be Congress legislating concerning the District of Columbia . . . or the States legislating concerning local affairs. . . . This principle admits of no exception merely because the power of eminent domain is involved. . . ."

The Court explicitly recognized the breadth of the principle it was announcing, noting:

"Once the object is within the authority of Congress, the right to realize it through the exercise of eminent domain is clear. For the power of eminent domain is merely the means to the end. . . . Once the object is within the authority of Congress, the means by which it will be attained is also for Congress to determine. Here one of the means chosen is the use of private enterprise for redevelopment of the area. Appellants argue that this makes the project a taking from one businessman for the benefit of another businessman. But the means of executing the project are for Congress and Congress alone to determine, once the public purpose has been established."

The "public use" requirement is thus coterminous with the scope of a sovereign's police powers.

There is, of course, a role for courts to play in reviewing a legislature's judgment of what constitutes a public use, even when the eminent domain power is equated with the police power. But the Court in *Berman* made clear that it is "an extremely narrow" one. The Court in *Berman* cited with approval the Court's decision in *Old Dominion Co. v. United*

States (1925), which held that deference to the legislature's "public use" determination is required "until it is shown to involve an impossibility." The *Berman* Court also cited to *United States ex rel. TVA v. Welch* (1946), which emphasized that "[a]ny departure from this judicial restraint would result in courts deciding on what is and is not a governmental function and in their invalidating legislation on the basis of their view on that question at the moment of decision, a practice which has proved impracticable in other fields." In short, the Court has made clear that it will not substitute its judgment for a legislature's judgment as to what constitutes a public use "unless the use be palpably without reasonable foundation."

To be sure, the Court's cases have repeatedly stated that "one person's property may not be taken for the benefit of another private person without a justifying public purpose, even though compensation be paid." Thus, in *Missouri Pacific R. Co. v. Nebraska* (1896), where the "order in question was not, *and was not claimed to be*, . . . a taking of private property for a public use under the right of eminent domain," the Court invalidated a compensated taking of property for lack of a justifying public purpose. But where the exercise of the eminent domain power is rationally related to a conceivable public purpose, the Court has never held a compensated taking to be proscribed by the Public Use Clause.

On this basis, we have no trouble concluding that the Hawaii Act is constitutional. The people of Hawaii have attempted, much as the settlers of the original 13 Colonies did, to reduce the perceived social and economic evils of a land oligopoly traceable to their monarchs. The land oligopoly has, according to the Hawaii Legislature, created artificial deterrents to the normal functioning of the State's residential land market and forced thousands of individual homeowners to lease, rather than buy, the land underneath their homes. Regulating oligopoly and the evils associated with it is a classic exercise of a State's police powers. We cannot disapprove of Hawaii's exercise of this power.

Nor can we condemn as irrational the Act's approach to correcting the land oligopoly problem. The Act presumes that when a sufficiently large number of persons declare that they are willing but unable to buy lots at fair prices the land market is malfunctioning. When such a malfunction is signalled, the Act authorizes HHA to condemn lots in the relevant tract. The Act limits the number of lots any one tenant can purchase and authorizes HHA to use public funds to ensure that the market dilution goals will be achieved. This is a comprehensive and rational approach to identifying and correcting market failure.

Of course, this Act, like any other, may not be successful in achieving its intended goals. But "whether *in fact* the provision will accomplish its objectives is not the question: the [constitutional requirement] is satisfied if . . . the . . . [state] Legislature *rationally could have believed* that the [Act] would promote its objective." When the legislature's purpose is legitimate and its means are not irrational, our cases make clear that empirical debates over the wisdom of takings—no less than debates over the wisdom of other kinds of socioeconomic legislation—are not to be carried out in the federal courts. Redistribution of fees simple to correct deficiencies in the market determined by the state legislature to be attributable to land oligopoly is a rational exercise of the eminent domain power. Therefore, the Hawaii statute must pass the scrutiny of the Public Use Clause. . . .

The mere fact that property taken outright by eminent domain is transferred in the first instance to private beneficiaries does not condemn that taking as having only a private purpose. The Court long ago rejected any literal requirement that condemned property be put into use for the general public. "It is not essential that the entire community, nor even any considerable portion, . . . directly enjoy or participate in any improvement in order [for it] to constitute a public use." As the unique way titles were held in Hawaii skewed the land market, exercise of the power of eminent domain was justified. The Act advances its purposes without the State's taking actual possession of the land. In such cases, government does not itself have to use property to legitimate the taking, it is only the taking's purpose, and not its mechanics, that must pass scrutiny under the Public Use Clause. . . .

The State of Hawaii has never denied that the Constitution forbids even a compensated taking of property when executed for no reason other than to confer a private benefit on a particular private party. A purely private taking could not withstand the scrutiny of the public use requirement; it would serve no legitimate purpose of government and would thus be void. But no purely private taking is involved in these cases. The Hawaii Legislature enacted its Land Reform Act not to benefit a particular class of identifiable individuals but to attack certain perceived evils of concentrated property ownership in Hawaii—a legitimate public purpose. Use of the condemnation power to achieve this purpose is not irrational. Since we assume for purposes of these appeals that the weighty demand of just compensation has been met, the requirements of the Fifth and Fourteenth Amendments have been satisfied. Accordingly, we reverse the judgment of the Court of Appeals, and remand these cases for further proceedings in conformity with this opinion.

It is so ordered.

Decisions such as *Berman* and *Midkiff* made significant changes in the way the Court dealt with Takings Clause appeals. No longer did the justices examine the nature of the public purpose of the taking. Instead, the Court gave wide latitude to legislatures to determine what constitutes public use. To this extent private property rights became political as well as legal questions, increasing the power of the legislature at the expense of traditional property considerations. These decisions also reduced the extent to which "public use" objections could be employed to thwart the legislative redistribution of wealth and property for the public good.[14]

RESURRECTING THE TAKINGS CLAUSE

The Court's Takings Clause jurisprudence began to change in 1986 when William Rehnquist was elevated to the chief justiceship and Antonin Scalia joined the Court. Both were strong advocates of private property rights. Rehnquist previously had been on the losing side of important Takings Clause cases. (See Box 11-1 for a review of Rehnquist's background and public service.) His dissenting opinion in the *Penn Central Transportation* case clearly indicated that he had views at odds with the way the majority was handling Takings Clause appeals. It was also an area of the law in which he had a special interest.

The signs of change began to appear in 1987, when the Court handed down three Takings Clause decisions. The first, decided in March, was ***Keystone Bituminous Coal Association v. DeBenedictis***. The majority upheld a state regulation of coal mining operations against Takings Clause and Contract Clause attacks, but a dissenting opinion by the new chief justice attracted the support of three other justices, indicating that the more conservative members of the Court were poised to make a major assault on existing Takings Clause interpretations. The second case, ***First English Evangelical Lutheran Church of Glendale v. County of Los Angeles***, was decided in June. Although this case involved a relatively minor point regarding the recovery of damages in Takings Clause cases, the Court voted 6–3 to support the property owners who claimed compensation. Chief Justice Rehnquist wrote the majority opinion in support of the property rights position. This decision was a clear signal that the Rehnquist Court was open to new Takings Clause appeals. This fact was acknowledged in Justice John Paul Stevens's dissenting opinion, in which he said: "One thing is certain. The Court's decision today will generate a great deal of litigation."

The third case, *Nollan v. California Coastal Commission*, decided in late June, was the most important indication that the Rehnquist Court was about to resurrect property rights under the Takings Clause.[15] The decision also illustrates how the justices' political philosophies influence case outcomes. Behind this dispute were California's regulations to increase the public's access to the ocean beaches. To help accomplish this objective, the state would allow the Nollans to construct a house on their beachfront property only if they granted the public the right to use a portion of their land to walk from one public beach to another. The five justices who were considered the Court's conservative bloc thought the state regulation was a taking of the Nollans' property. The four liberals said it was not. What do you think? Was the Nollan property partially taken from them by the public access requirement and, therefore, was California bound by the Fifth Amendment to pay just compensation?

---

14. Schultz, *Property, Power, and American Democracy*, 73–74.

15. To hear oral arguments, navigate to: *www.oyez.org/oyez/frontpage*.

BOX 11-1   WILLIAM HUBBS REHNQUIST

WILLIAM HUBBS REHNQUIST was born in Milwaukee, Wisconsin, October 1, 1924. After World War II service in the Army Air Corps, Rehnquist attended Stanford University, receiving B.A. and M.A. degrees in political science. He earned an additional master's degree in government at Harvard, before returning to Stanford to study law. He graduated first in his class in 1952. One of his classmates was Sandra Day, who would later join him on the Supreme Court.

After completing law school, Rehnquist clerked for Justice Robert Jackson. In 1952 he wrote a memorandum that became an issue during his Senate confirmation hearings. The memorandum favored separate but equal schools for blacks and whites. When questioned about these views, he repudiated them, claiming that they were Justice Jackson's beliefs at that time, not his own.

Following his clerkship, Rehnquist moved to Arizona and began the practice of law. He married Natalie Cornell, whom he had met at Stanford, and they had three children. Rehnquist immersed himself in Republican politics, especially the more conservative wing of the party. In 1957 he wrote an article for *U.S. News and World Report* in which he criticized the Warren Court's liberal rulings and suggested that the Court's political leanings might be the result of undue influence exerted by the Court's law clerks. During the 1964 presidential campaign, Rehnquist supported the unsuccessful Republican nominee Barry Goldwater, a U.S. senator from Arizona.

After Richard Nixon was elected to the presidency in 1968, Rehnquist received an appointment to the Justice Department's Office of Legal Counsel, largely because of his association with Deputy Attorney General Richard Kliendienst, a fellow Phoenix lawyer. Rehnquist became one of the Nixon administration's most influential spokesmen on Capitol Hill.

Nixon nominated Rehnquist to be an associate justice on the Supreme Court in 1971 after attempts to find a suitable replacement for the retiring John Marshall Harlan reached an impasse. Rehnquist was only forty-seven years old at the time and not politically well known. He was confirmed, 68–26, and began his service to the Court on January 7, 1972. During his fifteen years as an associate justice, Rehnquist voted in a predictably conservative fashion. He especially favored state interests in federalism disputes and law enforcement in criminal cases. His views were frequently in the minority.

In 1986 President Ronald Reagan nominated Rehnquist to replace Chief Justice Warren Burger, who was retiring. The nomination was controversial. Rehnquist's views on civil rights were questioned. He was accused of harassing black voters in Phoenix during the 1950s and early 1960s and was criticized for owning property with racially restrictive covenants. Liberal politicians and commentators branded him too extreme to lead the Court. In the end, however, the Senate majority considered the charges against him to be unproven or "ancient history." There was no evidence of misconduct during his tenure as associate justice. Rehnquist was confirmed by a 65–33 vote, becoming only the third sitting justice to be promoted to chief.

During his tenure as chief justice, Rehnquist continued his conservative voting record on federalism, civil liberties, criminal justice, and private property issues. With the Court gradually shifting in the conservative direction, Rehnquist more often than not found his views supported by a majority of his colleagues.

Rehnquist is the author of four books on Supreme Court history: *The Supreme Court: How It Was, How It Is* (1988), *Grand Inquests: The Historic Impeachments of Justice Samuel Chase and President Andrew Johnson* (1992), *Civil Liberty and the Civil War* (1996), and *All the Laws but One: Civil Liberties in Wartime* (1998). Rehnquist's research and writing on federal impeachments proved propitious when he was called upon to preside over the 1999 Senate impeachment trial of President Bill Clinton.

SOURCES: John Biskupic and Elder Witt, *Guide to the U.S. Supreme Court,* 3rd ed. (Washington, D.C.: Congressional Quarterly, 1997); and Clare Cushman, ed., *The Supreme Court Justices: Illustrated Biographies 1789–1993* (Washington, D.C.: Congressional Quarterly, 1993).

Nollan v. California Coastal Commission

483 U.S. 825 (1987)
http://laws.findlaw.com/US/483/825.html
Vote: 5 (O'Connor, Powell, Rehnquist, Scalia, White)
*   4 (Blackmun, Brennan, Marshall, Stevens)*
Opinion of the Court: Scalia
Dissenting opinions: Blackmun, Brennan, Stevens

James and Marilyn Nollan owned a beachfront lot in Ventura County, California. One-quarter mile north of their property was Faria County Park, an oceanside public beach and recreation area. Another public beach, known as the Cove, was located 1,800 feet south of the Nollan lot. A concrete sea wall, eight feet high, separated the beach part of the Nollan property from the rest of the land. Originally, a small bungalow that was rented to summer vacationers stood on the property. The house, however, fell into serious disrepair and could no longer be rented. The Nollans decided to replace the bungalow with a new structure, and, to do so, they needed a building permit from the California Coastal Commission.

The commission granted the Nollans permission to build their new house, but with one significant condition: a strip of their property was to be set aside for use by the public to move between the two public beaches. The Nollans protested. On rehearing, the commission reaffirmed the requirement, finding that the easement was necessary because the new house would reduce the view of the beach from the street and prevent the public "psychologically . . . from realizing a stretch of coastline exists nearby that they have every right to visit." The Nollans then filed suit claiming that the public access condition constituted a taking under the Fifth Amendment. The California Supreme Court ruled in favor of the coastal commission, and the Nollans took their case to the U.S. Supreme Court.

JUSTICE SCALIA delivered the opinion of the Court.

Had California simply required the Nollans to make an easement across their beachfront available to the public on a permanent basis in order to increase public access to the beach, rather than conditioning their permit to rebuild

their house on their agreeing to do so, we have no doubt there would have been a taking. To say that the appropriation of a public easement across a landowner's premises does not constitute the taking of a property interest but rather . . . "a mere restriction on its use" is to use words in a manner that deprives them of all their ordinary meaning. Indeed, one of the principal uses of the eminent domain power is to assure that the government be able to require conveyance of just such interests, so long as it pays for them. Perhaps because the point is so obvious, we have never been confronted with a controversy that required us to rule upon it, but our cases' analysis of the effect of other governmental action leads to the same conclusion. We have repeatedly held that, as to property reserved by its owner for private use, "the right to exclude [others is] 'one of the most essential sticks in the bundle of rights that are commonly characterized as property.' " In *Loretto [v. Teleprompter Manhattan CATV*, 1982] we observed that where governmental action results in "[a] permanent physical occupation" of the property, by the government or others, "our cases uniformly have found a taking to the extent of the occupation, without regard to whether the action achieves an important public benefit or has only minimal economic impact on the owner." We think a "permanent physical occupation" has occurred, for purposes of that rule, where individuals are given a permanent and continuous right to pass to and fro, so that the real property may continuously be traversed, even though no particular individual is permitted to station himself permanently upon the premises. . . .

Given, then, that requiring uncompensated conveyance of the easement outright would violate the Fourteenth Amendment, the question becomes whether requiring it to be conveyed as a condition for issuing a land-use permit alters the outcome. We have long recognized that land-use regulation does not effect a taking if it "substantially advance[s] legitimate state interests" and does not "den[y] an owner economically viable use of his land.". . . Our cases have not elaborated on the standards for determining what constitutes a "legitimate state interest" or what type of connection between the regulation and the state interest satisfies the requirement that the former "substantially advance" the latter. They have made clear, however, that a broad range of governmental purposes and regulations satisfies these requirements. The Commission argues that among these permissible purposes are protecting the public's ability to see the beach, assisting the public in overcoming the "psychological barrier" to using the beach created by a developed shorefront, and preventing congestion on the public beaches. We assume, without deciding, that this is so—in which case the Commission unquestionably would be able to deny the Nollans their permit outright if their new house (alone, or by reason of the cumulative impact produced in conjunction with other construction) would substantially impede these purposes, unless the denial would interfere so drastically with the Nollans' use of their property as to constitute a taking.

. . . Thus, if the Commission attached to the permit some condition that would have protected the public's ability to see the beach notwithstanding construction of the new house—for example, a height limitation, a width restriction or a ban on fences—so long as the Commission could have exercised its police power (as we have assumed it could) to forbid construction of the house altogether, imposition of the condition would also be constitutional. Moreover (and here we come closer to the facts of the present case), the condition would be constitutional even if it consisted of the requirement that the Nollans provide a viewing spot on their property for passersby with whose sighting of the ocean their new house would interfere. Although such a requirement, constituting a permanent grant of continuous access to the property, would have to be considered a taking if it were not attached to a development permit, the Commission's assumed power to forbid construction of the house in order to protect the public's view of the beach must surely include the power to condition construction upon some concession by the owner, even a concession of property rights, that serves the same end. If a prohibition designed to accomplish that purpose would be a legitimate exercise of the police power rather than a taking, it would be strange to conclude that providing the owner an alternative to that prohibition which accomplishes the same purpose is not.

The evident constitutional propriety disappears, however, if the condition substituted for the prohibition utterly fails to further the end advanced as the justification for the prohibition. . . . The purpose then becomes, quite simply, the obtaining of an easement to serve some valid governmental purpose, but without payment of compensation. Whatever may be the outer limits of "legitimate state inter-

ests" in the takings and land-use context, this is not one of them. In short, unless the permit condition serves the same governmental purpose as the development ban, the building restriction is not a valid regulation of land use but "an out-and-out plan of extortion.". . .

It is quite impossible to understand how a requirement that people already on the public beaches be able to walk across the Nollans' property reduces any obstacles to viewing the beach created by the new house. It is also impossible to understand how it lowers any "psychological barrier" to using the public beaches, or how it helps to remedy any additional congestion on them caused by construction of the Nollans' new house. We therefore find that the Commission's imposition of the permit condition cannot be treated as an exercise of its land-use power for any of these purposes. Our conclusion on this point is consistent with the approach taken by every other court that has considered the question, with the exception of the California state courts. . . .

California is free to advance its "comprehensive program," if it wishes, by using its power of eminent domain for this "public purpose," but if it wants an easement across the Nollans' property, it must pay for it.

Reversed.

JUSTICE BRENNAN, with whom JUSTICE MARSHALL joins, dissenting.

The Court's conclusion that the permit condition imposed on appellants is unreasonable cannot withstand analysis. First, the Court demands a degree of exactitude that is inconsistent with our standard for reviewing the rationality of a State's exercise of its police power for the welfare of its citizens. Second, even if the nature of the public-access condition imposed must be identical to the precise burden on access created by appellants, this requirement is plainly satisfied.

There can be no dispute that the police power of the States encompasses the authority to impose conditions on private development. It is also by now commonplace that this Court's view of the rationality of a State's exercise of its police power demands only that the State *"could rationally have decided"* that the measure adopted might achieve the State's objective. In this case, California has employed its police power in order to condition development upon preservation of public access to the ocean and tidelands. The Coastal Commission, if it had so chosen, could have denied the Nollans' request for a development permit, since the property would have remained economically viable without the requested new development. Instead, the State sought to accommodate the Nollans' desire for new development, on the condition that the development not diminish the overall amount of public access to the coastline. Appellants' proposed development would reduce public access by restricting visual access to the beach, by contributing to an increased need for community facilities, and by moving private development closer to public beach property. The Commission sought to offset this diminution in access, and thereby preserve the overall balance of access, by requesting a deed restriction that would ensure "lateral" access: the right of the public to pass and repass along the dry sand parallel to the shoreline in order to reach the tidelands and the ocean. In the expert opinion of the Coastal Commission, development conditioned on such a restriction would fairly attend to both public and private interests.

The Court finds fault with this measure because it regards the condition as insufficiently tailored to address the precise type of reduction in access produced by the new development. The Nollans' development blocks visual access, the Court tells us, while the Commission seeks to preserve lateral access along the coastline. Thus, it concludes, the State acted irrationally. Such a narrow conception of rationality, however, has long since been discredited as a judicial arrogation of legislative authority. . . .

Imposition of the permit condition in this case represents the State's reasonable exercise of its police power. The Coastal Commission has drawn on its expertise to preserve the balance between private development and public access, by requiring that any project that intensifies development on the increasingly crowded California coast must be offset by gains in public access. Under the normal standard for review of the police power, this provision is eminently reasonable. . . .

State agencies . . . require considerable flexibility in responding to private desires for development in a way that guarantees the preservation of public access to the coast. They should be encouraged to regulate development in the context of the overall balance of competing uses of the shoreline. The Court today does precisely the opposite, overruling an eminently reasonable exercise of an expert state agency's judgment, substituting its own narrow view of how this balance should be struck. Its reasoning is hardly suited to the complex reality of natural resource protection in the 20th century. I can only hope that today's decision is an aberration, and that the broader vision ultimately prevails.

I dissent.

Justice Brennan's hope that *Nollan* would be an aberration did not come to pass. In the years following this opinion the personnel on the Court continued to change. Justices Brennan and Marshall retired. Both had been firm supporters of public interests over private property rights. Joining the Court were two supporters of private property, Justices Anthony Kennedy and Clarence Thomas. These changes gave increased strength to the chief justice's efforts to breathe new life into the Constitution's private property protections.

The next major Takings Clause decision was *Lucas v. South Carolina Coastal Council* (1992), a case that pitted private property rights against a state's attempts to protect its coastal environment.[16] As might be predicted, the Court's conservative majority sided in favor of the landowner, holding that the state may not deprive the owner of the value of his property without proper compensation. In dissent, Justice Harry Blackmun decried the Court's changing policies.

Lucas v. South Carolina Coastal Council

505 U.S. 1003 (1992)
http://laws.findlaw.com/US/505/1003.html
Vote: 6 (Kennedy, O'Connor, Rehnquist, Scalia, Thomas, White)
    3 (Blackmun, Souter, Stevens)
Opinion of the Court: Scalia
Opinion concurring in the judgment: Kennedy
Dissenting opinions: Blackmun, Stevens
Separate statement: Souter

David Lucas owned two vacant oceanfront lots on the Isle of Palms, a barrier island near Charleston, South Carolina. He acquired the property with the intention

---

16. To hear oral arguments, navigate to: *www.oyez.org/oyez/frontpage.*

David Lucas purchased two oceanfront lots on the Isle of Palms with the intention of building houses on them. Shortly after the sale was completed, the South Carolina Coastal Council determined that building would be detrimental to the environment and prohibited future development. In 1992 the Supreme Court agreed with Lucas that the state's action violated the Takings Clause.

of building single-family homes similar to those already built on adjacent lots. When Lucas bought the land there were no regulations prohibiting such use. Shortly thereafter, however, the state passed the Beachfront Management Act, an environmental law that gave the state coastal council increased authority to protect certain shoreline areas against erosion and other dangers. The council decided that the Lucas lots were in a "critical area" and prohibited any new construction.

There is no doubt that under its police powers the state has the right to pass such legislation, but Lucas claimed that the new regulations amounted to a taking of his property for a public purpose. The Fifth Amendment, he argued, required the state to pay him for the loss of his property. A state trial judge agreed that the regulations had made the Lucas property essentially worthless and ordered the state to compensate him for his loss. On appeal the South Carolina Supreme Court reversed, holding that the environmental legislation was not a taking under the meaning of the Constitution. Lucas appealed to the U.S. Supreme Court.

JUSTICE SCALIA delivered the opinion of the Court.

Prior to Justice Holmes' exposition in *Pennsylvania Coal Co. v. Mahon* (1922), it was generally thought that the Takings Clause reached only a "direct appropriation" of property or the functional equivalent of a "practical ouster of [the owner's] possession." Justice Holmes recognized in *Mahon,* however, that if the protection against physical appropriations of private property was to be meaningfully enforced, the government's power to redefine the range of interests included in the ownership of property was necessarily constrained by constitutional limits. If, instead, the uses of private property were subject to unbridled, uncompensated qualification under the police power, "the natural tendency of human nature [would be] to extend the qualification more and more until at last private property disappear[ed]." These considerations gave birth in that case to the oft-cited maxim that, "while property may be regulated to a certain extent, if regulation goes too far it will be recognized as a taking."

Nevertheless, our decision in *Mahon* offered little insight into when, and under what circumstances, a given regulation would be seen as going "too far" for purposes of the Fifth Amendment. . . . We have, however, described at least two discrete categories of regulatory action as compensable without case-specific inquiry into the public interest advanced in support of the restraint. The first encompasses regulations that compel the property owner to suffer a physical "invasion" of his property. In general (at least with regard to permanent invasions), no matter how minute the intrusion, and no matter how weighty the public purpose behind it, we have required compensation. . . .

The second situation in which we have found categorical treatment appropriate is where regulation denies all economically beneficial or productive use of land. As we have said on numerous occasions, the Fifth Amendment is violated when land-use regulation "does not substantially advance legitimate state interests *or denies an owner economically viable use of his land.*". . .

We think . . . that there are good reasons for our frequently expressed belief that when the owner of real property has been called upon to sacrifice *all* economically beneficial uses in the name of the common good, that is, to leave his property economically idle, he has suffered a taking.

The trial court found Lucas's two beachfront lots to have been rendered valueless by respondent's enforcement of the coastal-zone construction ban. Under Lucas's theory of the case, which rested upon our "no economically viable use" statements, that finding entitled him to compensation. . . . The South Carolina Supreme Court, however, thought otherwise. In its view, the Beachfront Management Act was no ordinary enactment, but involved an exercise of South Carolina's "police powers" to mitigate the harm to the public interest that petitioner's use of his land might occasion. . . .

It is correct that many of our prior opinions have suggested that "harmful or noxious uses" of property may be proscribed by government regulation without the requirement of compensation. For a number of reasons, however, we think the South Carolina Supreme Court was too quick to conclude that that principle decides the present case. The "harmful or noxious uses" principle was the Court's early attempt to describe in theoretical terms why government may, consistent with the Takings Clause, affect property values by regulation without incurring an obligation to compensate—a reality we nowadays acknowledge explicitly with respect to the full scope of the State's police power. . . . "Harmful or noxious use" analysis was, in other words, sim-

ply the progenitor of our more contemporary statements that "land-use regulation does not effect a taking if it 'substantially advance[s] legitimate state interests'. . . ."

The transition from our early focus on control of "noxious" uses to our contemporary understanding of the broad realm within which government may regulate without compensation was an easy one, since the distinction between "harm-preventing" and "benefit-conferring" regulation is often in the eye of the beholder. It is quite possible, for example, to describe in *either* fashion the ecological, economic, and aesthetic concerns that inspired the South Carolina legislature in the present case. One could say that imposing a servitude on Lucas's land is necessary in order to prevent his use of it from "harming" South Carolina's ecological resources; or, instead, in order to achieve the "benefits" of an ecological preserve. . . . Whether Lucas's construction of single-family residences on his parcels should be described as bringing "harm" to South Carolina's adjacent ecological resources thus depends principally upon whether the describer believes that the State's use interest in nurturing those resources is so important that any competing adjacent use must yield.

When it is understood that "prevention of harmful use" was merely our early formulation of the police power justification necessary to sustain (without compensation) *any* regulatory diminution in value; and that the distinction between regulation that "prevents harmful use" and that which "confers benefits" is difficult, if not impossible, to discern on an objective, value-free basis; it becomes self-evident that noxious-use logic cannot serve as a touchstone to distinguish regulatory "takings"—which require compensation—from regulatory deprivations that do not require compensation. *A fortiori* the legislature's recitation of a noxious-use justification cannot be the basis for departing from our categorical rule that total regulatory takings must be compensated. If it were, departure would virtually always be allowed. . . .

Where the State seeks to sustain regulation that deprives land of all economically beneficial use, we think it may resist compensation only if the logically antecedent inquiry into the nature of the owner's estate shows that the proscribed use interests were not part of his title to begin with. This accords, we think, with our "takings" jurisprudence, which has traditionally been guided by the understandings of our citizens regarding the content of, and the State's power over, the "bundle of rights" that they acquire when they obtain title to property. It seems to us that the property owner necessarily expects the uses of his property to be restricted, from time to time, by various measures newly enacted by the State in legitimate exercise of its police powers; "[a]s long recognized, some values are enjoyed under an implied limitation and must yield to the police power." And in the case of personal property, by reason of the State's traditionally high degree of control over commercial dealings, he ought to be aware of the possibility that new regulation might even render his property economically worthless (at least if the property's only economically productive use is sale or manufacture for sale). In the case of land, however, we think the notion pressed by the Council that title is somehow held subject to the "implied limitation" that the State may subsequently eliminate all economically valuable use is inconsistent with the historical compact recorded in the Takings Clause that has become part of our constitutional culture.

Where "permanent physical occupation" of land is concerned, we have refused to allow the government to decree it anew (without compensation), no matter how weighty the asserted "public interests" involved. . . . We believe similar treatment must be accorded confiscatory regulations, *i.e.*, regulations that prohibit all economically beneficial use of land: Any limitation so severe cannot be newly legislated or decreed (without compensation), but must inhere in the title itself, in the restrictions that background principles of the State's law of property and nuisance already place upon land ownership. A law or decree with such an effect must, in other words, do no more than duplicate the result that could have been achieved in the courts—by adjacent landowners (or other uniquely affected persons) under the State's law of private nuisance, or by the State under its complementary power to abate nuisances that affect the public generally, or otherwise.

On this analysis, the owner of a lake bed, for example, would not be entitled to compensation when he is denied the requisite permit to engage in a landfilling operation that would have the effect of flooding others' land. Nor the corporate owner of a nuclear generating plant, when it is directed to remove all improvements from its land upon discovery that the plant sits astride an earthquake fault. Such regulatory action may well have the effect of eliminating the land's only economically productive use, but it does not proscribe a productive use that was previously permissible under relevant property and nuisance principles. The use of these properties for what are now expressly prohibited purposes was *always* unlawful, and (subject to other constitutional limitations) it was open to the State at any point to make the implication of those background principles of nuisance and property law explicit. . . . When, however, a regulation that declares "off-limits" all economically productive or beneficial uses of land goes beyond what the relevant background principles would dictate, compensation must be paid to sustain it.

The "total taking" inquiry we require today will ordinarily entail (as the application of state nuisance law ordinarily entails) analysis of, among other things, the degree of harm to public lands and resources, or adjacent private property, posed by the claimant's proposed activities, the social value of the claimant's activities and their suitability to the locality in question, and the relative ease with which the alleged harm can be avoided through measures taken by the claimant and the government (or adjacent private landowners) alike. The fact that a particular use has long been engaged in by similarly situated owners ordinarily imports a lack of any common-law prohibition (though changed circumstances or new knowledge may make what was previously permissible no longer so). So also does the fact that other landowners, similarly situated, are permitted to continue the use denied to the claimant.

It seems unlikely that common-law principles would have prevented the erection of any habitable or productive improvements on petitioner's land; they rarely support prohibition of the "essential use" of land. The question, however, is one of state law to be dealt with on remand. We emphasize that to win its case South Carolina must do more than proffer the legislature's declaration that the uses Lucas desires are inconsistent with the public interest, or the conclusory assertion that they violate a common-law maxim. . . . As we have said, a "State, by *ipse dixit*, may not transform private property into public property without compensation. . . ." Instead, as it would be required to do if it sought to restrain Lucas in a common-law action for public nuisance, South Carolina must identify background principles of nuisance and property law that prohibit the uses he now intends in the circumstances in which the property is presently found. Only on this showing can the State fairly claim that, in proscribing all such beneficial uses, the Beachfront Management Act is taking nothing.

The judgment is reversed and the cause remanded for proceedings not inconsistent with this opinion.

So ordered.

JUSTICE BLACKMUN, dissenting.

Today the Court launches a missile to kill a mouse.

The state of South Carolina prohibited petitioner Lucas from building a permanent structure on his property from 1988 to 1990. Relying on an unreviewed (and implausible) state trial court finding that this restriction left Lucas' property valueless, this Court granted review to determine whether compensation must be paid in cases where the State prohibits all economic use of real estate. According to the Court, such an occasion never has arisen in any of our prior cases, and the Court imagines that it will arise "relatively rarely" or only in "extraordinary circumstances." Almost certainly it did not happen in this case.

Nonetheless, the Court presses on to decide the issue, and as it does, it ignores its jurisdictional limits, remakes its traditional rules of review, and creates simultaneously a new categorical rule and an exception (neither of which is rooted in our prior case law, common law, or common sense). I protest not only the Court's decision, but each step taken to reach it. More fundamentally, I question the Court's wisdom in issuing sweeping new rules to decide such a narrow case. Surely, . . . the Court could have reached the result it wanted without inflicting this damage upon our Takings Clause jurisprudence. . . .

The Court makes sweeping and, in my view, misguided and unsupported changes in our takings doctrine. While it limits these changes to the most narrow subset of government regulation—those that eliminate all economic value from land—these changes go far beyond what is necessary to secure petitioner Lucas' private benefit. One hopes they do not go beyond the narrow confines the Court assigns them to today.

I dissent.

The Court's decision meant that David Lucas was entitled to compensation in return for being denied the right to develop his land *(see Box 11-2)*. But beyond the matter of Lucas's lots, what did the Court's decision

---

BOX 11-2 AFTERMATH . . .
LUCAS V. SOUTH CAROLINA COASTAL COUNCIL

IN 1986 DAVID LUCAS, a developer of residential properties, purchased two lots on the Isle of Palms in South Carolina for $975,000. He intended to build two houses on the land, keeping one for himself and selling the other. Because of environmental concerns, however, the state coastal council denied Lucas permission to build. In response, Lucas took legal action, demanding compensation for his economic loss. He won a $1.23 million judgment in the state trial court, but the state supreme court reversed that ruling. In 1992 the U.S. Supreme Court found that Lucas had been deprived of property for a public purpose and was entitled to be compensated. The justices remanded the case back to the South Carolina courts for further proceedings.

Additional court action was not required, however. The state had lost the essential issue presented in the case, and only the determination of adequate compensation remained to be decided. South Carolina was understandably eager to settle the dispute rather than to prolong the legal battle. Lucas and the state came to a quick out-of-court settlement, in which the state agreed to pay Lucas $1.5 million in return for the property.

To recoup the funds lost in the Lucas settlement and related litigation costs, the state decided to sell the properties. Ironically, to increase their value prior to sale, the state announced that the new owners would be allowed to build houses on the lots.

SOURCES: *Arizona Republic,* November 2, 1994; *Chicago Sun-Times,* July 28, 1995; *Christian Science Monitor,* September 27, 1993; *San Diego Union-Tribune,* July 21, 1993.

---

mean for future cases? Justice Blackmun expressed the hope that the Court's ruling would be interpreted narrowly and not be expanded to other Takings Clause disputes. His hopes were quickly dashed. In *Dolan v. City of Tigard* (1994), the Court again addressed a Takings Clause dispute.[17] At issue was the validity of municipal

---

17. To hear oral arguments, navigate to: *www.oyez.org/oyez/frontpage.*

land use regulations imposed for environmental, flood control, and recreational purposes. Was the city's attempt to force the property owner to devote a portion of her land to these purposes a legitimate land use regulation? Or was it a taking that required compensation? Chief Justice Rehnquist wrote for the majority.

Dolan v. City of Tigard

512 U.S. 374 (1994)
http:laws.findlaw.com/US/512/374.html
Vote: 5 (Kennedy, O'Connor, Rehnquist, Scalia, Thomas)
      4 (Blackmun, Ginsburg, Souter, Stevens)
Opinion of the Court: Rehnquist
Dissenting opinions: Souter, Stevens

In 1973 Oregon passed a comprehensive land use program that required cities and counties to adopt plans consistent with the state program. In response, the city of Tigard, a Portland suburb, adopted a local community development code (CDC) and related ordinances. Three provisions of this local legislation are relevant. First, the CDC required that 15 percent of land parcels in the central business district be left open and landscaped. Second, the city initiated a pedestrian/bicycle pathway program and mandated that any new development falling along the proposed pathway dedicate land for its development. Third, to combat flooding of Fanno Creek, the city adopted a master drainage plan that included expanded greenways.

Petitioner Florence Dolan owned a plumbing and electric supply store located in the central business district. The store covered approximately 9,700 square feet on the eastern side of a 1.67-acre parcel that included a gravel parking lot. Fanno Creek flows on the western border of the property, which falls within the CDC legislation. Dolan applied for a city permit to redevelop her business site by doubling the size of her store and paving the parking lot. In addition, Dolan proposed to add a second structure to the site for additional retail business. Dolan's proposal was consistent with the city's long-range development plan.

The City Planning Commission approved the application with the condition that Dolan dedicate a portion of her property for the improvement of the storm drainage system. This included converting a part of her property within the flood plain to a public green space. The commission also required that Dolan set aside a fifteen-foot strip across her property for the city's pedestrian/bicycle pathway. These conditions affected approximately 10 percent of Dolan's land, which could be credited toward the city's requirement that 15 percent of all property in the central business district be devoted to open space. In response Dolan requested a variance from the city standards. The commission denied the request, finding that the conditions were related to the improvements proposed. The pedestrian/bicycle pathway would increase customer traffic to Dolan's store, and the newly paved parking lot would necessitate the storm drainage improvements. The City Council approved the actions of the Planning Commission. Dolan appealed to the Land Use Board of Appeals claiming that the conditions imposed by the city constituted an uncompensated taking of property in violation of the Fifth Amendment. The appeals board rejected this argument, as did the Oregon Supreme Court.

CHIEF JUSTICE REHNQUIST delivered the opinion of the Court.

We granted certiorari to resolve a question left open by our decision in *Nollan v. California Coastal Comm'n* (1987) of what is the required degree of connection between the exactions imposed by the city and the projected impacts of the proposed development. . . .

The Takings Clause of the Fifth Amendment of the United States Constitution, made applicable to the States through the Fourteenth Amendment, *Chicago, B. & Q. R. Co. v. Chicago* (1897), provides: "[N]or shall private property be taken for public use, without just compensation." One of the principal purposes of the Takings Clause is "to bar Government from forcing some people alone to bear public burdens which, in all fairness and justice, should be borne by the public as a whole." *Armstrong v. United States* (1960). Without question, had the city simply required petitioner to dedicate a strip of land along Fanno Creek for public use, rather than conditioning the grant of her permit to redevelop her property on such a dedication, a taking would have occurred. *Nollan.* Such public access would deprive petitioner of the right to exclude others, "one of the most essential sticks in the bundle of rights that are commonly characterized as property." *Kaiser Aetna v. United States* (1979).

On the other side of the ledger, the authority of state and local governments to engage in land use planning has been sustained against constitutional challenge as long ago as our decision in *Euclid v. Ambler Realty Co.* (1926). "Government hardly could go on if to some extent values incident to property could not be diminished without paying for every such change in the general law." *Pennsylvania Coal Co. v. Mahon* (1922). A land use regulation does not effect a taking if it "substantially advance[s] legitimate state interests" and does not "den[y] an owner economically viable use of his land." *Agins v. Tiburon* (1980).

The sort of land use regulations discussed in the cases just cited, however, differ in two relevant particulars from the present case. First, they involved essentially legislative determinations classifying entire areas of the city, whereas here the city made an adjudicative decision to condition petitioner's application for a building permit on an individual parcel. Second, the conditions imposed were not simply a limitation on the use petitioner might make of her own parcel, but a requirement that she deed portions of the property to the city. In *Nollan*, we held that governmental authority to exact such a condition was circumscribed by the Fifth and Fourteenth Amendments. Under the well-settled doctrine of "unconstitutional conditions," the government may not require a person to give up a constitutional right—here the right to receive just compensation when property is taken for a public use—in exchange for a discretionary benefit conferred by the government where the property sought has little or no relationship to the benefit.

Petitioner contends that the city has forced her to choose between the building permit and her right under the Fifth Amendment to just compensation for the public easements. Petitioner does not quarrel with the city's authority to exact some forms of dedication as a condition for the grant of a building permit, but challenges the showing made by the city to justify these exactions. She argues that the city has identified "no special benefits" conferred on her, and has not identified any "special quantifiable burdens" created by her new store that would justify the particular dedications required from her which are not required from the public at large.

In evaluating petitioner's claim, we must first determine whether the "essential nexus" exists between the "legitimate state interest" and the permit condition exacted by the city. *Nollan*. If we find that a nexus exists, we must then decide the required degree of connection between the exactions and the projected impact of the proposed development. We were not required to reach this question in *Nollan*, because we concluded that the connection did not meet even the loosest standard. Here, however, we must decide this question.

We addressed the essential nexus question in *Nollan*. The California Coastal Commission demanded a lateral public easement across the Nollans' beachfront lot in exchange for a permit to demolish an existing bungalow and replace it with a three-bedroom house. The public easement was designed to connect two public beaches that were separated by the Nollans' property. The Coastal Commission had asserted that the public easement condition was imposed to promote the legitimate state interest of diminishing the "blockage of the view of the ocean" caused by construction of the larger house.

We agreed that the Coastal Commission's concern with protecting visual access to the ocean constituted a legitimate public interest. We also agreed that the permit condition would have been constitutional "even if it consisted of the requirement that the Nollans provide a viewing spot on their property for passersby with whose sighting of the ocean their new house would interfere." We resolved, however, that the Coastal Commission's regulatory authority was set completely adrift from its constitutional moorings when it claimed that a nexus existed between visual access to the ocean and a permit condition requiring lateral public access along the Nollans' beachfront lot. How enhancing the public's ability to "traverse to and along the shorefront" served the same governmental purpose of "visual access to the ocean" from the roadway was beyond our ability to countenance. The absence of a nexus left the Coastal Commission in the position of simply trying to obtain an easement through gimmickry, which converted a valid regulation of land use into "an out-and-out plan of extortion."

No such gimmicks are associated with the permit conditions imposed by the city in this case. Undoubtedly, the prevention of flooding along Fanno Creek and the reduction of traffic congestion in the Central Business District qualify as the type of legitimate public purposes we have upheld. It seems equally obvious that a nexus exists between preventing flooding along Fanno Creek and limiting development within the creek's 100-year floodplain. Petitioner proposes to double the size of her retail store and to pave her now-gravel parking lot, thereby expanding the impervious surface on the property and increasing the amount of stormwater run-off into Fanno Creek. The same may be said for the city's attempt to reduce traffic congestion by providing for alternative means of transportation. In theory, a pedestrian/bicycle pathway provides a useful alternative means of transportation for workers and shoppers. . . .

The second part of our analysis requires us to determine whether the degree of the exactions demanded by the city's permit conditions bear the required relationship to the projected impact of petitioner's proposed development. . . . Here the Oregon Supreme Court deferred to what it termed the "city's unchallenged factual findings" supporting the dedication conditions and found them to be reasonably related to the impact of the expansion of petitioner's business. . . .

The city made the following specific findings relevant to the pedestrian/bicycle pathway:

"In addition, the proposed expanded use of this site is anticipated to generate additional vehicular traffic thereby increasing congestion on nearby collector and arterial streets. Creation of a convenient, safe pedestrian/bicycle pathway system as an alternative means of transportation could offset some of the traffic demand on these nearby streets and lessen the increase in traffic congestion."

The question for us is whether these findings are constitutionally sufficient to justify the conditions imposed by the city on petitioner's building permit. Since state courts have been dealing with this question a good deal longer than we have, we turn to representative decisions made by them.

In some States, very generalized statements as to the necessary connection between the required dedication and the proposed development seem to suffice. We think this standard is too lax to adequately protect petitioner's right to just compensation if her property is taken for a public purpose.

Other state courts require a very exacting correspondence, described as the "specifi[c] and uniquely attributable" test. The Supreme Court of Illinois first developed this test. . . . Under this standard, if the local government cannot demonstrate that its exaction is directly proportional to the specifically created need, the exaction becomes "a veiled exercise of the power of eminent domain and a confiscation of private property behind the defense of police regulations." We do not think the Federal Constitution requires such exacting scrutiny, given the nature of the interests involved.

A number of state courts have taken an intermediate position, requiring the municipality to show a "reasonable relationship" between the required dedication and the impact of the proposed development. Typical is the Supreme Court of Nebraska's opinion in *Simpson v. North Platte* (1980), where that court stated:

"The distinction, therefore, which must be made between an appropriate exercise of the police power and an improper exercise of eminent domain is whether the requirement has some reasonable relationship or nexus to the use to which the property is being made or is merely being used as an excuse for taking property simply because at that particular moment the landowner is asking the city for some license or permit."

Thus, the court held that a city may not require a property owner to dedicate private property for some future public use as a condition of obtaining a building permit when such future use is not "occasioned by the construction sought to be permitted.". . .

We think the "reasonable relationship" test adopted by a majority of the state courts is closer to the federal constitutional norm than either of those previously discussed. But we do not adopt it as such, partly because the term "reasonable relationship" seems confusingly similar to the term "rational basis" which describes the minimal level of scrutiny under the Equal Protection Clause of the Fourteenth Amendment. We think a term such as "rough proportionality" best encapsulates what we hold to be the requirement of the Fifth Amendment. No precise mathematical calculation is required, but the city must make some sort of individualized determination that the required dedication is related both in nature and extent to the impact of the proposed development. . . .

It is axiomatic that increasing the amount of impervious surface will increase the quantity and rate of stormwater flow from petitioner's property. Therefore, keeping the floodplain open and free from development would likely confine the pressures on Fanno Creek created by petitioner's development. In fact, because petitioner's property lies within the Central Business District, the Community Development Code already required that petitioner leave 15% of it as open space and the undeveloped floodplain would have nearly satisfied that requirement. But the city demanded more—it not only wanted petitioner not to build in the floodplain, but it also wanted petitioner's property along Fanno Creek for its Greenway system. The city has never said why a public greenway, as opposed to a private one, was required in the interest of flood control.

The difference to petitioner, of course, is the loss of her ability to exclude others. As we have noted, this right to exclude others is "one of the most essential sticks in the bundle of rights that are commonly characterized as property." It is difficult to see why recreational visitors trampling along petitioner's floodplain easement are sufficiently related to the city's legitimate interest in reducing flooding problems along Fanno Creek, and the city has not attempted to make any individualized determination to support this part of its request.

The city contends that recreational easement along the Greenway is only ancillary to the city's chief purpose in controlling flood hazards. It further asserts that unlike the residential property at issue in *Nollan*, petitioner's property is commercial in character and therefore, her right to exclude others is compromised. . . .

Admittedly, petitioner wants to build a bigger store to attract members of the public to her property. She also wants, however, to be able to control the time and manner in which they enter. The recreational easement on the Greenway is different in character from the exercise of state-protected rights of free expression and petition that we permitted in *PruneYard* [*Shopping Center v. Robins*, 1980]. In *PruneYard*, we held that a major private shopping center that attracted more than 25,000 daily patrons had to provide access to persons exercising their state constitutional rights to distribute pamphlets and ask passersby to sign their petitions. We based our decision, in part, on the fact that the shopping center "may restrict expressive activity by adopting time, place, and manner regulations that will minimize any interference with its commercial functions." By contrast, the city wants to impose a permanent recreational easement upon petitioner's property that borders Fanno Creek. Petitioner would lose all rights to regulate the time in which the public entered onto the Greenway, regardless of any interference it might pose with her retail store. Her right to exclude would not be regulated; it would be eviscerated.

If petitioner's proposed development had somehow encroached on existing greenway space in the city, it would have been reasonable to require petitioner to provide some alternative greenway space for the public either on her property or elsewhere. . . . But that is not the case here. We conclude that the findings upon which the city relies do not show the required reasonable relationship between the floodplain easement and the petitioner's proposed new building.

With respect to the pedestrian/bicycle pathway, we have no doubt that the city was correct in finding that the larger retail sales facility proposed by petitioner will increase traffic on the streets of the Central Business District. The city estimates that the proposed development would generate roughly 435 additional trips per day. Dedications for streets, sidewalks, and other public ways are generally reasonable exactions to avoid excessive congestion from a proposed property use. But on the record before us, the city has not met its burden of demonstrating that the additional number of vehicle and bicycle trips generated by the petitioner's development reasonably relate to the city's requirement for a dedication of the pedestrian/bicycle pathway easement. . . .

. . . No precise mathematical calculation is required, but the city must make some effort to quantify its findings in support of the dedication for the pedestrian/bicycle pathway beyond the conclusory statement that it could offset some of the traffic demand generated.

Cities have long engaged in the commendable task of land use planning, made necessary by increasing urbanization particularly in metropolitan areas such as Portland. The city's goals of reducing flooding hazards and traffic congestion, and providing for public greenways, are laudable, but there are outer limits to how this may be done. "A strong public desire to improve the public condition [will not] warrant achieving the desire by a shorter cut than the constitutional way of paying for the change." *Pennsylvania Coal*.

The judgment of the Supreme Court of Oregon is reversed, and the case is remanded for further proceedings consistent with this opinion.

It is so ordered.

JUSTICE STEVENS, with whom JUSTICE BLACKMUN and JUSTICE GINSBURG join, dissenting.

The record does not tell us the dollar value of petitioner Florence Dolan's interest in excluding the public from the greenway adjacent to her hardware business. The mountain of briefs that the case has generated nevertheless makes it obvious that the pecuniary value of her victory is far less important than the rule of law that this case has been used to establish. It is unquestionably an important case. . . .

The Court is correct in concluding that the city may not attach arbitrary conditions to a building permit or to a variance even when it can rightfully deny the application outright. I also agree that state court decisions dealing with ordinances that govern municipal development plans provide useful guidance in a case of this kind. Yet the Court's description of the doctrinal underpinnings of its decision, the phrasing of its fledgling test of "rough proportionality," and the application of that test to this case run contrary to the traditional treatment of these cases and break considerable and unpropitious new ground. . . .

Not one of the state cases cited by the Court announces anything akin to a "rough proportionality" requirement. For the most part, moreover, those cases that invalidated municipal ordinances did so on state law or unspecified grounds roughly equivalent to *Nollan*'s "essential nexus" requirement. . . .

The Court's assurances that its "rough proportionality" test leaves ample room for cities to pursue the "commendable task of land use planning,"—even twice avowing that "[n]o precise mathematical calculation is required,"—are wanting given the result that test compels here. Under the Court's approach, a city must not only "quantify its findings" and make "individualized determination[s]" with respect to the nature and the extent of the relationship between the conditions and the impact, but also demonstrate "proportionality." The correct inquiry should instead concentrate on whether the required nexus is present and venture beyond considerations of a condition's nature or germaneness only if the developer establishes that a concededly germane condition is so grossly disproportionate to the proposed development's adverse effects that it manifests motives other than land use regulation on the part of the city. The heightened requirement the Court imposes on cities is even more unjustified when all the tools needed to resolve the questions presented by this case can be garnered from our existing case law. . . .

The Court has made a serious error by abandoning the traditional presumption of constitutionality and imposing a novel burden of proof on a city implementing an admittedly valid comprehensive land use plan. Even more consequential than its incorrect disposition of this case, however, is the Court's resurrection of a species of substantive due process analysis that it firmly rejected decades ago. . . .

In our changing world one thing is certain: uncertainty will characterize predictions about the impact of new urban developments on the risks of floods, earthquakes, traffic congestion, or environmental harms. When there is doubt concerning the magnitude of those impacts, the public interest in averting them must outweigh the private interest of the commercial entrepreneur. If the government can demonstrate that the conditions it has imposed in a land-use permit are rational, impartial and conducive to fulfilling the aims of a valid land-use plan, a strong presumption of validity should attach to those conditions. The burden of demonstrating that those conditions have unreasonably impaired the economic value of the proposed improvement belongs squarely on the shoulders of the party challenging the state action's constitutionality. That allocation of burdens has served us well in the past. The Court has stumbled badly today by reversing it.

I respectfully dissent.

The *Dolan* decision was cheered by advocates of private property rights and criticized by supporters of government policies to regulate land for the public good. It once again demonstrated Chief Justice Rehnquist's intention to put more life into the Takings Clause. As successful as Rehnquist's attempts have been, note that this case was decided by the narrowest of margins.

The Court's inability to reach consensus in Takings Clause cases reveals deep internal divisions between those justices who place primary value on the rights of individual property owners and those who place greater value on the interests of the larger community. These divisions have continued to plague the Court in recent cases, and they make outcomes somewhat difficult to predict. For example, a badly fractured Court in *City of Monterey v. Del Monte Dunes* (1999) expanded the rights of land owners to have jury trials in Takings Clause disputes. But in **Tahoe-Sierra Preservation Council v. Tahoe Regional Planning Agency** (2002), the Court, divided 6–3, ruled against private property interests. A regional planning agency had imposed a "temporary" moratorium on new construction in the Lake Tahoe Basin while it conducted a study of appropriate land use regulations. When the moratorium had lasted thirty-two months, the landowners objected, claiming that a taking had occurred. The Supreme Court held otherwise, ruling that the moratorium did not constitute a taking that required compensation.

Given that the justices are closely divided, the Court's Takings Clause jurisprudence is unstable and subject to modification. A single change in the Court's personnel could easily tip the balance. Thus, as retirements from the bench require appointments of new justices, this area of the law merits close watching.

READINGS

Ackerman, Alan T. *Current Condemnation Law: Takings, Compensation, and Benefits.* Chicago: American Bar Association, 1994.

Ackerman, Bruce. *Economic Foundations of Property Law.* Boston: Little, Brown, 1975.

———. *Private Property and the Constitution.* New Haven: Yale University Press, 1977.

Coyle, Dennis J. *Property Rights and the Constitution: Shaping Society Through Land Use Regulation.* Albany: State University of New York Press, 1993.

Eagle, Steven J. *Regulatory Takings.* Charlottesville, Va.: Lexis Publishing, 2001.

Ely, James W., Jr. *The Guardian of Every Other Right: A Constitutional History of Property Rights.* New York: Oxford University Press, 1992.

Epstein, Richard A. *Takings: Private Property and the Power of Eminent Domain.* Cambridge: Harvard University Press, 1985.

Fischel, William A. *Regulatory Takings: Law, Economics, and Politics.* Cambridge: Harvard University Press, 1995.

Mercuro, Nicholas. *Taking Property and Just Compensation.* Boston: Kluwer, 1992.

Miceli, Thomas J., and Kathleen Segerson. *Compensation for Regulatory Takings.* Greenwich, Conn.: JAI Press, 1996.

Nedelsky, Jennifer. *Private Property and the Limits of American Constitutionalism: The Madisonian Framework and Its Legacy.* Chicago: University of Chicago Press, 1990.

Olivetti, Alfred M. *This Land Is Your Land, This Land Is My Land: The Property Rights Movement and Regulatory Takings.* New York: LFB Scholarly Publishing, 2003.

Paul, Ellen Frankel. *Liberty, Property, and the Foundations of the American Constitution.* Albany: State University of New York Press, 1988.

———. *Property Rights and Eminent Domain.* New Brunswick, N.J.: Transaction Books, 1987.

Roberts, Thomas E., ed. *Taking Sides on Takings Issues: The Impact of Tahoe-Sierra.* Chicago: American Bar Association, 2003.

Schultz, David A. *Property, Power, and American Democracy.* New Brunswick, N.J.: Transaction Books, 1992.

Stoebuck, William B. *Nontrespassory Takings in Eminent Domain.* Charlottesville, Va.: Michie, 1977.

REFERENCE MATERIAL

APPENDIX 1
CONSTITUTION OF THE UNITED STATES

We the People of the United States, in Order to form a more perfect Union, establish Justice, insure domestic Tranquility, provide for the common defence, promote the general Welfare, and secure the Blessings of Liberty to ourselves and our Posterity, do ordain and establish this Constitution for the United States of America.

ARTICLE I

Section 1. All legislative Powers herein granted shall be vested in a Congress of the United States, which shall consist of a Senate and House of Representatives.

Section 2. The House of Representatives shall be composed of Members chosen every second Year by the People of the several States, and the Electors in each State shall have the Qualifications requisite for Electors of the most numerous Branch of the State Legislature.

No Person shall be a Representative who shall not have attained to the age of twenty five Years, and been seven Years a Citizen of the United States, and who shall not, when elected, be an Inhabitant of that State in which he shall be chosen.

[Representatives and direct Taxes shall be apportioned among the several States which may be included within this Union, according to their respective Numbers, which shall be determined by adding to the whole Number of free Persons, including those bound to Service for a Term of Years, and excluding Indians not taxed, three fifths of all other Persons.][1] The actual Enumeration shall be made within three Years after the first Meeting of the Congress of the United States, and within every subsequent Term of ten Years, in such Manner as they shall by Law direct. The Number of Representatives shall not exceed one for every thirty Thousand, but each State shall have at Least one Representative; and until such enumeration shall be made, the State of New Hampshire shall be entitled to chuse three, Massachusetts eight,

Rhode-Island and Providence Plantations one, Connecticut five, New-York six, New Jersey four, Pennsylvania eight, Delaware one, Maryland six, Virginia ten, North Carolina five, South Carolina five, and Georgia three.

When vacancies happen in the Representation from any State, the Executive Authority thereof shall issue Writs of Election to fill such Vacancies.

The House of Representatives shall chuse their Speaker and other Officers; and shall have the sole Power of Impeachment.

Section 3. The Senate of the United States shall be composed of two Senators from each State, [chosen by the Legislature thereof,][2] for six Years; and each Senator shall have one Vote.

Immediately after they shall be assembled in Consequence of the first Election, they shall be divided as equally as may be into three Classes. The Seats of the Senators of the first Class shall be vacated at the Expiration of the second Year, of the second Class at the Expiration of the fourth Year, and of the third Class at the Expiration of the sixth Year, so that one third may be chosen every second Year; [and if Vacancies happen by Resignation, or otherwise, during the Recess of the Legislature of any State, the Executive thereof may make temporary Appointments until the next Meeting of the Legislature, which shall then fill such Vacancies.][3]

No Person shall be a Senator who shall not have attained to the Age of thirty Years, and been nine Years a Citizen of the United States, and who shall not, when elected, be an Inhabitant of that State for which he shall be chosen.

The Vice President of the United States shall be President of the Senate, but shall have no Vote, unless they be equally divided.

The Senate shall chuse their other Officers, and also a President pro tempore, in the Absence of the Vice President, or when he shall exercise the Office of President of the United States.

---

1. The part in brackets was changed by section 2 of the Fourteenth Amendment.

2. The part in brackets was changed by the first paragraph of the Seventeenth Amendment.

3. The part in brackets was changed by the second paragraph of the Seventeenth Amendment.

The Senate shall have the sole Power to try all Impeachments. When sitting for that Purpose, they shall be on Oath or Affirmation. When the President of the United States is tried, the Chief Justice shall preside: And no Person shall be convicted without the Concurrence of two thirds of the Members present.

Judgment in Cases of Impeachment shall not extend further than to removal from Office, and disqualification to hold and enjoy any Office of honor, Trust or Profit under the United States: but the Party convicted shall nevertheless be liable and subject to Indictment, Trial, Judgment and Punishment, according to Law.

Section 4. The Times, Places and Manner of holding Elections for Senators and Representatives, shall be prescribed in each State by the Legislature thereof; but the Congress may at any time by Law make or alter such Regulations, except as to the Places of chusing Senators.

The Congress shall assemble at least once in every Year, and such Meeting shall [be on the first Monday in December],[4] unless they shall by Law appoint a different Day.

Section 5. Each House shall be the Judge of the Elections, Returns and Qualifications of its own Members, and a Majority of each shall constitute a Quorum to do Business; but a smaller Number may adjourn from day to day, and may be authorized to compel the Attendance of absent Members, in such Manner, and under such Penalties as each House may provide.

Each House may determine the Rules of its Proceedings, punish its Members for disorderly Behaviour, and, with the Concurrence of two thirds, expel a Member.

Each House shall keep a Journal of its Proceedings, and from time to time publish the same, excepting such Parts as may in their Judgment require Secrecy; and the Yeas and Nays of the Members of either House on any question shall, at the Desire of one fifth of those Present, be entered on the Journal.

Neither House, during the Session of Congress, shall, without the Consent of the other, adjourn for more than three days, nor to any other Place than that in which the two Houses shall be sitting.

Section 6. The Senators and Representatives shall receive a Compensation for their Services, to be ascertained by Law, and paid out of the Treasury of the United States. They shall in all Cases, except Treason, Felony and Breach of the Peace, be privileged from Arrest during their Attendance at the Session of their respective Houses, and in going to and returning from the same; and for any Speech or Debate in either House, they shall not be questioned in any other Place.

No Senator or Representative shall, during the Time for which he was elected, be appointed to any civil Office under the Authority of the United States, which shall have been created, or the Emoluments whereof shall have been encreased during such time;

4. The part in brackets was changed by section 2 of the Twentieth Amendment.

and no Person holding any Office under the United States, shall be a Member of either House during his Continuance in Office.

Section 7. All Bills for raising Revenue shall originate in the House of Representatives; but the Senate may propose or concur with Amendments as on other Bills.

Every Bill which shall have passed the House of Representatives and the Senate, shall, before it become a Law, be presented to the President of the United States; If he approve he shall sign it, but if not he shall return it, with his Objections to that House in which it shall have originated, who shall enter the Objections at large on their Journal, and proceed to reconsider it. If after such Reconsideration two thirds of that House shall agree to pass the Bill, it shall be sent, together with the Objections, to the other House, by which it shall likewise be reconsidered, and if approved by two thirds of that House, it shall become a Law. But in all such Cases the Votes of both Houses shall be determined by Yeas and Nays, and the Names of the Persons voting for and against the Bill shall be entered on the Journal of each House respectively. If any Bill shall not be returned by the President within ten Days (Sundays excepted) after it shall have been presented to him, the Same shall be a Law, in like Manner as if he had signed it, unless the Congress by their Adjournment prevent its Return, in which Case it shall not be a Law.

Every Order, Resolution, or Vote to which the Concurrence of the Senate and House of Representatives may be necessary (except on a question of Adjournment) shall be presented to the President of the United States; and before the Same shall take Effect, shall be approved by him, or being disapproved by him, shall be repassed by two thirds of the Senate and House of Representatives, according to the Rules and Limitations prescribed in the Case of a Bill.

Section 8. The Congress shall have Power To lay and collect Taxes, Duties, Imposts and Excises, to pay the Debts and provide for the common Defence and general Welfare of the United States; but all Duties, Imposts and Excises shall be uniform throughout the United States;

To borrow Money on the credit of the United States;

To regulate Commerce with foreign Nations, and among the several States, and with the Indian Tribes;

To establish an uniform Rule of Naturalization, and uniform Laws on the subject of Bankruptcies throughout the United States;

To coin Money, regulate the Value thereof, and of foreign Coin, and fix the Standard of Weights and Measures;

To provide for the Punishment of counterfeiting the Securities and current Coin of the United States;

To establish Post Offices and post Roads;

To promote the Progress of Science and useful Arts, by securing for limited Times to Authors and Inventors the exclusive Right to their respective Writings and Discoveries;

To constitute Tribunals inferior to the supreme Court;

To define and punish Piracies and Felonies committed on the high Seas, and Offences against the Law of Nations;

To declare War, grant Letters of Marque and Reprisal, and make Rules concerning Captures on Land and Water;

To raise and support Armies, but no Appropriation of Money to that Use shall be for a longer Term than two Years;

To provide and maintain a Navy;

To make Rules for the Government and Regulation of the land and naval Forces;

To provide for calling forth the Militia to execute the Laws of the Union, suppress Insurrections and repel Invasions;

To provide for organizing, arming, and disciplining, the Militia, and for governing such Part of them as may be employed in the Service of the United States, reserving to the States respectively, the Appointment of the Officers, and the Authority of training the Militia according to the discipline prescribed by Congress;

To exercise exclusive Legislation in all Cases whatsoever, over such District (not exceeding ten Miles square) as may, by Cession of particular States, and the Acceptance of Congress, become the Seat of the Government of the United States, and to exercise like Authority over all Places purchased by the Consent of the Legislature of the State in which the Same shall be, for the Erection of Forts, Magazines, Arsenals, dock-Yards, and other needful Buildings;—And

To make all Laws which shall be necessary and proper for carrying into Execution the foregoing Powers, and all other Powers vested by this Constitution in the Government of the United States, or in any Department or Officer thereof.

Section 9. The Migration or Importation of such Persons as any of the States now existing shall think proper to admit, shall not be prohibited by the Congress prior to the Year one thousand eight hundred and eight, but a Tax or duty may be imposed on such Importation, not exceeding ten dollars for each Person.

The Privilege of the Writ of Habeas Corpus shall not be suspended, unless when in Cases of Rebellion or Invasion the public Safety may require it.

No Bill of Attainder or ex post facto Law shall be passed.

No Capitation, or other direct, Tax shall be laid, unless in Proportion to the Census or Enumeration herein before directed to be taken.[5]

No Tax or Duty shall be laid on Articles exported from any State.

No Preference shall be given by any Regulation of Commerce or Revenue to the Ports of one State over those of another; nor shall Vessels bound to, or from, one State, be obliged to enter, clear, or pay Duties in another.

No Money shall be drawn from the Treasury, but in Consequence of Appropriations made by Law; and a regular Statement

5. The Sixteenth Amendment gave Congress the power to tax incomes.

and Account of the Receipts and Expenditures of all public Money shall be published from time to time.

No Title of Nobility shall be granted by the United States: And no Person holding any Office of Profit or Trust under them, shall, without the Consent of the Congress, accept of any present, Emolument, Office, or Title, of any kind whatever, from any King, Prince, or foreign State.

Section 10. No State shall enter into any Treaty, Alliance, or Confederation; grant Letters of Marque and Reprisal; coin Money; emit Bills of Credit; make any Thing but gold and silver Coin a Tender in Payment of Debts; pass any Bill of Attainder, ex post facto Law, or Law impairing the Obligation of Contracts, or grant any Title of Nobility.

No State shall, without the Consent of the Congress, lay any Imposts or Duties on Imports or Exports, except what may be absolutely necessary for executing it's inspection Laws: and the net Produce of all Duties and Imposts, laid by any State on Imports or Exports, shall be for the Use of the Treasury of the United States; and all such Laws shall be subject to the Revision and Controul of the Congress.

No State shall, without the Consent of Congress, lay any Duty of Tonnage, keep Troops, or Ships of War in time of Peace, enter into any Agreement or Compact with another State, or with a foreign Power, or engage in War, unless actually invaded, or in such imminent Danger as will not admit of delay.

ARTICLE II

Section 1. The executive Power shall be vested in a President of the United States of America. He shall hold his Office during the Term of four Years, and, together with the Vice President, chosen for the same Term, be elected, as follows

Each State shall appoint, in such Manner as the Legislature thereof may direct, a Number of Electors, equal to the whole Number of Senators and Representatives to which the State may be entitled in the Congress: but no Senator or Representative, or Person holding an Office of Trust or Profit under the United States, shall be appointed an Elector.

[The Electors shall meet in their respective States, and vote by Ballot for two Persons, of whom one at least shall not be an Inhabitant of the same State with themselves. And they shall make a List of all the Persons voted for, and of the Number of Votes for each; which List they shall sign and certify, and transmit sealed to the Seat of the Government of the United States, directed to the President of the Senate. The President of the Senate shall, in the Presence of the Senate and House of Representatives, open all the Certificates, and the Votes shall then be counted. The Person having the greatest Number of Votes shall be the President, if such Number be a Majority of the whole Number of Electors appointed; and if there be more than one who have such Majority, and have an equal Number of Votes, then the House of Representatives shall immediately chuse by Ballot one of them for President; and if no Person have a Majority, then from the five highest on the list the said House shall in like Manner chuse the President. But in chusing the President, the Votes shall be taken by States, the Representation from each State having one Vote; A quorum for this Purpose shall consist of a Member or Members from two thirds of the States, and a Majority of all the States shall be necessary to a Choice. In every Case, after the Choice of the President, the Person having the greatest Number of Votes of the Electors shall be the Vice President. But if there should remain two or more who have equal Votes, the Senate shall chuse from them by Ballot the Vice President.] [6]

The Congress may determine the Time of chusing the Electors, and the Day on which they shall give their Votes; which Day shall be the same throughout the United States.

No Person except a natural born Citizen, or a Citizen of the United States, at the time of the Adoption of this Constitution, shall be eligible to the Office of President; neither shall any Person be eligible to that Office who shall not have attained to the Age of thirty five Years, and been fourteen Years a Resident within the United States.

In Case of the Removal of the President from Office, or of his Death, Resignation, or Inability to discharge the Powers and Duties of the said Office,[7] the Same shall devolve on the Vice President, and the Congress may by Law provide for the Case of Removal, Death, Resignation or Inability, both of the President and Vice President, declaring what Officer shall then act as President, and such Officer shall act accordingly, until the Disability be removed, or a President shall be elected.

The President shall, at stated Times, receive for his Services, a Compensation, which shall neither be encreased nor diminished during the Period for which he shall have been elected, and he shall not receive within that Period any other Emolument from the United States, or any of them.

Before he enter on the Execution of his Office, he shall take the following Oath or Affirmation:—"I do solemnly swear (or affirm) that I will faithfully execute the Office of President of the United States, and will to the best of my Ability, preserve, protect and defend the Constitution of the United States."

Section 2. The President shall be Commander in Chief of the Army and Navy of the United States, and of the Militia of the several States, when called into the actual Service of the United States; he may require the Opinion, in writing, of the principal Officer in each of the executive Departments, upon any Subject relating to the Duties of their respective Offices, and he shall have Power to grant Reprieves and Pardons for Offences against the United States, except in Cases of Impeachment.

He shall have Power, by and with the Advice and Consent of the Senate, to make Treaties, provided two thirds of the Senators present concur; and he shall nominate, and by and with the Advice and Consent of the Senate, shall appoint Ambassadors, other public Ministers and Consuls, Judges of the supreme Court, and all other Officers of the United States, whose Appointments are not herein otherwise provided for, and which shall be established by Law: but the Congress may by Law vest the Appointment of such inferior Officers, as they think proper, in the President alone, in the Courts of Law, or in the Heads of Departments.

The President shall have Power to fill up all Vacancies that may happen during the Recess of the Senate, by granting Commissions which shall expire at the End of their next Session.

Section 3. He shall from time to time give to the Congress Information of the State of the Union, and recommend to their Consideration such Measures as he shall judge necessary and expedient; he may, on extraordinary Occasions, convene both Houses, or either of them, and in Case of Disagreement between them, with Respect to the Time of Adjournment, he may adjourn them to such Time as he shall think proper; he shall receive Ambassadors and other public Ministers; he shall take Care that the Laws be faithfully executed, and shall Commission all the Officers of the United States.

Section 4. The President, Vice President and all civil Officers of the United States, shall be removed from Office on Impeachment for, and Conviction of, Treason, Bribery, or other high Crimes and Misdemeanors.

ARTICLE III

Section 1. The judicial Power of the United States, shall be vested in one supreme Court, and in such inferior Courts as the Congress may from time to time ordain and establish. The Judges, both of the supreme and inferior Courts, shall hold their Offices during good Behaviour, and shall, at stated Times, receive for their Services, a Compensation, which shall not be diminished during their Continuance in Office.

Section 2. The judicial Power shall extend to all Cases, in Law and Equity, arising under this Constitution, the Laws of the United States, and Treaties made, or which shall be made, under their Authority;—to all Cases affecting Ambassadors, other public Ministers and Consuls;—to all Cases of admiralty and maritime Jurisdiction;—to Controversies to which the United States shall be a Party;—to Controversies between two or more States; —between a State and Citizens of another State;[8]—between Citizens of different States;—between Citizens of the same State claiming Lands under Grants of different States, and between a State, or the Citizens thereof, and foreign States, Citizens or Subjects.[8]

In all Cases affecting Ambassadors, other public Ministers and

---

6. The material in brackets has been superseded by the Twelfth Amendment.

7. This provision has been affected by the Twenty-fifth Amendment.

8. These clauses were affected by the Eleventh Amendment.

Consuls, and those in which a State shall be Party, the supreme Court shall have original Jurisdiction. In all the other Cases before mentioned, the supreme Court shall have appellate Jurisdiction, both as to Law and Fact, with such Exceptions, and under such Regulations as the Congress shall make.

The Trial of all Crimes, except in Cases of Impeachment, shall be by Jury; and such Trial shall be held in the State where the said Crimes shall have been committed; but when not committed within any State, the Trial shall be at such Place or Places as the Congress may by Law have directed.

Section 3. Treason against the United States, shall consist only in levying War against them, or in adhering to their Enemies, giving them Aid and Comfort. No Person shall be convicted of Treason unless on the Testimony of two Witnesses to the same overt Act, or on Confession in open Court.

The Congress shall have Power to declare the Punishment of Treason, but no Attainder of Treason shall work Corruption of Blood, or Forfeiture except during the Life of the Person attainted.

ARTICLE IV

Section 1. Full Faith and Credit shall be given in each State to the public Acts, Records, and judicial Proceedings of every other State. And the Congress may by general Laws prescribe the Manner in which such Acts, Records and Proceedings shall be proved, and the Effect thereof.

Section 2. The Citizens of each State shall be entitled to all Privileges and Immunities of Citizens in the several States.

A Person charged in any State with Treason, Felony, or other Crime, who shall flee from Justice, and be found in another State, shall on Demand of the executive Authority of the State from which he fled, be delivered up, to be removed to the State having Jurisdiction of the Crime.

[No Person held to Service or Labour in one State, under the Laws thereof, escaping into another, shall, in Consequence of any Law or Regulation therein, be discharged from such Service or Labour, but shall be delivered up on Claim of the Party to whom such Service or Labour may be due.][9]

Section 3. New States may be admitted by the Congress into this Union; but no new State shall be formed or erected within the Jurisdiction of any other State; nor any State be formed by the Junction of two or more States, or Parts of States, without the Consent of the Legislatures of the States concerned as well as of the Congress.

The Congress shall have Power to dispose of and make all needful Rules and Regulations respecting the Territory or other Property belonging to the United States; and nothing in this Constitution shall be so construed as to Prejudice any Claims of the United States, or of any particular State.

Section 4. The United States shall guarantee to every State in this Union a Republican Form of Government, and shall protect each of them against Invasion; and on Application of the Legislature, or of the Executive (when the Legislature cannot be convened) against domestic Violence.

ARTICLE V

The Congress, whenever two thirds of both Houses shall deem it necessary, shall propose Amendments to this Constitution, or, on the Application of the Legislatures of two thirds of the several States, shall call a Convention for proposing Amendments, which, in either Case, shall be valid to all Intents and Purposes, as Part of this Constitution, when ratified by the Legislatures of three fourths of the several States, or by Conventions in three fourths thereof, as the one or the other Mode of Ratification may be proposed by the Congress; Provided [that no Amendment which may be made prior to the Year One thousand eight hundred and eight shall in any Manner affect the first and fourth Clauses in the Ninth Section of the first Article; and][10] that no State, without its Consent, shall be deprived of its equal Suffrage in the Senate.

ARTICLE VI

All Debts contracted and Engagements entered into, before the Adoption of this Constitution, shall be as valid against the United States under this Constitution, as under the Confederation.

This Constitution, and the Laws of the United States which shall be made in Pursuance thereof; and all Treaties made, or which shall be made, under the Authority of the United States, shall be the supreme Law of the Land; and the Judges in every State shall be bound thereby, any Thing in the Constitution or Laws of any State to the Contrary notwithstanding.

The Senators and Representatives before mentioned, and the Members of the several State Legislatures, and all executive and judicial Officers, both of the United States and of the several States, shall be bound by Oath or Affirmation, to support this Constitution; but no religious Test shall ever be required as a Qualification to any Office or public Trust under the United States.

ARTICLE VII

The Ratification of the Conventions of nine States, shall be sufficient for the Establishment of this Constitution between the States so ratifying the Same. Done in Convention by the Unanimous Consent of the States present the Seventeenth Day of September in the Year of our Lord one thousand seven hundred and Eighty seven and of the Independence of the United States of America the Twelfth. IN WITNESS whereof We have hereunto subscribed our Names,

George Washington,
President and deputy from Virginia.

9. This paragraph has been superseded by the Thirteenth Amendment.

10. Obsolete.

New Hampshire: John Langdon,
Nicholas Gilman.
Massachusetts: Nathaniel Gorham,
Rufus King.
Connecticut: William Samuel Johnson,
Roger Sherman.
New York: Alexander Hamilton.
New Jersey: William Livingston,
David Brearley,
William Paterson,
Jonathan Dayton.
Pennsylvania: Benjamin Franklin,
Thomas Mifflin,
Robert Morris,
George Clymer,
Thomas FitzSimons,
Jared Ingersoll,
James Wilson,
Gouverneur Morris.
Delaware: George Read,
Gunning Bedford Jr.,
John Dickinson,
Richard Bassett,
Jacob Broom.
Maryland: James McHenry,
Daniel of St. Thomas Jenifer,
Daniel Carroll.
Virginia: John Blair,
James Madison Jr.
North Carolina: William Blount,
Richard Dobbs Spaight,
Hugh Williamson.
South Carolina: John Rutledge,
Charles Cotesworth Pinckney,
Charles Pinckney,
Pierce Butler.
Georgia: William Few,
Abraham Baldwin.

[The language of the original Constitution, not including the Amendments, was adopted by a convention of the states on September 17, 1787, and was subsequently ratified by the states on the following dates: Delaware, December 7, 1787; Pennsylvania, December 12, 1787; New Jersey, December 18, 1787; Georgia, January 2, 1788; Connecticut, January 9, 1788; Massachusetts, February 6, 1788; Maryland, April 28, 1788; South Carolina, May 23, 1788; New Hampshire, June 21, 1788.

Ratification was completed on June 21, 1788.

The Constitution subsequently was ratified by Virginia, June 25, 1788; New York, July 26, 1788; North Carolina, November 21, 1789; Rhode Island, May 29, 1790; and Vermont, January 10, 1791.]

AMENDMENTS

Amendment I

(First ten amendments ratified December 15, 1791.)

Congress shall make no law respecting an establishment of religion, or prohibiting the free exercise thereof; or abridging the freedom of speech, or of the press; or the right of the people peaceably to assemble, and to petition the Government for a redress of grievances.

Amendment II

A well regulated Militia, being necessary to the security of a free State, the right of the people to keep and bear Arms, shall not be infringed.

Amendment III

No Soldier shall, in time of peace be quartered in any house, without the consent of the Owner, nor in time of war, but in a manner to be prescribed by law.

Amendment IV

The right of the people to be secure in their persons, houses, papers, and effects, against unreasonable searches and seizures, shall not be violated, and no Warrants shall issue, but upon probable cause, supported by Oath or affirmation, and particularly describing the place to be searched, and the persons or things to be seized.

Amendment V

No person shall be held to answer for a capital, or otherwise infamous crime, unless on a presentment or indictment of a Grand Jury, except in cases arising in the land or naval forces, or in the Militia, when in actual service in time of War or public danger; nor shall any person be subject for the same offence to be twice put in jeopardy of life or limb; nor shall be compelled in any criminal case to be a witness against himself, nor be deprived of life, liberty, or property, without due process of law; nor shall private property be taken for public use, without just compensation.

Amendment VI

In all criminal prosecutions, the accused shall enjoy the right to a speedy and public trial, by an impartial jury of the State and district wherein the crime shall have been committed, which district shall have been previously ascertained by law, and to be informed of the nature and cause of the accusation; to be confronted with the witnesses against him; to have compulsory process for obtaining witnesses in his favor, and to have the Assistance of Counsel for his defence.

Amendment VII

In Suits at common law, where the value in controversy shall exceed twenty dollars, the right of trial by jury shall be preserved, and no fact tried by a jury, shall be otherwise re-examined in any Court of the United States, than according to the rules of the common law.

Amendment VIII

Excessive bail shall not be required, nor excessive fines imposed, nor cruel and unusual punishments inflicted.

Amendment IX

The enumeration in the Constitution, of certain rights, shall not be construed to deny or disparage others retained by the people.

Amendment X

The powers not delegated to the United States by the Constitution, nor prohibited by it to the States, are reserved to the States respectively, or to the people.

Amendment XI

(Ratified February 7, 1795)

The Judicial power of the United States shall not be construed to extend to any suit in law or equity, commenced or prosecuted against one of the United States by Citizens of another State, or by Citizens or Subjects of any Foreign State.

Amendment XII

(Ratified June 15, 1804)

The Electors shall meet in their respective states and vote by ballot for President and Vice-President, one of whom, at least, shall not be an inhabitant of the same state with themselves; they shall name in their ballots the person voted for as President, and in distinct ballots the person voted for as Vice-President, and they shall make distinct lists of all persons voted for as President, and of all persons voted for as Vice-President, and of the number of votes for each, which lists they shall sign and certify, and transmit sealed to the seat of the government of the United States, directed to the President of the Senate;—The President of the Senate shall, in the presence of the Senate and House of Representatives, open all the certificates and the votes shall then be counted;—The person having the greatest number of votes for President, shall be the President, if such number be a majority of the whole number of Electors appointed; and if no person have such majority, then from the persons having the highest numbers not exceeding three on the list of those voted for as President, the House of Representatives shall choose immediately, by ballot, the President. But in choosing the President, the votes shall be taken by states, the representation from each state having one vote; a quorum for this purpose shall consist of a member or members from two-thirds of the states, and a majority of all the states shall be necessary to a choice. [And if the House of Representatives shall not choose a President whenever the right of choice shall devolve upon them, before the fourth day of March next following, then the Vice-President shall act as President, as in the case of the death or other constitutional disability of the President.][11] The person hav-

ing the greatest number of votes as Vice-President, shall be the Vice-President, if such number be a majority of the whole number of Electors appointed, and if no person have a majority, then from the two highest numbers on the list, the Senate shall choose the Vice-President; a quorum for the purpose shall consist of two-thirds of the whole number of Senators, and a majority of the whole number shall be necessary to a choice. But no person constitutionally ineligible to the office of President shall be eligible to that of Vice-President of the United States.

Amendment XIII

(Ratified December 6, 1865)

Section 1. Neither slavery nor involuntary servitude, except as a punishment for crime whereof the party shall have been duly convicted, shall exist within the United States, or any place subject to their jurisdiction.

Section 2. Congress shall have power to enforce this article by appropriate legislation.

Amendment XIV

(Ratified July 9, 1868)

Section 1. All persons born or naturalized in the United States, and subject to the jurisdiction thereof, are citizens of the United States and of the State wherein they reside. No State shall make or enforce any law which shall abridge the privileges or immunities of citizens of the United States; nor shall any State deprive any person of life, liberty, or property, without due process of law; nor deny to any person within its jurisdiction the equal protection of the laws.

Section 2. Representatives shall be apportioned among the several States according to their respective numbers, counting the whole number of persons in each State, excluding Indians not taxed. But when the right to vote at any election for the choice of electors for President and Vice President of the United States, Representatives in Congress, the Executive and Judicial officers of a State, or the members of the Legislature thereof, is denied to any of the male inhabitants of such State, being twenty-one years of age,[12] and citizens of the United States, or in any way abridged, except for participation in rebellion, or other crime, the basis of representation therein shall be reduced in the proportion which the number of such male citizens shall bear to the whole number of male citizens twenty-one years of age in such State.

Section 3. No person shall be a Senator or Representative in Congress, or elector of President and Vice President, or hold any office, civil or military, under the United States, or under any State, who, having previously taken an oath, as a member of Congress, or as an officer of the United States, or as a member of any State legislature, or as an executive or judicial officer of any State, to support the Constitution of the United States, shall have engaged in insurrection or rebellion against the same, or given aid

11. The part in brackets has been superseded by section 3 of the Twentieth Amendment.

12. See the Nineteenth and Twenty-sixth Amendments.

or comfort to the enemies thereof. But Congress may by a vote of two-thirds of each House, remove such disability.

Section 4. The validity of the public debt of the United States, authorized by law, including debts incurred for payment of pensions and bounties for services in suppressing insurrection or rebellion, shall not be questioned. But neither the United States nor any State shall assume or pay any debt or obligation incurred in aid of insurrection or rebellion against the United States, or any claim for the loss or emancipation of any slave; but all such debts, obligations and claims shall be held illegal and void.

Section 5. The Congress shall have power to enforce, by appropriate legislation, the provisions of this article.

Amendment XV
(Ratified February 3, 1870)

Section 1. The right of citizens of the United States to vote shall not be denied or abridged by the United States or by any State on account of race, color, or previous condition of servitude.

Section 2. The Congress shall have power to enforce this article by appropriate legislation.

Amendment XVI
(Ratified February 3, 1913)

The Congress shall have power to lay and collect taxes on incomes, from whatever source derived, without apportionment among the several States, and without regard to any census or enumeration.

Amendment XVII
(Ratified April 8, 1913)

The Senate of the United States shall be composed of two Senators from each State, elected by the people thereof, for six years; and each Senator shall have one vote. The electors in each State shall have the qualifications requisite for electors of the most numerous branch of the State legislatures.

When vacancies happen in the representation of any State in the Senate, the executive authority of such State shall issue writs of election to fill such vacancies: *Provided,* That the legislature of any State may empower the executive thereof to make temporary appointments until the people fill the vacancies by election as the legislature may direct.

This amendment shall not be so construed as to affect the election or term of any Senator chosen before it becomes valid as part of the Constitution.

[Amendment XVIII
(Ratified January 16, 1919)

Section 1. After one year from the ratification of this article the manufacture, sale, or transportation of intoxicating liquors within, the importation thereof into, or the exportation thereof from the United States and all territory subject to the jurisdiction thereof for beverage purposes is hereby prohibited.

Section 2. The Congress and the several States shall have concurrent power to enforce this article by appropriate legislation.

Section 3. This article shall be inoperative unless it shall have been ratified as an amendment to the Constitution by the legislatures of the several States, as provided in the Constitution, within seven years from the date of the submission hereof to the States by the Congress.][13]

Amendment XIX
(Ratified August 18, 1920)

The right of citizens of the United States to vote shall not be denied or abridged by the United States or by any State on account of sex.

Congress shall have power to enforce this article by appropriate legislation.

Amendment XX
(Ratified January 23, 1933)

Section 1. The terms of the President and Vice President shall end at noon on the 20th day of January, and the terms of Senators and Representatives at noon on the 3d day of January, of the years in which such terms would have ended if this article had not been ratified; and the terms of their successors shall then begin.

Section 2. The Congress shall assemble at least once in every year, and such meeting shall begin at noon on the 3d day of January, unless they shall by law appoint a different day.

Section 3.[14] If, at the time fixed for the beginning of the term of the President, the President elect shall have died, the Vice President elect shall become President. If a President shall not have been chosen before the time fixed for the beginning of his term, or if the President elect shall have failed to qualify, then the Vice President elect shall act as President until a President shall have qualified; and the Congress may by law provide for the case wherein neither a President elect nor a Vice President elect shall have qualified, declaring who shall then act as President, or the manner in which one who is to act shall be selected, and such person shall act accordingly until a President or Vice President shall have qualified.

Section 4. The Congress may by law provide for the case of the death of any of the persons from whom the House of Representatives may choose a President whenever the right of choice shall have devolved upon them, and for the case of the death of any of the persons from whom the Senate may choose a Vice President whenever the right of choice shall have devolved upon them.

Section 5. Sections 1 and 2 shall take effect on the 15th day of October following the ratification of this article.

Section 6. This article shall be inoperative unless it shall have been ratified as an amendment to the Constitution by the legisla-

13. This Amendment was repealed by section 1 of the Twenty-first Amendment.
14. See the Twenty-fifth Amendment.

tures of three-fourths of the several States within seven years from the date of its submission.

Amendment XXI

(Ratified December 5, 1933)

Section 1. The eighteenth article of amendment to the Constitution of the United States is hereby repealed.

Section 2. The transportation or importation into any State, Territory, or possession of the United States for delivery or use therein of intoxicating liquors, in violation of the laws thereof, is hereby prohibited.

Section 3. This article shall be inoperative unless it shall have been ratified as an amendment to the Constitution by conventions in the several States, as provided in the Constitution, within seven years from the date of the submission hereof to the States by the Congress.

Amendment XXII

(Ratified February 27, 1951)

Section 1. No person shall be elected to the office of the President more than twice, and no person who has held the office of President, or acted as President, for more than two years of a term to which some other person was elected President shall be elected to the office of the President more than once. But this Article shall not apply to any person holding the office of President when this Article was proposed by the Congress, and shall not prevent any person who may be holding the office of President, or acting as President, during the term within which this Article become operative from holding the office of President or acting as President during the remainder of such term.

Section 2. This article shall be inoperative unless it shall have been ratified as an amendment to the Constitution by the legislatures of three-fourths of the several States within seven years from the date of its submission to the States by the Congress.

Amendment XXIII

(Ratified March 29, 1961)

Section 1. The District constituting the seat of Government of the United States shall appoint in such manner as the Congress may direct:

A number of electors of President and Vice President equal to the whole number of Senators and Representatives in Congress to which the District would be entitled if it were a State, but in no event more than the least populous State; they shall be in addition to those appointed by the States, but they shall be considered, for the purposes of the election of President and Vice President, to be electors appointed by a State; and they shall meet in the District and perform such duties as provided by the twelfth article of amendment.

Section 2. The Congress shall have power to enforce this article by appropriate legislation.

Amendment XXIV

(Ratified January 23, 1964)

Section 1. The right of citizens of the United States to vote in any primary or other election for President or Vice President, for electors for President or Vice President, or for Senator or Representative in Congress, shall not be denied or abridged by the United States or any State by reason of failure to pay any poll tax or other tax.

Section 2. The Congress shall have power to enforce this article by appropriate legislation.

Amendment XXV

(Ratified February 10, 1967)

Section 1. In case of the removal of the President from office or of his death or resignation, the Vice President shall become President.

Section 2. Whenever there is a vacancy in the office of the Vice President, the President shall nominate a Vice President who shall take office upon confirmation by a majority vote of both Houses of Congress.

Section 3. Whenever the President transmits to the President pro tempore of the Senate and the Speaker of the House of Representatives his written declaration that he is unable to discharge the powers and duties of his office, and until he transmits to them a written declaration to the contrary, such powers and duties shall be discharged by the Vice President as Acting President.

Section 4. Whenever the Vice President and a majority of either the principal officers of the executive departments or of such other body as Congress may by law provide, transmit to the President pro tempore of the Senate and the Speaker of the House of Representatives their written declaration that the President is unable to discharge the powers and duties of his office, the Vice President shall immediately assume the powers and duties of the office as Acting President.

Thereafter, when the President transmits to the President pro tempore of the Senate and the Speaker of the House of Representatives his written declaration that no inability exists, he shall resume the powers and duties of his office unless the Vice President and a majority of either the principal officers of the executive department or of such other body as Congress may by law provide, transmit within four days to the President pro tempore of the Senate and the Speaker of the House of Representatives their written declaration that the President is unable to discharge the powers and duties of his office. Thereupon Congress shall decide the issue, assembling within forty-eight hours for that purpose if not in session. If the Congress, within twenty-one days after receipt of the latter written declaration, or, if Congress is not in session, within twenty-one days after Congress is required to assemble, determines by two-thirds vote of both Houses that the President is unable to discharge the powers and duties of his office, the Vice

President shall continue to discharge the same as Acting President; otherwise, the President shall resume the powers and duties of his office.

Amendment XXVI
(Ratified July 1, 1971)

Section 1. The right of citizens of the United States, who are eighteen years of age or older, to vote shall not be denied or abridged by the United States or by any State on account of age.

Section 2. The Congress shall have power to enforce this article by appropriate legislation.

Amendment XXVII
(Ratified May 7, 1992)

No law varying the compensation for the services of the Senators and Representatives shall take effect, until an election of Representatives shall have intervened.

SOURCE: *United States Government Manual, 1993–94* (Washington, D.C.: Government Printing Office, 1993), 5–20.

APPENDIX 2
FEDERALIST PAPER, NO. 78

A VIEW OF THE CONSTITUTION OF THE JUDICIAL DEPARTMENT IN RELATION TO THE TENURE OF GOOD BEHAVIOUR

We proceed now to an examination of the judiciary department of the proposed government.

In unfolding the defects of the existing Confederation, the utility and necessity of a federal judicature have been clearly pointed out. It is the less necessary to recapitulate the considerations there urged as the propriety of the institution in the abstract is not disputed; the only questions which have been raised being relative to the manner of constituting it, and to its extent. To these points, therefore, our observations shall be confined.

The manner of constituting it seems to embrace these several objects: 1st. The mode of appointing the judges. 2nd. The tenure by which they are to hold their places. 3rd. The partition of the judiciary authority between different courts and their relations to each other.

First. As to the mode of appointing the judges: this is the same with that of appointing the officers of the Union in general and has been so fully discussed in the two last numbers that nothing can be said here which would not be useless repetition.

Second. As to the tenure by which the judges are to hold their places: this chiefly concerns their duration in office, the provisions for their support, the precautions for their responsibility.

According to the plan of the convention, all judges who may be appointed by the United States are to hold their offices *during good behavior;* which is conformable to the most approved of the State constitutions, and among the rest, to that of the State. Its propriety having been drawn into question by the adversaries of that plan is no light symptom of the rage for objection which disorders their imaginations and judgments. The standard of good behavior for the continuance in office of the judicial magistracy is certainly one of the most valuable of the modern improvements in the practice of government. In a monarchy it is an excellent barrier to the despotism of the prince; in a republic it is a no less excellent barrier to the encroachments and oppressions of the representative body. And it is the best expedient which can be devised in any government to secure a steady, upright, and impartial administration of the laws.

Whoever attentively considers the different departments of power must perceive that, in a government in which they are separated from each other, the judiciary, from the nature of its functions, will always be the least dangerous to the political rights of the Constitution; because it will be least in a capacity to annoy or injure them. The executive not only dispenses the honors but holds the sword of the community. The legislature not only commands the purse but prescribes the rules by which the duties and rights of every citizen are to be regulated. The judiciary, on the contrary, has no influence over either the sword or the purse; no direction either of the strength or of the wealth of the society, and can take no active resolution whatever. It may truly be said to have neither FORCE nor WILL but merely judgment; and must ultimately depend upon the aid of the executive arm even for the efficacy of its judgments.

This simple view of the matter suggests several important consequences. It proves incontestably that the judiciary is beyond comparison the weakest of the three departments of power; that it can never attack with success either of the other two; and that all possible care is requisite to enable it to defend itself against their attacks. It equally proves that though individual oppression may now and then proceed from the courts of justice, the general liberty of the people can never be endangered from that quarter; I mean so long as the judiciary remains truly distinct from both the legislature and the executive. For I agree that "there is no liberty if the power of judging be not separated from the legislative and executive powers." And it proves, in the last place, that as liberty can have nothing to fear from the judiciary alone, but would have everything to fear from its union with either of the other departments; that as all the effects of such a union must ensue from a dependence of the former on the latter, notwithstanding a nominal and apparent separation; that as, from the natural feebleness of the judiciary, it is in continual jeopardy of being overpowered, awed, or influenced by its co-ordinate branches; and that as nothing can contribute so much to its firmness and independence as permanency in office, this quality may therefore be justly regarded as an indispensable ingredient in its constitution, and, in a great measure, as the citadel of the public justice and the public security.

The complete independence of the courts of justice is peculiarly essential in a limited Constitution. By a limited Constitution, I understand one which contains certain specified exceptions to the legislative authority; such, for instance, as that it shall pass no bills of attainder, no *ex post facto* laws, and the like. Limitations of this kind can be preserved in practice no other way than through the medium of courts of justice, whose duty it must be to declare all acts contrary to the manifest tenor of the Constitution void. Without this, all the reservations of particular rights or privileges would amount to nothing.

Some perplexity respecting the rights of the courts to pronounce legislative acts void, because contrary to the Constitution, has arisen from an imagination that the doctrine would imply a superiority of the judiciary to the legislative power. It is urged that the authority which can declare the acts of another void must necessarily be superior to the one whose acts may be declared void. As this doctrine is of great importance in all the American constitutions, a brief discussion of the grounds on which it rests cannot be unacceptable.

There is no position which depends on clearer principles than that every act of a delegated authority, contrary to the tenor of the commission under which it is exercised, is void. No legislative act, therefore, contrary to the Constitution, can be valid. To deny this would be to affirm that the deputy is greater than his principal; that the servant is above his master; that the representatives of the people are superior to the people themselves; that men acting by virtue of powers may do not only what their powers do not authorize, but what they forbid.

If it be said that the legislative body are themselves the constitutional judges of their own powers and that the construction they put upon them is conclusive upon the other departments it may be answered that this cannot be the natural presumption where it is not to be collected from any particular provisions in the Constitution. It is not otherwise to be supposed that the Constitution could intend to enable the representatives of the people to substitute their *will* to that of their constituents. It is far more rational to suppose that the courts were designed to be an intermediate body between the people and the legislature in order, among other things, to keep the latter within the limits assigned to their authority. The interpretation of the laws is the proper and peculiar province of the courts. A constitution is, in fact, and must be regarded by the judges as, a fundamental law. It therefore belongs to them to ascertain its meaning as well as the meaning of any particular act proceeding from the legislative body. If there should happen to be an irreconcilable variance between the two, that which has the superior obligation and validity ought, of course, to be preferred: or, in other words, the Constitution ought to be preferred to the statute, the intention of the people to the intention of their agents.

Nor does this conclusion by any means suppose a superiority of the judicial to the legislative power. It only supposes that the power of the people is superior to both, and that where the will of the legislature, declared in its statutes, stands in opposition to that of the people, declared in the Constitution, the judges ought to be governed by the latter rather than the former. They ought to regulate their decisions by the fundamental laws rather than by those which are not fundamental.

This exercise of judicial discretion in determining between two contradictory laws is exemplified in a familiar instance. It not un-commonly happens that there are two statutes existing at one time, clashing in whole or in part with each other and neither of them containing any repealing clause or expression. In such a case, it is the province of the courts to liquidate and fix their meaning and operation. So far as they can, by fair construction, be reconciled to each other, reason and law conspire to dictate that this should be done; where this is impracticable, it becomes a matter of necessity to give effect to one in exclusion of the other. The rule which has obtained in the courts for determining their relative validity is that the last in order of time shall be preferred to the first. But this is a mere rule of construction, not derived from any positive law but from the nature and reason of the thing. It is a rule not enjoined upon the courts by legislative provision but adopted by themselves, as consonant to truth and propriety, for the direction of their conduct as interpreters of the law. They thought it reasonable that between the interfering acts of an *equal* authority that which was the last indication of its will should have the preference.

But in regard to the interfering acts of a superior and subordinate authority of an original and derivative power, the nature and reason of the thing indicate the converse of that rule as proper to be followed. They teach us that the prior act of a superior ought to be preferred to the subsequent act of an inferior and subordinate authority; and that accordingly, whenever a particular statute contravenes the Constitution, it will be the duty of the judicial tribunals to adhere to the latter and disregard the former.

It can be of no weight to say that the courts, on the pretense of a repugnancy, may substitute their own pleasure to the constitutional intentions of the legislature. This might as well happen in the case of two contradictory statutes; or it might as well happen in every adjudication upon any single statute. The courts must declare the sense of the law; and if they should be disposed to exercise WILL instead of JUDGMENT, the consequence would equally be the substitution of their pleasure for that of the legislative body. The observation, if it proved anything, would prove that there ought to be no judges distinct from that body.

If, then, the courts of justice are to be considered as the bulwarks of a limited Constitution against legislative encroachments, this consideration will afford a strong argument for the permanent tenure of judicial offices, since nothing will contribute so much as this to that independent spirit in the judges which must be essential to the faithful performance of so arduous a duty.

This independence of the judges is equally requisite to guard the Constitution and the rights of individuals from the effects of those ill humors which the arts of designing men, or the influence of particular conjunctures, sometimes disseminate among the people themselves, and which, though they speedily give place to better information, and more deliberate reflection, have a tendency, in the meantime, to occasion dangerous innovations in the government, and serious oppressions of the minor party in the community. Though I trust the friends of the proposed Constitution will never concur with its enemies in questioning that fundamental principle of republican government which admits the right of the people to alter or abolish the established Constitution whenever they find it inconsistent with their happiness; yet it is not to be inferred from this principle that the representatives of the people, whenever a momentary inclination happens to lay hold of a majority of their constituents incompatible with the provisions in the existing Constitution, would, on that account, be justifiable in a violation of those provisions; or that the courts would be under a greater obligation to connive at infractions in this shape than when they had proceeded wholly from the cabals of the representative body. Until the people have, by some solemn and authoritative act, annulled or changed the established form, it is binding upon themselves collectively, as well as individually; and no presumption, or even knowledge, of their sentiment can warrant their representatives in a departure from it prior to such an act. But it is easy to see that it would require an uncommon portion of fortitude in the judges to do their duty as faithful guardians of the Constitution, where legislative invasions of it had been instigated by the major voice of the community.

But it is not with a view to infractions of the Constitution only that the independence of the judges may be an essential safeguard against the effects of occasional ill humors in the society. These sometimes extend no farther than to the injury of the private rights of particular classes of citizens, by unjust and partial laws. Here also the firmness of the judicial magistracy is of vast importance in mitigating the severity and confining the operation of such laws. It not only serves to moderate the immediate mischiefs of those which may have been passed but it operates as a check upon the legislative body in passing them; who, perceiving that obstacles to the success of an iniquitous intention are to be expected from the scruples of the courts, are in a manner compelled, by the very motives of the injustice they meditate, to qualify their attempts. This is a circumstance calculated to have more influence upon the character of our governments than but few may be aware of. The benefits of the integrity and moderation of the judiciary have already been felt in more States than one; and though they may have displeased those whose sinister expectations they may have disappointed, they must have commanded the esteem and applause of all the virtuous and disinterested. Considerate men of every description ought to prize whatever will tend to beget or fortify that temper in the courts; as no man can be sure that he may not be tomorrow the victim of a spirit of injustice, by which he may be a gainer today. And every man must now feel that the inevitable tendency of such a spirit is to sap the foundations of public and private confidence and to introduce in its stead universal distrust and distress.

That inflexible and uniform adherence to the rights of the Constitution, and of individuals, which we perceive to be indispensable in the courts of justice, can certainly not be expected from judges who hold their offices by a temporary commission. Periodical appointments, however regulated, or by whomsoever made, would, in some way or other, be fatal to their necessary independence. If the power of making them was committed either to the executive or legislature there would be danger of an improper complaisance to the branch which possessed it; if to both, there would be an unwillingness to hazard the displeasure of either; if to the people, or to persons chosen by them for the special purpose, there would be too great a disposition to consult popularity to justify a reliance that nothing would be consulted but the Constitution and the laws.

There is yet a further and weighty reason for the permanency of the judicial offices which is deducible from the nature of the qualifications they require. It has been frequently remarked with great propriety that a voluminous code of laws is one of the inconveniences necessarily connected with the advantages of a free government. To avoid an arbitrary discretion in the courts, it is indispensable that they should be bound down by strict rules and precedents which serve to define and point out their duty in every particular case that comes before them; and it will readily be conceived from the variety of controversies which grow out of the folly and wickedness of mankind that the records of those precedents must unavoidably swell to a very considerable bulk and must demand long and laborious study to acquire a competent knowledge of them. Hence it is that there can be but few men in the society who will have sufficient skill in the laws to qualify them for the stations of judges. And making the proper deductions for the ordinary depravity of human nature, the number must be still smaller of those who unite the requisite integrity with the requisite knowledge. These considerations apprise us that the government can have no great option between fit characters; and that a temporary duration in office which would naturally discourage such characters from quitting a lucrative line of practice to accept a seat on the bench would have a tendency to throw the administration of justice into hands less able and less well qualified to conduct it with utility and dignity. In the present circumstances of this country and in those in which it is likely to be for a long time to come, the disadvantages on this score would be greater than they may at first sight appear; but it must be confessed that they are far inferior to those which present themselves under the other aspects of the subject.

Upon the whole, there can be no room to doubt that the convention acted wisely in copying from the models of those constitutions which have established *good behavior* as the tenure of their judicial offices, in the point of duration; and that so far from being blamable on this account, their plan would have been inexcusably defective if it had wanted this important feature of good government. The experience of Great Britain affords an illustrious comment on the excellence of the institution.

PUBLIUS [Hamilton]

U.S. PRESIDENTS

President	Political Party	Term of Service
George Washington	Federalist	April 30, 1789–March 4, 1793
George Washington	Federalist	March 4, 1793–March 4, 1797
John Adams	Federalist	March 4, 1797–March 4, 1801
Thomas Jefferson	Democratic Republican	March 4, 1801–March 4, 1805
Thomas Jefferson	Democratic Republican	March 4, 1805–March 4, 1809
James Madison	Democratic Republican	March 4, 1809–March 4, 1813
James Madison	Democratic Republican	March 4, 1813–March 4, 1817
James Monroe	Democratic Republican	March 4, 1817–March 4, 1821
James Monroe	Democratic Republican	March 4, 1821–March 4, 1825
John Q. Adams	Democratic Republican	March 4, 1825–March 4, 1829
Andrew Jackson	Democrat	March 4, 1829–March 4, 1833
Andrew Jackson	Democrat	March 4, 1833–March 4, 1837
Martin Van Buren	Democrat	March 4, 1837–March 4, 1841
W. H. Harrison	Whig	March 4, 1841–April 4, 1841
John Tyler	Whig	April 6, 1841–March 4, 1845
James K. Polk	Democrat	March 4, 1845–March 4, 1849
Zachary Taylor	Whig	March 4, 1849–July 9, 1850
Millard Fillmore	Whig	July 10, 1850–March 4, 1853
Franklin Pierce	Democrat	March 4, 1853–March 4, 1857
James Buchanan	Democrat	March 4, 1857–March 4, 1861
Abraham Lincoln	Republican	March 4, 1861–March 4, 1865
Abraham Lincoln	Republican	March 4, 1865–April 15, 1865
Andrew Johnson	Republican	April 15, 1865–March 4, 1869
Ulysses S. Grant	Republican	March 4, 1869–March 4, 1873
Ulysses S. Grant	Republican	March 4, 1873–March 4, 1877
Rutherford B. Hayes	Republican	March 4, 1877–March 4, 1881
James A. Garfield	Republican	March 4, 1881–Sept. 19, 1881
Chester A. Arthur	Republican	Sept. 20, 1881–March 4, 1885
Grover Cleveland	Democrat	March 4, 1885–March 4, 1889

President	Political Party	Term of Service
Benjamin Harrison	Republican	March 4, 1889–March 4, 1893
Grover Cleveland	Democrat	March 4, 1893–March 4, 1897
William McKinley	Republican	March 4, 1897–March 4, 1901
William McKinley	Republican	March 4, 1901–Sept. 14, 1901
Theodore Roosevelt	Republican	Sept. 14, 1901–March 4, 1905
Theodore Roosevelt	Republican	March 4, 1905–March 4, 1909
William H. Taft	Republican	March 4, 1909–March 4, 1913
Woodrow Wilson	Democrat	March 4, 1913–March 4, 1917
Woodrow Wilson	Democrat	March 4, 1917–March 4, 1921
Warren G. Harding	Republican	March 4, 1921–Aug. 2, 1923
Calvin Coolidge	Republican	Aug. 3, 1923–March 4, 1925
Calvin Coolidge	Republican	March 4, 1925–March 4, 1929
Herbert Hoover	Republican	March 4, 1929–March 4, 1933
Franklin D. Roosevelt	Democrat	March 4, 1933–Jan. 20, 1937
Franklin D. Roosevelt	Democrat	Jan. 20, 1937–Jan. 20, 1941
Franklin D. Roosevelt	Democrat	Jan. 20, 1941–Jan. 20, 1945
Franklin D. Roosevelt	Democrat	Jan. 20, 1945–April 12, 1945
Harry S. Truman	Democrat	April 12, 1945–Jan. 20, 1949
Harry S. Truman	Democrat	Jan. 20, 1949–Jan. 20, 1953
Dwight D. Eisenhower	Republican	Jan. 20, 1953–Jan. 20, 1957
Dwight D. Eisenhower	Republican	Jan. 20, 1957–Jan. 20, 1961
John F. Kennedy	Democrat	Jan. 20, 1961–Nov. 22, 1963
Lyndon B. Johnson	Democrat	Nov. 22, 1963–Jan. 20, 1965
Lyndon B. Johnson	Democrat	Jan. 20, 1965–Jan. 20, 1969
Richard Nixon	Republican	Jan. 20, 1969–Jan. 20, 1973
Richard Nixon	Republican	Jan. 20, 1973–Aug. 9, 1974
Gerald R. Ford	Republican	Aug. 9, 1974–Jan. 20, 1977
Jimmy Carter	Democrat	Jan. 20, 1977–Jan. 20, 1981
Ronald Reagan	Republican	Jan. 20, 1981–Jan. 20, 1985
Ronald Reagan	Republican	Jan. 20, 1985–Jan. 20, 1989
George Bush	Republican	Jan. 20, 1989–Jan. 20, 1993
William J. Clinton	Democrat	Jan. 20, 1993–Jan. 20, 1997
William J. Clinton	Democrat	Jan. 20, 1997–Jan. 20, 2001
George W. Bush	Republican	Jan. 20, 2001–

THUMBNAIL SKETCH OF THE SUPREME
COURT'S HISTORY

Court Era	Chief Justices	Defining Characteristics	Major Court Cases
Developmental Period (1789–1800)	John Jay (1789–1795) John Rutledge (1795) Oliver Ellsworth (1796–1800)	Low prestige: spotty attendance by justices, resignations for more "prestigious positions," hears about fifty cases Business of the Court: largely admiralty and maritime disputes Use of seriatim opinion practice	*Chisholm v. Georgia* (1793) *Hylton v. United States* (1796) *Ware v. Hylton* (1796)
The Marshall Court (1801–1835)	John Marshall (1801–1835)	Establishment of Court's role in governmental process Strong Court support for national powers (especially commerce) over states' rights Use of "Opinions of the Court," rather than seriatim practice Beginning of systematic reporting of Court opinions Despite the importance of its opinions interpreting the Constitution, the business of the Court continues to involve private law issues (maritime, property, contracts)	*Marbury v. Madison* (1803) *Fletcher v. Peck* (1810) *Dartmouth College v. Woodward* (1819) *McCulloch v. Maryland* (1819) *Cohens v. Virginia* (1821) *Gibbons v. Ogden* (1824)
Taney and Civil War Courts (1836–1888)	Roger Taney (1836–1864) Salmon Chase (1864–1873) Morrison Waite (1874–1888)	Continued assertion of federal power over states (with some accommodation for state police powers) Growing North–South splits on the Court Court showdowns with Congress at the onset and conclusion of the Civil War Growth of Court's caseload, with the majority of post–Civil War cases involving private law issues and war litigation Congress fixes Court size at nine	*Charles River Bridge v. Warren Bridge* (1837) *New York v. Miln* (1837) *Luther v. Borden* (1849) *Scott v. Sandford* (1857) *Ex parte Milligan* (1866) *Ex parte McCardle* (1869) *Civil Rights Cases* (1883)
Conservative Court Eras (1889–1937)	Melville Fuller (1888–1910) Edward White (1910–1921) William Howard Taft (1921–1930) Charles Evans Hughes (1930–1937)	But for a brief period reflecting progressivism, the Courts of this era tended to protect business interests over governmental police powers Court sets "civil rights" policy of "separate but equal" Congress relieves justices of circuit-riding duty	*United States v. E. C. Knight* (1895) *Pollock v. Farmers' Loan* (1895) *Plessy v. Ferguson* (1896) *Allgeyer v. Louisiana* (1897) *Lochner v. New York* (1905) *Hammer v. Dagenhart* (1918) *Schenck v. United States* (1919)

Court Era	Chief Justices	Defining Characteristics	Major Court Cases
		Congress, in 1925 Judiciary Act, gives Court greater discretion over its docket Despite Judiciary Act, Court's docket continues to grow, with many cases reflecting economic issues (e.g., congressional power under the Commerce Clause) Some important construction of Bill of Rights guarantees (protection of rights increases after WW I) Showdown with FDR over New Deal legislation: Court continues to strike down New Deal, leading the president to propose a Court-packing plan	*Adkins v. Children's Hospital* (1923) *Near v. Minnesota* (1931) *Powell v. Alabama* (1932) *Schechter Poultry v. United States* (1935)
The Roosevelt and World War II Court Eras (1937–1953)	Charles Evans Hughes (1937–1941) Harlan Fiske Stone (1941–1946) Fred Vinson (1946–1953)	With the "switch in time that saved nine" the Court begins to uphold federal regulations under the Commerce Clause, as well as state use of police powers Expansion of rights and liberties, until WW II and ensuing cold war Increases in nonconsensual behavior (dissents and concurrences) among the justices	*NLRB v. Jones & Laughlin Steel* (1937) *United States v. Carolene Products* (1938) *Korematsu v. United States* (1944) *Dennis v. United States* (1951) *Youngstown Sheet & Tube v. Sawyer* (1952)
The Warren Court Era (1953–1969)	Earl Warren (1953–1969)	Expansion of rights, liberties, and criminal justice Establishment of the right to privacy Emergence of Court as national policy maker Continued increase in Court's docket, with steady growth in the number of *in forma pauperis* petitions Growth in the percentage of constitutional cases on Court's plenary docket First black (Marshall) appointed to the Court	*Brown v. Board of Education* (1954) *Roth v. United States* (1957) *Mapp v. Ohio* (1961) *Baker v. Carr* (1962) *Abington School District v. Schempp* (1963) *Gideon v. Wainwright* (1963) *New York Times v. Sullivan* (1964) *Heart of Atlanta Motel v. United States* (1964) *Griswold v. Connecticut* (1965) *Miranda v. Arizona* (1966)
Republican Court Eras (1969–)	Warren Burger (1969–1986) William Rehnquist (1986–)	Attempts in some areas (e.g., criminal law) to limit or rescind Warren Court rulings Expansion of women's rights, including right to abortion Some attempt to increase state power Legitimation of affirmative action policies Court increasingly called on to resolve intergovernmental disputes, involving separation of powers or the authority of one branch of government over another Appointment of first woman (O'Connor) to the Court Rejection of race-based legislative districting Increased recognition of gay rights Intervention in the 2000 presidential election	*Reed v. Reed* (1971) *Miller v. California* (1973) *Roe v. Wade* (1973) *United States v. Nixon* (1974) *Buckley v. Valeo* (1976) *Gregg v. Georgia* (1976) *Regents of the University of California v. Bakke* (1978) *Garcia v. SAMTA* (1985) *Planned Parenthood of Southeastern Pennsylvania v. Casey* (1992) *Clinton v. Jones* (1997) *Alden v. Maine* (1999) *Boy Scouts of America v. Dale* (2000) *Bush v. Gore* (2000) *Zelman v. Simmons-Harris* (2002) *Grutter v. Bollinger* (2003) *Lawrence v. Texas* (2003)

THE JUSTICES

The justices of the Supreme Court are listed below in alphabetical order, with their birth and death years, state from which they were appointed, political party affiliation at time of appointment, educational institutions attended, appointing president, confirmation date and vote, date of service termination, and significant preappointment offices and activities.

Baldwin, Henry (1780–1844). Pennsylvania. Democrat. Yale. Nominated associate justice by Andrew Jackson; confirmed 1830 by 41–2 vote; died in office 1844. U.S. representative.

Barbour, Philip Pendleton (1783–1841). Virginia. Democrat. College of William and Mary. Nominated associate justice by Andrew Jackson; confirmed 1836 by 30–11 vote; died in office 1841. Virginia state legislator, U.S. representative, U.S. Speaker of the House, state court judge, federal district court judge.

Black, Hugo Lafayette (1886–1971). Alabama. Democrat. Birmingham Medical College, University of Alabama. Nominated associate justice by Franklin Roosevelt; confirmed 1937 by 63–16 vote; retired 1971. Alabama police court judge, county solicitor, U.S. senator.

Blackmun, Harry Andrew (1908–1999). Minnesota. Republican. Harvard. Nominated associate justice by Richard Nixon; confirmed 1970 by 94–0 vote; retired 1994. Federal appeals court judge.

Blair, John, Jr. (1732–1800). Virginia. Federalist. College of William and Mary; Middle Temple (England). Nominated associate justice by George Washington; confirmed 1789 by voice vote; resigned 1796. Virginia legislator, state court judge, delegate to Constitutional Convention.

Blatchford, Samuel (1820–1893). New York. Republican. Columbia. Nominated associate justice by Chester A. Arthur; confirmed 1882 by voice vote; died in office 1893. Federal district court judge, federal circuit court judge.

Bradley, Joseph P. (1813–1892). New Jersey. Republican. Rutgers. Nominated associate justice by Ulysses S. Grant; confirmed 1870 by 46–9 vote; died in office 1892. Private practice.

Brandeis, Louis Dembitz (1856–1941). Massachusetts. Republican. Harvard. Nominated associate justice by Woodrow Wilson; confirmed 1916 by 47–22 vote; retired 1939. Private practice.

Brennan, William Joseph, Jr. (1906–1997). New Jersey. Democrat. University of Pennsylvania, Harvard. Received recess appointment from Dwight Eisenhower to be associate justice 1956; confirmed 1957 by voice vote; retired 1990. New Jersey Supreme Court.

Brewer, David Josiah (1837–1910). Kansas. Republican. Wesleyan, Yale, Albany Law School. Nominated associate justice by Benjamin Harrison; confirmed 1889 by 53–11 vote; died in office 1910. Kansas state court judge, federal circuit court judge.

Breyer, Stephen G. (1938–). Massachusetts. Democrat. Stanford, Oxford, Harvard. Nominated associate justice by William Clinton; confirmed 1994 by 87–9 vote. Law professor; chief counsel, Senate Judiciary Committee; federal appeals court judge.

Brown, Henry B. (1836–1913). Michigan. Republican. Yale, Harvard. Nominated associate justice by Benjamin Harrison; confirmed 1890 by voice vote; retired 1906. Michigan state court judge, federal district court judge.

Burger, Warren Earl (1907–1995). Minnesota. Republican. University of Minnesota, St. Paul College of Law. Nominated chief justice by Richard Nixon; confirmed 1969 by 74–3 vote; retired 1986. Assistant U.S. attorney general, federal appeals court judge.

Burton, Harold Hitz (1888–1964). Ohio. Republican. Bowdoin College, Harvard. Nominated associate justice by Harry Truman; confirmed 1945 by voice vote; retired 1958. Ohio state legislator, mayor of Cleveland, U.S. senator.

Butler, Pierce (1866–1939). Minnesota. Republican. Carleton College. Nominated associate justice by Warren G. Harding; confirmed 1922 by 61–8 vote; died in office 1939. Minnesota county attorney, private practice.

Byrnes, James Francis (1879–1972). South Carolina. Democrat. Privately educated. Nominated associate justice by Franklin Roosevelt; confirmed 1941 by voice vote; resigned 1942. South Carolina local solicitor, U.S. representative, U.S. senator.

Campbell, John Archibald (1811–1889). Alabama. Democrat. Franklin College (University of Georgia), U.S. Military Academy. Nominated associate justice by Franklin Pierce; confirmed 1853 by voice vote; resigned 1861. Alabama state legislator.

Cardozo, Benjamin Nathan (1870–1938). New York. Democrat. Columbia. Nominated associate justice by Herbert Hoover; confirmed 1932 by voice vote; died in office 1938. State court judge.

Catron, John (1786–1865). Tennessee. Democrat. Self-educated. Nominated associate justice by Andrew Jackson; confirmed 1837 by 28–15 vote; died in office 1865. Tennessee state court judge, state chief justice.

Chase, Salmon Portland (1808–1873). Ohio. Republican. Dartmouth. Nominated chief justice by Abraham Lincoln; confirmed 1864 by voice vote; died in office 1873. U.S. senator, Ohio governor, U.S. secretary of the Treasury.

Chase, Samuel (1741–1811). Maryland. Federalist. Privately educated. Nominated associate justice by George Washington; confirmed 1796 by voice vote; died in office 1811. Maryland state legislator, delegate to Continental Congress, state court judge.

Clark, Tom Campbell (1899–1977). Texas. Democrat. University of Texas. Nominated associate justice by Harry Truman; confirmed 1949 by 73–8 vote; retired 1967. Texas local district attorney, U.S. attorney general.

Clarke, John Hessin (1857–1945). Ohio. Democrat. Western Reserve University. Nominated associate justice by Woodrow Wilson; confirmed 1916 by voice vote; resigned 1922. Federal district judge.

Clifford, Nathan (1803–1881). Maine. Democrat. Privately educated. Nominated associate justice by James Buchanan; confirmed 1858 by 26–23 vote; died in office 1881. Maine state legislator, state attorney general, U.S. representative, U.S. attorney general, minister to Mexico.

Curtis, Benjamin Robbins (1809–1874). Massachusetts. Whig. Harvard. Nominated associate justice by Millard Fillmore; confirmed 1851 by voice vote; resigned 1857. Massachusetts state legislator.

Cushing, William (1732–1810). Massachusetts. Federalist. Harvard. Nominated associate justice by George Washington; confirmed 1789 by voice vote; died in office 1810. Massachusetts state court judge, electoral college delegate.

Daniel, Peter Vivian (1784–1860). Virginia. Democrat. Princeton. Nominated associate justice by Martin Van Buren; confirmed 1841 by 22–5 vote; died in office 1860. Virginia state legislator, state Privy Council, federal district court judge.

Davis, David (1815–1886). Illinois. Republican. Kenyon College, Yale. Nominated associate justice by Abraham Lincoln; confirmed 1862 by voice vote; resigned 1877. Illinois state legislator, state court judge.

Day, William Rufus (1849–1923). Ohio. Republican. University of Michigan. Nominated associate justice by Theodore Roosevelt; confirmed 1903 by voice vote; resigned 1922. Ohio state court judge, U.S. secretary of state, federal court of appeals judge.

Douglas, William Orville (1898–1980). Connecticut. Democrat. Whitman College, Columbia. Nominated associate justice by Franklin Roosevelt; confirmed 1939 by 62–4 vote; retired 1975. Law professor, Securities and Exchange Commission.

Duvall, Gabriel (1752–1844). Maryland. Democratic/Republican. Privately educated. Nominated associate justice by James Madison; confirmed 1811 by voice vote; resigned 1835. Maryland state legislator, U.S. representative, state court judge, presidential elector, comptroller of the U.S. Treasury.

Ellsworth, Oliver (1745–1807). Connecticut. Federalist. Princeton. Nominated chief justice by George Washington; confirmed 1796 by 21–1 vote; resigned 1800. Connecticut state legislator, delegate to Continental Congress and Constitutional Convention, state court judge, U.S. senator.

Field, Stephen J. (1816–1899). California. Democrat. Williams College. Nominated associate justice by Abraham Lincoln; confirmed 1863 by voice vote; retired 1897. California state legislator, California Supreme Court.

Fortas, Abe (1910–1982). Tennessee. Democrat. Southwestern College, Yale. Nominated associate justice by Lyndon Johnson; confirmed 1965 by voice vote; resigned 1969. Counsel for numerous federal agencies, private practice.

Frankfurter, Felix (1882–1965). Massachusetts. Independent. College of the City of New York, Harvard. Nominated associate justice by Franklin Roosevelt; confirmed 1939 by voice vote; retired 1962. Law professor, War Department law officer, assistant to secretary of war, assistant to secretary of labor, War Labor Policies Board chairman.

Fuller, Melville Weston (1833–1910). Illinois. Democrat. Bowdoin College, Harvard. Nominated chief justice by Grover Cleveland; confirmed 1888 by 41–20 vote; died in office 1910. Illinois state legislator.

Ginsburg, Ruth Bader (1933–). New York. Democrat. Columbia. Nominated associate justice by William Clinton; confirmed 1993 by 96–3 vote. Professor, federal court of appeals judge.

Goldberg, Arthur J. (1908–1990). Illinois. Democrat. Northwestern. Nominated associate justice by John Kennedy; confirmed 1962 by voice vote; resigned 1965. Secretary of labor.

Gray, Horace (1828–1902). Massachusetts. Republican. Harvard. Nominated associate justice by Chester A. Arthur; confirmed 1881 by 51–5 vote; died in office 1902. Massachusetts Supreme Court.

Grier, Robert Cooper (1794–1870). Pennsylvania. Democrat. Dickinson College. Nominated associate justice by James Polk; confirmed 1846 by voice vote; retired 1870. Pennsylvania state court judge.

Harlan, John Marshall (1833–1911). Kentucky. Republican. Centre College, Transylvania University. Nominated associate justice by Rutherford B. Hayes; confirmed 1877 by voice vote; died in office 1911. Kentucky attorney general.

Harlan, John Marshall (1899–1971). New York. Republican. Princeton, Oxford, New York Law School. Nominated associate justice by Dwight Eisenhower; confirmed 1955 by 71–11 vote; retired 1971. Chief counsel for New York State Crime Commission, federal court of appeals.

Holmes, Oliver Wendell, Jr. (1841–1935). Massachusetts. Republican. Harvard. Nominated associate justice by Theodore Roosevelt; confirmed 1902 by voice vote; retired 1932. Law professor; justice, Supreme Judicial Court of Massachusetts.

Hughes, Charles Evans (1862–1948). New York. Republican. Colgate, Brown, Columbia. Nominated associate justice by William Howard Taft; confirmed 1910 by voice vote; resigned 1916; nominated chief justice by Herbert Hoover; confirmed 1930 by 52–26 vote; retired 1941. New York governor, U.S. secretary of state, Court of International Justice judge.

Hunt, Ward (1810–1886). New York. Republican. Union College. Nominated associate justice by Ulysses S. Grant; confirmed 1872 by voice vote; retired 1882. New York state legislator, mayor of Utica, state court judge.

Iredell, James (1751–1799). North Carolina. Federalist. English schools. Nominated associate justice by George Washington; confirmed 1790 by voice vote; died in office 1799. Customs official, state court judge, state attorney general.

Jackson, Howell Edmunds (1832–1895). Tennessee. Democrat. West Tennessee College, University of Virginia, Cumberland University. Nominated associate justice by Benjamin Harrison; confirmed 1893 by voice vote; died in office 1895. Tennessee state legislator, U.S. senator, federal circuit court judge, federal court of appeals judge.

Jackson, Robert Houghwout (1892–1954). New York. Democrat. Albany Law School. Nominated associate justice by Franklin Roosevelt; confirmed 1941 by voice vote; died in office 1954. Counsel for Internal Revenue Bureau and Securities and Exchange Commission, U.S. solicitor general, U.S. attorney general.

Jay, John (1745–1829). New York. Federalist. King's College (Columbia University). Nominated chief justice by George Washington; confirmed 1789 by voice vote; resigned 1795. Delegate to Continental Congress, chief justice of New York, minister to Spain and Great Britain, secretary of foreign affairs.

Johnson, Thomas (1732–1819). Maryland. Federalist. Privately educated. Nominated associate justice by George Washington; confirmed 1791 by voice vote; resigned 1793. Delegate to Annapolis Convention and Continental Congress, governor, state legislator, state court judge.

Johnson, William (1771–1834). South Carolina. Democratic/Republican. Princeton. Nominated associate justice by Thomas Jefferson; confirmed 1804 by voice vote; died in office 1834. South Carolina state legislator, state court judge.

Kennedy, Anthony McLeod (1936–). California. Republican. Stanford, London School of Economics, Harvard. Nominated associate justice by Ronald Reagan; confirmed 1988 by 97–0 vote. Federal appeals court judge.

Lamar, Joseph Rucker (1857–1916). Georgia. Democrat. University of Georgia, Bethany College, Washington and Lee. Nominated associate justice by William Howard Taft; confirmed 1910 by voice vote; died in office 1916. Georgia state legislator, Georgia Supreme Court.

Lamar, Lucius Quintus Cincinnatus (1825–1893). Mississippi. Democrat. Emory College. Nominated associate justice by Grover Cleveland; confirmed 1888 by 32–28 vote; died in office 1893. Georgia state legislator, U.S. representative, U.S. senator, U.S. secretary of the interior.

Livingston, Henry Brockholst (1757–1823). New York. Democratic/Republican. Princeton. Nominated associate justice by Thomas Jefferson; confirmed 1806 by voice vote; died in office 1823. New York state legislator, state court judge.

Lurton, Horace Harmon (1844–1914). Tennessee. Democrat. University of Chicago, Cumberland. Nominated associate justice by William Howard Taft; confirmed 1909 by voice vote; died in office 1914. Tennessee Supreme Court, federal court of appeals judge.

McKenna, Joseph (1843–1926). California. Republican. Benicia Collegiate Institute. Nominated associate justice by William McKinley; confirmed 1898 by voice vote; retired 1925. California state legislator, U.S. representative, federal court of appeals judge, U.S. attorney general.

McKinley, John (1780–1852). Alabama. Democrat. Self educated. Nominated associate justice by Martin Van Buren; confirmed 1837 by voice vote; died in office 1852. Alabama state legislator, U.S. senator, U.S. representative.

McLean, John (1785–1861). Ohio. Democrat. Privately educated. Nominated associate justice by Andrew Jackson; confirmed 1829 by voice vote; died in office 1861. U.S. representative,

Ohio Supreme Court, commissioner of U.S. General Land Office, U.S. postmaster general.

McReynolds, James Clark (1862–1946). Tennessee. Democrat. Vanderbilt, University of Virginia. Nominated associate justice by Woodrow Wilson; confirmed 1914 by 44–6 vote; retired 1941. U.S. attorney general.

Marshall, John (1755–1835). Virginia. Federalist. Privately educated, College of William and Mary. Nominated chief justice by John Adams; confirmed 1801 by voice vote; died in office 1835. Virginia state legislator, minister to France, U.S. representative, U.S. secretary of state.

Marshall, Thurgood (1908–1993). New York. Democrat. Lincoln University, Howard University. Nominated associate justice by Lyndon Johnson; confirmed 1967 by 69–11 vote; retired 1991. NAACP Legal Defense Fund, federal court of appeals judge, U.S. solicitor general.

Matthews, Stanley (1824–1889). Ohio. Republican. Kenyon College. Nominated associate justice by Rutherford B. Hayes; no Senate action on nomination; renominated associate justice by James A. Garfield; confirmed 1881 by 24–23 vote; died in office 1889. Ohio state legislator, state court judge, U.S. attorney for southern Ohio, U.S. senator.

Miller, Samuel Freeman (1816–1890). Iowa. Republican. Transylvania University. Nominated associate justice by Abraham Lincoln; confirmed 1862 by voice vote; died in office 1890. Medical doctor, private law practice, justice of the peace.

Minton, Sherman (1890–1965). Indiana. Democrat. Indiana University, Yale. Nominated associate justice by Harry Truman; confirmed 1949 by 48–16 vote; retired 1956. U.S. senator, federal court of appeals judge.

Moody, William Henry (1853–1917). Massachusetts. Republican. Harvard. Nominated associate justice by Theodore Roosevelt; confirmed 1906 by voice vote; retired 1910. Massachusetts local district attorney, U.S. representative, secretary of the navy, U.S. attorney general.

Moore, Alfred (1755–1810). North Carolina. Federalist. Privately educated. Nominated associate justice by John Adams; confirmed 1799 by voice vote; resigned 1804. North Carolina legislator, state attorney general, state court judge.

Murphy, William Francis (Frank) (1880–1949). Michigan. Democrat. University of Michigan, London's Inn (England), Trinity College (Ireland). Nominated associate justice by Franklin Roosevelt; confirmed 1940 by voice vote; died in office 1949. Michigan state court judge, mayor of Detroit, governor of the Philippines, governor of Michigan, U.S. attorney general.

Nelson, Samuel (1792–1873). New York. Democrat. Middlebury College. Nominated associate justice by John Tyler; confirmed 1845 by voice vote; retired 1872. Presidential elector, state court judge, New York Supreme Court chief justice.

O'Connor, Sandra Day (1930–). Arizona. Republican. Stanford. Nominated associate justice by Ronald Reagan; confirmed 1981 by 99–0 vote. Arizona state legislator, state court judge.

Paterson, William (1745–1806). New Jersey. Federalist. Princeton. Nominated associate justice by George Washington; confirmed 1793 by voice vote; died in office 1806. New Jersey attorney general, delegate to Constitutional Convention, U.S. senator, governor.

Peckham, Rufus Wheeler (1838–1909). New York. Democrat. Albany Boys' Academy. Nominated associate justice by Grover Cleveland; confirmed 1895 by voice vote; died in office 1909. New York local district attorney, city attorney, state court judge.

Pitney, Mahlon (1858–1924). New Jersey. Republican. Princeton. Nominated associate justice by William Howard Taft; confirmed 1912 by 50–26 vote; retired 1922. U.S. representative, New Jersey state legislator, New Jersey Supreme Court, Chancellor of New Jersey.

Powell, Lewis Franklin, Jr. (1907–1998). Virginia. Democrat. Washington and Lee, Harvard. Nominated associate justice by Richard Nixon; confirmed 1971 by 89–1 vote; retired 1987. Private practice, Virginia State Board of Education, American Bar Association president, American College of Trial Lawyers president.

Reed, Stanley Forman (1884–1980). Kentucky. Democrat. Kentucky Wesleyan, Yale, Virginia, Columbia, University of Paris. Nominated associate justice by Franklin Roosevelt; confirmed 1938 by voice vote; retired 1957. Federal Farm Board general counsel, Reconstruction Finance Corporation general counsel, U.S. solicitor general.

Rehnquist, William Hubbs (1924–). Arizona. Republican. Stanford, Harvard. Nominated associate justice by Richard Nixon; confirmed 1971 by 68–26 vote; nominated chief justice by Ronald Reagan; confirmed 1986 by 65–33 vote. Private practice, assistant U.S. attorney general.

Roberts, Owen Josephus (1875–1955). Pennsylvania. Republican. University of Pennsylvania. Nominated associate justice by Herbert Hoover; confirmed 1930 by voice vote; resigned 1945. Private practice, Pennsylvania local prosecutor, special U.S. attorney.

Rutledge, John (1739–1800). South Carolina. Federalist. Middle Temple (England). Nominated associate justice by George Washington; confirmed 1789 by voice vote; resigned 1791. Nominated chief justice by George Washington August 1795 and served as recess appointment; confirmation denied and service terminated December 1795. South Carolina legislator, state attorney general, governor, chief justice of South Carolina, delegate to Continental Congress and Constitutional Convention.

Rutledge, Wiley Blount (1894–1949). Iowa. Democrat. Maryville College, University of Wisconsin, University of Colorado. Nominated associate justice by Franklin Roosevelt; confirmed 1943 by voice vote; died in office 1949. Law professor, federal court of appeals judge.

Sanford, Edward Terry (1865–1930). Tennessee. Republican. University of Tennessee, Harvard. Nominated associate justice by Warren G. Harding; confirmed 1923 by voice vote; died in office 1930. Assistant U.S. attorney general, federal district court judge.

Scalia, Antonin (1936–). District of Columbia. Republican. Georgetown, Harvard. Nominated associate justice by Ronald Reagan; confirmed 1986 by 98–0 vote. Assistant U.S. attorney general, federal court of appeals judge.

Shiras, George, Jr. (1832–1924). Pennsylvania. Republican. Ohio University, Yale. Nominated associate justice by Benjamin Harrison; confirmed 1892 by voice vote; retired 1903. Private practice.

Souter, David Hackett (1939–). New Hampshire. Republican. Harvard, Oxford. Nominated associate justice by George Bush; confirmed 1990 by 90–9 vote. New Hampshire attorney general, state court judge, federal appeals court judge.

Stevens, John Paul (1920–). Illinois. Republican. Chicago, Northwestern. Nominated associate justice by Gerald Ford; confirmed 1975 by 98–0 vote. Federal court of appeals judge.

Stewart, Potter (1915–1985). Ohio. Republican. Yale, Cambridge. Received recess appointment from Dwight Eisenhower to be associate justice in 1958; confirmed 1959 by 70–17 vote; retired 1981. Cincinnati city council, federal court of appeals judge.

Stone, Harlan Fiske (1872–1946). New York. Republican. Amherst College, Columbia. Nominated associate justice by Calvin Coolidge; confirmed 1925 by 71–6 vote; nominated chief justice by Franklin Roosevelt; confirmed 1941 by voice vote; died in office 1946. Law professor, U.S. attorney general.

Story, Joseph (1779–1845). Massachusetts. Democratic/Republican. Harvard. Nominated associate justice by James Madison; confirmed 1811 by voice vote; died in office 1845. Massachusetts state legislator, U.S. representative.

Strong, William (1808–1895). Pennsylvania. Republican. Yale. Nominated associate justice by Ulysses S. Grant; confirmed 1870 by voice vote; retired 1880. U.S. representative, Pennsylvania Supreme Court.

Sutherland, George (1862–1942). Utah. Republican. Brigham Young, University of Michigan. Nominated associate justice by Warren G. Harding; confirmed 1922 by voice vote; retired 1938. Utah state legislator, U.S. representative, U.S. senator.

Swayne, Noah Haynes (1804–1884). Ohio. Republican. Privately educated. Nominated associate justice by Abraham Lincoln; confirmed 1862 by 38–1 vote; retired 1881. Ohio state legislator, local prosecutor, U.S. attorney for Ohio, Columbus city council.

Taft, William Howard (1857–1930). Ohio. Republican. Yale, Cincinnati. Nominated chief justice by Warren G. Harding; confirmed 1921 by voice vote; retired 1930. Ohio local prosecutor, state court judge, U.S. solicitor general, federal court of appeals judge, governor of the Philippines, secretary of war, U.S. president.

Taney, Roger Brooke (1777–1864). Maryland. Democrat. Dickinson College. Nominated associate justice by Andrew Jackson; nomination not confirmed 1835; nominated chief justice by Andrew Jackson; confirmed 1836 by 29–15 vote; died in office 1864. Maryland state legislator, state attorney general, acting secretary of war, secretary of the Treasury (nomination later rejected by Senate).

Thomas, Clarence (1948–). Georgia. Republican. Holy Cross, Yale. Nominated associate justice by George Bush; confirmed 1991 by 52–48 vote. Department of Education, Equal Employment Opportunity Commission, federal appeals court judge.

Thompson, Smith (1768–1843). New York. Democratic/Republican. Princeton. Nominated associate justice by James Monroe; confirmed 1823 by voice vote; died in office 1843. New York state legislator, state court judge, secretary of the navy.

Todd, Thomas (1765–1826). Kentucky. Democratic/Republican. Liberty Hall (Washington and Lee). Nominated associate justice by Thomas Jefferson; confirmed 1807 by voice vote; died in office 1826. Kentucky state court judge, state chief justice.

Trimble, Robert (1776–1828). Kentucky. Democratic/Republican. Kentucky Academy. Nominated associate justice by John Quincy Adams; confirmed 1826 by 27–5 vote; died in office 1828. Kentucky state legislator, state court judge, U.S. attorney, federal district court judge.

Van Devanter, Willis (1859–1941). Wyoming. Republican. Indiana Asbury University, University of Cincinnati. Nominated associate justice by William Howard Taft; confirmed 1910 by voice vote; retired 1937. Cheyenne city attorney, Wyoming territorial legislature, Wyoming Supreme Court, assistant U.S. attorney general, federal court of appeals judge.

Vinson, Frederick Moore (1890–1953). Kentucky. Democrat. Centre College. Nominated chief justice by Harry Truman; confirmed 1946 by voice vote; died in office 1953. U.S. representative, federal appeals court judge, director of Office of Economic Stabilization, secretary of the Treasury.

Waite, Morrison Remick (1816–1888). Ohio. Republican. Yale. Nominated chief justice by Ulysses S. Grant; confirmed 1874 by 63–0 vote; died in office 1888. Private practice, Ohio state legislator.

Warren, Earl (1891–1974). California. Republican. University of California. Recess appointment as chief justice by Dwight Eisenhower 1953; confirmed 1954 by voice vote; retired 1969. California local district attorney, state attorney general, governor.

Washington, Bushrod (1762–1829). Virginia. Federalist. College of William and Mary. Nominated associate justice by John Adams; confirmed 1798 by voice vote; died in office 1829. Virginia state legislator.

Wayne, James Moore (1790–1867). Georgia. Democrat. Princeton. Nominated associate justice by Andrew Jackson; confirmed 1835 by voice vote; died in office 1867. Georgia state legislator, mayor of Savannah, state court judge, U.S. representative.

White, Byron Raymond (1917–2002). Colorado. Democrat. University of Colorado, Oxford, Yale. Nominated associate justice by John Kennedy; confirmed 1962 by voice vote; retired 1993. Deputy U.S. attorney general.

White, Edward Douglass (1845–1921). Louisiana. Democrat. Mount St. Mary's College, Georgetown. Nominated associate justice by Grover Cleveland; confirmed 1894 by voice vote; nominated chief justice by William Howard Taft; confirmed 1910 by voice vote; died in office 1921. Louisiana state legislator, Louisiana Supreme Court, U.S. senator.

Whittaker, Charles Evans (1901–1973). Missouri. Republican. University of Kansas City. Nominated associate justice by Dwight Eisenhower; confirmed 1957 by voice vote; retired 1962. Federal district court judge, federal appeals court judge.

Wilson, James (1742–1798). Pennsylvania. Federalist. University of St. Andrews (Scotland). Nominated associate justice by George Washington; confirmed 1789 by voice vote; died in office 1798. Delegate to Continental Congress and Constitutional Convention.

Woodbury, Levi (1789–1851). New Hampshire. Democrat. Dartmouth, Tapping Reeve Law School. Nominated associate justice by James Polk; confirmed 1846 by voice vote; died in office 1851. New Hampshire state legislator, state court judge, governor, U.S. senator, secretary of the navy, secretary of the Treasury.

Woods, William B. (1824–1887). Georgia. Republican. Western Reserve College, Yale. Nominated associate justice by Rutherford B. Hayes; confirmed 1880 by 39–8 vote; died in office 1887. Ohio state legislator, Alabama chancellor, federal circuit court judge.

NATURAL COURTS

Natural Court[a]	Justices[b]	Dates	U.S. Reports[c]
Jay 1	Jay (*o* October 19, 1789), J. Rutledge (*o* February 15, 1790), Cushing (*o* February 2, 1790), Wilson (*o* October 5, 1789), Blair (*o* February 2, 1790)	October 5, 1789–May 12, 1790	2
Jay 2	Jay, Rutledge (*r* March 5, 1791), Cushing, Wilson, Blair, Iredell (*o* May 12, 1790)	May 12, 1790–August 6, 1792	2
Jay 3	Jay, Cushing, Wilson, Blair, Iredell, T. Johnson (*o* August 6, 1792; *r* January 16, 1793)	August 6, 1792–March 11, 1793	2
Jay 4	Jay (*r* June 29, 1795), Cushing, Wilson, Blair, Iredell, Paterson (*o* March 11, 1793)	March 11, 1793–August 12, 1795	2–3
Rutledge 1	J. Rutledge (*o* August 12, 1795; *rj* December 15, 1795), Cushing, Wilson, Blair (*r* January 27, 1796), Iredell, Paterson	August 12, 1795–February 4, 1796	3
No chief justice	Cushing, Wilson, Iredell, Paterson, S. Chase (*o* February 4, 1796)	February 4, 1796–March 8, 1796	3
Ellsworth 1	Ellsworth (*o* March 8, 1796), Cushing, Wilson (*d* August 21, 1798), Iredell, Paterson, S. Chase	March 8, 1796–February 4, 1799	3
Ellsworth 2	Ellsworth, Cushing, Iredell (*d* October 20, 1799), Paterson, S. Chase, Washington (*o* February 4, 1799)	February 4, 1799–April 21, 1800	3–4
Ellsworth 3	Ellsworth (*r* December 15, 1800), Cushing, Paterson, S. Chase, Washington, Moore (*o* April 21, 1800)	April 21, 1800–February 4, 1801	4
Marshall 1	Marshall (*o* February 4, 1801), Cushing, Paterson, S. Chase, Washington, Moore (*r* January 26, 1804)	February 4, 1801–May 7, 1804	5–6
Marshall 2	Marshall, Cushing, Paterson (*d* September 9, 1806), S. Chase, Washington, W. Johnson (*o* May 7, 1804)	May 7, 1804–January 20, 1807	6–7
Marshall 3	Marshall, Cushing, S. Chase, Washington, W. Johnson, Livingston (*o* January 20, 1807)	January 20, 1807–May 4, 1807	8
Marshall 4	Marshall, Cushing (*d* September 13, 1810), S. Chase (*d* June 19, 1811), Washington, W. Johnson, Livingston, Todd (*o* May 4, 1807)	May 4, 1807–November 23, 1811	8–10

Natural Court[a]	Justices[b]	Dates	U.S. Reports[c]
Marshall 5	Marshall, Washington, W. Johnson, Livingston, Todd, Duvall (*o* November 23, 1811)	November 23, 1811–February 3, 1812	11
Marshall 6	Marshall, Washington, W. Johnson, Livingston (*d* March 18, 1823), Todd, Duvall, Story (*o* February 3, 1812)	February 3, 1812–February 10, 1824	11–21
Marshall 7	Marshall, Washington, W. Johnson, Todd (*d* February 7, 1826), Duvall, Story, Thompson (*o* February 10, 1824)	February 10, 1824–June 16, 1826	22–24
Marshall 8	Marshall, Washington (*d* November 26, 1829), W. Johnson, Duvall, Story, Thompson, Trimble (*o* June 16, 1826; *d* August 25, 1828)	June 16, 1826–January 11, 1830	25–27
Marshall 9	Marshall, W. Johnson (*d* August 4, 1834), Duvall (*r* January 14, 1835), Story, Thompson, McLean (*o* January 11, 1830), Baldwin (*o* January 18, 1830)	January 11, 1830–January 14, 1835	28–33
Marshall 10	Marshall (*d* July 6, 1835), Story, Thompson, McLean, Baldwin, Wayne (*o* January 14, 1835)	January 14, 1835–March 28, 1836	34–35
Taney 1	Taney (*o* March 28, 1836), Story, Thompson, McLean, Baldwin, Wayne	March 28, 1836–May 12, 1836	35
Taney 2	Taney, Story, Thompson, McLean, Baldwin, Wayne, Barbour (*o* May 12, 1836)	May 12, 1836–May 1, 1837	35–36
Taney 3	Taney, Story, Thompson, McLean, Baldwin, Wayne, Barbour, Catron (*o* May 1, 1837)	May 1, 1837–January 9, 1838	36
Taney 4	Taney, Story, Thompson, McLean, Baldwin, Wayne, Barbour (*d* February 25, 1841), Catron, McKinley (*o* January 9, 1838)	January 9, 1838–January 10, 1842	37–40
Taney 5	Taney, Story, Thompson (*d* December 18, 1843), McLean, Baldwin (*d* April 21, 1844), Wayne, Catron, McKinley, Daniel (*o* January 10, 1842)	January 10, 1842–February 27, 1845	40–44
Taney 6	Taney, Story (*d* September 10, 1845), McLean, Wayne, Catron, McKinley, Daniel, Nelson (*o* February 27, 1845)	February 27, 1845–September 23, 1845	44
Taney 7	Taney, McLean, Wayne, Catron, McKinley, Daniel, Nelson, Woodbury (*o* September 23, 1845)	September 23, 1845–August 10, 1846	44–45
Taney 8	Taney, McLean, Wayne, Catron, McKinley, Daniel, Nelson, Woodbury (*d* September 4, 1851), Grier (*o* August 10, 1846)	August 10, 1846–October 10, 1851	46–52
Taney 9	Taney, McLean, Wayne, Catron, McKinley (*d* July 19, 1852), Daniel, Nelson, Grier, Curtis (*o* October 10, 1851)	October 10, 1851–April 11, 1853	53–55
Taney 10	Taney, McLean, Wayne, Catron, Daniel, Nelson, Grier, Curtis (*r* September 30, 1857), Campbell (*o* April 11, 1853)	April 11, 1853–January 21, 1858	56–61
Taney 11	Taney, McLean (*d* April 4, 1861), Wayne, Catron, Daniel (*d* May 31, 1860), Nelson, Grier, Campbell (*r* April 30, 1861), Clifford (*o* January 21, 1858)	January 21, 1858–January 27, 1862	61–66
Taney 12	Taney, Wayne, Catron, Nelson, Grier, Clifford, Swayne (*o* January 27, 1862)	January 27, 1862–July 21, 1862	66
Taney 13	Taney, Wayne, Catron, Nelson, Grier, Clifford, Swayne, Miller (*o* July 21, 1862)	July 21, 1862–December 10, 1862	67

Natural Court[a]	Justices[b]	Dates	U.S. Reports[c]
Taney 14	Taney, Wayne, Catron, Nelson, Grier, Clifford, Swayne, Miller, Davis (*o* December 10, 1862)	December 10, 1862– May 20, 1863	67
Taney 15	Taney (*d* October 12, 1864), Wayne, Catron, Nelson, Grier, Clifford, Swayne, Miller, Davis, Field (*o* May 20, 1863)	May 20, 1863– December 15, 1864	67–68
Chase 1	S. P. Chase (*o* December 15, 1864), Wayne (*d* July 5, 1867), Catron (*d* May 30, 1865), Nelson, Grier (*r* January 31, 1870), Clifford, Swayne, Miller, Davis, Field	December 15, 1864– March 14, 1870	69–76
Chase 2	S. P. Chase, Nelson (*r* November 28, 1872), Clifford, Swayne, Miller, Davis, Field, Strong (*o* March 14, 1870), Bradley (*o* March 23, 1870)	March 14, 1870– January 9, 1873	76–82
Chase 3	S. P. Chase (*d* May 7, 1873), Clifford, Swayne, Miller, Davis, Field, Strong, Bradley, Hunt (*o* January 9, 1873)	January 9, 1873– March 4, 1874	82–86
Waite 1	Waite (*o* March 4, 1874), Clifford, Swayne, Miller, Davis (*r* March 4, 1877), Field, Strong, Bradley, Hunt	March 4, 1874– December 10, 1877	86–95
Waite 2	Waite, Clifford, Swayne, Miller, Field, Strong (*r* December 14, 1880), Bradley, Hunt, Harlan I (*o* December 10, 1877)	December 10, 1877– January 5, 1881	95–103
Waite 3	Waite, Clifford, Swayne (*r* January 24, 1881), Miller, Field, Bradley, Hunt, Harlan I, Woods (*o* January 5, 1881)	January 5, 1881– May 17, 1881	103
Waite 4	Waite, Clifford (*d* July 25, 1881), Miller, Field, Bradley, Hunt, Harlan I, Woods, Matthews (*o* May 17, 1881)	May 17, 1881– January 9, 1882	103–104
Waite 5	Waite, Miller, Field, Bradley, Hunt (*r* January 27, 1882), Harlan I, Woods, Matthews, Gray (*o* January 9, 1882)	January 9, 1882– April 3, 1882	104–105
Waite 6	Waite, Miller, Field, Bradley, Harlan I, Woods (*d* May 14, 1887), Matthews, Gray, Blatchford (*o* April 3, 1882)	April 3, 1882– January 18, 1888	105–124
Waite 7	Waite (*d* March 23, 1888), Miller, Field, Bradley, Harlan I, Matthews, Gray, Blatchford, L. Lamar (*o* January 18, 1888)	January 18, 1888– October 8, 1888	124–127
Fuller 1	Fuller (*o* October 8, 1888), Miller, Field, Bradley, Harlan I, Matthews (*d* March 22, 1889), Gray, Blatchford, L. Lamar	October 8, 1888– January 6, 1890	128–132
Fuller 2	Fuller, Miller (*d* October 13, 1890), Field, Bradley, Harlan I, Gray, Blatchford, L. Lamar, Brewer (*o* January 6, 1890)	January 6, 1890– January 5, 1891	132–137
Fuller 3	Fuller, Field, Bradley (*d* January 22, 1892), Harlan I, Gray, Blatchford, L. Lamar, Brewer, Brown (*o* January 5, 1891)	January 5, 1891– October 10, 1892	137–145
Fuller 4	Fuller, Field, Harlan I, Gray, Blatchford, L. Lamar (*d* January 23, 1893), Brewer, Brown, Shiras (*o* October 10, 1892)	October 10, 1892– March 4, 1893	146–148
Fuller 5	Fuller, Field, Harlan I, Gray, Blatchford (*d* July 7, 1893), Brewer, Brown, Shiras, H. Jackson (*o* March 4, 1893)	March 4, 1893– March 12, 1894	148–151
Fuller 6	Fuller, Field, Harlan I, Gray, Brewer, Brown, Shiras, H. Jackson (*d* August 8, 1895), E. White (*o* March 12, 1894)	March 12, 1894– January 6, 1896	152–160

Natural Court[a]	Justices[b]	Dates	U.S. Reports[c]
Fuller 7	Fuller, Field (r December 1, 1897), Harlan I, Gray, Brewer, Brown, Shiras, E. White, Peckham (o January 6, 1896)	January 6, 1896–January 26, 1898	160–169
Fuller 8	Fuller, Harlan I, Gray (d September 15, 1902), Brewer, Brown, Shiras, E. White, Peckham, McKenna (o January 26, 1898)	January 26, 1898–December 8, 1902	169–187
Fuller 9	Fuller, Harlan I, Brewer, Brown, Shiras (r February 23, 1903), E. White, Peckham, McKenna, Holmes (o December 8, 1902)	December 8, 1902–March 2, 1903	187–188
Fuller 10	Fuller, Harlan I, Brewer, Brown (r May 28, 1906), E. White, Peckham, McKenna, Holmes, Day (o March 2, 1903)	March 2, 1903–December 17, 1906	188–203
Fuller 11	Fuller, Harlan I, Brewer, E. White, Peckham (d October 24, 1909), McKenna, Holmes, Day, Moody (o December 17, 1906)	December 17, 1906–January 3, 1910	203–215
Fuller 12	Fuller (d July 4, 1910), Harlan I, Brewer (d March 28, 1910), E. White, McKenna, Holmes, Day, Moody, Lurton (o January 3, 1910)	January 3, 1910–October 10, 1910	215–217
No chief justice	Harlan I, E. White (p December 18, 1910), McKenna, Holmes, Day, Moody (r November 20, 1910), Lurton, Hughes (o October 10, 1910)	October 10, 1910–December 19, 1910	218
White 1	E. White (o December 19, 1910), Harlan I (d October 14, 1911), McKenna, Holmes, Day, Lurton, Hughes, Van Devanter (o January 3, 1911), J. Lamar (o January 3, 1911)	December 19, 1910–March 18, 1912	218–223
White 2	E. White, McKenna, Holmes, Day, Lurton (d July 12, 1914), Hughes, Van Devanter, J. Lamar, Pitney (o March 18, 1912)	March 18, 1912–October 12, 1914	223–234
White 3	E. White, McKenna, Holmes, Day, Hughes, Van Devanter, J. Lamar (d January 2, 1916), Pitney, McReynolds (o October 12, 1914)	October 12, 1914–June 5, 1916	235–241
White 4	E. White, McKenna, Holmes, Day, Hughes (r June 10, 1916), Van Devanter, Pitney, McReynolds, Brandeis (o June 5, 1916)	June 5, 1916–October 9, 1916	241
White 5	E. White (d May 19, 1921), McKenna, Holmes, Day, Van Devanter, Pitney, McReynolds, Brandeis, Clarke (o October 9, 1916)	October 9, 1916–July 11, 1921	242–256
Taft 1	Taft (o July 11, 1921), McKenna, Holmes, Day, Van Devanter, Pitney, McReynolds, Brandeis, Clarke (r September 18, 1922)	July 11, 1921–October 2, 1922	257–259
Taft 2	Taft, McKenna, Holmes, Day (r November 13, 1922), Van Devanter, Pitney (r December 31, 1922), McReynolds, Brandeis, Sutherland (o October 2, 1922)	October 2, 1922–January 2, 1923	260
Taft 3	Taft, McKenna, Holmes, Van Devanter, McReynolds, Brandeis, Sutherland, Butler (o January 2, 1923)	January 2, 1923–February 19, 1923	260
Taft 4	Taft, McKenna (r January 5, 1925), Holmes, Van Devanter, McReynolds, Brandeis, Sutherland, Butler, Sanford (o February 19, 1923)	February 19, 1923–March 2, 1925	260–267
Taft 5	Taft (r February 3, 1930), Holmes, Van Devanter, McReynolds, Brandeis, Sutherland, Butler, Sanford, Stone (o March 2, 1925)	March 2, 1925–February 24, 1930	267–280
Hughes 1	Hughes (o February 24, 1930), Holmes, Van Devanter, McReynolds, Brandeis, Sutherland, Butler, Sanford (d March 8, 1930), Stone	February 24, 1930–June 2, 1930	280–281
Hughes 2	Hughes, Holmes (r January 12, 1932), Van Devanter, McReynolds, Brandeis, Sutherland, Butler, Stone, Roberts (o June 2, 1930)	June 2, 1930–March 14, 1932	281–285

Natural Court[a]	Justices[b]	Dates	U.S. Reports[c]
Hughes 3	Hughes, Van Devanter (*r* June 2, 1937), McReynolds, Brandeis, Sutherland, Butler, Stone, Roberts, Cardozo (*o* March 14, 1932)	March 14, 1932–August 19, 1937	285–301
Hughes 4	Hughes, McReynolds, Brandeis, Sutherland (*r* January 17, 1938), Butler, Stone, Roberts, Cardozo, Black (*o* August 19, 1937)	August 19, 1937 January 31, 1938	302–303
Hughes 5	Hughes, McReynolds, Brandeis, Butler, Stone, Roberts, Cardozo (*d* July 9, 1938), Black, Reed (*o* January 31, 1938)	January 31, 1938–January 30, 1939	303–305
Hughes 6	Hughes, McReynolds, Brandeis (*r* February 13, 1939), Butler, Stone, Roberts, Black, Reed, Frankfurter (*o* January 30, 1939)	January 30, 1939–April 17, 1939	306
Hughes 7	Hughes, McReynolds, Butler (*d* November 16, 1939), Stone, Roberts, Black, Reed, Frankfurter, Douglas (*o* April 17, 1939)	April 17, 1939–February 5, 1940	306–308
Hughes 8	Hughes (*r* July 1, 1941), McReynolds (*r* January 31, 1941), Stone (*p* July 2, 1941), Roberts, Black, Reed, Frankfurter, Douglas, Murphy (*o* February 5, 1940)	February 5, 1940–July 3, 1941	308–313
Stone 1	Stone (*o* July 3, 1941), Roberts, Black, Reed, Frankfurter, Douglas, Murphy, Byrnes (*o* July 8, 1941; *r* October 3, 1942), R. Jackson (*o* July 11, 1941)	July 3, 1941–February 15, 1943	314–318
Stone 2	Stone, Roberts (*r* July 31, 1945), Black, Reed, Frankfurter, Douglas, Murphy, R. Jackson, W. Rutledge (*o* February 15, 1943)	February 15, 1943–October 1, 1945	318–326
Stone 3	Stone (*d* April 22, 1946), Black, Reed, Frankfurter, Douglas, Murphy, R. Jackson, W. Rutledge, Burton (*o* October 1, 1945)	October 1, 1945–June 24, 1946	326–328
Vinson 1	Vinson (*o* June 24, 1946), Black, Reed, Frankfurter, Douglas, Murphy (*d* July 19, 1949), R. Jackson, W. Rutledge, Burton	June 24, 1946–August 24, 1949	329–338
Vinson 2	Vinson, Black, Reed, Frankfurter, Douglas, R. Jackson, W. Rutledge (*d* September 10, 1949), Burton, Clark (*o* August 24, 1949)	August 24, 1949–October 12, 1949	338
Vinson 3	Vinson (*d* September 8, 1953), Black, Reed, Frankfurter, Douglas, R. Jackson, Burton, Clark, Minton (*o* October 12, 1949)	October 12, 1949–October 5, 1953	338–346
Warren 1	Warren (*o* October 5, 1953), Black, Reed, Frankfurter, Douglas, R. Jackson (*d* October 9, 1954), Burton, Clark, Minton	October 5, 1953–March 28, 1955	346–348
Warren 2	Warren, Black, Reed, Frankfurter, Douglas, Burton, Clark, Minton (*r* October 15, 1956), Harlan II (*o* March 28, 1955)	March 28, 1955–October 16, 1956	348–352
Warren 3	Warren, Black, Reed (*r* February 25, 1957), Frankfurter, Douglas, Burton, Clark, Harlan II, Brennan (*o* October 16, 1956)	October 16, 1956–March 25, 1957	352
Warren 4	Warren, Black, Frankfurter, Douglas, Burton (*r* October 13, 1958), Clark, Harlan II, Brennan, Whittaker (*o* March 25, 1957)	March 25, 1957–October 14, 1958	352–358
Warren 5	Warren, Black, Frankfurter, Douglas, Clark, Harlan II, Brennan, Whittaker (*r* March 31, 1962), Stewart (*o* October 14, 1958)	October 14, 1958–April 16, 1962	358–369
Warren 6	Warren, Black, Frankfurter (*r* August 28, 1962), Douglas, Clark, Harlan II, Brennan, Stewart, B. White (*o* April 16, 1962)	April 16, 1962–October 1, 1962	369–370
Warren 7	Warren, Black, Douglas, Clark, Harlan II, Brennan, Stewart, B. White, Goldberg (*o* October 1, 1962; *r* July 25, 1965)	October 1, 1962–October 4, 1965	371–381

Natural Court[a]	Justices[b]	Dates	U.S. Reports[c]
Warren 8	Warren, Black, Douglas, Clark (*r* June 12, 1967), Harlan II, Brennan, Stewart, B. White, Fortas (*o* October 4, 1965)	October 4, 1965–October 2, 1967	382–388
Warren 9	Warren (*r* June 23, 1969), Black, Douglas, Harlan II, Brennan, Stewart, B. White, Fortas (*r* May 14, 1969), T. Marshall (*o* October 2, 1967)	October 2, 1967–June 23, 1969	389–395
Burger 1	Burger (*o* June 23, 1969), Black, Douglas, Harlan II, Brennan, Stewart, B. White, T. Marshall	June 23, 1969–June 9, 1970	395–397
Burger 2	Burger, Black (*r* September 17, 1971), Douglas, Harlan II (*r* September 23, 1971), Brennan, Stewart, B. White, T. Marshall, Blackmun (*o* June 9, 1970)	June 9, 1970–January 7, 1972	397–404
Burger 3	Burger, Douglas (*r* November 12, 1975), Brennan, Stewart, B. White, T. Marshall, Blackmun, Powell (*o* January 7, 1972), Rehnquist (*o* January 7, 1972)	January 7, 1972–December 19, 1975	404–423
Burger 4	Burger, Brennan, Stewart (*r* July 3, 1981), B. White, T. Marshall, Blackmun, Powell, Rehnquist, Stevens (*o* December 19, 1975)	December 19, 1975–September 25, 1981	423–453
Burger 5	Burger (*r* September 26, 1986), Brennan, B. White, T. Marshall, Blackmun, Powell, Rehnquist (*p* September 26, 1986), Stevens, O'Connor (*o* September 25, 1981)	September 25, 1981–September 26, 1986	453–478
Rehnquist 1	Rehnquist (*o* September 26, 1986), Brennan, B. White, T. Marshall, Blackmun, Powell (*r* June 26, 1987), Stevens, O'Connor, Scalia (*o* September 26, 1986)	September 26, 1986–February 18, 1988	478–484
Rehnquist 2	Rehnquist, Brennan (*r* July 20, 1990), B. White, T. Marshall, Blackmun, Stevens, O'Connor, Scalia, Kennedy (*o* February 18, 1988)	February 18, 1988–October 9, 1990	484–498
Rehnquist 3	Rehnquist, B. White, T. Marshall (*r* October 1, 1991), Blackmun, Stevens, O'Connor, Scalia, Kennedy, Souter (*o* October 9, 1990)	October 9, 1990–October 23, 1991	498–501
Rehnquist 4	Rehnquist, B. White (*r* July 1, 1993), Blackmun, Stevens, O'Connor, Scalia, Kennedy, Souter, Thomas (*o* October 23, 1991)	October 23, 1991–August 10, 1993	502–509
Rehnquist 5	Rehnquist, Blackmun (*r* August 3, 1994), Stevens, O'Connor, Scalia, Kennedy, Souter, Thomas, Ginsburg (*o* August 10, 1993)	August 10, 1993–August 3, 1994	510–512
Rehnquist 6	Rehnquist, Stevens, O'Connor, Scalia, Kennedy, Souter, Thomas, Ginsburg, Breyer (*o* August 3, 1994)	August 3, 1994–	513–

SOURCE: Lee Epstein, Jeffrey A. Segal, Harold J. Spaeth, and Thomas G. Walker, *The Supreme Court Compendium: Data, Decisions, and Developments,* 2d ed. (Washington, D.C.: Congressional Quarterly, 1996), Table 5-2.

NOTE: The term *natural court* refers to a period of time during which the membership of the Court remains stable. There are a number of ways to determine the beginning and end of a natural court. Here a natural court begins when a new justice takes the oath of office and continues until the next new justice takes the oath. When two or more justices join the Court within a period of fifteen or fewer days, we treat it as the beginning of a single natural court (for example, Marshall 9, Chase 2, White 1, and Stone 1).

a. Numbered sequentially within the tenure of each chief justice.

b. The name of the chief justice appears first, with associate justices following in order of descending seniority. In addition, the date a justice left the Court, creating a vacancy for the next justice to be appointed, is given, as well as the date the new justice took the oath of office. *o* = oath of office taken, *d* = died, *r* = resigned or retired, *rj* = recess appointment rejected by Senate, *p* = promoted from associate justice to chief justice.

c. Volumes of *United States Reports* in which the actions of each natural court generally may be found. Because of the way decisions were published prior to the twentieth century, these volume numbers may not contain all of the decisions of a given natural court. They do, however, provide a general guide to the location of each natural court's published decisions. Natural courts of short duration may have little business published in the reports.

SUPREME COURT CALENDAR

Activity	Time
Start of Term	First Monday in October
Oral Argument Cycle	October–April: Mondays, Tuesdays, Wednesdays in seven two-week sessions
Recess Cycle	October–April: two or more consecutive weeks after two weeks of oral argument; Christmas, Easter holidays
Conferences	Wednesday afternoon following Monday oral arguments (discussion of four Monday cases)
	Friday following Tuesday, Wednesday oral arguments (discussion of eight Tuesday–Wednesday cases; certiorari petitions)
	Friday before two-week oral argument period
Majority Opinion Assignment	Following oral arguments/conferences
Opinion Announcement	Throughout term with bulk coming in spring/summer
Summer Recess	Late June/early July until first Monday in October
Initial Conference	Late September (resolve old business, consider certiorari petitions from the summer)

APPENDIX 8
BRIEFING SUPREME COURT CASES

1. **What is the name of the case?**
   The name is important because it *generally* reveals which party is asking the Court to review the case. The name appearing first is usually (but not always) the appellant/petitioner, the party that lost in the court below.

2. **In what year did the Supreme Court decide the case?**
   The year is important because it will help to put the case into a legal and historical context. See Thumbnail Sketch of Supreme Court History for more detail.

3. **What circumstances triggered the dispute?**

4. **What statute or action triggered the dispute?**

5. **What provision of the Constitution is at issue?**

6. **What is the basic legal question(s) the Court is being asked to address?**

7. **What was the outcome of the dispute?**

8. **How did the majority reach its decision? What was its legal reasoning?**

9. **What legal doctrine, standards, or policy did the majority announce?**

10. **What other views (dissents, concurrences) were expressed?**

AN EXAMPLE: *Texas v. Johnson* (1989)

1. Case Name. *Texas v. Johnson*
2. Year Case Decided by Supreme Court. 1989
3. Facts that Triggered the Dispute. While the Republican National Convention was meeting in Dallas, Texas, in 1984, Gregory Johnson took part in a demonstration, protesting policies of the Reagan administration. During the demonstration, Johnson burned an American flag, and Dallas police arrested him.
4. Statute. Johnson was arrested and subsequently convicted under a Texas law that made it a criminal activity to desecrate a "venerable" object, including a state or a national flag.
5. Provision of the Constitution. Johnson alleged that his conviction, under the Texas state law, violated First Amendment guarantees of freedom of expression.
6. Legal Question. Is flag burning, in the context of this dispute, an activity protected by the First Amendment?
7. Outcome. In a 5–4 ruling, the Court held for Johnson.
8. Legal Reasoning of the Majority. In delivering the opinion of the Court, Justice William J. Brennan Jr. held that:

   a. Johnson's action constituted expressive conduct, allowing him to raise a First Amendment claim.

   b. Although governments have a "freer hand" in restricting "conduct" (as opposed to pure speech or writing), they still must demonstrate a sufficiently important governmental interest in regulating the activity in question.

   c. Texas's stated interests—preventing breaches of the peace and preserving the flag as a symbol of national unity—are insufficient to prohibit Johnson's expressive conduct.

9. Legal Doctrine. The majority:

   a. set policy in an area of the law that was previously murky. States may not "foster" their own view "of the flag by prohibiting expressive conduct relating to it."

   b. reaffirmed past precedents, suggesting that in such cases the Court will not only consider the nature of the expresion (whether it is verbal or nonverbal), but the governmental interest at stake.

   c. reaffirmed a general commitment to the fundamental nature of the First Amendment: "If there is a bedrock principle underlying the First Amendment, it is that the Government may not prohibit the expression of an idea simply because society finds that idea itself offensive or disagreeable."

10. Other Points of View.

   a. Justice Kennedy concurred: while the flag "holds a lonely place of honor," the Constitution mandates the outcome expressed by the majority. In short, sometimes justices "make decisions" they do not "like." But they make them "because they are right."

   b. Chief Justice Rehnquist (joined by White and O'Connor) dissented: freedom of expression is not absolute: conduct may be prohibited in light of legitimate governmental interests. Here, those interests outweigh the expression.

   i. Johnson's conduct had the tendency to incite a breach of the peace.

   ii. the American flag is a "visible symbol embodying our Nation"; it does not represent a political idea or philosophy, nor is it just "another symbol."

   c. Justice Stevens dissented: the question of flag desecration is unique. Cases involving other forms of symbolic expression are not dispositive of it. Our nation's flag symbolizes those values—liberty and equality—that "are worth fighting for." As such it cannot be "true that the flag . . . is not itself worthy of protection from unnecessary desecration.

Abstention A doctrine or policy of the federal courts to refrain from deciding a case so that the issues involved may first be definitively resolved by state courts.

Acquittal A decision by a court that a person charged with a crime is not guilty.

Advisory opinion An opinion issued by a court indicating how it would rule on a question of law should such a question come before it in an actual case. Federal courts do not hand down advisory opinions, but some state courts do.

Affidavit A written statement of facts voluntarily made under oath or affirmation.

Affirm To uphold a decision of a lower court.

A fortiori With greater force or reason.

Aggravating circumstances Conditions that increase the seriousness of a crime but are not a part of its legal definition.

Amicus curiae "Friend of the court." A person (or group), not a party to a case, who submits views (usually in the form of written briefs) on how the case should be decided.

Ante Prior to.

Appeal The procedure by which a case is taken to a superior court for a review of the lower court's decision.

Appellant The party dissatisfied with a lower court ruling who appeals the case to a superior court for review.

Appellate jurisdiction The legal authority of a superior court to review and render judgment on a decision by a lower court.

Appellee The party usually satisfied with a lower court ruling against whom an appeal is taken.

Arbitrary Unreasonable; capricious; not done in accordance with established principles.

Arguendo In the course of argument.

Arraignment A formal stage of the criminal process in which the defendants are brought before a judge, confronted with the charges against them, and they enter a plea to those charges.

Arrest Physically taking into custody or otherwise depriving freedom of a person suspected of violating the law.

Attainder, Bill of A legislative act declaring a person or easily identified group of people guilty of a crime and imposing punishments without the benefit of a trial. Such legislative acts are prohibited by the United States Constitution.

Attest To swear to; to be a witness.

Bail A security deposit, usually in the form of cash or bond, which allows those accused of crimes to be released from jail and guarantees their appearance at trial.

Balancing test A process of judicial decision making in which the court weighs the relative merits of the rights of the individual against the interests of the government.

Bench trial A trial, without a jury, conducted before a judge.

Bicameral A legislature, such as the U.S. Congress, with two houses.

Bona fide Good faith.

Brandeis brief A legal argument that stresses economic and sociological evidence along with traditional legal authorities. Named after Louis Brandeis, who pioneered its use.

Brief A written argument of law and fact submitted to the court by an attorney representing a party having an interest in a lawsuit.

Case A legal dispute or controversy brought to a court for resolution.

Case-in-chief The primary evidence offered by a party in a court case.

Case law Law that has evolved from past court decisions, as opposed to law created by legislative acts.

Case or controversy rule The constitutional requirement that courts may only hear real disputes brought by adverse parties.

Casus faederis In international law, the case of a treaty. The particular event contemplated by the treaty or stipulated for, or which comes within its terms.

Certification A procedure whereby a lower court requests that a superior court rule on specified legal questions so that the lower court may correctly apply the law.

Certiorari, Writ of An order of an appellate court to an inferior court to send up the records of a case that the appellate court has elected to review. The primary method by which the U.S. Supreme Court exercises its discretionary jurisdiction to accept appeals for a full hearing.

Civil law Law that deals with the private rights of individuals (e.g., property, contracts, negligence), as contrasted with criminal law.

Class action A lawsuit brought by one or more persons who represent themselves and all others similarly situated.

Collateral estoppel A rule of law that prohibits an already settled issue from being relitigated in another form.

Comity The principle by which the courts of one jurisdiction give respect and deference to the laws and legal decisions of another jurisdiction.

Common law Law that has evolved from usage and custom as reflected in the decisions of courts.

Compensatory damages A monetary award, equivalent to the loss sustained, to be paid to the injured party by the party at fault.

Concurrent powers Authority that may be exercised by both the state and federal governments.

Concurring opinion An opinion that agrees with the result reached by the majority, but disagrees as to the appropriate rationale for reaching that result.

Confrontation The right of a criminal defendant to see the testimony of prosecution witnesses and subject such witnesses to cross examination.

Consent decree A court-ratified agreement voluntarily reached by parties to settle a lawsuit.

Constitutional court A court created under authority of Article III of the Constitution. Judges serve for terms of good behavior and are protected against having their salaries reduced by the legislature.

Contempt A purposeful failure to carry out an order of a court (civil contempt) or a willful display of disrespect for the court (criminal contempt).

Contraband Articles that are illegal to possess.

Courts of appeals (federal) The intermediate level appellate courts in the federal system having jurisdiction over a particular region known as a circuit.

Criminal law Law governing the relationship between individuals and society. Deals with the enforcement of laws and the punishment of those who, by breaking laws, commit crimes.

Curtilage The land and outbuildings immediately adjacent to a home and regularly used by its occupants.

Declaratory judgment A court ruling determining a legal right or interpretation of the law, but not imposing any relief or remedy.

De facto In fact, actual.

Defendant A party at the trial level being sued in a civil case or charged with a crime in a criminal case.

De jure As a result of law or official government action.

De minimis Small or unimportant. A de minimis issue is considered one too trivial for a court to consider.

Demurrer A motion to dismiss a lawsuit in which the defendant admits to the facts alleged by the plaintiff but contends that those facts are insufficient to justify a legal cause of action.

De novo New, from the beginning.

Deposition Sworn testimony taken out of court.

Dicta; Obiter dicta Those portions of a judge's opinion that are not essential to deciding the case.

Directed verdict An action by a judge ordering a jury to return a specified verdict.

Discovery A pretrial procedure whereby one party to a lawsuit gains access to information or evidence held by the opposing party.

Dissenting opinion A formal written expression by a judge who disagrees with the result reached by the majority.

Distinguish A court's explanation of why a particular precedent is inapplicable to the case under consideration.

District courts The trial courts of general jurisdiction in the federal system.

Diversity jurisdiction The authority of federal courts to hear cases in which a party from one state is suing a party from another state.

Docket The schedule of cases to be heard by a court.

Double jeopardy The trying of a defendant a second time for the same offense. Prohibited by the Fifth Amendment to the Constitution.

Due process Government procedures that follow principles of essential fairness.

Eminent domain The authority of the government to take private property for public purpose.

En banc An appellate court hearing with all the judges of the court participating.

Enjoin An order from a court requiring a party to do or refrain from doing certain acts.

Entrapment Law enforcement officials inducing an otherwise innocent person into the commision of a criminal act.

Equity Law based on principles of fairness rather than strictly applied statutes.

Error, Writ of An order issued by an appeals court commanding a lower court to send up the full record of a case for review.

Exclusionary rule A principle of law that illegally gathered evidence may not be admitted in court.

Exclusive powers Powers reserved for either the federal government or the state governments, but not exercised by both.

Ex parte A hearing in which only one party to a dispute is present.

Ex post facto law A criminal law passed by the legislature and made applicable to acts committed prior to passage of the law. Prohibited by the U.S. Constitution.

Ex rel Upon information from. Used to designate a court case instituted by the government but instigated by a private party.

Ex vi termini From the force or very meaning of the term or expression.

Federal question A legal issue based on the U.S. Constitution, laws, or treaties.

Felony A serious criminal offense, usually punishable by incarceration of one year or more.

Gerrymander To construct political boundaries for the purpose of giving advantage to a particular political party or interest.

Grand jury A panel of twelve to twenty-three citizens who review prosecutorial evidence to determine if there are sufficient grounds to issue an indictment binding an individual over for trial on criminal charges.

Guilty A determination that a person accused of a criminal offense is legally responsible as charged.

Habeas corpus "You have the body." A writ issued to determine if a person held in custody is being unlawfully detained or imprisoned.

Harmless error An error occurring in a court proceeding that is insufficient in magnitude to justify the overturning of the court's final determination.

Hearsay Testimony not based on the personal knowledge of the witness, but a repetition of what the witness has heard others say.

Immunity An exemption from prosecution granted in exchange for testimony.

In camera A legal hearing held in the judge's chambers or otherwise in private.

Incorporation The process whereby provisions of the Bill of Rights are declared to be included in the due process guarantee of the

Fourteenth Amendment and made applicable to state and local governments.

Indictment A document issued by a grand jury officially charging an individual with criminal violations and binding the accused over for trial.

In forma pauperis "In the form of a pauper." A special status granted to indigents that allows them to proceed without payment of court fees and to be exempt from certain procedural requirements.

Information A document, serving the same purpose as an indictment, but issued directly by the prosecutor.

Infra Below.

Injunction A writ prohibiting the person to whom it is directed from committing certain specified acts.

In pari materia On the same subject.

In re "In the matter of." The designation used in a judicial proceeding in which there are no formal adversaries.

In rem An act directed against a thing and not against a person.

Inter alia Among other things.

Interlocutory decree A provisional action that temporarily settles a legal question pending the final determination of a dispute.

Ipse dixit A statement that depends for its persuasiveness on the authority of the one who said it.

Judgment of the court The final ruling of a court, independent of the legal reasoning supporting it.

Judicial activism A philosophy that courts should not be reluctant to review and if necessary strike down legislative and executive actions.

Judicial notice The recognition by a court of the truth of certain facts without requiring one of the parties to put them into evidence.

Judicial restraint A philosophy that courts should defer to the legislative and executive branches whenever possible.

Judicial review The authority of a court to determine the constitutionality of acts committed by the legislative and executive branches and to strike down acts judged to be in violation of the Constitution.

Jurisdiction The authority of a court to hear and decide legal disputes and to enforce its rulings.

Justiciable Capable of being heard and decided by a court.

Legislative court A court created by Congress under authority of Article I of the Constitution to assist in carrying out the powers of the legislature.

Litigant A party to a lawsuit.

Magistrate A low level judge with limited authority.

Mandamus "We command." A writ issued by a court commanding a public official to carry out a particular act or duty.

Mandatory jurisdiction A case that a court is required to hear.

Marque and reprisal An order from the government of one country requesting and legitimizing the seizure of persons and property of another country. Prohibited by the Constitution.

Merits The central issues of a case.

Misdemeanor A less serious criminal act, usually punishable by less than one year of incarceration.

Mistrial A trial that is prematurely ended by a judge because of procedural irregularities.

Mitigating circumstances Conditions that lower the moral blame of a criminal act, but do not justify or excuse it.

Moot Unsettled or undecided. A question presented in a lawsuit that cannot be answered by a court either because the issue has resolved itself or conditions have so changed that the court is unable to grant the requested relief.

Motion A request made to a court for a certain ruling or action.

Natural law Laws considered applicable to all persons in all nations because they are thought to be basic to human nature.

Nolle prosequi The decision of a prosecutor to drop criminal charges against an accused.

Nolo contendere No contest. A plea entered by a criminal defendant in which the accused does not admit guilt but submits to sentencing and punishment as if guilty.

Opinion of the court An opinion announcing the judgment and reasoning of a court endorsed by a majority of the judges participating.

Order A written command issued by a judge.

Original jurisdiction The authority of a court to try a case and to decide it, as opposed to appellate jurisdiction.

Per curiam An unsigned or collectively written opinion issued by a court.

Peremptory challenge Excusing a prospective juror without explaining the reasons for doing so.

Per se In and of itself.

Petitioner A party seeking relief in court.

Petit jury A trial court jury to decide criminal or civil cases.

Plaintiff The party who brings a legal action to court for resolution or remedy.

Plea bargain An arrangement in a criminal case in which the defendant agrees to plead guilty in return for the prosecutor reducing the criminal charges or recommending a lenient sentence.

Plurality opinion An opinion announcing the judgment of a court with supporting reasoning that is not endorsed by a majority of the justices participating.

Police powers The power of the state to regulate for the health, safety, morals, and general welfare of its citizens.

Political question An issue more appropriate for determination by the legislative or executive branch than the judiciary.

Precedent A previously decided case that serves as a guide for deciding a current case.

Preemption A doctrine under which an area of authority previously left to the states is, by act of Congress, brought into the exclusive jurisdiction of the federal government.

Prima facie "At first sight." A case that is sufficient to prevail unless effectively countered by the opposing side.

Pro bono publico "For the public good." Usually refers to legal representation done without fee for some charitable or public purpose.

Pro se A person who appears in court without an attorney.

Punitive damages A monetary award (separate from compensatory damages) imposed by a court for punishment purposes to be paid by the party at fault to the injured party.

Quash To annul, vacate, or totally do away with.

Ratio decidendi A court's primary reasoning for deciding a case the way it did.

Recuse The action of a judge not to participate in a case because of conflict of interest or other disqualifying condition.

Remand To send a case back to an inferior court for additional action.

Res judicata A legal issue that has been finally settled by a court judgment.

Respondent The party against whom a legal action is filed.

Reverse An action by an appellate court setting aside or changing a decision of a lower court.

Ripeness A condition in which a legal dispute has evolved to the point where the issues it presents can be effectively resolved by a court.

Selective incorporation The policy of the Supreme Court to decide incorporation issues on a case-by-case, right-by-right basis.

Show cause A judicial order commanding a party to appear in court and explain why the court should not take a proposed action.

Solicitor general Justice Department official whose office represents the federal government in all litigation before the U.S. Supreme Court.

Standing; standing to sue The right of parties to bring legal actions because they are directly affected by the legal issues raised.

Stare decisis "Let the decision stand." The doctrine that once a legal issue has been settled it should be followed as precedent in future cases presenting the same question.

State action An action taken by an agency or official of a state or local government.

Stay To stop or suspend.

Strict construction Narrow interpretation of the provisions of laws.

Subpoena ad testificandum An order compelling a person to testify before a court, legislative hearing, or grand jury.

Subpoena duces tecum An order compelling a person to produce a document or other piece of physical evidence that is relevant to issues pending before a court, legislative hearing, or grand jury.

Sub silentio "Under silence." A court action taken without explicit notice or indication.

Summary judgment A decision by a court made without a full hearing or without receiving briefs or oral arguments.

Supra Above.

Temporary restraining order A judicial order prohibiting certain challenged actions from being taken prior to a full hearing on the question.

Test A criterion or set of criteria used by courts to determine if certain legal thresholds have been met or constitutional provisions violated.

Three-judge court A special federal court made up of appellate and trial court judges created to expedite the processing of certain issues made eligible for such priority treatment by congressional statute.

Ultra vires Actions taken that exceed the legal authority of the person or agency performing them.

Usus loquendi The common usage of ordinary language.

Vacate To void or rescind.

Vel non "Or not."

Venireman A juror.

Venue The geographical jurisdiction in which a case is heard.

Voir dire "To speak the truth." The stage of a trial in which potential jurors are questioned to determine their competence to sit in judgment of a case.

Warrant A judicial order authorizing an arrest or search and seizure.

Writ A written order of a court commanding the recipient to perform or not to perform certain specified acts.

Excerpts from the cases below can be found at www.cqpress.com/clca. htm. The page number shown refers to the primary mention of the case in the text. Multiple page numbers are provided for those cases that receive significant attention in more than one chapter. This archive will be updated with additional case excerpts as the Supreme Court hands down important decisions.

SUBJECT INDEX

CASE INDEX

IMAGE CREDITS